ESSENTIALS OF
PSYCHOLOGY

ESSENTIALS of PSYCHOLOGY

Essentials of Psychology, Third Edition *offers an integrated pedagogical system designed to help students get the most out of their reading. Hallmark features include an outline, a preview statement, preview questions, instructional captions,* In Review *charts, and a marginal glossary. Each chapter ends with an* Active Review *that includes a* Linkages *diagram, chapter summary,* Learn by Doing *and* Step into Action *sections, a review of key terms, and multiple-choice questions.*

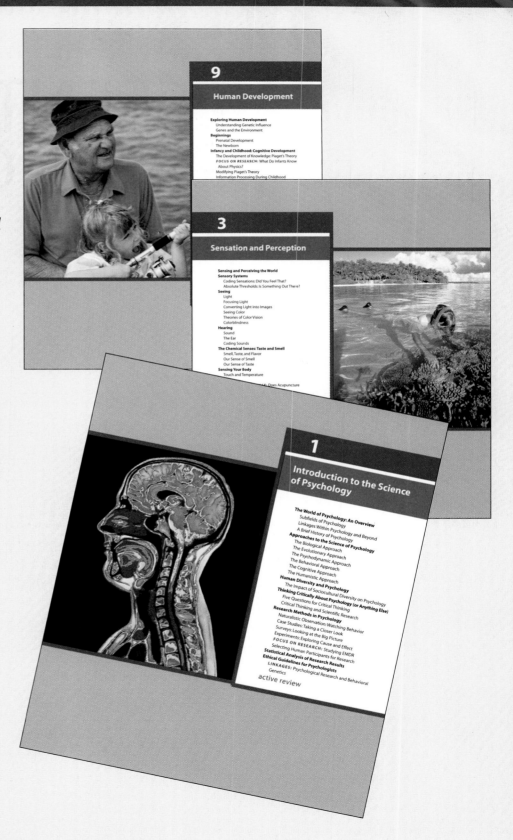

An Integrated Pedagogical System

Each chapter opens with a full **outline,** a brief **preview statement,** and a list of **preview questions** related to each main section of the chapter. The preview questions are repeated at the start of each section and within the chapter summary.

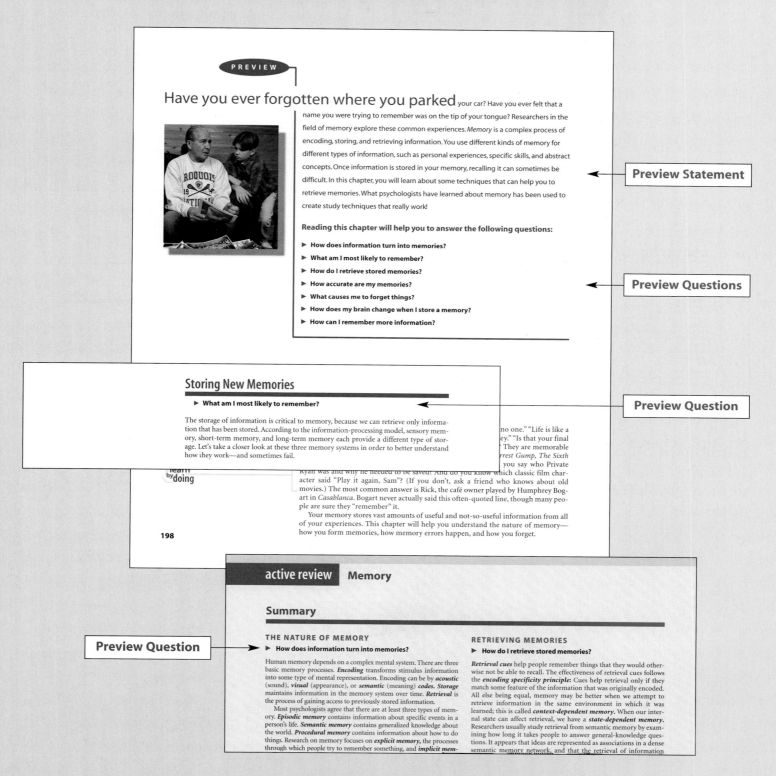

PREVIEW

Have you ever forgotten where you parked your car? Have you ever felt that a

name you were trying to remember was on the tip of your tongue? Researchers in the field of memory explore these common experiences. *Memory* is a complex process of encoding, storing, and retrieving information. You use different kinds of memory for different types of information, such as personal experiences, specific skills, and abstract concepts. Once information is stored in your memory, recalling it can sometimes be difficult. In this chapter, you will learn about some techniques that can help you to retrieve memories. What psychologists have learned about memory has been used to create study techniques that really work!

Reading this chapter will help you to answer the following questions:

▶ **How does information turn into memories?**
▶ **What am I most likely to remember?**
▶ **How do I retrieve stored memories?**
▶ **How accurate are my memories?**
▶ **What causes me to forget things?**
▶ **How does my brain change when I store a memory?**
▶ **How can I remember more information?**

Preview Statement ◀

Preview Questions ◀

Storing New Memories

▶ **What am I most likely to remember?**

Preview Question ◀

The storage of information is critical to memory, because we can retrieve only information that has been stored. According to the information-processing model, sensory memory, short-term memory, and long-term memory each provide a different type of storage. Let's take a closer look at these three memory systems in order to better understand how they work—and sometimes fail.

no one." "Life is like a
ey." "Is that your final
? They are memorable
rrest Gump, The Sixth
you say who Private
Ryan was and why he needed to be saved? And do you know which classic film character said "Play it again, Sam"? (If you don't, ask a friend who knows about old movies.) The most common answer is Rick, the café owner played by Humphrey Bogart in *Casablanca.* Bogart never actually said this often-quoted line, though many people are sure they "remember" it.

Your memory stores vast amounts of useful and not-so-useful information from all of your experiences. This chapter will help you understand the nature of memory—how you form memories, how memory errors happen, and how you forget.

learn
by doing

198

---

active review   Memory

Summary

THE NATURE OF MEMORY

▶ **How does information turn into memories?**

Preview Question ◀

Human memory depends on a complex mental system. There are three basic memory processes. *Encoding* transforms stimulus information into some type of mental representation. Encoding can be by *acoustic* (sound), *visual* (appearance), or *semantic* (meaning) *codes. Storage* maintains information in the memory system over time. *Retrieval* is the process of gaining access to previously stored information.

Most psychologists agree that there are at least three types of memory. *Episodic memory* contains information about specific events in a person's life. *Semantic memory* contains generalized knowledge about the world. *Procedural memory* contains information about how to do things. Research on memory focuses on *explicit memory,* the processes through which people try to remember something, and *implicit mem-*

RETRIEVING MEMORIES

▶ **How do I retrieve stored memories?**

Retrieval cues help people remember things that they would otherwise not be able to recall. The effectiveness of retrieval cues follows the *encoding specificity principle:* Cues help retrieval only if they match some feature of the information that was originally encoded. All else being equal, memory may be better when we attempt to retrieve information in the same environment in which it was learned; this is called *context-dependent memory.* When our internal state can affect retrieval, we have a *state-dependent memory.* Researchers usually study retrieval from semantic memory by examining how long it takes people to answer general-knowledge questions. It appears that ideas are represented as associations in a dense semantic memory network, and that the retrieval of information

An Integrated Pedagogical System

In Review Charts summarize information in a convenient format and offer a new fill-in-the-blank self-testing item to further aid student learning and review of the chapter material.

Instructional captions for all figures, tables, photographs, and cartoons reiterate core concepts and help to interpret visual material.

The **marginal glossary** found throughout the text defines key terms on the appropriate pages.

Active Review

*The **Active Review** at the end of each chapter acts as a built-in study guide.*

A **Linkages diagram** illustrates how material in the chapter is connected to other chapters. A **Chapter Summary,** two **Learn by Doing** activities, an opportunity to **Step into Action,** a **Review of Key Terms,** and a **Multiple-Choice Self-Test** all help students master the chapter material successfully.

Learn by Doing

Four features throughout the text underscore a commitment to active learning and applying psychology.

Figure and Photo Captions

Dozens of new figure and photo captions identified with a "Learn by Doing" symbol reinforce concepts by suggesting ways in which students can demonstrate the concepts for themselves.

Applying Psychology Photos

The Applying Psychology photos highlight the diversity of applied psychology.

Learn by Doing Marginal Callout

A symbol appears in the page margin where active learning opportunities occur in the narrative.

Put It in Writing and *Personal Learning Activity*

As part of the Active Review section, *Put It in Writing* invites readers to write about a specific chapter topic, and *Personal Learning Activity* provides another opportunity to *do* psychology— not just read about it.

Thinking Critically

A dedicated section in each chapter helps improve this vital skill.

Structured around five questions, these sections encourage readers to analyze material before drawing conclusions:

- What am I being asked to believe or accept?
- Is there evidence available to support the claim?
- Can that evidence be interpreted another way?
- What evidence would help to evaluate the alternatives?
- What conclusions are most reasonable?

THINKING CRITICALLY

Are Personality Traits Inherited?

Gray's approach-inhibition theory is one of several biologically oriented explanations of the origins of personality traits. A related explanation is that the big-five factors and other personality traits arise from our genes. Consider the case of identical twins who had been separated at five weeks of age and did not meet again for thirty-nine years. Both men drove Chevrolets, chain-smoked the same brand of cigarettes, had divorced a woman named Linda, were remarried to a woman named Betty, had sons named James Allan, had dogs named Toy, enjoyed similar hobbies, and had served as sheriff's deputies (Tellegen et al., 1988).

■ **What am I being asked to believe or accept?**

Cases like this have helped focus the attention of behavioral geneticists on the possibility that some core aspects of personality might be partly, or even largely, inherited (Krueger, Markon, & Bouchard, 2003; Plomin & Caspi, 1999).

■ **Is there evidence available to support the claim?**

The evidence and the arguments regarding this assertion are much like those presented in the chapter on thought, language, and intelligence, where we discuss the origins of differences in mental abilities. Stories about children who seem to "have" their parents' or grandparents' bad temper, generosity, or shyness are often presented to support the idea that personality is inherited. And in fact, family resemblances in personality do provide one important source of evidence. Several studies have found moderate, but significant, correlations between children's personality test scores and those of their parents and siblings (Davis, Luce, & Kraus, 1994; Loehlin, 1992).

Even stronger evidence comes from studies conducted around the world comparing identical twins raised together, identical twins raised apart, nonidentical twins raised together, and nonidentical twins raised apart (Grigorenko, 2002). Identical twins (who have exactly the same genes) tend to be more alike in personality than nonidentical twins

---

Thinking Critically

Focus on Research

Highlighting a particular study, these sections emphasize the value of research and the creativity with which it is often conducted.

These sections are organized around five questions:

- What was the researcher's question?
- How did the researcher answer the question?
- What did the researcher find?
- What do the results mean?
- What do we still need to know?

FOCUS ON RESEARCH

Self-Esteem and the Ultimate Terror

Why is self-esteem so important to so many people? An intriguing answer to this question comes from the *terror management theory* proposed by Jeff Greenberg, Tom Pyszczynski, and Sheldon Solomon. This theory is based on the notion that humans are the only creatures capable of thinking about the future and realizing that we will all eventually die. Terror management theory suggests that humans cope with anxiety, including the terror that thoughts about death might bring, by developing a variety of self-protective psychological strategies. One of these is the effort to establish and maintain high self-esteem (Greenberg, Pyszczynski, & Solomon, 2003; Pyszczynski, Greenberg, & Solomon, 2001).

■ What was the researchers' question?

In one series of experiments, Greenberg and his colleagues (1992) asked whether high self-esteem would, in fact, serve as a buffer against anxiety—specifically, the anxiety brought on by thoughts about death and pain.

■ How did the researchers answer the question?

About 150 students at several North American universities participated in one of three studies, each of which followed a similar format. The first step was to temporarily alter the participants' self-esteem. To do so, the researchers gave the students feedback on a personality or intelligence test they had taken earlier in the semester. Half the participants received positive feedback designed to increase their self-esteem. The other half received feedback that was neutral—it was neither flattering nor depressing. (Measurement of the students' self-esteem showed that the positive feedback actually did create higher self-esteem than the neutral feedback.) In the next phase of each experiment, the researchers used a film about death, or the (false) threat of a mild electric shock, to provoke some anxiety in half the participants in the positive feedback group and half the participants in the neutral feedback group. The amount of anxiety created was measured

---

Focus on Research

Linkages

*The **Linkages** feature reflects the relationships among the subfields of psychology.*

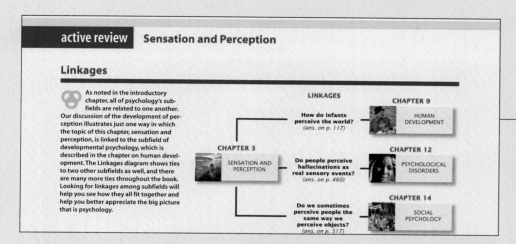

active review | **Sensation and Perception**

Linkages

As noted in the introductory chapter, all of psychology's subfields are related to one another. Our discussion of the development of perception illustrates just one way in which the topic of this chapter, sensation and perception, is linked to the subfield of developmental psychology, which is described in the chapter on human development. The Linkages diagram shows ties to two other subfields as well, and there are many more ties throughout the book. Looking for linkages among subfields will help you see how they all fit together and help you better appreciate the big picture that is psychology.

LINKAGES

How do infants perceive the world? (ans. on p. 117) — **CHAPTER 9** HUMAN DEVELOPMENT

CHAPTER 3 SENSATION AND PERCEPTION

Do people perceive hallucinations as real sensory events? (ans. on p. 460) — **CHAPTER 12** PSYCHOLOGICAL DISORDERS

Do we sometimes perceive people the same way we perceive objects? (ans. on p. 517) — **CHAPTER 14** SOCIAL PSYCHOLOGY

Linkages Diagram

In the *Active Review* section at the end of each chapter, a **Linkages diagram** presents three questions to illustrate how material in the chapter is related to other chapters in the book.

Marginal Callouts

The Linkages diagram directs students to the pages that carry further discussion of each question, where a **marginal callout** appears.

LINKAGES
How do infants perceive the world? (a link to Human Development)

We have seen that perception is influenced by the knowledge and experience we gain over time, but what perceptual abilities do we start with? To learn about infants' perception, psychologists have studied two inborn patterns called *habituation* and *dishabituation*. Infants stop looking when they repeatedly see stimuli perceived to be the same. This is habituation. If they see a stimulus that is perceived to be different, they resume looking. This is dishabituation. Using the habituation/dishabituation technique, researchers have found that newborns can perceive differences in stimuli showing various amounts of black-and-white contrast, but they cannot yet distinguish differences between colors (Burr, Morrone, & Fiorentini, 1996). Other studies using the same methods have shown that newborns can perceive differences in the angles of lines (Slater et al., 1991). Taken together, these studies suggest that we are born with the basic components of feature detection.

Are we also born with the ability to combine features into perceptions of whole objects? This is still a matter of debate. We know that at one month of age, infants concentrate their gaze on one part of an object, such as the corner of a triangle (Goldstein,

LINKAGES
Perception and Human Development

Linkages

Linkages Sections

One of the questions in the Linkages diagram is discussed at length in the chapter's special section titled *Linkages.*

NEW for Instructors!

Designed to enhance and maximize the teaching and learning experience, we have introduced two new powerful tools for Essentials, 3/e:

Psych in Film® DVD/VHS
contains 35 clips from Universal Studios films illustrating key concepts in psychology. Clips from films like *Apollo 13, Schindler's List, Snow Falling on Cedars,* and many others are combined with commentary, discussion questions, and teaching tips to help bring psychology alive for students.

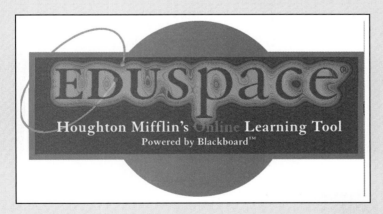

Ask your Houghton Mifflin sales representative for further details on these two new products.

Eduspace® is a powerful course management system powered by Blackboard that makes preparing, presenting, and managing courses easier. Use this distance-learning platform to manage large courses online, as well as to access, customize, create, and deliver course materials and tests online. You can easily maintain student portfolios using the gradebook where grades for all assignments are automatically scored, averaged, and saved. Our premium Eduspace content for *Essentials,* 3/e, includes our **new *Psych in Film®* video clips,** complete with **teaching tips, discussion questions,** and **trackable quizzing** (in addition to our computerized test bank material); **interactive practice tests** and **tools** (NetLabs, Personal Learning Activities, Web Tutorials, Flashcards) for your students; as well as high-quality **presentation tools** such as PowerPoints and art from the textbook. All in one easy-to-use platform!

ESSENTIALS *OF* PSYCHOLOGY

THIRD EDITION

Douglas A. Bernstein
University of South Florida
Southampton University

Peggy W. Nash
Broward Community College

with

Alison Clarke-Stewart
University of California, Irvine

Louis A. Penner
Wayne State University
University of Michigan

Edward J. Roy
University of Illinois at Urbana-Champaign

Houghton Mifflin Company   Boston   New York

To my dear wife, Lindsay N. Kennedy
     Doug Bernstein

to my family and sons, Rob and Jeff, with love
     Peggy Nash

Vice President & Publisher: Charles Hartford
Senior Sponsoring Editor: Kerry Baruth
Development Editor: Rita Lombard
Editorial Assistant: Caryn Yilmaz
Senior Project Editrix: Aileen Mason
Editorial Assistant: Neil Reynolds
Senior Production/Design Coordinator: Sarah Ambrose
Senior Manufacturing Manager: Florence Cadran
Senior Marketing Manager: Katherine Greig
Marketing Manager: Jane Potter

Cover illustration: Anson Liaw

For permission to use copyrighted materials, grateful acknowledgment is made to the copyright holders listed on pages A-74–A-76, which is hereby considered an extension of the copyright page.

Printed in the U.S.A.

Library of Congress Control Number: 2003110133

ISBN: 0-618-21329-5 (Student Edition)
     0-618-33599-4 (Instructor's Annotated Edition)

3 4 5 6 7 8 9-WC-08 07 06 05 04

BRIEF CONTENTS

FEATURES

CONTENTS

4   Consciousness   128

5   Learning   160

11 Personality 400

12 Psychological Disorders 432

13 Treatment of Psychological Disorders 477

PREFACE

PSYCHOLOGY IS A RICH and varied science, covering the breadth and depth of human behavior—everything from fleeting reflexes to enduring memories, from falling asleep to falling in love. In our experience, most students enter the introductory course thinking that psychology concerns itself mainly with personality, psychological testing, mental disorders, psychotherapy, and other aspects of clinical psychology. Many of these students are surprised, then, when they find themselves reading about such topics as the structure of the brain, optical illusions, the effect of jet lag on Olympic athletes, AIDS and the immune system, and prenatal risk factors, to name just a few. Yet these are all topics under the umbrella that is psychology.

For all its diversity, psychology is also a remarkably integrated discipline whose subfields are linked to one another through common interests and overarching research questions. As psychologists and scholars, we wrote this book to portray the wide range of topics that make up the science of psychology. As teachers, we focused on the essentials of the discipline, the core concepts of psychology that we hope will be especially accessible and interesting to students. We also tried to present these topics through an integrated, active pedagogical system designed to help students get the most out of the text.

In creating the third edition of *Essentials of Psychology*, we rededicated ourselves to presenting a textbook that is not only clear and enjoyable to read, but that also provides features to support the learning process in all students, regardless of their academic background. Specifically, we set these goals:

- To focus on topics that represent the full range of psychology, from cell to society, without overwhelming the reader with details.

- To provide many active learning exercises that invite students to work with the text material in ways that can help them understand and remember it.

- To help students develop their ability to think critically and scientifically by examining the ways that psychologists have solved, or failed to solve, fascinating puzzles of behavior and mental processes.

- To explain the content of psychology with an emphasis on the doing of psychology, grounding all discussions in current and classic research studies. (We help students appreciate the importance of research by exploring one study in detail in a special feature in each chapter).

Our discussion of research in psychology is also designed to remind students that although, in some ways, "people are people wherever you go," sociocultural factors—including gender, ethnicity, cultural background, and geography—often shape human behavior and mental processes. We repeatedly point out, therefore, that psychological research on the thinking styles, perceptual habits, psychological disorders, social pressures, and other phenomena seen in North America or Europe, for example, may not apply to other cultures—or even to subcultures within Western countries.

Rather than isolating discussion of sociocultural material in boxed features, we have woven it into every chapter so that students will encounter it repeatedly as they read. We introduce the importance of sociocultural factors in Chapter 1 and continue to reinforce it through coverage of such topics as the impact of culture and experience on perception (Chapter 3), classrooms across cultures (Chapter 5), ethnic differences in IQ (Chapter 7), social and cultural factors in sexuality (Chapter 8), gender differences in stress responses (Chapter 10), personality, culture, and human development (Chapter 11), gender and cultural differences in depression and suicide (Chapter 12), and cultural factors in aggression (Chapter 14), to cite just a few examples. (In the instructor's annotated edition of the book, each discussion of sociocultural factors is marked in the margin of the page where the discussion appears.)

WHAT'S NEW IN THIS EDITION?

Feedback from faculty colleagues and students suggests that the changes we made in the second edition of *Essentials* were well received. Accordingly, in creating the third edition, we have sought to update and upgrade all the book's best features, rather than change them for the sake of change. We hope that the result of our efforts is a book that offers even more of what faculty and students want and need.

Organization

Designed for presentation in a single semester, the book's fourteen-chapter organization has been retained, and the chapters appear in the same sequence as before. Have we arranged those fourteen chapters in an ideal sequence? The sequence reflects the way we teach our introductory courses, but we know that your preference for chapter sequencing may not match ours. Accordingly, we have again ensured that each of the fourteen chapters appears as a free-standing unit so that you may assign the chapters in whatever order you wish. For example, many instructors prefer to teach the material on human development relatively late in the course, which is why it appears as Chapter 9. However, the chapter can be just as comfortably assigned earlier in the course. For the third edition, we have also added an "optional" fifteenth chapter, Industrial/Organizational Psychology, which can be included in the textbook on request. Note that end-of-book materials for this chapter, such as answer keys, references, credits, and the combined index/glossary are printed in blue.

A Continued Emphasis on Learning by Doing

The added emphasis on active learning in the second edition was so popular with faculty and students that we have emphasized it again in the third edition. Three kinds of "Learn by Doing" features appear throughout the book.

- First, there are dozens of new or revised figure and photo captions that help students understand and remember a psychological principle or phenomenon by suggesting ways in which they can demonstrate it for themselves. In the memory chapter, for example, a photo caption suggests that students show the photo to a friend, then ask questions about it to illustrate the operation of constructive memory. These captions are all identified with a Learn by Doing symbol.

- Second, we have placed Learn by Doing symbols in page margins at even more places where active learning opportunities occur in the narrative. At these points, we ask students to stop reading and try *doing something* to illustrate or highlight the psychological principle or phenomenon under discussion. For example, in the sensation and perception chapter, we ask the student to focus attention on various targets as a way of appreciating the difference between overt and covert attention shifts.

- Finally, we have carried the active learning theme through to the end of each chapter, where—as part of the built-in study guide we call "Active Review"—students will find sections called "Put It in Writing" and "Personal Learning Activity." These sections invite students to (a) write about a specific chapter-related topic, and (b) collect, analyze, and discuss some data on a chapter-related principle or phenomenon.

Active Review

The Put It in Writing and Personal Learning Activity sections are just one part of our effort to add educational value to the built-in Active Review study guide. The Active Review's other features include

- A "Linkages" diagram, which helps students understand and appreciate the ways in which the chapter they have just read relates to other subfields of psychology.

- Twenty-item multiple-choice self-tests. We have revised some of the questions, but—as in the second edition—they are focused on the application, as well as the definition, of principles, concepts, and phenomena.

- A "Step into Action" section, which—to highlight our emphasis on active learning—lists the courses in which students can further pursue chapter-related study and provides a newly expanded and annotated list of movies and books related to each chapter. We also refer students to Houghton

Mifflin's textbook web site, where—as the result of a continuous updating and upgrading process—they can easily find the latest, most interesting, and most valuable web addresses related to chapter content, as well as a range of interactive activities and self-quizzes for each chapter.

- A Review of Key Terms section, which invites students to write their own definitions of the most important terms presented in the chapter. These lists have been updated to include all the key terms discussed in the new edition.

"Applying Psychology" Photos

As in the second edition, we continue to emphasize the many ways in which psychological theory and research results are being applied to benefit human welfare. We further highlight the diversity of applied psychology by including in each chapter at least one Applying Psychology photo that offers a memorable example. In the learning chapter, for example, a photo illustrates the use of classical conditioning principles in the humane control of predators that can threaten sheep ranchers' livelihoods. In the consciousness chapter, the Applying Psychology photo illustrates the value of stimulus control therapy for helping insomniacs get a better night's sleep.

Updated Content

As in the second edition, our goal in preparing this new edition of *Essentials* is to present the latest, most established results of basic and applied research, on topics that are both important to psychology and of high interest to students. Accordingly, we offer updated coverage of research on how drugs affect the brain (Chapter 2), the basis for optical illusions (Chapter 3), the effects of subliminal messages (Chapter 4), the importance of active learning in the classroom (Chapter 5), the accuracy of eyewitness testimony (Chapter 6), the origins of intelligence (Chapter 7), sources of sexual orientation (Chapter 8), the development of morals (Chapter 9), the effects of stress on health (Chapter 10), what determines and shapes our personalities (Chapter 11), the causes of multiple personality disorder (Chapter 12), the effects of psychotherapy (Chapter 13), and the development of ethnic prejudice (Chapter 14).

In this new edition, students will also encounter the latest evidence on topics such as

- The value of dietary supplements in improving memory and slowing memory loss (Chapter 2)

- Individual differences in taste abilities, including how to determine if one is a "supertaster" (Chapter 3)

- The role of expectations on the effects of psychoactive drugs (Chapter 4)

- The role of active learning processes in long-term retention of information (Chapter 5)

- Factors that may make people more susceptible to reporting false memories (Chapter 6)

- The process of acquiring language (Chapter 7)

- Factors that influence subjective well-being (Chapter 8)

- The origins of infantile amnesia (Chapter 9)

- The "tend and befriend" response to stressors, and its relationship to the traditional "fight-or-flight" syndrome (Chapter 10)

- Biological theories of personality (Chapter 11)

- The origins of schizophrenia, depression, and anxiety (Chapter 12)

- The current status of psychologists' efforts to gain the right to prescribe psychoactive drugs (Chapter 13)

- Social neuroscience, which lies at the interface between biological and social psychology (Chapter 14)

SPECIAL FEATURES

The third edition of *Essentials of Psychology* contains improved versions of a number of special features found in its predecessor. Designed to promote efficient learning and mastery of the material, these include, in each chapter, an integrated pedagogical system, as well as sections on Thinking Critically, Focus on Research, and Linkages, along with an Active Review section.

An Integrated Pedagogical System

Our integrated pedagogical system is designed to help students get the most out of their reading. Based on the PQ4R study system (discussed in detail in Chapter 6, "Memory"), learning aids in each chapter include the following elements.

Preview Questions To help students survey and question the material, each chapter opens with a full outline, a brief preview statement, and a list of questions related to the key topic of each main section of the chapter. Those questions are repeated within the chapter at the start of each corresponding main section, and they appear again in the Active Review, where they help organize the chapter summary.

Margin Glossary Key terms are defined in the margin of the page where they appear, reinforcing core concepts without interrupting the flow of reading. (For the third edition, we have revised many of our phonetic guides to make it even easier for students to correctly pronounce unfamiliar key terms—as well as other terms whose pronunciation is not immediately obvious.) In the Active Review section at the end of each chapter, a definition exercise encourages students to restate these core concepts in their own words.

Instructional Captions Captions to all figures, tables, photographs, and cartoons reiterate core concepts and help students learn to interpret visual information. And, as mentioned earlier, many of these captions prompt students to engage in various kinds of active learning experiences.

In Review Charts In Review study charts summarize information in a convenient tabular format. We have placed two or three In

Review charts strategically in each chapter to help students synthesize and assimilate large chunks of information—for example, on drug effects, key elements in personality theories, and stress responses and mediators. We have added a new fill-in-the-blank self-testing item at the bottom of each In Review chart to further aid student learning and review of the chapter material. The answer key is at the back of the book; answers printed in blue indicate those for the "optional" Industrial/Organizational Psychology chapter.

Active Review As mentioned earlier, the built-in Active Review study guide at the end of each chapter includes

- A *Linkages diagram* containing questions that illustrate three of the ways in which material in each chapter is connected to other chapters in the book.

- A *chapter summary* organized around major topic headings and the related preview questions. The summary is presented in short, easy-to-read paragraphs that are focused on subheadings.

- A *Learn by Doing* feature that is designed to promote active learning. Here, students will find Put It in Writing and Personal Learning Project sections that invite them to (a) write about a specific chapter-related topic, and (b) collect, analyze, and discuss some data on a chapter-related principle or phenomenon. For example, in the personality chapter, the Put It in Writing section suggests that students list a celebrity's personality traits, then summarize how various personality theories would account for the development of those traits. In the biology and behavior chapter, students are asked to write about how research on brain development might affect one's choice of an infant day care center. These Put It in Writing suggestions might be helpful as writing-across-the-curriculum assignments.

- Personal Learning Projects that suggest ways in which students can *do* psychology as well as read about it. In the motivation and emotion chapter, for example, the Personal Learning Project section suggests a way in which students can collect data on lie-detection skills. In the social psychology chapter, students are invited to test some assumptions of evolutionary theories of mate selection by analyzing personal ads in a local newspaper. Each Personal Learning Project section ends by referring the student to additional projects listed in the study guide that accompanies the book.

- A *Step into Action* section, which (a) suggests courses that students can take to pursue further chapter-related study, (b) presents an annotated list of movies and books related to each chapter, and (c) encourages students to visit Houghton Mifflin's textbook web site for resources related to the chapter, in the form of interactive activities, self-quizzes, and web links.

- A *Review of Key Terms*, which invites students to write their own definitions of the most important terms presented in the chapter. These lists have been updated to include all the key terms discussed in the new edition.

- A twenty-item *Multiple-Choice Self-Test* designed to help students assess their understanding of the chapter's key points prior to taking quizzes and exams. As before, we provide an answer key at the back of the book that identifies and briefly explains each correct answer, and refers students to the page on which the tested material was first discussed. Note that the answers printed in blue are for the "optional" Industrial/Organizational Psychology chapter.

Thinking Critically

A special Thinking Critically section in each chapter helps students hone their abilities in this vital skill. Our approach to writing centers on describing research on psychological phenomena in a way that reveals the logic of the scientific method, identifies possible flaws in design or interpretation, and leaves room for more questions and further research. In other words, as author-teachers, we try to model critical thinking processes for our readers. The Thinking Critically sections are designed to make these processes more explicit and accessible by providing readers with a framework for analyzing evidence before drawing conclusions. The framework is built around five questions that the reader should find useful in analyzing not only psychological research studies, but other forms of communication as well, including political speeches, advertising claims, and appeals for contributions. These five questions first appear in Chapter 1, when we introduce the importance of critical thinking, and they are repeated in every chapter's Thinking Critically section.

1. What am I being asked to believe or accept?

2. Is there evidence available to support the claim?

3. Can that evidence be interpreted another way?

4. What evidence would help to evaluate the alternatives?

5. What conclusions are most reasonable?

Using this simple yet powerful framework, we explore issues such as subliminal persuasion, pornography and aggression, recovered memories, and memory-enhancing dietary supplements, to name just a few. Page xiv includes a complete list of the Thinking Critically features.

Focus on Research

Scientists in psychology have helped us to better understand behavior and mental processes through their commitment to empirical research. They have posed vital questions about psychological phenomena and designed research that is capable of answering, or at least illuminating, those questions. In Chapter 1 we introduce readers to the methods of scientific research and to basic research designs in psychology. Every subsequent chapter features a Focus on Research section that highlights a particular research study to help students appreciate the value of research and the creativity with which psychologists have conducted it. Like the Thinking Critically sections, the Focus on Research features are organized around five questions designed to help readers organize their thinking about research questions and research results.

1. What was the researcher's question?

2. How did the researcher answer the question?

3. What did the researcher find?

4. What do the results mean?

5. What do we still need to know?

These Focus on Research sections help students to see how psychologists have used experiments, surveys, observations, and other designs to explore phenomena such as learned helplessness, infant cognition, evolutionary theories of helping, and human sexual behavior. A full list of the Focus on Research features appears on page xiv.

Linkages

In our experience, introductory psychology students are better able to appreciate the scope of our discipline when they look at it not as a laundry list of separate topics, but as an interrelated set of subfields, each of which contributes to—and benefits from—the work being done in all the others. To help students see these relationships, we have built into the book an integrating tool called Linkages. There are three elements in the Linkages program.

■ *Linkages diagrams* The first element of the chapter's Active Review is a Linkages diagram, which presents a set of questions that illustrate three ways in which material in the chapter is related to other chapters in the book. For example, the Linkages diagram in Chapter 2, "Biology and Behavior," contains questions that show how biological psychology is related to consciousness ("Does the brain shut down when we sleep?"), human development ("How do our brains change over a lifetime?"), and treatment of psychological disorders ("How do drugs help people who suffer from schizophrenia?"). These diagrams are designed to help students keep in mind how the content of each chapter fits into psychology as a whole. To introduce the concept of Linkages, the diagram in Chapter 1 appears within the body of the chapter.

■ *Cross-references* The page numbers following each question in the Linkages diagrams direct the student to pages that carry further discussion of that question. There, the linking question is repeated in the margin alongside the discussion.

■ *Linkages sections* One of the questions in each chapter's Linkages diagram reminds the student of the chapter's discussion of that question in a special section titled, appropriately enough, Linkages (see page xiv for a complete list of Linkages sections).

These three elements combine with the text narrative to highlight the network of relationships among psychology's subfields. This Linkages program is designed to help students see the "big picture" that is psychology—no matter how many chapters their instructor assigns or in what sequence.

TEACHING AND LEARNING SUPPORT PACKAGE

Many useful instructional and pedagogical materials have been developed to support the *Essentials of Psychology* textbook and the introductory course. Designed to enhance and maximize the teaching and learning experience, this third edition focuses on greater integration of the supplemental package components with the text itself. New features of several supplements reflect the text's emphasis on active learning and writing across the curriculum.

For the Instructor

Instructor's Annotated Edition To help instructors coordinate the many print, video, and software supplements available with the text, the *Instructor's Annotated Edition* shows which materials apply to the content on each page of the student text. The annotations coordinate learning objectives, test questions, discussion and lecture ideas, handouts, overhead transparencies, PowerPoint slides, active learning activities, video segments, and the like. As in the second edition, the third edition contains annotations marking passages in the text that cover multicultural topics. A key to the annotations appears on the inside front cover. An annotated optional Industrial/Organizational Psychology chapter is also available. See your Houghton sales representative for details.

Instructor's Resource Manual For each chapter of the textbook, the *Instructor's Resource Manual* includes learning objectives, a lecture outline, and numerous classroom "supplements"—that is, discussion, activity, and lecture suggestions and related handouts. The revised manual includes new Thinking Critically and Put It in Writing supplements similar to the exercises that appear in the textbook. The manual also includes a video guide and a pedagogical strategy section that covers active learning, critical thinking, using the Linkages feature, using the Research Focus supplements, and writing across the curriculum, as well as suggestions on how to build a syllabus. For instructors switching from the second to the third edition of the text, the manual includes a detailed transition guide for each chapter, outlining the key changes between editions. Note that this revised *Instructor's Resource Manual* comes with a **fifteenth** chapter offering supporting material on the optional Industrial/ Organizational Psychology chapter specially written for the third edition. As noted earlier, this chapter can be included in your text on request—see your Houghton Mifflin sales representative for details.

Test Bank The *Test Bank*, available in print or within a testing software program, includes 125 multiple-choice questions per chapter. Over one third of these are new, as are one third of the essay questions. Each multiple-choice question is keyed to pages in the student text and to the learning objectives that appear in the *Instructor's Resource Manual* and *Study Guide* and that are printed in the *Test Bank* as well. Each question is identified by whether it tests simple factual recall or deeper conceptual understanding. Over **45 percent** of the items have been class-tested with between 400 and 2,500 students. A statistical performance analysis is provided for those items. The computerized version allows instructors to edit questions, integrate their own, and generate paper or online exams.

The print *Test Bank* contains questions on the new optional Industrial/Organizational Psychology chapter.

PowerPoint Slides An extensively revised set of PowerPoint slides is available with the third edition. Each chapter's show includes dozens of slides featuring a lecture sequence that includes tables, figures, and photos from the textbook and other sources. Updates to this edition include more extensive information on the Thinking Critically and Focus on Research features, as well as hyperlinks that allow instructors to jump to illustrative slides when discussing a particular term. The slides are available on the instructor web site and the *Essentials* HMClass Prep CD-ROM (instructor CD-ROM).

Overhead Transparencies The *Essentials* transparency acetates include 100 four-color images from the text and other sources, organized by chapter.

HM Classprep CD-ROM with HMTesting (0-618-38113-9) This combined CD includes both the Computerized Test Bank and the HMClass Prep CD. Our HMTesting program offers delivery of test questions in an easy-to-use interface, compatible with both Mac and Windows platforms (and includes questions on the fifteenth chapter, Industrial/Organizational Psychology, that may be packaged with your text on request). The HMClass Prep instructor CD-ROM provides one location for all text-specific preparation materials that instructors might want to have available electronically. It contains PowerPoint lecture outlines and art from the textbook (including the In Review charts and the Linkages diagrams), as well as electronic versions of the *Instructor's Resource Manual* and other useful instructor materials such as the video guide and the third edition transition guide.

Textbook Web Site (0-618-38114-7) On the full-service, interactive web site accompanying *Essentials*, instructors have access to the PowerPoint slides and most elements of the *Instructor's Resource Manual,* described previously, as well as an online guide offering tips on how to use and assign the student activities available on the student side of the text-specific site. To view a sampling of instructor materials, point to **http://college.hmco. com,** select *Psychology,* then select this textbook.

Eduspace® is a powerful course management system powered by Blackboard that makes preparing, presenting, and managing courses easier. Using this distance-learning platform, you can not only easily manage large courses online, but you can also access, customize, create, and deliver course materials and tests online. You can easily maintain student portfolios using the gradebook, where grades for all assignments are automatically scored, averaged, and saved. Our premium Eduspace content for *Essentials* includes our **new *Psych in Film*® video clips,** complete with **teaching tips, discussion questions,** and **trackable quizzing** (in addition to our computerized test bank material); **interactive practice tests** and **tools** (NetLabs, Personal Learning Activities, Web Tutorials, Flashcards) for your students, as well as high-quality **presentation tools** such as PowerPoint slides and art from the textbook. And it all comes in one easy-to-use platform! You can also enable access to password-protected Houghton Mifflin student website resources directly from this course management solution.

Content for Course Management Software   *Blackboard* and *WebCT* course cartridges are available with *Essentials,* allowing instructors to use text-specific material to create an online course on their own campus course management system. The *Essentials* cartridges feature Ace quizzes, interactive NetLab exercises, PowerPoint slides, and other study materials all correlated to each chapter in the new edition of the text.

New! Houghton Mifflin Psych in Film® DVD   This DVD contains 35 clips from Universal Studios films illustrating key concepts in psychology. Clips from films like *Schindler's List, Snow Falling on Cedars,* and many others are combined with commentary and discussion questions to help bring psychology alive for students and demonstrate its relevance to contemporary life and culture. Teaching tips are correlated to specific text chapters and concepts on the instructor web site.

Lecture Starter Videos   Four videotapes featuring brief clips designed to launch lectures or discussions are available with *Essentials of Psychology.* The *Introductory Psychology Lecture Starter Video* includes approximately sixty-five short (two- to seven-minute) videoclips organized into thirty-four topical areas. An accompanying guide correlated to specific text chapters and concepts resides on the instructor web site. Also available are lecture starter videotapes covering child development, social psychology, and abnormal psychology.

The Psychology Show   This video supplement is available in both videodisc and VHS format. Featuring nineteen brief segments and numerous still images, *The Psychology Show* is designed to expand on the text's coverage of major topical areas and stimulate class discussion. The accompanying guide offers information on each motion segment and provides bar codes for videodisc use.

Media Policy   Ask your Houghton Mifflin sales representative about additional videos available for rental or purchase, including, among others, *The Brain, The Mind,* and *Discovering Psychology* modules.

For the Student

Textbook Web Site (0-618-381114-7)   The text-specific web site offers students a wide range of independent study resources including interactive NetLab exercises, Thinking Critically and Evaluating Research exercises, ACE self-quizzes, Flashcards and recommended web links, and articles on current events, books, and movies.

Student CD-ROM   The CD that accompanies every copy of the student text at no extra charge features study outlines corresponding to each chapter of the textbook, embedded with relevant interactive NetLab exercises, Evaluating Research and Critical Thinking exercises, ACE self-quizzes, a glossary, and a link to the textbook web site.

Study Guide (0-618-38110-4)   The *Study Guide* augments the Active Review study materials built into every chapter of the textbook. Introductory sections in the guide provide tips on developing critical thinking skills, studying Linkages, reading a textbook, and, new to this edition, developing writing skills. For each chapter of the text—including the optional Industrial/Organizational Psychology chapter—the guide includes learning objectives, key term hints and examples, a Concepts and Exercises section that shows students how to apply their knowledge of psychology to everyday issues and concerns, a Critical Thinking exercise, and several Personal Learning Activities of the same type as those in the text. In addition, each chapter concludes with two multiple-choice quizzes with wrong-answer rejoinders and a self-diagnostic quiz analysis to pinpoint weaknesses in topic and cognitive skill areas. A section of each chapter called "What Should I Write About?" provides advice on how to choose an appropriate term paper topic related to the chapter.

Psychology in Context: Voices and Perspectives, 2/e   The second edition of this exceptional reader, edited by David N. Sattler and Virginia Shabatay, may be shrinkwrapped with the text. It features engaging first-person narratives and essays by noted writers, with each article keyed to major psychological concepts.

Psychology: Fields of Application   This unique reader, edited by Astrid Stec and Douglas Bernstein, explores the most prominent areas of applied psychology. Each chapter features an expert's account of one area of application, including a brief history of the area's development, examples of research and how it has been applied, and the challenges facing the field.

ACKNOWLEDGMENTS

Many people provided us with the help, criticism, and encouragement we needed to create *Essentials of Psychology,* and to revise it into this third edition. We are of course indebted to our colleagues Louis Penner, Ed Roy, and Alison Clarke-Stewart, who, as co-authors of the Bernstein, Penner, Clarke-Stewart, and Roy textbook, *Psychology,* provided invaluable assistance in reviewing the revised *Essentials* manuscript as it developed. We also offer sincere thanks to Professor Paul Spector of the University of South Florida, who took the lead in helping us to create the new chapter, Industrial/Organizational Psychology, which is available on request for this edition. We are indebted, too, to a number of other colleagues for their expert help and advice on the revision of various chapters in the third edition of *Essentials.* These colleagues include, for Chapter 3, Melody Carswell, University of Kentucky; for Chapter 4, Joel Shenker, University of Virginia Medical School; for Chapter 5, J. Bruce Overmier, University of Minnesota; for Chapter 6, Kathleen McDermott, Washington University; for Chapter 7, Paul Whitney, Washington State University and Jeri Morris, Northwestern University Medical School; for Chapter 8, Tamera Schneider, Wright State University and Toru Shimizu, University of South Florida; and for Chapters 12 and 13, Geoff Kramer, Grand Valley State University.

Special thanks are also due to our dear friend and valued colleague, Sandra Goss Lucas, director of Introductory Psychology at the University of Illinois, who worked closely with us as we shaped and organized the new edition of *Essentials,* and who helped us to revise and improve the multiple-choice self-tests at the end of each chapter.

We also want to offer heartfelt thanks to our friends and colleagues who did such a wonderful job in creating revised versions of the ancillary materials for *Essentials*. Most of these people have worked with us for years, and many of them had been graduate student instructors in the University of Illinois Introductory Psychology program out of which this book emerged. They include Kelly Bouas Henry, Missouri Western State College; Sandra Goss Lucas, Amanda Allman, and Jonathan Nall, all of the University of Illinois; Linda Lebie and Travis Sola, both of Lakeland College; Elaine Cassel, Lord Fairfax Community College; Billa R. Reiss, St. Johns University; David B. Strohmetz, Monmouth University; and Bonnie Nichols, Missouri County Community College.

We also extend our deep appreciation to the *Essentials'* Board of Consultants, eight dedicated instructors whose involvement in focus groups and surveys, comments on manuscript chapters, and answers to development queries shaped the first edition of this text: Charles Blair-Broeker, Cedar Falls High School; Ken LeSure, Cuyahoga Community College; Barbara Lusk, Collin County Community College; Malinda Jo Muzi, Community College of Philadelphia; Nancy Simpson, Trident Technical College; Maggie Sokolik, University of California, Berkeley; Fred Whitford, Montana State University; and Robert Wildblood, Northern Virginia Community College.

We wish to thank several of our colleagues who helped us get the third edition off to a good start by reviewing and commenting on the strengths and weaknesses of the second edition.

James Bean, *Lock Haven University*

Doris A. Bitler, *George Mason University*

J. Peter Burton, *Santa Fe Community College*

Bernardo J. Carducci, *Indiana University Southeast*

Dwaine Cochran, *Stetson University*

Marcie N. Desrochers, *College of Charleston*

Kenneth C. Elliot, *University of Maine at Augusta*

Matthew Fanetti, *Southwest Missouri State University*

Leticia Y. Flores, *Southwest Texas State University*

Diane Herbert, *Hofstra University*

Jennifer M. Lancaster, *St. Francis College*

David S. Malcolm, *Fordham University*

Joseph G. Marrone, *Siena College*

Bonnie J. Nichols, *Missouri County Community College*

Arthur G. Olguin, *Santa Barbara City College*

Sheila O'Brien Quinn, *Salve Regina University*

Les Parrott, *Seattle Pacific University*

Elisabeth D. Sherwin, *University of Arkansas at Little Rock*

Jane A. Smith, *Concordia University*

Mary A. Waterstreet, *St. Ambrose University*

We owe an enormous debt as well to the colleagues listed next for their thoughtful reviews of the first and second edition manuscripts as they were being developed. Their advice and suggestions for improvement were responsible for many of the good qualities you will find in this book. If you have any criticisms, they probably involve areas our reviewers warned us about!

Patricia Abbot, *D'Youville College*

Gary Altmann, *York University, UK*

Robin A. Anderson, *St. Ambrose University*

Grace Auyang, *University of Cincinnati*

Alan Baxter, *Technical Career Institutes, New York*

Beth Benoit, *University of Massachusetts, Lowell,* and *Middlesex Community College*

Joseph J. Benz, *University of Nebraska at Kearney*

Winfield Brown, *Florence Darlington Technical College*

James F. Calhoun, *University of Georgia*

Yiwei Chen, *Bowling Green State University*

Saundra Ciccarelli, *Gulf Coast Community College*

Samuel Clay, *Heartland Community College*

Anne M. Cooper, *St. Petersburg Junior College*

Nat DeAnda, *Los Madanos College*

John R. Foust, *Parkland College*

Laura Freberg, *California Polytechnic State University, San Luis Obispo*

Grace Galliano, *Kennesaw State University*

Christopher Gilbert, *Bristol Community College*

Craig W. Gruber, *Walt Whitman High School*

Lynn Haller, *Morehead State University*

Wen Harris, *Lane Community College*

Debra Hollister, *Valencia Community College*

Gene Indenbaum, *SUNY Farmingdale*

John S. Klein, *Castleton State College*

Ronald Kleinknecht, *Western Washington University*

Janet L. Kottke, *California State University, San Bernardino*

Joseph A. Mayo, *Gordon College*

David Murphy, *Waubonsee College*

Sheila M. Murphy, *Mount Wachusett Community College*

Steve A. Nida, *Franklin University*

Christine Offutt Lingenfelter, *Lock Haven University*

Randall E. Osborne, *Indiana University East*

Ralph G. Pifer, *Sauk Valley Community College*

James S. Previte, *Victor Valley College*

Wayne J. Robinson, *Monroe Community College*

John L. Romanek, *Jefferson Community College*

Kenneth M. Rosenberg, *State University of New York, Oswego*

Cynthia J. Smith, *Wheeling Jesuit University*

Mitchell Speaks, *Keene State College*

Holly Straub, *University of South Dakota*

Linda K. Swindell, *Anderson University*

Parsram S. Thakur, *Community College of Rhode Island*

Inger Thompson, *Glendale Community College*

M. Lisa Valentino, *Seminole Community College*

Michael J. Wenger, *University of Notre Dame*

Gordon Whitman, *Sandhills Community College*

Jean M. Wynn, *Manchester Community College*

C. Van Youngman, *Art Institute of Philadelphia*

The process of creating *Essentials of Psychology* was greatly facilitated by the work of many dedicated people in the College Division at Houghton Mifflin Company. From the sales representatives and sales managers who reinforced our colleagues' requests for the text, to the marketing staff who worked to tell our colleagues what *Essentials* has to offer, it seems everyone in the division had a hand in shaping this book, and now in revising it into its third edition. Several people in the editorial and production areas at Houghton Mifflin deserve special mention, however, because they did an absolutely outstanding job in helping us develop and revise the *Essentials* manuscript and turn that manuscript into the beautiful book you are now holding. Senior Development Editor Jane Knetzger was involved in the shaping and development of *Essentials* from day one; her advice and suggestions were invariably helpful. For this third edition, our Developmental Editor Rita Lombard did a great job as we worked on the new manuscript and tried to meet the goal of focusing on the essentials of psychology. Thanks for all your help, Rita. And many thanks to Aileen Mason, Senior Produc-

tion Editrix, for once again coordinating the myriad production tasks associated with this project and for keeping them, and us, on schedule. We appreciate it very much. We also want to thank Ann Schroeder, Charlotte Miller, and Jessyca Broekman for their outstanding work in the creation of the photo and art programs of the book. And many thanks, too, to Mary Berry for her flawless copyediting of the final manuscript; Gertrude Wilkins, who proofread the pages; and Chris Arden, who created the combined Glossary/Index. We thank Sarah Ambrose for her work as Production/Design Coordinator. We extend our thanks to Editorial Assistants Caryn Yilmaz and Neil Reynolds for their assistance in managing the print supplements, and to Sarah Tasker; Technology Sponsor, for helping to refine and strengthen our technology offerings for this edition. To Kerry Baruth, Senior Sponsoring Editor; Katherine Greig, Senior Marketing Manager; Jane Potter, Marketing Manager; and Kathleen Mellon, Marketing Assistant, for their unfailing support in this project, we offer our sincere thanks. Without these people, and those who worked with them, the third edition of *Essentials of Psychology* would still be just an idea.

Finally, we want to express our thanks to our friends and our families who helped sustain us as we worked on this new edition. Your love and support mean more to us than we can ever express in words.

Doug Bernstein

Peggy Nash

Introduction to the Science of Psychology

Can you figure out what the following people have in common?

- **Kristen Beyer** works for the Federal Bureau of Investigation, where she develops questionnaires and conducts interviews aimed at identifying common features in the backgrounds of serial killers.

- **David Buss,** a professor at the University of Texas, conducts research and teaches courses on how evolution influences aggression, the choice of sexual partners, and other aspects of people's social behavior.

- **Anne Marie Apanovitch** is employed by a major drug company to study which of the company's marketing strategies are most effective in promoting sales.

- **Michael Moon's** job at a software company is to find new ways to make Internet web sites easier for consumers to use.

- **Marissa Reddy,** co-director of the U.S. Secret Service's Safe Schools Initiative, tries to identify risk factors for violent behavior in high school students.

- **Sharon Lundgren,** founder of Lundgren Trial Consulting, Inc., helps prepare witnesses to testify in court and teaches attorneys how to present their evidence in the most convincing way.

- **Evan Byrne** works at the U.S. National Transportation Safety Board, where he investigates the role of memory lapses, disorientation, errors, and other human factors in causing airplane crashes.

- **Capt. Karen Orts,** chief of mental health services at a U.S. Air Force base, provides psychotherapy to military personnel suffering combat-related stress disorders and teaches leadership courses to commissioned and noncommissioned officers.

Because Captain Orts offers psychotherapy, you probably guessed that she is a psychologist, but the fact is that *all* these people are psychologists! They may not all fit your image of what psychologists do, but as you will see in this chapter, and throughout this book, psychology is much broader and more diverse than you might have expected. We hope that reading this book will give you a fuller picture of psychology, and that you will find our field as fascinating as we do.

This chapter begins our exploration of psychology with a brief look at some of its interrelated specialty areas, or *subfields*. We then tell the story of how psychology came to be, and we review several theories and approaches that guide psychologists in their work. We also point out how the activities of psychologists in virtually every subfield are affected by human diversity, especially by age, gender, ethnicity, and other individual characteristics encountered in today's multicultural societies. Finally, we consider how critical thinking, scientific methods, and ethical standards guide psychologists as they conduct research and evaluate the evidence they collect.

Reading this chapter will help you to answer the following questions:

► **What is psychology, and how did it grow?**

► **Why don't all psychologists explain behavior in the same way?**

► **How does your cultural background influence your behavior?**

► **How can critical thinking save you money?**

► **How do psychologists learn about people?**

► **What does it mean when scientists announce that a research finding is "significant"?**

► **Do psychologists deceive people when they do research?**

The World of Psychology: An Overview

► **What is psychology, and how did it grow?**

Psychology is the science that seeks to understand behavior and mental processes, and to apply that understanding in the service of human welfare. So, although the people we described earlier are engaged in many different kinds of work, what makes them all psychologists is that they are all involved in studying, predicting, improving, or explaining some aspect of behavior and mental processes (Conner, 2001). But even this wide variety of jobs fails to capture the full scope of psychologists' interests. As a group, the world's half-million psychologists are interested in all the behaviors and mental processes that make you who you are, and make other people the way they are in every culture around the world.

Subfields of Psychology

To appreciate how many things come under the umbrella of *behavior and mental processes*, think for a moment about how you would answer the question, Who are you? Would you describe your personality, your 20/20 vision, your interests and goals, your job skills and accomplishments, your IQ, your cultural background, your social skills, or perhaps a physical or psychological problem you have? You could list these and dozens of other things about yourself, and every one of them would reflect some aspect of what psychologists mean by *behavior and mental processes*. When psychologists focus their work on particular aspects of behavior and mental processes, they enter one of psychology's many subfields. Let's take a quick look at the typical interests and activities of psychologists in these subfields now; we will focus on many of them in more detail in later chapters.

psychology The science that seeks to understand behavior and mental processes and to apply that understanding in the service of human welfare.

Source: Botwinick (1961).

figure 1.1

Husband and Father-in-Law

learn by doing This figure is called "Husband and Father-in-Law" (Botwinick, 1961) because you can see it as two different people, depending on how you mentally organize the features of the drawing. The elderly "father-in-law" faces to your right and is turned slightly toward you. He has a large nose, and the dark areas represent a coat pulled up to his chin. However, the tip of his nose can also be seen as the tip of a younger man's chin. The "husband" is in profile, also looking to your right, but away from you. The old man's mouth is the young man's neck band. Both men are wearing broad-brimmed hats. Can you see them? Cognitive psychologists point out that your ability to see two different figures in a drawing that does not physically change—and to choose which one to see at any given moment—means that you actively manipulate incoming information rather than just passively receiving it.

cognitive psychologists　Psychologists whose research focus is analysis of the mental processes underlying judgment, decision making, problem solving, imagining, and other aspects of human thought or cognition.

- **Cognitive psychologists** study basic mental processes such as sensation and perception (see Figure 1.1), learning and memory (including the question of whether people can repress and recover traumatic memories), and judgment, decision-making, and problem solving.

- **Biological psychologists,** also called *physiological psychologists* or *neuroscientists,* study topics such as the roles played by genetics and brain chemistry in causing schizophrenia, how brain cells communicate with each other, whether patterns of brain activity can reveal when a person is lying, and how stress hormones weaken the body's immune system. Biological psychologists have found, for example, that when mental patients "hear voices" or "see things" that are not really there, activity appears in regions of the brain that process information about real sounds and sights (Silbersweig et al., 1995).

- **Personality psychologists** study individuality—the unique features of each person. Your personality traits, like your fingerprints, are different from those of all other people. Some personality psychologists describe how one individual compares with others in terms of openness to experience, emotionality, reliability, agreeableness, and sociability. Others study particular combinations of personality traits that may predict particular patterns of behavior. For instance, personality psychologists interested in *positive psychology* are identifying the characteristics of people who can remain optimistic even in the face of stress or tragedy, and find happiness in life (Lucas, Diener, & Larson, 2003).

- **Developmental psychologists** study and describe changes in behavior and mental processes over the life span, trying to understand their causes and effects (see Figure 1.2). They explore areas such as the development of thought, friendship patterns, parenting styles, and whether everyone must face a midlife crisis. Some of their research has been used by judges and attorneys in deciding how old a child has to be in order to serve as a reliable witness in court, or to responsibly choose which divorcing parent to live with.

- **Quantitative psychologists** develop and use statistical methods to analyze vast amounts of data collected by their colleagues in other subfields. Later in this chapter we examine the correlation coefficient, a statistic these psychologists use to evaluate the *validity* of tests, as well as other mathematical methods they have developed to estimate the relative contributions of heredity and environment in determining our intelligence. Are people born brilliant, or is their brilliance created by their environment? This is one of the hottest topics in psychology today, and quantitative psychologists are right in the middle of it.

- **Clinical, counseling,** and **community psychologists** study the causes of behavior disorders and offer services to help troubled people overcome these disorders. Generally, **clinical psychologists** have a Ph.D. in psychology; most provide therapy services, and many conduct research as well. A **counseling psychologist** might work as a mental health counselor, for example, and have either a Ph.D. or a master's degree in psychology. **Community psychologists** offer psychological services to the homeless and others who need help but tend not to seek it. By working for changes in schools and other social systems, they also try to prevent poverty and other stressful conditions that so often lead to disorder. All of these psychologists differ from *psychiatrists,* who are medical doctors with a specialty in abnormal behavior (psychiatry) and are licensed to prescribe medications.

- **Educational psychologists** conduct research and develop theories about teaching and learning. The results of their work are applied in programs designed to improve teacher training, refine school curricula, reduce dropout rates, and help students learn more efficiently. For example, they have supported the use of the "jigsaw" technique, a type of classroom activity in which children from various ethnic groups must work together to complete a task or solve a problem. These cooperative experiences appear to promote learning, generate mutual respect, and reduce intergroup prejudice (Aronson, Wilson, & Akert, 2002).

- **School psychologists** traditionally specialized in IQ testing, diagnosing learning disabilities and other academic problems, and setting up programs to improve students' achievement and satisfaction in school. Today, however, they are also involved in early

figure 1.2

Where Would You Put a Third Eye?

In a study of how thinking processes develop, children were asked to show where they would place a third eye, if they could have one. Part A shows that nine-year-old children, who were still in an early stage of mental development, drew the extra eye between their existing eyes, "as a spare." Having developed more advanced thinking abilities, eleven-year-olds (Part B) drew the third eye in more creative places, such as the palm of their hand "so I can see around corners" (Shaffer, 1973).

Drawing by a nine-year-old

(A)

Drawing by an eleven-year-old

(B)

Source: Shaffer (1973), Box 4–2.

detection of students' mental health problems, in crisis intervention following school violence, and the like (DeAngelis, 2000).

Social psychologists study the ways that people influence one another. For example, they conduct research on social-influence strategies—such as the effectiveness of safe-sex advertising campaigns designed to halt the spread of AIDS. They also explore how peer pressure affects us, what determines whom we like (or even love), and why and how prejudice forms. They have found, for example, that although we may pride ourselves on not being prejudiced, we may actually hold unconscious beliefs about certain ethnic groups that negatively affect the way we relate to people from those groups (Banaji, Lemm, & Carpenter, 2001).

applying psychology   **APPLYING PSYCHOLOGY TO MATCHMAKING**   Some commercial dating services apply social psychologists' research on interpersonal attraction in an effort to pair up people whose characteristics are most likely to be compatible.

biological psychologists   Psychologists who analyze the biological factors influencing behavior and mental processes.

personality psychologists   Psychologists who focus on people's unique characteristics.

developmental psychologists   Psychologists who seek to understand, describe, and explore how behavior and mental processes change over the course of a lifetime.

quantitative psychologists   Psychologists who develop statistical methods for evaluating and analyzing data from psychological research.

clinical and counseling psychologists   Psychologists who seek to assess, understand, and modify abnormal behavior.

community psychologists   Psychologists who work to obtain psychological services for underserved client groups, and to prevent psychological disorders by working for changes in social systems.

educational psychologists   Psychologists who study methods by which instructors teach and students learn, and who apply their results to improving such methods.

school psychologists   Psychologists who test IQ, diagnose students' academic problems, and set up programs to improve students' achievement.

social psychologists   Psychologists who study how people influence one another's behavior and attitudes, especially in groups.

learn by doing   **UNDERSTANDING THE SCOPE OF PSYCHOLOGY**   Make a list of the questions that you think psychologists might ask about each of these photos. To help you get started, the wedding picture might prompt a psychologist to ask about the physical and personality characteristics that attracted this couple to each other, about how they went about deciding to marry, and about whether their relationship is strong enough to survive. Try to think of at least three more questions for that photo. What might psychologists ask about the picture of ground zero after the September 11 attacks on New York City's World Trade Center? The list you compile will represent just a few of the behaviors and mental processes that psychologists seek to understand. Throughout this book you will see how their research has provided knowledge and insights that are being used every day to promote human welfare.

industrial/organizational psychologists Psychologists who examine factors that influence people's performance in the workplace.

health psychologists   Psychologists who study the effects of behavior on health and the impact of illness on behavior and emotion.

sport psychologists   Psychologists whose research is aimed at maximizing athletic performance.

forensic psychologists   Psychologists who are involved in many aspects of psychology and law.

engineering psychologists   Psychologists who study, and try to improve, the relationships between human beings and the computers and other machines they use.

environmental psychologists   Psychologists who study the relationship between people's physical environment and their behavior.

■ **Industrial/organizational psychologists** study factors that affect the efficiency, productivity, and satisfaction of workers and the organizations that employ them. They conduct research on topics such as increasing the motivation of current employees and helping companies select the best new workers. They also explore the ways in which businesses and industrial organizations work—or fail to work—and they make recommendations for helping them to work better (Spector, 2003). Their role in understanding and improving the "health" of business organizations is likely to grow in light of recent disclosures about the shoddy business practices—and even outright fraud—by executives of some of the largest corporations in the United States.

Our list of psychology's subfields is still not complete. For example, **health psychologists** study the effects of behavior on health and the impact of illness on behavior and emotion; **sport psychologists** search for the keys to maximum athletic performance; and **forensic psychologists** create criminal profiles, assist in jury selection, and are involved in the legal aspects of insanity and psychology. **Engineering psychologists,** also known as *human factors psychologists,* study the relationships of human beings to the computers and other machines they use. Their research has been applied in the design of computer keyboards; Internet web sites; aircraft instrument panels; controls for hospital beds and nuclear power plants; and even on-screen programming systems for TV sets that are more logical, easier to use, and less likely to cause errors. Finally, **environmental psychologists** study the effects of the environment on people's behavior and mental processes. The results of their research are applied by architects and interior designers as they plan or remodel residence halls, shopping malls, auditoriums, hospitals, prisons, offices, and other spaces to make them more

Ψ applying psychology

APPLYING PSYCHOLOGY IN THE HOSPITAL Health psychologists have learned that when patients are mentally prepared for a surgical procedure, they are less stressed by it and recover more rapidly. Their research is now routinely applied in hospitals through programs in which children and adults are given clear information about what to expect before, during, and after their operations.

comfortable and functional for the people who will occupy them. (See Table 1.1 for a summary of the typical activities and work settings of psychologists in the United States.)

Linkages Within Psychology and Beyond

We have listed psychology's subfields as though they were separate, but they often overlap, as do the activities of the psychologists working in them. When developmental psychologists study the growth of children's thinking skills or friendships, for example, their research is linked to that of colleagues in cognitive or social psychology. Similarly, biological psychologists are working partly in clinical psychology when they study the possibility that faulty brain chemistry is a cause of mental disorder. And when social psychologists apply research on persuasion or cooperation to improve anti-smoking campaigns or group activities in the classroom, they are linking up with health psychology or educational psychology. Even when psychologists are not conducting research across subfields, they are likely to draw on, and contribute to, the knowledge developing in other subfields.

Hundreds of linkages among psychology's subfields appear throughout this book, and recognizing them is an important part of understanding psychology as a whole. To help you identify some of these linkages, we have placed a diagram similar to the one in Figure 1.3 near the end of every chapter. Each chapter's diagram contains questions that illustrate three relationships between the topics discussed in that chapter and the topics of other chapters. The page numbers after each question indicate where discussions related to them appear (look for "Linkages" symbols on those pages). There are many more linkages than could be included in the diagrams, so we hope that the diagrams will remind you to look for other linkages that we did not mention. This kind of detective work can actually help you to do better on exams and quizzes, because it may be easier for you to remember material in one chapter by relating it to linked material in other chapters.

Psychology itself is linked to other disciplines. Some of these connections occur because of common interests across disciplines, as when cognitive psychologists work with computer scientists to create computer programs that mimic human thinking. Other links occur when research in one discipline is applied in another. For example, economists are using research by psychologists (one of whom, Daniel Kahneman, recently won a Nobel Prize in economics for his work) to better understand the

WORKING UNDERGROUND Before putting its new data-processing center in the basement of its office building, a large corporation asked an environmental psychologist how employees' performance and morale would be affected by working in a windowless space. He described the possible negative effects and, to combat those effects, recommended the creation of shafts that let in natural light, as well as installation of plants and artwork depicting nature's beauty (Sommer, 1999).

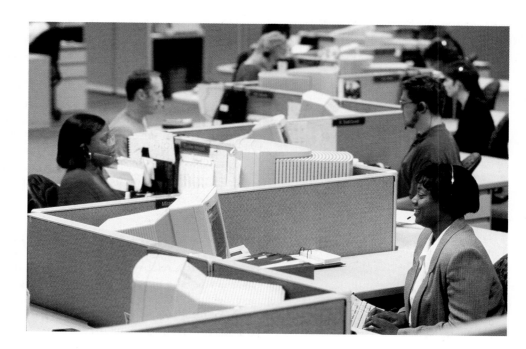

table 1.1 | Typical Activities and Work Settings for Psychologists

The fact that psychologists can work in such a wide variety of settings and do so many interesting—and often well-paying—jobs helps account for the ever-growing popularity of psychology as an undergraduate major (APA, 2000; Murray, 2002; National Center for Education Statistics, 2002; Williams, 2000). Psychology courses also provide excellent background for students planning to enter medicine, law, business, and many other fields.

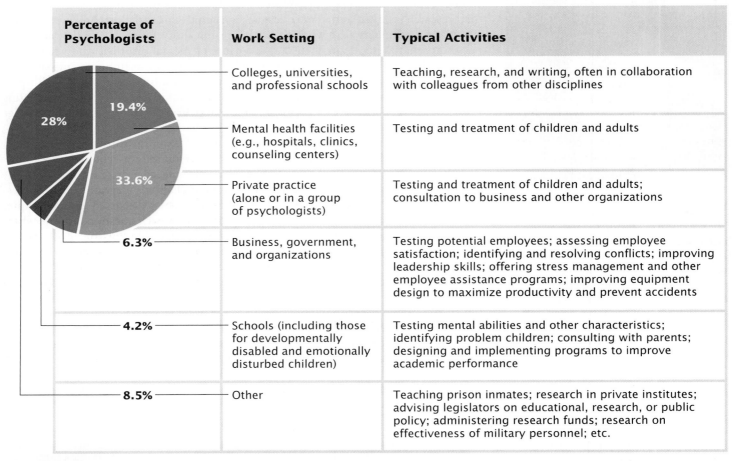

Percentage of Psychologists	Work Setting	Typical Activities
19.4%	Colleges, universities, and professional schools	Teaching, research, and writing, often in collaboration with colleagues from other disciplines
28%	Mental health facilities (e.g., hospitals, clinics, counseling centers)	Testing and treatment of children and adults
33.6%	Private practice (alone or in a group of psychologists)	Testing and treatment of children and adults; consultation to business and other organizations
6.3%	Business, government, and organizations	Testing potential employees; assessing employee satisfaction; identifying and resolving conflicts; improving leadership skills; offering stress management and other employee assistance programs; improving equipment design to maximize productivity and prevent accidents
4.2%	Schools (including those for developmentally disabled and emotionally disturbed children)	Testing mental abilities and other characteristics; identifying problem children; consulting with parents; designing and implementing programs to improve academic performance
8.5%	Other	Teaching prison inmates; research in private institutes; advising legislators on educational, research, or public policy; administering research funds; research on effectiveness of military personnel; etc.

Source: Data from 2001 APA Directory Survey.

thought processes influencing people's decisions about investments and other financial matters. And psychologists' memory research has influenced how lawyers and judges question witnesses and instruct juries. Throughout this book you'll encounter examples of other ways in which psychological theories and research have been applied to fields as diverse as medicine, law, business, engineering, architecture, aviation, public health, and sports.

A Brief History of Psychology

Psychology is a relatively new science, but its origins can be traced through centuries. Since at least the time of Socrates, Plato, and Aristotle in ancient Greece, philosophers have debated such psychological topics as where human knowledge comes from, the nature of mind and soul, the relationship of the mind to the body, and even the possibility of scientifically studying these matters (Wertheimer, 1987).

figure 1.3

Linkages to the Science of Psychology

The questions listed in this diagram highlight just three of the many ways in which research in psychology's subfields can be linked to one another. Three additional linking questions are listed in the Linkages diagram included in every chapter to come. Each diagram lists the page number on which each question is answered, and when you turn to that page, you will find a Linkages symbol in the margin where the answer is discussed. Sometimes the discussion is brief, but every chapter also contains a special Linkages section that examines linked research in more detail. By staying alert to linkages among psychology's subfields, you will come away from this course not only with threads of knowledge about each subfield but also with an appreciation of the fabric of psychology as a whole.

LINKAGES

CHAPTER 1
INTRODUCTION TO THE SCIENCE OF PSYCHOLOGY

Is behavior influenced more by our genes or by our environment?
(ans. on p. 36)

CHAPTER 2
BIOLOGY AND BEHAVIOR

Does psychotherapy work?
(ans. on p. 494)

CHAPTER 13
TREATMENT OF PSYCHOLOGICAL DISORDERS

Is it ethical to deceive people to learn about their social behavior?
(ans. on p. 538)

CHAPTER 14
SOCIAL PSYCHOLOGY

So scientific psychology has its roots in philosophy, and especially in a philosophical view called **empiricism.** To empiricists, knowledge comes through experience and observation, not through speculation. In the 1600s, empiricists such as John Locke, George Berkeley, and David Hume challenged the view—which had been held by philosophers as far back as Plato—that some of our knowledge is present at birth. Empiricists argued that at birth, our minds are actually like a blank slate (*tabula rasa* in Latin) on which experience writes a lifelong story.

By 1859, English naturalist Charles Darwin had published *The Origin of Species.* In this book, Darwin claimed that the forms of life we see today are the result of *evolution,* of changes in life forms that occur over many generations. He said that through *natural selection,* individuals whose behavior and appearance allow them to withstand the ele-

LINKING PSYCHOLOGY AND LAW
Cognitive psychologists' research on the quirks of human memory has led to new guidelines for police and prosecutors (U.S. Department of Justice, 1999). The guidelines note that asking crime witnesses leading questions (e.g., "Do you remember seeing a gun?") can distort their memory, and that innocent people are less likely to be accused if witnesses are told that the real criminal might not be in a lineup or set of "mug shots" (Foxhall, 2000).

empiricism   The view that knowledge comes from experience and observation.

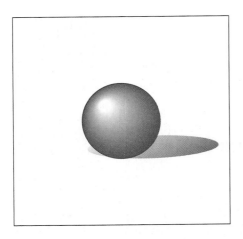

figure 1.4

A Stimulus for Introspection

learn by **doing**   Look at this object and try to describe not what it is, but only the intensity and clarity of the sensations and images (such as redness, brightness, and roundness) that make up your experience of it. If you succeeded, you would have been an excellent participant in Titchener's laboratory.

consciousness   The awareness of external stimuli and our own mental activity.

ments, to avoid predators, and to mate are able to survive and produce offspring with similar characteristics. Those less successful at adjusting, or *adapting,* to changing conditions die out of the species. Notice that Darwin included humans as one of the forms of life that evolved. His revolutionary ideas moved the entire field of biology into the forefront of research. When biological research expanded, psychology as a science was not far behind.

Wundt and the Structuralism of Titchener   The birth date of modern scientific psychology is usually given as 1879. This is the year in which Wilhelm Wundt (pronounced "voont") established the first formal psychology research laboratory, at the University of Leipzig, in Germany. Wundt was a physiologist, and like other physiologists of his day, he studied the abilities and limits of our sensory-perceptual systems. However, Wundt's more ambitious goal was to use the methods of laboratory science to study **consciousness**—the mental experience that arises from these systems. In doing so, Wundt changed psychology from the *philosophy* of mental processes to the *science* of mental processes.

Wundt wanted to describe the basic elements of consciousness, their organization, and their relation to one another (Schultz & Schultz, 2002). In an attempt to study conscious experience, Wundt used the technique of *introspection,* which means "inward looking." Edward Titchener, an American who had been a student of Wundt, later used introspection in his own laboratory at Cornell University to study sensations, feelings, and images associated with conscious experience. To understand introspection, look at the object in Figure 1.4, but try to describe not what it is but only how intensely and clearly you experience its sensations and images (such as redness, brightness, and roundness). This was the difficult task that Wundt and Titchener set for carefully trained "introspectors" in a search for the building blocks of consciousness. The term *structuralism* was used to describe Titchener's efforts to define the structure of consciousness. Wundt and Titchener were not the only scientific researchers in psychology, and their work was not universally accepted. Other scientific psychologists in Europe were studying sensory limits and the capability for learning and memory. They saw the structuralists' work as too simplistic.

Gestalt Psychology   Around 1912, another group of European psychologists led by Max Wertheimer, Kurt Koffka, and Wolfgang Köhler argued against the value of trying to break down human experience or consciousness into its component parts. They were called *Gestalt psychologists* because they pointed out that the whole (or *Gestalt,* in German) of conscious experience is not the same as the sum of its parts. Wertheimer noted, for example, that when two lights are placed near each other in a dark room and go on and off in just the right sequence, we experience not two lights but a single light "jumping" back and forth. This is called the *phi phenomenon,* and you have probably seen it at night in advertising signs that create the impression of a series of lights racing around a display. Similarly, consider how boring it would be to browse slowly through the thousands of still images that are the component parts of movies. Yet when those images are projected onto a screen at just the right speed, they combine to create a rich emotional experience. In other words, said the Gestaltists, consciousness should be studied in its entirety, not piece by piece.

Freud and Psychoanalysis   While Wundt was conducting scientific research on consciousness in Germany in the late 1800s, Sigmund Freud was in Vienna, Austria, exploring the unconscious. Freud, a physician, began to question the assumption that biological factors were behind all behavior and mental processes. Using hypnosis and other methods, Freud suggested that the cause of some people's physical ailments was not physical. The real cause, he said, was deep-seated problems that the patients had pushed out of consciousness (Friedman & Schustak, 2003). He eventually came to believe that all behavior—from everyday slips of the tongue to severe forms of mental disorder—is motivated by *psychological processes,* especially what he called *psychody-*

WILHELM WUNDT (1832–1920) In a classic experiment on the speed of mental processes, Wilhelm Wundt (third from left) first measured how quickly people could respond to a light by releasing a button they had been holding down. He then determined how much longer the response took when they held down one button with each hand and had to decide—based on the color of the light—which one to release. Wundt reasoned that the additional time taken reflected how long it took to perceive the color and decide which hand to move. In the chapter on thought, language, and intelligence, you will see that the logic behind this experiment remains a part of research on cognitive processes today.

namic conflicts within ourselves that occur without our awareness, at an unconscious level. He said that sexual and aggressive instincts, clashing with society's rules, generated many of these hidden conflicts. For nearly fifty years, Freud revised and expanded his ideas into a body of work known as *psychoanalysis*. This theory included his views on personality and mental disorder, as well as a set of treatment methods. Freud's ideas were (and still are) controversial. Even so, he was a groundbreaker whose psychodynamic theories had a significant influence on psychology and many other fields.

William James and Functionalism Psychology took root in North America at about the same time as Wundt was doing his work in Germany. In the late 1870s, William James founded the first psychology laboratory in the United States, at Harvard University. At the University of Toronto, James Mark Baldwin established the first Canadian laboratory in 1889.

James rejected both Wundt's approach and Titchener's structuralism. Influenced by Darwin's theory of evolution, James was more interested in understanding how consciousness *functions* to help people adapt to their environments (James, 1890, 1892). This idea came to be called *functionalism*. It focused on the ongoing "stream" of consciousness, the ever-changing pattern of images, sensations, memories, and other mental events that people experience. James wanted to know how the functions of consciousness could be applied, how they worked for the individual. He asked, for example, why most people remember recent events better than things that happened in the distant past. Other functionalists measured individual differences in learning, memory, and intelligence. They recommended improving educational practices in the schools, even assisting teachers with programs tailored to children with special needs (Nietzel et al., 2003).

John B. Watson and Behaviorism Darwin's theory also led psychologists, especially in North America after 1900, to study animals as well as humans. If all species evolved in adaptive ways, perhaps their behavior and mental processes would follow the same, or similar, laws. Psychologists observed animal behavior in mazes and other

WILLIAM JAMES'S LABORATORY
William James (1842–1910) established this psychology demonstration laboratory at Harvard University in the late 1870s. Like the Gestalt psychologists, James saw the approach used by Wundt and Titchener as a scientific dead end; he said that trying to understand consciousness by studying its components is like trying to understand a house by looking at individual bricks (James, 1884). He preferred to study instead the functions served by consciousness.

experimental situations. From these observations, they drew conclusions about conscious experience, learning, memory, intelligence, and other mental processes in animals and humans.

John B. Watson, a psychology professor at Johns Hopkins University, agreed that observable behavior in animals and humans was the most important source of scientific information for psychology. In 1913, Watson wrote an article called "Psychology as the Behaviorist Views It." In this article, he argued that psychologists should ignore mental events and concern themselves only with observable behavior (Watson, 1913, 1919). His approach, known as *behaviorism*, did not address consciousness, as structuralism and functionalism did, let alone consider the unconscious, as the Freudian view did. Preoccupation with consciousness, said Watson, would prevent psychology from ever being a true science. Watson believed that *learning* is the most important cause of behavior. He was famous for claiming that if he had enough control over the environment, he could create learning experiences that would turn any infant into a doctor, a lawyer, or even a criminal.

The American psychologist B. F. Skinner was another early champion of behaviorism. From the 1930s until his death in 1990, Skinner studied how rewards and punishments shape, maintain, and change behavior through what he termed *operant conditioning*. His *functional analysis of behavior* helped explain, for example, how parents and teachers can unknowingly encourage children's tantrums by rewarding them with attention. In functional analysis, you first discover what rewards or punishers shape the behavior. Then you can change the rewarding or punishing consequences to change the behavior. Watson's and Skinner's vision of psychology as the learning-based science of observable behavior found favor with many psychologists. Behaviorism dominated psychological research in North America from the 1920s through the 1960s. ("In Review: The Development of Psychology" summarizes the schools of thought that have influenced psychologists over the years.)

Psychology Today　By end of the 1960s, however, behaviorists' lack of attention to mental processes was seen by more and more psychologists as a serious limitation (e.g., Ericsson & Simon, 1994). As the computer age dawned, psychologists began to think about mental activity in a new way—as information processing. At the same time,

in review

THE DEVELOPMENT OF PSYCHOLOGY

School of Thought	Founders	Goals	Methods
Structuralism	Edward Titchener, trained by Wilhelm Wundt	To study conscious experience and its structure	Experiments; introspection
Gestalt psychology	Max Wertheimer	To describe organization of mental processes: "The whole is greater than the sum of its parts."	Observation of sensory/ perceptual phenomena
Psychoanalysis	Sigmund Freud	To explain personality and behavior; to develop techniques for treating mental disorders	Study of individual cases
Functionalism	William James	To study how the mind works in allowing an organism to adapt to the environment	Naturalistic observation of animal and human behavior
Behaviorism	John B. Watson; B. F. Skinner	To study only observable behavior and explain behavior via learning principles	Observation of the relation-ship between environmental stimuli and behavioral responses

? *In the history of psychology, _____ was the first school of thought to appear.*

figure 1.5

Visualizing Brain Activity

Magnetic resonance imaging (MRI) techniques allow biological psychologists to study the brain activity accompanying various mental processes. This study found that males (left) and females (right) show different patterns of brain activity (indicated by the brightly colored areas) while reading (Shaywitz et al., 1995).

progress in biotechnology began to offer psychologists new ways to study the biological bases of mental processes. Armed with ever more sophisticated research tools, many psychologists today are trying to do what Watson thought was impossible: to study mental processes and, as shown in Figure 1.5, even watch the brain perform them. So, psychology has come full circle, once again accepting consciousness, in the form of cognitive processes, as a legitimate topic for research (Kimble, 2000).

Approaches to the Science of Psychology

▶ **Why don't all psychologists explain behavior in the same way?**

We have seen that the history of psychology is, in part, the history of the differing ways in which psychologists have thought about, or "approached," behavior and mental processes. Today, psychologists no longer refer to themselves as structuralists or functionalists, but the psychodynamic and behavioral approaches remain, along with some newer ones known as the *biological, evolutionary, cognitive,* and *humanistic approaches.* Some psychologists adopt just one of these approaches, whereas others are *eclectic* (pronounced "ek-LECK-tick"). This means that they blend aspects of two or more approaches in an effort to more fully understand the behavior and mental processes in their subfield (e.g., Cacioppo et al., 2000). Some of these approaches are currently more influential than others, but we will review the main features of all of them so you can more easily understand why different psychologists may explain the same behavior or mental process in different ways.

The Biological Approach

As its name implies, the **biological approach** assumes that behavior and mental processes are largely shaped by biological processes. Psychologists who take this approach study the

THE BIOLOGY OF EMOTION   Robert Levenson, a psychologist at the University of California at Berkeley, takes a biological approach to the study of social interactions. He measures heart rate, muscle tension, and other physical reactions as couples discuss problems in their relationships. He then looks for patterns of physiological activity in each partner, such as overreactions to criticism, that might be related to success or failure in resolving such problems.

biological approach   The view that behavior is the result of physical processes, especially those relating to the brain, to hormones, and to other chemicals.

A FATHER'S LOVE   Mothers are solely responsible for the care and protection of their offspring in 95 percent of mammalian species. If all these species survive without male involvement in parenting, why are some human fathers so active in child rearing? Do evolutionary forces make fathering more adaptive for humans? Is it a matter of learning to care? Is it a combination of both? Psychologists who take an evolutionary approach study these questions and others relating to the origins of human social behavior.

psychological effects of hormones, genes, and the activity of the nervous system, especially the brain. When studying memory, for example, these researchers try to identify changes taking place in the brain as information is stored there. (Figure 6.13, in the chapter on memory, shows an example of these changes.) And when studying thinking, they might look for patterns of brain activity associated with, say, making quick decisions or reading a foreign language. Research discussed in nearly every chapter of this book reflects the enormous influence of the biological approach on psychology today.

The Evolutionary Approach

As mentioned earlier, Darwin's theory of evolution proposed that natural selection operates to promote the survival of the fittest individuals. Most evolutionists today see natural selection operating at the level of genes, but the process is the same. Genes that result in characteristics and behaviors that are adaptive and useful in a certain environment will enable the creatures that inherited them to survive and reproduce, thereby passing those genes on to subsequent generations. According to evolutionary theory, many (but not all) of the genes we possess today are the result of natural selection. This theory forms the foundation of the **evolutionary approach** to psychology, which assumes that the behavior of animals and humans today is largely the result of evolution through natural selection. Evolutionary psychologists see aggression, for example, as a form of territory protection, and they see gender differences in mate selection preferences as reflecting different ways of helping genes to survive in future generations (Buss, 1999; de Waal, 2002; Kurzban & Leary, 2001). You will encounter the evolutionary approach in later chapters in relation to topics such as mental disorders, temperament, interpersonal attraction, and helping.

The Psychodynamic Approach

The **psychodynamic approach** to psychology offers a different slant on the role of inherited characteristics in shaping behavior and mental processes. Rooted in the Freudian theory of psychoanalysis we described earlier, this approach assumes that behavior and mental processes reflect constant, and mostly unconscious, psychodynamic conflicts taking place in every human mind. According to Freud, these conflicts usually take place when our impulses to immediately and selfishly satisfy inherited instincts—such as for food, sex, or aggression—come up against what society has taught us about self-control,

evolutionary approach   A view that emphasizes the inherited, adaptive aspects of behavior and mental processes.

psychodynamic approach   A view developed by Freud emphasizing unconscious mental processes in explaining human thought, feelings, and behavior.

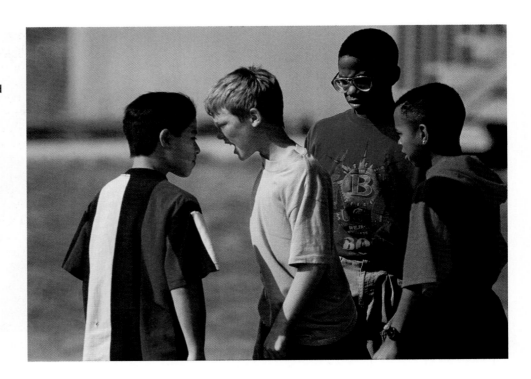

WHY IS HE SO AGGRESSIVE? Psychologists who take a cognitive-behavioral approach suggest that there are several ways in which children learn to be aggressive. They might see others being rewarded for acting aggressively, and then might be rewarded themselves when they do the same. Aggressiveness might also be made more likely if children hear that other people can be dangerous, and that aggression is the only way to deal with threats, disagreements, and other conflict situations (Shahinfar, Kupersmidt, & Matza, 2001).

consideration for others, and playing by the rules. Freud saw anxiety, depression, and other psychological disorders as the outward signs of this inner turmoil.

Freud's original theories are not as influential today as they once were (Robins, Gosling, & Craik, 1999), but in other chapters you will see that modern versions of the psychodynamic approach still appear in various theories of personality, psychological disorders, and psychotherapy.

The Behavioral Approach

The assumptions of the **behavioral approach** to psychology contrast sharply with those of the biological, evolutionary, and psychodynamic approaches. For one thing, the behavioral approach is rooted in the behaviorism of Watson and Skinner. As described earlier, behaviorism focused entirely on observable behavior in humans and animals, and on how it is learned. Accordingly, psychologists who take a behavioral approach concentrate on studying observable behavior. They want to know how life's rewards, punishments, and other learning experiences act on the "raw materials" provided by genes and evolution to shape our behavior into what it is today. So whether they are trying to understand a person's aggressiveness, fear of spiders, parenting methods, or tendency to abuse drugs, behaviorists look mainly at that person's learning history. They also believe that because people's behavior problems are learned, those problems can be changed or even prevented by unlearning old habits and learning new ones.

Recall, though, that behaviorism was criticized precisely because it ignored everything but observable behavior. That criticism has not been lost on the many behaviorists who now apply their learning-based approach in an effort to understand thoughts, or cognitions, as well as observable behavior. Those who take this *cognitive-behavioral,* or *social-cognitive,* approach explore such topics as the ways in which we learn our thoughts, attitudes, and beliefs and, in turn, how these learned cognitive patterns affect observable behavior.

The Cognitive Approach

The growth of the cognitive-behavioral perspective reflects the influence of a broader **cognitive approach** to psychology, which focuses on how behavior is affected by the ways in

behavioral approach A view based on the assumption that human behavior is determined mainly by what a person has learned in life, especially by rewards and punishments.

cognitive approach A view that emphasizes research on how the brain takes in information, creates perceptions, forms and retrieves memories, processes information, and generates integrated patterns of action.

which people take in, mentally represent, process, and store information. Here is an example of how the cognitive approach might help psychologists explain an aggressive incident outside a movie theater: A person in line for tickets (1) *perceived* that someone had cut into the theater line, (2) used information stored in memory to *judge* that this act was inappropriate, (3) *assumed* that the act was due to the other person's rudeness, (4) *considered* several possible responses and their likely consequences, (5) *decided* that punching the other person was the best response, and then (6) *executed* that response. Psychologists who take a cognitive approach focus on these and other mental processes to understand many kinds of individual and social behaviors, from decision making and problem solving to interpersonal attraction and intelligence. In the situation we just described, for example, the person's aggression would be seen as the result of poor problem solving, because there were probably several better ways to deal with the problem of line cutting. The cognitive approach is especially important in a relatively new field called *cognitive science,* in which researchers from psychology, computer science, biology, engineering, linguistics, and philosophy study intelligent systems in humans and computers.

The Humanistic Approach

Mental processes play a different role in the *humanistic approach* to psychology (sometimes known as the *phenomenological approach*). Psychologists who favor the **humanistic approach** see behavior as determined primarily by each person's capacity to choose how to think and act. And they see our choices being guided by our own individual perception of the world, not by instincts, biological processes, or rewards and punishments. If you perceive the world as a friendly place, you are likely to be optimistic and secure. If you perceive it as full of hostile people, you will probably be defensive and anxious, or perhaps unfriendly and aggressive. So humanistic psychologists would agree with their cognitively oriented colleagues that the incident outside that movie theater stemmed from one person's perception that aggression was justified. However, instead of trying to find general laws governing *all* people's thoughts and actions, humanistic psychologists try to understand how each

in review

APPROACHES TO PSYCHOLOGY	
Approach	**Characteristics**
Biological	Emphasizes activity of the nervous system, especially of the brain; the action of hormones and other chemicals; and genetics
Evolutionary	Emphasizes the ways in which behavior and mental processes are adaptive for survival
Psychodynamic	Emphasizes internal conflicts, mostly unconscious, which usually pit sexual or aggressive instincts against environmental obstacles to their expression
Behavioral	Emphasizes learning, especially each person's experience with rewards and punishments
Cognitive	Emphasizes mechanisms through which people receive, store, retrieve, and otherwise process information
Humanistic	Emphasizes individual potential for growth and the role of unique perceptions in guiding behavior and mental processes

humanistic approach A view of behavior as controlled by the decisions that people make about their lives based on their perceptions of the world.

? *Charles Darwin was not a psychologist, but his work influenced the _____ approach to psychology.*

individual's immediate and unique perceptions guide *that* person's thoughts and actions. In fact, many proponents of the humanistic approach say that behavior and mental processes can be fully understood only by appreciating the perceptions and feelings experienced by each individual. Humanistic psychologists also believe that people are essentially good, that they are in control of themselves, and that they seek to grow toward their fullest potential.

In the second half of the twentieth century, the humanistic approach to psychology in North America was promoted mainly by Carl Rogers and Abraham Maslow. As you will see in later chapters, their views have had a significant influence on the way some psychologists think about the development of personality, about how to conduct psychotherapy, and about why people are motivated to behave as they do. Overall, however, the humanistic approach to psychology is less influential today than the biological, cognitive, behavioral, and evolutionary approaches, mainly because many psychologists find humanistic concepts and predictions too vague to be expressed and tested scientifically. (All the approaches we have described are summarized in "In Review: Approaches to Psychology.")

Human Diversity and Psychology

► **How does your cultural background influence your behavior?**

The diversity we have seen in various approaches to psychology is matched by the diversity of psychologists' own backgrounds. As in other academic disciplines in the early twentieth century, most psychologists were white, middle-class men (Walker, 1991). Almost from the beginning, however, women and people of color were also part of the field (Schultz & Schultz, 2002). Throughout this book you will find the work of their modern counterparts, whose contributions to research, service, and teaching have all increased in tandem with their growing representation in psychology. In the United States, women now constitute about 46.1 percent of all psychologists holding doctoral degrees (National Science Foundation, 2001). Women are also earning 75 percent of the new master's degrees and 66.7 percent of the new doctoral degrees awarded in psychology each year (National Science Foundation, 2002). Moreover, about 17 percent of new doctoral degrees in psychology are being earned by members of ethnic minority groups (National Science Foundation, 2000). These num-

MARY WHITON CALKINS (1863–1930)
Mary Whiton Calkins studied psychology at Harvard University, where William James described her as "brilliant." Because she was a woman, though, Harvard refused to grant her a doctoral degree. They offered her the degree through Radcliffe, an affiliated school, but she refused it. She went on to do research on memory, and in 1905 she became the first woman president of the American Psychological Association (APA). Margaret Washburn (1871–1939) encountered similar sex discrimination at Columbia University, so she transferred to Cornell University, became the first woman to earn a doctorate in psychology, and in 1921 became the second woman president of the APA.

GILBERT HAVEN JONES (1883–1966)
When Gilbert Haven Jones graduated from the University of Jena in Germany in 1909, he became one of the first African Americans to earn a doctorate in psychology. Many others were to follow, including J. Henry Alston, who was the first African American to publish research in a major U.S. psychology journal (Alston, 1920).

table 1.2

Some Characteristics of Behavior and Mental Processes Typical of Individualist Versus Collectivist Cultures

Psychologists and anthropologists have noticed that cultures can create certain general tendencies in behavior and mental processes among the people living in them (Bhagat et al., 2002). As shown here, individualist cultures tend to support the idea of placing one's personal goals before the goals of the extended family or work group, whereas collectivist cultures tend to encourage putting the goals of those groups ahead of personal goals. Remember, however, that these labels represent very rough categories. Cultures cannot be pigeonholed as being either entirely individualist or entirely collectivist, and not everyone raised in a particular culture always thinks or acts in exactly the same way (Oyserman, Coon, & Kemmelmeier, 2002).

Variable	Individualist	Collectivist
Personal identity	Separate from others	Connected to others
Major goals	Self-defined; be unique; realize your personal potential; compete with others	Defined by others; belong; occupy your proper place; meet your obligations to others; be like others
Criteria for self-esteem	Ability to express unique aspects of the self; ability to be self-assured	Ability to restrain the self and be part of a social unit; ability to be self-effacing
Sources of success and failure	Success comes from personal effort; failure, from external factors	Success is due to help from others; failure is due to personal faults
Major frame of reference	Personal attitudes, traits, and goals	Family, work group

bers reflect continuing efforts by psychological organizations and governmental bodies, especially in the United States and Canada, to promote the recruitment, graduation, and employment of women and ethnic minorities in psychology.

The Impact of Sociocultural Diversity on Psychology

As diversity among psychologists has increased, so too has their interest in the diversity of people in general. This change is significant, because psychologists once presumed that all humans were essentially alike and that whatever principles emerged from research with one group would apply to people everywhere. They were partly right, because people around the world are alike in many ways. They tend to live in groups; have religious beliefs; and create rules, music, dances, and games. The principles of nerve cell activity or reactions to heat or a sour taste are the same in men and women everywhere, as is their recognition of a smile. This is not true of all characteristics, however. Research has shown that people's striving for achievement, their moral values, their styles of communicating, and many other aspects of behavior and mental processes are shaped by a variety of **sociocultural variables,** including gender, ethnicity, social class, and the culture in which they grow up (Miller, 2002).

Culture has been defined as the sum total of the values, rules of behavior, forms of expression, religious beliefs, occupational choices, and the like for a group of people who share a common language and environment (Fiske et al., 1998). Culture is an organizing and stabilizing influence. It encourages or discourages particular behaviors and ways of thinking; it also allows people to understand others in that culture, and to know what to expect from them. It is a kind of group adaptation, passed on by tradition and example rather than by genes from one generation to the next. Culture determines, for example, whether children's education will focus on skill at hunting or reading, how close people stand when they talk to each other, and whether or not they form lines in public places (Munroe & Munroe, 1994).

Cultures can differ in many ways (Abi-Hashem, 2000; Triandis, 1998). They may have strict or loose rules governing social behavior. They might place great value on achievement or on self-awareness. Some seek dominance over nature; others seek harmony with it. Time is of great importance in some cultures, but not in others. Psychologists have tended to focus above all on the differences between cultures that can best be described as individualist or collectivist (Smith & Bond, 1999; see Table 1.2). In *individualist* cultures, such as those typical of North America and Western Europe, people tend to focus on and value personal rather than

sociocultural variables Social identity and other background factors, such as gender, ethnicity, social class, and culture.

culture The accumulation of values, rules of behavior, forms of expression, religious beliefs, and occupational choices for a group of people who share a common language and environment.

THE IMPACT OF CULTURE   Culture helps shape virtually every aspect of our behavior and mental processes, from how we dress to how we think to what we think is important. Because most people grow up immersed in a particular culture, they may not notice its influence on their thoughts and actions until—like these young women who immigrated from Africa to Denmark—they encounter people whose culture has shaped them in different ways (Nisbett & Masuda, 2003).

group goals and achievement. Competitiveness to distinguish oneself from others is common, as is a sense of isolation. By contrast, in *collectivist* cultures like those found in Japan and other parts of Asia, people more often tend to think of themselves as part of family or work groups. Cooperative effort aimed at advancing the welfare of those groups is highly valued. And although loneliness is rarely a problem, fear of rejection by the group is common. Though we seldom think about it, many aspects of mainstream U.S. culture—from self-reliant cowboy heroes and bonuses for "top" employees to the invitation to "help yourself" at a buffet table—reflect its tendency toward an individualist orientation (see Table 1.3).

We often associate cultures with particular countries, but in reality, most countries are *multicultural*. In other words, they host many cultural groups within their borders. For instance, the United States encompasses African Americans, Hispanic Americans, Asian Americans, and American Indians, as well as European Americans with Italian, German, English, Polish, Irish, and other origins. In each of these groups, the individuals who

table 1.3

Cultural Values in Advertising

learn **by doing**   The statements listed here appeared in advertisements in Korea and the United States. Those from Korea reflect collectivist values, whereas those from the United States emphasize a more individualist orientation (Han & Shavitt, 1994). See if you can tell which are which; then check the bottom of the next page for the answers. You might want to follow up on this exercise by identifying the cultural values appearing in the ads you see in newspapers and magazines, and on billboards and television. By surfing the Web or scanning international newspapers, you can compare the values conveyed by ads in your culture with those in ads from other cultures.

1. "She's got a style all her own."
2. "You, only better."
3. "A more exhilarating way to provide for your family."
4. "We have a way of bringing people closer together."
5. "Celebrating a half-century of partnership."
6. "How to protect the most personal part of the environment: Your skin."
7. "Our family agrees with this selection of home furnishings."
8. "A leader among leaders."
9. "Make your way through the crowd."
10. "Your business success: Harmonizing with (company name)."

Source: Brehm, Kassin, & Fein (1999).

identify with their cultural heritage tend to share behaviors, values, and beliefs based on their culture of origin. In other words, they form a *subculture*.

Most of us don't realize how strongly our culture or subculture has shaped our thoughts and actions until we come in contact with people whose culture or subculture has shaped them differently. For example, an American teaching in Korea learned that some people there believe it is in poor taste to write a student's name in red ink (Stevens, 1999). Doing so, he discovered, conveys a prediction or wish that the person will die, because red ink was traditionally used to record names in official death registers. Similarly, the "thumbs-up" sign means that "everything is OK" to people in North America and Europe, but it is considered a rude gesture in Australia. Even some of the misunderstandings between people in the same culture are traceable to subtle, culturally influenced differences in communication (Tannen, 1994). In the United States, for instance, women's efforts to connect with others by talking may be perceived by many men as "pointless" unless the discussion is geared to solving a particular problem. As a result, women often feel frustrated and misunderstood by men, who tend to offer well-meant, but unwanted, advice instead of conversation.

For decades, the impact of culture on behavior and mental processes was of concern mainly to a relatively small group of researchers working in *cross-cultural* psychology (Miller, 2002). As you will see in the chapters to come, however, psychologists in almost every subfield are now looking at how ethnicity, gender, age, and many other sociocultural variables can influence the behavior and mental processes of the people they serve and the people they study. In short, psychology is striving to be the science of *all* behavior and mental processes, not just of those in the cultures where it began.

Thinking Critically About Psychology (or Anything Else)

▶ **How can critical thinking save you money?**

In order to appreciate the effects of sociocultural variables on behavior and mental processes, psychologists had to engage in some nontraditional thinking. For one thing, they had to question the assumption that studying people of just one gender, age range, ethnic group, or culture can tell us about people in general. This kind of "thinking outside the box" can lead to new insights, but it takes effort, and it sometimes upsets those who hold more traditional views. No wonder, then, that some people prefer to simply accept what they are told, especially when it comes from a believable source (see Table 1.4). Some advertisers, politicians, TV evangelists, and social activists hope for this kind of easy acceptance when they go after your money, vote, or loyalty. They want you to believe their promises or claims without careful thought. In other words, they don't want you to think critically.

Critical thinking is the process of assessing claims and making judgments on the basis of well-supported evidence (Wade, 1988). Let's consider some of the questions that arise from thinking critically about psychology (or anything else), and then review the scientific research methods that psychologists use to try to answer those questions.

Five Questions for Critical Thinking

Francine Shapiro, a clinical psychologist in northern California, had an odd experience while taking a walk one day in 1987. She had been thinking about some distressing events when she noticed that her emotional reaction to them was fading away. As she tried to figure out why this had happened, she realized she had been moving her eyes from side to side. Had the eye movements caused the emotion-reducing effect? When she made these same eye movements more deliberately, the effect was even stronger. Was this a fluke, or would the same thing happen to others? To find out, she tested the eye movement effect in friends and colleagues, and then with clients who had suffered childhood sexual abuse, military combat,

critical thinking The process of assessing claims and making judgments on the basis of well-supported evidence.

Answer key for Table 1.3: U.S. ads are numbers 1, 2, 6, 8, and 9.

table 1.4 Some Popular Myths

Ask several friends and relatives what they think about the statements listed in the left-hand column of this table. Most people you ask will probably agree with at least one of them, even though all of them are false. Perhaps you already knew that, but don't feel too smug. At one time or another, we all accept something we are told simply because the information seems to come from a reliable source or because "everyone knows" it is true (Losh et al., 2003).

Myth	Fact
Many children are injured each year in the United States when razor blades, needles, or poison is put in Halloween candy.	Reported cases are rare, most turn out to be hoaxes, and in the only documented case of a child dying from poisoned candy, the culprit was the child's own parent (Brunvald, 1989).
If your roommate commits suicide during the school term, you automatically get A's in all your classes for that term.	No college or university anywhere has ever had such a rule.
People have been known to burst into flames and die from fire erupting within their own bodies.	In rare cases, humans have been consumed by fires that caused little or no damage to the surrounding area. However, this phenomenon has been duplicated in a laboratory, and each alleged case of "spontaneous human combustion" has been traced to an external source of ignition (Benecke, 1999; Nienhuys, 2001).
Most big-city police departments rely on the advice of psychics to help them solve murders, kidnappings, and missing persons cases.	Only about 35% of urban police departments ever seek psychics' advice, and that advice is virtually never more helpful than other means of investigation (Nickell, 1997; Wiseman, West, & Stemman, 1996).
Murders, suicides, animal bites, and episodes of mental disorder are more likely to occur when the moon is full.	Records of crimes, dog bites, and mental hospital admissions do not support this common belief (Bickis, Kelly, & Byrnes, 1995; Chapman & Morrell, 2000; Rotton & Kelly, 1985).
You can't fool a lie detector.	Lie detectors can be helpful in solving crimes, but they are not perfect; their results can free a guilty person or send an innocent person to jail (see the chapter on motivation and emotion).
Viewers never see David Letterman walking to his desk after the opening monologue because his contract prohibits him from showing his backside on TV.	When questioned about this story on the air, Letterman denied it and, to prove his point, lifted his jacket and turned a full circle in front of the cameras and studio audience (Brunvald, 1989).
Psychics have special abilities to see into the future.	Even the most famous psychics are almost always wrong, as in these predictions for the year 2002: "Satan will be discovered working in a homeless shelter, reading to the blind and delivering Meals on Wheels," "The Super Bowl will be cancelled after the first half because team owners will refuse to cough up an extra $10,000 for each player," and "A time tunnel will be created to allow people to make a one-way trip back into time." No psychic's 2001 predictions included the September 11 terrorist attacks on New York and Washington. When psychics do appear to be correct it is usually because their forecasts are either vague ("Hilary Clinton will be much in the headlines with a scandal.") or easy to predict without special powers ("Prince Charles and Camilla Parker-Bowles will marry") (Emery, 2002).

rape, or other traumas. She asked the clients to recall these traumas while keeping their eyes focused on her finger as she moved it back and forth in front of their faces. Like her, they said that their emotional reactions to the memories faded. They also reported that trauma-related problems such as nightmares, fears, and emotional flashbacks decreased dramatically, often after only one session (Shapiro, 1989b). Shapiro called her new treatment *eye movement desensitization and reprocessing*, or *EMDR* (Shapiro, 1991, 2001). Today, Shapiro and 30,000 other therapists in 52 countries are using EMDR to treat an ever-widening range of anxiety-related problems in children and adults, from phobias and posttraumatic stress disorder to marital conflicts and skin rashes (Gupta & Gupta, 2002; Protinski, Sparks, & Flemke, 2001; Shapiro & Maxfield, 2002).

Would the phenomenal growth of EMDR be enough to convince you to spend your own money on it? If not, what would you want to know about EMDR before deciding? As a cautious person, you would probably ask some of the same questions that have occurred to many scientists in psychology: Are the effects of EMDR caused by the treatment itself, or by the faith that clients might have in any new and impressive treatment? And are EMDR's effects faster, stronger, and longer lasting than those of other treatments?

Questioning what we are told is an important part of a more general critical thinking process that can help us make informed decisions, not only about psychotherapy options but also about many other things—such as which pain reliever or Internet service to choose, which college to attend, what apartment to rent, which candidate to vote for, and whether we believe that cell phones can cause cancer or that shark cartilage can cure it. One way of applying critical thinking to EMDR or any other topic is to ask the following five questions:

▨ What am I being asked to believe or accept?

In this case, you are asked to believe that EMDR reduces or eliminates anxiety-related problems.

▨ Is there evidence available to support the claim?

Shapiro began her EMDR research on herself. When she found the same effects in others, coincidence became an unlikely explanation for the observed changes.

▨ Can that evidence be interpreted another way?

The dramatic effects that Shapiro's friends and clients experienced might have been due to their motivation to change or their desire to please her, not to EMDR. And who knows? They might have eventually improved on their own, without any treatment. In other words, even the most remarkable evidence cannot be accepted as confirming an assertion until all reasonable alternative explanations have been ruled out. Doing that leads to the next step in critical thinking: conducting scientific research.

▨ What evidence would help to evaluate the alternatives?

The ideal method for testing the value of EMDR would be to identify three groups of people who are identical in every way except for the anxiety treatment they receive. One group receives EMDR. The second group gets an equally motivating but useless treatment. The third group gets no treatment at all. If the EMDR group improves much more than the other two, then it is less likely that the changes following EMDR can be explained entirely by client motivation or the mere passage of time.

Uncritically accepting claims for the value of astrologers' predictions, "get-rich-quick" investments, unproven therapies, or proposed government policies can be embarrassing, expensive, and sometimes dangerous. Critical thinkers carefully evaluate evidence *for* and *against* such claims before reaching a conclusion about them.

DOONESBURY

TAKING YOUR LIFE IN YOUR HANDS?
Does exposure to microwave radiation from cell phone antennas cause brain tumors? Do the dangers outweigh the benefits of hormone replacement therapy (HRT) for postmenopausal women? And what about the value of herbal remedies, dietary supplements, and other controversial treatments for cancer, AIDS, and depression? These questions generate intense speculation, strong opinions, and a lot of wishful thinking, but the answers ultimately depend on scientific research based on critical thinking. So, even though there is no conclusive evidence that cell phones cause tumors, scientists continue to monitor the effects of long-term or heavy exposure (e.g., Carlo & Thibodeau, 2001; Inskip et al., 2001). Recent evidence that HRT may be related to breast cancer and heart disease has led to the cancellation of a large clinical trial in the United States (Kolata, 2003), and scientists are calling for new research on the safety of the testosterone replacement therapy that about 250,000 U.S. men receive each year (Groopman, 2002; Kolata, 2002).

■ What conclusions are most reasonable?

The evidence available so far has not yet ruled out alternative explanations for the effects of EMDR (e.g., Goldstein et al., 2000). And although those effects are often greater than no treatment at all, they appear to be no stronger than those of several other kinds of treatment (Davidson & Parker, 2001; Ironson et al., 2002; Taylor et al., 2003). Accordingly, the only reasonable conclusions to be drawn at this point are that (1) EMDR remains a controversial treatment, (2) it seems to have an impact on some clients, and (3) further research is needed in order to understand it (Herbert et al., 2000).

Does that sound wishy-washy? Critical thinking sometimes does seem to be indecisive thinking, but that's because scientific conclusions must be guided by the evidence available. In the long run, though, critical thinking also opens the way to understanding. (To help you sharpen your critical thinking skills, we have included in every chapter to come a feature in which our five critical thinking questions are applied to a particularly interesting topic in psychology.) Let's now consider how psychologists translate critical thinking into scientific research.

Critical Thinking and Scientific Research

Scientific research often begins with curious questions, such as, Can eye movements reduce anxiety? Like many seemingly simple questions, however, this one is actually rather complex. Are we talking about horizontal, vertical, or diagonal eye movements? How long do they continue? How many treatment sessions should there be? Are we referring to mild or severe anxiety, and how will we measure improvement? In other words, a scientist must ask *specific* questions in order to get meaningful answers.

Psychologists and other scientists clarify their questions about behavior and mental processes by phrasing them in terms of a **hypothesis**—a specific, testable statement or proposition about something they want to study. In the case of EMDR, the hypothesis might be as follows: *EMDR treatment causes a significant reduction in anxiety*. To make it easier to understand and objectively evaluate hypotheses, scientists employ **operational definitions,** which are statements describing the exact operations or methods they will use in their research. In the hypothesis we just proposed, "EMDR treatment" might be operationally defined as a certain number of back-and-forth eye movements per second for a particular period of time, whereas "significant reduction in anxiety" might be operationally defined as a decline of at least ten points on a test that measures anxiety. The kind of treatment a client is given (say, EMDR versus no treatment) and the results of that treatment (how much anxiety reduction occurred) are examples of research **variables,** the specific factors or characteristics that are altered and measured in research.

In addition to collecting evidence, scientists must also check on how good it is. Usually, the quality of evidence is evaluated in terms of two characteristics: reliability and validity. **Reliability** is the consistency of the evidence that is obtained. **Validity** is the degree to which the evidence accurately represents the topic being studied. For example, if Shapiro had not been able to repeat, or *replicate*, the eye movement effects with others, or if only a few clients had shown improvement, she would question the reliability of her evidence. If the clients' reports of improvement were not checked for accuracy through, say, supporting reports from family members, she would doubt their validity.

The Role of Theories After gathering a significant amount of research evidence, scientists may organize their explanations into a theory. A **theory** is an integrated set of statements designed to explain certain phenomena. For example, Shapiro's theory about EMDR suggests that eye movements activate parts of the brain where traumatic or unpleasant information has been stored but never fully processed (Shapiro, 2001; Stickgold, 2002). Theories are tentative explanations that must be subjected to scientific evaluation based on critical thinking and research findings. For example, Shapiro's theory about EMDR has been criticized as vague, lacking in supportive evidence, and having less plausibility than alternative explanations (e.g., Herbert et al., 2000). In other words, theories are based on research results, but they also generate questions to be asked in further research. Many psychologists will test predictions from a single theory. That theory will be revised or even abandoned if research does not support it.

The constant formulating, evaluating, reformulating, and abandoning of theories has generated many competing explanations of behavior and mental processes. As a result, we cannot offer as many definite conclusions about psychology as you might want. The conclusions we do draw about many of the phenomena described in this book are always based on what is known so far, and we always cite the need for additional research. This is because research often raises at least as many questions as it answers. For example, research on an herbal remedy for mild depression might show that it is effective, but would it work as well in cases of severe depression? Keep this point in mind the next time you hear self-proclaimed experts—called "pop" (for *popular*) psychologists by the scientific community—giving easy answers and simple formulas for complex problems. They tend to oversimplify issues, cite evidence for their views without concern for its reliability or validity, and ignore good evidence that contradicts the pet theories that they live on. Psychological scientists must be more cautious, often delaying final judgments about behavior and mental processes until they have collected better data. Still, psychological research has created an enormous body of knowledge that is being put to good use in many ways. And today's knowledge forms the foundation for future research that will further increase understanding. Let's look now at the scientific methods that psychologists use in their research and at some of the pitfalls that lie in their path.

Research Methods in Psychology

► **How do psychologists learn about people?**

Like other scientists, psychologists try to achieve four main goals in their research: to *describe* a phenomenon, to *make predictions* about it, and to introduce enough *control* in their research to allow them to *explain* the phenomenon with some degree of confidence. Four research methods have proven especially useful for gathering the evidence needed to reach each of these goals. They include *naturalistic observation, case studies, surveys,* and *experiments*.

Naturalistic Observation: Watching Behavior

The process of watching and recording a phenomenon as it naturally occurs, without interfering with it, is called **naturalistic observation** (Hoyle, Harris, & Judd, 2002). This method gathers descriptive data in situations where other techniques might be disruptive. For example, much of what we know about gender differences in how children play and communicate with one another has come from psychologists' observations in classrooms and playgrounds. Observations of adults, too, have suggested that childhood gender differences might underlie some of the conflict and miscommunication seen in marriages and other male-female intimate relationships.

Naturalistic observation can provide a lot of good information, but it is not without its problems (Nietzel et al., 2003). For one thing, people tend to act differently when they know they are being observed (and research ethics usually requires that they do know). To combat this problem, researchers typically observe people long enough for them to get used to the situation and begin behaving more naturally. Still, observations can be incomplete or misleading if the observers are not well trained or if they report what they expect to see rather than what actually occurs. Further, even the best observational methods do not allow researchers to draw conclusions about what is causing the behavior being observed.

Case Studies: Taking a Closer Look

Case studies intensively examine some event or phenomenon in a particular individual, group, or situation. Often, case studies combine observations; tests; interviews; and analysis of letters, school transcripts, or other written records. Case studies are especially

---

hypothesis   In scientific research, a specific, testable proposition about a phenomenon.

operational definitions   Statements that define phenomena or variables by describing the exact research operations or methods used in measuring or manipulating them.

variables   Specific factors or characteristics that can take on different numerical values in research.

reliability   The degree to which test results or other research evidence occurs repeatedly.

validity   The degree to which evidence from a test or other research method measures what it is supposed to measure.

theory   An integrated set of propositions used to explain certain phenomena, including behavior and mental processes.

naturalistic observation   The process of watching without interfering as a phenomenon occurs in the natural environment.

case studies   Research involving the intensive examination of some phenomenon in a particular individual, group, or situation.

learn **by doing**   **NATURALISTIC OBSERVATION**   Observing people in natural settings can provide important clues to understanding social interaction and other aspects of behavior and mental processes. It is harder than it looks. Imagine you are studying these children at play, and make a list of the *exact* behaviors you would count as "aggressive," "cooperative," and "competitive."

useful when a phenomenon is new, complex, or rare (Sacks, 2002). They have a long tradition in clinical psychology and psychiatry. Freud's development of psychoanalysis, for example, was based on case studies of people whose paralysis or other physical symptoms disappeared when they were hypnotized or asleep.

Case studies have played a special role in neuropsychology, which focuses on the relationships among brain activity, thinking, and behavior. Consider the case of Dr. P., a patient described by neurologist Oliver Sacks (1985). Dr. P. was a distinguished musician who began to show odd symptoms. He could not recognize familiar people or distinguish between people and things. For instance, while he and his wife were at the neurologist's office, Dr. P. mistook his foot for his shoe. When he rose to leave, he tried to lift off his wife's head as if it were a hat and put it on his own head. He could not name common objects, but he could describe them. When handed a glove, for example, he said, "A continuous surface, infolded on itself. It appears to have . . . five outpouchings, if this is the word . . . a container of some sort." Only later, when he put it on his hand, did he exclaim, "My God, it's a glove!" (Sacks, 1985, p. 13). Using case studies like this one, pioneers in neuropsychology noted the symptoms suffered by people with particular kinds of brain damage or disease (Banich, 2003). Eventually, neuropsychologists were able to tie specific disorders to certain types of injuries, poisons, and other causes. In Dr. P.'s case, it was probably a large brain tumor that caused his symptoms.

Case studies do have some limitations. They may not represent people in general, and they may contain only the evidence a particular researcher considered important, thus possibly reflecting the researcher's biases rather than the actual facts (Loftus & Guyer, 2002). Nonetheless, when conducted and used with care, case studies can provide valuable raw material for further research and can serve as the testing ground for new treatments, training programs, and other applications of research (Tavris, 2004).

Surveys: Looking at the Big Picture

surveys   Research that involves giving people questionnaires or interviews designed to describe their attitudes, beliefs, opinions, and intentions.

Whereas case studies give a close-up view of an individual, **surveys** give broad portraits of large groups. A survey uses interviews or questionnaires to ask people about

LEARNING FROM RARE CASES
Dustin Hoffman's character in the movie *Rain Man* was based on the case of "Joseph," an autistic man who can, for example, mentally multiply or divide six-digit numbers. Other case studies have described autistic savants who can correctly identify the day of the week for any date in the past or the future, or tell at a glance that, say, exactly 125 paper clips are scattered on the floor. By carefully studying such rare cases, cognitive psychologists are learning more about human mental capacities and how they might be maximized in everyone.

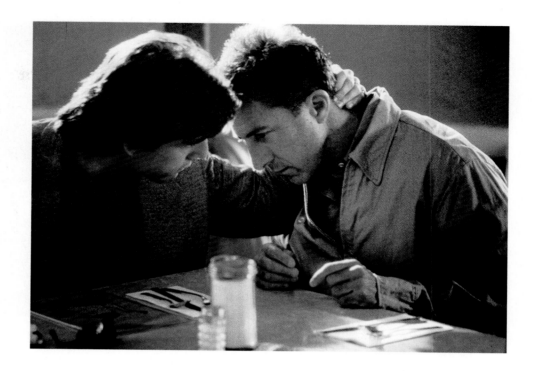

their behavior, attitudes, beliefs, opinions, or intentions. Just as politicians and advertisers rely on opinion polls to test the popularity of policies or products, psychologists use surveys to gather descriptive data on just about any behavior or mental process, from parenting practices to sexual behavior. However, the validity of survey data depends partly on the way the survey questions are asked (Visser, Krosnick, & Lavrakas, 2000). In one survey study at a health clinic, patients were asked how frequently they experienced headaches, stomachaches, and other symptoms of illness (Schwarz & Scheuring, 1992). If the question was worded in a way that suggested most people frequently experience such symptoms, the patients indicated that they frequently experienced them, too. But if the wording suggested that most people rarely experience these symptoms, the patients said they experienced the symptoms infrequently. For example, 75 percent of the patients said that the weather affected their health when the wording suggested this was a common phenomenon, but only 21 percent said so if the wording suggested that this was an uncommon phenomenon. Were the people in the first group actually sicker than the people in the second? Probably not. It is more likely that they reported more symptoms because of the way the question was worded.

A survey's validity also depends on who is surveyed. If the particular people surveyed do not represent the views of the entire population you are interested in, it is easy to be misled by survey results. For example, if you were interested in Americans' views on the prevalence of racial and ethnic prejudice, you would come to the wrong conclusion if you surveyed only African Americans or only European Americans. To get a complete picture, you would have to survey people from all ethnic groups so that each group's opinions could be fairly represented.

Other limitations of the survey method are more difficult to avoid. For example, the American Society for Microbiology (ASM) found that 95 percent of the 1,021 U.S. adults it surveyed said that they wash their hands after using toilet facilities. However, naturalistic observations of 7,836 people in public restrooms across the United States revealed that the figure is closer to 67 percent (ASM, 2000). In other words, people may be reluctant to admit undesirable or embarrassing things about themselves, or they may say what they believe they *should* say about an issue. And sometimes, those who respond to a survey hold views that differ from those who do

learn by doing **DESIGNING SURVEY RESEARCH** There is considerable controversy about whether gay men and lesbians should be allowed to serve openly in the U.S. military and about how best to keep terrorists from slipping through security screenings. To appreciate the difficulty of conducting survey research on such topics, try phrasing a question about each of these issues in a way that you think is clear enough and neutral enough to generate valid data. Show your work to some friends. Do they agree that your questions would be good ones?

not respond (Visser et al., 2000). Survey results—and the conclusions drawn from them—will be distorted to the extent that these tendencies distort people's responses and researchers' access to responses (Hoyle et al., 2002). Still, surveys provide an efficient way to gather large amounts of data about people's attitudes, beliefs, or other characteristics.

Experiments: Exploring Cause and Effect

Naturalistic observation, case studies, and surveys are valuable for describing and making predictions about behavior and mental processes, but they cannot offer explanations for the results. For example, observations that children who watch a lot of violence on television tend to be more aggressive than other children led to the hypothesis that exposure to TV violence can cause aggressiveness (see the chapter on learning). Does violent television actually cause the problems with which it is associated? It might, but the most obvious explanations of what is causing what in observational, case study, and survey results may not always be the correct ones. To make the best choice among alternative explanations and to determine what causes the phenomena they observe, psychological scientists must take control over certain factors, or variables, in their research. Controlled research usually takes the form of an experiment.

In an **experiment,** the researcher makes a change in one variable and then observes the effect of that change on another variable, while holding all the other variables constant. The variable that is changed, or manipulated, by the experimenter is called the **independent variable.** The variable that is measured following this manipulation is called the **dependent variable,** because it *depends* on the independent variable. So in an experiment on the effects of TV violence, the independent variable might be the amount of violence that different groups of children are allowed to watch: a lot, a little, or none at all. The **experimental group** is the group that is exposed to an experience of interest to the experimenter (a lot of violent TV, for example). A group that receives no such exposure, or a differing amount of exposure, is called the **control group.** Control groups provide baselines against which to compare the performance of the experimental group. If everything about the groups is exactly the same except for exposure to some experience, then any differences between groups at the end of the experiment should be due to that experience.

experiment A situation in which the researcher manipulates one variable and observes the effect of that manipulation on another variable, while holding all other variables constant.

independent variable In an experiment, the variable manipulated by the researcher.

dependent variable In an experiment, the factor affected by the independent variable.

experimental group The group that receives the experimental treatment.

control group The group that receives no treatment or provides some other baseline against which to compare the performance or response of the experimental group.

1. Preliminary screening of participants

Participants are interviewed by the researcher, and their baseline anxiety is established.

2. Random assignment to conditions

Experimental group

Control group

3. Treatment phase

Receives EMDR treatment

No EMDR

4. Posttreatment phase

Reports on anxiety

Reports on anxiety

figure 1.6

A Simple Two-Group Experiment

Ideally, the only difference between the experimental and control group in experiments like this one is whether the participants receive the treatment the experimenter wishes to evaluate. Under these ideal circumstances, at the end of the experiment any difference in the two groups' reported levels of anxiety (the dependent variable) should be attributable to whether or not they received treatment (the independent variable).

Let's consider how Francine Shapiro used the experimental method to explore whether her EMDR treatment was actually causing the improvements she observed in her clients' emotional problems. (Each chapter to follow contains a Focus on Research section like this one, which presents a different example of how researchers in psychology pose and answer questions about behavior and mental processes.)

FOCUS ON RESEARCH

Studying EMDR

■ What was the researcher's question?

Like other scientists, Shapiro phrased her question about the value of EMDR in the form of a hypothesis, namely that *EMDR treatment causes a significant reduction in anxiety.* Does it?

■ How did the researcher answer the question?

To find out, Shapiro operationally defined "EMDR treatment" as making a certain number of back-and-forth eye movements per second for a particular period of time. And "significant reduction in anxiety" was operationally defined as a certain amount of reduction in clients' self-reported discomfort.

Shapiro then identified twenty-two people who were suffering the ill effects of traumas such as rape or military combat. These were her research participants. As shown in Figure 1.6, she assigned these participants to two groups. The experimental group received one 50-minute session of EMDR. Members of the control group focused on their unpleasant memories for 8 minutes, but without moving their eyes back and forth (Shapiro, 1989a). The experimenter controlled whether EMDR treatment was given to each participant, so the presence or absence of treatment was the independent variable. The participants' anxiety level was the dependent variable. In Shapiro's experiment, having a control group allowed her to measure how much change in anxiety might be expected from exposure to bad memories, but without EMDR treatment.

■ What did the researcher find?

The results of Shapiro's experiment showed that participants receiving EMDR treatment experienced a complete and nearly immediate reduction in anxiety related to their traumatic memories. Those in the control group showed no such change.

■ What do the results mean?

At this point, you might be ready to believe that the treatment caused the difference. Before coming to that conclusion, though, look again at the structure, or *design,* of the experiment. The treatment group's session lasted fifty minutes. The control group focused on their memories for only eight minutes. Would the people in the control group have improved if they, too, had spent fifty minutes focusing on their memories? We don't know, because the experiment did not compare methods of equal length.

■ What do we still need to know?

Experiments are now being conducted that introduce enough control into the treatment situation to evaluate alternative explanations for the EMDR effect. Most of the controlled studies completed so far cast doubt on whether the eye movements in EMDR are causing clients' improvement (e.g., Davidson & Parker, 2001), but we still don't know for sure what is producing the effects that EMDR proponents report. As the research continues, it will be important for these proponents to avoid *confirmation bias,* the human tendency to look only for evidence that supports their hypotheses. In fact, all scientists have a responsibility to combat confirmation bias by looking for evidence *for* and *against* even their most cherished hypotheses.

Shapiro's (1989a) experiment reminds us to be on the lookout for flaws in experimental design and control that might affect the conclusions we can draw from research results. In fact, we have to consider anything that could confuse, or *confound,* our interpretation of those results. Any factor that might have affected the dependent variable, along with or instead of the independent variable, may operate as a **confounding variable.** When confounding variables are present, we can't tell whether it was the independent variable or the confounding variable that produced the results. Let's consider three sources of confounding variables: random variables, participants' expectations, and experimenter bias.

Random Variables   In an ideal research world, everything about experimental and control groups would be identical except for their exposure to the independent variable (such as whether or not they receive a treatment of some kind). In reality, however, there are always other differences in **random variables,** such as the conditions under which each experimental session takes place, and each participant's cultural background, personality, health, and sensitivity to stress. To minimize the effects of random variables, experimenters do all they can to keep constant the temperature, noise, and other environmental circumstances that might affect participants' behavior. And although they cannot create groups that are alike on all random variables, experimenters also flip a coin or use some other random process to assign each participant to experimental or control groups. Such procedures, called **random assignment,** tend to spread the effects of uncontrolled variables randomly (and probably about evenly) across groups. This minimizes the chance that they will distort the results of the experiment (Shadish, Cook, & Campbell, 2002).

Expectations: The Placebo Effect   Differences in what participants think about the experimental situation can act as another confounding variable. For example, if participants expect that a treatment will help them, they may try harder to improve than those in a control group who receive no treatment or a less impressive one. Improvement created by a participant's expectations is called the *placebo effect.* A **placebo** (pronounced "plah-SEE-boe") contains nothing known to be helpful, but nevertheless produces benefits because a person believes it will do so.

How can researchers determine the extent to which the results of an experiment were caused by the independent variable or by a placebo effect? One solution is to include a special control group that receives *only* a placebo. Then the researchers can compare results for the experimental group, the placebo group, and a group of participants receiving no treatment. In one stop-smoking study, for example, participants in a placebo group took sugar pills that the experimenter said would help them endure the stress of giving up cigarettes (Bernstein, 1970). These participants did as well at quitting as those in the experimental group, who had received extensive treatment. This result suggested that the experimental group's success may have been due largely to the participants' expectations, not to the treatment methods. Some studies suggest the same conclusion about the effects of EMDR, because significant anxiety reduction has been observed in clients who get a version of the treatment that does not involve eye move-

confounding variable   Any factor that affects the dependent variable along with, or instead of, the independent variable.

random variables   Uncontrolled or uncontrollable factors that affect the dependent variable along with, or instead of, the independent variable.

random assignment   A procedure through which random variables are evenly distributed in an experiment by placing participants in experimental and control groups on the basis of a coin flip or some other random process.

placebo   A treatment that contains no active ingredient but produces an effect because the person receiving it believes it will.

EVER SINCE I STARTED WEARING THESE MAGNETS . . . Placebo-controlled experiments are vital for establishing cause-effect relationships between treatments and outcomes with human participants. For example, many people swear that magnets held against their joints relieve the pain of sports injuries and even arthritis. But experiments show that magnets are no more effective than placebo treatment with an identical, but non-magnetic, metal object (e.g., Collacott et al., 2000).

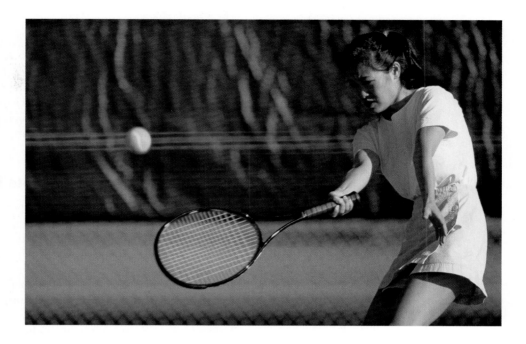

ments or even focusing on traumatic memories (Cahill, Carrigan, & Frueh, 1999; Cusack & Spates, 1999). In fact, although EMDR appears to have some positive effects on some clients, its failure to outperform impressive placebo treatments (or other established methods for helping clients deal with unpleasant images) has led many researchers to conclude that EMDR should not be a first-choice treatment for anxiety-related disorders (Davison & Parker, 2001; Goldstein et al., 2000; Herbert et al., 2000). Accordingly, mental health professionals volunteering to work with traumatized people in the days following the September 11, 2001, terrorist attack on the World Trade Center were asked by New York authorities not to use EMDR (P. Fraenkel, personal communication, October 28, 2001).

Experimenter Bias Sometimes experimenters themselves unintentionally affect their results. This **experimenter bias** may introduce another potential confounding variable. Robert Rosenthal (1966) was one of the first to demonstrate the power of experimenter bias. His participants were laboratory assistants who were asked to place rats in a maze. Rosenthal told some of the assistants that their rats were "maze-bright." He told the others that their rats were "maze-dull." In fact, though, both groups of rats were randomly drawn from the same population and had equal maze-learning capabilities. Still, the so-called maze-bright animals learned the maze significantly faster than the "maze-dull" ones. Why? Rosenthal concluded that the result had nothing to do with the rats and everything to do with the experimenters. He suggested that the assistants' expectations about their rats' supposedly superior (or inferior) capabilities caused them to slightly alter their training and handling techniques. This alteration, in turn, speeded or slowed the animals' learning. Similarly, when administering different kinds of anxiety treatments to different groups, experimenters who believe one treatment will be the best might do a slightly better job with that treatment and thus unintentionally improve its effects.

To prevent experimenter bias from confounding results, experimenters can use a **double-blind design.** In this design, the participants *and* those giving the treatments are unaware of, or "blind" to, who is receiving a placebo, and they do not know what results are to be expected of the various treatments. Only the director of the study, who makes no contact with participants, has this information, and the director does not reveal it until the end of the experiment. Double-blind studies have not yet been

experimenter bias A confounding variable that occurs when an experimenter unintentionally encourages participants to respond in a way that supports the hypothesis.

double-blind design A research design in which neither the experimenter nor the participants know who is in the experimental group and who is in the control group.

conducted with EMDR, which is another reason for caution in drawing conclusions about this treatment.

In summary, experiments are vital tools for examining cause-effect relationships between independent and dependent variables, but they are also vulnerable to error. To maximize the value of their experiments, scientists try to eliminate as many confounding variables as possible, repeat their work to ensure consistent results, and then carefully interpret results to take into account the limitations or problems that remain.

Selecting Human Participants for Research

Just as visitors from another planet would be wildly mistaken if they tried to describe the typical earthling after seeing only Eminem, Michael Jackson, Madonna, and a trained seal, psychologists can be misled if the participants they choose for their research are not typical of the people or animals about which they want to draw conclusions. In other words, the sample of participants studied must be representative of people in general if the researcher wants results that reveal something about people in general. So the process of selecting participants, a process called **sampling**, is a very important part of doing scientific research.

If chance alone determines who is chosen as a research participant, the individuals selected can be called a **random sample.** If factors other than chance determine who participates (e.g., knowing the researcher, or being willing to volunteer), the researcher has selected a **biased sample.** Because it is so difficult and expensive to select a truly random sample from, say, "all college students," "all Canadians," or any other large group, most researchers draw their participants, as randomly as possible, from the population available to them. This population might include, for example, all college students on a local campus or on several campuses around the country, all citizens in the Toronto phone book, or the like. Participants chosen in this way constitute a *representative sample* of the population from which they were selected. These samples might represent an even larger population as well, but researchers cannot merely assume that. They must conduct addi-

learn **by doing** **SELECTING RESEARCH PAR-TICIPANTS** Suppose that you want to study people's willingness to help each other. You have developed a way of measuring helpfulness, but now you need a sample of people to test. Take a minute to think about the steps necessary to select a truly random sample; then ask yourself how you might obtain a representative sample, instead. Remember that although the names are similar, *random sampling* is not the same as *random assignment*. Random sampling helps ensure that the people studied are representative of some larger group, whereas random assignment is used in experiments to create equivalence among various groups.

in review

METHODS OF PSYCHOLOGICAL RESEARCH

Method	Features	Strengths	Pitfalls
Naturalistic observation	Observation of human or animal behavior in the environment where it typically occurs	Provides descriptive data about behavior presumably uncontaminated by outside influences	Observer bias and participant self-consciousness can distort results.
Case studies	Intensive examination of the behavior and mental processes associated with a specific person or situation	Provide detailed descriptive analyses of new, complex, or rare phenomena	They may not provide representative picture of phenomena.
Surveys	Standard sets of questions asked of a large number of participants	Gather large amounts of descriptive data relatively quickly and inexpensively	Sampling errors, poorly phrased questions, and response biases can distort results.
Experiments	Manipulation of an independent variable and measurement of its effects on a dependent variable	Can establish a cause-effect relationship between independent and dependent variables	Confounding variables may prevent valid conclusions.

? *The _____ method is most likely to use a double-blind design.*

tional studies to show that their research conclusions apply to people of various ages, ethnic backgrounds, and other sociocultural characteristics (APA Office of Ethnic Minority Affairs, 2000; Case & Smith, 2000; Gray-Little & Hafdahl, 2000).

Sometimes, a representative sample of the general population may not be necessary or even desirable. For example, studying language development in the average child may be less valuable than studying the unfortunate child raised in solitary confinement by parents who provided no language instruction (Rymer, 1992). Also, if you want to learn about a specific group (male Asian American accountants, say), your participants should be selected from that group, not from the general population. For a recap of the strategies psychologists use in their research efforts, see "In Review: Methods of Psychological Research."

Statistical Analysis of Research Results

▶ **What does it mean when scientists announce that a research finding is "significant"?**

Regardless of the methods used, psychological research usually generates a large amount of data. **Data** are numbers that represent research findings and provide the basis for conclusions. Like other scientists, psychologists use statistics to summarize their data and interpret what they mean. As the name implies, *descriptive statistics* describe a set of data.

sampling   The process of selecting participants who are members of the population that the researcher wishes to study.

random sample   A group of research participants selected from a population each of whose members had an equal chance of being chosen.

biased sample   A group of research participants selected from a population each of whose members did not have an equal chance of being chosen for study.

data   Numbers that represent research findings and provide the basis for conclusions.

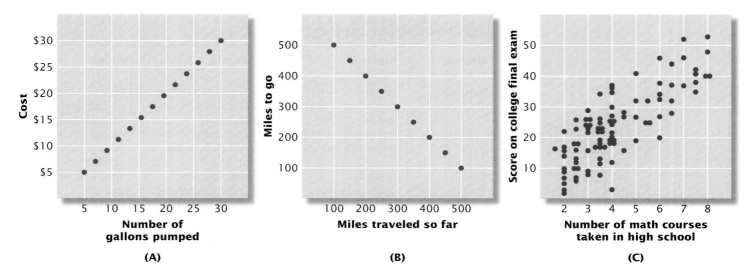

figure 1.7

Three Correlations

The strength and direction of the correlation between variables can be seen in a graph called a *scatterplot*. Here are three examples. In Part A, we have plotted the cost of a gasoline purchase against the number of gallons pumped. The number of gallons is *positively* and perfectly correlated with their cost, so the scatterplot appears as a straight line, and you can predict the value of either variable from a knowledge of the other. Part B shows a perfect *negative* correlation between the number of miles you have traveled toward a destination and the distance remaining. Again, one variable can be exactly predicted from the other. Part C illustrates a correlation of +.81 between the number of math courses students had taken in high school and their scores on a college math exam (Hays, 1981). As correlations decrease, they are represented by less and less organized scatterplots. A correlation of 0.00 would appear as a shapeless cloud.

correlation   The degree to which one variable is related to another.

Inferential statistics are mathematical procedures used to draw conclusions from data and to make assumptions about what they mean. We describe these methods of statistical analysis in the "Statistics in Psychological Research" appendix; here we explore another important statistical concept known as *correlation*.

Let's begin with a research question: Do the number of fears people have tend to decrease with age? In general, the answer is yes (Kleinknecht, 1991), but to test hypotheses about questions such as this, psychologists must have a way to measure how, and to what extent, variables such as age and fearfulness are related to each other. **Correlation** means just what it says: "co-relation." In statistics, it refers both to the strength of the relationship between two variables and to the direction of the relationship. A *positive correlation* means that the two variables increase together or decrease together. A *negative correlation* means that the variables move in opposite directions. When one increases, the other decreases. For example, James Schaefer observed 4,500 customers in 65 bars and found that the tempo of the jukebox music was negatively correlated with the rate at which the customers drank alcohol. The slower the tempo, the faster the drinking (Schaefer et al., 1988).

Does this mean Schaefer could have worn a blindfold and predicted exactly how fast people were drinking by timing the music? Could he have plugged his ears and determined the musical tempo just by watching people's sip rates? No, and no, because the accuracy of predictions about one variable from knowing the other depends on the *strength* of the correlation. Only a perfect correlation between two variables would allow you to predict the exact value of one from a knowledge of the other. The weaker the correlation, the less one variable can tell you about the other.

To statistically describe how two things co-relate, psychologists calculate a *correlation coefficient* (see the "Statistics in Psychological Research" appendix). The value of a correlation coefficient can vary from +1.00 to –1.00. The sign of a correlation indicates its direction. A plus sign signifies a *positive* correlation. A minus sign signifies a *negative* correlation. The size of a correlation indicates the strength of the relationship. A perfectly predictable relationship between two variables is indicated by +1.00 or –1.00 (see Figure 1.7). A correlation of 0.00 between people's shoe size and the age of their cars, for example, indicates that there is virtually no relationship between the variables.

Psychologists use correlation coefficients to help them describe the results of their research and to evaluate their hypotheses. However, they must be extremely careful when interpreting what correlations mean. Consider, for example, the positive correlation between watching violent television programs and behaving violently. Does seeing violence on TV cause viewers to be violent, or does being violent to begin with cause a preference for violent shows? Perhaps neither causes the other; violent behavior and TV choices could both be due to a third factor, such as personality. The mere fact that two variables are correlated does not mean that one is causing an effect on the other. And even if one variable actually does cause

Ice cream consumption

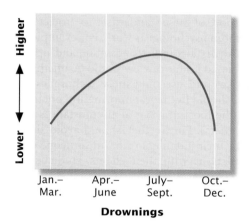

Drownings

figure 1.8

What Is Causing What?

As these graphs show, ice cream consumption and drownings in the United States tend to rise and fall together. Does this positive correlation mean that eating ice cream causes people to drown? No. The correlation probably reflects a third variable—time of year—that affects both ice cream sales and the likelihood of swimming and boating (Brenner et al., 2001).

statistically significant   Referring to a correlation, or a difference between two groups, that is larger than would be expected by chance.

an effect on the other, a correlation coefficient cannot say which variable is influencing which. In short, correlations can reveal and describe relationships, but correlations alone cannot explain them. Remember, correlation does not guarantee causation (see Figure 1.8).

When a correlation coefficient is larger than would be expected by chance alone, it is said to be **statistically significant** (see the "Statistics in Psychological Research" appendix). Statistical significance alone does not guarantee final "proof," but scientists do tend to pay more attention to correlations or other research findings that are statistically significant, especially when those results have been repeated, or *replicated,* in separate studies (Rosenthal, 1996). So, when thinking critically about research, part of the process of evaluating evidence about hypotheses is to ask whether a researcher's results are statistically significant and repeatable.

Ethical Guidelines for Psychologists

▶ **Do psychologists deceive people when they do research?**

Statistics can easily be misunderstood. They can also be manipulated. A few years ago newspaper headlines stated, "Hair dye causes cancer." Hairdressers were alarmed at first, then angry. The information given to the public was less than accurate. Rats—not humans—had been used in the research, and they only developed cancer after drinking the hair dye!

Spectacular headlines sell newspapers, but scientific psychologists have an ethical obligation not to manipulate, distort, or sensationalize their research results. The obligation to analyze and report research fairly and accurately is just one of the ethical standards that guide psychologists. Preservation of the welfare and dignity of their research participants is another. Although researchers could certainly measure anxiety by putting a loaded gun to people's heads, or study marital conflicts by telling one partner that the other has been unfaithful, such methods are potentially harmful and therefore unethical.

In each of these examples, the ethical course of action is obvious: The psychologist must find another way to conduct the research. To measure anxiety, for example, a researcher might ask people to enter a situation that is anxiety provoking, but not traumatic (e.g., approaching a feared animal or sitting in a dark room). And research on marital conflict usually involves observing couples as they discuss controversial issues in their relationship. In other words, experiments often reflect a compromise between the need to protect participants from harm and the need to learn about the unknown. Laws in the United States, Canada, and many other countries now require that any research involving human participants must be approved by an *Institutional Review Board (IRB)* whose members have no connection to the research. If a proposed study is likely to create risks or discomfort for participants, the IRB members weigh the potential benefits of the work in terms of knowledge and human welfare against any potential harm. They ensure that the researcher has minimized any discomfort and risk to the participants and that participants will not suffer any long-term negative consequences. Researchers must also inform potential participants about every aspect of the study that might influence their decision to participate and ensure that each individual's involvement is voluntary. But what if the purpose of the study is, say, to measure emotional reactions to being insulted? Participants might not react as they otherwise would if they knew ahead of time that an "insult" would be part of the experiment. When some deception is necessary to create certain experimental conditions, review committees and ethical standards require the researcher to "debrief" participants as soon as the study is over by revealing all relevant information about the research and correcting any false impressions it created.

The obligation to protect participants' welfare also extends to animals, which are used in about 8 percent of psychological research projects (Plous, 1996). Psychologists study animals partly because their behavior is interesting and partly because research with animals can provide information that would be impossible or unethical to collect from humans. For example, researchers can randomly assign animals to live alone, and then look at how these conditions affect later social interactions. The same thing could not ethically be done with people, but animal studies offer clues about how social isolation might affect humans (see the chapter on motivation and emotion).

Contrary to the allegations of some animal-rights activists, animals used in psychological research are not routinely subjected to extreme pain, starvation, or other inhumane conditions. Even in the small proportion of studies that require the use of electric shock, the discomfort created is mild, brief, and not harmful. The Animal Welfare Act, the *Guide for the Care and Use of Laboratory Animals* published by the National Institutes of Health, the American Psychological Association's *Guidelines for Ethical Conduct in the Care and Use of Animals,* and other laws and regulations set high standards for the care and treatment of animals in research. In those relatively rare studies that require animals to undergo short-lived pain, legal and ethical standards require the psychologist to explain to funding agencies and local animal research monitoring committees how the discomfort is justified by the expected benefits to human welfare.

The responsibility for conducting research in the most humane fashion is one aspect of the *Ethical Principles of Psychologists and Code of Conduct* developed by the American Psychological Association (2002). The main purpose of these standards is to protect and promote the welfare of society and those with whom psychologists work. For example, as teachers, psychologists should strive to give students a complete, accurate, and up-to-date view of each topic. Presenting narrow and biased points of view would be unethical. Psychologists should perform only those services and use only those techniques for which they are adequately trained. Psychologists should not reveal information obtained from clients or research participants, except in the most unusual of circumstances (see the chapter on treatment of psychological disorders). Finally, they should avoid situations in which a conflict of interest might impair their judgment or harm someone else. They should not, for example, have sexual relations with their clients, students, or employees.

Despite these guidelines, doubt and controversy arise in some cases about whether a proposed experiment or a particular practice, such as deceiving participants, is ethical. The American Psychological Association has published a casebook to help psychologists resolve such issues (Nagy, 1999). The ethical principles themselves must continually be updated to deal with complex new questions—such as how to protect the confidentiality of e-mail communications—that psychologists face in their ever-expanding range of work (APA, 2002; Smith, 2003b).

CARING FOR RESEARCH ANIMALS
Psychologists are careful to protect the welfare of the animals they study. They take no pleasure in animals' suffering, and besides, inflicting undue stress on research animals can create reactions that can act as confounding variables. For example, in a study of how learning is affected by the size of food rewards, the researcher could starve animals to make them hungry enough to want the rewards. But this would introduce discomfort, which would make it impossible to separate the effects of the reward from the effects of starvation.

LINKAGES
Is behavior influenced by our genes or by our environment?
(a link to Biology and Behavior)

LINKAGES

Psychological Research and Behavioral Genetics

One of the most fascinating and difficult challenges in psychology is to find research methods that can help us understand the ways in which people's genetic inheritance (their biological *nature*) intertwines with environmental events and conditions before and after birth (often called *nurture*) to shape their behavior and mental processes. Consider Mark and John, identical twins who were both adopted at birth because their parents were too poor to care for them. John grew up with a married couple who made him feel secure and loved. Mark went from orphanage to foster home to hospital and, finally, back to his natural father's second wife. In other words, these genetically identical people had encountered quite different environments. When they met for the first time at the age of twenty-four, they discovered similarities that went beyond physical appearance. They used the same aftershave, smoked the same brand of cigarettes, brushed with the same imported brand of toothpaste, and liked the same sports. They had joined the military within eight days of each other, and their IQ scores were nearly identical.

How had genetic influences operated in two different environments to shape such similarities? Exploring questions like these has taken psychologists into the field of *behavioral genetics,* the study of how genes and heredity affect behavior. They have discovered that most behavioral tendencies can be influenced by many different genes, but also by the environment. Accordingly, research in behavioral genetics is designed to explore the relative roles of genetic and environmental factors in creating differences among people in personality, mental ability, mental disorders, and other phenomena. It also seeks to identify specific genes that contribute to hereditary influences.

Research on behavioral genetics often relies on the selective breeding of animals. For example, Stephen Soumi (1999) identified monkeys whose genes predisposed them to react strongly or weakly to stress. He then mated strong reactors with other strong reactors, and mated weak reactors with other weak reactors. Within a few generations, descendants of the strong-reactor pairs reacted much more strongly to stressors than did the descendants of the weak-reactor pairs. Selective-breeding studies must be interpreted with caution, though, because it is not specific behaviors that are inherited. What is inherited are differing sets of physical structures and capacities that make certain behaviors more or less likely. These behavioral tendencies are often very specific, and they can be altered by the environment (Grigorenko, 2002). For example, when Soumi (1999) placed young, highly stress-reactive monkeys with unrelated "foster mothers," he discovered that the foster mothers' own stress reactivity amplified or dampened the youngsters' genetically influenced behavioral tendencies. If stress-reactive monkeys were placed with stress-reactive foster mothers, they tended to be fearful of exploring their environments and had strong reactions to stressors. But if equally stress-reactive young monkeys had calm, supportive foster mothers, they appeared eager to explore their environments and were much less upset by stressors than their peers with stress-reactive foster mothers.

Research on behavioral genetics in humans must be interpreted with even greater care. First, environmental influences can have an enormous impact on human behavior. Second, legal, moral, and ethical considerations obviously prohibit selective breeding, so research in human behavioral genetics depends on studies in which control is imperfect. Some of the most important research designs are family studies, twin studies, and adoption studies (Plomin et al., 2001; Rutter et al., 2001).

In *family studies,* researchers look at whether close relatives are more likely than distant ones to show similarities in behavior and mental processes. If increasing similarity is associated with closer family ties, the similarities might be inherited. For example, data from family studies suggest a genetic basis for schizophrenia, as Figure 1.9 shows. Remember,

Separated at birth, the Mallifert twins meet accidentally.

figure 1.9

Family and Twin Studies of Schizophrenia

The risk of developing schizophrenia, a severe mental disorder, is highest for the siblings and children of schizophrenia patients and lowest for those who are not genetically related to anyone with schizophrenia. Does this mean that schizophrenia is inherited? These results are consistent with that interpretation, but the question cannot be answered through family studies alone. Environmental factors, such as stressors that close relatives share, could also play an important role. Studies comparing identical and nonidentical twins also suggest genetic influence, but even twin studies do not eliminate the role of environmental influences.

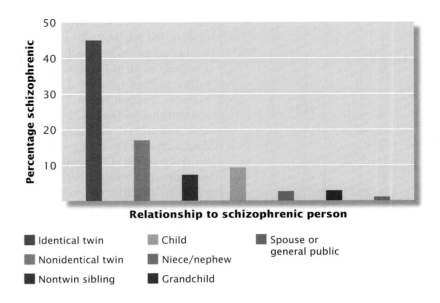

though, that correlation does not guarantee causation. Family studies alone cannot establish the role of genetic factors in mental disorders or other characteristics. Close relatives tend to share environments, as well as genes. Therefore, similarities and differences among close relatives might stem from environmental factors, as well as genetic ones.

Twin studies explore the nature-nurture mix by comparing similarities seen in identical twins with those of nonidentical twins. Twins usually share the same environment and may also be treated very much the same by parents and others. So, if identical twins—whose genes are the same—are more alike on some characteristics than nonidentical twins (whose genes are no more similar than those of other siblings), those characteristics may have a significant genetic component.

Adoption studies take advantage of the naturally occurring experiments that happen when babies are adopted. The logic of these studies is that if adopted children's characteristics are more like those of their biological parents than those of their adoptive parents, genetics probably plays a clear role in those characteristics. In fact, the personalities of young adults who were adopted at birth tend to be more like those of their biological parents than those of their adoptive parents. Especially valuable are adoption studies of identical twins who, like Mark and John, were separated soon after birth. If identical twins show similar characteristics after years of living in very different environments, the role of heredity in those characteristics is highlighted. Adoption studies of intelligence tend to support the role of genetics in variations in mental ability. However, environmental influences are important, too.

Remember that family, twin, and adoption studies explore the relative roles of heredity and environment that underlie *group* differences. These studies cannot determine the degree to which a *particular* person's behavior is due to heredity or environment. In the future, though, behavioral genetics research will be shaped by the results of the Human Genome Project, which has now deciphered the genetic code contained in the DNA that makes each human being unique (International Human Genome Sequencing Consortium, 2001; Venter et al., 2001). This achievement has allowed behavioral geneticists and other scientists to begin pinpointing some of the many genes that contribute to individual differences in disorders such as autism, learning disabilities, hyperactivity, and Alzheimer's disease, as well as to the differences in personality and mental abilities that we see all around us (Plomin et al., 2002). Finding the DNA differences responsible for certain personal attributes and behaviors will eventually make it possible to understand exactly how heredity interacts with the environment as development unfolds. Analysis of DNA—collected by rubbing a cotton swab inside an individual's cheek—may someday be used not only in behavioral genetics research but also in clinics, where it will help psychologists more precisely diagnose clients' problems and choose the most appropriate treatments (Plomin & Crabbe, 2000; Plomin et al., 2002).

active review Introduction to the Science of Psychology

Summary

THE WORLD OF PSYCHOLOGY: AN OVERVIEW

▶ **What is psychology, and how did it grow?**

Psychology is the science that seeks to understand behavior and mental processes. The broad concept of "behavior and mental processes" encompasses virtually all aspects of what it means to be a human being. Psychologists study a wide variety of topics, ranging from the activity of individual nerve cells; to the way people sense and perceive things, think, make decisions, and experience emotion; to the way people create, and interact in, societies.

Because the subject matter of psychology is so diverse, most psychologists work in particular subfields within the discipline. For example, *cognitive psychologists* focus on basic psychological processes such as learning, memory, and perception. *Biological psychologists* explore the influence of brain chemistry and other physiological factors on behavior and mental processes. *Personality psychologists* focus on characteristics that set people apart from one another. *Developmental psychologists* specialize in trying to understand the development of behavior and mental processes over a lifetime. *Quantitative psychologists* develop methods for statistical analysis of research data. *Clinical* and *counseling psychologists* provide direct service to troubled people and conduct research on abnormal behavior. *Community psychologists* work to prevent mental disorders and extend mental health services to those who need it. *Educational psychologists* conduct and apply research on teaching and learning, whereas *school psychologists* specialize in assessing and alleviating children's academic problems. *Social psychologists* examine questions regarding how people influence one another; *industrial/ organizational psychologists* conduct research on topics such as increasing the motivation of employees and helping companies select the best new workers. *Health psychologists, sport psychologists, forensic psychologists, engineering psychologists,* and *environmental psychologists* exemplify some of psychology's many other subfields. Psychology's subfields often overlap, and psychologists often work in more than one subfield, sharing knowledge with colleagues in other subfields and contributing to knowledge in other disciplines.

Scientific psychology has its roots in philosophy, and especially in a philosophical view called *empiricism.* The modern science of psychology began to emerge in the late nineteenth century as scientists in Germany and North America established laboratories to conduct research in psychology. In Germany, Wundt explored the building blocks of *consciousness*; Gestalt psychologists there later studied it as a whole. In Vienna, Freud explored the unconscious. At the same time in the United States, James was applying Darwin's theory of evolution to the

exploration of human behavior. In the early twentieth century, Watson argued that to be truly scientific, psychologists should focus only on observable behavior. He founded behaviorism, which dominated psychology for decades. Today, consciousness—in the form of cognitive processes—is being intensively studied once again.

APPROACHES TO THE SCIENCE OF PSYCHOLOGY

▶ **Why don't all psychologists explain behavior in the same way?**

Psychologists differ in their approaches to psychology—that is, in the assumptions, questions, and methods they believe will be most helpful in their work. Those psychologists adopting a *biological approach* examine how physiological factors shape behavior and mental processes. Darwin's theory helped stimulate the *evolutionary approach,* which emphasizes the inherited, adaptive aspects of behavior and mental processes. The *psychodynamic approach* sees behavior and mental processes as a struggle to resolve conflicts between impulses and the demands made by society to control those impulses. Psychologists who take the *behavioral approach* consider behavior to be determined primarily by learning based on experiences with rewards and punishments. The *cognitive approach* assumes that behavior can be understood through analysis of the basic mental processes that underlie it. The *humanistic approach* views behavior as controlled by the decisions that people make about their lives based on their perceptions of the world.

HUMAN DIVERSITY AND PSYCHOLOGY

▶ **How does your cultural background influence your behavior?**

Most of the prominent figures in psychology's history were white males, but women and people of color made important contributions from the start, and they continue to do so. Psychologists are increasingly taking into account the influence of *culture* and other *sociocultural variables* such as gender and ethnicity in shaping human behavior and mental processes.

THINKING CRITICALLY ABOUT PSYCHOLOGY (OR ANYTHING ELSE)

▶ **How can critical thinking save you money?**

Critical thinking is the process of assessing claims and making judgments on the basis of well-supported evidence. This process can unfold by asking five questions: What am I being asked to believe or accept? Is there evidence available to support the claim? Can that evidence be interpreted another way? What evidence would help to evaluate the alternatives? What conclusions are most reasonable?

Often, questions about psychological phenomena are phrased in terms of **hypotheses** about **variables** that are specified by **operational definitions.** Evidence for hypotheses must be evaluated for **reliability** and **validity.** After gathering research evidence, scientists may organize their findings into a **theory,** a set of statements designed to explain certain phenomena. Theories must be subjected to rigorous evaluation.

RESEARCH METHODS IN PSYCHOLOGY

▶ **How do psychologists learn about people?**

Research in psychology, as in other sciences, focuses on four main goals: description, prediction, control, and explanation. Psychologists have found several research methods especially useful in gathering the evidence needed to reach each of these goals. **Naturalistic observation** entails watching without interfering as behavior occurs in the natural environment. **Case studies** are intensive examinations of a particular individual, group, or situation. **Surveys** ask questions, through interviews or questionnaires, about behavior, attitudes, beliefs, opinions, and intentions. In **experiments,** researchers manipulate an **independent variable** and observe the effect of that manipulation on a **dependent variable.** Participants receiving experimental treatment are called the **experimental group.** Participants in comparison conditions are called **control groups.** Experiments can reveal cause-effect relationships between variables, but only if researchers use **random assignment** and other strategies (such as **placebo** conditions and **double-blind designs**) to avoid being misled by **random variables, experimenter bias,** and other **confounding variables.**

Psychologists' research can be limited if their **sampling** procedures do not give them a representative cross-section of the population they want to study and about which they want to draw conclusions. Letting chance determine who participates in a study produces a **random sample,** but deciding to include only certain people produces a **biased sample** of participants.

STATISTICAL ANALYSIS OF RESEARCH RESULTS

▶ **What does it mean when scientists announce that a research finding is "significant"?**

Psychologists use descriptive and inferential statistical analyses to summarize and analyze **data,** the numbers that represent research findings and provide the basis for conclusions. A **correlation** is the degree to which one variable is related to another. Although often valuable to research, correlations alone cannot establish that two variables are causally related; nor can they determine which variable might affect which, or why. When a correlation coefficient or other research finding is larger than would be expected by chance alone, it is said to be **statistically significant.**

ETHICAL GUIDELINES FOR PSYCHOLOGISTS

▶ **Do psychologists deceive people when they do research?**

Ethical guidelines promote the protection of human and animal participants in psychological research, and set the highest standards for behavior in all other aspects of psychologists' professional lives.

Learn by Doing

Put It in Writing

Choose one or two recent newspaper or magazine articles describing a research study in psychology, and then, based on the article alone, try to answer the five critical thinking questions we described earlier (*What am I being asked to believe or accept?, Is there evidence available to support the claim?, Can that evidence be interpreted another way?, What evidence would help to evaluate the alternatives?, and What conclusions are most reasonable?*). When you have finished, write a paragraph or two describing how well you think the popular press covers the results of scientific research in psychology, and how such coverage could be improved.

Personal Learning Activity

Try designing an experiment on a hypothesis of your choice. First, state your hypothesis as specifically as possible, being sure to include operational definitions of the independent and dependent variables. Then tell where you will get your research participants, what the experimental and control groups will experience, and what all your research procedures will be. For example, if your hypothesis is that rock music played during studying improves students' memory for the material, then you should decide what you mean by "rock music" and "improved memory," what the experimental and control groups will hear while studying, what they will study, and how you will measure the students' memory for what they learned. *For additional projects, see the Personal Learning Activities in the corresponding chapter of the study guide that accompanies this text.*

Step into Action

Courses

History and Systems of Psychology
Experimental Psychology

Movies

Gorillas in the Mist (naturalistic observation)
The Joy Luck Club (cultural influences on behavior)
Mr. Baseball (collectivist versus individualistic cultures)

Books

Ludy T. Benjamin and D. B. Baker, *From Seance to Science: A History of the Profession of Psychology in America* (Wadsworth, 2004) (the development of clinical, counseling, school, and industrial/organizational psychology)

Steve Jones, *Darwin's Ghost: The Origin of Species Updated* (Random House, 2000) (evolutionary theory explained with modern examples).

F. Barbara Orlans, Tom Beauchamp, Rebecca Dresser, and John Gluck (Eds.), *The Human Use of Animals: Case Studies in Ethical Choice* (Oxford University Press, 1998) (case studies related to animal research).

Peter Gay, *Freud: A Life for Our Time* (Norton, 1998) (comprehensive biography of the founder of psychoanalysis)

Roger Hock, *Forty Studies that Changed Psychology* (Prentice Hall, 1995) (reports of famous psychological studies)

Alice Wexler, *Mapping Fate* (University of California Press, 1996) (the story of Nancy Wexler's discovery of the gene for Huntington's disease)

The Web

The World Wide Web is a good source of additional information about the science of psychology, provided you use it carefully and think critically about the information you find. The web site that accompanies this text offers many resources relevant to this chapter. These resources include interactive NetLab exercises; Thinking Critically and Evaluating Research exercises; ACE chapter quizzes; recommended web links; and articles on current events, books, and movies. At http://college.hmco.com, select *Psychology* and then this textbook.

Review of Key Terms

Can you define each of the key terms in the chapter? Check your definitions against those on the pages listed in parentheses below or in the Glossary/Index at the end of the text.

behavioral approach (p. 16)
biased sample (p. 32)
biological approach (p. 14)
biological psychologists (p. 4)
case studies (p. 25)
clinical and counseling psychologists (p. 4)
cognitive approach (p. 16)
cognitive psychologists (p. 4)
community psychologists (p. 4)
confounding variable (p. 30)
consciousness (p. 10)
control group (p. 28)
correlation (p. 34)
critical thinking (p. 21)

culture (p. 19)
data (p. 33)
dependent variable (p. 28)
developmental psychologists (p. 4)
double-blind design (p. 31)
educational psychologists (p. 4)
empiricism (p. 9)
engineering psychologists (p. 6)
environmental psychologists (p. 6)
evolutionary approach (p. 15)
experiment (p. 28)
experimental group (p. 28)

experimenter bias (p. 31)
forensic psychologists (p. 6)
health psychologists (p. 6)
humanistic approach (p. 17)
hypothesis (p. 24)
independent variable (p. 28)
industrial/organizational psychologists (p. 6)
naturalistic observation (p. 25)
operational definitions (p. 24)
personality psychologists (p. 4)
placebo (p. 30)
psychodynamic approach (p. 15)
psychology (p. 3)
quantitative psychologists (p. 4)

random assignment (p. 30)
random sample (p. 32)
random variables (p. 30)
reliability (p. 24)
sampling (p. 32)
school psychologists (p. 4)
social psychologists (p. 5)
sociocultural variables (p. 19)
sport psychologists (p. 6)
statistically significant (p. 35)
surveys (p. 26)
theory (p. 24)
validity (p. 24)
variables (p. 24)

Multiple-Choice Self-Test

Select the best answer for each of the questions below. Then check your responses against the Answer Key at the end of the text.

1. Scientific psychology has its roots in
   a. philosophy.
   b. physiology.
   c. psychoanalysis.
   d. functionalism.

2. To understand what rewards a child receives for bullying other children, a behaviorist would use
   a. cognitive science.
   b. functional analysis of behavior.
   c. introspection.
   d. psychoanalysis.

3. Dr. Hemmings believes that human behavior is influenced by genetic inheritance, unconscious motivations, and environmental influences. Dr. Hemmings uses a(n) _____ approach.

   a. evolutionary
   b. eclectic
   c. humanistic
   d. behavioral

4. Dr. Foreman emphasizes the role of unconscious processes in explaining behavior. Dr. Foreman takes which approach to psychology?

   a. cognitive
   b. humanistic
   c. psychodynamic
   d. cognitive behavioral

5. Larry says that people act the way they learned to act. He believes that if others stop rewarding a person's annoying behavior, that behavior will lessen. Larry most likely takes a(n) _____ approach to psychology.

   a. behavioral
   b. cognitive
   c. evolutionary
   d. humanistic

6. Psychologists who focus on the role of such processes as perceptions, judgments, and assumptions in explaining behavior take a(n) _____ approach.

   a. evolutionary
   b. biological
   c. cognitive
   d. deterministic

7. Dr. Rose, a cross-cultural psychologist, is most likely to find which behavior to be similar in all of the groups she studies?

   a. striving for achievement
   b. rules governing social behavior
   c. styles of communication
   d. recognition of a smile

8. You are a wise consumer of therapy (and other products). Which of the following questions is not among the five critical thinking questions you usually ask yourself?"

   a. What am I being asked to believe or accept?
   b. Is there evidence available to support claims for this type of therapy?
   c. Are there other ways to interpret the claims made to support this type of therapy?
   d. Which celebrities have gone on record as endorsing this form of therapy?

9. Which of the following is the correct list of scientific research goals?

   a. adjudication, prediction, control, and explanation
   b. random guessing, understanding, reasoning, and control
   c. description, uncritical thinking, control, and explanation
   d. description, prediction, control, and explanation

10. Case studies are used to

    a. avoid a placebo effect.
    b. determine the effects of an independent variable.
    c. collect descriptive data.
    d. provide control in an experiment.

11. Before using survey results to support a hypothesis, we must be sure about which of the following?

    a. The questions are properly worded.
    b. The sample used is representative of the population of interest.
    c. The responses are not strongly biased by efforts to appear "socially acceptable."
    d. All of the above.

12. Which of the following is not a possible random variable?

    a. treatment given to participants
    b. room temperature
    c. time of day
    d. participants' personalities

13. Dr. Daneli believes that memory is aided by an increase in the brain chemical serotonin. To avoid the possibility that experimenter bias may confound the results of his experiment aimed at testing this hypothesis, he should use a(n) _____ design.

    a. operational
    b. naturalistic
    c. random
    d. double-blind

14. In Dr. Daneli's experiment, Group A receives serotonin before being given a memory test, whereas Group B takes the same test without being given serotonin. In this experiment, performance on the memory test is the _____ variable.

    a. dependent
    b. independent
    c. control
    d. random

15. Jeremy designed an experiment to test the effects of praise on the sharing behavior of children. Children in Group A will be praised after they share; children in Group B will only be observed. Group A is the _____ group.

    a. control
    b. experimental
    c. operational
    d. random

16. José wants to know if growing up in an abusive family causes children to become physically violent. Which of the following research methods would create the greatest ethical problems in trying to scientifically study this question?

    a. case studies
    b. experiments
    c. observations
    d. surveys

17. Choose the strongest correlation coefficient.

    a. +.75
    b. −.99
    c. +.01
    d. −.01

18. A correlation coefficient can tell us all of the following, except the _____ of a relationship between two variables.

    a. strength
    b. direction
    c. existence
    d. cause

19. Your psychology professor asks you to learn about the smoking habits of Asian American female students on your campus. To select your participants for this study, you would use a

    a. random sample.
    b. random population.
    c. representative sample.
    d. coin-flip.

20. Why do psychologists follow ethical guidelines?

    a. Psychologists would not want the cost of participating in an experiment to be too high in comparison with the information to be gained.
    b. The American Psychological Association has set standards for psychologists to follow when conducting research and treating clients.
    c. Stress and pain could act as confounding variables in an experiment.
    d. All of the above.

2

Biology and Behavior

Before you read the next sentence,

close your eyes and touch your nose. This task is easy, but it is not simple. To get the job done, your brain used specific nerves to tell your eyelids to close. It used other nerves to tell your hand to extend a finger and then sent a series of messages that moved your arm in just the right direction until it received a message that your finger and your nose were in contact. This example illustrates that everything you do—including how you feel and think—is based on some kind of biological activity in your body, especially in your brain. This chapter tells the story of that activity, beginning with a basic biological unit of the body, a specialized cell called the *neuron*. Collections of neurons form the systems that receive information from our senses; process that information; and translate it into behavior, thoughts, and biochemical changes.

Reading this chapter will help you to answer the following questions:

► **What are neurons, and what do they do?**

► **How do biochemicals affect my mood?**

► **How is my nervous system organized?**

► **How is my brain "wired"?**

► **How can my hormones help me in a crisis?**

W hat do Ronald Reagan, Muhammad Ali, Michael J. Fox, and Christopher Reeve all have in common? Each of these men has a nervous system disorder that affects his behavior. Former president Reagan has severe Alzheimer's disease; former heavyweight boxing champ Ali has severe Parkinson's syndrome; and Fox, who gave up his role in the TV show *Spin City*, has Parkinson's disease. Reeve, who starred in the Superman movies, was paralyzed as a result of damage to his spinal cord. Medical research has not yet found cures for these disorders, although it has developed treatments that attempt to reverse or minimize the symptoms and suffering. You may know of other people, perhaps in your own family, whose behavior has changed because of a devastating biological condition.

The fact is, biological factors are intimately related to *all* behavior and mental processes. The question of how they are related takes us into the realm of **biological psychology**—the study of cells, genes, and organs of the body and the physical, hormonal, and chemical changes involved in behavior and mental processes. Although all behavior and mental processes are based on biology, those processes are also influenced by the environment. We will see later, for example, that the experiences we have in the environment can change the chemistry, and even the structure, of our brain. Let's begin to consider in more detail the relationship between the body and mind, between the brain and behavior.

biological psychology The study of physical and chemical changes involved in behavior and mental processes.

45

Understanding how we think, feel, act, and react requires some knowledge of our body and how it works. Two primary systems—the nervous system and the endocrine system—direct the activities of the body. The nervous system receives information, sends messages from one part of the body to another, and begins actions. The endocrine system regulates internal activity of the body with glands that secrete chemicals, called *hormones*, into the bloodstream to control energy consumption, reactions to stress, sexual functioning, and the like. These are the basic pieces of the puzzle of the body. Putting the pieces together is the next step in understanding our complex behavior.

Cells of the Nervous System

▶ **What are neurons, and what do they do?**

Let's start by considering your **nervous system,** a vast network of cells that tells you what is going on inside and outside your body and allows you to make appropriate responses. For example, if you are jabbed with a pin, your nervous system gets the message and immediately causes you to flinch. But your nervous system can do far more than detect information and make responses. When information about the world reaches the brain, that information is *processed*—meaning that it is combined with information about past experiences and current wants and needs to make a decision about how to respond (see Figure 2.1). We begin our exploration of the nervous system at the "bottom," with a description of its individual cells. Later we consider how these cells are organized to form the structures of the human nervous system.

Neurons

As Figure 2.1 shows, your nervous system is actually an information-processing system with three functions: input, processing, and output. These functions are possible partly because the nervous system is made up of cells that communicate with each other. Two major types

figure 2.1

Three Functions of the Nervous System

The nervous system's three main functions are to receive information (input), integrate that information with past experiences (processing), and guide actions (output). When the alarm clock goes off, this person's nervous system, like yours, gets the message, recognizes what it means, and takes action—by getting out of bed or perhaps hitting the snooze button.

1. Input
The sound of the alarm clock is conveyed to your brain by your ears.

2. Processing
Your brain knows from past experience that it is time to get up.

3. Output
Your brain directs the muscles of your arm and hand to reach out and shut off the alarm clock.

nervous system   A network of billions of cells that detects what is going on inside and outside the body and guides appropriate responses.

figure 2.2

The Neuron

Part B shows the cell body of a nervous system cell known as a *neuron,* enlarged from the whole neuron shown in Part A. The cell body of a neuron includes an outer membrane, a nucleus, and mitochondria. Part A shows the fibers extending outward from the cell body. These fibers are called *axons* and *dendrites.*

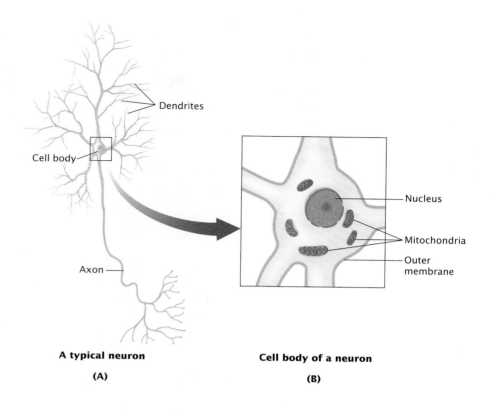

Dendrites

Cell body

Axon

Nucleus

Mitochondria

Outer membrane

A typical neuron

(A)

Cell body of a neuron

(B)

of cells, neurons and glial cells, allow the nervous system to carry out its complex signaling tasks efficiently. The specialized cells that send and receive signals are called **neurons.**

Most of our discussion of brain cells will be about neurons, but glial cells are important as well. *Glial* means "glue," and scientists had long believed that glial cells did no more than hold neurons together. Recent research shows, however, that **glial cells** also help neurons communicate by directing their growth, keeping their chemical environment stable, providing energy, secreting chemicals to help restore damage, and even responding to signals from neurons (Laming et al., 2000; Parish et al., 2002; Smit et al., 2001). Without glial cells, neurons could not function.

Every cell in the body has a skin called an *outer membrane;* a cell body that (with the exception of red blood cells) contains a core called the *nucleus;* and tiny "engines," called *mitochondria* (pronounced "my-toh-CON-dree-uh"). Neurons are no different. A neuron's outer membrane acts like a screen, letting some substances pass in and out while blocking others. In the neuron's cell body, the nucleus (or center) carries genetic information that tells the cell what to do. And neurons' mitochondria turn oxygen and glucose into energy. This process is especially vital to brain cells, because although the brain accounts for only 2 percent of the body's weight, it uses more than 20 percent of the body's oxygen. All of this energy is required because brain cells transmit signals among themselves to an even greater extent than do cells in the rest of the body.

Neurons have special structural and chemical features that allow them to communicate with each other. Let's first examine their structure. Although neurons come in many shapes and sizes, they all have long, thin fibers that reach outward from the cell body like arms (see Figure 2.2). When these fibers get close to other neurons, communication between the cells can occur. The interweaving of these fibers with fibers from other neurons allows each neuron to be close to thousands or even hundreds of thousands of other neurons.

Fibers extending from the cell body are called *axons* and *dendrites.* As shown in Figure 2.2, each neuron generally has only one **axon,** whose function is to carry signals away from the cell body. An axon may have many branches along its stem, much like a tree. At the end of each branch of the axon is a terminal region with pouch-like sacs called *vesicles* (pro-

neurons Specialized cells of the nervous system that send and receive messages.

glial cells Cells that hold neurons together, direct growth, and help restore damaged neurons.

axon A fiber that carries signals away from the cell body.

figure 2.3

Communication Between Neurons

When stimulation of a neuron reaches a certain level, the neuron fires, sending an action potential shooting to the end of its axon and triggering the release of a neurotransmitter into the synapse. This process stimulates neighboring neurons and may cause them to fire their own action potentials.

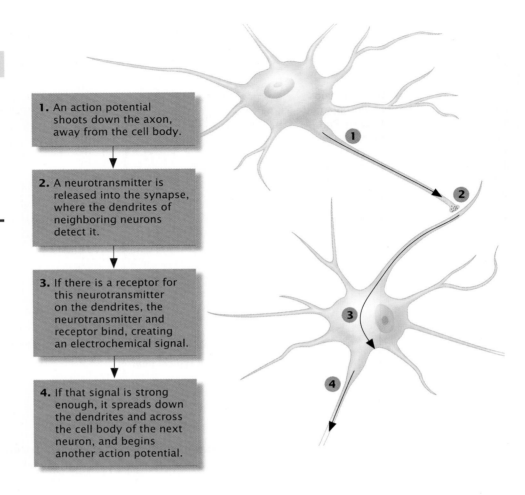

1. An action potential shoots down the axon, away from the cell body.

2. A neurotransmitter is released into the synapse, where the dendrites of neighboring neurons detect it.

3. If there is a receptor for this neurotransmitter on the dendrites, the neurotransmitter and receptor bind, creating an electrochemical signal.

4. If that signal is strong enough, it spreads down the dendrites and across the cell body of the next neuron, and begins another action potential.

dendrites   Fibers that receive signals from the axons of other neurons.

action potential   The electrochemical impulse or message that is sent down an axon and stimulates release of a neurotransmitter.

refractory period   A short recovery time after cell firing, during which the cell cannot fire again.

nounced "VESS-ick-els"). Axons can be short or long. In the brain, they may extend no more than a fraction of an inch, but the axon from your big toe to your spine is more than three feet long! **Dendrites** are the fibers that receive signals from the axons of other neurons and carry those signals to the cell body. As you can see in Figure 2.2, a neuron can have many dendrites, each of which usually has many branches. Remember that *a*xons carry signals *away* from the cell body, and *d*endrites *detect* those signals.

Action Potentials

The communication signal between neurons begins with an electrochemical pulse called an **action potential,** which shoots down the axon. Figure 2.3 shows this process. This is an "all-or-nothing" affair: The cell either fires its action potential at full strength or it does not fire at all. Once a cell has fired, there is a short recovery time called the **refractory period,** during which the cell cannot fire again. The speed of an action potential ranges from about 5 to about 260 miles per hour and depends on the thickness or diameter of the axon—larger ones are faster—and on the presence of myelin (pronounced "MY-a-lin"). *Myelin* is a fatty substance that wraps around some axons like a stocking and speeds up action potentials. When a neuron fires, dendrites in the next cell detect the message and send the signal to their cell body.

Synapses and Communication Between Neurons

How do the dendrites detect a signal from another neuron? It works a little like the game of tag you played as a child. In this neural communication tag game, however, one neuron "sends" a tag without actually touching the next neuron. When the action potential reaches the axon's terminal regions, the vesicles located there release a chemical substance called a **neurotransmitter.** Between the axon of one neuron and the dendrites of another is a tiny gap less than a millionth of an inch wide. This is the synaptic gap, often referred to simply as the **synapse.** The neurotransmitters flow across the gap. On the dendrite of the next cell, the neurotransmitters reach places where they chemically fit, or bind, to proteins called *receptors*. Like a key fitting into the right lock, a neurotransmitter snugly binds to its own receptors but not to receptors for other neurotransmitters. The receptors "recognize" only one type of neurotransmitter. In the dendrite, this binding creates an electrochemical signal that is called a *postsynaptic potential* because it occurs *after* the neurotransmitter has crossed the synapse. The postsynaptic potential, in turn, passes the message to the cell body for the signaling process to continue.

Generally, more than one message must go to a cell to make it fire. Signals from groups of cells often arrive at the same postsynaptic cell at about the same time. The messages from these many cells may conflict with one another. Some messages tell the cell to fire, whereas others tell the cell not to fire. Whether it actually does fire depends on which kind of signals are most numerous. So axons, neurotransmitters, synapses, and dendrites allow cells of the nervous system to communicate. If these components are damaged or disordered, however, serious problems can result. In the case of Christopher Reeve, for example, a spinal cord injury suffered in a riding accident damaged his nervous system to the point that its axons and dendrites could no longer send or receive the signals that had allowed him to feel most of his body and to move most of his muscles. ("In Review: Neurons, Neurotransmitters, and Receptors" summarizes the process of neural communication.)

in review

NEURONS, NEUROTRANSMITTERS, AND RECEPTORS

Part	Function	Type of Signal Carried
Axon	Carries signals away from the cell body	The action potential, an all-or-nothing electrochemical signal that shoots down the axon to vesicles at the tip of the axon, releasing neurotransmitters
Dendrite	Detects and carries signals to the cell body	The postsynaptic potential, an electrochemical signal moving toward the cell body
Synapse	Provides an area for the transfer of signals between neurons, usually between axon and dendrite	Chemicals that cross the synapse and reach receptors on another cell
Neurotransmitter	A chemical released by one cell that binds to the receptors on another cell	A chemical message telling the next cell to fire or not to fire its own action potential
Receptor	Proteins on the cell membrane that receive chemical signals	Recognizes certain neurotransmitters, thus allowing it to begin a postsynaptic potential in the dendrite

neurotransmitter A chemical that transfers messages across synapses.

synapse The tiny gap between the axon of one neuron and the dendrites of another.

? For one neuron to communicate with another, a _____ has to cross the _____ between them.

The Chemistry of Behavior: Neurotransmitters

▶ **How do biochemicals affect my mood?**

Different sets of neurons use different neurotransmitters. A group of neurons that communicate using the same neurotransmitter is called a *neurotransmitter system*. Chemical neurotransmission was first demonstrated, in frogs, by Otto Loewi in 1921. Since then, about 100 different neurotransmitters have been identified. Let's explore where these neurotransmitters operate and how they affect behavior.

Three Classes of Neurotransmitters

Three main classes of neurotransmitters are used in the nervous system: *small molecules, peptides,* and *gases.* Let's consider some examples of each.

Small Molecules   The most important of the small-molecule chemicals that act as neurotransmitters are acetylcholine, norepinephrine, serotonin, dopamine, GABA, and glutamate. *Acetylcholine* (pronounced "uh-see-tull-KO-leen") was the first to be identified as a neurotransmitter. Among the many neurons that communicate using acetylcholine are those active in controlling movement of the body, in making memories, and in slowing the heartbeat and activating the digestive system. No wonder, then, that disruption of acetylcholine systems can result in a wide variety of problems, including the memory loss and eventual loss of all mental powers seen in Alzheimer's disease.

Systems of neurons that use *norepinephrine* (pronounced "nor-eppa-NEF-rin") affect arousal, wakefulness, learning, and mood. This neurotransmitter is involved when your nervous system prepares you to fight or run away from a threat; changes in norepinephrine systems have also been implicated in depression.

The neurotransmitter *serotonin* (pronounced "sair-ah-TOE-nin") is similar to norepinephrine in that it affects both sleep and mood. Serotonin has also been implicated in aggression and impulsive behaviors. Unlike norepinephrine, though, what you eat can affect the amount of serotonin in your brain. For example, eating carbohydrates can increase serotonin, and the increase in serotonin normally reduces the desire for carbohydrates. Some researchers suspect that malfunctions in serotonin systems can result in the mood and appetite problems seen in some types of obesity, premenstrual tension, and depression (Oquendo & Mann, 2000; Wurtman & Wurtman, 1995). Antidepressant medications such as Prozac, Zoloft, and Paxil appear to relieve some of the symptoms of depression by acting on serotonin systems to maintain optimal levels of this neurotransmitter.

Dopamine (pronounced "DOPE-uh-meen") is a neurotransmitter that is important for movement. Malfunctions of dopamine systems contribute to movement disorders such as the shakiness experienced by people with Parkinson's disease. Parkinson's has been treated with some success using drugs that enable neurons to make more dopamine (Chase, 1998). Other dopamine systems are involved in the experiencing of reward, or pleasure, which is vital in shaping and motivating behavior (Spanagel & Weiss, 1999). Animals will work very hard to receive a direct dose of dopamine to a portion of the brain. These dopamine systems play a role in the rewarding properties of many drugs, including cocaine (Wise, 1998). Certain dopamine systems are also suspected to be partly responsible for the perceptual, emotional, and thought disturbances associated with schizophrenia, a severe mental disorder (Marenco & Weinberger, 2000).

GABA stands for gamma-amino butyric acid. Whereas most neurotransmitters excite neurons to fire action potentials, GABA *reduces* the likelihood that neurons will fire. In fact, it is the main neurotransmitter for slowing, or inhibiting, the brain's neural activity.

PROMOTING RESEARCH ON PARKINSON'S DISEASE Former heavyweight boxing champion Muhammad Ali suffers from Parkinson's disease, a condition related to malfunctioning of dopamine systems in the brain. Even though his shakiness is getting worse, he appeared before these U.S. senators and representatives and encouraged them to sponsor bills to fund more research on curing, and perhaps even preventing, Parkinson's disease.

When you fall asleep, neurons that use GABA deserve part of the credit. Drugs that cause reduced neural activity often do so by amplifying the inhibitory action of GABA. In the case of alcohol, for example, the result is an impairment of thinking, judgment, and motor skills. Drugs that interfere with GABA's inhibitory effects produce intense repetitive electrical discharges, known as *seizures*. Malfunctions of GABA systems contribute to severe anxiety and to Huntington's disease, an inherited disorder that causes its victims to suffer uncontrollable movement of the arms and legs, along with a progressive loss of thinking abilities. Researchers also suspect that impaired GABA systems contribute to epilepsy, another brain disorder associated with seizures and convulsive movements. Repeated or sustained seizures can result in permanent brain damage. Drug treatments can reduce seizure frequency and severity, but completely effective drugs are not yet available.

Glutamate (pronounced "GLOO-tuh-mate") is used by more neurons than any other neurotransmitter. Glutamate's importance comes from its role in enabling the brain to "strengthen" its synaptic connections. Such strengthening allows messages to cross the synaptic gap between neurons more easily. This process is necessary for normal development and may be at the root of learning and memory (Pennartz, McNaughton, & Mulder, 2000). Yet overactivity of glutamate synapses can cause neurons to die. This overactivity is the main cause of the brain damage that occurs when oxygen is cut off from neurons during a stroke. Glutamate can "excite neurons to death." Blocking glutamate receptors immediately after a brain trauma can prevent permanent brain damage (Dawson, Wadsworth, & Palmer, 2001). Glutamate may also contribute to the loss of brain cells that occurs in Alzheimer's disease (Cha et al., 2001).

Peptides Hundreds of chemicals called *peptides* have been found to act as neurotransmitters. The first of these, called *endorphins*, were discovered in the 1970s, when scientists were studying *opiates* such as morphine and heroin. Derived from poppy flowers, opiates can relieve pain; produce intense feelings of happiness; and in high doses, bring on sleep. After marking morphine with a radioactive agent, researchers traced where it became concentrated in the brain. They found that the opiates bound to receptors that had not been associated with any previously identified neurotransmitter. It is unlikely that the brain had developed opiate receptors just in case a person might want to use morphine or heroin, so researchers reasoned that the body must contain a substance that is similar to opiates. This hypothesis led to the search for a naturally occurring, or *endogenous*, morphine. (*Endogenous* is pronounced "en-DODGE-uh-niss"; *endorphin* is a contraction of the words *endogenous* and *morphine*.) As it turns out, there are many natural opiate-like compounds, and new ones are still being discovered. So the term *endorphin* refers to any neurotransmitter that can bind to the same receptors stimulated by opiates. Endorphins are used by neurons in several parts of the brain, including neuronal pathways that modify pain signals to the brain.

Gases   Ideas about what substances can act as neurotransmitters were radically altered following the recent discovery that these chemicals include *nitric oxide* and *carbon monoxide*—two toxic gases that contribute to air pollution (Baranano, Ferris, & Snyder, 2001; Boehning & Snyder, 2002). When nitric oxide or carbon monoxide is released by a neuron, it spreads to nearby neurons, sending a signal that affects chemical reactions inside those neurons rather than binding to receptors on their surface. Nitric oxide is not stored in vesicles, as most other neurotransmitters are; it can be released from any part of the neuron. Nitric oxide appears to be one of the neurotransmitters responsible for such diverse functions as penile erection and the formation of memories—not at the same site, obviously.

Neurotransmitters link biochemistry to behavior and mental processes. ("In Review: Classes of Neurotransmitters" summarizes the main neurotransmitters and the consequences of malfunctioning neurotransmitter systems.) Many drugs, like heroin and Prozac, have effects on various neurotransmitters or receptor sites. The intimate relationships among neurotransmitters, drugs, behavior, and mental processes suggest exciting research questions. For instance, can drugs be used to improve our memory?

in review

CLASSES OF NEUROTRANSMITTERS

Neurotransmitter Class	Normal Function	Disorder Associated with Malfunction
Small Molecules Acetylcholine	Memory, movement	Alzheimer's disease
Norepinephrine	Mood, sleep, learning	Depression
Serotonin	Mood, appetite, impulsivity	Depression
Dopamine	Movement, reward	Parkinson's disease, schizophrenia
GABA	Sleep, movement	Anxiety, Huntington's disease, epilepsy
Glutamate	Memory	Damage after stroke
Peptides Endorphins	Pain control	No established disorder
Gases Nitric oxide	Memory	No established disorder

?   *The main neurotransmitter for slowing, or inhibiting, brain activity is _____.*

As suggested by our discussion so far, if drugs could improve memory, they would probably work by altering the activity of memory-related neurotransmitters in the brain. Several drugs—including Cognex, Aricept, Exelon, Reminyl, Eldepryl, and memantine—are being prescribed for, or tested with, elderly people who suffer from Alzheimer's disease and other severe memory disorders. These patients are probably outnumbered, though, by the college students and other healthy younger people who buy a dizzying variety of over-the-counter dietary supplements that are supposed to improve memory. These include, among others, *Ginkgo biloba,* ginseng, vitamins C and E, *Bacopa monniera,* ashwaganda, docosahexaenoic acid (DHA), acetyl-L-carnitine, phosphatidylserine, phosphatidylcholine, piracetam, and vinpocetine. Several supplements are combined in "brain tonics" with names such as GinkoIQ, Thinker's Edge, BrainPower, Megamind, Remind, and Brain Booster. Some are even included in soft drinks marketed under the names Arizona and SoBe.

THINKING CRITICALLY

Are There Nutrients That Can Improve Your Memory?

■ What am I being asked to believe or accept?

"Smart drugs" are known as *nootropics* (pronounced "no-oh-TROH-pix"), a name derived from the Greek words *noos* and *tropein,* which mean "mind" and "toward." Proponents of supposedly nootropic dietary supplements say that these substances do, in fact, improve a variety of cognitive functions, including learning and memory (Gabryel & Trzeciak, 1994).

■ Is there evidence available to support the claim?

As you might expect, much of the evidence for the effects of these substances comes in the form of reports by satisfied users. One man claimed that after taking *Ginkgo biloba* for three months, "I'm able to find things faster—misplaced keys, papers I'm working on," and a person who took a combination of ginkgo and phosphatidylcholine said, "I passed my psychiatric board exams on these supplements!" (Fremerman, 1998). Sincere as they may be, such reports could easily reflect placebo effects, so it is important to determine whether evidence from placebo-controlled experiments supports users' testimonials.

Two reviews of evidence from such experiments suggest that dietary supplements can, in fact, enhance memory (Gold, Cahill, & Wenk, 2003; McDaniel, Maier, & Einstein, 2002). A few of the studies reviewed found that taking *Ginkgo biloba* was associated with small but significant improvement on some measures of cognitive ability in patients with mild cognitive impairment, such as early Alzheimer's disease. Other studies showed that ginkgo improved performance on cognitive tasks in healthy younger people, too. Still other studies found that aged animals performed more like young animals on some memory tasks after treatment with phosphatidylserine, piracetam, vinpocetine, and vitamin E. Similar results were found in humans. People who received these nutrients performed better on cognitive tasks than did people who received placebos, though the difference was most pronounced in people who had been suffering some degree of memory impairment.

■ Can that evidence be interpreted another way?

Most of the experimental evidence available suggests that the effects of nootropics are small, are confined to only certain cognitive tasks, and are most noticeable in people whose memories are somewhat impaired. In unimpaired people, the effects of nootropics may appear mainly when cognitive performance would normally have been poorest, such as in midafternoon (McDaniel, Maier, & Einstein, 2002; Wesnes et al., 2000). In other words, though some nootropics can produce effects that are superior to placebos, this does not mean that these substances offer a solution to all human memory problems, or that everyone should be taking them (McDaniel et al., 2002). In fact, the available evidence could be interpreted to mean that the average healthy person will be able to perform cognitive tasks at work and at school just as well without these supplements.

■ What evidence would help to evaluate the alternatives?

Those who have reviewed the research literature on nootropics suggest that final conclusions about the value of these substances be deferred until we have more experimental evidence about their effects on impaired and normal people of various ages. We will also need more detailed information about how varying doses of nootropics affect specific memory processes. Would higher doses or longer courses of treatment produce greater effects than those seen so far? How do nootropics work? Do they affect the making of memories, the recollection of memories, or both? Would the effects seen in the relatively small studies available today be replicated in larger studies with more participants from a wider range of sociocultural groups?

Some of this research has already been reported. In one double-blind, placebo-controlled study of memory enhancement, 230 healthy men and women over the age of sixty were randomly assigned to receive six weeks of treatment with either *Ginkgo biloba* or a placebo (Solomon et al., 2002). The treatment program followed the dosage, frequency, and duration recommended by the supplement's manufacturer. All the volunteers were tested on fourteen measures of cognitive ability before and after treatment began. In this study, the participants who took ginkgo did no better after treatment than the members of the placebo group. Other research is still under way. For example, the U.S. National Institutes of Health has recently allocated $15 million to fund a much larger study on the effects of ginkgo in normal and mildly impaired elderly people. The results will be available in 2006.

■ What conclusions are most reasonable?

The available evidence suggests that nootropic dietary supplements offer neither a cure for cognitive impairment nor a pathway to superhuman memory. But the evidence doesn't justify dismissing them as worthless. Although the supplements currently available for improving memory are limited in effectiveness, they appear to be worthy of further investigation. In the meantime, the strategies described in the chapter on memory are likely to be far more effective than nootropics in helping you remember information and do well in school. There is also evidence that "exercising your brain" and exercising your body have long-term benefits on memory and brain function. For example, educational pursuits, physical activity in middle age, and a life of working at a job that engages the mind have been associated with a lowered risk for Alzheimer's disease later on, perhaps because they all increase cerebral blood flow (Crawford, 1998; Evans et al., 1997; Friedland et al., 2001; Gatz et al., 2001; Wilson, Mendes de Leon, et al.; 2002).

The Peripheral Nervous System: Keeping in Touch with the World

▶ How is my nervous system organized?

The billions of neurons that make up your nervous system are organized into two main parts—the *central nervous system* and the *peripheral nervous system* (see Figure 2.4). We describe them in separate sections, but they work together closely to coordinate your behavior and mental processes. The **central nervous system (CNS)** consists of the brain and spinal cord, which are encased in bone for protection. Like the chief executive officer in a company, the CNS receives information, processes it, and determines what actions should result.

The **peripheral nervous system** sends sensory information from the eyes, ears, and other sense organs to the CNS. The peripheral nervous system also carries messages from the

central nervous system (CNS) The brain and spinal cord.

peripheral nervous system The part of the nervous system that sends messages to and from the central nervous system.

figure 2.4

Organization of the Nervous System

The brain and spinal cord make up the bone-encased central nervous system (CNS), the body's central information processor, decision maker, and director of actions. The peripheral nervous system, which is not housed in bone, functions mainly to carry messages. The somatic subsystem of the peripheral nervous system transmits information to the CNS from the outside world and conveys instructions from the CNS to the muscles. The autonomic subsystem conveys messages from the CNS that alter the activity of organs and glands, and it sends information about that activity back to the brain.

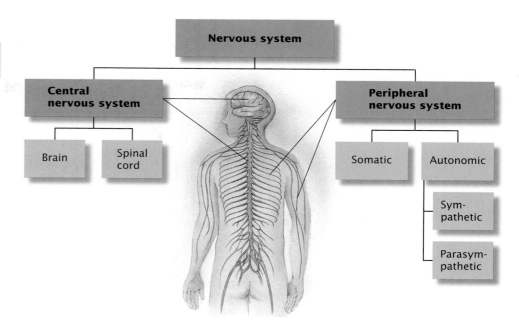

brain and spinal cord to the muscles, glands, and other parts of the body. In essence, the peripheral nervous system is an information relay system to and from the CNS. Unlike the CNS, it is not protected by bone. To accomplish its relay tasks, the peripheral nervous system has two subsystems—the autonomic nervous system and the somatic nervous system.

The Somatic Nervous System

Imagine that you are at the beach. It is hot, and the ocean smells salty. An attractive stranger approaches, catching your eye. The stranger smiles. You smile in return. The stranger continues walking away. In these few seconds, your nervous system has been busy. You feel the warmth of the sun and smell the ocean because your **somatic nervous system** takes in these pieces of sensory information and sends them to the central nervous system for processing. The CNS evaluates the warmth and the smells, sending messages through the somatic nervous system to the muscles that allow you to turn over, sit up, or put on more sunscreen. *Sensory neurons* bring information into the brain. *Motor neurons* carry information from the part of the brain that directs motion.

The Autonomic Nervous System

The **autonomic nervous system** carries messages back and forth between the CNS and the heart, lungs, and other organs and glands (Berthoud & Neuhuber, 2000). For example, the autonomic nervous system takes that passing stranger's "attractive" rating from the CNS and translates it into an increase in heart rate, pupil dilation, and perhaps a little blushing. This system is called "autonomic" because such activities are generally autonomous, or independent of your control. With training and practice, some people can use a technique called *biofeedback* to bring some of their involuntary responses, such as heart rate, under conscious (CNS) control.

As shown in Figure 2.4, the autonomic system has two subsystems of its own—the *sympathetic nervous system* and the *parasympathetic nervous system*. These two subsystems work like a seesaw on a playground. Generally, the **sympathetic nervous system** readies your body for action in the face of stress. The **parasympathetic nervous system**

somatic nervous system The subsystem of the peripheral nervous system that transmits information from the senses to the central nervous system and carries signals from the CNS to the muscles that move the skeleton.

autonomic nervous system The subsystem of the peripheral nervous system that carries messages between the central nervous system and the heart, lungs, and other organs and glands in the body.

sympathetic nervous system The subsystem of the autonomic nervous system that readies the body for vigorous activity.

parasympathetic nervous system The subsystem of the autonomic nervous system that typically influences activity related to the protection, nourishment, and growth of the body.

calms you down once the crisis has passed. So the sympathetic nervous system *spends* energy, whereas the parasympathetic nervous system *preserves* energy.

The Central Nervous System: Making Sense of the World

▶ How is my brain "wired"?

Researchers tend to think of the central nervous system as being like the central processor in a computer, but the CNS does not simply function as a high-powered computer. It certainly isn't laid out as neatly, either. The layout of the brain is more like what you would see on a college campus. There are clusters of offices for the administrators in one place, clusters of faculty offices in another place, and classrooms in yet another. Some of the sidewalks or hallways that connect these clusters are wide; others are narrow. There are many different but connected ways to get to the same place. Like a campus with its office clusters, the CNS has clusters of neuron cell bodies called **nuclei** (pronounced NUKE-lee-eye; *nuclei* is the plural of *nucleus*). The sidewalks and hallways of the CNS are axons that travel together in bundles called **fiber tracts** or *pathways*. The axon (hallway) from any given cell (office) may merge with and leave many fiber tracts (sidewalks) and send branches out to other tracts. Let's consider a practical example of nervous system functioning to begin learning our way around the "campus" of the brain.

It is 6 A.M and your alarm clock goes off, creating the simple case of information processing illustrated in Figure 2.1. Your ears receive sensory input in the form of sound from the alarm. The sound is converted into neural signals and sent to the brain. Your brain compares these signals with previous experiences stored in memory and correctly associates the sound with "alarm clock." Your muscle-guiding output is not yet at peak performance, though, because your brain activity has not yet reached the waking state. So you fumble to turn off the alarm, shuffle to the kitchen, and accidentally touch the coffeemaker's heating element. Things get more lively now. Heat energy activates sensory neurons in your fingers, generating action potentials that speed along fiber tracts going into the spinal cord. Your motor neurons are reflexively activated by the CNS, causing muscles in your arm to contract and quickly withdraw your hand.

applying psychology   **IS THAT YOUR FINAL ANSWER?**   The geographically largest U.S. state is (a) Montana, (b) Texas, (c) Alaska, (d) Wyoming. Like contestants on shows such as *Who Wants to Be a Millionaire*, you must rely on your central nervous system, and especially on the information-processing power of your brain, to understand the question, recognize the correct option, and direct movements of your vocal muscles to make your answer heard. (The correct choice in this case is *c*.)

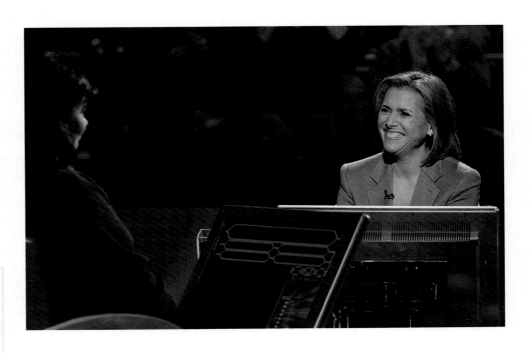

nuclei   Clusters of nerve cell bodies in the central nervous system.

fiber tracts   Bundles of axons that travel together.

figure 2.5

A Reflex Pathway

learn by **doing**   Sit on a chair, cross one leg over the other, and then use the handle of a butter knife or some other solid object to gently tap your top knee, just below the joint, until you get a "knee jerk" reaction. Tapping your knee at just the right spot sets off an almost instantaneous sequence of events that begins with stimulation of sensory neurons that respond to stretch. When those neurons fire, their axons, which end within the spinal cord, cause spinal neurons to fire. This, in turn, stimulates the firing of motor neurons with axons ending in your thigh muscles. The result is a contraction of those muscles and a kicking of the lower leg and foot. Information about the knee tap and about what the leg has done also goes to your cerebral cortex, but the reflex is completed without waiting for guidance from the brain.

spinal cord   The part of the central nervous system that receives information from the senses, passes these signals to the brain, and sends messages from the brain to the body.

reflexes   Simple, involuntary, unlearned behaviors directed by the spinal cord without instructions from the brain.

The Spinal Cord

The **spinal cord** receives signals such as pain and touch from the senses and passes those signals to the brain. Neuron fibers within the cord also carry signals downward from the brain to the muscles. Some cells of the spinal cord can direct simple behaviors without instructions from the brain. These behaviors are called **reflexes,** because the response to the incoming signal is directly "reflected" back out, as shown in Figure 2.5. Spinal reflexes, like the one that pulled your hand away from the heat, are very fast because they make few time-consuming synaptic links. Reflexes are called *involuntary* because they occur without instructions from the brain. As reflexes occur, though, action potentials are also sent along fiber tracts to the brain. So, you officially "know" you have been burned a fraction of a second after your reflex got you out of trouble. The spinal cord is an example of a *feedback system*. When touching something hot sets off a simple reflex, one set of arm muscles contracts, and an opposing set of muscles relaxes. If this did not happen, the arm would go rigid. The muscles also have receptors that send information to the spinal cord to let it know how extended they are so that adjustments can be made for a smooth contracting motion. Information about the consequences of an action goes back to the source of the action for further adjustment. That is a feedback system.

The Brain

Have you ever been bothered by a tune or a phrase that you "couldn't get out your head"? New techniques for monitoring the activity of various brain regions can actually "see" inside your head to locate where such persistent thoughts occur (Zungu-Dirwayi et al., 1999). The same techniques can be used to determine which parts of the brain are active when people are excited by sexually explicit images (Stoleru et al., 1999). These new techniques, combined with older techniques, have opened new doors to studying brain function in humans (Miller, 2003; see Table 2.1). Each technique can indirectly measure the activity of neurons firing, and each has different advantages and disadvantages. One of the earliest of these techniques, called the *electroencephalograph (EEG)*, measures general electrical activity of the brain. Electrodes are pasted on the scalp to detect the electrical fields resulting from the activity of billions of neurons. Although this tool can associate rapidly changing electrical activity with changes in the activity of the brain, it cannot tell us exactly where the active cells are.

A newer technique, called the *PET scan*, can locate cell activity by recording where radioactive substances become concentrated when injected into the bloodstream. *PET* stands for *positron emission tomography*. It records images from the brain that indicate

table 2.1	Techniques for Studying Human Brain Function and Structure

Technique	What It Shows	Advantages (+) and Disadvantages (−)
EEG (electroencephalograph): Multiple electrodes are pasted to the outside of the head	Lines that chart the summated electrical fields resulting from the activity of billions of neurons	+ Detects very rapid changes in electrical activity, allowing analysis of stages of cognitive processing − Provides poor spatial resolution of the source of electrical activity; EEG is sometimes combined with magnetoencephalography (MEG), which localizes electrical activity by measuring magnetic fields associated with it.
PET (positron emission tomography) and SPECT (single-photon emission computed tomography): Positrons and photons are emissions from radioactive substances	An image of the amount and localization of any molecule that can be injected in radioactive form, such as neurotransmitters, drugs, or tracers for blood flow or glucose use (which indicates specific changes in neuronal activity)	+ Allows functional and biochemical studies + Provides visual image corresponding to anatomy − Requires exposure to low levels of radioactivity − Provides spatial resolution better than that of EEG but poorer than that of MRI − Cannot follow rapid changes (faster than 30 seconds)
MRI (magnetic resonance imaging): Exposes the brain to a magnetic field and measures radiofrequency waves	Traditional MRI provides high-resolution image of brain anatomy. Functional MRI (fMRI) provides images of changes in blood flow (which indicate specific changes in neural activity). A new variant, diffusion tensor imaging (DTI), shows water flow in neural fibers, thus revealing the "wiring diagram" of neural connections in the brain.	+ Requires no exposure to radioactivity + Provides high spatial resolution of anatomical details (< 1 mm) + Provides high temporal resolution ($< \frac{1}{10}$ second)
TMS (transcranial magnetic stimulation): Temporarily disrupts electrical activity of a small region of brain by exposing it to an intense magnetic field.	Normal function of a particular brain region can be studied by observing changes after TMS is applied to a specific location.	+ Shows which brain regions are necessary for given tasks. − Long term safety not well established.

the location of the radioactivity as the brain performs various tasks. For instance, PET studies have revealed that specific brain regions are activated when we look at fearful facial expressions or engage in certain kinds of thoughts (Morris et al., 1998; Wharton et al., 2000). PET scans can tell us a lot about where changes in brain activity occur, but they can't reveal details of the brain's physical structure.

figure 2.6

Combining a PET Scan and Magnetic Resonance Imaging

Researchers have superimposed images from PET scans and MRI to construct a three-dimensional view of the living brain. This figure shows the brain of a young epileptic girl. The picture of the outer surface of the brain is from the MRI; the pink area is from the PET scan and shows the source of epileptic activity. To the right of the figure are separate MRI and PET images taken at one plane, or "slice," through the brain (indicated by the line on the brain at the left).

A detailed structural picture of the brain can be seen, however, using *magnetic resonance imaging*, or *MRI*. MRI exposes the brain to a magnetic field and measures the resulting radiofrequency waves to get amazingly clear pictures of the brain's anatomical details (see Figure 2.6). *Functional MRI*, or *fMRI*, combines the advantages of PET and MRI and is capable of detecting changes in blood flow that reflect ongoing changes in the activity of neurons—providing a sort of "moving picture" of the brain (e.g., Shu et al., 2002). The newest techniques offer even better insight into brain activity, structure, and functioning. These techniques include a variant on fMRI called *diffusion tensor imaging (DTI)*, as well as a procedure called *transcranial magnetic stimulation (TMS)*.

These tools have opened new frontiers for biological psychology, neuroscience, and medicine. Much of our growing understanding of how and why behavior occurs comes from research with these techniques (e.g., Goldstein & Volkow, 2002; Miller, 2003). Let's now explore some of the structures highlighted by these techniques, starting with three major subdivisions of the brain: the hindbrain, the midbrain, and the forebrain.

The Hindbrain

Figure 2.7 shows the major structures of the brain. The **hindbrain** lies just inside the skull and is actually a continuation of the spinal cord. Incoming signals from the spinal cord first reach the hindbrain. Many vital autonomic functions, such as heart rate, blood pressure, and breathing, are controlled by nuclei in the hindbrain, particularly in an area called the **medulla**.

Weaving throughout the hindbrain and into the midbrain is a mesh-like collection of cells called the **reticular formation** (*reticular* means "net-like"). This network is involved in arousal and attention. Cutting off fibers of the reticular system from the rest of the brain would put a person into a permanent coma. Some of the fibers carrying pain signals from the spinal cord connect in the reticular formation and immediately arouse the brain from sleep. Within seconds, the hindbrain causes your heart rate and blood pressure to increase. You are awake and aroused.

The **cerebellum** (pronounced "sair-a-BELL-um") is also part of the hindbrain. For a long time its primary function was thought to be control of finely coordinated movements, such as threading a needle. We now know that the cerebellum also allows the eyes to track a moving target accurately (Krauzlis & Lisberger, 1991) and that it may be the storehouse for well-rehearsed movements, such as those associated with dancing, piano playing, and athletics (McCormick & Thompson, 1984). The cerebellum might

hindbrain The portion of the brain that lies just inside the skull and is a continuation of the spinal cord.

medulla The area of the hindbrain that controls vital autonomic functions such as heart rate, blood pressure, and breathing.

reticular formation A collection of cells and fibers in the hindbrain and midbrain that are involved in arousal and attention.

cerebellum The part of the hindbrain that controls finely coordinated movements.

figure 2.7

Major Structures of the Brain

This side view of a section cut down the middle of the brain reveals the forebrain, midbrain, hindbrain, and spinal cord. Many of these subdivisions do not have clear-cut borders, because they are all interconnected by fiber tracts. The brain's anatomy reflects its evolution over millions of years. Newer structures (such as the cerebral cortex, which is the outer surface of the forebrain) that handle higher mental functions were built on older ones (such as the medulla) that coordinate heart rate, breathing, and other, more basic functions.

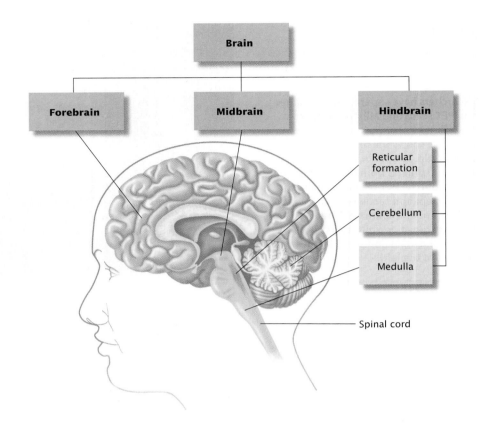

also be involved in the learning of these skills (Hazeltine & Ivry, 2002), as well as in more uniquely human tasks such as language and symbolic thought (Cabeza & Nyberg, 2000). For instance, abnormalities in the cerebellum have been associated with reading disabilities (Rae et al., 2002), and surgery that affects the cerebellum sometimes results in a syndrome called *cerebellar mutism,* in which patients become unable to speak for periods ranging from a few days to several years (Gelabert-Gonzalez & Fernandez-Villa, 2001).

Reflexes and feedback systems are important in the hindbrain. For example, if blood pressure drops, heart action reflexively increases to make up for that decrease. If you stand up very quickly, your blood pressure can drop so suddenly that you feel lightheaded until the hindbrain reflexively "catches up." You will faint if the hindbrain does not activate the autonomic nervous system to increase your blood pressure.

The Midbrain

A small structure called the **midbrain** lies above the hindbrain. If you focus your eyes on another person and then move your head, midbrain circuits allow you to move your eyes smoothly in the direction opposite from your head movement so you never lose focus. Did you ever swing a bat, swat a mosquito, or jump rope? Part of the midbrain and its connections to the forebrain allowed you to produce those movements smoothly. When a car backfires, causing you to reflexively turn your head and look in the direction of the sound, it is again the midbrain at work. Together, the midbrain and parts of the hindbrain other than the cerebellum are called the *brainstem.*

The Forebrain

In humans, the **forebrain** controls the most complex aspects of behavior and mental life. It folds back over and completely covers the rest of the brain. The outer surface

midbrain   A small structure between the hindbrain and the forebrain that helps produce smooth movements.

forebrain   The part of the brain responsible for the most complex aspects of behavior and mental life.

A FIELD SOBRIETY TEST The cerebellum is heavily involved in the balance and coordination required for walking and other well-rehearsed motor skills. When the cerebellum's activity is impaired by alcohol, these skills are disrupted, which is why the police ask people suspected of drunken driving to walk a straight line.

of the forebrain is called the *cerebral cortex*. Figure 2.8 shows some structures of the forebrain.

Two structures deep within the forebrain, the *hypothalamus* and the *thalamus*, help operate basic drives, emotion, and sensation. The **thalamus** acts as a relay station for pain and sense-organ signals (except smell) from the body to the upper levels of the brain. The thalamus also processes and makes sense of these signals. The **hypothalamus** lies under the thalamus (*hypo* means "under") and helps regulate hunger, thirst, and sex drives. The hypothalamus is well connected to the autonomic nervous system and to other parts of the brain. Damage to parts of the hypothalamus upsets normal appetite, thirst, and sexual behavior.

Can you set an "internal alarm clock" to wake up in the morning at whatever time you want? Some people can, with the help of a remarkable part of the hypothalamus that contains the brain's own clock: the *suprachiasmatic nuclei*. The suprachiasmatic

figure 2.8

Major Structures of the Forebrain

The structures of the forebrain are covered by an outer "bark" known as the *cerebral cortex*. This diagram shows some of the structures that lie deep within the forebrain. The amygdala, the hippocampus, and portions of the cerebral cortex are part of the limbic system.

thalamus A forebrain structure that relays messages from most sense organs to higher brain areas.

hypothalamus A forebrain structure that regulates hunger, thirst, and sex drives, with many connections to and from the autonomic nervous system and other parts of the brain.

(pronounced "soo-pra-kye-as-MAT-ik") nuclei operate on approximately a twenty-four-hour cycle, controlling daily biological rhythms such as waking and sleeping, as well as cycles of body temperature. Studies of the suprachiasmatic nuclei in animals suggest that having different night or morning energy times is biological and stable throughout a lifetime (Cofer et al., 1992). In humans, such differences may make some of us "morning people" and others "night people."

Other parts of the forebrain, especially the *amygdala* (pronounced "ah-MIG-duh-luh") and the *hippocampus,* help to regulate memory and emotion. The **amygdala** links different kinds of sensory information in memory, such as the shape and feel of objects (Murray & Mishkin, 1985). If you close your eyes and pick up an object, your amygdala helps you recognize it. The amygdala also plays a role in fear and other emotions (LeDoux, 1995; Whalen, 1998), connecting emotion to sensation. People who suffer from posttraumatic stress disorder have unusual amygdala activity (Pitman, Shin, & Rauch, 2001). The amygdala, hippocampus, and some portions of the cerebral cortex are part of a group of brain structures called the *limbic system,* which is activated when emotions are being generated.

The **hippocampus** also helps you form new memories. In one case, a patient known as R.B. suffered a stroke (an interruption of blood flow to the brain) that damaged only his hippocampus. Although his intelligence remained above average and he could recall old memories, he was almost totally unable to build new memories (Squire, 1986). Damage to the hippocampus within a day of a mildly painful event seems to erase memories of the experience. However, if the damage occurs several days after the event, the memory remains. It seems that memories are not permanently stored in the hippocampus but instead are transferred from there to somewhere else in the brain.

The hippocampus becomes smaller with age, and research shows that this shrinkage relates to the declining memory function that many elderly people experience (Golomb et al., 1996). On average, the hippocampus of a person with Alzheimer's disease has been found to be 40 percent smaller than that of a person without the disease. Alzheimer's disease is a major cause of senile dementia, which involves the decay of cognitive capabilities. About 10 percent of people over age sixty-five and 47 percent of people over eighty-five suffer from this disease (Kukull et al., 2002; U.S. Department of Health and Human Services, 2001a; U.S. Surgeon General, 1999). The financial cost of Alzheimer's disease is more than $100 billion a year in the United States (U.S. Department of Health and Human Services, 2001a). The cost in human suffering is incalculable.

The Cerebral Cortex

On the surface of the forebrain is the **cerebral cortex**. The total area of the cerebral cortex is one to two square feet, but it fits into the skull because it is somewhat wrinkled and folded. You can wad up a T-shirt and fit it into a bowl in much the same way. The cerebral cortex is much larger in humans than in most other animals (dolphins are an exception). Like a computer's central processing unit, the cerebral cortex is our primary processing area. It analyzes all information from the senses and controls voluntary movement, abstract thinking, and the other most complex aspects of our behavior and mental processes. The cerebral cortex looks somewhat round, with a long groove down the middle creating two halves, called *cerebral hemispheres*. The **corpus callosum,** a massive bundle of more than a million fibers, connects the two hemispheres.

The folds of the cerebral cortex give the surface of the human brain its wrinkled appearance, its ridges and valleys. The ridges are called *gyri* (pronounced "ji-rye"), and the valleys are known as *sulci* (pronounced "sulk-eye") or *fissures*. As you can see in Figure 2.9, several deep sulci divide the cortex into four areas: the frontal (front), parietal (top), occipital (back), and temporal (side) lobes. The gyri and sulci provide landmarks for describing the structure of the cortex, but the *functions* of the cortex do not follow these boundaries. When divided according to function, the cortex includes areas of sensory cortex, motor cortex, and association cortex. ("In Review: Organization of the Brain" summarizes the major structures and functions of the brain.)

amygdala   A forebrain structure that links information from various systems and plays a role in emotions.

hippocampus   A forebrain structure associated with the formation of new memories.

cerebral cortex   The outer surface of the forebrain.

corpus callosum   A massive bundle of fibers that connects the left and right cerebral hemispheres.

figure 2.9

The Cerebral Cortex (viewed from the left side)

The brain's ridges (gyri) and valleys (sulci) are landmarks that divide the cortex into four lobes: the frontal, parietal, occipital, and temporal. These terms describe where the regions are (the lobes are named for the skull bones that cover them), but the cortex is also divided in terms of function. These functional areas include the motor cortex (which controls movement), sensory cortex (which receives information from various senses), and association cortex (which integrates information). Also labeled are Wernicke's area and Broca's area, two regions that are found only on the left side of the cortex and that are vital to the interpretation and production of speech (Peña et al., 2003).

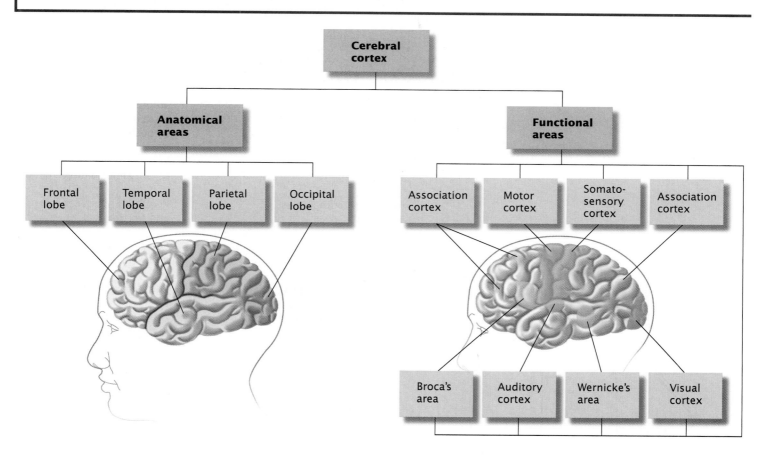

Sensory and Motor Cortex

The **sensory cortex** lies in the parietal, occipital, and temporal lobes. Different regions of the sensory cortex receive information from different senses. Occipital lobe cells called the *visual cortex* receive visual information. Temporal lobe cells called the *auditory cortex* receive information from the ears. And information from the skin, such as touch, pain, and temperature, is received by cells in the parietal lobe. These skin-related areas are called the *somatosensory cortex* (*soma* is Greek for "body"). Information about skin sensations from neighboring parts of the body comes to neighboring parts of the somatosensory cortex. It is as if the outline of a tiny person, dangling upside down, determined the location of the information (see Figure 2.10). This pattern is called the *homunculus* (Latin for "little man"). The amount of sensory cortex that responds to particular sensory stimulation can be modified by experience (Candia et al., 2003; Kilgard & Merzenich, 1998). For example, if a limb is lost, sensory cortex that had been stimulated by that limb will now be stimulated by other regions of skin. Similarly, practicing the violin will increase the number of sensory neurons that respond to touch; the same thing

sensory cortex The part of the cerebral cortex located in the parietal, occipital, and temporal lobes that receives stimulus information from the skin, eyes, and ears, respectively.

ORGANIZATION OF THE BRAIN

in review

Major Division	Some Major Structures	Some Major Functions
Hindbrain	Medulla	Regulates breathing, heart rate, and blood pressure
	Reticular formation (also extends into midbrain)	Regulates arousal and attention
	Cerebellum	Controls finely coordinated movements
Midbrain	Various nuclei	Relays sensory signals to forebrain; creates automatic responses to certain stimuli; initiates smooth movement
Forebrain	Thalamus	Interprets and relays sensory information
	Hypothalamus	Regulates hunger, thirst, and sex drives
	Amygdala	Connects sensations and emotions
	Hippocampus	Forms new memories
	Cerebral cortex	Analyzes sensory information; controls voluntary movements, abstract thinking, and other complex cognitive activity
	Corpus callosum	Transfers information between the two cerebral hemispheres

? *The oldest part of the brain is the _____.*

THE FAR SIDE® BY GARY LARSON

"Whoa! *That* was a good one! Try it, Hobbs—just poke his brain right where my finger is."

happens when blind people learn to read Braille with their fingertips (Pascual-Leone & Torres, 1993).

In the frontal lobe, specific neurons of the **motor cortex** control voluntary movements in specific parts of the body (Indovina & Sanes, 2001). The motor cortex's arrangement mirrors that of the somatosensory cortex. So the parts of the motor cortex that control hand movement are near parts of the sensory cortex that receive sensory information from the hands.

Seems easy, doesn't it? You have a map of your body parts in your cerebral cortex, and you activate cells in the hand region of the cortex if you want to move your hand. In fact, the actual process is quite complex. Recall again your sleepy reach for the coffee pot. To grasp its handle, your cortex must first translate the pot's location into a position relative to your body—to your left or right, for example. Next, the cortex must determine which muscles must be contracted to produce the desired movement toward that exact posi-

motor cortex The part of the cerebral cortex that controls voluntary movement.

figure 2.10

Motor and Somatosensory Cortex

The areas of cortex that move parts of the body (motor cortex) and receive sensory input from body parts (somatosensory cortex) appear in both hemispheres of the brain. Here we show cross-sections of only those on the left side, looking from the back of the brain toward the front. Areas controlling movement of neighboring parts of the body, such as the foot and leg, occupy neighboring parts of the motor cortex. Areas receiving input from neighboring body parts, such as the lips and tongue, are near one another in the sensory cortex. Notice that the size of these areas is uneven; the larger the area devoted to each body part, the larger that body part appears on the "homunculus."

Note: Did you notice the error in this classic drawing? (The figure shows the right side of the body, but the left hand and left side of the face.)
Source: Penfield & Rasmussen, 1968).

tion. Groups of neurons work together to produce just the right combinations of direction and force in particular muscle groups. Making these determinations involves many interconnected areas of the cortex. Computer models of neural networks are showing how these complex problem-solving processes might occur (Graziano, Taylor, & Moore, 2002; Krauzlis, 2002).

FOCUS ON RESEARCH

The Case of the Disembodied Woman

Neurologist Oliver Sacks described the case of "Christina," a woman who had somehow lost the ability to feel the position of her own body (Sacks, 1985). This case study led to important insights about biological psychology that could not be studied through controlled experiments. One such insight was the realization that the sense known as *kinesthesia* (pronounced "kin-es-THEE-see-uh") not only tells us where our body parts are but also plays an important role in our sense of self.

Christina was a healthy young woman who entered a hospital in preparation for some minor surgery. Before the surgery could be performed, however, she began to have difficulty holding onto objects. Then she had trouble moving. She would rise from bed and flop onto the floor like a rag doll. Christina seemed to have "lost" her body. She felt disembodied, like a ghost. On one occasion, for example, she became annoyed at a visitor she thought was tapping her fingers on a tabletop. But it was she, not the visitor, who was doing it. Her hands were acting on their own. Her body was doing things she did not know about.

■ What was the researcher's question?

Christina could not walk or use her hands and arms. Why was a seemingly normal, healthy young woman falling and dropping things?

■ How did the researcher answer the question?

A psychiatrist at the hospital thought that Christina was suffering from *conversion disorder,* a condition in which psychological problems cause physical disabilities (see the chapter on psychological disorders). Unconvinced, Dr. Sacks conducted a careful case study of Christina.

■ What did the researcher find?

It turned out that the psychiatrist's diagnosis was wrong. Dr. Sacks's examinations and tests revealed that Christina had lost all sensory feedback about her joints, muscle tone, and the position of her limbs. Christina had suffered a breakdown, or degeneration, of the sensory neurons that normally bring kinesthetic information to her brain. In other words, there was a biological reason why Christina could not walk or control her hands and arms.

■ What do the results mean?

In his analysis of this case, Dr. Sacks noted that the sense we have of our bodies is provided partly through our experience of seeing, but also partly through *proprioception* (sensing the self). Christina herself put it this way: "Proprioception is like the eyes of the body, the way the body sees itself. And if it goes, it's like the body's blind." With great effort and determination, Christina was ultimately able to regain some of her ability to move about. If she looked intently at her arms and legs, she could coordinate their movement somewhat. Eventually, she left the hospital and resumed many of her normal activities. But Christina never recovered her sense of self. She still feels like a stranger in her own body.

■ What do we still need to know?

Notice that Christina's case study did not confirm any hypotheses about kinesthesia in the way an experiment might. It did, however, focus attention on what it feels like to have lost this sense. It also highlighted a rare condition that, though almost unknown when Dr. Sacks reported it, has been observed more often in recent years, especially among people taking megadoses of vitamin B6, also known as *pyridoxine* (Sacks, 1985). These high doses—or even lower doses taken over a long period of time—can damage sensory neurons (Dordain & Deffond, 1994). How and why vitamin B6 does such damage still needs to be determined. Are there other causes of this kinesthetic disorder? What treatments might best combat it? Much research remains to be done, and pursuing that work is how psychologists and other scientists begin to unravel the mysteries of behavior and mental processes.

Association Cortex

Parts of the cortex that do not directly receive specific sensory information or control specific movements are referred to as **association cortex.** The term *association* describes these areas well, because they receive input from more than one sense or input that combines sensory and motor information. For instance, these areas associate words with images. Association cortex appears in all of the lobes and forms a large part of the cerebral cortex in humans. For this reason, damage to association areas can create serious problems in a wide range of mental abilities.

Consider language. Language information comes from the auditory cortex for spoken language or from the visual cortex for written language. Areas of the motor cortex produce speech. Putting it all together in the complex activity known as language involves activity in association cortex. In the 1860s, Paul Broca described the effects of damage to association cortex in the frontal lobe near motor areas that control face muscles. This part of the cortex is on the left side of the brain and is called *Broca's area* (see Figure 2.9). Damage to Broca's area disrupts speech organization, a condition called *Broca's aphasia.* Victims have difficulty speaking, often making errors in grammar. Each word comes out slowly. Surprisingly, when a person with Broca's aphasia sings, the words come easily and correctly. Apparently, words set to music are handled by a different part of the brain (Besson et al., 1998). Some speech therapists take advantage of this fact through "melodic intonation" therapy, which helps Broca's aphasia patients to gain fluency by speaking in a "singsong" manner (Lapointe, 1990).

Other language problems result from damage to a portion of association cortex described in the 1870s by Carl Wernicke (pronounced "VER-nick-ee"). Figure 2.9 shows that, like Broca's area, *Wernicke's area* is on the left side of the brain, but it is in the temporal lobe, near the area of the sensory cortex that receives information from the ears. Wernicke's area also receives input from the visual cortex and is involved in the interpretation of both speech and written words. Damage to Wernicke's area produces complicated symptoms. It can leave patients with the ability to speak but disrupts the ability to understand the meaning of words or to speak understandably.

One study illustrates the different effects of damage to each area (Lapointe, 1990). In response to the request "Tell me what you do with a cigarette," a person with Broca's aphasia replied, "Uh . . . uh . . . cigarette [pause] smoke it." Though halting and

**LINKAGES
Where are the brain's language centers?**
(a link to Thought, Language, and Intelligence)

learn **by doing**

LANGUAGE AREAS OF THE BRAIN Have you ever tried to write notes while you were talking to someone? Like this teacher, you can probably write and talk at the same time, because each of these language functions uses different areas of association cortex. However, stop reading for a moment, and try writing one word with your left hand and a different word with your right hand. If you had trouble, it is partly because you asked the same language area of your brain to do two things at once.

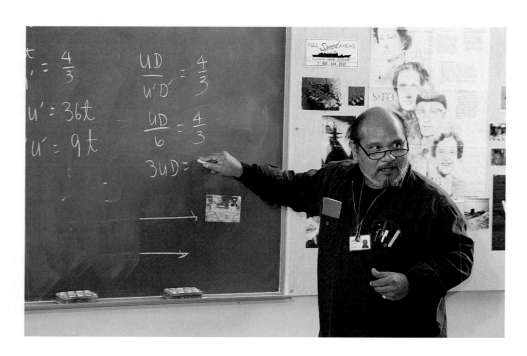

association cortex The parts of the cerebral cortex that integrate sensory and motor information and perform complex cognitive tasks.

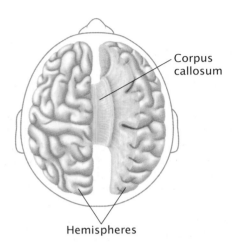

figure 2.11

The Brain's Left and Right Hemispheres

The brain's two hemispheres are joined by a core bundle of nerve fibers known as the *corpus callosum;* in this figure the hemispheres are separated so that the corpus callosum can be seen. The two cerebral hemispheres look nearly the same but perform somewhat different tasks. For one thing, the left hemisphere receives sensory input from, and controls movement on, the right side of the body. The right hemisphere senses and controls the left side of the body.

awkwardly phrased, this speech was meaningful. In response to the same request, a person with Wernicke's aphasia replied, "This is a segment of a pegment. Soap a cigarette." This speech, by contrast, was fluent but without meaning.

It appears that written language and spoken language require the use of different areas of association cortex. So does language involving specific grammatical or conceptual categories. For example, two women—H.W. and S.J.D—each had a stroke in 1985, causing damage to different language-related parts of their association cortex. Neither woman has difficulty speaking or writing nouns, but both have difficulty with verbs (Caramazza & Hillis, 1991). H.W. can write verbs but cannot speak them. S.J.D. can speak verbs but has difficulty writing them. Interestingly, H.W. has difficulty pronouncing *watch* when it is used as a verb in the sentence "I watch TV," but she speaks the same word easily when it appears as a noun in "My watch is slow."

The Divided Brain: Lateralization

A striking suggestion emerged from observations of people with damage to the language centers of the brain. Researchers noticed that damage to specific areas of the left hemisphere interfered with the use or comprehension of language. Corresponding damage to the right hemisphere usually did not. Could it be that the right and left hemispheres of the brain serve different functions?

This is not a new idea. It has long been understood that most sensory and motor pathways cross over from one hemisphere to the other as they enter or leave the brain. As a result, the left hemisphere receives information from, and controls movements of, the right side of the body. The right hemisphere receives input from and controls the left side of the body. Figure 2.11 shows the two hemispheres. The fact that language centers such as Broca's area and Wernicke's area almost always occur on the left side of the brain suggests that each hemisphere might be specialized to perform some functions almost independently of the other hemisphere (Stephan et al., 2003).

In the late 1800s there was great interest in the idea that the hemispheres might be specialized, but no techniques were available for testing it. Renewed interest grew out of studies during the 1960s by Roger Sperry, Michael Gazzaniga, and their colleagues.

Split-Brain Studies Sperry studied *split-brain* patients—people who had undergone surgery in an attempt to control the severe seizures of epilepsy. Before the surgery, their seizures began in one hemisphere and then spread throughout the brain. As a last resort, surgeons isolated the two hemispheres from each other by cutting the corpus callosum, which had connected them.

After the surgery, researchers used a special device like the one shown in Figure 2.12 to present visual images to only one side of these patients' split brains. They found that cutting the tie between the hemispheres had dramatically affected the way these people thought about and dealt with the world. For example, when the image of a spoon was presented to the left, language-oriented side of patient N.G.'s split brain, she could say what the spoon was. But when the spoon was presented to the right side of her brain, she could not describe the spoon in words. She still knew what the object was, because she could pick it out from a group of objects by feeling its shape with her left hand (controlled by the right hemisphere). When asked what she had just grasped, she replied, "A pencil." The right hemisphere recognized the object, but the patient could not say what it was because the left (language) half of her brain did not see or feel it (Sperry, 1968).

Although the right hemisphere has no control over spoken language in split-brain patients, it does have important capabilities related to nonspoken language. For example, a split-brain patient's right hemisphere can guide the left hand in spelling out words with Scrabble tiles (Gazzaniga & LeDoux, 1978). Thanks to this finding, researchers concluded that split-brain patients have self-awareness and normal learning abilities in their right hemispheres. In addition, these patients' right hemispheres did better than their left

figure 2.12

Apparatus for Studying Split-Brain Patients

When the person stares at the dot on the screen, images briefly presented on one side of the dot go to only one side of the brain. For example, a picture of a spoon presented on the left side of the screen goes to the right side of the brain. The right side of the brain can find the spoon and direct the left hand to touch it; but because the language areas on the left side of the brain did not see it, the person is not able to say what it is.

hemispheres at tasks involving spatial relationships (especially drawing three-dimensional shapes) and recognizing human faces.

Having these two somewhat specialized hemispheres allows the normal brain to perform some tasks more efficiently, particularly difficult ones (Hoptman & Davidson, 1994). But the differences between the hemispheres should not be exaggerated. Remember, the corpus callosum usually integrates the functions of the "two brains" (Rueckert et al., 1999). As a result, the hemispheres work closely together, each making up well for whatever lack of ability the other may have (Banich & Heller, 1998; Staudt et al., 2001).

Plasticity in the Brain and Spinal Cord

The central nervous system has a remarkable property called **plasticity,** which is the ability to strengthen neural connections at synapses, as well as to establish new connections (Cohen-Cory, 2002; Kolb, Gibb, & Robinson, 2003). As a result, even the simplest reflex in the spinal cord can be modified by experience (Feng-Chen & Wolpaw, 1996). In the brain, plasticity is the basis for our ability to form new memories and learn new things. For example, more cells in the brain's motor cortex become involved in controlling hand movements in people who have learned to play a musical instrument. The process can be seen in brain imaging studies; as nonmusicians get better at making rhythmic finger movements, the amount of motor cortex devoted to this task increases (Munte, Altenmuller, & Jancke, 2002). Even more amazing is that merely *imagining* practicing these movements causes changes in the motor cortex (Pascual-Leone, 2001). Brain imaging also shows neural connections changing when athletes visualize making skilled sports movements.

There are limits to plasticity, though, especially when it comes to repairing damage in the brain and spinal cord. Unlike the skin or the liver, the adult central nervous system does not automatically replace damaged cells and restore lost functions. As a result, most victims of severe stroke, Parkinson's disease, Alzheimer's disease, or spinal cord injury are permanently disabled in some way. Nevertheless, scientists are searching for ways to help a damaged central nervous system heal some of its own wounds.

plasticity A property of the central nervous system that has the ability to strengthen neural connections at synapses, as well as to establish new connections.

STILL A SUPER MAN   After a 1995 riding accident left actor/director Christopher Reeve paralyzed below his shoulders, he embarked upon a long, intense rehabilitation regimen. He received electrical stimulation to maintain muscle tone and was strapped to a tilting table to maintain bone density. He was suspended in a harness over a treadmill while his legs were put through walking movements. In 1999, he began using a functional electrical stimulation bicycle, which sends computer-controlled electrical impulses to his legs, causing the muscles to contract and move the bike's pedals. After a year of work on the bicycle, he found he could move a finger, so he increased the intensity of his exercise. By the end of 2002, he could move his fingers, right wrist, and upper legs. When in a swimming pool, he could move his knees and upper arms. He has also regained feeling in about 70 percent of his body.

One approach has been to transplant, or graft, tissue from the still-developing brain of a fetus into the brain of an adult animal. If the receiving animal does not reject it, the graft sends axons out into the brain and makes some functional connections. This treatment has reversed animals' learning difficulties, movement disorders, and other results of brain damage (Noble, 2000). The technique has also been used to treat a small number of people with Parkinson's disease—a disorder characterized by tremors, rigidity of the arms and legs, and poor balance (Lindvall & Hagell, 2001). At first, the results were encouraging, but improvement faded after a year, and some patients suffered serious side effects (Freed et al., 2001). Brain tissue transplants in humans are controversial because they require the use of tissue from aborted fetuses. As an alternative, some scientists have tried transplanting neural tissue from another species into humans. For example, Russian physicians transplanted neural tissue from fruit flies into the brains of Parkinson's patients. The results were beneficial, and there were no immediate side effects (Saveliev et al., 1997), but the fruit fly neurons were eventually rejected by the patients' bodies (Korochkin, 2000).

Other scientists are attempting to coax the brain to repair damage by making its own new neurons. This is a revolutionary idea, because it was long believed that once humans reached adulthood, the cells of the central nervous system stopped dividing, leaving each of us with a fixed set of neurons (Rakic, 2002). Then came research showing that cell division *does* take place in the adult central nervous systems of humans, nonhuman primates, and other animals (Blakeslee, 2000; Eriksson et al., 1998; Gould et al., 1999; Steindler & Pincus, 2002). It turns out that the adult brain contains *neural stem cells,* a special kind of glial cells that are capable of dividing to form new tissue, including new neurons (Alvarez-Buylla et al., 2001; Mezey et al., 2003). Many scientists now think that stem cells may hold the key to reversing the consequences of brain damage and neurodegenerative diseases. They hope that someday, patients suffering from spinal cord injuries, as well as Parkinson's disease and Alzheimer's disease, might be cured by treatments that replace damaged or dying neurons with new ones grown from the patients' own stem cells (Horner & Gage, 2002; Mezey et al., 2003; Pluchino et al., 2003; Sanchez-Ramos et al., 2000; Stewart & Przyborski, 2002; Teng et al., 2002; Woodbury et al., 2000; Zhao et al., 2003).

Generating new neurons is only half the battle, however. The new cells' axons and dendrites would have to reestablish all the synaptic connections that had been lost to damage or disease. Unfortunately, this process is hampered in the central nervous system by glial cells that actively suppress new connections between newly sprouted axons and other neurons (Olson, 1997). Several central nervous system proteins, including one aptly named *Nogo*, have the same suppressant effect.

Despite these challenges, scientists are reporting exciting results in their efforts to promote healing in damaged brains and spinal cords. They have found, for example, that blocking the action of Nogo in rats with spinal cord injuries allows surviving neurons to make new axonal connections and repair the damage (Watkins & Barres, 2002). Other research with animals has shown that both spontaneous recovery and the effectiveness of brain-tissue transplants can be greatly enhanced by naturally occurring proteins called *growth factors,* which promote the survival of neurons (Hoglinger et al., 2001). One of these proteins is called *nerve growth factor.* Another, called *glial cell line–derived neurotrophic factor,* or *GDNF,* actually causes neurons to produce the neurotransmitter needed to reverse the effects of Parkinson's disease (Kordower et al., 2000; Theofilopoulos et al., 2001). The best way to increase the amount of these growth factors in humans is still being studied. In one case, nerve growth factor was put directly into the brain of an Alzheimer's patient (Seiger et al., 1993). The early results seemed encouraging, but the continuous infusion of the protein into the brain caused unacceptable side effects (Nabeshima & Yamada, 2000). Another way to deliver growth factors is through gene therapy, in which a gene for the desired growth factor is inserted into a patient's neurons (Bomze et al., 2001; Condic, 2001; Tuszynski, et al., 2002). Future research will tell us more about the value of this promising high-tech treatment.

In the meantime, there are things that patients themselves can do to promote the neural plasticity needed to restore lost central nervous system functions. Special mental and physical exercise programs appear useful in "re-wiring" the brains of stroke victims

At birth

Six years old

Fourteen years old

Source: Conel (1939/1967).

figure 2.13

Changes in Neurons of the Cerebral Cortex During Development

During childhood, the brain overproduces neural connections, establishes the usefulness of certain connections, and then "prunes" the extra connections. Overproduction of synapses, especially in the frontal cortex, may be essential for infants to develop certain intellectual abilities. Some scientists believe that connections that are used survive, whereas others die.

LINKAGES
How do our brains change over a lifetime?
(a link to Human Development)

and spinal cord injury patients, thus reversing some forms of paralysis and improving some sensory and cognitive abilities (Blakeslee, 2001; Liepert et al., 2000; Robertson & Murre, 1999). Christopher Reeve is an inspiring case in point. After his spinal cord injury in 1995, Reeve was told he would never again be able to move or feel his body. He refused to accept this prediction, and after years of devoted adherence to an exercise-oriented rehabilitation program, he has regained some movement and is able to feel sensations from much of his body (Blakeslee, 2001).

LINKAGES

Human Development and the Changing Brain

Fortunately, most of the changes that take place in the brain are not the kind associated with damage and disease. How does the human brain change as we develop throughout our lives? Researchers are using PET scans and functional MRI to begin to answer that question. They have discovered interesting correlations between changes in neural activity and the behavior of newborns and infants. Among newborns, PET scans show that activity is relatively high in the thalamus but low in a portion of the forebrain related to smooth movement. This finding may be related to the way newborns move. They make random, sweeping movements of the arms and legs—much like patients with Huntington's disease, who have a hyperactive thalamus and a withering of the part of the forebrain that controls smooth movement (Chugani & Phelps, 1986). During the second and third months of life, activity increases in many regions of the cortex. This change is correlated with the loss of reflexes that are not under cortical control, such as the grasping reflex. At eight or nine months of age, infants show increased frontal cortex activity, which correlates well with the apparent beginnings of cognitive activity (Chugani & Phelps, 1986). The brain continues to mature even through adolescence, showing evidence of ever more efficient neural communication in its major fiber tracts (Paus et al., 1999; Thompson et al., 2000).

Most of these changes reflect plasticity—changes in axons and synapses—not the appearance of new cells. After birth, the number of dendrites and synapses increases. Although different areas of the cortex sprout at different rates, the number of synapses can increase tenfold in the first year after birth (Huttenlocher, 1990). In fact, by the time children are six or seven years old, their brains have more dendrites than those of adults, and they use twice as much energy. In early adolescence, the number of dendrites and neural connections actually drops, so the adult level is reached by about the age of fourteen. During childhood, the brain overproduces neural connections and then "prunes" the extra connections (Sowell et al., 2001). Figure 2.13 shows that as we grow, we develop more brainpower with less brain (Sowell et al., 2003).

As already mentioned, the brain's plasticity allows it to "re-wire" itself to form new connections throughout life. Genes apparently determine the basic pattern of growth and the major lines of connections. However, the details of the connections seem to depend on factors such as how interesting the environment is. For example, researchers have compared the brains of rats raised in individual cages with only a boring cage-side view to the brains of rats raised with toys and playmates. The cerebral cortex of those from the enriched environment had more and longer dendrites, as well as more synapses, than did the cortex of animals raised alone in bare cages (Klintsova & Greenough, 1999; Torasdotter et al., 1998). Furthermore, the number of synapses increased when old animals who had always lived in boring cages were moved to an enriched environment. Environmentally influenced neuronal changes may help explain why the maze-learning ability of genetically "maze-dull" rats raised in stimulating cages can equal that of genetically "maze-bright" animals.

Researchers have not yet determined whether an enriched environment stimulates the development of new connections or slows down normal pruning. Also not known is whether animals moved from a stimulating environment to a boring one will lose synaptic connections. If existing findings apply to humans, however, they have implications for how we raise children and treat the elderly. It is surely the case that within the limits set by genetics, interactions with the world mold the brain itself.

The Endocrine System: Coordinating the Internal World

▶ **How can my hormones help me in a crisis?**

Neurons are not the only cells that use chemicals to communicate with one another in ways that affect behavior and mental processes. Another kind of cell with this ability is found in the **endocrine system** (pronounced "EN-doh-krin"). Operating on orders from the brain, the endocrine system regulates growth, energy consumption, and sexual behavior, and it readies the body for action. The cells of the endocrine organs, or **glands,** communicate by secreting chemicals, much as neurons do. Figure 2.14 shows some major glands of the endocrine system. The chemicals that these glands secrete are called **hormones**.

Hormones from endocrine organs are similar to neurotransmitters. In fact, many such chemicals, including norepinephrine and endorphins, act both as hormones and as neurotransmitters. However, whereas neurons secrete neurotransmitters into synapses, endocrine organs put their chemicals into the bloodstream to be carried throughout the body. In this way, endocrine glands can stimulate cells with which they have no direct

figure 2.14

Some Major Glands of the Endocrine System

Each of the glands shown releases its hormones into the bloodstream. Even the hypothalamus, a part of the brain, regulates the nearby pituitary gland by secreting hormones.

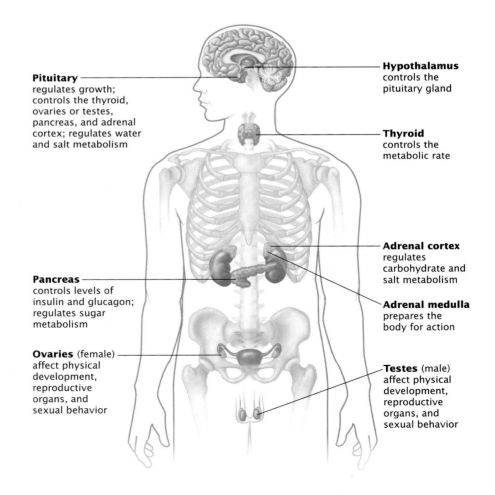

Pituitary
regulates growth; controls the thyroid, ovaries or testes, pancreas, and adrenal cortex; regulates water and salt metabolism

Hypothalamus
controls the pituitary gland

Thyroid
controls the metabolic rate

Adrenal cortex
regulates carbohydrate and salt metabolism

Pancreas
controls levels of insulin and glucagon; regulates sugar metabolism

Adrenal medulla
prepares the body for action

Ovaries (female)
affect physical development, reproductive organs, and sexual behavior

Testes (male)
affect physical development, reproductive organs, and sexual behavior

endocrine system   Cells that form organs called *glands* and that communicate with one another by secreting hormones.

glands   Organs that secrete hormones into the bloodstream.

hormones   Chemicals secreted by glands into the bloodstream, allowing stimulation of cells that are not directly connected.

fight-or-flight syndrome   Physical reactions initiated by the sympathetic nervous system that prepare the body to fight or to run from a threatening situation.

connection. Not all cells receive the hormonal message. Hormones, like neurotransmitters, can influence only those cells with receptors capable of receiving them (McEwen, 1991). *Target organs* are those whose cells have receptors for a particular hormone.

Each hormone acts on many target organs, producing coordinated effects throughout the body. For example, when a woman's ovaries secrete the sex hormone estrogen, it activates her reproductive system, causing the uterus to grow in preparation for nurturing an embryo. It enlarges the breasts to prepare them for nursing. It stimulates the brain to increase interest in sexual activity. And it stimulates the pituitary gland to release another hormone that causes a mature egg to be released by the ovary for fertilization. The brain, as a kind of "boss," has ultimate control over the secretion of hormones. The hypothalamus controls the pituitary gland, which in turn controls endocrine organs in the body. The brain is also a target organ for most hormones. In short, the endocrine system typically involves the brain, the pituitary gland, the endocrine organ, and the target organs (which include the brain). Each part in the system uses hormones to signal the next (Compagnone & Mellon, 2000).

The secretion of each hormone is increased or decreased by other hormones. Let's look, for example, at stress-hormone systems. When the brain interprets a situation as threatening, it stimulates the pituitary to release adrenocorticotropic hormone (ACTH), which causes the adrenal glands to release the hormone *cortisol* into the bloodstream. Cortisol, in turn, acts on cells throughout the body, including the brain. One effect of cortisol is to activate the emotion-related limbic system, making it more likely that you will remember stressful or traumatic events (Cahill & McGaugh, 1998). The combined effects of the adrenal hormones and the activation of the sympathetic nervous system result in the **fight-or-flight syndrome.** This set of responses prepares us for action in response to danger or other stress. The heart beats faster, the liver releases glucose into the bloodstream, fuels are mobilized from fat stores, and the body as a whole is placed in a state of high arousal. Without the endocrine system and the effects of its hormones on the brain, your life would not only be much less emotional, but you also would be less able to escape or avoid threatening experiences.

active review   Biology and Behavior

Linkages

As noted in the introductory chapter, all of psychology's subfields are related to one another. Our discussion of developmental changes in the brain illustrates just one way in which the topic of this chapter, biology and behavior, is linked to the subfield of developmental psychology, which is described in the chapter on human development. The Linkages diagram shows ties to two other subfields as well, and there are many more ties throughout the book. Looking for linkages among subfields will help you see how they all fit together and help you better appreciate the big picture that is psychology.

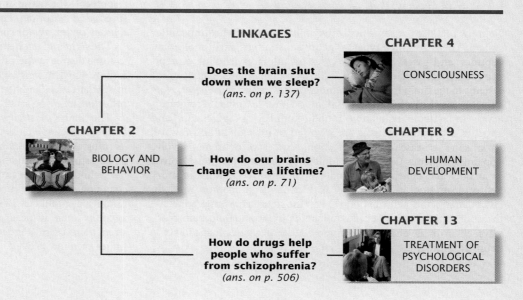

Summary

Biological psychology focuses on the biological aspects of our being, which provide the physical basis for behavior and mental processes. Included among these aspects is the *nervous system,* which is composed of billions of cells that allow humans and other organisms to gain information about what is going on inside and outside the body and to respond appropriately.

CELLS OF THE NERVOUS SYSTEM

▶ **What are neurons, and what do they do?**

Much of our understanding of the biological aspects of psychology has stemmed from research on animal and human nervous systems at levels ranging from single cells to complex organizations of cells, including the brain. The fundamental units of the nervous system are cells called *neurons* and *glial cells.* Neurons are especially good at receiving signals from, and transmitting signals to, other neurons. Neurons have cell bodies and two types of fibers, called *axons* and *dendrites.* Axons usually carry signals away from the cell body, whereas dendrites usually carry signals to the cell body.

Neurons can transmit signals because of the structure of the axons and dendrites, and the *synapses,* or gaps, between cells. A neuron can transmit, or fire, an *action potential* from one end of its axon to the other. The speed of the action potential is fastest in neurons sheathed in myelin. Between firings there is a very brief rest, called a *refractory period.*

When an action potential reaches the end of an axon, the axon releases a chemical called a *neurotransmitter.* This chemical crosses the synapse and interacts with the postsynaptic cell at receptors that make the postsynaptic cell either more likely or less likely to fire its own action potential. Because the fibers of neurons have many branches, each neuron can interact with thousands of other neurons. Each neuron constantly integrates signals received at its many synapses; the result of this integration determines how often the neuron fires an action potential.

THE CHEMISTRY OF BEHAVIOR: NEUROTRANSMITTERS

▶ **How do biochemicals affect my mood?**

Neurons that use the same neurotransmitter form a neurotransmitter system. There are three types of neurotransmitters: small molecules, peptides, and gases. Small molecules include acetylcholine, norepinephrine, serotonin, dopamine, GABA, and glutamate. Acetylcholine systems in the brain influence memory processes and movement. Norepinephrine is involved in arousal, mood, and learning. Serotonin is active in systems regulating mood, impulsivity, aggression, and appetite. Dopamine systems are involved in movement and reward; Parkinson's disease, drug addiction, and schizophrenia involve dopamine systems. GABA is an inhibitory neurotransmitter involved in anxiety and epilepsy. Glutamate is the most common excitatory neurotransmitter; it is involved in learning and memory and, in excess, may cause neuronal death. Peptide neurotransmitters include the endorphins, which act like morphine by modulating pain pathways. Nitric oxide and carbon monoxide are two gases that can act as neurotransmitters.

THE PERIPHERAL NERVOUS SYSTEM: KEEPING IN TOUCH WITH THE WORLD

▶ **How is my nervous system organized?**

Neurons are organized in networks of connected cells, forming sensory systems, which receive information from the environment, and motor systems, which influence the actions of muscles and other organs. The two major divisions of the nervous system are the *central nervous system (CNS),* which includes the brain and spinal cord, and the *peripheral nervous system.* The peripheral nervous system has two components. The first is the *somatic nervous system,* which transmits information from the senses to the CNS and carries signals from the CNS to muscles that move the skeleton. The second is the *autonomic nervous system,* whose subsystems, the *sympathetic nervous system* and the *parasympathetic nervous system,* carry messages back and forth between the CNS and the heart, lungs, and other organs and glands.

THE CENTRAL NERVOUS SYSTEM: MAKING SENSE OF THE WORLD

▶ **How is my brain "wired"?**

The CNS is laid out in interconnected groups of neuron cell bodies called *nuclei,* whose collections of axons travel together in *fiber tracts* or pathways. The *spinal cord* receives information from the peripheral senses and sends it to the brain; it also relays messages from the brain to the rest of the body. In addition, cells of the spinal cord can direct simple behaviors, called *reflexes,* without instructions from the brain. The brain's major subdivisions are the *hindbrain, midbrain,* and *forebrain.* The hindbrain includes the *medulla* and the *cerebellum.* The *reticular formation* is found in both the hindbrain and the midbrain.

The forebrain is the largest and most highly developed part of the brain. Its structures include the *hypothalamus* and *thalamus,* as well as the *hippocampus* and the *amygdala,* which form part of the limbic system. The suprachiasmatic nuclei, a part of the hypothalamus, maintain a clock that determines biological rhythms. The outer surface of the cerebral hemispheres is called the *cerebral cortex;* it is responsible for many of the higher functions of the brain, including speech and reasoning. The functional areas of the cortex consist of the *sensory cortex, motor cortex,* and *association cortex.*

The right and left hemispheres of the cerebral cortex are specialized to some degree in their functions. In most people, the left hemisphere is more active in language and logical tasks and the right hemisphere, in spatial tasks. The hemispheres are connected through the *corpus callosum,* allowing them to operate in a coordinated fashion.

The brain's *plasticity,* the ability to strengthen neural connections at its synapses as well as to establish new synapses, forms the basis for learning and memory. Scientists are studying ways to increase plasticity and stimulate formation of new neurons following brain damage.

A child's growing and changing intellectual abilities are based on changing synaptic connections in the brain, not on an increase in the number of brain cells. The brain produces many more synaptic connections than it needs, pruning extra connections as experience strengthens useful connections. The ability to form new synapses continues even into old age.

THE ENDOCRINE SYSTEM: COORDINATING THE INTERNAL WORLD

▶ **How can my hormones help me in a crisis?**

Like nervous system cells, the cells of the *endocrine system* communicate by releasing a chemical that signals other cells. However, the chemicals released by endocrine organs, or *glands,* are called *hormones* and are carried by the bloodstream to remote target organs. The brain is the main controller: Through the hypothalamus, it controls the pituitary gland, which in turn controls endocrine organs in the body. The brain is also a target organ for most endocrine secretions. The target organs often produce a coordinated response to hormonal stimulation. One of these responses is the *fight-or-flight syndrome,* which is set off by adrenal hormones that prepare for action in times of stress.

Learn by Doing

Put It in Writing

Suppose you are asked to help a young mother choose an infant care center that will be most likely to stimulate her one-year-old son's brain development. Write a page about what biological psychology research tells you about the role of environment on brain development. Does that research provide a useful guide for choosing the best day-care center? Why or why not?

Personal Learning Activity

To get a rough measure of the role played by your brain's left hemisphere in language, try the following test. First, see how long you can balance a yardstick on the tip of your right index finger, and then try the same task with your left hand. The difference in how long you can keep the stick balanced will probably be determined by whether you are right-handed or left-handed. Now try this balancing act eight more times, alternating hands on each trial so that you use your left index finger four times and your right index finger four times. Now here's where language might come in: On two of the four trials with each hand, count backward from 100 by 3s (100, 97, 94, 91, and so on) out loud while you try to keep the stick balanced. It has been suggested that this language task might interfere with your balancing skill, especially when you are using your right hand (Kemble, Filipi, & Gravlin, 1985; Kinsbourne & Cook, 1971). Why? If the left side of your brain is more involved with language, then counting backward while balancing with your right hand requires the left hemisphere to do two things at once. When counting while balancing with the left hand, the right hemisphere is handling the balancing, and the left hemisphere is dealing with the language task. Is this what happened in your case? Try the same tests on your friends, and summarize the results. *For additional projects, see the Personal Learning Activities in the corresponding chapter of the study guide that accompanies this text.*

Step into Action

Courses

Biological Bases of Behavior
Physiological Psychology
Biological Psychology
Brain and Behavior
Introduction to Neuroscience
Anatomy and Physiology

Movies

Awakenings (neurotransmitters and mental functioning)
Iris (coping with a spouse's Alzheimer's disease)

Books

William Calvin, *The Throwing Madonna: Essays on the Brain* (Bantam, 1991) (brain and behavior)
Steven Pinker, *How the Mind Works* (Norton, 1997) (brain and behavior)
V. S. Ramachandran, *Phantoms in the Brain: Probing the Mysteries of the Human Mind* (Quill, 1999) (a doctor explores neurological disorders)

The Web

The World Wide Web is a good source of additional information about the science of psychology, provided you use it carefully and think critically about the information you find. The web site that accompanies this text offers many resources relevant to this chapter. These resources include interactive NetLab exercises; Thinking Critically and Evaluating Research exercises; ACE chapter quizzes; recommended web links; and articles on current events, books, and movies. At http://college.hmco.com, select *Psychology* and then this textbook.

Review of Key Terms

Can you define each of the key terms in the chapter? Check your definitions against those on the pages listed in parentheses below or in the Glossary/Index at the end of the text.

action potential *(p. 48)*

amygdala *(p. 62)*

association cortex *(p. 67)*

autonomic nervous system *(p. 55)*

axon *(p. 47)*

biological psychology *(p. 45)*

central nervous system (CNS) *(p. 54)*

cerebellum *(p. 59)*

cerebral cortex *(p. 62)*

corpus callosum *(p. 62)*

dendrites *(p. 48)*

endocrine system *(p. 72)*

fiber tracts *(p. 56)*

fight-or-flight syndrome *(p. 73)*

forebrain *(p. 60)*

glands *(p. 72)*

glial cells *(p. 47)*

hindbrain *(p. 59)*

hippocampus *(p. 62)*

hormones *(p. 72)*

hypothalamus *(p. 61)*

medulla *(p. 59)*

midbrain *(p. 60)*

motor cortex *(p. 64)*

nervous system *(p. 46)*

neurons *(p. 47)*

neurotransmitter *(p. 49)*

nuclei *(p. 56)*

parasympathetic nervous system *(p. 55)*

peripheral nervous system *(p. 54)*

plasticity *(p. 69)*

reflexes *(p. 57)*

refractory period *(p. 48)*

reticular formation *(p. 59)*

sensory cortex *(p. 63)*

somatic nervous system *(p. 55)*

spinal cord *(p. 57)*

sympathetic nervous system *(p. 55)*

synapse *(p. 49)*

thalamus *(p. 61)*

Multiple-Choice Self-Test

Select the best answer for each of the questions below. Then check your responses against the Answer Key at the end of the text.

1. The genetic information that tells cells what to do is found

   a. in the outer membrane of the cells.
   b. in red blood cells.
   c. in the mitochondria.
   d. in the cell nucleus.

2. A nurse has mixed up some test results on neurotransmitter function for several patients at the hospital where you work. To help her out, you tell her that the depressed patient's chart will show malfunctions in _____ systems, and the Parkinson's patient's chart will show malfunctions in _____ systems.

   a. dopamine; norepinephrine
   b. dopamine; acetylcholine
   c. serotonin; dopamine
   d. acetylcholine; norepinephrine

3. Hannah had a stroke and suffered brain damage caused by over-activity of _____ when oxygen was cut off from neurons in her brain.

   a. glutamate
   b. dopamine
   c. acetylcholine
   d. serotonin

4. Research on nootropics, or "smart drugs," suggests that the best benefits for memory and brain function would result from

   a. taking *Ginkgo biloba* supplements.
   b. using a combination of ginkgo and phosphatidyl.
   c. making no drastic changes in your normal routine.
   d. exercising your brain.

5. In today's episode of your favorite soap opera, a doctor charges through the emergency room doors and tells a worried spouse that her husband has a neurological problem. "The nerves that carry signals to his muscles are not functioning," the doctor says, "which means the _____ nervous system has been damaged."

   a. central
   b. autonomic
   c. somatic
   d. sympathetic

6. Kalli finishes her exam and hurries home. When she arrives, she flops down on her bed to relax. As Kalli relaxes, her _____ nervous system becomes less active, whereas her _____ nervous system becomes more active.

   a. central; somatic
   b. somatic; central
   c. parasympathetic; sympathetic
   d. sympathetic; parasympathetic

7. When Karena accidentally touched a hot stove, she instantly jerked her hand away. This automatic response was directed by neurons entering and leaving the _____, which is part of the _____ nervous system.

   a. spinal cord; central
   b. spinal cord; autonomic
   c. hypothalamus; central
   d. hypothalamus; autonomic

8. Dr. Frankenstein is performing a new procedure on a patient. This procedure helps Dr. Frankenstein detect changes in blood flow that reflect ongoing changes in the activity of the patient's neurons. This procedure, which also provides a "moving picture" of the brain, is a(n)

   a. PET scan.
   b. MRI.
   c. fMRI.
   d. TMI.

9. The _____ is located in the hindbrain and helps to regulate heart rate, blood pressure, and breathing.

   a. medulla
   b. hypothalamus
   c. thalamus
   d. cerebellum

10. Lily had surgery on her hindbrain, because damage in that area caused her to lapse into a coma. The damage most likely occurred in the

    a. cerebellum.
    b. hippocampus.
    c. hypothalamus.
    d. reticular formation.

11. Riley was an excellent pianist until he suffered brain damage. Now, problems with fine motor skills make it impossible for him to play the piano. Riley most likely had damage to his

    a. cerebellum.
    b. hippocampus.
    c. hypothalamus.
    d. reticular formation.

12. The hippocampus has been found to be significantly smaller in patients who are suffering from which of the following problems?

    a. Parkinson's disease
    b. Alzheimer's disease
    c. depression
    d. eating disorder

13. A woman was rushed to an emergency room with severely burned hands. She had picked up an iron because she couldn't tell it was hot, and she still doesn't feel pain from her burns. The neurologist who examined her concluded that the woman's _____ system is malfunctioning.

    a. sensory
    b. motor
    c. autonomic
    d. parasympathetic

14. The occipital lobe receives sensory information about

    a. pain.
    b. body movement.
    c. vision.
    d. body temperature.

15. Elnora wants to hit a nail with a hammer so she can hang a picture on the wall. This involves voluntary movements that are controlled by neurons in the _____ cortex, which is located in the _____ lobe.

    a. motor; frontal
    b. motor; parietal
    c. association; temporal
    d. sensory; occipital

16. Roberto, an actor, is recovering following a freak accident on the set of his latest movie. When asked about the accident, Roberto, once a confident and fluent speaker, can now only say, "Noise . . . acting . . . hurts." The part of Roberto's brain most likely involved in this type of speech problem is _____ area.

    a. Broca's   c. Wernicke's
    b. Sperry's   d. Sylva's

17. Broca's area and Wernicke's area are located in the _____ cerebral hemisphere and are involved in _____.

    a. right; language
    b. left; language
    c. right; movement
    d. left; biological rhythms

18. Concerned about the health and development of your brain, you have done a great deal of research into changes that occur as you age. You have learned all of the following except

    a. using (and even imagining that you are using) specific body movements can increase the number of neurons in your motor cortex.
    b. transplanting tissue from a fetal brain can reverse the effects of Alzheimer's disease.
    c. contrary to what was previously believed, the adult brain contains neural stem cells that can form new neurons, even in older adults.
    d. mental and physical exercise programs can help reverse some of the effects of stroke and spinal cord injury.

19. Ted is creating a study sheet to help him learn the differences between neurotransmitters and hormones. Which of the following statements on his list is not correct?

    a. Neurotransmitters travel via the bloodstream, and hormones travel across synapses.
    b. Both hormones and neurotransmitters stimulate only those cells and organs that have receptors for them.
    c. Hormones and neurotransmitters regulate complex behaviors and mental processes.
    d. Hormones operate mainly in the endocrine system; neurotransmitters operate mainly in the nervous system.

20. When Mitch saw a woman who appeared to be drowning, he grabbed his life preserver and ran to save her. To prepare his body for running, Mitch's _____ released cortisol and other chemicals into his bloodstream.

    a. glands   c. synapses
    b. neurotransmitter systems d. target organs

3

Sensation and Perception

As you read and understand this sentence, you are performing a feat of

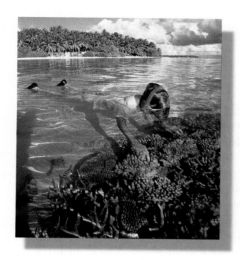

immense proportions as the lines and squiggles of the letters become meaningful words. This is what sensation and perception are all about. You translate incoming stimulation, such as the light bouncing off this page, into neural activity called *sensations*. Then you interpret these sensations as meaningful experiences—in this case, as letters and words. These processes are so quick and automatic that you probably take them for granted. In this chapter, we draw your attention to these amazing processes. You will learn about how our sensory systems receive stimulation and how that stimulation is coded into patterns of nerve activity for the brain to decode. The sensory systems include vision, hearing, taste, smell, and touch. You will also discover how the brain interprets, or perceives, this information from your senses. Principles for organizing the perceptual world allow you to recognize what you have seen, heard, tasted, smelled, or felt.

Reading this chapter will help you to answer the following questions:

► **What is the difference between sensation and perception?**

► **How does information from my eyes and ears get to my brain?**

► **Why do some people need eyeglasses?**

► **How would my voice sound on the moon?**

► **Why can't I taste anything when I have a cold?**

► **Which is the largest organ in my body?**

► **How do sensations become perceptions?**

► **What determines how I perceive my world?**

► **How do I recognize familiar people?**

► **Can you "run out" of attention?**

It has been years since Fred Aryee lost his right arm below the elbow in a boating accident, yet he still "feels" sensations from his missing arm and hand. Once, his doctor asked Aryee to reach for a cup on the table in front of him with his right arm. When asked what he felt, Aryee said, "I feel my fingers clasping the cup" (Shreeve, 1993). People like Fred may also feel intense pain that seems to be coming from a lost limb (Merzenich, 1998). Where do these "phantom limb" sensations and perceptions come from? Fred no longer has fingers to send messages to the brain, yet he experienced his "feeling" of the cup as real.

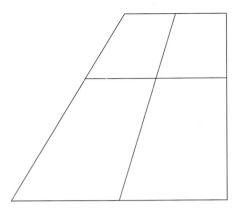

figure 3.1

What Do You See?

The question, then, is, What is reality? We tend to assume that everyone experiences the same reality, but sensory psychologists tell us that reality is not that simple. Every individual's senses actively shape information about the outside world to create a *personal reality*. Psychologists distinguish between sensation (the initial message coming from the senses) and perception (the process of giving meaning to that message). So you do not actually sense a cat lying on the sofa. You sense shapes and colors, the visual sensations. You then use your knowledge of the world to interpret, or perceive, these sensations as a cat. However, it is impossible to draw a clear line between sensation and perception, because the process of interpreting sensations begins in the sense organs themselves.

Sensing and Perceiving the World

▶ **What is the difference between sensation and perception?**

To understand how sensory systems help us create reality, we need basic information about the senses. A **sense** is a system that translates outside information into activity in the nervous system. For example, your eyes convert light into neural activity that tells the brain something about the source of the light or about the objects reflecting the light. Messages from the senses are called **sensations.** Sensations shape behaviors and mental processes by providing the vital link between the self and the world outside the brain.

Perception is the process of using information and your understanding of the world so that sensations become meaningful experiences. Perception is more than a passive process of absorbing and decoding incoming sensations. For example, look at Figure 3.1. It sends you only raw sensory information about a series of intersecting lines. But your perceptual system automatically interprets this image as a rectangle (or window frame) lying on its side. Perception is so quick and familiar that it is difficult to appreciate the processes that allow you to turn sensory signals into your personal experience of reality. By shaping experience, perceptions influence thoughts, feelings, and actions. But before something can be perceived, it must be sensed.

Sensory Systems

▶ **How does information from my eyes and ears get to my brain?**

Your senses gather information about the world by detecting various forms of energy, such as sound, light, heat, and physical pressure. Your eyes detect light energy, your ears detect the energy of sound, and your skin detects the energy of heat and pressure. Humans depend mainly on vision, hearing, and the skin senses to gain information about the world. We depend less than other animals on smell and taste. To your brain, "the world" also includes the rest of your body, so specific sensory systems provide information about the location and position of your body parts.

All of these senses must detect information about stimuli (the plural of *stimulus*), encode it into neural activity, and then transfer this coded information to the brain. Figure 3.2 illustrates these basic steps in sensation. At each step, sensory information is "processed" in some way. So the information that arrives at one point in the system is not exactly the same information that goes to the next step.

In some sensory systems, the first step in sensation involves **accessory structures,** which modify the incoming stimulus (Step 1 in Figure 3.2). For example, the lens of the eye is an accessory structure that changes incoming light by focusing it. The outer part of the ear is an accessory structure that collects sound.

sense A system that translates data from outside the nervous system into neural activity.

sensations Raw information from the senses.

perception The process through which people take raw sensations from the environment and give them meaning, using knowledge, experience, and understanding of the world.

accessory structures Structures, such as the outer part of the ear, that modify a stimulus.

figure 3.2

Elements of a Sensory System

Objects in the world generate energy that is focused by accessory structures and detected by sensory receptors, which convert the energy into neural signals. The signals are then relayed through parts of the brain, which processes them into perceptual experiences.

The second step in sensation is **transduction,** which is the process of converting incoming energy into neural activity (Step 2 in Figure 3.2). Your radio receives electromagnetic energy from your favorite station and transduces it into sounds. In much the same way, your ears receive sound energy and transduce it into neural activity that you recognize as voices and music. Transduction takes place at structures called **receptors,** specialized cells that detect certain forms of energy. These receptors respond to incoming energy by firing an action potential and releasing neurotransmitters that send signals to neighboring cells. Sensory receptors respond best to *changes* in energy (Graziano et al., 2002). A constant level of stimulation usually produces **adaptation,** a decreasing responsiveness to the stimulus over time. This is why the touch sensations you get from your glasses, watch, or earrings disappear shortly after you have put them on.

Sensory nerves carry information from receptors to the brain (Step 3 in Figure 3.2). For all the senses except smell, this information goes first to the thalamus, which does some initial processing before sending it on to the cerebral cortex (Step 4). The most complex processing occurs in the cortex (Step 5). (For a reminder of the location of these brain structures, see Figure 2.8.)

Coding Sensations: Did You Feel That?

When receptors transduce, or convert, energy, they must somehow *code* the physical properties of the stimulus into patterns of neural activity. When organized by the brain, those neural patterns allow you to make sense of the stimulus. This processing lets you determine whether you are looking at a cat, a dog, or your friend.

Each psychological dimension of a sensation, such as brightness or color, has a corresponding physical dimension that is encoded by the sensory receptors. In other words, **coding** translates the physical properties of a stimulus, such as the loudness of sound, into a pattern of neural activity that tells us what those physical properties are.

Absolute Thresholds: Is Something Out There?

How much stimulus energy is needed to trigger a conscious perceptual experience? Not much at all. Normal human vision can detect the light equivalent to a candle flame burning in the dark thirty miles away. The minimum detectable amount of light, sound, pressure, or other physical energy is called the *absolute threshold.* Table 3.1 lists absolute thresholds for human vision, hearing, taste, smell, and touch.

Psychologists discovered these thresholds by exploring *psychophysics,* the relationship between *physical* energy in the environment and your *psychological experience* of that energy. In a typical absolute threshold experiment, you would be seated in a darkened laboratory. After your eyes got used to the darkness, the researcher would show you brief flashes of light. These flashes would differ in brightness, or stimulus intensity. Each time, you'd be asked if you saw the light. Averaged over a large number of trials, your

transduction   The process of converting incoming physical energy into neural activity.

receptors   Cells specialized to detect certain types of energy and convert it into neural activity.

adaptation   Decreasing responsiveness to an unchanging stimulus.

coding   Translation of the physical properties of a stimulus into a specific pattern of neural activity.

table 3.1

Some Absolute Thresholds

learn by doing Absolute thresholds can be amazingly low. Here are examples of the stimulus equivalents at the absolute threshold for the five primary senses. Set up the conditions for testing the absolute threshold for sound, and see if you can detect this minimal amount of auditory stimulation. If you can't hear it, the signal-detection theory we discuss in this section may help explain why.

Human Sense	Absolute Threshold Is Equivalent to:
Vision	A candle flame seen at 30 miles on a clear night
Hearing	The tick of a watch under quiet conditions at 20 feet
Taste	One teaspoon of sugar in 2 gallons of water
Smell	One drop of perfume diffused into the entire volume of air in a 6-room apartment
Touch	The wing of a fly falling on your cheek from a distance of 1 centimeter

Source: Galanter (1962).

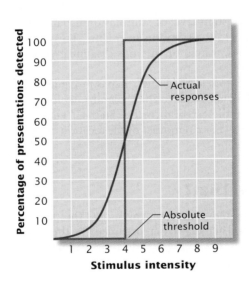

figure 3.3

The Absolute Threshold

The curved line shows the relationship between the physical intensity of a signal and the likelihood that it will be detected. If the absolute threshold were truly absolute, or exact, all signals at or above a particular intensity would always be detected, and no signal below that intensity would ever be detected (as shown by the red line). But this response pattern almost never occurs, so the "absolute" threshold is defined as the intensity at which the signal is detected 50 percent of the time.

responses would probably form a curve like the one shown in Figure 3.3. As you can see, the absolute threshold is not an all-or-nothing phenomenon. A stimulus at an intensity of 3, which is below the absolute threshold in the figure, will still be detected 20 percent of the time it occurs. Because of such variability, psychophysicists redefined the **absolute threshold** as the smallest amount of energy that can be detected 50 percent of the time. Why does a supposedly "absolute" threshold vary? The two most important reasons have to do with internal noise and our response criterion.

Internal noise is the random firing of cells in the nervous system that occurs to varying degrees whether or not you are stimulated by physical energy. This ongoing neural activity is a little like "snow" on a television screen or static between radio stations. If the amount of internal noise happens to be high at a particular moment, your sensory systems may mistakenly interpret the noise as an external stimulus.

The second source of variation in absolute threshold, the **response criterion,** reflects a person's willingness to respond to a stimulus. A person's *motivation*—wants and needs—as well as *expectancies* affect the response criterion. For example, if you were punished for reporting that a faint light appeared when it did not, then you might be motivated to raise your response criterion. That is, you would report the light only when you were quite sure you saw it. Similarly, expecting a faint stimulus to occur lowers the response criterion. Suppose, for example, that you worked at an airport security checkpoint, examining x-ray images of people's handbags, briefcases, and luggage. The signal to be detected in this situation is a weapon. If there has been a recent terrorist attack, or if a security warning has just been issued, your response criterion for saying that some questionable object on the x-ray image might be a weapon will be much lower than if terrorism were not so likely.

Signal-Detection Theory   Whether you detect a stimulus depends on its physical energy, the effects of internal noise, and your response criterion. Because all human beings experience these effects, researchers realized that the measurement of absolute thresholds could never be more precise than the 50 percent rule mentioned earlier. So they abandoned the effort to determine absolute thresholds and turned to signal-detection theory.

Signal-detection theory presents a mathematical model of how your personal sensitivity and response criterion combine to determine your decision about whether or not a near-threshold stimulus occurred (Green & Swets, 1966). **Sensitivity** refers to your ability to discriminate a stimulus from its background. It is influenced by internal noise, the intensity of the stimulus, and the capacity of your sensory systems. As already noted, the response criterion is the internal rule, also known as *bias*, that you use in deciding whether to report a signal. How likely is it that an airport security guard will spot a

DETECTING VITAL SIGNS According to signal-detection theory, the likelihood that security personnel will detect the outline of a bomb or other weapon in a passenger's luggage depends partly on the sensitivity of their visual systems as they look at x-ray images, and partly on their response criterion. That criterion is affected by their expectations that weapons might appear, as well as by how motivated they are to look carefully for them. To help keep inspectors' response criteria sufficiently low, airport security officials occasionally attempt to smuggle a simulated weapon through a checkpoint. This procedure evaluates the inspectors' performance, but also helps improve it by keeping inspectors more focused on their vital task.

weapon in a passenger's x-rayed luggage? Signal-detection theory provides a way to understand and predict such responses, because it allows precise measurement of sensitivity to stimuli of any kind (Swets, 1992, 1996).

Judging Differences Between Stimuli In many situations, you have to detect a stimulus and determine whether two stimuli are the same or different. When tuning up for a concert, musicians must decide if notes played by two instruments are the same. When repainting part of a wall, you have to decide if the new paint matches the old.

Your ability to judge differences between stimuli depends on the strength of the stimuli you are dealing with. The weaker the stimuli are, the easier it is to detect small differences between them. For example, if you are comparing the weight of two oranges, you will be able to detect a difference of as little as a fraction of an ounce. But if you are comparing two boxes weighing around fifty pounds each, you may not notice a difference unless it is a pound or more. One of the oldest laws in psychology, named after German physiologist Ernst Weber (pronounced "VAY-ber"), gives a precise description of this relationship. **Weber's law** states that the smallest detectable difference in stimulus energy is a constant fraction of the intensity of the stimulus. The smallest detectable difference in the stimulus is called the *difference threshold* or **just-noticeable difference (JND)**. According to this law, if an object weighs twenty-five pounds, the JND is only half a pound. So, if you added a container of yogurt to a grocery bag with three gallons of milk in it, you would not be able to tell the difference. But candy snatchers beware. It takes a change of only two-thirds of an ounce to determine that someone has been into a two-pound box of chocolates! Different senses have different JNDs. Vision, for instance, is very sensitive. Only a small change in the intensity of light is needed for a difference in its brightness to be noticeable.

Sensory Energy The sensory energies of light and sound vibrate as *waves* passing through space. These waves result from reflected light or from changes in air pressure caused when vocal cords and other objects move. The eye and ear detect the waves as light and sound. Waves of light and sound can be described in terms of wavelength, frequency, and amplitude, and it is these properties that determine what is sensed and perceived. **Wavelength** is the distance from one peak of the wave to the next. Wave **frequency** is the number of complete waves, or cycles, that pass a given point per unit of time. **Amplitude** is the height of the wave from baseline to peak (see Figure 3.4). Different wavelengths, frequencies, and amplitudes create different visual and sound experiences. Let's now consider how these physical properties of light and sound waves become sights and sounds.

---

absolute threshold   The minimum amount of stimulus energy that can be detected 50 percent of the time.

internal noise   The spontaneous, random firing of nerve cells that occurs because the nervous system is always active.

response criterion   The internal rule a person uses to decide whether or not to report a stimulus.

signal-detection theory   A mathematical model of what determines a person's report of a near-threshold stimulus.

sensitivity   The ability to detect a stimulus.

Weber's law   A law stating that the smallest detectable difference in stimulus energy (just-noticeable difference) is a constant fraction of the intensity of the stimulus.

just-noticeable difference (JND)   The smallest detectable difference in stimulus energy. Also called *difference threshold*.

wavelength   The distance between peaks in a wave of light or sound.

frequency   The number of complete waves, or cycles, that pass a given point per unit of time.

amplitude   The distance between the peak and the baseline of a wave.

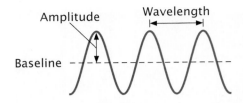

figure 3.4

The Dimensions of a Wave

Wavelength is the distance from one peak of a wave to the next. Frequency is the number of complete waves, or cycles, that pass a given point in a given amount of time, such as one second. Amplitude is the height of a wave from baseline to peak.

Seeing

▶ **Why do some people need eyeglasses?**

Soaring eagles have the incredible ability to see a mouse move in the grass from a mile away. Cats have special "reflectors" at the back of their eyes that help them to see even in very dim light. Nature has provided each species with a visual system uniquely adapted to its way of life. The human visual system is also adapted to do many things well. It combines great sensitivity with great sharpness, enabling people to see objects near and far, during the day and night. Our night vision is not as good as that of some animals, but our color vision is excellent. Not a bad tradeoff; after all, being able to experience a sunset's splendor seems worth an occasional stumble in the dark.

Light

Light is a form of energy known as *electromagnetic radiation*. Most electromagnetic radiation, including x-rays, radio waves, television signals, and radar, passes through space undetected by the human eye. You can see in Figure 3.5 that visible light is but a small portion of the spectrum, or range, of electromagnetic radiation. In fact, **visible light** is electromagnetic radiation with a wavelength ranging from just under 400 nanometers to about 750 nanometers. (A *nanometer* is one-billionth of a meter.) Light waves vibrate with a certain wavelength as they pass, like particles, through space. Light has some properties of waves and some properties of particles. It is correct to refer to light as either *light waves* or *light rays*.

Sensations of light depend on the intensity and wavelength of light waves. **Light intensity,** which refers to how much energy the light contains, determines the brightness of light. And what color you sense depends mainly on **light wavelength.** At a

figure 3.5

The Spectrum of Electromagnetic Energy

The human eye is sensitive to only a narrow range of electromagnetic wavelengths. To detect energy outside this range, we rely on radios, TV sets, radar detectors, infrared night-vision scopes, and other electronic instruments that can "see" this energy, just as the eye sees visible light.

figure 3.6

Major Structures of the Eye

As shown in this top view of the eye, light rays bent by the combined actions of the cornea and the lens are focused on the retina, where the light energy is converted into neural activity. Nerve fibers from the retina combine to form the optic nerve, which leaves the back of the eye and continues to the brain.

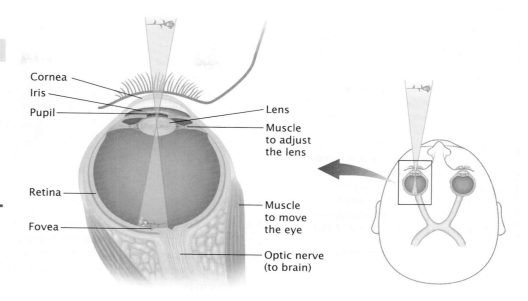

Cornea
Iris
Pupil
Lens
Muscle to adjust the lens
Retina
Muscle to move the eye
Fovea
Optic nerve (to brain)

given intensity, different wavelengths produce sensations of different colors. For instance, 440-nanometer light appears violet blue, and 600-nanometer light appears orangish red.

Focusing Light

The eye transduces light energy into neural activity. First, accessory structures of the eye modify incoming light rays. The light rays enter the eye by passing through the curved, transparent, protective layer called the **cornea.** As shown in Figure 3.6, the light then passes through the **pupil,** the opening just behind the cornea. The **iris,** which gives the eye its color, adjusts the amount of light allowed into the eye by constricting to reduce the size of the pupil or dilating to enlarge it. Directly behind the pupil is the **lens.** Both the cornea and lens of the eye are curved so that they bend light rays. (A camera lens works the same way.) This bending process focuses light rays coming from various angles into a sharp image on the inner surface at the back of the eye. This surface is called the **retina.** Light rays from the top of an object are focused at the bottom of the image on the retinal surface. Light rays from the right side of the object end up on the left side of the retinal image (see Figure 3.7). The brain rearranges this upside-down and reversed image so that we can see the object as it is.

The muscles that hold the lens adjust its shape so that either near or far objects can be focused on the retina. To illustrate this for yourself, try reading the next sentence while holding the book as close to your face as possible. To maintain a focused image at close range, your muscles have to tighten your lenses, making them more curved. This ability to change the shape of the lens to bend light rays is called **accommodation.** If accommodation is impaired, converging light rays will come into focus either before or after they reach the retina, causing images to be blurry. For example, as the lens loses some of its flexibility over the years, most older people become "farsighted," seeing distant objects clearly but needing glasses for reading or close work. A more common problem in younger people is "nearsightedness," in which close objects are in focus but distant ones are blurry. This condition has a genetic component, but it may be influenced by the environment, too (Quinn et al., 1999; Zadnik, 2001).

Converting Light into Images

The conversion of light energy into neural activity takes place in the retina, which contains neurons that are actually an extension of the brain. The word *retina* is Latin for "net," and the retina is in fact an intricate network of cells (Masland, 2001).

learn ^{by} doing

visible light   Electromagnetic radiation that has a wavelength of about 400 nanometers to about 750 nanometers.

light intensity   A physical dimension of light waves that refers to how much energy the light contains and that determines its brightness.

light wavelength   A physical dimension of light waves that refers to their length and that produces sensations of different colors.

cornea   The curved, transparent, protective layer through which light rays enter the eye.

pupil   An opening in the eye, just behind the cornea, through which light passes.

iris   The part of the eye that gives it its color and adjusts the amount of light entering it.

lens   The part of the eye directly behind the pupil.

retina   The surface at the back of the eye onto which the lens focuses light rays.

accommodation   The ability of the lens to change its shape and bend light rays so that objects are in focus.

figure 3.7

The Lens and the Retinal Image

To see objects as they are, your brain must rearrange the upside-down and reversed images that the lens focuses on the retina. If light rays are out of focus when they reach the retina, glasses usually correct the problem. In some older people, vision is impaired by *cataracts,* a condition in which a "cloudy" lens severely reduces incoming light. Cataracts can be cleared up with laser surgery or by replacing the natural lens with an artificial one (Snellingen et al., 2002).

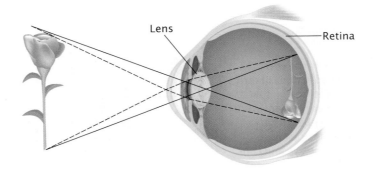

Rods and Cones   Specialized cells in the retina called **photoreceptors** convert light energy into neural activity. There are two main types of photoreceptors: rods and cones. **Rods** and **cones** are retinal cells that are named for their shapes and contain chemicals that respond to light. When light strikes these chemicals, they break apart, creating a signal that can be transferred to the brain.

The process of rebuilding these light-sensitive chemicals after they break down takes a little time. This explains why you cannot see when you first come from bright sunshine into a dark room. In the dark, as your rods build up their light-sensitive chemicals, your ability to see gradually increases. This increasing ability to see in the dark over time is called **dark adaptation.** You become about 10,000 times more sensitive to light after about half an hour in a darkened room.

There are three kinds of light-sensitive chemicals in cones, and they provide the basis for color vision. Rods have only one kind of chemical, so they cannot discriminate colors. However, rods are more sensitive to light than cones. Rods allow you to see in dim light, as on a moonlit night, but they don't allow you to see colors. It's only at higher light intensities that the cones, with their ability to detect colors, become most active. As a result, you might put on what looked like a matched pair of socks in a darkened bedroom, only to go outside and discover that one is dark blue and the other is dark green.

Cones are concentrated in the center of the retina, in a circular region called the **fovea,** which is where the eye focuses incoming light. Differences in the density of cones in the fovea probably account for differences in various people's visual *acuity,* or ability to see

learn *by* **doing**   **RODS AND CONES**   This electron microscope view of rods (blue) and cones (aqua) shows what your light receptors look like. Rods are more light-sensitive, but they do not detect color. Cones can detect color, but they require more light in order to be activated (Kefalov et al., 2003). To experience the difference in how these cells work, try looking at an unfamiliar color photograph in a room where there is barely enough light to see. This dim light will activate your rods and allow you to make out images in the picture. But because there is not enough light to activate your cones, you will not be able to see colors in the photo.

figure 3.8

Find Your Blind Spot

learn by doing There is a blind spot where the optic nerve exits the eye. To "see" your blind spot, cover your left eye and stare at the cross inside the circle. Move the page closer and farther away, and at some point the dot to the right should disappear from view. However, the vertical lines around the dot will probably look continuous, because the brain tends to fill in visual information at the blind spot. We are normally unaware of this "hole" in our vision because the blind spot of one eye is in the normal visual field of the other eye.

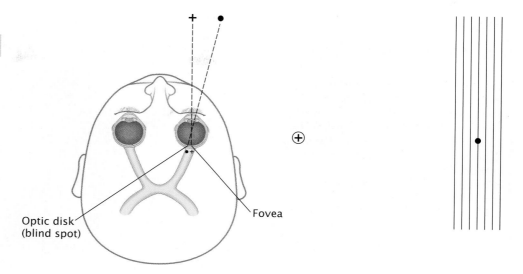

Optic disk (blind spot)

Fovea

photoreceptors   Specialized cells in the retina that convert light energy into neural activity.

rods   Photoreceptors in the retina that allow sight even in dim light, but that cannot discriminate colors.

cones   Photoreceptors in the retina that are less light-sensitive than rods, but that can distinguish colors.

dark adaptation   The increasing ability to see in the dark as time passes.

fovea   A region in the center of the retina.

optic nerve   A bundle of fibers that carries visual information to the brain.

blind spot   The point at which the optic nerve exits the eyeball.

feature detectors   Cells in the cortex that respond to a specific feature of an object.

details. There are no rods in the human fovea. With increasing distance from the fovea, though, the number of cones gradually decreases, and the proportion of rods gradually increases. So, if you are trying to detect a weak light, like the light from a faint star, it is better to look slightly away from where you expect to see it. This focuses the weak light on the very light-sensitive rods outside the fovea. Because cones do not work well in low light, looking directly at the star will make it seem to disappear.

From the Retina to the Brain   If the eye simply transferred to the brain the images it focused on the retina, we would experience something like a slightly blurry TV picture. Instead, the eye first sharpens visual images. How? The key lies in the interactions among cells of the retina.

Light rays pass through several layers of retinal cells before striking the rods and cones. Signals generated by the rods and cones then go back toward the surface of the retina, making connections with *bipolar cells* and *ganglion cells,* which allow the eye to begin analyzing visual information even before that information leaves the retina. Ganglion cells in the retina have axons that form the **optic nerve,** which then goes to the brain. Because there are no receptors for visual stimuli at the point where the optic nerve exits the eyeball, a **blind spot** is created, as Figure 3.8 demonstrates.

After leaving the retina, about half the optic nerve fibers cross over to the opposite side of the brain at a structure called the *optic chiasm.* (*Chiasm* means "cross" and is pronounced "KYE-az-um.") Fibers from the inside half of each eye, nearest to the nose, cross over. Fibers from the outside half of each eye do not. This arrangement brings all the visual information about the right half of the visual world to the left hemisphere of the brain and all the visual information from the left half of the visual world to the right hemisphere of the brain (Roth, Lora, & Heilman, 2002) .

The optic chiasm is part of the bottom surface of the brain. Beyond this chiasm, the fibers extend into the brain itself. The axons from most of the ganglion cells form synapses in the thalamus. Neurons there send the visual input to the primary visual cortex in the occipital lobe at the back of the brain. The primary visual cortex sends visual information to many association areas of the brain for processing (see Figures 2.8 and 2.9).

Certain cells in the brain's cerebral cortex are called **feature detectors** because they respond to specific characteristics of objects in the visual field (Hubel & Wiesel, 1979). For example, one type of feature detector specializes in responding to straight lines. Others respond to corners, to angles, or to some other feature. The combined responses of several types of feature-detecting cells allow us to sense the shapes of objects, such as rectangles or triangles. Most people can also detect color. Let's explore how color vision works.

figure 3.9

The Color Circle

Ordering colors according to their psychological similarities creates a color circle that predicts the result of additive mixing of two colored lights. For example, mixing equal amounts of pure green and pure red light will produce yellow, the color that lies at the midpoint of the line connecting red and green. (*Note: Nm* stands for *nanometers,* the unit in which light wavelengths are measured.)

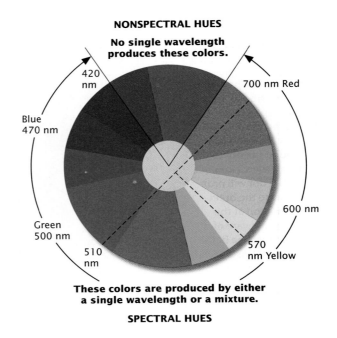

NONSPECTRAL HUES
No single wavelength produces these colors.

420 nm
Blue 470 nm
Green 500 nm
510 nm
570 nm Yellow
600 nm
700 nm Red

These colors are produced by either a single wavelength or a mixture.
SPECTRAL HUES

Seeing Color

Like beauty, color is in the eye of the beholder. Many animals see only shades of gray, even when they look at a rainbow, but for humans, color is an important feature of vision.

Wavelengths and Color Sensations   At a given intensity, each wavelength of light is sensed as a certain color. However, the eye rarely, if ever, encounters pure light of a single wavelength. Sunlight, for example, is a mixture of all wavelengths of light. When sunlight passes through a droplet of water, each different wavelength of light bends to a different degree, separating into a colorful rainbow. The spectrum of color found in the rainbow illustrates an important concept: The sensation produced by a *mixture* of different wavelengths of light is not the same as the sensations produced by separate wavelengths.

The sensation of a color results from features of the wavelength mixtures striking the eye. The three separate aspects of this sensation are hue, saturation, and brightness. These are *psychological* dimensions that correspond roughly to the physical properties of light. **Hue,** the essential "color," is determined by the dominant wavelength in the mixture of the light. Black, white, and gray are not considered hues, because they do not have a dominant wavelength. **Saturation** is related to the purity of the color. A color is more saturated (purer) if just one wavelength is more intense—contains more energy—than other wavelengths. The yellow of a school bus and the red of a stop sign are saturated colors. Add in many other wavelengths, and the color is said to be *desaturated*. Pastels are colors that have been desaturated by the addition of whiteness. **Brightness** refers to the overall intensity of the wavelengths making up light.

The *color circle* shown in Figure 3.9 arranges hues according to their perceived similarities. Mix two different light wavelengths of equal intensity, and the color you sense is midway between the two original colors. This process is known as *additive color mixing,* because the effects of the wavelengths are added together. Keep adding different colored lights and you eventually get white, which is the combination of all wavelengths. You are probably more familiar with a different form of color mixing, called *subtractive color mixing,* which occurs when paints are combined. Paint, like other physical objects, reflects certain wavelengths and absorbs others. Grass is green because it absorbs all wavelengths except wavelengths perceived as green. White objects appear white because they reflect all wavelengths.

hue   The essential color determined by the dominant wavelength of a light.

saturation   The purity of a color.

brightness   The overall intensity of the wavelengths making up light.

trichromatic theory   A theory of color vision stating that information from three types of visual elements combines to produce the sensation of color.

THE SENSATION OF COLOR The vivid array of colored powders offered by this vendor in India allows him to create virtually any combination of hue (color), saturation (purity), and brightness that a customer might request.

Theories of Color Vision

Psychologists have long tried to explain how color vision works, but only two theories have stood the test of time: trichromatic (or "three-color") theory and opponent-process theory.

The Trichromatic Theory of Color Vision In the early 1800s, Thomas Young and, later, Hermann von Helmholtz proved that by mixing pure versions of blue, green, and red light in different ratios, they could produce any other color. Their theory of color vision is called the **trichromatic theory.**

Support for trichromatic theory comes from research on cones in the retina. There are three types of cones, and each is most sensitive to particular wavelengths. *Short-wavelength* cones respond most to light in the blue range. *Medium-wavelength* cones are most sensitive to light in the green range. *Long-wavelength* cones respond best to light in the yellow range (by tradition, though, these are known as "red" cones). No single cone, by itself, can signal the color of a light. It is the *ratio* of the activities of the three types of cones that determines what color will be sensed. As you can see in Figure 3.10, the exact mixture of these three cone types can differ from person to person. The trichromatic theory was applied in the creation of

figure 3.10

Individual Differences in Cone Types

These photographs show that people can differ widely from one another in the distribution of blue, green, and red cones in their retinas (Roorda & Williams, 1999). J.W., whose retina is shown in Part A, has an especially high population of red cones, whereas green cones predominate in A.N., whose retina is shown in Part B. Both have normal color vision, but J.W. will be somewhat more sensitive to long wavelengths of light, whereas A.N. will be somewhat more sensitive to light of medium wavelengths.

(A)

(B)

figure 3.11

Afterimages Produced by the Opponent-Process Nature of Color Vision

learn **by doing** Stare at the black dot in the flag for at least thirty seconds, and then focus on the dot in the white space below it. The afterimage you will see can be explained by the opponent-process theory of color vision. What colors appeared in the afterimage you saw?

color television screens, which contain microscopic elements of red, green, and blue. A television broadcast excites these elements to varying degrees, mixing their colors to produce many other colors. You see color mixtures, not patterns of red, green, and blue dots, because the dots are too small and close together to be seen individually.

The Opponent-Process Theory of Color Vision Although essentially correct, the trichromatic theory cannot explain some aspects of color vision, such as afterimages. To see an afterimage, stare at the black dot in the flag in Figure 3.11 for thirty seconds, and then look at the black dot in the white space below it. What was yellow in the original image will be blue in the afterimage. What was green before will appear red, and what was black will now appear white.

This type of observation led Ewald Hering to offer another theory of color vision, called the **opponent-process theory.** Hering suggested that color-sensitive visual elements in the eye are arranged into three kinds of pairs and that the members of each pair oppose, or inhibit, each other. Each element signals one color or the other (red or green, blue or yellow, black or white), but never both. This theory explains color afterimages. When one member of an opponent pair is no longer stimulated, the other is activated. So, in Figure 3.11, if the original image you look at is green, the afterimage will be red.

Summing Up Together, the trichromatic and opponent-process theories encompass most of what we now know about the complex process of color vision. We see color because our three types of cones have different sensitivities to different wavelengths. We sense different colors when the three cone types are stimulated in different ratios. Because there are three types of cones, any color can be produced by mixing three pure wavelengths of light. But there is more to it than that. The cones connect to ganglion cells containing pairs of opposing elements that respond to different colors and inhibit each other. This arrangement provides the basis for afterimages. Therefore, the trichromatic theory explains color vision as it relates to rods and cones, whereas the opponent-process theory explains color vision as it relates to the ganglion cells. Both theories are needed to account for the complexity of our visual sensations of color. ("In Review: Seeing" summarizes our discussion of vision.)

in review — SEEING

Aspect of Sensory System	Elements	Key Characteristics
Energy	Visible light: electromagnetic radiation with a wavelength of about 400 nm to about 750 nm	The intensity, wavelength, and complexity of light waves determine the brightness, hue, and saturation of visual sensations.
Accessory structures of the eye	Cornea, pupil, iris, lens	Light rays are bent to focus on the retina.
Conversion of visual stimuli to neural activity	Photoreceptors (rods and cones) in the retina	Rods are more sensitive to light than cones, but cones discriminate among colors. Sensations of color depend first on the cones, which respond differently to different light wavelengths, and then on processing by ganglion cells.
Pathway to the brain	Optic nerve to optic chiasm to thalamus to primary visual cortex	Neurons in the brain respond to particular aspects of the visual stimulus, such as shape.

? *When you are able to see in very dim light, it is because of photoreceptors called _____.*

figure 3.12

Are You Colorblind?

learn by **doing** At the upper left is a photo as it appears to people whose cones have all three types of color-sensitive chemicals. The other photos simulate how colors appear to people who are missing chemicals for short wavelengths (lower left), long wavelengths (upper right), or medium wavelengths (lower right). If any of these photos look to you just like the one at the upper left, you may have a form of colorblindness.

Colorblindness

Cones normally contain three kinds of chemicals, each of which responds best to a particular wavelength of light. People who have cones containing only two of these three color-sensitive chemicals are described as *colorblind*. They are not really blind to all color, but they discriminate fewer colors than do other people, as Figure 3.12 shows. Red-green colorblindness, for example, means that reds and greens look the same brownish gray color. Colorblindness is more common in men than in women.

Hearing

▶ **How would my voice sound on the moon?**

When Neil Armstrong stepped onto the moon in 1969, millions of people back on earth heard his radio transmission: "That's one small step for a man, one giant leap for mankind." But if Armstrong had taken off his space helmet and shouted, "Whoo-ee! I can moonwalk!," not even an astronaut three feet away could have heard him. Why? Because he would have been speaking into airless, empty space. **Sound** is a repeating fluctuation in the pressure of a substance, such as air. Because the moon has almost no atmosphere and almost no air pressure, sound cannot exist there.

Sound

Vibrations of an object produce the fluctuations in pressure that make sound. When you speak, your vocal cords vibrate, causing fluctuations—rising and falling—in air pressure that spread as sound waves. Figure 3.13 shows how these changes in air pressure can be represented as sound waveforms. The waveforms are drawn in only two dimensions, but remember that the sound waves actually move through the air in all directions. This is why, when students talk to each other during a lecture, classmates all around them are distracted by the conversation.

Just as the amplitude and wavelength of light waves affect our experience of light, the characteristics of sound waves alter our experience of sound. The psychological dimen-

opponent-process theory   A theory of color vision stating that the visual elements sensitive to color are grouped into red-green, blue-yellow, and black-white pairs.

sound   A repetitive fluctuation in the pressure of a medium such as air.

figure 3.13

Sound Waves and Waveforms

Sound is produced when objects, such as a tuning fork, vibrate. The vibration creates alternating regions of greater and lesser compression of air molecules, which can be represented as a waveform. The point of greatest compression is the peak of the wave. The lowest point of the wave is where compression is least. In a given medium, such as air, a sound's wavelength (the distance between peaks) is related to its frequency (the number of waves per second). The longer the wavelength, the lower the sound frequency; the higher the frequency, the shorter the wavelength.

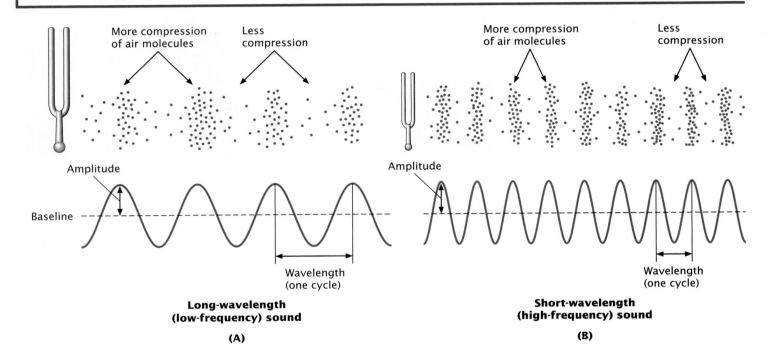

table 3.2

Intensity of Sound Sources

Sound intensity varies across an extremely wide range. A barely audible sound is, by definition, 0 decibels; every increase of 20 decibels reflects a tenfold increase in the amplitude of sound waves. Thus, the 40-decibels sounds of an office are actually 10 times as intense as a 20-decibels whisper; and traffic noise of 100 decibels is 10,000 times as intense as that whisper.

Source	Sound Level (decibels)
Spacecraft launch (from 45 meters)	180
Loudest rock band on record	160
Pain threshold (approximate)	140
Large jet motor (at 22 meters)	120
Loudest human shout on record	111
Heavy auto traffic	100
Conversation (at about 1 meter)	60
Quiet office	40
Soft whisper	20
Threshold of hearing	0

Source: Levine & Schefner (1981).

figure 3.14

Structures of the Ear

The outer ear (pinna and ear canal) channels sound waves into the middle ear, where the vibrations of the eardrum are amplified by the delicate bones that stimulate the cochlea. In the cochlea, in the inner ear, the vibrations are converted, or transduced, into changes in neural activity, which are sent along the auditory nerve to the brain.

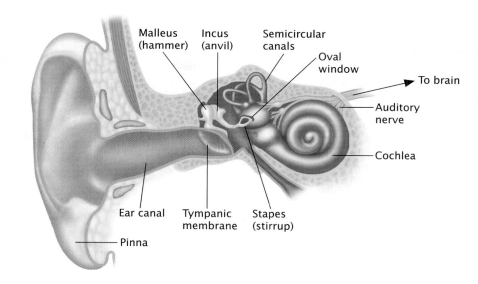

Malleus (hammer) Incus (anvil) Semicircular canals Oval window To brain Auditory nerve Cochlea Ear canal Tympanic membrane Stapes (stirrup) Pinna

sion of **loudness** is determined by the amplitude, or height, of the sound wave. The greater the amplitude, the louder the sensation of sound. Loudness is described in units called *decibels* (abbreviated *dB*). By definition, 0 decibels is the minimum detectable sound for normal hearing. Table 3.2 gives examples of the intensity, or loudness, of some common sounds.

The psychological dimension of **pitch**—how high or low a tone sounds—depends on the frequency of the sound wave. Frequency is the number of complete waves or cycles that pass a given point in one second. It is described in units called *hertz,* abbreviated *Hz* (for Heinrich Hertz, a nineteenth-century physicist). One cycle per second is 1 hertz. High-frequency waves are sensed as sounds of high pitch. The highest note on a piano has a frequency of about 4,000 hertz, and the lowest note has a frequency of about 50 hertz. Humans can hear sounds ranging from about 20 to 20,000 hertz.

Most sounds are a mixture of many frequencies and amplitudes, and this mixture creates a sound's **timbre** (pronounced "tamber"), the psychological dimension of sound quality. Complex wave patterns added to the *fundamental*, or lowest, frequency of sound determine its timbre. The extra waves allow you to tell the difference between, say, a note played on a flute and the same note played on a clarinet.

The Ear

The human ear converts sound energy into neural activity through a series of accessory structures and transduction mechanisms. The crumpled part of the ear on the side of the head, called the **pinna,** collects sound waves in the outer ear. (People trying to hear a faint sound may cup a hand to their ear, because this action tilts the pinna forward and enlarges the sound-collection area. Try this for a moment, and you will notice a clear difference in how sounds sound.) The pinna funnels sound down through the ear canal. At the end of the ear canal, the sound waves reach the middle ear (see Figure 3.14). There they strike the **eardrum,** a tightly stretched structure also known as the *tympanic membrane*. The sound waves set up vibrations in the eardrum. The *hammer,* the *anvil,* and the *stirrup,* three tiny bones named for their shapes, amplify these vibrations and direct them onto a smaller membrane called the *oval window.*

The Inner Ear   Sound vibrations passing through the oval window enter the inner ear, reaching the **cochlea** (pronounced "COK-lee-ah"), where transduction occurs. The cochlea is rolled into a coiled spiral. (*Cochlea* comes from the Greek word for

learn by doing

loudness   A psychological dimension of sound determined by the amplitude of a sound wave.

pitch   How high or low a tone sounds; pitch depends on the frequency of a sound wave.

timbre   The quality of a sound that identifies it.

pinna   The crumpled part of the outer ear that collects sound waves.

eardrum   A tightly stretched membrane in the middle ear that generates vibrations that match the sound waves striking it. Also known as the *tympanic membrane.*

cochlea   A fluid-filled spiral structure in the inner ear in which auditory transduction occurs.

figure 3.15

The Cochlea

The vibrations of the stirrup set up vibrations in the fluid inside the cochlea. The coils of the cochlea are unrolled in this illustration to show the path of the fluid waves along the basilar membrane. Movements of the basilar membrane stimulate hair cells, which transduce the vibrations into changes in neural firing patterns.

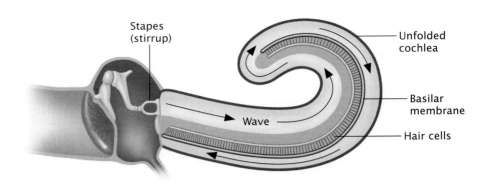

"snail.") A fluid-filled tube runs down its length. The **basilar membrane** forms the floor of this tube, as you can see in Figure 3.15. When a sound wave passes through the fluid in the tube, it moves the basilar membrane (Ren, 2002). This movement, in turn, bends *hair cells* on the membrane. These hair cells make connections with fibers from the **auditory nerve,** a bundle of axons that goes into the brain. Bending the hair cells stimulates the auditory nerve, which sends coded signals to the brain about the amplitude and frequency of the sound waves. These signals allow you to sense loudness, pitch, and timbre.

Deafness   The middle and inner ear are among the most delicate structures in the body, and damage to them can lead to deafness. One form of deafness is caused by problems with the bones of the middle ear. Over time they can fuse together, preventing accurate reproduction of vibrations. This condition is called *conduction deafness*. Surgical treatment may involve breaking the bones apart or replacing the natural bones with plastic ones; a hearing aid that amplifies vibrations can also be helpful.

Damage to the auditory nerve or the hair cells results in *nerve deafness*. Hair cell damage can be caused by very loud sounds, including amplified rock music (Goldstein, 1999). High-intensity sound can actually rip off the hair cells of the inner ear. Generally, any sound loud enough to produce ringing in the ears causes some damage. In humans, small amounts of damage accumulate to produce significant hearing loss by middle age—as many older rock musicians, and their fans, are finding out (Levine, 1999).

Hair cells can be regenerated in chickens' ears (Cotanche, 1997), and a related kind of inner-ear hair cell has been regenerated in mammals (Malgrange et al., 1999). Scientists hope that human hair-cell regeneration might someday be accomplished by treating damaged areas with growth factors similar to those being used to repair damaged brain cells (Shinohara et al., 2002; see the chapter on biology and behavior). This achievement could revolutionize the treatment of nerve deafness, which cannot be overcome by conventional hearing aids. In the meantime, scientists have developed an artificial cochlea that can be implanted in the human ear to stimulate the auditory nerve (Gates & Miyamoto, 2003; Lee et al., 2001; Rauschecker & Shannon, 2002).

Auditory Pathways to the Brain   Before sounds can be heard, the information coded in the firing of the many axons that make up the auditory nerve must be sent to the brain and processed further. This process begins when the auditory nerve conveys the information to the thalamus. From there, the information is relayed to the *primary auditory cortex,* an area in the temporal lobe of the brain (see Figure 2.9). Cells in the auditory cortex have *preferred frequencies*. That is, individual cells there respond most vigorously to sounds of a particular frequency. Each neuron in the auditory nerve also has a "favorite," or characteristic, frequency, though each also responds to some extent to a range of frequencies. The auditory cortex examines the pattern of activity of many neurons to determine the frequency of a sound. Some parts of the auditory cortex are devoted to processing certain types of sounds. One part, for example, specializes in information coming

basilar membrane   The floor of the fluid-filled duct that runs through the cochlea.

auditory nerve   The bundle of axons that carries messages from the hair cells of the cochlea to the brain.

place theory   A theory of hearing stating that hair cells at a particular place on the basilar membrane respond most to a particular frequency of sound.

from human voices (Belin et al., 2000; Belin, Zatorre, & Ahad, 2002). The auditory cortex receives information from other senses as well. For example, the primary auditory cortex is activated when you watch someone say words (but not when the person makes other facial movements). This is the biological basis for the lip reading that helps you to hear what people say (Calvert et al., 1997).

Coding Sounds

Most people can hear a wide range of sound intensities. The faintest sound that can be heard barely moves the ear's hair cells. Sounds more than a trillion times more intense can also be heard. Between these extremes, the auditory system codes intensity in a rather simple way: The more intense the sound, the more rapid the firing of a given neuron. We are also very good at detecting differences between sound frequencies that allow us to hear differences in pitch (Shera, Guinan, & Oxenham, 2002). Information about frequency differences appears to be coded in two ways: by their location on the basilar membrane and by the rate at which the auditory neurons fire.

As sound waves move down the basilar membrane, they reach a peak and then taper off, much like an ocean wave that crests and then dissolves. High-frequency sounds produce a wave that peaks soon after it starts down the basilar membrane. Lower-frequency sounds produce a wave that peaks farther down the basilar membrane. According to **place theory,** the greatest response by hair cells occurs at the peak of the wave. Because the location of the peak varies with the frequency of sound, it follows that hair cells at a particular place on the basilar membrane are most responsive to a particular frequency of sound. When cells with a particular characteristic frequency fire, we sense a sound of that frequency.

SHAPING THE BRAIN   The brain region known as the primary auditory cortex is larger in trained musicians than in people whose jobs are less focused on fine gradations of sound. How much larger this area becomes is correlated with how long the musicians have studied their art. This finding reminds us that, as described in the chapter on biology and behavior, the brain can literally be shaped by experience and other environmental factors.

in review

HEARING		
Aspect of Sensory System	**Elements**	**Key Characteristics**
Energy	Sound: pressure fluctuations of air produced by vibrations	Amplitude, frequency, and complexity of sound waves determine the loudness, pitch, and timbre of sounds.
Accessory structures of the ear	Pinna, eardrum, hammer, anvil, stirrup, oval window, basilar membrane	Changes in pressure produced by the original wave are amplified.
Conversion of sound frequencies into neural activity	Hair cells in the inner ear	Frequencies are coded by the location of the hair cells receiving the greatest stimulation (place theory) and by the combined firing rate of neurons (volley theory).
Pathway to the brain	Auditory nerve to thalamus to primary auditory cortex	Auditory cortex examines patterns of information from the auditory nerve, allowing us to sense loudness, pitch, and timbre.

? *The basilar membrane can be found inside a fluid-filled tube in the _____ ear, where sound energy is converted into neural activity.*

Place theory cannot explain the coding of very low frequencies, such as deep bass notes, because there are no auditory nerve fibers that have very low preferred frequencies. Humans can hear frequencies as low as twenty hertz, though, so they must be coded somehow. The answer appears to be *frequency matching,* a process in which the firing rate of a neuron in the auditory nerve matches the frequency of a sound wave. Frequency-matching theory is sometimes called the **volley theory** of frequency coding, because the outputs of many cells can combine to create a *volley* of firing.

The nervous system apparently uses more than one way to code the range of audible frequencies. The lowest frequencies are coded by frequency matching. Low to moderate frequencies are coded by frequency matching, as well as by the place on the basilar membrane where the wave peaks. And high frequencies are coded solely by the place where the wave peaks. ("In Review: Hearing" summarizes the coding process and other aspects of the auditory system.)

The Chemical Senses: Taste and Smell

▶ **Why can't I taste anything when I have a cold?**

There are animals without vision and animals without hearing, but there are no animals without some form of chemical sense. Chemical senses arise from the interaction of chemicals and receptors. Our **sense of smell** (olfaction) detects chemicals that are airborne, or volatile. Our **sense of taste** (gustation) detects chemicals in solution that come into contact with receptors inside the mouth. These systems are connected.

Smell, Taste, and Flavor

If you have a stuffy nose, everything tastes like cardboard. Why? Because smell and taste act as two components of a single system, known as *flavor* (Rozin, 1982). Most of the properties that make food taste good are actually odors detected by the olfactory system, not chemicals detected by the taste system. The scent and taste pathways converge in the cerebral cortex (Rolls et al., 1998), which is how smell and taste come to seem like one sensation.

Both tastes and odors prompt strong emotional responses. People have an inborn dislike of bitter flavors, but we have to learn to associate emotions with odors (Bartoshuk, 1991). Many animals easily learn taste aversions to particular foods when the taste is associated with nausea, but humans learn aversions to odors more readily than to tastes (Bartoshuk & Wolfe, 1990).

Variations in our nutritional state also affect our experience of taste and flavor, as well as our motivation to eat particular foods. Food deprivation or salt deficiency makes sweet or salty things taste better. Influences on protein and fat intake are more indirect. Protein and fat molecules have no particular taste or smell. So preferring or avoiding foods that contain these nutrients is based on associations between scent cues from other volatile substances in food and on the nutritional results of eating the foods (Bartoshuk, 1991; Schiffman et al., 1999).

We experience warm foods as sweeter, but temperature does not alter our experience of saltiness (Cruz & Green, 2000). Warming releases aromas that rise from the mouth into the nose and create more flavor sensations. This is why some people find hot pizza delicious and cold pizza disgusting. Spicy "hot" foods actually stimulate pain fibers in the mouth, because they contain a substance called *capsaicin* (pronounced "kap-SAY-uh-sin").

Our Sense of Smell

Pinching your nose prevents you from smelling odors, and taping a nasal dilator strip over the bridge of your nose intensifies odors (Raudenbush & Meyer, 2002). These effects

volley theory   A theory of hearing stating that the firing rate of an auditory nerve matches a sound wave's frequency. Also called *frequency-matching theory.*

sense of smell   The sense that detects chemicals that are airborne. Also called *olfaction.*

sense of taste   The sense that detects chemicals in solution that come into contact with receptors inside the mouth. Also called *gustation.*

occur because the nose (and the mouth, to some extent) acts as an accessory structure that collects airborne odor molecules for coding and analysis by the olfactory system (see Figure 3.16). As odor molecules pass into the moist lining of the upper part of the nose—called the *mucous membrane*—they bind to receptors on the dendrites of olfactory neurons, causing a biochemical change. This change, in turn, leads to changes in the firing rates of these neurons, whose axons combine to form the *olfactory nerve* (Dionne & Dubin, 1994). It only takes a single molecule of an odorous substance to cause a change in the activity of an olfactory neuron, but detection of the odor by a human requires about fifty such molecules (Menini, Picco, & Firestein, 1995).

There are thousands of different receptors for odors, but there are even more possible odors in the world. Any particular odor is sensed as a particular *pattern* of responses by these odorant receptors (Duchamp-Viret, Chaput, & Duchamp, 1999). So a rose, a pizza, and your favorite cologne each have a different smell because they stimulate their own unique pattern of activity in your odorant receptors.

Unlike other senses, our sense of smell does not send its messages through the thalamus. Instead, axons from olfactory neurons in the nose extend through a bony plate and directly into the brain, where they have a synapse in a structure called the **olfactory bulb.** Connections from the olfactory bulb spread throughout the brain, but they are especially plentiful in the amygdala, a part of the brain involved in emotional experience and learning. In humans, the amygdala is especially active in response to disgusting odors (Zald & Pardo, 1997).

The unique anatomy of the olfactory system may help account for the unique relationship between smells and memory. Associations between a certain experience and a particular odor are not weakened much by time or later experiences (Lawless & Engen, 1977). So catching a whiff of the cologne once worn by a lost loved one can reactivate intense feelings of love or sadness associated with that person. Odors can also be better than sights or sounds at bringing back accurate memories of experiences linked with them, especially positive experiences (Engen, Gilmore, & Mair, 1991; Mohr et al., 2001).

figure 3.16

The Olfactory System: The Nose and the Rose

Airborne odor molecules reach the olfactory area either through the nose or through an opening in the palate at the back of the mouth. This opening allows us to sample odors from our food as we eat. Nerve fibers pass directly from the olfactory area to the olfactory bulb in the brain, and from there signals pass to areas that are involved in emotion. This arrangement helps explain why odors often trigger strong emotional memories.

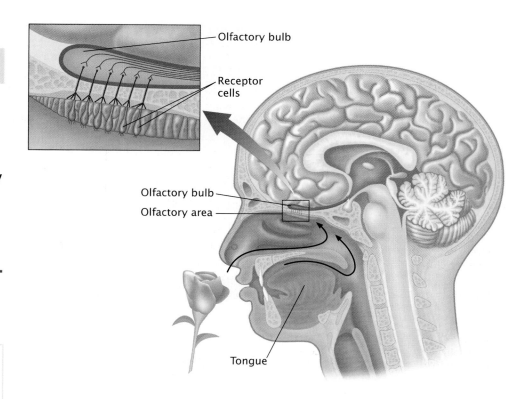

olfactory bulb   A brain structure that receives messages regarding smell.

figure 3.17

Are You a Supertaster?

learn by doing This photo shows papillae on the tongue of a "supertaster." If you don't mind a temporary stain on your mouth and teeth, you can look at your own papillae by painting the front of your tongue with a cotton swab soaked in blue food coloring. Distribute the dye by moving your tongue around and swallowing; then look into a magnifying mirror as you shine a flashlight on your tongue. The pink circles you see against the blue background are papillae, each of which has about six taste buds buried in its surface. Get several friends to do this test, and you will see that genes create wide individual differences in taste bud density.

Species ranging from humans to worms have remarkably similar neural mechanisms for sensing smell. Different species vary considerably, however, in their sensitivity to odor and in the degree to which they depend on it for survival. Whereas humans have about 9 million olfactory neurons, dogs have about 225 million. No wonder dogs are so dependent on smell to identify food, territory, and receptive mates. Dogs and many other species also have an accessory olfactory system that detects pheromones. **Pheromones** (pronounced "FAIR-oh-mohns") are chemicals that, when released by one animal and detected by another, can shape the second animal's behavior. For example, when a male snake detects a chemical on the skin of a female snake, it is stimulated to "court" the female (Mason et al., 1989).

The role of pheromones in humans is much less clear, but it appears that we do have some sort of pheromone-like system. For one thing, pheromonal signals secreted in women's perspiration can influence nearby women's menstrual cycles. As a result, women living together eventually tend to menstruate at about the same time (Stern & McClintock, 1998). Furthermore, odorants that cannot be consciously detected can nevertheless influence mood and stimulate activity in nonolfactory areas of the brain (Jacob & McClintock, 2000; Jacob et al., 2001; Savic et al., 2001). Despite steamy ads for cologne and perfume, however, there is not yet any solid evidence that humans give off or can detect pheromones that act as sexual attractants. If a certain scent does enhance a person's readiness for sex, it is probably because the person has learned to associate that scent with previous sexual experiences. There are many other examples of people using olfactory information in social situations. For instance, after just a few hours of contact with their newborn babies, mothers can usually identify them by the infants' smell. And if infants are breastfed, they can discriminate their own mother's odor from that of other breastfeeding women and appear to be comforted by it (Porter, 1998/1999). Recognizing this odor may help establish the mother-infant bond discussed in the chapter on human development.

Our Sense of Taste

Our receptors for taste are in the taste buds, which are grouped together in structures called **papillae** (pronounced "puh-PILL-ee"). Normally, there are about ten thousand

pheromones Chemicals that are released by one animal and detected by another, shaping the second animal's behavior or physiology.

papillae Structures in the mouth, on which taste buds are grouped.

somatic senses Senses including touch, temperature, pain, and kinesthesia that are spread throughout the body rather than located in a specific organ. Also called *somatosensory systems*.

in review

SMELL AND TASTE		
Aspect of Sensory System	**Elements**	**Key Characteristics**
Energy	Smell: volatile chemicals Taste: chemicals in solution	The amount, intensity, and location of the chemicals determine taste and smell sensations.
Structures of taste and smell	Smell: chemical receptors in the mucous membrane of the nose Taste: taste buds grouped in papillae in the mouth	Odor and taste molecules stimulate chemical receptors.
Pathway to the brain	Olfactory bulb and taste buds	Axons from the nose and mouth bypass the thalamus and extend directly to the olfactory bulb.

?   *The flavor of food arises from a combination of _____ and _____.*

taste buds in a person's mouth, mostly on the tongue but also on the roof of the mouth and on the back of the throat.

The human taste system detects only a few basic sensations: sweet, sour, bitter, and salty. Each taste bud responds best to one or two of these categories (Zhang et al., 2003) but it also responds weakly to others. Research has also revealed two additional taste sensations (Rolls, 1997). One, called *umami,* enhances other tastes and is produced by certain proteins, as well as by monosodium glutamate (MSG). The other, called *astringent,* is the taste produced by tannins, which are found in tea, for example. Scientists have only recently begun to identify how chemical interactions between foods and taste receptors signal various tastes (Herness & Gilbertson, 1999; Small et al., 2003). They do know, however, that about 25 percent of us are "supertasters"—individuals whose genes have given them an especially large number of papillae on their tongues (Bartoshuk, 2000; see Figure 3.17). Supertasters are more sensitive than other people to bitterness, as revealed in their reaction to foods such as broccoli, soy products, and grapefruit. ("In Review: Smell and Taste" summarizes our discussion of these senses.)

Sensing Your Body

▶ **Which is the largest organ in my body?**

Some senses are not located in a specific organ, such as the eye or the ear. These are the **somatic senses,** also called *somatosensory systems,* which are spread throughout the body. The somatic senses include the skin senses of touch, temperature, and pain, as well as a body sense, called *kinesthesia,* that tells the brain where the parts of the body are. Kinesthesia is closely related to our sense of balance. Although balance is not strictly a somatosensory system, we will describe it here.

Touch and Temperature

People can function and prosper without vision, hearing, or smell. But a person without a sense of touch would have difficulty surviving. Without this sense, you could not even swallow food, because you could not tell where it was in your mouth and throat. You receive touch sensations through your skin, which is the body's largest organ. The skin covers nearly two square yards of surface area, weighs more than twenty pounds, and has hair virtually everywhere on it. The hairs on your skin do not sense anything directly. However, when the hairs are bent, they push against the skin beneath them. Receptors in, and just below, the skin send the "touch" message to the brain.

Coding Touch Information   The sense of touch codes information about two aspects of an object contacting the skin: its weight and its location. The *intensity* of the stimulus—how heavy it is—is coded both by the firing rate of individual neurons and by the number of neurons stimulated. A heavy object triggers a higher rate of firing and stimulates more neurons than a light object. The brain "knows" where the touch occurs based on the *location* of the nerves that sense the touch information.

Adapting to Touch Stimuli   Constant input from all your touch neurons would provide a lot of unnecessary information. Once you get dressed, you do not need to be constantly reminded that you are wearing clothes. Partly because of the process of adaptation, you do not continue to feel your clothes against your skin.

Changes in touch (as when your belt or shoe suddenly feels loose) provide the most important sensory information. The touch sense emphasizes these changes and filters out the excess information. How? Typically, a touch neuron responds with a burst of

learn by doing **TOUCH AND VISION**   Just as taste and smell interact, so do touch and vision. To experience an example of this interaction, ask someone sitting across a table from you to stroke the tabletop while stroking your knee under the table in exactly the same way, in exactly the same direction. If you watch the person's hand stroking the table, you will soon experience the touch sensations coming from the table, not your knee! If the person's two hands do not move in synch, however, the illusion will not occur.

firing when a stimulus is applied, then quickly returns to its baseline firing rate, even though the stimulus may still be in contact with the skin. If the touch pressure increases, the neuron again responds by increasing its firing rate, then slowing down. A few neurons adapt more slowly, however, continuing to fire as long as pressure is applied. By attending to this input, you can sense a constant stimulus (try doing this by focusing on touch sensations from your glasses or shoes).

Sensing Temperature   Some of the skin's sensory neurons respond to a change in temperature but not to simple contact. "Warm fibers" and "cold fibers" respond to specific temperature changes only. However, many fibers that respond to temperature also respond to touch, so these sensations sometimes interact. For example, if you touch an object made up of alternating warm and cool sections, you will have the sensation of intense heat (Thunberg, 1896, cited in Craig & Bushnell, 1994). Different firing patterns in a single nerve fiber in the skin can code different stimuli, but just how these different stimuli can create differing patterns of firing is not yet known.

Pain

Touch can feel pleasurable, but if the intensity of stimulation increases too much, it can turn into a pain sensation. Pain tells you about the impact of the world on your body. It also has a distinctly negative emotional component that interrupts whatever you are doing (Eccleston & Crombez, 1999).

Pain as an Information Sense   The information-carrying aspect of pain is very similar to that of touch and temperature. The receptors for pain are free nerve endings, which come from the spinal cord, enter the skin, and then simply end. Painful stimuli cause the release of chemicals that fit into these specialized receptors in pain neurons, causing them to fire. The axons of pain-sensing neurons release neurotransmitters not only near the spinal cord (thus sending pain information to the brain) but also near the skin (causing swelling).

Two types of nerve fibers carry pain signals from the skin to the spinal cord. *A-delta* fibers carry sharp, pricking pain sensations; *C-fibers* carry continuous, dull aches and burning sensations. When you stub your toe, for example, that immediate wave of sharp, intense pain is signaled by A-delta fibers, whereas that slightly delayed wave of gnawing, dull pain is signaled by C-fibers. When pain impulses reach the spinal cord, they form synapses with neurons that relay the pain signals to the thalamus and other parts of the brain. Different pain neurons are activated by different types and degrees of painful stimulation (Ploner et al., 2002).

Emotional Aspects of Pain   There are specific pathways that carry the emotional component of a painful stimulus to areas of the hindbrain, reticular formation, and cortex via the thalamus (Johansen, Fields, & Manning, 2001). However, our overall emotional response to pain depends greatly on how we think about it (Flor, 2002; Keefe & France, 1999; Pincus & Morley, 2001). In one study, some participants were told about the kind of painful stimulus they were to receive and when to expect it. Others were not informed. Those who knew what to expect objected less to the pain, even though the sensation was reported to be equally noticeable in both groups (Mayer & Price, 1982). People can lessen their emotional responses to pain by using pain-reducing strategies (such as distracting thoughts), especially if they expect these strategies to succeed (Young et al., 1995).

Modulating Pain: The Gate Control Theory   Pain is useful because it can protect you from harm. There are times, though, when enough is enough. Fortunately, the nervous system has several mechanisms for controlling the experience of pain. One theory about how these mechanisms work is called the **gate control theory** (Melzack & Wall, 1965). This theory suggests that there is a "gate" in the spinal cord that either allows pain signals to reach the brain or prevents their passage. Some details of the original theory were incorrect, but more recent work supports the idea that natural mechanisms can indeed block pain sensations (Stanton-Hicks & Salamon, 1997).

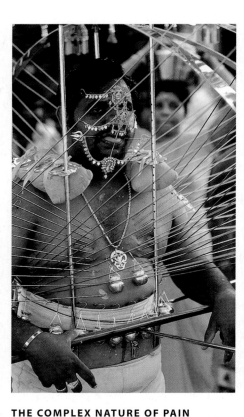

THE COMPLEX NATURE OF PAIN
If pain were based only on the nature of incoming stimuli, this participant in a purification ceremony in Singapore would be hurting. However, the experience of pain is a complex phenomenon that is affected by psychological and biological variables that can make it more or, as in this case, less intense.

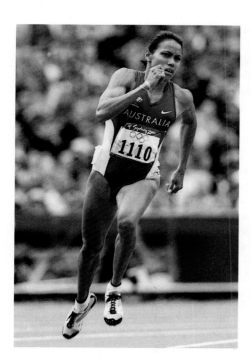

NATURAL ANALGESIA The stress of athletic exertion causes the release of endorphins, natural painkillers that have been associated with pleasant feelings called "runner's high."

For example, input from other skin senses can come into the spinal cord at the same time the pain gets there and "take over" the pathways that the pain impulses would have used. This appears to be the reason we can relieve pain by rubbing the skin around a wound or using creams that produce temperature sensations. It also helps explain why scratching relieves itching; itchy sensations involve activity in fibers located close to pain fibers (Andrew & Craig, 2001).

Alternatively, the brain can close the gate to pain impulses by sending signals down the spinal cord. These messages from the brain block incoming pain signals at spinal cord synapses. The result is **analgesia** (pronounced "ann-nuhl-JEE-zhah"), a reduction in pain sensation in the presence of a normally painful stimulus. Drugs that dull pain sensations, such as aspirin, are called *analgesics*.

Natural Analgesics As we saw in the chapter on biology and behavior, natural opiates called *endorphins* play a role in the brain's ability to block pain signals. Endorphins are natural painkillers that act as neurotransmitters at many levels of the pain pathway. In the spinal cord, for example, they block the synapses of the fibers that carry pain signals. Endorphins may also relieve pain when the adrenal and pituitary glands secrete them into the bloodstream as hormones. The more endorphin receptors a person has inherited, the more pain tolerance that person has (Kest, Wilson, & Mogil, 1999; Uhl, Sora, & Wang, 1999).

Several conditions can cause the body to ease its own pain. For example, endorphins are released where inflammation occurs (Cabot, 2001). During the late stages of pregnancy, a spinal cord endorphin system develops to reduce the mother's labor pains (Dawson-Basoa & Gintzler, 1997). An endorphin system may also be activated when we eat spicy chili peppers. People who like "hot" foods can no longer tolerate them when they receive naloxone, a drug that blocks the action of endorphins (Estcorn, 1992, cited in Stern & Stern, 1992). An endorphin system is also activated when people believe they are receiving a painkiller, even when they are not (Benedetti & Amanzio, 1997); this may be one reason for the placebo effect, discussed in the introductory chapter (Petrovic et al., 2002). Interestingly, the resulting pain inhibition is experienced in the part of the body where it was expected to occur, but not elsewhere (Benedetti, Arduino, & Amanzio, 1999). Physical or psychological stress can also activate natural analgesic systems. Stress-induced release of endorphins may account for the fact that injured soldiers and athletes sometimes continue to perform in the heat of battle or competition with no apparent pain.

gate control theory A theory suggesting the presence of a "gate" in the spinal cord that either permits or blocks the passage of pain impulses to the brain.

analgesia Reduction in the sensation of pain in the presence of a normally painful stimulus.

A cupuncture is an ancient and widely used treatment in Asian medicine that is alleged to relieve pain (Ulett, 2003). The method is based on the idea that body energy flows along lines called *channels* (Vincent & Richardson, 1986). According to this theory, there are fourteen main channels, and a person's health depends on the balance of energy flowing in them. Stimulating the channels by inserting fine needles into the skin and twirling them is said to restore a balanced flow of energy. The needles produce an aching and tingling sensation called *Teeh-ch'i* at the site of stimulation, and they relieve pain at distant, seemingly unrelated parts of the body.

THINKING CRITICALLY

Does Acupuncture Relieve Pain?

■ **What am I being asked to believe or accept?**

Acupuncturists assert that twirling needles in the skin can relieve pain caused by everything from tooth extraction to cancer.

■ **Is there evidence available to support the claim?**

There is evidence from magnetic resonance imaging (MRI) studies that stimulating acupuncture sites changes activity in brain regions related to the targets of treatment

(Cho et al., 1998; Cho, Wong, & Fallon, 2001). Numerous studies also show positive results in 50 to 80 percent of patients treated by acupuncture for various kinds of pain (Richardson & Vincent, 1986). In one controlled study of headache pain, 53 percent of the participants reported reduced pain following real acupuncture, whereas only 33 percent of placebo group members improved following fake electrical stimulation (Dowson, Lewith, & Machin, 1985). This latter figure is about the usual proportion of people responding to a placebo.

Another headache study found both acupuncture and drugs to be superior to a placebo. Each reduced the frequency of headaches, but the drugs were more effective than acupuncture at reducing the severity of headache pain (Hesse, Mogelvang, & Simonsen, 1994). Unfortunately, such well-controlled studies are rare, and their results are often contradictory (Ter Riet, Kleijnen, & Knipschild, 1990). More recent studies of patients with back or neck pain, for example, found acupuncture to be no better than a placebo or massage therapy (Cherkin et al., 2001; Irnich et al., 2001).

Drugs that slow the breakdown of opiates also prolong the analgesia produced by acupuncture (He, 1987). The pain-reducing effects of acupuncture during electrical stimulation of a tooth can be reversed by naloxone, a substance mentioned earlier as blocking the painkilling effects of endorphins and other opiate drugs. These findings suggest that acupuncture somehow activates endorphins, the body's natural painkillers. Is this activation brought about only by a placebo effect? Probably not entirely, because acupuncture produces naloxone-reversible analgesia even in monkeys and rats, who obviously have no expectations about acupuncture (Ha et al., 1981; Kishioka et al., 1994).

■ Can that evidence be interpreted another way?

Yes. Evidence about acupuncture might be interpreted as simply confirming that the body's painkilling system can be stimulated by external means. Acupuncture may merely provide one activating method. There may be other, even more efficient methods for doing so (Ulett, 2003). We already know, for example, that successful placebo treatments for human pain appear to operate by activating the endorphin system.

■ What evidence would help to evaluate the alternatives?

More placebo-controlled studies of acupuncture are needed, but it is difficult to control for the placebo effect in acupuncture treatment, especially in double-blind fashion (e.g., Kaptchuk, 2001). (How could a therapist not know whether the treatment being given was acupuncture or not? And from the patient's perspective, what placebo treatment could look and feel like having a needle inserted and twirled in the skin?) Nevertheless, researchers have tried to separate the psychological and physical effects of acupuncture—for example, by using phony needles, mock electrical nerve stimulation (in which electrodes are attached to the skin but no electrical stimulation is given), or stimulation at other sites on the skin (Park, White, & Ernst, 2001).

Researchers must also learn more about what factors govern whether acupuncture will activate the endorphin system. Other important unknowns include the types of pain for which acupuncture is most effective, the types of patients who respond best, and the precise procedures that are most effective. Knowing more about the general relationship between internal painkilling systems and external methods for stimulating them would also be valuable.

■ What conclusions are most reasonable?

There seems little doubt that, in some circumstances, acupuncture relieves pain. Acupuncture is not a cure-all, however. For example, committees convened in the United States and the United Kingdom have concluded that acupuncture can be useful in the treatment of pain and nausea (British Medical Association, 2000; National Institutes of Health, 1998), but more than $2 million in research has failed to show that acupuncture is better than new antinausea drugs or conventional painkilling procedures (Taub, 1998). Further studies are likely to continue; the quality of their methodology and the nature of their results will determine whether acupuncture finds a more prominent place in Western medicine.

Sensing Body Position

Most sensory systems receive information from the external world, such as the light reflected from a flower or the feeling of cool water. But as far as the brain is concerned, the rest of the body is "out there," too. You know about the position of your body and what each of its parts is doing only because sensory systems provide this information to your brain. These sensory systems are described as **proprioceptive** ("received from one's own," pronounced "pro-pree-oh-SEP-tiv").

Kinesthesia Remember Christina, the woman described in the biology and behavior chapter who did not recognize her own body? She had lost her sense of **kinesthesia** (pronounced "kin-es-THEE-see-uh"), which tells us where the parts of the body are in relation to one another. Try this: Close your eyes; then hold your arms out in front of you and touch your two index fingers together. You probably did this well, because your kinesthetic sense told you where each finger was with respect to your body. You also depend on kinesthetic information to guide all your movements, from walking to complex athletic actions such as running down a basketball court while dribbling a ball and avoiding an opposing player. These movement patterns become simple and fluid because, with practice, the brain uses kinesthetic information automatically. Normally, kinesthetic information comes primarily from the joints and muscles. Receptors in muscle fibers send information to the brain about the stretching of muscles. When the position of the bones changes, receptors in the joints set off neural activity. This coded information goes to the spinal cord and then to the thalamus, along with sensory information from the skin. Finally it goes to the cerebellum and to the somatosensory cortex, both of which help coordinate movements.

Balance Have you ever been on a roller coaster? How did you feel when the ride ended? The **vestibular sense** (pronounced "ves-TIB-u-ler") tells the brain about the position of the head (and therefore the body) in space and about its general movements. You have probably heard it referred to as the *sense of balance.* People usually become aware of the vestibular sense only when they overstimulate it and become dizzy or motion sick.

The inner ear contains the organs for the vestibular sense. Each ear has two *vestibular sacs* filled with fluid and containing small crystals called *otoliths* ("ear stones") that rest on hair endings. Three arc-shaped tubes, called the *semicircular canals,* are also fluid filled (see Figure 3.14). Tiny hairs extend into the fluid in the canals. When your head moves, the otoliths shift in the vestibular sacs and the fluid moves in the semicircular canals, stimulating hair endings. This process activates neurons that travel along the auditory nerve, signaling the brain about the amount and direction of head movement.

Neural connections from the vestibular system to the cerebellum help coordinate bodily movements. Connections to the part of the autonomic nervous system that affects the digestive system help create the nausea that may follow overstimulation of the vestibular system—by a roller coaster ride, for instance. Finally, connections to the eye muscles produce *vestibular-ocular reflexes,* which cause your eyes to move opposite to your head movements. These reflexes allow you to focus on one spot even when your head is moving. You can dramatize these reflexes by having a friend spin you around on a stool for a while. When you stop, try to fix your gaze on one point in the room. You'll be

proprioceptive Referring to sensory systems that tell us about the location of our body parts and what each is doing.

kinesthesia The proprioceptive sense that tells us where the parts of the body are with respect to one another.

vestibular sense The proprioceptive sense that provides information about the position of the head and its movements.

in review

BODY SENSES

Sense	Energy	Conversion of Physical Energy to Nerve Activity	Pathways and Characteristics
Touch	Mechanical deformation of skin	Skin receptors (may be stimulated by hair on the skin)	Nerve endings respond to changes in weight (intensity) and location of touch.
Temperature	Heat	Sensory neurons in the skin	Changes in temperature are detected by warm-sensing and cool-sensing fibers. Temperature interacts with touch.
Pain	Increases with intensity of touch or temperature	Free nerve endings in or near the skin surface	Changes in intensity cause the release of chemicals detected by receptors in pain neurons. Some fibers convey sharp pain; others convey dull aches and burning sensations.
Kinesthesia	Mechanical energy of joint and muscle movement	Receptors in muscle fibers	Information from muscle fibers is sent to the spinal cord, thalamus, cerebellum, and cortex.

?   *Gate control theory offers an explanation of why we sometimes do not feel _____ .*

unable to do so, because the excitation of the vestibular system will cause your eyes to move repeatedly in the direction opposite from the way you were spinning. (See "In Review: Body Senses" for a summary of our discussion of touch, temperature, pain, and kinesthesia.)

Perception

▶ **How do sensations become perceptions?**

So far, we have explored how sensory information reaches the brain. Let's now consider the processes of perception that allow the brain to make sense of that information. These perceptual processes can sometimes make the difference between life and death. For example, at a traffic circle in Scotland, fourteen fatal accidents occurred in one year, partly because drivers did not slow down as they approached the circle. After warning signs failed to solve the problem, Gordon Denton, a British psychologist, found a clever solution. He recommended that white lines be painted across the road leading to the circle, in a pattern something like this:

/   /   /   / / / //

Crossing these lines, which were spaced progressively more closely, gave drivers the impression that they were speeding up, so their automatic response was to slow down. During the fourteen months after Denton's idea was implemented, there were only two fatalities at the traffic circle! Similar kinds of striping patterns are now widely used throughout Britain, and on approaches to some towns and intersections in the United States, too (Associated Press, 1999). Denton's solution depended partly on his knowledge of sensation, but mostly on the principles of human perception.

figure 3.18

Misperceiving Reality

learn by **doing** Measure lines A-C and A-B. They are exactly the same length, but you probably perceived A-C as longer. Why? Partly because your visual system tries to interpret all stimuli as three-dimensional, even when they are not. A three-dimensional interpretation of this drawing would lead you to see the two lines as the edges of two parallel paths, one of which ends closer to you than the other. Your eyes tell you that the two paths originate from about the same point (the castle entrance), so you assume that the closer line must be the longer of the two.

Source: Gardner (1988).

Some perceptual tasks take attention and effort, as when a child struggles to recognize printed letters. But as experienced readers know, a lot of the perceptual work that transforms sensory information into meaningful experiences happens automatically, without conscious awareness. To illustrate the workings of these complex processes, psychologists draw attention to *perceptual failures*—cases in which we perceive stimuli incorrectly. Just as drivers at the traffic circle incorrectly perceived themselves as speeding up, you will probably perceive the two lines in Figure 3.18 as differing in length, even though they are the same.

Organizing the Perceptual World

▶ **What determines how I perceive my world?**

To further appreciate the wonder of the complicated perceptual work you do every day, imagine yourself driving on a busy road searching for Barney's Diner, an unfamiliar restaurant where you are to meet a friend. The roadside is crammed with signs of all shapes and colors, some flashing, some rotating. If you are ever to recognize the sign that says "Barney's Diner," you must impose some sort of organization on this overwhelming mixture of visual information. How do you do this? How do you know where one sign ends and another begins? And how do you know that an apparently tiny sign is not really tiny, but just far away?

Principles of Perceptual Organization

Before you can recognize the "Barney's Diner" sign, your perceptual system must separate that sign from its background of lights, colors, letters, and other competing stimuli. Two basic principles—*figure-ground perception* and *grouping*—guide this initial organization.

(A)

(B)

figure 3.19

Reversible Images

learn by **doing**   These reversible images can be organized by your perceptual system in two ways. Try perceiving Part A as the word *figure,* and the space around the letters becomes meaningless background. Now emphasize the word *ground,* and what had stood out a moment ago now becomes background. You can do the same in Part B. When you emphasize the vase, the faces become background; if you organize the faces as the figure, what had been a vase now becomes background.

figure   The part of the visual field that has meaning.

ground   The contourless part of the visual field; the background.

Figure and Ground   When you look at a complex scene or listen to a noisy environment, your perceptual apparatus automatically picks out certain features, objects, or sounds to emphasize. The emphasized features become the **figure.** This part of the visual field has meaning, stands in front of the rest, and always seems to include contours or edges. These contours and edges separate the figure from the less relevant background, called the **ground** (Rubin, 1915). So, as you drive toward an intersection, a stop sign becomes a figure, standing out clearly against the background of trees, houses, and cars.

To experience how perception creates figure and ground, look at Figure 3.19. Notice that you can decide how to organize the stimuli in the drawings. You can repeatedly reverse figure and ground to see faces, then a vase, then faces again, or to see the word *figure* or the word *ground.* These "reversible" images show that your perceptual systems are not just video cameras that passively record incoming sensations; you play an active part in organizing what you perceive. However, you usually organize sensory stimulation into only one perceptual category at a time. This is why it is difficult to see both a vase and two faces—or the words *figure* and *ground*—at the same time.

Grouping   Why is it that certain parts of the world become figure and others become ground, even when nothing in particular stands out in the pattern of light that falls on the retina? The answer is that certain properties of stimuli lead you to group them together, more or less automatically.

In the early 1900s, several German psychologists described the principles behind this grouping of stimuli. They argued that people perceive sights and sounds as organized wholes. These wholes, they said, become different from, and more than, the sum of the individual sensations, just as water becomes something more than just an assortment of hydrogen and oxygen atoms. Because the German word meaning (roughly) "whole figure" is *Gestalt* (pronounced "ge-SHTALT"), these researchers became known as *Gestalt psychologists.* They proposed a number of principles that describe how the perceptual system "glues" raw sensations together in particular ways:

1. *Proximity.* The closer objects or events are to one another, the more likely they are to be perceived as belonging together, as Figure 3.20(A) illustrates.

2. *Similarity.* Similar elements are perceived to be part of a group, as in Figure 3.20(B). This is why students wearing the same school colors at a stadium will be perceived as belonging together even if they are not seated close together.

3. *Continuity.* Sensations that appear to create a continuous form are perceived as belonging together, as in Figure 3.20(C).

4. *Closure.* We tend to mentally "fill in" missing parts of incomplete objects, as in Figure 3.20(D). The gaps are easy to see, but the tendency to link disconnected parts can be so strong that you may perceive faint connections that are not actually there.

5. *Texture.* When basic features of stimuli have the same texture (such as the angle of several elements), we tend to group those stimuli together. So we group standing trees together and perceive them as separate from their fallen neighbors.

6. *Simplicity.* We tend to group features of a stimulus in a way that provides the simplest interpretation of the world. You can see the simplicity principle in action in Figure 3.20(D), where it is simpler to see a single cube than an assortment of separate, unrelated arrows and Ys.

7. *Common fate.* Sets of objects that move in the same direction at the same speed are perceived together. So a flock of birds, though separated in space, will be perceived as a group. Choreographers and marching-band directors use the principle of common fate when they arrange for groups of dancers or musicians to move identically, causing the audience to perceive waves of motion or large moving objects.

figure 3.20

Gestalt Principles of Perceptual Grouping

We tend to perceive Part A as two groups of two circles plus one single circle, rather than as, say, five circles. In Part B, we see two columns of Xs and two columns of Os, not four rows of XOXO. We see the X in Part C as being made out of two continuous lines, not a combination of the odd forms shown. In Part D, we fill gaps so as to perceive a hollow cube. In Part E, we tend to pair up dots in the same oval even though they are far apart. Part F shows that connected objects are grouped together.

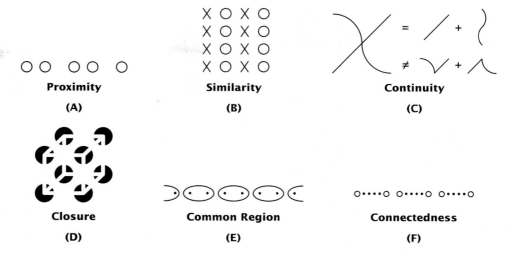

Stephen Palmer (1999) has proposed some important additional grouping principles:

1. *Synchrony.* Stimuli that occur at the same time are likely to be perceived as coming from the same source. For example, if you see a car up ahead stop violently at the same instant you hear a crash, you will probably perceive these visual and auditory stimuli as part of the same event.

2. *Common region.* Stimuli located within some boundary tend to be grouped together. The boundary can be created by an enclosing perimeter, as in Figure 3.20(E), a region of color, or other factors.

3. *Connectedness.* Stimuli that are connected by other elements tend to be grouped together. In Figure 3.20(F), the circles connected by dotted lines seem to go together even though they are farther apart than some pairs of unconnected circles. Here, the principle of connectedness appears more important than the principle of proximity.

Perception of Depth and Distance

We are able to experience the world in three-dimensional depth even though the visual information we receive from it is projected onto two-dimensional retinas. This is possible because of **depth perception,** our ability to perceive distance. Depth perception, in turn, is made possible partly by *stimulus cues* provided by the environment and partly by the properties of our visual system.

Stimulus Cues   To some extent, people perceive depth through the same cues that artists use to create the impression of depth and distance on a two-dimensional canvas. Figure 3.21 demonstrates several of these cues:

■ The two people at the far left of Figure 3.21 illustrate the principle of *relative size:* If two objects are assumed to be the same size, the object producing a larger image on the retina is perceived as closer than the one producing a smaller image.

■ Another cue comes from *height in the visual field:* On the ground, more-distant objects are usually higher in the visual field than those nearby. Because the buildings in Figure 3.21 are higher than the people in the foreground, the buildings appear to be farther away from you. This is one reason why objects higher in the visual field are more likely to be interpreted as the background for objects that are lower in a scene (Vecera, Vogel, & Woodman, 2002).

depth perception   Perception of distance, allowing us to experience the world in three dimensions.

figure 3.21

Stimulus Cues for Depth Perception

learn by **doing**   See if you can identify the cues of relative size, interposition, linear perspective, height in the visual field, textural gradient, and shadows that combine to create a sense of three-dimensional depth in this drawing.

convergence   A depth cue resulting when the eyes rotate to project the image of an object on each retina.

binocular disparity   A depth cue based on the difference between the retinal images received by each eye.

looming   A motion cue whereby rapid expansion in the size of an image fills the available space on the retina.

▪ The person walking near the car in the middle of Figure 3.21 illustrates another depth cue, called *interposition*. Closer objects block the view of things farther away.

▪ The tiny figure near the dotted center line of the road in Figure 3.21 is seen as very far away because she is near a point in the road where its edges, like all parallel lines that recede into the distance, appear to converge toward a single point. This apparent convergence provides a cue called *linear perspective*. The closer together two converging lines are, the greater the perceived distance.

▪ Notice that the road in Figure 3.21 disappears into a hazy background. Increased distance usually produces less clarity, and this *reduced clarity* is interpreted as a cue for greater distance. (Hazy, distant objects also tend to take on a bluish tone, which is why art students are taught to add a little blue when mixing paint for deep background features.)

▪ *Light and shadow* also contribute to the perception of three dimensions (Kingdom, 2003; Ramachandran, 1988). The buildings in the background of Figure 3.21 are seen as three-dimensional, not flat, because of the shadows on their right faces. Figure 3.22 shows a more dramatic example.

▪ An additional stimulus-based depth cue comes from continuous changes across the visual field, called *gradients*. For example, a *textural gradient* is a graduated change in the texture, or "grain," of the visual field, as you can see in the sidewalk, the grass, and the road in Figure 3.21. Texture appears finer as distance increases. So, as the texture of a surface changes across the retinal image, you perceive a change in distance.

figure 3.22

Light, Shadow, and Depth Perception

learn **by doing** The shadows cast by these protruding rivets and deep dents make it easy to see them in three dimensions. But if you turn the book upside down, the rivets now look like dents, and the dents look like bumps. This reversal in depth perception occurs partly because people normally assume that illumination comes from above and interpret the pattern of light and shadow accordingly. With the picture upside down, light coming from the top would produce the observed pattern of shadows only if the circles were dents, not rivets.

A CASE OF DEPTH MISPERCEPTION
The runner in this photo is actually farther away than the man on the pitcher's mound. But because he is lower, not higher, in the visual field—and because his leg can be seen as in front of, not behind, the pitcher's leg—the runner appears smaller than normal rather than farther away.

Cues Based on Properties of the Visual System   Some depth cues result from the way human eyes are built and positioned. Recall that to bring an image into focus on the retina, the lens of the eye changes shape, or *accommodates.* Information about the muscle activity involved is relayed to the brain, and this accommodation cue helps create the perception of distance.

Two other depth cues are produced by the relative location of our two eyes. One is **convergence.** Each eye is located at a different place on the skull, so the eyes must converge, or rotate inward, to project the same image on each retina. The closer the object, the more the eyes must converge. Eye muscles send information about this convergence to the brain, which processes it as a distance cue.

Second, because they are in slightly different locations, each eye sees the world from a slightly different angle. The difference between these different retinal images is called **binocular disparity.** The difference, or disparity, between images gets smaller for objects that are far away, and larger for objects that are nearby. The brain not only combines the two images of an object but also takes into account how much they differ. This information helps to generate the impression of a single object located at a particular distance. View-Master slide viewers, 3-D movies, and some virtual reality systems also use binocular disparity cues to create the appearance of depth in a two-dimensional stimulus. They show each eye an image of a scene as viewed from a slightly different angle.

In short, many cues—some present in the environment and in retinal images, others arising from the structure of the visual system—combine to give us a powerful and accurate sense of depth and distance.

Perception of Motion

Sometimes the most important property of an object is its motion—how fast it is going and where it is heading. Usually motion perception occurs as visual patterns from objects move across the surface of the retina. As in the case of depth perception, you automatically translate this two-dimensional information into a three-dimensional experience. One example is the response to **looming,** which is a rapid expansion in the size of an image so that it fills the retina. When an image looms, there is an automatic tendency to perceive it as an approaching stimulus. If the expansion is as fast to the right as to the left, and as fast above as below, this information signals that the object is directly approaching the eyes. In other words: Duck!

We are lucky that movement of the retinal image is not the only factor contributing to motion perception. If it were, everything in sight would appear to move every time you

BINOCULAR DISPARITY AND DISTANCE   There is less difference between each eye's view of an object when the object is far away than when it is close by. The amount of this binocular disparity helps us estimate the object's distance from us. To see for yourself how binocular disparity changes with distance, hold a pencil vertically about six inches in front of your nose; then close one eye and notice where the pencil is in relation to the background. Now open that eye, close the other one, and notice how much the pencil "shifts." These are the two different views your eyes have of the pencil. Repeat this procedure while holding the pencil at arm's length. Notice that there is now less disparity or "shift," because there is less difference in the angles from which your two eyes see the pencil.

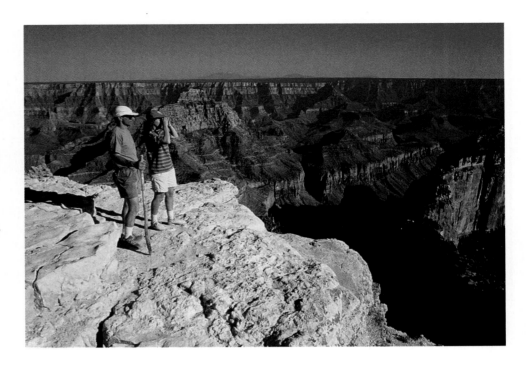

moved your eyes and head (Ölveczky, Baccus, & Meister, 2003). This does not happen, because as noted earlier, the brain receives and processes information about the motion of the eyes and head. So if head or eye movements occur while images of fixed objects move across the retina, you will perceive those objects as stationary. If the images move but the eyes and head do not, you will perceive the objects as moving (Goltz et al., 2003). To demonstrate this, scan the room with your eyes. Stationary objects will not appear to move. Now close one eye, and carefully move your open eyeball by gently pushing on its lower eyelid. Because your brain receives no signals that your eye is being moved by its own muscles, you will perceive objects in the room as moving.

When your body is moving, as in a car, the flow of visual information across the retina combines with information from the vestibular and touch senses to give you the experience of being in motion. So if the car accelerates, you feel pressure from the back of the seat and feel your head tilting backward. If visual flow is perceived without appropriate sensations from other parts of the body, particularly the vestibular senses, motion sickness may result. This explains why you might feel nauseous while operating motion simulators or playing some video games, especially those with virtual reality technology. The images suggest that you are moving through space when there is no real motion.

Other illusions of motion are far less unpleasant. The most important of these occurs when still images appear, one at a time, in rapid succession, as they do on films, videos, and DVDs. Because each image differs slightly from the preceding one, the brain sees the people and objects in each image appearing in one place for only a fraction of a second before they disappear and then quickly reappear in a slightly different location. The entertaining result is the illusion of **stroboscopic motion;** when objects disappear and then quickly reappear nearby, the brain assumes that they have moved smoothly from one location to another. The same illusion is at work when it appears that flashing lights on a theater or casino sign are moving around the sign.

Perceptual Constancy

stroboscopic motion   An illusion in which lights or images flashed in rapid succession are perceived as moving.

Suppose that one sunny day you are watching someone walking toward you along a tree-lined sidewalk. The visual sensations produced by this person are actually very strange.

applying
psychology

A FAILURE OF SHAPE CONSTANCY When certain stimuli are viewed from an extreme angle, the brain's ability to maintain shape constancy can break down. British traffic engineers have taken this phenomenon into account in the design of road markings. The arrow in the top photo appears to be about the same height as the lettering below it, but it isn't. The arrow had to be greatly elongated, as shown in the side view, so that approaching drivers would see its shape clearly. If the arrow had been painted to match the height of the accompanying letters, it would appear "squashed," and only half as tall as the lettering.

learn
by doing

For one thing, the size of the image on your retinas keeps getting larger as the person gets closer. To see this for yourself, hold out a hand at arm's length and look at someone far away. The retinal image of that person will be so small that you can cover it with your hand. If you do the same thing when the person is three feet away, the retinal image will be too large to be covered by your hand, yet you perceive the person as being closer now, not bigger. Similarly, if you watch a person pass from bright sunshine through the shadows of trees, your retinas receive images that shift back and forth from dark to light. Still, you perceive the person's coloring as staying the same.

These examples illustrate **perceptual constancy**, the perception that objects maintain their size, shape, color, and other properties despite changes in their retinal image. Without this aspect of perception, you would experience the world as a place where solid objects continuously changed their properties.

Size Constancy Why does an object's perceived size stay more or less constant, regardless of changes in the size of its retinal image? One reason is that the brain perceives a change in the distance of an object and automatically adjusts the perception of size. Specifically, the *perceived size* of an object is equal to the size of the retinal image multiplied by the perceived distance (Holway & Boring, 1941). As an object moves closer, the size of its retinal image increases, but the perceived distance decreases at the same rate.

perceptual constancy The perception of objects as retaining the same size, shape, color, and other properties despite changes in their retinal image.

figure 3.23

Brightness Contrast

 At first glance, the inner rectangle on the left probably looks lighter than the inner rectangle on the right. But carefully examine the inner rectangles alone (covering their surroundings), and you will see that both are of equal intensity. The brighter surround in the right-hand figure leads you to perceive its inner rectangle as relatively darker.

So, the perceived size remains constant. If a balloon is inflated in front of your eyes, perceived distance remains constant, and the perceived size (correctly) increases as the size of the retinal image increases.

Shape Constancy   The principles behind shape constancy are closely related to those of size constancy. To see shape constancy at work, remember what page you are on, close this book, and tilt it toward and away from you several times. The book will continue to look rectangular, even though the shape of its retinal image changes dramatically as you move it. Your brain automatically integrates information about retinal images and distance as movement occurs. In this case, the distance information had to do with the difference in distance between the near and far edges of the book.

Brightness Constancy   Even with dramatic changes in the amount of light striking an object, the object's perceived brightness remains relatively constant. Place a piece of charcoal in sunlight and a piece of white paper in nearby shade. The charcoal will look very dark and the paper very bright, yet a light meter would tell you that much more light energy is reflected from the sun-bathed coal than from the shaded paper. Why? Partly because the charcoal is the darkest object relative to its sunlit background, and the paper is the brightest object relative to its background of shade. As shown in Figure 3.23, the brightness of an object is perceived in relation to its background.

Optical Illusions

Usually, the perceptual system works automatically and perfectly to create correct perceptions of depth, distance, and size. Sometimes, though, it can fail, resulting in *optical illusions* such as the ones shown in Figure 3.24. Why does the monster that is placed higher in Figure 3.24(A) look larger than the lower one, even though they are equal in size? The converging lines in the tunnel provide depth cues telling you that the higher monster is farther away. Because the retinal image of the "distant" monster is the same size as the "closer" one, your perceptual system calculates that the more distant monster must be bigger. This

figure 3.24

Three Optical Illusions

These illusions are named for the scientists who described them. In Part A, a version of the *Ponzo illusion,* the upper monster looks bigger but is actually the same size as the lower one. In the *Müller-Lyer illusion* (Part B), both vertical lines are actually of equal length; in the *Ebbinghaus illusion* shown in Part C, both center circles are exactly the same size. To prove that you can't always believe your eyes, measure these drawings for yourself.

(A)   **(B)**   **(C)**

PRINCIPLES OF PERCEPTUAL ORGANIZATION AND CONSTANCY

Principle	Description	Example
Figure-ground	Certain objects or sounds automatically become identified as figure, whereas others become meaningless background.	You see a person standing against a building, not a building with a person-shaped hole in it.
Grouping	Properties of stimuli lead us to automatically group them together. These include proximity, similarity, continuity, closure, texture, simplicity, common fate, synchrony, common region, and connectedness.	People who are sitting together, or who are dressed similarly, are perceived as a group.
Depth perception	The world is perceived as three-dimensional, with help from stimulus cues (such as relative size, height in the visual field, interposition, linear perspective, reduced clarity, light and shadow, and gradients) and from visual system cues (such as accommodation, convergence, and binocular disparity).	A person who looks tiny and appears high in the visual field will be perceived as being of normal size, but at a great distance.
Perceptual constancy	Objects are perceived as constant in size, shape, color, and other properties despite changes in their retinal images.	A train coming toward you is perceived as getting closer, not larger; an advertising sign is perceived as rotating, not changing shape.

? *The movement we see in movies, videos, and DVDs is due to a perceptual illusion called _____.*

is the principle of size constancy at work: When two objects have retinal images of the same size, you perceive the one that seems farther away as larger. Now look at Figure 3.24(B). The two vertical lines are the same length, but the one on the right looks longer. Why? One possible reason is that the perceived length of an object is based on what frames it. When the frame is perceived as larger, as on the right side of Figure 3.24(B), so is the line segment within it (Rock, 1978). In Figure 3.24(C), the inner circle at the left looks smaller than the one at the right because, like the brightness of the center rectangles in Figure 3.23, the inner circles are judged in relation to what surrounds them. Because perception is based on many principles, illusions like these probably reflect the violation of more than one of them. (See "In Review: Principles of Perceptual Organization and Constancy.")

Culture, Experience, and Perception

We have talked as if all aspects of perception appear at birth and work or fail in the same way for everyone, everywhere. However, some perceptual abilities appear later than others (see this chapter's Linkages section), and virtually all of them are shaped by experience in the world.

For example, people are better at judging the size and distance of familiar objects than those of unfamiliar ones. This fact suggests that size constancy depends not only on judging image sizes and distances but also on knowledge and experience that tell us that most objects (aside from balloons) do not suddenly change size. As with size constancy, much of the ability to judge shape constancy depends on automatic processes, but our expectations that books and other solid objects do not suddenly change shape also play a role. The knowledge-based nature of perception can also be seen in brightness constancy: Part of the reason you perceive charcoal to be darker than a sheet of paper, no matter how much light it reflects, is that you know charcoal is black.

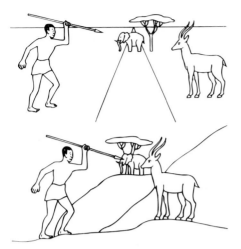

Source: Hudson (1960).

figure 3.25

Culture and Depth Cues

In research on the influence of experience on perception, people are shown drawings like these and asked to say which animal is closest to the hunter. Those in cultures where pictured depth cues are familiar choose the antelope, which is at the same distance from the viewer as the hunter. Those in cultures less familiar with such cues may choose the elephant, which, though closer on the page, is more distant when depth cues are considered.

top-down processing Aspects of recognition guided by higher-level cognitive processes and psychological factors such as expectations.

bottom-up processing Aspects of recognition that depend first on information about stimuli that come up to the brain from the sensory systems.

schemas Mental representations of what we know and expect about the world.

If experience can affect perception, having differing experiences can, too. For example, people in cultures that do and do not use pictures and paintings to represent reality show differing responses to pictures containing depth cues (Derogowski, 1989). People in the Me'n or the Nupa cultures of Africa, who have little experience with pictorial representation, have a more difficult time judging distances shown in pictures than do people in picture-oriented cultures (see Figure 3.25). These individuals also tend to have a harder time sorting pictures of three-dimensional objects into categories, even though they can easily sort the objects themselves (Derogowski, 1989). So, although the structure and principles of human perceptual systems tend to create generally similar views of the world for all of us, our perception of reality is also shaped by experience, including the experience of living in a particular culture.

Recognizing the Perceptual World

▶ **How do I recognize familiar people?**

So far, we have ignored a vital question about perception: How do you recognize what objects are? If you are driving in search of Barney's Diner, exactly what happens when your eyes finally locate the pattern of light that spells out its name? How do you recognize it as the place you are seeking?

The answer is that your brain analyzes the incoming pattern of information and compares that pattern to information stored in your memory. If it finds a match, recognition takes place, and the stimulus is put into a *perceptual category.* Once recognition occurs, your perception of the stimulus may never be the same again. Look at Figure 3.26. Do you see anything familiar? If not, turn to Figure 3.27; then look at Figure 3.26 again. You should now see it in an entirely new light. The difference between your "before" and "after" experiences is the difference between the sensory world before and after a perceptual match occurs and recognition takes place.

How does this matching process occur? Some aspects of recognition begin at the "top." That is, they are guided by knowledge, expectations, and other psychological factors. This phenomenon is called **top-down processing,** because it involves high-level, knowledge-based information. Other aspects of recognition begin at the "bottom," relying on specific, detailed information from the sensory receptors and assembling them into a whole. This latter phenomenon is called **bottom-up processing,** because it begins with basic information units that serve as a foundation for recognition.

Bottom-Up Processing

All along the path from the eye to the brain, certain cells respond to selected features of a stimulus. The stimulus is first analyzed into these *basic features,* which are then recombined to create the perceptual experience.

What are these features? As mentioned earlier, certain cells specialize in responding to lines, edges, corners, and stimuli having specific orientations in space (Hubel & Wiesel, 1979). For example, cells in the cerebral cortex that fire only in response to a diagonal line act as *feature detectors* for diagonal lines. The analysis by such feature detectors, early in the sensation-perception sequence, may contribute to recognition of letters or judgments of shape. Color and motion are other sensory features that appear to be analyzed separately, in different parts of the brain, prior to full perceptual recognition (Beatty, 1995; Cowey, 1994).

The brain also apparently analyzes patterns of light and darkness in the visual scene. Analyzing these patterns may help us to perceive textural gradients, which in turn help us to judge depth and recognize the general shape of blurry images.

Top-Down Processing

Bottom-up feature analysis can explain why you recognize the letters in a sign for Barney's Diner. But why is it that you can recognize the sign more easily if it appears where

figure 3.26

Categorizing Perceptions

learn
by doing

What do you see here? For the identity of this figure, turn to Figure 3.27.

©2001 stellarimages.com/Mark D. Phillips

learn
by doing

WHAT DOES IT LOOK LIKE TO YOU? Some people have reported seeing a demonic face in the smoke pouring from New York City's World Trade Center after terrorists attacked it on September 11, 2001. This perception results from a combination of bottom-up and top-down recognition processes. Feature detectors automatically register the edges and colors of images, whereas knowledge, beliefs, and expectancies give meaning to these features. A person who does not expect to see a face in the smoke might not see one until that interpretation is suggested. To test this possibility, ask some people who have not seen the photo before what they see in the smoke. How many identified a demonic face before you mentioned it?

you were told to expect it rather than a block earlier? And why can you recognize it even if a few letters are missing from the sign? Top-down processing seems to be at work in those cases. In top-down processing, people rely on their knowledge in making inferences, or "educated guesses," that help them recognize objects, words, or melodies, especially when sensory information is vague or ambiguous (DeWitt & Samuel, 1990; Rock, 1983). For example, once you knew that there was a dog in Figure 3.26, it became much easier for you to perceive one. Similarly, police officers find it easy to recognize familiar people on blurry security camera videos, but it is much more difficult for them to recognize strangers (Burton et al., 1999).

Top-down processing illustrates that our experiences create **schemas,** mental representations of what we know and expect about the world. Schemas can bias our perception toward one recognition or another by creating a *perceptual set*—that is, a readiness to perceive a stimulus in a certain way. Expectancy can be shaped by the *context* in which a stimulus occurs. For example, we know of a woman who saw a masked man in the darkened hallway of a house she was visiting. Her first perception was that the man who lived there was playing a joke; in fact, she had confronted a burglar. Context has biasing effects for sounds as well as sights. When shots are heard on a downtown street, they are often perceived as firecrackers or a car backfiring; at a pistol range, the same sound would immediately be interpreted as gunfire.

Motivation is another aspect of top-down processing that can affect perception. A hungry person, for example, might initially mistake a sign for "Burger's Body Shop" as indicating a place to eat. Similarly, you may remember a time when an obviously incompetent referee incorrectly called a penalty on your favorite sports team. You knew the call was wrong because you clearly saw the other team's player at fault. But suppose you had been cheering for that other team. The chances are good that you would have seen the referee's call as the right one. (See "In Review: Mechanisms of Pattern Recognition" for a summary of bottom-up and top-down processing.)

Top-Down and Bottom-Up Processing Together

Bottom-up and top-down processing usually work together to help us recognize the perceptual world. This interaction is beautifully illustrated by the process of reading. When the quality of the raw stimulus on the page is poor, as in Figure 3.28, top-down processes compensate to make continued reading possible. They allow you to fill in where words are not well perceived and processed, thus giving you a general idea of the meaning of the text.

figure 3.27

Another Version of Figure 3.26

learn by doing Now that you can identify a dog in this figure, it should be much easier to recognize when you look back at the original version.

You can fill in the gaps because the world is *redundant;* it provides multiple clues about what is going on. So even if you lose or miss one stimulus in a pattern, other clues can help you recognize the pattern. There is so much redundancy in written language, for instance, that many of the words and letters you see are not needed. Fo- ex-mp-e, y-u c-n r-ad -hi- se-te-ce -it- ev-ry -hi-d l-tt-r m-ss-ng. Similarly, vision in three dimensions normally provides multiple cues to depth, making recognition of distance easy and clear. It is when many of these cues are eliminated that ambiguous stimuli create the sorts of depth illusions discussed earlier.

In hearing, too, top-down processing can compensate for ambiguous stimuli. In one experiment, participants heard strings of five words in meaningless order, such as "wet brought who socks some." There was so much background noise, however, that only about 75 percent of the words could be recognized (Miller, Heise, & Lichten, 1951). The words were then read to a second group of participants in a meaningful order (e.g., "who brought some wet socks"). The second group was able to recognize almost all of the words, even under the same noisy conditions. In fact, it took twice as much noise to reduce their performance to the level of the first group. Why? When the words were in

in review

MECHANISMS OF PATTERN RECOGNITION

Mechanism	Description	Example
Bottom-up processing	Raw sensations from the eye or the ear are analyzed into basic features, such as edges, color or movement; these features are then recombined at higher brain centers, where they are compared with stored information about objects or sounds.	You recognize a dog as a dog because its features—four legs, barking, panting—match your perceptual category for "dog."
Top-down processing	Knowledge of the world and experience in perceiving allow people to make inferences about the identity of stimuli, even when the quality of raw sensory information is low.	On a dark night, a small, vaguely seen blob pulling on the end of a leash is recognized as a dog because the stimulus occurs at a location where we would expect a dog to be.

? *Your ability to read a battered old sign that has some letters missing is a result of _____ processing.*

figure 3.28

Interaction of Top-Down and Bottom-Up Processing

 learn by doing Which obscured line do you find easier to read: the one on the top or the one on the bottom? Top-down processing should help you read the obscured text on the top line. However, in the bottom line, the words are not related, so top-down processing cannot operate.

it is very easy to read this redundant sentence
BUT NOT
better resist ... grammar ... (...)

meaningless order, only bottom-up processing was available. Recognizing one word was no help in identifying the next. Meaningful sentences, however, provided a more familiar context and allowed for some top-down processing. Hearing one word helped the listener make a reasonable guess (based on knowledge and experience) about the others.

LINKAGES
How do infants perceive the world? (a link to Human Development)

We have seen that perception is influenced by the knowledge and experience we gain over time, but what perceptual abilities do we start with? To learn about infants' perception, psychologists have studied two inborn patterns called *habituation* and *dishabituation*. Infants stop looking when they repeatedly see stimuli perceived to be the same. This is habituation. If they see a stimulus that is perceived to be different, they resume looking. This is dishabituation. Using the habituation/dishabituation technique, researchers have found that newborns can perceive differences in stimuli showing various amounts of black-and-white contrast, but they cannot yet distinguish differences between colors (Burr, Morrone, & Fiorentini, 1996). Other studies using the same methods have shown that newborns can perceive differences in the angles of lines (Slater et al., 1991). Taken together, these studies suggest that we are born with the basic components of feature detection.

Are we also born with the ability to combine features into perceptions of whole objects? This is still a matter of debate. We know that at one month of age, infants concentrate their gaze on one part of an object, such as the corner of a triangle (Goldstein, 1999). By two months, though, their eyes systematically scan the perimeter of the object. This change suggests that they are now perceiving the pattern, or shape, of the object, not just its component features. However, other researchers have found that newborns show dishabituation (that is, they pay attention) when a familiar set of features are combined in a new way. So even newborns appear to notice, and keep track of, the way some stimulus features are put together (Slater et al., 1991).

Infants may also be innately tuned to perceive at least one important complex pattern of features: the human face. In one study of newborns, patterns like those in Figure 3.29 were moved slowly past the infants' faces (Johnson et al., 1991). The infants

LINKAGES

Perception and Human Development

figure 3.29

Infants' Perceptions of Human Faces

Newborns show significantly greater interest in the face-like pattern at the far left than in any of the other patterns. Evidently, some aspects of face perception are innate.

Face   **Configuration**   **Linear**   **Scrambled**

Source: Johnson et al. (1991).

figure 3.30

The Visual Cliff

The *visual cliff* is a glass-topped table that creates the impression of a sudden drop-off. A ten-month-old placed at what looks like the edge will calmly crawl across the shallow side to reach a parent but will hesitate and cry rather than crawl over the "cliff" (Gibson & Walk, 1960). Changes in heart rate show that infants too young to crawl also perceive the depth but are not frightened by it. Here is another example of the adaptive interaction of nature and nurture: Depth perception appears shortly after birth, but fear and avoidance of dangerous depth do not develop until an infant is old enough to crawl into trouble.

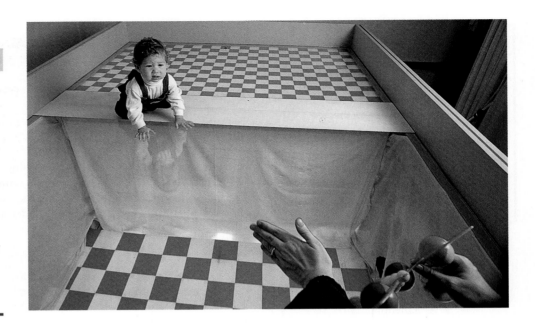

moved their heads and eyes to follow these patterns. But they tracked the face-like pattern shown on the left side of Figure 3.29 significantly farther than any of the nonfaces. The difference in tracking indicates that infants can tell faces from nonfaces and are more interested in faces. In a more recent experiment, infants looked more at a face-like pattern drawn especially for the newborn visual system (Valenza et al., 1996). Why should this be? Investigators suggest that interest in human faces is adaptive, in evolutionary terms. It helps newborns focus on their only source of food and care.

Other research on perceptual development suggests that our ability to accurately perceive depth and distance develops more slowly than our ability to recognize shapes (see Figure 3.30). For example, infants' ability to use binocular disparity and motion cues to judge depth appears to develop sometime after about three months of age. And infants do not use textural gradients and linear perspective as cues to depth until they are five to seven months old (Arterberry, Craton, & Yonas, 1993).

In summary, there is little doubt that many of the basic building blocks of perception are present within the first few days after birth. The basics include such organ-based cues to depth as accommodation and convergence. Maturation of the visual system adds to these basics as time goes by. Over the first few months after birth, the eye's fovea gradually develops the number of cone cells necessary for high visual acuity and perception of fine details (Goldstein, 1999). Visual experience is also necessary. Experience teaches the infant to recognize unified patterns and objects, to interpret depth and distance cues, and to use them in moving safely through the world. Like so many aspects of human psychology, perception is the result of a blending of heredity and environment. From infancy onward, the perceptual system creates a personal reality.

Attention

▶ **Can you "run out" of attention?**

attention The process of directing and focusing certain psychological resources to enhance perception.

Believe it or not, you still haven't found Barney's Diner! By now, you understand *how* you will recognize the right sign when you perceive it. But how can you be sure you *will* perceive it? The diner's sign will appear as one small piece of a sensory puzzle that also includes road signs, traffic lights, sirens, talk radio, and dozens of other stimuli. You can't perceive all of them at once. So, to find Barney's, you are going to have to be sure that the information you process includes the stimuli that will help you reach your goal. In short, you are going to have to pay attention.

Attention is the process of directing and focusing certain psychological resources to enhance perception, performance, and mental experience. We use attention to *direct* our sensory and perceptual systems toward certain stimuli, to *select* specific information for further processing, to *allocate* the mental energy required to do that processing, and to *regulate* the flow of resources necessary for performing a task or coordinating several tasks at once (Wickens & Carswell, 1997).

Psychologists have discovered three important characteristics of attention. First, it *improves mental processing*. You often need to concentrate attention on a task to do your best at it. Second, attention takes *effort*. Prolonged concentration of attention can leave you drained (McNay, McCarty, & Gold, 2001). When you are tired, focusing attention on anything becomes more difficult. Third, attention is *limited*. When your attention is focused on your reading, for instance, you will have less attention left over to listen to a conversation in the next room.

The Process of Attention

learn
by doing

To experience attention as a process, try "moving it around" a bit. When you finish reading this sentence, look at something behind you, then face forward and notice the next sound you hear, then visualize your best friend, then focus on how your tongue feels. You just used attention to direct your perceptual systems toward different aspects of your external and internal environments. When you looked behind you, shifting attention involved *overt orienting*—pointing sensory systems at a particular stimulus. But you were able to shift attention to an image of your friend's face without having to move a muscle. This is called *covert orienting*. (We have heard a rumor that students sometimes use covert orienting to shift their attention from their lecturer to thoughts that have nothing to do with the lecture.)

Your search for Barney's Diner will be aided by your ability to overtly allocate attention to a certain part of the environment. It would be made even easier if Barney's had the only flashing sign on the road. As the most intense stimulus around you, it would attract your attention automatically. Psychologists describe this ability to search for targets rapidly and automatically as *parallel processing*. It is as if you can examine all nearby locations at once (in parallel) and rapidly detect the target no matter where it appears.

BLUE	GREEN
GREEN	ORANGE
PURPLE	ORANGE
GREEN	BLUE
RED	RED
GRAY	GRAY
RED	BLUE
BLUE	PURPLE

figure 3.31

The Stroop Task

learn
by doing

Look at this list of words and, as rapidly as possible, call out *the color of the ink* in which each word is printed. How did you do?

Dividing and Focusing Attention

Often you can divide your attention efficiently enough to allow you to perform more than one activity at a time (Damos, 1992). You can drive a car, listen to the radio, sing along, and keep a beat by drumming on the steering wheel. However, your attention cannot be divided beyond a certain point without a loss in performance and mental-processing ability. The reason is that attention is a limited resource. If you try to spread it over too many targets, you "run out" of attention.

Still, it can sometimes be hard to keep your attention focused rather than divided. Look at the list of words in Figure 3.31 and, as rapidly as possible, call out *the color of the ink* in which each word is printed. This *Stroop task* (Stroop, 1935) is not easy, because your brain automatically processes the meanings of the familiar words in the list. These meanings then compete for attention with the responses you are supposed to give. To do well, you must focus on the ink color and not allow your attention to be divided between color and meaning. Children just learning to read have far less trouble with this task, because they do not yet process the meanings of words as automatically as experienced readers do.

Attending to some stimuli makes us less able to attend to others. In other words, attention is selective. It is like a spotlight that can illuminate only a part of the external or internal environment at any particular moment. So if you focus intently on your reading or a computer game, you may fail to perceive even dramatic changes in other parts of your environment. This phenomenon has been called *inattentional blindness* (Mack & Rock, 1998). In one study, a researcher asked college students for directions to a campus building (Simons & Levin, 1997). During each conversation, two other researchers dressed as workmen passed between the first researcher and the student, carrying a large door. As the door hid the researcher from the student's view, one of the "workmen" took his place. This new person then resumed the conversation with the student as though nothing had happened. Amazingly, only half of the students noticed that they were suddenly talking to a new person! The rest had apparently been paying so much attention to the researcher's question, or to the map he was showing, that they did not notice what he looked like. Magicians take advantage of inattentional blindness when they use sudden movements or other attention-grabbing stimuli to draw our attention away from the actions that lie behind their tricks.

How do you control, or allocate, your attention? Research shows that control over attention can be voluntary or involuntary (Yantis, 1993). *Voluntary*, or goal-directed, control over attention occurs when you purposely focus so that you can perform a task. Voluntary control reflects top-down processing, because attention is guided by knowledge-based factors such as intention, beliefs, expectations, and motivation. As people learn certain skills, they voluntarily direct their attention to information they once ignored. For example, the experienced driver notices events taking place farther down the road than the first-time driver does.

When some aspect of the environment—such as a loud noise—diverts your attention, control is said to be *involuntary,* or stimulus driven. Stimulus characteristics that tend to capture attention include abrupt changes in lighting or color (such as flashing signs), movement, and the appearance of unusual shapes (Folk, Remington, & Wright, 1994). Engineering psychologists' research on which stimuli are most likely to attract attention—and distract attention—has been used in the design of everything from Internet web sites and billboard ads to operator warning devices for airliners, nuclear power plants, and other complex systems (Clay, 2000; Laughery, 1999).

Although you can walk while talking, or drive while listening to music, you would find it virtually impossible to read and talk at the same time. Why is it sometimes so easy and at other times so difficult to do two things at once? When one task is so automatic as to require little or no attention, it is usually easy to do something else at the same time (Schneider, 1985). Even when two tasks require attention, it may still be possible to perform them simultaneously, as long as each taps into different kinds of attention (Wickens, 2002; Wickens et al., 1992). Some types of attention are devoted to perceiving incoming stimuli. Others handle making responses. This specialization of attention allows a skilled pianist to read musical notes and press keys simultaneously the first time through a piece. Apparently, the human brain can manage more than one type of attention and more than one spotlight of attention (Wickens, 1989). This notion of different types of attention also helps explain why an experienced driver can listen to the radio while steering safely.

FOCUS ON RESEARCH

Attention and the Brain

We have seen that if you divide your attention among too many tasks, you may not do equally well at all of them. Some researchers have documented this phenomenon by looking at what happens in the brain as people attend to more than one source of information at once.

■ **What was the researchers' question?**

If directing attention to more than one task causes extra mental work to be done, there should be evidence of that work in brain activity. One possibility is that information-processing activity in the brain should slow down. Does it? This was the question asked by one research team.

■ **How did the researchers answer the question?**

Allan J. Nash and Mercedes Fernandez (1996) examined the brain processing speed of participants engaged in various tasks. Sixteen college students heard high and low tones and saw red and green light flashes. They were asked to respond as quickly as possible to the identified target stimulus. On some trials they were to ignore tones and respond only to one of the lights, and on other trials they were to respond to one light and keep a running count of one of the tones. In short, the participants either attended to one task (responding to a light) or split their attention between two tasks (responding to a light and counting tones). The speed of the participants' reactions to the flashing light was measured throughout the experiment.

■ **What did the researchers find?**

When attention had to be shared between information required for two tasks, reaction times were slower than they were in response to the single-attention task.

■ **What do the results mean?**

The finding that reaction times were slower on split-attention trials suggests that information processing in the brain was slower, too. Further evidence for this conclusion has been provided by positron emission tomography (PET) scans. They reveal increased blood flow to regions of the brain where mental processing is taking place (Corbetta et al., 1991; Just et al., 2001). When attention is focused on only one stimulus feature, increased blood flow appears only in the part of the brain where that feature is analyzed. But when attention is divided, the added supply of blood is shared between two locations.

■ **What do we still need to know?**

Still to be determined are the limits of attention and processing; the means by which attention is shared; and the specific parts of the brain that are involved in attention, whether divided or undivided. Other research using PET scans, surgery on animals, and case studies of humans with brain damage has shown that switching the spotlight of visual attention involves at least three different parts of the brain (e.g., Braver, Reynolds, & Donaldson, 2003; Posner & Raichle, 1994). Attention appears to be a linked set of resources that improve mental processing at several levels and locations in the brain. No single brain region has yet been identified as an "attention center" (Posner & Peterson, 1990; Sasaki et al., 2001).

Linkages

As noted in the introductory chapter, all of psychology's subfields are related to one another. Our discussion of the development of perception illustrates just one way in which the topic of this chapter, sensation and perception, is linked to the subfield of developmental psychology, which is described in the chapter on human development. The Linkages diagram shows ties to two other subfields as well, and there are many more ties throughout the book. Looking for linkages among subfields will help you see how they all fit together and help you better appreciate the big picture that is psychology.

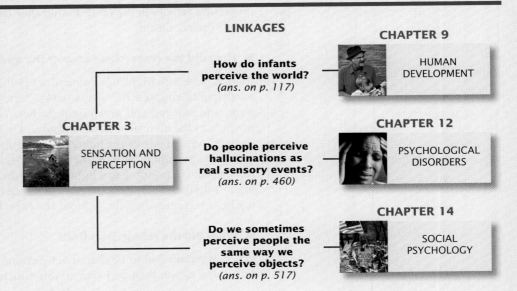

LINKAGES

CHAPTER 3
SENSATION AND PERCEPTION

How do infants perceive the world? *(ans. on p. 117)*

CHAPTER 9
HUMAN DEVELOPMENT

Do people perceive hallucinations as real sensory events? *(ans. on p. 460)*

CHAPTER 12
PSYCHOLOGICAL DISORDERS

Do we sometimes perceive people the same way we perceive objects? *(ans. on p. 517)*

CHAPTER 14
SOCIAL PSYCHOLOGY

Summary

SENSING AND PERCEIVING THE WORLD

▶ **What is the difference between sensation and perception?**

A *sense* is a system that translates information from outside the nervous system into neural activity. Messages from the senses are called *sensations. Perception* is the process through which people actively use knowledge and understanding of the world to interpret sensations as meaningful experiences.

SENSORY SYSTEMS

▶ **How does information from my eyes and ears get to my brain?**

The first step in sensation involves *accessory structures,* which collect and modify sensory stimuli. The second step is *transduction,* the process of converting incoming energy into neural activity; it is accomplished by sensory *receptors,* neural cells specialized to detect energy of some type. *Adaptation* takes place when receptors receive unchanging stimulation. Except in the case of smell, neural activity is transferred through the thalamus, which relays it to the cerebral cortex.

   Coding is the translation of physical properties of a stimulus into a pattern of neural activity that specifically identifies those physical properties. It is the language that the brain uses to describe sensations.

   The minimum amount of light, sound, pressure, or other physical energy that can be detected 50 percent of the time is called the *absolute threshold. Internal noise* is the spontaneous, random firing of cells in the nervous system that occurs whether or not you are stimulated by physical energy. The *response criterion* reflects your willingness to respond to a stimulus or ignore it. *Signal-detection theory* addresses whether you will perceive a stimulus. *Sensitivity* refers to your ability to discriminate a stimulus from its background. *Weber's law* states that the smallest detectable difference in stimulus energy is a constant fraction of the intensity of the stimulus. This smallest detectable difference in a stimulus is called the difference threshold or *just-noticeable difference (JND). Wavelength* is the distance from one peak of a sound wave or light wave to the next. Wave *frequency* is the number of complete waves, or cycles, that pass a given point per unit of time. *Amplitude* is the height of the wave from baseline to peak.

SEEING

▶ **Why do some people need eyeglasses?**

Visible light is electromagnetic radiation with a wavelength of about 400 to about 750 nanometers. *Light intensity,* or the amount of energy in light, determines its brightness. Differing *light wavelengths* are sensed as different colors.

   Accessory structures of the eye include the *cornea, pupil, iris,* and *lens.* Through *accommodation* and other means, these structures focus light rays on the *retina* (the net-like structure of cells at the back of the eye).

   Photoreceptors in the retina—*rods* and *cones*—convert light into neural activity. Rods and cones differ in shape, sensitivity to light, ability to discriminate colors, and distribution across the retina. Photoreceptors, especially rods, contribute to *dark adaptation.* The *fovea,* the area of highest acuity, has only cones, which are color sensitive. Rods are more sensitive to light but do not discriminate colors; they are distributed in areas around the fovea. From the photoreceptors, neural activity is transferred to bipolar cells and then to ganglion cells. A *blind spot* is created at the point where axons of ganglion cells leave the eye as a bundle of fibers called the *optic nerve.* Half of these fibers cross over at the optic chiasm. *Feature detectors* are cells in the cerebral cortex that respond to specific characteristics of objects in the visual field. The color of an object depends on which of the wavelengths striking it are absorbed and which are reflected. The sensation of color has three psychological dimensions: *hue, saturation,* and *brightness.*

According to the *trichromatic* (or Young-Helmholtz) *theory,* color vision results from the fact that the eye includes three types of cones, each of which is most sensitive to short, medium, or long wavelengths; information from the three types combines to produce the sensation of color. According to the *opponent-process* (or Hering) *theory,* there are red-green, blue-yellow, and black-white visual elements, and the members of each pair inhibit each other so that only one member of a pair may produce a signal at a time. Opponent-process theory explains color afterimages.

HEARING

▶ **How would my voice sound on the moon?**

Sound is a repetitive fluctuation in the pressure of a medium such as air; it travels in waves. The frequency (which is related to wavelength) and amplitude of sound waves produce the psychological dimensions of *pitch* and *loudness,* respectively. *Timbre,* the quality of sound, depends on complex wave patterns added to the basic frequency of sound.

The energy from sound waves is collected and transmitted to the *cochlea* through a series of accessory structures, including the *pinna, eardrum,* hammer, anvil, stirrup, and oval window. Transduction occurs when sound energy stimulates hair cells on the *basilar membrane* of the cochlea, which in turn stimulate the *auditory nerve.* Auditory information is relayed through the thalamus to the primary auditory cortex.

The intensity of a sound stimulus is coded by the firing of auditory neurons. *Place theory* describes the coding of high frequencies. They are coded by the place on the basilar membrane where the sound wave peaks. Each neuron in the auditory nerve is most sensitive to a specific frequency (its preferred frequency). According to *volley theory,* some frequencies may be matched by the firing rate of a group of neurons.

THE CHEMICAL SENSES: TASTE AND SMELL

▶ **Why can't I taste anything when I have a cold?**

The chemical senses include smell (olfaction) and taste (gustation). Our *sense of smell* detects volatile chemicals that come into contact with olfactory receptors in the nose. Olfactory signals are sent through the olfactory nerve to the *olfactory bulb* in the brain without passing through the thalamus. *Pheromones* are odors from one animal that change the physiology or behavior of another animal. Our *sense of taste* detects chemicals that come into contact with taste receptors in *papillae* in the mouth, especially on the tongue. The basic taste sensations are sweet, sour, bitter, salty, umami, and astringent. The senses of smell and taste interact to produce flavor.

SENSING YOUR BODY

▶ **Which is the largest organ in my body?**

The *somatic senses,* also called somatosensory systems, include the skin senses and the *proprioceptive* senses. The skin senses detect touch, temperature, and pain. When they are mechanically stimulated, nerve endings in the skin generate touch sensations. Some nerve endings are sensitive to temperature, and some respond to both temperature and touch.

Pain provides information about intense stimuli. Sharp pain is carried by A-delta fibers; dull, chronic pain is carried by C-fibers. The emotional response to pain depends on how the painful stimulus is interpreted. According to the *gate control theory,* pain signals can be blocked on their way to the brain, sometimes by messages sent from the brain down the spinal cord, resulting in *analgesia.* Endorphins act at several levels in pain systems to reduce sensations of pain.

The proprioceptive senses are *kinesthesia,* which provides information about the position of body parts with respect to one another, and the *vestibular sense* (balance), which provides information about the position of the head in space.

PERCEPTION

▶ **How do sensations become perceptions?**

Perception is the knowledge-based interpretation of sensations. Much of this interpretation takes place automatically, but sometimes conscious effort is required to translate sensations into meaningful experience.

ORGANIZING THE PERCEPTUAL WORLD

▶ **What determines how I perceive my world?**

Our perceptual systems automatically discriminate *figure* from *ground.* They also automatically group stimuli into patterns on the basis of the Gestalt principles of proximity, similarity, continuity, closure, texture, simplicity, common fate, and three others known as synchrony, common region, and connectedness.

The perception of distance, or *depth perception,* depends partly on stimulus cues and partly on the physical structure of the visual system. Stimulus cues include relative size, height in the visual field, interposition, linear perspective, reduced clarity, light and shadow, and textural gradients. Cues based on the structure of the visual system include *convergence* of the eyes (the fact that the eyes must move to focus on the same object), *binocular disparity* (the fact that the eyes are set slightly apart), and accommodation (changes in the shape of the lenses as objects are brought into focus).

The perception of motion results, in part, from the movement of stimuli across the retina. Expanding or *looming* stimulation is perceived as an approaching object. Movement of the retinal image is interpreted along with information about movement of the head, eyes, and other body parts, so that one's own movement can be discriminated from the movement of external objects. *Stroboscopic motion* is a movement illusion arising when a series of slightly different still images are seen in rapid succession.

Because of *perceptual constancy,* the brightness, size, and shape of objects can be seen as constant despite changes in the sensations received from those objects. Size constancy and shape constancy depend on the relationship between the retinal image of the object and the knowledge-based perception of its distance. Brightness constancy depends on the perceived relationship between the brightness of an object and its background.

Optical illusions are distortions of reality that result when principles of perception are applied inappropriately. Many illusions are caused by misreading depth cues and by evaluating stimuli in the context of their surroundings.

To the extent that the visual environments of people in different cultures differ, their perceptual experiences—and their responses to perceptual illusions—may differ as well.

RECOGNIZING THE PERCEPTUAL WORLD

▶ **How do I recognize familiar people?**

Both *bottom-up processing* and *top-down processing* contribute to recognition of the world. The ability to recognize objects is based on finding a match between the pattern of sensations organized by the perceptual system and a pattern that is stored in memory. Bottom-up processing seems to be accomplished by the analysis of features, or combinations of features, such as form, color, motion, and depth. Top-down processing is influenced by expectancy and motivation. *Schemas* based on past experience can create a perceptual set, the readiness or predisposition to perceive stimuli in certain ways. Expectancies can also be created by the context in which a stimulus appears. Top-down and bottom-up processing commonly work

together to create recognition. Top-down processing can fill in gaps in physical stimuli, in part because the environment provides redundant stimuli.

The abilities to perceive color, basic shape features, and possibly the human face are present at or near birth. Other abilities, such as recognition of form, develop later. Depth, too, is perceived early, but its meaning is learned later. Perceptual abilities are modified by both experience and maturation.

ATTENTION

▶ **Can you "run out" of attention?**

Attention is the process of focusing psychological resources to enhance perception, performance, and mental experience. We can shift attention overtly (by moving the eyes, for example) or covertly (without any movement of sensory systems). Attention is selective; it is like a spotlight that illuminates different parts of the external environment or specific mental processes. Control over attention can be voluntary and knowledge based or involuntary and driven by environmental stimuli. People can sometimes attend to two tasks at once, but there are limits to how much they can divide their attention.

Learn by Doing

Put It in Writing

Which of your five sensory systems—vision, hearing, touch, taste, or smell—do you think you could most easily do without? Which could you least easily do without? Write a page describing why you chose each of these sensory systems and listing what you would do to try to make up for the loss of each of these two systems.

Personal Learning Activity

Have you ever noticed how big the moon appears to be when it has just risen above the horizon? Some researchers suggest that the moon appears larger on the horizon than overhead because the horizon moon—seen across a space filled with houses, trees, and terrain—appears to be farther away than when it is overhead (Kaufman & Kauf-

man, 2000). According to principles of size constancy discussed in this chapter, the greater perceived distance causes the horizon moon to be perceived as larger. This explanation has been questioned, though, because the horizon moon sometimes seems larger even when the observer cannot see the intervening terrain. The next time you see what appears to be a bigger-than-normal full moon just above the horizon, turn your back to it, and then bend over and look at the moon, upside down, between your legs. Does the so-called moon illusion remain, or is it destroyed when you look at the moon so that terrain appears above it rather than below it? What do you think causes the moon illusion? *For additional projects, see the Personal Learning Activities in the corresponding chapter of the study guide that accompanies this text.*

Step into Action

Courses

Sensation and Perception
Speech and Hearing
Biological Psychology
Vision
Artificial Intelligence

Movies

The Miracle Worker (the story of Helen Keller, who was both deaf and blind)

Home Before Dark (a thriller about a blind girl menaced by a killer)

Children of a Lesser God (set in a school for the deaf)

At First Sight (changes and problems that occur when a man, blind from birth, can suddenly see)

The Matrix (a futuristic film that raises the question, What is reality?)

Rashomon (focuses on a single event perceived in vastly different ways by different people)

The Five Senses (main characters have heightened sensory powers)

Books

Chandler Burr, *The Emperor of Scent* (Random House, 2003) (about the perfume industry and a scientist who is testing a new theory of smell)

Henry Grunwald, *Twilight: Losing Sight, Gaining Insight* (Knopf, 1999) (former editor-in-chief of *Time* writes about going blind)

Michael Posner and Marcus Raichle, *Images of Mind* (W. H. Freeman, 1997) (brain imaging)

Richard. L. Gregory and J. Harris (Eds.), *The Artful Eye* (Oxford University Press, 1995) (visual perception)

Richard. L. Gregory and Andrew M. Colman (Eds.), *Sensation and Perception* (Longman, 1995) (the senses and psychophysics)

Oliver Sacks, *The Island of the Colorblind* (Knopf, 1997) (about a Pacific island where colorblindness is common)

Oliver Sacks, *The Man Who Mistook His Wife for a Hat* (Touchstone Books, 1998) (descriptions of patients with sensory and perceptual disorders)

Oliver Sacks, *Seeing Voices: A Journey into the World of the Deaf* (Vintage, 2000) (how deaf people experience the world)

Roger Shepard, *Mind Sights* (W. H. Freeman, 1990) (visual illusions, ambiguous figures)

J. Richard Block and Harold Yuker, *Can You Believe Your Eyes?* (Gardner Press, 1989) (more illusions and visual oddities)

The Web

The World Wide Web is a good source of additional information about the science of psychology, provided you use it carefully and think critically about the information you find. The web site that accompanies this text offers many resources relevant to this chapter. These resources include interactive NetLab exercises; Thinking Critically and Evaluating Research exercises; ACE chapter quizzes; recommended web links; and articles on current events, books, and movies. At http://college.hmco.com, select *Psychology* and then this textbook.

Review of Key Terms

Can you define each of the key terms in the chapter? Check your definitions against those on the pages listed in parentheses below or in the Glossary/Index at the end of the text.

absolute threshold *(p. 82)*
accessory structures *(p. 80)*
accommodation *(p. 85)*
adaptation *(p. 81)*
amplitude *(p. 83)*
analgesia *(p. 101)*
attention *(p. 119)*
auditory nerve *(p. 94)*
basilar membrane *(p. 94)*
binocular disparity *(p. 109)*
blind spot *(p. 87)*
bottom-up processing *(p. 114)*
brightness *(p. 88)*
cochlea *(p. 93)*
coding *(p. 81)*
cones *(p. 86)*
convergence *(p. 109)*
cornea *(p. 85)*
dark adaptation *(p. 86)*

depth perception *(p. 107)*
eardrum *(p. 93)*
feature detectors *(p. 87)*
figure *(p. 106)*
fovea *(p. 86)*
frequency *(p. 83)*
gate control theory *(p. 100)*
ground *(p. 106)*
hue *(p. 88)*
internal noise *(p. 82)*
iris *(p. 85)*
just-noticeable difference (JND) *(p. 83)*
kinesthesia *(p. 103)*
lens *(p. 85)*
light intensity *(p. 84)*
light wavelength *(p. 84)*
looming *(p. 109)*
loudness *(p. 93)*

olfactory bulb *(p. 97)*
opponent-process theory *(p. 90)*
optic nerve *(p. 87)*
papillae *(p. 98)*
perception *(p. 80)*
perceptual constancy *(p. 111)*
pheromones *(p. 98)*
photoreceptors *(p. 86)*
pinna *(p. 93)*
pitch *(p. 93)*
place theory *(p. 95)*
proprioceptive *(p. 103)*
pupil *(p. 85)*
receptors *(p. 81)*
response criterion *(p. 82)*
retina *(p. 85)*
rods *(p. 86)*
saturation *(p. 88)*

schemas *(p. 115)*
sensations *(p. 80)*
sense *(p. 80)*
sense of smell *(p. 96)*
sense of taste *(p. 96)*
sensitivity *(p. 82)*
signal-detection theory *(p. 82)*
somatic senses *(p. 99)*
sound *(p. 91)*
stroboscopic motion *(p. 110)*
timbre *(p. 93)*
top-down processing *(p. 114)*
transduction *(p. 81)*
trichromatic theory *(p. 89)*
vestibular sense *(p. 103)*
visible light *(p. 84)*
volley theory *(p. 96)*
wavelength *(p. 83)*
Weber's law *(p. 83)*

Multiple-Choice Self-Test

Select the best answer for each of the questions below. Then check your responses against the Answer Key at the end of the text.

1. _____ is the process of using information and your understanding of the world so that messages from the senses become meaningful experiences.

   a. Perception
   b. Sensation
   c. Transduction
   d. Absolute threshold

2. The process of converting incoming energy into neural activities is

   a. focusing.
   b. transduction.
   c. adaptation.
   d. reception.

3. In an experiment, Dante raises his hand each time he hears a tone through a set of headphones. The tone gets quieter and quieter until he fails to hear it half the time. After repeating the same procedure many times, the researcher ends the experiment, because she has found Dante's

   a. absolute threshold.
   b. difference threshold.
   c. internal noise.
   d. response criterion.

4. Expecting to see a stimulus will _____ your response criterion.

   a. raise
   b. lower
   c. not influence
   d. be influenced by

5. Participants in a study are comparing the weight of 2 pay envelopes, one containing 10 bills and the other containing 15 bills. They also compare the weight of 2 bags, one of which contains 1,000 coins and the other of which contains 1,100 coins. Which difference will be easier to detect?

   a. Both differences will be equally noticeable and detectable.
   b. The difference in the bags of coins will be easier to detect.
   c. The difference in the envelopes will be easier to detect.
   d. Neither difference is likely to be detected.

6. Bianca wants Bruce to see the distant star she wishes on every night. Because it is so faint, to have him see the star she should have him look

   a. directly at the star.
   b. slightly away from where the star is expected to be.
   c. at the star's reflection in a mirror.
   d. at the star when there is a full moon.

7. A projection-screen TV aims green, red, and blue lights at a screen. Because the TV can show a full range of colors by combining the green, red, and blue lights in differing amounts, it best illustrates the _____ theory of color vision.

   a. convergence
   b. frequency-matching
   c. opponent-process
   d. trichromatic

8. After tying 100 yellow ribbons into bows for party decorations, Aparna saw blue afterimages. "I had no idea that would happen," she said. Having read the chapter on sensation and perception, she correctly comments, "This is clearly an example of the _____ theory."

   a. opponent-process
   b. simultaneous processing
   c. trichromatic
   d. top-down processing

9. Mick has been a rock musician for forty years. The constant loud noise from his band has caused hair cell damage, literally ripping off hair cells from his inner ear. We would expect that Mick now has

   a. extremely acute hearing.
   b. conduction deafness.
   c. nerve deafness.
   d. normal hearing loss for someone his age.

10. The frequency of a sound wave determines its

   a. pitch.
   b. loudness.
   c. timbre.
   d. intensity.

11. Rashid rated the taste of several liquids on the basis of how salty, sweet, or sour each one was. This procedure most likely tested Rashid's

   a. analgesia.
   b. gustation.
   c. kinesthesia.
   d. vestibulation.

12. In cooking school, Natalie studied flavor. She learned that the flavor of food can be altered by

   a. nutritional state.
   b. changing its temperature.
   c. changing its color.
   d. both a and b.

13. Which statement about human olfaction and pheromones is *not* correct?

    a. Women who live together tend to menstruate at about the same time.
    b. Humans give off and detect pheromones that act as sexual attractants.
    c. After a few hours of contact with their newborn babies, mothers can usually identify them by smell.
    d. Breastfed infants can discriminate their own mother's odor form that of other breastfeeding women.

14. Ally has lost her kinesthetic sense. She will most likely be unable to

    a. know that her hand is raised without looking at it.
    b. identify the flavor of her ice cream cone.
    c. feel the warmth of the sun on her face.
    d. feel pain.

15. Shanelle is planning to take a group of children on a field trip to a big-city museum. She wants all the children to wear identical T-shirts. That way, a stray child will still be recognized as part of the group. This example demonstrates the principle of

    a. similarity.
    b. proximity.
    c. orientation.
    d. textural gradients.

16. Four swimmers practicing their synchronized swimming routine are perceived as a group because they are performing the same movements at the same speed. This is an example of

    a. synchrony.
    b. common fate.
    c. orientation.
    d. interposition.

17. When you perceive an object as being closer to you because it blocks out part of the background, you are using the depth cue called

    a. linear perspective.
    b. reduced clarity.
    c. interposition.
    d. movement gradient.

18. As Cliff walks out his front door, he sees a snowball coming straight at him. The retinal image of the snowball is increasing, and he realizes that the snowball is approaching, not getting larger. This example illustrates

    a. induced motion.
    b. looming.
    c. the movement gradient.
    d. stroboscopic motion.

19. As an example of top-down and bottom-up processing working together, most students are able to read the example in the text, "Fo- ex-mp-e, y-u c-n r-ad -hi- se-te-ce -it- ev-ry -hi-d l-tt-r m-ss-ng." This is because there is so much _____ in written language.

    a. redundancy
    b. ambiguity
    c. meaning
    d. expectancy

20. Although José appears to be listening as Rich talks about his new clothes, vacation plans, and exercise routine, José is thinking about the list of errands he has to run. José is

    a. covertly orienting.
    b. overtly orienting.
    c. using parallel distributed processing.
    d. using serial processing.

4

Consciousness

Have you ever "spaced out" while driving on a boring highway? Has your mind wandered far and wide during a boring lecture? These experiences contrast sharply with how it feels to focus your attention on playing a video game or to concentrate on a complicated recipe, but all of them represent differing versions of consciousness. In this chapter, we delve into both "normal" and altered states of consciousness. Most of the altered states—sleep, dreaming, hypnosis, meditation—differ psychologically and physiologically from normal waking consciousness. We'll examine how they differ, and we'll look at the effects of psychoactive drugs, which, in addition to altering consciousness, have complex physiological effects.

Reading this chapter will help you to answer the following questions:

▶ **Can unconscious thoughts affect your behavior?**

▶ **Does your brain go to sleep when you do?**

▶ **Can you be hypnotized against your will?**

▶ **How do drugs affect the brain?**

KEEPING AN EYE OUT Humans are not the only creatures capable of processing information while apparently unconscious. While ducks sleep, one hemisphere of their brains can process visual information from an eye that remains open. Birds positioned where they are most vulnerable to predators, such as at the end of a row, may spend twice as much time in this "alert" sleep than do birds in more protected positions (Rattenborg, Lima, & Amlaner, 1999).

There is an old *Sesame Street* episode in which Ernie is trying to find out whether Bert is asleep or awake. In other words, Ernie is trying to determine Bert's state of consciousness. Ernie observes that Bert's eyes are closed, and he comments that Bert usually closes his eyes when he is asleep. Ernie also notes that when Bert is asleep, he does not respond to pokes, so naturally, he delivers a few pokes. At first, Bert does not respond; but after being poked a few times, he awakes, very annoyed, and yells at Ernie for waking him. Ernie then informs Bert that he just wanted to let him know it was time for his nap.

Doctors face a similar situation in dealing with the more than 30 million people each year who receive general anesthesia during surgery. All these patients certainly appear to go to sleep, but there is no reliable way of knowing whether they are actually unconscious. It turns out that about 1 percent of them retain some degree of consciousness during the surgical procedure (Ranta, Jussila, & Hynynen, 1990; Sandin et al., 2000). In rare cases, patients have conscious awareness of pain and remember the trauma. Although their surgical wounds heal, these people may be psychologically scarred by the experience and may even show symptoms of posttraumatic stress disorder (Schwender et al., 1995).

The fact that people can be conscious while "asleep" under the influence of powerful anesthetic drugs makes defining consciousness quite difficult (Edelman, 2003). In fact, after decades of discussion and research by philosophers, psychologists, and even physicists, some believe that consciousness is still not yet understood well enough to be precisely defined (Crick & Koch, 1998; King & Pribram, 1995). Given the ethical and legal concerns raised by the need to ensure that patients are not subjected to pain during surgery, doctors tend to define *consciousness* as awareness that is demonstrated by either explicit or implicit recall (Schwender et al., 1995). In psychology, the definition is

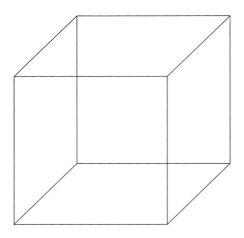

figure 4.1

The Necker Cube

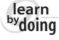

Each of the two squares in the Necker cube can be perceived as either the front or rear surface of the cube. Try to make the cube switch back and forth between these two orientations. Now try to hold only one orientation. You probably cannot maintain the whole cube in consciousness for longer than about three seconds before it "flips" from one orientation to the other.

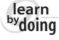

consciousness   The awareness of external stimuli and our own mental activity.

state of consciousness   The characteristics of consciousness at any particular moment.

conscious level   The level of consciousness at which mental activities accessible to awareness occur.

nonconscious level   The level of consciousness at which reside processes that are totally inaccessible to conscious awareness.

somewhat broader: **Consciousness** is generally defined as your awareness of the outside world and of your mental processes, thoughts, feelings, and perceptions (Metzinger, 2000; Zeman, 2001). Let's see how this definition applies as we explore the scope of consciousness and various states of consciousness.

The Scope of Consciousness

▶ **Can unconscious thoughts affect your behavior?**

Mental activity changes constantly. The features of consciousness at any instant—what reaches your awareness, the decisions you are making, and so on—make up your **state of consciousness** at that moment (Tassi & Muzet, 2001). Possible states include coma, deep sleep, hypnosis, meditation, daydreaming, and alert wakefulness. Consciousness can also be altered by drugs and other influences.

States of Consciousness

States of consciousness can be viewed as different points on a continuum of consciousness. For example, suppose you were aboard an airliner flying from New York to Los Angeles. The pilot calmly scans instrument displays while talking to an air-traffic controller. In the seat next to you, a lawyer finishes her second cocktail while planning a courtroom strategy. Across the aisle, a young father gazes out the window, daydreaming, while his small daughter sleeps in his lap, dreaming dreams of her own. All these people are experiencing different states of consciousness. Some states are active, and some are passive. The daydreaming father lets his mind wander, passively noticing images, memories, and other mental events that come to mind. Like the pilot, the lawyer actively directs her mental processes. In her case, though, as she evaluates various options and considers their likely outcomes, she is altering her state of consciousness by sipping alcohol.

Generally, people spend most of their time in a *waking* state of consciousness. Mental processing in this state varies with changes in attention or arousal (Taylor, 2002). While reading, for example, you may temporarily ignore sounds around you. Similarly, if you are upset or bored, you may tune out important cues from the environment, making it dangerous to perform complex activities like driving a car.

Levels of Consciousness

At any moment, the events and mental processes that you are aware of exist at the **conscious level.** For example, look at the Necker cube in Figure 4.1. If you are like most people, you can hold the cube in one orientation for only a few seconds before the other version "pops out" at you. The version that you experience at any moment is at your conscious level of awareness for that moment.

Some events, however, cannot be experienced consciously. For example, you are not directly aware of your brain regulating your blood pressure. Such mental processing occurs at the **nonconscious level,** totally removed from conscious awareness. Some people can learn to alter a nonconscious process through *biofeedback training*. In this training, you receive information about your biological processes and try to change them. Usually, special equipment is required, but you can approximate a biofeedback session by having a friend take your pulse at one-minute intervals while you sit quietly. First, establish a baseline pulse; then imagine a peaceful scene, or think about lowering your pulse rate. Then, ask your friend to softly say whether your pulse is higher or lower compared with the baseline. After four or five minutes of having this information "fed back" to you, you will probably be able to keep your pulse below the original baseline. Yet the pulse-regulating processes themselves remain out of consciousness.

Evidence for subconscious mental processing includes research showing that some surgery patients later comply with instructions or suggestions given while they were under anesthesia and that they do not recall hearing that information (Bennett, Giannini, & Davis, 1985). Another study found that people displayed physiological arousal to emotionally charged words even when they were not paying attention to them (Von Wright, Anderson, & Stenman, 1975).

BLOOM COUNTY by Berke Breathed

Reprinted by permission of International Creative Management, Inc. Copyright © 1996 by Berke Breathed

Some mental events are not conscious but can become so or can influence conscious experience. These mental events make up the *cognitive unconscious* (Reber, 1992), which includes the preconscious and the subconscious. Mental events that are outside awareness, but can easily be brought into awareness, exist at the **preconscious level.** What did you have for dinner last night? The information you needed to answer this question was probably not already in your conscious awareness, but it was at the preconscious level. So when you read the question, you could answer it immediately. Similarly, when you play trivia games, you draw on your large storehouse of preconscious memories to come up with obscure facts.

Other mental activities can alter thoughts, feelings, and actions but are more difficult to bring into awareness (Ratner, 1994). Sigmund Freud suggested that these **unconscious** activities, especially those involving unacceptable sexual and aggressive urges, are actively kept out of consciousness. Most psychologists do not accept Freud's view, but they still use the term *unconscious,* or **subconscious,** to describe mental activity that influences us in various ways but occurs outside of awareness.

Mental Processing Without Awareness

Research with surgery patients provided one demonstration of mental processing without awareness. After their operations, but while the patients were still unconscious from the anesthesia, an audiotape of fifteen word pairs was played over and over for them in the recovery room. After regaining consciousness, the patients could not say what words were on the tape, or even if a tape had been played at all. However, when given one word from each of the word pairs and asked to say the first word that came to mind, the patients were able to come up with the other member of the word pair from the tape (Cork, Kihlstrom, & Hameroff, 1992).

Even when conscious and alert, you can sometimes process and use information without being aware of it (Ward, 1997). In one study, participants watched a computer screen as an X flashed in one of four locations. The task was to indicate where the X appeared. The X's location seemed to vary randomly but was actually determined by a set of complex rules. (One such rule was "If the X moves horizontally twice in a row, then it will move vertically next.") Participants' responses became progressively faster and more accurate. Then, unknown to the participants, the rules were abandoned, and the X appeared in *truly* random locations. Participants' accuracy and speed deteriorated instantly. Apparently, the participants had learned the rules without being aware of them and had applied them to improve their performance. However, even when offered $100 to state the rules that had guided the location sequence, they could not do so, nor were they sure any such rules existed (Lewicki, 1992).

Visual processing without awareness may even occur in certain cases of blindness. When blindness is caused by damage only to the brain's primary visual cortex, fibers from the eyes are still connected to other brain areas that process visual information. Some of these surviving pathways may permit visual processing, but without visual awareness—a condition known as *blindsight* (Gazzaniga, Fendrich, & Wessinger, 1994).

preconscious level The level at which reside mental events that are not currently conscious but can become conscious at will.

unconscious The term used to describe a level of mental activity said by Freud to contain unacceptable sexual, aggressive, and other impulses of which an individual is unaware.

subconscious Another term describing the mental level at which influential, but normally inaccessible, mental processes take place.

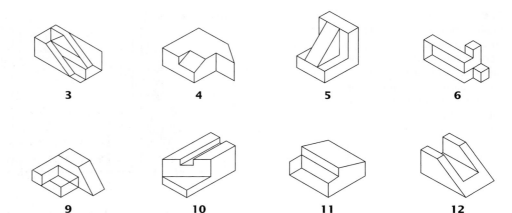

Source: D. L. Schacter et al. (1991).

figure 4.2

Stimuli Used in a Priming Experiment

 learn by **doing**   Look at these figures and decide, as quickly as you can, whether each can actually exist. Priming studies show that this task would be easier for figures you have seen in the past, even if you don't recall seeing them. How did you do? The correct answers appear on page 134.

So though patients say they see nothing, if forced to guess, they can still locate visual targets, identify the direction and orientation of moving images, reach for objects, name the color of lights, and even discriminate happy from fearful faces (Morris et al., 2001).

Priming research also demonstrates mental processing without awareness. In a typical priming study, people tend to respond faster or more accurately to stimuli they have seen before. This is true even when they cannot consciously recall having seen those stimuli (Abrams & Greenwald, 2000; Arndt et al., 1997; Bar & Biederman, 1998; Schacter & Cooper, 1993). In one study, for example, people looked at figures like those in Figure 4.2. They had to decide which figures could actually exist in three-dimensional space and which figures could not. The participants were better at classifying pictures they had seen before, even when they could not remember having seen them (Cooper et al., 1992; Schacter et al., 1991).

Similar results occur in experiments on the *mere-exposure effect,* the tendency for people to like previously encountered stimuli more than new ones. In one such experiment, participants first viewed a series of unfamiliar block figures similar to those in Figure 4.2. Next, they were shown several pairs of figures and asked to say which member came from the series they had seen earlier. They also stated which figure in each pair they liked better. Their choice about the previously seen figure was correct about half the time, as would be expected by chance alone. However, they tended to like best the figures they had seen before, even when they did not remember having seen them. These responses demonstrated the mere-exposure effect, revealing a memory of their prior experience with the figures that was not reflected in their conscious awareness (Seamon et al., 1995). In the chapter on social psychology, we consider how subconscious processes might alter people's reactions to one another.

C an something you perceive at a *subliminal* level—that is, below your conscious awareness—affect your thoughts, emotions, and actions? In 1957, an adman named James Vicary claimed that a New Jersey theater flashed messages such as "buy popcorn" and "drink Coke" on a movie screen, too briefly to be noticed, while customers watched the movie *Picnic.* He said that these subliminal messages caused a 15 percent rise in sales of Coca-Cola and a 58 percent increase in popcorn sales. Can such "mind control" really work? Many people seem to think so. Millions of dollars each year are spent on audiotapes, CDs, and videos whose subliminal messages are supposed to help people lose weight, raise self-esteem, quit smoking, make more money, or achieve other goals.

THINKING CRITICALLY

Can Subliminal Messages Change Your Behavior?

■ **What am I being asked to believe or accept?**

The claim underlying the alleged value of subliminal tapes is that information can be detected, perceived, and acted upon without our being aware of it. The strong version of this claim implies that people's buying habits, political decisions, and other actions can be secretly influenced without their awareness.

■ Is there evidence available to support the claim?

Studies that present visual stimuli too briefly to be perceived consciously provide some evidence that subliminal messages can affect conscious judgments. In one such study, participants viewed slides showing people performing ordinary acts like washing dishes. Unknown to the participants, each slide was preceded by a subliminal exposure to a photo of "positive" stimuli (such as a child playing) or "negative" stimuli (such as a monster). Later, participants rated the people on the visible slides as more likable, polite, friendly, successful, and reputable when their images had been preceded by a positive subliminal photo (Krosnick et al., 1992). The subliminal photos not only affected participants' liking of the people they saw but also shaped beliefs about their personalities.

In another study, participants were shown written messages at subliminal speed while researchers recorded their physiological arousal. Although the slides were flashed too quickly to be consciously perceived, the participants' physiological arousal increased after messages such as "no one loves me," but not after nonemotional messages such as "no one lifts it" (Masling & Bornstein, 1991). Researchers have also exposed participants to subliminal presentations of slides showing snakes, spiders, flowers, and mushrooms. Even though the slides were impossible to perceive at a conscious level, participants who were afraid of snakes or spiders showed physiological arousal (and reported feeling fear) in response to slides of snakes and spiders (Öhman & Soares, 1994).

The results of studies like these confirm that subliminal information can have an impact on judgments and emotion, but they say little or nothing about the value of subliminal tapes for achieving self-help goals. In fact, no laboratory evidence exists to support the effectiveness of these tapes. Their promoters offer only the reports of satisfied customers.

■ Can that evidence be interpreted another way?

Many claims for subliminal persuasion—including the New Jersey theater case mentioned earlier—have turned out to be publicity stunts using phony data (Pratkanis, 1992). Other claims appear to reflect the fact that if enough data are collected, almost any desired result will eventually appear by chance. But it is misleading to publicize one positive result without mentioning all the negative results.

Further, testimonials from satisfied customers could be biased by what these people would like to believe about the subliminal tapes they bought. There is strong evidence to support this alternative interpretation. In one study, half the participants were told that they would be listening to tapes containing subliminal messages for improving memory. The other half were told that the subliminal messages would promote self-esteem. However, the participants were not necessarily exposed to the subliminal messages they were expecting. Half the participants in the memory group got self-esteem messages, and half of the self-esteem group got memory messages. Regardless of which version they actually got, participants who thought they had heard memory enhancement messages reported improved memory; those who thought they had received self-esteem messages said their self-esteem had improved (Pratkanis, Eskenazi, & Greenwald, 1994). In other words, the effects of the tapes were determined by the listeners' expectations—not by the tapes' subliminal content. This result suggests that customers' reports about the value of subliminal self-help tapes may reflect placebo effects based on optimistic expectations rather than the effects of subliminal messages.

■ What evidence would help to evaluate the alternatives?

The effects of subliminal messages must be assessed through controlled experiments like the ones described in the introductory chapter. Those advocating the development and use of subliminal methods must provide supporting evidence from such research.

■ What conclusions are most reasonable?

The available evidence suggests that subliminal perception occurs, but that it has no potential for "mind control" (Greenwald, Klinger, & Schuh, 1995). Subliminal effects are usually small and short-lived, and they affect only general measures of overall arousal. Most researchers agree that subliminal messages have no special power to create needs, goals, skills, or actions (Pratkanis, 1992). In fact, it is the advertisements, political speeches, and other messages that we *can* perceive consciously that have the strongest persuasive effects.

Subliminal Messages in Rock Music

Would the persuasive power of subliminal messages be increased if they were presented at normal speed, but in reverse so we could not consciously understand them? According to numerous Internet web sites, this is exactly how satanic or drug-related messages have been hidden in the recorded music of rock bands such as Marilyn Manson, Nine Inch Nails, Judas Priest, Led Zeppelin, and the Rolling Stones. These alleged "backmasked" subliminal messages are said to have influenced listeners to commit suicide or murder.

■ What was the researchers' question?

There is no compelling evidence that backward messages are actually present in most of the music cited. However, John R. Vokey and J. Don Read (1985) asked a more important question: Could a backward message even be perceived and understood when the music was playing forward? They also asked whether such a message, if perceived at all, would have any effect on the listener's behavior.

■ How did the researchers answer the question?

First, Vokey and Read made tape recordings of a person reading portions of the Twenty-third Psalm and Lewis Carroll's poem "Jabberwocky." This poem includes many nonsense words, but it follows the rules of grammar (e.g., "'Twas brillig, and the slithy toves . . . "). These recordings were then played backward to groups of college students. The students were asked to judge whether what they heard would have been nonsensical or meaningful if played forward.

SUBLIMINAL MESSAGES IN ROCK MUSIC?　These picketers are protesting outside a Marilyn Manson concert. Some people claim that Manson's music, as well as that of rock stars ranging from Michael Jackson to Madonna, contains subliminal messages advocating drug use, violence, and satanism.

Answer key for Figure 4.2: Figures 1, 4, 5, 7, 10, and 12 can exist in three-dimensional space.

■ What did the researchers find?

When the students heard the readings played backward, they could not discriminate sense from nonsense. They could not tell the difference between declarative sentences and questions. They could not even identify the original material on which the recordings were based. In short, the participants could not make sense of the backward messages at a conscious level. Could they do so subconsciously? To find out, the researchers asked the participants to sort the backward statements they heard into one of five categories: nursery rhymes, Christian, satanic, pornographic, or advertising. They reasoned that if some sort of meaning could be subconsciously understood, the participants would be able to sort the statements nonrandomly. As it turned out, however, the accuracy of the participants' category judgments was no better than chance.

But perhaps backward messages might alter people's behavior even if the messages were not perceived consciously. To check on this possibility, Vokey and Read conducted another study. This time, they presented a backward version of a message whose sentences contained homophones (words that sound alike but have two spellings and two different meanings, such as *feat* and *feet*). When heard in the normal forward direction, such messages affect people's spelling of ambiguous words that are read aloud to them at a later time. (For example, they tend to spell out *f-e-a-t* rather than *f-e-e-t* if they previously heard the sentence "It was a great feat of strength.") This example of priming occurs even if people do not recall having heard the message. After hearing a *backward* version of the message, however, the participants in this study did not produce the expected spelling bias.

■ What do the results mean?

Obviously, it wasn't possible for the participants to subconsciously understand meaning in the backward messages. Backward messages are evidently not consciously or unconsciously understood, nor do they influence behavior.

■ What do we still need to know?

Researchers would like to understand why the incorrect idea persists that backward messages can influence behavior. Beliefs and suspicions do not simply disappear in the face of contrary scientific evidence (Vyse, 2000; Winer et al., 2002). Perhaps such evidence needs to be publicized more widely in order to lay the misconceptions to rest, but it seems likely that some people so deeply want to believe in the existence and power of backward messages in rock music that such beliefs will forever hold the status of folk myths in Western culture.

Altered States of Consciousness

When changes in mental processes are great enough for you or others to notice significant differences in how you function, you have entered an **altered state of consciousness.** In an altered state, mental processing shows distinct changes unique to that state. Cognitive processes or perceptions of yourself or the world may change, and normal inhibitions or self-control may weaken (Martindale, 1981).

The phrase *altered states of consciousness* recognizes waking consciousness as the most common state, a baseline against which "altered" states are compared. However, this is not to say that waking consciousness is universally considered more normal, proper, or valued than other states. In fact, value judgments about different states of consciousness vary considerably across cultures (Ward, 1994).

Consider, for instance, *hallucinations,* which are perceptual experiences (such as hearing voices) that occur without sensory stimuli. In the United States, hallucinations are viewed as undesirable. Mental patients who hallucinate often feel stress and self-blame. They may avoid reporting their hallucinations, and they tend to receive poorer prognoses and more drastic treatments than patients who do not hallucinate. Among the Moche of

altered state of consciousness A condition that exists when changes in mental processes are extensive enough to produce noticeable differences in psychological and behavioral functioning.

Peru, however, hallucinations have a culturally approved place. When someone experiences illness or misfortune, a healer conducts an elaborate ritual to find causes and treatments. During the ceremony, the healer ingests mescaline, a drug that causes hallucinations. These hallucinations are thought to give the healer spiritual insight into the patient's problems (de Rios, 1989). In the context of many other tribal cultures, too, purposeful hallucinations are respected, not rejected (Grob & Dobkins-de-Rios, 1992).

In other words, states of consciousness differ not only in their characteristics but also in their value to members of particular cultures. In the sections that follow, we describe some of the most interesting altered states of consciousness, beginning with the most common one: sleep.

ALTERED STATES AND CULTURAL VALUES   Cultures differ in their definitions of which altered states of consciousness are approved and which are inappropriate. The top photo shows members of a Brazilian spirit possession cult in various stages of trance. The bottom photo depicts a Moche *curandero,* or "curer," in Peru who is attempting to heal an ailing patient by using fumes from a potion—and a drug derived from the San Pedro cactus—to put himself in an altered state of consciousness.

Sleeping and Dreaming

▶ **Does your brain go to sleep when you do?**

According to ancient myths, sleepers lose control of their minds and flirt with death as their souls wander freely. Early researchers thought sleep was a time of mental inactivity. In fact, sleep is an active, complex state.

Stages of Sleep

LINKAGES
Does the brain shut down when we sleep? (a link to Biology and Behavior)

Sleep researchers use an *electroencephalograph,* or *EEG,* to record the brain's electrical activity during sleep. EEG recordings, often called *brain waves,* vary in height (amplitude) and speed (frequency) as behavior or mental processes change. The brain waves of an awake, alert person have high frequency and low amplitude. They appear as small, closely spaced, irregular EEG spikes. A relaxed person with closed eyes shows slower, more rhythmic brain waves at speeds of eight to twelve cycles per second (cps). During a normal night's sleep, brain waves show distinctive and systematic changes in amplitude and frequency as the person passes through various stages of sleep (Guevara et al., 1995).

Slow-Wave Sleep   Imagine that you are participating in a sleep study. You are hooked up to an EEG and various monitors, and videotaped as you sleep through the night. If you were to watch that video, here's what you'd see: At first, you are relaxed, with eyes closed, but awake. At this point, your muscle tone and eye movements are normal, and your EEG shows the slow brain waves associated with relaxation. As you then drift into sleep, your breathing deepens, your heartbeat slows, and your blood pressure drops. Over the next half hour, you descend through four stages of sleep that are characterized by even slower brain waves with even higher amplitude (see Figure 4.3). The last two of these, stages 3 and 4, are called **slow-wave sleep.** When you reach stage 4, the deepest stage of slow-wave sleep, it is quite difficult to be awakened. If you were roused from this stage of deep sleep, you would be groggy and confused.

REM Sleep   After thirty to forty-five minutes in stage 4, you quickly return to stage 2 and then enter a special stage in which your eyes move rapidly under your closed eyelids. This is called **rapid eye movement (REM) sleep**, or *paradoxical sleep.* It is called *paradoxical* because its characteristics contain a paradox, or contradiction. In REM sleep, your EEG resembles that of an awake, alert person, and your physiological arousal—heart rate, breathing, and blood pressure—is also similar to when you are awake. However, your muscles are nearly paralyzed. Sudden, twitchy spasms appear, especially in your face and hands, but your brain actively suppresses other movements (Blumberg & Lucas, 1994). In other words, there are two distinctly different types of sleep, REM sleep and *non-REM,* or *NREM,* sleep.

A Night's Sleep   Most people pass through the cycle of sleep stages four to six times each night. Each cycle lasts about ninety minutes, but with a somewhat changing pattern of stages and stage duration. Early in the night, most of the time is spent in slow-wave sleep, with only a few minutes in REM (see Figure 4.4). As sleep continues, though, it is dominated by stage 2 and REM sleep, from which sleepers finally awaken.

Sleep patterns change with age. The average infant sleeps about sixteen hours a day, and the average seventy-year-old sleeps only about six hours (Roffwarg, Muzio, & Dement, 1966). The composition of sleep changes, too. REM accounts for half of total sleep at birth but less than 25 percent in young adults. Individuals vary widely from these averages, though. Some people feel well rested after four hours of sleep, whereas others of similar age require ten hours to feel satisfied (Clausen, Sersen, & Lidsky, 1974). To some extent, too, sleep patterns are a matter of choice or necessity. For example, North American college students get less sleep than other people their age (Hicks, Fernandez, & Pellegrini, 2001). This trend has grown over the last thirty years as students deal with

slow-wave sleep   Sleep stages 3 and 4, which are accompanied by slow, deep breathing; a calm, regular heartbeat; and reduced blood pressure.

rapid eye movement (REM) sleep   The stage of sleep during which the EEG resembles that of someone who is awake, but muscle tone decreases dramatically.

figure 4.3

EEG During Sleep

learn by **doing** EEG recordings of brain wave activity show four relatively distinct stages of sleep. Notice the regular patterns of brain waves that occur just before a person goes to sleep, followed by the slowing of brain waves as sleep becomes deeper (stages 1 through 4). In REM (rapid eye movement) sleep, the frequency of brain waves increases dramatically. In some ways the brain waves of REM sleep resemble those of people who are awake.

Source: Horne (1988).

academic and job responsibilities, along with family obligations and a variety of social and recreational activities—including those late-night sessions playing computer games or surfing the Internet. You have probably noticed the results of sleep deprivation as your classmates (or you?) struggle to stay awake during lectures.

Sleep Disorders

Sometime in life, most people experience sleep-related problems (Silber, 2001). These can range from occasional nights of tossing and turning to more serious and long-term sleep disorders. The most common sleep disorder is **insomnia,** in which one feels daytime fatigue due to trouble falling asleep or staying asleep. If you have difficulty getting to sleep or staying asleep that persists for longer than one month at a time, you may be suffering from insomnia. Besides being tiring, insomnia is tied to mental distress and impairment of functioning. Insomnia is especially associated with depressive and anxiety disorders (U.S. Surgeon General, 1999). Overall, insomniacs are three times more likely to show a mental disorder than individuals with no sleep complaints (Ford & Kamerow, 1989). It is unclear from such correlations, however, whether insomnia causes mental disorders, mental disorders cause insomnia, or some other factor causes both.

Sleeping pills can relieve insomnia. However, they interact dangerously with alcohol, disturb REM sleep, and may eventually lead to increased sleeplessness (Ashton, 1995). In the long run, learning-based treatments may be more helpful (Perlis et al., 2001). Stress-management techniques such as relaxation training have been shown to help reduce tension and other stress reactions, thus allowing sleep (Bernstein, Borkovec, & Hazlett-Stevens, 2000). Short daytime naps and moderate evening exercise have also been shown to help elderly insomniacs fall asleep more easily at night, sleep better, and feel better the next day (Tanaka et al., 2001).

insomnia   A sleep disorder in which a person feels tired during the day because of trouble falling asleep or staying asleep at night.

narcolepsy   A daytime sleep disorder in which a person suddenly switches from an active waking state into REM sleep.

sleep apnea   A sleep disorder in which people briefly but repeatedly stop breathing during the night.

sudden infant death syndrome (SIDS) A disorder in which a sleeping baby stops breathing but does not awaken and suffocates.

figure 4.4

A Night's Sleep

learn **by doing** During a typical night, a sleeper goes through this sequence of EEG stages. Notice that sleep is deepest during the first part of the night and more shallow later on, when REM sleep becomes more prominent.

Source: Cartwright (1978).

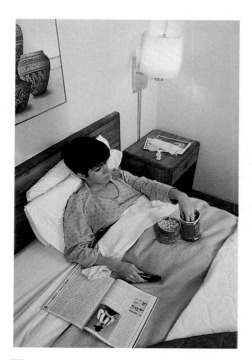

applying psychology **STIMULUS CONTROL THERAPY** Insomnia can often be reduced through a combination of relaxation techniques and *stimulus control therapy,* in which the person goes to bed only when sleepy and gets out of bed if sleep does not come within fifteen to twenty minutes. The goal is to have the bed become a stimulus associated with sleeping, and perhaps sex, but not with reading, eating, watching television, worrying, or anything else that is incompatible with sleep (Edinger et al., 2001).

Narcolepsy is a disturbing daytime sleep disorder that is typically first seen in people who are from fifteen to twenty-five years old (Choo & Guilleminault, 1998). People with narcolepsy abruptly enter REM sleep directly from the waking state, usually as they are laughing or experiencing some other emotional state. Because of the loss of muscle tone in REM, narcoleptics may experience *cataplexy,* meaning that they collapse and remain briefly immobile even after awakening. The most common cause of narcolepsy appears to be the absence or deficiency of a recently discovered neurotransmitter called *orexin,* which is also known as *hypocretin* (Beuckmann & Yanagisawa, 2002; Peyron et al., 2000; Sinton & McCarley, 2000). A combination of regular naps and stimulant drugs can be a helpful treatment (Rogers, Aldrich, & Lin, 2001).

People who suffer from **sleep apnea** briefly stop breathing hundreds of times each night, waking each time long enough to resume breathing. In the morning, victims do not recall the awakenings. However, they feel tired and tend to show impaired attention and learning ability (Naëgelé et al., 1995). In one tragic case, two members of a train crew—both of whom had apnea—fell asleep on the job, resulting in a collision that killed two people (Pickler, 2002). Apnea has many causes, including genetic predisposition, obesity, problems with brain mechanisms that control breathing, and compression of the windpipe (Dixon, Schachter, & O'Brien, 2001; Kadotani et al., 2001; Macey et al., 2002; Richards et al., 2002). Effective treatments include weight loss and use of a mask that provides a steady stream of air; in some cases surgery may be required to widen the air passageway in the upper throat (Davies & Stradling, 2000; Patel et al., 2003; Vilaseca et al., 2002).

In cases of **sudden infant death syndrome (SIDS),** sleeping infants stop breathing and die. In the United States, SIDS strikes about two of every thousand infants, especially very low birthweight babies, usually when they are two to four months old (Hirschfeld, 1995; Vernacchio et al., 2003). Some SIDS cases may stem from problems with brain systems regulating breathing, from exposure to cigarette smoke, or possibly from genetic causes (Ackerman et al., 2001; Guntheroth & Spiers, 2002; Harper et al., 1988; Klonoff-Cohen & Edelstein, 1995; Narita et al., 2001). Because SIDS is less common in cultures where infants and parents sleep in the same bed, it may also be that sleeping position is involved in sudden infant death (Gessner, Ives, & Perham-Hester, 2001; Li et al., 2003). Correlational evidence suggests that about half of apparent SIDS cases might actually be accidental suffocations caused when infants sleep face down on a soft surface (Guntheroth & Spiers, 1992). For example, SIDS in the United States is more common in families where babies are placed in the face-down position (Corwin et al., 2003; Hauck et al.,

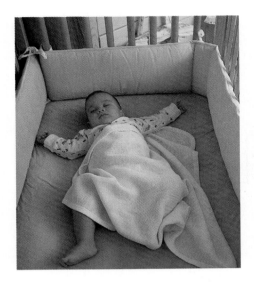

SUDDEN INFANT DEATH SYNDROME (SIDS)   In SIDS cases, seemingly healthy infants stop breathing while asleep in their cribs. All the causes of SIDS are not known, but health authorities now suggest that infants should sleep on their backs, as this baby demonstrates.

2002; Spiers & Guntheroth, 2001). Further, ever since doctors began a "back to sleep" program, which advises parents to be sure their babies sleep face-up, the number of infants dying from SIDS in the United States has dropped by 40 percent (Gibson et al., 2000; Pollack & Frohna, 2002; Rasinski et al., 2003).

Sleepwalking occurs in non-REM sleep, usually in childhood (Guilleminault et al., 2003; Masand, Popli, & Welburg, 1995). By morning, most sleepwalkers have forgotten their travels. Despite myths to the contrary, waking a sleepwalker is not harmful. Drugs help, but most children simply outgrow the problem. One adult sleepwalker was cured when his wife blew a whistle whenever he began a nighttime stroll (Meyer, 1975).

Nightmares are frightening REM dreams (Zadra & Donderi, 2000). **Night terrors** are horrific dream images during stage 4 sleep. Sleepers often awaken from a night terror with a bloodcurdling scream and remain intensely afraid for up to thirty minutes. Yet they may not recall the episode in the morning. Night terrors are especially common in boys, but adults can suffer milder versions. The condition is sometimes treatable with drugs (Lillywhite, Wilson, & Nutt, 1994).

People with **REM behavior disorder** do not experience the near-paralysis that normally accompanies rapid eye movement sleep. They move as if acting out their dreams (Watanabe & Sugita, 1998). If the dreams are violent, the disorder can be dangerous to the dreamer or those nearby. One nine-year-old boy in New York City was seriously injured when he jumped from a third-floor window while dreaming that his parents were being murdered. In another case, a Minnesota man grabbed his wife's throat while dreaming about breaking a deer's neck (Brown, 2003). REM behavior disorder sometimes occurs along with daytime narcolepsy (Schenck & Mahowald, 1992), and in one case study was caused by a brain tumor (Zambelis, Paparrigopoulos, & Soldatos, 2002). Fortunately, drug treatments are usually effective (Takeuchi et al., 2001).

Why Do People Sleep?

People need a certain amount of uninterrupted sleep to function normally. In fact, most living creatures sleep. In trying to understand why people sleep, psychologists have studied both the functions of sleep and the ways in which brain mechanisms shape its characteristics.

Sleep as a Circadian Rhythm   Humans and almost all animals display cycles of behavior and physiology that repeat about every twenty-four hours. This pattern is called a **circadian rhythm.** (*Circadian* is pronounced "sir-KAY-dee-en." It comes from the Latin *circa dies,* meaning "about a day.") Longer and shorter rhythms also occur, but they are less common. These rhythms are linked to signals such as the light of day and the dark of night.

Some rhythms continue without such time cues, though. Volunteers living for months without external light and dark cues maintain daily rhythms in sleeping and waking, eating, urination, hormone release, and other physiological functions. Under such conditions, these cycles repeat about every twenty-four hours (Czeisler et al., 1999). The sleep-wake cycle is just one example of the rhythmic nature of life.

Disruption of the sleep-wake cycle can create problems. For example, air travel across several time zones often causes **jet lag,** a pattern of fatigue, irritability, inattention, and sleeping problems. The traveler's body feels ready to sleep at the wrong time for the new location. It tends to be easier to stay awake longer than usual than to go to sleep earlier than usual. That's why changing time zones causes more intense symptoms of jet lag after eastward travel (when time is lost) than after westward travel (when time is gained) (Lemmer et al., 2002). Symptoms similar to those of jet lag also appear in workers who repeatedly change between day and night shifts, and in people who try to go to sleep early on a Sunday night after a weekend of later-than-usual bedtimes. For these people, Monday morning "blues" may actually be symptoms of a disrupted sleep-wake cycle (Yang & Spielman, 2001).

The length of circadian sleep rhythms can vary from person to person such that some have a natural tendency to stay up later at night ("owls") or to wake up earlier in the

sleepwalking   A phenomenon that starts primarily in non-REM sleep, especially in stage 4, and involves walking while asleep.

nightmares   Frightening dreams that take place during REM sleep.

night terrors   Horrific dream images during stage 4 sleep, followed by a rapid awakening and a state of intense fear.

REM behavior disorder   A sleep disorder in which a person fails to show the decreased muscle tone normally seen in REM sleep, thus allowing the person to act out dreams.

circadian rhythm   A cycle, such as waking and sleeping, that repeats about once a day.

jet lag   Fatigue, irritability, inattention, and sleeping problems caused by air travel across several time zones.

figure 4.5

Sleep, Dreaming, and the Brain

learn by doing This diagram shows the location of some of the brain structures thought to be involved in sleep and dreaming, as well as in other altered states discussed later in the chapter. For example, one area near the suprachiasmatic nuclei acts as a "master switch" to promote sleep (Saper, Chou, & Scammell, 2001). If it is damaged, sleep may be nearly impossible. Another nearby area promotes wakefulness; individuals with damage to this area sleep virtually all the time (Salin-Pascual et al., 2001).

Suprachiasmatic nuclei

Locus coeruleus

Pineal gland

Cerebellum

Hindbrain

morning ("larks"). Because our sleep-wake rhythms stay about the same even without external cues about light and dark, we must have an internal "biological clock" that keeps track of time. This clock is in the *suprachiasmatic nuclei (SCN)* of the hypothalamus, as shown in Figure 4.5. The SCN receives light information from a special set of photoreceptors in the eyes, and then sends signals to hindbrain areas that initiate sleep or wakefulness (Berson, Dunn, & Takao, 2002; Lee et al., 2003). When animals with SCN damage receive transplanted SCN cells, their circadian rhythms become like those of the donor animal (Menaker & Vogelbaum, 1993). SCN neurons also regulate the release of the hormone *melatonin*. Melatonin, in turn, appears to be important in maintaining circadian rhythms. Taken about an hour before you want to fall asleep, melatonin reduces disorientation from jet lag or other sleep-wake cycle changes by acting on melatonin receptors in the SCN (Herxheimer & Petrie, 2002; Liu et al., 1997; Sack et al., 1997).

The Functions of Sleep Examining the effects of sleep deprivation may help explain why people sleep at all. People who go without sleep for as long as a week usually do not suffer serious long-term effects. However, extended sleeplessness leads to fatigue, irritability, and inattention (Drummond et al., 2000; Smith & Maben, 1993). Short-term sleep deprivation can also be dangerous (Stapleton, 2001). Most fatal auto accidents in the United States occur during the "fatigue hazard" hours of midnight to 6 A.M. (Coleman, 1992), leading some researchers to consider "sleepy driving" to be as dangerous as drunk driving (Dawson & Reid, 1997). Fatigue may be the primary cause of up to 25 percent of all auto accidents (Garbarino et al., 2001; Philip et al., 2001) and of many injuries suffered by sleepy young children at play or in day care (Valent, Brusaferro, & Barbone, 2001). Learning, too, is more difficult after sleep deprivation; but certain parts of the cerebral cortex actually increase their activity when a sleep-deprived person faces a learning task, so the person is able to compensate for a while (Drummond et al., 2000).

Some researchers believe that non-REM sleep helps to restore the body and the brain's energy stores for the next day's activity (Beuckmann & Yanagisawa, 2002; Porkka-Heiskanen et al., 1997). In fact, most people get their non-REM sleep first (Hartman, Baekeland, & Zwilling, 1972). After total sleep deprivation, people do not make up lost sleep hour for hour. Instead, they sleep about 50 percent more than usual, then wake up feeling rested. But if people are deprived *only* of REM sleep, they later compensate more directly. In one study, participants were awakened whenever their EEG showed REM.

When allowed to sleep uninterrupted the next night, they "rebounded," nearly doubling the percentage of time spent in REM (Dement, 1960). This apparent need for REM sleep suggests that REM has special functions.

What these special functions might be is still unclear, but there are several interesting possibilities. First, REM may improve the functioning of neurons that use norepinephrine (Siegel & Rogawski, 1988). Norepinephrine is a neurotransmitter released by cells in the *locus coeruleus* (pronounced "lo-kus seh-ROO-lee-us"; see Figure 4.5). During waking hours, it affects alertness and mood. But the brain's neurons do not fully respond to norepinephrine if it is released continuously for too long. The locus coeruleus is almost completely inactive during REM sleep, leading researchers to suggest that REM helps restore sensitivity to norepinephrine and thus its ability to keep us alert (Steriade & McCarley, 1990). Animals deprived of REM sleep show unusually high norepinephrine levels and decreased daytime alertness (Brock et al., 1994).

REM sleep may also be a time for developing, checking, and expanding the brain's nerve connections (Graves, Pack, & Abel, 2001; Maquet, 2001; Peigneux et al., 2001). This notion would explain why, as mentioned earlier, infants—whose brains are still developing—spend so much time in REM. In contrast, guinea pigs and other animals born with well-developed brains spend very little sleep time in REM early in their lives (Cartwright, 1978). REM sleep may also help to solidify and absorb the day's experiences and skills (Fischer et al., 2002; Sejnowski & Destexhe, 2000; Stickgold et al., 2000). In one study, people who were REM deprived showed poorer retention of a skill learned the day before when compared with people who were either deprived of non-REM sleep or allowed to sleep normally (Karni et al., 1994). Another study found that establishing memories of emotional information was particularly dependent on REM sleep (Wagner, Gais, & Born, 2001). Even 60- to 90-minute naps in which REM sleep appears can be enough to solidify the learning of visual information (Mednick, Nakayama, & Stickgold, 2003).

Dreams and Dreaming

The brain is active in all sleep stages, and some of this activity is experienced as the sensations and perceptions known as **dreams.** Some dreaming occurs during non-REM sleep, but most dreams—and the most bizarre and vivid dreams—occur during REM (Casagrande et al., 1996; Dement & Kleitman, 1957; Stickgold, Rittenhouse, & Hobson, 1994). Dreams may be as short as a few seconds or last for many minutes. They may be organized or chaotic, realistic or fantastic, boring or exciting (Hobson & Stickgold, 1994).

Although they may seem senseless, dreams often contain a certain amount of logic. For example, when people read dream reports whose segments had been randomly reordered, they could correctly say which had been rearranged and which were intact. And although dreams often involve one person transforming into another or one object turning into another object, it is rare that objects become people or vice versa (Stickgold, Rittenhouse, & Hobson, 1994).

Daytime activities may have some influence on dream content, though their impact is probably minor (Foulkes, 1985). In one study, people wore red-tinted goggles for a few minutes just before going to sleep. Although they didn't know the purpose of the study, the next morning they reported more red images in their dreams than people who had not worn the goggles (Roffwarg, Hermann, & Bowe-Anders, 1978). It is also sometimes possible to intentionally direct dream content. This is called **lucid dreaming,** because the sleeper is aware of dreaming while a dream is occurring (Stickgold et al., 2000).

Research leaves little doubt that everyone dreams during every night of normal sleep. Even blind people dream, although their perceptual experiences are usually not visual. Whether you remember a dream depends on how you sleep and wake up. Recall is better if you awaken abruptly and lie quietly while writing or tape-recording your recollections.

Why do we dream? Theories abound (Antrobus, 2001; Domhoff, 2001). Some see dreaming as a fundamental process through which all species with complex brains analyze and consolidate information (Porte & Hobson, 1996). This view is supported by the fact that dreaming appears to occur in most mammals, as indicated by the appearance of

dreams   Story-like sequences of images, sensations, and perceptions that last from several seconds to many minutes and occur mainly during REM sleep.

lucid dreaming   Being aware that a dream is a dream while it is occurring.

REM sleep. For example, after researchers disabled the neurons that cause REM sleep paralysis, sleeping cats ran around and attacked, or seemed alarmed by, unseen objects, presumably the images from dreams (Winson, 1990).

According to Freud (1900), dreams are a disguised form of *wish fulfillment.* They are a way to satisfy unconscious urges or resolve unconscious conflicts that are too upsetting to deal with consciously. So sexual desires might appear in a dream as the rhythmic motions of a horseback ride. Conflicting feelings about a parent might appear as a dream about a fight. Seeing his patients' dreams as a "royal road to a knowledge of the unconscious," Freud interpreted their meaning as part of his psychoanalytic treatment (see the chapter on the treatment of psychological disorders).

In contrast, the *activation-synthesis theory* sees dreams as the meaningless, random byproducts of REM sleep (Hobson, 1997). According to this theory, hindbrain arousal during REM creates random messages that *activate* the brain, especially the cerebral cortex. Dreams result as the cortex connects, or *synthesizes,* these random messages as best as it can, using stored memories and current feelings to translate random brain activity into something more coherent. From this perspective, dreams represent the brain's attempt to make sense of meaningless stimulation during sleep, much as we might try to find meaningful shapes in cloud formations (Bernstein & Roberts, 1995; Rittenhouse, Stickgold, & Hobson, 1994).

Even if dreams arise from random brain activity, their content may still have psychological significance. For example, the mental style or current concerns of the dreamer can affect the ways in which dreams are organized and recalled (Domhoff, 1996; Stevens, 1996). There are also similarities between the emotions and thoughts experienced in dreams and in recent waking life (Domhoff, 1999). However, research using brain imaging techniques shows that while we are asleep, brain areas involved in emotion tend to be overactivated, whereas those areas controlling logical thought tend to be suppressed (Braun, Balkin, & Wesensten, 1998; Hobson et al., 1998). In fact, as we reach deeper sleep stages, and then enter REM sleep, thinking subsides and hallucinations increase (Fosse, Stickgold, & Hobson, 2001). This is probably why dreams rarely provide realistic, logical solutions to our problems (Blagrove, 1996).

INDUCING HYPNOSIS In the late 1700s, Austrian physician Franz Anton Mesmer used a forerunner of hypnosis to treat physical disorders. His procedure, known as *mesmerism,* included elaborate trance-induction rituals, but we now know that hypnosis can be induced far more easily, often simply by staring at an object, as this woman did.

Hypnosis

▶ **Can you be hypnotized against your will?**

The word *hypnosis* comes from the Greek word *hypnos,* meaning "sleep." However, hypnotized people are not sleeping. Describing their hypnotic experiences, these people say that although their bodies were deeply relaxed, their minds were active and alert. **Hypnosis** has been defined as an altered state of consciousness brought on by special techniques and producing responsiveness to suggestions for changes in experience and behavior (Kirsch, 1994a). Most hypnotized people do not feel forced to follow the hypnotist's instructions. They simply see no reason to refuse (Hilgard, 1965). In fact, the more that people want to cooperate with the hypnotist, the more likely it is they will experience hypnosis (Lynn et al., 2002). People cannot be hypnotized against their will.

Experiencing Hypnosis

Usually, hypnosis begins with suggestions that the person feels relaxed and sleepy. The hypnotist then gradually focuses the person's attention on a restricted, often monotonous set of stimuli, such as a swinging pendant. The hypnotist suggests that the individual ignore everything else and imagine certain feelings.

Not everyone can be hypnotized. Special tests measure **hypnotic susceptibility,** the degree to which people respond to hypnotic suggestions (Gfeller, 1994). These tests show

hypnosis An altered state of consciousness brought on by special techniques, characterized by varying degrees of responsiveness to suggestions for changes in experience and behavior.

hypnotic susceptibility The degree to which a person responds to hypnotic suggestion.

that about 10 percent of adults are difficult or impossible to hypnotize (Hilgard, 1982). People who can easily be hypnotized typically differ from others in having a better ability to focus attention and ignore distraction (Crawford, Brown, & Moon, 1993). They have more active imaginations (Spanos, Burnley, & Cross, 1993), a tendency to fantasize (Lynn & Rhue, 1986), a capacity for processing information quickly and easily (Dixon, Brunet, & Laurence, 1990), a tendency to be suggestible (Kirsch & Braffman, 2001), and positive attitudes toward hypnosis (Gfeller, 1994).

The results of hypnosis can be fascinating. People told that their eyes are locked shut may struggle unsuccessfully to open them. They may appear deaf or blind or insensitive to pain. They may forget their own names. Some appear to remember forgotten things. Others show *age regression*, apparently recalling or reenacting their childhood (see Figure 4.6). Hypnotic effects can last for hours or days through *posthypnotic suggestions*, which are instructions about how to behave after hypnosis has ended (such as smiling whenever someone says "England"). Some individuals show *posthypnotic amnesia*, an inability to recall what happened while they were hypnotized, even after being told what happened (Barnier, 2002).

Ernest Hilgard (1965, 1992) described the main changes that people display during hypnosis. First, hypnotized people *tend not to begin actions on their own*, waiting instead for the hypnotist's instructions. One participant said, "I was trying to decide if my legs were crossed, but I couldn't tell, and didn't quite have the initiative to move to find out" (Hilgard, 1965). Second, hypnotized people tend to ignore all but the hypnotist's voice and whatever it points out: Their *attention is redistributed*. Third, hypnosis *enhances the ability to fantasize*. Participants more vividly imagine a scene or relive a memory. Fourth, hypnotized people *readily take on roles*. They more easily act like a person of a different age or a member of the opposite sex than nonhypnotized people do. Fifth, hypnotized individuals show *reduced reality testing*. They tend not to question whether statements are true, and they are more willing to accept apparent distortions of reality. So a hypnotized person might shiver in a warm room if a hypnotist says it is snowing.

Explaining Hypnosis

Hypnotized people look and act different from nonhypnotized people (Hilgard, 1965). Do these differences indicate an altered state of consciousness?

Advocates of **state theory** say that they do. They point to the dramatic effects that hypnosis can produce, including insensitivity to pain and the disappearance of warts (Noll, 1994). They also note that there are subtle differences in the way hypnotized and nonhypnotized people carry out suggestions. In one study, hypnotized people and those who had been asked to simulate hypnosis were told to run their hands through their hair whenever they heard the

---

Source: Hilgard (1965).

figure 4.6

Hypnotic Age Regression

learn by **doing** Here are the signatures of two adults before hypnotically induced age regression (top of each pair) and while age regressed (bottom of each pair). The lower signatures in each pair look less mature, but was the change due to hypnosis? To find out, ask a friend to write his or her name on a blank sheet of paper, first as usual, and then as if he or she were five years old. If the two signatures look significantly different, what does this say about the cause of certain age-regression effects?

---

figure 4.7

Reports of Pain in Hypnosis

This graph compares the intensity of pain reported by three groups of participants while their hands were immersed in ice water. The orange line represents nonhypnotized participants. The blue line represents hypnotized participants who were told they would feel no pain. The purple line shows the reports of hypnotized participants who were told they would feel no pain but were asked to press a key if "any part of them" felt pain. The key pressing by this "hidden observer" suggests that under hypnosis, the experience of pain was dissociated from conscious awareness (Hilgard, 1977).

SURGERY UNDER HYPNOSIS Bernadine Coady, of Wimblington, England, has a condition that makes general anesthesia dangerous for her. In April 1999, she faced a foot operation that would have been extremely painful without anesthesia. She arranged for a hypnotherapist to help her through the procedure, but when he failed to show up, she was forced to rely on self-hypnosis as her only anesthetic. She said she imagined the pain as "waves lashing against a sea wall . . . [and] going away, like the tide." Coady's report that the operation was painless is believable because, in December 2000, she underwent the same operation on her other foot, again using only self-hypnosis for pain control (Morris, 2000).

word *experiment* (Orne, Sheehan, & Evans, 1968). Simulators did so only when the hypnotist said the cue word. Hypnotized participants complied no matter who said it. Another study found that hypnotized people complied more often than simulators with a posthypnotic suggestion to mail postcards to the experimenter. (Barnier & McConkey, 1998).

Supporters of **role theory** maintain that hypnosis is *not* a special state of consciousness. Rather, they say, hypnotized people are merely complying with social demands and acting in accordance with a special social role (Kirsch, 1994b). From this perspective, hypnosis simply provides a socially acceptable reason to follow someone's suggestions. Support for role theory comes from several sources. First, nonhypnotized people sometimes display behaviors that are usually associated with hypnosis. For example, contestants on television game shows and reality shows do lots of odd, silly, gross, or even dangerous things without first being hypnotized. Second, laboratory studies show that motivated, but nonhypnotized, volunteers can duplicate many aspects of hypnotic behavior, from arm rigidity to age regression (Dasgupta et al., 1995; Orne & Evans, 1965). Other studies have found that people rendered blind or deaf by hypnosis can still see or hear, even though their actions and beliefs suggest that they cannot (Bryant & McConkey, 1989).

Hilgard (1992) proposed a **dissociation theory** to blend role and state theories. He suggested that hypnosis is not one specific state but a general condition that temporarily reorganizes or breaks down our normal control over thoughts and actions. Hypnosis, he said, activates a process called *dissociation,* meaning a split in consciousness (Hilgard, 1979). Dissociation allows body movements normally under voluntary control to occur on their own, and normally involuntary processes (such as overt reactions to pain) to be controlled voluntarily.

Hilgard argued that this relaxation of control is possible because of a social agreement between the hypnotized person and the hypnotist to share control. In other words, people usually decide for themselves how to act or what to attend to, perceive, or remember. During hypnosis, the hypnotist is given permission to control some of these experiences and actions. Compliance with a social role may tell part of the story, Hilgard said, but hypnosis also leads to significant changes in mental processes.

Support for dissociation theory comes from a study in which hypnotized participants immersed one hand in ice water (Hilgard, Morgan, & MacDonald, 1975). They were told that they would feel no pain, but they were asked to press a key with their other hand if "any part of them" felt pain. As shown in Figure 4.7, these participants said they felt almost no pain, but their key pressing told a different story. Hilgard concluded that a "hidden observer" was reporting on pain that was reaching the person but that had been separated, or dissociated, from conscious awareness (Hilgard, 1977).

Much remains to be learned about the nature of hypnosis as contemporary research continues to test the various explanatory theories (Green & Lynn, 1995). However, traditional distinctions between state and role theories have become less important as researchers focus on larger questions, such as why people are susceptible to hypnosis and what roles social and cognitive factors may play in it.

Applications of Hypnosis

Whatever hypnosis is, it has proven useful, especially in relation to pain (Patterson & Jensen, 2003). Magnetic resonance imaging (MRI) studies of hypnotized pain patients show altered activity in the anterior cingulate cortex, a brain region associated with the emotional component of pain (Faymonville et al., 2000). Hypnosis seems to be the only anesthetic some people need to block the pain of dental work, childbirth, burns, and surgery (Van Sickel, 1992). For others, hypnosis relieves chronic pain from arthritis, nerve damage, migraine headaches, and cancer (Nolan et al., 1995; Patterson, Goldberg, & Ehde, 1996). Hypnotic suggestion can reduce nausea and vomiting due to chemotherapy (Redd, 1984). It can also help reduce surgical bleeding (Gerschman, Reade, & Burrows, 1980).

Other applications of hypnosis are more controversial, especially the use of hypnosis to aid memory. For example, hypnotic age regression is sometimes used in an attempt to help people recover lost memories. However, age-regressed memories may actually be

state theory A theory proposing that hypnosis creates an altered state of consciousness.

role theory A theory proposing that hypnotized people act in accordance with a social role that demands compliance.

dissociation theory A theory proposing that hypnosis is a socially agreed-upon opportunity to display one's ability to let mental functions become dissociated.

less accurate than those of nonhypnotized individuals (Lynn et al., 1997). Similarly, it is doubtful that hypnosis can help witnesses to recall the details of a crime (Lynn, Myers, & Malinoski, 1997). Like nonhypnotized crime witnesses, hypnotized witnesses may unintentionally distort information or reconstruct memories for the events in question (Garry & Loftus, 1994; Weekes et al., 1992). Unfortunately, being hypnotized may make them more confident about their reports, even if they are inaccurate.

LINKAGES
Does meditation relieve stress? (a link to Health, Stress, and Coping)

LINKAGES

Meditation, Health, and Stress

Meditation provides a set of techniques intended to create an altered state of consciousness characterized by inner peace and tranquility (Shapiro & Walsh, 1984). Some people claim that meditation increases their awareness and understanding of themselves and their environment. Others claim that it reduces anxiety, improves health and immune system functioning, and aids performance in everything from work to tennis (Bodian, 1999; Davidson et al., 2003; Mahesh Yogi, 1994).

Techniques to achieve a meditative state differ, depending on belief and philosophy (e.g., Eastern meditation, Sufism, yoga, or prayer). However, in the most common meditation methods, attention is focused on just one thing until the meditator stops thinking about anything else and experiences nothing but "pure awareness" (Benson, 1975). In this way, the individual becomes more fully aware of the present moment rather than being caught up in the past or the future.

To organize their attention, meditators may focus on the sound or tempo of their breathing, or slowly repeat a *mantra*, which is a soothing word or phrase. During a typical meditation session, breathing, heart rate, muscle tension, blood pressure, and oxygen consumption decrease (Wallace & Benson, 1972). Most forms of meditation induce EEG activity similar to that seen in a relaxed, eyes-closed, waking state (see Figure 4.3). Meditation also increases the brain's level of dopamine, the same neurotransmitter thought to be involved in the experience of reward or pleasure (Kjaer et al., 2002).

Meditators often report significant reductions in stress-related problems such as anxiety, high blood pressure, and insomnia (Beauchamp-Turner & Levinson, 1992). More generally, meditators' scores on personality tests indicate increases in overall mental health, self-esteem, and social openness (Janowiak & Hackman, 1994; Sakairi, 1992). Exactly how meditation produces its effects is unclear. Many of its effects can also be achieved by biofeedback, hypnosis, or just relaxing (Beyerstein, 1999).

---

psychoactive drugs   Chemical substances that act on the brain to create psychological effects.

psychopharmacology   The study of psychoactive drugs and their effects.

blood-brain barrier   A feature of blood vessels in the brain that prevents some substances from entering brain tissue.

agonists   Drugs that bind to a receptor and mimic the effects of the neurotransmitter that normally fits that receptor.

antagonists   Drugs that bind to a receptor and prevent the normal neurotransmitter from binding.

substance abuse   The use of psychoactive drugs in ways that deviate from cultural norms.

Psychoactive Drugs

▶ **How do drugs affect the brain?**

The altered states we have discussed so far serve a biological need (sleep) or rely on the chemistry of the brain and body (hypnosis and meditation). Other altered states are brought on by outside agents: drugs. Every day, most people in the world use drugs that alter brain activity and consciousness (Levinthal, 1996). For example, 80 to 90 percent of people in North America use caffeine, the stimulant found in coffee and tea. A *drug* is a chemical that is not required for normal physiological functioning, yet has an effect on the body. You may say that you "need" a cup of coffee in the morning, but you will wake up without it; accordingly, the caffeine in coffee is defined as a drug. Drugs that affect the brain, changing consciousness and other psychological processes, are called **psychoactive drugs.** The study of psychoactive drugs is called **psychopharmacology.**

Psychopharmacology

Most psychoactive drugs affect the brain by altering the interactions between neuro-transmitters and their receptors, as described in the chapter on biology and behavior. To create their effects, these drugs must cross the **blood-brain barrier,** a feature of blood vessels in the brain that prevents some substances from entering brain tissue. Once past this barrier, a psychoactive drug's effects depend on several factors: With which neuro-transmitter systems does the drug interact? How does the drug affect those neurotrans-mitters or their receptors? What psychological functions are performed by the brain sys-tems that use those neurotransmitters?

Drugs can affect neurotransmitters or their receptors through several mechanisms. Neurotransmitters fit into their own receptors, as Figure 4.8 shows. Some drugs, such as morphine, are similar enough to a particular neurotransmitter to fool its receptors. These drugs, called **agonists,** bind to receptors and mimic the effects of the normal neu-rotransmitter. Other drugs, called **antagonists,** are similar enough to a neurotransmitter to occupy its receptors but cannot mimic its effects. When they bind to receptors, they prevent the normal neurotransmitter from binding. Still other drugs work by increasing or decreasing the release of a specific neurotransmitter. Finally, some drugs work by speeding or slowing the *removal* of a neurotransmitter from synapses.

Predicting a psychoactive drug's behavioral effects is complicated. For one thing, most of these drugs interact with many neurotransmitter systems. Also, the nervous system may compensate for a given drug's effects. For instance, repeated exposure to a drug that blocks receptors for a certain neurotransmitter often leads to an increase in the number of receptors available to accept that neurotransmitter.

The Varying Effects of Drugs

Unfortunately, chemical properties that give drugs their medically desirable main effects, such as pain relief, often create undesirable side effects as well.

Substance Abuse   One side effect may be the potential for abuse. **Substance abuse** is a pattern of use that causes serious social, legal, or interpersonal problems for the user

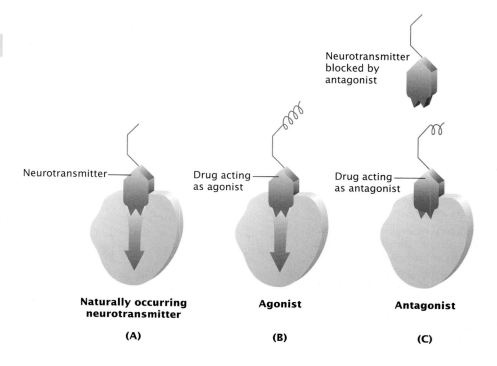

figure 4.8

Agonists and Antagonists

In Part A, a molecule of neurotransmitter interacts with a receptor on a neuron's dendrites by fitting into and stimulating it. Part B shows a drug molecule acting as an *agonist,* affecting the receptor in the same way a neurotransmitter would. Part C depicts an *antagonist* drug molecule blocking a natural neurotransmitter from reaching and acting on the receptor.

Neurotransmitter blocked by antagonist

Neurotransmitter—

Drug acting as agonist—

Drug acting as antagonist—

Naturally occurring neurotransmitter

Agonist

Antagonist

(A)

(B)

(C)

figure 4.9

Changing Definitions of Illicit Drugs

The definition of an "inappropriate" drug can vary across cultures and over time (Weiss & Moore, 1990). For example, in the United States cocaine was once a respectable, commercially available drug; today it is illegal. And alcohol, which is legal in the United States and many other nations, is banned in some countries, such as Kuwait, Iran, and Saudi Arabia.

psychological dependence   A condition in which a person continues drug use despite adverse effects, needs the drug for a sense of well-being, and becomes preoccupied with obtaining the drug if it is unavailable.

addiction   Development of a physical need for a psychoactive drug.

withdrawal syndrome   A set of symptoms associated with discontinuing the use of an addictive substance.

tolerance   A condition in which increasingly larger drug doses are needed to produce a given effect.

depressants   Psychoactive drugs that inhibit the functioning of the central nervous system.

(American Psychiatric Association, 1994, 2000). Of course, as a culture changes, the drugs that cause a person social and legal problems may also change, as Figure 4.9 illustrates.

Substance abuse can lead to psychological or physical dependence. People displaying **psychological dependence** on a drug will continue to use it despite its adverse effects. They need the drug for a sense of well-being and become preoccupied with getting the drug if it is no longer available. However, they can still function without the drug. Psychological dependence can occur with or without *physical dependence,* also known as *addiction.* **Addiction** is a physiological state in which there is not only a strong craving for the drug, but in which using the drug becomes necessary to prevent an unpleasant **withdrawal syndrome.** Withdrawal symptoms vary depending on the drug, but they often include an intensification of craving for the drug and physical effects generally opposite to those of the drug itself.

Physical dependence can develop gradually, without a person's awareness. As the addiction progresses, the person may also develop drug **tolerance,** a condition in which increasingly larger drug doses are required to produce the same effect (Gilman et al., 1985; Sokolowska, Siegel, & Kim, 2002). Scientists believe that the changes in the brain that underlie addiction may be similar to those that occur during learning (Nestler, 2001; Overton et al., 1999). With the development of tolerance, many addicts need the drug just to prevent the negative effects of not taking it. However, most researchers believe that a craving for the positive effects of drugs is what keeps addicts coming back to drug use (George et al., 2001; Schulteis et al., 2000; Weiss et al., 2001).

It is tempting to think of "addicts" as being unlike ourselves, but we should never underestimate the potential for "normal" people to develop drug dependence. (If you're a coffee or tea drinker, think about how you'd feel without that morning "jolt.") All addictive drugs stimulate the brain's "pleasure centers," regions that are sensitive to the neurotransmitters dopamine and endorphin. Neuron activity in these areas of the brain produces intensely pleasurable feelings. It also helps generate the pleasant feelings of a good meal, a "runner's high," or sex (Grunberg, 1994; Harris & Aston-Jones, 1995). It is no wonder, then, that addictive drugs have the capacity for creating tremendously rewarding effects in most people (Kelley & Berridge, 2002).

Expectations and Drug Effects   Drug effects are determined by more than biochemistry. *Learned expectations* also play a role (Cumsille, Sayer, & Graham, 2000; Goldman, Del Boca, & Darkes, 1999; Stein, Goldman, & Del Boca, 2000). Several experiments have shown that research participants who consume alcohol-free drinks that they *think* contain alcohol are likely to behave in line with their expectations about alcohol's effects. So they tend to feel drunk, and to become more aggressive, more interested in violent and sexual material, and more easily sexually aroused (Darkes & Goldman, 1993; George & Marlatt, 1986; Lang et al., 1975; Lansky & Wilson, 1981). And because they know that alcohol impairs memory, these participants are more vulnerable to developing false memories about a crime they witnessed on videotape (Assefi & Garry, 2003).

Expectations about drug effects develop in part as people watch other people react to drugs (Sher et al., 1996), and can influence how much of a drug they themselves consume (see Figure 4.10). What they see can differ from one individual and culture to the next, so drug effects vary considerably throughout the world (MacAndrew & Edgerton, 1969). In the United States, for example, loss of inhibition, increased anger and violence, and sexual promiscuity are commonly associated with drinking alcohol. These effects are not seen in all cultures, however. In Bolivia's Camba culture, people sometimes engage in extended bouts of drinking a brew that is 89 percent alcohol (178 proof). During their binges, the Camba repeatedly pass out, wake up, and start drinking again—all the while maintaining tranquil social relations. Other studies have shown that learned expectations also contribute to the effects of heroin, cocaine, and marijuana (Robbins & Everitt, 1999; Schafer & Brown, 1991; Smith et al., 1992).

In short, the effects of psychoactive drugs are complex and variable. Here, we consider several major categories of psychoactive drugs that people use primarily to produce altered states of consciousness. They include depressants, stimulants, opiates, and hallucinogens.

Depressants

Depressants, such as alcohol and barbiturates, reduce or depress central nervous system activity, partly by increasing activity of the inhibitory neurotransmitter GABA (discussed in the chapter on biology and behavior). Because GABA reduces neuron activity, drugs that enhance GABA's functions heighten its inhibitory effects, creating feelings of relaxation, drowsiness, and sometimes depression (Hanson & Venturelli, 1995).

Alcohol   The most common depressant drug by far is alcohol. In the United States, more than 100 million people drink alcohol. It is equally popular worldwide (Alvarez, Delrio, & Prada, 1995). Alcohol's physiological effects involve the neurotransmitters GABA, endorphins, and dopamine, among others (Koob et al., 1998). The GABA effect is notable; drugs that interact with GABA receptors can block some of alcohol's effects (Suzdak et al., 1986).

Alcohol also enhances the effect of endorphins, the body's natural painkillers. The fact that endorphins produce a sense of well-being may explain why people initially feel "high" when drinking alcohol. It may also explain why drugs that block endorphins are better than placebos at reducing alcohol cravings and relapse rates in recovering alcoholics (Salloum et al., 1998). Alcohol also interacts with dopamine systems, which are part of the brain's reward mechanisms (Thanos et al., 2001). Prolonged alcohol use can have lasting effects on the brain's ability to regulate dopamine levels (Tiihonen et al., 1995). Dopamine agonists reduce alcohol cravings and withdrawal effects (Lawford et al., 1995).

Alcohol affects specific brain regions. It depresses activity in the locus coeruleus, an area described in our discussion of sleep that helps activate the cerebral cortex (Koob & Bloom, 1988). This reduced activity, in turn, tends to cause cognitive changes and a release of culturally prescribed inhibitions (Casbon et al., 2003). Some drinkers begin talking loudly, acting silly, or telling others what they think of them. Emotional reactions range from euphoria (happiness) to despair. Normally shy people may become impulsive or violent. Alcohol also impairs the hippocampus, making it more difficult to process information and form new memories (Givens, 1995). And it suppresses the cerebellum, causing poor motor coordination, stumbling, and falling (Rogers et al., 1986). Alcohol's ability to depress hindbrain mechanisms required for breathing and heartbeat can make overdoses fatal.

Some effects of alcohol—such as anger and aggressiveness—depend on both biochemical factors and learned expectations (Goldman, Darkes, & Del Boca, 1999; Kushner et al., 2000). Disruptions in motor coordination, speech, and thought result mainly from

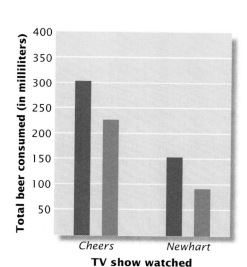

figure 4.10

Expectancies and Alcohol Consumption

People may drink more when their expectancies about the positive effects of alcohol have been primed. In this study, some participants watched *Cheers* (a TV show depicting people enjoying themselves while drinking alcohol) and were exposed to adjectives associated with positive expectancies about alcohol. They later drank more (nonalcoholic) beer than participants who were not exposed to the adjectives and who watched a non-alcohol-related show (Roehrich & Goldman, 1995).

DRINKING AND DRIVING DON'T MIX
Though practice makes it seem easy, driving a car is a complex information-processing task. As described in the chapter on thought, language, and intelligence, such tasks require constant vigilance, quick decisions, and skillful execution of responses. Alcohol can impair all these processes, as well as the ability to judge the degree of impairment—thus making drinking and driving a deadly combination that results in 275,000 injuries and almost 18,000 deaths each year in the United States alone (National Highway Traffic Safety Administration, 2003).

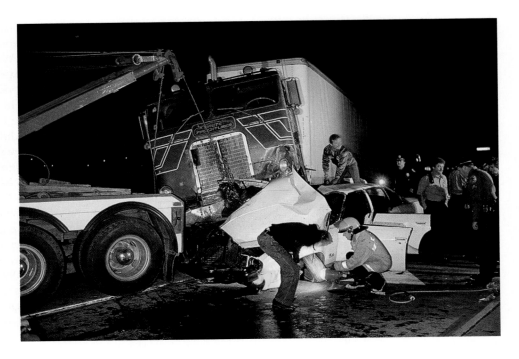

biochemical factors. These biological effects depend on the amount of alcohol the blood carries to the brain. Because it takes the liver about an hour to break down one ounce of alcohol (the amount in one typical drink), alcohol has milder effects if consumed slowly. Faster drinking or drinking on an empty stomach speeds absorption of alcohol into the blood and heightens its effects. Even after allowing for differences in average male and female body weight, researchers have found metabolic differences that make male bodies able to tolerate somewhat greater amounts of alcohol. So a given quantity of alcohol may have a stronger effect on a woman than on a man (York & Welte, 1994).

Genetics also seems to play a role in determining the biochemical effects of alcohol. Evidence suggests that particular ethnic groups have a genetic predisposition toward alcohol dependence (Agarwal, 1997), though the genes involved have not yet been identified (Holden, 1998). Other groups (the Japanese, for example) may have inherited metabolic characteristics that enhance alcohol's adverse effects, possibly inhibiting the development of alcohol abuse (Iwahashi et al., 1995).

Barbiturates   Sometimes called "downers" or sleeping pills, *barbiturates* are highly addictive. In small doses, their psychoactive effects include relaxation, mild pleasure, loss of muscle coordination, and lowered attention. Higher doses cause deep sleep, but continued use actually distorts sleep patterns (Kales & Kales, 1973). So long-term use of barbiturates as sleeping pills is unwise. Overdoses can be fatal. Withdrawal symptoms are among the most severe for any drug and can include intense agitation, violent outbursts, convulsions, hallucinations, and even sudden death.

GHB   *Gamma hydroxybutyrate (GHB)* is a naturally occurring substance similar to the neurotransmitter GABA. In recent years, a laboratory-manufactured version of GHB (also known as "G") has become a popular "club drug" known for creating relaxation, feelings of euphoria, loss of inhibitions, and increased sex drive. Unfortunately, it can also cause nausea and vomiting, headaches, memory loss, dizziness, loss of muscle control or paralysis, breathing problems, loss of consciousness, and even death—especially when combined with alcohol or other drugs (Miotto et al., 2001; Stillwell, 2002). As with other depressants, long-term use of GHB can lead to dependence. If dependent users abruptly stop taking the drug, they may experience a withdrawal syndrome that can include seizures, hallucinations, agitation, and even coma or death (Catakano et al., 2001).

DEADLY DRUG USE In his short career as a comedian, Chris Farley starred on *Saturday Night Live* and in several movies. At the age of thirty-three, he died from an overdose of cocaine and opium.

Stimulants

Whereas depressants slow down central nervous system activity, **stimulants** speed it up. Amphetamines, cocaine, caffeine, and nicotine are all examples of stimulants.

Amphetamines Often called "uppers" or "speed," *amphetamines* increase the release of norepinephrine and dopamine into synapses, affecting sleep, learning, and mood (Kolb et al., 2003). Amphetamines also slow the removal of both substances at synapses, leaving more of them there, ready to work. The increased activity at these neurotransmitters' receptors results in alertness, arousal, and appetite suppression. These effects are further enhanced by the fact that amphetamines also reduce activity of the inhibitory neurotransmitter GABA (Centonze et al., 2002). Amphetamines' rewarding properties are probably associated with their effect on dopamine activity, because taking dopamine antagonists reduces amphetamine use (Holman, 1994).

People who abuse amphetamines usually begin taking these drugs in an effort to lose weight, stay awake, or obtain a "high." Continued use leads to anxiety, insomnia, heart problems, confusion, paranoia, nonstop talking, and psychological and physical dependence (Volkow et al., 2001). In some cases, the symptoms of amphetamine abuse appear virtually identical to those of paranoid schizophrenia, a serious mental disorder linked to dopamine malfunction.

Cocaine Like amphetamines, *cocaine* increases norepinephrine and dopamine activity and decreases GABA activity, so it produces many amphetamine-like effects (Kolb et al., 2003). Cocaine's particularly powerful and rapid effect on dopamine activity may underlie its remarkably addictive nature (Holman, 1994; Ungless et al., 2001). In fact, most drugs with rapid onset and short duration are more addictive than others (Kato, Wakasa, & Yamagita, 1987), which helps explain why *crack*—a purified, fast-acting, highly potent, smokable form of cocaine—is especially addictive.

Cocaine stimulates self-confidence, a sense of well-being, and optimism. Continued use brings nausea, overactivity, insomnia, paranoia, a sudden depressive "crash," hallucinations, sexual dysfunction, and seizures (Lacayo, 1995). Overdoses, especially overdoses of crack cocaine, can be deadly. Even small doses can cause a fatal heart attack or stroke (Marzuk et al., 1995). There is now little doubt that a pregnant woman who uses cocaine harms her fetus (Hurt et al., 1995). However, many of the severe, long-term behavioral problems seen in "cocaine babies" may have as much to do with poverty and neglect after birth as with the mother's cocaine use beforehand. Early intervention can reduce the effects of both cocaine and the hostile environment that confronts most cocaine babies (Wren, 1998).

Caffeine *Caffeine* may be the world's most popular drug. It is found not only in coffee and tea, but in chocolate, and many soft drinks. Caffeine reduces drowsiness and can enhance cognitive performance, including problem solving and vigilance (Beaumont et al., 2001). It also increases the capacity for physical work and raises urine production (Warburton, 1995). At high doses it causes anxiety and tremors. People can develop tolerance to caffeine, and it can be physically addictive (Strain et al., 1994). Withdrawal symptoms—including headache, fatigue, anxiety, shakiness, and craving—appear on the first day of abstinence and last about a week (Silverman et al., 1992). Caffeine may make it harder for women to become pregnant and may increase the risk of miscarriage or stillbirth (Alderete, Eskenazi, & Sholtz, 1995; Cnattingius et al., 2000; Wisborg et al., 2003). Overall, however, moderate daily caffeine use appears to have few, if any, negative effects (Kawachi, Colditz, & Stone, 1994; Thompson, 1995).

Nicotine A powerful autonomic nervous system stimulant, *nicotine* is the main psychoactive ingredient in tobacco. It is an acetylcholine agonist that also increases the availability of glutamate, the brain's primary excitatory neurotransmitter, and activates the brain's dopamine-related pleasure systems (Balfour, 2002; McGehee et al., 1995). Nicotine has many psychoactive effects, including elevated mood and improved memory and

stimulants Psychoactive drugs that have the ability to increase behavioral and mental activity.

attention (Ernst et al., 2001). Like heroin and cocaine, nicotine can be physically addictive (White, 1998). The nicotine withdrawal syndrome includes craving, anxiety, irritability, lowered heart rate, and weight gain (Epping-Jordan et al., 1998; Hughes, Higgins, & Bickel, 1994). Some smokers appear to develop only a psychological dependence on nicotine (Robinson & Pritchard, 1995), but whether the dependence is physiological or psychological, there is no doubt that tobacco smoking is usually a difficult habit to break (Shiffman et al., 1997). It is also clearly recognized as a major risk factor for cancer, heart disease, and respiratory disorders (U.S. Department of Health and Human Services, 2001c).

MDMA   The stimulant "ecstasy," or *MDMA* (short for 3,4-methylenedioxymethamphetamine), is becoming increasingly popular on campuses in the United States (Strote, Lee, & Wechsler, 2002). It creates euphoria, increased sex drive, visual hallucinations, and a feeling of greater closeness to others, but also increased blood pressure, fever, dry mouth, hyperactivity, jaw muscle spasms that may result in "lockjaw," and dangerously abnormal heart rhythms (Smith, Larive, & Romanelli, 2002). On the day after using MDMA—also known as "XTC," "clarity," "essence," "E," and "Adam"—people often experience muscle aches, fatigue, depression, and poor concentration (Peroutka, Newman, & Harris, 1988). Because MDMA increases the activity of dopamine-releasing neurons, it leads to some of the same effects as those produced by cocaine and amphetamines (Steele, McCann, & Ricaurte, 1994). MDMA is a serotonin agonist and also causes neurotransmitter release, which may account for the drug's hallucinatory effects (Green, Cross, & Goodwin, 1995). Even though it does not appear to be physically addictive, MDMA is a dangerous, potentially deadly drug with many negative psychological and biochemical consequences (National Institute on Drug Abuse, 2000). These consequences, including impaired decision making, elementary hallucinations, and depressed mood 24 hours after taking the drug are especially pronounced in women, even when the dosage is corrected for differences in body weight between men and women (Liechti, Gamma, & Vollenweider, 2001). MDMA permanently damages the brain, killing serotonin-sensitive neurons (Green, Cross, & Goodwin, 1995), as well as neurons that use dopamine. As you might expect, the danger of brain damage increases with higher doses and continued use (Battaglia, Yeh, & DeSouza, 1988).

Opiates

The **opiates** (opium, morphine, heroin, and codeine) are unique in their capacity for inducing sleep and relieving pain (Julien, 2001). *Opium,* derived from the poppy plant, relieves pain and causes feelings of well-being and dreamy relaxation (Cowan et al., 2001). One of its most active ingredients, *morphine,* was first isolated in the early 1800s. It is used worldwide for pain relief. Percodan and Demerol are some common morphine-like drugs. *Heroin* is derived from morphine but is three times more powerful, causing intensely pleasurable reactions. Opiates have complex effects on consciousness. Drowsy, cloudy feelings occur because opiates depress activity in some areas of the cerebral cortex. They also create excitation in other parts, causing some users to experience euphoria (Bozarth & Wise, 1984). Opiates exert many of their effects by stimulating the receptors normally stimulated by endorphins, the body's own painkillers. This action "tricks" the brain into activating its painkilling and mood-altering systems (Julien, 2001).

Opiates are highly addictive, partly because they stimulate a type of glutamate receptor in the brain's neurons that causes physical changes in these neurons. It may be, then, that opiates alter neurons so that they come to require the drug to function properly. Beyond the hazard of addiction itself, heroin addicts risk death through overdoses, contaminated drugs, or AIDS contracted by sharing needles (Hser et al., 2001).

Hallucinogens

Hallucinogens, also called *psychedelics,* create a loss of contact with reality and alter other aspects of emotion, perception, and thought. They can cause distortions in body image (one

opiates   Psychoactive drugs that have the ability to produce both sleep-inducing and pain-relieving effects.

hallucinogens   Psychoactive drugs that alter consciousness by producing a temporary loss of contact with reality and changes in emotion, perception, and thought.

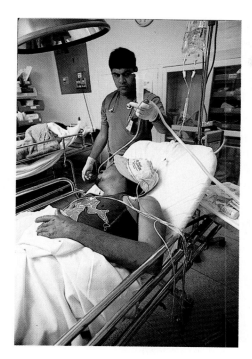

A NEW DRUG DANGER Oxycodone, a morphine-like drug prescribed by doctors under the label OxyContin, has recently become popular among recreational substance abusers. It was designed as a timed-release painkiller, but when people crush OxyContin tablets and then inject or inhale the drug, they get a much stronger and potentially lethal dose. Deaths from Oxy-Contin abuse are already on the rise in the United States (National Drug Intelligence Center, 2001).

may feel gigantic or tiny), loss of identity (confusion about who one actually is), dream-like fantasies, and hallucinations. Because these effects resemble many severe forms of mental disorder, hallucinogens are also called *psychotomimetics* ("mimicking psychosis").

LSD One of the most powerful hallucinogens is *lysergic acid diethylamide,* or *LSD*. It was first synthesized from a rye fungus by a Swiss chemist, Albert Hofmann. In 1938, after Hofmann accidentally ingested a minuscule amount of the substance, he discovered the drug's strange effects in the world's first LSD "trip" (Julien, 2001). LSD hallucinations can be quite bizarre. Time may seem distorted, sounds may cause visual sensations, and users may feel as if they have left their bodies. These experiences probably result from LSD's action as a serotonin agonist, because serotonin antagonists greatly reduce LSD's hallucinatory effects (Carlson, 1998; Leonard, 1992).

The precise effects of LSD are unpredictable. Unpleasant hallucinations and delusions can occur during a person's first—or two hundredth—LSD experience. Although LSD is not addictive, tolerance to its effects does develop. Some users suffer lasting side effects, including severe short-term memory loss, paranoia, violent outbursts, nightmares, and panic attacks (Gold, 1994). Sometimes "flashbacks" can occur, in which a person suddenly returns to an LSD-like state of consciousness weeks or even years after using the drug.

Ketamine *Ketamine* is an anesthetic used by veterinarians to ease pain in animals, but because it also has hallucinogenic effects, it is being stolen and sold as a recreational drug known as "Special K." Its effects include dissociative feelings that create what some users describe as an "out-of-body" or "near-death" experience. Unfortunately, ketamine can lead to enduring memory loss (Curran & Monaghan, 2001; Smith, Larive, & Romananelli, 2002), possibly because it damages memory-related brain structures such as the hippocampus (Jevtovic-Todorovic et al., 2001).

Marijuana A mixture of crushed leaves, flowers, and stems from the hemp plant (*Cannabis sativa*) makes up *marijuana*. The active ingredient is *tetrahydrocannabinol,* or *THC* (Wachtel et al., 2002). When inhaled, THC is absorbed in minutes by many organs, including the brain, and it continues to affect consciousness for a few hours (O'Leary et al., 2002). THC tends to collect in fatty deposits of the brain and reproductive organs, where it can be detected for weeks. Low doses of marijuana may initially create restlessness and hilarity, followed by a dreamy, carefree relaxation, an expanded sense of space and time, more vivid sensations, food cravings, and subtle changes in thinking (Kelly et al., 1990).

There is an ongoing debate about the dangers and potential benefits of marijuana (Iversen & Snyder, 2000; Strang, Witten, & Hall, 2000). Its dangers are suggested by the fact that a mild withdrawal syndrome has been reported in rats; in humans, withdrawal from marijuana may be accompanied by increases in anxiety, depression, irritablity, restlessness, and aggressiveness (Budney et al., 2001, 2003; Haney et al., 1999; Kouri, Pope, & Lukas, 1999; Rodriguez de Fonseca et al., 1997; Smith, 2002). Further, marijuana interacts with the same dopamine and opiate receptors that heroin acts on (Tanda, Pontieri, & Di Chiara, 1997), leading some researchers to speculate that marijuana might be a "gateway" to the use of opiates (Lynskey et al., 2003). Other researchers have cautioned that the interpretation of these results is not clear-cut (Grinspoon, 1999), because sex and chocolate have their rewarding effects by activating those same neurotransmitter receptors—and few people would want to outlaw those pleasures!

Regardless of whether marijuana is addicting or leads to the use of opiates, it can create a number of problems. It disrupts memory formation, making it difficult to carry out mental or physical tasks; and despite users' impressions, it actually reduces creativity (Bourassa & Vaugeois, 2001; Pope & Yurgelun-Todd, 1996). And because marijuana disrupts muscle coordination, driving while under its influence can be dangerous. In fact, motor impairment continues well after the subjective effects of the drug have worn off. As one study demonstrated, pilots had difficulty landing a simulated aircraft even a full day after smoking a single marijuana cigarette (Yesavage et al., 1985). Marijuana easily

MAJOR CLASSES OF PSYCHOACTIVE DRUGS

Drug	Trade/Street Name	Main Effects	Potential for Physical/ Psychological Dependence
Depressants		Relaxation, anxiety	High/high
Alcohol	"booze"	reduction, sleep	High/high
Barbiturates	Seconal, Tuinal, Nembutal ("downers")	Relaxation, euphoria	High/high
GHB	G, Jib, Scoop, GH Buddy		
Stimulants			Moderate/high
Amphetamines	Benzedrine, Dexedrine, Methadrine ("speed,""uppers,""ice")	Alertness, euphoria	
Cocaine	"coke,""crack"		Moderate to high/high
Caffeine		Alertness	Moderate/moderate
Nicotine	"smokes,""coffin nails"	Alertness	High (?)/high
MDMA	"ecstasy,""clarity"	Hallucinations	Low/(?)
Opiates		Euphoria	High/high
Opium		Euphoria, pain control	High/high
Morphine	Percodan, Demerol	Euphoria, pain control	High/high
Heroin	"junk,""smack"		
Hallucinogens		Altered perceptions,	Low/low
LSD/ketamine	"acid"/"Special K"	hallucinations	
Marijuana (cannabis)	"pot,""dope,""reefer"	Euphoria, relaxation	Low/moderate

? *Physical dependence on a drug is a condition more commonly known as _____.*

reaches a developing fetus and therefore should not be used by pregnant women (Fried, Watkinson, & Gray, 1992). Finally, long-term use can lead to psychological dependence (Stephens, Roffman, & Simpson, 1994), as well as to impairments in reasoning and memory that last for months or years after marijuana use stops (Bolla et al., 2002; Solowij et al., 2002). Research has also shown that adults who frequently used marijuana scored lower than equal-IQ nonusers on a twelfth-grade academic achievement test (Block & Ghoneim, 1993), and that heavier use in teenagers is associated with the later appearance of anxiety, depression, and other symptoms of mental disorder (Patton et al., 2002; Zammit et al., 2002).

Marijuana may have considerable value in some domains, however. Doctors have successfully used it in the treatment of asthma, glaucoma, epilepsy, chronic pain, and nausea from cancer chemotherapy; it may even help in treating some types of cancer (Parolaro et al., 2002; Tramer et al., 2001; Voelker, 1997). Critics say that medical legalization of marijuana should not occur until controlled research more firmly establishes its medicinal value compared with existing treatments (Campbell et al., 2001). However, in Canada, it is legal to grow and use marijuana for medicinal purposes, and despite federal laws to the contrary, the same is true in eight U.S. states. Although the American Medical Association has recently rejected the idea of medical uses for marijuana, scientists are intent on objectively studying its potential value in the treatment of certain diseases, as well as its dangers (or lack thereof). Their work is being encouraged by bodies such as the National Institute of Medicine (Joy, Watson, & Benson, 1999), and a British company is working on new cannabis-based medicines (Altman, 2000). The United Nations, too, has recommended that governments worldwide sponsor additional work on the medical uses of marijuana (Wren, 1999). ("In Review: Major Classes of Psychoactive Drugs" summarizes our discussion of these substances.)

Linkages

As noted in the introductory chapter, all of psychology's subfields are related to one another. Our discussion of meditation, health, and stress illustrates just one way in which the topic of this chapter, consciousness, is linked to the subfield of health psychology, which is described in the chapter on health, stress, and coping. The Linkages diagram shows ties to two other subfields as well, and there are many more ties throughout the book. Looking for linkages among subfields will help you see how they all fit together and help you better appreciate the big picture that is psychology.

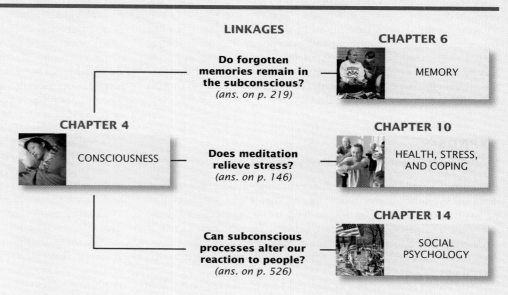

LINKAGES

CHAPTER 4
CONSCIOUSNESS

Do forgotten memories remain in the subconscious?
(ans. on p. 219)

CHAPTER 6
MEMORY

Does meditation relieve stress?
(ans. on p. 146)

CHAPTER 10
HEALTH, STRESS, AND COPING

Can subconscious processes alter our reaction to people?
(ans. on p. 526)

CHAPTER 14
SOCIAL PSYCHOLOGY

Summary

Consciousness can be defined as awareness of the outside world and of one's own thoughts, feelings, perceptions, and other mental processes.

THE SCOPE OF CONSCIOUSNESS

▶ **Can unconscious thoughts affect your behavior?**

A person's *state of consciousness* is constantly changing. When the changes are particularly noticeable, they are called *altered states of consciousness.* Examples of altered states include sleep, hypnosis, meditation, and some drug-induced states. Cultures vary considerably in the value placed on different states of consciousness.

Variations in how much awareness you have for a mental function are described by different levels of consciousness. The *preconscious level* includes mental activities that are outside of awareness but can easily be brought to the *conscious level. Subconscious* and *unconscious* mental activity involves thoughts, memories, and processes that are more difficult to bring to awareness. Mental processes that cannot be brought into awareness occur at the *nonconscious level.*

Awareness is not always required for mental operations. For example, the priming phenomenon shows that people's responses to stimuli speed up and improve as stimuli are repeated, even when there is no conscious memory of which stimuli are old and which are new. And the mere-exposure effect shows that people tend to judge previously encountered stimuli more favorably, even when they are unaware of having seen those stimuli before.

SLEEPING AND DREAMING

▶ **Does your brain go to sleep when you do?**

Sleep is an active and complex state. Different stages of sleep are defined on the basis of changes in brain activity (as measured by an electroencephalograph, or EEG) and physiological arousal. Sleep normally begins with stage 1 sleep and progresses gradually to stage 4 sleep. Sleep stages 3 and 4 constitute *slow-wave sleep,* which is part of non-REM sleep. After passing back to stage 2, people enter *rapid eye movement (REM) sleep,* or paradoxical sleep. The sleeper passes through these stages several times each night, gradually spending more time in stage 2 and REM sleep later in the night.

Sleep disorders can disrupt the natural rhythm of sleep. Among the most common is *insomnia,* in which one feels tired because of trouble falling asleep or staying asleep. *Narcolepsy* produces sudden daytime sleeping episodes. In cases of *sleep apnea,* people briefly but repeatedly stop breathing during sleep. *Sudden infant death syndrome (SIDS)* may be due to brain abnormalities or accidental suffocation. *Sleepwalking* happens most frequently during childhood. *Nightmares* and *night terrors* are different kinds of frightening dreams. *REM behavior disorder* is potentially dangerous because it allows people to act out REM dreams. The cycle of waking and sleeping is a natural *circadian rhythm,* controlled by the suprachiasmatic nuclei of the brain. *Jet lag* can be one result of disrupting the normal sleep-wake cycle.

The purpose of sleep is still unclear. Non-REM sleep may aid bodily rest and repair. REM sleep may help maintain activity in brain areas that provide daytime alertness, or it may allow the brain to "check circuits," eliminate useless information, and solidify learning from the previous day.

Most dreaming occurs during REM sleep. *Dreams* are story-like sequences of images, sensations, and perceptions that occur during sleep. Evidence from research on *lucid dreaming* suggests that people may be able to control their own dreams. Some claim that dreams are the meaningless byproducts of brain activity, but our recall of dreams may still have psychological significance.

HYPNOSIS

▶ Can you be hypnotized against your will?

Hypnosis is a well-known but still poorly understood phenomenon. Tests of *hypnotic susceptibility* suggest that some people cannot be hypnotized. Hypnotized people tend to focus attention on the hypnotist and passively follow instructions. They become better at fantasizing and role taking. They may exhibit apparent age regression, experience posthypnotic amnesia, and obey posthypnotic suggestions.

State theory sees hypnosis as a special state of consciousness. *Role theory* suggests that hypnosis creates a special social role that gives people permission to act in unusual ways. *Dissociation theory* combines aspects of role and state theories, suggesting that hypnotized individuals enter into a social contract with the hypnotist to allow normally integrated mental processes to become dissociated and to share control over these processes.

Hypnosis is useful in the control of pain and the reduction of nausea associated with cancer chemotherapy. Meditation is a set of techniques designed to create an altered state of consciousness characterized by inner peace and increased awareness. The consistent practice of meditation has been associated with reductions in stress-related problems such as anxiety and high blood pressure.

PSYCHOACTIVE DRUGS

▶ How do drugs affect the brain?

Psychoactive drugs affect the brain, changing consciousness and other psychological processes. *Psychopharmacology* is the field that studies drug effects and their mechanisms. Psychoactive drugs exert their effects primarily by influencing specific neurotransmitter systems and, hence, certain brain activities. To reach brain tissue, drugs must cross the *blood-brain barrier.* Drugs that mimic the receptor effects of a neurotransmitter are called *agonists*; drugs that block the receptor effects of a neurotransmitter are called *antagonists.* Some drugs alter the release or removal of specific neurotransmitters, thus affecting the amount of neurotransmitter available for receptor effects.

Adverse effects such as *substance abuse* often accompany the use of psychoactive drugs. *Psychological dependence, addiction* (physical dependence), *tolerance,* and a *withdrawal syndrome* may result. Drugs that produce dependence share the property of directly stimulating certain dopamine-sensitive areas of the brain known as pleasure centers. The consequences of using a psychoactive drug depend both on how the drug affects neurotransmitters and on the user's expectations.

Alcohol and barbiturates are examples of *depressants.* They reduce activity in the central nervous system, often by enhancing the action of inhibitory neurotransmitters. They have considerable potential for producing both psychological and physical dependence.

Stimulants, such as amphetamines and cocaine, increase behavioral and mental activity mainly by increasing the action of dopamine and norepinephrine. These drugs can produce both psychological and physical dependence. Caffeine, one of the world's most popular stimulants, may also create dependence. Nicotine is a potent stimulant. And MDMA, which has both stimulant and hallucinogenic properties, is one of several psychoactive drugs that can permanently damage brain tissue.

Opiates such as opium, morphine, and heroin are highly addictive drugs that induce sleep and relieve pain.

LSD and marijuana are examples of *hallucinogens,* or psychedelics. They alter consciousness by producing a temporary loss of contact with reality and changes in emotion, perception, and thought.

Learn by Doing

Put It in Writing

Watch a prime-time television program, and make notes on how alcohol, nicotine, cocaine, or other drugs played a role in the story. Now think about what you saw, and write a one-page paper describing the messages the show sent to viewers about drugs. Did it directly or indirectly approve or disapprove of drug use? Did it lead viewers to expect particular effects from particular drugs? Conclude by considering what effects these drug-related messages might have on viewers, especially young children.

Personal Learning Activity

For the next two weeks, keep a note pad or tape recorder by your bed, and write down or record your dreams as soon as you awaken. During this same period, use a diary or calendar to jot down significant events, problems, and emotional reactions in your waking life. Then compare the two sets of information. Do you see any correlation? For example, did any of your life events appear in your dreams? Did any dreams contain wished-for solutions to the problems or challenges you were facing at the time? What do you think your own data might say about the meaning of dreams in general? *For additional projects, see the Personal Learning Activities in the corresponding chapter of the study guide that accompanies this text.*

Step into Action

Courses

History of Psychology
Neuropsychology
Cognitive Psychology
Psychopharmacology
Computational Neuroscience
Sleep

Movies

An American Werewolf in London (nightmares)
Boyz N the Hood (role of drugs and alcohol in adolescent development)
Days of Wine and Roses, Leaving Las Vegas; When a Man Loves a Woman (alcoholism)
Deadly Dreams (portrayal of dreams as glimpses of the future)
Rush; Trainspotting; Basketball Diaries (drug addiction)
Stir of Echoes; Hypnosis (myths and misconceptions about hypnosis)
Sacred Sleep: The Power of Dreams (various cultures view the meaning of dreams)

Books

Susan Cheever, *Note Found in a Bottle: My Life as a Drinker* (Washington Square Press, 2000) (memoir of an alcoholic)
Barnaby Conrad, *Time Is All We Have* (Cameron, 1992) (a month at the Betty Ford Treatment Center)
Nicholas Humphrey, *A History of the Mind: Evolution and the Birth of Consciousness* (Copernicus, 1999) (description of how consciousness has arisen from brain activity)
Ernest Keen, *Chemicals for the Mind: Pharmacology and Human Consciousness* (Praeger, 2000) (theories of consciousness and drugs' effects on it)

Caroline Knapp, *Drinking: A Love Story* (Delta, 1997) (a woman explores the roots of her alcohol addiction)
Robert M. Julien, *A Primer of Drug Action: A Concise, Nontechnical Guide to the Actions, Uses, and Side Effects of Psychoactive Drugs* (Rev. ed.) (W. H. Freeman, 2001) (the title says it all)
Daniel Goleman, *The Meditative Mind: Varieties of Meditative Experience* (J. P. Tarcher, 1996) (meditation and its effects)
Steven J. Lynn, Irving Kirsch, and Judith W. Rhue (Eds.), *Casebook of Clinical Hypnosis* (American Psychological Association, 1996) (summary of clinical cases by distinguished hypnotherapists)
Joseph Barber (Ed.), *Hypnosis and Suggestion in the Treatment of Pain* (Norton, 1996) (case studies in pain management using hypnosis)
Stanley Coren, *Sleep Thieves: An Eye-Opening Exploration into the Science and Mysteries of Sleep* (Free Press, 1996) (an introduction to sleep research)
Mary A. Carskadon (Ed.), *Encyclopedia of Sleep and Dreaming* (Macmillan, 1996) (a comprehensive set of research articles on sleep and dreaming)

The Web

The World Wide Web is a good source of additional information about the science of psychology, provided you use it carefully and think critically about the information you find. The web site that accompanies this text offers many resources relevant to this chapter. These resources include interactive NetLab exercises; Thinking Critically and Evaluating Research exercises; ACE chapter quizzes; recommended web links; and articles on current events, books, and movies. At http://college. hmco.com, select *Psychology* and then this textbook.

Review of Key Terms

Can you define each of the key terms in the chapter? Check your definitions against those on the pages listed in parentheses below or in the Glossary/Index at the end of the text.

addiction *(p. 148)*
agonists *(p. 147)*
altered state of consciousness *(p. 135)*
antagonists *(p. 147)*
blood-brain barrier *(p. 147)*
circadian rhythm *(p. 140)*
conscious level *(p. 130)*
consciousness *(p. 130)*
depressants *(p. 149)*
dissociation theory *(p. 145)*
dreams *(p. 142)*

hallucinogens *(p. 152)*
hypnosis *(p. 143)*
hypnotic susceptibility *(p. 143)*
insomnia *(p. 138)*
jet lag *(p. 140)*
lucid dreaming *(p. 142)*
narcolepsy *(p. 139)*
night terrors *(p. 140)*
nightmares *(p. 140)*
nonconscious level *(p. 130)*
opiates *(p. 152)*
preconscious level *(p. 131)*

psychoactive drugs *(p. 146)*
psychological dependence *(p. 148)*
psychopharmacology *(p. 146)*
rapid eye movement (REM) sleep *(p. 137)*
REM behavior disorder *(p. 140)*
role theory *(p. 145)*
sleep apnea *(p. 139)*
sleepwalking *(p. 140)*

slow-wave sleep *(p. 137)*
state of consciousness *(p. 130)*
state theory *(p. 144)*
stimulants *(p. 151)*
subconscious *(p. 131)*
substance abuse *(p. 147)*
sudden infant death syndrome (SIDS) *(p. 139)*
tolerance *(p. 148)*
unconscious *(p. 131)*
withdrawal syndrome *(p. 148)*

Multiple-Choice Self-Test

Select the best answer for each of the questions below. Then check your responses against the Answer Key at the end of the text.

1. Tyrrell is undergoing biofeedback training to help him regulate his blood pressure, a bodily function typically regulated at which level of consciousness?

    a. nonconscious
    b. preconscious
    c. subconscious
    d. unconscious

2. Sylandra hates her brother, but her therapist suggests that she is unable to let herself experience this unacceptable feeling. According to Freud, Sylandra's hatred for her brother most likely resides at the _____ level.

    a. conscious
    b. unconscious
    c. nonconscious
    d. preconscious

3. During her first semester at college, Zandra never noticed the framed Rembrandt prints in the hallway of her classroom building. Then, in an art appreciation class the next semester, she found that she liked Rembrandt paintings more than those by other artists, although she'd never had a preference for his work before. Zandra has experienced

    a. the prosopagnosia effect.
    b. the mere-exposure effect.
    c. binocular priming.
    d. visual masking.

4. Edie has purchased a tape that supposedly contains subliminal messages to help her lose weight. According to the Thinking Critically section in this chapter, Edie's success in losing weight most likely depends on

    a. the content of the subliminal messages.
    b. her expectation that the subliminal messages will help.
    c. how relaxed the subliminal messages make her feel.
    d. the number of times the subliminal messages occur.

5. Mitch, a well-behaved adolescent, smoked marijuana after being encouraged to do so by his friends. After watching his friends tip over garbage cans, he began to engage in the same behavior—something he had never done before and normally would not do. This suggests that Mitch is

    a. in an altered state of consciousness.
    b. in a preconscious state.
    c. under the influence of priming.
    d. under the influence of a stimulant.

6. In an experiment, Leroy is connected to an EEG machine and a muscle tension monitor as he sleeps. When his brain waves are similar to those of an awake person, but there is near-paralysis in his muscles, the researcher can conclude that Leroy is in _____ sleep.

    a. stage 1
    b. stage 2
    c. stage 4
    d. REM

7. Alena, a legal aid attorney, often drops her head on her desk and falls into a deep sleep in the middle of the day while working on a case. This occurs most often when she has a deep emotional involvement with a particular case. Her doctor attributes her _____ to a deficiency of the neurotransmitter orexin.

    a. hypersomnia
    b. narcolepsy
    c. insomnia
    d. night terrors

8. The "back to sleep" program, which advises parents to have their babies sleep face-up, has greatly reduced the incidence of _____ in the United States.

    a. SIDS
    b. night terrors
    c. REM behavior disorder
    d. insomnia

9. Benjamin Franklin said, "Early to bed and early to rise, makes a man healthy, wealthy, and wise." A psychologist who knows about circadian rhythms would probably make which statement instead?

    a. "Whenever you bed, whenever you rise, a change in your rhythm will be your demise."
    b. "Bed when you will, rise when you wish, it just doesn't make that big of a diff."
    c. "Early to bed, early to rise, makes a man grisly and grumpy, but wise."
    d. "Bed after midnight will make you uptight."

10. Sleep research suggests that REM sleep may be important for all of the following except

    a. improving the functioning of neurons that use norepinephrine.
    b. developing, checking, and expanding the brain's nerve connections.
    c. restoring the body's and brain's energy stores for the next day's activity.
    d. establishing memories of emotional information

11. According to the activation-synthesis theory, dreams

    a. help our brain analyze and consolidate information.
    b. satisfy unconscious urges and resolve unconscious conflicts.
    c. are hallucinations.
    d. are meaningless, random byproducts of REM sleep.

12. Lavonne volunteered to participate in a hypnosis study. After being hypnotized, she put her hand in painfully cold ice water. She said she felt no pain, but she pressed a button indicating that "some part of her" was experiencing pain. This result supports the _____ theory of hypnosis.

    a. role
    b. state
    c. dissociation
    d. James-Lange

13. Hypnosis has been especially effective in

    a. connecting with past lives.
    b. improving memory.
    c. pain control.
    d. lowering cholesterol.

14. Norman has found himself a quiet spot, settled into a comfortable position, started using his mantra, and assumed a passive attitude. He is most likely about to

    a. meditate.
    b. enter self-hypnosis.
    c. go to sleep.
    d. daydream.

15. Dr. Lyman has developed a new drug that treats movement disorders by blocking dopamine receptors. Dr. Lyman's new drug is a dopamine

    a. agonist.
    b. antagonist.
    c. reuptake blocker.
    d. placebo.

16. Vincent has been using cocaine because he says it gives him an edge that helps him focus. Lately, though, he finds he needs larger amounts of the drug to achieve the same effect. Vincent has developed a(n) _____ cocaine.

    a. tolerance for
    b. aversion to
    c. withdrawal syndrome for
    d. synaptic potential for

17. Which of the following is true about alcohol?

    a. A given amount of alcohol will affect a man more than a woman.
    b. Alcohol's effects are the same whether it is consumed slowly or quickly.
    c. There are no genetic predispositions toward alcohol abuse.
    d. Dopamine agonists reduce alcohol cravings.

18. A young man experiencing hallucinations is brought to a hospital emergency room. Which of the following drugs could his doctor rule out as a likely cause of the hallucinations?

    a. MDMA
    b. cocaine
    c. caffeine
    d. LSD

19. Abel took a drug to reduce the pain in his broken arm. The drug Abel took to reduce his pain would be classified as a(n)

    a. depressant.
    b. opiate.
    c. hallucinogen.
    d. stimulant.

20. Yeh is doing research for a term paper about legalizing the use of marijuana in the United States. If her research is accurate, she is likely to learn all of the following except which one?

    a. Marijuana has been used successfully in treating asthma, glaucoma, chronic pain, and nausea from chemotherapy.
    b. Marijuana increases memory function and creativity.
    c. It is legal to grow and use marijuana for medicinal purposes in Canada.
    d. Doctors have found that marijuana may help treat some types of cancer.

5

Learning

Live and learn. This simple phrase captures the idea that learning is a lifelong

process that affects our behavior every day. Understanding how learning takes place is an important part of understanding ourselves. Sometimes, learning involves linking signals, as when we learn to associate wailing sirens with ambulances. Other times, learning depends on what happens after we do something—whether we receive praise or punishment, for example. But learning is more than these kinds of associations. What we think and how we feel about life's signals and consequences also have an impact on what we learn to do, and not do. Blend in practice and feedback about our behavior, mix well, and you have all the ingredients of the learning process.

Reading this chapter will help you to answer the following questions:

► **How did Russian dogs teach psychologists about learning?**

► **How do reward and punishment work?**

► **Can people learn to be helpless?**

► **What should teachers learn about learning?**

Like most newborn babies, Jeffrey cried until he was fed. He awakened at 3 A.M. nearly every morning, hungry and crying for food. And as she had done every day since he was born, his mother would put on her slippers and walk down the tile hallway to his bedroom. After a quick change of his diaper came the feeding. By the time he was four months old, Jeffrey would cry for about a minute and then quietly wait a few more minutes for his mother to arrive for his feeding. One particular morning, as his mother was halfway down the hall, she stopped in her tracks as she felt a sneeze coming. She pinched her nostrils together, and the urge to sneeze passed. However, she noticed that Jeffrey had begun to cry again. This was unusual. She began to walk again, and he quieted. Her scientific curiosity aroused, she walked a few steps, then stopped, then started, then stopped. She discovered that Jeffrey stopped crying when he heard her footsteps but resumed crying when he did not hear her coming.

Jeffrey had learned a lot in the four months since his birth. He could anticipate events and predict outcomes based on the meaning of certain sounds. Like all of us, he showed an ability to learn about relationships in the environment and to adjust to them. This adjustment to changes in the environment is called *adaptation*. Along with adaptation comes expectations and predictions about what is and what is not likely to occur in our world. The entire process of development, from birth to death, involves adapting to increasingly complex, ever-changing environments, using continuously updated knowledge and skills gained through experience.

All species exhibit, to some degree, the ability to adapt to changing environments. Individual variability in this ability shapes the evolution of behavior and appearance in animals and humans. As Charles Darwin noted, individuals who don't adapt may not survive to reproduce. Many forms of adaptation follow the principles of learning.

Learning is a relatively permanent change in behavior or knowledge due to experience. We are born with some behaviors and knowledge, acquire others through maturation, and learn still others. Some of our sayings, such as "Once burned, twice shy" and "Fool me once, shame on you; fool me twice, shame on me," reflect this vital learning process. In fact, learning plays a central role in most aspects of human behavior. If you want to know who you are and how you became the person you are today, examining what and how you have learned is a good place to start.

You learn primarily by identifying relationships between events and noting the regularity of patterns in the world around you. When two events repeatedly take place together, you can predict that one will occur based on what you know about the other. Jeffrey predicted his feeding from hearing his mother's footsteps. You have learned that a clear blue sky means dry weather, that too little sleep makes you irritable, that you can reach someone on the telephone by pressing certain buttons, and that yelling orders motivates some people and angers others. Some learning takes place consciously, as when you study for an exam, but as mentioned later, you can also learn things without being aware you are doing so (Watanabe, Náñez, & Sasaki, 2001).

This chapter describes what psychologists now know about the fundamental principles of learning. These include a form of learning called *operant conditioning*, in which rewards and punishments alter the frequency of observable behavior. There is also *classical conditioning*, a form of learning in which specific signals come to trigger behavior. In addition, there are cognitive processes that underlie some of the most complex forms of learning, such as the ability to learn from watching others. Let's begin by considering classical conditioning.

Classical Conditioning: Learning Signals and Associations

▶ **How did Russian dogs teach psychologists about learning?**

At the first notes of the national anthem, a young athlete's heart may begin to pound. Those sounds signal that the game is about to begin. Similarly, a flashing red light on your car's instrument panel might make your adrenaline flow, because it means that something is wrong with the engine. People are not born with these reactions. They have learned them from associations between events in the world. The experimental study of this kind of learning was begun, almost by accident, by Ivan Petrovich Pavlov.

Pavlov's Discovery

Pavlov is one of the best-known figures in psychology, but he was not a psychologist. He was a Russian physiologist who won the Nobel Prize in 1904 for his research on the digestive system of dogs. In the course of this research, Pavlov noticed a strange phenomenon. His dogs sometimes salivated, or drooled, when no food was present. For instance, they salivated when they saw the assistant who normally brought their food, even if he was empty-handed.

Pavlov devised a simple experiment to determine how salivation could occur without an obvious physical cause, such as food. First he performed an operation to divert a dog's saliva into a container, allowing him to measure precisely how much was secreted. Next he placed the dog in an apparatus similar to the one shown in Figure 5.1.

The experiment had three phases. In the first phase, Pavlov and his associates confirmed that when meat powder was placed on the dog's tongue, the dog automatically salivated (Anrep, 1920). They also confirmed that the dog did not automatically salivate in response to neutral stimuli, such as a white lab coat or a tone. The researchers thus established the existence of the two basic components for Pavlov's experiment: (1) a natural reflex (in this case, automatic salivation to meat powder placed on the dog's

learning   The modification of pre-existing behavior and understanding.

classical conditioning   A procedure in which a neutral stimulus is paired with a stimulus that elicits a reflexive response until the neutral stimulus alone comes to elicit a similar response.

figure 5.1

Apparatus for Measuring Conditioned Responses

In this more elaborate version of Pavlov's original apparatus, the amount of saliva flowing from a dog's mouth is measured and then recorded on a slowly revolving drum of paper.

Pen recording on cylinder

tongue) and (2) a neutral stimulus (the sound of a tone, which by itself would cause no salivation). A *reflex* is a swift, automatic response to a stimulus, such as shivering in the cold or jumping when you are jabbed with a needle. A neutral stimulus is one that does not elicit the reflex being studied.

In the second phase of Pavlov's experiment, the tone sounded, and meat powder was placed in the dog's mouth. The dog salivated. This pairing of the tone and the meat powder was repeated several times. Then, in the third phase, the tone was sounded, but no meat powder was presented. The dog again salivated. The tone by itself now made the dog salivate. The tone had come to predict the presentation of the meat powder. You may have seen the same principle in action when you open a can of pet food with an electric can opener. The sound of the can opener may bring your pet running. It means that food is coming.

Pavlov's experiment demonstrated what we now call **classical conditioning**. In this procedure, a neutral stimulus is repeatedly paired with a stimulus that already triggers a reflexive response, until the previously neutral stimulus alone provokes a similar response. Figure 5.2 shows the basic elements of classical conditioning. The stimulus that

figure 5.2

Classical Conditioning

Before classical conditioning has occurred, meat powder on a dog's tongue produces salivation, but the sound of a tone—a neutral stimulus—does not. During the process of conditioning, the tone is repeatedly paired with the meat powder. After classical conditioning has taken place, the sound of the tone alone acts as a conditioned stimulus, producing salivation.

PHASE 1: Before conditioning has occurred

UCS (meat powder) → UCR (salivation)

Neutral stimulus (tone) → Orienting response

PHASE 2: The process of conditioning

Neutral stimulus (tone) followed by UCS (meat powder) → UCR (salivation)

PHASE 3: After conditioning has occurred

CS (tone) → CR (salivation)

figure 5.3

Changes over Time in the Strength of a Conditioned Response

As the conditioned stimulus (CS) and the unconditioned stimulus (UCS) are repeatedly paired during initial conditioning, the strength of the conditioned response (CR) increases. During extinction, the strength of the CR decreases as more trials occur in which the CS is presented without the UCS. Eventually the CR disappears. However, after a brief period, the CR reappears if the CS is again presented.

naturally elicits a response *without* conditioning, such as the meat powder in Pavlov's experiment, is called the **unconditioned stimulus (UCS).** The automatic, unlearned, reflexive response to this stimulus is called the **unconditioned response (UCR).** The neutral stimulus (tone), after being paired with the unconditioned stimulus (meat powder), is called the **conditioned stimulus (CS),** and the response it comes to trigger is a learned or **conditioned response (CR).**

Conditioned Responses over Time: Extinction and Spontaneous Recovery

If a barking dog bit you in the past, you may be afraid whenever you hear a dog barking now. The more bad experiences you have had with dogs, the stronger will be your learned distress in response to the sound of barking. In the language of classical conditioning, continued pairings of a conditioned stimulus (CS/bark) with an unconditioned stimulus (UCS/bite) strengthen the conditioned response (CR/distress). The curve on the left side of Figure 5.3 shows an example: Repeated associations of a tone (CS) with meat powder (UCS) caused Pavlov's dogs to increase their salivation (CR) to the tone alone.

What if the meat powder (UCS) is no longer given? In general, the conditioned response will gradually disappear through a process known as **extinction** (see the center section of Figure 5.3). Extinction is the result of eliminating the UCS (meat powder) and repeatedly presenting the CS (tone) alone. Eventually, the CS (tone) will no longer elicit the CR (salivation). If the CS (tone) and the UCS (meat powder) are again paired after the conditioned response has been extinguished, the conditioned response returns to its original strength very quickly. This quick relearning of a conditioned response after extinction is called **reconditioning.** Because reconditioning takes much less time than the original conditioning, extinction must not have completely erased the association between the conditioned stimulus and the conditioned response.

The right side of Figure 5.3 shows additional evidence for this conclusion. An extinguished conditioned response will temporarily reappear if, after some time delay, the conditioned stimulus occurs without the unconditioned stimulus. This is called **spontaneous recovery,** the temporary reappearance of a conditioned response after extinction (and without further CS-UCS pairings). In general, the longer the time between extinction and the reappearance of the CS, the stronger the recovered conditioned response. However, unless the UCS is again paired with the CS, extinction rapidly occurs again. So, if you hear a song or smell the cologne associated with a former lover, there is a ripple of emotion—a conditioned response. Through its association with that person, the song or fragrance, which once had no particular significance, has become a conditioned stimulus. Even years later, it can provoke conditioned emotional reactions.

unconditioned stimulus (UCS)   A stimulus that elicits a response without conditioning.

unconditioned response (UCR)   The automatic, unlearned, reflexive reaction to a stimulus.

conditioned stimulus (CS)   An originally neutral stimulus that now elicits a conditioned response.

conditioned response (CR)   The response elicited by the conditioned stimulus.

extinction   The gradual disappearance of a conditioned response.

reconditioning   The relearning of a conditioned response following extinction.

spontaneous recovery   The temporary reappearance of a conditioned response after extinction.

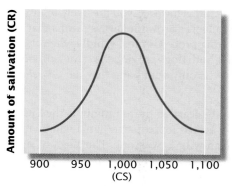

figure 5.4

Stimulus Generalization

The strength of a conditioned response (CR) is greatest when the original conditioned stimulus (CS) occurs, but the CR also appears following stimuli that closely resemble the CS. Here, the CS is the sound of a buzzer at a frequency of 1,000 hertz (Hz), and the CR is salivation. Notice that the CR generalizes well to stimuli at 990 or 1,010 Hz, but that it gets weaker and weaker following stimuli that are less and less similar to the CS.

stimulus generalization A process in which a conditioned response is elicited by stimuli similar to the original conditioned stimulus.

stimulus discrimination A process through which people learn to differentiate among similar stimuli and respond appropriately to each one.

Stimulus Generalization and Discrimination

After a conditioned response is learned, stimuli similar to the conditioned stimulus will also trigger the response. This phenomenon, called **stimulus generalization,** is illustrated by the fact that a person who was bitten by one particular dog may now show some fear of all dogs. Usually, the greater the similarity between a new stimulus and the original conditioned stimulus, the stronger the conditioned response will be. If the person was bitten by a small, curly-haired dog, fear responses would be strongest to other small dogs with similar hairstyles. Figure 5.4 shows an example involving sounds.

Stimulus generalization has some obvious advantages. For example, it is important for survival that if you get sick after drinking sour-smelling milk, you now avoid dairy products that have a similar odor. Generalization would be a problem if it had no limits, however. You would probably be justifiably frightened if you found a lion in your home, but imagine the problems if your fear response generalized so widely that you were panicked by a picture of a lion, or even by reading the word *lion*.

Stimulus generalization does not run wild, because it is usually balanced by a process called **stimulus discrimination**. Through stimulus discrimination you learn to differentiate among similar stimuli. You should be afraid of the dog that bit you, but not necessarily of every other dog in the world.

The Signaling of Significant Events

Classical conditioning allows one stimulus (the conditioned stimulus, or CS) to substitute for another (the unconditioned stimulus, or UCS) in producing a reflexive response. In this way, an animal or person can prepare for the arrival of the UCS. It is certainly adaptive to prepare for the arrival of food, for example. Having saliva automatically flowing in advance makes it easier to swallow food. Early research on classical conditioning focused on its role in controlling such automatic, involuntary behavior. However, psychologists now recognize the wider implications of classical conditioning. For example, some argue that organisms learn conditioned responses when one event reliably predicts, or *signals,* the appearance of another. These psychologists believe that classical conditioning does not simply produce robot-like, reflexive responses. Instead, they say, it provides a means through which animals and people develop *mental representations* of the relationships between events in their environment. These representations aid in adaptation and survival.

What determines whether and how a conditioned response is learned? Some important factors are the timing, predictability, and strength of signals. Others include how much attention signals receive and how easily they can be associated with other stimuli.

Timing If your teacher dismisses class every day at 9:59 and a bell rings at 10:00, the bell cannot prepare you for the dismissal. It comes too late to be a useful signal. For the same reason, classical conditioning works best when the conditioned stimulus precedes the unconditioned stimulus. This arrangement is adaptive. Normally, the presence of food, predators, or other significant stimuli is most reliably signaled by smells, sounds, or other events that come just before their appearance (Einhorn & Hogarth, 1982). So it is logical that the brain should be "wired" to form associations most easily between things that occur at about the same time. How close together do they have to be? There is no single "best" interval for every situation. Classical conditioning can occur when the interval between the CS and the UCS is less than a second or more than a minute. It all depends on the particular CS, UCS, and UCR that are involved (Longo, Klempay, & Bitterman, 1964; Pavlov, 1927). However, classical conditioning will always be weaker if the interval between the CS and the UCS is longer than what is ideal for the stimuli and responses in a given situation.

Predictability It is not enough for the CS merely to come before the UCS. Suppose your dogs, Moxie and Fang, have very different personalities. When Moxie growls, she sometimes bites, but sometimes she doesn't. Fang growls *only* before biting. Your conditioned fear response to Moxie's growl will probably occur slowly, because her growl does not reliably predict or signal the danger of a bite. However, you are likely to quickly develop a classically conditioned fear response to Fang's growl. It always means that you are in danger of being bitten. Classical conditioning proceeds most rapidly when the CS *always* signals the UCS, and *only* the UCS. Even if both dogs provide the same number of pairings of the CS (growl) and the UCS (bite), it is only with Fang that the CS *reliably* predicts the UCS (Rescorla, 1968).

Signal Strength   A conditioned response will be learned more rapidly if the UCS is strong than if it is weak. For example, a CS that acts as a predictive signal will be more rapidly associated with a strong shock (UCS) than with a weak one. The effect of signal strength on classical conditioning makes adaptive sense. It is more important to be prepared for major events than for those that have little impact.

   The same principle holds true for the strength of the conditioned stimulus. A conditioned response will be learned more quickly if the cue or CS attracts your attention. Louder tones, brighter lights, or other more noticeable events tend to get attention, so they are more rapidly associated with a UCS.

Attention   Many stimuli might occur just before a UCS in the natural environment. For instance, suppose you are at the beach eating a tasty apple, reading a magazine, listening to an Eminem CD, and enjoying the smell of suntan lotion just before being stung by a bee. Which of these stimuli is most likely to become a conditioned stimulus for fear? It depends partly on where you were focusing your attention when you were stung. The stimulus you most closely attended to—the one you most fully perceived—is most likely to become a CS that later triggers a conditioned response.

Second-Order Conditioning   Sometimes a learned signal (CS) can function as if it were an unlearned signal (UCS). For instance, suppose that a painful medical procedure (UCS) at the doctor's office becomes associated with the doctor's white coat. The white coat might then become a conditioned stimulus (CS) that can evoke a conditioned fear response. Once the white coat can trigger a conditioned fear response, it may take on some properties of an unconditioned stimulus. So at future visits, just the sight of the doctor's waiting room can become a conditioned stimulus for fear because it signals the appearance of the doctor's white coat, which in turn signals pain. When a conditioned stimulus acts like an unconditioned stimulus, creating conditioned stimuli out of events associated with it, the process is called **second-order conditioning.** This process is an adaptive "early warning system." It prepares us for damaging or life-threatening events (UCS) that are signaled not only by a CS but also by events that precede, and thus predict, that CS.

THE POWER OF SECOND-ORDER CONDITIONING   Cancer patients may feel queasy when they enter a chemotherapy room because they have associated the room with nausea-producing treatment. Through second-order conditioning, almost anything associated with the room can also become a conditioned stimulus for nausea. One cancer patient, flying out of town on a business trip, became nauseated just by seeing her hospital from the air.

second-order conditioning   A process in which a conditioned stimulus acts like an unconditioned stimulus, creating conditioned stimuli out of events associated with it.

© Herb Lingl/aerialarchives.com

TASTE AVERSIONS Humans can develop classically conditioned taste aversions, even to preferred foods. For example, Ilene Bernstein (1978) gave one group of cancer patients Mapletoff ice cream an hour before they received nausea-provoking chemotherapy. A second group ate this same distinctively flavored ice cream on a day they did not receive chemotherapy. A third group got no ice cream. Five months later, the patients were asked to taste several ice cream flavors. Those who had never tasted Mapletoff and those who had not eaten it in association with chemotherapy chose it as their favorite. Those who had eaten Mapletoff before receiving chemotherapy found it very distasteful.

Unfortunately, second-order conditioning can result in incorrect diagnoses of high blood pressure (hypertension). For some patients, the mere presence of a doctor or nurse becomes a conditioned stimulus for fear, and these patients' blood pressure rises as part of a conditioned fear response. Doctors call these people *white coat hypertensives* (Myers et al., 1996).

Biopreparedness Certain signals or events are especially likely to form associations with other signals or events (Logue, 1985). This apparently natural tendency for certain events to become linked suggests that organisms are "biologically prepared" or "genetically tuned" to develop certain conditioned associations.

The most dramatic example of this *biopreparedness* phenomenon is seen in conditioned taste aversions. In one study, rats were either shocked or made nauseous in the presence of a light, a buzzer, and flavored water. The rats formed only certain conditioned associations. Those that had been shocked developed a conditioned fear response to the light and the buzzer, but not to the flavored water. And those that had been made nauseous developed a conditioned avoidance of the flavored water, but they showed no particular response to the light or buzzer (Garcia & Koelling, 1966). These results reflect an adaptive process. Something we eat or drink will more likely produce nausea than will a noise or light. So nausea is more likely to become a conditioned response to an internal stimulus, such as a flavor, than to an external stimulus. In contrast, the sudden pain of a shock is more likely to have been caused by an external stimulus, so it makes evolutionary sense that the organism should be "tuned" to associate shock or sudden pain with a sight or sound.

Conditioned taste aversion illustrates that for certain kinds of stimuli, classical conditioning can occur even when there is a considerable delay between the CS (taste) and the UCS (nauseous sensations). Poisons do not usually produce their effects until minutes or hours after being ingested. However, people who have experienced food poisoning may never again eat the type of food that made them ill. Organisms that are biologically prepared to link taste signals with illness, even a delayed illness, are more likely to survive than organisms not so prepared.

Other evidence for biopreparedness comes from research showing that people are much more likely to develop a conditioned fear of harmless dogs or nonpoisonous snakes than of electrical outlets, knives, or other more dangerous objects (Öhman & Mineka, 2001, 2003). And experiments with animals suggest that they tend to learn the type of associations that are most relevant to survival in their environment (Staddon & Ettinger, 1989). Birds of prey, which strongly depend on vision to find food, may develop taste aversions on the basis of appearance. Coyotes and rats depend more on their sense of smell, so they tend to develop aversions related to odor.

applying psychology **PREDATOR CONTROL THROUGH CONDITIONING** In the western United States, some ranchers lace a sheep carcass with enough lithium chloride to make wolves and coyotes nauseous. The predators associate nausea with the smell and taste of sheep and afterward stay away from the ranchers' flocks. A similar program supported by the government of India has greatly reduced the human death toll from tiger attacks. Stuffed dummies are connected to a shock generator and placed in areas where tigers have killed people. When the animals approach the dummies, they receive a shock (UCS). After learning to associate shock with the human form (CS), the tigers tend to avoid people (CR).

Some Applications of Classical Conditioning

The principles of classical conditioning are summarized in "In Review: Basic Processes of Classical Conditioning." These principles have proven useful in many areas, including overcoming fears and diagnosing Alzheimer's disease.

Phobias   *Phobias* are intense, irrational fears of objects or situations. Either the objects or situations are not dangerous, or they are less dangerous than the fear response would suggest. Classical conditioning often plays a role in the development of such fears (Bouton, Mineka, & Barlow, 2001). As mentioned earlier, a person frightened by a dog may learn a fear that is so intense and generalized that it leads the person to avoid all dogs and all situations where dogs might be encountered. Classically conditioned fears can be extremely long-lasting, especially when they are based on experiences with strong unconditioned stimuli. Combat veterans and victims of violent crime, terrorism, or other traumatic events may show intense fear responses to trauma-related stimuli for many years afterward.

Classical conditioning has also been used to treat phobias (see the chapter on treatment of psychological disorders). Joseph Wolpe (1958) pioneered the development of this methodology. He showed that irrational fears could be relieved through *systematic desensitization,* a procedure that associates a new response, such as relaxation, with a feared stimulus. To treat a thunderstorm phobia, for instance, a therapist might first teach the client to relax deeply and then associate that relaxation with increasingly intense sights and sounds of thunderstorms presented on videotape (Öst, 1978). Because, as Wolpe noted, a person cannot be relaxed and afraid at the same time, the new conditioned response (relaxation) to thunderstorms replaces the old one (fear).

Diagnosis of Alzheimer's Disease   A puff of air directed at your eye is an unconditioned stimulus that causes a reflexive unconditioned response, namely an eye blink. If each air puff is preceded by a flash of light, the light will become a conditioned stimulus

in review

BASIC PROCESSES OF CLASSICAL CONDITIONING

Process	Description	Example
Acquisition	A neutral stimulus and an unconditioned stimulus (UCS) are paired. The neutral stimulus becomes a conditioned stimulus (CS), eliciting a conditioned response (CR).	A child learns to fear (conditioned response) the doctor's office (conditioned stimulus) by associating it with the reflexive emotional reaction (unconditioned response) to a painful injection (unconditioned stimulus).
Stimulus generalization	A conditioned response is elicited not only by the conditioned stimulus but also by stimuli similar to the conditioned stimulus.	A child fears most doctors' offices and places that smell like them.
Stimulus discrimination	Generalization is limited so that some stimuli similar to the conditioned stimulus do not elicit the conditioned response.	A child learns that his mother's doctor's office is not associated with the unconditioned stimulus.
Extinction	The conditioned stimulus is presented alone, without the unconditioned stimulus. Eventually the conditioned stimulus no longer elicits the conditioned response.	A child visits the doctor's office several times for a checkup, but does not receive a shot. Fear may eventually cease.

?   *If your conditioned fear of spiders is triggered by the sight of other creatures that look like spiders, you are demonstrating stimulus _____.*

that can cause an eye blink on its own. Research with animals has demonstrated that the hippocampus, a brain structure that is damaged in the early stages of Alzheimer's disease, is involved in the development of this type of conditioned response (Green & Woodruff-Pak, 2000). That research is now being applied to help identify people who are at high risk for this devastating brain disorder. One study found that elderly people whose eye blink conditioning was impaired were the ones most likely to develop Alzheimer's disease within two or three years (Downey-Lamb & Woodruff-Pak, 1999). Knowing who is at high risk for Alzheimer's is important because it allows doctors to offer these people medication that might delay the emergence of the disease.

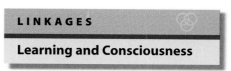

LINKAGES

Learning and Consciousness

People appear to be genetically "wired" to attend to, and orient toward, certain kinds of events. Loud noises and pain attract immediate attention. New stimuli are also very likely to attract attention. When a new stimulus is repeated often, though, it isn't new anymore. It no longer grabs our attention, and we stop focusing on it. We learn not to respond. This reduced responsiveness to a repeated stimulus, called **habituation,** is perhaps the simplest form of learning. It has been observed in organisms ranging from sea snails to humans (Gottfried, O'Doherty, & Dolan, 2003; Pinel, 1993). It provides another example of how learning helps organisms adapt to their environments (Schwartz & Reisberg, 1991). A theory proposed by Richard Solomon suggests that habituation has a direct connection to classical conditioning and to certain drug effects.

According to Solomon's (1980) *opponent-process theory,* habituation is the result of two processes. These processes balance each other, like a seesaw. The first process is a relatively automatic, involuntary response—essentially an unconditioned response (UCR). The second, or opponent, process is a learned or conditioned response (CR) that follows and counteracts the first. For example, an injection of adrenaline produces an increase in heart rate (UCR), the first process. Then the opponent process decreases the heart rate somewhat. This second, counterbalancing process is a learned response (CR). If the UCS (injection) is repeated many times, the learned opposing response, or CR (slowed heart rate), occurs more quickly and with greater intensity. As the CR more strongly counteracts the UCR over time, the rise in heart rate caused by the injection gets smaller and smaller, resulting in the phenomenon we call *habituation.*

What would you expect to happen in the case of extended use of heroin, according to Solomon's theory? Initially, the first process (UCR) produces an intensely pleasurable "high." But with repeated use of the drug, the high is countered or neutralized as the opponent process (unpleasantness) becomes quicker and stronger. As a result, progressively larger doses of the drug are required to obtain the same drug high. According to Solomon, opponent processes could be the basis for the development of drug tolerance and addiction, described in the chapter on consciousness.

LINKAGES
Can learning shape the effect of a drug on consciousness?
(a link to consciousness)

Instrumental and Operant Conditioning: Learning the Consequences of Behavior

▶ **How do reward and punishment work?**

Classical conditioning is an important form of learning, but it cannot explain most of what you learn on a daily basis. In classical conditioning, neutral and unconditioned stimuli are predictably paired. The result is an association of the two. This association is

habituation   Reduced responsiveness to a repeated stimulus.

figure 5.5

Thorndike's Puzzle Box

This drawing illustrates the kind of puzzle box used in Thorndike's research. His cats learned to open the door and reach food by stepping on the pedal, but the learning occurred gradually. Some cats actually took longer to get out of the box on one trial than on a previous trial.

figure 5.6

B. F. Skinner (1904–1990)

In the operant conditioning chamber shown here, the rat can press a bar to obtain food pellets from a tube. Operant and instrumental conditioning are similar in most respects, but they do differ in one way. Instrumental conditioning is measured by how long it takes for a response (such as a bar press) to occur. Operant conditioning is measured by the rate at which responses occur. In this chapter, the term *operant conditioning* refers to both.

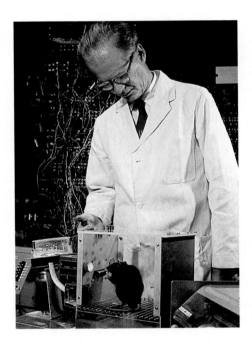

reflected in the fact that the conditioned stimulus now triggers the conditioned response. Notice that both stimuli occur before, or along with, the conditioned response. But you also learn many associations between responses and the stimuli that *follow* them, between behavior and its consequences. A child learns to say "please" to get a piece of candy. A headache sufferer learns to take a pill to escape the pain. A dog learns to "shake hands" to get a treat.

From the Puzzle Box to the Skinner Box

Edward L. Thorndike, an American psychologist, did much of the fundamental research on the consequences of behavior. Whereas Pavlov explored classical conditioning, Thorndike studied the ability of animals to think and reason. For example, he placed a hungry cat in a *puzzle box* like the one in Figure 5.5. The cat had to learn some response—such as stepping on a pedal—to unlock the door and get food. During the first few trials in the puzzle box, the cat explored and prodded until it finally hit the pedal. The animal eventually solved the puzzle, but very slowly. It did not appear to understand, or suddenly gain insight into, the problem (Thorndike, 1898). After many trials, though, the cat learned to solve the puzzle quickly each time it was placed in the box. What was it learning? Thorndike argued that any response (such as pacing or meowing) that did not produce a satisfying effect (opening the door) gradually became weaker. And any response (pressing the pedal) that did have a satisfying effect gradually became stronger. The cat's learning, said Thorndike, is governed by the **law of effect.** According to this law, if a response made to a particular stimulus is followed by a satisfying effect (such as food or some other reward), that response is more likely to occur the next time the stimulus is present. In contrast, responses that produce discomfort are less likely to be performed again. Thorndike described this kind of learning as *instrumental conditioning*, because responses are strengthened when they are instrumental in producing rewards (Thorndike, 1905).

About forty years after Thorndike published his work, B. F. Skinner extended and formalized many of Thorndike's ideas. Skinner noted that, during instrumental conditioning, an organism learns a response by *operating on* the environment. So he used the term **operant conditioning** to refer to the learning process in which observable behavior is changed by its consequences, specifically by rewards and punishments. To study operant conditioning, Skinner devised new tools. One of these was a small chamber that, despite Skinner's objections, came to be known as the *Skinner box* (see Figure 5.6).

figure 5.7

Positive and Negative Reinforcement

learn by doing   Remember that behavior is strengthened through positive reinforcement when something pleasant or desirable occurs following the behavior. Behavior is strengthened through negative reinforcement when the behavior results in the removal or termination of something unpleasant. To see how these principles apply in your own life, list two examples of situations in which your behavior was affected by positive reinforcement and two in which you were affected by negative reinforcement.

POSITIVE REINFORCEMENT

| **Behavior** You put coins into a vending machine. | → | **Presentation of a pleasant or positive stimulus** You receive a cold can of soda. | → | **Frequency of behavior increases** You put coins in vending machines in the future. |

NEGATIVE REINFORCEMENT

| **Behavior** In the middle of a boring date, you say you have a headache. | → | **Termination of an unpleasant stimulus** The date ends early. | → | **Frequency of behavior increases** You use the same tactic on future boring dates. |

Basic Components of Operant Conditioning

The chamber Skinner designed allowed researchers to arrange relationships between a particular response and its consequences. If a laboratory animal pressed a lever in the chamber, for example, it might receive a food pellet. The researchers could then analyze how consequences affect behavior. The phenomena seen in classical conditioning (stimulus generalization, stimulus discrimination, extinction, and spontaneous recovery) also appear in operant conditioning. In operant conditioning, however, the focus is on operants, reinforcers, and discriminative stimuli.

Operants and Reinforcers   Skinner coined the term *operant* or *operant response* to distinguish the responses in operant conditioning from those in classical conditioning. In classical conditioning, the conditioned response does not affect whether or when the stimulus occurs. Pavlov's dogs salivated when a buzzer sounded. The salivation had no effect on the buzzer or on whether food was presented. In contrast, an **operant** has some effect on the world. It is a response that operates on the environment. When a child says, "Momma, I'm hungry" and is then fed, the child has made an operant response that influences when food will appear.

A **reinforcer** is a stimulus event that increases the probability that the operant behavior will occur again. There are two main types of reinforcers: positive and negative. **Positive reinforcers** strengthen a response if they are presented after that response occurs. The food given to a hungry pigeon after it pecks a key is a positive reinforcer for key pecking. Among people, positive reinforcers can include food, smiles, money, and other desirable outcomes. Presentation of a positive reinforcer after a response is called *positive reinforcement*. **Negative reinforcers** are the *removal* of unpleasant stimuli, such as pain or noise. For example, the disappearance of headache pain after you take a pain reliever acts as a negative reinforcer that strengthens the taking of that pain reliever in the future. The process of strengthening behavior (taking pain relievers) that terminates an aversive stimulus (pain) is called *negative reinforcement*.

Notice that reinforcement always increases the likelihood of the behavior that precedes it, whether the reinforcer is adding something pleasant or removing something unpleasant. Figure 5.7 shows this relationship.

Escape and Avoidance Conditioning   The effects of negative reinforcement can be seen in both escape conditioning and avoidance conditioning. **Escape conditioning** occurs when we learn to behave in a way that stops an aversive stimulus. The

law of effect   A law stating that if a response made in the presence of a particular stimulus is rewarded, the same response is more likely to occur when that stimuus is encountered again.

operant conditioning   A process in which responses are learned on the basis of their rewarding or punishing consequences.

operant   A response that has some effect on the world.

reinforcer   A stimulus event that increases the probability that the response immediately preceding it will occur again.

positive reinforcers   Stimuli that strengthen a response if they follow that response.

negative reinforcers   The removal of unpleasant stimuli, such as pain, that strengthens responses that precede the removal.

escape conditioning   The process of learning responses that terminate an aversive stimulus.

left-hand panel of Figure 5.8 shows an example from an animal laboratory, but escape conditioning operates in humans, too. We not only learn to take pills to stop pain, but some parents learn to stop their child's annoying demands for a toy by agreeing to buy it. And television viewers learn to use the mute button to shut off obnoxious commercials.

When an animal or person responds to a signal in a way that *avoids* an aversive stimulus that has not yet arrived, **avoidance conditioning** has occurred (see the right-hand sections of Figure 5.8). Avoidance conditioning is an important influence on everyday behavior. We go to work even when we would rather stay in bed, we stop at red lights even when we are in a hurry, and we apologize for our mistakes even before they are discovered. Each of these behaviors helps us avoid a negative consequence, such as lost pay, a traffic ticket, or a scolding.

Avoidance conditioning often represents a marriage of classical and operant conditioning. If, as shown in Figure 5.8, a buzzer predicts shock (an unconditioned stimulus), the buzzer becomes a conditioned stimulus (CS). Through classical conditioning, the buzzer (now a CS) elicits a conditioned fear response (CR). Like the shock itself, conditioned fear is an unpleasant internal sensation. The animal then learns the instrumental response of jumping the barrier. The instrumental response (jumping) is reinforced because it reduces fear.

Once learned, avoidance is a difficult habit to break (Solomon, Kamin, & Wynne, 1953). Fear-reducing avoidance responses continue to be reinforced by fear reduction, even if the aversive stimulus that was originally avoided is no longer a threat. This continued avoidance prevents the opportunity to learn that the "rules" may have changed and that avoidance is no longer necessary. If you fear elevators and avoid them, you will never discover that they are safe. Avoidance conditioning may also prevent people from learning new, more desirable behaviors. Fear of doing something embarrassing may cause people with limited social skills to shy away from social situations, but it also prevents them from learning how to be successful in those situations.

The study of avoidance conditioning has not only expanded our understanding of negative reinforcement, but also has led some psychologists to consider more complex cognitive processes in learning. These psychologists suggest, for example, that in order for people to learn to avoid an unpleasant event (such as getting fired or paying a fine), they must have established an expectancy or other mental representation of that event. The role of such mental representations is emphasized in the cognitive theories of learning described later in this chapter.

Discriminative Stimuli and Stimulus Control   Even if you have been reinforced for telling jokes, you are not likely to do so when you are alone. Pigeons show similar wisdom. If they are reinforced for pecking at a button when a red light is on, but there is no reinforcement when a green light is on, they will eventually peck only when they see a red light. This behavior demonstrates the effect of **discriminative stimuli,** which are stimuli that signal whether reinforcement is available if a certain response is made. *Stimulus discrimination* occurs when an organism learns to make a particular response in the presence of one stimulus but not another (see Figure 5.9). The response is then said to be under *stimulus control*. Stimulus discrimination allows people or animals to learn what is appropriate (reinforced) and inappropriate (not reinforced) in particular situations.

Stimulus generalization also occurs in operant conditioning. That is, an animal or person will perform a response in the presence of a stimulus that is similar to, but not exactly like, a stimulus that has signaled reinforcement in the past. The more similar the new stimulus is to the old one, the more likely it is that the response will be performed. Suppose you ate a wonderful meal at a restaurant called "Captain Jack's," which was decorated to look like the inside of a sailing ship. You might later be attracted to other restaurants with nautical names or with interiors that look something like the one where you had that great meal.

Stimulus generalization and stimulus discrimination complement each other. In one study, for example, pigeons received food for pecking a key, but only when they saw certain kinds of artwork (Watanabe, Sakamoto, & Wakita, 1995). As a result, these birds

avoidance conditioning   The process of learning particular responses that avoid an aversive stimulus.

discriminative stimuli   Stimuli that signal whether reinforcement is available if a certain response is made.

Escape conditioning

Avoidance conditioning

Source: Adapted from Hintzman (1978).

figure 5.8

A Shuttle Box

A shuttle box has two sections, usually separated by a barrier, and its floor is an electric grid. Shock can be administered through the grid to either section. The left-hand panel shows escape conditioning, in which an animal learns to get away from a mild shock by jumping over the barrier when the electricity is turned on. The next two panels show avoidance conditioning. Here, the animal has learned to avoid shock altogether by jumping over the barrier when it hears a warning buzzer that sounds just before shock occurs.

learned to *discriminate* the works of the impressionist painter Claude Monet from those of the cubist painter Pablo Picasso. Later, when the birds were shown new paintings by other impressionist and cubist artists, they were able to *generalize* from the original artists to other artists who painted in the same style, as if they had learned the conceptual categories of "impressionism" and "cubism." We humans learn to place people and objects into even more finely detailed categories, such as "honest," "dangerous," or "tax deductible." We discriminate one stimulus from another and then, through generalization, respond similarly to all those we perceive to be in a particular category. As we'll see in the chapter on social psychology, prejudice is an example of category discrimination and then generalization about categories of people.

Forming and Strengthening Operant Behavior

Your daily life is full of examples of operant conditioning. You go to movies, parties, classes, and jobs primarily because doing so brings reinforcement. What is the effect of the type or timing of your reinforcers? How do you learn new behaviors? How can you get rid of old ones?

Shaping   Let's say you want to train your dog, Sugar, to sit and "shake hands." You figure that positive reinforcement should work, so you decide to give Sugar a treat every time she sits and shakes hands. But there's a problem with this plan. Smart as Sugar is, she

figure 5.9

Stimulus Discrimination

In this experiment, the rat could jump from a stand through any of three doors, but it was reinforced only if it jumped through the door that differed from the other two. The rat learned to do this quite well: On this trial, it discriminated vertical from horizontal stripes.

may never spontaneously make the desired response, in which case you'd never be able to give the reinforcer. The way around this problem is to shape Sugar's behavior. **Shaping** is the process of reinforcing *successive approximations* to the target behavior. For example, you might first give Sugar a treat whenever she sits down. Next, you might reinforce her only when she sits and partially lifts a paw. Finally, you might reinforce only complete paw lifting. Eventually, you would require Sugar to perform the entire sit-lift-shake sequence before giving the treat. Shaping is a powerful tool. Animal trainers have used it to teach chimpanzees to roller-skate, dolphins to jump through hoops, and pigeons to play Ping-Pong (Coren, 1999).

Secondary Reinforcement   Operant conditioning often begins using **primary reinforcers,** which are events or stimuli—such as food or water—that satisfy needs basic to survival. The effects of primary reinforcers are powerful and automatic. But constantly giving Sugar food as a reward can disrupt training, because she will stop to eat after every response. Also, once she gets full, food will no longer act as an effective reinforcer. To avoid these problems, parents and animal trainers capitalize on the principle of secondary reinforcement.

Secondary reinforcers are previously neutral stimuli that take on reinforcing properties after being paired with stimuli that are already reinforcing. In other words, they are rewards that people or animals learn to like. If you say "Good girl!" just before feeding Sugar, those words will become reinforcing after a few pairings. "Good girl!" can then be used alone to reinforce Sugar's behavior. It helps if the words are again paired with food every now and then. This process is actually another application of classical conditioning. The primary reinforcer (food) is the unconditioned stimulus. And because "Good girl!" has been repeatedly paired with the food, these sounds become a predictable signal for food. In short, the sound of the words becomes a conditioned stimulus (CS). For this reason, secondary reinforcers are sometimes called *conditioned reinforcers.*

Secondary reinforcement greatly expands the power of operant conditioning (Schwartz & Reisberg, 1991). Money is a prime example of a secondary reinforcer. Some people will do almost anything for it despite the fact that it tastes terrible and won't quench your thirst. Its reinforcing power lies in its association with the many rewards it can buy. Smiles and other forms of social approval (like the words "Good job!") are also

shaping   The reinforcement of responses that come successively closer to some desired response.

primary reinforcers   Events or stimuli that satisfy physiological needs basic to survival.

secondary reinforcers   Rewards that people or animals learn to like.

*"Oh, not bad. The light comes on, I press the bar, they write me a check.
How about you?"*

Although the artist may not have intended it, this cartoon nicely illustrates one way in which discriminative stimuli can affect behavior.

GETTING THE HANG OF IT Learning to eat with a spoon is, as you can see, a hit-and-miss process at first. However, this child will learn to hit the target more and more often as the food reward gradually shapes a more efficient, and far less messy, pattern of behavior.

important secondary reinforcers for human beings. However, what becomes a secondary reinforcer can vary widely from person to person and culture to culture. Tickets to a rock concert may be an effective secondary reinforcer for some people, but not others. A ceremony honoring outstanding job performance might be strongly reinforcing in an individualist culture, but the same experience might be embarrassing for a person in a collectivist culture, where group cooperation is given greater value than personal distinction (Miller, 2001). When carefully chosen, however, secondary reinforcers can build or maintain behavior, even when primary reinforcement is absent for long periods.

Delay and Size of Reinforcement Much of our behavior is learned and maintained because it is regularly reinforced. But many of us overeat, smoke, drink too much, or procrastinate, even though we know these behaviors are bad for us. We may want to eliminate them, but they are hard to change. We seem to lack "self-control." If behavior is controlled by its consequences, why do we do things that are ultimately self-defeating?

Part of the answer lies in the timing of reinforcers. For example, the good feelings (positive reinforcers) that follow excessive drinking are immediate. But because hangovers and other negative consequences are usually delayed, their effects on future drinking are weakened. In other words, operant conditioning is stronger when there is little delay in receiving a reinforcer. Under some conditions, delaying a positive reinforcer for even a few seconds can decrease the effectiveness of positive reinforcement. (An advantage of praise and other secondary reinforcers is that they can easily be delivered as soon as the desired response occurs.) The size of the reinforcer is also important. In general, conditioning is faster when the reinforcer is large than when it is small.

Schedules of Reinforcement When a *continuous reinforcement schedule* is in effect, a reinforcer is delivered every time a particular response occurs. This schedule can be helpful when teaching someone a new skill, but it can be impractical in the long run. Imagine how inefficient it would be, for example, if an employer had to deliver praise or pay following every little task employees performed all day long. In most cases, reinforcement is given only some of the time, on a *partial,* or *intermittent, reinforcement schedule.* Intermittent schedules are described in terms of when and how reinforcers are given. "When" refers to the number of responses that have to occur, or the amount of time that must pass, before a reinforcer will occur. "How" refers to whether the reinforcer will be delivered in a predictable or unpredictable way.

1. *Fixed-ratio (FR) schedules* provide reinforcement following a fixed (unchanging) number of responses. Rats might receive food after every tenth time they press a bar (FR 10) or after every twentieth time (FR 20). Factory workers might be paid for every five computers they assemble.

2. *Variable-ratio (VR) schedules* also call for reinforcement after a certain number of responses, but that number varies. As a result, it is impossible to predict which particular response will bring reinforcement. On a VR 30 schedule, for example, a rat will be reinforced after an *average* of thirty bar presses. This means that the reward sometimes comes after ten presses, sometimes after fifteen, and other times after fifty or more. Gambling offers humans a similar variable-ratio schedule. Slot machines pay off only after a frustratingly unpredictable number of lever pulls, averaging perhaps one in twenty.

3. *Fixed-interval (FI) schedules* provide reinforcement for the first response that occurs after some fixed time has passed since the last reward. On an FI 60 schedule, for instance, the first response after sixty seconds has passed will be rewarded, regardless of how many responses have been made during that interval. You may have noticed that some radio stations make use of fixed-interval schedules. Listeners who have won a call-in contest might have to wait at least ten days before they are eligible to win again.

learn by**doing**

REINFORCEMENT SCHEDULES ON THE JOB Make a list of all the jobs you have ever held, along with the reinforcement schedule on which you received your pay for each. Now consider which of the four types of schedules (fixed ratio, fixed interval, variable ratio, or variable interval) was most common, and which was most satisfying to you.

4. *Variable-interval (VI) schedules* reinforce the first response after some period of time, but the amount of time varies unpredictably. So on a VI 60 schedule, the first response that occurs after an *average* of 60 seconds is reinforced, but the actual time between reinforcements might vary anywhere from 1 to 120 seconds or more. Police in Illinois once used a VI schedule to encourage seat belt use. They stopped drivers at random times and awarded prizes to those who were buckled up (Mortimer et al., 1988). Kindergarten teachers, too, use VI schedules when they give rewards to children who are in their seats when a chime sounds at random intervals.

As shown in Figure 5.10, different schedules of reinforcement produce different patterns of responding (Skinner, 1961). Both fixed-ratio and variable-ratio schedules produce especially high response rates overall. The reason, in both cases, is that the frequency of reward depends directly on the rate of responding. Under a fixed-interval schedule, it does not matter how many responses are made during the time between rewards. Because the timing of the reinforcement is so predictable, the rate of responding typically drops immediately after reinforcement, then increases as the time for another reward approaches. When teachers schedule quizzes on the same day each week, most students will study just before each quiz and then almost cease studying immediately afterward. By contrast, the possibility of unpredictable "pop" quizzes (on a variable-interval schedule) typically generates more consistent studying patterns.

Schedules and Extinction   Ending the relationship between an operant response and its consequences weakens that response. In fact, failure to reinforce a response eventually *extinguishes* it. The response occurs less and less often and eventually may disappear. If you keep sending e-mail to someone who never replies, you eventually stop trying. Extinction in operant conditioning does not totally erase learned relationships, though. If a discriminative stimulus for reinforcement reappears

figure 5.10

Results of Four Partial Reinforcement Schedules

These curves illustrate the patterns of behavior typically seen under different reinforcement schedules. The steeper the curve, the faster the response rate; the thin diagonal lines crossing the curves show when reinforcement was given. In general, the rate of responding is higher under ratio schedules than under interval schedules.

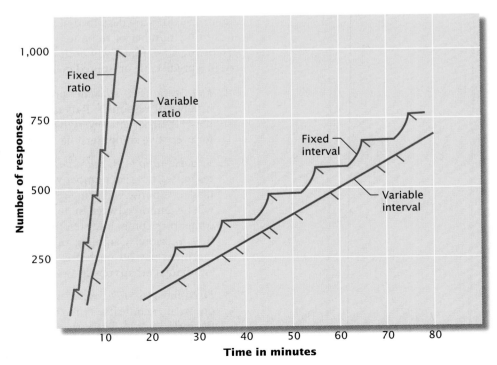

Source: Adapted from Skinner (1961).

SUPERSTITION AND PARTIAL REINFORCEMENT Partial reinforcement helps to sustain superstitious athletic rituals—such as a fixed sequence of actions prior to hitting a golf ball or shooting a free throw in a basketball game. If the ritual has preceded success often enough, failure to execute it may upset the player and disrupt performance. Boston Red Sox shortstop Nomar Garciaparra, shown here, tugs, loosens, and retightens each batting glove after every pitch. Those who watch sports have their superstitious rituals, too. One Green Bay Packers football fan said, "I have a certain outfit I wear. I will not drink anything but water when I'm watching. . . . And I have a touchdown dance I *have* to do or they won't score again" (Pearson, 2000).

partial reinforcement extinction effect A phenomenon in which behaviors learned under a partial reinforcement schedule are more difficult to extinguish than those learned on a continuous reinforcement schedule.

punishment The presentation of an aversive stimulus or the removal of a pleasant one following some behavior.

some time after an operant response has been extinguished, that response may recur (spontaneously recover). And if again reinforced, the response will be relearned rapidly.

In general, behaviors learned under a partial reinforcement schedule are far more difficult to extinguish than those learned on a continuous reinforcement schedule. This phenomenon is called the **partial reinforcement extinction effect.** Imagine, for example, that you are in a gambling casino, standing near a broken candy machine and a broken slot machine. You might deposit money in the broken candy machine once, but this behavior will probably stop (extinguish) very quickly. The candy machine should deliver its goodies on a continuous reinforcement schedule, so you can easily tell that it is not going to provide a reinforcer. But slot machines are known to offer rewards on an intermittent and unpredictable schedule. You might put in coin after coin, unsure of whether the machine is broken or is simply not paying off at that particular moment.

Partial reinforcement helps to explain why superstitious behavior is so resistant to extinction (Vyse, 2000). Suppose you had been out for a run just before hearing that you passed an important exam. The run did nothing to cause this outcome. The reward followed it through sheer coincidence. Still, for some people, this kind of *accidental reinforcement* can strengthen the behavior that appeared to "cause" good news. Those people might decide that it is "lucky" to go running after taking an exam. Similarly, someone who wins the lottery or a sports bet while wearing a particular shirt may begin wearing the "lucky shirt" more often. Of course, if the person wears the shirt often enough, something good is bound to follow every now and then, thus further strengthening the superstitious behavior on a sparse partial schedule.

Why Reinforcers Work

What makes a reinforcer reinforcing? For primary reinforcers, at least, the reason could be that they satisfy basic physiological needs for survival. Yet stimuli like saccharin, which have no nutritional value, can be as powerfully reinforcing as sugar, which is nutritious. And what about addictive drugs, which are also powerful reinforcers, even though they threaten the health of those who use them?

Research by biological psychologists suggests that reinforcers may work by exerting particular effects on the brain. In their classic study on this point, James Olds and Peter Milner (1954) discovered that mild electrical stimulation of certain areas of the hypothalamus can be a powerful reinforcer. Hungry rats will ignore food if they can press a lever that stimulates these "pleasure centers" in the brain (Olds, 1973). It is not yet clear whether physiological mechanisms underlie the power of all reinforcers, but evidence available so far certainly suggests that these mechanisms are important components of the process (Waelti, Dickinson, & Schultz, 2001). We already know, for example, that activation of dopamine systems is associated with the pleasure of many stimuli, including food, music, sex, the uncertainty of gambling, and some addictive drugs such as cocaine (Berns et al., 2001; Blood & Zatorre, 2001; Breiter et al., 2001; Cardinal et al., 2001; Ciccocioppo, Sanna, & Weiss, 2001).

Punishment and Learning

Positive and negative reinforcement *increase* the frequency of a response, either by presenting something pleasurable or by stopping something that is unpleasant. In contrast, **punishment** presents an aversive stimulus or terminates a pleasant one and *decreases* the frequency of the immediately preceding response. Swatting your cat with a newspaper when it begins chewing on your plants presents an aversive stimulus following a response. And taking away a child's TV privileges because of rude behavior is

figure 5.11

Two Kinds of Punishment

In one form of punishment, a behavior is followed by an aversive or unpleasant stimulus. In a second form of punishment, sometimes called *penalty,* a behavior is followed by termination of a pleasant stimulus. In either case, punishment decreases the chances that the behavior will occur in the future. Now you decide: A toddler reaches toward an electric outlet, and her father says "NO!" and gently taps her hand. Is that punishment or negative reinforcement? If you said *punishment,* you are right, because it will reduce the likelihood of the behavior that preceded it.

PUNISHMENT 1

Behavior You touch a hot iron.	→	**Presentation of an unpleasant stimulus** Your hand is burned.	→	**Frequency of behavior decreases** You no longer touch hot irons.

PUNISHMENT 2 (Penalty)

Behavior You're careless with your ice cream cone.	→	**Removal of a pleasant stimulus** The ice cream falls on the ground.	→	**Frequency of behavior decreases** You're not as careless with the next cone.

a kind of punishment—sometimes called *penalty*—that removes a positive stimulus (see Figure 5.11).

Punishment is often confused with negative reinforcement, but they are quite different. Just remember that reinforcement of any type always *strengthens* behavior, whereas punishment always *weakens* behavior. If shock is *turned off* when a rat presses a lever, that is negative reinforcement. It increases the probability that the rat will press the lever when shock occurs again. But if shock is *turned on* when the rat presses the lever, that is punishment. The rat will be less likely to press the lever again.

Although punishment can change behavior, it has some drawbacks (Gershoff, 2002). First, it does not "erase" an undesirable habit. It merely lowers the probability that it will occur again right way. In fact, children often repeat punished acts when they think they can do so without getting caught. Second, punishment can produce unwanted side effects. If you punish a child for swearing, the child may associate the punisher with the punishment and end up being afraid of you. Third, punishment is often ineffective unless it is given immediately after the undesirable behavior and each time that behavior occurs. If a child gets into the cookie jar and enjoys a few cookies before being discovered and punished, the effect of the punishment will be greatly reduced. Fourth, physical punishment can become aggression, even abuse, when given in anger. Because children tend to imitate what they see, frequent punishment may lead them to behave aggressively themselves (Gilbert, 1997). Finally, although punishment signals that inappropriate behavior has occurred, it does not specify what should be done instead. An "F" on a term paper indicates that the assignment was poorly done, but the grade alone tells the student nothing about how to improve.

figure 5.12

Life-Saving Punishment

This child suffered from chronic ruminative disorder, a condition in which he regurgitated all food. At left, the boy was approximately one year old and had been vomiting for four months. At right is the same child thirteen days after punishment with electric shock had eliminated the vomiting response; his weight had increased 26 percent. He was physically and psychologically healthy when tested six months, one year, and two years later (Lang & Melamed, 1969).

Source: Lang & Melamed (1969).

When used properly, however, punishment can be a valuable tool (Baumrind, Larzelere, & Cowan, 2002). As shown in Figure 5.12, for example, it can help children who suffer from certain developmental disorders or who engage in self-injurious behavior (Flavell et al., 1982). Punishment is especially effective when a few guidelines are followed. First, to prevent the development of a general fear of the punisher, specify why punishment is being given. Second, emphasize that the behavior, not the person, is being punished. Third, without being abusive, make sure the punishment is immediate and noticeable enough to eliminate the undesirable response. A half-hearted "Quit it" may actually reinforce a child's misbehavior, because almost any attention is rewarding to some children. And once a child gets used to overly mild punishment, the parent may resort to punishment that is far more severe than would have been necessary if stern, but moderate, punishment had been used in the first place. (You may have witnessed this *escalation effect* in grocery stores or restaurants when children ignore their parents' initially weak efforts to stop their misbehavior.) Fourth, identify and positively reinforce more appropriate responses.

When these guidelines are not followed, the beneficial effects of punishment may be wiped out or may be only temporary. As demonstrated in the U.S. prison system, punishment alone does not usually lead to rehabilitation. Following their release, about two-thirds of prison inmates are rearrested for felonies or serious misdemeanors within three years, and about 50 percent will go back to prison (Cassel & Bernstein, 2001; U.S. Department of Justice, 2002).

Some Applications of Operant Conditioning

Although the principles of operant conditioning were originally worked out with animals in the laboratory, they are valuable for understanding human behavior in an endless variety of everyday situations. ("In Review: Reinforcement and Punishment"

in review

REINFORCEMENT AND PUNISHMENT

Concept	Description	Example or Comment
Positive reinforcement	Increasing the frequency of behavior by following it with the presentation of a positive reinforcer—a pleasant, positive stimulus or experience	You say "Good job" after someone works hard to perform a task.
Negative reinforcement	Increasing the frequency of behavior by following it with the removal of an unpleasant stimulus or experience	You press the "mute" button on a TV remote control to remove the sound of an obnoxious commercial.
Escape conditioning	Learning to make a response that removes an unpleasant stimulus	A little boy learns that crying will cut short the time that he must stay in his room.
Avoidance conditioning	Learning to make a response that prevents exposure to an unpleasant stimulus	You slow your car to the speed limit when you spot a police car, thus avoiding being stopped and reducing the fear of a fine. Very resistant to extinction.
Punishment	Decreasing the frequency of behavior by either presenting an unpleasant stimulus or removing a pleasant one (penalty)	You swat the dog after she steals food from the table or take a favorite toy away from a child who misbehaves. A number of cautions should be kept in mind before using punishment.

? *Taking an aspirin can relieve headache pain, so people learn to do so through the process of _____ reinforcement.*

summarizes some key concepts of operant conditioning.) Effective use of reinforcements and punishments by parents, teachers, and peers is vital to helping children learn what is and is not appropriate behavior at the dinner table, in the classroom, or at a birthday party. People learn how to be "civilized" in their culture partly through experiencing positive and negative responses from others. And differing patterns of rewards and punishments for boys and girls underlie the development of behavior that fits culturally approved *gender roles,* a topic explored in more detail in the chapter on human development.

The scientific study of operant conditioning has led to numerous treatment programs for altering problematic behavior. Behavior modification programs that combine the use of rewards and extinction (or carefully administered punishment) have helped countless mental patients, mentally retarded or brain-damaged individuals, autistic children, and hard-to-manage youngsters to develop the behaviors they need to live happier and more productive lives (e.g., Alberto, Troutman, & Feagin, 2002; Pear & Martin, 2002). These programs include establishing goal behaviors, choosing reinforcers and punishers, and developing a systematic plan for applying them to achieve desired changes. Many self-help books also incorporate principles of positive reinforcement, recommending self-reward following each small victory in people's efforts to lose weight, stop smoking, avoid procrastination, or reach other goals (e.g., Grant & Kim, 2002; Rachlin, 2000).

When people cannot do anything to alter the consequences of a behavior, discriminative stimuli may hold the key to changing that behavior. For example, people trying to quit smoking often find it easier to abstain if, at first, they stay away from bars and other places where there are discriminative stimuli for smoking. Old cues can trigger old behavior, so they should avoid the old cues until new behavior can be established. Stimulus control can also help alleviate insomnia. Insomniacs tend to use their beds for activities such as watching television, writing letters, reading magazines, worrying, and so on. Soon the bedroom becomes a discriminative stimulus for so many activities that relaxation and sleep become less and less likely. *Stimulus control therapy* encourages insomniacs to use their beds only for sleeping, and perhaps sex, making it more likely that they will sleep better when in bed (Edinger et al., 2001).

LEARNING CULTURAL VALUES   The prevalence of aggressive behavior varies considerably from culture to culture, in part because some cultures reward it more than others. In some Inuit cultures, for example, aggressive behavior is actively discouraged and extremely rare (Banta, 1997). In many other cultures, it is all too common.

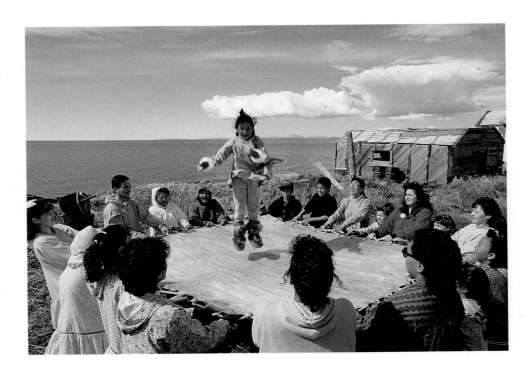

Cognitive Processes in Learning

▶ **Can people learn to be helpless?**

In the first half of the twentieth century, psychologists in North America tended to see classical and operant conditioning coming about through the automatic, unthinking formation or modification of associations between observable stimuli and observable responses. They gave little consideration to the role of mental activity that might accompany the learning process.

This strictly behavioral view of classical and operant conditioning is challenged by the cognitive approach, which has become increasingly influential in recent decades. Cognitive psychologists see a common thread in these two forms of learning. Both classical and operant conditioning, they argue, help animals and people to detect and understand what causes what (Young, 1995). By extension, both types of conditioning may result not only from automatic associations but also from more complex mental processes that underlie our adaptation to, and understanding of, the world around us (Dickinson, 2001). The importance of these cognitive processes—of how people represent, store, and use information—has been demonstrated in research on learned helplessness, latent learning, cognitive maps, insight, and observational learning.

Learned Helplessness

Babies learn that crying attracts attention. Children learn how to make the TV louder. Adults learn what it takes to succeed in the workplace. In other words, people learn to expect that certain actions on their part will cause certain consequences. But some events are beyond our control. What happens when actions have no effect on events, and especially when escape or avoidance behaviors fail? If such ineffectiveness is prolonged, one result may be **learned helplessness,** a tendency to give up on efforts to control the environment (Overmier, 2002; Seligman, 1975).

Learned helplessness was first demonstrated in animals. As described earlier, dogs in a shuttle box will learn to jump over a partition to escape a shock (see Figure 5.8). But if the dogs are first placed in a restraining harness and receive shocks that they cannot escape, they later do not even try to escape when the shock is turned on in the shuttle box (Overmier & Seligman, 1967). It is as if the animals had learned that "shock happens, and there is nothing I can do about it." Do people learn the same lesson?

learned helplessness A process in which a person or animal stops trying to exert control after experience suggests that no control is possible.

What lessons do abused and neglected children learn about their ability to get what they need from the environment? Do they learn that even their best efforts result in failure? Do they give up even trying? Why would a student with above-average ability tell a counselor, "I can't do math"? How do people develop an "I can't do it" attitude?

FOCUS ON RESEARCH

The "I Can't Do It" Attitude

■ **What was the researcher's question?**

Can lack of control over the environment lead to helplessness in humans? Donald Hiroto (1974) conducted an experiment to test the hypothesis that people develop learned helplessness either after experiencing lack of control or after simply being told that their control is limited.

■ How did the researcher answer the question?

Hiroto assigned research participants to one of three groups. One group heard a series of thirty random bursts of loud, obnoxious noise and, like dogs receiving inescapable shock, had no way to stop it. A second group could control the noise by pressing a button to turn it off. The third group heard no noise at all. After this preliminary phase, all three groups were exposed to eighteen additional bursts of noise, each preceded by a red warning light. During this second phase, *all* participants could stop the noise by moving a lever. However, they did not know whether to push the lever left or right on any given trial. Still, they could prevent the noise if they acted quickly enough. Before these new trials began, the experimenter told half the participants in each group that avoiding or escaping the noise depended on their skill. The other half were told that their success would be a matter of chance.

■ What did the researcher find?

The people who had previously experienced lack of control now failed to control noise on about four times as many trials as did those who had earlier been in control (50 percent versus 13 percent). This finding was similar to that of the research with dogs and inescapable shock. When the dogs were later placed in a situation where they could escape or avoid shock, they did not even try. Humans, too, seem to use prior experiences to guide later efforts to try, or not to try, to control their environment.

Expectation of control, whether accurate or not, also had an effect on behavior. In Hiroto's study, those participants who expected that skill could control the noise exerted control on significantly more trials than did those who expected chance to govern the result. This outcome occurred regardless of whether the participants had experienced control before.

■ What do the results mean?

These results support Hiroto's hypothesis that people, like animals, tend to make less effort to control their environment when prior experience suggests that those efforts will be in vain. But unlike animals, humans need only be *told* that they have no control or are powerless in order for this same effect to occur.

Hiroto's (1974) results appear to reflect a general phenomenon. When prior experience leads people to *believe* that there is nothing they can do to change their lives or control their destiny, they may stop trying to improve their lot (Faulkner, 2001; LoLordo, 2001; Peterson, Maier, & Seligman, 1993). Instead, they may passively endure painful situations. Has this ever happened to you?

■ What do we still need to know?

Further research is needed on when and how learned helplessness affects people's thoughts, feelings, and actions. For example, could learned helplessness explain why some battered women remain with abusive partners? We do know that learned-helplessness experiences are associated with the development of a generally pessimistic way of thinking that can produce depression and other mental disorders (Peterson & Seligman, 1984). People with this *pessimistic explanatory style* see the good things that happen to them as temporary and due to chance, and the bad things as permanent and due to internal factors (e.g., lack of ability). This explanatory style has, in fact, been associated with poor grades, inadequate sales performance, health problems, and other negative outcomes (Bennett & Elliott, 2002; Seligman & Schulman, 1986; Taylor, 2002). The exact mechanisms responsible for this connection are still unknown, but understanding how pessimistic (or optimistic) explanatory styles can lead to negative (or positive) consequences remains an important focus of research (e.g., Brennan & Charnetski, 2000). Research is also focusing on how best to minimize learned helplessness and maximize learned optimism in areas such as education, parenting, and psychotherapy (e.g., Jackson, Sellers, & Peterson, 2002).

latent learning   Learning that is not demonstrated at the time it occurs.

cognitive map   A mental representation of the environment.

Latent Learning and Cognitive Maps

Decades ago, Edward Tolman studied cognitive processes in learning by watching rats try to solve mazes. The rats' task was to find the goal box where food awaited. At first, the rats took many wrong turns. Over time, though, they made fewer and fewer mistakes. The behavioral interpretation of this result was that the rats learned a long chain of turning responses that were reinforced by food. Tolman disagreed and offered evidence for a cognitive interpretation.

In one of Tolman's studies, three groups of rats were placed in the same maze once a day for several consecutive days (Tolman & Honzik, 1930). For Group A, food was placed in the goal box of the maze on each trial. As shown in Figure 5.13, these rats gradually improved their performance. Group B also ran the maze once a day, but there was never any food in the goal box. The animals in Group B continued to make many errors. Neither of these results is surprising.

The third group of rats, Group C, was the critical one. For the first ten days, they received no reinforcement for running the maze and continued to make many mistakes. On the eleventh day, food was placed in the goal box for the first time. What do you think happened? On the day after receiving reinforcement, these rats made almost no mistakes (again, see Figure 5.13). In fact, their performance was as good as that of the group that had been reinforced every day. The single reinforcement trial on day 11 produced a dramatic change in their performance the next day.

Tolman argued that these results support two conclusions. First, because the rats in Group C improved their performance the first time they ran the maze after being reinforced, the reinforcement on day 11 could not have significantly affected their *learning* of the maze. Rather, the reinforcement simply changed their subsequent *performance*. They must have learned the maze earlier as they wandered around making mistakes on their way to the end of the maze. These rats demonstrated **latent learning**—learning that is not evident when it first occurs. (Latent learning occurs in humans, too; for example, after years of experience in your neighborhood, you could probably tell a visitor that the corner drugstore is closed on Sundays, even if you had never tried to go there on a Sunday yourself.) Second, the rats' sudden improvement in performance after the first reinforcement trial could have occurred only if the rats had earlier developed a cognitive map of the maze. A **cognitive map** is a mental representation of some physical arrangement—in this case, a maze.

Tolman concluded that cognitive maps develop naturally through experience, even in the absence of any overt response or reinforcement. Research on learning in the natural

figure 5.13

Latent Learning

This graph shows the average number of wrong turns that Tolman's rats made on their way to the goal box of a maze. Notice that when rats in Group C did not receive food reinforcement, they continued to make many errors. The day after first finding food in the goal box, however, they took almost no wrong turns! The reinforcement, argued Tolman, affected only the rats' performance; they must have learned the maze earlier, without reinforcement.

Source: Köhler (1976).

figure 5.14

Insight

Here are three impressive examples of problem solving by chimpanzees. At left, a chimp fixed a fifteen-foot pole in the ground, climbed to the top, and dropped down after grabbing a piece of fruit. In the center photo, the animal stacked two boxes from different areas of the compound, climbed to the top, and used a pole to knock down the fruit. The chimp at right stacked three boxes and climbed them to reach the fruit.

environment has supported this view. We develop mental maps of shopping malls and city streets, even when we receive no direct reward for doing so (Tversky & Kahneman, 1991). Having such a map allows you to tell that neighborhood visitor exactly how to get to the corner drugstore from where you are standing.

Much as Gestalt psychologists believe that a whole perception is more than the sum of its parts (see the chapter on sensation and perception), cognitive psychologists see learning as more than the sum of reinforcement effects and automatic associations. And just as our perceptions depend on the meaning we attach to sensations, some forms of learning require higher mental processes and depend on how the learner attaches meaning to events. To take just one example, being praised by a boss we respect may be more reinforcing than getting the same good evaluation from a boss we hate.

Insight and Learning

Wolfgang Köhler was a psychologist whose work on the cognitive aspects of learning happened almost by accident. He was visiting Tenerife, an island in the Atlantic Ocean, when World War I broke out in 1914. As a German in territory controlled by Germany's enemy, Britain, Köhler was confined there until the war ended in 1918. He used this time to study problem solving in a colony of local chimpanzees (Köhler, 1924).

For example, Köhler would put a chimpanzee in a cage and place a piece of fruit where the chimp could see it but not reach it. He sometimes hung the fruit too high to be reached, or placed it on the ground too far outside the animal's cage to be retrieved. Many of the chimps overcame these obstacles easily. If the fruit was out of reach beyond the cage, some chimps looked around, found a long stick, and used it to rake in the fruit. Surprised that the chimpanzees could solve these problems, Köhler tried more difficult tasks. Again, the chimps quickly got to the fruit, as Figure 5.14 illustrates.

Köhler's research convinced him that animals' problem solving does not have to depend on automatic associations developing slowly through trial and error. He used three particular observations to support this claim. First, once a chimpanzee solved one type of problem, it would immediately do the same thing in a similar situation. In other words, it acted as if it understood the problem. Second, Köhler's chimpanzees rarely tried a solution that did not work. Apparently, the solution was not discovered randomly, but "thought out" ahead of time and then acted out successfully. Third, the chimps often reached a solution quite suddenly. When confronted with a piece of fruit hanging from a string, for instance, a chimp would jump for it several times. Then it would stop jumping, look up, and pace back and forth. Finally it would run over to a wooden crate, place it directly under the fruit, and climb on top of it to reach the fruit. Once, when there were no other objects in the cage, a chimp went over to Köhler, dragged him by the arm until he stood beneath the fruit, and then started climbing up his back!

Köhler believed that the only explanation for these results was that the chimpanzees suddenly had insight into the problem as a whole. They did not, he said, solve the problem simply through forming associations between responses and consequences. Some psychologists have argued that insight does not develop as quickly as Köhler's descriptions suggest. They see **insight** as the result of actual trial-and error-experimentation (Harlow, 1949) or of an extended "mental trial-and-error" process in which people (and some animals) envision a course of action, mentally simulate its results, compare them with the imagined outcome of other alternatives, and then settle on the course of action most likely to aid complex problem solving and decision making (Klein, 1993).

Observational Learning: Learning by Imitation

People learn a lot from personal experience, but they can also learn by observing what others do, and what happens to them when they do it. Learning by watching others—a process called **observational learning,** or *social learning*—is efficient and adaptive. We don't have to find out for ourselves that a door is locked or an iron is hot if we have just seen someone else try the door or suffer a burn.

Modeling and Vicarious Conditioning   Children are particularly influenced by the adults and peers who act as *models* for appropriate behavior. In a classic experiment,

learn by doing   **LEARNING BY IMITATION**
Much of our behavior is learned by imitating others, especially those who serve as role models. To appreciate the impact of social learning in your life, list five examples of how your own actions, speech, appearance, or mannerisms have come to match those of a parent, a sibling, a friend, a teacher, or even a celebrity.

insight   An understanding about what is required to produce a desired effect.

observational learning   Learning by watching the behavior of others.

Albert Bandura showed nursery school children a film starring an adult and a large, inflatable, bottom-heavy "Bobo" doll (Bandura, 1965). The adult in the film punched the Bobo doll in the nose, kicked it, threw things at it, and hit its head with a hammer while saying things like "Sockeroo!" There were different endings to the film. Some children saw an ending in which the aggressive adult was called a "champion" by a second adult and rewarded with candy and soft drinks. Some saw the aggressor scolded and called a "bad person." Some saw a neutral ending in which there was neither reward nor punishment. After the film, each child was allowed to play alone with a Bobo doll. The way they played in this and similar studies led to some important conclusions about learning and the role of cognitive factors in it.

Bandura found that children who saw the adult rewarded for aggression showed the most aggressive acts in play (see Figure 5.15). They had received **vicarious conditioning,** a kind of observational learning through which a person is influenced by watching or hearing about the consequences of others' behavior. The children who had seen the adult punished for aggressive acts initially showed less aggression, but they still learned something. When later offered rewards for all the filmed aggressive acts they could perform, these children displayed just as many of these acts as the children who watched the adult being rewarded. Observational learning can occur even when there are no vicarious consequences; many children in the neutral condition also imitated the model's aggression.

Observational learning is a powerful source of human socialization throughout development (Bandura, 1999). Experiments show that children are more willing to help and share after seeing a demonstration of helping by an impressive model. This effect is observed even when several months have elapsed since the demonstration (Schroeder et al., 1995). Fears, too, can be learned by watching fearfulness in others (Kleinknecht, 1991).

figure 5.15

Observational Learning

Bandura found that after observing an aggressive model, many children imitate the model's acts precisely, especially if the model's aggression was rewarded.

Source: Bandura, Ross, & Ross (1963).

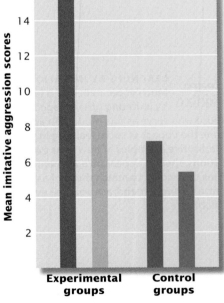

Mean imitative aggression scores

Experimental groups   Control groups

■ Aggressive model rewarded
■ Aggressive model punished
■ Nonaggressive model
■ No model

vicarious conditioning   A kind of observational learning through which a person is influenced by watching or hearing about the consequences of others' behavior.

If observational learning is important, then surely television—and televised violence—must teach children a great deal. It is estimated that the average child in the United States spends about two and a half hours each day watching television (Annenberg Public Policy Center, 2000). Much of what children see is violent. Prime-time programs in the United States present an average of 5 violent acts per hour. Some Saturday morning cartoons include more than 20 per hour (American Psychological Association, 1993; Gerbner, Morgan, & Signorielli, 1994). As a result, the average child will have witnessed at least 8,000 murders and more than 100,000 other acts of televised violence before finishing elementary school, and twice that number by age 18 (Annenberg Public Policy Center, 1999; Kunkel et al., 1996).

Psychologists have long speculated that watching so much violence might be emotionally arousing, making viewers more likely to react violently to frustration (Huston & Wright, 1989). In fact, there is evidence that exposure to media violence can trigger or amplify viewers' aggressive thoughts and feelings, thus increasing the likelihood that they will act aggressively (Anderson & Dill, 2000; Bushman, 1998). Televised violence might also provide models that viewers imitate, particularly if the violence is carried out by the "good guys" (Bandura, 1983; Huesmann et al., 2003). Finally, prolonged viewing of violent TV programs might "desensitize" viewers, making them less distressed when they see others suffer and less disturbed about inflicting pain on others (Aronson, 1999b; Smith & Donnerstein, 1998). Concern over the influence of violence on television has led to the development of a violence-blocking "V-Chip" for new television sets in the United States.

THINKING CRITICALLY

Does Watching Violence on Television Make People More Violent?

■ What am I being asked to believe or accept?

Many have argued that watching violence on television *causes* violent behavior in viewers (Anderson & Bushman, 2002; Eron et al., 1996; Huesmann, 1998). In 1993, a National Academy of Sciences report concluded that "overall, the vast majority of studies, whatever their methodology, showed that exposure to television violence resulted in increased aggressive behavior, both contemporaneously and over time" (Reiss & Roth, 1993, p. 371). The American Psychological Association Commission on Violence and Youth reached the same conclusion (American Psychological Association, 1993).

■ Is there evidence available to support the claim?

Three types of evidence back up the claim that watching violent television programs increases violent behavior. First, there are anecdotes and case studies. Children have poked one another in the eye after watching the Three Stooges appear to do so on television. And adults have claimed that watching TV shows prompted them to commit murders or other violent acts matching those seen on the shows (Werner, 2003).

Second, many correlational studies have found a strong link between watching violent television programs and later acts of aggression and violence (Johnson et al., 2002). One such study tracked people from the time they were six or seven (in 1977) until they reached their early twenties (in 1992). Those who watched more violent television as children were significantly more aggressive as adults (Huesmann et al., 1997, 2003) and more likely to engage in criminal activity (Huesmann, 1995). They were also more likely to use physical punishment on their own children, who themselves tended to be much more aggressive than average. These latter results were found not only in the United States but also in Israel, Australia, Poland, the Netherlands, and even Finland, where the number of violent TV shows is very small (Centerwall, 1990; Huesmann & Eron, 1986).

Finally, the results of numerous experiments support the view that TV violence increases aggression among viewers (American Psychological Association, 1993; Paik &

Comstock, 1994; Reiss & Roth, 1993). In one study, groups of boys watched violent or nonviolent programs in a controlled setting and then played floor hockey (Josephson, 1987). Boys who had watched the violent shows were more likely than those who had watched nonviolent programs to behave aggressively on the hockey floor. This effect was greatest for boys who had the most aggressive tendencies to begin with. More extensive experiments in which children are exposed for long periods to carefully controlled types of television programs also suggest that exposure to large amounts of violent activity on television results in aggressive behavior (Eron et al., 1996).

■ Can that evidence be interpreted another way?

Anecdotal reports and case studies are certainly open to different interpretations. If people face imprisonment or execution for their violent acts, how much credibility can we give to their claims that their actions were triggered by television programs? How many other people might say that the same programs made them *less* likely to be violent? Anecdotes alone do not provide a good basis for drawing solid scientific conclusions.

What about the correlational evidence? Recall that a *correlation* between two variables does not necessarily mean that one caused the other. Both might be caused by a third factor. In fact, at least two possible "third factors" might account for the observed relationship between watching TV violence and acting aggressively.

First, certain people may prefer to watch more violent TV programs and to behave aggressively toward others. In other words, personality may partly account for the observed correlations (e.g., Aluja-Fabregat & Torrubia-Beltri, 1998). Second, perhaps poverty, unemployment, or the effects of drugs and alcohol leave certain people more time to watch television and leave them with frustration or other stressors that trigger aggressive behavior.

Finally, some researchers question whether the results of controlled experiments on the effects of televised violence extend beyond the experimental situation (Anderson, Lindsay, & Bushman, 1999). Who is to say, for example, whether an increase in aggressive acts during a hockey game has any later bearing on a child's tendency to commit an act of violence?

■ What evidence would help to evaluate the alternatives?

By their nature, correlational studies of the role of TV violence in violent behavior can never be conclusive. As we've pointed out, a third, unidentified causal variable could always be responsible for the results. More important would be further evidence from controlled experiments in which equivalent groups of people were given different, long-term "doses" of TV violence, and its effects on their subsequent behavior were observed. Such experiments could also explore the circumstances under which different people (for example, children versus adults) are affected by various forms of violence. However, studies like these create an ethical dilemma. If watching violent television programs really does cause violent behavior, are psychologists justified in creating conditions that might lead some people to be more violent? If such violence occurred, would the researchers be partly responsible to the victims and to society? If some participants commit violent acts, should the researchers continue the experiment to establish a pattern, or should they terminate the participation of those individuals? Difficulty in answering questions like these is partly responsible for the use of short-term experiments and correlational designs in this research area, as well as for some of the remaining uncertainty about the effects of television violence.

■ What conclusions are most reasonable?

The evidence collected so far makes it reasonable to conclude that watching TV violence is one cause of violent behavior, especially in some children (Anderson & Bushman, 2002; Bushman & Anderson, 2001; Robinson et al., 2001; Huesmann et al., 1997; Smith & Donnerstein, 1998). Playing violent video games may be another (Anderson & Bushman, 2001). But any cause-effect relationship between watching

TV violence and acting violently is not an inevitable one. There are many circumstances in which the effect does not occur (Charleton, Gunter, & Coles, 1998; Freedman, 1992). Parents, peers, and other environmental influences, along with personality factors, may dampen or amplify the effect of watching televised violence. Indeed, not every viewer interprets violence in the same way, and not every viewer is equally vulnerable (Ferguson, 2002; Wood, Wong, & Chachere, 1991). The most vulnerable may be those who are most aggressive or violence-prone in the first place, a trait that could well have been acquired by observing the behavior of parents or peers (Huesmann et al., 1997).

Still, the fact that violence on television *can* have a causal impact on violent behavior is reason for serious concern. This issue continues to influence public debate about what should, and should not, be aired on television.

Using Research on Learning to Help People Learn

► **What should teachers learn about learning?**

Teaching and training—explicit efforts to assist learners in mastering a skill—are major aspects of socialization in virtually every culture. The study of how people learn obviously has important implications for improved teaching in our schools (Azar, 2002; Lambert, 1999; Woolfolk-Hoy, 1999) and for helping people develop skills.

Classrooms Across Cultures

Many people have expressed concern that schools in the United States are not doing a very good job (Associated Press, 1997; Carnegie Task Force, 1996; Penner et al., 1994). The average performance of U.S. students on tests of reading, math, and other basic academic skills has tended to fall short of that of youngsters in other countries, especially Asian countries (International Association for the Evaluation of Education Achievement, 1999; National Center for Education Statistics, 2000, 2002). In one comparison study, Harold Stevenson (1992) followed a sample of pupils in Taiwan, Japan, and the United States from first grade, in 1980, to eleventh grade, in 1991. In the first grade, the Asian students scored no higher than their U.S. peers on tests of mathematical aptitude and skills, nor did they enjoy math more. However, by the fifth grade the U.S. students had fallen far behind. Corresponding differences were seen in reading skills.

Some possible causes of these differences were found in the classroom itself. In a typical U.S. classroom, teachers talked to students as a group; then students worked at their desks independently. Reinforcement or other feedback about performance on their work was usually delayed until the next day or, often, not provided at all. In contrast, the typical Japanese classroom placed greater emphasis on cooperative work among students (Kristof, 1997). Teachers provided more immediate feedback on a one-to-one basis. And there was an emphasis on creating teams of students with varying abilities, an arrangement in which faster learners help teach slower ones. However, before concluding that the differences in performance are the result of social factors alone, we must consider another important distinction: The Japanese children practiced more. They spent more days in school during the year and, on average, spent more hours doing homework.

Although the significance of these cultural differences in learning and teaching is not yet clear, the educational community in the United States is paying attention to them (e.g., Felder & Brent, 2001). Psychologists and educators are also considering how various principles of learning can be applied to improve education (Azar, 2002; Woolfolk-Hoy, 1999). For example, anecdotal and experimental evidence suggests that some of the most successful educational techniques are those that apply basic principles of operant

applying psychology **RECIPROCAL TEACHING** Ann Brown and her colleagues (1992) have demonstrated the success of reciprocal teaching, in which children take turns teaching each other. This technique is similar to the cooperative arrangements seen in Japanese education.

conditioning, offering frequent testing, positive reinforcement for correct performance, and immediate corrective feedback following mistakes (Kass, 1999; Oppel, 2000; Walberg, 1987).

Further, research in cognitive psychology (e.g., Bjork, 1979, 1999) suggests that students will retain more of what they learn if they study in several sessions distributed over time rather than in a single "cramming" session on the night before a test. To encourage this kind of "distributed practice," researchers say, teachers should give enough exams and quizzes (some unannounced, perhaps) that students will be reading and studying more or less continuously. And because learning is aided by repeated opportunities to use new information, these exams and quizzes should cover material from throughout the term, not just from recent classes. These recommendations are not necessarily popular with students, but there is good evidence that they promote long-term retention of course material (e.g., Bjork, 1999).

Active Learning

The importance of cognitive processes in learning is apparent in instructional methods that emphasize *active learning* (Bonwell & Eison, 1991). These methods take many forms, including, for example, small-group problem-solving tasks, discussion of "one-minute essays" written in class, use of "thumbs up" or "thumbs down" to indicate agreement or disagreement with the instructor's assertions, and multiple-choice questions that give students feedback about their understanding of the previous fifteen minutes of a lecture (Heward, 1997). Students typically find classes that include active learning experiences to be interesting and enjoyable (Moran, 2000; Murray, 2000). In addition, active learning methods help students go beyond memorizing isolated facts; these methods encourage students to think more deeply, consider how new material relates to what they already know, and apply it in new situations. This kind of thinking also makes the material easier to remember, which is why we have included so many opportunities for you to actively learn, rather than just passively read, the material in this book.

Studies of students in elementary schools, high schools, community colleges, and universities have found that active learning approaches result in better test performance and greater class participation compared with more passive instructional techniques (e.g., Hake, 1998; Kellum, Carr, & Dozier, 2001; Meyers & Jones, 1993). In one study, a fifth-grade teacher spent some days calling only on those students whose hands were raised. The rest listened passively. On other days, all students were required to answer every question by holding up a card with their response written on it. Scores on next-day quizzes and biweekly tests showed that students remembered more of the material covered on the active learning days than on the "passive" days (Gardner, Heward, & Grossi, 1994). In another study of two consecutive medical school classes taught by the same instructor, scores on the final exam were significantly higher when students learned mainly through small-group discussions and case studies than when they were taught mainly through lectures (Chu, 1994). Similarly, among adults being taught to use a new computer program, active learning with "hands-on" practice was more effective than passively watching a demonstration video (Kerr & Payne, 1994). Finally, high school and college students who passively listened to a physics lecture received significantly lower scores on a test of lecture content than did those who participated in a virtual reality lab that allowed them to "interact" with the physical forces covered in the lecture (Brelsford, 1993).

Results like these have fueled the development of other science education programs that place students in virtual laboratory environments where they actively manipulate materials and test hypotheses (e.g., Horwitz & Christie, 2000). Despite the enthusiasm generated by active learning methods, rigorous experimental research is still needed to compare their short- and long-term effects with those of more traditional methods in teaching various kinds of course content.

VIRTUAL SURGERY   Using a virtual reality system called "Surgery in 3-D," this medical student can actively learn and practice eye surgery skills before working with real patients.

Skill Learning

The complex action sequences, or *skills*, that people learn to perform in everyday life develop through learning processes that include feedback and, of course, lots of practice. In fact, *practice*—the repeated performance of a skill—is critical to mastery (Howe, Davidson, & Sloboda, 1998). For perceptual-motor skills such as playing pool or piano, both physical and mental practice are beneficial (Druckman & Bjork, 1994). To be most effective, practice should continue past the point of correct performance until the skill can be performed automatically, with little or no attention. Feedback about the correctness of the response is also necessary. As with any learning process, the feedback should come soon enough to be effective, but not so quickly that it interferes with the learner's efforts to learn independently.

Large amounts of guidance may produce very good performance during practice, but too much guidance may impair later performance (Kluger & DeNisi, 1998; Wickens, 1992). For instance, coaching students about correct responses in math may impair their ability later to retrieve the correct response from memory on their own. Independent practice at retrieving previously learned responses or information requires more effort, but it is critical for skill development (Ericsson & Charness, 1994). There is little or no evidence to support "sleep learning" or similar schemes designed to make learning effortless (Druckman & Bjork, 1994). In short, "no pain, no gain."

active review   Learning

Linkages

As noted in the introductory chapter, all of psychology's subfields are related to one another. Our discussion of opponent-process theory and drug effects illustrates just one way in which the topic of this chapter, learning, is linked to the subfield of consciousness, which is described in the chapter by that name. The Linkages diagram shows ties to two other subfields as well, and there are many more ties throughout the book. Looking for linkages among subfields will help you see how they all fit together and help you better appreciate the big picture that is psychology.

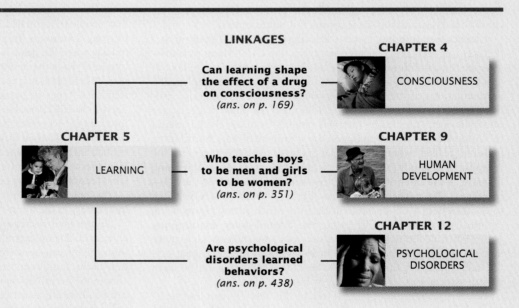

LINKAGES

CHAPTER 5
LEARNING

Can learning shape the effect of a drug on consciousness?
(ans. on p. 169)

CHAPTER 4
CONSCIOUSNESS

Who teaches boys to be men and girls to be women?
(ans. on p. 351)

CHAPTER 9
HUMAN DEVELOPMENT

Are psychological disorders learned behaviors?
(ans. on p. 438)

CHAPTER 12
PSYCHOLOGICAL DISORDERS

Summary

Individuals adapt to changes in the environment through the process of *learning,* which is the modification, through experience, of preexisting behavior and understanding.

CLASSICAL CONDITIONING: LEARNING SIGNALS AND ASSOCIATIONS

▶ **How did Russian dogs teach psychologists about learning?**

One form of learning is *classical conditioning.* It occurs when a previously neutral *conditioned stimulus,* or *CS* (such as a tone), is repeatedly paired with an *unconditioned stimulus,* or *UCS* (such as meat powder on a dog's tongue), which naturally brings about an *unconditioned response,* or *UCR* (such as salivation). Eventually the conditioned stimulus will elicit a response, known as the *conditioned response,* or *CR,* even when the unconditioned stimulus is not presented.

In general, the strength of a conditioned response grows as CS-UCS pairings continue. If the UCS is no longer paired with the CS, the conditioned response eventually disappears; this is *extinction.* After extinction, the conditioned response often reappears if the CS is presented after some time; this is *spontaneous recovery.* In addition, if the conditioned and unconditioned stimuli are paired once or twice after extinction, *reconditioning* occurs; that is, the conditioned response reverts to its original strength.

Because of *stimulus generalization,* conditioned responses occur to stimuli that are similar, but not identical to, conditioned stimuli. Generalization is limited by *stimulus discrimination,* which prompts conditioned responses to some stimuli but not to others.

Classical conditioning involves learning that the CS is an event that predicts the occurrence of another event, the UCS. Many psychologists see the conditioned response not just as an automatic reflex but also as a means through which animals and people develop mental representations of the relationships between events. Classical conditioning works best when the conditioned stimulus precedes the unconditioned stimulus by intervals ranging from less than a second to a minute or more, depending on the stimuli involved. Conditioning is also more likely when the CS reliably signals the UCS. In general, the strength of a conditioned response and the speed of conditioning increase as the intensity of the UCS—and the strength of the CS—increases. The particular stimulus likely to become a CS linked to a subsequent UCS depends in part on which stimulus was being attended to when the UCS occurred. *Second-order conditioning* occurs when a conditioned stimulus becomes powerful enough to make CSs out of stimuli associated with it. Some stimuli are easier to associate than others; organisms seem to be biologically prepared to learn certain associations, as exemplified by taste aversions.

Classical conditioning plays a role in the development and treatment of phobias and in procedures for identifying people at risk for Alzheimer's disease.

Habituation is reduced responsiveness to a repeated stimulus. According to Solomon's opponent-process theory, habituation is the result of two processes that balance each other. The first process is a relatively automatic, involuntary response—essentially a UCR. The second, or opponent, process is a learned or conditioned response that follows and counteracts the first. This theory may help explain drug tolerance.

INSTRUMENTAL AND OPERANT CONDITIONING: LEARNING THE CONSEQUENCES OF BEHAVIOR

▶ **How do reward and punishment work?**

Learning occurs not only through associating stimuli but also through associating behavior with its consequences. Thorndike's *law of effect* holds that any response that produces satisfaction becomes more likely to occur again, and any response that produces discomfort becomes less likely to recur. Thorndike referred to this type of learning as *instrumental conditioning.* Skinner called the process *operant conditioning.*

An *operant* is a response that has some effect on the world. A *reinforcer* increases the probability that the operant preceding it will occur again. There are two types of reinforcers: *positive reinforcers,* which are desirable stimuli that strengthen a response if they are presented after that response occurs, and *negative reinforcers,* which are the removal of an unpleasant stimulus following some response. Both kinds of reinforcers strengthen the behaviors that precede them. *Escape conditioning* results when a behavior terminates an unpleasant stimulus. *Avoidance conditioning* results when behavior avoids an unpleasant stimulus; it reflects both classical and operant conditioning. Behaviors learned through avoidance conditioning are very resistant to extinction. *Discriminative stimuli* indicate whether reinforcement is available for a particular behavior.

Complex responses can be learned through *shaping,* which involves reinforcing successive approximations of the desired response. *Primary reinforcers* are inherently rewarding; *secondary reinforcers* are rewards that people or animals learn to like because of their association with primary reinforcers. In general, operant conditioning proceeds more quickly when the delay in receiving reinforcement is short rather than long, and when the reinforcer is large rather than small. Reinforcement may be delivered on a continuous reinforcement schedule or on one of four basic types of partial, or intermittent, reinforcement schedules: fixed-ratio (FR), variable-ratio (VR), fixed-interval (FI), and variable-interval (VI) schedules. Ratio schedules lead to a rapid rate of responding. Behavior learned through partial reinforcement is very resistant to extinction; this phenomenon is called the *partial reinforcement extinction effect.* Partial reinforcement is involved in superstitious behavior, which results when a response is coincidentally followed by a reinforcer.

Psychologists are not certain what makes reinforcers rewarding, but activity in the brain's "pleasure centers" is one possibility.

Punishment decreases the frequency of a behavior by following it either with an unpleasant stimulus or with the removal of a pleasant one. Punishment can be useful when performed properly, but it can have drawbacks. It only suppresses behavior; fear of punishment may generalize to the person doing the punishing; it is ineffective when delayed; it can be physically harmful and may teach aggressiveness; and it teaches only what not to do, not what should be done to obtain reinforcement.

The principles of operant conditioning have been applied in many areas, from teaching social skills to treating sleep disorders.

COGNITIVE PROCESSES IN LEARNING

▶ **Can people learn to be helpless?**

Cognitive processes—how people represent, store, and use information—play an important role in learning. *Learned helplessness* appears to result when people believe that their behavior has no effect on the world. Both animals and humans display *latent learning.* They also form *cognitive maps* of their environments, even in the absence of any reinforcement for doing so. Experiments on *insight* also suggest that cognitive processes play an important role in learning, even by animals. The process of learning by watching others is called *observational learning,* or social learning. Some observational learning occurs through *vicarious conditioning,* in which one is influenced by seeing or hearing about the consequences of others' behavior. Observational learning is more likely to occur when the person observed is rewarded for the observed behavior. It is a powerful source of socialization.

USING RESEARCH ON LEARNING TO HELP PEOPLE LEARN

▶ **What should teachers learn about learning?**

Research on how people learn has implications for improved teaching and for the development of a wide range of skills. The degree to which learning principles, such as immediate reinforcement, are used in teaching varies considerably from culture to culture. The importance of cognitive processes in learning is seen in active learning methods designed to encourage people to think deeply about and apply new information instead of just memorizing isolated facts. Observational learning, practice, and corrective feedback play important roles in the learning of skills.

Learn by Doing

Put It in Writing

Imagine that you have inherited a circus from a long-lost relative, but you discover that all of the animal acts are stale and out of date. At a meeting with your employees, you explain that the principles of classical and operant conditioning could be used to improve these acts. Write a one-page paper describing how classical conditioning could be used to teach elephants a new trick, and how operant conditioning could be used to spice up a trained seal act. Be sure to label all the concepts and principles you use (such as "conditioned stimulus," "conditioned response," "shaping," and the like).

Personal Learning Activity

Select a pair of friends or relatives of about the same age and intelligence, and try teaching each of them something that is new to them but that you know well—perhaps the words to a song; a popular dance; or how to operate a digital camera, tie a tie, hit a tennis ball, or use a skateboard. Teach one person simply by telling or showing what you want him or her to learn, but work out a set of active learning methods to use with the second person. (Recall that active learning requires the learner to get involved in the learning process by doing something other than just listening to a lesson.) Keep a record of which student did better at this learning task and how long it took each student to learn. Which method was more efficient, and which student do you think enjoyed the learning process more? Did your results confirm or conflict with research on active learning in the classroom? *For additional projects, see the Personal Learning Activities in the corresponding chapter of the study guide that accompanies this text.*

Step into Action

Courses

Learning
Animal Behavior
Behavior Modification

Movies

The Deer Hunter; Schindler's List (learned helplessness)
The Miracle Worker (shaping and reinforcement)
A Clockwork Orange; The Manchurian Candidate (misconceptions about the power of classical conditioning)
Free Willy (reinforcement and animal behavior)
The War (observational learning, modeling)

Books

Kieran Egan, *The Educated Mind: How Cognitive Tools Shape Our Understanding* (University of Chicago Press, 1997) (how children learn)
James Garbarino, *Lost Boys: Why Our Sons Turn Violent and How We Can Save Them* (Free Press, 1999) (development of violence examined from several perspectives, including learning theories)
Linda Metcalf, *Parenting Toward Solutions: How Parents Can Use Skills They Already Have to Raise Responsible, Loving Kids* (Prentice Hall, 1996) (learning-based parenting skills)

Martin Seligman, *What You Can Change and What You Can't: The Complete Guide to Successful Self-Improvement* (Fawcett Books, 1995) (using learning principles for self-improvement)

Martin Seligman, with Karen Reivich, Lisa Jaycox, and Jane Gillham, *The Optimistic Child* (Harper Perennial Library, 1996) (the role of cognitive processes in learning and behavior)

The Web

The World Wide Web is a good source of additional information about the science of psychology, provided you use it carefully and think critically about the information you find. The web site that accompanies this text offers many resources relevant to this chapter. These resources include interactive NetLab exercises; Thinking Critically and Evaluating Research exercises; ACE chapter quizzes; recommended web links; and articles on current events, books, and movies. At http://college.hmco.com, select *Psychology* and then this textbook.

Review of Key Terms

Can you define each of the key terms in the chapter? Check your definitions against those on the pages listed in parentheses below or in the Glossary/Index at the end of the text.

avoidance conditioning *(p. 172)*

classical conditioning *(p. 163)*

cognitive map *(p. 183)*

conditioned response (CR) *(p. 164)*

conditioned stimulus (CS) *(p. 164)*

discriminative stimuli *(p. 172)*

escape conditioning *(p. 171)*

extinction *(p. 164)*

habituation *(p. 169)*

insight *(p. 185)*

latent learning *(p. 183)*

law of effect *(p. 170)*

learned helplessness *(p. 181)*

learning *(p. 162)*

negative reinforcers *(p. 171)*

observational learning *(p. 185)*

operant *(p. 171)*

operant conditioning *(p. 170)*

partial reinforcement extinction effect *(p. 177)*

positive reinforcers *(p. 171)*

primary reinforcers *(p. 174)*

punishment *(p. 177)*

reconditioning *(p. 164)*

reinforcer *(p. 171)*

second-order conditioning *(p. 166)*

secondary reinforcers *(p. 174)*

shaping *(p. 174)*

spontaneous recovery *(p. 164)*

stimulus discrimination *(p. 165)*

stimulus generalization *(p. 165)*

unconditioned response (UCR) *(p. 164)*

unconditioned stimulus (UCS) *(p. 164)*

vicarious conditioning *(p. 186)*

Multiple-Choice Self-Test

Select the best answer for each of the questions below. Then check your responses against the Answer Key at the end of the text.

1. Which saying best reflects learning?

   a. "A watched pot never boils."
   b. "A stitch in time saves nine."
   c. "Once burned, twice shy."
   d. "If you will it, it is no dream."

2. In a classical conditioning experiment, a puff of air was blown into Ralph's eye, and he reflexively blinked. The experimenter then began flashing a green light just before presenting the puff of air. After many pairings of the green light and the puff of air, Ralph began to blink as soon as the green light appeared, whether or not the air puff followed. In this experiment, the green light is the

   a. unconditioned stimulus.
   b. conditioned stimulus.
   c. conditioned response.
   d. unconditioned response.

3. To best obtain classical conditioning in the experiment described in the previous question, the experimenter should present the puff of air _____ presenting the green light.

   a. after
   b. just before
   c. at the same time as
   d. hours before

4. Suppose that the experimenter in Question 2 continues presenting the green light, but never again follows it with the puff of air. Ralph will soon _____ through the process of _____.

   a. blink faster; reconditioning
   b. stop blinking in response to the green light; extinction
   c. blink slower; stimulus control
   d. stop blinking; spontaneous recovery

5. After being bitten by a dog at a young age, Najla became fearful of all dogs. Now, when Najla sees a dog, her heart races and she feels like running away. Which of the following is a conditioned stimulus for Najla?

   a. dog bite
   b. fear
   c. running away
   d. seeing a dog

6. Anya moved away from her abusive parents and did not see them for many years. Through therapy, she finally felt strong enough to face them at her sister's wedding. However, when she saw them in the church, all of her fearful and angry feelings flooded back. This is an example of

   a. reconditioning.
   b. spontaneous recovery.
   c. stimulus generalization.
   d. stimulus discrimination.

7. Just as "Little Albert" was shown a white lab rat, a loud noise startled him and made him cry. After several such incidents, Albert cried whenever he saw the white rat. Later, when his mother took him to a petting zoo, Albert cried when he saw a white rabbit. This is an example of

   a. stimulus generalization.
   b. stimulus discrimination.
   c. vicarious learning.
   d. observational learning.

8. Laverne lost control and ate an entire coconut cream pie. Later that day she got the flu, complete with nausea and vomiting. After this experience, Laverne associated coconut cream pie with being sick, and now she can't even stand the smell of it. This is an example of _____, which supports the concept of _____.

   a. escape conditioning; spontaneous recovery
   b. discriminative conditioning; biopreparedness
   c. taste aversion; biopreparedness
   d. latent learning; spontaneous recovery

9. The fact that you didn't notice the feeling of your watch or your glasses or your tongue until you read this sentence is an example of

   a. habituation.
   b. stimulus generalization.
   c. stimulus discrimination.
   d. spontaneous recovery.

10. Manuel has learned that every time he cleans his room, his mother makes his favorite dessert. This is an example of

    a. classical conditioning.
    b. negative reinforcement.
    c. operant conditioning.
    d. extinction.

11. Loretta gets a backache every day, but if she sits in a hot bath, the pain goes away. So she decides to take a hot bath every day. She has learned to do this through

    a. positive reinforcement.
    b. negative reinforcement.
    c. stimulus discrimination.
    d. shaping.

12. A problem with _____ conditioning is that once learned, it can be difficult to change. The resulting _____ may keep a person from learning new, more desirable behaviors.

    a. escape; avoidance
    b. avoidance; avoidance
    c. avoidance; escape
    d. discriminative; discrimination

13. Ten minutes before a movie starts, the theater is filled with people who are talking and laughing. As soon as the lights go out, everyone becomes quiet. Sudden darkness serves as a _____ in this example of operant conditioning.

    a. positive reinforcer
    b. negative reinforcer
    c. punishment
    d. discriminative stimulus

14. Craig wanted to teach his dog, JoJo, to sit up and beg using operant conditioning principles. He started by giving JoJo a treat when she was simply standing. Then he gave her a treat only if she was sitting. Next, he gave her a treat only if she was sitting and had raised one paw, and so on. This is an example of

    a. stimulus discrimination.
    b. stimulus generalization.
    c. negative reinforcement.
    d. shaping.

15. Every fifth time Jamey washes the dishes, his mom gives him a candy bar. Once a week, on average, Susan's dad gives her a cookie for washing the dishes. What schedules of reinforcement are Jamey and Susan on, respectively?

    a. fixed interval; variable interval
    b. fixed ratio; variable interval
    c. variable ratio; fixed interval
    d. variable interval; fixed ratio

16. Which of the following is a potential problem with using punishment to change behavior?

    a. It can produce unwanted side effects.
    b. Frequent punishment can teach children to behave aggressively.
    c. Although it may signal that inappropriate behavior has occurred, it does not indicate what should be done instead.
    d. These are all potential problems with using punishment.

17. Whenever Javier attempted to ask his teacher a question or get help from her, he was told to "shut up and listen." After a while, he did "shut up." Although initially he was a good, interested student, after a while Javier just gave up. This demonstrates

a. latent learning.
b. learned helplessness.
c. observational learning.
d. trial and error.

18. When Kenzi got a flat tire not far from campus, he walked down the street to a service station he drove by every day, but had never visited. The fact that he immediately knew where it was illustrates

a. insight learning.
b. observational learning.
c. latent learning.
d. vicarious learning.

19. After watching a number of people petting and playing with a dog, Najla decides that dogs aren't as scary as she'd thought. The next day, at her neighbors' house, she pets their dog. Najla's fear has been reduced through

a. classical conditioning.
b. operant conditioning.
c. spontaneous recovery.
d. observational learning.

20. According to the discussion in this chapter, teachers should do which of the following to bring about the most improvement in students' ability to recall course material?

a. lecture more slowly
b. hand out lecture outlines before class begins
c. encourage students to recopy their notes
d. have students work in groups to solve problems

6

Memory

Have you ever forgotten where you parked your car? Have you ever felt that a

name you were trying to remember was on the tip of your tongue? Researchers in the field of memory explore these common experiences. *Memory* is a complex process of encoding, storing, and retrieving information. You use different kinds of memory for different types of information, such as personal experiences, specific skills, and abstract concepts. Once information is stored in your memory, recalling it can sometimes be difficult. In this chapter, you will learn about some techniques that can help you to retrieve memories. What psychologists have learned about memory has been used to create study techniques that really work!

Reading this chapter will help you to answer the following questions:

► **How does information turn into memories?**

► **What am I most likely to remember?**

► **How do I retrieve stored memories?**

► **How accurate are my memories?**

► **What causes me to forget things?**

► **How does my brain change when I store a memory?**

► **How can I remember more information?**

learn by**doing**

I'll make him an offer he can't refuse." "I'll be back." "Trust no one." "Life is like a box of chocolates." "I see dead people." "Show me the money." "Is that your final answer?" Do you remember where you heard these words? They are memorable lines from *The Godfather, The Terminator, The X-Files, Forrest Gump, The Sixth Sense, Jerry McGuire,* and *Who Wants to Be a Millionaire.* Can you say who Private Ryan was and why he needed to be saved? And do you know which classic film character said "Play it again, Sam"? (If you don't, ask a friend who knows about old movies.) The most common answer is Rick, the café owner played by Humphrey Bogart in *Casablanca.* Bogart never actually said this often-quoted line, though many people are sure they "remember" it.

Your memory stores vast amounts of useful and not-so-useful information from all of your experiences. This chapter will help you understand the nature of memory—how you form memories, how memory errors happen, and how you forget.

The Nature of Memory

► **How does information turn into memories?**

Memory is a funny thing. You might be able to remember the name of your first-grade teacher, but not the name of someone you met five minutes ago. Mathematician John Griffith estimated that in an average lifetime, a person stores roughly five hundred times as much information as can be found in all the volumes of the *Encyclopaedia Britannica* (Hunt, 1982). Keep in mind, however, that although we retain a great deal of information, we also lose a great deal (Bjork & Vanhuele, 1992). Consider Tatiana Cooley. She was the U.S. National Memory Champion for three years in a row, but confesses that she is so absent-minded that she relies on Post-it Notes to remember everyday errands (Schacter, 2001). Obviously, memory is made up of many component abilities, some of which may operate more efficiently than others.

Memory plays a critical role in your life. Without memory, you would not know how to shut off your alarm, take a shower, get dressed, recognize objects, or communicate. You would be unaware of your own likes and dislikes. You would have no idea of who you are (Craik et al., 1999). The impressive capacity of human memory depends on the operation of a complex mental system (Schacter, 1999).

Basic Memory Processes

In February 2002, prison warden James Smith lost his set of master keys to the Westville Correctional Facility. As a result, 2,559 inmates were kept under partial lockdown for eight days while the Indiana Department of Correction spent $53,000 to change locks in the affected areas. As it turned out, the warden had put the keys in his pocket when he went home, forgot he had done so, and reported the keys "missing" when they were not in their usual place in his office the next day (Associated Press, 2002). What went wrong? There are several possibilities. Memory depends on three basic processes: encoding, storage, and retrieval (see Figure 6.1). Our absent-minded warden might have had problems with any one of these processes.

First, information must be put into memory, a step that requires encoding. **Encoding** is a process that puts information to be remembered into a form that our memory system can accept and use. We use *memory codes* to translate information from the senses into mental representations of that information. **Acoustic codes** represent information as sequences of sounds, such as a tune or a rhyme. **Visual codes** represent stimuli as pictures, such as the image of a person's face. **Semantic codes** represent the general meaning of an experience. So if you see a billboard that reads "Huey's Going-Out-of-Business Sale," you might encode the sound of the words as if they had been spoken (acoustic coding), the image of the letters as they were arranged on the sign (visual coding), or the fact that you recently saw an ad for Huey's (semantic coding). The type of coding we use influences what we remember. Semantic coding might allow you to remember that an unfamiliar car was parked in your neighbors' driveway just before their house was robbed. If there were little or no other coding, however, you might not be able to remember the make, model, or color of the car.

The second basic memory process is storage. **Storage** refers to the holding of information in your memory over time. When you recall a vacation you took in childhood or find it possible to use a pogo stick many years after you last played with one, you are depending on the storage capacity of your memory.

The third memory process, **retrieval,** occurs when you find information stored in memory and bring it into consciousness. Retrieving stored information such as your current address or telephone number is usually so fast and effortless that it seems automatic. The search-and-retrieval process becomes more noticeable, however, when you read a quiz question but cannot quite recall the answer. Retrieval involves both recall and

encoding   The process of putting information into a form that the memory system can accept and use.

acoustic codes   Mental representations of stimuli as sounds.

visual codes   Mental representations of stimuli as pictures.

semantic codes   Mental representations of experiences by their general meaning.

storage   The process of maintaining information in the memory system over time.

retrieval   The process of recalling information stored in memory.

figure 6.1

Basic Memory Processes

Remembering something requires, first, that the item be encoded—put in a form that can be placed in memory. It must then be stored and, finally, retrieved, or recovered. If any of these processes fails, forgetting will occur.

Encoding Code and put into memory	**Storage** Maintain in memory	**Retrieval** Recover from memory
Types of memory codes ■ Acoustic ■ Visual ■ Semantic	**Types of long-term memory** ■ Episodic ■ Procedural ■ Semantic	**Types of retrieval** ■ Recall ■ Recognition

recognition. To *recall* information, you have to retrieve it from memory without much help; this is what is required when you answer an essay test question or play *Jeopardy!* In *recognition*, retrieval is aided by clues, such as the response alternatives given on multiple-choice tests and the questions on *Who Wants to Be a Millionaire*. Accordingly, recognition tends to be easier than recall.

Types of Memory

In which hand does the *Statue of Liberty* hold her torch? When was the last time you made a phone call? What part of speech is used to modify a noun? Your attempt to answer the first question is likely to involve a visual image. To answer the second, you must remember a particular event in your life. The third question requires general knowledge that is unlikely to be tied to a specific event. Some psychologists suggest that answering each of these questions requires a different type of memory (Baddeley, 1998). How many types of memory are there? No one is sure, but most research suggests that there are at least three basic types. Each is named for the kind of information it handles: episodic, semantic, and procedural (Best, 1999).

Any memory of a specific event that happened while you were present is an **episodic memory** (Tulving, 2002). It is a memory of an episode in your life. What you had for dinner yesterday, what you did last summer, or where you were last Friday night are episodic memories. **Semantic memory** contains generalized knowledge of the world—such as that twelve items make a dozen—that does not involve memory of a specific event. So you would answer the question "Are wrenches pets or tools?" using your semantic memory, because you don't have to remember a specific episode in which you learned that wrenches are tools. As a general rule, people convey episodic memories by saying, "I remember when . . . " whereas they convey semantic memories by saying, "I know that . . . " (Tulving, 1995). **Procedural memory** involves knowledge of how to do things, such as riding a bike, folding a map, or playing golf. A procedural memory often consists of a complicated sequence of movements that cannot be described adequately in words. For instance, a gymnast might find it impossible to describe the exact motions in a particular routine.

Many activities require all three types of memory. Consider the game of tennis. Knowing the official rules or the number of sets needed to win a match involves semantic memory. Remembering who served last requires episodic memory. And knowing how to hit the ball involves procedural memory.

Recalling these three kinds of memories can be either intentional or unintentional. When you deliberately try to remember something, such as where you went on your last vacation, you are relying on **explicit memory**. In contrast, **implicit memory** involves the unintentional recollection and influence of prior experiences (McDermott, 2002; Nelson, 1999). For example, if you were to read this chapter a second time, implicit memories of its content would help you to read it more quickly than you did the first time. For the same reason, you can solve a puzzle faster if you have solved it in the past. This

learn by doing

HOW DOES SHE DO THAT? As she practices, this young violinist is developing procedural memories of how to play her instrument that may be difficult to put into words. To appreciate the special nature of procedural memory, try writing a step-by-step description of *exactly* how you tie a shoe.

improvement of performance—often called *priming*—is automatic, and it occurs without conscious effort. In fact, people are often unaware that their actions have been influenced by previous events (see the chapter on consciousness). Because some influential events cannot be recalled even when people try to do so, implicit memory has been said to involve "retention without remembering" (Roediger, Guynn, & Jones, 1995).

Models of Memory

Your explicit memory for some information is far better and lasts far longer than for other information. Suppose your friends throw a surprise party for you. When you enter the room, you might barely notice the flash of a camera. Later, you cannot recall it at all. And you might forget in a few seconds the name of a person you met at the party. But if you live to be a hundred, you will never forget where the party took place or how surprised and pleased you were. Why do some things stay in memory forever, whereas others barely make an impression? Each of four ways of thinking about memory, called *models* of memory, provides a somewhat different explanation. Let's see what the levels-of-processing, transfer-appropriate processing, parallel distributed processing, and information-processing models have to say about memory.

Levels of Processing   The **levels-of-processing model** suggests that memory depends on the extent to which you encode and process information when you first receive it. Consider, for example, the task of remembering a phone number you just heard in a radio commercial. If you were unable to write it down, you would probably repeat the number over and over to yourself until you could get to a phone. This repetition process is called **maintenance rehearsal.** It can be an effective method for encoding information temporarily, but what if you need to remember something for hours, months, or years? In such cases, you would be better off using **elaborative rehearsal,** a process in which you relate new material to information you already have stored in memory. For example, instead of trying to remember a new person's name by simply repeating it to yourself, try thinking about how the name is related to something you know well. Let's say you are introduced to a man named John Crews. You might think, "He is as tall as my Uncle John, who always wears a crew cut."

   Study after study has shown that memory is improved when people use elaborative rather than maintenance rehearsal (Jahnke & Nowaczyk, 1998). Why? According to the levels-of-processing model, the reason is that material is processed more "deeply" when elaborative rehearsal is used (Lockhart & Craik, 1990; Roediger & Gallo, 2001). The more you think about new information, organize it, and relate it to something you already know, the "deeper" the processing, and the better your memory of the information becomes. Teachers use this idea when they ask their students not only to define a new word but also to use it in a sentence. Figuring out how to use the new word takes deeper processing than does merely defining it. (The next time you come across an unfamiliar word in this book, don't just read its definition. Try to use the word in a sentence by coming up with an example of the concept that relates to your knowledge and experience.)

Transfer-Appropriate Processing   Level of processing is not the only factor that affects memory (Baddeley, 1992). Another critical factor, suggested by the **transfer-appropriate processing model** of memory, is how the encoding process matches up with what is later retrieved. In one study, for example, half the students in a class were told that an upcoming exam would contain multiple-choice questions. The rest of the students were told to expect essay questions. Only half the students actually got the type of exam they expected, however. These students did much better on the exam than those who took an unexpected type of exam. Apparently, in studying for the exam, the two groups used encoding strategies that were most appropriate to the type of exam they expected. Those who tried to retrieve the information in a way that did not match their encoding method had a harder time (d'Ydewalle & Rosselle, 1978). Results like these indicate that how well the encoding method transfers to the retrieval task is just as important as the depth of processing.

---

episodic memory   A person's recall of a specific event that happened while the person was present.

semantic memory   A type of memory containing generalized knowledge of the world.

procedural memory   A type of memory containing information about how to do things.

explicit memory   The process through which people deliberately try to remember something.

implicit memory   The unintentional recollection and influence of prior experiences.

levels-of-processing model   A model of memory suggesting that differences in how well something is remembered reflect the degree or depth of mental processing.

maintenance rehearsal   A memorization method that involves repeating information over and over to keep it in memory.

elaborative rehearsal   A memorization method that relates new information to information already stored in memory.

transfer-appropriate processing model   A model suggesting that memory depends on how the encoding process matches up with what is later retrieved.

| EXTERNAL STIMULI | → | **Sensory memory** Briefly retains the information picked up by the sensory organs | → | **Short-term memory** Temporarily holds information in consciousness | → | **Long-term memory** Can retain information for long periods of time, often until the person dies |

figure 6.2

Three Stages of Memory

This traditional information-processing model describes three stages in the memory system.

Parallel Distributed Processing   A third way of thinking about memory is based on **parallel distributed processing (PDP) models** (Rumelhart & McClelland, 1986). These models of memory suggest that new experiences do more than store facts that are later retrieved individually. The experiences also change your knowledge base in ways that alter your overall understanding of the world and how it operates. For example, when you first arrived at college, you learned specific facts, such as where classes are held, what time the library closes, and where to get the best pizza. Over time, these and many other facts about college life form a network of information that creates a more general understanding of how the whole college system works. Developing this network makes experienced students not only more knowledgeable but also more sophisticated. It allows them to, say, allocate their study time so as to do well in their most important classes, and to plan a schedule that avoids conflicts between work and recreational activities.

Using this network concept, PDP models of memory see each unit of knowledge as connected with every other unit. The connections between units become stronger as they are experienced together more frequently. In other words, your knowledge about the world is distributed across a network of associations that allows you to quickly and efficiently draw inferences and generalizations. For example, because of your network of associations, just seeing the word *chair* allows you to know immediately what a chair looks like, what it is used for, where it tends to be located, who might buy one, and the like. PDP models of memory explain this process very effectively.

Information Processing   The **information-processing model** is probably the most influential and comprehensive model of memory. It suggests that for information to be firmly implanted in memory, it must pass through three stages of mental processing: sensory memory, short-term memory, and long-term memory (see Figure 6.2).

parallel distributed processing (PDP) models   Models of memory suggesting that new experiences provide specific information, but also become part of, and alter, a whole network of associations in a person's knowledge base.

information-processing model   A model suggesting that information must pass through sensory memory, short-term memory, and long-term memory in order to become firmly embedded in memory.

in review

MODELS OF MEMORY

Model	Assumptions
Levels of processing	The more deeply material is processed, the better our memory of it.
Transfer-appropriate processing	Retrieval is improved when we try to recall material in a way that matches how the material was encoded.
Parallel distributed processing (PDP)	New experiences add to and alter our overall knowledge base; they are not separate, unconnected facts. Networks of associations allow us to draw inferences and make generalizations about the world.
Information processing	Information is processed in three stages: sensory memory, short-term memory, and long-term memory.

? *The value of elaborative rehearsal over maintenance rehearsal has been cited as evidence for the _____ model of memory.*

SENSORY MEMORY AT WORK Turn on a small flashlight, stand in front of a full-length mirror in a dark room, and move the light very slowly in a circle. You will see a single point of light moving in a circle. If it appears to have a "tail," like a comet, that is your sensory memory of the light before it fades. Now move the light faster and faster. You should now see a complete circle of light, because as the light moves, its impression on your sensory memory does not have time to fade before the circle is completed. A similar process allows us to see "sparkler circles" and still images that appear to move as we watch films, videos, or DVDs (see our discussion of stroboscopic motion in the chapter on sensation and perception).

In **sensory memory,** information from the senses—sights or sounds, for example—is held very briefly, often for less than one second, before being lost. But if information in sensory memory is attended to, analyzed, and encoded as a meaningful pattern, we say that it has been *perceived* (see the chapter on sensation and perception). Information in sensory memory that has been perceived can now enter *short-term memory.* If nothing further is done with it, that information will disappear in less than twenty seconds. However, if the information in short-term memory is further processed, it may be encoded into *long-term memory,* where it may remain indefinitely.

The act of reading illustrates all three stages of memory processing. As you read any sentence in this book, for example, light energy reflected from the page reaches your eyes, where it is converted to neural activity and registered in your sensory memory. If you pay attention to these visual stimuli, your perception of the patterns of light can be held in short-term memory. This stage of memory holds the early parts of the sentence so that they can be integrated and understood as you read the rest of the sentence. As you read, you are constantly recognizing words by matching your perceptions of them with the patterns and meanings you have stored in long-term memory. In short, all three stages of memory are necessary for you to understand a sentence.

"In Review: Models of Memory" summarizes the four memory models we have discussed. Each of these models provides an explanation of why we remember some things and forget others, but which model offers the best explanation? The answer is that more than one model may be required to understand memory. Just as it is helpful for physicists to characterize light in terms of both waves and particles, psychologists find it useful to think of memory as both a sequential process, as suggested by the information-processing model, and as a parallel process, as suggested by parallel distributed processing models.

Storing New Memories

▶ **What am I most likely to remember?**

The storage of information is critical to memory, because we can retrieve only information that has been stored. According to the information-processing model, sensory memory, short-term memory, and long-term memory each provide a different type of storage. Let's take a closer look at these three memory systems in order to better understand how they work—and sometimes fail.

Sensory Memory

To recognize incoming stimuli, the brain must analyze and compare them with what is already stored in long-term memory. Although this process is very quick, it still takes time. The major function of *sensory memory* is to hold information long enough for it to be processed further. This "holding" function is the job of the **sensory registers,** which act as temporary storage bins. There is a separate register for each of the five senses. Every register is capable of storing an almost complete representation of a sensory stimulus (Best, 1999). However, the sensory registers hold this representation for only a very brief period of time, often less than one second.

Sensory memory helps us experience a constant flow of information, even if that flow is interrupted. To appreciate this fact, move your head and eyes slowly from left to right. Although it seems to you that your eyes are moving smoothly, like a movie camera scanning a scene, this is not what happens. Your eyes fixate at one point for about one-fourth of a second and then rapidly jump to a new position. You perceive smooth motion because you hold the scene in your visual sensory register until your eyes fixate again. Similarly, when you listen to someone speak, your auditory sensory register allows you to experience a smooth flow of information, even though there are actually short silences between or within words.

sensory memory A type of memory that is very brief, but lasts long enough to connect one impression to the next.

sensory registers Memory systems that briefly hold incoming information.

The fact that sensory memories fade quickly if they are not processed further is actually an adaptive characteristic of this memory system (Baddeley, 1998). You simply cannot deal with all of the sights, sounds, odors, tastes, and touch sensations that come to your sense organs at any given moment. Using **selective attention,** you focus your mental resources on only part of the stimuli around you, thus controlling what information is processed further in short-term memory.

Short-Term Memory and Working Memory

The sensory registers allow your memory system to develop a representation of a stimulus. However, they do not allow the more thorough analysis needed if the information is going to be used in some way. That function is accomplished by short-term memory and working memory.

Short-term memory (STM) is the part of your memory system that stores limited amounts of information for up to about eighteen seconds. When you check the newspaper or an on-screen guide for the channel number of a TV show you want to watch and then keep that number in mind as you switch channels, you are using short-term memory. **Working memory** is the part of the memory system that allows us to mentally work with, or manipulate, the information being held in short-term memory. So short-term memory is actually a component of working memory.

Together, working memory and short-term memory enable us to do many kinds of mental work (Baddeley, 2000; Engle & Oransky, 1999). Suppose you are buying something for eighty-three cents. You go through your change and pick out two quarters, two dimes, two nickels, and three pennies. To do this you use both short-term memory and working memory to remember the price, retrieve the rules of addition from long-term memory, and keep a running count of how much change you have so far. Now try to recall how many windows there are on the front of the house or apartment where you grew up. In answering this question, you probably formed a mental image of the building. You used one kind of working-memory process to form that image, and then you maintained the image in short-term memory while you "worked" on it by counting the windows. So working memory has at least two components: *maintenance* (holding information in short-term memory) and *manipulation* (working on that information).

Encoding in Short-Term Memory   The encoding of information in short-term memory is much more elaborate and varied than encoding in the sensory registers (Brandimonte, Hitch, & Bishop, 1992). *Acoustic coding* (by sound) seems to dominate short-term memory. This conclusion comes from research on the mistakes people make when encoding information in short-term memory. These mistakes tend to involve the substitution of similar sounds. For instance, Robert Conrad (1964) showed people strings of letters and asked them to repeat the letters immediately. Among their most common mistakes was the replacement of the correct letter with another that sounded like it. For example, the correct letter *C* was replaced with a *D*, *P*, or *T*. The participants made these mistakes even though the letters were presented visually, without any sound. Studies in several cultures have also shown that items are more difficult to remember if they sound similar. For example, native English speakers perform more poorly when they must remember a string of letters like *ECVTGB* (which all have similar sounds) than when asked to remember one like *KRLDQS* (which have distinct sounds).

Encoding in short-term memory is not always acoustic, however. Information in short-term memory also can be encoded visually, semantically, and even kinesthetically (in terms of physical movements) (Best, 1999). In one study, deaf people were shown a list of words and then asked to immediately write down as many as they could remember (Shand, 1982). When these participants made errors, they wrote words that are expressed through similar *hand movements* in American Sign Language, rather than words that *sounded* similar to the correct words. Apparently, these individuals had encoded the words on the basis of the movements they would use when signing them.

```
9 2 5
8 6 4 2
3 7 6 5 4
6 2 7 4 1 8
0 4 0 1 4 7 3
1 9 2 2 3 5 3 0
4 8 6 8 5 4 3 3 2
2 5 3 1 9 7 1 7 6 8
8 5 1 2 9 6 1 9 4 5 0
9 1 8 5 4 6 9 4 2 9 3 7
```

Source: Howard (1983).

figure 6.3

The Capacity of Short-Term Memory

learn by **doing**   Here is a test of your immediate memory span (Howard, 1983). Ask someone to read to you the numbers in the top row at the rate of about one per second; then try to repeat them back in the same order. Then try the next row, and the one after that, until you make a mistake. Your immediate memory span is the maximum number of items you can repeat back perfectly.

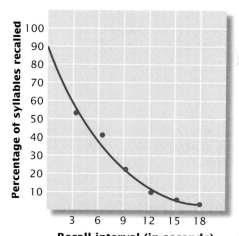

Recall interval (in seconds)

Source: Data from Peterson & Peterson (1959).

figure 6.4

Forgetting in Short-Term Memory

This graph shows the percentage of non-sense syllables recalled after various intervals during which rehearsal was prevented. Notice that virtually complete forgetting occurred after a delay of eighteen seconds.

selective attention The process of focusing mental resources on only part of the stimulus field.

short-term memory (STM) A stage of memory in which information normally lasts less than twenty seconds; a component of working memory.

working memory The part of the memory system that mentally works with, or manipulates, information being held in short-term memory.

immediate memory span The maximum number of items a person can recall perfectly after one presentation of the items.

chunks Stimuli that are perceived as units or meaningful groupings of information.

Brown-Peterson procedure A method for determining how long unrehearsed information remains in short-term memory.

Storage Capacity of Short-Term Memory How much information can you hold in short-term memory? The simple test presented in Figure 6.3 will help you determine your **immediate memory span,** which is the largest number of items you can recall perfectly after one presentation. If your memory span is like most people's, you can repeat six or seven items from the test in this figure. And you should come up with about the same result whether you use digits, letters, words, or virtually any type of unit (Pollack, 1953). George Miller (1956) noticed that many studies using a variety of tasks showed the same limit on the ability to process information. This "magic number," which is seven plus or minus two, appears to be the immediate memory span or capacity of short-term memory, at least in laboratory settings. It is generally considered to be somewhat less in more naturalistic situations (Martindale, 1991). The "magic number" refers to meaningful *groupings* of information, called **chunks,** not to a certain number of discrete elements.

To see the difference between discrete elements and chunks, read the following letters to a friend, pausing at each dash: *FB-IAO-LM-TVI-BMB-MW.* The chances are very good that your friend will not be able to repeat this string of letters perfectly. Why? There are fifteen letters, which exceeds most people's immediate memory span. Now, give your friend the test again, but group the letters like this: *FBI-AOL-MTV-IBM-BMW.* Your friend will probably repeat the string easily. Although the same fifteen letters are involved, they will be processed as only five meaningful chunks of information.

The Power of Chunking Chunks of information can be quite complex. If you heard someone say, "The boy in the red shirt kicked his mother in the shin," you could probably repeat the sentence perfectly. Yet, it contains twelve words and forty-three letters. How can you repeat the sentence so effortlessly? The answer is that you are able to build bigger and bigger chunks of information (Ericsson & Staszewski, 1989). In this case, you might represent "the boy in the red shirt" as one chunk of information rather than as six words or nineteen letters. Similarly, "kicked his mother" and "in the shin" represent separate chunks of information.

Learning to use bigger and bigger chunks of information can greatly benefit short-term memory. This effect can easily be seen in children. Their short-term memories improve partly because they become able to hold as many as seven chunks in memory, but also because they get better at grouping information into chunks (Servan-Schreiber & Anderson, 1990). Adults also can greatly increase the capacity of their short-term memory by using more appropriate chunking. For example, after extensive training, one college student increased his immediate memory span from seven to eighty digits (Neisser, 2000a). So although the capacity of short-term memory is more or less constant (from five to nine chunks of meaningful information), the size of those chunks can vary tremendously.

Duration of Short-Term Memory Why don't you remember every phone number you ever called or every conversation you ever had? The answer is that unless you do something to retain it, information in short-term memory is soon forgotten. This adaptive feature of short-term memory gets rid of a lot of useless information, but it can also be inconvenient. You may have discovered this if you ever looked up a phone number, got distracted before you could call it, and then forgot the number.

How long does information remain in short-term memory if you don't keep rehearsing it? John Brown (1958) and Lloyd and Margaret Peterson (1959) devised the **Brown-Peterson procedure** to measure the duration of short-term memory when no rehearsal is allowed. In this procedure, participants are presented with a group of three letters, such as *GRB.* They then count backward by threes from some number until they get a signal. Counting prevents the participants from rehearsing the letters. At the signal, they stop counting and try to recall the letters. By varying the number of seconds spent counting backward, the experimenter can determine how much forgetting takes place over time. As you can see in Figure 6.4, information in short-term memory is forgotten gradually, but rapidly: After only eighteen seconds, participants can remember almost nothing.

Evidence from other such experiments also suggests that unrehearsed information can be held in short-term memory for no more than about eighteen seconds. However, if the information is rehearsed or processed further in some other way, it may be encoded into long-term memory.

Long-Term Memory

When people talk about memory, they are usually referring to long-term memory. **Long-term memory (LTM)** is the part of the memory system whose encoding and storage capabilities can produce memories that last a lifetime.

Encoding in Long-Term Memory   Some information is encoded into long-term memory automatically, without any conscious attempt to memorize it (Ellis, 1991). However, placement of information into long-term memory is often the result of more elaborate and conscious processing that usually involves *semantic coding*. As we mentioned earlier, semantic encoding often leaves out details in favor of the more general, underlying meaning of the information.

The notion that semantic encoding dominates in LTM was demonstrated in a classic study by Jacqueline Sachs (1967). Her participants first listened to tape recordings of people reading from books. Then Sachs showed them sets of sentences with the same meaning and asked whether each exact sentence had been read on the tape. Participants did very well when tested immediately, using mainly short-term memory. After only twenty-seven seconds, though, they could not be sure which of two sentences they had heard. For example, they could not remember whether they had heard "He sent a letter about it to Galileo, the great Italian scientist" or "A letter about it was sent to Galileo, the great Italian scientist." Why did this happen? It occurred because the delay was long enough that the participants had to recall the information from long-term memory, where they had encoded the *general meaning* of what they had heard, but not the exact wording.

Perhaps you are thinking, "So what?" After all, the two sentences mean the same thing. Unfortunately, when people encode the general meaning of information they hear or read, they can make mistakes about the details of that information (Brewer, 1977). This can be a problem when recalling exact words is important—such as in the courtroom, during business negotiations, and in discussions between students and teachers about previous agreements. Later in this chapter we will show that such mistakes occur partly because people encode into long-term memory not only the general meaning of information but also what they think and assume about that information (Hannigan & Reinitz, 2001).

Counterfeiters depend on the fact that people encode the general meaning of visual stimuli rather than specific details. For example, look at Figure 6.5, and find the correct drawing of a U.S. penny (Nickerson & Adams, 1979). Most people from the United States are unsuccessful at this task. People from other countries do poorly at recognizing their country's coins, too (Jones, 1990). Research showing that people fail to remember specific details about visual information has prompted the U.S. Treasury to begin using more distinctive drawings on the paper currency it distributes.

figure 6.5

Encoding into Long-Term Memory

 Which is the correct image of a U.S. penny? (See p. 208 for the answer.)

(A)   (B)   (C)   (D)   (E)

Source: Nickerson & Adams (1979).

learn ^{by}**doing**

PHOTOGRAPHIC MEMORY
Using only his long-term memory, Franco Magnani created amazingly accurate paintings of his hometown in Italy even though he had not seen it for more than thirty years (see comparison photo, at right; Sacks, 1992). People like Magnani display *eidetic imagery,* commonly called *photographic memory.* About 5 percent of school-age children have photographic memory, but it is very rare in adults (Haber, 1979). You can test yourself for eidetic imagery by drawing a detailed picture or map of a place that you know well but have not seen recently. How did you do?

Storage Capacity of Long-Term Memory The capacity of long-term memory is extremely large. In fact, many psychologists believe that it is literally unlimited (Matlin, 1998). There is no way to prove this, but we do know that people store vast quantities of information in long-term memory that can be remembered remarkably well after long periods of time. For example, people are amazingly accurate at recognizing the faces of their high school classmates after having not seen them for over twenty-five years (Bruck, Cavanagh, & Ceci, 1991). They also do surprisingly well on tests of a foreign language or high school algebra fifty years after having formally studied these subjects (Bahrick & Hall, 1991; Bahrick et al., 1994). And college students are reasonably accurate in remembering their high school grades—especially if they were good grades (Bahrick, Hall, & Berger, 1996).

But long-term memories are also subject to distortion. In one study illustrating this point, students were asked to describe where they were and what they were doing at the moment they heard about the verdict in the O. J. Simpson murder trial (Schmolck, Buffalo, & Squire, 2000). The students first reported their recollections three days after the verdict, and then again after either fifteen or thirty-two months. Only half the recollections reported at fifteen months were accurate, and 11 percent contained major errors or distortions. Among those reporting after thirty-two months, 71 percent of their recollections were inaccurate, and just over 40 percent contained major errors or distortions. Here is just one example: Three days after the verdict, a student said he heard about it while in a campus lounge with many fellow students around him. Thirty-two months later, this same person recalled hearing the news in the living room of his home with his father and sister. Amazingly, most of the students whose memories had been substantially distorted over time were unaware that this distortion had occurred; they were very confident that the reports were accurate. Later, we will see that such overconfidence can also appear in courtroom testimony by eyewitnesses to crime.

Distinguishing Between Short-Term and Long-Term Memory

Some psychologists argue that short-term memory and long-term memory have different features and obey different laws (Cowan, 1988). ("In Review: Storing New Memories" summarizes the characteristics of these systems.) Evidence that information is

long-term memory (LTM) The stage of memory for which the capacity to store new information is believed to be unlimited.

in review

STORING NEW MEMORIES			
Storage System	**Function**	**Capacity**	**Duration**
Sensory memory	Briefly holds representations of stimuli from each sense for further processing	Large: absorbs all sensory input from a particular stimulus	Less than 1 second
Short-term and working memory	Holds information in awareness and manipulates it to accomplish mental work	Five to nine distinct items or chunks of information	About 18 seconds
Long-term memory	Stores new information indefinitely	Unlimited	Unlimited

? *If you looked up a phone number, but forgot it before you could call it, the information was probably lost from _____ memory.*

learn by doing

transferred from short-term memory to a distinct storage system comes primarily from experiments on recall.

You can conduct your own recall experiment. Look at the following list of words for thirty seconds, and then look away and write down as many of the words as you can, in any order: desk, chalk, pencil, chair, paperclip, book, eraser, folder, briefcase, essays. Which words you recall depends in part on their serial position, or where the words are in the list. The *serial-position curve* in Figure 6.6 shows this effect. From this curve you can see the chances of recalling words appearing in each position in a list. For the first two or three words in a list, recall tends to be very good. This phenomenon is called the **primacy effect.** The probability of recall decreases for words in the middle of the list and then rises dramatically for the last few words. The ease of recalling words near the end of the list is called the **recency effect.** The primacy effect may reflect the rehearsal that puts early words into long-term memory. The recency effect may occur because the last few words are still in short-term memory when you try to recall the list (Glanzer & Cunitz, 1966; Koppenaal & Glanzer, 1990).

Retrieving Memories

▶ **How do I retrieve stored memories?**

Most people have trouble remembering things at one time or another. Have you ever been unable to recall the name of a musical group or movie star, only to think of it the next day? Remembering requires not only the appropriate coding and storing of information but also the ability to bring it into consciousness. In other words, you have to be able to *retrieve* it.

Retrieval Cues and Encoding Specificity

Retrieval cues are stimuli that help you retrieve information from long-term memory. As mentioned earlier, retrieval cues are what make recognition tasks (such as multiple-choice tests) easier than recall tasks (such as essay exams).

The effectiveness of retrieval cues depends on the extent to which they tap into information that was encoded at the time of learning (Tulving, 1983). This rule is known as the **encoding specificity principle.** Because long-term memories are often encoded in terms of their general meaning, cues that trigger the meaning of the stored information tend to work best. Imagine that you have learned a long list of sentences, one of which

figure 6.6

A Serial-Position Curve

The probability of recalling an item is plotted here as a function of its serial position in a list of items. Generally, the first several items and the last several items are most likely to be recalled.

Drawing A in Figure 6.5 shows the correct penny image.

CONTEXT-DEPENDENT MEMORIES
Many people attending a reunion at their old high school find that being in the building again provides context cues that help bring back memories of their school days.

was either (1) "The man lifted the piano" or (2) "The man tuned the piano." Now suppose that on a later recall test, you were given the retrieval cue "something heavy." This cue would probably help you to remember the first sentence (because you probably encoded something about the weight of a piano as you read it) but not the second sentence (because it has nothing to do with weight). Similarly, the cue "makes nice sounds" would probably help you recall the second sentence, but not the first (Barclay et al., 1974).

Context and State Dependence

Have you ever taken a test in a classroom other than the one in which you learned the material for that test? If so, your performance may have been affected. Research has shown that people tend to recall more of what they have learned when they are in the place in which they learned it. Why? Because if they have encoded features of the environment where the learning occurred, these features can later act as retrieval cues (Richardson-Klavehn & Bjork, 1988). In one experiment, people studied a series of photos while in the presence of a particular odor. Later, they reviewed a larger set of photos and tried to recognize the ones they had seen earlier. Half of the people were exposed to the original odor while taking the recognition test. The other half were tested in the presence of another odor. Those who smelled the same odor during learning and testing did significantly better on the recognition task than those tested in the presence of a different odor. The matching odor served as a powerful retrieval cue (Cann & Ross, 1989).

Context-dependent memories are those that are helped or hindered by similarities or differences in environmental context. This context-dependency effect is not always strong (Smith, Vela, & Williamson, 1988), but some students do find it helpful to study for a test in the classroom where the test will be given.

Sometimes, we also encode information about how we were feeling during a learning experience, and this information, too, can act as a retrieval cue. When our internal state influences retrieval, we have a **state-dependent memory.** For example, if people learn new material while under the influence of marijuana, they tend to recall it better if they are also tested under the influence of marijuana (Eich et al., 1975). Similar effects have been found with alcohol (Overton, 1984), other drugs (Eich, 1989), and various mood states (Eich & Macaulay, 2000). College students are more likely to remember positive incidents from the past when they are feeling good at the time of recall (Bower, 1981; Ehrlichman & Halpern, 1988). Negative events are more likely to be recalled when people are feeling sad or angry

primacy effect   A phenomenon whereby recall for the first two or three items in a list is particularly good.

recency effect   A phenomenon whereby recall for the last few items in a list is particularly good.

retrieval cues   Stimuli that allow or help people to recall information.

encoding specificity principle   A principle stating that the ability of a cue to aid retrieval depends on whether it taps into information that was originally encoded.

context-dependent memories   Memories that are helped or hindered by similarities or differences between the contexts in which they are learned and recalled.

state-dependent memory   Memory that is helped or hindered by similarities or differences in a person's internal state during learning versus recall.

(Lewinsohn & Rosenbaum, 1987). These *mood congruency* effects are strongest when people try to recall personally meaningful episodes (Eich & Metcalfe, 1989). The more meaningful the experience, the more likely it is that the memory has been colored by their mood. (See "In Review: Factors Affecting Retrieval from Long-Term Memory.")

Retrieval from Semantic Memory

The retrieval situations we have discussed so far are relevant to episodic memory—our memory for events. What factors affect our ability to retrieve information from semantic memory, where we store general knowledge about the world? Researchers studying this question typically ask participants general-knowledge questions, such as (1) Are fish minerals? (2) Is a beagle a dog? (3) Do birds fly? and (4) Does a car have legs? As you might imagine, most people respond correctly to such questions. But by measuring how long it takes to answer them, psychologists gain important clues about how semantic memory is organized and how we retrieve information from it.

Semantic Networks   One explanation of semantic memory suggests that concepts such as "bird" or "animal" are represented in a dense network of associations (Churchland, 1989). Figure 6.7 presents a fragment of what a *semantic memory network* might look like. In general, semantic network theories suggest that information is retrieved from memory through the principle of **spreading activation** (Medin, Ross, & Markman, 2001). In other words, when you think about some concept, it becomes activated in the network, and this activation begins to "spread" down all the paths related to it. For example, if you are asked whether the statement "A robin is a bird" is true or false, the concepts of both "robin" and "bird" will become activated, and the spreading activation from each will intersect somewhere in these paths.

Some associations within the network are stronger than others, and spreading activation travels more quickly along stronger paths than along weaker ones. For instance, you probably have a stronger association between "bat" and "wings" than between "bat" and "mammal." As a result, you'd probably respond more quickly to "Can a bat fly?" than to "Is a bat a mammal?"

Because of the tight organization of semantic networks and the speed at which activation spreads through them, people can gain access to an enormous body of knowledge about the world quickly and effortlessly. They retrieve not only facts that they have learned directly but also knowledge that allows them to infer other facts about the world (Matlin, 1998). For example, imagine answering the following two questions: (1) Is a

in review

FACTORS AFFECTING RETRIEVAL FROM LONG-TERM MEMORY	
Process	**Effect on Memory**
Encoding specificity	Retrieval cues are effective only to the extent that they tap into information that was originally encoded.
Context dependence	Retrieval is most successful when it occurs in the same environment in which the information was originally learned.
State dependence	Retrieval is most successful when people are in the same psychological state as when they originally learned the information.

? *Stimuli called _____ help you recall information stored in long-term memory. They are more plentiful on _____ tests than on _____ tests.*

spreading activation   In semantic network theories of memory, a principle that explains how information is retrieved.

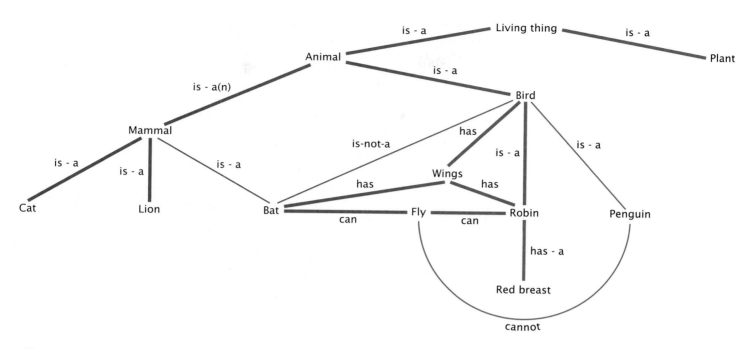

figure 6.7

Semantic Memory Networks

This drawing represents just a small part of a network of semantic associations. Semantic network theories of memory suggest that networks like these allow us to retrieve specific pieces of previously learned information and to make new inferences about the world.

robin a bird? and (2) Is a robin a living thing? You can probably answer the first question "directly," because you probably learned this fact at some point in your life. However, you may never have consciously thought about the second question, so answering it requires some inference. Figure 6.7 illustrates the path to that inference. Because you know that a robin is a bird, a bird is an animal, and animals are living things, you infer that a robin must be a living thing. As you might expect, however, it takes slightly longer to answer the second question than the first.

Retrieving Incomplete Knowledge   Concepts such as "bird" or "living thing" are represented in semantic memory as unique sets of features or attributes. What if you can retrieve some features of a concept from your semantic network, but not enough of them to identify what the concept is? For example, you might know that there is an animal that has wings, can fly, and is not a bird, and yet be unable to retrieve its name (Connor, Balota, & Neely, 1992). When this happens, you are retrieving *incomplete knowledge*. (The animal in question is a bat.)

The *tip-of-the-tongue phenomenon* is a common example of incomplete knowledge. In a typical experiment on this phenomenon, participants listen as dictionary definitions are read to them. They are then asked to identify the word being defined (Brown & McNeill, 1966). If they cannot recall a defined word, they are asked if they can recall any feature of it, such as its first letter or how many syllables it has. People are surprisingly good at this task, indicating that they are able to retrieve at least some knowledge of the word (Brennen et al., 1990). Most people experience the tip-of-the-tongue phenomenon about once a week; older people tend to experience it more often than younger people (Brown, 1991; Brown & Nix, 1996).

Constructing Memories

▶ **How accurate are my memories?**

Our memories are affected not only by what we perceive but also by what we already know about the world (Schacter, Norman, & Koutstaal, 1998). We use that existing knowledge to organize new information as we receive it, and we fill in gaps in the information that we encode and retrieve (Sherman & Bessennoff, 1999). This process is called *constructive memory*.

In one study of constructive memory, undergraduates were asked to wait for several minutes in the office of a graduate student (Brewer & Treyens, 1981). Later, they were asked to recall everything that was in the office. Most of the students mistakenly "remembered" seeing books, even though there were none. Apparently, the general knowledge that graduate students read many books influenced the participants' memory of what was in the room.

I Could Swear I Heard It!

By constructing our own versions of what we have seen and heard, we may experience an event differently from the way it actually happened. These errors, called *false memories,* can occur in relation to anything from the objects present in a room to the identity of an armed robber (Clancy et al., 2000). Later, we discuss how false memories might color eyewitness testimony and reports of sexual abuse in childhood. For now, though, let's take a look at how researchers study false memories about less dramatic, everyday experiences.

■ What was the researchers' question?

How easy is it for people to form false memories? Henry Roediger and Kathleen McDermott (1995) addressed this question in an experiment to test for false memories as people recalled lists of words that had been read to them.

■ How did the researchers answer the question?

On each of sixteen trials, college students heard a different list of words. Each list related to a particular theme. For example, the "snow" list featured fifteen words such as *sleet,*

learn by doing **CONSTRUCTIVE MEMORY** Ask a friend to examine this photo for a minute or so (cover the caption). Then close the book and ask whether each of the following items appeared in the office: chair, wastebasket, bottle, typewriter, coffeepot, and book. If your friend reports having seen a wastebasket or a book, you will have demonstrated constructive memory.

slush, frost, white, cold, and so on. Yet the list's theme word—in this case, *snow*—was never included. On half the trials, the students were simply asked to recall as many words from the list as they could. But on the other half, the students did math problems before trying to recall the words. Working the math problems prevented them from rehearsing the words, as they had been able to do with the previous lists. When all sixteen lists had been presented, the students were given a new list of words and asked to say which of them had been on the lists they had heard earlier and which had not. Some of the words on this new list were theme words, such as *snow,* that had never been presented. Would the students "remember" having heard the theme words? How confident would they be about their "memory" of these words?

■ What did the researchers find?

The students falsely, but confidently, recalled hearing the theme words on 55 percent of the lists. In fact, theme words were falsely remembered as often as listed words were correctly remembered. As you might expect, accurate recall of the listed words was greater when the students had been allowed to say them shortly after hearing them rather than after first doing math problems. However, false memory of never-presented theme words occurred in both conditions.

■ What do the results mean?

The results of this study suggest that the participants could not always distinguish words they had heard from those they had not heard. Why? The never-presented theme words "belonged" with the lists of presented words and apparently were "remembered" because they fit logically into the gaps in the students' memories. In short, the students' knowledge of words that "should" have been included on the lists created a "memory" that they *were* presented.

   Given that rehearsal is known to improve short-term memory, why did these false memories appear even when the participants could both rehearse the listed words and quickly try to recall them? Perhaps the association between the never-presented theme words and the listed words was strong enough that rehearsing the listed words "pulled" the theme words along with them.

■ What do we still need to know?

Studies like this one make it clear that memory is constructive, and that memory distortion and inaccuracy are commonplace (Schacter, Norman, & Koutstaal, 1998; Schmolck, Buffalo, & Squire, 2000). We still need to identify the processes behind such distortion. In addition, we are not yet sure why false memories can seem as real to us as our memories of actual events. Perhaps the more frequently we recall an event (as when students were allowed to rehearse some lists), the stronger is our belief that we have accurately recalled it. There is also evidence that merely thinking about or hearing sounds associated with certain objects or events appears to make false memories of them more likely (Henkel, Franklin, & Johnson, 2000). Questions about how false memories are created lead to even deeper questions about the degree to which our imperfect memory processes might distort our experiences of reality. Is there an objective reality, or do we each experience our own version of reality?

Constructive Memory and PDP Models

Parallel distributed processing models of memory offer one way of explaining how semantic and episodic information become integrated in constructive memories. As mentioned earlier, PDP models suggest that newly learned facts alter our general knowledge of the world. In these network models, learned associations between specific facts

figure 6.8

The Effect of Schemas on Recall

In a classic study, people were shown figures like these, along with labels designed to activate certain schemas (Carmichael, Hogan, & Walter, 1932). For example, when showing the top figure, the experimenter said either "This resembles eyeglasses" or "This resembles a dumbbell." When the participants were asked to reproduce the figures from memory, their drawings tended to resemble the items mentioned by the experimenter. In other words, their memory had been altered by the schema-activating labels.

Figure shown to participants	Group 1		Group 2	
	Label given	Figure drawn by participants	Label given	Figure drawn by participants
◯—◯	Eyeglasses	◯◯	Dumbbell	◯—◯
⋈	Hourglass	⋈	Table	⋈
フ	Seven	7	Four	4
◁—	Gun	⟞⟵	Broom	🧹

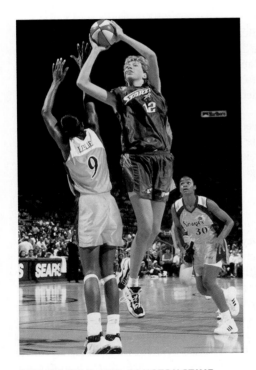

PDP MODELS AND CONSTRUCTIVE MEMORY If you were to hear that "our basketball team won last night," your schema about basketball might prompt you to encode, and later retrieve, the fact that the players were men. Such spontaneous, though often incorrect, generalizations associated with PDP models of memory help account for constructive memory.

schemas Mental representations of categories of objects, places, events and people.

come together. Let's say, for example, that your own network "knows" that your friend Joe is a male European American student who is a business major. It also "knows" that Claudia is a female African American student. However, your network has never learned Claudia's major. Now suppose that every other student you know is a business major. In this case, the connection between "students you know" and "business majors" would be so strong that you would conclude that Claudia is a business major, too. You would be so confident in this belief that it would take overwhelming evidence for you to change your mind (Rumelhart & McClelland, 1986). In short, you would have constructed a memory about Claudia.

PDP networks also produce *spontaneous generalizations*. So if your friend tells you that she just bought a new car, you would know without asking that, like all other cars you have experienced, it has four wheels. This is a spontaneous generalization from your knowledge base. Such spontaneous generalizations are obviously helpful, but they can also create significant errors if the network is based on limited or biased experience with a class of objects or people.

If it occurs to you that ethnic prejudice can result from spontaneous generalization errors, you are right (Greenwald & Banaji, 1995). But ironically, researchers are encouraged by this prejudicial aspect of PDP networks, because it is an accurate reflection of human thought and memory. Virtually all people make spontaneous generalizations about males, females, European Americans, African Americans, the young, the old, and many other categories (Rudman et al., 1999). Is prejudice, then, a process that we have no choice in or control over? Not necessarily. Relatively unprejudiced people tend to recognize that they are making generalizations and consciously try to ignore or suppress them (Monteith, Sherman, & Devine, 1998).

Schemas   PDP models also help us understand constructive memory by explaining the operation of the schemas that guide it. As described in the chapters on social psychology and on thought, language, and intelligence, **schemas** are mental representations of categories of objects, places, events, and people. For example, most Americans have a schema for *baseball game*, so simply hearing these words is likely to activate whole clusters of information in long-term memory, including the rules of the game and images of players, bats, balls, a green field, summer days, and perhaps hot dogs and stadiums. The generalized knowledge contained in schemas provides a basis for making inferences about incoming information during the encoding stage. So if you hear that a baseball player was injured, your schema about baseball might prompt you to encode the incident as game related, even though the cause was not mentioned. Later, you are likely to recall the injury as having occurred during a game (see Figure 6.8 for another example).

LINKAGES

How accurate is eyewitness testimony?

(a link to Sensation and Perception)

There are few situations in which accurate retrieval of memories is more important—and constructive memory is more dangerous—than when an eyewitness testifies in court about a crime. Let's consider the accuracy of eyewitness memory and how it can be distorted. The most compelling evidence a lawyer can provide is that of an eyewitness, but eyewitnesses make many mistakes (Loftus & Ketcham, 1991; Wells, Olson, & Charman, 2002). In 1984, for example, North Carolina college student Jennifer Thompson confidently identified Ronald Cotton as the man who had raped her at knifepoint. Mainly on the basis of Thompson's eyewitness testimony, Cotton was convicted of rape and sentenced to life in prison. He was released eleven years later, when DNA evidence revealed that he was innocent (and identified another man as the rapist). The eyewitness/victim's certainty had convinced a jury, but her memory had been faulty (O'Neill, 2000).

Like the rest of us, eyewitnesses can remember only what they perceive, and they can perceive only what they attended to (Backman & Nilsson, 1991). The witnesses' task is to report as accurately as possible what they saw or heard. But no matter how hard they try to be accurate, there are limits to how valid their reports can be (Kassin, Rigby, & Castillo, 1991). For example, hearing new information about a crime, including the form of a lawyer's question, can alter a witness's memory (Belli & Loftus, 1996). Experiments show that when witnesses are asked "How fast were the cars going when they *smashed into* each other?" they are likely to recall a higher speed than when asked "How fast were the cars going when they *hit* each other?" (Loftus & Palmer, 1974; see Figure 6.9). There is also evidence that an object or event mentioned after the fact is often mistakenly remembered as having been seen (Dodson & Reisberg, 1991). For example, if a lawyer says that a screwdriver was lying on the ground (when it was not), witnesses may recall with great certainty having seen it (Ryan & Geiselman, 1991). This *misinformation effect* can occur in several ways (Loftus & Hoffman, 1989). In some cases, hearing new information can make it harder to retrieve the original memory (Tversky & Tuchin, 1989). In others, the new information may be integrated into the old memory, making it impossible to distinguish from what was originally seen (Loftus, 1992). In still others, an eyewitness report might be influenced by the person's assumption that if a lawyer or police officer says an object was there, or that something happened, it must be true.

LINKAGES

Memory and Perception in the Courtroom

figure 6.9

The Impact of Questions on Eyewitness Memory

After seeing a filmed traffic accident, people were asked, "About how fast were the cars going when they (smashed into, hit, or contacted) each other?" As shown here, the witnesses' responses were influenced by the verb used in the question; *smashed* was associated with the highest average speed estimates. A week later, people who heard the question using *smashed* remembered the accident as being more violent than did people in the other two groups (Loftus & Palmer, 1974).

Original information

External information

About how fast were the cars going when they SMASHED INTO each other?

The "memory"

HERMAN

8-10   © Jim Unger/dist. by United Media, 2001

**"Can you identify the man who
punched you in the knee?"**

**This is exactly the sort of biased lineup that
*Eyewitness Evidence: A Guide for Law
Enforcement* (U.S. Department of Justice,
1999) is designed to avoid. Based on
research in memory and perception, this
guide recommends that no suspect should
stand out from all the others in a lineup,
that witnesses should not assume the real
criminal is in the lineup, and that they
should not be encouraged to base identification on their "best guess."**

Jurors' belief in a witness's testimony often depends as much (or even more) on *how*
the witness presents evidence as on the content or relevance of that evidence. For example, many jurors are particularly impressed by witnesses who give lots of details about
what they saw. Extremely detailed testimony from prosecution witnesses is especially
likely to lead to guilty verdicts, even when the details reported are irrelevant (Bell & Loftus, 1989). Apparently, when a witness reports details, such as the exact time of the crime
or the color of the criminal's shoes, jurors assume that the witness had paid especially
close attention or has a particularly good memory. This assumption seems reasonable,
but there are limits on how much people can pay attention to, particularly when they are
emotionally aroused and there is not much time to scan the scene. So especially when
crimes happen quickly, witnesses whose attention was drawn to details such as shoe color
might not have accurately perceived the criminal's facial features (Backman & Nilsson,
1991). The fact that an eyewitness reports many details does not guarantee that all of
them were remembered correctly.

Jurors also tend to believe witnesses who are confident about their testimony (Leippe,
Manion, & Romanczyk, 1992). Unfortunately, research shows that witnesses' confidence
is frequently much higher than the accuracy of their reports (Shaw, 1996; Wells, Olson, &
Charman, 2002). Why? In some cases, inflated confidence may stem from repeated exposure to misinformation and the repeated recall of that misinformation, both of which
can make witnesses more sure of themselves even when they are giving incorrect testimony (Lamb, 1998; Mitchell & Zaragoza, 1996; Roediger, Jacoby, & McDermott, 1996).
In short, as in the Jennifer Thompson case, witnesses who are confident about their testimony are not always correct.

The weaknesses inherent in eyewitness memory can be amplified by the use of police
lineups and certain other criminal identification procedures (Wells & Olson, 2003). In one
study, for example, participants watched a videotaped crime and then tried to identify the
criminal from a set of photographs (Wells & Bradfield, 1999). None of the photos showed
the person who had committed the crime, but some participants nevertheless identified one
of them as the criminal they saw on tape. When these mistaken participants were led to
believe that they had correctly identified the criminal, they became even more confident in
the accuracy of their false identification (Wells, Olson, & Charman, 2003). These incorrect,
but confident, witnesses became more likely than other participants to claim that it had
been easy for them to identify the criminal from the photos because they had had a good
view of him and had paid careful attention to him.

As of 2003, over 100 people, including Ronald Cotton, have been released from
U.S. prisons after DNA tests or other evidence revealed that they had been falsely convicted—mostly on the basis of faulty eyewitness testimony (Death Penalty Information Center, 2002; Scheck, Neufeld, & Dwyer, 2000; Wells et al., 2000). DNA evidence
freed Charles Fain, who had been convicted of murder and spent almost 18 years on
death row in Idaho (Bonner, 2001). Maryland officials approved $900,000 in compen-
sation for Bernard Webster, who served 20 years in prison for rape before DNA
revealed that he was innocent (Associated Press, 2003). Frank Lee Smith, too, would
have been set free after the sole eyewitness at his murder trial retracted her testimony,
but he had already died of cancer while awaiting execution in a Florida prison.
Research on memory and perception helps explain how these miscarriages of justice
can occur, and it is also guiding efforts to prevent such errors in the future. The U.S.
Department of Justice has acknowledged the potential for errors in eyewitness evidence, as well as the dangers of asking witnesses to identify suspects from lineups and
photo arrays. The result is *Eyewitness Evidence: A Guide for Law Enforcement* (U.S.
Department of Justice, 1999), the first-ever guide for police and prosecutors involved
in obtaining eyewitness evidence. The guide warns these officials that asking leading
questions about what witnesses saw can distort their memory, that witnesses should
examine photographs of possible suspects one at a time, and that false identifications
are less likely if witnesses viewing suspects in a lineup are told that the real perpetrator might not be included (Wells & Olson, 2003; Wells et al., 2000).

method of savings   A method for measuring forgetting.

Forgetting

► **What causes me to forget things?**

The frustrations of forgetting—where you left your keys, the answer to a test question, an anniversary—are apparent to most people nearly every day (Neisser, 2000b). Let's look more closely at the nature of forgetting and what causes it.

How Do We Forget?

Hermann Ebbinghaus, a German psychologist, began the systematic study of memory and forgetting in the late 1800s, using only himself as a research participant. He read aloud a list of nonsense syllables, such as *POF, XEM,* and *QAL,* at a constant pace, and then tried to recall the syllables.

Ebbinghaus devised the **method of savings** to measure how much he forgot over time. This method computes the difference between the number of repetitions (or trials) needed to learn a list of items and the number of repetitions needed to relearn it after some period of time has passed. This difference represents the *savings* from one learning to the next. If it took Ebbinghaus ten trials to learn a list and ten more trials to relearn it, there would be no savings. Forgetting would have been complete. If it took him ten trials to learn the list and only five trials to relearn it, there would be a savings of 50 percent.

Ebbinghaus's research produced two lasting discoveries. One is the shape of the forgetting curve shown in Figure 6.10. Even when psychologists have substituted words, sentences, and stories for nonsense syllables, the forgetting curve shows the same strong initial drop in memory, followed by a more moderate decrease over time (Slamecka & McElree, 1983). Of course, we remember sensible stories better than nonsense syllables, but the shape of the curve is the same no matter what type of material is involved (Davis & Moore, 1935). Even the forgetting of events from daily life tends to follow Ebbinghaus's forgetting curve (Thomson, 1982).

Ebbinghaus also discovered just how long-lasting "savings" in long-term memory can be. Psychologists now know from the method of savings that information about everything from algebra to bike riding is often retained for decades (Matlin, 1998). So, although you may forget something you have learned if you do not use the information, it is very easy to relearn the material if the need arises, indicating that the forgetting was not complete (Hall & Bahrick, 1998).

figure 6.10

Ebbinghaus's Curve of Forgetting

learn by **doing** Select thirty words at random from a dictionary, and spend a few minutes memorizing them. After an hour has passed, write down as many words as you can remember, but don't look at the original list again. Test yourself again eight hours later, a day later, and two days later. Now look at the original list, and see how well you did on each recall test. Ebbinghaus found that most forgetting occurs during the first nine hours after learning, and especially during the first hour. If this was not the case for you, why do you think you got different results?

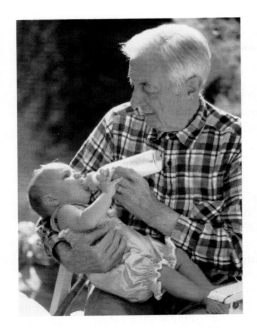

IT'S ALL COMING BACK TO ME This grandfather has not fed an infant for decades, but his memory of how to do it is not entirely gone. He showed some "savings"; it took him less time to relearn the skill than it took him to learn it initially.

Why Do We Forget?

We have seen *how* forgetting occurs, but *why* does it happen? In principle, one of two processes can be responsible (Best, 1999). One process is **decay,** the gradual disappearance of the information from memory. Decay occurs in memory in much the same way as the inscription on a ring or bracelet wears away and becomes less distinct over time. Forgetting might also occur because of interference. Through **interference,** either the storage or the retrieval of information is impaired by the presence of other information. Interference might occur because one piece of information actually displaces other information, pushing it out of memory. It might also occur because one piece of information makes storing or recalling other information more difficult.

In the case of short-term memory, if an item is not rehearsed or thought about, memory of it decreases consistently over the course of eighteen seconds or so. Simple decay appears to play a big role in the forgetting of information in short-term memory. But interference through displacement can also be operating. Like a desktop, short-term memory can hold only so much. When additional items are added, the old ones tend to "fall off" and are no longer available (Haberlandt, 1999). Displacement is one reason why the phone number you just looked up is likely to drop out of short-term memory if you read another number immediately afterward. Rehearsal prevents displacement by continually reentering the same information into short-term memory.

The cause of forgetting from long-term memory appears to be more directly tied to interference, but it is also more complicated. In long-term memory there can be **retroactive interference,** in which learning of new information interferes with recall of older information. There can also be **proactive interference,** in which old information interferes with learning or remembering new information. Retroactive interference would help explain why studying French vocabulary this term might make it more difficult to remember the Spanish words you learned last term. And because of proactive interference, the French words you are learning now might make it harder to learn German next term. Figure 6.11 outlines the types of experiments used to study the influence of each form of interference in long-term memory.

figure 6.11

Procedures for Studying Interference

To remember the difference between the two types of interference, keep in mind that the prefixes—*pro* and *retro*—indicate directions in time. *Pro* means "forward," and *retro* means "backward." In proactive interference, previously learned material "comes forward" to interfere with new learning; retroactive interference occurs when new information "goes back" to interfere with the recall of past learning.

PROACTIVE INTERFERENCE

Group	Time 1	Time 2	Time 3	Result
Experimental	Learn list A	Learn list B	Recall list B	The experimental group will suffer from proactive interference, and the control group will be able to recall more material from list B.
Control		Learn list B	Recall list B	

RETROACTIVE INTERFERENCE

Group	Time 1	Time 2	Time 3	Result
Experimental	Learn list A	Learn list B	Recall list A	The experimental group will suffer from retroactive interference, and the control group will be able to recall more material from list A.
Control	Learn list A		Recall list A	

Source: Tulving & Psotka (1971).

figure 6.12

Retrieval Failures and Forgetting

On the initial test in Tulving and Psotka's experiment, people's ability to recall a list of items was strongly affected by the number of other lists they learned before being tested on the first one. When item-category (retrieval) cues were provided on a second test, however, retroactive interference from the intervening lists almost disappeared.

LINKAGES
Do forgotten memories remain in the subconscious?
(a link to Consciousness)

decay The gradual disappearance of information from memory.

interference The process through which storage or retrieval of information is impaired by the presence of other information.

retroactive interference A cause of forgetting whereby new information placed in memory interferes with the ability to recall information already in memory.

proactive interference A cause of forgetting whereby previously learned information interferes with the ability to remember new information.

Does interference push information out of memory, or does it merely hinder the ability to retrieve the information? To find out, Endel Tulving and Joseph Psotka (1971) presented people with different numbers of word lists. Each list contained words from six categories, such as types of buildings (*hut, cottage, cabin, hotel*) or earth formations (*cliff, river, hill, volcano*). Some people learned a list and then recalled as many of the words as possible. Other groups learned the first list and then learned different numbers of other lists before trying to recall the first one.

The results were dramatic. As the number of additional lists increased, the number of words that people could recall from the original list consistently decreased. This finding reflected strong retroactive interference. Then the researchers gave a second test, in which they provided people with a retrieval cue by telling the category of the words (such as "types of buildings") to be recalled. Now the number of additional lists had almost no effect on the number of words recalled from the original list, as Figure 6.12 shows. These results indicate that the words were still represented in long-term memory; they had not been pushed out, but the participants could not remember them without appropriate retrieval cues. In short, faulty retrieval caused the original forgetting. Putting more and more information in long-term memory may be like placing more and more CDs in a storage case. Although none of the CDs disappears, it becomes increasingly difficult to find the one you are looking for.

Some theorists have concluded that all forgetting from long-term memory is due to some form of retrieval failure (Ratcliff & McKoon, 1989). Does this mean that everything in long-term memory remains there until death, even if you cannot always, or ever, recall it? No one yet knows for sure, but as described in the next section, this question lies at the heart of some highly controversial court cases.

In 1989, Eileen Franklin told California police that when she looked into her young daughter's eyes one day, she suddenly remembered seeing her father kill her childhood friend more than twenty years earlier. On the basis of her testimony about this memory, her father, George Franklin, Sr., was sent to prison for murder (Loftus & Ketcham, 1994).

THINKING CRITICALLY

Can Traumatic Memories Be Repressed, Then Recovered?

■ What am I being asked to believe or accept?

The prosecution in the Franklin case successfully argued that Eileen had repressed, and then recovered, her memory of a murder. Similar arguments in other cases tried in the early 1990s also resulted in imprisonment as now-adult children claimed to have recovered childhood memories of physical or sexual abuse at the hands of their parents. The juries in these trials accepted the assertion that all memory of shocking events can be repressed, or pushed into an inaccessible corner of the mind where, for decades, subconscious processes keep it out of awareness, yet potentially subject to recall (Hyman, 2000). And juries are not the only believers. A few years ago a large American news organization reported that the United States had illegally used nerve gas during the war in Vietnam. This story was based, in part, on a Vietnam veteran's account of recovered memories of having been subjected to a nerve gas attack.

■ Is there evidence available to support the claim?

Proponents of the repressed memory argument point to several lines of evidence to support their claims. First, as discussed in the chapter on consciousness, a substantial amount of mental activity occurs outside of awareness (Kihlstrom, 1999). Second, research on implicit memory shows that our behavior can be influenced by information of which we are unaware (Schacter, Chiu, & Ochsner, 1993). Third, retrieval cues can help people recall memories that had previously been inaccessible to conscious aware-ness (Andrews et al., 2000; Landsdale & Laming, 1995). For example, carefully docu-mented cases report that these cues have helped soldiers remember for the first time the circumstances under which they had been wounded many years before (Karon & Wide-ner, 1997). Fourth, research on *motivated forgetting* suggests that people are able to will-fully suppress information so that it is no longer accessible on a later memory test (Anderson & Green, 2001). Even suppressing one's emotional reactions to events can interfere with memories of those events (Richards & Gross, 2000). And people appear more likely to forget unpleasant rather than pleasant events (Erdelyi, 1985). In one study, a psychologist kept a detailed record of his daily life over a six-year period. When he later tried to recall these experiences, he remembered more than half of the positive events but only one-third of the negative ones (Waagenaar, 1986). In another study, 38 percent of women who, as children, had been brought to a hospital because of sexual abuse did not report the incident as adults (Williams, 1994). Finally, there is the confidence with which people report recovered memories; they say they are just too vivid to be anything but real.

■ Can that evidence be interpreted another way?

Those who are skeptical about repressed memories do not deny that subconscious mem-ory and retrieval processes exist (Kihlstrom, 1999). They also recognize that, sadly, child abuse and other traumas are all too common. But these facts do not eliminate the possi-bility that any given "recovered" memory may actually be a distorted, or constructed, memory (Clancy et al., 2000). Our recall of past events is affected by what happened at the time, what we knew beforehand, and everything we have experienced since. The peo-ple who "remembered" nonexistent books in an office inadvertently used their prior knowledge of what is usually in graduate students' offices to construct a false memory for the books. Similarly, the "recovered memory" of the Vietnam veteran mentioned earlier appears to have no basis in fact; the news story about the alleged nerve gas attack was later retracted.

As we saw in the Focus on Research section, false memories—distortions of actual events and the recall of events that didn't actually happen—can be just as vivid as real, accurate memories, and people can be just as confident in them (Brainerd & Reyna, 1998; Pezdek, Finger, & Hodge, 1997; Roediger & McDermott, 2000). In one case study, for example, a teenager named Chris was given descriptions of four incidents from his childhood and asked to write about each of them every day for five days (Loftus, 1997a). One of these incidents—being lost in a shopping mall at age five—never really hap-pened. Yet Chris eventually "remembered" this event, and he even added many details about the mall and the stranger whose hand he was supposedly found holding. He also rated this (false) memory as being more vivid than two of the other three (real) incidents he wrote about. A more recent study found similar results in about half of seventy-seven child participants (Porter, Yuille, & Lehman, 1999). The same pattern of results has appeared in formal experiments on the planting of emotion-laden false memories (Hyman & Pentland, 1996; Loftus & Pickrell, 1995). Researchers have been able to create vivid and striking, but completely false, memories of events that people thought they experienced when they were one day old (DuBreuil, Garry, & Loftus, 1998). In other experiments, children who were repeatedly asked about a nonexistent trauma (getting a hand caught in a mousetrap) eventually developed a vivid and unshakable false memory of experiencing it (Ceci et al., 1994). In other words, people sometimes have a difficult time distinguishing between what has happened to them and what they have only imag-ined, or have come to believe, has happened (Garry & Polaschek, 2000; Johnson & Raye, 1998; Mazzoni & Memon, 2003; Zaragoza et al., 2001).

Some studies have found that people who are fantasy-prone and tend to have lapses in attention and memory are more likely than others to develop false memories and possi-bly more likely to report the recovery of repressed memories (McNally, 2003; McNally et al., 2000b; Porter et al., 2000). Two other studies have found that women who have suf-fered physical or sexual abuse are more likely to falsely remember words on a laboratory

applying psychology

EXPLORING MEMORY PROCESSES Research by Elizabeth Loftus (shown here with a student) and other cognitive psychologists has demonstrated mechanisms through which false memories can be created. They have shown, for example, that false memories appear even in research participants who are told about them and asked to avoid them (McDermott & Roediger, 1998). Their work has helped to focus scientific scrutiny on reports of recovered memories, especially those arising from contact with therapists who assume that most people have repressed memories of abuse.

recall test (Bremner, Shobe, & Kihlstrom, 2000; Zoellner et al., 2000). This tendency appears strongest among abused women who show signs of posttraumatic stress disorder (Bremner, Shobe, & Kihlstrom, 2000). Another study found that the tendency to have false memories on a word recall task was greater in women who reported recovered memories of sexual abuse than in nonabused women or in those who had always remembered the abuse they suffered (Clancy et al., 2000). False memories on this laboratory recall task are also more common among people who claim to have been abducted by space aliens than among other people (Clancy et al., 2002).

Why would anyone "remember" a trauma that did not actually occur? Elizabeth Loftus (1997b) suggests that for one thing, popular books such as *The Courage to Heal* (Bass & Davis, 1994) and *Secret Survivors* (Blume, 1998) may lead people to believe that anyone who experiences guilt, depression, low self-esteem, overemotionality, or any of a long list of other problems is harboring repressed memories of abuse. This message, says Loftus, is reinforced and elaborated by some therapists, particularly those who specialize in using guided imagination, hypnosis, and other methods to "help" clients recover repressed memories (Polusny & Follette, 1996; Poole et al., 1995). In so doing, these therapists may influence their clients to construct false memories by encouraging them to imagine experiencing events that might never have actually occurred, or that occurred only in a dream (Mazzoni & Loftus, 1996; Olio, 1994). As one client described her therapy, "I was rapidly losing the ability to differentiate between my imagination and my real memory" (Loftus & Ketcham, 1994, p. 25). To such therapists, a client's failure to recover memories of abuse, or refusal to accept that they exist, is evidence of "denial" (Loftus, 1997a; Tavris, 2003).

The possibility that recovered memories might actually be false memories has led to dismissed charges or not-guilty verdicts for defendants in some repressed memory cases. In other cases, previously convicted defendants have been released. (George Franklin's conviction was overturned, but only after he spent five years in prison.) Concern over the potential damage resulting from false memories prompted the establishment in 1992 of the False Memory Syndrome Foundation, an organization of families affected by abuse allegations. In cooperation with a scientific and professional advisory board, this organization seeks to educate the public about the problems created by accusations stemming from allegedly repressed memories. More than a hundred of these families (including George Franklin's) have filed lawsuits against hospitals and therapists. In 1994, California winery executive Gary Ramona received $500,000 in damages from two therapists who had "helped" his daughter recall alleged sexual abuse at his hands. A more recent suit led to a $2 million judgment against a Minnesota therapist whose client discovered that her "recovered" memories of childhood were false; a similar case in Wisconsin brought a $5 million judgment against two therapists. And an Illinois case resulted in a $10.6 million settlement and the suspension of the license of the psychiatrist who had "found" his patient's lost memories (Loftus, 1998).

■ What evidence would help to evaluate the alternatives?

Evaluating reports of recovered memories would be easier if we had more information about whether it is possible for people to repress memories of traumatic events. If it is possible, we also need to know how common it is and how accurate recovered memories might be. So far, we know that some people apparently forget intense emotional experiences, but that most have vivid and long-lasting memories of them (Goodman et al., 2003; Pope et al., 1998; Strongman & Kemp, 1991). Some are called *flashbulb memories* because they preserve particular experiences in great detail (Brown & Kulik, 1977). In fact, many people who live through trauma are *unable* to forget it. In the sexual abuse study mentioned earlier, for example (Williams, 1994), 62 percent of the victims recalled as adults the trauma that had been documented in their childhoods. A similar study of a different group of adults found that 81 percent of them recalled their documented childhood abuse (Goodman et al., 2003). The true recall figures might actually be higher in such studies, because some people who remember abuse may not wish to talk about it. In any case, additional studies like these—studies that track the fate of memories in known abuse cases—would not only help estimate the prevalence of this kind of forgetting but also might offer clues as to the kinds of people and events most likely to be associated with it.

It would also be valuable to know more about the processes through which repression might occur. Is there a mechanism that specifically pushes traumatic memories out of awareness, then keeps them at a subconscious level for long periods? So far, cognitive psychologists have not found evidence for such a mechanism (Loftus, 1997a; McNally, Clancy, & Schacter, 2001; McNally, 2003; McNally et al., 2000a; Pope et al., 1998).

■ What conclusions are most reasonable?

An objective reading of the research evidence suggests that the recovery of traumatic memories is not impossible, but that the implantation of false memories is clearly possible—and has been demonstrated repeatedly in numerous controlled experiments (Brainerd & Reyna, 2002). With this in mind, it is not easy to decide whether any particular case is an instance of recovered memory or false memory, especially when there is no objective corroborating evidence.

The intense conflict between those who uncritically accept claims of recovered memories and those who are more wary about the accuracy of such claims reflects a fundamental disagreement about evidence (Tavris, 2003). To many therapists who deal daily with victims of sexual abuse and other traumas, clients' reports constitute stronger "proof" of recovered memories than do the results of laboratory experiments. Those reports are viewed with considerably more skepticism by psychologists who engage in, or rely on, empirical research on the processes of memory and forgetting (Loftus, 2003; Pope, 1998).

So whether you believe a claim of recovered memory may be determined by the relative weight you assign to personal experiences and intuition versus evidence that comes from controlled experiments. Still, the apparent ease with which false memories can be created should lead judges, juries, and the general public to exercise great caution before accepting unverified memories of traumatic events as the truth. At the same time, we should not automatically reject the claims of people who appear to have recovered memories. Perhaps the wisest course is to use all the scientific and circumstantial evidence available to carefully and critically examine claims of recovered memories while keeping in mind the possibility that constructive memory processes *might* have influenced those memories. This careful, scientific approach is vital if we are to protect the rights of those who report recovered memories, as well as those who face accusations arising from them.

Biological Bases of Memory

▶ How does my brain change when I store a memory?

Many psychologists who study memory focus on explicit and implicit mental processes. Others explore the physical, electrical, and chemical changes that take place in the brain when people encode, store, and retrieve information (Cavallaro et al., 2002; Mitchell, Heatherton, & Macrae, 2002; Otten, Hensen, & Rugg, 2002).

The Biochemistry of Memory

As described in the chapter on biology and behavior, communication among brain cells takes place at the synapses between axons and dendrites, using chemicals called *neurotransmitters* that are released at the synapses. The formation and storage of new memories are associated with at least two kinds of changes in synapses.

figure 6.13

Building Memories

These models of synapses are based on electron microscope images of neurons in the brain. Notice that, before signals were repeatedly sent across the synapse, just one spine (shown in white) appears on this part of the dendrite. Afterward, there are two spines, which helps improve communication across the synapse. The creation and changing of many individual synapses in the brain appears to underlie the formation and storage of new memories.

 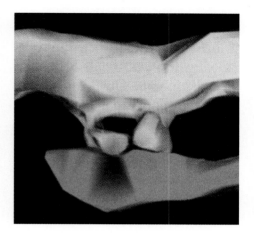

Source: Toni et al. (1999).

The first kind of change occurs when stimulation from the environment promotes the formation of *new* synapses. Scientists can now actually see this process occur. As shown in Figure 6.13, repeatedly sending signals across a particular synapse increases the number of special little branches, called *spines,* that appear on the receiving cell's dendrites (Toni et al., 1999). The second kind of change occurs as new experiences alter the functioning of *existing* synapses. For example, when two neurons fire at the same time and together stimulate a third neuron, that other neuron will later be more responsive than before to stimulation by either neuron alone. This process of "sensitizing" synapses is called *long-term potentiation* (Li et al., 2003; Rioult-Pedotti, Friedman, & Donoghue, 2000). Changing patterns of electrical stimulation can also weaken synaptic connections (Malenka, 1995). Such changes in sensitivity could account for the development of conditioned responses and other types of learning.

In the hippocampus (see Figure 6.14), these changes appear to occur at synapses that use the neurotransmitter *glutamate* (Malenka & Nicoll, 1999). Other neurotransmitters, such as *acetylcholine,* also play important roles in memory formation (e.g., Furey, Pietrini, & Haxby, 2000; Li et al., 2003). The memory problems seen in Alzheimer's patients are related to a deficiency in neurons that use acetylcholine and send fibers to the hippocampus and the cortex (Muir, 1997). Drugs that interfere with the action of acetylcholine impair memory, and drugs that increase the amount of acetylcholine in

figure 6.14

Brain Structures Involved in Memory

Combined neural activity in many parts of the brain allows us to encode, store, and retrieve memories. The complexity of the biological bases of these processes is underscored by research showing that different aspects of a memory—such as the sights and sounds of some event—are stored in different parts of the cerebral cortex.

Cerebral cortex

Thalamus

Hippocampus

Cerebellum

synapses improve memory in aging animals and humans (Pettit, Shao, & Yakel, 2001; Sirvio, 1999).

In summary, research has shown that the formation of memories is associated with changes in many individual synapses that, together, strengthen and improve the communication in networks of neurons (Malleret et al., 2001; Rosenzweig & Bennett, 1996).

LINKAGES
Where are memories stored?
(a link to Biology and Behavior)

Brain Structures and Memory

Are the biochemical processes involved in memory concentrated in certain brain regions, or are they distributed throughout the brain? The latest research suggests that memory involves both specialized regions for various types of memory formation and widespread areas for storage.

The Impact of Brain Damage   Studies of how brain injuries affect memory provide evidence about which parts of the brain are involved in various kinds of memory. For example, damage to the hippocampus, nearby parts of the cerebral cortex, and the thalamus often results in **anterograde amnesia,** a loss of memory for any event occurring after the injury. People who suffer this kind of damage are unable to form new memories.

The case of H.M. provides a striking example of anterograde amnesia (Milner, 1966). When H.M. was twenty-seven years old, part of his hippocampus was removed to end his severe epileptic seizures. After the operation, both his long-term and short-term memory appeared normal, but something was wrong. Two years later, he still believed that he was twenty-seven. When his family moved into a new house, he could not remember the new address or how to get there. When his uncle died, he grieved in a normal way; but soon after, he began to ask why his uncle had not visited him. He had to be repeatedly reminded of the death and, each time, H.M. began the mourning process all over again. The surgery had apparently destroyed the mechanism that transfers information from short-term to long-term memory. Now in his seventies, H.M. lives in a nursing home, where his only long-term memories are from fifty years ago, before the operation. He is still unable to recall events and facts he has experienced since then—not even the names of people he sees every day (Hathaway, 2002).

Although patients with damage to the hippocampus cannot form new episodic memories, they may still be able to form implicit memories. For example, H.M.'s performance on a complicated puzzle improved steadily over several days, just as it does with normal people, and eventually it became virtually perfect. But each time he tried the puzzle, he insisted that he had never seen it before (Cohen & Corkin, 1981). A musician with a similar kind of brain damage was able to use his implicit memory to continue leading choral groups (Vattano, 2000). So it appears that the hippocampus is crucial in the formation of new episodic memories, but that implicit memory, procedural memory, and working memory are governed by other regions of the brain (Squire, 1992).

Retrograde amnesia involves loss of memory for events *prior* to some brain injury. Often, a person with this type of amnesia can't remember anything that took place in the months or years before the injury (Kapur, 1999). In 1994, head injuries from a car crash left thirty-six-year-old Perlene Griffith-Barwell with retrograde amnesia so severe that she forgot virtually everything she had learned about everything and everybody over the previous twenty years. She thought she was still sixteen and did not recognize her husband, Malcolm, or her four children. She said, "The children were sweet, but they didn't seem like mine," and she "didn't feel anything" for Malcolm. Her memories of the last twenty years have never fully returned. She is divorced, but she still lives with her children and holds a job in a bank (Weinstein, 1999).

Unlike Perlene, most victims of retrograde amnesia gradually recover their memories (Riccio, Millin, & Gisquet-Verrier, 2003). The most distant events are recalled first; then the person gradually regains memory for events leading up to the injury.

anterograde amnesia   A loss of memory for events that occur after a brain injury.

retrograde amnesia   A loss of memory for events that occurred prior to a brain injury.

Recovery is seldom complete, however, and the person may never remember the last few seconds before the injury. One man received a severe blow to the head after being thrown from his motorcycle. Upon regaining consciousness, he claimed that he was eleven years old. Over the next three months, he slowly recalled more and more of his life. He remembered when he was twelve, thirteen, and so on—right up until the time he was riding his motorcycle the day of the accident. But he was never able to remember what happened just before the accident (Baddeley, 1982). Those final events were probably encoded into short-term memory, but apparently they were never transferred into long-term memory.

Other conditions that suppress neural activity in the brain can also disrupt the transfer of information from short-term to long-term memory. These conditions include anesthetic drugs, poisoning by carbon monoxide or other toxins, and strong electrical impulses such as those in the electroconvulsive therapy that is sometimes used to treat cases of severe depression (see the chapter on treatment of psychological disorders).

Multiple Storage Areas   Obviously, the hippocampus does not permanently store long-term memories (Bayley, Hopkins & Squire, 2003; Rosenbaum et al., 2000). (If it did, H.M. would not have retained memories from the years before part of his hippocampus was removed.) The hippocampus and thalamus send nerve impulses to the cerebral cortex, and it is in the cortex that long-term semantic and episodic memories are probably stored (Gabrieli, 1998)—but not just in one place. As we saw in the chapter on biology and behavior, different regions of the cortex receive messages from different senses. Specific aspects of an experience are probably stored near these regions. For example, damage to the auditory association cortex disrupts memory for sounds (Colombo et al., 1990). A memory, however, involves more than one sensory system. Even in the simple case of a rat remembering a maze, the experience of the maze involves vision, smell, movements, and emotions, each of which may be stored in different regions of the brain (Gallagher & Chiba, 1996). So memories are both localized and distributed. Certain brain areas store specific aspects of each remembered event, but many brain systems are involved in experiencing a whole event. For example, the cerebellum (see Figure 6.14) is involved in the storage of procedural memories, such as dance steps and other movements.

What happens in the brain as we retrieve memories? Functional neuroimaging studies show that the hippocampus, as well as various regions of the cerebral cortex, are active during memory retrieval (Buckner & Wheeler, 2001; Cabeza et al., 2001; Davachi, Mitchell, & Wagner, 2003; McDermott & Buckner, 2001; Rugg & Wilding, 2000). There is also evidence to suggest that retrieving memories of certain experiences, such as a conversation or a tennis game, reactivates the sensory and motor regions of the brain that had been involved during the event itself (Nyberg et al., 2001). Research shows, too, that when an emotional (fear-related) memory is recalled, it may be subject to a biological restorage process during which it is open to alteration (Eisenberg et al., 2003; Nader, Schafe, & Le Doux, 2000). Cognitive neuroscientists are also trying to determine whether different patterns of brain activity are associated with the retrieval of accurate versus inaccurate memories (Gonsalves & Paller, 2000). Future research in these areas will have obvious applications in areas such as lie detection, the understanding of false memory processes, and the evaluation of claims of recovered memories.

A CASE OF RETROGRADE AMNESIA
Trevor Rees-Jones, a bodyguard for Diana, Princess of Wales, is the sole survivor of the 1997 car crash that killed her; her companion, Dodi al-Fayed; and her driver. The head injury Rees-Jones received left him with retrograde amnesia. It was months before he could begin to recall anything about the events leading up to the accident, and he still cannot remember the accident itself. This type of amnesia is relatively common following concussions, so if you ride a bicycle or a motorcycle, wear that helmet!

Improving Your Memory

▶ **How can I remember more information?**

Although many basic questions about what memory is and how it works remain, psychologists know a great deal about how people can improve their memories (Neisser, 2000a).

Mnemonics

One way to improve your memory is to employ mnemonics (pronounced "nee-MON-ix"). **Mnemonics** are strategies for putting information into an organized context in order to remember it more easily. To remember the names of the Great Lakes, for example, you could use the acronym HOMES (for Huron, Ontario, Michigan, Erie, and Superior). Verbal organization is the basis for many mnemonics. You can link items by weaving them into a story, a sentence, or a rhyme. To help customers remember where they have parked their cars, some large garages have replaced section designations such as "A1" or "G8" with the names of colors, months, or animals. Customers can then tie the location of their cars to information already in long-term memory—for example, "I parked in the month of my mother's birthday."

One simple but powerful mnemonic is called the *method of loci* (pronounced "LOW-sigh"), or the "method of places." To use this method, first think about a set of familiar locations. Use your home, for example. You might imagine walking through the front door, around all four corners of the living room, and through each of the other rooms. Next, imagine each item to be remembered in one of these locations. Whenever you want to remember a list, use the same locations, in the same order. Creating vivid or unusual images of how the items appear in each location seems to be particularly effective (Kline & Groninger, 1991). For example, tomatoes smashed against the front door or bananas hanging from the bedroom ceiling might be helpful in recalling these items on a grocery list.

Guidelines for More Effective Studying

The success of mnemonic strategies demonstrates again the importance of relating new information to knowledge already stored in memory. All mnemonic systems require that you have a well-learned body of knowledge (such as locations) that can be used to provide a context for organizing incoming information (Hilton, 1986).

When you want to remember more complex material, such as a textbook chapter, the same basic principle applies (Palmisano & Herrmann, 1991).You can improve your memory for text material by first creating an outline or other overall context for learning, rather than by just reading and rereading (Glover et al., 1990). For retaining information over long periods, maintenance rehearsal alone tends to be ineffective, no matter how much time you spend on it (Bjorklund & Green, 1992). In short, "work smarter, not harder."

In addition, spend your time wisely. *Distributed practice* is much more effective than *massed practice* for learning, and retaining, new information. If you are going to spend ten hours studying for a test, you will be much better off studying for ten 1-hour blocks, separated by periods of sleep and other activity. "Cramming" for one 10-hour block will not be as successful. By scheduling more study sessions, you will stay fresh and be able to think about the material from a new perspective during each session. This method will help you elaborate on the material, as in elaborative rehearsal, and thus remember it better.

Reading a Textbook   More specific advice for remembering textbook material comes from a study that examined how successful and unsuccessful college students approached their reading (Whimbey, 1976). Unsuccessful students tended to read the material straight through. They did not slow down when they reached a difficult section. They kept going even when they did not understand what they were reading. In contrast, successful college students monitored their understanding, reread difficult sections, and periodically stopped or reviewed what they had learned. In short, effective learners engage in a deep level of processing. They are active learners. They think of each new fact in relation to other material, and they develop a context in which many new facts can be organized effectively.

mnemonics   Strategies for organizing information in order to remember it.

Research on memory suggests two specific guidelines for reading a textbook. First, make sure that you understand what you are reading before moving on (Herrmann & Searleman, 1992). Second, try the *PQ4R method* (Thomas & Robinson, 1972). *PQ4R* stands for six activities to engage in when you read a chapter: preview, question, read, reflect, recite, and review. These activities are designed to increase the depth to which you process the information you read (Anderson, 1990b; Chastain & Thurber, 1989):

1. *Preview.* Take a few minutes to skim the chapter. Look at the section headings and any boldfaced or italicized terms. Get a general idea of what material will be discussed, the way it is organized, and how its topics relate to one another and to what you already know. Some people find it useful to survey the entire chapter once and then survey each major section in a little more detail before reading it.

2. *Question.* Before reading each section, ask yourself what content will be covered and what information should be extracted from it.

3. *Read.* Read the text, but think about the material as you read. Are the questions you raised earlier being answered? Do you see the connections between and among the topics?

4. *Reflect.* As you read, think of your own examples—and create visual images—of the concepts and phenomena you encounter. Ask yourself what the material means, and consider how each section relates to other sections in the chapter, and other chapters in the book (this book's Linkages features are designed to promote this kind of reflection).

5. *Recite.* At the end of each section, recite the major points. Resist the temptation to be passive and say, "Oh, I remember that." Be active. Put the ideas into your own words by reciting them aloud.

6. *Review.* Finally, at the end of the chapter, review all the material. You should see connections not only within each section but also among sections. The objective is to see how the material is organized. Once you grasp the organization, the individual facts will be far easier to remember.

By following these procedures, you will learn and remember the material better. You will also save yourself considerable time.

Lecture Notes   Students and employees often have to learn and remember material from lectures or other presentations. Taking notes will help, but doing so effectively is an acquired skill. Research on memory suggests some simple strategies for taking and using notes effectively.

Realize first that in note taking, more is not necessarily better. Taking detailed notes on everything requires that you pay close attention to unimportant as well as important content, leaving little time for thinking about the material. Note takers who concentrate on expressing the major ideas in relatively few words remember more than those who try to catch every detail (Pauk, 2002; Pauk & Fiore, 2000). In short, the best way to take notes is to think about what is being said. Draw connections with other material in the presentation. Then summarize the major points clearly and concisely.

Once you have a set of lecture notes, review them as soon as possible after the lecture so that you can fill in missing details. (Remember: Most forgetting from long-term memory occurs during the first hour after learning.) When the time comes for serious study, use your notes as if they were a chapter in a textbook. Write a detailed outline. Think about how various points are related. Once you have organized the material, the details will make more sense and will be much easier to remember. ("In Review: Improving Your Memory" summarizes tips for studying.)

UNDERSTAND AND REMEMBER
Research on memory suggests that students who simply read their textbooks will not remember as much as those who, like this woman, read for understanding using strategies such as the PQ4R method. Further, memory for the material is likely to be better if you read and study it over a number of weeks rather than in one marathon session on the night before a test.

in review

IMPROVING YOUR MEMORY

Goal	Helpful Techniques
Remembering lists of items	Use mnemonics. Look for meaningful acronyms. Try the method of loci.
Remembering textbook material	Follow the PQ4R system. Allocate your time to allow for distributed practice. Read actively, not passively.
Taking lecture notes	Take notes, but record only the main points. Think about the overall organization of the material. Review your notes as soon after the lecture as possible in order to fill in missing points.
Studying for exams	Write a detailed outline of your lecture notes rather than passively reading them.

? *Using mnemonics and the PQ4R system to better remember course material are examples of the value of _____ rehearsal.*

active review   Memory

Linkages

As noted in the introductory chapter, all of psychology's subfields are related to one another. Our discussion of eyewitness testimony illustrates just one way in which the topic of this chapter, memory, is linked to the subfield of sensation and perception, as discussed in the chapter by that name. The Linkages diagram shows ties to two other subfields as well, and there are many more ties throughout the book. Looking for linkages among subfields will help you see how they all fit together and help you better appreciate the big picture that is psychology.

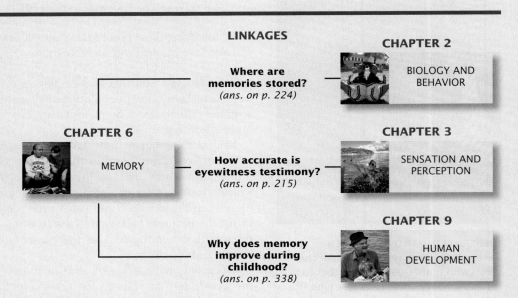

LINKAGES

CHAPTER 6

MEMORY

Where are memories stored?
(ans. on p. 224)

CHAPTER 2
BIOLOGY AND BEHAVIOR

How accurate is eyewitness testimony?
(ans. on p. 215)

CHAPTER 3
SENSATION AND PERCEPTION

Why does memory improve during childhood?
(ans. on p. 338)

CHAPTER 9
HUMAN DEVELOPMENT

Summary

THE NATURE OF MEMORY

▶ **How does information turn into memories?**

Human memory depends on a complex mental system. There are three basic memory processes. **Encoding** transforms stimulus information into some type of mental representation. Encoding can be by **acoustic** (sound), **visual** (appearance), or **semantic** (meaning) **codes. Storage** maintains information in the memory system over time. **Retrieval** is the process of gaining access to previously stored information.

Most psychologists agree that there are at least three types of memory. **Episodic memory** contains information about specific events in a person's life. **Semantic memory** contains generalized knowledge about the world. **Procedural memory** contains information about how to do things. Research on memory focuses on **explicit memory,** the processes through which people try to remember something, and **implicit memory,** the unintentional recollection and influence of prior experiences.

Four models of memory have guided most research. The **levels-of-processing model** suggests that the most important determinant of memory is how extensively information is encoded or processed when it is first received. In general, **elaborative rehearsal** is more effective than **maintenance rehearsal** in learning new information, because it represents a deeper level of processing. According to the **transfer-appropriate processing model,** the critical determinant of memory is not how deeply information is encoded but whether the processes used during retrieval match those used during encoding. **Parallel distributed processing (PDP) models** of memory suggest that new experiences not only provide specific information but also become part of, and alter, a whole network of associations. The **information-processing model** suggests that for information to become firmly embedded in memory, it must pass through three stages of processing: sensory memory, short-term memory, and long-term memory.

STORING NEW MEMORIES

▶ **What am I most likely to remember?**

Sensory memory maintains incoming stimulus information in the **sensory registers** for a very brief time. **Selective attention,** which focuses mental resources on only part of the stimulus field, controls what information in the sensory registers is actually perceived and transferred to short-term memory.

Working memory is a system that allows us to store, organize, and manipulate information in order to think, solve problems, and make decisions. The storage, or maintenance, component of working memory is referred to as **short-term memory (STM).** Various memory codes can be used in short-term memory, but acoustic codes seem to be preferred in most verbal tasks. Studies of the **immediate memory span** indicate that the capacity of short-term memory is approximately seven **chunks,** or meaningful groupings of information. Studies using the **Brown-Peterson procedure** show that information in short-term memory is usually forgotten in about eighteen seconds if it is not rehearsed.

Long-term memory (LTM) normally involves semantic coding, which means that people tend to encode the general meaning of information, not specific details, into long-term memory. The capacity of long-term memory to store new information is extremely large, and perhaps unlimited. The appearance of a **primacy effect** and a **recency effect** suggests that short-term and long-term memory may be distinct systems.

RETRIEVING MEMORIES

▶ **How do I retrieve stored memories?**

Retrieval cues help people remember things that they would otherwise not be able to recall. The effectiveness of retrieval cues follows the **encoding specificity principle:** Cues help retrieval only if they match some feature of the information that was originally encoded. All else being equal, memory may be better when we attempt to retrieve information in the same environment in which it was learned; this is called **context-dependent memory.** When our internal state can affect retrieval, we have a **state-dependent memory.** Researchers usually study retrieval from semantic memory by examining how long it takes people to answer general-knowledge questions. It appears that ideas are represented as associations in a dense semantic memory network, and that the retrieval of information occurs by a process of **spreading activation.** Each concept in the network is represented as a unique collection of features or attributes. The tip-of-the-tongue phenomenon represents the retrieval of incomplete knowledge.

CONSTRUCTING MEMORIES

▶ **How accurate are my memories?**

In the process of constructive memory, people use generalized knowledge, or **schemas,** to fill in gaps in the information they encode and retrieve. PDP models provide one explanation of how people make spontaneous generalizations about the world.

Eyewitnesses can remember only what they perceive, and they can perceive only what they attended to. As a result, eyewitness testimony is often much less accurate than witnesses, and jurors, think it is.

FORGETTING

▶ **What causes me to forget things?**

In his research on long-term memory and forgetting, Ebbinghaus introduced the **method of savings.** He found that most forgetting from long-term memory occurs during the first hour after learning and that savings can be extremely long-lasting. **Decay** and **interference** are two mechanisms of forgetting. There is evidence of both decay and interference in short-term memory; it appears that most forgetting from long-term memory is due to either **retroactive interference** or **proactive interference.**

BIOLOGICAL BASES OF MEMORY

▶ **How does my brain change when I store a memory?**

Research has shown that memories can result from new synapses forming in the brain and improved communication at existing synapses. Studies of **anterograde amnesia, retrograde amnesia,** and other consequences of brain damage provide information about the brain structures involved in memory. For example, the hippocampus and thalamus are known to play a role in the formation of memories. These structures send nerve impulses to the cerebral cortex, and it is there that memories are probably stored. Memories appear to be both localized and distributed throughout the brain.

IMPROVING YOUR MEMORY

► **How can I remember more information?**

Mnemonics are strategies that are used to remember things better. One of the simplest but most powerful mnemonics is the method of loci. It is useful because it provides a context for organizing material

effectively. The key to remembering textbook material is to read actively rather than passively. One way to do this is to follow the PQ4R method: preview, question, read, reflect, recite, and review. Similarly, to take lecture notes or to study them effectively, organize the points in a meaningful framework, and think about how each main point relates to the others.

Learn by Doing

Put It in Writing

Write a paragraph describing your views on claims of recovered memories of childhood abuse. Be sure to mention what evidence leads you to think as you do about this topic. For example, indicate whether you tend to give more weight to the testimony of clients who say they have recovered traumatic memories or to the results of scientific research on memory and repression. Be sure to say why you prefer one kind of evidence over another, and whether you think the debate over recovered memories will ever be resolved to everyone's satisfaction.

Personal Learning Activity

When you study for your next quiz or exam, try using some of the memory tips contained in this chapter. For example, use one or more mnemonic devices to help you to remember lists of information, and try the PQ4R method with the next chapter you read. Did these memory-enhancing methods make it easier for you to study and to do well on your next quiz or exam? Why or why not? *For additional projects, see the Personal Learning Activities in the corresponding chapter of the study guide that accompanies this text.*

Step into Action

Courses

Cognitive Psychology
Social Cognition
Experimental Psychology
Learning and Memory

Movies

The Bourne Identity (amnesia)
Memento; The Lazarus Man; Anastasia; Blackout; Lapse of Memory; Regarding Henry (memory loss)
Rashoman; Stagecoach (constructive memory)
On Golden Pond (memory and aging)
Total Recall (futuristic images of constructing memories)

Books

Douglas J. Herrmann, Cathy McEvoy, and Christopher Hertzog (Eds.), *Basic and Applied Memory Research: Theory in Context* (Lawrence Erlbaum Associates, 1996) (overview of memory research)
Steven Pinker, *How the Mind Works* (Norton, 1997) (biology of memory and thought)
William H. Calvin, *The Cerebral Code: Thinking a Thought in the Mosaics of the Mind* (MIT Press, 1996) (brain function and memory)
Akira Miyake and Priti Shah (Eds.), *Models of Working Memory* (Cambridge University Press, 1999) (theories of short-term memory)
Elizabeth Loftus and Katherine Ketcham, *The Myth of Repressed Memory* (St. Martin's Press, 1996) (research casting doubt on the validity of some recovered memories)

E. Sue Blume, *Secret Survivors: Uncovering Incest and Its Aftereffects in Women* (Ballantine, 1998) (presents the position of some therapists who believe in the validity of all reports of recovered memories)
Elizabeth Loftus, *Eyewitness Testimony* (Harvard University Press, 1996) (summarizes research on limitations of eyewitness testimony)
Lawrence Wright, *Remembering Satan: A Tragic Case of Recovered Memory* (Vintage, 1994) (false memories led to convictions of sexual abuse for Paul Ingram)
Kathryn Lyon, *Witch Hunt* (Avon, 1998) (sexual abuse hysteria in Washington State in the 1990s led to dozens of false convictions)
Moira Johnson, *Spectral Evidence* (Westview, 1997) (the Gary Ramona case that found a therapist liable for inducing false memories of sexual abuse)

The Web

The World Wide Web is a good source of additional information about the science of psychology, provided you use it carefully and think critically about the information you find. The web site that accompanies this text offers many resources relevant to this chapter. These resources include interactive NetLab exercises; Thinking Critically and Evaluating Research exercises; ACE chapter quizzes; recommended web links; and articles on current events, books, and movies. At http://college.hmco.com, select *Psychology* and then this textbook.

Review of Key Terms

Can you define each of the key terms in the chapter? Check your definitions against those on the pages listed in parentheses below or in the Glossary/Index at the end of the text.

acoustic codes (p. 199)

anterograde amnesia (p. 224)

Brown-Peterson procedure (p. 205)

chunks (p. 205)

context-dependent memories (p. 209)

decay (p. 218)

elaborative rehearsal (p. 201)

encoding (p. 199)

encoding specificity principle (p. 208)

episodic memory (p. 200)

explicit memory (p. 200)

immediate memory span (p. 205)

implicit memory (p. 200)

information-processing model (p. 202)

interference (p. 218)

levels-of-processing model (p. 201)

long-term memory (LTM) (p. 206)

maintenance rehearsal (p. 201)

method of savings (p. 217)

mnemonics (p. 226)

parallel distributed processing (PDP) models (p. 202)

primacy effect (p. 208)

proactive interference (p. 218)

procedural memory (p. 200)

recency effect (p. 208)

retrieval (p. 199)

retrieval cues (p. 208)

retroactive interference (p. 218)

retrograde amnesia (p. 224)

schemas (p. 214)

selective attention (p. 204)

semantic codes (p. 199)

semantic memory (p. 200)

sensory memory (p. 203)

sensory registers (p. 203)

short-term memory (STM) (p. 204)

spreading activation (p. 210)

state-dependent memory (p. 209)

storage (p. 199)

transfer-appropriate processing model (p. 201)

visual codes (p. 199)

working memory (p. 204)

Multiple-Choice Self-Test

Select the best answer for each of the questions below. Then check your responses against the Answer Key at the end of the text.

1. Ludwig had an extraordinary memory for sound. Even when he lost his hearing in his later years, he was still able to create beautiful music. This demonstrates his well-developed _____ codes.

   a. acoustic
   b. visual
   c. semantic
   d. auditory

2. Henry clearly remembers his seventh birthday. When he woke up, he saw a shiny new bicycle standing in his bedroom. His father had spent hours putting it together the previous night. Henry's memory of this event is _____ memory; his father's knowledge of how to put the bicycle together is _____ memory.

   a. procedural; episodic
   b. episodic; semantic
   c. episodic; procedural
   d. semantic; procedural

3. Riesa was uncomfortable when she was introduced to her roommate's cousin. She was not aware of it, but the cousin reminded her of a hated classmate in elementary school. This incident provides an example of the operation of _____ memory.

   a. procedural
   b. semantic
   c. implicit
   d. explicit

4. Raquel was still studying ten minutes before her test. As she entered the classroom, she kept repeating the last sentence she had read: "Henry VIII had six wives." She was using _____ to keep this information in mind.

   a. elaborative rehearsal
   b. maintenance rehearsal
   c. mnemonics
   d. retrieval

5. In a memory study, half the students in a class were told to expect multiple-choice questions on their upcoming exam, and the other half were told to expect essay questions. Students did better if they got the type of exam they expected, which is consistent with the _____ model of memory.

   a. levels-of-processing
   b. transfer-appropriate processing
   c. parallel distributed processing
   d. information-processing

6. Reepal listens as her father describes a party the family is planning. She also smells popcorn from the kitchen, hears the radio playing, notices flashes of lightning outside, and feels too warm in her sweater. Yet Reepal is able to transfer the information about the party to her short-term memory, primarily because of

   a. elaborative rehearsal.
   b. implicit memory cues.
   c. selective attention.
   d. transfer-appropriate processing.

7. Larry was thrilled when he met the girl of his dreams at the mall. She gave him her phone number before she left, but if Larry doesn't use any rehearsal methods, he will only remember the number for about

   a. one second.
   b. eighteen seconds.
   c. one minute.
   d. five minutes.

8. Remembering your bank account number (2171982) as your birthday (February 17, 1982) is an example of

   a. chunking.
   b. the Brown-Peterson technique.
   c. the PQ4R method.
   d. the method of loci.

9. Lisbeth was trying to recall a phrase that her mother always used, but all she could remember was the gist of it, not the exact wording. Her problem in recalling the exact words is probably due to the fact that encoding in long-term memory is usually

   a. acoustic.
   b. visual.
   c. semantic.
   d. state dependent.

10. Research on long-term memory has found which of the following?

   a. It is almost always highly accurate.
   b. It is subject to distortion, especially in males.
   c. It is subject to distortion, especially in females.
   d. It is subject to distortion in everyone, even those who are confident about the accuracy of their recollections.

11. Before Nesta went to the library, she wrote a list of twenty CDs that she wanted to check out. Unfortunately, she lost the list and can now remember only the first few titles on it. This case illustrates the _____ effect.

   a. primacy
   b. recency
   c. fatigue
   d. parallel processing

12. Because of context dependence, people may remember material better when they

   a. organize it in an outline.
   b. are in the same place as when they learned the material.
   c. are in the same frame of mind as when they learned the material.
   d. use mnemonics.

13. Molly knows that she knows the name of her kindergarten teacher, but she couldn't quite remember it when asked. This tip-of-the-tongue phenomenon is caused by retrieval of incomplete information from her

   a. constructive memory.
   b. sensory memory.
   c. semantic networks.
   d. schemas.

14. When asked if there was a fever thermometer in her doctor's office, Careen says she remembers seeing one, even though it wasn't actually there. This is an example of

   a. the tip-of-the-tongue phenomenon.
   b. forgetting.
   c. constructive memory.
   d. the primacy effect.

15. Recent use of DNA evidence has had what effect on the U.S. legal system's view of eyewitness testimony?

   a. It has tended to back up eyewitness testimony.
   b. It has demonstrated that eyewitness testimony, though not always accurate, is much better than anyone thought it was.
   c. It has revealed that eyewitness testimony has put many people in prison for crimes they did not commit.
   d. It has had little effect.

16. Robin memorized the names of all of the U.S. presidents when she was ten. Two years later, she had forgotten most of them, but she was pleasantly surprised that she could learn them a second time much more quickly than the first. This is an example of what Ebbinghaus called

   a. mnemonics.
   b. state dependence.
   c. savings.
   d. context dependence.

17. Berean studied French during his first year at college, and then started learning Spanish in his second year. Now he is having difficulty remembering his Spanish vocabulary because the French words keep popping into his mind. This is an example of _____ interference.

   a. retrograde
   b. anterograde
   c. proactive
   d. retroactive

18. The hippocampus is crucial in the formation of _____ memories?

   a. episodic
   b. implicit
   c. procedural
   d. working

19. Jerry, a factory worker, suffered a brain injury when a steel beam fell on his head. Jerry cannot remember anything that happened since the accident. Jerry is experiencing _____ amnesia.

   a. retrograde
   b. anterograde
   c. proactive
   d. retroactive

20. Loretta wanted to remember the names of famous psychologists, so she pictured them all being in her apartment. She imagined Elizabeth Loftus playing video games in the living room, Hermann Ebbinghaus taking a nap in the bathtub, Sigmund Freud scrubbing the kitchen floor, and so on. Loretta is using the memory strategy called

   a. the method of loci.
   b. procedural memorization.
   c. encoding cues.
   d. context dependence.

Thought, Language, and Intelligence

"Say what you mean, and mean what you say."

This is good advice, but following it is not always easy, partly because our thoughts don't always come to us in clear, complete sentences. We have to construct those sentences—using the language we have learned—from the words, images, ideas, and other mental materials that reside in our minds. Often, the complexity of that material makes it difficult to accurately express what we are thinking. We all manage to do it, but with varying degrees of success. In this chapter, we explore what thoughts are, what language is, and how people translate one into the other. We also consider how thinking guides decision making and problem solving and how psychologists measure individual differences in these and other mental abilities that are commonly described as *intelligence*.

Reading this chapter will help you to answer the following questions:

▶ **What good is thinking, anyway?**

▶ **What are thoughts made of?**

▶ **Do people always think logically?**

▶ **What's the best way to solve a problem?**

▶ **How can I become a better decision maker?**

▶ **How do babies learn to talk?**

▶ **How is intelligence measured?**

▶ **How good are IQ tests?**

▶ **Is there more than one type of intelligence?**

---

r. Joyce Wallace, a New York City internist, was having trouble figuring out what was the matter with a forty-three-year-old patient, "Laura McBride." Laura reported pain in her stomach and abdomen, aching muscles, irritability, occasional dizzy spells, and fatigue (Rouéché, 1986). The doctor's first hypothesis was iron-deficiency anemia, a condition in which there is not enough oxygen-carrying hemoglobin in the blood. There was some evidence to support that hypothesis. A physical examination revealed that Laura's spleen was somewhat enlarged, and blood tests showed low hemoglobin and high production of red blood cells, suggesting that her body was attempting to compensate for the loss of hemoglobin. However, other tests revealed normal iron levels. Perhaps she was losing blood through internal bleeding, but other tests ruled that out. Had Laura been vomiting blood? She said no. Blood in the urine? No. Abnormally heavy menstrual flow? No.

As Dr. Wallace puzzled over the problem, Laura's condition worsened. She reported more intense pain, cramps, shortness of breath, and severe loss of energy. Her blood was becoming less and less capable of sustaining her; but if it was not being lost, what was happening to it? Finally, the doctor looked at a smear of Laura's blood on a microscope slide. What she saw indicated that a poison was destroying Laura's red blood cells. What could it be? Laura spent most of her time at home, but her teenage daughters, who lived with her, were perfectly healthy. Dr. Wallace asked herself, "What does Laura do that the girls do not?" She repairs and restores paintings. Paint. Lead! She might be suffering from lead poisoning! When the next blood test showed a lead level seven times higher than normal, Dr. Wallace knew she had found the answer at last.

To solve this medical mystery, Dr. Wallace relied on her intelligence, part of which can be seen in her ability to think, solve problems, and make judgments and decisions. She put these vital mental abilities to use in weighing the pros and cons of various hypotheses and in reaching decisions about what tests to order and how to interpret them. In consulting with the patient and other physicians, she relied on another remarkable human mental ability known as *language*. Let's take a look at what psychologists have discovered about these complex mental processes, how to measure them, and how to compare people in terms of intelligence. We begin by examining a general framework for understanding human thinking and then go on to look at some specific cognitive processes.

Basic Functions of Thought

▶ **What good is thinking, anyway?**

The main functions, or purposes, of human thinking are to *describe, elaborate, decide, plan,* and *guide action.* You might imagine these functions as forming a circle of thought (see Figure 7.1).

The Circle of Thought

Consider how the circle of thought operated in Dr. Wallace's case. It began when she received the information about Laura's symptoms that allowed her to *describe* the problem. Next, Dr. Wallace *elaborated* on this information by using her knowledge,

figure 7.1

The Circle of Thought

The circle of thought begins as our sensory systems take in information from the world. Our perceptual system describes and elaborates this information, which is represented in the brain in ways that allow us to make decisions, formulate plans, and guide our actions. As those actions change our world, we receive new information— and the circle of thought begins again.

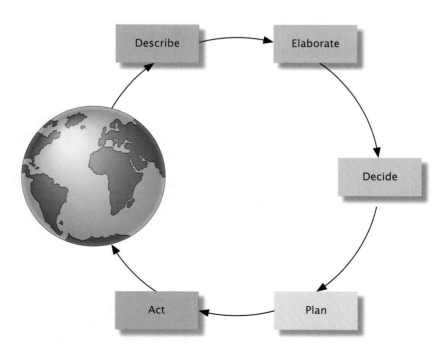

experience, and powers of reasoning to consider what disorders might cause such symptoms. Then she made a *decision* to investigate a possible cause, such as anemia. To implement this decision, she formulated a *plan*—and then *acted* on that plan. But the circle of thought did not stop there. Information from the blood test provided new descriptive information, which Dr. Wallace elaborated further to reach another decision, create a new plan, and guide her next action. Each stage in the circle of thought was also influenced by her *intention*—in this case, to find and cure her patient's problem.

Usually, the circle of thought spins so quickly, and its processes are so complex, that slowing it down for careful analysis might seem like trying to nail Jell-O to a tree. Some psychologists approach this task by studying thought processes as if they were part of a computer-like information-processing system. An **information-processing system** receives information, represents the information with symbols, and then manipulates those symbols. According to this model, then, **thinking** is defined as the manipulation of mental representations. Figure 7.2 shows how an information-processing model might view one spin around the circle of thought. Notice that information from the world is somewhat transformed as it passes through each stage of processing (Wickens, Gordon, & Liu, 1998).

In the first stage, information about the world reaches your brain through the senses we discussed in the chapter on sensation and perception. This stage does not require attention. In the second stage, you must perceive and recognize the information—processes that do require attention. In this stage, you also consciously elaborate information using the short-term and working memory processes described in the memory chapter. These processes allow you to think about new information in relation to knowledge stored in your long-term memory. Once the information has been elaborated in this way, you must decide what to do with it. This third stage—decision making—demands attention, too. You may decide to store the information or to take some action. It's in this stage that you plan what action you might take. In the fourth and fifth stages, the action is carried out. This action usually affects the environment, providing new information that is "fed back" to the system for processing in the ongoing circle of thought.

figure 7.2

An Information-Processing Model

Some stages in the information-processing model depend heavily on both short-term and long-term memory and require some attention—that limited supply of mental resources required for information processing to be carried out efficiently.

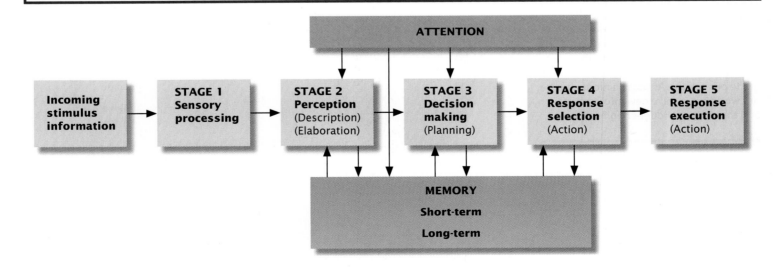

"AUTOMATIC" THINKING The sensory, perceptual, decision-making, and response-planning components of the circle of thought can occur so rapidly that—as when playing a video game—we may only be aware of the incoming information and our quick response to it. In such cases, our thinking processes become so well practiced that they are virtually automatic.

Mental Representations: The Ingredients of Thought

► **What are thoughts made of?**

Just as measuring, stirring, and baking are only part of the story of cookie making, describing the processes of thinking tells only part of the story behind the circle of thought. Psychologists usually describe the ingredients of thought as *information*. But that is like saying you make cookies with "stuff." What specific forms can information take in our minds? Cognitive psychologists have found that information can be mentally represented in many ways, including as *concepts, propositions, schemas, scripts, mental models, images,* and *cognitive maps.* Let's explore these ingredients of thought and how people manipulate them as they think.

Concepts

When you think about anything—dogs, happiness, sex, movies, pizza—you are manipulating a basic ingredient of thought called *concepts.* **Concepts** are categories of objects, events, or ideas with common properties. Some concepts, such as "round" and "red," are visual and concrete. Concepts like "truth" and "justice" are more abstract. "To have a concept" is to recognize the properties, or *features,* that tend to be shared by members of a category. For example, the concept of "bird" includes such properties as having feathers, laying eggs, and being able to fly. The concept of "scissors" includes such properties as having two blades, a connecting hinge, and a pair of finger holes. Concepts allow you to relate each object or event you encounter to a category that you already know. Using concepts, you can say, "No, that is not a dog," or "Yes, that is a car." Concepts also make it possible for you to think logically. If you have the concepts "whale" and "bird," you can decide whether a whale is a bird without having either creature in the room with you.

Types of Concepts Some concepts—called **formal concepts**—clearly define objects or events by a set of rules and properties, such that each member of the concept has all of the defining properties and no nonmember does. For instance, the concept "square" can be defined as "a shape with four equal sides and four right-angle corners." Any object that does not have all of these features is simply not a square. Formal concepts are often used

---

information-processing system Mechanisms for receiving information, representing it with symbols, and manipulating it.

thinking The manipulation of mental representations.

concepts Categories of objects, events, or ideas that have common properties.

formal concept A concept that can be clearly defined by a set of rules or properties.

to study concept learning in the laboratory, because the members of these concepts can be neatly defined (Trabasso & Bower, 1968).

In contrast, try to define the concepts "home" or "game." You might say that "home" is the place where you live, and that a "game" is a competition between players. However, some people define "home" as the place they were born, and solitaire is a card game even though it involves only one player. These are just two examples of **natural concepts,** concepts that have no fixed set of defining features. Instead, they share a set of *characteristic features*. Members of a natural concept need not have all of these characteristic features. The ability to fly is a characteristic feature of the natural concept "bird," but an ostrich is a bird even though it cannot fly. It is a bird because it possesses enough other characteristic features of "bird" (such as feathers and wings). Having just one bird property is not enough, though. A snake lays eggs and a bat can fly, but neither animal is a bird. It is usually a combination of properties that defines a concept. Outside the laboratory, most of the concepts people use in thinking are natural rather than formal concepts. Natural concepts include object categories, such as "bird" or "house." They also include goal-related categories, such as "things to pack in a suitcase," that help us to make plans (Barsalou, 1993).

The boundaries of natural concepts are fuzzy (Rosch, 1975), so some members are better examples of the concept than others. A robin, a chicken, an ostrich, and a penguin are all birds. But the robin is a better example than the others, because it is closer to what most people have learned to think of as a typical bird. A member of a natural concept that possesses all or most of its characteristic features is called a **prototype.** The robin is a *prototypical* bird. The more prototypical of a concept something is, the more quickly you can decide if it is an example of the concept. This is why people can answer more quickly when asked "Is a robin a bird?" than when asked "Is a penguin a bird?"

Propositions

We often combine concepts in units known as propositions. A **proposition** is a mental representation that expresses a relationship between concepts. Propositions can be true or false. Suppose you hear someone say that your friend Heather broke up with her boyfriend, Jason. Your mental representation of this event will include a proposition that links your concepts of "Heather" and "Jason" in a particular way. This proposition could be diagrammed (using unscientific terms) as follows: Heather→dumped→Jason.

The diagram looks like a sentence, but it is not. Propositions can be expressed as sentences, but they are actually general ideas that can be conveyed in any number of specific ways. In this case, the words "Jason was dumped by Heather" and "Heather is not willing to date Jason anymore" would all express the same proposition. If you later discovered that it was Jason who caused the breakup, the diagram of your proposition about the event would change to reflect this new information, shown here as reversed arrows: Heather←dumped←Jason.

Schemas, Scripts, and Mental Models

Sets of propositions are often so closely associated that they form more complex mental representations called *schemas*. As mentioned in the chapters on sensation and perception, memory, and human development, **schemas** are generalizations that we develop about categories of objects, places, events, and people. Our schemas help us to understand the world. If you borrow a friend's car, your "car" schema will give you a good idea of where to put the ignition key, where the accelerator and brake are, and how to raise and lower the windows. Schemas also generate expectations about objects, places, events, and people—telling us that stereo systems have speakers, that picnics occur in the summer, that rock concerts are loud, and so on.

Scripts   Schemas about familiar activities, such as going to a restaurant, are known as **scripts** (Anderson, 2000). Your "restaurant" script represents the sequence of events you

---

natural concepts   Concepts that have no fixed set of defining features but instead share a set of characteristic features.

prototype   A member of a natural concept that possesses all or most of its characteristic features.

propositions   Mental representations that express a relationship between concepts.

schemas   Generalizations about categories of objects, places, events, and people.

scripts   Mental representations of familiar sequences of activity.

mental models   Sets of propositions that represent people's understanding of how things look and work.

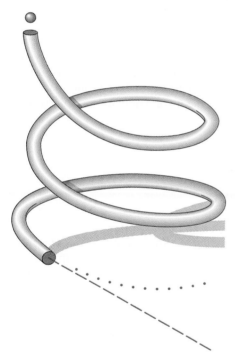

figure 7.3

Applying a Mental Model

learn by doing   Try to imagine the path that the marble will follow when it leaves the curved tube. In one study, most people drew the incorrect (curved) path indicated by the dotted line, rather than the correct (straight) path indicated by the dashed line (McCloskey, 1983). Their error was based on the construction of a faulty mental model of the behavior of physical objects.

can expect when you go out to eat. That script tells you what to do when you are in a restaurant and helps you to understand stories involving restaurants (Whitney, 2001). Scripts also shape your interpretation of events. For example, on your first day of college, you no doubt assumed that the person standing at the front of the class was a teacher, not a mugger.

If our scripts are violated, however, it is easy to misinterpret events. In 1993, a heart attack victim in London lay for nine hours in the hallway of an apartment building after an ambulance crew smelled alcohol on his breath and assumed he was "sleeping it off." The crew's script for what happens in the poorer sections of big cities told them that someone slumped in a hallway is drunk, not sick. Because script-violating events are unexpected, our reactions to them tend to be slower and less effective than are our reactions to expected events. Your "grocery shopping" script, for example, probably includes pushing a cart, putting items in it, going to the checkout stand, and paying for your purchases. But suppose you are at the back of the store when a robber near the entrance fires a gun and shouts at the manager to open the safe. People sometimes ignore these script-violating events, interpreting gunshots as a car backfiring and shouted orders as "someone fooling around." Others simply "freeze," unsure of what to do.

Mental Models   Sets of propositions can be organized not only as schemas and scripts but also as **mental models** (Johnson-Laird, 1983). For example, suppose someone tells you, "My living room has blue walls, a white ceiling, and an oval window across from the door." You will mentally represent this information as propositions about how the concepts "wall," "blue," "ceiling," "white," "door," "oval," and "window" are related. However, you will also combine these propositions to create in your mind a three-dimensional model of the room. As more information about the world becomes available, either from existing memories or from new information we receive, our mental models become more complete.

Accurate mental models are excellent guides for thinking about, and interacting with, many of the things we encounter (Galotti, 1999). If a mental model is incorrect, however, we are likely to make mistakes (see Figure 7.3). For example, people who hold an incorrect mental model of how physical illness is cured might stop taking an antibiotic when their symptoms begin to disappear, well before the bacteria causing those symptoms have been eliminated (Medin, Ross, & Markman, 2001). Others overdose on

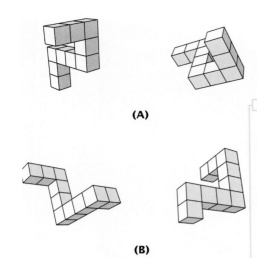

(A)

(B)

Source: Shepard & Metzler (1971).

figure 7.4

Manipulating Images

 learn by **doing** Are these pairs of objects the same or different? To decide, you will have to rotate one member of each pair. Because manipulating mental images, like manipulating actual objects, takes some time, the speed of your decision will depend on how far you have to mentally rotate one object to line it up with the other for comparison. (The top pair matches; the bottom pair does not.) Brain imaging studies have confirmed that manipulating mental images activates some of the same visual and spatial areas of the brain that are active during comparable tasks with real objects (Farah, 2000; Mazoyer et al., 2002).

learn by **doing**

medication because according to their faulty mental model, "if taking three pills a day is good, taking six would be even better."

Images and Cognitive Maps

Think about how your best friend would look in a clown suit. The "mental picture" you just got illustrates that thinking often involves the manipulation of **images**—which are mental representations of visual information. We can manipulate these images in a way that is similar to manipulating the objects themselves (Reed, 2000; see Figure 7.4). Our ability to think using images extends beyond the manipulation of stimuli like those in Figure 7.4. We also create mental images from written or spoken descriptions (Mazoyer et al., 2002), as you probably did a minute ago when you read about that blue-walled room.

The same thing happens when someone gives you directions to that new pizza place in town. In this case, you scan your **cognitive map**—a mental representation of familiar parts of your world—to find the location. In doing so, you use a mental process similar to the visual process of scanning a paper map (Anderson, 2000; Taylor & Tversky, 1992). Manipulating images on a different cognitive map would help you if a power failure left your home pitch dark. Even though you couldn't see a thing, you could still find a flashlight or candle, because your cognitive map would show the floor plan, furniture placement, door locations, and other physical features of your home. You would not have this mental map in an unfamiliar house; there, you would have to walk slowly, arms outstretched, to avoid wrong turns and painful collisions. In the chapter on learning we describe how experience shapes cognitive maps that help animals navigate mazes and people navigate shopping malls. ("In Review: Ingredients of Thought" summarizes the ways in which we mentally represent information.)

Thinking Strategies

▶ **Do people always think logically?**

We have seen that our thinking capacity is based largely on our ability to manipulate mental representations—the ingredients of thought—much as a baker manipulates the ingredients of cookies. The baker's food-processing system combines and transforms these ingredients into a delicious treat. Our information-processing system combines, transforms, and elaborates mental representations in ways that allow us to engage in reasoning, problem solving, and decision making. Let's begin our discussion of these thinking strategies by considering *reasoning,* the process through which we generate and evaluate arguments, as well as reach conclusions about them.

Formal Reasoning

Astronomers say that the temperature at the core of the sun is about 27 million degrees Fahrenheit. How do they know this? It is not possible to place a temperature probe inside the sun, so their estimate is based on *inferences* from other things that they know about the sun and about physical objects in general. For example, telescopic observations allowed astronomers to calculate the energy coming from one small part of the sun. They then used what geometry told them about the surface area of spheres to estimate the sun's total energy output. Further calculations told them how hot a body would have to be to generate that much energy.

In other words, astronomers' highly educated guess about the sun's core temperature is based on **formal reasoning** (also called *logical reasoning*)—the process of following a set of rigorous steps for reaching valid, or correct, conclusions. Some of these steps included the application of specific mathematical formulas to existing data in order to

in review

INGREDIENTS OF THOUGHT

Ingredient	Description	Examples
Concepts	Categories of objects, events, or ideas with common properties; basic building blocks of thought	"Square" (a formal concept); "game" (a natural concept).
Propositions	Mental representations that express relationships between concepts; can be true or false	Assertions such as "The cow jumped over the the moon."
Schemas	Sets of propositions that create generalizations and expectations about categories of objects, places, events, and people	A schema might suggest that all grandmothers are elderly, are gray haired, and bake a lot of cookies.
Scripts	Schemas about familiar activities and situations; guide behavior in those situations	You pay before eating in fast-food restaurants and after eating in fancier restaurants.
Mental models	Sets of propositions about how things relate to each other in the real world; can be correct or incorrect	Mistakenly assuming that airflow around an open car will send thrown objects upward, a driver tosses a lighted cigarette butt overhead, causing it to land in the back seat.
Images	Mental representations of visual information	Hearing a description of your blind date creates a mental picture of him or her.
Cognitive maps	Mental representations of familiar parts of the world	You can get to class by an alternate route even if your usual route is blocked by construction.

? *Thinking is the manipulation of _____.*

---

images Mental representations of visual information.

cognitive map A mental representation of the environment.

formal reasoning A set of rigorous procedures for reaching valid conclusions.

algorithms Systematic procedures that cannot fail to produce a correct solution to a problem.

rules of logic A set of statements that provide a formula for drawing vaild conclusions.

---

generate new data. Such formulas are examples of **algorithms**—systematic methods that always reach a correct solution to a problem, if a correct solution exists.

The astronomers also followed the **rules of logic,** a set of statements that provide a formula for drawing valid conclusions about the world. For example, each step in the astronomers' thinking took the form of "if-then" propositions: If we know how much energy comes from one part of the sun's surface, and if we know how big the whole surface is, then we can calculate the total energy output. You use the same logical reasoning processes when you conclude, for example, that if your friend José is two years older than you are, then his twin brother, Juan, will be two years older, too. This kind of reasoning is called *deductive reasoning,* because it takes a general rule (e.g., twins are the same age) and applies it to deduce conclusions about specific cases (e.g., José and Juan).

Most of us try to use logical or deductive reasoning to reach valid conclusions and avoid invalid ones (Rips, 1994). However, even when our logic is perfect, we can make mistakes if we base our reasoning on false assumptions. Likewise, correct assumptions combined with faulty logic can lead to errors. Do you think the following example leads to a valid conclusion?

Assumption 1: *All women want to be mothers.*

Assumption 2: *Jill is a woman.*

Conclusion: *Jill wants to be a mother.*

If you said that the first assumption is not necessarily correct, you're right. Now consider this example:

PITFALLS IN LOGICAL REASONING
"Elderly people cannot be astronauts; this is an elderly man; therefore, he cannot be an astronaut." The logic is correct, but because the first statement is wrong, so is the conclusion. In 1962, John Glenn became the first American astronaut to orbit the earth. Here he is in 1998, at the age of seventy-seven, just before he returned to space as a full-fledged member of the crew of the space shuttle *Discovery*.

Assumption 1: *All gun owners are people.*

Assumption 2: *All criminals are people.*

Conclusion: *All gun owners are criminals.*

Here, the assumptions are correct, but the logic is faulty. If "all A's are B" and "all C's are B," it does not follow that "all A's are C."

Psychologists have discovered that both kinds of pitfalls we just described can lead people to make errors in logical reasoning. This finding is one reason why misleading advertisements or speeches can still attract sales and votes (Cialdini, 2001).

Informal Reasoning

Using the rules of formal logic to deduce answers about specific cases is an important kind of reasoning, but it is not the only kind. We also use **informal reasoning** to decide whether a general statement is valid based on the evidence available to support it. Informal reasoning is also known as *inductive reasoning*, because its goal is to induce a general conclusion to appear on the basis of specific facts or examples. Psychologists use informal reasoning when they design experiments and other research methods whose results will provide evidence for (or against) their theories. Jurors use informal reasoning when weighing evidence for the guilt or innocence of a defendant. And investigators used it in their efforts to discover what caused the space shuttle *Columbia* to disintegrate as it returned to Earth in February 2003, killing all seven astronauts aboard (Broad & Revkin, 2003).

Formal reasoning is guided by algorithms, or formulas, but there are no foolproof methods for informal reasoning. For instance, how many white swans would you have to see before concluding that all swans are white? Fifty? A hundred? A million? Formal logic would require that you observe every swan in existence. A more practical approach is to base your conclusion on the number of observations that some mental rule of thumb leads you to believe is "enough." In other words, you would take a mental "shortcut" to reach a conclusion that is probably, but not necessarily, correct. Such mental shortcuts are called **heuristics** (pronounced "hyoor-IST-ix").

Heuristics can be helpful, but they can also bias our thinking and cause errors. Suppose your rule of thumb is to vote for all the candidates in a particular political party instead of researching the views of each individual. You might end up voting for someone with whom you strongly disagree on some issues. The extent to which heuristics are responsible for important errors in judgment and decision making is still being studied and debated by cognitive psychologists (e.g., Hilton, 2002; Medin & Bazerman, 1999). Nevertheless, Amos Tversky and Daniel Kahneman have described three potentially problematic heuristics that seem to affect people's judgments (Tversky & Kahneman, 1993).

The Anchoring Heuristic   People use the **anchoring heuristic** when they estimate the probability of an event by adjusting an earlier estimate, not by starting from scratch

informal reasoning   Assessment of a conclusion's validity based on the evidence available to support it.

heuristics   Mental shortcuts or rules of thumb.

anchoring heuristic   A shortcut in the thought process that involves adding new information to existing information to reach a judgment.

Formal reasoning follows the rules of logic, but there are no foolproof rules for informal reasoning, as this fool demonstrates.

DILBERT reprinted by permission of United Feature Syndicates, Inc.

(Rottenstreich & Tversky, 1997). This strategy sounds reasonable, but the starting point biases the final estimate. Once people have established (or "anchored to") that starting point, their adjustments of the initial judgment tend to be too small. Suppose you think that the chance of being mugged in Los Angeles is 90 percent, but then you see evidence that the figure is closer to 1 percent. You might reduce your estimate, but only to 80 percent; your new estimate is still way off. The anchoring heuristic presents a challenge for defense attorneys in U.S. criminal courts, because the prosecution presents its evidence first. That evidence always suggests that the defendant is guilty, so even if the judge throws some of it out, the initial impression it creates may establish in jurors' minds an unshakable belief in the defendant's guilt (Hogarth & Einhorn, 1992). Similarly, first impressions of people are not easily shifted by later evidence (see the chapter on social psychology).

The Representativeness Heuristic   People use the **representativeness heuristic** when they conclude that something belongs in a certain class based on how similar it is to other items in that class. For example, consider this personality sketch:

> *Tom W. is of high intelligence, although lacking in true creativity. He has a need for order and clarity, and for neat and tidy systems in which every detail finds its appropriate place. His writing is rather dull and mechanical, occasionally enlivened by somewhat corny puns and by flashes of imagination of the sci-fi type. He has a strong drive for competence. He seems to have little feel and little sympathy for other people and does not enjoy interacting with others. Self-centered, he nonetheless has a deep moral sense.*

Do you think it is more likely that Tom is majoring in computer science or psychology? Research by Kahneman and Tversky (1973; Tversky & Kahneman, 1974) showed that most people would choose *computer scientist*. But this answer would probably be wrong. True, the description given is more similar to the prototypical computer science major than to the prototypical psychology major. However, there are many more psychology majors than computer science majors in the world. So there are probably more psychology majors than computer science majors who match this description. In fact, almost any personality sketch is more likely to describe a psychology major than a computer science major.

The Availability Heuristic   People use the **availability heuristic** when they judge the likelihood of an event or the correctness of a hypothesis by how easy it is to think of that event or hypothesis (Reed, 2000). In other words, they tend to choose the hypothesis or predict the event that is most mentally "available," much as they might select the quart of milk that happens to be at the front of the supermarket shelf. Although the availability heuristic tends to work well, it, too, can lead to biased judgments—especially when the mental availability of events and their actual frequency do not match. For example, news reports about shark attacks and urban shootings lead many people to overestimate how often these memorable, but relatively rare, events actually occur. As a result, people may suffer undue anxiety over swimming in the ocean or being in certain cities (Bellaby, 2003).

These three heuristics represent only a few of the many mental shortcuts that people use more or less automatically in making judgments, and they describe only some of the biases and limitations evident in human reasoning (Hogarth & Einhorn, 1992). Other biases and limitations are described in the following sections as we consider two important goals of thinking: problem solving and decision making.

representativeness heuristic   A mental shortcut that involves judging whether something belongs in a given class on the basis of its similarity to other members of that class.

availability heuristic   A mental shortcut through which judgments are based on information that is most easily brought to mind.

Problem Solving

▶ **What's the best way to solve a problem?**

Suppose that you're lost, you don't have a map or navigation system, and there's nobody around to ask for directions. You have a *problem*. The circle of thought suggests that the most efficient approach to solving it would be to first diagnose the problem in the elaboration stage, then formulate a plan for solving it, then execute the plan, and finally evaluate the results to determine whether the problem remains (Bransford & Stein, 1993). But people's problem-solving efforts are not always so systematic. This is one reason why medical tests are sometimes given unnecessarily, diseases are sometimes misdiagnosed, and auto parts are sometimes replaced when there is nothing wrong with them.

Strategies for Problem Solving

When you are trying to get from one place to another, the best path may not necessarily be a straight line. In fact, obstacles may dictate going in the opposite direction. So it is with problem solving. Sometimes, the best strategy does not involve mental steps aimed straight at your goal. For example, when a problem is especially difficult, it can sometimes be helpful to allow it to "incubate" by setting it aside for a while. A solution that once seemed out of reach may suddenly appear after you think about other things for a time. The benefits of *incubation* probably arise from forgetting incorrect ideas that may have been blocking the path to a correct solution (Anderson, 2000). Other effective problem-solving strategies are more direct.

One of these strategies is called *means-end analysis*. It involves continuously asking where you are in relation to your final goal, and then deciding on the means by which you can get one step closer to that goal (Newell & Simon, 1972). In other words, rather than trying to solve the problem all at once, you identify a subgoal that will take you toward a solution (this process is also referred to as *decomposition*). After reaching that subgoal, you identify another one that will get you even closer to the solution, and you continue this step-by-step process until the problem is solved. Some students apply this approach to the problem of writing a major term paper. The task might seem overwhelming at first, but their first subgoal is simply to write an outline of what they think the paper should cover. When the outline is complete, they decide whether a paper based on it will satisfy the assignment. If so, the next subgoal might be to search the library and the Internet for information about each section. If they decide that this information is adequate, the next subgoal would be to write a rough draft of the introduction, and so on.

A second strategy in problem solving is to *work backward*. Many problems are like a tree. The trunk is the information you are given; the solution is a twig on one of the branches. If you work forward by taking the "givens" of the problem and trying to find the solution, it's easy to branch off in the wrong direction. Sometimes the more efficient approach is to start at the end, working backward from your goal (Galotti, 1999). Consider the problem of planning a climb to the summit of Mount Everest. The best strategy is to figure out, first, what equipment and supplies are needed at the highest camp on the

Calvin and Hobbes   by Bill Watterson

Simply knowing about problem-solving strategies, such as decomposition, is not enough. As described in the chapter on motivation and emotion, people must perceive the effort involved as being worth the rewards it is likely to bring.

night before the attempt to reach the summit, then how many people are needed to stock that camp the day before, then how many people are needed to supply those who must stock the camp, and so on until a plan for the entire expedition is established. People often overlook the working-backward strategy because it runs counter to the way they have learned to think. It is hard for them to imagine that the first step in solving a problem could be to assume that you have already solved it. Sadly, it was partly because of failure to apply this strategy that six climbers died on Mount Everest in 1996 (Krakauer, 1997).

A third problem-solving strategy is to try to find *analogies,* or similarities, between today's problem and others you have encountered before. A supervisor may discover that a seemingly hopeless problem between co-workers can be resolved by the same compromise that worked during a recent family squabble. Of course, to take advantage of analogies, you must first recognize the similarities between current and previous problems. Then you will be in a position to recall the solution that worked before. Most people are surprisingly poor at seeing the similarities between new and old problems (Anderson, 2000). They tend to concentrate on the surface features that make problems appear different.

FOCUS ON RESEARCH

Problem-Solving Strategies in the Real World

The value of using analogies in problem solving was beautifully illustrated in relation to the Hubble Space Telescope. In 1990, this telescope was placed in an earth orbit to take detailed photographs of distant galaxies, but because its main mirror was not focusing light properly, the pictures were blurry. When NASA engineer James Crocker happened to notice the way a hotel room showerhead pivoted, it gave him the idea for a system of movable mirrors to correct for the flaw in the Hubble's mirror. Shuttle astronauts installed these mirrors in 1993, and the problem was solved (Stein, 1993).

How do people use the other problem-solving strategies we have described to solve other real-world problems? To explore this question, researchers have reconstructed problem-solving strategies associated with major inventions and scientific discoveries (Klahr & Simon, 1999; Weber, 1992).

■ What was the researcher's question?

On December 17, 1903, Wilbur and Orville Wright successfully flew the first heavier-than-air flying machine. Gary Bradshaw (1993a, 1993b) was interested in identifying the problem-solving strategies that led to this momentous event. He found that forty-nine individuals or teams had worked on the problem of heavier-than-air flight, but only the

WORKING BACKWARD TO FORGE AHEAD Whether you are organizing a family vacation or sailing alone in an around-the-world race, as Ellen MacArthur did, working backward from the final goal through all the steps necessary to reach that goal is a helpful approach to solving complex problems.

Wright brothers were successful. In fact, it took them only four years to develop the airplane, whereas others worked for decades without success. Bradshaw asked, How did the Wright brothers solve the problem of creating a heavier-than-air flying machine when so many others had failed?

■ How did the researcher answer the question?

Bradshaw compared the written records left by all the individuals and teams who had worked on an airplane design. Using this "comparative case study" method, he was able to see patterns in the ways they approached the flying machine problem.

■ What did the researcher find?

Bradshaw found several factors that might have contributed to the Wright brothers' success. First, as bachelors, they had a lot of spare time to work on their designs. Second, they owned a bicycle shop, so they were familiar with lightweight, but sturdy, structures. Third, they were brothers who had a good working relationship. And finally, as mechanics, they were good with their hands. But were any of these features causally related to their successful invention of the airplane?

Perhaps, but Bradshaw's use of the comparative case study method revealed that everyone else working on the problem of flight shared at least one of these features with the Wright brothers. For instance, an engineer named Octave Chanute was good with his hands and familiar with lightweight, sturdy structures. And two other pairs of brothers had worked together to try to invent a flying machine.

However, Bradshaw found one feature that was unique to the Wright brothers' approach. Of all the inventors working on the problem, only the Wrights spent considerable time and energy testing aircraft components before field-testing complete machines. This feature was important because even the best designs of the day flew for only a few seconds—far too briefly to reveal what was working and what was not. As a result, inventors had to guess about what to fix and often ended up with an "improved" model that was worse than the previous one.

■ What do the results mean?

Bradshaw's comparative case study method suggested that the problem-solving strategy of decomposition was the basis for the Wright brothers' success. By testing components, they obtained the information they needed to develop an efficient propeller, improve the shape of the wings for maximum lift, and refine other vital components of their aircraft.

■ What do we still need to know?

Decomposition is a strategy often seen in the laboratory, and as demonstrated by the case of the Wright brothers, it is a potentially important aspect of major inventions and discoveries beyond the laboratory. But is decomposition used in other real-world settings as well? To find out, researchers will need to conduct additional studies of people's mental strategies as they attempt to solve problems ranging from how to connect a new computer to how to efficiently search the Internet.

Obstacles to Problem Solving

The failure of the Wright brothers' competitors to use decomposition is just one example of the obstacles that face problem solvers every day. Difficulties frequently occur at the start, during the diagnosis stage, when a person forms and then tests hypotheses about a problem.

As a case in point, consider the following true story: In September 1998, John Gatiss was in the kitchen of his rented house in Cheltenham, England, when he heard a faint "meowing" sound. Worried that a kitten had become trapped somewhere, he called for the fire brigade to rescue the animal. The sound seemed to be coming from the electric stove, so the rescuers dismantled it, disconnecting the power cord in the process. The sound stopped, but everyone assumed that wherever the kitten was, it was now too frightened to meow. The search was reluctantly abandoned, and the stove was reconnected; four days later, however, the meowing began anew. This time, Gatiss and his landlord called the Royal Society for the Prevention of Cruelty to Animals (RSPCA), whose inspectors heard the kitten in distress and asked the fire brigade to come back. They spent the next three days searching for the cat. First, they dismantled parts of the kitchen walls and ripped up the floorboards. Next, they called in plumbing and drainage specialists, who used cables tipped with fiber-optic cameras to search remote cavities where a kitten might hide. Rescuers then brought in a disaster search team, which tried to find the kitten with acoustic and ultrasonic equipment normally used to locate victims trapped under earthquake debris. Not a sound was heard. Increasingly concerned about how much longer the kitten could survive, the fire brigade tried to coax it from hiding with the finest-quality fish, but to no avail. Suddenly, there was a burst of "purring" that, to everyone's surprise (and the landlord's dismay), was traced by the ultrasonic equipment to the clock in the electric stove! Later, the landlord commented that everyone assumed Gatiss's original hypothesis was correct—that the "meowing" came from a cat trapped in the kitchen. "I just let them carry on. If there is an animal in there, you have to do what it takes. The funniest thing was that it seemed to reply when we called out to it" (*The Daily Telegraph*, 1998).

How could fifteen fire-rescue workers, three RSPCA inspectors, four drainage workers, and two acoustics experts waste eight days and cause nearly $2,000 in damage to a house in pursuit of a nonexistent kitten? The answer lies in the fact that they, like the rest of us, were prone to four main obstacles to efficient problem solving, described in the following sections.

Multiple Hypotheses   Often, we begin to solve a problem with only a hazy notion of which hypotheses to test. Suppose you heard a strange sound in your kitchen. It could be caused by several different things, but which hypotheses should you test, and in what order?

People have a difficult time working with more than two or three hypotheses at a time (Mehle, 1982). The limited capacity of short-term memory may be part of the reason. As discussed in the memory chapter, a person can hold only about seven chunks of information in short-term memory. Because a single hypothesis, let alone two or three, might include more than seven chunks, it may be difficult or impossible to keep them all in mind at once. As a result, the correct hypothesis is often neglected. The one that is chosen may be influenced by the availability heuristic. In other words, it may be the one that most easily comes to mind, rather than the one that's most likely to be correct (Tversky & Kahneman, 1974). So Gatiss diagnosed the sound he heard as coming from a kitten, not a clock, because such sounds usually come from kittens, not clocks.

Mental Sets   Sometimes people are so blinded by one hypothesis or strategy that they stick with it even when better alternatives should be obvious. This is a clear case of the anchoring heuristic at work. Once Gatiss reported hearing a "trapped kitten," his description created an assumption that everyone else accepted and that no one challenged. Figure 7.5 shows a problem-solving situation in which such errors often appear. In the first problem, the object is to obtain 21 quarts of liquid by using 3 jars that have capacities of 8, 35, and 3 quarts, respectively. Can you figure out how to do it?

The solution is to fill Jar B to its capacity, 35 quarts, and then use its contents to fill Jar A to its capacity of 8 quarts, leaving 27 quarts in Jar B. Then pour from Jar B to fill Jar C twice, leaving 21 quarts in Jar B [$27 - (2 \times 3) = 21$]. Now solve the remaining problems before you read any further.

If you solved all the problems in Figure 7.5, you found that a similar solution worked each time. But what happened with Problem 7? If you are like most people, you

learn by**doing**

figure 7.5

The Jar Problem

learn by doing The problem is to obtain the number of quarts of liquid shown in the first column by filling jars with the capacities shown in the next three columns. Each line represents a different problem. See if you can solve the first six without looking at the answer in the text; then try the last one. In dealing with such problems, people often fall prey to mental sets that prevent them from using the most efficient solution (Luchins, 1942).

Quantity	Jar A	Jar B	Jar C
1. 21 quarts	8	35	3
2. 10 quarts	6	18	1
3. 19 quarts	5	32	4
4. 21 quarts	20	57	8
5. 18 quarts	8	40	7
6. 6 quarts	7	17	2
7. 15 quarts	12	33	3

Problem: Measure out the quantities listed in the first column using jars with the stated capacities (in quarts).

figure 7.6

The Nine-Dot Problem

learn by doing The problem is to draw no more than four straight lines that run through all nine dots on the page without lifting your pencil from the paper. Figure 7.8 shows two ways of solving this problem that ignore its apparent limitations.

mental set   The tendency for old patterns of problem solving to persist.

functional fixedness   The tendency to think about familiar objects in familiar ways.

confirmation bias   The tendency to pay more attention to evidence in support of one's hypothesis about a problem than to evidence that refutes that hypothesis.

artificial intelligence (AI)   The field that studies how to program computers to imitate the products of human perception, understanding, and thought.

developed a **mental set**, the tendency for old patterns of problem solving to persist (Sweller & Gee, 1978). Your mental set may have caused you to use the same solution formula (B − A − 2C) for Problem 7 even though a simpler one (A + C) would have worked just as well. Figures 7.6 and 7.8 show another way in which a mental set can restrict our perception of the possible solutions to a problem.

Another restriction on problem solving may come from experience with objects. Once people become familiar with using an object for one type of function, they may be blinded to other ways of using it. Long experience may produce **functional fixedness,** a tendency to use familiar objects in familiar, rather than creative, ways. Figure 7.7 provides an example. An incubation strategy often helps to break mental sets.

Confirmation Bias   Anyone who has had a series of medical tests knows that diagnosis is not a one-shot decision. Instead, physicians choose an initial hypothesis on the basis of observed symptoms and then order tests or evaluate additional symptoms to confirm or eliminate that hypothesis (Trillin, 2001). This process can be distorted by a **confirmation bias:** Humans have a strong bias to confirm rather than to refute the hypothesis they have chosen, even in the face of strong evidence against the hypothesis. In other words, people are quite willing to perceive and accept data that support their hypothesis, but they tend to ignore information that is inconsistent with it (Groopman, 2000). Confirmation bias may be seen as a form of the anchoring heuristic. Once you've "anchored" to an initial hypothesis, you may be unwilling to abandon it. The would-be rescuers of John Gatiss's "trapped kitten" were so intent on their efforts to pinpoint its location that they never stopped to question its existence. Confirmation bias has been found operating, too, in expectations of students' performance, leading teachers to presume that good students will continue to perform well, and that poorer students will not improve much (Fiedler et al., 2002).

Ignoring Negative Evidence   On September 26, 1983, Lt. Col. Stanislav Petrov was in command of a secret facility that analyzed information from Soviet early-warning satellites. Suddenly, alarms went off as computers found evidence of five U.S. missiles being launched toward the Soviet Union. Tension between the two countries was high at the time, so based on the availability heuristic, Petrov hypothesized that a nuclear attack was under way. He was about to alert his superiors to launch a counterattack on the United States when it occurred to him that if this were a real nuclear attack, there should be evidence of many more than five missiles. Fortunately for everyone, he realized that the "attack" was a false alarm (Hoffman, 1999). As this near-disaster shows, the absence of symptoms or events can sometimes provide important evidence for or against a

figure 7.7

An Example of Functional Fixedness

learn ^by^**doing** Before reading further, ask yourself how you would fasten together two strings that are hanging from the ceiling but are out of reach of each other. Several tools are available, yet most people do not think of attaching, say, a pair of pliers to one string and swinging it like a pendulum until it can be reached while holding the other string. This solution is not obvious because we tend to fixate on the function of pliers as a tool rather than as a weight. People are more likely to solve this problem if the tools are scattered around the room. When the pliers are in a toolbox, their function as a tool is emphasized, and functional fixedness becomes nearly impossible to break.

hypothesis. Compared with evidence that is present, however, symptoms or events that do not occur are less likely to be noticed (Hunt & Rouse, 1981). People have a difficult time using the absence of evidence to help eliminate hypotheses from consideration (Ashcraft, 1989). In the "trapped kitten" case, when the "meowing" stopped for several days after the stove was unplugged and reconnected, rescuers assumed that the animal was frightened into silence. They ignored the possibility that their hypothesis was incorrect in the first place. (For a summary of problem solving and its pitfalls, see "In Review: Solving Problems.")

Problem Solving by Computer

Medical and scientific researchers have created artificial limbs, retinas, cochleas, and even hearts to help people with disabilities move, see, hear, and live more normally. Researchers are developing artificial brains, too, in the form of computer systems that not only see, hear, and manipulate objects but also reason and solve problems. These systems are the product of research in **artificial intelligence (AI),** a field that seeks to develop computers that imitate the processes of human perception and thought. For problems such as those involved in making certain kinds of medical diagnoses, computers using relatively simple formulas can already perform just as well as humans, if not better (Khan et al., 2001). However, humans and computers seem to work better together than alone. The human's role is to establish the presence and nature of a patient's symptoms. The computer then combines this information in a completely unbiased way to identify the most likely diagnosis (Swets, Dawes, & Monahan, 2000). Such teamwork can also help in the diagnosis of psychological problems (Nietzel et al., 2003).

Symbolic Reasoning and Computer Logic   An IBM computer known as Deep Blue has won chess games against the world's best chess masters. This result is not surprising, given that chess is a clearly defined, logical game at which computers can perform effectively. However, it is precisely their reliance on logic and formulas that accounts for the limitations of artificial intelligence systems. For example, these systems are successful in only very narrowly defined fields, not in general problem solving. This limitation stems from the fact that AI systems are based on logical symbolic manipulations that depend

in review

SOLVING PROBLEMS

Steps	Pitfalls	Remedies
Define the problem.	Inexperience: the tendency to see each problem as unique	Gain experience and practice in seeing the similarity between present problems and previous problems.
Form hypotheses about solutions.	Availability heuristic: the tendency to recall the hypothesis or solution that is most available to memory	Force yourself to write down, and carefully consider, many different hypotheses.
	Anchoring heuristic, or mental set: the tendency to anchor on the first solution or hypothesis, and not adjust your beliefs in light of new evidence or failures of the current approach	Break the mental set, stop, and try a fresh approach.
Test hypotheses.	The tendency to ignore negative evidence	In evaluating a hypothesis, consider the things you should see (but don't) if the hypothesis were true.
	Confirmation bias: the tendency to seek only evidence that confirms your hypothesis	Look for disconfirming evidence that, if found, would show your hypothesis to be false.

? *If you were lost and thirsty on a barren plain, but it doesn't occur to you to use your shoes to collect water during a sudden shower, you would be the victim of an obstacle to problem solving called _____.*

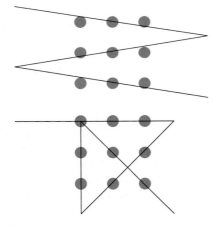

figure 7.8

Two Creative Solutions to the Nine-Dot Problem

Many people find puzzles like this difficult because mental sets create artificial limits on the range of solutions. In this case, the mental sets involve the tendency to draw within the frame of the dots and to draw through the middle of each dot. As shown here, however, there are other possibilities.

on "if-then" rules. Unfortunately, it is difficult to tell a computer how to recognize the "if" condition in the real world (Dreyfus & Dreyfus, 1988). Consider this simple "if-then" rule: "If it is a clock, then set it." Humans recognize all kinds of clocks because they have the natural concept of "clock," but computers are still not very good at forming natural concepts. Doing so requires putting into the same category many examples that have very different physical features, from a bedside digital alarm clock to Big Ben.

Neural Network Models Recognizing the problems posed by the need to teach computers to form natural concepts, many researchers in AI have moved toward the *connectionist,* or *neural network,* approach (Anderson, 1995). The neural network approach simulates the information processing taking place at many different, but interconnected, locations in the brain. This approach has contributed to the development of computers that are able to recognize voices, understand speech, read print, guide missiles, forecast solar flares, and perform many other complex tasks. Some of these computer simulations are being used to test theories of how infants learn to recognize speech (e.g., Roy & Pentland, 2002); others have been used to improve on human decision making. One program, called PAPNET, actually outperforms human technicians at detecting abnormal cells in smears collected during cervical examinations (Kok & Boon, 1996).

ARTIFICIAL INTELLIGENCE   Chess master Garry Kasparov had his hands full in May 1997, when he was challenged by "Deep Blue," a chess-playing computer that was programmed so well that it has won games against the world's best competitors, including Kasparov. Still, even the most sophisticated computers cannot perceive and think about the world in general anywhere near as well as humans can. Some observers believe that this situation will eventually change as progress in computer technology—and a deepening understanding of human cognitive processes—leads to dramatic breakthroughs in artificial intelligence.

Unfortunately, however, most computer models of neural networks still fall well short of the capacities of the human perceptual system. For example, computers are slow to learn how to classify visual patterns, and they do not show sudden insight when a key common feature is identified. But even though neural networks are far from perfect "thinking machines," they are sure to play an important role in psychologists' efforts to build ever more intelligent systems and to better understand the principles of human problem solving.

Creative Thinking

One of the greatest challenges in the development of artificial intelligence will be to program computers in a way that allows their thinking and problem solving to be as creative as that of humans. Consider the case that opened this chapter. It was Dr. Wallace's knowledge of the chemicals in paint—which has no obvious connection to human body chemistry—that led her to figure out what was causing Laura McBride's illness. Computers are still not nearly as good as humans are at recognizing that information from one area can be used to solve a problem in a seemingly unrelated area.

The ability to blend knowledge from many different domains is only one aspect of the creative thinking that humans display every day. People demonstrate **creativity** by producing original, but useful, solutions to all sorts of challenges (Simonton, 1999; Sternberg, 2001). Executives and homemakers, scientists and artists—all may be creative to varying degrees (Klahr & Simon, 1999). How do we know when people are thinking creatively? Psychologists have defined *creativity* as mental activity that can be inferred from performance on certain tests, as well as from the writings, computer programs, artwork, and other products resulting from the creative process (Sternberg & Dess, 2001). To measure creativity, some psychologists have generated tests of **divergent thinking**—the ability to think along many paths to generate multiple solutions to a problem (Diakidoy & Spanoudis, 2002). The Consequences Test is an example. It contains items such as "Imagine all of the things that might possibly happen if all national and local laws were suddenly abolished" (Guilford, 1959). Divergent thinking tests are scored by counting the number of sensible responses that a person can give to each item, and how many of these responses differ from those given by most people.

Only sensible responses to creativity tests are counted, because creativity involves divergent thinking that is appropriate for a given problem or situation. To be productive rather than just weird, a creative person must be firmly anchored in reality, understand society's needs, and learn from the experience and knowledge of others (Sternberg & Lubert, 1992). Theresa Amabile has identified three kinds of cognitive and personality

creativity   The capacity to produce original solutions or novel compositions.

divergent thinking   The ability to generate many different solutions to a problem.

characteristics necessary for creativity (Amabile, 1996; Amabile, Hennessey, & Grossman, 1986):

1. *Expertise* in the field of endeavor, which is directly tied to what a person has learned. For example, a painter or composer must know the paints, techniques, or instruments available.

2. A set of *creative skills,* including persistence at problem solving, capacity for divergent thinking, ability to break out of old problem-solving habits (mental sets), and willingness to take risks. Amabile believes that training can influence many of these skills, some of which are closely linked to the strategies for problem solving discussed earlier.

3. The *motivation* to pursue creative work for internal reasons, such as satisfaction, rather than for external reasons, such as prize money. In fact, Amabile and her colleagues found that external rewards can deter creativity. They asked groups of children and adults to create artistic products such as paintings or stories. Some were simply asked to work on the project. Others were informed that their project would be judged for its creativity and excellence and that rewards would be given or winners announced. Experts, who had no idea which products were created by which group, judged those from the "reward" group to be significantly less creative. Similar effects have been found in many other studies (Deci, Koestner, & Ryan, 1999, 2001).

Is creativity inherited? To some extent, perhaps it is; but evidence suggests that the social, economic, and political environment in which a person grows and lives also influences creative behavior (Amabile, 2001; Nakamura & Csikszentmihalyi, 2001). Do you have to be smart to be creative? Creativity does appear to require a certain degree of intelligence, but you don't have to be a genius (Simonton, 1984, 2002; Sternberg, 2001). In fact, although correlations between scores on creativity tests and intelligence tests are almost always positive, they are relatively modest (Simonton, 1999). This finding is not surprising, because creativity involves divergent thinking about many solutions to a problem. As described later, high scores on most intelligence tests require **convergent thinking,** which uses logic and knowledge to narrow down the number of possible solutions to a problem. Research on creativity and its relationship to intelligence has intensified in recent years (Sternberg & Dess, 2001). One result of that research has been to define the combination of intelligence and creativity in the same person as *wisdom* (Sternberg, 2001; Sternberg & O'Hara, 1999).

Decision Making

▶ **How can I become a better decision maker?**

Paper or plastic? Do I watch TV or study for the test? Should I get out of this relationship? Is it time to start thinking about a nursing home for Mom? Life is full of decisions. Some are easy to make; others are painfully difficult and require considerable time, planning, and mental effort. Even carefully considered decisions can lead to undesirable outcomes, though, because the world is an uncertain place. Decisions made when the outcome is uncertain are called *risky decisions* or *decisions under uncertainty.* Chance aside, psychologists have discovered reasons why human decisions sometimes lead to unsatisfactory outcomes. Let's consider some of these reasons.

Evaluating Options

Suppose that you must choose between (1) an academic major that fascinates you but is unlikely to lead to steady employment or (2) a major that is less interesting but virtu-

convergent thinking   The ability to apply the rules of logic and what one knows about the world to narrow down the possible solutions to a problem.

utility   In decision making, any subjective measure of value.

expected value   The total benefit to be expected of a decision if it were repeated on several occasions.

ally guarantees a high-paying job. The fact that each option has positive and negative features greatly complicates decision making. Deciding which car to buy, which college to attend, or even how to spend the evening are all examples of choices that require you to weigh several options. Such choices are often based on the positive or negative value, or **utility,** that you, personally, place on each feature of each option. Listing the pros and cons of each option is a helpful way of keeping them all in mind as you think about your decisions. You also have to estimate the probabilities and risks associated with the possible outcomes of each choice. For example, you must consider how likely it is that job opportunities in your chosen major will have faded by the time you graduate. In studying risky decision making, some psychologists begin with the assumption that the best decision maximizes expected value. The **expected value** of a decision is the total amount of benefit you could expect to receive if the decision were repeated on several occasions.

Biases and Flaws in Decision Making

Most people think of themselves as logical and rational, but they do not always act in ways that maximize expected value (Arkes & Ayton, 1999; Gilovich, 1997; Shiller, 2001). Why not?

Gains, Losses, and Probabilities   For one thing, the pain people feel about losing a certain amount is usually greater than the pleasure they feel about gaining the same amount. This phenomenon is known as *loss aversion* (Dawes, 1998; Tversky & Kahneman, 1991). So you might go to more trouble to collect a $100 debt than to win a $100 prize. In addition, the value of a specific gain doesn't depend on the amount of the gain but on what you start with. Suppose you could have a $10 gift certificate from a restaurant, but you have to drive 10 miles to pick it up. This gain has the same monetary value as having an extra $10 added to your paycheck. However, most people tend to behave as if the difference between $0 and $10 is greater than the difference between, say, $300 and $310. So the same person who may refuse to drive across town after work to add a $10 bonus to next week's paycheck might gladly make the same trip to pick up a $10 gift certificate. Understanding these biases, and how they affect people's purchasing patterns and other economic decisions, has proven so important that Daniel Kahneman received the 2002 Nobel Prize in economics for his research in this area.

People are also biased in how they perceive probability. For example, they tend to overestimate the probability of rare events and to underestimate the probability of frequent ones (Kahneman & Tversky, 1984). This bias helps explain why people gamble in casinos and enter lotteries, even though the odds are against them and the decision to do so has a negative expected value. People overestimate the probability of winning, especially in a casino, so they associate a positive expected value with gambling. The tendency to overestimate rare events is amplified by the availability heuristic: Vivid memories of rare gambling successes and the publicity given to lottery winners encourage people to recall gains rather than losses.

Another bias in estimating probability is called the *gambler's fallacy:* People believe that the probability of future events in a random process will change depending on past events. This belief is false. For example, if you flip a coin and it comes up heads ten times in a row, what is the likelihood of tails on the next flip? Although some people think otherwise, the chance that it will come up tails on the eleventh try is still 50 percent, just as it was for the first ten flips. Yet, many gamblers continue feeding a slot machine that has not paid off much for hours, assuming it is "due."

Poor decision making can also stem from the human tendency to be unrealistically confident in the accuracy of our predictions. Baruch Fischoff and Donald MacGregor (1982) devised a clever way to study this bias. People were asked whether they believed a certain event would occur and then were asked to say how confident they were about their prediction. For example, they were asked whether a particular sports team would win an upcoming game. After the events were over, the accuracy of the people's forecasts was compared with their level of confidence. Sure enough, their confidence in their predictions was

applying psychology   **A HIGHLY UNLIKELY OUTCOME**   By focusing the public's attention on the very few people who win big lottery prizes, state lottery agencies take advantage of the general human tendency to overestimate the probability of rare events. Lottery ads never show any of the millions of people whose tickets turn out to be worthless.

consistently greater than their accuracy. This overconfidence operates even when people make predictions concerning the accuracy of their own memory (Bjork, 1998).

Overconfidence about knowledge and judgments appears in many cultures, and in some more than others. In one study, students in China and the United States were asked to say how confident they were about their answers to general-knowledge questions (Wright & Phillips, 1980). Both groups were overconfident, but the Chinese were especially so. A study comparing Chinese, Japanese, and North American students found the same result (Yates et al., 1989). Why? Cultural traditions that strongly discourage Chinese students from challenging what they are told by teachers may make them less likely than Americans to question what they tell themselves, and thus more likely to be overconfident. This possibility is supported by the fact that compared with American and Japanese students, Chinese students were able to list the fewest arguments against their own judgments (Yates, Lee, & Shinotsuka, 1992). The moral of the story is to be wary when people in any culture express confidence that a forecast or decision is correct. They will be wrong more often than they think.

How Biased Are We?   Almost everyone makes decisions they later regret, but these outcomes may not be due entirely to biased thinking about gains, losses, and probabilities. Some decisions are not intended to maximize expected value but rather to satisfy other goals, such as minimizing expected loss, producing a quick and easy resolution, or preserving a moral principle (Arkes & Ayton, 1999; Zsambok & Klein, 1997). Often, decisions depend not just on how likely we are to gain or lose a particular amount of something but also on what that something is. A decision that could cost or save a human life may be made differently than one that could cost or gain a few dollars, even though the probabilities of each outcome are exactly the same in both cases.

Even the "goodness" or "badness" of decisions is often difficult to assess. Many of them depend on personal values (utilities), which can vary from person to person and from culture to culture. People in individualist cultures, for example, may tend to assign high utilities to attributes that promote personal goals, whereas people in collectivist cultures might place greater value on attributes that bring group harmony and the approval of family and friends (Markus, Kitayama, & Heiman, 1996).

LINKAGES
Do groups solve problems more effectively than individuals?
(a link to Social Psychology)

LINKAGES

Group Processes in Problem Solving and Decision Making

Problem solving and decision making often take place in groups. The factors that influence an individual's problem solving and decision making continue to operate when the individual is in a group, but group interactions also shape the outcome.

When groups are trying to choose from among several options, for example, the discussion tends to follow a consistent pattern (Hastie, Penrod, & Pennington, 1983). First, various options are proposed and debated until the group sees that no one has strong objections to one option; that option becomes the *minimally acceptable solution*. From then on, the group criticizes any other proposal and argues more and more strongly for the minimally acceptable solution, which is likely to become the group's decision. In other words, the order in which options are considered can determine the outcome (Wittenbaum & Stasser, 1996). (This phenomenon is an example of the anchoring heuristic operating in a group situation.)

Group discussion often results in decisions that are more extreme than the group members would make individually. This tendency toward extreme decisions is called *group polarization* (Kaplan, 1987). Two mechanisms appear to underlie group polarization. First, most arguments presented during the discussion favor the majority view, most criticisms are directed at the minority view, and confirmation bias leads group members to seek additional information that supports the majority position (Schulz-Hardt et al., 2000). In this atmosphere, it seems rational to those favoring the majority view to adopt an even stronger version of it (Stasser, 1991). Second, once some group members begin to agree that a particular decision is desirable, other members may try to associate themselves with it, perhaps by advocating an even more extreme version (Kaplan & Miller, 1987).

Are people better at problem solving and decision making when they work in groups than when on their own? This is one of the questions about human thinking that is studied by social psychologists. In a typical experiment, a group of people is asked to solve a problem like the one in Figure 7.6 or to decide the guilt or innocence of the defendant in a fictional court case. Each person is asked to work alone and then to join with the others to try to agree on a decision. These studies have found that when correct solutions can be made obvious to everyone, groups usually outperform individuals (Laughlin, 1999). When problems have less obvious solutions, groups may be somewhat better at solving them than their average member, but usually no better than their most talented member (Hackman, 1998). And because of a phenomenon called *social loafing* (discussed in the social psychology chapter), people working in a group are often less productive than people working alone (Williams & Sommer, 1997).

Other research suggests that a critical element in successful group problem solving is the sharing of individual members' unique information and expertise (e.g., Stasser, Stewart, & Wittenbaum, 1995). For example, when asked to diagnose an illness, groups of physicians were much more accurate when they pooled their knowledge (Larson et al., 1998). However, *brainstorming,* a popular strategy that supposedly encourages group members to generate new and innovative solutions to a problem, may actually produce fewer ideas than are generated by individuals working alone (Levine & Moreland, 1998), possibly because some individuals' creative processes may be impaired by comments from other group members. Further, group members who are confident or have high status are most likely to influence a group's deliberations (Levine & Moreland, 1998), but whether these people will help or hurt the group's efforts depends on whether they express good ideas (Hinsz, 1990). Unfortunately, there is little evidence that members with the best ideas or greatest competence (as opposed to the highest status) always contribute more to group deliberations (Littlepage et al., 1995).

As they work to solve a problem, group members experience their own thoughts as propositions, images, or other mental representations. How does each member share these private events to help the group perform its task? The answer lies in the use of language.

Language

▶ **How do babies learn to talk?**

Many pet owners swear that their animals "talk" to them. Maybe Duchess barks in a particular way when she wants to go outside, or Cleo meows to be fed. But are Duchess's barks and Cleo's meows really language? Probably not. These pets are surely communicating something to their owners, but the noises they make lack many of the components of human language (Rendall, Cheney, & Seyfarth, 2000). So although Duchess may let out, say, three high-pitched yelps when she wants to go outside, she may bark in exactly the same way when her owner asks her whether she agrees with the local leash laws. For this reason, we wouldn't call her barking "language." Humans, however, can use language to express everything from simple requests to abstract principles. They can create stories that pass on cultural information and traditions from one generation to the next.

A **language** has two basic elements: symbols, such as words, and a set of rules, called **grammar,** for combining those symbols. With their knowledge of approximately 50,000 to 100,000 words (Miller, 1991), humans can create and understand an infinite number

language   Symbols, and a set of rules for combining them, used as a means of communicating.

grammar   A set of rules for combining the symbols, such as words, used in a given language.

of sentences. Yet all of the sentences ever spoken are created from just a few dozen categories of sounds. The power of language comes from the way these rather unimpressive raw materials are organized according to certain rules.

Learning to Speak: Stages of Language Development

Children the world over develop language with impressive speed; the average six-year-old already has a vocabulary of about 13,000 words (Pinker, 1994). But acquiring language involves more than just learning vocabulary. We also have to learn how words are combined and how to produce and understand sentences. Psychologists who study the development of language have found that the process begins in the earliest days of a child's life and follows some predictable steps (Saffran, Senghas, & Trueswell, 2001).

The First Year   In their first year, infants become more and more attuned to the sounds that will be important in acquiring their native language. The first year is also the time when babies begin to produce **babblings,** which are patterns of meaningless sounds that first resemble speech. These alternating consonant and vowel sounds (such as "bababa," "dadada," and "mamimamima") appear at about four months of age, once the infant has developed the necessary coordination of the tongue and mouth. Though meaningless to the baby, babblings are a delight to parents. Infants of all nationalities begin with the same set of babbling sounds, but at about nine months of age, they begin to produce only the sounds that occur in the language they hear the most. At about the same time, their babbling becomes more complex and begins to sound like "sentences" in the babies' native language (Goldstein, King, & West, 2003). Infants who hear English begin to shorten some of their vocalizations to "da," "duh," and "ma." They use these sounds to convey joy, anger, interest, and other messages in specific contexts and with obvious purpose (Blake & de Boysson-Bardies, 1992).

By ten to twelve months of age, babies can understand several words—certainly more words than they can say (Fenson et al., 1994). Proper names and object words—such as *mama, daddy, cookie, doggy,* and *car*—are among the earliest words they understand. These are also the first words children are likely to say when, at around twelve months of age, they begin to talk (some talk a little earlier and some a little later). Nouns for simple object categories *(dog, flower)* are acquired before more general nouns *(animal, plant)* or more specific names *(collie, rose)* (Rosch et al., 1976).

GETTING READY TO TALK   Long before they say their first words, babies are getting ready to talk (Dehaene-Lambertz, Dehaene, & Hertz-Pannier, 2002). Experiments in Patricia Kuhl's laboratory show that even six-month-olds tend to look longer at faces whose lip movements match the sounds of spoken words. This tendency reflects babies' abilities to focus on, recognize, and discriminate the sounds of speech, especially in their native language. These abilities are crucial to the development of language (Mayberry, Lock, and Kazmi, 2002).

Of course, these early words do not sound exactly like adult language. English-speaking babies usually reduce them to a shorter, easier form, like "duh" for *duck* or "mih" for *milk*. Children make themselves understood, however, by using gestures, voice tones, facial expressions, and endless repetitions. Once they have a word for an object, they may "overextend" it to cover more ground. So they might use *doggy* to refer to cats, bears, and horses; they might use *fly* for all insects and perhaps for other small things like raisins and M&Ms (Clark, 1983, 1993). Children make these "errors" because their vocabularies are limited, not because they fail to notice the difference between dogs and cats or because they want to eat a fly (Fremgen & Fay, 1980; Rescorla, 1981). Being around people who don't understand these overextensions encourages children to learn and use more precise words (Markman, 1994). During this period, children build up their vocabularies one word at a time. They also use their limited vocabulary one word at a time; they cannot yet put words together into sentences.

The Second Year Then, sometime around eighteen months of age, children's vocabularies expand dramatically (Gleitman & Landau, 1994). They may learn several new words each day, and by the age of two, most youngsters can use fifty to well over one hundred words. They also start using two-word combinations to form efficient little sentences. These two-word sentences are called **telegraphic** because, like telegrams or text messages on a mobile phone, they are brief and to the point, leaving out anything that is not absolutely essential. So if she wants her mother to give her a book, a twenty-month-old might first say, "Give book," then "Mommy give," and if that does not work, "Mommy book." The child also uses rising tones to indicate a question ("Go out?") and emphasizes certain words to indicate location ("Play *park*") or new information ("*Big* car").

Three-word sentences come next in the development of language. They are still telegraphic, but more nearly complete: "Mommy give book." The child's sentences now begin to have the subject-verb-object form typical of adult sentences. Other words and word endings begin appearing, too. In English, these include the suffix *-ing*, the prepositions *in* and *on*, the plural *-s*, and irregular past tenses ("It broke," "I ate") (Brown, 1973; Dale, 1976). Children learn to use the suffix *-ed* for the past tense ("I walked"), but they often overapply this rule to irregular verbs that they previously used correctly, saying, for example, "It breaked," "It broked," or "I eated" (Marcus, 1996). Children also expand their sentences with adjectives, although at first they make some mistakes. For example, they are likely to use both *less* and *more* to mean "more" (Smith & Sera, 1992).

The Third Year and Beyond By age three or so, children begin to use auxiliary verbs ("Adam is going") and to ask questions using *what, where, who,* and *why.* They begin to put together clauses to form complex sentences ("Here's the ball I was looking for"). By age five, children have acquired most of the grammatical rules of their native language.

How Is Language Acquired?

Despite all that has been learned about the steps children follow in learning language, mystery and debate still surround the question of just how they learn it. We know that children pick up the specific content of language from the speech they hear around them: English children learn English; French children learn French. But how do children learn the rules of grammar?

Conditioning, Imitation, and Rules Perhaps children learn grammar because their parents reward them for using it. This idea sounds reasonable, but observations suggest that positive reinforcement (which we describe in the learning chapter) does not tell the whole story. Parents are usually more concerned about what is said than about its grammatical form (Hirsch-Pasek, Treiman, & Schneiderman, 1984). So when the little boy with chocolate crumbs on his face says, "I not eat cookie," his mother is more likely to

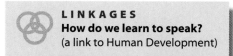

LINKAGES
How do we learn to speak?
(a link to Human Development)

babblings Repetitions of syllables; the first sounds infants make that resemble speech.

telegraphic A term referring to young children's utterances that are brief and to the point and that leave out non-essential words.

respond, "Yes, you did" than to ask the child to say, "I did not eat the cookie" and then reinforce him for grammatical correctness.

Learning through modeling, or imitation, appears to be more influential. Children learn grammar most rapidly when adults demonstrate the correct form in the course of conversation. For example:

Child: Mommy fix.
Mother: Okay, Mommy will fix the truck.
Child: It breaked.
Mother: Yes, it broke.

But if children learn grammar by imitation, why do children who at one time said "I went" later say "I goed"? Adults do not use this form of speech, so neither imitation nor reward can account for its sudden appearance. It must be that children analyze for themselves the underlying patterns in the language they hear around them and then learn the rules governing those patterns (Bloom, 1995).

Biological Bases for Language Acquisition   The ease with which children everywhere discover these patterns and learn language has led some to argue that language acquisition is at least partly innate, or automatic. Noam Chomsky (1965) believes that we are born with a built-in *universal grammar,* a mechanism that allows us to identify the basic dimensions of language (Baker, 2002; Chomsky, 1986; Nowak, Komarova, & Niyogi, 2001). According to Chomsky, a child's universal grammar might tell the child that word order is important to the meaning of a sentence. In English, for example, word order tells us who is doing what to whom (the sentences "Heather dumped Jason" and "Jason dumped Heather" contain the same words, but they have different meanings). In Chomsky's view, then, we don't entirely learn language—we develop it as genetic predispositions interact with experience (Senghas & Coppola, 2001). So a child's innate assumption that word order is important to grammar would change if the child heard language in which word order did not have much effect on the meaning of a sentence.

Other theorists disagree with Chomsky, arguing that the development of language reflects the development of more general cognitive skills rather than innate, language-specific mechanisms (e.g., Bates, 1993). Still, there is other evidence to support the existence of biological factors in language acquisition. For example, the unique proper-

LEARNING A SECOND LANGUAGE   As these international students are discovering, people who learn a second language as adults do so more slowly, and with less proficiency, than younger people (Johnson & Newport, 1989; Patkowski, 1994) and virtually never learn to speak it without an accent (Lenneberg, 1967). Still, the window of opportunity for learning a second language is open far beyond the critical period in childhood during which first-language acquisition must occur (Hakuta, Bialystok, & Wiley, 2003).

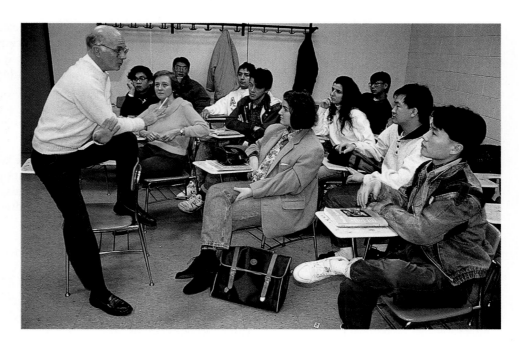

ANIMAL LANGUAGE? Several chimpanzees and gorillas have been taught to use American Sign Language (ASL). Here, Koko the gorilla signs "smoke" as Penny Patterson holds Smoky the cat. Are such primates' remarkable accomplishments with ASL the same as human language abilities? Research continues to reveal the similarities and differences and suggests that with the right tools and training, these animals can master language-like skills (Sevcik & Savage-Rumbaugh, 1994).

ties of the human mouth and throat, the language-related brain regions described in the chapter on biology and behavior, and recent genetic research all suggest that humans are innately "prewired," or biologically programmed, for language (Buxhoeveden et al., 2001; Lai et al., 2001). In addition, there appears to be a period in childhood during which we can learn language more easily than at any other time (Ridley, 2000). The existence of this *critical period* is supported by evidence from cases in which unfortunate children spent their early years in isolation from human contact and the sound of adult language. Even after years of therapy and language training, these individuals are not able to combine ideas into sentences (Rymer, 1993b). Such cases suggest that in order to acquire the complex features of language, we must be exposed to speech before a certain age.

Bilingualism   Does trying to learn two languages at once, even before the critical period for language learning is over, impair the learning of either? Research suggests just the opposite. Like some children in any situation, the early language of children from a bilingual environment may be confused or delayed, but they eventually show enhanced performance in each language (de Houwer, 1995). There is also some evidence that *balanced bilinguals*—those who have roughly equal mastery of two languages in childhood—are superior to other children in cognitive flexibility, concept formation, and creativity. It is as if each language offers a slightly different perspective on thinking, and this dual perspective makes the brain more flexible (Hong et al., 2000).

Testing Intelligence

▶ **How is intelligence measured?**

People who are good at using and understanding language, and skilled at thinking, problem-solving, and decision-making are likely to be seen as *intelligent*. But intelligence is not limited to these abilities alone. Over the years, psychologists studying people in various cultures around the world have proposed that the concept of "intelligence" is a broad umbrella that can also include attributes such as efficiently storing and retrieving memories; effectively focusing—or dividing—attention; rapidly processing information; quickly learning new things; profiting from experience; adapting well to changing environments; having a good sense of direction; appreciating patterns in nature; being good at music, dance, or athletics; showing eye-hand coordination; understanding oneself and others; and displaying polished social skills (Berry & Bennett, 1992; Eysenck, 1986; Gardner, 1999; Hunt, 1983; Meyer & Salovey, 1997; Sternberg, 1996; Sternberg, Lautrey, & Lubart, 2003).

So what, exactly, is intelligence? Psychologists have never been able to agree on an answer to this question, but many of them accept a working definition proposed by Robert Sternberg (1985, 1997b). According to Sternberg, **intelligence** can be described in terms of three characteristics: the possession of knowledge, the ability to efficiently use that knowledge to reason about the world, and the ability to use that reasoning adaptively in various environments.

Standard tests of intelligence measure some of these characteristics, but they don't address all of them. Accordingly, some psychologists argue that these tools are not able to capture all that should be tested if we want to get a complete picture of someone's intelligence in its broadest sense. To better understand the controversy, let's take a look at how standard intelligence tests were created, what they are designed to measure, and how well they do their job. Later, we will consider some alternative intelligence tests that have been proposed by those who find fault with traditional ones.

A Brief History of Intelligence Tests

In 1904 the French government asked psychologist Alfred Binet (pronounced "bih-NAY") to join a committee whose job was to identify, study, and provide special educational programs for children who were not doing well in school. As part of his work, Binet developed a set of mental tasks that provided the model for today's intelligence tests. Binet assumed that reasoning, thinking, and problem solving all depend on intelligence, so he chose tasks that would highlight individual differences in children's ability to do these things (Binet & Simon, 1905). Children taking Binet's test were asked to unwrap a piece of candy, repeat numbers or sentences from memory, identify familiar objects, and the like (Rogers, 1995).

Binet also assumed that children's mental abilities increase with age. So after trying out test items on children of various ages, he categorized each item according to how old a child had to be to get the item right. For example, a "six-year-old item" was one that a large majority of six-year-olds could answer correctly. In other words, Binet's test contained a set of *age-graded* items. It measured a child's "mental level," later called *mental age,* by determining the age level of the most advanced items that the child could consistently answer correctly. Children whose mental age equaled their actual age, or *chronological age,* were considered to be of "regular" intelligence (Schultz & Schultz, 2000).

About a decade after Binet published his test, Lewis Terman at Stanford University developed an English version, known as the **Stanford-Binet** test (Terman, 1916). Table 7.1 gives examples of the kinds of items included on the test. Terman added items to measure the intelligence of adults and revised the scoring procedure. Mental age was divided by chronological age, and the result was multiplied by 100. This figure was called the *intelligence quotient,* or *IQ.* So a child whose mental age and chronological age were equal would have an IQ of 100, which is considered "average" intelligence. A ten-year-old who scored at the mental age of twelve would have an IQ of $12/10 \times 100 = 120$. From this method of scoring came the term **IQ test,** a name now widely used for any test designed to measure intelligence on an objective, standardized scale.

The method used to score the Stanford-Binet allowed testers to rank people based on their IQs. This goal was important to Terman and others who popularized the test in the United States. Terman believed that IQ tests could pinpoint who did and who did not have a suitable "amount" of intelligence. These beliefs were controversial and, in some instances, led to prejudice and discrimination as enthusiasm for testing outpaced under-

intelligence   The possession of knowledge, the ability to efficiently use that knowledge to reason about the world, and the ability to use that reasoning adaptively in different environments.

Stanford-Binet   A test for determining a person's intelligence quotient, or IQ.

IQ test   A test designed to measure intelligence on an objective, standardized scale.

table 7.1

The Stanford-Binet

Here are samples of the type of items included on Lewis Terman's original Stanford-Binet test. As in Binet's test, an age level was assigned to each item.

Age	Task
2	Place geometric shapes into corresponding openings; identify body parts; stack blocks; identify common objects.
4	Name objects from memory; complete analogies (e.g., fire is hot; ice is _____); identify objects of similar shape; answer simple questions (e.g., "Why do we have schools?").
6	Define simple words: explain differences (e.g., between a fish and a horse); identify missing parts of a picture; count out objects.
8	Answer questions about a simple story; identify absurdities (e.g., in statements like "John had to walk on crutches because he hurt his arm"); explain similarities and differences among objects; tell how to handle certain situations (e.g., finding a stray puppy).
10	Define more difficult words; give explanations (e.g., about why people should be quiet in a library); list as many words as possible; repeat 6-digit numbers.
12	Identify more difficult verbal and pictured absurdities; repeat 5-digit numbers in reverse order; define abstract words (e.g., *sorrow*); fill in a missing word in a sentence.
14	Solve reasoning problems; identify relationships among points of the compass; find similarities in apparently opposite concepts (e.g., "high" and "low"); predict the number of holes that will appear when folded paper is cut and then opened.
Adult	Supply several missing words for incomplete sentences; repeat 6-digit numbers in reverse order; create a sentence using several unrelated words (e.g., *forest, businesslike,* and *dismayed*); describe similarities between concepts (e.g., "teaching" and "business").

Source: Nietzel & Bernstein (1987).

standing of what was being tested. For example, when the United States entered World War I in 1917, a team of psychologists was asked to develop group-administered tests that could identify the mental ability of army recruits and guide their assignment to appropriate jobs. Soldiers who could speak and read English were tested on mental tasks that required verbal skills, such as defining words, whereas the rest were asked to visualize objects and perform other nonverbal tasks. Unfortunately, the verbal tests contained items that were unfamiliar to many recruits. Further, tests were often given under stressful conditions in crowded rooms where instructions were not always audible or, for non-English speakers, understandable. As a result, almost half of the soldiers tested appeared to have a mental age of thirteen or lower (Yerkes, 1921), leading testers to draw seriously incorrect conclusions about their lack of intelligence—especially in the cases of those who did not speak English (Brigham, 1923). Later tests developed by David Wechsler (1939, 1949) were designed to correct some of the weaknesses of earlier ones.

IQ Tests Today

Today's editions of the Wechsler tests and the Stanford-Binet are the most widely used of all individually administered intelligence tests. The Wechsler Adult Intelligence Scale (WAIS-III) includes fourteen subtests. Seven of them require verbal skills and make up

figure 7.9

Sample Items from the Wechsler Intelligence Scale for Children (WISC)

Items like these are designed to measure aspects of intelligence that involve little or no verbal ability. The latest edition of the Wechsler Intelligence Scale for Children (called the WISC-IV) contains both verbal and performance subtests. Comparing scores on the two kinds of subtests can provide valuable information. For example, a child who does far better on nonverbal subtests than on verbal ones might have a language problem that prevents the overall IQ score from accurately describing the child's mental abilities (Lezak, 1995).

Picture completion
What part is missing from this picture?

Picture arrangement
These pictures tell a story, but they are in the wrong order. Put them in the right order so that they tell a story.

Block design

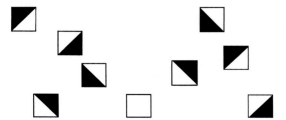

Put the blocks together to make this picture.

Source: Simulated items similar to those in the *Wechsler Intelligence Scales for Adults and Children.* Copyright © 1949, 1955, 1974, 1981, 1991, 1997, 2003 by the Psychological Corporation, a Harcourt Assessment Company. Reproduced by permission. All rights reserved. "Wechsler" is a trademark of The Psychological Corporation registered in the United States of America and/or other jurisdictions.

verbal scale Subtests in Wechsler tests that measure verbal skills as part of a measure of overall intelligence.

performance scale Subtests in Wechsler tests that measure spatial ability and the ability to manipulate materials as part of a measure of overall intelligence.

intelligence quotient (IQ score) A number that reflects the degree to which a person's score on an intelligence test differs from the average score of others in his or her age group.

test A systematic observation of behavior in a standard situation, described by a numerical scale or category.

norms Descriptions of the frequency of particular scores on a test.

reliability The degree to which test results or other research evidence occurs repeatedly.

the **verbal scale** of the test. These subtests include such items as remembering a series of digits, solving arithmetic problems, defining vocabulary words, and understanding and answering general-knowledge questions. The other seven subtests have little or no verbal content and make up the **performance scale.** They include tasks that require understanding the relationships between objects and manipulation of various materials—tasks such as assembling blocks, solving mazes, arranging pictures to form a story, and completing unfinished pictures. Testers using the WAIS-III can compute a verbal IQ, a performance IQ, and an overall IQ, as well as "index" scores that reflect a person's mental processing speed, memory ability, perceptual skills, and understanding of verbal information. The latest edition of the Wechsler Intelligence Scale for Children (WISC-IV) yields four similar index scores, along with an overall IQ score (see Figure 7.9 for examples of items from an earlier version of the WISC).

The latest edition of the Stanford-Binet (SB5) also contains subtests (Roid, 2003). It provides scores on verbal IQ, nonverbal IQ, and overall IQ, along with measures of verbal reasoning (e.g., How are a pen and a pencil alike?), quantitative reasoning (e.g., math problems), general knowledge (e.g., explaining why we wear coats in cold weather), working memory (e.g., repeating numbers), and ability to process visual information.

Calculating IQ

IQ scores are no longer calculated by dividing mental age by chronological age. If you take an IQ test today, the points you earn for each correct subtest or age-level answer are

figure 7.10

The Distribution of IQ Scores in the Population

When the IQ scores in the general population are plotted on a graph, a bell-shaped curve appears. The average IQ score of any given age group is 100. Half of the scores are higher than 100, and half are below 100. Approximately 68 percent of the IQ scores of any age group fall between 84 and 116; about 16 percent fall below 84, and about 16 percent fall above 116.

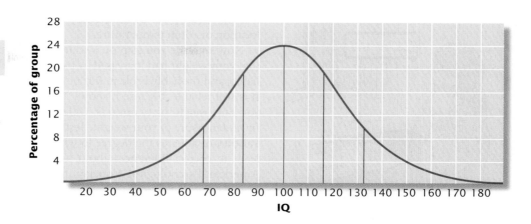

summed. Your total score is then compared with the scores earned by other people. The average score obtained by people at each age level is given the IQ value of 100. Other scores are given IQ values that reflect how much each score differs from the average. So if you do better on the test than the average person in your age group, you will receive an IQ score above 100. How far above depends on how much better than average you do. Similarly, a person scoring below the age-group average will have an IQ below 100. This procedure is based on a well-supported assumption about many characteristics: Most people's scores fall in the middle of the range of possible scores, creating a bell-shaped curve that approximates the normal distribution (see Figure 7.10). Half of those tested score below 100, the average for any given age group. The other half score above 100. In short, your **intelligence quotient,** or **IQ score,** reflects your relative standing within a population of your age.

Evaluating IQ Tests

▶ **How good are IQ tests?**

We have said that no IQ test can accurately measure all aspects of what various people think of as intelligence. So what does your IQ score say about you? Can it predict your performance in school or on the job? Is it a fair summary of your mental abilities? To scientifically answer questions like these, we have to measure the quality of the tests that yield IQ scores, using the same criteria that apply to tests of personality, language skills, driving, or anything else. Let's review these criteria and then see how they are used to evaluate IQ tests.

Any **test** is a systematic procedure for observing behavior in a standard situation and describing it with the help of a numerical scale or system of categories (Cronbach, 1990). Tests are *standardized,* meaning that they present the same tasks, under similar conditions, to each person who takes them. Standardization helps ensure that test results will not be significantly affected by factors such as who gives and scores the test. To the extent that the biases of those giving a test do not influence the results, the test is said to be *objective.* Testers can use test scores to calculate **norms,** which are descriptions of the frequency of particular scores. Norms tell us, for example, what percentage of high school students obtained each possible score on a college entrance exam. They also allow us to say whether a particular IQ score or entrance-exam score is above or below the average score.

The two most important measures of a test's value are its reliability and its validity. A test is said to have high **reliability** if its results are repeatable or stable. The test must measure the same thing in the same way every time it is used. Let's suppose you receive a very high score on a test of reasoning. If you re-take the test the next day and get a very low score, the test is probably unreliable. The higher the reliability of a test, the less likely

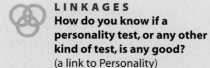

LINKAGES
How do you know if a personality test, or any other kind of test, is any good?
(a link to Personality)

If only measuring intelligence were this easy!

it is that scores will be affected by irrelevant environmental factors, such as hunger or location or room temperature.

Now suppose you step on a scale, check your weight, step off, step back on, and find that your weight had increased by twenty pounds. You would know that the scale is unreliable, and probably broken. But now imagine that the scale is broken in a different way. It is still reliable, because it shows the same weight every time you step on it, but it says you only weigh thirty pounds! Unless you are a small child, this scale would provide an *invalid* measure of your weight. Tests, like scales, can be reliable and still not be valid. The **validity** of a test is the degree to which it measures what it is supposed to measure and leads to correct inferences about people (American Educational Research Association, American Psychological Association, and National Council on Measurement in Education, 1999; Dooley, 2001).

Researchers evaluate the reliability of a test by obtaining two sets of scores on the same test from the same people. They then calculate a correlation coefficient between the two sets of scores (see the introductory chapter). When the correlation is high and positive (usually above +.80), the test is considered reliable. Evaluating a test's validity usually means calculating a correlation coefficient between test scores and something else. What that "something else" is depends on what the test is designed to measure. Suppose, for example, you wanted to know if a creativity test is valid for identifying creative people. You could do so by computing the correlation between people's scores on the creativity test and experts' judgments about the quality of those same people's artistic creations. If the correlation is high, the test has high validity as a measure of creativity. Notice that a test's validity cannot be said to be high or low until you know how the test is to be used. Measuring how long someone can keep a bare hand in ice water might be a valid test of pain tolerance, but not of intelligence. So a test can be valid for one purpose but not valid for another.

The Reliability and Validity of IQ Tests

The reliability of IQ tests is generally evaluated on the basis of their stability, or consistency. The validity of IQ tests is usually based on their accuracy in making statements and predictions about people's intellectual abilities.

Reliability   IQ scores obtained before the age of seven typically do not correlate very highly with scores on IQ tests given later. There are two key reasons. First, test items used with very young children are different from those used with older children. Second, cognitive abilities change rapidly in the early years (see the chapter on human development). During the school years, however, IQ scores tend to remain stable (Mayer & Sutton, 1996). For teenagers and adults, then, the reliability of IQ tests is high, generally above +.90.

Of course, a person's score may vary from one occasion to another if there are significant changes in motivation, anxiety, health, or other factors. Overall, though, modern IQ tests usually provide exceptionally consistent results, especially compared with most other kinds of mental tests.

Validity   If everyone agreed on exactly what intelligence is (having a good memory, for example), we could evaluate the validity of IQ tests simply by correlating people's IQ scores with their performance on various tasks (in this case, memory tasks). IQ tests whose scores correlated most highly with scores on memory tests would be the most valid measures of intelligence. But because psychologists do not fully agree on a single definition of intelligence, they don't have a single standard against which to compare IQ tests. Therefore, they cannot say whether IQ tests are valid measures of intelligence. They can only assess the validity of IQ tests for specific purposes.

The results of their research suggest that IQ tests are most valid for assessing aspects of intelligence that are related to schoolwork, such as abstract reasoning and understanding verbal material. Their validity—as measured by correlating IQ scores with high school grades—is reasonably good, about +.50 (Brody & Erlichmann, 1998).

validity   The degree to which a test measures what it is supposed to measure and leads to correct inferences about people.

In addition, there is evidence that employees who score high on tests of verbal and mathematical reasoning tend to perform better on the job than those who earn lower scores (Borman, Hanson, & Hedge, 1997; Johnson & Neal, 1998; Pulakos et al., 2002). Later we describe a study that kept track of people for sixty years and found that those who had high IQ scores as children tended to be well above average in terms of academic and financial success in adulthood (Cronbach, 1996; Oden, 1968; Terman & Oden, 1947). IQ scores also appear to be highly correlated with performance on routine tasks such as reading medicine labels and using a telephone book (Gottfredson, 1997).

So, by the standard measures for judging psychological tests, IQ tests have good reliability and reasonably good validity for predicting certain criteria, such as success in school. However, an IQ score is not a perfect measure of how "smart" a person is. Because IQ tests do not measure the full array of cognitive abilities, a particular test score tells only part of the story, and even that part may be distorted. Many factors other than mental ability, including reactions to the tester, can influence test performance. For example, children who are suspicious of strangers, and adults who fear making mistakes, may become anxious and fail even to try answering some questions, thus artificially lowering their IQ scores (Fagan, 2000; Steele, 1997).

IQ Scores as a Measure of Innate Ability

Alfred Binet believed that intelligence could be improved with training and practice at mental tasks. Lewis Terman saw it as an inherited characteristic. Both were partly right. Years of research has led psychologists to conclude that hereditary and environmental factors interact to influence intelligence.

To explore the influence of genetics on individual differences in IQ scores, psychologists have compared the correlations in scores between people who share varying degrees of similarity in genetic makeup and environment. For example, they have examined the IQ scores of identical twins (pairs with exactly the same genes) who were separated when very young and raised in different environments. They have also examined the scores of identical twins raised together. (Research designs used in behavioral genetics studies are described in the introductory chapter.)

These studies find, first, that genetic factors are strongly related to IQ scores. When identical twins who were separated at birth and adopted by different families are tested many years later, the correlation between their scores is usually high and positive, at least +.60 (Bouchard, 1999). If one twin receives a high IQ score, the other probably will, too; if one is low, the other is likely to be low as well. However, studies of IQ correlations also highlight the importance of the environment (Scarr, 1998). Consider any two people—twins, nontwin siblings, or unrelated children—brought up together in a foster home. No matter what the degree of genetic similarity in these pairs, the correlation between their IQ scores is higher if they share the same home than if they are raised in different homes, as Figure 7.11 shows (Scarr & Carter-Saltzman, 1982).

The role of environmental influences is also seen in studies that compare children's IQ scores before and after environmental changes such as adoption. Generally, when children from relatively impoverished backgrounds were adopted into homes offering a more enriching intellectual environment—including interesting materials and experiences, as well as a supportive, responsive adult—they showed modest increases in their IQ scores (Weinberg, Scarr, & Waldman, 1992).

A study of French children who were adopted soon after birth demonstrates the importance of both genetic and environmental influences. These children were tested after years of living in their adopted homes. Those whose biological parents were from higher socioeconomic groups (where higher IQs are more common) had higher IQ scores than those whose biological parents came from lower socioeconomic groups, regardless of the socioeconomic status of the adopted homes (Capron & Duyme, 1989, 1996). These findings are supported by data from the Colorado Adoption Project (Cardon & Fulker, 1993; Cardon et al., 1992), and they suggest that a genetic component of

figure 7.11

Correlations of IQ Scores

The correlation in IQ between pairs increases with increasing similarity in heredity or environment.

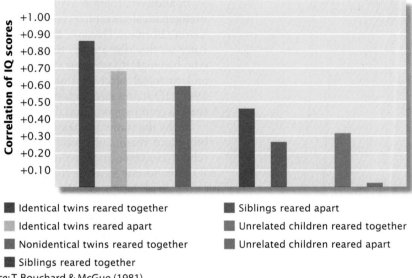

■ Identical twins reared together   ■ Siblings reared apart

■ Identical twins reared apart   ■ Unrelated children reared together

■ Nonidentical twins reared together   ■ Unrelated children reared apart

■ Siblings reared together

Source: T. Bouchard & McGue (1981).

the children's mental abilities continued to exert an influence in the adoptive environment. At the same time, when children from low socioeconomic backgrounds were adopted by parents who provided academically enriched environments, their IQ scores rose by twelve to fifteen points (Capron & Duyme, 1989).

Programs designed to enhance young children's school readiness and academic ability have also been associated with improved scores on tests of intelligence (Neisser et al., 1996; Ripple et al., 1999). These early-intervention programs may be partly responsible for the steady increase in average IQ scores seen throughout the world over the past six decades (Flynn, 1999; Neisser, 1998).

Some researchers have concluded that the influences of genetic and environmental factors on intelligence appear to be about equal. Others see a somewhat larger role for genetic factors (Herrnstein & Murray, 1994; Loehlin, 1989; Petrill et al., 1998; Plomin, 1994). One research team has even suggested that specific genes are associated with extremely high IQs (Chorney et al., 1998). Still, it must be emphasized that the relative contributions of heredity and environment apply only to groups, not to individuals. It would be inaccurate to say that 50 percent of your IQ score is inherited and 50 percent learned. It is more accurate to say that about half of the variability in the IQ scores of a group of people can be attributed to genetic influences, and about half can be attributed to environmental influences. (As discussed in the appendix, *variability* is the degree to which scores spread out around an average score.)

Group Differences in IQ Scores

Much of the controversy over the roles played by genes and the environment in intelligence has been sparked by efforts to explain differences in the average IQ scores earned by particular groups of people. For example, the average scores of Asian Americans are typically the highest among various ethnic groups, followed, in order, by European Americans, Hispanic Americans, and African Americans (e.g., Fagan, 2000; Lynn, 1996; Taylor & Richards, 1991). Further, the average IQ scores of people from high-income areas in the United States and elsewhere are consistently higher than those of people from low-income communities with the same ethnic makeup (Jordan, Huttenlocher, & Levine, 1992; McLoyd, 1998; Rowe, Jacobson, & Van den Oord, 1999).

To understand these differences and where they come from, we have to remember two things. First, group scores are just that; they do not describe individuals. Although the mean IQ score of Asian Americans is higher than the mean IQ score of European Americans, there will still be large numbers of European Americans who score well above the Asian American mean and large numbers of Asian Americans who score below the European American mean (see Figure 7.12). Second, inherited characteristics are not necessarily fixed. A favorable environment can improve a child's intellectual performance, even if the inherited influences on that child's IQ are negative (Flynn, 1999; Humphreys, 1984; Neisser, 1998).

Socioeconomic Differences   Why is there a relationship between IQ scores and family income? Four factors seem to account for the correlation. First, parents' jobs and status depend on characteristics related to their own intelligence. And this intelligence is partly determined by a genetic component that, in turn, contributes to their children's IQ scores. Second, parents' income affects their children's environment in ways that can increase or decrease the children's IQ scores (Bacharach & Baumeister, 1998). Third, motivational differences may play a role. Parents in upper- and middle-income families tend to provide more financial and psychological support for their children's motivation to succeed and excel in academic endeavors (Atkinson & Raynor, 1974; Nelson-LeGall & Resnick, 1998). Perhaps these families influence their children to be more highly motivated to succeed on IQ tests. If so, children from middle- and upper-class families may exert more effort and therefore obtain higher scores (Bradley-Johnson, Graham, & Johnson, 1986; Zigler & Seitz, 1982). Fourth, because colleges, universities, and businesses usually select people with higher scores on various cognitive ability tests, those with higher IQs—who tend to do better on such tests—may have greater opportunities to earn more money (Sackett et al., 2001).

Ethnic Differences   Some have argued that the average differences in IQ among various ethnic groups in the United States are due mostly to heredity. However, the existence of hereditary differences among individuals *within* groups does not indicate whether differences *between* groups result from similar genetic causes (Lewontin, 1976). Notice again in Figure 7.12 that variation within ethnic groups is much greater than variation among the mean scores of those groups (Zuckerman, 1990).

We must also take into account the large differences among the environments in which the average African American, Hispanic American, and European American child grows up. To take only the most blatant evidence, the latest U.S. Census Bureau figures show 24 percent of African American families and 21.8 percent of Hispanic American families living below the poverty level, compared with 10.2 percent of Asian American families and 8 percent of European American families (U.S. Census Bureau, 2003). Compared with European Americans, African American children are more likely to have parents with poor educational backgrounds, as well as inferior nutrition, health care, and

LINKAGES
How does motivation affect IQ scores?
(a link to Motivation and Emotion)

figure 7.12

A Representation of Ethnic Group Differences in IQ Scores

The average IQ score of Asian Americans is about four to six points higher than the average score of European Americans, who average twelve to fifteen points higher than African Americans and Hispanic Americans. Notice, however, that the variation within these groups is much greater than the variation between them.

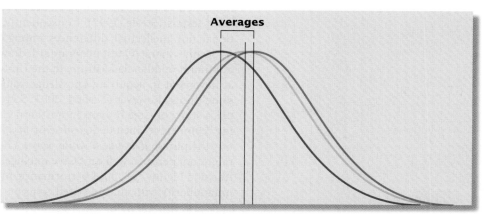

—— African Americans and Hispanic Americans
—— European Americans
—— Asian Americans

schools. All of these conditions are likely to pull down scores on IQ tests (Brooks-Gunn, Klebanov, & Duncan, 1996).

Evidence for the influence of environmental factors on the average black-white IQ difference is supported by adoption studies. One such study involved African American children from disadvantaged homes who were adopted by middle- to upper-income European American families in the first years of their lives (Scarr & Weinberg, 1976). When measured a few years later, the mean IQ score of these children was 110. A comparison of this mean score with that of nonadopted children from similar backgrounds suggests that the new environment raised the children's IQ scores at least ten points. A ten-year follow-up study of these youngsters showed that their average IQ scores were still higher than the average scores of African American children raised in disadvantaged homes (Weinberg, Scarr, & Waldman, 1992).

If environmental factors such as poverty and inferior educational opportunities are partly responsible for the lower average IQ scores seen in children from disadvantaged groups, is it fair to compare all children on traditional IQ tests? After all, success on these tests depends heavily on knowledge and skills that disadvantaged youngsters may not have had an equal chance to develop.

■ What am I being asked to believe or accept?

Some critics claim that, indeed, standard IQ tests are not fair. They argue that a disproportionately large number of people in some ethnic minority groups score low on IQ tests for reasons that are unrelated to mental ability, job potential, or other criteria that the tests are supposed to predict (Helms, 1992, 1997; Kwate, 2001). They say that using IQ tests to make decisions about people—such as assigning them to particular jobs or special classes—causes members of certain groups to be unfairly deprived of equal employment or educational opportunities.

■ Is there evidence available to support the claim?

Research reveals several possible sources of bias in tests of cognitive abilities. First, as mentioned earlier, noncognitive factors can influence a person's performance on IQ tests and may put certain groups at a disadvantage. We have seen, for example, that children from some ethnic and socioeconomic groups may be less likely than other children to be motivated to perform well on standardized tests. They may also be less likely to trust adult testers (Steele, 1997). Consequently, differences in IQ scores may reflect motivational, not intellectual, differences among various groups.

Second, many IQ test items are still drawn from the vocabulary and experiences of the dominant middle-class culture in the United States. As a result, these tests often measure achievement in acquiring knowledge valued by that culture. Not all cultures value the same things, however (Nisbett, 2003; Serpell, 1994; Yang & Sternberg, 1997). For example, a study of Cree Indians in northern Canada revealed that words and phrases meaning "competent" included *good sense of direction*. At the "incompetent" end of the scale was the phrase *lives like a white person* (Berry & Bennett, 1992). A European American might not perform well on a Cree intelligence test based on these criteria. In fact, as illustrated in Figure 7.13, poor performance on a culture-specific test is probably due more to unfamiliarity with culture-based concepts than to lack of mental ability.

Third, some tests may reward those who interpret questions as expected by the test designer. Conventional IQ tests have clearly defined "right" and "wrong" answers. Yet a person may interpret test questions in a manner that is "intelligent" or "correct," but that produces a "wrong" answer. For example, when one child was asked, "In what way are a

figure 7.13

An Intelligence Test?

learn by **doing**

How did you do on this "intelligence test"? If, like most people, you are unfamiliar with the concepts being tested by these rather obscure questions, your score was probably low. Would it be fair to say, then, that you are not very intelligent?

Take a minute to answer each of these questions, and check your answers against the key below.

1. What fictional detective was created by Leslie Charteris?
2. What planet travels around the sun every 248 years?
3. What vegetable yields the most pounds of produce per acre?
4. What was the infamous pseudonym of broadcaster Iva Toguri d'Aquino?
5. What kind of animal is Dr. Dolittle's Pushmi-Pullyu?

Answers: (1) Simon Templar (2) Pluto (3) Cabbage (4) Tokyo Rose (5) A two-headed llama

pen and a pencil alike?" he replied, "They can both poke holes in paper." And the fact that you don't give the answer that the test designer was looking for does not mean that you *can't.* When Liberian rice farmers were asked to sort objects, they tended to put a knife in the same group as vegetables. This was the clever way to do it, they said, because the knife is used to cut vegetables. When asked to sort the objects as a "stupid" person would, the farmers grouped the cutting tools together, the vegetables together, and so on, as most North Americans would (Segall et al., 1990).

■ Can that evidence be interpreted another way?

The evidence might be interpreted as showing that although traditional IQ tests do not provide a complete and unbiased measure of "intelligence," they do provide a fair test of whether a person is likely to succeed in school or in certain jobs. In short, they may be biased, but not in a way that discriminates *unfairly* between groups. Perhaps familiarity with the culture reflected in IQ tests is just as important for success at school or work in that culture as it is for success on the tests themselves. After all, the ranking among various ethnic groups on measures of academic achievement is similar to the ranking for mean IQ scores (Sue & Okazaki, 1990). According to this view, it doesn't matter very much if IQ tests measure culture-related achievement, as long as they are useful in predicting whatever criterion is of interest.

■ What evidence would help to evaluate the alternatives?

Some psychologists have developed "culture-fair" intelligence tests (Bracken & McCallum, 1998), which result in smaller average differences among ethnic groups. Unfortunately, these tests do not predict academic achievement as well as conventional IQ tests do (Aiken, 1994). Other alternative tests are also being explored, including some that assess problem-solving skills and other abilities not measured by most IQ tests (e.g., Sternberg & Kaufman, 1998). If these new tests prove to be less biased than traditional tests but have equal or better predictive validity, many of the issues discussed in this section will have been resolved.

■ What conclusions are most reasonable?

The American Psychological Association and other organizations set demanding standards for the reliability, validity, fairness, and use of all psychological tests, including IQ tests (American Educational Research Association, American Psychological Association, & National Council on Measurement in Education, 1999). "Summarizing" a person through an IQ score runs the risk of oversimplifying reality and making errors, but the use of standard intelligence tests can also prevent errors. If boredom makes a child appear mentally slow, or even retarded, an IQ test conducted under the right

INFLUENCES ON IQ SCORES		
Source of Effect	**Description**	**Examples of Evidence for Effect**
Genetics	Genes appear to play a significant role in IQ test performance.	The IQ scores of siblings who share no common environment are positively correlated. There is a greater correlation between scores of identical twins than between those of nonidentical twins.
Environment	Environmental conditions interact with genetic inheritance. Nutrition, medical care, sensory and intellectual stimulation, interpersonal relations, and influences on motivation are all significant features of the environment.	IQ scores have risen among children who are adopted into homes that offer a stimulating, enriching environment. Correlations between IQs of twins reared together are higher than for those reared apart.

? *Intelligence is determined by both _____ and _____.*

circumstances is likely to reveal the child's potential. And, as Binet had hoped, IQ tests have been enormously helpful in identifying children who need special educational attention. So despite their limitations, IQ tests can minimize the likelihood of assigning children to remedial work they do not need, or to advanced work they cannot yet handle.

Nevertheless, efforts to reduce cultural bias in intelligence tests are well founded, as long as the resulting tests objectively measure the knowledge and skills people need to succeed in the culture where they live and work. The problem of test bias would best be solved, though, by addressing the poverty, inferior schools, poor nutrition, lack of health care, and other conditions that result in lower average IQ scores and reduced economic opportunities for certain groups of people. ("In Review: Influences on IQ Scores" summarizes our discussion of environmental and genetic factors affecting performance on intelligence tests.)

Diversity in Intelligence

▶ **Is there more than one type of intelligence?**

IQ scores can tell us some things—and predict some things—about people, but we have seen that they don't tell the whole story of intelligence. Let's see how diverse intelligence can be by looking at some nontraditional aspects of intelligence, and at some people whose intellectual abilities are unusually high or low.

Multiple Intelligences

Many people with only average scores on IQ tests have exceptional ability in specific areas. Even those with very low IQ scores have been known to show incredible ability in narrowly defined skills (Miller, 1999). One such child, whose IQ was only 50, could instantly and correctly state the day of the week for any date between 1880 and 1950 (Scheerer, Rothmann, & Goldstein, 1945). He could also play melodies on the piano by ear and sing Italian operatic pieces he had heard. He could spell—forward or backward—any word spoken to him and could memorize long speeches. However, he had no understanding of what he was doing.

Cases like this are part of the evidence that led Howard Gardner to propose his theory of *multiple intelligences* (Gardner, 1993, 2002). Gardner focused on how people learn and use symbol systems like language, mathematics, and music. He asked, Do these systems all require the same abilities and processes—the same "intelligence"? According to Gardner, the answer is no. He believes that everyone possesses a number of intellectual potentials, or "intelligences," each of which involves a somewhat different set of skills. Biology, he says, provides raw capacities for each of these intelligences; cultures provide symbolic systems—such as language—that enable people to use their raw capacities. Although the various intelligences normally interact, they can function with some independence, and individuals may develop certain intelligences further than others.

The specific intelligences that Gardner (1999) proposes are (1) *linguistic* intelligence (reflected in good vocabulary and reading comprehension), (2) *logical-mathematical* intelligence (as indicated by skill at arithmetic and certain kinds of reasoning), (3) *spatial* intelligence (seen in understanding relationships between objects), (4) *musical* intelligence (as in abilities involving rhythm, tempo, and sound identification), (5) *body-kinesthetic* intelligence (reflected in skill at dancing, athletics, and eye-hand coordination), (6) *intrapersonal* intelligence (displayed by self-understanding), (7) *interpersonal* intelligence (seen in the ability to understand and interact with others), (8) *naturalistic* intelligence (the ability to see patterns in nature), and (9) *existential* intelligence (the tendency to ponder the meaning of life, death, and the nature of reality). Other researchers have suggested that people also possess *emotional* intelligence, which involves the capacity to perceive emotions and to link them to one's thinking (Meyer & Salovey, 1997).

Gardner says that standard IQ tests sample only the first three of these diverse intelligences, mainly because they are the forms of intelligence most valued in school. To measure specific intelligences that are not tapped by standard IQ tests, Gardner suggests collecting samples of children's writing, assessing their ability to appreciate or produce music, and obtaining teacher reports of their strengths and weaknesses in athletic and social skills.

Gardner's view of intelligence is appealing, partly because it allows virtually everyone to be highly intelligent in at least one way. However, his critics argue that including athletic or musical skill as part of intelligence dilutes the usefulness of the concept, especially as it is applied to school and in many kinds of jobs. Nevertheless, Gardner and his colleagues are working on new ways of assessing "multiple intelligences" (Gardner, 2002; Kornhaber, Krechevsky, & Gardner, 1990). The value of these methods will be determined by further research.

Practical and Creative Intelligence

In contrast to Gardner, Robert Sternberg (1988, 1999) sees only three types of intelligence: analytic, creative, and practical. *Analytic* intelligence, the kind that is measured by traditional IQ tests, helps you to solve a physics problem; *creative* intelligence is what you would use to compose music; and you would draw on *practical* intelligence to figure out what to do if you were stranded on a lonely road during a storm. (His view is known as the *triarchic theory* of intelligence.)

Sternberg recognizes the importance of analytic intelligence for success in academics and other areas, but he argues that universities and companies should not select people solely on the basis of tests of this kind of intelligence (Sternberg, 1996; Sternberg & Williams, 1997). Why? Because the tasks posed by tests of analytic intelligence are often of little interest to the people taking them, and these tasks typically have little relationship to their daily experience. In contrast, the practical problems people face every day are generally of personal interest and are related to their actual experiences (Sternberg et al., 1995). It is no wonder, then, that children who do poorly in school and on IQ tests can nevertheless show high degrees of practical intelligence. Some Brazilian street children, for example, are capable of doing the math required for their street business, despite having failed mathematics in school (Carraher, Carraher, & Schliemann, 1985). In other words, their practical intelligence is unrelated to measures of their IQ. There is some evidence that scores on tests of practical and creative intelligence predict success at some jobs at least as well as standard IQ test scores (Leonhardt, 2000; Sternberg & Kaufman, 1998; Sternberg et al., 1995). (See Figure 7.14.)

Unusual Intelligence

Psychologists' understanding of intelligence has been advanced by studying people whose mental abilities are unusual—especially the gifted and the mentally retarded (Robinson, Zigler, & Gallagher, 2000).

Giftedness   People with especially high IQ scores are often referred to as *gifted,* but this does not mean that they share the same pattern of exceptional cognitive abilities. In one study, Sternberg (2000) found that gifted people can display at least seven different combinations of the analytic, creative, and practical skills measured by his Triarchic Abilities Test.

Do all people with unusually high IQs become famous and successful in their chosen fields? Do their remarkable intellectual abilities hurt their chances of "fitting in" with the social world? One of the best-known studies of the intellectually gifted was conducted by Lewis Terman and his colleagues (Oden, 1968; Sears, 1977; Terman & Oden, 1947, 1959). This study began in 1921 with the identification of more than 1,500 children whose IQ scores were very high—most higher than 135 by age ten. Periodic interviews and tests over the next sixty years revealed that few, if any, became world-famous scientists, inventors, authors, artists, or composers. But only 11 failed to graduate from high school, and more than two-thirds graduated from college. Ninety-seven earned Ph.D.'s; 92, law degrees; and 57, medical degrees. In 1955 their median family income was well above the national average (Terman & Oden, 1959). In general, they were physically and mentally healthier than the nongifted and appeared to have led happier, or at least more fortunate, lives (Cronbach, 1996).

In other words, high IQ scores tend to predict success in life (Whalley & Deary, 2001), but an extremely high IQ does not guarantee special distinction. Some research suggests that gifted children are not fundamentally different kinds of people. They just have "more" of the same basic mental abilities seen in all children (Dark & Benbow, 1993). Other work suggests that gifted people may be different in other ways, too, such as having unusually intense motivation to master certain tasks or areas of intellectual endeavor (Lubinski et al., 2001; Winner, 2000).

Mental Retardation   People whose IQ is less than about 70 *and* who fail to display the skills at daily living, communication, and other tasks that are expected of those their age have traditionally been described as *mentally retarded* (American Psychiatric Association, 1994). They are now often referred to as *developmentally disabled* or *mentally challenged.* People within this very broad category differ greatly in their mental abilities, and in their ability to function independently in daily life (see Table 7.2).

Some cases of mental retardation have a clearly identifiable cause. The best-known example is *Down syndrome,* which occurs when an abnormality during conception results in an extra copy of chromosome 21 (Hattori et al., 2000). Children with Down syndrome typically have IQ scores in the range of 40 to 55, though some may score higher than that. There are also several inherited causes of mental retardation. The most common of these is *fragile X syndrome,* a defect on chromosome 23 (known as the *X chromosome*). Retardation can also result from environmental causes, such as exposure to German measles (rubella), alcohol, or other toxins before birth; oxygen deprivation during birth; and head injuries, brain tumors, and infectious diseases (such as meningitis or encephalitis) in childhood (U.S. Surgeon General, 1999).

THE EAGLE HAS LANDED   In February 2000, Richard Keebler, twenty-seven, became an Eagle Scout in the Boy Scouts of America. His achievement is notable not only because a mere 4 percent of all Scouts ever reach this rank but also because Keebler has Down syndrome. As we come to better understand the potential, and not just the limitations, of mentally retarded people, their opportunities and their role in society will continue to expand.

figure 7.14

Testing for Practical and Creative Intelligence

learn by doing Robert Sternberg notes that traditional IQ tests measure mainly analytic intelligence. Here are sample items from tests he developed that test practical and creative intelligence as well. The answers are given at the bottom of the figure. How did you do?

PRACTICAL

1. Think of a problem that you are currently experiencing in real life. Briefly describe the problem, including how long it has been present and who else is involved (if anyone). Then describe three different practical things you could do to try to solve the problem. *(Students are given up to 15 minutes and up to 2 pages.)*

2. Choose the answer that provides the **best** solution, given the specific situation and desired outcome.

   John's family moved to Iowa from Arizona during his junior year in high school. He enrolled as a new student in the local high school two months ago but still has not made friends and feels bored and lonely. One of his favorite activities is writing stories. What is likely to be the most effective solution to this problem?

   A. Volunteer to work on the school newspaper staff.

   B. Spend more time at home writing columns for the school newsletter.

   C. Try to convince his parents to move back to Arizona.

   D. Invite a friend from Arizona to visit during Christmas break.

3. Each question asks you to use information about everyday things. Read each question carefully and choose the best answer.

   Mike wants to buy two seats together and is told there are pairs of seats available only in Rows 8, 12, 49, and 95–100. Which of the following is not one of his choices for the total price of the two tickets?

   A. $10.   **B.** $20.   **C.** $30.   **D.** $40.

CREATIVE

1. Suppose you are the student representative to a committee that has the power and the money to reform your school system. Describe your ideal school system, including buildings, teachers, curriculum, and any other aspects you feel are important. *(Students are given up to 15 minutes and up to 2 pages.)*

2. Each question has a "Pretend" statement. You must suppose that this statement is true. Decide which word goes with the third underlined word in the same way that the first two underlined words go together.

   Colors are audible.

   flavor is to tongue as shade is to

   A. ear.   **B.** light.   **C.** sound.   **D.** hue.

3. First, read how the operation is defined. Then, decide what is the correct answer to the question.

   *There is a new mathematical operation called **flix**.*
   It is defined as follows:

   $A \text{ flix } B = A + B, \text{ if } A > B$

   but $A \text{ flix } B = A \times B, \text{ if } A < B$

   and $A \text{ flix } B = A / B, \text{ if } A = B$

   How much is 4 flix 7?

   A. 28.   **B.** 11.   **C.** 3.   **D.** −11.

ANSWERS. Practical: (2) A, (3) B. Creative: (2) A, (3) A.

Source: Sternberg (1996).

table 7.2

Categories of Mental Retardation

These categories are approximate. Especially at the upper end of the scale, many retarded persons can be taught to handle tasks well beyond what their IQ scores might suggest. Furthermore, IQ is not the only diagnostic criterion for retardation. Many people with IQs lower than 70 can function adequately in their everyday environment and so would not be classified as mentally retarded.

Level of Retardation	IQ Scores	Characteristics
Mild	50–70	A majority of all the mentally retarded. Usually show no physical symptoms of abnormality. Individuals with higher IQs can marry, maintain a family, and work in unskilled jobs. Abstract reasoning is difficult for those with the lower IQs of this category. Capable of some academic learning to a sixth-grade level.
Moderate	35–49	Often lack physical coordination. Can be trained to take care of themselves and to acquire some reading and writing skills. Abilities of a 4- to 7-year-old. Capable of living outside an institution with their families.
Severe	20–34	Only a few can benefit from any schooling. Can communicate vocally after extensive training. Most require constant supervision.
Profound	Below 20	Mental age less than 3. Very limited communication. Require constant supervision. Can learn to walk, utter a few simple phrases, and feed themselves.

Familial retardation refers to the 30 to 40 percent of (usually mild) cases of mental retardation in which there is no obvious genetic or environmental cause (American Psychiatric Association, 1994). These cases appear to result from a complex, and as yet unknown, interaction between heredity and environment that researchers are continuing to explore (Croen, Grether, & Selvin, 2001).

People who are mildly retarded differ from other people in three important ways (Campione, Brown, & Ferrara, 1982):

1. They perform certain mental operations more slowly, such as retrieving information from long-term memory. When asked to repeat something they have learned, they are not as quick as a person of normal intelligence.

2. They simply know fewer facts about the world. It is likely that this deficiency is a consequence of the problem listed next.

3. They are not very good at using certain mental strategies that may be important in learning and problem solving. For example, they do not spontaneously rehearse material that must be held in short-term memory.

Despite such difficulties, the intellectual abilities of mentally retarded people can be improved to some extent. One program emphasizing positive parent-child communications began when the children were as young as two and a half years old. It helped children with Down syndrome to eventually master reading skills at a second-grade level, providing the foundation for further achievement (Rynders & Horrobin, 1980). However, designing effective programs for children who are retarded is complicated by the fact that learning does not depend on cognitive skills alone. It also depends on social and emotional factors, including where children learn. Much debate has focused on *mainstreaming,* the policy of teaching children with disabilities, including those who are retarded, in regular classrooms along with those without disabilities. Is mainstreaming good for retarded children? A number of studies comparing the cognitive and social skills of children who have been mainstreamed and those who were separated show few significant differences overall. However, it does appear that students at higher ability levels may gain more from being mainstreamed than their less mentally able peers (Cole et al., 1991; Mills et al., 1998).

familial retardation   Cases of mild retardation for which no environmental or genetic cause can be found.

Linkages

As noted in the introductory chapter, all of psychology's subfields are related to one another. Our discussion of group problem solving illustrates just one way in which the topic of this chapter, thought, language, and intelligence, is linked to the subfield of social psychology, which is described in the chapter by that name. The Linkages diagram shows ties to two other subfields as well, and there are many more ties throughout the book. Looking for linkages among subfields will help you see how they all fit together and help you better appreciate the big picture that is psychology.

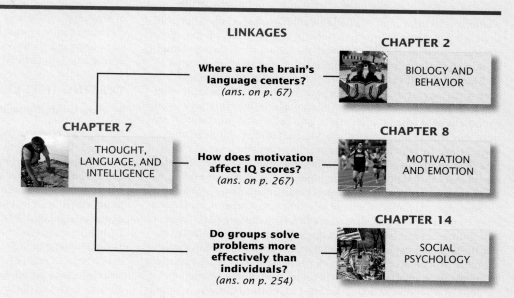

LINKAGES

CHAPTER 7
THOUGHT, LANGUAGE, AND INTELLIGENCE

Where are the brain's language centers?
(ans. on p. 67)

CHAPTER 2
BIOLOGY AND BEHAVIOR

How does motivation affect IQ scores?
(ans. on p. 267)

CHAPTER 8
MOTIVATION AND EMOTION

Do groups solve problems more effectively than individuals?
(ans. on p. 254)

CHAPTER 14
SOCIAL PSYCHOLOGY

Summary

BASIC FUNCTIONS OF THOUGHT

▶ **What good is thinking, anyway?**

The five core functions of thought are to describe, elaborate, decide, plan, and guide action. Many psychologists think of the components of this circle of thought as constituting an *information-processing system* that receives, represents, transforms, and acts on incoming stimuli. *Thinking,* then, is defined as the manipulation of mental representations by this system.

MENTAL REPRESENTATIONS: THE INGREDIENTS OF THOUGHT

▶ **What are thoughts made of?**

Mental representations take the form of concepts, propositions, schemas, scripts, mental models, images, and cognitive maps. *Concepts* are categories of objects, events, or ideas with common properties. They may be formal or natural. *Formal concepts* are precisely defined by the presence or absence of certain features. *Natural concepts* are fuzzy; no fixed set of defining properties determines membership in a natural concept. A member of a natural concept that displays all or most of the concept's characteristic features is called a *prototype.*

Propositions are assertions that state how different concepts are related. Propositions can be true or false. *Schemas* serve as generalized mental representations of concepts and also generate expectations about them. *Scripts* are schemas about familiar sequences of events or activities. Experience creates accurate or inaccurate *mental models* that help to guide our understanding of, and interaction with, the world. Mental *images* may also be manipulated when people think. *Cognitive maps* are mental representations of familiar parts of one's world.

THINKING STRATEGIES

▶ **Do people always think logically?**

By combining and transforming mental representations, our information-processing system makes it possible for us to reason, solve problems, and make decisions. *Formal reasoning* seeks valid conclusions through the application of rigorous procedures. It is guided by *algorithms,* systematic methods that always reach a correct result. To reach a sound conclusion, people should consider both the truth or falsity of their assumptions and whether the argument follows the *rules of logic.* Unfortunately, people are prone to logical errors.

People use *informal reasoning* to assess the validity of a conclusion based on the evidence for it. Errors in informal reasoning often stem from the use of *heuristics,* which are mental shortcuts or rules of thumb. Three important heuristics are the *anchoring heuristic* (estimating the probability of an event by adjusting a starting value), **the** *representativeness heuristic* (basing conclusions about whether something belongs in a certain class on how similar it is to other items in that class), and the *availability heuristic* (estimating probability by how available an event is in memory).

PROBLEM SOLVING

▶ **What's the best way to solve a problem?**

Steps in problem solving include diagnosing the problem and then planning, executing, and evaluating a solution. Especially when solutions are not obvious, problem solving can be aided by the use of strategies such as means-end analysis (also called *decomposition*), working backward, finding analogies, and allowing for incubation.

Many of the difficulties that people experience in solving problems arise when they are dealing with hypotheses. People do not easily entertain multiple hypotheses. Because of *mental sets,* they may stick to one hypothesis even when it is incorrect and, because of *functional fixedness,* may tend to miss opportunities to use familiar objects in unusual ways. People are reluctant to revise or change hypotheses on the basis of new data, partly because *confirmation bias* may focus their attention on evidence that supports their hypotheses. They may also fail to use the absence of symptoms or events as evidence in solving problems.

Some specific problems can be solved by computer programs developed by researchers in the field of *artificial intelligence (AI).* There are two approaches to AI. One focuses on programming computers to imitate the logical manipulation of symbols that occurs in human thought; the other (involving connectionist, or neural network, models) attempts to imitate the connections among neurons in the human brain.

Tests of *divergent thinking* are used to measure differences in *creativity.* In contrast, intelligence tests require *convergent thinking.* Although creativity and intelligence are not highly correlated, creative behavior requires a certain amount of intelligence, along with expertise in a creative field, skill at problem solving and divergent thinking, and motivation to pursue a creative endeavor for its own sake.

DECISION MAKING

▶ **How can I become a better decision maker?**

Decisions are sometimes difficult because there are too many alternatives and too many features of each alternative to consider at one time. Furthermore, decisions often involve comparisons of subjective *utility,* not of objective value. Decision making is also complicated by the fact that the world is unpredictable, which makes decisions risky.

People should act in ways that maximize the *expected value* of their decisions. But they often fail to do so because losses are perceived differently from gains of equal size and because people tend to overestimate the probability of rare events, underestimate the probability of frequent events, and feel overconfident about the accuracy of their forecasts. The gambler's fallacy leads people to believe that events in a random process are affected by previous events. People also make decisions aimed at goals other than maximizing expected value; these goals may be determined by personal and cultural factors.

Group decisions tend to show group polarization, the selection of more extreme outcomes than would have been chosen by the average group member. Group performance in problem solving and decision making can be effective, but depending on the problem and the people involved, it may be less efficient than when individuals work alone.

LANGUAGE

▶ **How do babies learn to talk?**

Language consists of words or word symbols and rules for their combination—a *grammar.* Children develop grammar according to an orderly pattern. *Babblings* come first, then *telegraphic* two-word sentences. Next come three-word sentences and certain grammatical forms that appear in a somewhat predictable order. Once children learn certain regular verb forms and plural endings, they may overgeneralize rules. Children acquire most of the syntax of their native language by the time they are five years old.

Both conditioning and imitation play a role in a child's acquisition of language, but neither can provide a complete explanation of how children acquire syntax. Humans may be biologically programmed to learn language. In any event, it appears that language must be learned during a certain critical period if normal language is to occur.

TESTING INTELLIGENCE

▶ **How is intelligence measured?**

Intelligence refers to the possession of knowledge, the ability to reason, and the capacity to adapt to different environments. Binet's pioneering test of intelligence included questions that required reasoning and problem solving at varying levels of difficulty, graded by age. Terman developed a revision of Binet's test that became known as the *Stanford-Binet;* it included items designed to assess the intelligence of adults as well as that of children, and it became the model for *IQ tests.* Early IQ tests in the United States required not just mental ability but also knowledge of U.S. culture. Wechsler's tests remedied some of the deficiencies of earlier IQ tests. Made up of subtests, including a *verbal scale* but also a *performance scale* with little verbal content, these tests allowed testers to obtain scores for different aspects of mental ability.

In schools, the Stanford-Binet and Wechsler tests are the most popular individually administered intelligence tests. Both include subtests and provide scores for parts of the test, as well as an overall score. Currently, a person's *intelligence quotient,* or *IQ score,* reflects how much the person's performance on the test deviates from the average performance of people in the same age group. An average performance is assigned an IQ of 100.

EVALUATING IQ TESTS

▶ **How good are IQ tests?**

Tests are standardized, so the performance of different people can be compared; they also produce scores that can be compared with *norms.* A good test must have *reliability,* which means that the results for each person are consistent, or stable. A test is said to have *validity* if it measures what it is supposed to measure and leads to correct inferences about people.

IQ tests are quite reliable and do a reasonable job of predicting academic success. However, IQ tests assess only some of the abilities that might be considered aspects of intelligence, and they may favor people most familiar with middle-class culture. Nonetheless, this familiarity is important for academic and occupational success in that culture.

Both genes and the environment influence IQ scores, and their effects interact. Genetic influences are reflected in the high correlation between IQ scores of identical twins raised in separate households and in the similarity between the IQ scores of children adopted at birth and those of their biological parents. The influence of the environment is revealed by the higher correlation of IQ between siblings who share the same environment than between those who do not and by the effects of environmental changes such as adoption.

Different socioeconomic and ethnic groups have somewhat different mean IQ scores. These differences appear to be due to numerous factors, including differences in motivation, family support, educational opportunity, and other environmental conditions. An enriched environment sometimes raises IQ scores. Despite their limitations, IQ tests can help educators to identify a student's strengths and weaknesses and to offer the curriculum that will best serve that student.

DIVERSITY IN INTELLIGENCE

▶ **Is there more than one type of intelligence?**

According to Gardner, biology equips us with the capacities for several intelligences that can function with some independence—specifically, linguistic, logical-mathematical, spatial, musical, body-kinesthetic, intrapersonal, interpersonal, naturalistic, and existential intelligences. Sternberg sees three types of intelligence: analytic, practical, and creative. He says that scores on tests of practical intelligence predict job success as well as traditional IQ test scores do.

Knowledge about mental abilities has been expanded by research on giftedness and mental retardation. People with very high IQ scores tend to be successful in life but are not necessarily geniuses. People are considered retarded if their IQ score is below about 70 and if their communication and daily living skills are less than expected of people their age. In cases of *familial retardation,* no genetic or environmental causes are evident. Compared with people of normal intelligence, people who are retarded process information more slowly, know fewer facts, and are deficient at knowing and using mental strategies. Special teaching programs can, to some extent, improve the intellectual abilities of some people who are mentally retarded.

Learn by Doing

Put It in Writing

Try writing your own definition of *intelligence.* Make a list of at least seven behaviors or characteristics that you feel represent intelligence, and then decide how they could best be tested in children and adults from your own culture and other cultures. Describe the kinds of difficulties you encountered in making your list and designing your assessment devices.

Personal Learning Activity

Consider a problem that you are facing at the moment, or one that is being faced by someone you know. In accordance with the problem-solving section of this chapter, write down all the alternative solutions you can think of to solve this problem; then list the pros and cons of each option. Which alternative comes out on top? Does the alternative that seems best on paper also strike you as the best solution to try? Why or why not? *For additional projects, see the Personal Learning Activities in the corresponding chapter of the study guide that accompanies this text.*

Step into Action

Courses

Experimental Psychology
Cognitive Psychology
Psycholinguistics
Engineering Psychology (also called Human Factors)
Tests and Measurement (sometimes called Psychometrics)
Behavioral Genetics

Movies

Nell; Dances with Wolves; Clan of the Cave Bear (language development)
Gorillas in the Mist (animal communication)
Apollo 13; The Negotiator; K-19: The Widowmaker (problem solving)
2001: A Space Odyssey (artificial intelligence)
My Left Foot (assessment of ability)
Forrest Gump; Of Mice and Men; The Other Sister; Charly; Rain Man; Little Man Tate (diversity of intelligence)
Cast Away (problem solving, creativity, intelligence)
Hilary and Jackie (story of the child prodigy cellist Jacqueline du Pré)
Pi (the darker side of genius)
Searching for Bobby Fischer (story of a gifted child chess player)

Books

Gerd Gigerenzer, Peter M. Todd, and ABC Research Group, *Simple Heuristics That Make Us Smart* (Oxford University Press, 2000) (research on, and ideas for using, mental shortcuts)
Peter Bernstein, *Against the Gods: The Remarkable Story of Risk* (Wiley, 1998) (history of efforts to understand risk and probability in decision making)
Howard Gardner, *Intelligence Reframed: Multiple Intelligences for the 21st Century* (Basic Books, 1999) (theory of multiple intelligences)
Nicholas Lemann, *The Big Test: The Secret History of American Meritocracy* (Farrar, Straus and Giroux, 1999) (history of testing in the United States)
Hans Eysenck, with Darrin Evans, *Test Your IQ* (Penguin, 1995) (self-testing)
Steven Fatsis, *Word Freak* (Houghton Mifflin, 2002) (inside the high-stakes world of professional Scrabble)
Richard Herrnstein and Charles Murray, *The Bell Curve* (Free Press, 1994) (controversial book about group differences in intelligence)
Daniel Seligman, *A Question of Intelligence: The IQ Debate in America* (Citadel Press, 1994) (nature, nurture, and IQ)
Steven Fraser (Ed.), *The Bell Curve Wars* (Basic Books, 1995) (essays critical of *The Bell Curve*)

The Web

The World Wide Web is a good source of additional information about the science of psychology, provided you use it carefully and think critically about the information you find. The web site that accompanies this text offers many resources relevant to this chapter. These resources include interactive NetLab exercises; Thinking Critically and Evaluating Research exercises; ACE chapter quizzes; recommended web links; and articles on current events, books, and movies. At http://college.hmco.com, select *Psychology* and then this textbook.

Review of Key Terms

Can you define each of the key terms in the chapter? Check your definitions against those on the pages listed in parentheses below or in the Glossary/Index at the end of the text.

algorithms *(p. 241)*
anchoring heuristic *(p. 242)*
artificial intelligence (AI) *(p. 249)*
availability heuristic *(p. 243)*
babblings *(p. 256)*
cognitive map *(p. 240)*
concepts *(p. 237)*
confirmation bias *(p. 248)*
convergent thinking *(p. 252)*
creativity *(p. 251)*
divergent thinking *(p. 251)*

expected value *(p. 253)*
familial retardation *(p. 274)*
formal concept *(p. 237)*
formal reasoning *(p. 240)*
functional fixedness *(p. 248)*
grammar *(p. 255)*
heuristics *(p. 242)*
images *(p. 240)*
informal reasoning *(p. 242)*
information-processing system *(p. 236)*
intelligence *(p. 260)*

intelligence quotient (IQ score) *(p. 263)*
IQ test *(p. 260)*
language *(p. 255)*
mental models *(p. 239)*
mental set *(p. 248)*
natural concepts *(p. 238)*
norms *(p. 263)*
performance scale *(p. 262)*
propositions *(p. 238)*
prototype *(p. 238)*
reliability *(p. 263)*

representativeness heuristic *(p. 243)*
rules of logic *(p. 241)*
schemas *(p. 238)*
scripts *(p. 238)*
Stanford-Binet *(p. 260)*
telegraphic *(p. 257)*
test *(p. 263)*
thinking *(p. 236)*
utility *(p. 253)*
validity *(p. 264)*
verbal scale *(p. 262)*

Multiple-Choice Self-Test

Select the best answer for each of the questions below. Then check your responses against the Answer Key at the end of the text.

1. *Thinking* is defined as the manipulation of

   a. concepts.
   b. mental models.
   c. heuristics.
   d. mental representations.

2. Jarrod is in his bedroom when the power fails and the lights go off. He can't see a thing, but he is still able to walk confidently through his apartment to get a flashlight. Jarrod used a(n) _____ to find his way.

   a. hypothesis
   b. cognitive map
   c. heuristic
   d. algorithm

3. Clint is frustrated. His uncle has been winning at checkers all night. During the next game he is going to base his strategy on an algorithm, not a heuristic. What problem will this strategy cause?

   a. Clint still may not win the game.
   b. Clint and his uncle may be playing the same game of checkers for a long time.
   c. Clint will be ignoring overall probabilities.
   d. The representativeness heuristic will bias Clint's choice of strategy.

4. Alicia is telling her friend Mona about the new apartment she has rented. As she describes the layout, Mona will construct a _____ of the apartment, probably as a three-dimensional representation.

   a. concept schema
   b. mental model
   c. proposition
   d. script

5. Stephanie has worked for hours on a biochemistry problem without success. She decides to put it aside and work on her psychology homework in the hope that a solution might occur to her while she is thinking about something else. Stephanie is trying the _____ strategy to solve her problem.

   a. decomposition
   b. incubation
   c. working backward
   d. analogies

6. Ebony wanted to leave a note for her husband but couldn't find a pen, so she wrote the note with her lipstick. Ebony was able to overcome the obstacle to problem solving called

   a. absence of information.
   b. multiple hypotheses.
   c. confirmation bias.
   d. functional fixedness.

7. Because Dr. Sand is convinced that Ahmed has appendicitis, he pays more attention to test results that indicate appendicitis than to test results that don't support his original belief. Dr. Sand is displaying

   a. functional fixedness.
   b. a mental model.
   c. confirmation bias.
   d. the availability heuristic.

8. Each time Richard pulls a card from the deck, he has a one-in-fifty-two chance of selecting the queen of spades (assuming he replaces the selected card and shuffles before drawing again). After drawing the queen of spades twice in a row, he says, "There is no way I will draw the queen of spades next time!" Richard is being influenced by

   a. the gambler's fallacy.
   b. loss aversion.
   c. a disregard of negative evidence.
   d. confirmation bias.

9. The fact that children learning language sometimes make errors, such as saying "I goed" instead of "I went," has been used to suggest which of the following?

   a. There is a critical period in language development.
   b. Children are born with a knowledge of grammar.
   c. Children do not learn language entirely through imitation.
   d. Speech is learned mainly through imitation.

10. Children who spend their early years isolated from human contact and the sound of adult language are unable to develop adult language skills despite extensive training efforts later. This phenomenon provides evidence for the notion that

    a. there is a critical period in language development.
    b. children are born with a language acquisition device.
    c. there are no fixed stages in language acquisition.
    d. speech is acquired only through imitation.

11. The earliest IQ test was developed to

    a. identify children who needed special educational programs.
    b. help the armed forces make appropriate assignments of recruits.
    c. identify which immigrants were mentally defective and thus should not be allowed into the United States.
    d. help employers decide which employees were most appropriate for the available jobs.

12. "All monsters are ugly. The Creature from the Black Lagoon is a monster. Therefore, the Creature is ugly." Together, these three statements are an example of

    a. a premise.
    b. a proposition.
    c. a natural concept.
    d. formal reasoning.

13. Jonah just took an IQ test. According to the scoring method used today, his IQ score will reflect

    a. his mental age divided by his chronological age, times 100.
    b. how quickly he completed the test.
    c. the degree to which his score differs from the average of other people his age.
    d. his raw score, adjusted for how long he has lived in his present culture.

14. Correlating people's job success with their pre-employment test scores is one way of measuring a test's

    a. reliability.
    b. standardization.
    c. validity.
    d. norms.

15. When Jerrica first took the Handy Dandy Intelligence test, her score was 140. When she took the same test six weeks later, her score was only 102. If other people showed similarly changing score patterns, the Handy Dandy Intelligence test would appear to lack

    a. reliability.
    b. validity.
    c. standardization.
    d. norms.

16. Research shows that today's standardized IQ tests

    a. have good reliability and reasonably good validity for predicting success in school.
    b. do not do a good job of predicting success on the job.
    c. are not correlated with performance on "real-life" tasks.
    d. measure the full array of mental abilities.

17. There are two sets of twins in the Mullis family. Louise and Lanie are identical twins; Andy and Adrian are not. According to research on heredity and IQ, which pair of twins is likely to show the most similarity in IQ scores?

    a. Andy and Adrian, because they are male siblings.
    b. Andy and Adrian, because they are fraternal twins.
    c. Louise and Lanie, because they are female siblings.
    d. Louise and Lanie, because they are identical twins.

18. Rowena is mildly mentally retarded. This means that she

    a. probably has a specific genetic defect.
    b. is quicker than others to remember information, but then forgets it more rapidly.
    c. knows fewer facts about the world than others.
    d. has no potential for employment.

19. Betsy's musical intelligence and body-kinesthetic intelligence are being evaluated by her teacher, who believes that these are important abilities not measured by standard intelligence tests. Her teacher obviously believes in

    a. inherited intelligence.
    b. multiple intelligences.
    c. environmentally determined intelligence.
    d. Wechsler's IQ tests.

20. Theresa Amabile identified cognitive and personality characteristics necessary for creativity. Which of the following is not one of these characteristics?

    a. A capacity for focusing on the most important element in a problem, which is tied to convergent thinking.
    b. Expertise in the field of endeavor, which is tied to learning.
    c. A set of creative skills, including the capacity for divergent thinking.
    d. The motivation to pursue creative work for internal reasons.

8

Motivation and Emotion

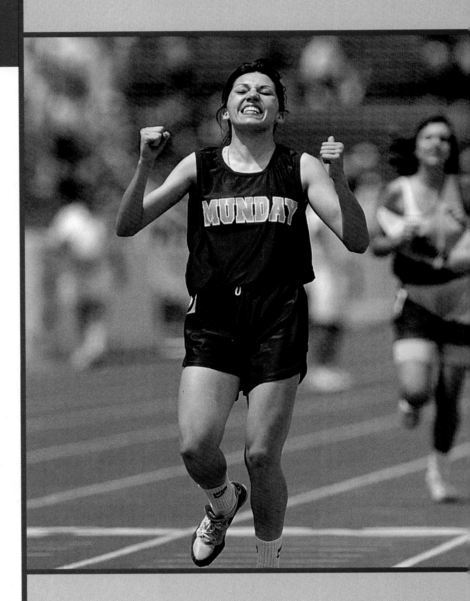

When your alarm clock goes off in the morning, do you jump out of bed,

eager to face the day, or do you bury your head in the blankets, trying to avoid all that's ahead of you? Once you're out of bed, do you eat a big breakfast, or just have coffee or tea—no matter how hungry you feel? As you leave home, do you notice your attractive neighbor and find yourself wondering if the two of you might someday have a romantic relationship? Or, if you're in a long-term relationship, do you find yourself thinking fond thoughts of your partner? Once you're at your job or on campus, do you always try to do your best, or do you work just hard enough to get by? And how do you feel about your life? Are you generally happy? Do you sometimes worry, or experience sadness or anxiety? In this chapter, we explore the physical, mental, and social factors that motivate human behavior in areas ranging from eating to sexuality to achievement. We also examine what emotions are and how they are expressed.

Reading this chapter will help you to answer the following questions:

▶ **Where does motivation come from?**

▶ **What makes me start eating, and stop eating?**

▶ **How often does the average person have sex?**

▶ **Why do some people try harder than others to succeed?**

▶ **Which motives move me most?**

▶ **How do feelings differ from thoughts?**

▶ **Is emotion in the heart, in the head, or both?**

▶ **Which emotional expressions are innate, and which are learned?**

When Tiger Woods won the British Open in July 2000, he became the youngest man to win all four tournaments that make up the Grand Slam in men's professional golf. He remains the world's best golfer today. Lance Armstrong, a bicyclist who had overcome cancer to win the Tour de France bicycle race in 1999, won it again in 2000, 2001, 2002, and 2003. Serena Williams captured both the 2002 and 2003 women's singles tennis championship at Wimbledon by winning in the finals against her sister, Venus Williams.

Success did not come easily to these athletes; it took years of effort and unwavering determination. Why did they work so hard in the face of daunting challenges and tough competitors to rise to the top of their fields? For that matter, what prompts any of us to excel, to perform acts of kindness, to look for food, to take dancing lessons, to go bungee jumping, to become violent, or to act in any other particular way? What makes some

MOTIVATION AND EMOTION The link between motivation and emotion can be seen in many situations. For example, being motivated to win the U.S. National Spelling Bee creates strong emotions as this contestant struggles with a tough word. And the link works both ways. Often, emotions create motivation, as when anger leads a person to become aggressive toward a child or when love leads a person to provide for that child.

motivation The influences that account for the initiation, direction, intensity, and persistence of behavior.

motive A reason or purpose for behavior.

instinct theory A view that explains human behavior as motivated by automatic, involuntary, and unlearned responses.

instincts Innate, automatic dispositions to respond in particular ways to specific stimuli.

people go all out to reach a goal, whereas others try only halfheartedly and quit at the first obstacle? These are all questions about **motivation,** the factors that influence the initiation, direction, intensity, and persistence of behavior (Reeve, 1996).

Like the study of *how* people behave and think, the puzzle of *why* they do so has intrigued psychologists for many decades. Part of the motivation for behavior is to feel certain emotions, such as the joy of finishing a race or of becoming a parent. Motivation also affects emotion, as when hunger makes you more likely to become angry if people annoy you. In this chapter we review several aspects of motivation. We also examine the features of emotions and consider their value to humans.

Concepts and Theories of Motivation

▶ **Where does motivation come from?**

Suppose that a woman works two jobs, refuses party invitations, wears old clothes, drives a beat-up car, eats food left behind by others, never gives to charity, and keeps her house at sixty degrees all winter. Why does she do these things? You could propose a separate explanation for each of these behaviors: Perhaps she likes to work hard, hates parties, doesn't care about new clothes and new cars, enjoys other people's leftovers, has no concern for the poor, and likes cold air. Or, you could suggest a **motive,** a reason or purpose that provides a single explanation for all these different behaviors. That unifying motive might be the woman's desire to save as much money as possible. This example illustrates the fact that motivation itself cannot be directly observed. Its presence is inferred from what we can observe.

Motivation helps explain why behavior changes over time. For example, many people are unable to lose weight, quit smoking, or exercise until they experience a heart attack or other serious health problem. At that point, they may suddenly be motivated to eat a heathier diet, give up tobacco, and start an exercise program. In other words, a change in motivation can change a person's responses to stimuli such as ice cream, cigarettes, and health clubs.

Sources of Motivation

Human motivation stems from four main sources. First, we can be motivated by *biological factors,* such as the need for food, water, sex, and temperature regulation (Tinbergen, 1989). Second, *emotional factors* can motivate behavior (Izard, 1993). Panic, fear, anger, love, and hatred can underlie behavior ranging from selfless giving to brutal murder. *Cognitive factors* provide a third source of motivation (Weiner, 1993). Your perceptions of the world, your beliefs about what you can do, and your expectation of how others will respond generate certain behaviors. You are more likely to try for a role in a play, for example, if you have confidence in your acting ability. Fourth, motivation can stem from *social factors,* including reactions to parents, teachers, siblings, friends, television, and other sociocultural forces. Have you ever bought a jacket or tried a particular hairstyle, not because you liked it but because it was in fashion? This is just one example of how social factors can affect almost all human behavior (Baumeister & Leary, 1995).

Four main theories have been proposed to explain motivation. They include instinct theory, drive reduction theory, arousal theory, and incentive theory. Each of these theories has proven helpful in accounting for some aspects of behavior.

Instinct Theory and Its Descendants

Early in this century, many psychologists favored an **instinct theory** of motivation. **Instincts** are automatic, involuntary, and unlearned behavior patterns consistently "released" or triggered by particular stimuli (Tinbergen, 1989). For example, the male stickleback fish attacks when it sees the red underbelly of another male. Such behaviors are called *fixed action patterns* because they are unlearned, genetically coded responses to specific "releaser" stimuli.

William McDougall (1908) argued that human behavior, too, is motivated by instincts. He began by listing eighteen human instincts, including self-assertion, reproduction, pugnacity (eagerness to fight), and gregariousness (sociability). Within a few years, McDougall and other theorists had named more than 10,000 instincts, prompting one critic to suggest that his colleagues had "an instinct to produce instincts" (Bernard, 1924). The problem was that instincts had become meaningless labels that described human behavior without explaining it. Saying that people gamble because of a gambling instinct, or work hard because of a work instinct, explains nothing about why these behaviors appear in some people and not others, or about how they developed. Applying instinct theory to human motivation also appeared problematic because people display few, if any, instinctive fixed-action patterns.

Still, psychologists continued to explore the possibility that at least some aspects of human motivation are innate. They noticed, for example, that sucking, grasping, and other reflexes, as well as certain facial expressions such as smiling, are present at birth. And babies do not have to learn to be hungry or thirsty. Further, as discussed in the chapter on learning, humans appear to be biologically prepared to fear snakes and other potential dangers. Psychologists who take an evolutionary approach to behavior suggest that these actions and tendencies have evolved because, over the centuries, they were adaptive for individual survival. Those who possessed these adaptive predispositions were more likely than others to live long enough to father or give birth to offspring. We are descendants of these human survivors. So to the extent that their behavioral predispositions were transmitted genetically, we should have inherited similar predispositions. Evolutionary psychologists also argue that many aspects of human social behavior—including helping, aggression, and the choice of sexual or marriage partners—are motivated by inborn factors, especially by the desire to maximize our genetic contribution to the next generation (Buss, 1999). We may not be consciously aware of this desire (Geary, 2000), so you are more likely to hear someone say "I can't wait to have children" than to say "I want to pass on my genes."

By emphasizing genetic predispositions and innate tendencies to promote the survival of our genes, modern versions of instinct theory seek to identify the ultimate, long-term reasons behind much human behavior. The theories of motivation discussed next highlight influences that serve as more immediate causes of behavior (Alcock, 2001).

Drive Reduction Theory

Like instinct theory, drive reduction theory emphasizes innate biological factors, but it focuses mainly on how these factors serve to maintain homeostasis. **Homeostasis** (pronounced "ho-me-oh-STAY-sis") is the tendency for organisms to make constant adjustments to maintain body temperature, blood pressure, and other physiological systems at a steady level, or *equilibrium*—much as a thermostat functions to maintain a constant temperature in a home.

According to **drive reduction theory**, any imbalance in homeostasis creates a **need,** which is a biological requirement for well-being. In responding to needs, the brain tries to restore homeostasis by creating a psychological state called **drive**—a feeling that prompts an organism to take action to fulfill the need and thus return to a balanced state. For example, if you have had nothing to drink for some time, the chemical balance of your bodily fluids will be disturbed, creating a biological need for water. One consequence of this need is a drive—thirst—that motivates you to find and drink water. After you drink, the need for water is met, so the drive to drink is reduced. In other words, drives push people to satisfy needs, thus reducing the drives that have been created. This cycle is shown in Figure 8.1.

homeostasis The tendency for physiological systems to remain at a stable, steady level by constantly adjusting themselves in response to change.

drive reduction theory A theory stating that motivation arises from imbalances in homeostasis.

need A biological requirement for well-being.

drive A physiological state that arises from an imbalance in homeostasis and prompts action to fulfill a need.

figure 8.1

Drive Reduction Theory and Homeostasis

The mechanisms of homeostasis, such as the regulation of body temperature or food and water intake, are often compared to home thermostats. If the temperature in a house drops below the thermostat setting, the furnace comes on and brings the temperature up to that preset level, achieving homeostasis. When the temperature reaches the preset point, the furnace shuts off.

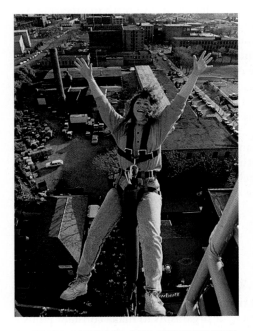

OPTIMAL AROUSAL AND PERSONALITY People whose optimal level of arousal is high are more likely to smoke, drink alcohol, engage in frequent sexual activity, listen to loud music, eat "hot" foods, and do other things that are stimulating, novel, and risky (Farley, 1986; Zuckerman, 1993). Those with lower optimal arousal tend to behave in ways that bring less intense stimulation; they also take fewer risks. As discussed in the personality chapter, differences in optimal arousal may help shape other characteristics, such as whether we are introverted or extraverted.

Proponents of drive reduction theory describe two types of drives. **Primary drives** stem from biological needs, such as the need for food or water. People do not have to learn either these basic biological needs or the primary drives to satisfy them (Hull, 1951). However, we do learn other drives, called *secondary drives*. Once learned, **secondary drives** motivate us to act as if we have unmet basic needs. For example, as people learn to associate money with the ability to buy things to satisfy primary drives for food, shelter, and so on, having money may become a secondary drive. Having too little money then motivates many behaviors—from hard work to stealing—to obtain more funds. By recognizing secondary as well as primary drives, drive reduction theory can account for an extremely wide range of behaviors.

Arousal Theory

Still, humans and animals often go to great lengths to do things that do not appear to reduce any drive. Consider curiosity. Animals explore and manipulate their surroundings even though these activities do not satisfy a primary drive. They will also work hard simply to enter a new environment, especially if it is complex and full of novel objects (Loewenstein, 1994). People are no less curious. Most of us cannot resist checking out whatever is new and unusual. We go to the mall, surf the Internet, and travel the world just to see what there is to see.

People also go out of their way to ride roller coasters, skydive, eat spicy food, and do countless other things that do not reduce any known drive (Zuckerman, 1996). In fact, these behaviors actually increase their **arousal**—the general level of activation in physiological systems (Plutchik & Conte, 1997). Recognizing that people sometimes try to reduce arousal and sometimes try to increase it led some psychologists to suggest that we are motivated to regulate our level of arousal.

A person's level of arousal is reflected in heart rate, muscle tension, brain activity, and many other functions (Deschaumes et al., 1991). Normally, arousal is lowest during deep sleep and highest during panic or great excitement. Many factors increase arousal, including hunger, thirst, intense stimuli, unexpected events, and stimulant drugs.

People perform best, and may feel best, when arousal is moderate (Teigen, 1994). Too much arousal can harm performance, as when anxiety causes a student to forget familiar material on a test. Overarousal can also cause an athlete to "choke," and thus miss an easy catch or a simple shot (Smith et al., 2000; Wright et al., 1995).

Arousal theory suggests that people are motivated to behave in ways that keep themselves at their own *optimal level* of arousal (Hebb, 1955). This optimal level is higher for some people than for others (Zuckerman, 1984). These differences in optimal arousal tend to have a strong biological basis and may help shape broader differences in personality, such as boldness or shyness. In general, though, arousal theory predicts that people will be motivated to increase arousal when it is too low and to decrease it when it is too high. They seek excitement when they are bored and relaxation when they are stressed or overstimulated.

in review

THEORIES OF MOTIVATION	
Theory	**Main Points**
Instinct	Innate biological instincts guide behavior.
Drive reduction	Behavior is guided by biological needs and learned ways of reducing drives arising from those needs.
Arousal	People seek to maintain an optimal level of physiological arousal, which differs from person to person. Maximum performance occurs at optimal arousal levels.
Incentive	Behavior is guided by the lure of rewards and the threat of punishment. Cognitive factors influence expectations of the value of various rewards and the likelihood of attaining them.

? *The fact that some people like roller coasters and other scary amusement park rides has been cited as evidence for the _____ theory of motivation.*

Incentive Theory

Instinct, drive reduction, and arousal theories of motivation all focus on internal processes that prompt people to behave in certain ways. In contrast, **incentive theory** emphasizes the role of external stimuli that motivate behavior. According to this view, people are pulled toward behaviors that offer positive incentives and pushed away from behaviors associated with negative incentives. In other words, differences in behavior from one person to another, or from one situation to another, should be traceable to the incentives available and the value a person places on those incentives at the time. If you expect that some behavior (such as buying a lottery ticket) will lead to a valued outcome (winning money), you will be motivated to perform that behavior. The value of incentives can be influenced by biological, as well as cognitive, factors. For example, food is a more motivating incentive when you are hungry than when you are full (Balleine & Dickinson, 1994).

"In Review: Theories of Motivation" summarizes the theoretical approaches we have outlined. Each theory has helped to guide research on motivated behaviors such as eating, sex, and work, which we consider in the sections that follow.

Hunger and Eating

▶ What makes me start eating, and stop eating?

At first glance, hunger seems a simple example of drive reduction theory at work. You get hungry when you do not eat. Much as a car needs gasoline, you need fuel from food. But what actually causes hunger? What bodily mechanism acts as a "gauge" to signal the need for fuel? What determines which foods you eat, and how do you know when to stop? The answers to these questions involve complex interactions between the brain and the rest of the body, as well as the operation of learning and social factors (Hill & Peters, 1998).

Biological Signals for Hunger and Satiety

A variety of mechanisms underlie **hunger,** the general state of wanting to eat, and **satiety** (pronounced "seh-TYE-eh-tee"), the general state of no longer wanting to eat.

primary drives   Drives that arise from basic biological needs.

secondary drives   Stimuli that take on the motivational properties of primary drives through learning.

arousal   A general level of activation reflected in several physiological systems.

arousal theory   A theory stating that people are motivated to maintain what is, for them, an optimal level of arousal.

incentive theory   A theory stating that people are pulled toward behaviors offering positive incentives and pushed away from behaviors associated with negative incentives.

hunger   The general state of wanting to eat.

satiety   The condition of no longer wanting to eat.

Signals from the Stomach   The stomach would seem to be a logical source of signals for hunger and satiety. You have probably felt "hunger pangs" from an "empty" stomach and felt "stuffed" after overeating. In fact, the stomach does contract during hunger pangs, and increased pressure within the stomach can reduce appetite (Cannon & Washburn, 1912; Houpt, 1994). But people who have lost their stomachs due to illness still get hungry when they don't eat, and they still eat normal amounts of food (Janowitz, 1967). So stomach cues can affect eating, but they do not always control it. These cues appear to operate mainly when you are very hungry or very full.

Signals from the Blood   More precise signals about the body's fuel level and nutrient needs are sent to the brain from the blood. The brain's ability to "read" blood-borne signals about the body's nutritional needs was discovered when researchers deprived rats of food for a long period and then injected some of the rats with blood from rats that had just eaten. When offered food, the injected rats ate little or nothing (Davis et al., 1969). Something in the injected blood of the well-fed animals apparently signaled the hungry rats' brains that there was no need to eat. What sent that satiety signal? Research has shown that the brain constantly monitors both the level of *food nutrients* absorbed into the bloodstream from the stomach and the level of *hormones* released into the blood in response to those nutrients (Korner & Leibel, 2003).

The nutrients that the brain monitors include *glucose* (the main form of sugar used by body cells), *fatty acids* (from fat), and *amino acids* (from protein). When the level of blood glucose drops, eating increases sharply (Mogenson, 1976). When large doses of glucose are injected into the blood of even a food-deprived animal, it refuses to eat.

The brain also monitors hormone levels to regulate hunger and satiety. For example, when glucose levels rise, the pancreas releases *insulin,* a hormone that most body cells need in order to use the glucose they receive. Insulin itself may also provide a satiety signal by acting directly on brain cells (Brüning et al., 2000; Schwartz et al., 2000).

The hormone *leptin* (from the Greek word for "thin") also appears to provide a satiety signal to the brain (Farooqi et al., 2001; Margetic et al., 2002). Unlike glucose and insulin, whose satiety signals help us know when to end a particular meal, leptin appears involved mainly in the long-term regulation of body fat (Huang & Li, 2000). The process works like this: Cells that store fat normally have genes that produce leptin. As the fat supply in these cells increases, leptin is released into the blood, helping to reduce food intake. Animals with defects in these genes make no leptin and are obese. When these animals are given leptin injections, though, they rapidly lose weight and body fat, but not muscle tissue (Forbes et al., 2001). Leptin injections can produce the same changes in normal animals, too (Fox & Olster, 2000). These results initially raised hope that leptin might be a "magic bullet" for treating human obesity, but this is not the case. Although it can help those rare individuals whose fat cells make no leptin (Farooqi et al., 1999), injections of leptin are far less effective in people who are obese because they eat a high-fat diet (Gura, 1999; Heymsfield et al., 1999). In these far more common cases of obesity, the brain appears to have become less sensitive to leptin's satiety signals (Ahima & Flier, 2000; Lin et al., 2000).

LINKAGES
How does the brain know when we are hungry?
(a link to Biology and Behavior)

Hunger and the Brain

Many parts of the brain contribute to the control of hunger and eating. However, research has focused on regions of the hypothalamus that may play primary roles in detecting and reacting to the blood's signals about the need to eat. As shown in Figure 8.2, the hypothalamus influences both how much food is taken in and how quickly its energy is used, or metabolized.

Some regions of the hypothalamus detect leptin and insulin; these regions generate signals that either increase hunger and reduce energy expenditure, or reduce hunger and increase energy expenditure. There are at least twenty neurotransmitters that convey these signals to networks in other parts of the hypothalamus and in the rest of the brain (Woods et al., 1998, 2000).

figure 8.2

The Hypothalamus and Hunger

Regions of the hypothalamus generate signals that either increase hunger and reduce energy expenditure, called *anabolic effects,* or reduce hunger and increase energy expenditure, called *catabolic effects.*

Source: Adapted from Schwartz et al. (2000).

ONE FAT MOUSE   After surgical damage to its ventromedial nucleus, this mouse began to eat far more than usual—enough to triple its body weight. Results like this initially led many psychologists to conclude that food intake is regulated by a combination of "start-eating" signals from the lateral hypothalamus and "stop-eating" signals from the ventromedial nucleus. We now know that the regulation process is far more complex, and involves more than just these two brain regions.

Activity in one part of the network that passes through the *ventromedial nucleus* in the hypothalamus tells an animal that there is no need to eat. So, if a rat's ventromedial nucleus is stimulated, the animal will stop eating (Kent et al., 1994). However, if the ventromedial nucleus is destroyed, the animal will eat continuously, increasing its weight up to threefold.

In contrast, the *lateral hypothalamus* contains networks that prompt eating to begin. So when the lateral hypothalamus is stimulated, rats begin to eat huge quantities, even if they have just had a large meal (Stanley et al., 1993). When the lateral hypothalamus is destroyed, however, rats stop eating almost entirely.

Years ago, these findings generated an explanation of eating in which the two hypothalamic regions interact to maintain some homeostatic level, or *set point,* based on food intake, body weight, or other eating-related signals (Powley & Keesey, 1970). According to this application of drive reduction theory, normal animals eat until their set point is reached, then stop eating until desirable intake falls below the set point (Cabanac & Morrissette, 1992).

This theory turned out to be too simplistic. More recent research shows that the brain's control of eating involves more than just the interaction of a pair of "stop-eating" and "start-eating" areas (Winn, 1995). For example, the *paraventricular nucleus* in the hypothalamus also plays an important role. As with the ventromedial nucleus, stimulating the paraventricular nucleus results in reduced food intake. Damaging it causes animals to become obese (Leibowitz, 1992). In addition, hunger—and the eating of particular types of food—is related to the effects of various neurotransmitters on certain neurons in the brain (Lee, Schiffman, & Pappas, 1994; Woods et al., 1998). One of these neurotransmitters, called *neuropeptide Y,* stimulates increased eating of carbohydrates (Jhanwar et al., 1993; Schwartz et al., 2000), whereas another one, *serotonin,* suppresses carbohydrate intake. *Galanin* motivates eating of high-fat food (Krykouli et al., 1990), whereas *enterostatin* reduces it (Lin et al., 1998). *Endocannabinoids* stimulate eating in general. They affect the same hypothalamic receptors as does the active ingredient in

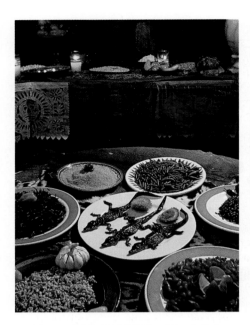

learn **by doing**   **BON APPÉTIT!**   The definition of *delicacy* differs from culture to culture. At this elegant restaurant in Mexico, diners pay to feast on baby alligators, insects, and other dishes that some people from other cultures would not eat even if the restaurant paid *them*. To appreciate your own food culture, make a list of foods that are traditionally valued by your family or cultural group but that people from other groups do not, or might even be unwilling to, eat.

marijuana, which may account for "the munchies," a sudden hunger that marijuana use often creates (Cota et al., 2003; Di Marzo et al., 2001). *Peptide YY3–36* causes a feeling of fullness and reduced food intake (Batterham et al., 2002, 2003).

In other words, several brain regions and many brain chemicals help to regulate hunger and eating. These regulatory processes are not set in stone, however. They can easily be overridden by other, nonbiological factors.

Flavor, Cultural Learning, and Food Selection

One of these factors is the *flavor* of food—the combination of its taste and smell (Carlson, 2001). In general, people eat more when differently flavored foods are served, as in a multi-course meal, than when only one food is served (Raynor & Epstein, 2001). Apparently the flavor of a food becomes less enjoyable as more of it is eaten (Swithers & Hall, 1994). In one study, for example, people rated how much they liked four kinds of food; then they ate one of the foods and rated all four again. The food they had just eaten now got a lower rating, whereas liking increased for all the rest (Johnson & Vickers, 1993).

Another factor that can override biological signals about satiety is *appetite*, the motivation to seek food's pleasures. The appearance and smell of certain foods come to elicit conditioned physiological responses—including the secretion of saliva, digestive juices, and insulin—in anticipation of eating those foods. Such conditioned responses, which are described in the chapter on learning, then increase appetite. So merely seeing a pizza on television may prompt you to order one. And if you see a delicious-looking cookie, you do not have to be hungry to start eating it. In other words, people eat not just to satisfy nutritional needs but also to experience enjoyment.

Social rules and cultural traditions are forms of learning that also influence eating. In North American culture, having lunch at noon, munching popcorn at movies, and eating hot dogs at ball games are common examples of how certain social situations can stimulate appetite for particular items at particular times. How much you eat may also depend on what others do. Politeness or custom might prompt you to try foods you would otherwise have avoided. Generally, the mere presence of others, even strangers, tends to increase food consumption. Most people consume 60 to 75 percent more food when they are with others than when eating alone (Clendenen, Herman, & Polivy, 1995).

Celebrations, holidays, vacations, and even daily family interactions often revolve around food and what some call a *food culture* (Rozin, 1996). There are wide cultural variations in food use and selection. For example, chewing coca leaves is popular in the Bolivian highlands but illegal in the United States (Burchard, 1992). And insects called palm weevils, a delicacy for people in Papua New Guinea (Paoletti, 1995), are regarded by many westerners as disgusting (Springer & Belk, 1994). Even within the same general culture, different groups may have sharply contrasting food traditions. Squirrel brains won't be found on most dinner tables in the United States, but some people in the rural South consider them to be a tasty treat. In short, eating serves functions beyond nutrition—functions that help to remind us of who we are and with whom we identify.

Eating Disorders

Problems in the processes regulating hunger and eating may cause an *eating disorder*. The most common and dangerous examples are obesity, anorexia nervosa, and bulimia nervosa.

Obesity   The World Health Organization defines **obesity** as a condition in which a person's body-mass index, or BMI, is greater than 30 (WHO, 1998). BMI is determined by dividing a person's weight (in kilograms) by the square of the person's height (in meters). So someone who is 5 feet 2 inches and weighs 164 pounds would be classified as obese, as would someone 5 feet 10 inches who weighs 207 pounds. (People whose BMI is 25 to 29.9 are considered to be overweight, but not obese. You will find quick BMI calculators

obesity   A condition in which a person is severely overweight.

at web sites such as www.consumer.gov/weightloss/bmi.htm.) Using this BMI criterion, 21 to 30 percent of adults in the United States are obese (Flegal et al., 2002; Mokdad et al., 2003). And obesity appears to be on the rise, not only in the United States but also in regions as diverse as Asia, Europe, South America, and Africa (e.g., McCarthy, Ellis, & Cole, 2003; Rolland-Cachera et al., 2002; Sturm, 2003; World Health Organization, 2002a). Obesity is associated with health problems such as diabetes, high blood pressure, an increased risk of heart attack, and possibly Alzheimer's disease (Gustafson et al., 2003). With nearly 300,000 deaths in the United States alone attributed to obesity each year, it has been described as at least as dangerous as smoking and alcohol abuse (Calle et al., 2003; Fontaine et al., 2003; Peeters et al., 2003).

Why do some people become obese? Body weight is determined by a combination of food intake and energy output (Keesey & Powley, 1986). Obese people get more energy from food than their body metabolizes, or "burns up." The excess energy, measured in calories, is stored as fat. Obese people tend to eat above-average amounts of high-calorie, tasty foods but below-average amounts of less tasty foods (Kauffman, Herman, & Polivy, 1995). Further, they may be less active than lean people, a pattern that often begins in childhood (Strauss & Pollack, 2001). Spending long hours watching television or playing computer games is a major cause of the inactivity seen in overweight children (Hu et al., 2003; Vioque, Torres, & Quiles, 2000).

In short, inadequate physical activity, combined with overeating—especially of the high-fat foods so prevalent in most Western cultures—has a lot to do with obesity. But not everyone who is inactive and eats a high-fat diet becomes obese, and some obese people are as active as lean people, so other factors must also be involved (Blundell & Cooling, 2000). Some people probably have a genetic predisposition toward obesity (Arner, 2000; Branson et al., 2003; Rosmond, Bouchard, & Björntorp, 2001). Brain-imaging studies also suggest that obese people's brains may be slower to "read" satiety signals coming from their blood, so they continue eating when leaner people would have stopped (Liu et al., 2000). These factors, along with the presence of one or more recently discovered viruses in the body (Dhurandhar et al., 2000), may help explain obese people's tendency to eat more, to accumulate fat, and to feel more hunger than lean people.

Losing weight and keeping it off for at least five years is extremely difficult for many people, especially those who are obese (Lewis et al., 2000; McGuire et al., 1999). Part of the problem may be due to metabolic changes that accompany weight loss. When food intake is reduced, the body's efforts to maintain its weight (homeostasis) lead to a drop in metabolic rate, which saves energy and curbs weight loss (Leibel, Rosenbaum, & Hirsch, 1995). This response makes evolutionary sense: Conserving energy during famine, for example, is adaptive for survival. But when obese people try to lose weight, their metabolic rate drops below normal. As a result, they can gain weight even while eating amounts that would maintain constant weight in others. These facts suggest that attempts to lose a great deal of weight quickly will be offset by changes in metabolism (Brownell & Rodin, 1994).

Several anti-obesity drugs have been developed, including one that prevents fat in foods from being digested (e.g., Finer et al., 2000; Hauptman et al., 2000). Another drug has been found to interfere with an enzyme that forms fat. This "fatty acid synthase inhibitor" not only caused rapid weight loss in mice but also reduced their hunger (Loftus et al., 2000). The drug has not yet been tested for safety and effectiveness in humans, but researchers hope that it may someday be possible to give obese people medications that alter brain mechanisms involved in overeating and fat storage (Abu-Elheiga et al., 2001; Arterburn & Noël, 2001).

Millions of people are taking anti-obesity medications in the United States alone (Stafford & Radley, 2003), but even the best drug treatments are unlikely to solve the problem of obesity on their own. To achieve the kind of gradual weight loss that is most likely to last, obese people are advised to increase regular exercise, because it burns calories without slowing metabolism. In fact, regular aerobic exercise raises the metabolic rate (Binzen, Swan, & Manore, 2001). The most effective weight-loss programs include components designed to reduce food intake, change eating habits and attitudes toward

THIN IS IN   In Western cultures today, thinness is a much-sought-after ideal, especially among young women. This ideal is seen in fashion models, as well as in Miss America pageant winners, whose body mass index has decreased from the "normal" range of 20 to 25 in the 1920s to an "undernourished" 18.5 in recent years (Rubinstein & Caballero, 2000; Voracek & Fisher, 2002). In the United States, 35 percent of normal-weight girls—and 12 percent of underweight girls!—begin dieting when they are as young as nine or ten. Many of these children try to lose weight in response to criticism by their mothers (Schreiber et al., 1996); for some, the result is anorexia.

anorexia nervosa   An eating disorder characterized by self-starvation and dramatic weight loss.

bulimia nervosa   An eating disorder that involves eating massive quantities of food and then eliminating the food by self-induced vomiting or laxatives.

food, and increase energy expenditure through exercise (Bray & Tartaglia, 2000; National Task Force on the Prevention and Treatment of Obesity, 2000; Wadden et al., 2001).

Anorexia Nervosa   At the opposite extreme of eating disorders is **anorexia nervosa** (pronounced "ann-or-EX-ee-ah nuhr-VO-suh"). It is characterized by some combination of self-starvation, self-induced vomiting, and laxative use that results in weight loss to below 85 percent of normal (Kaye et al., 2000). About 95 percent of people who suffer from anorexia are female. Anorexics often feel hungry, and many are obsessed with food and its preparation, yet they refuse to eat. Anorexic self-starvation causes serious, often irreversible, physical damage, including reduction in bone density that enhances the risk of fractures (Grinspoon et al., 2000). It is estimated that as many as 6 percent of those suffering severe anorexia eventually die of starvation, biochemical imbalances, or suicide; their risk of death is twelve times higher than for other young women (Herzog et al., 2000; National Association of Anorexia Nervosa and Associated Disorders, 2002; Sullivan, 1995). Anorexia tends to appear in adolescence, when concern over appearance becomes intense. It affects about 1 percent of young women in the United States and is a growing problem in many other industrialized nations as well (American Psychiatric Association Work Group on Eating Disorders, 2000; Rome et al., 2003).

The causes of anorexia are not yet clear, but they probably involve a combination of factors, including genetic predispositions, biochemical imbalances, social influences, and psychological characteristics (Bulik et al., 2000; Kaye et al., 2000; Keel & Klump, 2003; Vink et al., 2001). Psychological factors that may contribute to the problem include a self-punishing, perfectionistic personality and a culturally reinforced obsession with thinness and attractiveness (Bulik et al., 2003; Thompson & Stice, 2001; Thompson et al., 1999). Anorexics appear to develop a fear of being fat, which they take to dangerous extremes (de Castro & Goldstein, 1995). Many anorexics continue to view themselves as fat or misshapen even as they are wasting away (Feingold & Mazzella, 1998).

Drugs, hospitalization, and psychotherapy are all used to treat anorexia. In most cases, some combination of treatment and the passage of time bring partial or full recovery (Herzog et al., 1999; National Institutes of Health, 2001).

Bulimia Nervosa   Like anorexia, bulimia nervosa (pronounced "bu-LEE-mee-uh nuhr-VO-suh") involves intense fear of being fat, but the person may be thin, normal in weight, or even overweight (U.S. Surgeon General, 1999). **Bulimia nervosa** involves eating huge amounts of food (say, several boxes of cookies, a half-gallon of ice cream, and a bucket of fried chicken) and then getting rid of the food through self-induced vomiting or strong laxatives. These "binge-purge" episodes may occur as often as twice a day (Weltzin et al., 1995).

Like people with anorexia, bulimic individuals are usually female, and like anorexia, bulimia usually begins with a desire to be slender. However, bulimia and anorexia are separate disorders (Pryor, 1995). For one thing, most bulimics see their eating habits as problematic, whereas most anorexics do not. In addition, bulimia nervosa is usually not life-threatening (Hall et al., 1989). There are consequences, however, including dehydration, nutritional problems, and intestinal damage. Many bulimics develop dental problems from the acids associated with vomiting. Frequent vomiting, and the insertion of objects to cause it, can also damage the throat.

Estimates of the prevalence of bulimia in the United States range from 1 to 3 percent of adolescent and college-age women (National Institutes of Health, 2001; U.S. Surgeon General, 1999). It appears to be caused by a combination of factors, including perfectionism, low self-esteem, overconcern with thinness and attractiveness, and depression and other emotional problems, along with as-yet-undetermined biological problems that might include defective satiety mechanisms (Crowther et al., 2001; Steiger et al., 2001; Stice, 2001). Treatment for bulimia, which typically includes individual or group psychotherapy and, sometimes, anti-depressant drugs, can help most bulimic people to eat more normally (Herzog et al., 1999; Wilson et al., 1999).

MAJOR FACTORS CONTROLLING HUNGER AND EATING

Theory	Stimulate Eating	Inhibit Eating
Biological factors	Levels of glucose and insulin in the blood provide signals that stimulate eating; neurotransmitters that affect neurons in different regions of the hypothalamus also stimulate food intake and influence hungers for specific kinds of foods, such as fats and carbohydrates. Stomach contractions are associated with subjective feelings of hunger, but they do not play a substantial role in the stimulation of eating.	Hormones released into the bloodstream produce signals that inhibit eating; hormones such as leptin and insulin affect neurons in the hypothalamus and inhibit eating.
Nonbiological factors	Sights and smells of particular foods elicit eating because of prior associations; family customs and social occasions often include norms for eating in particular ways.	Values in contemporary U.S. society encourage thinness, and thus can inhibit eating.

? *Many people eat dessert after dinner even when they are already "full," suggesting that eating is controlled not only by hunger but by _____.*

For a summary of the processes involved in hunger and eating, see "In Review: Major Factors Controlling Hunger and Eating."

Sexual Behavior

▶ **How often does the average person have sex?**

Unlike food, sex is not necessary for an individual's survival. A strong desire for reproduction does help ensure the survival of a species, however (Keeling & Roger, 1995). The various factors shaping sexual motivation and behavior differ in strength across species. They often include a combination of the individual's physiology, learned behavior, and the physical and social environment. For example, one species of desert bird requires adequate sex hormones, a suitable mate, and a particular environment before it engages in sexual behavior. As long as the dry season lasts, it shows no interest in sex, but within ten minutes of the first rainfall, the birds vigorously copulate.

Rainfall is obviously much less influential as a sexual trigger for humans. In fact, people show an amazing diversity of *sexual scripts,* or patterns of behavior that lead to sex. One survey of college-age men and women identified 122 specific acts and 34 different tactics used for promoting sexual encounters (Greer & Buss, 1994). What happens next? The matter is exceedingly difficult to address scientifically, partly because most people are reluctant to allow researchers to observe their sexual behavior. Many even resist responding to specific questions about their sexual practices (Bancroft, 1997). Yet having valid information about the nature of human sexual behavior is a vital first step for psychologists and other scientists who study such topics as individual differences in sexuality, gender differences in sexual motivation and behavior (Peplau, 2003), sources of sexual orientation, types of sexual dysfunctions, and pathways through which AIDS and other sexually transmitted diseases (STDs) reach new victims. This information also has important implications for helping people understand themselves ("Is my sexual behavior common?"), alleviating sexual problems, and curbing the spread of STDs.

FOCUS ON RESEARCH

Tell Me About Your Sex Life

The first extensive studies of sexual behavior in the United States were completed by Alfred Kinsey (Kinsey, Pomeroy, & Martin, 1948; Kinsey et al., 1953) and by William Masters and Virginia Johnson (1966). In the Kinsey studies, volunteers were asked about their sexual practices, whereas Masters and Johnson actually measured physiological responses as volunteers received natural or mechanical sexual stimulation in a laboratory. Together, these pioneering studies broke new ground in the exploration of human sexuality. Critics have argued that the people who volunteered for such studies probably were not a representative sample of humankind. Accordingly, the results, and any conclusions drawn from them, might not apply to people in general. Further, the data are now so old that they may not reflect sexual practices today. Unfortunately, the results of more recent surveys, such as reader polls in *Cosmopolitan* and other magazines, are also flawed by the use of unrepresentative samples.

■ What was the researchers' question?

Is there a way to gather data on sexual behavior that is more representative and therefore more revealing about people in general? A team of researchers at the University of Chicago believe there is, so they undertook the National Health and Social Life Survey, the first extensive survey of sexual behavior in the United States since the Kinsey studies (Laumann et al., 1994).

■ How did the researchers answer the question?

This survey included important design features that had been neglected in most other surveys of sexual behavior. First, the study did not depend on self-selected volunteers. The researchers sought out a particular sample of 3,432 people, ranging in age from eighteen to fifty-nine. Second, the sample was carefully constructed so as to reflect the sociocultural diversity of the U.S. population in terms of gender, ethnicity, socioeconomic status, geographical location, and the like. Third, unlike previous surveys, the Chicago study was based on face-to-face interviews. This approach made it easier to ensure that the participants understood each question and allowed them to explain their responses. To encourage honesty, the researchers allowed participants to answer some of the survey's questions anonymously, by placing written responses in a sealed envelope.

■ What did the researchers find?

For one thing, the researchers found that people in the United States have sex less often and with fewer partners than many had assumed. For most, sex occurs about once a week, and only with a partner with whom they share a stable relationship. About a third of the participants reported having sex only a few times, or not at all, in the past year. And in contrast to various celebrities' splashy tales of dozens, even hundreds, of sexual partners per year, the average male survey participant had only six sexual partners in his entire life. The average female respondent reported a lifetime total of two. Further, the survey data suggested that people in committed, one-partner relationships had the most frequent and the most satisfying sex. And although a wide variety of specific sexual practices were reported, the overwhelming majority of heterosexual couples said they tend to engage mainly in penis-vagina intercourse.

■ What do the results mean?

The Chicago survey challenges some of the cultural and media images of sexuality in the United States. In particular, it suggests that people in the United States may be more sexually conservative than one might think on the basis of magazine reader polls and the testimony of guests on daytime talk shows.

■ What do we still need to know?

Many questions remain. The Chicago survey did not ask about some of the more controversial aspects of sexuality, such as the effects of pornography, the nature and prevalence of pedophilia (sexual attraction to children), and the role in sexual activity of sexual fetishes such as shoes or other clothing. Had the researchers asked about such topics, their results might have painted a less conservative picture. Further, because the Chicago survey focused on people in the United States, it told us little or nothing about the sexual practices, traditions, and values of people in the rest of the world.

The Chicago team has continued to conduct interviews, and the results are beginning to fill in the picture about sexual behavior in the United States and around the world (Youm & Laumann, 2002). They have found, for example, that nearly one-quarter of U.S. women prefer to achieve sexual satisfaction without partners of either sex. And although people in the United States tend to engage in a wider variety of sexual behaviors than those in Britain, there is less tolerance in the United States of disapproved sexual practices (Laumann & Michael, 2000; Michael et al., 1998). Other researchers have found a number of consistent gender differences in sexuality. For example, men tend to have a stronger interest in and desire for sex than women, whereas women are more likely than men to associate sexual activity with a committed relationship (Baumeister, Catanese, & Vohs, 2001; Peplau, 2003; Peplau, Fingerhut, & Beals, in press; Regan & Berscheid, 1999).

Even the best survey methods—like the best of all other research methods—usually yield results that raise as many questions as they answer. When do people become interested in sex, and why? How do they choose to express these desires, and why? What determines their sexual likes and dislikes? How do learning and sociocultural factors modify the biological forces that seem to provide the raw material of human sexual motivation? These are some of the questions about human sexual behavior that a survey cannot easily or accurately explore (Benson, 2003).

The Biology of Sex

Some aspects of the sexual behavior observed in Masters and Johnson's laboratory may not have reflected exactly what goes on when people have sex in more typical surroundings. Still, those observations led to important findings about the **sexual response cycle,** the pattern of physiological arousal before, during, and after sexual activity (see Figure 8.3). Masters and Johnson (1966) found that men show one primary pattern of sexual response and that women display at least three different patterns from time to time. In both men and women, the first, or *excitement,* phase begins with sexually stimulating input from the environment or from one's own thoughts. Further stimulation leads to intensified excitement in the second, or *plateau,* phase. If stimulation continues, the person reaches the third, or *orgasmic,* stage. Although orgasm lasts only a few seconds, it provides an intensely pleasurable release of physical and psychological tension. The *resolution* phase follows, during which the person returns to a state of relaxation. At this point, men enter a *refractory period,* during which they are temporarily unable to be aroused. Women are capable of immediately repeating the cycle if stimulation continues.

People's motivation to engage in sexual activity has biological roots in **sex hormones.** The female sex hormones are **estrogens** and **progestins;** the main ones are *estradiol* and *progesterone.* The male hormones are **androgens;** the principal example is *testosterone.* Each sex hormone flows in the blood of both sexes, but males have relatively more androgens, and women have relatively more estrogens and progestins.

Sex hormones have both organizing and activating effects. Their *organizing effects* are permanent changes in the brain that occur around the time of birth and influence it to respond to sex hormones in specific ways. Their *activating effects* are temporary behavioral changes that last only while a sex hormone's level is elevated. As a result of the organizing effects, certain brain areas are sculpted into a "male-like" or "female-like" pattern.

sexual response cycle The pattern of arousal before, during, and after sexual activity.

sex hormones Chemicals in the blood that organize and motivate sexual behavior.

estrogens Feminine hormones that circulate in the bloodstream.

progestins Feminine hormones that circulate in the bloodstream.

androgens Masculine hormones that circulate in the bloodstream.

figure 8.3

The Sexual Response Cycle

Masters and Johnson (1966) found that men show one primary pattern of sexual response, depicted in Part A, and that women display at least three different patterns from time to time—labeled A, B, and C in Part B. For both men and women, sexual stimulation begins with the excitement phase, which is followed by intensified excitement in the plateau phase, and the pleasurable release of tension in the orgasmic stage. During the resolution phase, both men and women return to a state of relaxation. Following resolution, men (but not women) enter a refractory phase, during which they are unresponsive to sexual stimulation.

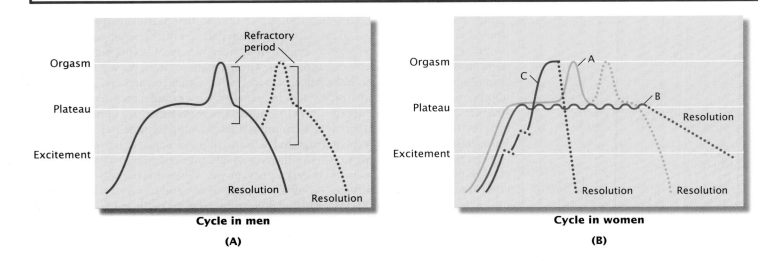

Cycle in men
(A)

Cycle in women
(B)

For example, a brain area called *BnST* is generally smaller in women than in men. Its possible role in some aspects of human sexuality was suggested by a study of transsexual men, genetic males who feel like women and who may request sex-change surgery in order to "be" female. The BnST in these men was smaller than in other men. In fact, it was about the size usually seen in women (Zhou et al., 1995).

Rising levels of sex hormones during puberty activate increased sexual desire and interest in sexual behavior. Generally, estrogens stimulate females' sexual interest (Burleson, Gregory, & Trevarthen, 1995). Androgens raise males' sexual interest (Davidson, Camargo, & Smith, 1979), but they may also do so in females (Sherwin & Gelfand, 1987). The ongoing activating effects of hormones are confirmed by the reduced sexual motivation and behavior seen in people whose hormone-secreting ovaries or testes have been removed for medical reasons. Injections of hormones help restore these people's sexual interest and activity (Sherwin, Gelfand, & Brender, 1985).

Generally, hormones affect sexual desire, not the physical ability to have sex (Wallen & Lovejoy, 1993). This fact may explain why castration (removal of the testes) does not prevent sex crimes in male offenders. Men with low testosterone levels due to medical problems or castration show less sexual desire, but they still have erections in response to erotic stimuli (Kwan et al., 1983). So a sex offender treated with chemical or physical castration would be less likely to seek out sex, but he would still respond as before to his favorite sexual stimuli (Wallen & Lovejoy, 1993; Wickham, 2001).

Social and Cultural Factors in Sexuality

Human sexuality is profoundly shaped by a lifetime of learning and thinking that modifies the biological "raw materials" provided by hormones. For example, children learn some of their sexual attitudes and behaviors as part of the development of *gender roles*, as described in the human development chapter. The specific attitudes and behaviors they learn depend partly on the nature of gender roles in their culture (Baumeister, 2000; Hyde & Durik, 2000; Peplau, 2003).

Sexual behavior is shaped by other sociocultural forces as well. In the United States, concern over sexual transmission of the AIDS virus has prompted mass-media campaigns and school-based educational programs to encourage sexual abstinence prior to marriage or "safe sex" using condoms (e.g., Smith & DiClemente, 2000). These efforts seem to be altering young people's sexual attitudes and practices. At the beginning of one sex education program, only 36 percent of 1,800 students in grades 7 through 10 thought premarital sex was a bad idea, and only 35 percent saw many benefits in premarital abstinence from sex. By the end of the semester-long program, these figures had risen to 66 percent and 58 percent, respectively (Eisenman, 1994). Another survey of 1,100 adolescents and young adults in the United States found that prior to 1985, first-time heterosexual intercourse seldom included the use of a condom or other contraceptive. With growing AIDS awareness since 1985, however, condom use has become far more common in first-time heterosexual intercourse and in subsequent sexual activity (American Academy of Pediatrics, 2001; Everett et al., 2000).

Sexual Orientation

Sexual orientation refers to the nature of a person's enduring emotional, romantic, or sexual attraction to others (American Psychological Association, 2002; Ellis & Mitchell, 2000). The most common sexual orientation is **heterosexual,** in which the attraction is to members of the opposite sex. When attraction focuses on members of one's own sex, the orientation is called **homosexual.** People who are attracted to members of both sexes are said to have a **bisexual** orientation. Sexual orientation involves feelings that may or may not be translated into corresponding patterns of sexual behavior. For example, some people whose orientation is homosexual or bisexual may have sex only with opposite-sex partners. Similarly, people whose orientation is heterosexual may have had one or more homosexual encounters.

In many cultures, heterosexuality has long been regarded as a moral norm, and homosexuality seen as a disease, a disorder, or even a crime (Hooker, 1993). Yet attempts to alter the sexual orientation of homosexuals—using psychotherapy, brain surgery, or electric shock—have usually been ineffective (American Psychiatric Association, 1999; Haldeman, 1994). In 1973 the American Psychiatric Association dropped homosexuality from the *Diagnostic and Statistical Manual of Mental Disorders,* thus ending its official status as a mental disorder. The same change was made by the World Health Organization in its *International Classification of Diseases* in 1993, by Japan's psychiatric organization in 1995, and by the Chinese Psychiatric Association in 2001.

Nevertheless, some people still disapprove of homosexuality. Because homosexuals and bisexuals are often the victims of discrimination and even hate crimes, many are reluctant to let their sexual orientation be known (Bernat et al., 2001). It is difficult, therefore, to obtain an accurate picture of the mix of heterosexual, homosexual, and bisexual orientations in a population. In the Chicago sex survey mentioned earlier, 1.4 percent of women and 2.8 percent of men identified themselves as exclusively homosexual (Laumann et al., 1994), figures much lower than the 10 percent found earlier in Kinsey's studies. However, the Chicago survey's face-to-face interviews did not allow respondents to give anonymous answers to questions about sexual orientation. Some researchers suggest that if anonymous responses to those questions had been permitted, the prevalence figures for homosexual and bisexual orientations would have been higher (Bullough, 1995). In fact, studies that have allowed anonymous responding estimate that homosexual people make up between 2 and 15 percent of the population in the United States, Canada, and Western Europe (Aaron et al., 2003; Bagley & Tremblay, 1998; Binson et al., 1995; Sell, Wells, & Wypij, 1995).

heterosexual   Referring to sexual desire or behavior that is focused on members of the opposite sex.

homosexual   Referring to sexual desire or behavior that is focused on members of a person's own sex.

bisexual   Referring to sexual desire or behavior that is focused on members of both sexes.

The question of where sexual orientation comes from is a topic of intense
debate in scientific circles, on talk
shows, in everyday conversation, and even in
the halls of the U.S. Congress.

■ **What am I being asked to believe or accept?**

One point of view suggests that genes dictate sexual orientation. According to this view,
we do not learn a sexual orientation but, rather, are born with it.

■ **Is there evidence available to support the claim?**

In 1995, a report by a respected research group suggested that one kind of sexual orientation—namely, homosexuality in males—was associated with a particular gene on the X
chromosome (Hu et al., 1995). This finding was not supported by later studies (Rice et al.,
1999), but a growing body of evidence from research in behavioral genetics suggests that
genes might indeed influence sexual orientation in humans (Kendler et al., 2000; Pillard &
Bailey, 1998). One study examined pairs of monozygotic male twins (whose genes are identical), nonidentical twin pairs (whose genes are no more alike than those of any brothers),
and pairs of adopted brothers (who are genetically unrelated). To participate in this study, at
least one brother in each pair had to be homosexual. As it turned out, the other brother was
also homosexual or bisexual in 52 percent of the identical-twin pairs, but in only 22 percent
of the nonidentical pairs and in just 11 percent of the adoptive pairs (Bailey & Pillard, 1991).
Similar findings have been reported for male identical twins raised apart. In such cases, a
shared sexual orientation cannot be attributed to the effects of a shared environment
(Whitam, Diamond, & Martin, 1993). The few available studies of female sexual orientation
have yielded similar results (Bailey & Benishay, 1993; Bailey, Dunne, & Nicholas, 2000).

   Other evidence for the role of biological factors in sexual orientation comes from
research on the impact of sex hormones. In adults, differences in the level of these hormones
is not generally associated with differences in sexual orientation. However, hormonal differences during prenatal development might be involved in the shaping of sexual orientation
(Lalumière et al., 2000; Lippa, 2003; Williams et al., 2000). For example, one study found
that women who had been exposed to high levels of androgens during their fetal development were much more likely to become lesbians than their sisters who were not similarly
exposed (Meyer et al., 1995). In animals, such hormonal influences alter the structure of the
hypothalamus, a brain region known to underlie some aspects of sexual functioning (Swaab
& Hofman, 1995). In humans, hormones may likewise be responsible for anatomical differences in the hypothalamus. These differences are seen not only in males versus females but
in homosexual versus heterosexual men as well (LeVay, 1991; Swaab et al., 2001).

   Finally, a biological basis for sexual orientation is suggested by the relatively weak
effects of the environment on sexual orientation. For example, the sexual orientation of
children's caregivers has little or no effect on those children's own orientation. Several
studies have shown that children adopted by homosexual parents are no more or less
likely to display a homosexual orientation than are children raised by heterosexual parents (Anderssen, Amlie, & Ytteroy, 2002; Bailey et al., 1995; Tasker & Golombok, 1995).

■ **Can that evidence be interpreted another way?**

Like all correlational data, correlations between genetics and sexual orientation are open
to alternative interpretations. As discussed in the introductory chapter, a correlation
describes the strength and direction of the relationship between two variables, but it does
not guarantee that one variable actually influences the other. Consider again the data
showing that the brothers who shared the most genes were also most likely to share a
homosexual orientation. It is possible that what they shared was not a gene for homosexuality but, rather, a set of genes that influenced the boys' activity levels, emotionality,

A COMMITTED RELATIONSHIP, WITH CHILDREN Like heterosexual relationships, homosexual relationships can be brief and stormy, or stable and long-lasting. These gay men are committed to each other for the long haul, as evidenced by their decision to adopt two children together. The strong role of biological factors in sexual orientation is seen in research showing that these children's orientation will not be influenced much, if at all, by that of their adopted parents (Bailey et al., 1995; Stacey & Biblarz, 2001; Tasker & Golombok, 1995).

aggressiveness, or other general aspects of their temperament or personality. It could have been these characteristics, and other people's reactions to them, that increased the likelihood of a particular sexual orientation. In other words, sexual orientation could arise as a reaction to the way people respond to a genetically determined, but nonsexual, aspect of personality. The influence of prenatal hormone levels could also influence sexual orientation by shaping aggressiveness or other nonsexual aspects of behavior.

It is also important to look at behavioral genetics evidence for what it can tell us about the role of *environmental* factors in sexual orientation. When we read a study showing that 52 percent of the time, both members of identical-twin pairs have a homosexual or bisexual orientation, it is easy to ignore the fact that the sexual orientation of the twin pair members *differed* in 48 percent of the cases. Viewed in this way, the results suggest that genes do not tell the entire story of sexual orientation. In other words, even if sexual orientation has a biological base, it is probably not determined solely by unlearned, genetic forces. As described in the chapter on biology and behavior, the bodies we inherit are quite responsive to environmental input. In fact, the behaviors we engage in and the experiences we have often result in physical changes in the brain and elsewhere (Wang et al., 1995). For example, physical changes occur in the brain's synapses as we form new memories. So differences in the brains of people with differing sexual orientations could be the effect, not the cause, of their behavior or experiences.

■ What evidence would help to evaluate the alternatives?

Much more evidence is needed regarding the extent to which genetic characteristics directly determine sexual orientation. We also need more data on the extent to which genes and hormones shape physical and psychological characteristics that lead to the social construction of various sexual orientations. In studying these topics, researchers will want to learn more about the genetic makeup, mental style, and behavioral characteristics of people with different sexual orientations. Are there personality characteristics associated with particular sexual orientations? If so, do those characteristics have a strong genetic component? To what extent are heterosexuals, bisexuals, and homosexuals similar—and different—in terms of biases, coping skills, developmental histories, and the like (Bailey, Dunne, & Martin, 2000)? The more we learn about sexual orientation in general, the easier it will be to interpret data relating to its origins.

Yet, even classifying sexual orientation is not simple, because people do not always fall into sharply defined categories (American Psychological Association, 2002). Should a man who identifies himself as gay be considered bisexual because he occasionally has heterosexual daydreams? What sexual orientation label would be appropriate for a forty-year-old woman who experienced a few lesbian encounters in her teens but has engaged in exclusively heterosexual sex since then? Progress in understanding the origins of sexual orientation would be enhanced by a generally accepted system for describing exactly what is meant by the term *sexual orientation* (Stein, 1999).

■ What conclusions are most reasonable?

Given the antagonism and physical danger often faced by people with nonheterosexual orientations, it seems unlikely that sexual orientation is entirely a matter of choice. In fact, much of the evidence reviewed suggests that our sexual orientation chooses us, rather than the other way around. In light of this evidence, a reasonable hypothesis is that genetic factors, probably operating via prenatal hormones, create differences in the brains of people with different sexual orientations. Even if this hypothesis is correct, however, the manner in which a person expresses a genetically influenced sexual orientation will be profoundly shaped by what that person learns through social and cultural experiences (Bancroft, 1994). In short, sexual orientation most likely results from the complex interplay of both genetic and nongenetic mechanisms—both nature and nurture. People who characterize sexual orientation as being either "all in the genes" or entirely a matter of choice are probably wrong.

Sexual Dysfunctions

The same biological, social, and psychological factors that shape human sexual behavior can also result in **sexual dysfunctions,** problems in a person's desire for, or ability to have, satisfying sexual activity (Goldstein & Rosen, 2002). Fortunately, most of these problems—which affect 30 to 50 percent of adults in the U.S. and Britain (Heiman, 2002; Laumann, Paik, & Rosen, 1999; Mercer et al., 2003)—respond to psychotherapy, drugs, or both (de Silva, 1994). For men, a common problem is *erectile disorder* (once called *impotence*), a persistent inability to have or maintain an erection adequate for sex. Physical causes—such as fatigue, diabetes, hypertension, and the use of alcohol or other drugs—account for some cases. Psychological causes such as anxiety are also common (Everaerd & Laan, 1994; Heiman, 2002). Viagra, a drug that affects blood flow in the penis, is effective in treating many cases of erectile disorder, and newer drugs are being developed (Lue, 2000; Nehra & Kulaksizoglu, 2002). As its name implies, *premature ejaculation* is a recurring tendency to ejaculate during sex sooner than the man or his partner desires. Most men experience episodes of at least one of these problems at some point in their lives. These episodes are considered dysfunctions only if they become a distressing obstacle to sexual functioning (American Psychiatric Association, 1994; Mercer et al., 2003).

For women, the most common sexual dysfunction is *sexual arousal disorder* (once called *frigidity*), which involves a recurring inability to become aroused during sexual activity (Phillips, 2000; Wilson et al., 1996). Sexual arousal disorder can stem from inadequate genital stimulation, hormonal imbalances, insufficient vaginal lubrication, or inadequate blood flow to the clitoris (Anastasiadis et al., 2002; Mansfield, Voda, & Koch, 1995; Wilson et al., 1996). However, it is also often tied to psychological factors such as guilt or self-consciousness, which can affect men as well as women (Davidson & Moore, 1994; Laan et al., 1993).

sexual dysfunctions   Problems with sexual motivation, arousal, or orgasmic response.

Source: Murray (1971).

figure 8.4

Assessing Achievement Motivation

This picture is similar to those included in the Thematic Apperception Test, or TAT (Morgan & Murray, 1935). The strength of people's achievement motivation is inferred from the stories they tell about TAT pictures. A response like "The young woman is hoping that she will be able to make her grandmother proud of her" would be seen as reflecting high achievement motivation.

need achievement A motive reflected in the degree to which a person establishes specific goals, cares about meeting those goals, and experiences feelings of satisfaction by doing so.

Achievement Motivation

► **Why do some people try harder than others to succeed?**

This sentence was written at 6 A.M. on a beautiful Sunday in June. Why would someone get up that early to work on a weekend? Why do people take their work seriously and try to do the best that they can? People work hard partly due to *extrinsic motivation*, a desire for external rewards such as money. But work and other human behaviors also reflect *intrinsic motivation,* a desire for internal satisfaction.

The next time you visit someone's home or office, notice the mementos displayed there. Perhaps there are framed diplomas and awards, trophies and ribbons, pictures of memorable personal events, and photos of children and grandchildren. These badges of achievement affirm that a person has accomplished tasks that merit approval or establish worth. Much of human behavior is motivated by a desire for approval, admiration, and a sense of achievement—in short, for esteem—from others and from oneself. In this section, we examine two of the most common avenues to esteem: achievement in general and achievement in one's work.

Need for Achievement

Many athletes who already hold world records still train intensely; many people who have built multimillion-dollar businesses still work fourteen-hour days. What motivates these people? A possible answer is a motive called **need achievement** (Murray, 1938). People with a high need for achievement seek to master tasks—such as sports, business ventures, occupational skills, intellectual puzzles, or artistic creation—and feel intense satisfaction from doing so. They work hard at striving for excellence, enjoy themselves in the process, take great pride in achieving at a high level, and often experience success.

Individual Differences How do people with strong achievement motivation differ from others? To find out, researchers gave children a test to measure their need for achievement and then asked them to play a ring-toss game. Most of the children who scored low on the need-for-achievement test stood either so close to the ring-toss target that they couldn't fail or so far away that they could not succeed. In contrast, children scoring high on the need-for-achievement test stood at a moderate distance from the target, making the game challenging but not impossible (McClelland, 1958).

Experiments with adults and children suggest that people with high achievement needs tend to set challenging, but realistic, goals. They actively seek to do well, make careful plans, can wait for rewards, and are intensely satisfied with success (Mayer & Sutton, 1996). Yet if they feel they have tried their best, people with high achievement motivation are not too upset by failure. Those with low achievement motivation also like to succeed, but success tends to bring them not joy but relief at having avoided failure (Winter, 1996). Figure 8.4 shows a test that is sometimes used to measure achievement motivation in adults.

Differences in achievement motivation also appear in the kinds of goals people seek in achievement-related situations (Molden & Dweck, 2000). Some tend to adopt *learning goals.* When they play golf, take piano lessons, work at problems, go to school, and engage in other achievement-oriented activities, they do so mainly to develop competence in those activities. They realize that they may not yet have the skills necessary to achieve at a high level, so they tend to learn by watching others and to struggle with problems on their own rather than asking for help (Mayer & Sutton, 1996). When they do seek help, people with learning goals are likely to ask for explanations, hints, and other forms of task-related information, not for quick, easy answers that remove the challenge from the situation. In contrast, people who adopt *performance goals* are usually more concerned with demonstrating the competence they believe they already possess. They tend to seek information about how well they have performed compared with others rather than about how to improve their performance (Butler, 1999). When they seek help, it is usually to ask for "the right answer" rather than for tips on how to find the answer themselves. Because their primary goal is to display competence, people with performance goals tend to avoid new challenges if they are not confident that they will be successful, and they tend to quit in response to failure (Grant & Dweck, 2003; Weiner, 1980).

Development of Achievement Motivation Achievement motivation tends to be learned in early childhood, especially from parents. Evidence suggesting parental influence comes from a study in which young boys were given a task so difficult that they were sure to fail. Fathers whose sons scored low on achievement motivation tests often became annoyed as they watched their boys work on the task, discouraged them from continuing, and interfered or even completed the task themselves (Rosen & D'Andrade, 1959). A quite different response pattern emerged among parents of children who scored high on tests of achievement motivation. Those parents tended to (1) encourage the child to try difficult tasks, especially new ones; (2) give praise and other rewards for success; (3) encourage the child to find ways to succeed rather than merely complaining about failure; and (4) prompt the child to go on to the next, more difficult challenge (McClelland, 1985). Other research with adults shows that even the slightest cues that bring a parent to mind can boost people's efforts to achieve a goal (Shah, 2003).

More general cultural influences also affect achievement motivation. Subtle messages about a culture's view of the importance and value of achievement often appear in the books children read, the stories they hear, and the programs they see on television. Does the story's main character work hard and overcome obstacles, thus creating expectations of a payoff for persistence? Or does a lazy main character win the lottery, suggesting that rewards come randomly, regardless of effort? And if the main character succeeds, is it the result of personal effort, as is typical of stories in individualist cultures? Or is success based on ties to a cooperative and supportive group, as is typical of stories in collectivist cultures? Such themes appear to act as blueprints for reaching one's goals. It is not surprising, then, that ideas about achievement motivation differ from culture to culture. In one study, individuals from Saudi Arabia and from the United States were asked to comment on short stories describing people succeeding at various tasks. Saudis tended to see the people in the stories as having succeeded because of the help they got from others, whereas Americans tended to attribute success to the internal characteristics of each story's main character (Zahrani & Kaplowitz, 1993).

HELPING THEM DO THEIR BEST Learning-oriented goals are especially appropriate in classrooms, where students typically have little knowledge of the subject matter. This is why most teachers tolerate errors and reward gradual improvement. They do not usually encourage performance goals, which emphasize doing better than others and demonstrating immediate competence (Reeve, 1996). Still, to help students do their best in the long run, teachers may promote performance goals, too. The proper combination of both kinds of goals may be more motivating than either kind alone (Barron & Harackiewicz, 2001).

Further evidence of social influences on achievement motivation comes from research with people whose cultural training in childhood did not encourage achievement (McClelland, 1985). In one study, high school and college students with low achievement motivation were helped to develop fantasies about their own success. They imagined setting goals that were difficult, but not impossible. Then they imagined themselves breaking a complex problem into small, manageable steps. They fantasized about working hard, failing but not being discouraged, continuing to work, and finally feeling great about achieving success. Afterward, the students' grades and academic success improved, suggesting an increase in their achievement motivation (McClelland, 1985). In short, achievement motivation is strongly influenced by social and cultural learning experiences, and by the beliefs about oneself that these experiences help to create. People who come to believe in their ability to achieve are more likely to do so than those who expect to fail (Butler, 1998; Dweck, 1998; Wigfield & Eccles, 2000).

Achievement and Success in the Workplace

In the workplace, there is usually more concern with employees' motivation to work hard during business hours than with their general level of need achievement. In fact, employers tend to set up jobs in accordance with their ideas about how intrinsic and extrinsic motivation combine to shape employees' performance (Riggio, 1989). Employers who see workers as lazy, untrustworthy, and lacking ambition tend to offer highly structured, heavily supervised jobs. They give the employees little say in deciding what to do or how to do it. These employers assume that workers are motivated mainly by extrinsic rewards—especially money. So they are often surprised when their employees are dissatisfied with their jobs and show little motivation to work hard (Amabile et al., 1994; Igalens & Roussel, 2000).

If good pay and benefits alone do not bring job satisfaction and the desire to excel on the job, what does? Research suggests that low worker motivation in Western cultures comes largely from negative thoughts and feelings about having little or no control over the work environment (Rosen, 1991). Compared with those in highly structured jobs, workers tend to be happier, more satisfied, and more productive if they are (1) encouraged to participate in decisions about how work should be done; (2) given problems to solve, without being told how to solve them; (3) taught more than one skill; (4) given

Children raised in environments that support the development of strong achievement motivation tend not to give up on difficult tasks—even if all the king's horses and all the king's men do!

"Maybe they didn't try hard enough."

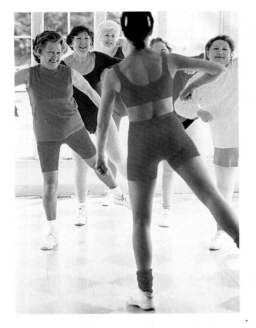

GOAL SETTING AND ACHIEVEMENT MOTIVATION   Clear and specific goals motivate the most persistent efforts at achievement on the job, and in other areas, too (Locke & Latham, 2002). These women are more likely to stick with their exercise program if they are pursuing the goal of "losing twenty pounds" or "doing aerobics three times a week," rather than the vague goal of "getting in shape." Similarly, you are more likely to keep reading this chapter if your goal is to "read the motivation section of the motivation and emotion chapter today" than if it is to "do some studying." Clarifying your goal makes it easier to know when you have reached it, and when it is time to stop. Without clear goals, a person can be more easily distracted by fatigue, boredom, or frustration and more likely to give up before completing a task.

subjective well-being   A combination of a cognitive judgment of satisfaction with life, the frequent experiencing of positive moods and emotions, and the relatively infrequent experiencing of unpleasant moods and emotions.

individual responsibility; and (5) given public recognition, not just money, for good performance (Fisher, 2000).

Allowing people to set and achieve clear goals increases both job performance and job satisfaction (Abramis, 1994). Goals that most effectively maintain work motivation have three features (Katzell & Thompson, 1990). First, they are personally meaningful. When a memo from a high-level administrator tells employees that their goal should be to increase production, they tend to feel unfairly pressured and not particularly motivated to meet the goal. Second, effective goals are specific and concrete (Locke & Latham, 2002). The goal of "doing better" is usually not a strong motivator. A specific target, such as increasing sales by 10 percent, is a far more motivating goal. It is there for all to see, and whether the goal has been reached is easily determined. Finally, goals are most effective if management supports the workers' own goal setting, offers special rewards for reaching goals, and gives encouragement after failure.

To summarize, motivating jobs offer personal challenges, independence, and both intrinsic and extrinsic rewards. They provide enough satisfaction for people to feel excitement and pleasure in working hard. For employers, the rewards are more productivity, less absenteeism, and fewer resignations (Ilgen & Pulakos, 1999).

Achievement and Subjective Well-Being

Some people believe that the more they achieve, and the more money and other material goods they acquire as a result, the happier they will be. Do you agree? Researchers studying *positive psychology* (Seligman & Csikszentmihalyi, 2000; Sheldon & King, 2001) have become increasingly interested in the systematic study of what it actually takes to achieve happiness, or more formally, subjective well-being (Lyubomirsky, 2001). **Subjective well-being** is a combination of a cognitive judgment of satisfaction with life, the frequent experiencing of positive moods and emotions, and the relatively infrequent experiencing of unpleasant moods and emotions (Diener, 2000; Diener & Biswas-Diener, 2002).

Research on subjective well-being indicates that, as you might expect, people living in extreme poverty or in war-torn or politically chaotic countries are less happy than people in better circumstances. And people everywhere react to good or bad events with corresponding changes in mood. As described in the chapter on health, stress, and coping, for example, severe or long-lasting stressors—such as the death of a loved one—can lead to psychological and physical problems. But although events do have an impact, the saddening or elevating effects of major changes, such as being promoted or fired, or even being imprisoned or seriously injured, tend not to last as long as we might think they would. In other words, how happy you are may have less to do with what happens to you than you might expect (Gilbert & Wilson, 1998; Lyubomirsky, 2001).

Most event-related changes in mood subside within days or weeks, and most people then return to their previous level of happiness (Suh, Diener, & Fujita, 1996). Even when events create permanent changes in circumstances, most people adapt by changing their expectancies and goals, not by radically and permanently changing their baseline level of happiness. For example, people may be thrilled after getting a big salary increase, but as they get used to having it, the thrill fades, and they may eventually feel just as underpaid as before. In fact, people's level of subjective well-being tends to be remarkably stable throughout their lives. This stable baseline may be related to temperament, or personality, and it has been likened to homeostatic processes that maintain body temperature or weight (Lykken, 1999). Like many other aspects of temperament, our baseline level of happiness may be influenced by genetics. Twin studies have shown, for example, that individual differences in happiness are more strongly associated with inherited personality characteristics than with environmental factors such as money, popularity, or physical attractiveness (Lykken, 1999; Tellegen et al., 1988).

Beyond inherited tendencies, the things that appear to matter most in generating happiness are close social ties (especially a satisfying marriage or partnership and good friends), religious faith, and having the resources necessary to allow progress toward one's goals (Diener, 2000; Myers, 2000a). So you don't have to be a rich, physically attractive high-achiever to be happy, and it turns out that most people in Western cultures are relatively happy (Diener & Diener, 1995). These results are consistent with the views expressed over many centuries by philosophers, psychologists, and wise people in all cultures. For example, decades ago, Abraham Maslow (1970) noted that when people in Western cultures experience unhappiness and psychological problems, those problems can often be traced to a *deficiency orientation* (see the personality chapter). That is, these people tend to seek happiness by trying to acquire the goods and status they don't have—but think they need—rather than by appreciating life itself and the value of the material and nonmaterial riches they already have. Others have amplified this point, suggesting that our efforts to get more of the things we think will bring happiness may actually contribute to unhappiness if what we get is never "enough" (Csikszentmihalyi, 1999; Myers, 2000b; Srivastava, Locke, & Bartol, 2001).

Relations and Conflicts Among Motives

▶ **Which motives move me most?**

It is far too early to tell whether research on subjective well-being will help to channel people's achievement motivation toward a more balanced set of goals, but there is no doubt that people will continue striving to meet whatever needs they perceive to be important. What are those needs?

Maslow's Hierarchy

Maslow (1970) suggested that human behavior is influenced by a hierarchy, or ranking, of five classes of needs, or motives (see Figure 8.5). He said that needs at the lowest level of the hierarchy must be at least partially satisfied before people can be motivated by higher-level goals. From the bottom to the top of Maslow's hierarchy, these five motives are as follows:

1. *Physiological,* such as the need for food, water, oxygen, activity, and sleep.

2. *Safety,* such as the need to be cared for as a child and have a secure income as an adult.

3. *Belongingness and love,* such as the need to be part of groups and to participate in affectionate sexual and nonsexual relationships.

figure 8.5

Maslow's Hierarchy of Motives

learn by **doing** Abraham Maslow saw motives as organized in a hierarchy in which motives at lower levels come before those at higher levels. According to this view, self-actualization is the essence of mental health; but Maslow recognized that only rare individuals, such as Mother Teresa or Martin Luther King, Jr., approach full self-actualization. Take a moment to consider which level of Maslow's hierarchy you are focused on at this point in your life. Which level do you ultimately hope to reach?

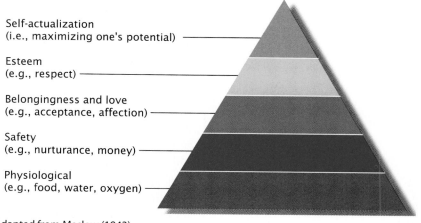

Self-actualization
(i.e., maximizing one's potential)

Esteem
(e.g., respect)

Belongingness and love
(e.g., acceptance, affection)

Safety
(e.g., nurturance, money)

Physiological
(e.g., food, water, oxygen)

Source: Adapted from Maslow (1943).

4. *Esteem*, such as the need to be respected as a useful, honorable individual.

5. *Self-actualization*, which means reaching one's full potential. People motivated by this need explore and enhance relationships with others; follow interests for intrinsic pleasure rather than for money, status, or esteem; and are concerned with issues affecting all people, not just themselves.

Maslow's hierarchy has been very influential over the years, but critics see it as far too simplistic (Hall, Lindzey, & Campbell, 1998; Neher, 1991). It does not predict or explain, for example, the motivation of people who starve themselves to death to draw attention to political or moral causes. Further, people may not have to satisfy one kind of need before addressing others; we can seek to satisfy several needs at once. And though the needs associated with basic survival and security do generally take precedence over those related to self-enhancement or personal growth (Baumeister & Leary, 1995; Oishi et al., 1999), the needs that are most important to people's satisfaction with life do not always correspond to Maslow's hierarchy. One set of studies with college students found that the needs for autonomy (independence), relatedness to others, competence, and self-esteem were more important than the need for luxury or self-actualization (Sheldon et al., 2001). Further, the ordering of needs within the survival/security and enhancement/growth categories differs from culture to culture, suggesting that there may not be a single, universal hierarchy of needs.

LINKAGES
Can motivational conflicts cause stress?
(a link to Health, Stress, and Coping)

LINKAGES

Conflicting Motives and Stress

As in the case of hunger strikes, when the desire to promote a cause is pitted against the desire to eat, human motives can sometimes conflict. The usual result is some degree of discomfort. For example, imagine that you are alone and bored on a Saturday night and decide to go to the store for a snack. What are your motives? Hunger might prompt you to go out. So might the prospect of the increased arousal and decreased boredom that a change of scene will provide. Even sexual motivation might be involved, as you consider the chances of meeting someone exciting in the snack-food aisle. But safety-related motives may also kick in: What if you get mugged? Even an esteem motive might come into play, making you hesitate to be seen alone on a weekend night.

These are just a few motives that may shape a trivial decision. When the decision is more important, the number and strength of motivational pushes and pulls are often greater, creating far more internal conflict. There are four basic types of motivational conflicts (Miller, 1959):

1. *Approach-approach conflicts.* When we must choose only one of two desirable activities—say, going to a movie or to a concert—an *approach-approach conflict* exists. As the importance of the choice increases, so does the difficulty of making it.

2. *Avoidance-avoidance conflicts.* An *avoidance-avoidance conflict* arises when we must select one of two undesirable alternatives. Someone forced either to sell the family home or to declare bankruptcy faces an avoidance-avoidance conflict. Such conflicts are very difficult to resolve and often create intense emotions.

3. *Approach-avoidance conflicts.* If someone you couldn't stand had tickets to your favorite group's sold-out concert and invited you to come along, what would you do? When a particular event or activity has both attractive and unattractive features, an *approach-avoidance* conflict is created. Conflicts of this type are also difficult to resolve and often result in long periods of indecision.

4. *Multiple approach-avoidance conflicts.* Suppose you must choose between two jobs. One offers a high salary with a well-known company, but it requires long working hours and relocation to a miserable climate. The other boasts good advancement opportunities, fringe benefits, and a better climate, but it doesn't pay as much and involves an unpredictable work schedule. This is an example of a *multiple approach-avoidance*

learn by **doing**

A STRESSFUL CONFLICT
Think back to the time when you were deciding which college to attend. Was the decision easy and obvious, or did it create a motivational conflict? If there was a conflict, was it an approach-approach, approach-avoidance, or multiple approach-avoidance conflict? What factors were most important in deciding how to resolve the conflict, and what emotions and signs of stress did you experience during and after the decision-making process?

conflict, in which two or more alternatives each have both positive and negative features. Such conflicts are difficult to resolve, partly because the features of each option are usually difficult to compare. For example, how many dollars a year does it take to compensate you for living in a bad climate?

Each of these conflicts can create stress, a topic we explore at length in the chapter on health, stress, and coping. Most people in motivational conflict are tense, irritable, and particularly vulnerable to physical and psychological problems. These reactions are especially likely when there is no obvious "right" choice, when varying motives have approximately equal strength, and when a choice can have serious consequences (as in decisions to marry, to divorce, or to approve disconnecting a terminally ill relative's life-support system). People may devote a lot of time and thought to resolving these conflicts, or they may make the decision quickly and impulsively, if only to end the discomfort of uncertainty. Even after resolving the conflict, people may continue to experience stress responses, such as worrying about whether they made the right decision or engaging in self-blame over bad choices. These and other consequences of conflicting motives can even lead to depression or other serious disorders.

The emotions associated with motivational conflicts provide just one example of the close links between human motivation and emotion. Motivation can intensify emotion, as when hunger leads a restaurant customer to angrily complain about slow service. But emotions can also create motivation. Happiness, for example, is an emotion that people want to feel, so they engage in whatever behaviors—studying, artwork, beachcombing—they think will achieve it. Similarly, as an emotion that most people want to avoid, anxiety prompts many behaviors, from leaving the scene of an accident to avoiding poisonous snakes. Let's now take a closer look at emotions.

The Nature of Emotion

▶ **How do feelings differ from thoughts?**

Everyone seems to agree that joy, sorrow, anger, fear, love, and hate are emotions. However, it is often hard to identify the shared features that make these experiences emotions rather than, say, thoughts or impulses.

Defining Characteristics

Most psychologists in Western cultures tend to see emotions as organized psychological and physiological reactions to changes in our relationship to the world. These reactions are partly inner, or *subjective,* experiences and partly measurable patterns of behavior and physiological arousal. The subjective experience of emotion has several characteristics:

1. Emotion is usually *temporary.* In other words, it tends to have a relatively clear beginning and end and a relatively short duration. Moods, by contrast, tend to last longer.

2. Emotional experience is either *positive* or *negative,* pleasant or unpleasant.

3. Emotional experience is triggered partly by a *mental assessment* of how a situation relates to your goals. The same event can bring on different emotions depending on how you interpret what the event means. An exam score of 75 percent may thrill you if your previous score had been 50 percent, but it may upset you if you had never before scored below 90 percent.

WINNERS AND LOSERS Emotional experiences depend in part on our interpretation of situations and how those situations relate to our goals. A single stimulus—the announcement of the results of a cheerleading contest—triggered drastically different emotional reactions in these women, depending on whether they perceived it as making them winners or losers.

emotion A temporary positive or negative experience that is felt as happening to the self, that is generated partly by mental assessment of situations, and accompanied by learned and innate physical responses.

parasympathetic nervous system The subsystem of the autonomic nervous system that typically influences activity related to the protection, nourishment, and growth of the body.

sympathetic nervous system The subsystem of the autonomic nervous system that readies the body for vigorous activity.

fight-or-flight syndrome Physical reactions initiated by the sympathetic nervous system that prepare the body to fight or to run from a threatening situation.

4. Emotional experience *alters thought processes,* often by directing attention toward some things and away from others (Craske, 1999). The anguish of parents whose child is killed by a drunken driver, for example, might focus far more attention than ever before on the importance of drunk-driving laws.

5. Emotional experience brings on an *action tendency,* a motivation to behave in certain ways. The grieving parents' anger, for example, might motivate them to harm the driver or spend countless hours working for stronger penalties for drunk driving.

6. Emotional experiences are *passions* that happen to you, usually whether you want them to happen or not. However, you can exert some control over emotions, because they depend partly on how you interpret situations (Gross, 2001). For example, your emotional reaction might be less extreme after a house fire if you remind yourself that no one was hurt and you are insured. Still, you cannot just rationally *decide* what emotions you experience; instead, you "fall in love" or "explode in anger" or are "overcome by grief." So emotional experiences have a different relation to the self than do conscious thoughts.

In other words, the subjective aspects of emotions are experiences that are both triggered by the thinking self and felt as happening to the self. The extent to which we are "victims" of our passions versus rational controllers of our emotions is a central dilemma of human existence.

The objectively measurable aspects of emotion include learned and innate *expressive displays* and *physiological responses.* Expressive displays—such as a smile or a frown—communicate feelings to others. Physiological responses—changes in heart rate, for example—provide the biological adjustments needed to perform actions generated by the emotional experience. If you throw a temper tantrum, for instance, your heart must deliver additional oxygen and fuel to your muscles.

In summary, an **emotion** is a temporary experience with either positive or negative qualities. It is felt with some intensity as happening to the self, generated in part by a mental assessment of situations, and accompanied by both learned and innate physical responses. Through emotion, people communicate their internal states and intentions to others, but emotion also functions to motivate a person's thoughts and actions.

The Biology of Emotion

The biological systems described in the chapter on biology and behavior play a major role in emotion. In the *central nervous system,* specific brain areas are involved in the generation of emotions, as well as in our experience of those emotions. The *autonomic nervous system* gives rise to many of the physiological changes associated with emotional arousal.

Brain Mechanisms Although many questions remain, researchers have described three basic features of the brain's control of emotion. First, it appears that activity in the *limbic system,* especially in the *amygdala,* is central to various aspects of emotion (Anderson & Phelps, 2001; LeDoux, 1996; see Figure 2.8 in the chapter on biology and behavior). Disruptions in the amygdala appear to contribute to the emotional problems associated with certain kinds of brain damage (Aggleton, 1993). For example, victims of a disease that destroys only the amygdala cannot judge other people's emotional state by looking at their facial expressions (Adolphs, Tranel, & Damasio, 1998).

A second aspect of the brain's involvement in emotion is seen in its control over emotional and nonemotional facial expressions (Rinn, 1984). Take a moment to look in a mirror, and put on your best fake smile. The voluntary facial movements you just made, like all voluntary movements, are controlled by the *pyramidal motor system,* a brain system that includes the motor cortex. However, a smile that expresses genuine happiness is involuntary. That kind of smile, like the other facial movements associated with emotions, is governed by the *extrapyramidal motor system,* which depends on areas beneath

figure 8.6

Control of Voluntary and Emotional Facial Movements

This man has a tumor in his motor cortex that prevents him from voluntarily moving the muscles on the left side of his face. In the top photograph he is trying to smile in response to instructions from the examiner. He cannot smile on command, but he can smile with happiness, as the bottom photograph shows, because the movements associated with genuine emotion are controlled by the extrapyramidal motor system, which is beneath the motor cortex.

the cortex. Brain damage can disrupt either system (see Figure 8.6). People with pyramidal motor system damage show normal facial expressions during genuine emotion, but they cannot fake a smile. In contrast, people with damage to the extrapyramidal system can pose facial expressions at will, but they remain straight-faced even when feeling genuine joy or profound sadness (Hopf, Muller, & Hopf, 1992).

A third aspect of the brain's role in emotion is revealed by research on the differing contributions of its two cerebral hemispheres to the perception, experience, and expression of emotion (Davidson, 2000). For example, after suffering damage to the right, but not the left, hemisphere, people no longer laugh at jokes—even though they can still understand the jokes' words, the logic (or illogic) underlying them, and the punch lines (Critchley, 1991). And compared with nondepressed people, depressed people display greater electrical activity in the right frontal cortex (Schaffer, Davidson, & Saron, 1983) and perform more poorly on tasks that depend especially on the right hemisphere (Banich et al., 1992; Heller, Etienne, & Miller, 1995).

There is still some debate about the relationship between hemispheric differences and emotion (Vingerhoets, Berckmoes, & Stroobant, 2003). However, research has generally shown that the following aspects of emotion depend more on the right hemisphere than on the left: (1) the experiencing of negative emotion, (2) the perception of any emotion exhibited in faces or other stimuli, and (3) the facial expression of any emotion (Heller, Nitschke, & Miller, 1998; Kawasaki et al., 2001).

If the right hemisphere is relatively dominant in emotion, which side of the face would you expect to be somewhat more involved in expressing emotion? If you said the left side you are correct, because as described in the chapter on biology and behavior, movements of each side of the body are controlled by the opposite side of the brain.

Mechanisms of the Autonomic Nervous System   The autonomic nervous system (ANS) triggers many of the physiological changes that accompany emotions (Vernet, Robin, & Dittmar, 1995; see Figure 8.7). If your hands get cold and clammy when you are nervous, it is because the ANS has increased perspiration and decreased the blood flow in your hands.

As described in the chapter on biology and behavior, the ANS carries information between the brain and most organs of the body—the heart and blood vessels, the digestive system, and so on. Each of these organs has its own ongoing activity, but ANS input affects this activity, too, either by increasing it or decreasing it. By affecting the activity of organs, the ANS coordinates their functioning to meet the body's general needs and to prepare the body for change (Porges, Doussard, & Maita, 1995). If you are aroused to take action, such as running to catch a bus, you need more glucose to fuel your muscles. The ANS frees needed energy by stimulating secretion of glucose-generating hormones and promoting blood flow to the muscles.

Figure 8.7 shows that the autonomic nervous system is organized into two parts: the sympathetic nervous system and the parasympathetic nervous system. Emotions can activate either part, both of which send axon fibers to each organ in the body. Generally, the sympathetic and parasympathetic fibers have opposite effects on these *target organs*. Axons from the **parasympathetic nervous system** release the neurotransmitter *acetylcholine* onto target organs, leading to activity related to the protection, nourishment, and growth of the body. Axons from the **sympathetic nervous system** release a different neurotransmitter, *norepinephrine*, onto target organs, helping to prepare the body for vigorous activity. It is this system that stimulates the **fight-or-flight syndrome**, a pattern of increased heart rate and blood pressure, rapid or irregular breathing, dilated pupils, perspiration, dry mouth, increased blood sugar, "goose bumps," and other changes that help prepare the body to confront or run from a threat.

The ANS is not directly connected to brain areas involved in consciousness, so information about organ activity reaches the brain at a nonconscious level. You may hear your stomach "grumble," but you can't actually feel it secrete acids. Similarly, you cannot consciously experience the brain mechanisms that alter the activity of your autonomic nervous system. This is why most people cannot exert direct, conscious control over blood pressure or other aspects of ANS activity. However, you can do things that have indirect

Parasympathetic functions   **Sympathetic functions**

figure 8.7

The Autonomic Nervous System

learn **by doing** Emotional responses involve activation of the autonomic nervous system, which is organized into sympathetic and parasympathetic subsystems. Which of the bodily responses depicted do you associate with emotional experiences?

effects on the ANS. For example, to create autonomic arousal of your sex organs, you might imagine an erotic situation. To raise your blood pressure, you might hold your breath or strain your muscles. And to lower your blood pressure, you can lie down, relax, and think calming thoughts.

Theories of Emotion

▶ **Is emotion in the heart, in the head, or both?**

Are the physiological responses associated with emotion sufficient to create an emotional experience? Or are these responses simply the results of an emotional experience that is created when we mentally interpret events? Questions about the roles played by physiological and mental activity in the experience of emotion have been the focus of research for over a century—and they have generated several important theories of emotion.

James's Peripheral Theory

Suppose you are camping in the woods when a huge bear approaches your tent in the middle of the night. Scared to death, you run for dear life. Do you run because you are afraid, or are you afraid because you run? This was the question posed by William James, one of the first psychologists to offer a formal account of how physiological responses relate to emotional experience. He argued that you are afraid because you run. Your running and the physiological responses associated with it, he said, follow directly from your perception of the bear.

At first, James's claim sounds ridiculous; it would be silly to run from something unless you already feared it. James concluded otherwise after examining his own mental processes. He decided that once you strip away all physiological responses—such as changes in heart rate, breathing, and other peripheral nervous system activity—nothing remains of the experience of an emotion (James, 1890). Without these responses, he said, you would feel no fear, because it is the experiencing of physiological responses that creates fear and other emotions. The same argument was made by Carle Lange, a Danish physician, so James's view is sometimes called the *James-Lange theory* of emotion. It is also known as a *peripheral theory* of emotion, because it emphasizes activity in the peripheral nervous system, not in the central nervous system, as the main cause of emotional experience.

Observing Peripheral Responses Figure 8.8 outlines the components of emotional experience, including those emphasized by James. First, perception affects the cerebral cortex. The brain interprets a situation and automatically directs a particular set of physiological changes, such as increased heart rate, sinking stomach, perspiration, and certain patterns of blood flow. It is when we become *aware* of these physiological changes, said James, that we experience an emotion. According to this view, each particular emotion is created by a particular pattern of physiological responses.

figure 8.8

Components of Emotion

Emotion is associated with activity in the brain, as well as with responses elsewhere in the body (called *peripheral* responses). Emotion theorists have argued about which of these components are essential for emotion. William James emphasized the perception of peripheral responses, such as changes in heart rate. Stanley Schachter emphasized the cognitive interpretation and labeling of peripheral responses. Walter Cannon asserted that emotion could occur entirely within the brain.

1. **Sensation/perception**
(It's a bear!)

2. **Cognitive interpretation**
(That bear can kill me!)

3. **Activation of CNS and peripheral nervous system**
(Cannon)

4. **Peripheral responses**
(e.g., increase in heart rate, change in facial expression)

5. **Perception of peripheral responses**
(James)

6. **Cognitive interpretation of peripheral responses**
(Schachter)

Notice that according to James's theory, emotional experience is not generated by the brain alone. There is no special "emotion center" in the brain where the firing of neurons creates a direct experience of emotion. If this theory is accurate, it might account for the difficulty we sometimes have in knowing our true feelings: We must figure out what emotions we feel by perceiving small differences in specific physiological response patterns (Katkin, Wiens, & Öhman, 2001).

Evaluating James's Theory   Research shows that certain emotional states are indeed associated with particular patterns of autonomic changes (Damasio et al., 2000; Kelter & Buswell, 1996; Sinha & Parsons, 1996). For example, blood flow to the hands and feet increases in association with anger and declines in association with fear (Levenson, Ekman, & Friesen, 1990). So fear involves "cold feet"; anger does not. A pattern of activity associated with disgust includes increased muscle activity but no change in heart rate. And when people mentally relive different kinds of emotional experiences, they show different patterns of autonomic activity (Ekman, Levenson, & Friesen, 1983). These emotion-specific patterns of physiological activity have been found in widely different cultures (Levenson et al., 1992). It also turns out that people who are more keenly aware of physiological changes in their body are likely to experience emotions more intensely than those who are less aware of such changes (Schneider, Ring, & Katkin, 1998; Wiens, Mezzacappa, & Katkin, 2000).

Furthermore, different patterns of autonomic activity are closely tied to specific emotional facial expressions, and vice versa. When research participants were asked to make various facial movements (Ekman, Levenson, & Friesen, 1983), these movements led to autonomic changes resembling those normally accompanying emotion (see Figure 8.9). In addition, almost all of the participants reported feeling the emotion associated with

figure 8.9

Patterns of Physiological Change Associated with Different Emotions

In this experiment, facial movements characteristic of different emotions produced different patterns of change in (A) heart rate; (B) peripheral blood flow, as measured by finger temperature; (C) skin conductance; and (D) muscle activity (Levenson, Ekman, & Friesen, 1990). For example, making an angry face caused heart rate and finger temperature to rise, whereas making a fearful face raised heart rate but lowered finger temperature.

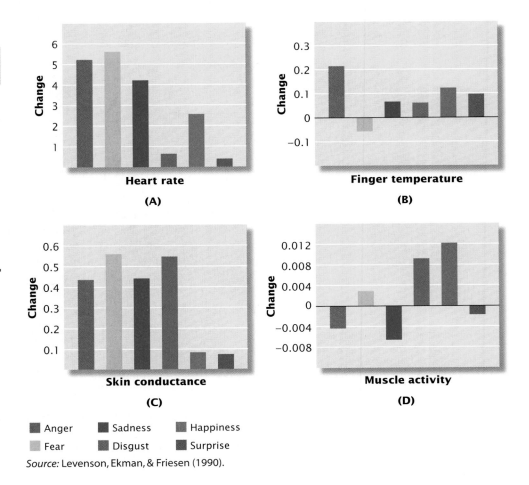

Source: Levenson, Ekman, & Friesen (1990).

the expression they had created, even though they could not see their own expressions and did not realize that a specific emotion was being portrayed.

Other studies, too, have shown that people feel emotions such as happiness, anger, or sadness, for example, when simply making an "angry" or "sad" face (Schnall & Laird, 2003). They can also ease these feelings just by relaxing their faces (Duclos & Laird, 2001). The emotional effects of this "face making" appear strongest in people who are the most sensitive to internal bodily cues. To get an idea of how facial expressions can alter, as well as express, emotion, look at a photograph of someone whose face is expressing a strong emotion, and try your best to imitate it. Doing this may create in you the same feelings and autonomic responses that the other person is experiencing.

learn *by* **doing**

In fact, a variant of James's theory, the *facial feedback hypothesis,* maintains that involuntary facial movements provide enough information about the body to drive emotional experience (Ekman & Davidson, 1993). This hypothesis predicts that feeling yourself smile should make you feel happy. It also helps to explain the results mentioned earlier suggesting that voluntarily posed facial expressions create the emotions normally associated with them. The next time you want to cheer yourself up, it might help to smile—even though you don't feel like it (Fleeson, Malanos, & Achille, 2002)!

Lie Detection   James's view that different patterns of physiological activity are associated with different emotions forms the basis for the lie detection industry. If people experience anxiety or guilt when they lie, specific patterns of physiological activity accompanying these emotions should be detectable on instruments, called *polygraphs,* that record heart rate, breathing rate, perspiration, and other autonomic responses.

To identify the perpetrator of a crime using the *control question test,* a polygraph tester might ask questions specific to the crime, such as "Did you stab someone on May 31, 2003?" Responses to such *relevant questions* are then compared with responses to *control questions,* such as "Have you ever lied to get out of trouble?" Innocent people might have lied at some time in the past and might feel guilty when asked about it, but they should have no reason to feel guilty about what they did on May 31, 2003. Accordingly, an innocent person should have a stronger emotional response to control questions than to relevant questions (Rosenfeld, 1995). Another approach, called the *directed lie test,* compares a person's physiological reactions when asked to lie about something and when telling what is known to be the truth. Finally, the *guilty knowledge test* seeks to determine if a person reacts in a notable way to information about a crime that only the perpetrator would know (Ben-Shakhar, Bar-Hillel, & Kremnitzer, 2002).

Most people do have emotional responses when they lie, but statistics about the accuracy of polygraphs are difficult to obtain. Estimates vary widely, from those suggesting that polygraphs detect 90 percent of guilty, lying individuals (Honts & Quick, 1995; Kircher, Horowitz, & Raskin, 1988; Raskin, 1986) to those suggesting that polygraphs mislabel as many as 40 percent of truthful, innocent persons as guilty liars (Ben-Shakhar & Furedy, 1990; Saxe & Ben-Shakhar, 1999). Obviously, the results of a polygraph test are not determined entirely by whether a person is telling the truth. What people think about the act of lying, and about the value of the test, can also influence the accuracy of its results. For example, people who consider lying to be acceptable and who do not believe in the power of polygraphs are unlikely to display emotion-linked physiological responses while lying during the test. However, an innocent person who believes in such tests and who thinks that "everything always goes wrong" might show a large fear response when asked about a crime, thus wrongly indicating "guilt."

Polygraphs can catch some liars, but most researchers agree that a guilty person can "fool" a polygraph lie detector, and that some innocent people can be mislabeled as guilty. After reviewing the relevant research literature, a panel of distinguished psychologists and other scientists in the United States expressed serious reservations about the value of polygraph tests in detecting deception and argued against their use as evidence in court or in employee screening and selection (Committee to Review the Scientific Evidence on the Polygraph, 2002). Other lie-detecting devices now being investigated focus on brain

SEARCHING FOR THE TRUTH   Polygraph tests are not foolproof, though they may intimidate people who believe that they are. In one small town where the police could not afford a polygraph, a guilty suspect confessed his crime when a "lie detector" consisting of a kitchen colander was placed on his head and attached by wires to a copy machine (Shepard, Kohut, & Sweet, 1989).

activity and other measures that do not depend on a link between deception and autonomic nervous system responses (Lee et al., 2002; Preston, 2002; Zhou et al., 2000).

Cannon's Central Theory

For James, the experience of emotion depends on feedback from physiological responses occurring outside the brain, but Walter Cannon disagreed (Cannon, 1927/1987). According to Cannon, you feel fear at the sight of a wild bear even before you start to run because emotional experience starts in the brain—specifically, in the thalamus, the brain structure that relays information from most sense organs to the cortex.

According to Cannon's *central theory* of emotion (called the *Cannon-Bard theory,* in recognition of Philip Bard's contribution), sensory information about emotional situations first reaches the thalamus. The thalamus then sends signals to the autonomic nervous system and—at the same time—to the cerebral cortex, where the emotion becomes conscious. So when you see a bear, the brain receives sensory information about it, interprets that information as a bear, and instantly creates the experience of fear while at the same time sending messages to the heart, lungs, and legs to get you out of the situation. According to Cannon's theory, then, there is a *direct,* central nervous system experience of emotion, with or without feedback about bodily responses (see Figure 8.8).

Updating Cannon's Theory   Later research indicates that the thalamus is not the "seat" of emotion, as Cannon had suggested. Still, the thalamus does participate in some aspects of emotional processing (Lang, 1995). For example, studies in animals and humans show that the emotion of fear is generated by connections from the thalamus to the amygdala (Anderson & Phelps, 2000; LeDoux, 1995). The implication is that strong emotions can sometimes bypass the cortex without requiring conscious thought to activate them—thus possibly explaining why people find it so difficult to overcome an intense fear, or phobia, even though they may consciously know the fear is irrational.

An updated version of Cannon's theory suggests that specific brain areas produce the feelings of pleasure or discomfort associated with emotion. This idea arose from studies showing that electrical stimulation of certain parts of the brain is rewarding. Researchers found that rats kept returning to the place in their cage where they received stimulation through electrodes in their brains. When these animals were allowed to control delivery of the stimulation by pressing a lever, they pressed it until they were physically exhausted, ignoring even food and water (Olds & Milner, 1954). The brain areas in which stimulation is experienced as especially pleasurable include the dopamine systems, which, as described in the chapter on consciousness, are activated by cocaine and other psychoactive drugs (Bardo, 1998). In contrast, stimulation of other brain regions is so unpleasant that animals work hard to avoid it.

Presumably, part of the direct central experience of emotion involves areas of the brain whose activity is experienced as either pleasant or aversive. The areas of the brain activated by the kind of events that elicit emotion in humans have widespread connections throughout the brain. So the central nervous system experience of emotion is probably widely distributed, not narrowly localized in any one emotion "center" (Derryberry & Tucker, 1992).

Cognitive Theories

Suppose you are about to be interviewed for your first job, or go out on a blind date, or take your first ride in a hot-air balloon. In such situations, it is not always easy to be sure of what you are feeling. Is it fear, excitement, anticipation, worry, happiness, dread, or what? Stanley Schachter suggested that the emotions we experience every day are shaped partly by how we interpret the arousal we feel. His cognitive theory of emotion is known as the *Schachter-Singer theory* in recognition of the contributions of Jerome Singer. The theory took shape in the early 1960s, when many psychologists were raising questions

attribution   The process of explaining the cause of some event.

excitation transfer   The process by which arousal is carried over from one experience to an independent situation.

about the validity of James's theory of emotion. Schachter argued that the theory was essentially correct—but required a few modifications (Cornelius, 1996).

According to the Schachter-Singer theory, emotions result from a combination of feedback from the body's responses and our mental interpretation of what caused those responses. So cognitive interpretation comes into play twice: first when you perceive the situation that leads to bodily responses and again when you interpret those responses as a particular emotion (see Figure 8.8). Schachter said that a given pattern of physiological responses can be interpreted in many different ways, and so might give rise to many different emotions. According to Schachter, then, the emotion you experience when that bear approaches your campsite might be fear, excitement, astonishment, or surprise, depending on how you mentally label your bodily reactions to seeing it (Schachter & Singer, 1962).

Schachter also said that how we label arousal depends on **attribution,** the process of identifying the cause of some event. We attribute our physiological arousal to different emotions depending on the information available about the situation. For example, if you are watching the final seconds of a close ball game, you might attribute your racing heart, rapid breathing, and perspiration to excitement; but you might attribute the same physiological reactions to anxiety if you are waiting for a big exam to begin. Schachter predicted that our emotional experiences will be less intense if we attribute arousal to a nonemotional cause. So if you notice your heart pounding before an exam but say to yourself, "Sure my heart's pounding—I just drank five cups of coffee!" then you should feel "wired" from caffeine rather than afraid or worried. This prediction has received some support (Mezzacappa, Katkin, & Palmer, 1999; Sinclair et al., 1994), but other aspects of Schachter's theory have not.

Few researchers today fully accept the Schachter-Singer theory. However, it did stimulate an enormous amount of valuable research, including studies of **excitation transfer,** a phenomenon in which physiological arousal from one experience carries over to affect emotion in an independent situation (Reisenzein, 1983; Zillmann, 1984). For example, people who have been aroused by physical exercise become more angry when provoked, and experience more intense sexual feelings when in the company of an attractive person, than do people who have been less physically active (Allen et al., 1989). Arousal from fear, like arousal from exercise, can also enhance emotions, including sexual feelings. One study of this transfer took place in Canada, near a deep river gorge. The gorge could be crossed either by a shaky swinging bridge or by a more stable wooden structure. A female researcher asked men who had just crossed each bridge to fill out a questionnaire that included a measure of sexual imagery. The men who met the woman after crossing the more dangerous bridge had much higher sexual imagery scores than the men who had crossed the stable bridge. Furthermore,

LABELING AROUSAL Schachter's cognitive theory of emotion predicts that these people will attribute their physiological arousal to the game they are watching and will label their emotion "excitement." Further, as described in the chapter on health, stress, and coping, the emotions they experience will also depend partly on their cognitive interpretation of the outcome (Lazarus & Folkman, 1984). Those who see their team's defeat as a disaster will experience more negative emotions than those who think of it as a challenge to improve.

they were more likely to rate the researcher as attractive (Dutton & Aron, 1974). When the person giving out the questionnaire was a male, however, the type of bridge crossed had no impact on sexual imagery. To test the possibility that the men who crossed the dangerous bridge were simply more adventurous in both bridge crossing and heterosexual encounters, the researcher repeated the study, but with one change. This time, the woman approached the men farther down the trail, long after arousal from the bridge crossing had subsided. Now, the apparently adventurous men were no more likely than others to rate the woman as attractive. So it was probably excitation transfer, not just adventurousness, that produced the original result.

Schachter focused his theory of emotion on the way we cognitively interpret our bodily responses to events. Other cognitive theorists have argued that it is our interpretation of events themselves that are most important in shaping emotional experiences. For example, as we mentioned earlier, a person's emotional reaction to receiving exam results can depend partly on whether the score is seen as a sign of improvement or as a disaster. According to Richard Lazarus's (1966, 1991) *cognitive appraisal theory* of emotion, these differing reactions can be best explained by how we think exam scores, job interviews, blind dates, bear sightings, and other events will affect our personal well-being. According to Lazarus, the process of cognitive appraisal, or evaluation, begins when we decide whether or not an event is relevant to our well-being; that is, do we even care about it? If we don't, as might be the case if an exam doesn't count toward our grade, we are unlikely to have an emotional experience when we get the results. If the event is relevant to our well-being, we will experience an emotional reaction to it. That reaction will be positive or negative, said Lazarus, depending on whether we appraise the event as advancing our personal goals or obstructing them. The *specific* emotion we experience depends on our individual goals, needs, standards, expectations, and past experiences. As a result, a second-place finisher in a marathon race might experience bitter disappointment at having "lost," whereas someone at the back of the pack may be thrilled just to have completed the race alive.

"In Review: Theories of Emotion" summarizes key elements of the theories we have discussed. It appears that both bodily responses (including facial responses) and the cognitive interpretation of those responses add to emotional experience. In addition, the

THEORIES OF EMOTION

Theory	Source of Emotions	Example
James-Lange	Emotions are created by awareness of specific patterns of peripheral (autonomic) responses.	Anger is associated with increased blood flow in the hands and feet; fear is associated with decreased blood flow in these areas.
Cannon-Bard	The brain generates direct experiences of emotion.	Stimulation of certain brain areas can create pleasant or unpleasant emotions.
Cognitive (Schachter-Singer and Lazarus)	Cognitive interpretation of events, and of physiological reactions to them, shapes emotional experiences.	Autonomic arousal can be experienced as anxiety or excitement, depending on how it is labeled. A single event can lead to different emotions, depending on whether it is perceived as threatening or challenging.

? *Research showing that there are pleasure centers in the brain has been cited in support of the _____ theory of emotion.*

brain itself can apparently generate emotional experience, independent of physiological arousal. So emotion is probably both in the heart and in the head (including the face). The most basic emotions probably occur directly within the brain, whereas the many shades of emotion probably arise from attributions, including evaluations of physiological responses. No theory has completely resolved the issue of which, if any, component of emotion is primary. However, the theories we have discussed have helped psychologists better understand how these components interact to produce emotional experience.

Communicating Emotion

▶ **Which emotional expressions are innate, and which are learned?**

So far, we have described emotion from the inside, as people experience their own emotions. Let's now consider how people communicate emotions to one another.

One way they do this is, of course, through words. Some people describe their feelings relatively simply, and mainly in terms of pleasantness or unpleasantness; others include information about the intensity of their emotions (Barrett, 1995; Barrett et al., 2001). In general, women are more likely than men to talk about their emotions and the complexity of their feelings (Barrett et al., 2000; Kring & Gordon, 1998). But humans also communicate emotion through the movement and posture of their bodies, through their tone of voice, and especially through their facial movements and expressions. Imagine a woman watching television. You can see her face, but not what she sees on the screen. She might be engaged in complex thought, perhaps comparing her investment decisions with those of the experts being interviewed on CNBC. Or she might be thinking of nothing at all as she loses herself in a rerun of *Seinfeld*. In other words, you can't tell much about what she is thinking just by looking at her. If the television program creates an emotional experience, however, you will be able to make a reasonably accurate guess about which emotion she is feeling based on her facial expressions. The human face can create thousands of different expressions, and people—especially females—are good at detecting them (McClure, 2000; Zajonc, 1998). Observers can see even very small facial movements: A twitch of the mouth can carry a lot of information. Are emotional facial expressions innate, or are they learned? And how are they used in communicating emotion?

Innate Expressions of Emotion

Charles Darwin observed that some facial expressions seem to be universal (Darwin, 1872/1965). He proposed that these expressions are genetically determined, passed on biologically from one generation to the next. The facial expressions seen today, said Darwin, are those that have been most effective at telling others something about how a person is feeling. If someone is scowling with teeth clenched, for example, you will probably assume that the person is angry. And you will be unlikely to choose that particular moment to ask for a loan.

Infants provide one source of evidence that some facial expressions are innate. Newborns do not have to be taught to grimace in pain, to smile in pleasure, or to blink when startled (Balaban, 1995). Even blind infants, who cannot imitate adults' expressions, show the same emotional expressions as do sighted infants (Goodenough, 1932).

A second line of evidence for innate facial expressions comes from studies showing that for the most basic emotions, people in all cultures show similar facial responses to similar emotional stimuli (Hejmadi, Davidson, & Rozin, 2000; Zajonc, 1998). Participants in these studies looked at photographs of people's faces and then tried to name the emotion each person was feeling. The pattern of facial movements we call a smile, for example, is universally related to positive emotions. Sadness is almost

learn by doing **WHAT ARE THEY FEELING?** People's emotions are usually "written on their faces." Jot down what emotions you think these people are feeling, and then look at the footnote on page 316 to see how well you "read" their emotions.

THE UNIVERSAL SMILE   The idea that some emotional expressions are inborn is supported by the fact that the facial movement pattern we call a smile is related to happiness, pleasure, and other positive emotions in human cultures throughout the world.

always accompanied by slackened muscle tone and a "long" face. Likewise, in almost all cultures, people contort their faces in a similar way when shown something they find disgusting. And a furrowed brow is frequently associated with frustration or unpleasantness (Ekman, 1994).

Anger is also linked with a facial expression recognized by almost all cultures. One study examined ceremonial masks of various Western and non-Western cultures (Aronoff, Barclay, & Stevenson, 1988). The angry, threatening masks of all eighteen cultures contained similar elements, such as triangular eyes and diagonal lines on the cheeks. In particular, angular and diagonal elements carry the impression of threat (see Figure 8.10).

Social and Cultural Influences on Emotional Expression

Some basic emotional expressions are innate, but many others are neither innate nor universal (Ekman, 1993). Even innate expressions are flexible, changing as necessary in the social situations in which they occur (Fernández-Dols & Ruiz-Belda, 1995). For example, facial expressions become more intense and change more frequently when people are imagining social scenes as opposed to solitary scenes (Fridlund et al., 1990). Similarly, facial expressions in response to odors tend to be more intense when others are watching than when people are alone (Jancke & Kaufmann, 1994).

Further, although a core group of emotional responses is recognized by all cultures (Hejmadi, Davidson, & Rozin, 2000), there is a certain degree of cultural variation in recognizing some emotions (Russell, 1995). In one study, for example, Japanese and North American people agreed about which facial expressions signaled happiness, surprise, and sadness, but they frequently disagreed about which faces showed anger, disgust, and fear (Matsumoto & Ekman, 1989). Members of cultures such as the Fore of New Guinea agree even less with people in Western cultures on the labeling of facial expressions (Russell, 1994). In addition, there are variations in the ways that cultures interpret emotions expressed by tone of voice (Mesquita & Frijda, 1992). An example is provided by a study showing that Taiwanese participants were best at recognizing a sad tone of voice, whereas Dutch participants were best at recognizing happy tones (Van Bezooijen, Otto, & Heenan, 1983).

People learn how to express certain emotions in ways specified by cultural rules. Suppose you say, "I just bought a new car," and all your friends stick their tongues out at you. In North America, this may mean they are envious or resentful. But in some regions of China, such a display expresses surprise.

Even smiles can vary as people learn to use them to communicate certain feelings. Paul Ekman and his colleagues categorized seventeen types of smiles, including "false smiles," which fake enjoyment, and "masking smiles," which hide unhappiness. They

The picture on page 315 shows the wife and daughter of a U.S. Marine helicopter pilot waving goodbye as he departs for deployment in the Persian Gulf in December 2002. Their emotions at the moment probably included sadness, anxiety, worry, dread, uncertainty, hope, and perhaps anger.

figure 8.10

Elements of Ceremonial Facial Masks That Convey Threat

learn by doing Certain geometric patterns are common to threatening masks in many cultures. "Scary" Halloween pumpkins tend to have such elements as well. When people in various cultures were asked which member of each of these pairs was more threatening, they consistently chose those, shown here on the left, containing triangular and diagonal elements. Cover this caption, then ask a few friends to try the same task. How many of them chose the left-hand elements as being more threatening?

called the smile that occurs with real happiness the *Duchenne smile* (pronounced "do-SHEN"), after the French researcher who first noticed a difference between spontaneous, happy smiles and posed smiles. A genuine, Duchenne smile includes contractions of the muscles around the eyes (creating a distinctive wrinkling of the skin in these areas), as well as contractions of the muscles that raise the lips and cheeks. Few people can successfully contract the muscles around the eyes during a posed smile, so this feature can be used to distinguish "lying smiles" from genuine ones (Frank, Ekman, & Friesen, 1993). In one study, the Duchenne smile was highly correlated with reports of positive emotions experienced while people watched a movie, as well as with a pattern of brain waves known to be associated with positive emotions. These relationships did not appear for other types of smiles (Ekman, Davidson, & Friesen, 1990).

Learning About Emotions The effects of learning are seen in a child's growing range of emotional expressions. Although infants begin with a set of innate emotional responses, they soon learn to imitate facial expressions and use them to express more and more emotions. In time, these expressions become more precise and personalized so that a particular expression conveys a clear message to anyone who knows that person well.

If facial expressions become too personalized, however, no one will know what the expressions mean, and they will fail to bring responses from others. Operant shaping, described in the chapter on learning, probably helps keep emotional expressions within certain limits. If you could not see other people's facial expressions or observe their responses to yours, you might show fewer, or less intense, facial signs of emotion. In fact, as congenitally blind people grow older, their facial expressions tend to become less animated (Izard, 1977).

As children grow, they learn an *emotion culture*—rules that govern what emotions are appropriate in what circumstances and what emotional expressions are allowed. These rules can vary between genders and from culture to culture (LaFrance, Hecht, & Paluck, 2003). For example, TV news cameras showed that men in the U.S. military being deployed to the Persian Gulf tended to keep their emotions in check as they said goodbye to wives, girlfriends, and parents. However, many male soldiers in Italy—where mother-son ties are particularly strong—wailed with dismay and wept openly as they left for duty in Kosovo. In a laboratory study, when viewing a distressing movie with a group of peers, Japanese students exerted much more control over their facial expressions than did North American students. When they watched the film while alone, however, the Japanese students' faces showed the same emotional expressions as those of the North American students (Ekman, Friesen, & Ellsworth, 1972).

Emotion cultures shape how people describe and categorize feelings, resulting in both similarities and differences across cultures (Russell, 1991). At least five of the seven basic emotions listed in an ancient Chinese book called the *Li Chi*—joy, anger, sadness, fear, love, disliking, and liking—are considered primary emotions by most Western theorists. Yet while English has over 500 emotion-related words, some emotion words in other languages have no English meaning. The Czech word *litost* apparently has no English word equivalent: "It designates a feeling that is the synthesis of many others; grief, sympathy, remorse, and an indefinable longing. . . . Litost is a state of torment caused by a sudden insight into one's own miserable self" (Russell, 1991). The Japanese word *ijirashii* also has no English equivalent; it describes the feeling of seeing a praiseworthy person overcoming an obstacle (Russell, 1991).

Similarly, other cultures have no equivalent for some English emotion words. Many cultures do not see anger and sadness as different, for example. The Ilongot, a head-hunting group in the Philippines, have only one word, *liget*, for both anger and grief (Russell, 1991). Tahitians have different words for forty-six types of anger, but no word for sadness and, apparently, no concept of it. One westerner described a Tahitian man as being sad over separation from his wife and child. The man himself said that he felt *pe'a pe'a*—a general word for feeling ill, troubled, or fatigued—and did not attribute it to the separation.

Social Referencing Facial expressions, tone of voice, body postures, and gestures not only communicate information about the emotion someone is experiencing; they can also influence others' behavior, especially the behavior of people who are not sure what to do. An inexperienced chess player, for instance, might reach out to move the queen, catch sight of a spectator's grimace, and infer that another move would be better. The process of letting another person's emotional state guide our own behavior is called **social referencing** (Campos, 1980). This process begins early; even three-month-old infants will look in the direction in which an adult's eyes have moved (Hood, Willen, & Driver, 1998).

social referencing   A phenomenon in which other people's facial expressions, tone of voice, and bodily gestures serve as guidelines for how to behave in uncertain situations.

The visual cliff studies described in the sensation and perception chapter have been used to create an uncertain situation for infants. To reach its mother, an infant in these experiments must cross the visual cliff. If the apparent drop-off is very small or very large, there is no doubt about what to do. One-year-olds crawl across in the first case and stay put in the second case. However, if the apparent drop-off is shallow enough to create uncertainty (say, two feet), the infant relies on its mother's facial expressions to decide what to do. In one study, mothers were asked to make either a fearful or a joyful face. When the mothers made a fearful face, no infant crossed the glass floor. But when they made a joyful face, most infants crossed (Sorce et al., 1981). Here is yet another example of the adaptive value of sending, and receiving, emotional communications.

active review Motivation and Emotion

Linkages

As noted in the introductory chapter, all of psychology's sub-fields are related to one another. Our discussion of motivational conflicts and stress illustrates just one way in which the topic of this chapter, motivation and emotion, is linked to the subfield of health psychology, discussed in the chapter on health, stress, and coping. The Linkages diagram shows ties to two other subfields as well, and there are many more ties throughout the book. Looking for linkages among subfields will help you see how they all fit together and help you better appreciate the big picture that is psychology.

Summary

Motivation refers to factors that influence the initiation, direction, intensity, and persistence of behavior. Emotion and motivation are often linked: Motivation can influence emotion, and people are often motivated to seek certain emotions.

CONCEPTS AND THEORIES OF MOTIVATION

▶ **Where does motivation come from?**

Focusing on a *motive* often reveals a single theme within apparently diverse behaviors. The many sources of motivation fall into four categories: biological factors, emotional factors, cognitive factors, and social factors.

An early argument held that motivation follows from *instincts*—automatic, involuntary, and unlearned behavior patterns consistently "released" by particular stimuli. Modern versions of *instinct theory* are seen in evolutionary accounts of helping, aggression, mate selection, and other aspects of social behavior. *Drive reduction theory* is based on *homeostasis,* a tendency to maintain equilibrium in a physical or behavioral process. When disruption of equilibrium creates a *need* of some kind, people are motivated to reduce the resulting *drive* by behaving in some way that satisfies the need and restores balance. *Primary drives* are unlearned; *secondary drives* are learned. According to the *arousal theory* of motivation, people are motivated to behave in ways that maintain a level of *arousal* that is optimal for their functioning. Finally, *incentive theory* highlights behaviors that are motivated by attaining desired stimuli (positive incentives) and avoiding undesirable ones (negative incentives). Each of these theories has contributed to our understanding the basis for various kinds of motivated behavior.

HUNGER AND EATING

▶ **What makes me start eating, and stop eating?**

Hunger and eating are controlled by a complex mix of learning, culture, and biology. The desire to eat *(hunger)* or to stop eating *(satiety)* depends on signals from the stomach and from blood-borne substances such as glucose, fatty acids, amino acids, insulin, and leptin. Activity in the ventromedial nucleus of the hypothalamus results in satiety, whereas activity in the lateral hypothalamus results in hunger. However, the control of eating is more complicated than that. Other areas of the hypothalamus, such as the paraventricular nucleus, are also involved. Further, several neurotransmitters act in various regions of the hypothalamus to create hunger for specific types of foods. Eating may also be influenced by the flavor of food and by appetite for the pleasure of food. Food selection is influenced by many factors, including social contexts and cultural traditions.

Obesity has been linked to overconsumption of certain kinds of foods, low energy metabolism, genetic factors, and even viruses. People suffering from *anorexia nervosa* starve themselves to avoid becoming fat. Those who suffer from *bulimia nervosa* engage in binge eating, followed by purging through self-induced vomiting or laxatives.

SEXUAL BEHAVIOR

▶ **How often does the average person have sex?**

Sexual motivation and behavior result from a rich interplay of biology and culture. Sexual stimulation produces a *sexual response cycle,* a predictable pattern of physiological arousal before, during, and after sexual activity. *Sex hormones,* which include male hormones *(androgens)* and female hormones *(estrogens* and *progestins),* occur in different relative amounts in both sexes. They can have organizing effects, which create physical differences in the brain, and activating effects, which temporarily increase the desire for sex.

Gender-role learning, educational experiences, media influences, and family dynamics are examples of cultural factors that can bring about variations in sexual attitudes and behaviors. Sexual orientation—*heterosexual, homosexual,* or *bisexual*—is increasingly viewed as a sociocultural variable that affects many other aspects of behavior and mental processes. Although undoubtedly shaped by a lifetime of learning, sexual orientation appears to have strong biological roots.

Common male *sexual dysfunctions* include erectile disorder and premature ejaculation. Females may experience such problems as sexual arousal disorder.

ACHIEVEMENT MOTIVATION

▶ **Why do some people try harder than others to succeed?**

People gain esteem from achievement in many areas, including the workplace. The motive to succeed is called *need achievement.* Individuals with high achievement motivation strive for excellence; persist despite failures; and set challenging, but realistic, goals.

Workers are most satisfied when they are working toward their own goals and getting concrete feedback. Jobs that offer clear and specific goals, a variety of tasks, individual responsibility, and other intrinsic rewards are the most motivating. People tend to have a characteristic level of happiness, or *subjective well-being,* which is not necessarily related to the attainment of money, status, or other material goals.

RELATIONS AND CONFLICTS AMONG MOTIVES

▶ **Which motives move me most?**

People's behavior reflects many motives, some of which may be in conflict. Maslow proposed a hierarchy of five types of human motives, from meeting basic physiological needs to attaining self-actualization. Motives at the lowest levels, according to Maslow, must be at least partially satisfied before people can be motivated by higher-level goals.

Four basic types of motivational conflict have been identified: approach-approach, avoidance-avoidance, approach-avoidance, and multiple approach-avoidance conflicts. These conflicts act as stressors, and people caught in them often experience physical and psychological problems.

THE NATURE OF EMOTION

▶ **How do feelings differ from thoughts?**

An *emotion* is a temporary experience with negative or positive qualities that is felt with some intensity as happening to the self, is generated in part by a mental assessment of a situation, and is accompanied by both learned and innate physical responses.

Several brain mechanisms are involved in emotion, including the amygdala, in the limbic system. The expression of emotion through involuntary facial movement is controlled by the extrapyramidal motor system. Voluntary facial movements are controlled by the pyramidal motor system. The brain's right and left hemispheres play somewhat different roles in emotional expression. In addition to specific brain mechanisms, both the *sympathetic nervous system* and the *parasympathetic nervous system,* which are divisions of the autonomic nervous system, are involved in physiological changes that accompany emotional activation. The *fight-or-flight syndrome,* for example, follows from activation of the sympathetic nervous system.

THEORIES OF EMOTION

▶ **Is emotion in the heart, in the head, or both?**

James said that peripheral physiological responses are the primary source of emotion and that awareness of these responses constitutes emotional experience. James's peripheral theory is supported by evidence that, at least for several basic emotions, physiological responses are distinguishable enough for emotions to be generated in this way. Distinct facial expressions are linked to particular patterns of physiological change.

Cannon's central theory of emotion proposes that emotional experience is independent of bodily responses and that there is a direct experience of emotion based on activity of the central nervous system. Updated versions of this theory suggest that various parts of the central nervous system may be involved in different emotions and different aspects of emotional experience. Some pathways in the brain, such as the pathway from the thalamus to the amygdala, allow strong emotions to occur before conscious thought can take place. Specific parts of the brain appear to be responsible for the feelings of pleasure or pain in emotion.

Cognitive theories of emotion include the Schachter-Singer theory. It suggests that physiological responses are primary sources of emotion but that mental interpretation of these responses in light of the situation is required to label the emotion. This interpretation process depends on **attribution.** Attributing arousal from one situation to stimuli in another situation can produce **excitation transfer,** intensifying the emotion experienced in the second situation. Cognitive theorists such as Lazarus have argued that emotional experience is significantly affected by how we interpret events themselves, not just by how we interpret physiological responses to those events.

COMMUNICATING EMOTION

▶ **Which emotional expressions are innate, and which are learned?**

In humans, words, voice tones, postures, bodily movements, and facial movements and expressions are involved in communicating emotions. Darwin suggested that certain facial expressions of emotion are innate and universal, and that these expressions evolved because they effectively communicate one creature's emotional condition to other creatures. Some facial expressions of basic emotions do appear to be innate, and certain facial movements are universally associated with certain emotions.

Other emotional expressions are learned, and even innate expressions are modified by learning and social contexts. As children grow, they learn an emotion culture, the rules of emotional expression appropriate to their culture. Accordingly, the same emotion may be communicated by different facial expressions in different cultures. Especially in ambiguous situations, other people's emotional expressions may serve as a guide about what to do or what not to do, a phenomenon called **social referencing.**

Learn by Doing

Put It in Writing

Write a page or two about what goals you hope to achieve in life, what motivates you to strive for them, and how important it is for you to reach them. In light of our discussion about achievement and subjective well-being, consider the question of whether reaching your goals will make you happy and contented, or leave you always wanting more.

Personal Learning Activity

Videotape a session in which you ask a friend four questions such as "Who was the best teacher you ever had?" "What's the strangest thing that ever happened to you?" "What is your most surprising talent?" or "Where would you most like to live?" Ask your friend to give truthful answers to two of these questions, but to lie as convincingly as possible while answering the other two. Now play the tape for a group of people, and ask them to say which answers are true and which are lies. How well did your participants do? If they are like most people, they probably were right about half the time on this lie detection task (DePaulo, 1994). Did those who knew the person on the tape do any better than those who did not? If so, why do you think that happened? *For additional projects, see the Personal Learning Activities in the corresponding chapter of the study guide that accompanies this text.*

Step into Action

Courses

Health Psychology
Motivation and Emotion
Human Sexuality
Personality
Industrial-Organizational Psychology

Movies

Entrapment; The Edge; Rudy (motivation and motivational conflict)
The Heidi Chronicles (secondary drives)
La Cage aux Folles, Wild Reeds; Wilde (sexual orientation)
Wall Street (greed as motivation)
The Family Man (goal-driven behavior)

Books

Gelsey Kirkland, *Dancing on My Grave* (Doubleday, 1987) (eating disorders)
Joyce Murdoch and Deb Price, *Courting Justice: Gay Men and Lesbians v. the Supreme Court* (Basic Books, 2001) (homosexuality and the law)
Lillian Rubin, *Intimate Strangers: Men and Women Together* (Harper, 1983) (gender differences in intimacy and sexuality)
David C. Edwards, *Motivation and Emotion: Evolutionary, Physiological, Cognitive, and Social Influences* (AltaMira Press, 1998) (a basic introduction to the field of motivation and emotion)
Steven Pinker, *The Blank Slate: The Modern Denial of Human Nature* (Viking Press, 2002) (wide-ranging description of evolutionary and genetic explanations of motivation)

David Goldstein (Ed.), *The Management of Eating Disorders and Obesity* (Humana Press, 1999) (a summary of research and treatment of eating disorders)

William H. Masters, Virginia E. Johnson, and Robert C. Kolodny, *Heterosexuality* (Grammercy Press, 1998) (an overview of sexuality between males and females)

Jan Clausen and Martin Duberman, *Beyond Gay or Straight: Understanding Sexual Orientation* (Chelsea House, 1996) (an overview of the origins of sexual orientation)

Aldert Vrij, *Detecting Lies and Deceit: The Psychology of Lying and Implications for Professional Practice* (Wiley, 2000) (a summary of various approaches)

David Lykken, *Happiness: The Nature and Nurture of Joy and Contentment* (Griffin, 2000) (a summary of research on the "happiness set point" and other aspects of subjective well-being)

Antonia Damasio, *Looking for Spinoza* (Harcourt, 2003) (a neurologist takes the position that emotions are primarily bodily sensations)

The Web

The World Wide Web is a good source of additional information about the science of psychology, provided you use it carefully and think critically about the information you find. The web site that accompanies this text offers many resources relevant to this chapter. These resources include interactive NetLab exercises; Thinking Critically and Evaluating Research exercises; ACE chapter quizzes; recommended web links; and articles on current events, books, and movies. At http://college.hmco.com, select *Psychology* and then this textbook.

Review of Key Terms

Can you define each of the key terms in the chapter? Check your definitions against those on the pages listed in parentheses below or in the Glossary/Index at the end of the text.

androgens *(p. 293)*
anorexia nervosa *(p. 290)*
arousal *(p. 284)*
arousal theory *(p. 284)*
attribution *(p. 313)*
bisexual *(p. 295)*
bulimia nervosa *(p. 290)*
drive *(p. 283)*
drive reduction theory *(p. 283)*
emotion *(p. 306)*

estrogens *(p. 293)*
excitation transfer *(p. 313)*
fight-or-flight syndrome *(p. 307)*
heterosexual *(p. 295)*
homeostasis *(p. 283)*
homosexual *(p. 295)*
hunger *(p. 285)*
incentive theory *(p. 285)*
instinct theory *(p. 282)*
instincts *(p. 282)*

motivation *(p. 282)*
motive *(p. 282)*
need *(p. 283)*
need achievement *(p. 299)*
obesity *(p. 288)*
parasympathetic nervous system *(p. 307)*
primary drives *(p. 284)*
progestins *(p. 293)*
satiety *(p. 285)*

secondary drives *(p. 284)*
sex hormones *(p. 293)*
sexual dysfunctions *(p. 298)*
sexual response cycle *(p. 293)*
social referencing *(p. 318)*
subjective well-being *(p. 302)*
sympathetic nervous system *(p. 307)*

Multiple-Choice Self-Test

Select the best answer for each of the questions below. Then check your responses against the Answer Key at the end of the text.

1. Although most researchers do not believe in instinct theories of motivation, psychologists who advocate _____ theory argue that many aspects of human behavior are motivated by efforts to pass on our genes to the next generation.

   a. drive reduction
   b. evolutionary
   c. arousal
   d. incentive

2. Steve is cold, so he turns up the heat in his house. Soon it gets too warm, so he turns the heat down. This process is similar to the concept of

   a. homeostasis.
   b. secondary drive.
   c. incentive.
   d. arousal.

3. Lisbeth and Harriet work as instructors in an exercise class. After class, Lisbeth prefers to go home and read quietly, whereas Harriet is ready to party. Which theory of motivation best explains the difference between these two women?

   a. drive reduction
   b. incentive
   c. evolutionary
   d. arousal

4. Monica wants her daughter to get high grades, so she offers her $10 for each A that she earns and $5 for each B. Monica appears to believe in the _____ theory of motivation.

   a. drive reduction
   b. incentive
   c. evolutionary
   d. arousal

5. Ahmed is desperate to lose weight. To keep from eating, he buys an electrical device that allows him to stimulate various areas of his brain. Which areas should he stimulate if he wants his brain to help him reduce food intake?

   a. ventromedial nucleus and paraventricular nucleus
   b. lateral hypothalamus and ventromedial nucleus
   c. lateral hypothalamus and paraventricular nucleus
   d. thalamus and pineal gland

6. Ronia is on a diet, again! She is most likely to eat more food if she

   a. eats with a group of friends.
   b. eats by herself.
   c. knows her food culture.
   d. is guided by hunger rather than her appetite.

7. Dr. Stefan is working in the emergency room when a very dehydrated young woman comes in. She is of normal weight, but a medical exam reveals nutritional imbalances and intestinal damage. Which eating disorder is she most likely suffering from?

   a. anorexia nervosa   c. obesity
   b. bulimia nervosa   d. ventromedial destruction

8. The University of Chicago's National Health and Social Life Survey found that people in the United States

   a. are more sexually active than previously thought.
   b. have sex more often if they are not in an exclusive relationship.
   c. have sex less often and with fewer people than previously thought.
   d. do not enjoy sex very much.

9. Immediately after having orgasms, which of the following will Jim, but not Charlene, be most likely to experience?

   a. another orgasm   c. a refractory period
   b. a plateau   d. excitement

10. Edwina wants her son, Egbert, to develop high need achievement and to be successful in life. According to research on need achievement, Edwina should do all of the following except

    a. encourage Egbert to try difficult tasks.
    b. encourage Egbert to avoid failure at all costs.
    c. give praise and rewards for success.
    d. read achievement-oriented stories to him.

11. Liang was playing a basketball-shooting game at the school fair. Because there were no prizes, he was allowed to shoot the ball from any distance between two and fifteen feet from the basket. The fact that Liang chose to shoot from six feet away suggests that he most likely has

    a. high need achievement.   c. high need to avoid success.
    b. low need achievement.   d. high need for affiliation.

12. According to Maslow, which of the following would you most likely do first if you were shipwrecked on a desert island?

    a. look for food and fresh water
    b. look for firewood
    c. start keeping a diary
    d. build a place to live

13. Jill would like to buy an expensive new stereo, but this would create a financial hardship for her. Jill is faced with a(n) _____ motivational conflict.

    a. approach-approach   c. approach-avoidance
    b. avoidance-avoidance   d. multiple approach-avoidance

14. When Debbie received bad news from her fiancé, she experienced the fight-or-flight syndrome. In other words, Debbie's

    a. parasympathetic nervous system was activated.
    b. sympathetic nervous system was activated.
    c. digestion and salivation were stimulated.
    d. respiration and heart rate slowed.

15. When people are afraid to do something, they are said to have "cold feet." The fact that fear is associated with decreased blood flow to the feet and hands supports _____ theory of emotion.

    a. James's peripheral   c. Schachter's cognitive
    b. Cannon's central   d. Lazarus's cognitive

16. After she finished a vigorous workout, Lydia saw Thaddeus walk into the gym, and she instantly fell in love. This is an example of _____, which is consistent with _____ theory of emotion.

    a. social referencing; James's
    b. social referencing; Schachter's
    c. excitation transfer; James's
    d. excitation transfer; Schachter's

17. When Yatsira saw someone trying to open her car door while she was stopped at a light, her heart raced, and at the exact same time she felt fear. This is most consistent with _____ theory of emotion.

    a. James's   c. Schachter's
    b. Cannon's   d. Lazarus's

18. As Jarrod got older, he learned that he could not express his anger by throwing his toys. Jarrod is learning

    a. to use facial feedback.
    b. Darwin's universal rules.
    c. to use social referencing.
    d. his emotion culture.

19. Suppose that Dick, Sally, Harry, and Tommy, the space aliens on the TV show *Third Rock from the Sun*, first came to earth in your backyard. They tell you they want to learn how to communicate their emotions so that humans will understand them. What should you focus on teaching them?

    a. body postures   c. hand gestures
    b. facial movements   d. voice inflections

20. Sam is unsure how to react to a comment from one of his friends, so he glances at his girlfriend, Diane, to see what her reaction is. In doing so, he is using

    a. facial feedback.   c. attribution.
    b. social referencing.   d. excitation transfer.

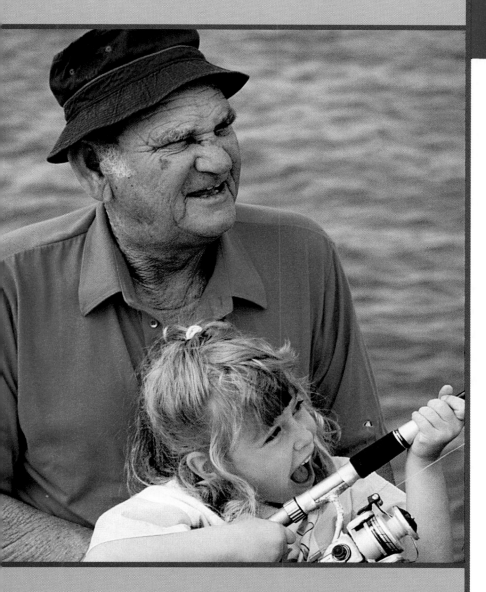

9

Human Development

PREVIEW

A colt begins walking within an hour of being born, but it typically takes a human baby

about a year to reach this milestone—a year in which the baby also first smiles, eats solid food, learns to recognize familiar people and objects, and gets ready to talk, to name just a few accomplishments. Four years later, the child is entering school, where learning, development, and change continue. Ten years after that, the adolescent is still changing and developing, becoming more independent and mature with each passing day. In young adulthood, change and development take the form of decisions about jobs, families, and relationships—decisions whose effects echo throughout adulthood. Development occurs in late adulthood, too, as the person adjusts to the joys and challenges of growing older. Developmental psychologists explore how people change, grow, and achieve continuity over the course of the life span.

Reading this chapter will help you to answer the following questions:

▶ **What does "genetic influence" mean?**

▶ **Why should pregnant women stay away from tobacco and alcohol?**

▶ **How do babies think?**

▶ **How do infants become attached to their caregivers?**

▶ **What threatens adolescents' self-esteem?**

▶ **What developmental changes occur in adulthood?**

Over the last several years, the tragedy of school shooting sprees has plagued all too many towns and cities in the United States and Canada. And though the number of school homicides has been dropping, this trend is of little solace to the friends and families of the more than one hundred students or teachers who have died or been injured in these horrific events. Why do these things happen? In each case, the killers were boys ranging in age from six to eighteen. Had they watched too many violent movies and television shows? Were their actions the fault of a "gun culture" that allows children access to firearms? Had they been victims of abuse and neglect? Were their parents too strict—or not strict enough? Did they come from "broken homes" or witness physical violence within their own families? Did they behave violently because they were going through a difficult "stage," because they had not been taught right from wrong, because they wanted to impress their peers, because males are more aggressive in general, or because their brains were "defective"? Or were they just "bad kids"?

These are the kinds of questions for which developmental psychologists try to find answers. They look into when certain kinds of behavior first appear, how those behaviors change with age, and whether the changes are sudden or gradual. They explore how development in one area, such as moral reasoning, relates to development in other areas, such as aggressive behavior. Developmental psychologists attempt to discover whether

A DEADLY CHILD Andrew Golden was barely out of diapers when he was given camouflage clothing and taught to fire a hunting rifle. In March 1998, at the age of eleven, he and a thirteen-year-old friend, Mitchell Johnson, used their rifles to kill four classmates and a teacher at their elementary school in Jonesboro, Arkansas. Many youngsters learn to hunt; what led these two to commit murder? Researchers in developmental psychology study the genetic and environmental factors that underlie violent aggression and many other patterns of behavior and mental processes.

developmental psychology The psychological specialty that documents the course of people's social, emotional, moral, and intellectual development over the life span.

maturation Natural growth or change triggered by biological factors independent of the environment.

everyone develops at the same rate and, if not, whether slow starters ever catch up to early bloomers. They ask how and why some children develop into well-adjusted, socially competent, caring individuals, whereas others become murderers; or why some adolescents go on to win honors in college and others drop out of high school. They seek to explain how development through infancy, childhood, and adolescence is affected by both genetics and the environment. They analyze the extent to which development is a product of what we arrive with at birth (our inherited, biological *nature*) and the extent to which it is a product of what the world provides (the *nurture* of the environment). And, of course, they also study the development that occurs over the years of adulthood and try to determine how these changes are related to earlier abilities and the events of life. In short, **developmental psychology** is concerned with the course and causes of developmental changes over a person's entire lifetime.

This chapter focuses on many of these changes, beginning with the physical and biological changes that take place from the moment of conception to the moment of birth.

Exploring Human Development

▶ **What does "genetic influence" mean?**

Arguments about how nature and nurture affect development can be traced back through centuries of philosophy. In essays published in the 1690s, the British empiricist philosopher John Locke argued for the dominance of nurture. He believed that what happens in childhood has a profound and permanent effect on the individual. Empiricists saw the newborn as a blank slate, or *tabula rasa*. Adults write on that slate, said Locke, as they teach children about the world and how to behave in it. About seventy years later, Jean-Jacques Rousseau (pronounced "roo-SOH"), a French philosopher, argued just the opposite, claiming that children are capable of discovering how the world operates and how they should behave without instruction from adults. According to Rousseau, children should be allowed to grow as nature commands, with little guidance or pressure from parents.

The first American psychologist to investigate systematically the role of nature in behavior was Arnold Gesell (pronounced "geh-ZELL"). In the early 1900s, Gesell made many observations of children of all ages. He found that motor skills, such as standing and walking, picking up a cube, and throwing a ball, develop in a fixed sequence of stages in all children, as illustrated in Figure 9.1. Gesell argued that the order of the stages and the age at which they appear are determined by nature and relatively unaffected by nurture. Only under extreme conditions, such as famine, war, or poverty, he claimed, are children thrown off their biologically programmed timetable. This type of natural growth or change, which unfolds in a fixed sequence relatively independent of the environment, is called **maturation.** The broader term *development* encompasses not only maturation but also the behavioral and mental processes that are influenced by learning.

John B. Watson disagreed with Gesell's views. He argued that the environment, not nature, molds and shapes development. As described in the introductory chapter, Watson founded the behaviorist approach to psychology. In the early 1900s he began conducting experiments with children. From these experiments Watson inferred that children learn *everything,* from skills to fears. In his words, "There is no such thing as an inheritance of capacity, talent, temperament, mental constitution and characteristics. These things . . . depend on training that goes on mainly in the cradle" (Watson, 1925, pp. 74–75).

The Swiss psychologist Jean Piaget (pronounced "p-ah-ZHAY") was the first to suggest that nature and nurture work together, and that their influences are inseparable and interactive. Through a series of books published from the 1920s until his death in 1980, Piaget's ideas influenced the field of developmental psychology more than those of any other person before or since (Flavell, 1996).

figure 9.1

Motor Development

When did you start walking? The left end of each bar indicates the age at which 25 percent of the infants tested were able to perform a particular behavior; 50 percent of the babies were performing the behavior at the age indicated by the vertical line in the bars; the right end indicates the age at which 90 percent could do so (Frankenberg & Dodds, 1967). Although different infants, especially in different cultures, achieve milestones of motor development at slightly different ages, all infants—regardless of their ethnicity, social class, or temperament—achieve them in the same order.

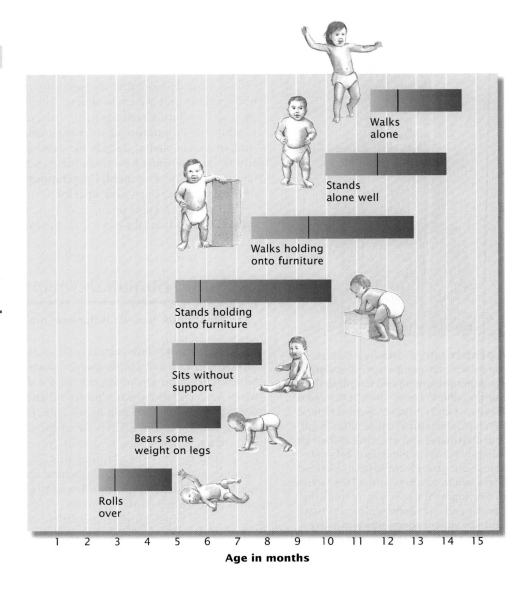

Age in months

Understanding Genetic Influence

Most developmental psychologists now accept Piaget's idea that both nature and nurture contribute to development. Guided by research in **behavioral genetics,** the study of how genes affect behavior, they explore how genes and the environment influence specific aspects of development. Their studies have demonstrated that nature and nurture jointly contribute to development in two ways. First, nature and nurture operate together to make all people *similar* in some respects. For example, nature influences all of us to achieve milestones of motor development in the same order and at roughly the same rate. But supportive nurture, in the form of proper nutrition and exercise, is also necessary to allow normal maturation to unfold. Second, nature and nurture operate together to make each person *unique.* The nature of inherited genes and the nurture of widely different family and cultural environments produce differences among individuals in athletic abilities, intelligence, speech patterns, personality, and many other dimensions (Cross & Markus, 1999; Plomin et al., 2002).

Behavioral geneticists are concerned with these *differences* between individuals or groups of individuals, not with the characteristics of a single individual. Consider height. Whether raised together or apart, identical twins (who have identical genes) are much more similar in height than fraternal twins (who share no more genes than other sib-

behavioral genetics   The study of the effect of genes on behavior.

lings) or unrelated individuals. This finding suggests that height is more strongly influenced by genes than by the environment. Does this mean that a person who is six feet tall grew, say, four of those feet because of genes and the other two feet because of environment? No. It means that more of the variability in height that we see among people can be explained by the genetic differences among them than by the environmental differences. In fact, genes do account for about 80 to 95 percent of the variability in height. If a person is, say, shorter than average, genetic reasons are probably the primary cause. We say "probably" because determination of a genetic influence on height refers only to the origins of average individual differences in the population. So even though the differences in people's heights are due mainly to genetic factors, a particular person's height could be due mainly to an early illness or other growth-stunting environmental factors.

To see how the logic of behavioral genetics applies to conclusions about psychological characteristics, suppose a researcher discovered that a certain personality trait is 50 percent heritable. This finding would mean that approximately half of the *differences between people* on that trait can be explained by genetic factors. It would not mean that each person inherits half of the trait and gets the other half from environmental influences. In other words, the results of behavioral genetics research allow us to draw general conclusions about the influence of nature and nurture on certain characteristics, but those conclusions do not necessarily apply to the origins of a *particular person's* characteristics. Keep in mind, too, that the effects of genes on our traits and behaviors are not always simple or inevitable. Complex traits such as intelligence and personality are influenced by many genes, as well as by many environmental factors. So genetic influence means just that: *influence* (Plomin et al., 2002). Genes can affect a trait without completely determining whether that trait will actually appear in a particular individual.

Genes and the Environment

The relative contributions of nature and nurture differ for specific aspects of development, but their influences on all human characteristics are forever intertwined. They are also mutually influential. Just as the environment encourages or discourages the expression of an individual's inherited characteristics, those inherited characteristics determine the individual's environment to some extent. In short, heredity creates predispositions that interact with the immediate environment, including family and teachers, books and computers (Caspi et al., 2002). This interaction is what produces developmental outcomes. Let's now consider how it all begins.

A TIGER IN TRAINING The development of human behavior is shaped by both heredity and environment—by nature and nurture. The joint and inseparable influence of these two factors in development is perfectly illustrated in the case of professional golfer Tiger Woods, shown here as a youngster with his father, who not only provided some of Tiger's genes but also served as his golf teacher.

Beginnings

▶ **Why should pregnant women stay away from tobacco and alcohol?**

Nowhere are the intertwined contributions of heredity and environment clearer than during the eventful nine months before birth, when a single fertilized egg develops into a functioning newborn infant.

Prenatal Development

The process of development begins when sperm from a father-to-be fertilizes the egg of a mother-to-be and forms a brand-new cell. Most human cells contain forty-six **chromosomes** (pronounced "KROH-muh-sohmz"), arranged in twenty-three matching pairs. Each chromosome is made up of thousands of **genes,** the biochemical units of heredity that govern the development of an individual. Genes, in turn, are composed of **deoxyribonucleic acid (DNA).** (*Deoxyribonucleic* is pronounced "dee-OKS-ee-rye-boh-noo-KLAY-ic.") The DNA in genes provides coded messages that serve as blueprints for

chromosomes Long, thin structures in every biological cell that contain genetic information in the form of genes.

genes Hereditary units, located on chromosomes, that contain biological instructions inherited from both parents, providing the blueprint for physical development.

deoxyribonucleic acid (DNA) The molecular structure of a gene that provides the genetic code.

A FETUS AT TWELVE WEEKS   At this point in prenatal development, the fetus can kick its legs, curl its toes, make a fist, turn its head, squint, open its mouth, swallow, and take a few "breaths" of amniotic fluid.

embryo   The developing individual from two weeks to two months after fertilization.

fetus   The developing individual from the third month after conception until birth.

teratogens   Harmful substances, such as alcohol and other drugs, that can cause birth defects.

critical period   An interval during which certain kinds of growth must occur if development is to proceed normally.

constructing every aspect of a physical human being, including eye color, height, blood type, inherited disorders, and the like. All of this information fits in less space than the period that ends this sentence.

New cells in the body are constantly being produced by the division of existing cells. Most of the body's cells divide through a process called *mitosis* (pronounced "mye-TOH-sis"), in which the cell's chromosomes duplicate themselves so that each new cell contains copies of the twenty-three pairs of chromosomes in the original cell.

A different kind of cell division occurs when a male's sperm cells and a female's egg cells, called *ova*, are formed. This process is called *meiosis* (pronounced "mye-OH-sis"). In meiosis, the chromosome pairs are not copied. Instead, they are randomly split and rearranged, leaving each new sperm and egg cell with just one member of each chromosome pair, or twenty-three *single* chromosomes. No two of these special new cells are quite the same, and none contains an exact copy of the person who produced it. So, at conception, when a male's sperm penetrates, or *fertilizes,* the female's ovum, a truly new cell is formed. The fertilized cell, called a *zygote,* carries the usual twenty-three pairs of chromosomes, but half of each pair comes from the mother and half from the father. The zygote represents a unique heritage—a complete genetic code for a new person that combines randomly selected aspects from both parents. The zygote divides first into copies of itself; then it divides and redivides into the billions of specialized cells that form a complete new human being.

Stages of Prenatal Development   The first two weeks after conception are called the *germinal,* or *zygotic,* stage of development. During this stage, rapidly dividing cells form a neural tube, which will become the central nervous system. By the end of the second week of cell division, the zygote has become a cell mass called an **embryo** (pronounced "EM-bree-oh"). During the *embryonic stage* of development, the heart, nervous system, stomach, esophagus, and ovaries or testes form. By two months, when the embryonic stage ends, the embryo looks decidedly human, with eyes, ears, nose, jaw, mouth, and lips. The tiny arms have elbows, hands, and stubby fingers; the legs have knees, ankles, and toes.

The seven-month period remaining until birth is called the *fetal stage* of prenatal development. During this stage, the various organs grow and function more efficiently. By the end of the third month, the **fetus** can kick, make a fist, turn its head, open its mouth, swallow, and frown. In the sixth month, the eyelids, which have been sealed, open. The fetus is now capable of making sucking movements and has a well-developed grasp, taste buds, eyebrows, and eyelashes.

By the end of the seventh month, the organ systems, though immature, are all functional. In the eighth and ninth months, the fetus becomes sensitive to a variety of outside sounds and responds to light and touch. Studies show, for example, that fetuses can recognize their mother's voice and that newborns prefer to listen to recordings in the same language—Spanish or English—that they heard from inside the womb as their parents spoke (Kisilevsky et al., 2003; Moon, Cooper, & Fifer, 1993).

Prenatal Risks   During prenatal development, a spongy organ called the *placenta* sends nutrients from the mother to the developing baby and carries away wastes. It also screens out many potentially harmful substances, including most bacteria. This screening is imperfect, however: Gases, viruses, nicotine, alcohol, and other drugs can pass through. Severe damage can occur if the baby's mother takes certain drugs, is exposed to certain toxic substances such as mercury, or has certain illnesses while organs are forming in the embryonic stage. A baby whose mother has rubella (German measles) during the third or fourth week after conception has a 50 percent chance of being born blind, deaf, or mentally retarded or of having a heart malformation. If the mother has rubella later in the pregnancy, after the eyes, ears, brain, and heart have formed, the likelihood that the baby will have one of these defects is substantially less.

Harmful substances, such as drugs or radiation, that invade the womb and result in birth defects are called **teratogens** (pronounced "tuh-RAT-uh-jens"). Teratogens are especially damaging in the embryonic stage, because it is a **critical period** in prenatal development, a time during which certain kinds of growth must occur if development is to proceed normally. If the heart, eyes, ears, hands, and feet do not appear during the embryonic stage, they cannot form later on. And if they form incorrectly, the defects will be permanent. Because the embryonic stage begins just two weeks after conception, the organ systems of the embryo can be forming even before the mother is aware of being pregnant. Nevertheless, even accidental exposure to teratogens during the embryonic stage can have devastating effects on the embryo. Later, during the fetal stage, the environment provided by the mother affects the baby's size, behavior, intelligence, and health rather than the formation of organs and limbs.

Critical factors for embryonic and fetal development include the mother's health and age; her nutrition before and during pregnancy; the emotional and physical stresses she experiences; and the nicotine, alcohol, and other drugs she may consume. For example, when a mother-to-be smokes cigarettes, she constricts the flow of blood and oxygen to her baby. The baby's delicate lungs, heart, and circulatory system suffer with each cigarette. Nicotine, a drug contained in tobacco, causes irregular heartbeat and many other harmful effects on the developing baby. No wonder that maternal smoking during pregnancy has been identified as a potential risk factor for low birth weight, respiratory problems, irritability, and attention deficit hyperactivity disorder (Gilliland, Li, & Peters, 2001; Law et al., 2003; Milberger et al., 1997).

Alcohol also threatens normal prenatal development. Babies born to women who abuse alcohol have a 44 percent chance of suffering from **fetal alcohol syndrome,** a pattern of defects that includes mental retardation and malformations of the face. Fetal alcohol syndrome is linked to heavy drinking, but even moderate drinking—a glass or two of wine a day—can harm infants' intellectual functioning (Streissguth et al., 1999).

Of special concern today are the effects of other drugs on infants' development (e.g., Mereu et al., 2003). Pregnant women who use substances such as cocaine create a substantial risk for their fetuses, which do not yet have the enzymes necessary to break down the drug. "Cocaine babies," also called "crack babies," may be born premature, underweight, tense, and fussy (Inciardi, Surratt, & Saum, 1997). They may also suffer delayed physical growth. Their kidneys, genitals, or other organs may be malformed because the mothers' use of cocaine led to a loss of blood to these developing structures. Research also suggests that, like other premature and underweight babies, "cocaine babies" are more likely than full-term, normal-weight babies to develop cognitive, behavioral, and learning problems (Bhutta et al., 2002; Jefferis, Power, & Hertzman, 2002; Singer et al., 2001, 2002). However, it may be possible to reverse these effects; how well "cocaine babies" ultimately do in school may depend on how supportive their environment turns out to be (Begley, 1997).

The likelihood that harmful conditions and substances will affect a particular infant depends on a combination of (1) the infant's inherited strengths or weaknesses, (2) the stage of prenatal development during which the infant was exposed to a teratogen, and (3) the intensity of the teratogen. Defects are most likely when the negative effects of nature and nurture combine. The worst-case scenario is one in which a genetically vulnerable infant receives a strong dose of a damaging substance during a critical period of prenatal development.

Despite these dangers, mental or physical problems resulting from all harmful factors affect fewer than 10 percent of the babies born in the United States. The vast majority of fetuses are born at the end of their nine-month gestation averaging a healthy seven pounds and ready to continue a normal course of development in the world.

The Newborn

Determining what newborns can see, hear, or do is one of the most fascinating and frustrating challenges for researchers in developmental psychology. Babies are extremely difficult to study because they sleep about 70 percent of the time. When they are not sleeping, they are drowsy, crying, awake and active, or awake and inactive. It is only when they are in this last state, which is infrequent and lasts only a few minutes, that researchers can assess the infants' abilities.

fetal alcohol syndrome A pattern of defects found in babies born to women who drink heavily during pregnancy.

A BABY'S-EYE VIEW OF THE WORLD The top photograph simulates what a mother looks like to her infant at three months of age. Although their vision is blurry, infants particularly seem to enjoy looking at faces.

To do so, psychologists show infants objects or pictures and record where they look and for how long. They film the infants' eye movements and note changes in heart rates, sucking rates, brain waves, bodily movements, and skin conductance (a measure of perspiration that accompanies emotion) when objects are shown or sounds are made. From studies using these techniques, researchers have pieced together a fair picture of infants' sensory and motor abilities (Kellman & Banks, 1998).

Vision and Other Senses   At birth, infant vision is limited by immaturities in both the eye and the brain. Infants' eyes do not yet have a fovea, which is the retinal area on which images are focused. Their eye movements are slow and jerky. And pathways in the nervous system connecting the eye to the brain remain inefficient, as does the processing of visual information within the brain. Researchers estimate that newborns have 20:300 eyesight; that is, an object 20 feet away looks the same to a newborn as it would if viewed from 300 feet by an adult with normal vision. So infants cannot see small objects across the room, and their vision is blurry. However, they can see large objects up close—the distance at which most interactions with caregivers take place. Infants look longest at what they can see best: large patterns with the most elements, the most movement, the clearest contours, and the greatest amount of contrast.

Newborns actively use their senses to explore the world around them. At first they attend to sights and sounds for only short periods, but gradually their attention span lengthens, and their exploration becomes more systematic. In the first two months, they focus only on the edges of objects, but after two months of age, they scan whole objects (Banks & Salapatek, 1983). Then, when they see an object, they get all the information they can from it before going on to something new (Hunter & Ames, 1988). Newborns stare at human faces longer than at other figures (Valenza et al., 1996). They are particularly interested in eyes, as shown in their preference for faces that are looking directly at them (Farroni et al., 2002).

At two or three days of age, newborns can hear soft voices and notice differences between tones about one note apart on the musical scale (Aslin, Jusczyk, & Pisoni, 1998). In addition, they turn their heads toward sounds (Clifton, 1992). But their hearing is not as sharp as that of adults' until well into childhood. This condition is not merely a hearing problem; it also reflects an inability to listen selectively to some sounds over others (Bargones & Werner, 1994). As infants grow, they develop sensory capacities and the skill to use them.

Infants pay special attention to speech. When they hear someone talking, they open their eyes wider and search for the speaker. Infants also prefer certain kinds of speech. They like rising tones spoken by women or children (Sullivan & Horowitz, 1983). They also like high-pitched, exaggerated, and expressive speech. In other words, they like to hear the "baby talk" used by most adults in all cultures when talking to babies (Fernald, 1990).

Newborns also like certain smells and tastes better than others. When given something sweet to drink, they suck longer and slower, pause for shorter periods, and smile and lick their lips (Ganchrow, Steiner, & Daher, 1983). Within a few days after birth, breastfed babies prefer the odor of their own mother to that of another mother (Porter et al, 1992).

Reflexes and Motor Skills   In the first weeks and months after birth, babies show involuntary, unlearned reactions called **reflexes.** These swift, automatic movements occur in response to external stimuli. Figure 9.2 illustrates the *grasping reflex,* one of more than twenty reflexes that have been observed in newborn infants. Another is the *rooting reflex,* whereby the infant turns its mouth toward a finger or nipple that touches its cheek. And the newborn exhibits the *sucking reflex* in response to anything that touches its lips. Many of these reflexive behaviors evolved because they help infants to survive. The absence of reflexes in a newborn signals problems in brain development. So does a failure of reflexes to disappear as brain development during the first three or four months allows the infant to control muscles voluntarily.

Voluntary control permits the development of motor skills, allowing the infant to roll over, sit up, crawl, stand, and walk. Until a few years ago, most developmental psychologists accepted Gesell's view that, except under extreme environmental conditions, these motor abilities occur spontaneously as the central nervous system and muscles mature.

reflexes   Simple, involuntary, unlearned behaviors directed by the spinal cord without instructions from the brain.

figure 9.2

Reflexes in the Newborn

When a finger is pressed into a newborn's palm, the *grasping reflex* causes the infant to hold on tightly enough to suspend its entire weight. And when a newborn is held upright over a flat surface, the *stepping reflex* leads to walking movements.

Research demonstrates, however, that maturation does not tell the whole story, even in normal environments (Thelen, 1995).

Psychologists have discovered, for example, that motor development depends on infants' active experimentation. In one study, researchers observed six infants as they learned to crawl on their hands and knees (Freedland & Bertenthal, 1994). Once they had developed sufficient muscle strength to support their abdomens, the infants tried various crawling styles—moving backward, moving one limb at a time, using the arms only, and so on. After a week or two of trial and error, all six infants arrived at the same method: moving the right arm and left leg together, then the left arm and right leg. This pattern turned out to be the most efficient way of getting around quickly without tipping over. Such observations suggest that the brain does not have a "crawling generator" that programs exactly how and when infants crawl. Instead, as maturation increases infants' strength and readiness, they try out various motor patterns and select the ones that work best (Nelson, 1999).

We know of a mother who tried to teach her infant, Rob, to crawl because he was not learning on his own. First she built a ramp surrounded by pillows for him to inch down. Placing Rob at the top of the gentle slope, she hoped gravity would help him move. No luck. Then she built a padded skateboard and put Rob on it with a safety belt so that his arms dangled to the floor. Did he paddle along and get the mobility idea? No, he threw up on the skateboard. In desperation, his mother asked her pediatrician why Rob did not crawl. The answer: Rob was at the 90th percentile for height and the 95th percentile for weight, so his body was simply too heavy for his immature arm muscles to support. His maturation had increased his readiness, but he didn't have the strength to try out motor patterns for crawling. This was one milestone he (and his mother) would just have to miss. Rob never crawled, but he started walking—and running—on his first birthday! Except for the skateboard, perhaps, Rob's story is not that unusual. Many children—especially those who sleep on their backs, as doctors recommend—go from sitting to walking without ever crawling first (Kolata & Maekel, 2001).

In other words, milestones of motor development result from a combination of maturation and experience, not from the unfolding of a sequence that is genetically etched in the brain. And, as always, nature and nurture influence each other. The brain controls developing behavior, but its own development is affected by experience, including efforts at building motor skills.

Infancy and Childhood: Cognitive Development

► **How do babies think?**

In a relatively short time, a tiny infant becomes a person who can read a book, write a poem, and argue logically for access to the family's new computer. What leads to the dramatic shifts in thinking, knowing, and remembering that occur between early infancy and later childhood? Researchers studying *cognitive development* try to answer this question.

The Development of Knowledge: Piaget's Theory

Foremost among these researchers was Jean Piaget, who dedicated his life to a search for the origins of intelligence and the factors that lead to changes in knowledge over the life span. Piaget was the first to chart the journey from the simple reflexes of the newborn to the complex understandings of the adolescent. Although his theory turned out to be incomplete, and in some respects incorrect, his ideas about cognitive development are still guiding research (Fischer & Hencke, 1996).

Intensive observations of infants (including his own) and extensive interviews with children led Piaget to propose that cognitive development proceeds in a series of distinct stages, or periods. He believed that all children's thinking goes through the same stages, in the same order, without skipping. (Table 9.1 outlines these stages.) According to Piaget, the thinking of infants is different from the thinking of children, which in turn is different from that of adolescents. He said that children are not just miniature adults, and they are not dumber than adults; they just think in completely different ways at different stages of development. In other words, entering each stage involves a *qualitative* change from whatever preceded it, much as a caterpillar is transformed into a butterfly.

Building Blocks of Development   To explain how infants and children move to ever higher stages of understanding and knowledge, Piaget introduced the concept of *schemas* as the basic units of knowledge, the building blocks of intellectual development. As noted in the chapters on sensation and perception and on learning, **schemas** are the mental images or generalizations that form as people experience the world. Schemas, in other words, organize past experiences and provide a framework for understanding future experiences.

At first, infants form simple schemas. For example, a sucking schema consolidates their experiences of sucking into images of what objects can be sucked on (bottles, fingers, pacifiers) and what kinds of sucking can be done (soft and slow, speedy and vigorous). Later, children form more complex schemas, such as a schema for tying a knot or making a bed. Still later, adolescents form schemas about what it is to be in love.

table 9.1

Piaget's Periods of Cognitive Development

According to Piaget, a predictable set of features characterizes each period of children's cognitive development. The ages associated with the stages are approximate; Piaget realized that some children move through the stages slightly faster or slower than others.

Period	Activities and Achievements
Sensorimotor Birth–2 years	Infants discover aspects of the world through their sensory impressions, motor activities, and coordination of the two. They learn to differentiate themselves from the external world. They learn that objects exist even when they are not visible and that they are independent of the infants' own actions. Infants gain some appreciation of cause and effect.
Preoperational 2–4 years 4–7 years	Children cannot yet manipulate and transform information in logical ways, but they now can think in images and symbols. They become able to represent something with something else, acquire language, and play games of pretend. Intelligence at this stage is said to be intuitive, because children cannot make general, logical statements.
Concrete operational 7–11 years	Children can understand logical principles that apply to concrete external objects. They can appreciate that certain properties of an object remain the same, despite changes in appearance, and they can sort objects into categories. They can appreciate the perspective of another viewer. They can think about two concepts, such as longer and wider, at the same time.
Formal operational Over 11 years	Only adolescents and adults can think logically about abstractions, can speculate, and can consider what might or what ought to be. They can work in probabilities and possibilities. They can imagine other worlds, especially ideal ones. They can reason about purely verbal or logical statements. They can relate any element or statement to any other, manipulate variables in a scientific experiment, and deal with proportions and analogies. They can reflect on their own activity of thinking.

schemas   Mental representations of what we know and expect about the world.

assimilation   The process of taking in new information about objects by using existing schemas on objects that fit those schemas.

accommodation   The process of modifying schemas as an infant tries out familiar schemas on objects that do not fit them.

sensorimotor period   According to Piaget, the first stage of cognitive development, when the infant's mental activity is confined to sensory perception and motor skills.

object permanence   The knowledge that an object exists even when it is not in view.

figure 9.3

Accommodation

Because the bars of the playpen are in the way, this child discovers that her schema for grasping and pulling objects toward her will not work. So she adjusts, or accommodates, her schema to achieve her goal.

Two complementary processes guide this development: assimilation and accommodation. In **assimilation,** infants and children take in information about new objects by trying out existing schemas and finding schemas that the new objects will fit. They *assimilate* the new objects into their existing schemas. So when an infant is given a new toy, he will suck on it, thus assimilating it into the sucking schema he has developed with his bottle and pacifier. In the same way, a toddler who sees a butterfly for the first time may assimilate it into her "birdie" schema, because, like a bird, it's colorful and it flies. Now suppose an older toddler encounters a large dog. How she assimilates this new experience depends on her existing schema of dogs. If she has had positive experiences with the family dog, she will have a positive schema, and expecting the dog to behave like her pet, she will greet it happily. In other words, past experiences affect what and how children think about new ones.

Sometimes, like Cinderella's sisters squeezing their oversized feet into the glass slipper, people distort information about a new object to make it fit an existing schema. When squeezing won't work, though, people are forced to change, or accommodate, their schemas to the new objects. In **accommodation,** the person tries out familiar schemas on a new object, finds that the schemas cannot be made to fit the object, and changes the schemas so that they will fit (see Figure 9.3). So if we give a baby boy a cup, he will try to suck on it and wave it. But he soon discovers that he can put only the edge in his mouth, and to wave it, it is best to hold onto the handle. Similarly, the toddler will refine her "doggie" schema if she meets a snarling stray and discovers that her original schema does not extend to all dogs.

Sensorimotor Development Piaget (1952) called the first stage of cognitive development the **sensorimotor period,** a time when mental activity is confined to schemas about sensory functions, such as seeing and hearing, and to schemas about motor skills, such as grasping and sucking. As motor skills develop and voluntary actions replace reflexes, babies elaborate these simple schemas into complex ones, such as waving and shaking. Later schemas include inserting and building.

Piaget believed that during the sensorimotor stage, infants can form schemas only of objects and actions that are present—things they can see, hear, or touch. They cannot think about absent objects, he said, because they cannot act on them; thinking, for infants, is doing. They do not lie in the crib thinking about Mother or their teddy bear, because they are not yet able to form schemas that are mental representations of objects and actions that are not present.

The sensorimotor period ends when infants become able to form such mental representations. At that point, they can think about objects or actions when the objects are not visible or the actions are not occurring. This milestone, according to Piaget, frees the child from the here-and-now of the sensory environment. It allows for the development of thought. One sign of this milestone is the child's ability to find a hidden object. This behavior reflects the infant's knowledge that an object exists even if it cannot be seen, touched, or sucked. Piaget called this knowledge **object permanence.**

Piaget believed that before infants acquire a knowledge of object permanence, they do not search for objects that are placed out of sight. For infants, out of sight is literally out of mind. The first evidence that object permanence is developing, he said, appears when infants are four to eight months old. At this age, for the first time, they can recognize a familiar object even if part of it is hidden: They know it's their bottle even if they can see only the nipple peeking out from under the blanket. Infants now have some primitive mental representations of objects. If an object is completely hidden, however, they will not search for it.

Several months later, infants will search briefly for a hidden object, but their search is haphazard and ineffective. Not until they are about eighteen to twenty-four months old, said Piaget, do infants appear able to picture and follow events in their minds. They look for the object in places other than where they saw it last, sometimes in completely new places. According to Piaget, their concept of object permanence is now fully developed. They have a mental representation of the object that is completely separate from their immediate perception of it.

New Views of Infants' Cognitive Development In the years since Piaget's death, researchers have discovered that infants know a lot more, and know it sooner, than Piaget thought they did. It isn't that infants are smarter now; rather, psychologists have found smarter ways to measure what is going on in infants' minds. Modern advances allow researchers to use infrared photography to record infants' eye movements, time-lapse photography to detect slight hand movements, special equipment to measure and analyze infants' sucking rates, and computer technology to track and analyze it all.

Their research shows that infants in the sensorimotor period are doing more than just sensing and moving; they are thinking as well. They are not just experiencing isolated sights and sounds but combining these experiences. In one study, for example, infants were shown two different videotapes at the same time, while the soundtrack for only one of them came from a speaker placed between the two TV screens. The infants tended to look at the video that went with the soundtrack—at a toy bouncing in synch with a tapping sound, at Dad's face when his voice was on the audio, or at an angry face when an angry voice was heard (Soken & Pick, 1992). Infants remember, too. Babies as young as two to three months of age can recall a mobile that was hung over their crib a few days before (Rovee-Collier, 1999; see Figure 9.4).

Young babies even seem to have a sense of object permanence. Piaget had required infants to demonstrate object permanence by making effortful responses, such as removing a cover that had been placed over an object. Today, researchers recognize that finding a hidden object under a cover requires several abilities: mentally representing the hidden object, figuring out where it might be, and pulling off the cover. Piaget's tests did not allow for the possibility that infants know a hidden object still exists but do not have adequate strategies for finding it. In research situations where infants merely have to stare to indicate that they know where an object is hidden, they demonstrate this cognitive ability even before the age of one (Ahmed & Ruffman, 1998; Hespos & Baillargeon, 2001). And when experimenters simply turn off the lights in a room, infants as young as five months of age may reach for now-unseen objects in the dark (Clifton et al., 1991).

Developmental psychologists generally agree that infants develop some mental representations earlier than Piaget suggested. However, they disagree about whether this knowledge is "programmed" in infants (Spelke et al., 1992), develops quickly through interactions with the world (Baillargeon, 1995), or is constructed by combining old schemas into new ones (Fischer & Bidell, 1991).

figure 9.4

Infant Memory

This infant has learned to move a mobile by kicking her left foot, which is connected to the mobile by a ribbon. Even a month later, the baby will show recognition of this particular mobile by kicking more vigorously when she sees it than when she sees another one.

FOCUS ON RESEARCH

What Do Infants Know About Physics?

To explore how infants develop mental representations, Renee Baillargeon (pronounced "by-ar-ZHAN") investigated infants' early understanding of the principles of physics. Whether you realize it or not, you have quite a storehouse of knowledge about physics. You know about gravity and balance, for example. At what age did you understand that "what goes up must come down" and that an unbalanced tray will tip over?

■ **What was the researcher's question?**

Baillargeon wanted to know when and how babies first develop knowledge about balance and gravity—specifically, about the tendency of unsupported objects to fall.

■ **How did the researcher answer the question?**

In one series of creative experiments, Baillargeon (1994a, 1994b) showed infants a red-gloved hand pushing a box from left to right along the top of a platform. On some trials, they saw physically possible events, as when the hand pushed the box to the edge of the platform or held onto the object as it went beyond the edge of the platform (see events A and D in Figure 9.5). On other trials, they saw physically impossible events, as when the

(A) **(B)**

Source: Baillargeon (1992). **(C)** **(D)**

figure 9.5

Events Demonstrating Infants' Knowledge of Physics

Infants look longer at things that interest them—that is, at new things rather than things they have seen before and find boring. In her research on the development of knowledge, Renee Baillargeon (1995) has found that physically impossible events B and C—made possible by an experimenter's reaching through a hidden door to support a moving box—attract the most attention from infants. These results suggest that humans understand some basic laws of physics quite early in life.

hand pushed the box until only the end of its bottom surface rested on the platform or went beyond the platform (see events B and C in the figure). Baillargeon measured the length of time the infants looked at the objects in each event. Trials continued until the infants had seen at least four pairs of possible and impossible events in alternating order.

■ What did the researcher find?

Baillargeon found that three-month-old infants looked longest at impossible event C, in which the box was entirely off the platform. They were not particularly interested in either event D (box held by the gloved hand) or event A (box still on the platform). But at six and a half months, infants stared intently at both event C (box off the platform) and event B (in which only the end of the box was resting on the platform).

■ What do the results mean?

According to Baillargeon (1998), these results suggest that three-month-old babies know something about physical support. They expected the box to fall if it was entirely off the platform and acted surprised when it did not. But they did not yet know that a box should fall if its center of gravity is unsupported, as in event B. By six and a half months of age, they had apparently developed this understanding.

■ What do we still need to know?

Baillargeon may have demonstrated that very young infants possess fundamental knowledge about the world that implies an understanding of complex physical principles. But a question remains: Does an infant's tendency to stare longer at a particular sight necessarily indicate "surprise," or could it mean that babies simply recognize that certain images are different from, or more interesting than, things they have seen before (Bogartz, Shinskey, & Speaker, 1997)? The answer to this question will require further research using varied visual stimuli that allow researchers to determine whether infants stare longer at physically possible events that are just as novel and vivid as physically impossible events.

Researchers also want to discover *how* babies know about physics (Johnson, Amso, & Slemmer, 2003). Does their knowledge develop from their experience with objects, or is it innate? In an attempt to answer this question, Baillargeon conducted another experiment with infants ranging from three to six and a half months old. Half the children were randomly selected to receive extra experience watching objects falling when unsupported. After only a few demonstrations of such events, infants in the extra-experience group stared longer than the other babies when an unsupported object did *not* fall. Other studies found similar results (Needham & Baillargeon, 1999). It is still too early to say for sure whether Baillargeon's hypothesis about the importance of experience in developing knowledge is correct. However, the next time you see an infant stacking blocks and watching them fall, consider the possibility that you are watching a little scientist testing hypotheses about the workings of the universe.

Preoperational Development   According to Piaget, the **preoperational period** follows the sensorimotor stage of development. During the first half of this period, he observed, children begin to understand, create, and use *symbols* that represent things that are not present. They draw, pretend, and talk.

Using and understanding symbols opens up a new world for two- to four-year-olds. At two, for the first time, children are able to play "pretend." They make their fingers "walk" or "shoot" and use a spoon to make a bridge. By the age of three or four, children can symbolize complex roles and events as they play "house," "doctor," or "superhero." They also can use drawing symbolically: Pointing to their scribble, they might say, "This is Mommy and Daddy and me going for a walk."

During the second half of the preoperational stage, according to Piaget, four- to seven-year-olds begin to make intuitive guesses about the world. However, Piaget observed that they cannot tell the difference between imagination and reality. In interviews with Piaget, children in this age range claimed that dreams are real and take place outside of themselves as "pictures on the window," "a circus in the room," or "something from the sky." They described inanimate objects as being alive and having intentions, feelings, and consciousness. For example, the children said that the clouds go slowly because they have no paws or legs. Flowers grow because they want to, and empty cars feel lonely. Children in the preoperational period are also *egocentric,* meaning that they assume their own view of the world is shared by everyone else. (This helps to explain why they stand between you and the TV screen and assume you can still see it, or ask "What's this?" as they look at a picture book in the back seat of the car you're driving.)

Children's thinking at this stage is so dominated by what they can see and touch for themselves that they do not realize something is the same if its appearance is changed. In one study, for example, preoperational children thought that a cat wearing a dog mask was actually a dog, because that's what it looked like (DeVries, 1969). In short, these children do not yet have what Piaget called **conservation,** the ability to recognize that important properties of a substance or a person remain the same despite changes in shape or appearance.

In one test of conservation, Piaget showed children water from each of two equal-sized glasses being poured into either a tall, thin glass or a short, wide one. They were then asked if one glass contained more water than the other. Children at the preoperational stage of development said that one glass (usually the taller one) contained more. They were dominated by the evidence of their eyes. If the glass looked bigger, then they thought it contained more.

Children at this stage do not understand the logic of *reversibility*—that if you just poured the water from one container to another, you can pour it back, and it will be the same amount. Nor do they understand the concept of *complementarity*—that one glass is taller but narrower, and the other is shorter but wider. They focus on only one dimension at a time—the most obvious or important one—and make their best intuitive guess. In fact, Piaget named this stage *preoperational* because children at this stage do not yet understand logical mental *operations* such as reversibility and complementarity.

Concrete Operational Thought   At some time around the age of six or seven, Piaget observed, children do develop conservation. When they do so, they enter what he called the stage of **concrete operations.** Now, he said, they can count, measure, add, and subtract. Their thinking is no longer dominated by the appearance of things. They can use simple logic and perform simple mental manipulations and mental operations on things. They can sort objects into classes (such as tools, fruit, and vehicles) or series (such as largest to smallest) by systematic searching and ordering.

THE FAMILY CIRCUS®   **By Bil Keane**

Reprinted with special permission of King Features Syndicate.

"I think the moon likes us. It keeps on followin' us."

During the second half of the preoperational period, according to Piaget, children believe that inanimate objects are alive and have intentions, feelings, and consciousness.

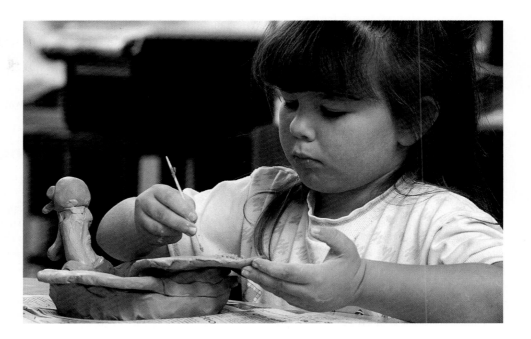

learn **by doing**

TESTING FOR CONSERVATION If you know a child who is between the ages of four and seven, get parental permission to test the child for conservation. Show the child two identical lumps of clay, and ask which lump is bigger. The child will probably say they are the same. Now roll one lump into a long "rope," and again ask which lump is bigger. If the child says that they are still the same, this is evidence of conservation. If the longer one is seen as bigger, conservation has not yet developed—at least not for this task. The older the child, the more likely it is that conservation will appear, but some children display conservation much earlier than Piaget thought was possible.

Still, concrete operational children can perform their logical operations only on real, concrete objects, such as sticks, glasses, tools, and fruit—not on abstract concepts, such as justice or freedom. They can reason only about what is, not about what is possible. The ability to think logically about abstract ideas comes in the next stage of cognitive development. This *formal operational period* occurs during adolescence, which we discuss later in the chapter.

Modifying Piaget's Theory

Piaget's observations and demonstrations of children's cognitive development are vivid and fascinating. He was right in pointing out that there are significant shifts with age in children's thinking and that thinking becomes more systematic, consistent, and integrated as children get older. His idea that children are active explorers and constructors of knowledge, not passive recipients of input from the environment, influenced our contemporary views of child development. Piaget also inspired other psychologists to test his findings and theory with experiments of their own. The results of these experiments suggest that Piaget's theory needs some modification.

What needs to be modified most is Piaget's notion of developmental stages. Several studies have shown that changes from one stage to the next are less consistent and global than Piaget had described them. For example, three-year-olds can sometimes make the distinction between physical and mental phenomena; they know the characteristics of real dogs versus pretend dogs (Woolley, 1997). And they are not always egocentric. In one study, children of this age knew that a white card, which looked pink to them because they were wearing rose-colored glasses, looked white to someone who was not wearing the glasses (Liben, 1978). Preoperational children can even succeed at conservation tasks if they are allowed to count the number of objects or have been trained to focus on relevant dimensions such as number, height, and width (Gelman & Baillargeon, 1983).

Taken together, these studies suggest that children's knowledge and mental strategies develop at different ages in different areas, and in "pockets" rather than at global levels of understanding. Knowledge in particular areas is demonstrated sooner in children who are given specific experience in those areas or who are faced with very simple questions and tasks. In other words, children's reasoning depends not only on their general level of development but also on (1) how easy the task is, (2) how familiar they are with the objects involved, (3) how well they understand the language being used, and (4) what experiences they have had in similar situations (Siegal, 1997). Research has also shown

preoperational period According to Piaget, the second stage of cognitive development, during which children begin to understand, create, and use symbols that represent things that are not present.

conservation The ability to recognize that the important properties of a substance, such as number, volume, or weight, remain constant despite changes in shape, length, or position.

concrete operations According to Piaget, the third stage of cognitive development, during which children can learn to count, measure, add, and subtract.

that the level of a child's thinking varies from day to day and may even shift when the child solves the same problem twice in the same day (Siegler, 1994).

In summary, psychologists now tend to think of cognitive development as occurring in rising and falling "waves" rather than in fixed stages characterized by permanent shifts from one way of thinking to another (Chen & Siegler, 2000). These waves reflect increases and decreases in how often children use various ways of thinking as development proceeds.

Information Processing During Childhood

An alternative to Piaget's theory of cognitive development is based on the concept of information processing described in the chapters on memory and on thought, language, and intelligence. The **information-processing** approach to development describes cognitive activities in terms of how people take in information, use it, and remember it. Developmental psychologists taking this approach focus on gradual quantitative changes in children's mental capacities, rather than on qualitative advances or stages in development.

LINKAGES
Why does memory improve during childhood?
(a link to Memory)

Research by these psychologists demonstrates that as children get older, their information-processing skills gradually get better. Older children have longer attention spans. They take in information and shift their attention from one task to another more rapidly. They are also more efficient in processing information once it is received (Miller & Vernon, 1997). Children's memory storage capacity also markedly improves (Schneider & Bjorklund, 1998). Preschoolers can keep only two or three pieces of information in mind at the same time; older children can hold four or five.

We don't yet know exactly what causes these increases in children's attention, information-processing, and memory capacities. A full explanation will undoubtedly include both nature (specifically, maturation of the brain) and nurture (including increased familiarity with the information to be processed and memorized). Researchers have observed that the cognitive abilities of children improve dramatically when they are dealing with familiar rather than unfamiliar material. In one experiment, Mayan children in Mexico lagged behind their age-mates in the United States on standard memory tests of pictures and nouns. But they did a lot better when researchers gave them a more familiar task, such as recalling miniature objects in a model of a Mayan village (Rogoff & Waddell, 1982).

Better memorization strategies may also help account for the improvement in children's memories. To a great extent, children learn these strategies in school. They learn how to memorize and how to study. They learn to repeat information over and over to help fix it in memory, to place information into categories, and to use other memory aids to help them remember.

After about age seven, schoolchildren are also better at remembering more complex and abstract information. Their memories are more accurate, extensive, and well organized. The knowledge they have accumulated allows them to draw more inferences and to integrate new information into a more complete network of facts. (See "In Review: Milestones of Cognitive Development in Infancy and Childhood.")

LINKAGES
What happens to our memories of infancy?
(a link to Memory)

learn
by doing

LINKAGES

Development and Memory

The ability to remember facts, figures, pictures, and objects improves as we get older and more expert at processing information. But take a minute right now and try to recall anything that happened to you when you were, say, one year old. Most people can accurately recall a few autobiographical memories from age five or six but remember virtually nothing from before the age of three (Bruce, Dolan, & Phillips-Grant, 2000).

Psychologists have not yet found a fully satisfactory explanation for this "infantile amnesia." Some have suggested that young children lack the memory encoding and storage processes described in the chapter on memory. Yet children of two or three can clearly recall experiences that happened weeks or even months earlier (Bauer, 1996, 2002). Others suggest

MILESTONES OF COGNITIVE DEVELOPMENT IN INFANCY AND CHILDHOOD

Age*	Achievement	Description
3–4 months	Maturation of senses	Immaturities that limit the newborn's vision and hearing are overcome.
	Voluntary movement	Reflexes disappear, and infants begin to gain voluntary control over their movements.
12–18 months	Mental representation	Infants can form images of objects and actions in their minds.
	Object permanence	Infants understand that objects exist even when out of sight.
18–24 months	Symbolic thought	Young children use symbols to represent things that are not present in their pretend play, drawing, and talk.
4 years	Intuitive thought	Children reason about events, real and imagined, by guessing rather than by engaging in logical analysis.
6–7 years	Concrete operations	Children can apply simple logical operations to real objects. For example, they recognize that important properties of a substance, such as number or amount, remain constant despite changes in shape or position.
	Conservation	
7–8 years	Information processing	Children can remember more information; they begin to learn strategies for memorization.

 Research in cognitive development suggests that children form mental representations _____ than Piaget thought they did.

*These ages are approximate; they indicate the order in which children first reach these milestones of cognitive development rather than the exact ages.

that infantile amnesia occurs because very young children lack a sense of self. Because they don't even recognize themselves in the mirror, they may not have a framework for organizing memories about what happens to them (Howe, 1995, 2003). However, this explanation would hold for only the first two years or so, because after that, children do recognize their own faces, and even their taped voices (Legerstee, Anderson, & Schaffer, 1998).

Another possibility is that early memories, though "present," are implicit rather than explicit. As mentioned in the memory chapter, *implicit memories* form automatically and can affect our emotions and behavior even when we do not consciously recall them. Note, however, that children's implicit memories of their early years, like their explicit memories, are quite limited. One study found that when ten-year-old children were shown photographs of preschool classmates they hadn't seen in five years, the children had little implicit or explicit memory of them (Newcombe & Fox , 1994). In contrast, adults can correctly identify 90 percent of photographs of high-school classmates they have not seen for thirty years (Bahrick, Bahrick, & Wittlinger, 1975).

information processing The process of taking in, remembering or forgetting, and using information.

Other explanations of infantile amnesia suggest that our early memories are lost because we do not yet have the language skills to talk about, and thus solidify, those memories. This possibility was explored in a study in which two- to three-year-old children played with a machine that supposedly shrunk toys (Simcock & Hayne, 2002). Six months later, they were asked what they remembered about this event. If they had not yet developed language at the time they played with the machine, the children were now able to say little or nothing about the experience. However, most of these same children could correctly identify pictures of the machine and act out what they had done with it. It appears that they had memories of the event that could be recalled nonverbally, but not in words. Another possibility is that early experiences tend to be fused into *generalized event representations,* such as "going to Grandma's" or "playing at the beach," so it becomes difficult to remember any specific event.

Research on hypotheses such as these is beginning to unravel the mystery of infantile amnesia (Howe, 2003; Newcombe et al., 2000; Rovee-Collier, 1999; Simcock & Hayne, 2003).

Culture and Cognitive Development

Whereas Piaget focused on the physical world of objects in explaining development, Russian psychologist Lev Vygotsky (pronounced "vah-GOT-skee") focused on the social world of people. He viewed the human mind as a product of cultural history. The child's mind, said Vygotsky, grows through contact with other minds. It is through interaction with parents, teachers, and other representatives of their culture that children acquire the ideas of that culture (Vygotsky, 1991).

Researchers in the West have pursued Vygotsky's ideas by studying the effects of the social world on children's development (Gauvain, 2001). For example, Katherine Nelson (1986) has studied how participation in social routines affects children's developing knowledge of the world. In North American culture, such routines include shopping, eating at McDonald's, going to birthday parties, and attending religious services. In another culture they might include helping to make pottery, going hunting, and weaving baskets (Larson & Verma, 1999). Quite early, children develop mental representations, called *scripts,* for these activities (see the chapter on thought, language, and intelligence). By the time they are three, children can describe routine activities quite accurately. Scripts, in turn, affect children's knowledge and understanding of cognitive tasks.

Children's cognitive abilities are also influenced by the language of their culture. Korean and Chinese children, for instance, show exceptional ability at adding and subtracting large numbers (Miller et al., 1995). As third-graders, they do in their heads three-digit problems (such as 702 minus 125) that their peers in the United States labor over or fail to solve. The difference seems traceable in part to the clear and explicit words that Asian languages use for the numbers from eleven to nineteen. In English, the meaning of the words *eleven* and *twelve,* for instance, is not as clear as the Asian *ten-one* and *ten-two.* Moreover, Asians use the abacus and the metric system of measurement, both of which are structured around the number ten. Korean math textbooks emphasize this tens structure by presenting the ones digits in red, the tens in blue, and the hundreds in green. Above all, for children in Asian cultures, educational achievement, especially in mathematics, is emphatically encouraged in school (Naito & Miura, 2001). Children's cognitive development is thereby affected in ways large and small by the culture in which they live (Tomasello, 2000).

Individual Variations in Cognitive Development

Even within a single culture, some children are mentally advanced while others lag behind their peers. Why? As already suggested, heredity is an important factor, but experience also plays a role. To explore how significant that role is, psychologists have studied the cognitive development of children raised in many different environments.

Cognitive development is profoundly delayed if children are raised in environments where they are deprived of the everyday sights, sounds, and feelings provided by conversation and loving interaction with family members; by pictures and books; and even by television, radio, and the Internet. Children subjected to severe deprivation show significant impairment in intellectual development by the time they are two or three years old (O'Conner et al., 2000; Rymer, 1993). "Genie" was one such child. When discovered at age fourteen, she weighed only fifty-nine pounds. The only things she could say were "stop it" and "no more." Investigators discovered that she had spent her life confined to a small bedroom, harnessed to a potty chair during the day and caged in a crib at night. She had not been permitted to hear or make many sounds. Although scientists and therapists worked intensively with Genie in the years after her discovery, she never learned to speak in complete sentences, and she remains in an adult care facility.

Cognitive development may also be impaired by less extreme conditions of deprivation, including the neglect, malnourishment, noise, and chaos that occur in some homes. A study of the effects of poverty found that by the time they were five years old, children raised in poverty scored nine points lower on IQ tests than did children in families whose incomes were twice the poverty level—even after the researchers had controlled for all other family variables, such as family structure and parents' education (Duncan, Brooks-Gunn, & Klebanov, 1994). A more recent study of more than 10,000 children found that the economic status of the family into which a child is born is a much better predictor of the child's later cognitive development than are physical risk factors, such as low birth weight (Jefferis, Power, & Hertzman, 2002).

Irrespective of their family's economic status, children's cognitive development is related to their surroundings and experiences. Parents can often make the difference between a child's getting A's or getting C's. To help children achieve those A's, adults can expose them, from the early years, to a variety of interesting materials and experiences—though not so many that the child is overwhelmed. Children's cognitive development is also enhanced when parents read and talk to them, encourage and help them to explore, and actively teach them (Gottfried, 1997)—in short, when they provide both support and challenge for their children's talents (Wong & Csikszentmihalyi, 1992). Although no substitute for adult attention, electronic games also provide opportunities for school-age children to hone attentional and spatial skills that can help improve their performance in math and science (Green & Bavelier, 2003; Greenfield et al., 1994).

To improve the cognitive skills of children who do not get these kinds of stimulation, developmental psychologists have provided some children with extra lessons, materials,

BABIES AT RISK The cognitive development of infants raised in this understaffed Russian orphanage will be permanently impaired if they are not given far more stimulation in the orphanage or, better yet, adopted into a loving family at a young age.

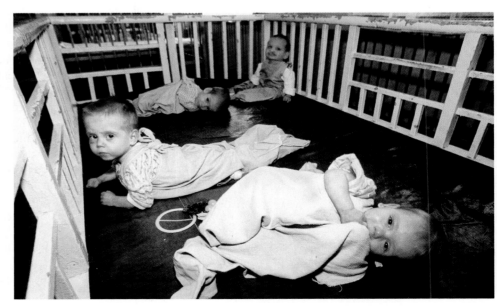

PROJECT HEAD START This teacher is working in Project Head Start, a program funded by the U.S. government to enrich the academic environments of preschoolers from lower-income backgrounds. The program has brought measurable benefits to children's academic and intellectual skills (Barnett, 1998; Lee, Brooks-Gunn, & Schnur, 1988; Ramey, 1999). Similar programs for infants at risk because of low birth weight, low socioeconomic status, or low parental IQ scores appear to enhance IQ scores by as much as nine points by the age of three. The effects appear to be especially strong for the infants of mothers with a high school education or less (Ramey et al., 2000).

and educational contact with sensitive adults. In the United States, the most comprehensive effort to provide this kind of help has been through Project Head Start, a preschool program for poor children. Many smaller, more intensive programs have also been carried out. In a variety of such programs, children's cognitive abilities have been enhanced (Ramey & Ramey, 1998), demonstrating that the environment can directly affect cognitive development.

Infancy and Childhood: Social and Emotional Development

▶ **How do infants become attached to their caregivers?**

Life for the child is more than learning about objects, doing math problems, and getting good grades. From the first months onward, infants are attracted by people—and most of them are very attractive creatures themselves, with their tiny bodies, large eyes, chubby cheeks, rosebud mouths, and soft gurgles. These qualities exert a powerful pull on people around them, especially parents and other caregivers.

Mutual attraction begins immediately. During the first hour or so after birth, babies are usually awake and, if they are with their mother, they gaze at her face while she gazes back and gives gentle touches (Klaus & Kennell, 1976). This is the first opportunity for the mother to display her *bond* to her infant—an emotional tie that begins even before the baby is born. Psychologists once believed that this immediate contact was critical—that the mother-infant bond would never be strong if the opportunity for early interaction was missed. Research has revealed, however, that such interaction is a luxury, not a requirement for a close relationship (Myers, 1987). Mothers and fathers, whether biological or adoptive, gradually form close attachments to their infants by interacting with them day after day.

From an early age, infants are sensitive to the people around them (Mumme & Fernald, 2003). They gaze at beaming faces and smile at toothy grins (Malatesta & Izard, 1984). In one study, researchers tested the ability of three-month-olds to respond to emotional cues from their mothers (Cohn & Tronick, 1983). Some mothers acted nor-

FORMING A BOND   Mutual eye contact, exaggerated facial expressions, and shared "baby talk" are an important part of the early social interactions that promote an enduring bond of attachment between parent and child.

mally, whereas others were asked to act depressed. Babies of the "depressed" mothers spent more time protesting, reacting warily, looking away, or giving only fleeting smiles. By the time they are a year old, children use their mothers' emotional expressions to guide their own behavior when they are uncertain (Saarni, Mummer, & Campos, 1998; Thompson, 1998). They tend to avoid a stranger, for example, if they see their mother look angry or afraid when the stranger approaches.

Individual Temperament

From the moment infants are born, they differ from one another in the emotions they express. Some infants are happy, active, and vigorous; they splash, thrash, and wriggle. Others lie still most of the time. Some infants approach new objects with enthusiasm; others turn away or fuss. Some infants whimper; others kick, scream, and wail. Characteristics like these make up the infant's temperament. **Temperament** refers to the infant's individual style and frequency of expressing needs and emotions; it is constitutional, biological, and genetically based. Although temperament mainly reflects nature's contribution to the beginning of an individual's personality, it can also be affected by the prenatal environment, including—as noted earlier—the mother's smoking and drug use.

In some of the earliest research on infant temperament, Alexander Thomas and Stella Chess (1977) found three main temperament patterns. *Easy babies,* the most common kind, get hungry and sleepy at predictable times, react to new situations cheerfully, and seldom fuss. *Difficult babies* are irregular and irritable. Those in the third group, *slow-to-warm-up babies,* react warily to new situations but eventually come to enjoy them.

Traces of early temperamental characteristics weave their way throughout childhood (Rothbart, Ahadi, & Evans, 2000). Easy infants usually stay easy, and difficult infants often remain difficult, sometimes developing attention and aggression problems in childhood (Guerin, Gottfried, & Thomas, 1997). Timid toddlers tend to become shy preschoolers, restrained and inhibited eight-year-olds, and somewhat anxious teenagers (Roberts, Caspi, & Moffitt, 2001). However, in temperament, as in cognitive development, nature interacts with nurture. Many events take place between infancy and adulthood that can shift the individual's development in one direction or the other.

One influential factor suggested by Thomas and Chess is the match between the infant's temperament and the parents' expectations, desires, and personal styles. When parents believe they are responsible for the infant's behavior, an easy child might reassure them. If parents are looking for signs of assertiveness, a difficult child might be just what they want.

If parent and infant are in tune, chances increase that temperamental qualities will be stable. Consider the temperament patterns of Chinese American and European American children. At birth, Chinese American infants are calmer, less changeable, less excitable, and more easily comforted when upset than European American infants (Kagan et al., 1994). This tendency toward self-control is powerfully reinforced by the Chinese culture. Compared with European American parents, Chinese parents are less likely to reward and stimulate babbling and smiling, and more likely to maintain close control of their young children. The children, in turn, are more dependent on their mothers and less likely to play by themselves. They are less vocal, noisy, and active than European American children (Smith & Freedman, 1983).

These temperamental differences between children in different ethnic groups illustrate the combined contributions of nature and nurture. Mayan infants, for example, are relatively inactive from birth. The Zinacantecos, a Mayan group in southern Mexico, reinforce this innate predisposition toward restrained motor activity by tightly wrapping their infants and by nursing at the slightest sign of movement (Greenfield & Childs, 1991). This combination of genetic predisposition and cultural reinforcement is adaptive. Quiet infants do not kick off their covers at night, which is important in the cold highlands where they live. Inactive infants are able to spend long periods on their mothers' backs as the mothers work. And infants who do not begin to walk until they can understand some language do not wander into the open fire at the center of the house. This adaptive interplay of innate and cultural factors in the development of temperament operates in all cultures.

temperament   An individual's basic, natural disposition, evident from infancy.

The Infant Grows Attached

As infants and caregivers respond to one another in the first year, the infant begins to form an **attachment**—a deep, affectionate, close, and enduring relationship—to these important figures. John Bowlby, a British psychoanalyst, drew attention to the importance of attachment after he observed children who had been orphaned in World War II. These children's depression and other emotional scars led Bowlby to propose a theory about the importance of developing a strong attachment to one's primary caregivers—a tie that normally keeps infants close to those caregivers and, therefore, safe (Bowlby, 1951, 1973). Soon after Bowlby first described his theory, researchers in the United States began to investigate how such attachments are formed and what happens when they fail to form or are broken by loss or separation. The most dramatic of these studies was conducted with monkeys by Harry Harlow.

Motherless Monkeys—and Children   Harlow (1959) separated newborn monkeys from their mothers and raised them in cages containing two artificial mothers. One "mother" was made of wire with a rubber nipple from which the infant could get milk (see Figure 9.6). It provided food but no physical comfort. The other artificial mother had no nipple but was made of soft, comfortable terry cloth. If attachments form entirely because caregivers provide food, the infants would be expected to prefer the wire mother. In fact, they spent most of their time with the terry cloth mother. And when they were frightened, the infants immediately ran to their terry cloth mother and clung to it. Harlow concluded that the monkeys were motivated by the need for comfort. The terry cloth mother provided feelings of softness and cuddling, which were things the infants needed when they sensed danger.

Harlow also investigated what happens when attachments do not form. He isolated some monkeys from all social contact from birth. After a year of this isolation, the monkeys showed dramatic disturbances. When visited by normally active, playful monkeys, they withdrew to a corner, huddling or rocking for hours. These monkeys' problems continued into adulthood. The males seldom got further than touching a potential sexual partner; the females quickly ran from any male who made a sexual advance. When some of the females were made pregnant through artificial means, their maternal behaviors were woefully inadequate. In most cases, these mothers ignored their infants. When the infants began to send distress signals, the mothers physically abused and sometimes even killed them.

Tragically, humans who spend their first few years without a consistent caregiver react in a similar manner. In Romanian and Russian orphanages, children who have been abandoned by their mothers and neglected by orphanage workers become withdrawn and engage in constant rocking—just like Harlow's deprived monkeys (Holden, 1996). These effects tend to remain even after the children are adopted. In one study, researchers observed the behavior of four-year-old children who had been in a Romanian orphanage for at least eight months before being adopted (Chisholm, 1997). Compared with children who had been adopted before they were four months old, the late-adopted children were found to have many more serious problems. Depressed or withdrawn, they stared blankly, demanded attention, and could not control their tempers. Although interacting poorly with their adoptive mothers, they were friendly with strangers, usually trying to cuddle and kiss them. Neurologists suggest that the dramatic problems seen in isolated monkeys, as well as humans, are the result of developmental brain dysfunction and damage brought on by a lack of touch and body movement in infancy (Prescott, 1996).

Forming an Attachment   Researchers would never even consider putting human babies in the socially isolated conditions Harlow's monkeys experienced. However, they have studied the development of attachment in humans as it occurs under naturally varying conditions. In most cultures where the attachment process has been studied, the mother is usually the first person to whom the baby forms an attachment. By the age of six or seven months, infants show signs of preferring the mother to anyone else. They crawl after her, call out to her, hug her, climb into her lap, and protest when she leaves (Ainsworth & Marvin, 1995). Babies who recognize and prefer their mothers even earlier—at three months—may be especially bright. One study found that such babies even-

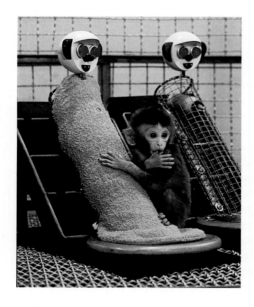

figure 9.6

Wire and Terry Cloth "Mothers"

Here are the two types of artificial mothers used in Harlow's research. Although baby monkeys received milk from the wire mother, they spent most of their time with the terry cloth version, and they clung to it when frightened.

tually achieve higher-than-average grades in high school, score higher on college entrance exams, and complete more years of education (Roe, 2001).

Infants also develop attachments to their fathers, but usually a little later (Lamb, 1997). Father-infant interaction is also less frequent than mother-infant interaction, and most studies show that it has a somewhat different nature (Parke, 2002). Mothers tend to feed, bathe, dress, cuddle, and talk to their infants, whereas fathers are more likely to play with, jiggle, and toss them, especially sons. In addition, although fathers are usually just as sensitive and responsive as mothers to their infants' expressions while the baby is happy, they may not do as well as mothers when the baby gets bored or distressed.

Variations in Attachment   The amount of closeness and contact the infant seeks with either mother or father depends to some extent on the infant. Babies who are ill, tired, or slow to warm up may require more closeness. Closeness also depends to some extent on the parent. An infant whose parent has been absent or unresponsive is likely to need more closeness than one whose parent is accessible and responsive.

Researchers have studied the differences in infants' attachments through a procedure that simulates the natural comings and goings of parents and infants—the so-called *Strange Situation Test* (Ainsworth et al., 1978). This test occurs in an unfamiliar playroom where the infant interacts with the mother and an unfamiliar woman in brief episodes: The infant plays with the mother and the stranger, the mother leaves the baby with the stranger for a few minutes, the mother and the stranger leave the baby alone in the room briefly, and the mother returns to the room.

Researchers have found that most infants in the United States display a *secure attachment* to the mother in the Strange Situation Test (Thompson, 1998). Their urge to be close is balanced by their urge to explore the environment. In the unfamiliar room, the infant uses the mother as a home base, leaving her side to explore and play but returning to her periodically for comfort or contact. Securely attached children can tolerate the brief separation from their mother, but they are always happy to see her return, and they are always receptive to her offers of contact. These mother-child pairs, researchers have found, tend to have harmonious interactions from the earliest months. The mothers themselves tend to be sensitive and responsive (DeWolff & van IJzendoorn, 1997).

Some infants, however, form an *insecure attachment*. If the relationship is *avoidant,* they avoid or ignore the mother when she approaches or when she returns after the brief separation. If the relationship is *ambivalent,* they are upset when their mother leaves, but when she returns they act angry and reject her efforts at contact, and when picked up they squirm to get down. If the relationship is *disorganized,* their behavior is inconsistent, disturbed, and disturbing; they may begin to cry again after the mother has returned and comforted them, or they may reach out for the mother while looking away from her.

The nature of a child's attachment to caregivers can have long-term and far-reaching effects. Compared with insecurely attached children, those who are securely attached tend to be more socially and emotionally competent. They are more cooperative, enthusiastic, and persistent; better at solving problems; more compliant and controlled; and more popular and playful (Thompson, 1998). First-graders with secure attachments report less loneliness than do those with insecure attachments (Berlin, Cassidy, & Belsky, 1995), and they also have better relationships with their peers when they reach adolescence (Schneider, Atkinson, & Tradif, 2001). Patterns of child care and attachment vary widely in different parts of the world. In northern Germany, for example, where parents are quite strict, the proportion of infants who display avoidant attachments is much higher than in the United States (Spangler, Fremmer-Bombik, & Grossman, 1996). Kibbutz babies in Israel, who sleep in infant houses away from their parents, are relatively likely to show insecure attachments and other related problems (Aviezer et al., 1999). In Japan, where mothers are expected to be completely devoted to their children and are seldom apart from them, even at night, children develop an attachment relationship that emphasizes harmony and union (Rothbaum et al., 2000). These attachment patterns differ from the secure one that is most common in the United States: With their parents' encouragement, U.S. children balance closeness and proximity with exploration and autonomy.

attachment   A deep, affectionate, close, and enduring relationship with a person with whom a baby has shared many experiences.

With about 60 percent of mothers of infants in the United States working outside the home, concern has been expressed about how daily separations from their mothers might affect children, especially infants. Some have argued that putting infants in day care, with a baby sitter or in a day-care center, damages the quality of the mother-infant relationship and increases the babies' risk for psychological problems later on (Gallagher, 1998).

■ What am I being asked to believe or accept?

The claim is that daily separations created by day care damage the formation of an attachment between the mother and infant and harm the infant's emotional development.

■ Is there evidence available to support the claim?

There is clear evidence that separation from the mother is painful for young children. If separation lasts a week or more, children who have formed an attachment to their mother tend to protest, then become apathetic and mournful, and finally seem to lose interest in the missing mother (Robertson & Robertson, 1971). But day care does not involve such lasting separations. Research has shown that infants who are in day care do form attachments to their mothers. In fact, they prefer their mothers to their daytime caregivers (Clarke-Stewart & Fein, 1983).

Are these attachments as secure as the attachments formed by infants whose mothers do not work outside the home? Researchers have examined this question by comparing how infants react to brief separations from their mother in the Strange Situation Test. A review of about twenty studies done in the 1980s revealed that infants in full-time day care were somewhat more likely to be classified as insecurely attached. About 36 percent of them were classified as insecure; only 29 percent of the infants who were not in full-time day care were counted as insecure (Clarke-Stewart, 1989). These results appear to support the suggestion that day care harms infants' attachments to their mothers.

■ Can that evidence be interpreted another way?

Perhaps factors other than day care could explain the difference between infants in day care and those at home with their mothers. What could these other factors be? One factor is the method that was used to assess attachment. Infants in these studies were judged insecure if they were relatively comfortable with a brief separation from their mothers in an unfamiliar room with an unfamiliar woman. Maybe infants who routinely experienced separations from their mothers when they were left in day care felt more comfortable in this situation and therefore sought out less closeness with their mothers. A second factor concerns the possible differences between the infants' mothers. Perhaps mothers who value independence in themselves and in their children are more likely to be working and to place their children in day care, whereas mothers who emphasize closeness with their children are more likely to stay home.

■ What evidence would help to evaluate the alternatives?

Finding insecure attachment to be more common among the infants of working mothers does not, by itself, demonstrate that day care is harmful. To judge the effects of day care, we must consider other measures of emotional adjustment as well. If day-care infants showed consistent signs of impaired emotional relations in other situations (at home, say) and with other caregivers (such as the father), this evidence would support the argument that day care harms children's emotional development. Another useful method would be to statistically control for differences in the behavior and attitudes of parents who do and do not put their infants in day care.

THE EFFECTS OF DAY CARE   Parents are understandably concerned that leaving their infants in a day-care center all day long might interfere with the mother-infant attachment, or with other aspects of the child's development. Research shows that most infants in day care do form healthy bonds with their parents, but that if children spend many hours in day care between infancy and kindergarten, they are more likely to have behavior problems in school, such as talking back to the teacher or getting into fights with other children (NICHD Early Child Care Research Network, 2001). Time will tell if other problems develop in the future.

In fact, this research design has already been employed. In 1990, the U.S. government funded a study of infant day care in ten sites around the country. The psychological and physical development of more than 1,300 randomly selected infants was tracked from birth through age three. The results available so far show that when factors such as parents' education, income, and attitudes were statistically controlled, infants in day care were no more likely to have emotional problems or to be insecurely attached to their mothers than infants not in day care (NICHD Early Child Care Research Network, 1997, 1998, 1999). However, in cases where infants were placed in poor-quality day care, where the caregivers were insensitive and unresponsive, and where the mothers were insensitive to the infants' needs at home, the infants were less likely to develop a secure attachment to their mothers (NICHD Early Child Care Research Network, 2002).

■ **What conclusions are most reasonable?**

Based on available evidence, the most reasonable conclusion appears to be that day care by itself does not lead to insecure attachment. But if that day care is of poor quality, it can worsen a risky situation at home and increase the likelihood that infants will have problems forming a secure attachment to their mothers. The U.S. government study is still under way, and the children's progress is being followed into elementary school.

Relationships with Parents and Peers

Erik Erikson (1968) saw the first year of life as a time when infants develop a feeling of trust (or mistrust) about the world. According to his theory, an infant's first year represents the first of eight stages of lifelong psychosocial development (see Table 9.2). Each stage focuses on an issue, or "crisis," that is especially important at that time of life. Erikson believed that the ways in which people resolve these crises shape their personalities and social relationships. Resolving a crisis in a positive way provides the foundation for characteristics such as trust, autonomy, initiative, or industry. But if the crisis is not resolved positively, according to Erikson, the person will be psychologically troubled and cope less effectively with later crises. In Erikson's theory, trusting caregivers during infancy forms the bedrock for all future social and emotional development.

table 9.2

Erikson's Stages of Psychosocial Development

In each of Erikson's stages of development, a different psychological issue presents a new crisis for the person to resolve. The person focuses attention on the issue and, by the end of the period, has worked through the crisis and resolved it either positively, in the direction of healthy development, or negatively, hindering further psychological development.

Age	Central Psychological Issue or Crisis
First Year	**Trust versus mistrust** Infants learn to trust that their needs will be met by the world, especially by the mother—or they learn to mistrust the world.
Second year	**Autonomy versus shame and doubt** Children learn to exercise will, to make choices, and to control themselves—or they become uncertain and doubt that they can do things by themselves.
Third to fifth year	**Initiative versus guilt** Children learn to initiate activities and enjoy their accomplishments, acquiring direction and purpose—or, if they are not allowed initiative, they feel guilty for their attempts at independence.
Sixth year through puberty	**Industry versus inferiority** Children develop a sense of industry and curiosity and are eager to learn—or they feel inferior and lose interest in the tasks before them.
Adolescence	**Identity versus role confusion** Adolescents come to see themselves as unique and integrated persons with an ideology—or they become confused about what they want out of life.
Early adulthood	**Intimacy versus isolation** Young people become able to commit themselves to another person—or they develop a sense of isolation and feel they have no one in the world but themselves.
Middle age	**Generativity versus stagnation** Adults are willing to have and care for children and to devote themselves to their work and the common good—or they become self-centered and inactive.
Old age	**Integrity versus despair** Older people enter a period of reflection, becoming assured that their lives have been meaningful and becoming ready to face death with acceptance and dignity—or they are in despair for their unaccomplished goals, failures, and ill-spent lives.

After children have formed strong emotional attachments to their parents, their next psychological task is to develop a more independent relationship with them. In Erikson's theory, this task is reflected in the second stage (again, see Table 9.2). Children begin to exercise their wills, to develop some independence from their parents, and to initiate activities on their own. According to Erikson, children who are not allowed to exercise their wills or initiate their own activities will feel uncertain about doing things for themselves and guilty about seeking independence. The extent to which parents allow or encourage their children's independence is related to their parenting style.

socialization The process by which parents, teachers, and others teach children the skills and social norms necessary to be well-functioning members of society.

Parenting Styles Most parents try to channel children's impulses into socially accepted outlets and teach them the skills and rules needed to function in their society. Cultural values strongly shape this **socialization** process. Parents in Hispanic cultures of Mexico, Puerto Rico, and Central America, for example, tend to be influenced by the collectivist tradition discussed in the introductory chapter, in which family and community interests are emphasized over individual goals. Children in these cultures are expected to respect and obey their elders, and they are taught to do less of the questioning, negotiating, and arguing that is encouraged—or at least tolerated—in many middle-class European American families (Greenfield, 1995).

European American parents tend to employ one of three distinct parenting styles, as described by Diana Baumrind (1991). **Authoritarian parents** tend to be strict, punishing, and unsympathetic. They value obedience from children and try to shape their children's behavior to meet a set standard and to curb the children's wills. They do not encourage independence. They are detached and seldom praise their youngsters. In contrast, **permissive parents** give their children complete freedom and provide little discipline. **Authoritative parents** fall between these two extremes. They reason with their children, encouraging give and take. They allow children increasing responsibility as they get older and better at making decisions. They are firm but understanding. They set limits but also encourage independence. Their demands are reasonable, rational, and consistent.

In her research with middle-class parents, Baumrind found these three parenting styles to be consistently related to young children's social and emotional development. Authoritarian parents had children who were unfriendly, distrustful, and withdrawn. The children of permissive parents were immature, dependent, and unhappy; they were likely to have tantrums or to ask for help when they encountered even slight difficulties. Children raised by authoritative parents were friendly, cooperative, self-reliant, and socially responsible. A follow-up study of the same children at age nine showed that the advantages of authoritative discipline were still present (Baumrind, 1986).

Other researchers following Baumrind's lead found that authoritative parenting styles were associated with additional positive outcomes, including better school achievement, greater popularity, and better psychological adjustment to parental divorce (Hetherington & Clingempeel, 1992; Hinshaw et al., 1997; Steinberg et al., 1994). Parenting styles may also help mold children's moral behavior. Children who are given orders, threats, and punishments are more likely than others to cheat and less likely to experience guilt or to accept blame after doing something wrong (Eisenberg & Fabes, 1998).

The results of these parenting studies are interesting, but they are limited in several ways. First, they are based on correlations, which, as discussed in the introductory chapter, do not prove causation. Finding consistent correlations between parents' and children's behavior does not establish that the parents are *creating* the differences seen in their children. Even evidence that differences between the children of authoritative and nonauthoritative parents tend to increase over time can only show that parents' socialization styles *might* have a direct influence on children's behavior (Steinberg et al., 1994). It is also possible, for example, that parents' behavior might be shaped to some extent by their children, especially by their children's temperaments (Bugental & Johnston, 2000).

Second, some developmental psychologists suggest that it is not the parents' socialization practices that influence children but, rather, how the children perceive the discipline they receive—as stricter or more lenient than what an older sibling received, for example (Reiss et al., 2000). A third limitation of parenting studies is that the correlations between parenting styles and children's behavior, though statistically significant, are not terribly strong. Expected outcomes do not always appear. For example, Baumrind (1971) found a small group of families in which discipline was never observed, yet the children were thriving.

In all likelihood, it is the "fit" between parenting style and children's characteristics that affects children the most. There is no universally "best" style of parenting (Parke & Buriel, 1998, 2002). So authoritative parenting, which is so consistently linked with positive outcomes in European American families, may not be the ideal parenting style for everyone. It was not, for example, related to better school performance among African American or Asian American youngsters (Steinberg, Dornbusch, & Brown, 1992). One reason for this lack of relationship could be that different disciplinary styles have different meanings in different cultures. When Chinese American parents use authoritarian discipline—which they do to a greater extent than European American parents—their goal is usually to "train" *(chiao shun)* and "govern" *(guan)* children so that they will know what is expected of them (Chao, 1994). By contrast, European American parents who use

authoritarian parents Parents who are firm, punitive, and unsympathetic.

permissive parents Parents who give their children complete freedom and lax discipline.

authoritative parents Parents who reason with their children and are firm but understanding.

authoritarian discipline are more likely to do so to "break the child's will." In other words, each parenting style must be evaluated in its cultural context.

Some people have suggested that parenting styles are a less significant influence on children's social development than are the influences they encounter outside the home—especially peer influences (Harris, 1995, 1998). Research evidence does not justify dismissing the impact of parenting styles, but there is no denying the impact of peer influences, either (Collins et al., 2000; Leventhal & Brooks-Gunn, 2000).

Relationships with Peers   Social development over the years of childhood spans an ever-enlarging social world that broadens to include brothers and sisters, playmates and classmates. Psychologists have observed that from a remarkably early age—as young as one year—children are interested in the behavior of other children (usually their siblings), and by the time they are a year and a half old, they know how to hurt or comfort other children (Rubin, Bukowski, & Parker, 1998).

It takes time for children to learn how to interact with other children. Two-year-olds in Western cultures are only able to exchange or fight over toys. By the time they are three, they can use toys to get a response from peers. At age four, children converse about the toys they are playing with, and at the end of the preschool period, they are able to share toys and tasks cooperatively. This kind of play is important because it shows children how to communicate what they are feeling and gives them the chance to form their first friendships (Dunn & Hughes, 2001).

In the school years, peer interaction becomes more complex and structured as children play games with rules, play on teams, tutor each other, and cooperate—or compete—in achieving goals. The school years are also the time when friends become important and friendships become long-lasting (Hartup & Stevens, 1997). At this age, the most important aspects of friendship are companionship and fun; psychological intimacy does not enter the picture until children become teenagers (Parker et al., 2001).

CHILDREN'S FRIENDSHIPS   Although relationships with peers may not always be this cordial, they are often among the closest and most positive in a child's life. Friends are more interactive than nonfriends; they smile and laugh together more, pay closer attention to equality in their conversations, and talk about mutual goals. Having at least one close friend in childhood predicts good psychological functioning later on.

Social Skills

The changes in peer interactions and relationships over the years of childhood reflect children's increasing social competence and understanding. *Social skills,* like cognitive skills, must be learned. Very young children do not yet have the social skills necessary to sustain responsive interactions with other children, but parents can help their children develop these skills (Parke & O'Neil, 2000). They can engage in lots of "pretend" play and other positive social behaviors with their children (Kahen, Katz, & Gottman, 1994), and they can help children to constructively express and deal with their emotions (Eisenberg, 1998).

Parents and other adults can also help children detect and interpret emotional signals from others. Three- or four-year-old children can name typical facial expressions of happiness, sadness, anger, and fear; girls can do this at younger ages than boys (Dunn et al., 1991). As children get older, they learn to recognize a wider range of emotions and to predict how a person will feel in emotion-provoking situations (Brown & Dunn, 1996). These abilities are important: Much as children's school performance depends on processing academic information, their social performance depends on processing information about other people (Slomkowski & Dunn, 1996). Children whose social skills allow them to understand another person's perspective, appreciate how that person might be feeling, and offer sympathy, cooperation, and help tend to be the most popular members of a peer group (Izard et al., 2001). Children without these skills tend to be rejected or neglected; they may become bullies or the victims of bullies.

Gender Roles

gender roles   Patterns of work, appearance, and behavior that society associates with being male or female.

An important aspect of understanding other people is knowing about social roles, including those linked to being male or female. All cultures establish expectations about **gender roles,** the general patterns of work, appearance, and behavior associated with

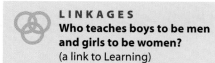

LINKAGES
Who teaches boys to be men and girls to be women?
(a link to Learning)

being a man or a woman. Gender roles appear in every culture, but they are more pronounced in some cultures than others. One recent analysis revealed, for example, that where there are smaller male-female differences in social status, gender-role differences are smaller as well (Wood & Eagly, 2002). In North America, some roles—such as homemaker and firefighter—have traditionally been tied to gender, although these traditions are weakening. Research by Deborah Best suggests that children show gender-role expectations earliest in Muslim countries (where the roles are perhaps most extreme), but children in all twenty-five countries she studied eventually developed them (Best, 1992; Williams & Best, 1990).

Gender roles appear and persist because they are deeply rooted in both nature and nurture. Small physical and behavioral differences between the sexes appear early on and tend to increase over the years. For example, girls suffer less often than boys from speech, learning, and behavior disorders; mental retardation; emotional problems; and sleep disorders. They tend to speak and write earlier and to be better at grammar and spelling (Halpern, 1997). They nurture others more than boys do and show more emotional empathy. Their play tends to be more orderly. At the same time, boys tend to be more skilled than girls at manipulating objects, constructing three-dimensional forms, and mentally manipulating complex figures and pictures. They are more physically active and aggressive and more inclined to hit obstacles or people. They play in larger groups and spaces and enjoy noisier, more strenuous physical games (Eisenberg & Fabes, 1998).

A biological contribution to these male-female differences is supported by studies of differences in anatomy, hormones, and brain organization and functioning (Geary, 1999; Ruble & Martin, 1998). A biological basis for male-female differences is also supported by cross-cultural research showing consistency in gender patterns despite differing socialization (Simpson & Kenrick, 1997). In virtually every culture, for example, males are more violent than females. In one survey, there was not a single culture in which the number of women who killed women was even one-tenth as great as the number of men who killed men. On average, men's homicides outnumbered women's by more than thirty to one (Cassel & Bernstein, 2001).

Some researchers question whether these sex differences have a direct biological cause (Wood & Eagly, 2002). The uncertainty arises because it is difficult, if not impossible, to untangle biologically based gender differences from socially created ones. From the moment they are born, boys and girls are treated differently. Adults usually play more gently with, and talk more to, infants they believe to be girls than infants they believe to be boys (Culp, Cook, & Housley, 1983). They often shower their daughters with dolls and tea sets, their sons with trucks and tools. They tend to encourage boys to achieve, compete, and explore; to control their feelings; to be independent; and to assume personal responsibility. They more often encourage girls to be expressive, nurturant, reflective, dependent, domestic, obedient, and unselfish (Ruble & Martin, 1998). In short, parents, teachers, and television role models consciously or inadvertently pass on their ideas about "appropriate" behaviors for boys and girls (Witt, 1997).

Children also pick up ideas about gender-appropriate behavior from their peers (Martin & Fabes, 2001). Peer pressure exaggerates whatever differences may already exist. For example, boys tend to be better than girls at computer or video games (Greenfield, 1994). However, this difference stems partly from the fact that boys encourage and reward each other for skilled performance at these games more than girls do (Law, Pellegrino, & Hunt, 1993). Children are also more likely to play with children of the same sex, and in gender-typical ways, on the playground than they are in private, at home, or in the classroom (Luria, 1992). An analysis of 143 studies of sex differences in aggression showed that boys acted significantly and consistently more aggressively than girls, but especially so when they knew they were being watched (Hyde, 1986). Among girls, aggression is less obvious; it is usually "relational aggression" that shows up in nasty words, not punching (Crick et al., 1999; Zuger, 1998).

In short, social and cultural training tends to support and amplify any biological predispositions that distinguish boys and girls. Gender roles reflect a mix of nature and

LEARNING GENDER ROLES   In every culture, socialization by parents and others typically encourages the interests, activities, and other characteristics traditionally associated with a child's own gender.

SOCIAL AND EMOTIONAL DEVELOPMENT DURING INFANCY AND CHILDHOOD

Age	Relationships with Parents	Relationships with Other Children	Social Understanding
Birth–2 years	Infants form an attachment to the primary caregiver.	Play focuses on toys, not on other children.	Infants respond to emotional expressions of others.
2–4 years	Children become more independent and no longer need their parents' constant attention.	Toys are a way of eliciting responses from other children.	Young children can recognize emotions of others.
4–10 years	Parents actively socialize their children.	Children begin to cooperate, compete, play games, and form friendships with peers.	Children learn social rules, like politeness, and roles, like being a male or female.

? *As part of their social development, children learn _____, which tell them what patterns of appearance and behavior are associated with being male or female.*

nurture. (Gender roles and other elements of early development are summarized in "In Review: Social and Emotional Development During Infancy and Childhood.")

The efforts of some parents to de-emphasize gender roles in their children's upbringing may be helping to reduce the magnitude of gender differences in areas such as verbal and quantitative skills. However, the evolutionary approach to psychology suggests that other gender differences are unlikely to change much. These differences include males' greater ability to visualize the rotation of objects in space and females' greater ability to read facial expressions. Evolutionary psychologists see these differences as deeply rooted reflections of gender-related hunting versus child-rearing duties that were adaptive eons ago for the survival of both sexes (Buss, 1999). This view is challenged by psychologists who see such differences as reflecting social inequality, not just biological destiny (Wood & Eagly, 2002).

Adolescence

▶ **What threatens adolescents' self-esteem?**

The years of middle childhood usually pass smoothly, as children busy themselves with schoolwork, hobbies, friends, and clubs. But in adolescence, things change dramatically. All adolescents undergo significant changes in size, shape, and physical capacities. In Western cultures, many adolescents also experience huge changes in their social lives, reasoning abilities, and views of themselves.

The Challenges of Change

A sudden spurt in physical growth is a visible signal that adolescence has begun. This growth spurt peaks at about age twelve for girls and at about age fourteen for boys (Tanner, 1978) (see Figure 9.7). Suddenly, adolescents find themselves in new bodies. At the

figure 9.7

Physical Changes in Adolescence

At about ten and a half years of age, girls begin their growth spurt, and by age twelve, they are taller than their male peers. When boys, at about twelve and a half years of age, begin their growth spurt, they usually grow faster and for a longer period of time than girls. Adolescents may grow as much as five inches a year. The development of sexual characteristics accompanies these changes in height. The ages at which these changes occur vary considerably across individuals, but the sequence of changes is the same.

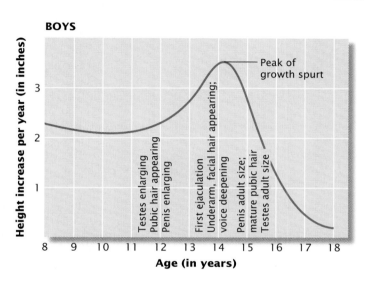

end of the growth spurt, menstruation begins in females, and live sperm are produced in males. This condition of being able for the first time to reproduce is called **puberty.**

In Western cultures, *early adolescence* (the period from age eleven to fourteen or so) is filled with challenges. Sexual interest stirs, and there are opportunities to smoke, drink alcohol, and take other drugs (Kazura et al., 2002; White & Pandina, 2002). All of this can be disorienting. Adolescents may experience bouts of depression and are vulnerable to other psychological difficulties as well (Ge, Conger, & Elder, 2001).

Some of these problems appear as adolescents begin to face challenges to their *self-esteem,* their sense of being worthy, capable, and deserving of respect—especially if other stressors occur at the same time (Ohring, Graber, & Brooks-Gunn, 2002.). Researchers have found that youths who experience more or stronger stressors, such as inadequate study space at home or parental divorce or unemployment, have more difficulty adapting to adolescence (Kling et al., 1999). The switch from elementary school to middle school is particularly challenging for young adolescents. Declining grades are especially likely among students who were already having trouble in school or who don't have confidence in their own abilities (Rudolph et al., 2001). But grades do not affect self-esteem in all teens; many base their self-esteem primarily on what others think of them or on other social factors that might affect their feelings of self-worth (Crocker & Wolfe, 2001).

The changes and pressures of adolescence are often played out at home. Many teenagers become discontented with their parents' rules and values, leading to arguments over everything from taking out the garbage to who left the gallon of milk on top of the refrigerator. Serious conflicts may lead to serious problems, including running away, pregnancy, stealing, drug taking, or even suicide—especially among teens who do not feel close to their parents (Blum, Beuhring, & Rinehart, 2000). In most families, however, the level of conflict is moderate (Steinberg, 1990). Especially in European American families, adolescents whose parents retain an authoritative disciplinary style and maintain a

puberty   The condition of being able, for the first time, to reproduce.

balance between being too strict (authoritarian) and too lax (permissive) tend to remain well adjusted (Bronstein et al., 1998).

In fact, research suggests that in Western cultures, more than half of today's teens find early adolescence relatively trouble-free (Arnett, 1999). Only about 15 percent of the adolescents studied experience serious turmoil, and most actually maintain relatively good and stable relationships with their parents (Steinberg, 1990; van Wal, ter Bogt, & Raaijmakers, 2002). However, if adolescents do experience problems, sexuality is often involved. Surveys suggest that almost half of North America's youth have had sexual intercourse by age sixteen (Klerman, 2002; National Center for Chronic Disease Prevention and Health Promotion, 2002). Fifty years ago, the comparable figure was less than 10 percent (Resnick, 1997).

Teens who have sex differ from those who do not in a number of ways. They hold less conventional attitudes and values, and they are more likely to smoke, drink alcohol, and use other drugs. Their parents tend to be less educated, less likely to exert control over them, and less likely to talk openly with them. Sexual activity in adolescence is also related to ethnicity. For instance, teens from Asian American families are less likely to be sexually active than those from European American families (McLaughlin et al., 1997).

Too often, sexual activity leads to declining school achievement and interest, sexually transmitted diseases, and unplanned and unwanted pregnancies. Teenagers have the highest rates of sexually transmitted diseases (such as gonorrhea, chlamydia, and pelvic inflammatory disease) of any age group (National Center for Health Statistics, 2000; Ross, 2002). One-fifth of all AIDS cases start in adolescence, and although teenage pregnancy rates have been declining of late, nearly 10 percent of all teenage girls in the United States get pregnant before they reach age nineteen (National Center for Health Statistics, 2000; Starkman & Rajani, 2002). More than half of the U.S. adolescents who become pregnant elect to keep their babies and become single mothers. A teenage pregnancy can wreak havoc for the baby, as well as for the parents. Teenage parents tend to be less positive and stimulating with their children than older parents (Brooks-Gunn & Chase-Lansdale, 2002); they are also more likely to abuse them (Coley & Chase-Lansdale, 1998). The children of teenage parents, in turn, are more likely to develop behavior problems and to do poorly in school than those whose parents are older (Moffitt, 2002; National Center for Health Statistics, 2000).

Identity and Development of the Self

In many less economically developed nations today, and in the United States during earlier times, the end of early adolescence (around the age of fourteen) marks the onset of adulthood—a time when work, parenting, and grown-up responsibilities begin. In modern North America, the transition from childhood to adulthood often lasts well into the twenties. Adolescents spend a lot of time being students or trainees. This lengthened adolescence has created special problems—among them, the matter of finding or forming an identity.

Forming a Personal and Ethnic Identity Preschool children asked to describe themselves often mention a favorite or habitual activity: "I watch TV" or "I play in the yard." At eight or nine, children identify themselves by giving facts such as their sex, age, name, physical appearance, and likes and dislikes. They may still describe themselves in terms of what they do, but they now include how well they do it compared with other children. Then, at about age eleven, children begin to describe themselves in terms of social relationships, personality traits, and other general, stable psychological characteristics such as "smart" or "friendly" (Shaffer, 1999). These changes in the way children and adolescents describe themselves suggest changes in the way they think about themselves. As they become more self-conscious, they gradually develop a personal identity as unique individuals.

Their personal identity may be affected by their **ethnic identity**—the part of a person's identity that reflects the racial, religious, or cultural group to which he or she belongs. In melting-pot nations such as the United States, some members of ethnic minorities may identify with their ethnic group—Chinese, Mexican, or Italian, for example—even more than with being Americans. Children are aware of ethnic cues such as skin color before they reach the age of three. Minority-group children notice these cues

ethnic identity The part of a person's identity that reflects the racial, religious, or cultural group to which he or she belongs.

earlier than other children and prefer to play with children from their own group (Milner, 1983). In high school, most students hang out with members of their own ethnic group. They tend not to know classmates in other ethnic groups well, seeing them more as members of those groups than as individuals (Steinberg, Dornbusch, & Brown, 1992). These social processes may solidify ethnic identity. A positive ethnic identity contributes to self-esteem, partly because seeing their own group as superior makes people feel good about themselves (Fiske, 1998). However, as described in the chapter on social psychology, the same processes that foster ethnic identity can also sow the seeds of ethnic prejudice. Adolescents who regularly interact with members of other ethnic groups usually become less prejudiced adults (Phinney, Ferguson, & Tate, 1997).

Facing the Identity Crisis   Identity formation is the central task of adolescence in Erikson's theory of psychosocial development. According to Erikson (1968), events of late adolescence—graduating from high school, going to college, and forging new relationships—challenge the adolescent's self-concept, precipitating an **identity crisis** (see Table 9.2). In this crisis, the adolescent must develop an integrated self-image as a unique person by pulling together self-knowledge acquired during childhood. If infancy and childhood brought trust, autonomy, and initiative, according to Erikson, the adolescent will resolve the identity crisis positively, feeling self-confident and competent. If infancy and childhood resulted in feelings of mistrust, shame, guilt, and inferiority, the adolescent will be confused about his or her identity and goals.

In Western cultures there is some limited empirical support for Erikson's ideas about the identity crisis. In late adolescence, young people do consider alternative identities (Waterman, 1982). They may "try out" being rebellious, studious, or detached as they attempt to resolve questions about sexuality, self-worth, industriousness, and independence, but late adolescence is also a time when many people become more aware of their obligations to their families (Fulgini & Pedersen, 2002). By the time they are twenty-one, about half of the adolescents studied have resolved the identity crisis in a way that is consistent with their self-image and the historical era in which they are living. They enter young adulthood with self-confidence. Basically the same people who entered adolescence, they now have more mature attitudes and behavior, more consistent goals and values, and a clearer idea of who they are (Savin-Williams & Demo, 1984). For those who fail to resolve identity issues—either because they avoided the identity crisis by accepting the identity their parents set for them or because they postponed dealing with the crisis and remain uncommitted and lacking in direction—there are often problems ahead (Lange & Byrd, 2002).

learn **by doing**   **HANGING OUT, SEPARATELY** Ethnic identity is that part of our personal identity that reflects the racial, religious, or cultural group to which we belong. Ethnic identity often leads people to interact mainly with others who share that same identity. To what extent is this true of you? You can get a rough idea by jotting down the ethnicity of all the people you chose to spend time with over the past week or so.

identity crisis   The phase during which an adolescent attempts to develop an integrated self-image as a unique person by pulling together self-knowledge acquired during childhood.

Abstract Thought and Moral Reasoning

Adolescents are able to develop a conscious identity partly because, for the first time, they can think and reason about abstract concepts. For many young people in Western cultures, adolescence begins a stage of cognitive development that Piaget called the **formal operational period,** a stage marked by the ability to engage in hypothetical thinking, including the imagining of logical consequences. For instance, adolescents who have reached the level of formal operations can consider various strategies for finding a part-time job and recognize that some methods are more likely to be successful than others. They can form general concepts and understand the impact of the past on the present and the present on the future. They can question social institutions; think about the world as it might be and ought to be; and consider the consequences of love, morality, work, politics, philosophy, and religion. They can think logically and systematically about symbols and assertions.

Piaget explored adolescents' formal operational abilities by asking them to perform science experiments that involved formulating and systematically investigating hypotheses. Research indicates that only about half the people in Western cultures ever reach the formal operational level necessary to succeed in Piaget's experiments. Those without high school science and math are less likely to succeed (Keating, 1990). In other cultures, too, people who have not gone to school are less likely to exhibit formal operations. Consider the following conversation, in which a researcher tests the formal operations of an illiterate Kpelle farmer in a Liberian village (Scribner, 1977):

> *Researcher*: All Kpelle men are rice farmers. Mr. Smith is not a rice farmer. Is he a Kpelle man?
> *Kpelle Farmer*: I don't know the man. I have not laid eyes on the man myself.

Kpelle villagers who had had formal schooling answered the question logically by saying, "No, Mr. Smith is not a Kpelle man."

Even people who have been to school do not use a single way of thinking in all situations. In adulthood, people are more likely to use formal operations for problems based on their own occupations. This is one reason why people whose logic is impeccable at work may still become victims of a home-repair or investment scam (Cialdini, 2001).

Kohlberg's Stages of Moral Reasoning   Adolescents often find themselves applying their advanced cognitive skills to questions of morality. To examine how people think about morality, psychologists have asked them how they would resolve moral dilemmas, and why. Perhaps the most famous of these is the "Heinz dilemma," in which people must decide whether a man named Heinz should steal a rare and unaffordably expensive drug in order to save his wife from cancer.

Posing moral dilemmas like this one to males between the ages of ten and twenty-six, Lawrence Kohlberg found that the reasons given for moral choices change systematically and consistently with age (Kohlberg & Gilligan, 1971). Young children make moral judgments that differ from those of older children, adolescents, or adults. Kohlberg proposed that moral reasoning develops in six stages, which are summarized in Table 9.3. These stages, he said, are not tightly linked to a person's chronological age. Instead, there is a range of ages for reaching each stage, and not everyone reaches the highest level.

Stage 1 and Stage 2 moral judgments, which are most typical of children under the age of nine, tend to be selfish in nature. Kohlberg called this level of moral reasoning **preconventional,** because it is not based on the conventions or rules that guide social interactions in society. People at this level of moral development are mainly concerned with avoiding punishment or following rules when it is to their own advantage. At the **conventional** level of moral reasoning, Stages 3 and 4, people care about other people. They think that morality consists of following rules and conventions such as duty to the family, to marriage vows, and to the country. The moral reasoning of children from nine to nineteen is most often at this level. Stages 5 and 6 represent the highest level of moral reasoning, which Kohlberg called **postconventional** because it occurs after conventional

---

formal operational period   According to Piaget, the fourth stage of cognitive development, characterized by the ability to engage in hypothetical thinking.

preconventional   Referring to moral reasoning that is not based on the conventions or rules that guide social interactions in a society.

conventional   Referring to moral reasoning that reflects a concern about other people, as well as the belief that morality consists of following rules and conventions.

postconventional   Referring to moral reasoning that reflects moral judgments based on personal standards or universal principles of justice, equality, and respect for human life.

table 9.3

Kohlberg's Stages of Moral Development

Kohlberg's stages of moral reasoning describe differences in how people think about moral issues. Here are some examples of answers that people at different stages might give to the "Heinz dilemma" described in the text. This dilemma is more realistic than you might think. In 1994, a man was arrested for robbing a bank after being turned down for a loan to pay for his wife's cancer treatments.

Stage	What Is Right?	Should Heinz Steal the Drug?
Preconventional 1	Obeying and avoiding punishment from a superior authority	"Heinz should not steal the drug, because he will be jailed."
2	Making a fair exchange, a good deal	"Heinz should steal the drug, because his wife will repay him later."
Conventional 3	Pleasing others and getting their approval	"Heinz should steal the drug, because he loves his wife and because she and the rest of the family will approve."
4	Doing your duty, following rules and social order	"Heinz should steal the drug for his wife, because he has a duty to care for her," or "Heinz should not steal the drug, because stealing is illegal."
Postconventional 5	Respecting rules and laws, but recognizing that they may have limits	"Heinz should steal the drug, because life is more important than property."
6	Following universal ethical principles, such as justice, reciprocity, equality, and respect for human life and rights	"Heinz should steal the drug because of the principle of preserving and respecting life."

reasoning. Moral judgments at this level are based on personal standards or universal principles of justice, equality, and respect for human life, not just on the demands of authority figures or society. People who have reached this level view rules and laws as arbitrary but respect them because they protect human welfare. They believe that individual rights can sometimes justify violating these laws if the laws become destructive. People do not usually reach this level until sometime after the end of adolescence. Stage 6 is seen only rarely, in extraordinary individuals. Studies of Kohlberg's stages have generally supported the sequence he proposed (Walker, 1989).

Limitations of Kohlberg's Stages   Do Kohlberg's stages appear across cultures? In general, yes. Forty-five studies in twenty-seven cultures from Alaska to Zambia showed that people do tend to make upward progress through Kohlberg's stages, without reversals (Snarey, 1987). Stages 5 and 6 did not always appear, but Stages 1 through 4 did and thus appear universal. The reason may be that these lower levels of reasoning are more closely linked to cognitive development than is the highest level.

However, moral judgments made in some cultures do not always fit neatly into Kohlberg's stages. For example, some people in collectivist cultures such as Papua New Guinea, Taiwan, and Israeli kibbutzim, for example, explained their answers to moral dilemmas by pointing to the importance of the community. And people in India included in their moral reasoning the importance of acting in accordance with one's caste (social class) and with maintaining personal purity (Shweder et al., 1994). In shaping moral judgments, as in other areas, culture plays a significant role.

Gender may also play a role. Carol Gilligan (1982, 1993) has suggested that Kohlberg's research documented mainly the abstract, impersonal concept of justice typically seen in males. When Gilligan asked people about moral conflicts, the majority of men focused on justice, but only half of the women did. The other half focused on caring. This finding supports Gilligan's belief that, for North American females, the moral ideal is to protect enduring relationships and fulfill human needs. This difference between men and women has not been found consistently, however (Jaffee & Hyde, 2000). In fact, it appears that males and females are capable of using either approach to moral reasoning (Johnston, 1988). The tendency for females to focus on caring more than males and for males to focus on justice more than females appears most clearly when they are resolving hypothetical moral dilemmas (Turiel, 1998). When resolving real-life moral issues, both men and women focus more on caring than on justice (Walker, 1995).

Taken together, the results of research in different countries and with both genders suggest that moral ideals are not absolute and universal. Moral development is apparently an adaptation to the moral world—and the specific situations in which one finds oneself (Bersoff, 1999). Formal operational reasoning may be necessary for people to reach the highest level of moral reasoning, but formal operational reasoning alone is not sufficient. To some extent, at the highest levels, moral reasoning is a product of culture and history.

Adulthood

► **What developmental changes occur in adulthood?**

Development does not end with adolescence. Adults, too, go through transitions and experience physical, cognitive, and social changes. It has been suggested that adulthood emerges as early as eighteen (Arnett, 2000), but for our purposes, adulthood can be divided into three periods: *early adulthood* (ages twenty to thirty-nine), *middle adulthood* (ages forty to sixty-five), and *late adulthood* (beyond age sixty-five).

Physical Changes

In early adulthood, physical growth continues. Shoulder width, height, and chest size increase, and people continue to develop their athletic abilities. By their mid-thirties nearly everyone shows some hearing impairment, but for most people, the years of early adulthood are the prime of life.

In middle adulthood, other physical changes slowly emerge. The most common of these involve the further loss of sensory sharpness (Fozard et al., 1977). People become less sensitive to light, less accurate at perceiving differences in distance, and slower and less able at seeing details. At about age forty, increased farsightedness is common, and glasses may be necessary to correct for it. In their late forties or early fifties, women generally experience *menopause,* the shutdown of reproductive capability. Estrogen and progesterone levels drop, and the menstrual cycle eventually ceases.

Most people are well into late adulthood before their bodily functions show noticeable impairment. However, inside the body, bone mass is dwindling, and the risk of heart disease is increasing. Men shrink about an inch in height, and women about two inches, as their posture changes and cartilage disks between the spinal vertebrae become thinner. Older adults tend to go to sleep earlier, but may find it harder to sleep through the night without awakening to use the bathroom (Park et al., 2002). Hardening of the arteries and a buildup of fat deposits on the artery walls may lead to heart disease. The digestive system slows down and becomes less efficient. Both digestive disorders and heart disease sometimes result from problems of diet—too little fluid, too little fiber, too much fat—

and inactivity. In addition, the brain shrinks during late adulthood. The few reflexes that remained after infancy, such as the knee-jerk reflex, weaken or disappear. The flow of blood to the brain slows. As in earlier years, many of these changes can be delayed or diminished by a healthy diet and exercise (Seeman & Chen, 2002).

Cognitive Changes

Despite the aging of the brain, cognition undergoes little change for the worse until late adulthood. Before that time, alert older people may function as well as alert younger people. In fact, older adults may perform even better than younger adults in situations that tap their long-term memories and well-learned skills (Park et al., 2002). The experienced teacher may deal with an unruly child more skillfully than the novice, and the senior lawyer may understand the implications of a new law better than the recent graduate. Their years of accumulating and organizing information can make older adults practiced, skillful, and wise.

Early and Middle Adulthood   Until age sixty at least, important cognitive abilities improve. During this period, adults do better on tests of vocabulary, comprehension, and general knowledge—especially if they use these abilities in their daily lives or engage in enriching activities such as travel or reading (Park, 2001). Young and middle-aged adults learn new information and new skills; they remember old information and hone old skills. In fact, it is in their forties through their early sixties that people tend to put in the best performance of their lives on complex mental tasks such as reasoning, verbal memory, and vocabulary (Willis & Schaie, 1999).

The nature of thought may also change during adulthood. Adult thought is often more complex and adaptive than adolescent thought (Labouvie-Vief, 1992). Unlike adolescents, adults understand the contradictions inherent in thinking. They see both the possibilities and the problems in every course of action—in deciding whether to start a new business, back a political candidate, move to a new place, or change jobs. Middle-aged adults are more expert than adolescents or young adults at making rational decisions and at relating logic and abstractions to actions, emotions, social issues, and personal relationships (Tversky & Kahneman, 1981). As they appreciate these relationships, their thought becomes more global, more concerned with broad moral and practical issues (Labouvie-Vief, 1982). It has been suggested that the achievement of these new kinds of thinking reflects a stage of cognitive development that goes beyond Piaget's formal operational period (Lutz & Sternberg, 1999). In this stage, people's thinking becomes *dialectical,* which means they understand that knowledge is relative, not absolute—such that what is seen as wise today may have been thought foolish in times past. They see life's contradictions as an inevitable part of reality, and they tend to weigh various solutions to problems rather than just accepting the first one that springs to mind.

Late Adulthood   It is not until late in adulthood, after the age of sixty-five or so, that some intellectual abilities decline in some people. Generally, these are abilities that require rapid and flexible manipulation of ideas and symbols, active thinking and reasoning, and sheer mental effort (Baltes, 1993; Craik, 1994) (see Figure 9.8). Older adults do just as well as younger ones at tasks they know well, like naming familiar objects (Radvansky, 1999). However, when asked to perform an unfamiliar task or to solve a complex problem they have not seen before, older adults are generally slower and less effective than younger ones (Craik & Rabinowitz, 1984). When faced with complex problems, older people apparently suffer from having too much information to sift through. They have trouble considering, choosing, and executing solutions (Arenberg, 1982). As people age, they grow less efficient at organizing the elements of a problem and at holding and mentally manipulating more than one idea at a time. They have difficulty doing tasks that require them to divide their attention between two activities and are slower at

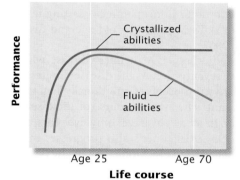

Performance

Crystallized abilities

Fluid abilities

Age 25   Age 70
Life course

Source: Adapted from Baltes (1994).

figure 9.8

Mental Abilities over the Life Span

Mental abilities collectively known as "fluid" intelligence—speed and accuracy of information processing, for example—begin to decline quite early in adult life. Changes in these biologically based aspects of thinking are usually not noticeable until late adulthood, however. "Crystallized" abilities learned over a lifetime—such as reading, writing, comprehension of language, and professional skills—do not normally diminish significantly, even in old age (Freedman, Aykan, & Martin, 2001).

shifting their attention back and forth between those activities (Korteling, 1991; Smith et al., 2001). If older adults have enough time, though, and can separate the two activities, they can perform just as well as younger adults (Hawkins, Kramer, & Capaldi, 1993).

Usually, the loss of intellectual abilities is slow and need not cause severe problems (Bashore & Ridderinkoff, 2002). A study of Swedish older adults (Nilsson, 1996) showed, for example, that their memory problems were largely confined to *episodic memory* (e.g., remembering what they had for lunch yesterday) rather than *semantic memory* (remembering general information, such as the capital of Italy).

In other words, everyday abilities that involve verbal processes are likely to remain intact into advanced old age (Freedman, Aykan, & Martin, 2001). Further, the risk of cognitive decline is significantly lower for people who are healthy and psychologically flexible; who have a high level of education, income, and occupation; and who live in an intellectually stimulating environment with mentally able spouses or companions (Albert et al., 1995; Chadosh et al., 2002; Shimamura et al., 1995). Continued mental exercise—such as doing puzzles, painting, and having intellectually stimulating conversations with friends—can help older adults think and remember effectively and creatively (Verghese et al., 2003; Wilson, Beckett et al., 2002). Maintaining physical fitness through dancing or other forms of aerobic exercise has also been associated with better maintenance of skills on a variety of mental tasks, including those involving reaction time, reasoning, and divided attention (Colcombe & Kramer, 2003; Tabbarah, Crimmins, & Seeman, 2002).

Research on people tested repeatedly since 1956 shows that scores on mental ability tests decline less rapidly in old age now than they did before 1970 (Schaie, 1993). Even at age eighty-one, fewer than half of the participants exhibited losses in mental abilities over the preceding seven years. This finding is probably due to the improved physical health and longer involvement in work and other mental activities seen in older adults over the last fifty years. Other research demonstrates that it is never too late to work at preserving mental ability. Practice at memory and other information-processing tasks, for example, may lead to some improvement in skills impaired by old age and disuse (Kramer & Willis, 2002; Rapp, Brenes, & Marsh, 2002).

The greatest threat to cognitive abilities in late adulthood is Alzheimer's disease, which strikes 3 percent of the world's population by age seventy-five. As the disease progresses, it leaves even the brightest minds incapable. The victim becomes emotionally flat, then disoriented, then incontinent, then mentally vacant. The average course of the disease, from onset to death, is seven years, but it can vary. In men, it averages only five years, and in women, eight (Molsa, Marttila, & Rinne, 1995). Alzheimer's also progresses more rapidly, and is more severe, the earlier it starts (Jagger, Clarke, & Stone, 1995). The disease tends to appear later in more educated people (Stern et al., 1995).

Social Changes

Adulthood is a time when changes occur in social relationships and positions. These changes do not come in neat, predictable stages but instead follow various paths, depending on individual experiences. Transitions involving divorce, being fired, going back to school, remarrying, losing a spouse to death, being hospitalized, getting arrested, moving back home, or retiring are just a few of the turning points that can redirect a person's life path (Caspi, 1998).

Early Adulthood   Men and women in Western cultures usually enter the adult world in their twenties. They decide on an occupation, or at least take a job, and often become preoccupied with their careers. They also become more concerned with matters of love. Recall the sixth of Erikson's stages of psychosocial development noted in Table 9.2: intimacy versus isolation. This intimacy may include sexual intimacy, friendship, or mutual intellectual stimulation. It may lead to marriage or some other form of committed relationship. All this comes at a time when, having separated from their parents, young adults may also be experiencing isolation and loneliness. They may view the future with a mixture of anticipation, fear, and insecurity.

STAYING ALERT, STAYING ACTIVE, STAYING ALIVE   Sisters Alcantara, 91, Claverine, 87, and Nicolette, 94, of the School Sisters of Notre Dame convent, stay alert by reading, solving puzzles, playing cards, and participating in vocabulary quizzes. The nuns at this convent are participating in a study of aging and the brain.

Just how willing and able people are to make intimate commitments may depend on their earlier attachment relationships (Conger et al., 2000). Researchers have discovered that young adults' views of intimate relationships parallel the patterns of infant attachment that we described earlier (Horowitz, Rosenberg, & Bartholomew, 1993). If their view reflects a secure attachment, they tend to feel valued and worthy of support and affection; develop closeness easily; and have relationships characterized by joy, trust, and commitment. If their view reflects an insecure attachment, however, they tend to be preoccupied with relationships and may feel misunderstood, underappreciated, and worried about being abandoned; their relationships are often negative, obsessive, and jealous. Alternatively, they may be aloof and unable to trust, or commit themselves to, a partner. Researchers have videotaped young adult dating partners in situations producing slight anxiety that somewhat resemble the Strange Situation Test used with infants (Simpson, Rholes, & Nelligan, 1992). The tapes reveal that as anxiety increases, people with a secure attachment style increase their requests for support from their partners, whereas those with an insecure style decrease support-seeking behaviors. In another study, insecurely attached individuals were found to engage in more one-night stands and less cuddling than did those whose attachment style was secure (Tidwell, Reis, & Shaver, 1996).

During young adulthood, the experience of becoming parents represents entry into a major new developmental phase often accompanied by personal, social, and occupational changes (Palkovitz, Copes, & Woolfolk, 2001). For many couples, marital satisfaction declines, and about half of all marriages break under the strain (Belsky & Kelly, 1994; National Center for Health Statistics, 2001). Young mothers experience particular dissatisfaction—especially if they resent the constraints an infant brings, if they see their career as important, if the infant is temperamentally difficult, and if their partner is not supportive (Shapiro, Gottman, & Carrere, 2000). When the father does not do his share of caring for the baby, both mothers and fathers are dissatisfied (Levy-Shiff, 1994). Research indicates that gay and lesbian parents tend to share duties more equally—and to be more satisfied with the division of labor—than is typically the case in heterosexual families (Patterson, 2002).

Relationship difficulties uncovered during the transition to parenthood not only threaten marriages but can interfere with child care (Erel & Burman, 1995). The quality of that care is also related to young parents' own attachment histories. New mothers whose attachment to their own mother is secure tend to be more responsive to their infants, and the infants, in turn, are more likely to develop secure attachments to them (van IJzendoorn, 1995).

The challenges of young adulthood are complicated by the nature of family life today. Forty years ago, about half of North American households consisted of married couples in their twenties and thirties—a breadwinner husband and a homemaker wife—raising at least two children together. This picture now describes only about 10 percent of households (Demo, Allen, & Fine, 2000; Hernandez, 1997). Parents are older now because young adults are delaying marriage longer and waiting longer to have children. Many are having children without marrying, or choosing to raise children on their own (Weinraub, Horvath, & Gringlas, 2002). Those who divorce face many unanticipated stressors, including money problems, changes in living circumstances and working hours, loneliness, anxiety, and for custodial parents, a dramatic increase in housework and child-care tasks (De Vaus, 2002; Hetherington & Stanley-Hagan, 2002). In short, the changes seen in families and family life over the past several decades have made it more challenging than ever to successfully navigate the years of early adulthood.

Middle Adulthood   By their forties, people become concerned with producing something that will outlast them, usually through parenthood and/or job achievements (Sheldon & Kasser, 2001; Zucker, Ostrove, & Stewart, 2002). Erikson called this concern the crisis of **generativity,** because people are focused on producing or generating something. If people do not resolve this crisis, he suggested, they stagnate.

For many North American adults, however, the greatest tension occurs between two types of generativity: parenthood versus achievement. The demands of children and career often pull in opposite directions. Devotion to a job may lead to guilt about depriving children of attention; too much emphasis on home life may impair productivity at work (Booth et al., 2002). This stressful balancing act can lead to anxiety, frustration, and conflicts at home and on the job.

Sometime around age forty, people go through a **midlife transition.** They may reappraise and modify their lives and relationships. Many people may feel invigorated and liberated and see midlife as an opportunity for personal development (Sampselle et al., 2002), but others may feel upset and have a "midlife crisis." No one knows how many people experience a crisis during the midlife transition, but researchers suspect that these people are in the minority (Beck, 1992). The contrast between youth and middle age may be especially upsetting for men who matured early in adolescence and were sociable and athletic rather than intellectual (Block, 1971). Some women who chose a career over a family may feel conflict and distress as their last childbearing years pass. Women who have had children, however, often become more independent, confident, and oriented

BUILDING MONUMENTS   Middle adulthood tends to be a time during which people become deeply committed to building personal monuments, either by raising children or through achievements outside the home. This parent seems to have accomplished both goals.

generativity   The concern of adults in their forties with generating something enduring.

midlife transition   A point at around age forty when adults take stock of their lives.

THE "SANDWICH" GENERATION   During their midlife transition, many people feel "sandwiched" between generations—pressured by the social, emotional, and financial needs of their children on one side and of their aging parents on the other.

toward achievement and events outside the family (Helson & Moane, 1987). For both men and women who are parents, the emerging sexuality of their teenage children, the emptiness of the nest as children leave home, or the declining health of a parent may precipitate a crisis. The transition is easier for those who can accept the idea that life may not turn out as planned—or whose lives *have* turned out as planned.

Results from one study of more than 7,000 adults suggest that the happiness and healthiness of people in midlife depend on how much control they feel they have over their job, finances, marriage, children, and sex life; the level of education they have attained; and the type of work they are doing (Azar, 1996). Once the midlife transition is past, the middle years of adulthood are usually a time of satisfaction and happiness (Brim et al., 2000; MacArthur Foundation, 1999).

Late Adulthood   Most people between sixty-five and seventy-five years of age think of themselves as middle-aged, not old (Neugarten, 1977). They are active and influential politically and socially; they often are physically vigorous. Ratings of life satisfaction and self-esteem are, on average, as high in old age as during any other period of adulthood (Ben-Zur, 2002b; Charles, Mather, & Carstensen, 2003; Hamarat et al., 2002). Men and women who have been employed usually retire from their jobs during this period. They adjust most easily to retirement if they view it as a choice (Swan, 1996).

Today, more people than ever are reaching old age. In fact, those over 75 make up the fastest-growing segment of the population, a group that is 25 times larger than it was a century ago. Today, 77,000 people in the United States are over 100, and the Census Bureau predicts that number will rise to 834,000 by 2050 (Volz, 2000). Old age is not necessarily a time of loneliness and desolation, but it is a time when people generally become more inward looking, cautious, and conforming (Reedy, 1983). It is a time when people develop coping strategies that increasingly take into account the limits of their control—accepting what they cannot change, such as chronic health problems (Brandtstadter & Renner, 1990). Although they interact with others less frequently, older adults enjoy these interactions more (Carstensen, 1997). They find relationships more satisfying, supportive, and fulfilling than earlier in life. As they sense that time is running out, they value positive interactions and become selective about their social partners. As long as they have a network of at least three close relatives or friends, they are usually content.

The many changes associated with adolescence and adulthood are summarized in "In Review: Milestones of Adolescence and Adulthood."

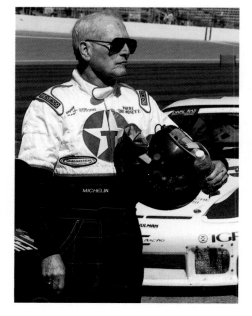

STILL ON A ROLL   Actor Paul Newman is a famous example of the many people whose late adulthood is healthy and vigorous. In January 2000, at the age of seventy, Newman received bruised ribs in a minor accident while preparing to drive his race car in the 24 Hours of Daytona. He was racing again the following month, and he is still racing today.

in review

MILESTONES OF ADOLESCENCE AND ADULTHOOD

Age	Physical Changes	Cognitive Changes	Social Events and Psychological Changes
Early adolescence (11–15 years)	Puberty brings reproductive capacity and marked bodily changes.	Formal operations and principled moral reasoning become possible for the first time. (This occurs only for some people.)	Social and emotional changes result from growing sexual awareness; adolescents experience mood swings, physical changes, and conflicts with parents.
Late adolescence (16–19 years)	Physical growth continues.	Formal operations and principled moral reasoning become more likely.	An identity crisis accompanies graduation from high school.
Early adulthood (20–39 years)	Physical growth continues.	Increases continue in knowledge, problem-solving ability, and moral reasoning.	People choose a job and often a mate; they may become parents.
Middle adulthood (40–65 years)	Size and muscle mass decrease; fat increases; eyesight declines; reproductive capacity in women ends.	Thought becomes more complex, adaptive, and global.	Midlife transition may lead to change; for most, the middle years are satisfying.
Late adulthood (over 65 years)	Size decreases; organs become less efficient.	Reasoning, mathematical ability, comprehension, novel problem solving, and memory may decline.	Retirement requires adjustments; people look inward; awareness of death precipitates life review.

? *The greatest threat to cognitive abilities in late adulthood is _____ disease.*

Death and Dying

With the onset of old age, people become aware that death is approaching. They watch as their friends disappear. They feel their health deteriorating, their strength waning, and their intellectual capabilities declining. A few years or a few months before death, some people experience a sharp decline in mental functioning known as **terminal drop** (Small & Bäckman, 1999).

The awareness of impending death brings about the last psychological crisis, according to Erikson's theory. During this stage, people evaluate their lives and accomplishments and affirm them as meaningful (leading to a feeling of integrity) or meaningless (leading to a feeling of despair). They tend to become more philosophical and reflective. They attempt to put their lives into perspective. They reminisce, resolve past conflicts, and integrate past events. They may also become more interested in the religious and spiritual side of life. This "life review" may trigger anxiety, regret, guilt, and despair; the risk of suicide does increase with age (Anderson & Conwell, 2002). But it may also help people to face their own death and the deaths of friends and relatives with a feeling of peace and acceptance (Lieberman & Tobin, 1983).

Even the actual confrontation with death does not have to bring despair and depression. When death finally is imminent, old people strive for a death with dignity, love, affection, physical contact, and no pain (Schulz, 1978). As they think about death, they are comforted by their religious faith, their achievements, and the love of their friends and family (Kastenbaum, Kastenbaum, & Morris, 1989).

terminal drop　A sharp decline in mental functioning that tends to occur in late adulthood, a few months or years before death.

Longevity   Facing death with dignity and openness helps people to complete the life cycle with a sense of life's meaningfulness, but most of us want to live as long as possible. How can we do so? Research suggests that people live longer if they do not have a history of heavy drinking and if they live independently in old age rather than in nursing homes. Longevity is not related to higher levels of education, income, or occupation—you can't buy long life (Jagger, Clarke, & Stone, 1995). However, certain personality characteristics and attitudes are associated with longer lives. These include being curious, being conscientious, and having positive feelings about getting older (Levy et al., 2002; Peterson et al., 1998). Having a strong marriage may also contribute to longer life for both spouses (Tower, Kasl, & Darefsky, 2002). Older adults also tend to live longer if they eat a low-calorie diet, get regular physical and mental exercise, and retain a sense of control over their lives (Krause & Shaw, 2000).

So eat your veggies, keep fit, and continue to think actively. You will live better now, and you may also live longer.

active review   Human Development

Linkages

As noted in the introductory chapter, all of psychology's subfields are related to one another. Our discussion of infantile amnesia illustrates just one way in which the topic of this chapter, human development, is linked to the subfield of memory, which is discussed in the chapter on memory. The Linkages diagram shows ties to two other subfields as well, and there are many more ties throughout the book. Looking for linkages among subfields will help you see how they all fit together and help you better appreciate the big picture that is psychology.

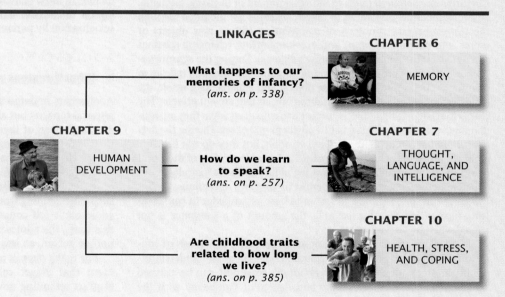

LINKAGES

CHAPTER 9
HUMAN DEVELOPMENT

What happens to our memories of infancy? (ans. on p. 338)

CHAPTER 6
MEMORY

How do we learn to speak? (ans. on p. 257)

CHAPTER 7
THOUGHT, LANGUAGE, AND INTELLIGENCE

Are childhood traits related to how long we live? (ans. on p. 385)

CHAPTER 10
HEALTH, STRESS, AND COPING

Summary

Developmental psychology is the study of the course and causes of systematic, sequential, age-related changes in mental abilities, social relationships, emotions, and moral understanding over the life span.

EXPLORING HUMAN DEVELOPMENT

▶ **What does "genetic influence" mean?**

A central question in developmental psychology concerns the relative influences of nature and nurture. Gesell stressed nature in his theory of development, proposing that development is *maturation*—the natural unfolding of abilities with age. Watson took the opposite view, claiming that development is learning, as shaped by the external environment. In his theory of cognitive development, Piaget described how nature and nurture work together. Today we accept the notion that both nature and nurture affect development and ask not whether, but how and to what extent, each contributes. Research in *behavioral genetics* shows that complex traits, such as intelligence and personality, are influenced by many genes, as well as by many environmental factors.

BEGINNINGS

▶ **Why should pregnant women stay away from tobacco and alcohol?**

Development begins with the union of an ovum and a sperm to form a zygote, which develops into an *embryo. Genes,* which consist of *deoxyribonucleic acid (DNA),* make up the **chromosomes** that are in each body cell. The embryonic stage is a **critical period** for development, a time when certain organs must develop properly or they never will. The development of organs at this stage is permanently affected by harmful **teratogens** such as tobacco, alcohol, or other drugs. After the embryo develops into a *fetus,* adverse conditions may harm the infant's size, behavior, intelligence, or health. Babies born to women who drink heavily are at risk for *fetal alcohol syndrome*.

Newborns have limited, but effective, senses of vision, hearing, taste, and smell. They exhibit many **reflexes**—swift, automatic responses to external stimuli. Motor development proceeds as the nervous system matures, muscles grow, and the infant experiments with and selects the most efficient movement patterns.

INFANCY AND CHILDHOOD: COGNITIVE DEVELOPMENT

▶ **How do babies think?**

Cognitive development refers to the development of thinking, knowing, and remembering. According to Piaget, *schemas* are modified through the complementary processes of *assimilation* (fitting new objects or events into existing schemas) and *accommodation* (changing schemas when new objects will not fit existing schemas). During the *sensorimotor period,* infants progress from using only simple senses and reflexes to forming mental representations of objects and actions. As a result, the child becomes capable of thinking about objects that are not present. The ability to recognize that objects continue to exist even when they are hidden from view is what Piaget called *object permanence.* During *the preoperational period,* children can use symbols, but they do not have the ability to think logically and rationally. Their understanding of the world is intuitive. When children develop the ability to think logically about concrete objects, they enter the period of *concrete operations.* At this time they can solve simple problems and have a knowledge of *conservation,* recognizing that, for example, the amount of a substance is not altered when its shape changes.

Today, developmental psychologists believe that new levels of cognition do not appear in sharply separated stages of global understanding but more gradually, and that children's reasoning can be affected by factors such as task difficulty and degree of familiarity with the objects and language involved.

Psychologists who explain cognitive development in terms of *information processing* have documented age-related improvements in children's attention, their abilities to explore and focus on features of the environment, and their memories. "Infantile amnesia" leaves us with virtually no memory of events from before the age of three. Several explanations have been suggested, but this phenomenon is not yet fully understood.

The specific content of cognitive development, including the development of scripts, depends on the cultural context in which children live. How fast children develop cognitive abilities depends to some extent on how stimulating and supportive their environments are. Children growing up in poverty are likely to have delayed or impaired cognitive abilities.

INFANCY AND CHILDHOOD: SOCIAL AND EMOTIONAL DEVELOPMENT

▶ **How do infants become attached to their caregivers?**

Infants and their caregivers, from the early months, respond to each other's emotional expressions. Most infants can be classified as having easy, difficult, or slow-to-warm-up **temperaments.** Whether they retain these temperamental styles depends to some extent on their parents' expectations and demands. Over the first year of life, infants form a deep, long-lasting emotional **attachment** to their mother or other primary caregiver. This attachment may be secure or insecure, depending largely on whether the caregiver is responsive and loving, or rejecting. The process of **socialization** begins as parents teach their children the skills and rules needed in their culture, using parenting styles described as **authoritarian, permissive,** or **authoritative.** Among European American parents, those with an authoritative style tend to have more competent and cooperative children. Patterns of socialization depend on the culture and conditions in which parents find themselves.

Over the childhood years, interactions with peers are increasingly characterized by cooperation and competition. Children come to base their friendships on feelings, not things. Changes in children's relationships are in part related to their growing social competence. Children become increasingly able to interpret and understand social situations and emotional signals. They also learn social rules and roles, including those related to gender. *Gender roles* are based both on biological differences between the sexes and on implicit and explicit socialization by parents, teachers, and peers.

ADOLESCENCE

▶ **What threatens adolescents' self-esteem?**

Adolescents undergo significant changes not only in size, shape, and physical capacity but also, typically, in their social lives, reasoning abilities, and views of themselves. *Puberty* brings about physical changes that lead to psychological changes. Early adolescence is a period of shaky self-esteem. It is also a time when conflict with parents, as well as closeness and conformity to friends, is likely to arise. Later adolescence focuses on finding an answer to the question, Who am I? Events such as graduating from high school and going to college challenge the adolescent's self-concept, precipitating an *identity crisis.* To resolve this crisis, the adolescent must develop an integrated self-image as a unique person, an image that often includes *ethnic identity.*

For many people, adolescence begins a stage of cognitive development that Piaget called the *formal operational period.* Formal abstract reasoning now becomes more sophisticated, and moral reasoning progresses from *preconventional* to *conventional* and, possibly, *postconventional* stages. Principled moral judgment—shaped by gender and culture—becomes possible for the first time.

ADULTHOOD

▶ **What developmental changes occur in adulthood?**

Physical, cognitive, and social changes occur throughout adulthood. Middle adulthood sees changes that include decreased sharpness of the senses, increased risk of heart disease, and declining fertility. Nevertheless, most people do not experience major health problems until late adulthood.

The cognitive changes that occur in early and middle adulthood are generally positive, including improvements in reasoning and problem-solving ability. In late adulthood, some intellectual abilities decline—especially those involved in tasks that are unfamiliar, complex, or difficult. Other abilities, such as recalling facts or making wise decisions, tend not to decline.

In their twenties, young adults make occupational choices and form intimate commitments. By the end of their thirties, they settle down and decide what is important. They become concerned with **generativity**—with producing something that will outlast them. Sometime around age forty, adults experience a **midlife transition,** which may or may not be a crisis. The forties and fifties are often a time of satisfaction. In their sixties, people contend with the issue of retirement. They generally become more inward looking, cautious, and conforming. In their seventies, eighties, and beyond, people confront their own mortality. They may become more philosophical and reflective as they review their lives. A few years or months before death, many experience a sharp decline in mental functioning known as **terminal drop**. Still, they strive for a death with dignity, love, and no pain.

Learn by Doing

Put It in Writing

Write a short paper describing some of the ways in which you have developed over the last five years. Include comments on physical changes, as well as changes in your thoughts, feelings, and behavior. Imagine yourself in another five years, and describe what further changes you expect in your physical condition, lifestyle, relationships, ideas, emotional state, and behavior. Compare the changes that have taken place in your life with those we have described in this chapter for the average person of your age.

Personal Learning Activity

Ask several of your friends about the way their parents raised them, and especially about how strict or permissive they were in providing discipline. Take notes on these interviews, and then try to categorize your friends' parents as either authoritarian, permissive, or authoritative. (You might try categorizing your own parents, as well.) Was it easy to decide which category to use in each case? Do you think that additional categories are necessary to describe parenting styles? Do you think that your friends' personalities reflect the effects of the parenting styles described in this chapter? *For additional projects, see the Personal Learning Activities in the corresponding chapter of the study guide that accompanies this text.*

Step into Action

Courses

Infancy
Child Development
Adolescence
Life-Span Development
Social Development
Cognitive Development
Death and Dying

Movies

Antwone Fisher (overcoming abuse and abandonment)
Wrestling Ernest Hemingway (aging)
About Schmidt (aging, Erikson's stage of generativity versus stagnation)
The War (parenting styles)
Schindler's List (moral development)
Lord of the Flies (nature-nurture)
Stand by Me; A Christmas Story (childhood)
Parenthood (child rearing)
Little Man Tate; Searching for Bobby Fischer; What's Eating Gilbert Grape (raising special children)
Revenge of the Nerds; Ferris Bueller's Day Off; The Breakfast Club; My Life in Pink; Rushmore (adolescence)
St. Elmo's Fire; Good Will Hunting; Reality Bites; Clerks; Chasing Amy (young adulthood)
The Big Chill; American Beauty; Same Time, Next Year (adulthood)
City Slickers (midlife transition)
On Golden Pond; Cocoon; Space Cowboys (aging)
Do the Right Thing (moral reasoning and moral action)
The Color Purple (development of self-esteem)

Books

Deborah Blum, *Love at Goon Park: Harry Harlow and the Science of Affection* (Perseus, 2002) (study of Harlow's famous research)
Sampson Davis, George Jenkins, and Rameck Hunt, *The Pact: Three Young Men Make a Promise and Fulfill a Dream* (Penguin/Putnam, 2002) (how three young men overcame their criminogenic backgrounds and became doctors)
Lawrence J. Friedman, *Identity's Architect: A Biography of Erik H. Erikson* (Scribner's, 1999) (focusing on Erikson's own identity crisis)
Thomas Hine, *The Rise and Fall of the American Teenager* (Avon, 1999) (social and cultural history of adolescence)
Jeffrey W. Trawick-Smith, *Early Childhood Development: A Multicultural Perspective* (Prentice Hall, 1999) (introduction to cultural influences on development)
Alison Gopnik, Andrew N. Meltzoff, and Patricia K. Kuhl, *The Scientist in the Crib: Minds, Brains, and How Children Learn* (William Morrow, 1999) (readable summary of research in cognitive development)
Richard Shulz and Timothy A. Salthouse, *Adult Development and Aging: Myths and Emerging Realities* (Prentice Hall, 1998) (the title says it all)
Rachel Simmons, *Odd Girl Out: The Hidden Culture of Aggression in Girls* (Harcourt Books, 2002) (study of girls' relational aggression)
Robin Karr-Morse and Meredith S. Wiley, *Ghosts from the Nursery: Tracing the Roots of Violence* (Grove/ Atlantic, 1999) (how biological predispositions may lead to violence)
Robert Karen, *Becoming Attached: First Relationships and How They Shape Our Capacity to Love* (Oxford University Press, 1995) (emotional development)

The Web

The World Wide Web is a good source of additional information about the science of psychology, provided you use it carefully and think critically about the information you find. The web site that accompanies this text offers many resources relevant to this chapter. These resources include interactive NetLab exercises; Thinking Critically and Eval-

uating Research exercises; ACE chapter quizzes; recommended web links; and articles on current events, books, and movies. At http://college.hmco.com, select *Psychology* and then this textbook.

Review of Key Terms

Can you define each of the key terms in the chapter? Check your definitions against those on the pages listed in parentheses below or in the Glossary/Index at the end of the text.

accommodation *(p. 333)*

assimilation *(p. 333)*

attachment *(p. 344)*

authoritarian parents *(p. 349)*

authoritative parents *(p. 349)*

behavioral genetics *(p. 326)*

chromosomes *(p. 327)*

concrete operations *(p. 336)*

conservation *(p. 336)*

conventional *(p. 356)*

critical period *(p. 328)*

deoxyribonucleic acid (DNA) *(p. 327)*

developmental psychology *(p. 325)*

embryo *(p. 328)*

ethnic identity *(p. 354)*

fetal alcohol syndrome *(p. 329)*

fetus *(p. 328)*

formal operational period *(p. 356)*

gender roles *(p. 350)*

generativity *(p. 362)*

genes *(p. 327)*

identity crisis *(p. 355)*

information processing *(p. 338)*

maturation *(p. 325)*

midlife transition *(p. 362)*

object permanence *(p. 333)*

permissive parents *(p. 349)*

postconventional *(p. 356)*

preconventional *(p. 356)*

preoperational period *(p. 336)*

puberty *(p. 353)*

reflexes *(p. 330)*

schemas *(p. 332)*

sensorimotor period *(p. 333)*

socialization *(p. 348)*

temperament *(p. 343)*

teratogens *(p. 328)*

terminal drop *(p. 364)*

Multiple-Choice Self-Test

Select the best answer for each of the questions below. Then check your response against the Answer Key at the end of the text.

1. Which of the following is *not* true? Research in behavioral genetics

   a. explores how nature and nurture contribute to make all people alike as human beings.
   b. explores how nature and nurture operate together to make people unique.
   c. is concerned with differences between individuals or groups, not with the characteristics of a single individual.
   d. can determine what percentage of your intelligence is due to heredity.

2. When she became pregnant, Alyse was advised to avoid teratogens. These include all of the following except

   a. alcohol.   c. smoking.
   b. drugs.   d. exercise.

3. Like most other children his age, Ty is proceeding through a natural unfolding of development: He first began to crawl, then to stand by holding onto furniture, then to stand alone, and now he is walking all by himself. This fixed sequence of development is referred to as

   a. biogenetic development.   c. maturation.
   b. behavioral development.   d. genetic influence.

4. Keshawn is one month old. He is most likely to look longest at

   a. small figures on the wallpaper.
   b. a ribbon hanging above his crib.
   c. colorful figures.
   d. a nearby human face.

5. At six months of age, Jacob still demonstrates the grasping and rooting reflexes. This could signal that Jacob

   a. has advanced motor skills.
   b. has muscles that cannot support his body.
   c. has a problem with brain development.
   d. needs less environmental stimulation than the average baby.

6. When two-year old Jessie sees a scuba diver emerge on the beach, he says "Big fish!" According to Piaget, Jessie used _____ to try to understand the new stimulus of a scuba diver.

   a. assimilation   c. object permanence
   b. accommodation   d. conservation

7. Adriana is crying because her teddy bear, Boyd, has fallen off the table and landed on his face. She insists that her mother put a bandage on Boyd's nose. According to Piaget's theory, Adriana is most likely in the _____ stage of cognitive development.

   a. sensorimotor   c. concrete operational
   b. preoperational   d. formal operational

8. Renee Baillargeon's research focused on infants' understanding about objects and gravity. Baillargeon found that infants

   a. looked longer at "possible" events that they had experienced many times.
   b. looked longer at "impossible" events that defied physical principles.

c. have no knowledge of physical principles until they have actual experience with such principles.

d. do not improve their understanding of physical principles between the age of three months and one year.

9. According to research on information processing and memory, when you try to recall your first birthday, you are likely to

a. recall a general schema of "birthday," as well as details about your first one.

b. be unable to recall anything about your first birthday due to infantile amnesia.

c. recall information about your first birthday if you are shown pictures of yourself taken that day.

d. recall information about the birthday if you hear a tape recorded at your party.

10. Tara is an infant who goes to sleep at fairly predictable times and cries only when she is hungry or uncomfortable. She is generally cheerful and is happy when taken new places. According to research on temperament, Tara would be described as a(n) _____ infant.

a. easy
b. slow-to-warm-up
c. difficult
d. dependent

11. Harlow's research with infant monkeys and artificial mothers demonstrated that

a. infant monkeys become attached to the "mothers" that feed them.

b. infant monkeys become attached to the "mothers" that provide contact comfort.

c. attachment is entirely innate, with no learned component.

d. "mothering" is instinctive, with no learned component.

12. When young Habib's mother drops him off at the day care center, he always cries when she leaves. When his mother returns and lifts him up, Habib tries to squirm away and refuses to be held by her. Habib is demonstrating a(n) _____ attachment to his mother.

a. secure
b. anxious insecure
c. avoidant insecure
d. ambivalent insecure

13. Sam and Alex are sixteen and want to drive to a rock concert in a big city, five hours from their home. Sam's parents explain that it is too dangerous for him to drive that distance and be in a major city without an adult. They offer to drive him and Alex to the concert. Alex's parents tell him that it is no problem if he wants to drive their car and stay in the city overnight. According to Baumrind's research, Sam's parents are displaying a(n) _____ style of parenting, whereas Alex's parents are displaying a(n) _____ style.

a. authoritative; authoritarian
b. authoritarian; authoritative
c. authoritative; permissive
d. authoritarian; permissive

14. Pat is seven years old and lives in the midwestern United States. Pat's parents encourage Pat to achieve, be independent, explore the environment, and assume personal responsibility. From this information we can conclude that Pat is most likely

a. female.
b. male.
c. African American.
d. androgenous.

15. Ludmilla recently graduated from high school but can't decide whether to attend a local community college or work full-time. She doesn't know what career she would like to pursue, and she is also uncertain whether she should stay with her current boyfriend. According to Erikson, Ludmilla is most likely experiencing the psychosocial crisis characterized by

a. trust versus mistrust.
b. initiative versus guilt.
c. identity versus role confusion.
d. integrity versus despair.

16. According to research on adolescence, which of the following is *not true* of teens who engage in sexual activity? They are

a. more likely to hold unconventional attitudes and values.
b. more likely to smoke and drink.
c. more likely to be Asian American.
d. less likely to have highly educated parents.

17. Jeanine and Helen are in a drugstore when Jeanine suggests that they steal some candy. Helen argues that they should not steal the candy because they might get caught and be put into jail. According to Kohlberg's theory, Helen is at the _____ stage of moral reasoning.

a. preconventional
b. conventional
c. postconventional
d. universal

18. In the past ten years, Vernon has gained weight, especially around the middle. He also now needs glasses. If he is typical of most people his age, Vernon has most likely reached

a. adolescence.
b. early adulthood.
c. middle adulthood.
d. old age.

19. Verna is sixty-five years old. Based on developmental research, we would assume that Verna

a. is slower at solving complex new problems than younger people.

b. has better mathematical skills than younger people.

c. finds her mental abilities improving every day.

d. will do better at mental tasks if her mind has "rested" as a result of being retired and inactive for many years.

20. Patrice is eighty years old and has recently been unable to read her books and comprehend what they say. She can't make sense of her checkbook, even though she was once an expert accountant. Her health is deteriorating, and her strength waning. Patrice is most likely experiencing

a. cognitive dissonance.
b. terminal drop.
c. the crisis of initiative versus guilt.
d. androgyny.

10

Health, Stress, and Coping

In North America, people are living longer than ever. In fact, those over 100 constitute the fastest-growing age group in the United States. Will you eventually join them? To some extent, the answer lies in your genes, but how long you live is also determined in large measure by how you behave, how you think, and what stressors you face. Health psychologists explore how illness and death are related to these behavioral, psychological, and social factors, and they apply their research to preventing illness and promoting health. They develop programs to help people make lifestyle changes that can lower their risk of illness and premature death. And they study how stress affects people's mental and physical health. Of particular importance is the immune system's response to stress. In this chapter, you will learn about several kinds of stressors, how people respond to them, and the relationship between stress reactions and illness. You will also discover what you can do to protect your own health and change risky behaviors that may affect it.

Reading this chapter will help you to answer the following questions:

▶ **What do health psychologists do?**

▶ **How do psychological stressors affect physical health?**

▶ **How do people react to stressors?**

▶ **Why doesn't everyone react to stressors in the same way?**

▶ **How does stress affect your immune system?**

▶ **Who is most likely to adopt a healthy lifestyle?**

I n Bangor, Maine, where snow and ice have paralyzed the community, Angie's headache gets worse as her four-year-old daughter and six-year-old son start bickering again. The day-care center and elementary school are closed, so Angie must stay home from her job at the grocery store. She probably couldn't have gotten there anyway, because the buses have stopped running. During the latest storm the power went out, and the house is now almost unbearably cold; the can of spaghetti Angie opens is nearly frozen. Worry begins to creep into her head: "If I can't work, how will I pay for rent and day care?" Her parents have money problems, too, so they can't offer financial help, and her ex-husband rarely makes his child-support payments. On top of everything else, Angie is coming down with the flu.

How do people manage such adversity, and what are its consequences for the individual? Psychologists who study questions like these have established a specialty known as **health psychology,** "a field within psychology devoted to understanding psychological influence on how people stay healthy, why they become ill, and how they respond when they do get ill" (Taylor, 1999, p. 4).

health psychology   A field in which psychologists conduct and apply psychological research to promote human health and prevent illness.

371

Health Psychology

▶ **What do health psychologists do?**

The themes underlying health psychology date back to ancient times. For thousands of years, in many cultures around the world, people have believed that their mental state, their behavior, and their health are linked. Today, there is scientific evidence to support this belief (Booth et al., 2001; Taylor, 2002). We now know that the stresses of life influence health through their impact on psychological and physical processes. Researchers have also associated anger, hostility, pessimism, depression, and hopelessness with the appearance of physical illnesses. Traits such as optimism are associated with good health. Similarly, poor health has been linked to behavioral factors such as lack of exercise, inadequate diet, smoking, and abuse of alcohol and other drugs. Good health has been associated with behaviors such as adequate exercise and following medical advice.

Health psychology has become increasingly prominent in North America, in part because of changing patterns of illness. Until the middle of the twentieth century, acute infectious diseases such as influenza, tuberculosis, and pneumonia were the major causes of illness and death in the United States and Canada. With these deadly diseases now tamed, chronic illnesses—such as coronary heart disease, cancer, and diabetes—have joined accidents and injury as the leading causes of disability and death (Guyer et al., 2000). Compared with acute diseases, these chronic diseases develop more slowly and are more strongly associated with people's psychological makeup, lifestyle, and environment (Centers for Disease Control and Prevention, 2001; D'Agostino et al., 2001) (see Table 10.1). The psychological and behavioral factors that contribute to these illnesses can be changed by intervention programs such as those that promote non-smoking, exercise, and healthy eating (e.g., Bazzano et al., 2003; Kraus et al., 2002). In fact, about half the deaths in the United States are due to potentially preventable health-risky behaviors (Greenland et al., 2003; Khot et al., 2003; Taylor, 2002).

One goal of health psychology is to help people understand the role they can play in controlling their own health and life expectancy (Baum, Revenson, & Singer, 2001; Nash et al., 2003). For example, health psychologists have been active in educating people about the warning signs of cancer, heart disease, and other serious illnesses, encouraging them to engage in self-examinations, and emphasizing the importance of seeking medical attention while life-saving treatment is still possible. Health psychologists also study, and help people to understand, the role played by stress in physical health and illness.

table 10.1

Lifestyle Behaviors That Affect the Leading Causes of Death in the United States

This table shows five of the leading causes of death in the United States today, along with behavioral factors that contribute to their development.

Cause of Death	Alcohol	Smoking	Diet	Exercise	Stress
Heart disease	x	x	x	x	x
Cancer	x	x	x		?
Stroke	x	x	x	?	?
Lung disease		x			
Accidents and injury	x	x			x

Source: Data from Centers for Disease Control and Prevention (2001).

Understanding Stress and Stressors

▶ **How do psychological stressors affect physical health?**

You have probably heard that death and taxes are the only two things guaranteed in life. If there is a third, it surely must be stress. Stress is woven into the fabric of life. No matter how wealthy, powerful, attractive, or happy you might be, stress happens. It comes in many forms: a difficult exam, an automobile accident, standing in a long line, reading about frightening world events, or just having a day when everything goes wrong. Mild stress, like waiting to be with that special person, can be stimulating, motivating, and even desirable, but as stress becomes more severe, it can bring on physical, psychological, and behavioral problems. To take just one example, surveys indicate that stress in the workplace costs U.S. businesses more than $150 billion each year as a result of employee absenteeism, reduced productivity, and health care costs (Sauter et al., 1999; Spector, 2002).

Stress is the negative emotional and physiological process that occurs as individuals try to adjust to or deal with environmental circumstances that disrupt, or threaten to disrupt, their daily functioning (Taylor, 2002). The environmental circumstances (such as exams or accidents) that cause people to make adjustments are called **stressors. Stress reactions** are the physical, psychological, and behavioral responses (such as nervousness, nausea, or fatigue) displayed in the face of stressors.

Some people are more strongly affected by stressors than other people, and they are more strongly affected on some occasions than on others. Why? As described in more detail later, several *mediating factors* influence the relationship between people and their environments. These mediating factors include (1) the extent to which people can *predict* and *control* their stressors, (2) how they *interpret* the threat involved, (3) the *social support* they get, and (4) their *stress-coping skills*. Mediating factors can either dampen or magnify a stressor's impact. In other words, as shown in Figure 10.1, stress is not a specific event but a transaction between people and their environments. It is a process in which the nature and intensity of stress responses depend on what stressors occur and how they are mediated by factors such as they way people think about them and the skills and resources they have to cope with them.

figure 10.1

The Process of Stress

Stressful events, stress reactions, and stress mediators are all important components of the stress process. Notice that the process involves many two-way relationships. For example, if a person has effective coping skills, stress responses will be less severe. Having milder stress responses will act as a "reward" that will strengthen those skills. Further, as coping skills (such as refusing unreasonable demands) improve, certain stressors (such as a boss's unreasonable demands) may become less frequent.

stress The process of adjusting to circumstances that disrupt, or threaten to disrupt, a person's daily functioning.

stressors Events or situations to which people must adjust.

stress reactions Physical and psychological responses to stressors.

Stressors	Stress mediators	Stress responses
Life changes and strains Catastrophic events Daily hassles Chronic stressors	Cognitive appraisal Predictability Control Coping resources and methods Social support	Physical Psychological • Emotional • Cognitive • Behavioral

Psychological Stressors

Most of the stressors people face have both physical and psychological components. Because these components overlap, it is often difficult to separate them for analysis. For example, students are challenged by psychological demands to do well in their courses, as well as by physical fatigue resulting from a heavy load of classes, and maybe a job and family responsibilities, too. So although we focus here on psychological stressors, remember that physical stressors almost always accompany them.

Any event that forces a person to change or adapt can be a psychological stressor. Even pleasant events can qualify as stressful. For example, a vacation is supposed to be relaxing, but it can be exhausting as well. And though the higher pay of a new job may be desirable, the change may also bring new pressures (Schaubroeck, Jones, & Xie, 2001). Still, it is usually unpleasant circumstances that produce the most adverse psychological and physical effects (Kessler, 1997). These circumstances include catastrophic events, life changes and strains, chronic stressors, and daily hassles (Baum, Gatchel, & Krantz, 1997).

Catastrophic events are sudden, unexpected, potentially life threatening experiences or traumas. Physical or sexual assault, military combat, natural disasters, terrorist attacks, and accidents fall into this category. *Life changes* and *strains* include divorce, illness in the family, difficulties at work, moving to a new place, and other circumstances that create demands to which people must adjust (Price, 1992; see Table 10.2). *Chronic stressors*—those that continue over a long period of time—include such circumstances as living near a noisy airport, having a serious illness, being unable to earn a decent living, residing in a high-crime neighborhood, being the victim of discrimination, and even enduring years of academic pressure (Evans, Hygge, & Bullinger, 1995; Levenstein, Smith, & Kaplan, 2001). Finally, *daily hassles* involve irritations, pressures, and annoyances that may not be major stressors by themselves but whose effects add up to become significant (Evans & Johnson, 2000). The frustrations of daily commuting in heavy traffic, for example, can become so intense for some drivers that they display a pattern of aggression called "road rage" (Levy et al., 1997; Rathbone & Huckabee, 1999).

Measuring Stressors

Which stressors are the most harmful? To study stress more precisely, psychologists have tried to measure the impact of particular stressors. In 1967, Thomas Holmes and Richard Rahe (pronounced "ray") pioneered the effort to find a standard way of measuring the stress in a person's life. Working on the assumption that both positive and negative

table 10.2

The Undergraduate Stress Questionnaire

Here are some items from the Undergraduate Stress Questionnaire, which asks students to indicate whether various stressors have occurred during the previous week.

Has this stressful event happened to you at any time during the last week? If it has, please check the space next to it. If it has not, please leave it blank.

_____ 1. Assignments in all classes due the same day

_____ 2. Having roommate conflicts

_____ 3. Lack of money

_____ 4. Trying to decide on major

_____ 5. Can't understand your professor

_____ 6. Stayed up late writing a paper

_____ 7. Sat through a boring class

_____ 8. Went into a test unprepared

_____ 9. Parents getting divorced

_____ 10. Incompetence at the registrar's office

Source: Crandall, Preisler, & Aussprung (1992).

COPING WITH CATASTROPHE Catastrophic events such as terrorism, explosions, hurricanes, plane crashes, school shootings, and other traumas are stressors that can be psychologically devastating for victims, their families, and rescue workers (Cohan & Cole, 2002; North & Pfefferbaum, 2002; Schlenger et al., 2002). As was the case in the wake of the terrorist attacks on the World Trade Center and the Pentagon, health psychologists and other professionals provide on-the-spot counseling and follow-up sessions to help people deal with the consequences of trauma.

changes produce stress, they asked a large number of people to rate—in terms of *life-change units,* or *LCUs*—the amount of change and demand for adjustment caused by events such as divorcing, being fired, retiring, losing a loved one, or becoming pregnant. On the basis of these ratings, Holmes and Rahe created the *Social Readjustment Rating Scale,* or *SRRS.* People taking the SRRS receive a stress score equal to the sum of the LCUs for all the stressful events they have recently experienced. Numerous studies showed that people scoring high on the SRRS and other life-change scales are more likely to suffer physical illness, mental disorder, or other problems than those with lower scores (e.g., Monroe, Thase, & Simons, 1992).

Some researchers wondered, though, whether life changes alone tell the whole story about the impact of stressors. Accordingly, some investigators have used face-to-face interviews to more precisely measure stressors and their impact (e.g., Dohrenwend et al., 1993). Others developed scales such as the *Life Experiences Survey,* or *LES* (Sarason, Johnson, & Siegal, 1978), which measure not just which life events occurred but also people's perceptions of how positive or negative the events were, and how well they were able to cope with the events. The LES also allows respondents to write in and rate any stressors they have experienced that are not on the printed list. This individualized approach can capture the differing impact and meaning that certain experiences might have for men compared with women and for members of various cultural or subcultural groups. Divorce, for example, may have different meanings to people of different religious and cultural backgrounds. And members of some ethnic groups may experience prejudice and discrimination that is not felt by other groups (Contrada et al., 2000; Steffen et al., 2003).

Different stress measurements yield somewhat differing results (McQuaid et al., 2000; Steffen et al., 2003), but as you might expect, they generally show that negative events have a stronger negative impact on health than do positive events (De Benedittis, Lornenzetti, & Pieri, 1990).

Stress Responses

▶ **How do people react to stressors?**

Physical and psychological stress reactions often occur together, especially as stressors become more intense. Furthermore, one type of stress response can set off a stress response in another dimension. For example, a physical stress reaction such as mild chest pains might trigger the psychological stress response of worrying about a heart attack. Still, it is useful to consider each category of stress responses one at a time.

Physical Responses

If you have experienced a near accident or some other sudden, frightening event, you know that the physical responses to stressors include rapid breathing, increased heartbeat, sweating, and a little later, shakiness. These reactions make up a general pattern known as the *fight-or-flight syndrome*. As described in the chapters on biology and behavior and on motivation and emotion, this syndrome prepares the body to face or to flee an immediate threat. Once the danger passes, fight-or-flight responses subside.

When stressors are longer-lasting, however, the fight-or-flight syndrome is only the beginning of a longer sequence of reactions. Careful observation of animals and humans led Hans Selye (pronounced "SELL-yay") to suggest that this extended sequence of physical stress responses occurs in a consistent pattern. He called this sequence the **general adaptation syndrome,** or **GAS** (Selye, 1956, 1976). The GAS occurs in three stages (see Figure 10.2), and it is activated by efforts to adapt to any stressor, whether it is physical or psychological.

The first stage, called the *alarm reaction,* involves some version of the fight-or-flight syndrome. The alarm reaction to a mild stressor, such as a hot room, might simply involve changes in heart rate, respiration, and perspiration that help the body regulate its temperature. More severe stressors prompt more dramatic alarm reactions, rapidly mobilizing the body's adaptive energy, much as a burglar alarm alerts the police to take action (Kiecolt-Glaser et al., 1998).

Alarm reactions are controlled by the sympathetic nervous system through organs and glands that make up the *sympatho-adreno-medullary (SAM) system.* As shown on the right side of Figure 10.3, stressors trigger a process that begins when the brain's hypothalamus activates the sympathetic branch of the autonomic nervous system (ANS), which stimulates the medulla (inner part) of the adrenal glands. The adrenals, in turn, secrete *catecholamines* (pronounced "kat-uh-KOH-luh-meens")—especially adrenaline and noradrenaline—which circulate in the bloodstream, activating the liver, kidneys, heart, lungs, and other organs. The result is increased blood pressure, muscle tension, and blood sugar, along with other physical changes needed to cope with stressors. Even brief exposure to a stressor can produce major changes in these coordinated regulatory body systems (Cacioppo et al., 1995).

As shown on the left side of Figure 10.3, stressors also activate the *hypothalamic-pituitary-adrenocortical (HPA) system,* in which the hypothalamus stimulates the pituitary gland in the brain. The pituitary, in turn, secretes hormones such as adrenocorti-

figure 10.2

The General Adaptation Syndrome

Hans Selye found that physical reactions to stressors include an initial alarm reaction, followed by resistance and then exhaustion. During the alarm reaction, the body's resistance to stress temporarily drops below normal as it absorbs a stressor's initial impact. Resistance increases and then levels off in the resistance stage, but it ultimately declines if the exhaustion stage is reached.

Source: Adapted from Selye (1974).

figure 10.3

Organ Systems Involved in the GAS

Stressors produce a variety of physiological responses that begin in the brain and spread to organs throughout the body. For example, the pituitary gland triggers the release of endorphins, the body's natural painkillers. It also stimulates the release of corticosteroids, which help resist stress but, as described later, also tend to suppress the immune system. Some of these substances may interact with sex hormones to create different physical stress responses and coping methods in men and women (Taylor et al., 2000).

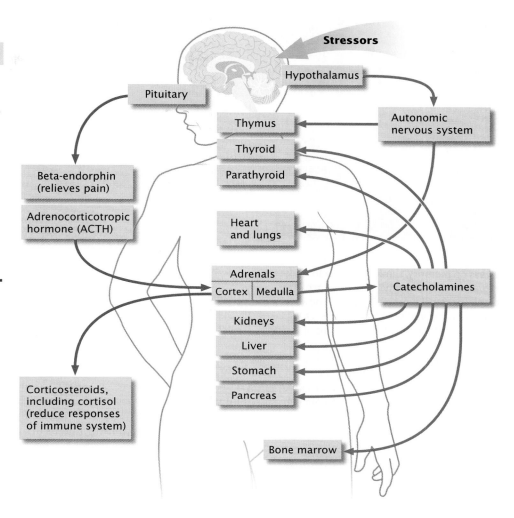

cotropic hormone (ACTH). Among other things, ACTH stimulates the cortex (outer surface) of the adrenal glands to secrete *corticosteroids;* these hormones release the body's energy supplies and fight inflammation. The pituitary gland also triggers the release of *endorphins,* the body's natural painkillers.

The overall effect of these stress systems is to generate emergency energy. The more stressors there are and the longer they last, the more resources the body must spend in responding to them.

If the stressors persist, the *resistance stage* of the GAS begins. Here, obvious signs of the initial alarm reaction fade as the body settles in to resist the stressor on a long-term basis. The drain on adaptive energy is less during the resistance stage compared with the alarm stage, but the body is still working hard to cope with stress.

This continued campaign of biochemical resistance is costly. It slowly but surely uses up the body's reserves of adaptive energy until the capacity to resist is gone. The body then enters the third GAS stage, known as *exhaustion.* In extreme cases, such as prolonged exposure to freezing temperatures, the result is death. More commonly, the exhaustion stage brings signs of physical wear and tear. Especially hard-hit are the organ systems that were weak to begin with or were heavily involved in the resistance process. For example, if adrenaline and cortisol (which help fight stressors during the resistance stage) remain elevated for an extended time, the result can be damage to the heart and blood vessels; suppression of the body's disease-fighting immune system; and vulnerability to illnesses such as heart disease, high blood pressure, arthritis, colds, and flu (e.g., Carney et al., 1998; Light et al., 1999; McEwen, 1998). Selye referred to illnesses caused or worsened by stressors as **diseases of adaptation.**

general adaptation syndrome (GAS) A three-stage pattern of responses triggered by the effort to adapt to stressors.

diseases of adaptation Illnesses caused or worsened by stressors.

STRESS FOR $500, ALEX   The effects of stress on memory, thinking, decision making, and other cognitive functions are often displayed by players on TV game shows like *Jeopardy!* and *Who Wants to be a Millionaire.* Under the intense pressure of time, competition, and the scrutiny of millions of viewers, contestants may miss questions that seem ridiculously easy to those calmly recalling the correct answers at home. The hosts of some shows, such as *The Weakest Link,* add to this pressure for the sake of entertainment.

Psychological Responses

Selye's research focused mainly on the physiological aspects of stress responses, but stressors also create a variety of psychological responses, including changes in emotion and cognition (thinking), and accompanying changes in behavior.

Emotional Changes   The physical stress responses we have described are usually accompanied by emotional stress responses. If someone pulls a gun and demands your money, you will most likely experience the GAS alarm reaction. You will also feel some strong emotion—probably fear, maybe anger. In describing stress, people tend to say, "I was angry and frustrated!" rather than "My heart rate increased, and my blood pressure went up." In other words, they tend to mention changes in the emotions they are experiencing.

In most cases, emotional stress reactions fade soon after the stressors are gone. Even severe emotional stress responses ease eventually. However, if stressors continue for a long time or if many occur in a short time, emotional stress reactions may persist. When people don't have a chance to recover their emotional equilibrium, they feel tense, irritable, short-tempered, or anxious, and they may experience increasingly intense feelings of fatigue, depression, and hopelessness. These reactions can become severe enough to be diagnosed as major depressive disorder, generalized anxiety disorder, or other stress-related mental problems discussed in the chapter on psychological disorders.

Cognitive Changes   In 1995, in the busy, noisy intensive care unit of a London hospital, a doctor misplaced a decimal point while calculating the amount of morphine a one-day-old premature baby should receive. The child died of a massive overdose (Davies, 1999). Reductions in the ability to concentrate, to think clearly, or to remember accurately are typical cognitive stress reactions (Hygge, Evans, & Bullinger, 2002). These problems appear partly because of *ruminative thinking,* the recurring intrusion of thoughts about stressful events (Lyubomirsky & Nolen-Hoeksema, 1995). Ruminative thoughts about relationship problems, for example, can seriously interfere with studying for a test. A related phenomenon is *catastrophizing,* which means dwelling on and overemphasizing the possible negative consequences of events. During exams, test-anxious college students are likely to say to themselves, "I'm falling behind" or "Everyone is doing better than I am." As catastrophizing or ruminative thinking impairs cognitive functioning, resulting feelings of anxiety and other emotional arousal add to the total stress response, further hampering performance (Mendl, 1999).

Overarousal created by stressors also tends to narrow the scope of attention, making it harder to scan the full range of possible solutions to complex problems (Craske, 1999; Keinan, Friedland, & Ben-Porath, 1987). In addition, stress-narrowed attention may increase the problem-solving errors described in the chapter on thought, language, and intelligence. People under stress are more likely to cling to *mental sets,* which are well-learned, but not always efficient, approaches to problems. Stress may also intensify *functional fixedness,* the tendency to use objects for only one purpose. Victims of hotel fires, for example, sometimes die trapped in their rooms because, in the stress of the moment, it did not occur to them to use the telephone or a piece of furniture to break a window.

Stressors may also impair decision making. Under stress, people who normally consider all aspects of a situation before making a decision may act impulsively and sometimes foolishly (Keinan, Friedland, & Ben-Porath, 1987). High-pressure salespeople often take advantage of this stress response by creating time-limited offers or by telling indecisive customers that others are waiting to buy the item they are considering (Cialdini, 2001).

Behavioral Responses   Clues about people's physical and emotional stress reactions come from changes in how they look, act, or talk. Strained facial expressions, a shaky voice, tremors, and jumpiness are common behavioral stress responses. Posture can also convey information about stress, a fact well known to skilled interviewers.

Even more obvious behavioral stress responses appear as people attempt to escape or avoid stressors. Some people quit their jobs, drop out of school, turn to alcohol, or even attempt suicide. Unfortunately, as discussed in the chapter on learning, escape and avoid-

burnout   A pattern of physical and psychological dysfunctions in response to continuous stressors.

posttraumatic stress disorder (PTSD)   A pattern of adverse reactions following a traumatic event, commonly involving re-experiencing the event through nightmares or vivid memories.

ance tactics deprive people of the opportunity to learn more adaptive ways of coping with stressful environments, including college (Cooper et al., 1992a). Aggression is another common behavioral response to stressors. All too often, this response is directed at members of one's own family (Polusny & Follette, 1995). For instance, in the wake of hurricanes and other natural disasters, it is not uncommon to see dramatic increases in the rate of domestic-violence reports in the devastated area (Curtis, Miller, & Berry, 2000; Rotton, 1990).

LINKAGES
When do stress responses become mental disorders?
(a link to Psychological Disorders)

P hysical and psychological stress responses sometimes appear together in patterns known as *burnout* and *posttraumatic stress disorder*. **Burnout** is an increasingly intense pattern of physical and psychological dysfunction in response to a continuous flow of stressors or to chronic stress (Maslach & Goldberg, 1998). As burnout nears, previously reliable workers or once-attentive spouses become indifferent, disengaged, impulsive, or accident-prone. They miss work frequently; oversleep; perform their jobs poorly; abuse alcohol or other drugs; and become irritable, suspicious, withdrawn, and depressed (Taylor, 2002). Burnout is particularly common among those who do "people work," such as teachers and nurses, and those who perceive themselves as being treated unjustly by employers (Elovainio, Kivimäki, & Vahtera, 2002; Schultz & Schultz, 1998).

LINKAGES

Stress and Psychological Disorders

A different pattern of severe stress reactions is illustrated by the case of Mary, a thirty-three-year-old nurse who was raped at knifepoint by an intruder in her apartment. In the weeks following this trauma, she became afraid of being alone and was preoccupied with the attack and with the fear that it might happen again. She installed additional locks on her doors and windows but experienced difficulty concentrating and could not immediately return to work. The thought of sex repelled her.

Mary suffered from **posttraumatic stress disorder (PTSD),** a pattern of severe negative reactions following a traumatic event (American Psychiatric Association, 1994). Among the characteristic reactions are anxiety, irritability, jumpiness, inability to concentrate or work productively, sexual dysfunction, and difficulty in getting along with others. PTSD sufferers also experience sleep disturbances and intense startle responses to noise or other sudden stimuli (e.g., Goenjian et al., 2001; Johnson et al., 2002; Kawamura, Kim, & Asukai, 2001). The most common feature of posttraumatic stress disorder

LIFE HANGING IN THE BALANCE
Symptoms of burnout and posttraumatic stress disorder often plague firefighters, police officers, emergency medical personnel, and others who are repeatedly exposed to time pressure, trauma, danger, and other stressors. Posttraumatic stress disorder can also occur following a single catastrophic event. Surveys taken in the weeks and months following the terrorist attacks on the World Trade Center revealed that 7.5 percent of adults who lived near the devastated area experienced symptoms of PTSD, and over half experienced significant symptoms of emotional distress (DeLisi et al., 2003; Galea et al., 2002; Simeon et al., 2003).

is re-experiencing the trauma through nightmares or vivid memories. In rare cases, *flash-backs* occur in which the person behaves for minutes, hours, or days as if the trauma were occurring again.

Posttraumatic stress disorder is most commonly associated with events such as war, terrorism, assault, or rape (e.g., Galea et al., 2002; Schnurr et al., 2000), but researchers now believe that some PTSD symptoms can be triggered by any major stressor, from car accidents to being stalked (Ironson et al., 1997; Kamphuis & Emmelkamp, 2001). PTSD may appear immediately following a trauma, or it may not occur until weeks, months, or even years later (Gilboa-Schechtman & Foa, 2001; Heim et al., 2000; Port, Engdahl, & Frazier, 2001). The majority of those affected require professional help, although some seem to recover without it. For most, improvement takes time; for nearly all, the support of family and friends is vital to recovery (Foa et al., 1999; LaGreca et al., 1996).

Stressors have also been implicated in the development of many other psychological disorders, including depression and schizophrenia. This point is emphasized in the chapter on psychological disorders, especially in relation to the *diathesis-stress approach* to psychopathology. This approach suggests that certain individuals may be predisposed to develop certain disorders, but that whether or not these disorders actually appear depends on the frequency, nature, and intensity of the stressors the people encounter in life.

Stress Mediators

▶ **Why doesn't everyone react to stressors in the same way?**

The ways in which particular people interact with particular stressors can be seen in many areas of life, from dealing with tough exams to coping with combat. For example, in Afghanistan in 2001, three U.S. special forces soldiers and several anti-Taliban fighters were killed when an error in communicating target coordinates caused a U.S. B-52 to drop a bomb on their position. During the war in Iraq in 2003, a U.S. warplane mistakenly bombed a convoy of Kurdish allies, killing 17 of them, and wounding 45 others. The stress of combat is partly responsible for the fact that "friendly fire" deaths and injuries occur in almost every military operation (Adler, 1993). But not everyone makes such mistakes in combat. Why does stress disrupt the performance of some individuals and not others? And why does one individual survive, and even thrive, under the same circumstances that lead another to break down, give up, and burn out? The answer may lie in *psychobiological models,* which recognize the importance of psychological as well as biological factors in the stress process (Folkman et al., 2000; Lazarus & Folkman, 1984; Taylor, 2002). These models emphasize that, as shown in Figure 10.1, the impact of stressors depends not only on the stressors themselves but on several important mediating factors as well (McEwen & Seeman, 1999).

How Stressors Are Perceived

As described in the chapter on sensation and perception, our view of the world depends on which stimuli we attend to and how we interpret them, a process known as *cognitive appraisal*. Similarly, our physical and psychological reactions to stressors depend somewhat on how we think about them. A potential stressor usually has a stronger negative impact on those who perceive it as a threat than on those who see it as a challenge (Goode et al., 1998; Lazarus, 1999). This holds true whether the stressor is a long line at the airport or a deskful of work.

Evidence for the effects of cognitive factors on stress responses comes from both laboratory experiments and surveys. Figure 10.4 shows the results of a classic experiment by

figure 10.4

Cognitive Influences on Stress Responses

Richard Lazarus and his colleagues found that students' physiological stress reaction to a film showing bloody industrial accidents was affected by the way they thought about what they saw. Those who had been instructed to remain detached from the film (the "intellectualizers") or to think of it as unreal (the "denial" group) were less upset—as measured by sweat-gland activity—than those in an "unprepared" group. These results were among the first to show that people's cognitive appraisal of stressors can affect their responses to those stressors.

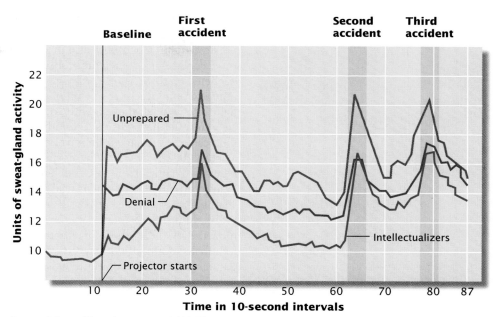

Source: Adapted from Lazarus et al. (1965).

Richard Lazarus that demonstrated these effects. He gave differing instructions to three groups of students who were about to watch a film showing bloody industrial accidents (Lazarus et al., 1965). One group (the "intellectualizers") was instructed to remain mentally detached from the bloody scenes; a second group (the "denial" group) was instructed to think of the scenes as unreal; and a third group (the "unprepared" group) was not told anything about the film. As Figure 10.4 shows, the intensity of physiological arousal during the film, as measured by sweat-gland activity, depended on how the viewers were instructed to think about the film. The unprepared students were more upset than either of the other two groups. Similarly, physical and psychological symptoms associated with the stress of airport noise, of learning about toxins in local soil, or of bioterrorism threats are more common in people who engage in more catastrophic thinking about these problems (Kjellberg et al., 1996; Lerner et al., 2003; Matthies, Hoeger, & Guski, 2000; Speckhard, 2002).

The influence of cognitive factors weakens somewhat as stressors become extreme. Still, even the impact of major stressors such as natural disasters or divorce may be less severe for those who think of them as challenges to be overcome. In other words, many stressful events are not inherently stressful; their impact depends partly on how people perceive them. An important part of this appraisal is the degree to which the stressors are perceived to be predictable or controllable.

Predictability and Control

One reason that the threat of terrorism is so terrorizing is that knowing that a stressor might occur but being uncertain whether, or when, it will occur tends to increase the stressor's impact (Boss, 1999; Lerner et al., 2003; Sorrentino & Roney, 2000). In other words, *unpredictable* stressors tend to have more impact than those that are predictable (Lazarus & Folkman, 1984; Pham, Taylor, & Seeman, 2001)—especially when the stressors are intense and occur for relatively short periods. For example, people whose spouses died suddenly tend to display more immediate disbelief, anxiety, and depression than those who had weeks or months to prepare for the loss (Parkes & Weiss, 1983; Schulz et al., 2001). However, predictability does not provide full protection against stressors. Research with animals shows that predictable stressors can be more damaging than unpredictable ones if they occur over long periods of time (Abbott, Schoen, & Badia, 1984).

The *perception of control* also mediates the effects of stressors. If people feel they have some control over stressors, those stressors usually have less impact (Christensen, Stephens, & Townsend, 1998; Krause & Shaw, 2000). For example, studies of several thousand employees in the United States, Sweden, and the United Kingdom have found that those who felt they had little or no control over their work environment were more likely to suffer heart disease and other health problems than workers with a high degree of perceived control over their work environment (Bosma et al., 1997; Cheng et al., 2000; Spector, 2002). And at many hospitals, it is now standard practice to help patients to manage or control the stress of emergency treatment or the side effects of surgery, because doing so helps them heal faster and go home sooner (Broadbent et al., 2003; Chamberlin, 2000; Kiecolt-Glaser et al., 1998).

Simply *believing* that a stressor is controllable, even if it isn't, can also reduce its impact. This effect was demonstrated in a study in which participants with panic disorder inhaled a mixture of oxygen and carbon dioxide that typically causes a panic attack (Sanderson, Rapee, & Barlow, 1989). Half the participants were led to believe (falsely) that they could control the concentration of the mixture. Compared with those who believed they had no control, significantly fewer of the "in-control" participants experienced full-blown panic attacks during the session, and their panic symptoms were fewer and less severe.

People who feel they have no control over negative events appear especially prone to physical and psychological problems. They often experience feelings of helplessness and hopelessness that, in turn, may promote depression or other mental disorders (Taylor & Aspinwall, 1996).

Coping Resources and Coping Methods

People usually suffer fewer ill effects from a stressor if they have adequate coping resources and effective coping methods. *Coping resources* include, among other things, the money and time to deal with stressful events. For example, the physical and psychological responses you experience if your car breaks down tend to be more negative if you are broke and pressed for time than if you have the money for repairs and the freedom to take a day off from work.

The impact of stressors can also be reduced by effective coping methods (Benight et al., 1999; Cote & Pepler, 2002; Poczwardowski & Conroy, 2002). Most of these methods can be classified as either problem focused or emotion focused. *Problem-focused* coping methods involve efforts to alter or eliminate a source of stress, whereas *emotion-focused* techniques attempt to regulate the negative emotional consequences of stressors (Folkman et al., 1986). These two forms of coping sometimes work together. For example, you might deal with the problem of noise from a nearby airport by forming a community action group to push for tougher noise-reduction laws and, at the same time, calm your anger when noise occurs by mentally focusing on the group's efforts to improve the situation (Folkman & Moskowitz, 2000; Hatfield et al., 2002). Susan Folkman and Richard Lazarus (1988) devised a widely used questionnaire to assess the specific ways in which people cope with stressors; Table 10.3 shows some examples from their questionnaire.

Particularly when a stressor is difficult to control, it is sometimes helpful to fully express and think about the emotions you are experiencing in relation to the stressful event (Bower et al., 1999; Niederhoffer & Pennebaker, 2002). The benefits of this coping strategy have been observed among many individuals whose religious beliefs allow them to bring meaning to the death of a loved one or the devastation of natural disasters that might otherwise seem senseless tragedies (Powell, Shahabi, & Thoreson, 2003; VandeCreek et al., 2002). Some individuals who use humor to help them cope also show better adjustment and lower physiological reactivity to stressful events (Martin, 2001; Moran, 2002).

table 10.3

Ways of Coping

learn by **doing** *Coping* is defined as cognitive and behavioral efforts to manage specific demands that people perceive as taxing their resources (Folkman et al., 1986). This table illustrates two major approaches to coping measured by the Ways of Coping Questionnaire: problem focused and emotion focused. Ask yourself which approach you usually take when faced with stressors. Now rank-order the coping skills under each major approach in terms of how often you tend to use each. Do you rely on just one or two, or do you adjust your coping strategies to fit different kinds of stressors?

Coping Skills	Example
Problem-focused coping	
Confronting	"I stood my ground and fought for what I wanted."
Seeking social support	"I talked to someone to find out more about the situation."
Planful problem solving	"I made a plan of action, and I followed it."
Emotion-focused coping	
Self-controlling	"I tried to keep my feelings to myself."
Distancing	"I didn't let it get to me; I tried not to think about it too much."
Positive reappraisal	"I changed my mind about myself."
Accepting responsibility	"I realized I brought the problem on myself."
Escape/avoidance (wishful thinking)	"I wished that the situation would go away or somehow be over with."

Source: Adapted from Folkman et al. (1986); Taylor (1995).

Social Support

Has a good friend ever given you comfort and reassurance during troubled times? If so, you have experienced the value of social support in easing the impact of stressful events. Social support consists of resources provided by other people; the friends and social contacts on whom you can depend for support make up your **social support network** (Burleson, Albrecht, & Sarason, 1994). The support can take many forms, from eliminating a stressor (as when a friend helps you fix your car) to lessening a stressor's impact by providing companionship, ideas for coping, or reassurance that you are cared about and valued and that everything will be all right (Sarason, Sarason, & Gurung, 1997).

The stress-reducing effects of social support have been documented in people dealing with a wide range of stressors, including cancer, military combat, loss of loved ones, natural disasters, arthritis, AIDS, and even ethnic discrimination (e.g., Foster, 2000; Jason, Witter, & Torres-Harding, 2003; Penner, Dovidio, & Albrecht, 2001; Savelkoul et al., 2000). Students, too, benefit from social support. Compared with those who are part of a supportive network, students with the least adequate social support have been found to

applying psychology **YOU'VE GOT A FRIEND** Even when social support cannot eliminate stressors, it can help people, such as these breast cancer survivors, to feel less anxious, more optimistic, more capable of control, and more willing to try new ways of dealing with stressors (Trunzo & Pinto, 2003).

social support network The friends and social contacts on whom one can depend for help and support.

suffer the most emotional distress and to be more vulnerable to upper respiratory infections during times of high academic stress (LePore, 1995a). Some researchers suggest that the comforting experience of social support actually enhances the body's ability to resist the effects of stressors (Taylor, Dickerson, & Klein, 2002). Others have concluded that having inadequate social support can be as dangerous as smoking, obesity, or lack of exercise in that it nearly doubles a person's risk of dying from disease, suicide, or other causes (House, Umberson, & Landis, 1988; Kiecolt-Glaser & Newton, 2001).

Having strong social support can reduce the likelihood of illness, improve recovery from existing illness, and promote healthier behaviors (Grassi et al., 2000; Taylor, 2002). However, the relationship between social support and the impact of stressors is not a simple one. First, just as the quality of social support can influence your ability to cope with stress, the reverse may also be true: Your ability to cope may determine the quality of the social support you receive (McLeod, Kessler, & Landis, 1992). For example, people who complain endlessly about stressors but never do anything about them may discourage social support, whereas those with an optimistic, action-oriented approach may attract support.

Second, *social support* refers not only to your relationships with others but also to the recognition that others care and will help (Demaray & Malecki, 2002). Some relationships in a seemingly strong social network can be stormy, fragile, or shallow, resulting in interpersonal conflicts that can have an adverse effect on health (Ben-Ari & Gil, 2002; Malarkey et al., 1994).

Third, having too much support or the wrong kind of support can be as bad as not having enough. People whose friends and family overprotect them may actually put less energy into coping efforts or have less opportunity to learn effective coping strategies. Further, if the efforts of people in our social support network become annoying, disruptive, or interfering, they can increase stress and intensify psychological problems (Newsome, 1999; Newsome & Schulz, 1998).

Finally, the value of social support may depend on the kind of stressor being encountered. So although having a friend nearby might reduce the impact of some stressors, it might amplify the impact of others. In one study, for example, participants who were about to make a speech experienced the task as more threatening—and showed stronger physical and psychological stress responses—when a friend was watching than when they were alone (Stoney & Finney, 2000).

Stress, Personality, and Gender

The impact of stress on health appears to depend not only on how people think about particular stressors, but also to some extent on how they think about, and react to, the world in general. For instance, stress-related health problems tend to be especially common among people whose "disease-prone" personalities lead them to (1) try to ignore stressors when possible; (2) perceive stressors as long-term, catastrophic threats that they brought on themselves; and (3) be pessimistic about their ability to overcome stressors or other negative situations (e.g., Penninx et al., 2001; Peterson et al., 1998; Segerstrom et al., 1998; Suinn, 2001).

Other cognitive styles, such as those characteristic of "disease-resistant" personalities, help insulate people from the ill effects of stress. These people tend to think of stressors as temporary challenges to be overcome, not catastrophic threats. And they do not constantly blame themselves for causing these stressors. One particularly important component of the "disease-resistant" personality seems to be *dispositional optimism,* the belief or expectation that things will work out positively (Folkman & Moskowitz, 2000; Taylor et al., 2000). For example, optimistic students experience fewer physical symptoms at the end of the academic term (Aspinwall & Taylor, 1992; Ebert, Tucker, & Roth, 2002). Optimistic coronary bypass surgery patients tend to heal faster than pessimists (Scheier et al., 1989) and perceive their quality of life following coronary surgery to be higher than do patients with less optimistic outlooks (Fitzgerald et al., 1993). And among HIV-positive men, dispositional optimism has been associated with lower psychological distress, fewer worries, and lower perceived risk of acquiring full-blown AIDS (Johnson & Endler, 2002; Taylor et al., 1992). These effects appear due in part to optimists' tendency to use challenge-oriented, problem-focused coping strategies that attack stressors directly, in contrast to pessimists' tendency to use emotion-focused coping strategies, such as denial and avoidance (Bosompra et al., 2002; Brenes et al., 2002).

There is also evidence that gender may play a role in responses to stressors. In a review of 200 studies of stress responses and coping methods, Shelley Taylor and her colleagues found that males under stress tended to get angry, avoid stressors, or both, whereas females were more likely to help others and to make use of their social support network (Taylor et al., 2000, 2002). This was not true in every case, of course, but why should a significant difference show up at all? The gender-role learning discussed in the human development chapter surely plays a part (Eagly & Wood, 1999). But Taylor also proposes that women's "tend and befriend" style differs from the "fight-or-flight" pattern so often seen in men because of gender differences in how hormones combine under stress. For example, oxytocin (pronounced "ox-see-TOH-sin"), a hormone released in both sexes as part of the general adaptation syndrome, interacts differently with male and female sex hormones—amplifying men's physical stress responses and reducing women's. This difference could lead to the more intense emotional and behavioral stress responses typical of men, and it might be partly responsible for men's greater vulnerability to heart disease and other stress-related illnesses. If that is the case, gender differences in stress responses may help to explain why women live an average of 7.5 years longer than men.

LINKAGES
Are childhood traits related to how long we live?
(a link to Human Development)

The way people think and act in the face of stressors, the ease with which they attract social support, and their tendency to be optimists or pessimists are but a few aspects of *personality,* as discussed in the personality chapter.

FOCUS ON RESEARCH

Personality and Health

■ What was the researchers' question?

Are there other personality characteristics that protect or threaten people's health? This was the question asked by Howard Friedman and his associates (1995a, 1995b). In particular, they attempted to identify aspects of personality that increase the likelihood that people will develop heart disease or high blood pressure and die prematurely from these disorders.

■ How did the researchers answer the question?

Friedman suspected that an answer might lie in the results of the Terman Life Cycle Study of Intelligence, which was named after Louis Terman, author of the Stanford-Binet intelligence test. As described in the chapter on thought, language, and intelligence, the study was originally designed to measure the long-term development of 1,528 gifted California children (856 boys and 672 girls)—nicknamed the "Termites" (Terman & Oden, 1947).

Starting in 1921, and every five to ten years thereafter, Terman's research team had gathered information about the Termites' personality traits, social relationships, stressors, health habits, and many other variables. The data were collected through questionnaires and interviews with the Termites themselves, as well as with their teachers, parents, and other family members. By the early 1990s, about half of the Termites had died. It was then that Friedman realized that the Terman Life Cycle Study could shed light on the relationship between personality and health, because the personality traits identified in the Termites could be related to how long they lived. So he examined the Termites' death certificates, noting the dates and causes of death, and then looked for associations between their personalities and the length of their lives.

■ What did the researchers find?

Friedman and his colleagues found that one of the most important predictors of long life was a dimension of personality known as *conscientiousness,* or social dependability (described in the personality chapter). Termites who, in childhood, had been seen as truthful, prudent, reliable, hard working, and humble tended to live longer than those whose parents and teachers had identified them as impulsive and lacking in self-control.

Friedman also examined the Terman Life Cycle Study for what it suggested about the relationship between health and social support. In particular, he compared Termites whose parents had divorced or who had been in unstable marriages themselves with those who grew up in stable homes and who had stable marriages. He discovered that people who had experienced parental divorce during childhood, or who themselves had unstable marriages, died an average of four years earlier than those whose close social relationships had been less stressful.

■ What do the results mean?

Did these differences in personality traits and social support actually cause some Termites to live longer than others? Friedman's research is based mainly on correlational analyses, so it was difficult for the investigators to draw conclusions about what caused the relationships they observed. Still, Friedman and his colleagues searched the Terman data for clues to mechanisms through which personality and other factors might have exerted a causal influence on how long the Termites lived (Peterson et al., 1998). For example, they evaluated the hypothesis that conscientious, dependable Termites who lived socially stable lives might have followed healthier lifestyles than those who were more impulsive and socially stressed. They found that people in the latter group did, in fact, tend to eat less healthy diets and were more likely to smoke, drink to excess, or use drugs. But health behaviors alone did not fully account for their shorter average life spans. Another possible explanation is that conscientiousness and stability in social relationships reflect a general attitude of caution that goes

in review

STRESS RESPONSES AND STRESS MEDIATORS

Category	Examples
Responses	
Physical	Fight-or-flight syndrome (increased heart rate, respiration, and muscle tension; sweating; pupillary dilation); SAM and HPA activation (involving release of catecholamines and corticosteroids); eventual breakdown of organ systems involved in prolonged resistance to stressors
Psychological	*Emotional:* anger, anxiety, depression, and other emotional states. *Cognitive:* inability to concentrate or think logically, ruminative thinking, catastrophizing. *Behavioral:* aggression and escape/avoidance tactics (including suicide attempts)
Mediators	
Appraisal	Thinking of a difficult new job as a challenge will create less discomfort than focusing on the threat of failure
Predictability	A tornado that strikes without warning may have a more devastating emotional impact than a long-predicted hurricane
Control	Repairing a disabled spacecraft may be less stressful for the astronauts doing the work than for their loved ones on earth, who can do nothing to help
Coping resources and methods	Having no effective way to relax after a hard day may prolong tension and other stress responses
Social support	Having no one to talk to about a rape or other trauma may amplify the negative impact of the experience

? *The friends and family we can depend on to help us deal with stressors are called our _____ system.*

beyond eating right and avoiding substance abuse. Friedman found some support for this idea in the Terman data. Termites who were impulsive or low on conscientiousness were somewhat more likely to die from accidents or violence than those who were less impulsive.

■ What do we still need to know?

The Terman Life Cycle Study does not provide final answers about the relationship between personality and health. However, it has generated some important clues and a number of intriguing hypotheses to be evaluated in future research with more representative samples of participants. Further, Friedman's decision to reanalyze a set of data on psychosocial development as a way of exploring issues in health psychology stands as a fine example of how a creative researcher can pursue answers to complex questions that are difficult or impossible to study via controlled experiments.

Our discussion of personality and other factors that can alter the impact of stressors should make it obvious that what is stressful for a given individual is not determined fully and simply by predispositions, coping styles, or situations. (See "In Review: Stress Responses and Stress Mediators.") Even more important are interactions between the person and the situation, the mixture of each individual's coping resources with the specific characteristics of the situation encountered.

The Physiology and Psychology of Health and Illness

► How does stress affect your immune system?

Several studies mentioned so far have suggested that stress shapes the development of physical illness by affecting our thoughts, our organ systems, and our behavior. In the following sections we focus on some of the ways in which stress can, directly or indirectly, lead to physical illnesses by affecting the immune system and the cardiovascular system.

Stress, Illness, and the Immune System

LINKAGES
Can stress give you the flu?
(a link to Biology and Behavior)

On March 19, 1878, at a seminar before the Académie de Médecine de Paris, Louis Pasteur showed his distinguished audience three chickens. One bird had been raised normally and was healthy. A second bird had been intentionally infected with bacteria but given no other treatment; it was also healthy. The third chicken that Pasteur presented was dead. It had been infected with the same bacteria as the second bird, but it had also been physically stressed by being exposed to cold temperatures; as a result, the bacteria killed it (Kelley, 1985).

Research conducted since Pasteur's time has greatly expanded knowledge about how stressors affect the body's reaction to disease. **Psychoneuroimmunology** is the field that examines the interaction of psychological and physiological processes that alter the body's ability to defend itself against disease (Ader, 2001).

psychoneuroimmunology The field that examines the interaction of psychological and physiological processes affecting the body's ability to defend itself against disease.

immune system The body's first line of defense against invading substances and microorganisms.

The Immune System and Illness The body's first line of defense against invading substances and microorganisms is the **immune system.** The immune system is perhaps as complex as the nervous system, and it contains as many cells as the brain (Guyton, 1991). Some of these cells are in organs such as the thymus and spleen, whereas others circulate in the bloodstream, entering tissues throughout the body. Components of the immune system kill or inactivate foreign or harmful substances in the body such as viruses and bacteria (Simpson, Hurtley, & Marx, 2000). If the immune system is impaired—by stressors, for example—a person is left more vulnerable to colds, mononucleosis, and many other infectious diseases (Potter & Zautra, 1997). It is by disabling the immune system that the human immunodefi-

THE FIRST LINE OF DEFENSE
A patrolling immune system cell sends out an extension known as a *pseudopod* (pronounced "SUE-doh-pod") to engulf and destroy a bacterial cell before alerting more defenders. These scavengers are able to squeeze out of the bloodstream and enter organs, where they destroy foreign cells.

ciency virus (HIV) leads to AIDS and leaves the HIV-infected person defenseless against other infections or cancers. The immune system can also become overactive, with devastating results. Many chronic, progressive diseases—including arthritis, diabetes, and lupus erythematosus—are now recognized as *autoimmune disorders*. In these cases, cells of the immune system begin to attack and destroy normal body cells (Oldenberg et al., 2000).

One important facet of the human immune system is the action of the white blood cells, called *leukocytes* (pronounced "LU-koh-sites"), which are formed in the bone marrow and serve as the body's mobile defense units. Leukocytes are called to action when foreign substances are detected. Among the varied types of leukocytes are *B-cells*, which produce *antibodies* to fight foreign toxins; *T-cells*, which kill other cells; and *natural killer cells*, which destroy a variety of foreign organisms and have particularly important antiviral and antitumor functions. The brain can influence the immune system indirectly by altering the secretion of adrenal hormones, such as cortisol, that modify the circulation of T-cells and B-cells. The brain can also influence the immune system directly by making connections with the immune organs, such as the thymus, where T-cells and B-cells are stored (Felten et al., 1991; Maier & Watkins, 2000).

The Immune System and Stress　Researchers have found that people under stress are more likely than less-stressed people to develop infectious diseases and to experience flare-ups of the latent viruses responsible for oral herpes (cold sores) or genital herpes (Cohen & Herbert, 1996).

These findings are supported by other studies showing more directly that a variety of stressors lead to suppression of the immune system. The effects are especially strong in the elderly, but they occur in everyone (Kiecolt-Glaser & Glaser, 2001; Kiecolt-Glaser et al., 2002). For example, a study of first-year law students found that as these students participated in class, took exams, and experienced other stressful aspects of law school, they showed a decline in several measures of immune functioning (Segerstrom et al., 1998). Similarly, decreases in natural killer cell activity have been observed in both men and women following the death of their spouses (Irwin et al., 1987), and a variety of immune system impairments have been found in people suffering the effects of divorce or of extended periods of caring for elderly relatives (Cacioppo et al., 1998; Kiecolt-Glaser et al., 2003; Wu et al., 1999).

The relationship between stress and the immune system can be critical to people who are HIV-positive but do not yet have AIDS. Because their immune system is already fragile, further stress-related impairments could be life-threatening. Research indicates that psychological stressors are associated with the progression of HIV-related illnesses (e.g., Antoni et al., 2000; Nott & Vedhara, 2000). Unfortunately, people with HIV (and AIDS) face a particularly heavy load of immune-suppressing psychological stressors, including grief, unemployment, uncertainty about the future, and daily reminders of serious illness. A lack of perceived control and resulting depression and anxiety can further magnify their stress responses (e.g., Sewell et al., 2000).

Moderators of Immune Functioning　Just as stressors can suppress the immune system, social support and other stress-mediating factors can help to sustain it. For example, students who get emotional support from friends during stressful periods appear to have better immune system functioning than those with less adequate social support (Cohen & Herbert, 1996).

James Pennebaker (1995, 2000) has suggested that social support may help prevent illness by providing the person under stress with an opportunity to express pent-up thoughts and emotions. Keeping important things to oneself, says Pennebaker, is itself a stressor. In a laboratory experiment, for example, participants who were asked to deceive an experimenter showed elevated physiological arousal (Pennebaker & Chew, 1985). Further, the spouses of suicide or accidental-death victims who do not or cannot confide their feelings to others are especially likely to develop physical illness during the year following the death (Pennebaker & O'Heeron, 1984). Disclosing, even anonymously, the stresses and traumas one has experienced is associated with enhanced immune functioning, reduced physical symptoms, and decreased use of health services (Campbell & Pennebaker, 2003; Niederhoffer & Pennebaker, 2002; Richards et al., 2000; Rosenberg et al., 2002). This may explain why support groups for problems ranging from bereavement to overeating to alcohol and drug abuse tend to promote participants' physical health (Taylor, Dickerson, & Klein, 2002). Future research in psychoneuroimmunology promises to reveal vital links in the complex chain of mental and physical events that determine whether people become ill or stay healthy.

Stress, Illness, and the Cardiovascular System

Earlier we mentioned the role of the sympatho-adreno-medullary (SAM) system in mobilizing the body during times of threat. Because the SAM system is linked to the cardiovascular system, its repeated activation in response to stressors has been linked to the development of coronary heart disease (CHD), high blood pressure (hypertension), and stroke (Krantz & McCeney, 2002). The link appears especially strong in people who display strong physical reactions to stressors (Andre-Petersson et al., 2001; Kamarck et al., 1997; Stoney & Matthews, 1988; Treiber et al., 2001). For example, among healthy young adult research participants, those whose blood pressure rose most dramatically in response to a mild stressor were the ones most likely to develop hypertension over the next three decades (Kasagi, Akahoshi, & Shimaoki, 1995; Light et al., 1999; Menkes et al., 1989).

As also mentioned earlier, these physical reactions to stressors—and the chances of suffering stress-related health problems—depend partly on personality, especially on how people tend to think about stressors and about life in general. For example, the trait of *hostility*—especially when accompanied by irritability and impatience—has been associated with the appearance of coronary heart disease (Day & Jreige, 2002; Friedman & Rosenman, 1974; Krantz & McCeney, 2002; Smith, 2003a; Smith & Ruiz, 2002).

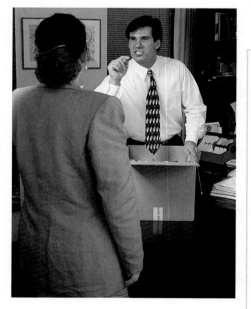

YOU CAN'T FIRE ME—I QUIT! For a time, researchers believed that anyone who displayed the pattern of aggressiveness, competitiveness, and nonstop work known as Type A behavior was at elevated risk for heart disease. More recent research shows, however, that the danger lies not in these characteristics alone, but in hostility, impatience, and irritability, which are seen in some, but not all, Type A people (e.g., Ben-Zur, 2002a).

THINKING CRITICALLY

Does Hostility Increase the Risk of Heart Disease?

Health psychologists see hostility as characterized by suspiciousness, resentment, frequent anger, antagonism, and distrust of others (Helmers & Krantz, 1996; Krantz & McCeney, 2002; Williams, 2001). The identification of hostility as a risk factor for coronary heart disease and heart attack may be an important breakthrough in understanding these illnesses, which remain chief causes of death in the United States and most other Western nations (Centers for Disease Control and Prevention, 2001; Hu et al., 2000). But is hostility as dangerous as health psychologists suspect?

■ What am I being asked to believe or accept?

Many researchers claim that individuals displaying hostility increase their risk for coronary heart disease, heart attack, and even heart failure (e.g., Krantz & McCeney, 2002; MacMahon & Lip, 2002). This risk, they say, is independent of other risk factors such as heredity, diet, smoking, and drinking.

■ Is there evidence available to support the claim?

There is evidence that hostility and heart disease are related, but scientists are still not sure about what causes the relationship. Some suggest that the risk of coronary heart disease and heart attack is elevated in hostile people because these people tend to be unusually reactive to stressors, especially when challenged. During interpersonal conflicts, for example, people predisposed to hostile behavior display not only overt hostility but also unusually large increases in blood pressure, heart rate, and other aspects of autonomic reactivity (Suls & Wan, 1993). In addition, it takes hostile individuals longer than normal to get back to their resting levels of autonomic functioning. Like a driver who damages a car by flooring the accelerator and applying the brakes at the same time, these "hot reactors" may create excessive wear and tear on the arteries of the heart as their increased heart rate forces blood through constricted vessels. Increased sympathetic nervous system activation not only puts stress on the coronary arteries but also leads to surges of stress-related hormones from the adrenal glands. High levels of these hormones are associated with increases in cholesterol and other fatty substances that are deposited in arteries and contribute to coronary heart disease (Bierhaus et al., 2003; Stoney & Hughes, 1999; Stoney et al., 1999a, 1999b). Cholesterol levels do appear to be elevated in the blood of hostile people (Dujovne & Houston, 1991; Engebretson & Stoney, 1995).

Hostility may affect heart disease risk less directly as well, through its impact on social support. Some evidence suggests that hostile people get fewer benefits from their social support network (Lepore, 1995b). Failure to use this support—and possibly offending potential supporters in the process—may intensify the impact of stressful events on hostile people. The result may be increased anger, antagonism, and ultimately, additional stress on the cardiovascular system.

■ Can that evidence be interpreted another way?

Studies suggesting that hostility causes coronary heart disease are not true experiments. Researchers cannot manipulate the independent variable by creating hostility in randomly selected people in order to assess its effects on heart health. Accordingly, we have to consider other possible explanations of the observed relationship between hostility and heart disease.

For example, some researchers suggest that higher rates of heart problems among hostile people are not due entirely to the impact of hostility on blood pressure, heart rate, and hormone surges. It may also be that a genetically determined tendency toward autonomic reactivity increases the likelihood of both hostility and heart disease (Cacioppo et al., 1998; Krantz et al., 1988). If this is the case, then the fact that hostility and coronary heart disease often appear in the same people might reflect not just the effects of hostility, but also a third factor—autonomic reactivity—that contributes to both of them.

■ What evidence would help to evaluate the alternatives?

One way to test whether hostile people's higher rates of heart disease are related specifically to their hostility or to a more general tendency toward intense physiological arousal is to examine how these individuals react to stress when they are not angry. Some researchers have done this by observing the physiological reactions of hostile people during the stress of surgery. One study found that even under general anesthesia, such people show unusually strong autonomic reactivity (Krantz & Durel, 1983). Because these patients were not conscious, it appears that oversensitivity to stressors, not hostile thinking, caused their exaggerated stress responses.

■ What conclusions are most reasonable?

Most studies continue to find that hostile individuals stand a greater risk of heart disease and heart attacks than their nonhostile counterparts (Krantz & McCeney, 2002; Stansfeld & Marmot, 2002). But the relationship between hostility and heart disease is probably more complex than any current theory suggests; it appears that many factors underlie this relationship.

A more elaborate psychobiological model may be required—one that takes into account that (1) some individuals may be biologically predisposed to react to stress with hostility and increased cardiovascular activity, each of which can contribute to heart disease; (2) hostile people help to create and maintain stressors through aggressive thoughts and actions, which can provoke others to be aggressive; and (3) hostile people are more likely than others to smoke, drink to excess, overeat, fail to exercise, and engage in other heart-damaging behaviors.

We must also keep in mind that the relationship between heart problems and hostility may not be universal. Although some evidence suggests that this relationship may hold for women as well as men, and for individuals in various ethnic groups (e.g., Davidson, Hall, & MacGregor, 1996; Nakano & Kitamura, 2001; Powch & Houston, 1996; Yoshimasu et al., 2002), final conclusions must await further research that examines the relationship between hostility and heart disease in other cultures.

Risking Your Life: Health-Endangering Behaviors

As we have seen, many major health problems are caused or aggravated by preventable behaviors such as those listed in Table 10.1.

Smoking   Smoking is the most significant preventable risk factor for fatal illnesses in the United States (Centers for Disease Control and Prevention, 2002a). It accounts for 430,000 deaths each year—which is 20 percent of all U.S. deaths, and more than those caused by all other drugs, car accidents, suicides, homicides, and fires combined (Centers for Disease Control and Prevention, 2002a; U.S. Department of Health and Human Services, 2001c). Even nonsmokers who inhale "secondhand" smoke face an elevated risk for lung cancer and other respiratory diseases (Je et al., 1999; Otsuka et al., 2001).

Although smoking has declined in the United States overall—only about 23.5 percent of adults now smoke—the rate is slightly higher (about 24.3 percent) in some groups, especially young European American and African American men, and much higher (40.8 percent) among American Indians and Alaskan Natives (Centers for Disease Control and Prevention, 2002a; American Lung Association, 2002). Conversely, Hispanic Americans and Asian Americans are less likely than other groups to smoke. In general, poorer, less educated people are particularly likely to smoke. In many other countries, particularly in less developed countries, smoking is still the rule rather than the exception. Breaking the smoking habit is difficult (Riemsma et al., 2003). In North America, only about 4 percent of smokers who try to quit on their own remain abstinent, and only 27 to 30 percent of those using nicotine replacement and/or behavior modification programs achieve long-term success (American Lung Association, 2002). Still, persistence can pay off: There are more than 45 million former smokers in the United States alone.

Alcohol   Like tobacco, alcohol is a potentially addicting substance that can lead to major health problems. Alcohol abuse is associated with most leading causes of death, including heart disease, stroke, cancer, and liver disease (Centers for Disease Control and Prevention, 1999b). It also contributes to irreversible damage to brain tissue, to

A DEADLY HABIT   Today, about 23.5 percent of U.S. adults are smokers, though the figure is almost 28 percent for those between 18 and 24 years old. Health authorities estimate that 25 million smokers will die of smoking-related illnesses unless they quit (Centers for Disease Control and Prevention, 2002a).

gastrointestinal illnesses, and to many other conditions. Both male and female abusers may experience disruption of their reproductive functions, such as early menopause in women and erectile disorder in men. And, as noted in the chapter on human development, alcohol consumption by pregnant women is the most preventable cause of birth defects.

Unsafe Sex   According to the Joint United Nations Programme on HIV/AIDS, about 40 million people worldwide are HIV-positive, and about 21 million have died from AIDS (Centers for Disease Control and Prevention, 2002b). As of December 2001, almost 817,000 people in the United States had been diagnosed as having AIDS, about 468,000 had died, and as many as 900,000 more had been infected with HIV (Centers for Disease Control and Prevention, 2002b). With growing public awareness of how to prevent HIV infection, the number of new AIDS cases, as well as AIDS deaths, began to fall in the United States during the 1990s, but the rate of infection is now holding steady at about 40,000 cases per year (Centers for Disease Control and Prevention, 2002b). In short, not everyone is getting the message.

Unsafe sex—especially sexual relations without the use of a condom—greatly increases the risk of contracting HIV. Yet many adolescents and adults continue this dangerous practice (Centers for Disease Control and Prevention, 1999a; Dodds et al., 2000). Like smoking and many other health-threatening behaviors, unprotected sex is more common among low-income individuals, many of whom belong to ethnic minority groups (St. Lawrence, 1993). Among African American men, the risk of contracting AIDS is three times greater than among European American men. The risk for African American women is fifteen times higher than for European American women (Centers for Disease Control, 2002b).

Promoting Healthy Behavior

> ▶ **Who is most likely to adopt a healthy lifestyle?**

Health psychologists are deeply involved in the development of smoking cessation programs, in campaigns to prevent young people from taking up smoking, in alcohol-education efforts, and in the fight against the spread of HIV and AIDS (e.g., Langenberg et al., 2000; Latkin, Sherman, & Knowlton, 2003; Taylor, 2002). They have also helped promote early detection of disease. Encouraging women to perform breast self-examinations and men to do testicular self-examinations are just two examples of health psychology programs that can save thousands of lives each year (Taylor, 2002).

Efforts to reduce, eliminate, or prevent behaviors that pose health risks and to encourage healthy behaviors are called **health promotion** (Taylor, 2002). As part of these efforts, health psychologists are trying to understand the thought processes that lead people to engage in health-endangering behaviors and, then, to create intervention programs that can alter those thought processes, or at least take them into account (Klepp, Kelder, & Perry, 1995).

Health Beliefs and Health Behaviors

This cognitive approach to health psychology appears in various *health-belief models.* Irwin Rosenstock (1974) developed one of the most influential and extensively tested of these models (e.g., Aspinwall & Duran, 1999). Rosenstock based his model on the assumption that people's decisions about health-related behaviors (such as smoking) are guided by four main factors:

1. A perception of personal threat or susceptibility to contracting a specific illness. (Do you believe that *you* will get lung cancer from smoking?)

2. A perception of the seriousness of the illness and the severity of the consequences of having it. (How serious do you think lung cancer is? What will happen to you if you get it?)

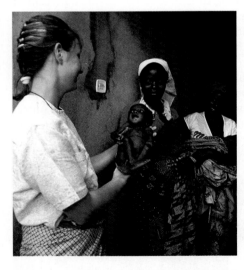

DOCTOR'S ORDERS   Despite physicians' instructions, many patients fail to take their blood pressure medication and continue to eat an unhealthy diet. Noncompliance with medical advice is especially common when cultural values and beliefs conflict with that advice. Aware of this problem, health psychologists are developing culture-sensitive approaches to health promotion and disease prevention (Kazarian & Evans, 2001).

©Steve Kelly/Copley News Service

As described in the chapter on thought, language, and intelligence, humans tend to underestimate the likelihood of common outcomes and to overestimate the likelihood of rare events. When this tendency causes people to ignore the dangers of smoking or other health-risky behaviors, the results can be disastrous.

3. The belief that a particular practice will reduce the threat. (Will stopping smoking prevent you from getting lung cancer?)

4. The balance between the perceived costs of starting a health practice and the benefits expected from this practice. (Will the reduced risk of getting cancer in the future be worth the discomfort and loss of pleasure from not smoking?)

This health-belief model suggests that the people most likely to quit smoking would be those who believe that they are susceptible to getting cancer from smoking, that cancer is serious and life-threatening, and that the benefits of preventing cancer clearly outweigh the difficulties associated with quitting.

Other important cognitive factors not included in Rosenstock's model are emphasized in other health-belief models. For example, people generally do not try to quit smoking unless they believe they can succeed. So *self-efficacy,* the belief that one is able to perform some behavior, is an additional determinant of decisions about health behaviors (Bandura, 1992; Dijkstra, DeVries, & Bakker, 1996). A related factor is the *intention* to engage in a healthy behavior (Albarracin et al., 2001; Schwarzer, 2001). Health-belief models help predict a variety of health behaviors, including exercise (McAuley, 1992), safe-sex practices (Fisher, Fisher, & Rye, 1995), adherence to doctors' orders among diabetic adolescents (Bond, Aiken, & Somerville, 1992), and the decision to undergo mammogram screening for breast cancer (Champion & Huster, 1995).

Changing Health Behaviors: Stages of Readiness

Knowing who is most likely to practice healthy behaviors is important, but health psychologists have also tried to understand how people change their health habits. According to James Prochaska and his colleagues, successful change involves five stages (Prochaska, DiClemente, & Norcross, 1992):

1. *Precontemplation.* The person does not perceive a health-related problem and has no intention of changing in the foreseeable future.

2. *Contemplation.* The person is aware of a problem behavior and is seriously thinking about changing it.

3. *Preparation.* The person has a strong intention to change and has made specific plans to do so.

4. *Action.* The person is engaging successfully in behavior change.

5. *Maintenance.* The healthy behavior has continued for at least six months, and the person is using newly learned skills to prevent relapse.

The path from precontemplation through maintenance can be a rough one (Prochaska, 1994). Usually, people relapse and go through the stages repeatedly until they finally

health promotion The process of altering or eliminating behaviors that pose risks to health and, at the same time, fostering healthier behavior patterns.

TAKING TIME OUT   The workplace is the number one source of stress for many people in the United States. On January 1, 2000, Raymond Fowler, who was then chief executive officer of the American Psychological Association, joined the ranks of those whose elevated blood pressure, heart problems, and other physical stress responses necessitated a temporary leave of absence from highly stressful jobs (Fowler, 2000). The National Institute for Occupational Safety and Health (1999) suggests a wide range of other behavioral coping options for stressed employees who cannot afford to take time off.

achieve stability in the healthy behavior they desire (Polivy & Herman, 2002). Smokers, for example, typically require three to four cycles through the stages and up to seven years before they finally reach the maintenance stage.

Programs for Coping with Stress

An important aspect of health psychologists' health promotion activities has been to improve people's stress-coping skills. Let's consider a few specific procedures and programs associated with this effort.

Planning to Cope   Just as people with extra money in the bank have a better chance of weathering a financial crisis, people with effective coping skills have a better chance of escaping some of the more harmful effects of intense stress. Like family money, the ability to handle stress appears to come naturally to some people, but coping strategies can also be learned. Programs for teaching these strategies include several stages, which are summarized in Table 10.4.

Bear in mind, however, that no single method of coping with stressors is universally successful. For example, denying the existence of an uncontrollable stressor may be fine in the short run but may lead to problems if no other coping method is used. Similarly, people who rely exclusively on an active, problem-focused approach to coping may handle controllable stressors well but find themselves nearly helpless in the face of uncontrollable ones (Murray & Terry, 1999). Individuals who are most successful at stress management may be those who are best able to adjust their coping methods to the demands of changing situations and differing stressors (Taylor, 2002).

Developing Coping Strategies   Strategies for coping with stress can be cognitive, emotional, behavioral, or physical. *Cognitive coping strategies* change how people interpret stimuli and events. They help people think more calmly, rationally, and constructively in the face of stress and may generate a more hopeful emotional state. For example, students with heavy course loads may experience anxiety, confusion, discouragement, lack of motivation, and the desire to run away from it all. Frightening, catastrophizing thoughts (such as "What if I fail?") magnify stress responses. Cognitive coping strategies replace catastrophic thinking with thoughts in which stressors are viewed as challenges rather than threats. This substitution process is called *cognitive restructuring* (Lazarus, 1971; Meichenbaum, 1977). It involves first identifying upsetting thoughts (such as "I'll never figure this out!") and then developing and

table 10.4

Stages in Coping with Stress

Many successful programs for systematically coping with stress guide people through several stages and are aimed at removing stressors that can be changed and at reducing responses to stressors that cannot be changed (Taylor, 2002).

Stage	Task
1. Assessment	Identify the sources and effects of stress.
2. Goal setting	List the stressors and stress responses to be addressed. Designate which stressors are and are not changeable.
3. Planning	List the specific steps to be taken to cope with stress.
4. Action	Implement coping plans.
5. Evaluation	Determine the changes in stressors and stress responses that have occurred as a result of coping methods.
6. Adjustment	Alter coping methods to improve results, if necessary.

in review · METHODS FOR COPING WITH STRESS

Type of Coping Method	Examples
Cognitive	Thinking of stressors as challenges rather than as threats; avoiding perfectionism
Emotional	Seeking social support; getting advice
Behavioral	Implementing a time-management plan; where possible, making life changes to eliminate stressors
Physical	Progressive relaxation training; exercise; meditation

? Reminding yourself that you have prepared for the exam you are about to take, that everyone makes mistakes now and then, and that you will do better if you remain calm are all examples of _____ stress coping strategies.

LINKAGES
How can people manage stress?
(a link to Treatment of Psychology Disorders)

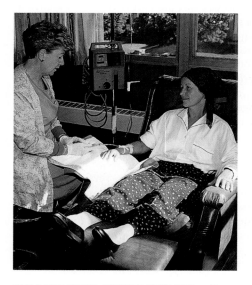

DEALING WITH CHEMOTHERAPY Progressive relaxation training involves briefly tensing groups of muscles throughout the body, one at a time, then releasing the tension and focusing on the resulting feelings of relaxation. It can be used to ease a variety of health-related problems, including the anxiety, physiological arousal, and nausea associated with cancer chemotherapy (Bernstein, Borkovec, & Hazlette-Stevens, 2000).

practicing more constructive thoughts (such as "All I can do is the best I can") when under stress. Cognitive coping does not eliminate stressors, but it can help people perceive them as less threatening and therefore make them less disruptive (Antoni et al., 2000).

Seeking and obtaining social support from others are effective *emotional coping strategies.* The perception that one has emotional support and is cared for and valued by others tends to be an effective buffer against the ill effects of many stressors. Having enhanced emotional resources is associated with improved functioning of the immune system (Kiecolt-Glaser & Newton, 2001) and more rapid recovery from illness (Taylor, 2002).

Behavioral coping strategies involve changing behavior to minimize the impact of stressors. Time management is one example. You might keep track of your time for a week and start a time-management plan. The first step is to set out a schedule that shows how your time is typically spent; then decide how to allocate your time in the future. A time-management plan can help control catastrophizing thoughts by providing reassurance that there is enough time for everything and a plan for handling it all.

Physical coping strategies can be used to alter one's physical responses before, during, or after stressors occur. The most common physical coping strategy is some form of drug use. Prescription medications are sometimes an appropriate coping aid, especially when stressors are severe and acute, such as the sudden death of one's child. However, people who depend on prescribed or other drugs, including alcohol, to help them face stressors often attribute any success to the drug, not to their own skill. Furthermore, the drug effects that blunt stress responses may also interfere with the ability to apply coping strategies. The resulting loss of perceived control over stressors may make those stressors even more threatening and disruptive.

Nonchemical methods of reducing physical stress reactions and improving functioning include progressive relaxation training (Bernstein, Borkovec, & Hazlette-Stevens, 2000; Scheufele, 2000), physical exercise (Anshel, 1996), biofeedback (Sarafino & Goehring, 2000), and meditation and tai chi (Li et al., 2001), among others (Taylor, 2002).

"In Review: Methods for Coping with Stress" summarizes our discussion of stress-coping methods.

Linkages

As noted in the introductory chapter, all of psychology's subfields are related to one another. Our discussion of how stressors can lead to the development of mental disorders illustrates just one way in which the topic of this chapter, health, stress, and coping, is linked to the subfield of abnormal psychology, which is described in the chapter on psychological disorders. The Linkages diagram shows ties to two other subfields as well, and there are many more ties throughout the book. Looking for linkages among subfields will help you see how they all fit together and help you better appreciate the big picture that is psychology.

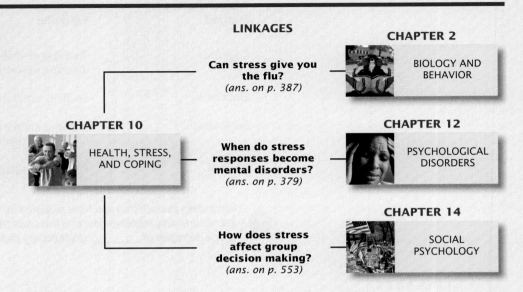

LINKAGES

CHAPTER 10

HEALTH, STRESS, AND COPING

Can stress give you the flu?
(ans. on p. 387)

When do stress responses become mental disorders?
(ans. on p. 379)

How does stress affect group decision making?
(ans. on p. 553)

CHAPTER 2

BIOLOGY AND BEHAVIOR

CHAPTER 12

PSYCHOLOGICAL DISORDERS

CHAPTER 14

SOCIAL PSYCHOLOGY

Summary

HEALTH PSYCHOLOGY

▶ **What do health psychologists do?**

The development of *health psychology* was prompted by recognition of the link between stress and illness, and of the role of behaviors such as smoking in increasing the risk of illness. Health psychologists work to understand how psychological factors are related to physical disease and to help people behave in ways that prevent or minimize disease and promote health.

UNDERSTANDING STRESS AND STRESSORS

▶ **How do psychological stressors affect physical health?**

The term *stress* refers in part to *stressors,* which are physical or psychological events and situations to which people must adjust. The term is also used to refer to *stress reactions.* Most generally, however, stress is viewed as an ongoing, interactive process that takes place as people adjust to, and cope with, their environment. Psychological stressors include catastrophic events, life changes and strains, chronic stressors, and daily hassles. Stressors can be measured by tests like the Social Readjustment Rating Scale (SRRS) and the Life Experiences Survey (LES), but scores on such tests provide only a partial picture of the stress in a person's life.

STRESS RESPONSES

▶ **How do people react to stressors?**

Responses to stressors can be physical and psychological. These stress responses can occur alone or in combination, and the appearance of one can often stimulate others.

Physical stress responses include changes in heart rate, respiration, and many other processes that are part of a pattern known as the *general adaptation syndrome,* or *GAS.* The GAS has three stages: alarm reaction, resistance, and exhaustion. The GAS helps people resist stress but, if present too long, can lead to impairment of immune system functions, as well as to physical illnesses, which Selye called *diseases of adaptation.*

Psychological stress responses can be emotional, cognitive, and behavioral. Anxiety, anger, and depression are among the most common emotional stress reactions. Cognitive stress reactions include ruminative thinking; catastrophizing; and disruptions in the ability to think clearly, remember accurately, and solve problems efficiently. Behavioral stress responses include changes in posture, as well as facial expressions, tremors, or jumpiness, that reflect physical tension or emotional stress reactions. More global behavioral stress responses include irritability, absenteeism, and even suicide attempts. Patterns of response to severe or long-lasting stressors can lead to *burnout* or to psychological disorders such as *posttraumatic stress disorder (PTSD).*

STRESS MEDIATORS

▶ **Why doesn't everyone react to stressors in the same way?**

The key to understanding stress appears to lie in observing the interaction of specific stressors with particular people. Stressors are likely to have greater impact if they are appraised as threats, or if they are unpredictable or uncontrollable. The people most likely to react strongly to a stressor are those whose coping resources, coping methods, and *social support networks* are inadequate.

THE PHYSIOLOGY AND PSYCHOLOGY OF HEALTH AND ILLNESS

▶ **How does stress affect your immune system?**

Psychoneuroimmunology is the field that examines the interaction of psychological and physiological processes that affect the body's ability to defend itself against disease. When a person is under stress, some of the hormones released from the adrenal glands, such as cortisol, reduce the effectiveness of the cells of the *immune system* (T-cells, B-cells, and natural killer cells) in combating foreign invaders, such as viruses and cancer cells.

People who are hostile appear at greater risk for heart disease than other people. The heightened reactivity to stressors that these people experience may damage their cardiovascular system.

Most of the major health problems in Western cultures are related to preventable behaviors such as smoking and drinking alcohol. Having unsafe sex is a major risk factor for contracting HIV.

PROMOTING HEALTHY BEHAVIOR

▶ **Who is most likely to adopt a healthy lifestyle?**

The process of altering or eliminating health-risky behaviors and fostering healthy behavior patterns is called **health promotion.** People's health-related behaviors are partly guided by their beliefs about health risks and what they can do about them.

The process of changing health-related behaviors appears to involve several stages, including precontemplation, contemplation, preparation, action, and maintenance. Understanding which stage people are in, and helping them move through these stages, is an important task in health psychology.

To cope with stress, people must recognize the stressors affecting them and develop a plan for coping with these stressors. Important coping skills include cognitive restructuring, acting to minimize the number or intensity of stressors, and using progressive relaxation training and other techniques for reducing physical stress reactions.

Learn by Doing

Put It in Writing

What is stress like for you? To help you understand the role of stress in your life, write a page or two describing a stressful incident that you had to face in the recent past. Identify what the stressors were, and classify each of them as physical or psychological. List your physical, emotional, cognitive, and behavioral responses to these stressors, and how long the responses lasted. Include a brief summary of how you coped with these stressors and how successful your coping efforts were. Some research suggests that writing about stressful experiences can help people to deal with those experiences. Did this writing project have any such benefits for you?

Personal Learning Activity

To get an idea of how much people differ in their approach to coping with stressors, create a one-paragraph story of a stressful situation (such as losing a job, having one's home destroyed by fire, working for an obnoxious boss, or being overburdened by schoolwork). Now show this description to ten people, and ask each of them to tell you how they would cope with the situation if it happened to them. Classify their responses in terms of whether they were problem-focused or emotion-focused coping methods. Did you notice any relationships between the kind of coping responses these people chose and characteristics such as age, gender, ethnicity, or experience with stress? If so, why do you think those relationships appeared? *For additional projects, see the Personal Learning Activities in the corresponding chapter of the study guide that accompanies this text.*

Step into Action

Courses

Biological Psychology
Health Psychology
Stress Management
Stress and Coping

Movies

Black Hawk Down (general adaptation syndrome)
Falling Down (behavioral stress responses)
The Deer Hunter (posttraumatic stress disorder)
Do the Right Thing (social support networks)
Women on the Verge of a Nervous Breakdown (impact of sudden stressor)
Glengarry Glen Ross (effects of stress in the workplace)
Angela's Ashes (impact of stress on development)
Saving Private Ryan (individual differences in responses to traumatic stress)

Books

David J. Mahoney, *The Longevity Strategy: How to Live to 100 Using the Brain-Body Connection* (Wiley, 1998) (the origins of longevity)
Lance Armstrong and Sally Jenkins, *It's Not About the Bike: My Journey Back to Life* (Berkley Books, 2001) (Armstrong focuses on the origins of his survival of a deadly form of cancer)
Lewis B. Puller, *Fortunate Son* (Bantam, 1996) (son of a famous Marine deals with posttraumatic stress and multiple amputations after the Vietnam War)
Richard Sorrentino and Christopher Roney, *The Uncertain Mind: Individual Differences in Facing the Unknown* (Psychology Press, 2000) (discusses the impact of uncertainty on physical and mental health)
Tony Cassidy, *Stress, Cognition, and Health* (Routledge, 1999) (summarizes research on the effects of stress on thinking and physical well-being)

Jerrold Greenberg, *Comprehensive Stress Management* (McGraw-Hill, 1999) (ideas for stress management)

James W. Pennebaker, *Opening Up: The Healing Power of Expressing Emotions* (Guilford, 1997) (describes research on the benefits of self-disclosure).

The Web

The World Wide Web is a good source of additional information about the science of psychology, provided you use it carefully and think critically about the information you find. The web site that accompanies this text offers many resources relevant to this chapter. These resources include interactive NetLab exercises; Thinking Critically and Evaluating Research exercises; ACE chapter quizzes; recommended web links; and articles on current events, books, and movies. At http://college.hmco.com, select *Psychology* and then this textbook.

Review of Key Terms

Can you define each of the key terms in the chapter? Check your definitions against those on the pages listed in parentheses below or in the Glossary/Index at the end of the text.

burnout *(p. 379)*

diseases of adaptation *(p. 377)*

general adaptation syndrome (GAS) *(p. 376)*

health promotion *(p. 392)*

health psychology *(p. 371)*

immune system *(p. 387)*

posttraumatic stress disorder (PTSD) *(p. 379)*

psychoneuroimmunology *(p. 387)*

social support network *(p. 383)*

stress *(p. 373)*

stress reactions *(p. 373)*

stressors *(p. 373)*

Multiple-Choice Self-Test

Select the best answer for each of the questions below. Then check your response against the Answer Key at the end of the text.

1. According to health psychology research,

   a. acute diseases cause more U.S. deaths than chronic ones.
   b. psychological methods cannot change behaviors that contribute to illness.
   c. teaching people to take an active role in protecting their own health has not had a major impact on the death rate.
   d. the stresses of life influence health through their impact on psychological and physical processes.

2. Lila got married, moved to a new city, and took a new job, all in the same month. We would expect Lila to

   a. display physical or psychological stress responses, or both.
   b. experience little stress, because these are all desirable changes.
   c. experience little stress, because these are not chronic stressors.
   d. experience physical stress responses only.

3. Psychological stressors

   a. always stem from a lack of social support.
   b. are by definition long term, or chronic.
   c. result mainly from catastrophic events.
   d. include anything that forces a person to change or adapt.

4. It is 2:00 a.m., and Aaron is lost in a big city with no money. His sympathetic nervous system has initiated the fight-or-flight syndrome. Which stage of the general adaptation syndrome (GAS) is he experiencing?

   a. alarm
   b. resistance
   c. exhaustion
   d. precontemplative

5. According to Hans Selye, diseases of adaptation occur when the body enters the _____ stage of the GAS.

   a. alarm
   b. resistance
   c. exhaustion
   d. precontemplative

6. While watching TV, taking a shower, or even having dinner with his girlfriend, Enrico finds that he can't stop thinking about all the stressful things happening in his life. Enrico is experiencing

   a. catastrophizing.
   b. ruminative thinking.
   c. functional fixedness.
   d. cognitive restructuring.

7. Caitlin just failed her high school math test. She says to herself, "Mom is going to be furious with me! She will probably ground me, which means I won't be able to go to the prom. If I don't go to the prom, I will be a social outcast, and no one will talk to me. I'll never have any friends or find a partner, and no one will ever love me!" This is an example of

   a. cognitive restructuring.
   b. catastrophizing.
   c. posttraumatic stress disorder.
   d. the fight-or-flight syndrome.

8. Dr. Angelica's teenage patient, Juan, is under a lot of stress. If the doctor is most worried about Juan's behavioral stress responses, she would focus mainly on his

   a. depression.
   b. catastrophic thoughts.
   c. blood pressure.
   d. aggressiveness.

9. Shane, a veteran, occasionally experiences flashbacks involving vivid recollections of his wartime experiences. Flashbacks are associated with

   a. generalized anxiety disorder.
   b. posttraumatic stress disorder.
   c. the general adaptation syndrome.
   d. the fight-or-flight syndrome.

10. Robin, Sarah, and Travis all work in the same office complex, which is plagued by temperature-regulation problems. Based on research on stress mediators, which of the three workers will display the most stress responses?

    a. Robin, whose office is always too warm
    b. Sarah, whose office is always too cold
    c. Travis, whose office changes from hot to cold without warning
    d. There is no way to predict who will be most stressed

11. When postsurgery patients are allowed to adjust their own level of painkillers, they tend to self-administer less pain medication than patients who must ask for it. This phenomenon is consistent with research showing that

    a. social support can mediate stress.
    b. predictable stressors are easier to manage.
    c. the perception of control reduces the impact of stressors.
    d. thinking of stressors as threats amplifies their effects.

12. Laton, the head of human resources at his company, knows that the employees have stressful jobs. So he schedules group picnics and lunches to help employees get better acquainted. Laton is trying to ease the employees' stressors by

    a. promoting cognitive restructuring.
    b. improving social support networks.
    c. increasing employees' sense of control.
    d. helping employees think of their stressors as challenges rather than threats.

13. In the Focus on Research section of this chapter, on the relationship between personality and life expectancy, the researchers found

    a. no relationship between the two.
    b. that conscientiousness was associated with longer life.
    c. that social relationships had no impact on longevity.
    d. that impulsiveness was associated with longer life.

14. Dr. Porter studies immune system cells that have antiviral properties and help prevent tumors. What type of cells does he study?

    a. B-cells   c. natural killer cells
    b. T-cells   d. macrophages

15. Fred is at high risk for coronary heart disease. As his friend, you tell him that current research suggests that he could lower his risk if he

    a. takes up fishing as a hobby.
    b. works at being less hostile.
    c. reduces his workload.
    d. restructures his thinking about stress.

16. The most significant preventable risk factor for fatal illness in the United States is

    a. smoking.
    b. consumption of alcohol.
    c. illegal drug use.
    d. unsafe sex.

17. According to Rosenstock's health-belief model, which of the following would most help Bridgit decide to quit smoking?

    a. perceiving a personal threat of getting cancer from her smoking
    b. knowing that smoking causes cancer
    c. knowing that quitting can lower people's risk of cancer
    d. carefully reading the statistics on smoking and health in general

18. Amanda is severely overweight. She knows that for her health's sake, she needs to limit her caloric intake, but she loves to eat and has made no specific plans to go on a diet. Amanda is at the _____ stage of readiness to change a health-risky behavior.

    a. precontemplation   c. preparation
    b. contemplation   d. maintenance

19. Sayumi is trying to control her stress. In response to a hurtful comment from a friend, Sayumi thinks to herself, "Don't jump to conclusions; he probably didn't mean it the way it sounded," instead of "That jerk! Who does he think he is?" Sayumi is using the coping strategy of

    a. cognitive restructuring.
    b. emotional restructuring.
    c. catastrophizing.
    d. contemplation.

20. Loretta, a marriage counselor, finds her job very stressful. She has found that physical coping strategies help her the most. Loretta most likely engages in

    a. cognitive restructuring.
    b. emotional restructuring.
    c. progressive relaxation training.
    d. problem-focused coping.

11

Personality

If you have ever been in a car

in heavy traffic, you have probably noticed dramatic differences in how drivers deal with the situation. Some are tolerant and calm; others become so cautious that they worsen the congestion; still others react with such impatience and anger that they may endanger others. Variations in how people handle traffic jams and other frustrating situations reflect just one aspect of their *personality*—the consistent patterns of thinking, feeling, and behaving that make each person different from, and in some ways similar to, others. In this chapter, we examine four views of personality and review some of the personality tests that psychologists have developed to measure and compare people's personalities. We also examine some of the ways in which personality theory and research are being applied in areas such as diagnosing mental disorders and screening potential employees.

Reading this chapter will help you to answer the following questions:

▶ **How did paralyzed patients lead Freud to psychoanalysis?**

▶ **What personality traits are most basic?**

▶ **Do we learn our personality?**

▶ **Is everyone basically good?**

▶ **How do psychologists measure personality?**

learn **by doing**

Take out your wallet, look through it, and select the four most important things you carry with you. One person we know picked a driver's license, a credit card, a friend's phone number, and a witty prediction from a fortune cookie. The driver's license describes his physical traits. The credit card represents information about his buying history and responsibility in paying debts. His friends provide support, affection, and intimacy. And the fortune cookie prediction says something about his wishes, beliefs, or hopes. In other words, the selected items form a crude personality sketch.

There is no universally accepted definition, but psychologists generally view **personality** as the unique pattern of enduring psychological and behavioral characteristics by which each person can be compared and contrasted with other people. Personality research, in turn, focuses on understanding the consistent patterns of cognition, emotion, and behavior that make people both different from and similar to one another.

To gain a full understanding of just one individual's personality, a researcher would have to learn about many things, including the person's developmental experiences and cultural influences, genetic and other biological characteristics, perceptual and other information-processing habits and biases, typical patterns of emotional expression, and social skills. Psychologists also want to know about personality in general, such as how it develops and changes across the life span. They ask why some people are usually optimistic, whereas others are usually pessimistic, and whether people respond consistently or inconsistently from one situation to the next.

personality The pattern of psychological and behavioral characteristics by which each person can be compared and contrasted with other people.

401

Conscious

Preconscious   EGO

Unconscious   SUPEREGO   ID

Source: Adapted from Liebert & Spiegler (1994).

figure 11.1

Freud's Conception of the Personality Structure

According to Freud, some parts of the personality are conscious, whereas others are unconscious. Between these levels is the preconscious, which Freud saw as the location of memories and other material not usually in awareness but that can be brought into consciousness with little or no effort.

psychodynamic approach   A view developed by Freud emphasizing unconscious mental processes in explaining human thought, feelings, and behavior.

id   According to Freud, a personality component containing basic instincts, desires, and impulses with which all people are born.

pleasure principle   The operating principle of the id, which guides people toward whatever feels good.

ego   According to Freud, the part of the personality that makes compromises and mediates conflicts between and among the demands of the id, the superego, and the real world.

reality principle   The operating principle of the ego, which takes into account the constraints of the social world.

The specific questions psychologists ask and the methods they use to investigate personality often depend on which of the four main approaches to personality they take. These four are known as the *psychodynamic, trait, social-cognitive,* and *humanistic* approaches.

The Psychodynamic Approach

▶ **How did paralyzed patients lead Freud to psychoanalysis?**

People often think they can understand personality by simply watching others behave. A person with an "obnoxious personality" shows it by acting obnoxiously. But is that all there is to personality? Not according to Sigmund Freud, who compared personality to an iceberg, whose tip is clearly visible but whose bulk is hidden underwater.

As a physician in Vienna, Austria during the 1890s, Freud specialized in treating "neurotic" disorders such as blindness or paralysis for which there was no physical cause and that hypnosis could often remove. One patient sleepwalked on legs that were paralyzed during the day. These cases led Freud to believe in *psychic determinism,* the idea that personality and behavior are determined more by psychological factors than by biological conditions or current events (Schultz & Schultz, 2001). He proposed that people may not know why they feel, think, or act the way they do, because they are partly controlled by the unconscious portion of the personality—the part of which people are normally unaware (Funder, 2001a). From these ideas Freud created *psychoanalysis,* a theory of personality and a way of treating mental disorders. Freud's theory became the basis of the **psychodynamic approach** to personality, which assumes that various unconscious psychological processes interact to determine our thoughts, feelings, and behavior.

The Structure of Personality

Freud believed that people are born with basic needs or instincts—not only for food and water, but also for sex and aggression. He believed that needs for love, knowledge, security, and the like arise from these more fundamental desires. Each person faces the task of figuring out how to meet his or her needs in a world that often frustrates these efforts. According to Freud, personality develops out of each person's struggle with this task and is reflected in how the person carries it out.

Id, Ego, and Superego   Freud described the personality as having three major components: the id, the ego, and the superego (Allen, 2003; see Figure 11.1). The **id** represents the inborn, unconscious portion of the personality where life and death instincts reside. The *life instincts* promote positive, constructive behavior; the *death instincts* are responsible for human aggression and destructiveness. The id operates on the **pleasure principle,** seeking immediate satisfaction of both kinds of instincts, regardless of society's rules or the rights and feelings of others. The hungry person who pushes to the front of the line at Burger King would be satisfying an id-driven impulse.

As parents, teachers, and others place greater restrictions on the expression of id impulses, a second part of the personality, called the *ego* (or "self"), evolves from the id. The **ego** is responsible for organizing ways to get what a person wants in the real world, as opposed to the fantasy world of the id. Operating on the **reality principle,** the ego makes compromises between the id's unreasoning demands for immediate satisfaction and the restrictions of the social world. The ego would influence that hungry person at Burger King to wait in line and think about what to order rather than risk punishment by pushing ahead.

As children gain experience with the rules and values of society, they tend to adopt them. This process of *internalizing* parental and societal values creates the third component of personality, the **superego,** which tells us what we should and should not do. The superego represents our sense of morality and is just as relentless and unreasonable as the id in its demands to be obeyed. It would make the pushy person at Burger King feel guilty for even thinking about violating culturally approved rules about standing in line and taking turns.

Conflicts and Defenses   Freud described the inner clashes among id, ego, and superego as *intrapsychic,* or *psychodynamic, conflicts.* He believed that each individual's personality is shaped by the number, nature, and outcome of these conflicts. Freud said that the ego works to prevent the anxiety or guilt that would arise if we became conscious of socially unacceptable id impulses, especially those that would violate the superego's rules (Engler, 2003). Sometimes, the ego guides realistic actions, as when a parent asks for help because of impulses to abuse a child. At other times, the ego uses **defense mechanisms,** which are unconscious tactics that either prevent threatening material from surfacing or disguise it when it does (see Table 11.1).

table 11.1

Ego Defense Mechanisms

learn **by doing**   According to Freud, defense mechanisms prevent anxiety or guilt in the short run, but they sap energy. Further, using them to avoid dealing with the source of problems can make those problems worse in the long run. Try listing some incidents in which you or someone you know might have used each of the defenses described here. What questions would a critical thinker ask to determine whether these behaviors were unconscious defense mechanisms or actions motivated by conscious intentions?

superego   According to Freud, the component of personality that tells people what they should and should not do.

defense mechanisms   Unconscious tactics that either prevent threatening material from surfacing or disguise it when it does.

Defense Mechanism	Description
Repression	Unconsciously pushing threatening memories, urges, or ideas from conscious awareness: A person may experience loss of memory for unpleasant events.
Rationalization	Attempting to make actions or mistakes seem reasonable: The reasons or excuses given (e.g., "I spank my children because it is good for them") sound rational, but they are not the real reasons for the behavior.
Projection	Unconsciously attributing one's own unacceptable thoughts or impulses to another person: Instead of recognizing that "I hate him," a person may feel that "He hates me."
Reaction formation	Defending against unacceptable impulses by acting opposite to them: Sexual interest in a married friend might appear as strong dislike instead.
Sublimation	Converting unacceptable impulses into socially acceptable actions, and perhaps symbolically expressing them: Sexual or aggressive desires may appear as artistic creativity or devotion to athletic excellence.
Displacement	Deflecting an impulse from its original target to a less threatening one: Anger at one's boss may be expressed through hostility toward a clerk, a family member, or even the dog.
Denial	Simply discounting the existence of threatening impulses: A person may vehemently deny ever having had even the slightest degree of physical attraction to a person of the same sex.
Compensation	Striving to make up for unconscious impulses or fears: A business executive's extreme competitiveness might be aimed at compensating for unconscious feelings of inferiority.

THE ORAL STAGE   According to Freud, personality develops in a series of psychosexual stages. At each stage, a different part of the body becomes the primary focus of pleasure. This baby would appear to be in the oral stage.

psychosexual stages   In Freud's psychodynamic theory, periods of personality development in which internal and external conflicts focus on particular issues.

oral stage   The first of Freud's psychosexual stages, occurring during the first year of life, in which the mouth is the center of pleasure.

anal stage   The second of Freud's psychosexual stages, occurring during the second year of life, in which the focus of pleasure shifts from the mouth to the anus.

phallic stage   The third of Freud's psychosexual stages, lasting from approximately ages three to five, in which the focus of pleasure shifts to the genital area.

Stages of Personality Development

Freud proposed that personality develops during childhood through a series of **psychosexual stages.** Failure to resolve the conflicts that appear at any of these stages can leave a person *fixated*—that is, unconsciously preoccupied with the area of pleasure associated with that stage. Freud believed that the stage at which a person became fixated in childhood can be seen in the person's adult personality characteristics.

The Oral Stage   In Freud's theory, a child's first year or so is called the **oral stage** because the mouth—which infants use to eat and to explore everything from toys to their own hands and feet—is the center of pleasure associated with this period. Personality problems arise, said Freud, when oral needs are either neglected or overindulged. For example, early or late weaning from breastfeeding or bottle feeding may leave a child fixated at the oral stage, resulting in adult characteristics such as talking too much, overeating, smoking, drinking excessively, or using "biting" sarcasm. Childlike dependence on others is another possible sign of oral fixation.

The Anal Stage   The **anal stage** occurs during the second year, when the child's ego develops to cope with parental demands for socially appropriate behavior. For example, in most Western cultures, toilet training clashes with the child's enjoyment in having bowel movements at will. Freud said that if toilet training is too harsh or begins too early, it can produce a kind of anal fixation that appears in adulthood as stinginess or preoccupation with neatness (thus symbolically withholding feces). If toilet training is too late or too lax, however, the result could be another kind of anal fixation, which is reflected in adults who are disorganized or impulsive (symbolically expelling feces).

The Phallic Stage   According to Freud, between the ages of three and five, the focus of pleasure shifts to the genital area. Because he emphasized the psychosexual development of boys, Freud called this period the **phallic stage** (*phallus* is another word for *penis*). It is during this stage, he claimed, that the boy experiences sexual feelings for his mother and a desire to eliminate, or even kill, his father, with whom the boy competes for the mother's affection. Freud called this set of impulses the **Oedipus complex,** because it reminded him of the plot of the classical Greek play *Oedipus Rex.* (In the play, Oedipus unknowingly kills his father and marries his mother.) The boy's fantasies create so much fear, however, that the ego represses his incestuous desires, and he seeks to "identify" with his father and be like him. In the process, the child's superego begins to develop.

According to Freud, the female child begins the phallic stage with a strong attachment to her mother; but when she realizes that boys have penises and girls do not, she supposedly develops *penis envy* and transfers her love to the father. (This sequence has been called the **Electra complex** because it echoes the plot of *Electra,* another classical Greek play, but Freud never used this term.) To avoid her mother's disapproval, the girl identifies with and imitates her, thus forming the basis for her own superego.

Freud believed that unresolved conflicts during the phallic stage create a fixation that is reflected in various problems in adulthood. These problems can include difficulties with authority figures and an inability to maintain a stable love relationship.

The Latency Period   As the phallic stage draws to a close and its conflicts are coped with by the ego, an interval of psychological peace ensues. During this **latency period**, which lasts through childhood, sexual impulses stay in the background as the youngster focuses on education, same-sex peer play, and the development of social skills.

The Genital Stage   During adolescence, when sexual impulses reappear at the conscious level, the genitals again become the focus of pleasure. Thus begins what Freud called the **genital stage,** which lasts for the rest of the person's life. The quality of relationships and the degree of fulfillment experienced during this stage, he claimed, are directly affected by how intrapsychic conflicts were resolved during the earlier stages.

FOUNDER OF THE PSYCHODYNAMIC APPROACH Here is Sigmund Freud with his daughter, Anna, who became a psychoanalyst herself and eventually developed a revised version of her father's theories.

Oedipus complex The notion that young boys' impulses involve sexual feelings for the mother and the desire to eliminate the father.

Electra complex The notion that young girls develop an attachment to the father and compete with the mother for the father's attention.

latency period The fourth of Freud's psychosexual stages, usually beginning during the fifth year of life, in which sexual impulses become dormant and the child focuses on education and other matters.

genital stage The fifth and last of Freud's psychosexual stages, which begins during adolescence, when sexual impulses begin to appear at the conscious level.

Variations on Freud's Personality Theory

Freud's ideas—especially those concerning infantile sexuality and the Oedipus complex—were, and still are, controversial. Even many of Freud's followers eventually disagreed with him. Some of these followers are known as *neo-Freudian* theorists, because they maintained many of the basic ideas in Freud's theory but developed their own approaches. Others are known as *ego-psychologists*, because their theories focus more on the ego than on the id (Mischel, Shoda, & Smith, 2004).

Jung's Analytic Psychology Carl Jung (pronounced "yoong") was the most prominent dissenter among Freud's early followers. Jung (1916) argued that people are born with a general life force that, in addition to a sex drive, includes a drive for creativity, for growth-oriented resolution of conflicts, and for the productive blending of basic impulses with real-world demands. Jung did not identify specific stages in personality development. He suggested instead that people gradually develop differing degrees of *introversion* (a tendency to reflect on one's own experiences) or *extraversion* (a tendency to focus on the social world), along with differing tendencies to rely on specific psychological functions, such as thinking or feeling. The combination of these tendencies and functions, said Jung (1933), creates personalities that show distinctive and predictable patterns of behavior.

Other Neo-Freudian Theorists Alfred Adler, one of Freud's first followers, also questioned his theories. Adler came to believe that the most important innate factor driving the development of personality was not id impulses but a desire to overcome infantile feelings of helplessness and gain some control over the environment. Other prominent neo-Freudians emphasized social relationships in the development of personality. Some, including Erik Erikson, Erich Fromm, and Harry Stack Sullivan, argued that once biological needs are met, the attempt to meet social needs (to feel protected, secure, and accepted, for example) is the main shaper of personality. According to these theories, the strategies that people use to meet social needs, such as dominating other people or being dependent on them, become core features of their personalities.

The first feminist personality theorist, Karen Horney (pronounced "horn-eye"), challenged Freud's view that women's lack of a penis causes them to envy men and feel inferior to them. Horney (1937) argued that it is men who envy women. Realizing that they cannot bear children, males see their lives as having less meaning and substance than women's. Horney called this condition *womb envy*. She believed that when women feel inferior, it is because of cultural factors—such as the personal and political restrictions that men have placed on them—not because of penis envy (Feist & Feist, 2002).

Contemporary Psychodynamic Theories

Today, some of the most influential psychodynamic approaches to personality focus on *object relations*—that is, on how people's perceptions of themselves and others influence their view of, and reactions to, the world (Westen & Gabbard, 1999). According to object relations theorists, early relationships between infants and their love objects (usually the mother and other primary caregivers) are vital influences on the development of personality (Greenberg & Mitchell, 1983; Klein, 1975; Kohut, 1984; Sohlberg & Jansson, 2002). These relationships, they say, shape our thoughts and feelings about social relationships in later life.

As described in the chapter on human development, children ideally form a secure early bond to the mother or other caregiver; gradually tolerate separation from this "object" of attachment; and finally develop the ability to relate to others as independent, secure individuals (Ainsworth & Bowlby, 1991). Object relations theorists explore how an infant's experience of a primary caregiver's protection, acceptance, and recognition influences development of the child's self-image, identity, security, social relationships, and other aspects of personality (Mikelson, Kessler, & Shaver,

1997; Simpson & Roles, 2000). In one study, women who had been securely attached to their parents in childhood were more likely to have happy marriages than women whose childhood attachment had been insecure (Klohnen & Bera, 1998). Another study found that people with secure attachments were less likely to abuse alcohol or other drugs (Mikelson, Kessler, & Shaver, 1997). Still other research suggests that children who, because of abuse, neglect, or rejection, miss the opportunity to become securely attached to their mother or other love "object" may suffer severe disturbances in their later relationships (Aizawa, 2002).

Evaluating the Psychodynamic Approach

Freud's personality theory is probably the most comprehensive and influential personality theory ever proposed. His ideas have shaped a wide range of psychotherapy techniques (see the chapter on treatment of psychological disorders) and stimulated the development of several personality assessments, including the projective tests described later in this chapter. Some of Freud's ideas have found support in research on cognitive processes, especially social cognition (Anderson & Chen, 2002). There is evidence, for example, that events and experiences that people are unable to recall can influence their thoughts, their actions, and even their health (Andersen & Miranda, 2000; Arndt et al., 2000).

However, there are several problems and weaknesses in Freud's psychodynamic theory (Crews, 1996). For one thing, his conclusions about personality are based almost entirely on case studies of a few individuals. As discussed in the introductory chapter, conclusions drawn from case studies may not apply to people in general. Freud's sample of cases was certainly not representative of people in general. Most of his patients were upper-class Viennese women who not only had psychological problems but also were raised in a society that considered the discussion of sex to be uncivilized. Second, Freud's theory reflected Western European and North American cultural values, which may or may not be helpful in understanding people in other cultures (Feist & Feist, 2002). For example, the concepts of ego and self that are so central to Freud's personality theory are based on the self-oriented values of individualist cultures and thus may be less descriptive of personality development in collectivist cultures, such as those of Asia and South America (Matsumoto, 2000).

Freud's conclusions may have been distorted by other biases as well. Some Freud scholars believe he might have (perhaps unconsciously) modified reports of what happened during therapy to better fit his theory (Esterson, 2001; MacMillan, 1997). He may also have asked leading questions that influenced patients to "recall" events from their childhood that never happened (Esterson, 2001). Today, as described in the memory chapter, there are similar concerns that some patients who recover allegedly repressed memories about childhood sexual abuse may actually be reporting false memories implanted by their therapists (Peiffer & Trull, 2000).

Freud's belief that women envy male anatomy and his focus on male psychosexual development have also been attacked. In the tradition of Horney, some contemporary neo-Freudians have proposed theories that focus specifically on the psychosexual development of women (Sayers, 1991).

Finally, as judged by modern standards, Freud's theory is not very scientific. His definitions of *id, ego, unconscious conflict,* and other concepts lack the precision required for scientific measurement and testing (Feist & Feist, 2002). Further, his belief that unconscious desires drive most human behavior ignores evidence showing that much of that behavior goes beyond impulse gratification. For example, the conscious drive to attain personal, social, and spiritual goals is an important determinant of behavior, as is learning from others. Taken together, these shortcomings have made the psychodynamic approach to personality less popular today than it was in past decades (Mischel, 2002; Robins, Gosling, & Craik, 2000).

The Trait Approach

> ▶ **What personality traits are most basic?**

If you were to describe the personality of someone you know, you would probably make a small number of descriptive statements. For example, you might say,

> *She's a really caring person, and very outgoing. She's generous with her time, and she works very hard at everything she does. Yet, sometimes I think she also lacks self-confidence. She always gives in to other people's demands because she wants to be accepted by them.*

In other words, most people describe others by referring to the kind of people they are ("outgoing"); to the thoughts, feelings, and actions that are most typical of them ("caring," "lacks self-confidence"); or to their needs ("wants to be accepted"). Together, these statements describe personality *traits*—the tendencies that help direct how a person usually thinks and behaves (Pervin & John, 2001).

The trait approach to personality makes three main assumptions:

1. Personality traits remain relatively stable, and therefore predictable, over time. So a gentle person tends to stay that way day after day, year after year (Costa & McCrae, 2002).

2. Personality traits remain relatively stable across situations, and they can explain why people act in predictable ways in many different settings. A person who is fiercely competitive at work will probably also be competitive on the tennis court or at a party.

3. People differ from one another in how much of a particular personality trait they possess; no two people are exactly alike on all traits. The result is an endless variety of unique personalities.

In short, psychologists taking the **trait approach** see personality as the combination of stable internal characteristics that people display consistently over time and across situations (Pervin, 2003). Trait theorists seek to measure the relative strength of the many personality characteristics appearing in each individual (see Figure 11.2).

Allport's Trait Theory

Gordon Allport (1961) spent thirty years searching for the traits that combine to form the normal personality. When he listed the nearly 18,000 dictionary terms used to describe human behavior, he noticed that many of these terms referred to the same thing (Hergenhahn & Olson, 1999). For example, *hostile, nasty,* and *mean* all convey a similar meaning. To better understand this clustering, think of a close relative, and jot down all the personality traits that describe this person. If you are like most people, you were able to capture your relative's personality using only a few trait labels. Allport believed that the set of labels chosen to describe a particular person reflects that person's *central traits*, those that organize and control behavior in many different situations and that are usually apparent to others. Central traits are roughly equivalent to the descriptive terms used in letters of recommendation (*reliable* or *distractible*, for example) that are meant to tell what can be expected from a person most of the time (Schultz & Schultz, 2001). Allport also believed that people possess *secondary traits*, those that are more specific to certain situations and control far less behavior. "Dislikes crowds" is an example of a secondary trait.

Allport's research helped to lay the foundation for modern research on personality traits. However, his focus on the uniqueness of each individual personality makes it difficult to draw general conclusions about the structure of human personality.

learn
by doing

trait approach   A perspective on personality that views it as the combination of stable characteristics that people display over time and across situations.

figure 11.2

Two Personality Profiles

learn **by doing** Trait theory describes personality in terms of the strength of particular dimensions, or traits. Here are trait profiles for Rodney, an inner-city social worker, and James, a sales clerk in a department store. Compared with James, Rodney is about equally industrious; more generous; and less nervous, extraverted, and aggressive. Just for fun, mark this figure to indicate how strong you think you are on each of the listed traits. Trait theorists suggest that this should be easy for you to do because, they say, virtually everyone displays a certain amount of almost any personality characteristic.

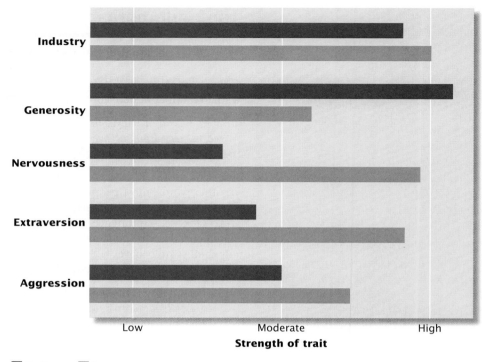

■ Rodney   ■ James

Source: Costa & McCrae (1992).

The Big-Five Model of Personality

In recent years, trait approaches have continued to focus on describing the structure of personality. Building on the work of Allport and other early trait theorists such as Raymond Catell, today's trait theorists have used statistical techniques such as *factor analysis* to discover which personality traits are correlated with one another. Factor analysis can reveal, for example, whether people who are anxious are also moody, and whether optimistic people are usually also friendly.

The results of this research have led many researchers to conclude that personality is organized around five basic factors (McCrae & Costa, 1999). The components of this so-

applying psychology **SELECTING A JURY** Some psychologists employ trait theories of personality in advising prosecution or defense attorneys about which potential jurors are most likely to be sympathetic to their side of a court case.

big-five model A view based on factor-analytic studies suggesting the existence of five basic components of human personality: neuroticism, extraversion, openness, agreeableness, and conscientiousness. Also called the *five-factor model*.

table 11.2

The Big-Five Personality Dimensions

Here is a list of the adjectives that define the big-five personality factors. You can more easily remember the names of these factors by noting that their first letters spell the word *ocean*.

Dimension	Defining Descriptors
Openness	Artistic, curious, imaginative, insightful, original, wide interests, unusual thought processes, intellectual interests
Conscientiousness	Efficient, organized, planful, reliable, thorough, dependable, ethical, productive
Extraversion	Active, assertive, energetic, outgoing, talkative, gesturally expressive, gregarious
Agreeableness	Appreciative, forgiving, generous, kind, trusting, noncritical, warm, compassionate, considerate, straightforward
Neuroticism	Anxious, self-pitying, tense, emotionally unstable, impulsive, vulnerable, touchy, worrying

Source: Adapted from McCrae & John (1992).

called **big-five model,** or **five-factor model,** of personality are *openness, conscientiousness, extraversion, agreeableness,* and *neuroticism* (see Table 11.2). Several different investigators have found these factors (or a set very similar to them) when they analyzed data from numerous sources, including personality inventories, peer ratings of personality characteristics, and checklists of descriptive adjectives (Costa & McCrae, 1995; John & Sirvasta, 1999). The fact that some version of the big-five factors reliably appear in many countries and cultures—including Canada, China, Germany, Finland, India, Japan, South Korea, the Philippines, and Poland (McCrae et al., 1998, 2000; Narayann, Menon, & Levine, 1995)—provides further evidence that these factors may represent the most important components of human personality.

The emergence of the big-five model is considered by many trait theorists to be a major breakthrough in personality research (Funder, 2001a). Identification of the big-five traits provides a standard way of examining the personalities of all people, regardless of where they live or the nature of their economic, social, and cultural backgrounds. The big-five model also allows researchers to precisely describe the similarities and differences in people's personalities, and to explore how these factors are related to everything from personality disorders to happiness, or subjective well-being (e.g., Diener, 2000; Lynam & Widiger, 2001).

ANIMAL PERSONALITIES The idea that personality can be described in terms of five main dimensions seems to hold for some animals, as well as humans. The five animal dimensions differ from, but are still related to, human traits. For example, hyenas vary in terms of dominance, excitability, agreeableness (toward people), sociability (toward each other), and curiosity. Some of these same traits have been observed in a wide variety of other species, including chimpanzees and other primates (Gosling, 2001), and dog and cat lovers often report such traits in their pets.

Biological Trait Theories

Some personality theorists are interested not only in what traits form the core of human personality, but also in why people differ on these traits. Their research suggests that differences in traits might be due to biological factors.

Eysenck's Biological Trait Theory   Like other trait theorists, British psychologist Hans Eysenck (pronounced "eye-sink") used factor analysis to study personality. His research convinced him that personality can be described in terms of two main factors or dimensions: *introversion-extraversion* and *emotionality-stability* (Eysenck, 1990a, 1994):

LINKAGES
Why do some people take more risks that others?
(a link to Motivation and Emotion)

1. *Introversion-extraversion.*   Extraverts are sociable and outgoing, enjoy parties and other social activities, take risks, and love excitement and change. Introverts tend to be quiet, thoughtful, and reserved, enjoying solitary pursuits and avoiding excitement and social involvement.

2. *Emotionality-stability.*   At one extreme of this dimension are people who exhibit such characteristics as moodiness, restlessness, worry, anxiety, and other negative emotions. People at the opposite end are calm, even-tempered, relaxed, and emotionally stable. (This dimension is also often called *neuroticism.*)

According to Eysenck, personality can be described in terms of where a person falls along these two dimensions. For example, an introverted but stable person is likely to be controlled and reliable. An introverted but emotional person is likely to be rigid and anxious (see Figure 11.3). Eysenck presented data to show that scores on tests measuring these dimensions—such as the Eysenck Personality Inventory—can predict people's key characteristics, including specific behavior disorders.

Eysenck argued that variations in personality characteristics among individuals can be traced to inherited differences in their nervous systems, especially in their brains. These biological differences, he said, explain why some people are more physiologically aroused than others. For example, people who inherit a nervous system with a consistently low level of arousal will be relatively insensitive to the effects of rewards and punishments, and therefore will not readily develop conditioned

figure 11.3

Eysenck's Personality Dimensions

learn by doing   According to Eysenck, varying degrees of emotionality-stability and introversion-extraversion combine to produce predictable trait patterns. Which section of the figure do you think best describes your personality? How about those of a friend or a relative? Did you find it any easier to "place" other people's personalities in a particular section compared with placing your own personality? If so, why do you think that might be?

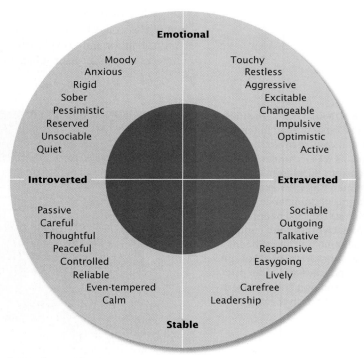

Source: Eysenck & Rachman (1965).

responses, including conditioned fears. Without such conditioned responses, said Eysenck, they will not easily learn to play by society's rules. Further, having a low arousal level may lead such people to look constantly for excitement and change in order to increase their arousal; in short, they will be extraverted. In contrast, Eysenck's theory predicts that people with more sensitive, "overaroused" nervous systems are likely to be strongly affected by rewards and punishments, to readily develop conditioned fear responses, and to avoid excessive stimulation—in other words, to be introverted.

Other Biological Trait Theories   Some researchers have challenged Eysenck's explanation of the biological origins of differences in personality traits. For example, another British psychologist, Jeffrey Gray, believes that differences in introversion-extraversion and emotionality-stability stem from two related systems in the brain, called the *behavioral approach system* and the *behavioral inhibition system.* The behavioral approach system affects people's sensitivity to rewards and their motivation to seek these rewards. The behavioral inhibition system affects sensitivity to punishment and the motivation to avoid punishment (Pickering & Gray, 1999). Gray says that people with an active behavioral approach system tend to experience positive emotions; people with an active behavioral inhibition system are more likely to experience negative ones (Zelenski & Larsen, 1999). Gray's theory is now more widely accepted than Eysenck's theory—primarily because it is supported by what neuroscientists have learned about brain structures, neurotransmitters, and how they operate (Larsen & Buss, 2002).

THINKING CRITICALLY

Are Personality Traits Inherited?

Gray's approach-inhibition theory is one of several biologically oriented explanations of the origins of personality traits. A related explanation is that the big-five factors and other personality traits arise from our genes. Consider the case of identical twins who had been separated at five weeks of age and did not meet again for thirty-nine years. Both men drove Chevrolets, chain-smoked the same brand of cigarettes, had divorced a woman named Linda, were remarried to a woman named Betty, had sons named James Allan, had dogs named Toy, enjoyed similar hobbies, and had served as sheriff's deputies (Tellegen et al., 1988).

■ **What am I being asked to believe or accept?**

Cases like this have helped focus the attention of behavioral geneticists on the possibility that some core aspects of personality might be partly, or even largely, inherited (Krueger, Markon, & Bouchard, 2003; Plomin & Caspi, 1999).

■ **Is there evidence available to support the claim?**

The evidence and the arguments regarding this assertion are much like those presented in the chapter on thought, language, and intelligence, where we discuss the origins of differences in mental abilities. Stories about children who seem to "have" their parents' or grandparents' bad temper, generosity, or shyness are often presented to support the idea that personality is inherited. And in fact, family resemblances in personality do provide one important source of evidence. Several studies have found moderate, but significant, correlations between children's personality test scores and those of their parents and siblings (Davis, Luce, & Kraus, 1994; Loehlin, 1992).

Even stronger evidence comes from studies conducted around the world comparing identical twins raised together, identical twins raised apart, nonidentical twins raised together, and nonidentical twins raised apart (Grigorenko, 2002). Identical twins (who have exactly the same genes) tend to be more alike in personality than nonidentical twins (whose genes are no more similar than those of other siblings)—regardless of whether they are raised apart or together. This research also shows that identical twins are more alike than nonidentical twins in general temperament, such as how active, sociable, anxious, and emotional they are (Pickering & Gray, 1999; Borkenau et al., 2002). On the basis of such twin studies, behavioral geneticists have concluded that at least 30 percent, and perhaps as much as 60 percent, of the variability in adult personality traits is due to genetic factors (Borkenau et al., 2001).

■ Can that evidence be interpreted another way?

Family resemblances in personality could reflect inheritance or social influence. So an obvious alternative interpretation of this evidence might be that family similarities come not from common genes but from a common environment. Children learn many rules, skills, and behaviors by watching parents, siblings, and others; perhaps they learn their personalities as well (Funder, 2001b). And the fact that nontwin siblings are less alike than twins may well result from what is called *nonshared environments* (Plomin & Caspi, 1999). A child's place in the family birth order, differences in the way parents treat each of their children, and accidents, illnesses, or events that alter a particular child's life or health are all examples of nonshared factors (Paulhus, Trapnell, & Chen, 1999). Each nonshared factor can have a different impact on each individual. Compared with twins, nontwins tend to be affected by more of these nonshared environmental factors.

■ What evidence would help to evaluate the alternatives?

One way to evaluate the degree to which personality is inherited would be to study people in infancy, before the environment has had a chance to exert its influence. If the environment were entirely responsible for personality, newborn infants should be essentially alike. However, as discussed in the chapter on human development, newborns do show differences in activity level, sensitivity to the environment, the tendency to cry, and interest in new stimuli (Matthews & Dreary, 1998). These differences in *temperament* suggest biological, and perhaps genetic, influences.

FAMILY RESEMBLANCE   Do children inherit personality traits in the same direct way as they inherit facial features, coloration, and other physical characteristics? Research in behavioral genetics suggests that personality is the joint product of genetically influenced behavioral tendencies and the environmental conditions each child encounters.

To evaluate the relative contributions of nature and nurture beyond infancy, psychologists have examined characteristics of adopted children. If adopted children are more like their biological than their adoptive parents, this suggests the influence of heredity in personality. If they are more like their adoptive family, a strong role for environmental factors in personality is suggested. In actuality, adopted children's personalities tend to resemble the personalities of their biological parents and siblings more than those of the families in which they are raised (Plomin et al., 1998).

Further research will determine more clearly what aspects of the environment are most important in shaping personality (Turkheimer & Waldron, 2000). So far, the evidence suggests that personality is not influenced very strongly by elements of the shared environment—such as socioeconomic status—that equally affect all children in the same family. However, nonshared environmental influences, at home and elsewhere, appear to be very important in personality development (Loehlin, Neiderhiser, & Reiss, 2003; Harris, 2000). We need to know more about the exact impact on personality development of nonshared environmental factors that may be different for twins and nontwin siblings.

■ What conclusions are most reasonable?

Even those researchers, such as Robert Plomin, who support genetic theories of personality caution that we should not replace "simple-minded environmentalism" with the equally incorrect view that personality is almost completely biologically determined (Plomin & Crabbe, 2000). It is pointless to talk about heredity *versus* environment as causes of personality, because nature and nurture always intertwine to exert joint and simultaneous influences (Cacioppo et al., 2000; Caspi et al., 2002).

With this caution in mind, we would be well advised to draw rather tentative conclusions about the origins of personality differences. The evidence available so far suggests that genetic influences do appear to contribute significantly to the differences among people in many personality traits (Plomin & Crabbe, 2000). However, there is no evidence of a specific gene for any specific personality trait. The genetic contribution to personality most likely comes as genes influence people's nervous systems and general predispositions toward certain temperaments (Arbelle et al., 2003; Grigorenko, 2002). Temperamental factors (e.g., emotionality and sociability) then interact with environmental factors, such as family experiences, to produce specific features of personality (Caspi & Roberts, 1999). For example, children who inherit a tendency toward emotionality might play less with other children, withdraw from social interactions, and thus tend to fail to learn important social skills (Eisenberg, Fabes, & Murphy, 1995). These experiences and tendencies, in turn, might foster the self-consciousness and shyness seen in introverted personalities.

Notice, though, that genetic predispositions toward particular personality characteristics may or may not appear in behavior, depending on whether the environment supports or suppresses them. Changes in genetically predisposed traits are not only possible but may actually be quite common as children grow (Cacioppo et al., 2000). Rather than inheriting specific traits, people appear to inherit raw materials that are then shaped by the world into individual personalities.

Evaluating the Trait Approach

The trait approach, especially the big-five model, tends to dominate contemporary research in personality. Yet there are several problems and weaknesses associated with this approach.

For one thing, trait theories are better at describing people than at explaining them. They say a lot about how people behave, but they don't always explain why (Pervin, 2003). In addition, trait theories tell little about how traits relate to the thoughts and feelings that precede, accompany, and follow behavior. Do introverts and extraverts decide to act as they do? Can they behave otherwise? And how do they feel about their actions and experiences (Cervone & Shoda, 1999)? Some personality psychologists are linking their research with that of cognitive psychologists in an effort to better understand how thoughts and emotions influence, and are influenced by, personality traits (Shoda & Tiernan, 2002).

The trait approach has also been criticized for offering a short list of traits that provides, at best, a fixed and rather shallow description of personality that doesn't capture how traits combine to form a complex and dynamic individual (Block, 2001; Funder, 2001a). Even if the big-five model of personality proves to be correct and universal, its factors are not all-powerful; situations, too, affect behavior. For example, people high in extraversion are not always sociable. Whether they behave sociably depends, in part, on where they are and who else is present.

In fairness, early trait theorists such as Allport acknowledged the importance of situations in influencing behavior, but it is only recently that consideration of person-situation interactions has become an important part of trait-based approaches to personality. This change is largely the result of research conducted by psychologists who have taken a social-cognitive approach to personality, which we describe next.

The Social-Cognitive Approach

▶ **Do we learn our personality?**

social-cognitive approach An approach to personality that views personality as a label summarizing the unique patterns of thinking and behavior that a person learns.

According to the psychodynamic and trait approaches, personality consists of inner dynamics or traits that guide thinking and behavior. In contrast, researchers who take a **social-cognitive approach** see personality as a set of behaviors that people acquire through learning and then display in particular situations. Some aspects of this approach

- ■ B = Behavior
- ▢ E = The external environment
- ■ P = Personal factors, such as thoughts, feelings, and biological events

figure 11.4

Reciprocal Determinism

Bandura's notion of reciprocal determinism suggests that thoughts, behavior, and the environment are constantly affecting each other. For example, a person's hostile thoughts might lead to hostile behavior, which generates even more hostile thoughts. At the same time, the hostile behavior offends other people, which creates a threatening environment that causes the person to think and act in even more negative ways. As increasingly negative thoughts alter the person's perceptions of the environment, it seems to be more threatening than ever.

self-efficacy   According to Bandura, the learned expectation of success in given situations.

reflect the view of traditional behaviorists, namely that all behavior is learned through classical and operant conditioning (see the chapter on learning). However, the social-cognitive approach expands that view by emphasizing (1) the role played by *learned patterns of thinking* in guiding behavior and (2) the fact that personality is learned in social situations as people observe and interact with other people (Bandura & Walters, 1963; Funder, 2001a; Kimble, 1999). The social-cognitive approach is sometimes called the *social-learning approach* because it defines personality as the sum of the behaviors and cognitive habits that develop as people learn through experience in the social world. Social-cognitive theorists are interested in how our thinking affects our behavior, as well as how our behavior and its consequences affect our thinking and our future actions.

Prominent Social-Cognitive Theories

Julian Rotter, Albert Bandura, and Walter Mischel rank among the most influential social-cognitive personality theorists.

Rotter's Expectancy Theory   Julian Rotter (1982) argued that learning creates cognitions known as *expectancies,* and that these expectancies guide behavior. He suggested that a person's decision to engage in a behavior is determined by (1) what the person expects to happen following the behavior and (2) the value the person places on the outcome. For example, people spend a lot of money on clothes to be worn at job interviews because past learning leads them to expect that doing so will help get them the job, and they place a high value on having the job. To Rotter, then, behavior is shaped by the positive or negative consequences it brings, and also by the expectancy that a particular behavior will be rewarded or punished (Mischel, Shoda, & Smith, 2004).

Personality researchers influenced by Rotter have suggested that in addition to learning expectancies about particular behaviors in particular situations, we also learn more general expectancies, especially about how life's rewards and punishments are controlled (e.g., Phares, 1976). Some people (called *internals*) come to expect that events are controlled mainly by their own efforts. These people assume that what they achieve and the rewards they get result from efforts they make themselves. Others (*externals*) tend to expect events to be controlled by external forces over which they have no control. When externals succeed, they tend to believe that their success occurred due to chance or luck.

Research on differences in generalized expectancies does show that they are correlated with differences in behavior. When confronted with a personal problem, for example, internals are more likely than externals to work on solving it. Externals are more likely to see the problem as unsolvable (Gianakos, 2002). Internals also tend to work harder than externals at staying physically healthy. They are more likely to exercise and wear seat belts, and less likely to smoke, drink alcohol, or—if they do drink—to drive while intoxicated (Cavaiola & Desordi, 2000; Maddux, 1993; Phares, 1991). Among college students, internals tend to be better informed about the courses they take, including what they need to do to get a high grade. Perhaps as a result, internals tend to get better grades than externals (Dollinger, 2000).

Bandura and Reciprocal Determinism   In his social-cognitive theory, Albert Bandura (1999) sees personality as shaped by the ways in which thoughts, behavior, and the environment interact and influence one another. He points out that whether people learn through direct experience with reward and punishment or by watching what happens to others (observational learning), their behavior tends to affect their environment. Observing these effects may, in turn, affect people's cognitions, which affects their behavior, and so on. According to Bandura (1999), then, personality is the result of *reciprocal determinism,* the complex and constant interaction among thoughts, the environment, and behavior (see Figure 11.4).

One especially important cognitive element in this mutual-influence system is perceived **self-efficacy,** the learned expectation of success. Bandura says that our behavior is largely controlled by our perception or belief that we can successfully perform

THE IMPACT OF SITUATIONS Like the rest of us, Jesse Ventura's behavior differs in different situations, including in the ring during his career as a professional wrestler, in the office where he served as the governor of Minnesota, and in the studio of his talk show. Mischel's theory of personality emphasizes that person-situation interactions are important in determining behavior.

that behavior. People with a high degree of perceived self-efficacy believe that they can successfully perform a behavior regardless of past failures or current obstacles. The higher your self-efficacy regarding a particular situation, the greater will be your actual accomplishments in that situation (Bandura, 2000, 2002). So going into a job interview believing that you have the skills for the job may help you to get the job or, at least, blunt the impact of rejection if you do not. (Perhaps you recall the classic children's story *The Little Engine That Could*. Trying to get up a steep hill, the scared little engine starts by saying "I think I can, I think I can" and ends up saying "I know I can, I know I can." And it did.)

According to Bandura, self-efficacy interacts with expectancies about the outcome of behavior in general, and the result of this interplay helps to shape a person's psychological well-being (Bandura, 1997). For example, if a person has low self-efficacy and also expects that nothing anyone does has much effect on the world, apathy may result. But if a person with low self-efficacy believes that other people enjoy the benefits of their efforts, the result may be self-criticism and depression.

Mischel's Cognitive/Affective Theory   Social-cognitive theorists believe that learned beliefs, feelings, and expectancies characterize each individual and make that individual different from others. Walter Mischel calls these characteristics *cognitive person variables*. He believes that they outline the dimensions along which individuals differ (Mischel & Shoda, 1999).

According to Mischel, the most important cognitive person variables are (1) *encodings* (the person's beliefs about the environment and other people), (2) *expectancies* (including self-efficacy and what the person expects to follow from various behaviors), (3) *affects* (feelings and emotions), (4) *goals and values* (the things a person believes in and wants to achieve), and (5) *competencies and self-regulatory plans* (the things the person can do, and the ability to thoughtfully plan behaviors) (Mischel & Shoda, 1999).

To predict how a person might behave in a particular situation, says Mischel, we need to know about these cognitive person variables and about the features of that situation. In short, the person and the situation interact to produce behavior. Mischel's ideas have been called an "if-then" theory, because he proposes that *if* people encounter a particular situation, *then* they will engage in the behaviors that they typically show in this situation (Mischel, Shoda, & Mendoza-Denton, 2002).

Mischel was once highly critical of the trait approach to personality, but now he sees his own theory as generally consistent with that approach. And trait theorists have come to accept many of Mischel's ideas. This search for similarities between the trait approach and the social-cognitive approach has helped to clarify the relationship between personal and situational variables and how they affect behavior under various conditions. Many of the conclusions that have emerged are consistent with Bandura's concept of reciprocal determinism:

1. Personal dispositions (which include traits and cognitive person variables) influence behavior only in relevant situations. The trait of anxiousness, for example, may predict anxiety, but mainly in situations where an anxious person feels threatened.

2. Personal dispositions can lead to behaviors that alter situations that, in turn, promote other behaviors. For example, a hostile child can trigger aggression in others and thus start a fight.

3. People choose to be in situations that are in accord with their personal dispositions. Introverts, for instance, are likely to choose quiet environments, whereas extraverts tend to seek out livelier, more social circumstances.

4. Personal dispositions are more important in some situations than in others. Where many different behaviors would be appropriate—at a picnic, for example—what people do can usually be predicted from their dispositions (extraverts will probably play games and socialize while introverts watch). However, in situations such as a funeral, where fewer options are socially acceptable, personal dispositions will not differentiate one person from another; everyone is likely to be quiet and somber.

Today, social-cognitive theorists are attempting to discover how person variables develop, how they relate to stress and health, and how they interact with situational variables to affect behavior.

Evaluating the Social-Cognitive Approach

The social-cognitive approach to personality is valuable because it blends behavioral learning theories with concepts from cognitive psychology and applies them to such socially important topics as aggression, the effects of mass media on children, and the development of techniques that enhance personal control over behavior. Social-cognitive principles have also been translated into cognitive-behavioral treatment procedures (O'Donohue, Fisher, & Hayes, 2003; see the chapter on treatment of psychological disorders).

The social-cognitive approach has not escaped criticism, however. Psychodynamic theorists point out that social-cognitive theories leave no role for unconscious thoughts and feelings in determining behaviors (e.g., Westen, 1998). Some advocates of trait theory complain that social-cognitive theorists have focused more on explaining why traits are unimportant than on why situations are important, and that they have failed to identify what it is about specific situations that brings out certain behaviors (Friedman & Schustack, 2003). Finally, some critics feel that the social-cognitive approach cannot really capture the complexities, richness, and uniqueness that is inherent in human personality (Hall, Lindzey, & Campbell, 1998). For these critics, a preferable alternative is the humanistic approach to personality.

The Humanistic Approach

▶ **Is everyone basically good?**

Unlike theories that emphasize the instincts and learning processes that humans seem to share with other animals, the humanistic approach to personality focuses on mental capabilities that set humans apart: self-awareness, creativity, planning, decision making, and responsibility. Those who adopt the **humanistic approach** view human behavior as motivated mainly by an innate drive toward growth that prompts people to fulfill their unique potential. And like the planted seed whose natural potential is to become a flower, people are seen as naturally inclined toward goodness, creativity, love, and joy. Humanistic psychologists also believe that to explain people's actions, it is more important to understand their view of the world than their instincts, traits, or learning experiences. To humanists, that world view is a bit different for each of us, and it is this unique way of perceiving and interpreting the world that shapes personality and guides behavior (Kelly, 1980). This emphasis on the importance of looking at people's perceptions is the reason why this approach is also sometimes referred to as the *phenomenological approach*.

Major Humanistic Theories

The most prominent humanistic theories of personality are those of Carl Rogers and Abraham Maslow.

Rogers's Self Theory   In his extensive writings, Carl Rogers (1942, 1951, 1961, 1970, 1980) emphasized the **actualizing tendency,** which he described as an innate inclination toward growth and fulfillment that motivates all human behavior (Raskin & Rogers, 2001). To Rogers, personality is the expression of that actualizing tendency as it unfolds in each person's uniquely perceived reality (Feist & Feist, 2002).

Central to Rogers's theory is the *self,* the part of experience that a person identifies as "I" or "me." According to Rogers, those who accurately experience the self—with all its

---

humanistic approach   A view of behavior as controlled by the decisions that people make about their lives based on their perceptions of the world.

actualizing tendency   An innate inclination toward growth and fulfillment that motivates all human behavior.

self-concept   The way one thinks of oneself.

conditions of worth   According to Rogers, circumstances in which an individual experiences positive regard from others only when displaying certain behaviors or attitudes.

"Just remember, son, it doesn't matter whether you win or lose—unless you want Daddy's love."

Parents are not usually this obvious about creating conditions of worth, but according to Rogers, the message gets through in many more subtle ways.

preferences, abilities, fantasies, shortcomings, and desires—are on the road to *self-actualization*. The progress of those whose experiences of the self become distorted, however, is likely to be slowed or stopped.

Rogers saw personality development beginning early, as children learn to need the approval, or *positive regard,* of others. Evaluations by parents, teachers, and others soon begin to affect children's self-evaluations. When these evaluations by others are in agreement with a child's own self-evaluations, the child reacts in a way that matches, or is *congruent* with, self-experience. The child not only feels the other person's positive regard but also evaluates the self as "good" for having earned approval. The result is a clearly identified and positively evaluated experience of the self. This self-experience becomes part of the **self-concept,** which is the way one thinks of oneself. Unfortunately, things may not always go so smoothly. If a pleasurable self-experience is evaluated negatively by others, the child must either do without their positive regard or reevaluate the experience. So a little boy who is teased by his father for having fun playing with dolls might adopt a distorted self-experience—deciding, perhaps, that "I don't like dolls" or that "Feeling good is bad."

In other words, said Rogers, personality is shaped partly by the actualizing tendency and partly by other people's evaluations. In this way, people come to like what they are "supposed" to like and to behave as they are "supposed" to behave. Although this socialization process helps people to get along in society, it often requires that they suppress their self-actualizing tendency and distort their experience. Rogers argued that psychological discomfort, anxiety, or mental disorder can result when the feelings people experience or express are *incongruent,* or at odds, with their true feelings.

Incongruence is likely, Rogers said, when parents and teachers lead children to believe that their worth as a person depends on displaying the "right" attitudes, behaviors, and values. These **conditions of worth** are created whenever people are evaluated instead of their behavior. For example, parents who find their child drawing on the wall with crayons are unlikely to say, "I love you, but I don't approve of this behavior." They are more likely to shout, "Bad boy!" or "Bad girl!" This reaction suggests that the child is lovable and worthwhile only when well-behaved. As a result, the child's self-experience is not "I like drawing on the wall, but Mom and Dad don't approve," but instead, "Drawing on the wall is bad, and I am bad if I like it, so I don't like it." The child may eventually show overly neat and tidy behaviors that do not reflect the real self but, rather, are part of an ideal self that is dictated by the parents.

Like Freud's concept of superego, conditions of worth are initially set up by external pressure but eventually become part of the person's belief system. To Rogers, then, rewards and

SEEKING SELF-ACTUALIZATION
According to Rogers, conditions of worth can make it harder for children to become aware of and accept aspects of themselves that conflict with their parents' values. Progress toward self-actualization can be enhanced by associating with those whose positive regard is not conditional on displaying any particular pattern of behavior.

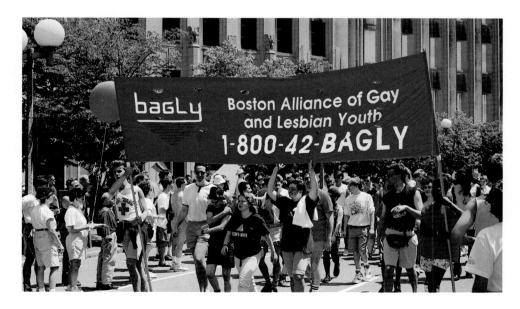

punishments are important in personality development not just because they shape behavior but also because they so easily create distorted self-perceptions and incongruence.

Maslow's Growth Theory   Like Rogers, Abraham Maslow (1954, 1971) viewed personality as the expression of a basic human tendency toward growth and self-actualization. In fact, Maslow believed that self-actualization is not just a human capacity but a human need; as described in the chapter on motivation and emotion, he placed self-actualization as the highest in a hierarchy of needs. Yet, said Maslow, people are often distracted from seeking self-actualization because they focus on needs that are lower in the hierarchy.

Maslow saw most people as controlled by a *deficiency orientation,* a preoccupation with perceived needs for material things. Ultimately, he said, deficiency-oriented people come to see life as a meaningless exercise in disappointment and boredom, and they may begin to behave in problematic ways. For example, in an attempt to satisfy the need for love, many people focus on what love can give them (security), not on what they can give to another. This deficiency orientation may lead a person to be jealous and to focus on what is missing in relationships; as a result, the person will never truly experience love or security.

In contrast, people with a *growth orientation* do not focus on what is missing but draw satisfaction from what they have, what they are, and what they can do. This orientation opens the door to what Maslow called *peak experiences,* in which people feel joy, and even ecstasy, in the mere fact of being alive, being human, and knowing that they are utilizing their fullest potential.

Evaluating the Humanistic Approach

The humanistic approach to personality is consistent with the way many people view themselves. It gives a central role to immediate experience and emphasizes each person's uniqueness. The best-known application of the humanistic approach is the client-centered therapy of Carl Rogers, which is discussed in the chapter on treatment of psychological disorders. The humanistic approach has also inspired other therapies, as well as short-term personal growth experiences, such as sensitivity training and encounter groups, designed to help people become more aware of themselves and the way they relate to others (e.g., Cain & Seeman, 2002). In addition, the approach has created techniques for teaching parents how to avoid creating conditions of worth while maximizing their children's potential.

To its critics, though, the humanistic approach is naive, romantic, and unrealistic. Are people all as inherently good and "growth oriented" as this approach suggests? Critics wonder about that, and they also fault humanists for paying too little attention to the role of inherited characteristics, learning, situational influences, and unconscious motivation in shaping personality. Further, the idea that personality development is directed only by an innate growth potential is seen by many as an oversimplification. So, too, is the humanistic assumption that all human problems stem from blocked self-actualization. Personality researchers also see many humanistic concepts as too vague to be tested empirically. Accordingly, the humanistic approach is not popular among those who conduct empirical research to learn about personality (Friedman & Schustack, 2003).

Finally, humanists' tendency to define ideal personality development in terms of personal growth, independence, and self-actualization has been criticized for emphasizing culture-specific concepts about mental health that may not apply outside of North American and other Western cultures (Heine, 2003). As discussed in the Linkages section of this chapter, the foundations of humanistic self theories may be in direct conflict with the values of non-Western, collectivist cultures. ("In Review: Major Approaches to Personality" summarizes key features of the humanistic approach, along with those of the other approaches we have described.)

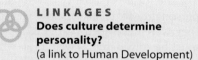

in review

MAJOR APPROACHES TO PERSONALITY

Approach	Basic Assumptions About Behavior	Typical Research Method
Psychodynamic	Determined by largely unconscious intrapsychic conflicts	Case studies
Trait	Determined by traits or needs	Analysis of tests for basic personality dimensions
Social-cognitive	Determined by learning, cognitive factors, and specific situations	Analysis of interactions between people and situations
Humanistic	Determined by innate growth tendency and individual perception of reality	Studies of relationships between perceptions and behavior

? *Tests that measure the big-five dimensions of personality are based on the _____ approach to personality.*

LINKAGES
Does culture determine personality?
(a link to Human Development)

LINKAGES

Personality, Culture, and Human Development

In many Western cultures, people encourage others to "stand up for yourself" or to "blow your own horn" in order to "get what you have coming to you." In middle-class North America, the values of achievement and personal distinction are taught to children, particularly male children, very early in life (Markus & Kitayama, 1997). North American children are encouraged to feel special, to want self-esteem, and to feel good about themselves, partly because these characteristics are associated with happiness, popularity, and superior performance in school. Whether self-esteem is the cause or the result of these good outcomes (Baumeister et al., 2003), children who learn and display these values nevertheless tend to receive praise for doing so. (The goal of esteem building is clear in day-care centers, summer camps, and other children's programs with names such as Starkids, Little Wonders, Superkids, and Precious Jewels.)

As a result of this cultural training, many people in North America and Europe develop personalities that are largely based on a sense of high self-worth. In a study by Hazel Markus and Shinobu Kitayama (1991), for example, 70 percent of a sample of U.S. students believed they were superior to their peers. In addition, 60 percent believed they were in the top 10 percent on a wide variety of personal attributes! This tendency toward self-enhancement is evident as early as age four.

It is no wonder that many Western personality theorists see a sense of independence, uniqueness, and self-esteem as fundamental to mental health. As noted in the chapter on human development, for example, Erik Erikson included the appearance of personal identity and self-esteem as part of normal psychosocial development. Middle-class North Americans who fail to value and strive for independence, self-promotion, and unique personal achievement may be seen as having a personality disorder, some form of depression, or other psychological problems.

Do these ideas reflect universal truths about personality development or, rather, the influence of the cultures that generated them? It is certainly clear that people in many non-Western cultures develop personal orientations that are quite different from those of North Americans and Europeans (Cross & Markus, 1999). In China and Japan, for example, an independent, unique self is not emphasized (Ho & Chiu, 1998). In fact, children there are encouraged to develop and maintain pleasant, respectful relations with others and not to stand out from the crowd, lest they diminish someone else. So in the United States, one often hears that "the squeaky wheel gets the grease" (meaning that you don't get what you want unless you make your needs known); in Japan, you are more likely to hear that "the nail that stands up gets pounded down" (meaning that it is not a good idea to draw attention to yourself). In Japanese, the word for "different" *(tigau)* also means "wrong" (Kitayama & Markus, 1992). From a very young age, Japanese children are taught to be modest, to play down the value of personal contributions, and to appreciate the joy and value of group work (Kitayama & Markus, 1992).

In contrast to the *independent* self-system common in individualist cultures such as Great Britain, Switzerland, and the United States, cultures with a more collectivist orientation (such as Brazil, China, Japan, and Nigeria) promote an *interdependent* self-system through which people see themselves as a fraction of the social whole. Each person has little or no meaningful definition without reference to the group. These differences in self-systems may produce differences in what gives people a sense of well-being and satisfaction. For example, in the United States, a sense of well-being is usually associated with *having positive attributes,* such as intelligence, creativity, competitiveness, persistence, and so on. In Japan, feelings of well-being are more likely to be associated with *having no negative attributes* (Eliot et al., 2001). Studies of thousands of people all over the world indicate that in collectivist cultures, those who are most satisfied with their lives are those whose behavior brings social approval and harmonious relations with others. In individualist cultures, life satisfaction is highest among those who experience high self-esteem and who feel good about their personal accomplishments (Uchida et al., 2001).

Because cultural factors shape ideas about how the ideal personality develops, it is important to evaluate various approaches to personality in terms of how well they apply to cultures other than the one in which they were developed (Cross & Markus, 1999). Their applicability to males and females must be considered as well. Even within North American cultures, for example, there are gender differences in the development of self-esteem. Females tend to show an interdependent self-system, achieving their sense of self and self-esteem from attachments to others. By contrast, males' self-esteem tends to develop in relation to personal achievement, in a manner more in keeping with an independent self-system (Cross & Madson, 1997). Cross-gender and cross-

learn *by* **doing** **CULTURE AND PERSONALITY** In individualist cultures, most children learn that personal distinction is valued by parents, teachers, and peers. In collectivist cultures, having a strong sense of self-worth may be seen as less important. In short, "normal" personality development differs from culture to culture. Make a list of the core values you have learned. Which of them are typical of individualist cultures, which are typical of collectivist cultures, and which reflect a combination of both?

cultural differences in the nature and determinants of a sense of self underscore the widespread effects of gender and culture on the development of many aspects of human personality.

Psychologists have long been interested in how people's personalities differ, but they also want to know why those differences appear. Some search for the source of personality differences by looking at infants' differing temperaments. As noted in the chapter on human development, temperament is reflected in the unlearned, generalized patterns of emotional expression and other behavior that humans display from birth (Buss, 1997).

■ What was the researchers' question?

Can young children's temperaments predict their personality characteristics and behaviors as adults?

■ How did the researchers answer the question?

To try to answer this question, Avshalom Caspi and his colleagues conducted a longitudinal study in which the same people were assessed at several different times in their lives (Caspi, 2000; Caspi & Silva, 1995; Caspi et al., 1997; Caspi et al., 1995, 2003a). The research sample included all the children born in Dunedin, New Zealand, between April 1972 and March 1973—a total of about 1,000 people. When these children were three years old, research assistants observed them in a standard situation and rated them on a number of dimensions, including the degree to which they showed explosive or uncontrolled behavior, interacted easily with others, or acted withdrawn and unresponsive. These observations were used to place each child into one of five temperament categories: *undercontrolled* (irritable, impatient, emotional), *inhibited* (shy, fearful, easily distracted), *confident* (eager to perform, responsive to questions), *reserved* (withdrawn, uncomfortable), and *well adjusted* (friendly, well controlled). The children were observed and categorized again when they were five, seven, and nine years old. If it occurs to you that seeing a child at one point in life might bias an observer's ratings of that child later on, you are right. To ensure that ratings would not be influenced by this kind of observer bias, the researchers arranged for different people to make the ratings at each point in time. These ratings indicated that the children's temperaments stayed about the same over the years from age three to age nine.

When the research participants were twenty-one, they were interviewed about their involvement in risky and unhealthy behaviors, such as excessive drinking, violent criminal activities, unprotected sex, and unsafe driving habits. To avoid bias, the interviewers were given no information about the participants' childhood temperament. At age twenty-six, they took a standard personality test, and were rated by friends on the Big-Five personality dimensions.

■ What did the researchers find?

Several significant differences were found in the personality test results of the five original temperament groups. For example, the average test scores of twenty-six-year-olds who had been classified as "undercontrolled" in childhood showed that they were more alienated, uninhibited, and stressed than the other temperament groups. Further, people who had been classified as "confident" or "well adjusted" as children tended to be better adjusted and more extraverted at twenty-six than people who had been classified as "inhibited" or "reserved." These findings held true for males and females alike.

There were also small, but significant, correlations between childhood temperament and risky behavior in young adulthood. For example, "undercontrolled" children were about twice as likely as others to develop personalities that are associated with violence, excessive drinking, and other health-risky behaviors (Caspi et al., 2003a).

■ What do the results mean?

The results of this research indicate that we can make relatively accurate predictions about people's personality and behavior as adults if we know about their temperament as children. But as critical thinkers, we must be careful not to overstate the strength of these results. Although the correlations between temperament and personality, and between temperament and health-risky behaviors, were statistically significant, they were also relatively small. In other words, not all children classified as "undercontrolled" at age three turned out to be aggressive or violent at eighteen. So it is more accurate to say that personality may be influenced and shaped by temperament, but not completely determined by it.

■ What do we still need to know?

Valuable as it is, this study leaves a number of unanswered questions about the relationship between temperament and personality (Roberts & DelVecchio, 2000). For example, why is there a connection between temperament as a child and personality as an adult? The link is probably a complex one, involving both nature and nurture. Caspi and his colleagues (1989) offered one explanation that draws heavily on Bandura's concept of reciprocal determinism. They proposed that long-term consistencies in behavior result from the mutual influence that temperament and environmental events have on one another. For example, undercontrolled people might choose to spend time with people who accept, and even encourage, rude or impolite behavior. When such behavior brings negative reactions, the world seems that much more hostile, and the undercontrolled people become even more aggressive and negative. Caspi and his colleagues see the results of their studies as evidence that this process of mutual influence between personality and situations can continue over a lifetime (Caspi et al., 2003a).

Assessing Personality

▶ How do psychologists measure personality?

Suppose you are an industrial-organizational psychologist whose job is to ensure that your company hires only honest, cooperative, and hard-working employees. How would you know which candidates had these characteristics? There are four basic methods of assessing and describing personality (Ozer, 1999): *life outcomes* (such as records of education, income, or marital status), *situational tests* (observations of behavior in situations designed to measure personality), *observer ratings* (judgments about a person made by friends or family), and *self-reports* (responses to interviews and personality test items). Data gathered through these methods assist in employee selection, in the diagnosis of psychological disorders, in making predictions about a convict's or mental patient's dangerousness, and in other risky decision situations (Meyer et al., 2001; Nietzel et al., 2003).

Life outcomes, observer ratings, and situational tests allow direct assessment of many aspects of personality and behavior, including how often, how effectively, and how consistently various actions occur. Self-reports provide information about personality from the person's own point of view, sometimes during *interviews*. Interviews can be *open-ended*, meaning that questions are tailored to the intellectual level, emotional state, and special needs of the person being assessed. Others are *structured*, meaning that the interviewer asks a fixed set of questions about specific topics in a particular order. Structured interviews are routinely used in personality research because they are sure to cover matters of special interest to the researcher.

Personality tests offer a way to gather self-report information that is more standardized and economical than interviews. To be useful, however, a personality test must be reliable and valid. As described in the chapter on thought, language, and intelligence, *reliability* refers to how stable or consistent the results of a test are; *validity* reflects the degree to which a test measures what it is intended to measure and leads to correct inferences about people. The many personality tests available today are traditionally classified as either *objective* or *projective*.

Objective Personality Tests

Objective personality tests ask clear questions about a person's thoughts, feelings, or behavior (such as "Do you like parties?"). The answers are used to draw conclusions about the individual's personality. These self-report tests are usually set up in a multiple-choice or true-false format that allows them to be given individually or to many people at once, much like the academic tests used in many classrooms. And as in the classroom, objective personality tests can be scored by machine and then compared mathematically. For example, before interpreting your score on an objective test of anxiety, a psychologist would compare your score with *norms*, or average scores from others of your age and gender. Only if you were well above these averages would you be considered unusually anxious.

Some objective personality tests focus on one particular trait, such as optimism (Scheier et al., 1989). Others measure a small group of related traits, such as empathy and social responsibility (Penner, 2002). Still other objective tests measure the strength of a wider variety of traits to reveal general psychological functioning. For example, the *Neuroticism Extraversion Openness Personality Inventory, Revised*, or *NEO-PI-R* (Costa & McCrae, 1992), is designed to measure the big-five personality traits described earlier. Table 11.3 shows how the test's results are presented. The NEO-PI-R is quite reliable (Viswesvaran & Ones, 2000), and people's scores on its various scales have been successfully used to predict a number of criteria, including performance on specific jobs and overall career success (Barrick & Mount, 1991; Siebert & Kraimer, 2001), social status (Anderson et al., 2001), and the likelihood of continued criminal behavior (Clower & Bothwell, 2001).

When the goal of personality assessment is to diagnose psychological disorders, the most commonly used objective test is the *Minnesota Multiphasic Personality Inventory*, better known as the *MMPI* (Butcher & Rouse, 1996). This 556-item true-false test was developed during the 1930s at the University of Minnesota by Starke Hathaway and J. C. McKinley. It has since been revised and updated in the MMPI-2 (National Computer Systems, 1992).

The MMPI is organized into ten groups of items called *clinical scales*. Certain patterns of responses to the items on these scales have been associated with people who display particular psychological disorders or personality characteristics. The MMPI and MMPI-2 also contain four *validity scales*. Responses to these scales detect whether respondents are distorting their answers, misunderstanding the items, or being uncooperative. For example, someone who responds "true" to items such as "I never get angry" may not be giving honest answers to the test as a whole.

LINKAGES
Can personality tests be used to diagnose mental disorders?
(a link to Psychological Disorders)

objective personality test   A form listing clear, specific questions, statements, or concepts to which people are asked to respond.

table 11.3

Sample Summary of Results from the NEO-PI-R

The NEO-PI-R is one of the most popular ways of assessing the big-five personality dimensions. In this example of the results a person might receive, the marked box in each row represents the person's score on (starting from the top row): neuroticism, extraversion, openness, agreeableness, and conscientiousness (Trull & Sher, 1994).

Compared with the responses of other people, your responses suggest that you can be described as:

☐ Sensitive, emotional, and prone to experience feelings that are upsetting.	☒ Generally calm and able to deal with stress, but you sometimes experience feelings of guilt, anger, or sadness.	☐ Secure, hardy, and generally relaxed even under stressful conditions.
☐ Extraverted, outgoing, active, and high-spirited. You prefer to be around people most of the time.	☐ Moderate in activity and enthusiasm. You enjoy the company of others, but you also value privacy.	☒ Introverted, reserved, and serious. You prefer to be alone with a few close friends.
☐ Open to new experiences. You have broad interests and are very imaginative.	☐ Practical but willing to consider new ways of doing things. You seek a balance between the old and the new.	☒ Down-to-earth, practical, traditional, and pretty much set in your ways.
☐ Compassionate, good-natured, and eager to cooperate and avoid conflict.	☒ Generally warm, trusting, and agreeable, but you can sometimes be stubborn and competitive.	☐ Hardheaded, skeptical, proud, and competitive. You tend to express your anger directly.
☒ Conscientious and well organized. You have high standards and always strive to achieve your goals.	☐ Dependable and moderately well organized. You generally have clear goals but are able to set your work aside.	☐ Easygoing, not very well organized, and sometimes careless. You prefer not to make plans.

To interpret the meaning of MMPI test results, a person's scores on the ten clinical scales are plotted as a *profile* (see Figure 11.5). This profile is then compared with the profiles of persons who are known to have certain personality characteristics or problems. Test-takers are presumed to be most like those whose profiles are most similar to theirs. An extremely high score on a particular clinical scale, such as depression, might suggest a problem in that area, but those who interpret the MMPI usually focus on the overall pattern in the clinical scales scores—particularly on the combination of two or three scales on which a person's scores are unusually high.

There is considerable evidence for the reliability and validity of MMPI clinical scales, but even the latest editions of the test are far from perfect measurement tools (McIntire & Miller, 2000). The validity of MMPI interpretations may be particularly suspect when—because of cultural factors—the perceptions, values, and experiences of the respondent are notably different from those of the test developers and the people with whom the respondent's results are compared. So a profile that appears similar to that of people with a certain disorder might actually reflect the culture-specific way the respondent interpreted the test items, not a mental problem (Groth-Marnat, 1997). Even though the MMPI-2 uses comparison norms that represent a more culturally diverse population than did those of the original MMPI, psychologists must still be cautious when interpreting the profiles of people who identify with minority subcultures.

figure 11.5

The MMPI: Clinical Scales and Sample Profiles

A score of 50 on the MMPI's clinical scales is average. Scores at or above 65 mean that responses on that scale are more extreme than at least 95 percent of the normal population. The red line represents the profile of Kenneth Bianchi, the "Hillside Strangler" who murdered thirteen women in the late 1970s. His profile is characteristic of a shallow person with poor self-control and little personal insight who is sexually preoccupied and unable to reveal himself to others. The profile in green comes from a more normal man, but it is characteristic of someone who is self-centered, passive, unwilling to accept personal responsibility for his behavior, and who, when under stress, complains of numerous vague physical symptoms.

The clinical scales abbreviated in the figure are as follows:

1. **Hypochondriasis (Hs)** (concern with bodily functions and symptoms)
2. **Depression (D)** (pessimism, hopelessness, slowed thinking)
3. **Hysteria (Hy)** (use of physical or mental symptoms to avoid problems)
4. **Psychopathic deviate (Pd)** (disregard for social customs, emotional shallowness)
5. **Masculinity/femininity (Mf)** (interests associated with a particular gender)
6. **Paranoia (Pa)** (delusions, suspiciousness)
7. **Psychasthenia (Pt)** (worry, guilt, anxiety)
8. **Schizophrenia (Sc)** (bizarre thoughts and perceptions)
9. **Hypomania (Ma)** (overactivity, excitement, impulsiveness)
10. **Social introversion (Si)** (shy, insecure)

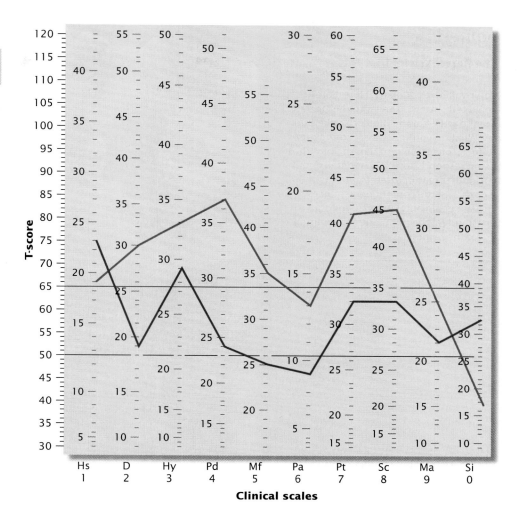

projective personality tests Personality tests made up of relatively unstructured stimuli in which responses are seen as reflecting the individuals' unconscious needs, fantasies, conflicts, thought patterns, and other aspects of personality.

Projective Personality Tests

Unlike the clearly stated items found in objective tests, the items used in **projective personality tests** are ambiguous, meaning that they can be perceived in more than one way. People taking these tests are asked to draw items such as a house, a person, or a tree; to fill in the missing parts of incomplete pictures or sentences; to say what they associate with particular words; or to report what they see in a drawing or picture. Advocates of projective tests tend to take a psychodynamic approach to personality. They believe that unconscious needs, motives, fantasies, conflicts, and thoughts guide people's responses to projective test stimuli.

One prominent projective test, called the *Thematic Apperception Test,* or *TAT,* is described in the motivation and emotion chapter as a measure of need for achievement. Henry Murray and Christina Morgan developed this test to assess the needs they saw as the basis of personality. Another well-known projective test, the *Rorschach Inkblot Test,* features a series of ten inkblots like the one in Figure 11.6. The respondent is asked to tell what the blot might be and then to explain why.

In comparison to objective test results, responses to projective tests are much more difficult to translate into numerical scores. However, projective personality tests are designed to keep respondents from knowing what is being measured and what the "best" answers might be. Those who favor projective tests argue, therefore, that these tests can measure aggressiveness, sexual impulses, and other personality features that the respondent might be able to hide on an objective test. They also point to specific instances, as in

figure 11.6

The Rorschach Inkblot Test

People taking the Rorschach test are shown ten patterns similar to this one and asked to tell what the blot looks like, and why. What do you see? Most scoring methods focus on (1) what part of the blot the person responds to; (2) what details, colors, or other features determine each response; (3) the content of responses (such as seeing animals, maps, or body parts); and (4) the popularity or commonness of the responses.

studies assessing achievement motivation with the TAT, in which projective tests show acceptable reliability and validity (Schultheiss & Brunstein, 2001).

Overall, however, projective personality tests are substantially less reliable and valid than objective tests (Garb, Florio, & Grove, 1998; Hunsley & Bailey, 1999; Lilienfeld, Wood, & Garb, 2000; Wood et al., 2003). In fact, because of their generally poor ability to predict behavior, they often add little information about people beyond what might be inferred from interviews or other sources (Lilienfeld, Wood, & Garb, 2000). "In Review: Personality Tests" summarizes the characteristics of objective and projective personality tests, along with some of their advantages and disadvantages.

Personality Tests and Employee Selection

How good are objective personality tests at selecting people for jobs? Most industrial/organizational psychologists believe that they are valuable tools for the selection of good employees. Tests such as the MMPI (and even some projective tests) are sometimes used to help guide hiring decisions, but large organizations usually choose objective tests that are designed to measure the big-five personality dimensions or related characteristics (Borman, Hanson, & Hedge, 1997; Costa, 2001). Several researchers have found significant relationships between scores on the big-five dimensions and overall job performance (Barrick & Mount, 1991; Ones, Viswesvaran, & Schmidt, 1993; Silverthorne, 2001). A more general review of studies involving thousands of people has shown

in review

PERSONALITY TESTS

Type of Test	Characteristics	Advantages	Disadvantages
Objective	Paper-and-pencil format; quantitatively scored	Efficiency, standardization	Subject to deliberate distortion
Projective	Ambiguous stimuli create maximum freedom of response; scoring is relatively subjective	"Correct" answers not obvious; designed to tap unconscious impulses; flexible use	Reliability and validity lower than those of objective tests

? *Projective personality tests are based on the _____ approach to personality.*

that objective personality tests are of value in helping businesses reduce thefts and other disruptive employee behaviors (Ones & Viswesvaran, 2001).

Still, personality tests are far from perfect tools for employee selection. For one thing, some of these tests measure traits that are too general to predict specific aspects of job performance (Furnham 2001). Second, personality traits may influence performance in some job situations but not in others (Ones & Viswesvaran, 2001). Third, some employees see personality tests as an invasion of their privacy. They worry, too, that test results in their personnel files might later be misinterpreted and hurt their chances for promotion or for employment by other companies. Lawsuits have resulted in a ban on the use of personality tests in the selection of U.S. federal employees. Concerns about privacy and other issues surrounding personality testing have also led the American Psychological Association and related organizations to publish ethical standards relating to procedures for the development, distribution, and use of all psychological tests (American Educational Research Association, American Psychological Association, and National Council on Measurement in Education, 1999; American Psychological Association, 2002). The goal is not only to improve the reliability and validity of tests but also to ensure that their results are properly used and do not infringe on individuals' rights (Turner et al., 2001).

active review Personality

Linkages

As noted in the introductory chapter, all of psychology's subfields are related to one another. Our discussion of personality, culture, and human development illustrates just one way in which the topic of this chapter, personality, is linked to the subfield of developmental psychology, which is described in the chapter on human development. The Linkages diagram shows ties to two other subfields as well, and there are many more ties throughout the book. Looking for linkages among subfields will help you see how they all fit together and help you better appreciate the big picture that is psychology.

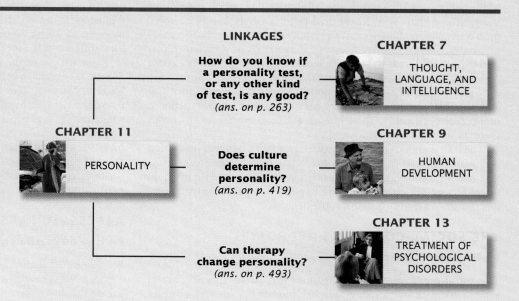

LINKAGES

CHAPTER 11
PERSONALITY

How do you know if a personality test, or any other kind of test, is any good? (ans. on p. 263)

CHAPTER 7
THOUGHT, LANGUAGE, AND INTELLIGENCE

Does culture determine personality? (ans. on p. 419)

CHAPTER 9
HUMAN DEVELOPMENT

Can therapy change personality? (ans. on p. 493)

CHAPTER 13
TREATMENT OF PSYCHOLOGICAL DISORDERS

Summary

Personality refers to the unique pattern of psychological and behavioral characteristics by which each person can be compared and contrasted with other people. The four main theoretical approaches to personality are the psychodynamic, trait, social-cognitive, and humanistic approaches.

THE PSYCHODYNAMIC APPROACH

▶ **How did paralyzed patients lead Freud to psychoanalysis?**

The *psychodynamic approach,* pioneered by Freud, assumes that personality arises out of unconscious psychological processes that interact to determine our thoughts, feelings, and behavior. Freud believed that personality has three components—the *id,* which operates according to the *pleasure principle*; the *ego*, which operates according to the *reality principle*; and the *superego*, **which internalizes society's rules and values. The ego uses *defense mechanisms* to prevent** unconscious conflicts among these components from becoming conscious and causing anxiety or guilt.

Freud proposed that the focus of conflict changes as the child passes through *psychosexual stages* of development. These include the *oral stage,* the *anal stage,* the *phallic stage* (during which the *Oedipus* or *Electra complex* occurs), the *latency period,* and the *genital stage.*

Many of Freud's followers developed new theories that differed from his. Among these theorists were Jung, Adler, and Horney. They tended to downplay the role of instincts and the unconscious, emphasizing instead the importance of conscious processes, ego functions, and social and cultural factors. Horney also challenged the male-oriented nature of Freud's original theory.

Current psychodynamic theories reflect the neo-Freudians' emphasis on family and social relationships. According to object relations theorists, personality development depends mainly on the nature of early interactions between individuals and their caregivers.

The psychodynamic approach is reflected in many forms of psychotherapy, but critics fault the approach for its lack of a scientific base and for its view of human behavior as driven by unmeasurable forces.

THE TRAIT APPROACH

▶ **What personality traits are most basic?**

The *trait approach* assumes that personality is created by a small set of central traits in each individual. Allport studied unique patterns of traits, whereas later researchers used factor analysis to explore common traits or core dimensions of personality. Most recently, these factor analyses have identified five basic dimensions of personality, collectively referred to as the *big-five model* or *five-factor model.* These dimensions, which have been found in many different cultures, may arise partly from inherited differences in temperament and other biological factors that provide the raw materials out of which experience molds each personality. These biological factors are the focus of trait theories proposed by Eysenck and by Gray.

The trait approach has been criticized for being better at describing personality than at explaining it, for failing to consider mechanisms that motivate behavior, and for underemphasizing the role of situational factors. Nevertheless, the trait approach—particularly the big-five model—currently dominates the field.

THE SOCIAL-COGNITIVE APPROACH

▶ **Do we learn our personality?**

The *social-cognitive approach* assumes that personality is a set of unique patterns of thinking and behavior that a person acquires through learning and then displays in particular situations. The social-cognitive approach has expanded on traditional behavioral approaches by emphasizing the role of cognitive factors, such as observational learning, in personality development.

Rotter's theory focuses on expectancies that guide behavior, and it generated interest in assessing general beliefs about whether rewards occur because of personal efforts (internal control) or chance (external control). Bandura believes that personality develops largely through cognitively mediated learning, including observational learning. He sees personality as reciprocally determined by interactions among cognition, environmental stimuli, and behavior. *Self-efficacy*—the belief in one's ability to accomplish a given task—is an important determinant of behavior. Mischel emphasizes the importance of situations—and their interactions with cognitive person variables—in determining behavior. According to Mischel, we must look at both cognitive person variables and situational variables in order to understand human consistencies and inconsistencies.

The social-cognitive approach has led to new forms of psychological treatment and many other applications. However, critics of this approach consider even its latest versions to be incapable of capturing all the unlearned factors that some psychologists see as important in personality.

THE HUMANISTIC APPROACH

▶ **Is everyone basically good?**

The *humanistic approach,* also called the *phenomenological approach,* is based on the assumption that personality is determined by the unique ways in which each individual views the world. These perceptions form a personal version of reality and guide people's behavior as they strive to reach their fullest potential.

Rogers believed that personality development is driven by an innate *actualizing tendency,* but also that one's *self-concept* is shaped by social evaluations. He proposed that *conditions of worth* imposed on children by parents and others interfere with personal growth and can lead to psychological problems. Maslow saw self-actualization as the highest in a hierarchy of needs. Personality development is healthiest, he said, when people have a growth orientation rather than a deficiency orientation.

Applications of the humanistic approach include certain forms of psychotherapy and group experiences designed to enhance personal growth. This approach has considerable popularity, but it has been faulted for being too idealistic, for failing to explain personality development, for being vague and unscientific, and for underplaying cultural differences in "ideal" personalities.

Many people in the individualist cultures of North America and Europe are taught to believe in the importance of self-worth and personal distinction. This independent self-system contrasts with the interdependent self-system often fostered in collectivist cultures, where the self is defined mainly in relation to family or other groups. Contrasting definitions of the self in different cultures, and among males versus females, tend to exert differing influences on the development of personality.

Research suggests that temperament in childhood may influence personality development into adulthood.

ASSESSING PERSONALITY

▶ **How do psychologists measure personality?**

Personality is usually assessed through some combination of life outcomes, observer ratings, situational tests, and self-reports. To be useful, personality assessments must be both reliable and valid.

Objective personality tests usually present clear, direct items; their scores can be compared with group norms. The NEO-PI-R and the MMPI are examples of objective personality tests.

Based on psychodynamic theories, *projective personality tests* present ambiguous stimuli in an attempt to tap unconscious personality characteristics. Two popular projective tests are the TAT and the Rorschach. In general, projective personality tests are less reliable and valid than objective personality tests.

Objective personality tests are often used to identify the people best suited for certain occupations. Although such tests can be helpful in this regard, those who use them must be aware of the tests' limitations and take care not to violate the rights of test respondents.

Learn by Doing

Put It in Writing

Choose a well-known person who interests you. It could be a rock star; an actor; a television personality; a political, religious, or business figure; or even a famous criminal. Write a one-paragraph description of this individual's personality traits as they seem to you. Now continue by writing a page or two about how you think the development of these traits would be explained by psychodynamic, social-cognitive, and humanistic personality theories.

Personal Learning Activity

To get an idea of the problems involved in scoring projective personality tests, try creating your own projective test that contains vague pictures, drawings, or other stimuli that can be interpreted in many different ways. Administer your test to some friends, and record their responses to each stimulus (in writing or on tape). How will you decide what your friends' responses tell you about their personalities? Do you think your conclusions about their personalities were affected mainly by their test responses or by what you already knew about them? Now give your test to someone you don't know. Was it easier or harder to draw conclusions about this person's personality? How will you know if your conclusions about this new person are correct, or valid? *For additional projects, see the Personal Learning Activities in the corresponding chapter of the study guide that accompanies this text.*

Step into Action

Courses

Personality Psychology
Personality Research Methods
Personality Theories
History and Systems of Psychology

Movies

Good Will Hunting; *Unforgiven*; *The Cider House Rules* (personality development)
Hoop Dreams (self-efficacy)
Freud (development of psychoanalytic theory)
Girl, Interrupted; *Bridget Jones's Diary* (conditions of worth and self-concept)
Gandhi (self-actualization)

Books

David C. Funder et al. (Eds.), *Studying Lives Through Time* (American Psychological Association, 1996) (famous studies in personality and development)
Harry Stack Sullivan, *The Interpersonal Theory of Psychiatry* (Norton, 1968) (Sullivan's neo-Freudian theory)

Frank J. Sulloway, *Born to Rebel: Birth Order, Family Dynamics and Creative Lives* (Vintage, 1997) (psychodynamics in personality development)
Duane P. Schultz and Sydney E. Schultz, *Theories of Personality* (Brooks-Cole, 2001) (summary of personality theories)
Stella Chess and M. D. Alexander, *Temperament: Theory and Practice* (Brunner/Mazel, 1996) (differences in temperament)

The Web

The World Wide Web is a good source of additional information about the science of psychology, provided you use it carefully and think critically about the information you find. The web site that accompanies this text offers many resources relevant to this chapter. These resources include interactive NetLab exercises; Thinking Critically and Evaluating Research exercises; ACE chapter quizzes; recommended web links; and articles on current events, books, and movies. At http://college.hmco.com, select *Psychology* and then this textbook.

Review of Key Terms

Can you define each of the key terms in the chapter? Check your definitions against those on the pages listed in parentheses below or in the Glossary/Index at the end of the text.

actualizing tendency *(p. 416)*
anal stage *(p. 404)*
big-five model *(p. 409)*
conditions of worth *(p. 417)*
defense mechanisms *(p. 403)*
ego *(p. 402)*
Electra complex *(p. 404)*
five-factor model *(p. 409)*

genital stage *(p. 404)*
humanistic approach *(p. 416)*
id *(p. 402)*
latency period *(p. 404)*
objective personality tests *(p. 423)*
Oedipus complex *(p. 404)*
oral stage *(p. 404)*
personality *(p. 401)*

phallic stage *(p. 404)*
pleasure principle *(p. 402)*
projective personality tests *(p. 425)*
psychodynamic approach *(p. 402)*
psychosexual stages *(p. 404)*
reality principle *(p. 402)*

self-concept *(p. 417)*
self-efficacy *(p. 414)*
social-cognitive approach *(p. 413)*
superego *(p. 403)*
trait approach *(p. 407)*

Multiple-Choice Self-Test

Select the best answer for each of the questions below. Then check your responses against the Answer Key at the end of the text.

1. When psychologists talk about the unique pattern of enduring psychological and behavioral characteristics by which each person can be compared and contrasted with other people, they are referring to

   a. motivation.
   b. personality.
   c. reciprocal determinism.
   d. conditions of worth.

2. As Jared is jostled by a passerby he thinks, "I'd like to hit that guy!" Freud would say that this impulse comes from Jared's _____, which operates on the _____ principle.

   a. id; pleasure
   b. id; reality
   c. ego; pleasure
   d. ego; reality

3. Nine-year-old Jeffrey has just bounded into the room with his latest artistic creation. He chatters about his friends at school and how much he likes reading and working math problems. According to Freud, Jeffrey is most likely in the _____ stage of psychosexual development.

   a. oral
   b. anal
   c. phallic
   d. latency

4. Elizabeth's boss yells at her for something that wasn't her fault, but Elizabeth is unable to yell back at him. When Elizabeth gets home, her husband asks, "What's for dinner?" and Elizabeth shouts at him for being insensitive. Her response illustrates which ego defense mechanism?

   a. rationalization
   b. displacement
   c. reaction-formation
   d. projection

5. Oscar never cleans up after himself. He is disorganized and impulsive. Freud would say that Oscar is fixated at the anal stage, which means that

   a. his parents did not toilet train him appropriately.
   b. his parents did not wean him appropriately.
   c. he uses defense mechanisms to relieve anxiety.
   d. his progress toward self-actualization is blocked.

6. Which of the following is not a common criticism of Freud's psychodynamic approach to personality?

   a. His sample of patients was small and unrepresentative of the general population.
   b. His theory reflects Western European and North American cultural values.
   c. The theory was not developed scientifically and thus is subject to bias.
   d. The theory was not comprehensive and has had little influence on psychology.

7. Dr. Rajeem believes that each person is unique because we each possess differing combinations of internal characteristics that don't change much as we age. Dr. Rajeem believes in the _____ approach to personality.

   a. psychodynamic
   b. trait
   c. social-cognitive
   d. humanistic

8. A politician is described by her critics as dishonest, intelligent, industrious, extraverted, aggressive, generous, and charming. This method of describing personality most closely matches _____ model of personality.

   a. Eysenck's biological
   b. Rotter's expectancy
   c. Allport's trait
   d. the big-five

9. Tamerika has been described as high on openness (very curious and imaginative), low in conscientiousness (disorganized and unproductive), high in extraversion (very active, talkative, and energetic), high in agreeableness (generous, kind, and trusting), and high in neuroticism (impulsive, touchy, and vulnerable). This description reflects _____ model of personality

   a. Eysenck's biological trait
   b. Rotter's expectancy
   c. Allport's trait
   d. the big-five

10. One criticism of trait theories of personality is that they

    a. put too much emphasis on unconscious wishes.
    b. put too much emphasis on the influence of situations.
    c. are better at describing personality than at explaining it.
    d. have no scientific basis.

11. According to the Thinking Critically section of this chapter, research on the question of whether or not personality is inherited concludes that

    a. there are specific genes for specific personality traits.
    b. there are genetic predispositions toward particular personality characteristics.
    c. the environment is the strongest influence on personality development.
    d. personality is essentially determined by the age of six months.

12. Sandy believes that if she works hard, she will be rewarded. So when she gets a D on her psychology test, she decides that she didn't study hard enough. When she wins the "Outstanding Senior of the Month" award, she believes that she earned it. According to one type of social-cognitive personality theory, Sandy would be described as

    a. internal.
    b. external.
    c. deficiency oriented.
    d. growth oriented.

13. Darma was standing in line at a movie theater, thinking about how her boyfriend had dumped her, when she was accidentally shoved from behind. She shouted "Hey! Back off, you jerks!" This prompted angry comments from the people behind her, which made Darma even angrier, so she refused to move forward in line. This case is an example of

    a. conditions of worth.
    b. growth orientation.
    c. reciprocal determinism.
    d. internal locus of control.

14. At college basketball games, Melinda jumps up and down and yells and screams continuously. Otherwise, however, she is a quiet person who chooses peaceful environments without much social stimulation. She finds that when she is around other people, they often become quiet, too. Melinda's personality can best be explained by _____ theory.

    a. psychodynamic
    b. Allport's trait
    c. Rotter's expectancy
    d. Mischel's person-situation

15. Rolf believes that his children's personalities are shaped by the way he rewards and punishes them. He thinks that most of each child's personality is learned in social situations where the child interacts with others and observes others' behavior. Rolf's beliefs most closely match the _____ approach to personality.

    a. psychodynamic
    b. trait
    c. social-cognitive
    d. humanistic

16. When Lizzie finger-paints on the wall, her mother gets angry and shouts, "You are a very bad girl!" Rogers would say that Lizzie's mother is creating

    a. a growth orientation.
    b. a deficiency orientation.
    c. conditions of worth.
    d. a psychodynamic conflict.

17. Ruben is constantly thinking about what he doesn't have. He has a good job, and just got a raise, but he still feels underpaid. He has a great wife, but he wishes she were more attractive. He bought a new car, but he just saw a bigger one that has become his latest obsession. Maslow would say that Ruben is controlled by

    a. growth orientation.
    b. deficiency orientation.
    c. conditions of worth.
    d. self-actualization.

18. Which of the following techniques would a psychodynamic psychologist be most likely to use to assess personality?

    a. behavioral observation
    b. an objective test
    c. measurement of physiological activity
    d. projective test

19. Paul is an undercontrolled boy who regularly has tantrums. Based on the longitudinal study described in this chapter, which of the following life outcomes is most likely? Paul will

    a. reach a high rank if he joins the military.
    b. have outgrown his lack of control by adulthood.
    c. be aggressive as an adult.
    d. keep jobs longer than most other men.

20. In an effort to summarize her clients' personality traits, Peggy administers tests that present a long series of true-false items. She is using a(n) _____ personality test.

    a. multifaceted
    b. objective
    c. projective
    d. social-cognitive

12

Psychological Disorders

A man sits alone in a restaurant booth, giving his order to a waitress. But when she

leaves, he continues talking and laughing as though someone were sitting with him. When his lunch arrives he thanks the waitress, then continues his "conversation." Later, he pays his bill, leaves a tip, and walks outside, chatting to his invisible companion all the while. Is this person crazy or just eccentric? When does oddness become abnormality? When does sadness become depression? What are psychological disorders? In this chapter, we describe the major categories of psychological disorders, discuss some of their possible causes, consider how they have been explained over the centuries, and examine their role in the insanity defense.

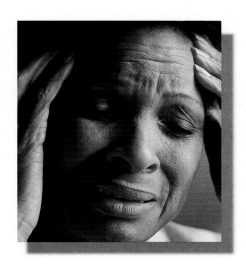

Reading this chapter will help you to answer the following questions:

▶ **How do psychologists define abnormal behavior?**

▶ **What causes abnormality?**

▶ **How many psychological disorders have been identified?**

▶ **What is a phobia?**

▶ **Can mental disorder cause blindness?**

▶ **What disorders create sudden memory loss?**

▶ **How common is depression?**

▶ **Is schizophrenia the same as "split personality"?**

▶ **Which personality disorder often leads to crime?**

▶ **How do children's disorders differ from adults' disorders?**

▶ **Can insanity protect criminals from punishment?**

José is a fifty-five-year-old electronics technician. A healthy and vigorous father of two adult children, he was recently forced to take medical leave because of a series of sudden, uncontrollable panic attacks in which dizziness, a racing heart, sweating, and other terrifying symptoms made him fear that he was about to die. José's case provides an example of someone who suffers from a psychological disorder, also called a *mental disorder* or *psychopathology*. **Psychopathology** involves patterns of thought, emotion, and behavior that are maladaptive, disruptive, or uncomfortable either for the person affected or for others.

The number of people who exhibit some form of psychological disorder is staggering. Surveys reveal that in any given year in the United States alone, about 86 million people, or about 30 percent of the adult population, have displayed some form of mental disorder, and that as many as 48 percent have experienced a disorder at some point in their

psychopathology Patterns of thinking and behaving that are maladaptive, disruptive, or uncomfortable for the affected person or for others.

433

figure 12.1

Incidence of Specific Psychological Disorders

Several large-scale surveys of adults in the United States revealed that about 30 percent of them experience some form of mental disorder in any given year, and that almost half of them have displayed a disorder at some time in life. The data shown here summarize these findings by category of disorder. The same general patterns appear among the more than 400 million people worldwide who suffer from some form of psychological disorder (Andrade et al., 2002; Bjil et al., 2003; Liu et al., 2002; World Health Organization, 2002b).

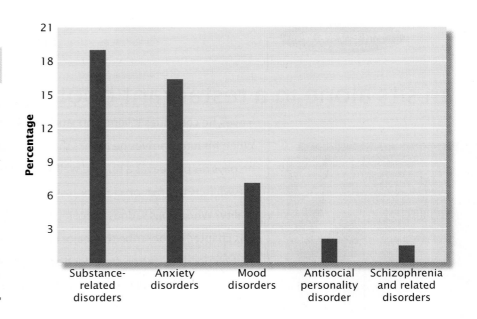

lives (Bjil et al., 2003; Kessler et al., 1996; Narrow et al., 2002; Regier, Farmer, et al., 1993; Regier, Narrow, et al., 1993; Robins & Regier, 1991; U.S. Surgeon General, 1999; see Figure 12.1). In addition, about 20 percent of U.S. children display significant mental disorder in any given year (Costello et al., 2003; U.S. Surgeon General, 1999). These overall rates of mental disorder are found, with only minor variations, in all segments of U.S. society, including males and females in all ethnic groups (Peterson et al., 1993). And the actual rates may be higher than the percentages just cited, because major survey studies have examined fewer than half of all known psychological disorders. In short, psychological disorders are enormously costly in terms of human suffering, wasted potential, economic burden, and lost resources (Druss, Rosenheck, & Sledge, 2000; Lyons & McLoughlin, 2001; Marcotte & Wilcox-Goek, 2001; Stewart et al., 2003).

Defining Psychological Disorders

▶ **How do psychologists define abnormal behavior?**

A woman's husband dies. In her grief, she stays in bed all day, weeping, refusing to eat, at times holding "conversations" with him. In India, a Hindu holy man on a pilgrimage rolls along the ground for more than 1,000 miles of deserts and mountains, in all kinds of weather, until he reaches the sacred place he seeks. Eight percent of U.S. adults surveyed say they have seen a UFO (CNN/Time, 1997), and hundreds claim to have been abducted by space aliens (Appelle Lynn & Newman , 2000). These examples and countless others raise the question of where to draw the line between normality and abnormality, between eccentricity and mental disorder (Kanner, 1995).

What Is Abnormal?

There are several criteria for judging whether a person's thinking, emotions, or behaviors are abnormal. Each criterion has value, but also some flaws.

If we define *normality* as what most people do, then the criterion for abnormality becomes *statistical infrequency,* or that which is unusual or rare. By this criterion, the few people who believe that space aliens steal their thoughts would be judged as abnormal; the many people who worry about becoming victims of crime or terrorism would not.

impaired functioning   Difficulty in fulfilling appropriate and expected social roles.

IS THIS PERSON ABNORMAL? This photo might have made you cringe. But whether unusual individuals are labeled "abnormal" and perhaps given treatment for psychological disorders depends on a number of factors, including how *abnormality* is defined by the culture in which they live, who is most directly affected by their behavior, and how much distress they suffer or cause.

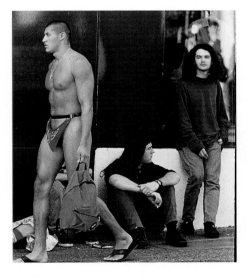

learn by doing **SITUATIONAL FACTORS IN DEFINING *ABNORMALITY*** When this college student attended classes virtually nude to protest "social repression," complaints from other students led to his dismissal. Yet if he lived in a nudist colony, he might be seen as "overdressed." Make a list of the reasons you would give in support of, or in opposition to, his having been labeled as "abnormal." Which criteria for abnormality did you use in making your list?

But statistical infrequency alone is a poor criterion for abnormality, because any rare quality or characteristic, including creative genius or world-class athletic ability, would be considered abnormal. Further, because this definition implies that conformity with the majority is normal, equating rarity with abnormality may result in the oppression of nonconformists who express unusual or unpopular views or ideas. Finally, just how rare must a behavior be in order to call it "abnormal"? The dividing line is not easy to locate.

Another possible criterion for abnormality is the violation of social norms—the cultural rules that tell us how we should and should not behave in various situations, especially in relation to others. According to this *norm violation* criterion, when people behave in ways that are unusual or disturbing enough to violate social norms, they may be described as abnormal. However, norm violation alone is an inadequate measure of abnormality. For one thing, some norm violations are better characterized as eccentric or illegal than as abnormal (Weeks & Weeks, 1995). People who bathe infrequently or who stand too close during conversation violate social norms, but are they abnormal or merely annoying? Further, whose norms are we talking about? Social norms vary across cultures, subcultures, and historical eras, so the behaviors that qualify as abnormal in one part of the world might be perfectly acceptable elsewhere (Giosan, Glovsky, & Haslam, 2001; Phelan et al., 2000).

Abnormality can also be described in terms of *personal suffering*. In fact, experiencing distress is the criterion that people often use in deciding that their psychological problems are severe enough to require treatment. But personal suffering alone is not an adequate criterion for abnormality. For one thing, it does not take into account the fact that people are sometimes distressed about behaviors (e.g., homosexuality) that are not mental disorders. Second, some people display serious psychological disorders, but experience little or no distress. Those who sexually abuse children, for example, create far more distress in victims and their families than they suffer themselves.

Behavior in Context: A Practical Approach

Obviously, no single criterion fully defines abnormality. So mental health practitioners and researchers tend to adopt a *practical approach* that combines aspects of all the criteria we've discussed. They consider the *content* of behavior (that is, what the person does), the sociocultural *context* in which the person's behavior occurs, and the *consequences* of the behavior for that person and for others. This practical approach pays special attention to whether a person's thoughts, behavior, or emotions cause **impaired functioning**—that is, difficulty in fulfilling appropriate and expected roles in family, social, and work-related situations (U.S. Surgeon General, 1999; Wakefield, 1999).

What is "appropriate" and "expected" depends on age, gender, culture, and the particular situation and historical era in which the individual lives. For example, the same short attention span considered normal in a two-year-old would be considered inappropriate and problematic in an adult. There are gender-specific norms, too. In the United States, many people consider it more appropriate for women than for men to display emotion. So kisses, tears, and long embraces are common when women greet each other after a long absence; men tend to simply shake hands or hug briefly. And because of cultural differences, hearing a dead relative's voice calling from the afterlife would be more acceptable in certain American Indian tribes than among, say, the families of suburban Toronto. Situational factors are important as well. Falling to the floor and "speaking in tongues" is considered appropriate, and even desirable, during the worship services of some religious groups; but the same behavior would be considered inappropriate, and possibly a sign of disorder, in a college classroom. Finally, judgments about behavior are shaped by changes in social trends and cultural values. For example, the American Psychiatric Association once listed homosexuality as a mental disorder but dropped this category from its official list of disorders in 1973. In taking this step, it was responding to changing views of homosexuality prompted in part by the political and educational efforts of gay and lesbian rights groups.

In summary, it is difficult, and probably impossible, to define a specific set of behaviors that everyone, everywhere, will agree constitutes abnormality (Lilienfeld & Marino, 1999; Wakefield, 1999). Instead, the practical approach sees abnormality as including those patterns of thought, behavior, and emotional reaction that impair functioning, cause discomfort, and/or disrupt the lives of others.

Explaining Psychological Disorders

▶ **What causes abnormality?**

Since the dawn of civilization, people have tried to understand the causes of psychological disorder. Centuries ago, explanations of abnormal behavior focused on gods or demons. Disordered people were seen either as innocent victims of evil spirits or as social or moral deviants suffering supernatural punishment. In Europe during the late Middle Ages, for example, people who engaged in threatening or unusual behavior were seen as controlled by the devil or other evil beings. Supernatural explanations of psychological disorders are still invoked today in many cultures around the world—including certain ethnic and religious subcultures in North America (Nickell, 2001; Tagliabue, 1999).

The Biopsychosocial Model

More generally, however, mental health researchers in Western cultures attribute the appearance of psychopathology to three other causes: biological factors, psychological processes, and sociocultural contexts. For many decades, there was controversy over which of these three causes was most important, but most researchers now agree that they can all be important. They have adopted a **biopsychosocial model** in which mental disorders are seen as caused by the combination and interaction of biological, psychological, and sociocultural factors, each of which contributes in varying degrees to particular problems in particular people (U.S. Surgeon General, 1999).

Biological Factors The biological factors thought to be involved in causing mental disorders include physical illnesses and disruptions or imbalances of bodily processes. This *medical model* of psychological disorder has a long history. For example, Hippocrates, a physician in ancient Greece, said that psychological disorders result from imbalances among four *humors*, or bodily fluids (blood, phlegm, black bile, and yellow

AN EXORCISM Supernatural explanations of mental disorder, and supernaturally oriented cures, such as the exorcism being performed by this Buddhist monk in Thailand, remain influential among religious groups in many cultures and subcultures around the world—including some in the United States and other Western countries (Fountain, 2000).

biopsychosocial model Explaining mental disorders as the combined result of biological, psychological, and sociocultural factors.

bile). In ancient Chinese cultures, psychological disorders were seen as arising from an imbalance of *yin* and *yang,* the dual forces of the universe flowing in the physical body.

As the medical model gained prominence in Western cultures after the Middle Ages, special hospitals for the insane were established throughout Europe. Treatment in these early asylums consisted mainly of physical restraints, laxative purges, bleeding of "excess" blood, and induced vomiting. Cold baths, fasts, and other physical discomforts were also used in efforts to "shock" patients back to normality.

The medical model gave rise to the concept of abnormality as *mental illness*—and in fact, most people in Western cultures today still tend to seek medical doctors and hospitals for the diagnosis and treatment of psychological disorders. The medical model is now more properly called the **neurobiological model,** because it explains psychological disorders in terms of particular disturbances in the anatomy and chemistry of the brain and in other biological processes, including genetic influences. Neuroscientists and others who adopt a neurobiological approach investigate these disorders as they would investigate any physical illness, seeing problematic symptoms stemming primarily from an underlying illness that can be diagnosed, treated, and cured.

Psychological Processes   If biological factors provide the "hardware" of mental disorders, the "software" includes psychological processes, such as our wants, needs, and emotions; our learning experiences; and our way of looking at the world. The roots of this **psychological model** of disorder can be found in ancient Greek literature and drama dealing with *psyche,* or mind—and especially with the problems people experience as they struggle to resolve inner conflicts or to overcome the effects of stressful events.

These ideas took center stage in the late 1800s, when Sigmund Freud challenged the assumption that psychological disorders had only physical causes. As described in the chapter on personality, Freud viewed psychological disorders as resulting mainly from the effects of unresolved, mostly unconscious clashes between people's inborn impulses and the limits placed on those impulses by the environment. These conflicts, he said, begin early in childhood. As also described in the personality chapter, today's versions of this psychodynamic model focus less on instinctual urges and more on the role of attachment and other early interpersonal relationships (Schultz & Schultz, 2001).

Other theories discussed in the personality chapter suggest still other psychological processes that can contribute to the appearance of mental disorders. For example, *social-cognitive* theorists, also known as *social-learning* theorists, see most psychological disorders as the result of past learning and current situations. These theorists say that just as

VISITING BEDLAM   As shown in William Hogarth's portrayal of "Bedlam" (the local name for London's Saint Mary's of Bethlehem hospital), most asylums of the 1700s were little more than prisons. Notice the well-dressed visitors; in those days, the public could buy tickets to look at mental patients, much as people go to the zoo today.

neurobiological model   A view of mental disorder as caused by physical illness or an imbalance in bodily processes, including disturbances in the anatomy and chemistry of the brain.

psychological model   An approach that views mental disorder as arising from inner turmoil or other psychological processes.

LINKAGES
Are psychological disorders learned behaviors?
(a link to Learning)

LINKAGES
How do societies define what is abnormal?
(a link to Social Psychology)

people learn to avoid touching hot stoves after being burned, bad experiences in school or a dental office can "teach" people to fear such places. Social-cognitive theorists also emphasize the effects of expectancies and other mental processes. They see depression, for example, as stemming from negative events, such as losing a job, and from learned patterns of thoughts about these events, such as "I never do anything right."

According to the *humanistic,* or phenomenological, approach to personality, behavior disorders appear when a person's actualizing tendency is blocked, usually by a failure to be aware of and to express true feelings. When this happens, the person's perceptions of reality become distorted. The greater the distortion, the more serious the psychological disorder.

Sociocultural Context   Together, neurobiological and psychological factors can go a long way toward explaining many forms of mental disorder. Still, they focus mainly on causes residing within the individual. The **sociocultural model** of disorder suggests that we cannot fully explain all forms of psychopathology without also looking outside the individual—at the social and cultural factors that form the context, or background, of abnormal behavior. Looking for causes of disorders in this *sociocultural context* means paying attention to factors such as gender, age, and marital status; the physical, social, and economic situations in which people live; and the cultural values, traditions, and expectations in which they are immersed (Evans et al., 2000; Johnson et al., 1999; Whisman, 1999). Sociocultural context influences not only what is and is not labeled "abnormal" but also who displays what kind of disorder.

Consider gender, for instance. The greater tolerance in many cultures for open expression of emotional distress among women, but not men, may contribute to the higher rates of depression reported by women compared with men (Nolen-Hoeksema, Larson, & Grayson, 1999). Similarly, the view held in many cultures that excessive alcohol consumption is less appropriate for women than for men is a sociocultural factor that may set the stage for higher rates of alcohol abuse in men (Helzer et al., 1990).

Sociocultural factors also influence the form that abnormality takes (Kyrios et al., 2001). For example, depression is considered a *culture-general* disorder because it appears virtually everywhere in the world. However, specific symptoms tend to differ depending on a person's cultural background (Hopper & Wanderling, 2000). In Western cultures, where the emotional and physical components of disorders are generally viewed separately, symptoms of depression tend to revolve around despair and other signs of emotional distress (Kleinman, 1991). But in China and certain other Asian cultures where emotional and physical experiences tend to be viewed as one, depressed people are as likely to report stomach or back pain as to complain of sadness (Parker, Gladstone, & Chee, 2001).

There are also *culture-specific* forms of disorder. For instance, Puerto Rican and Dominican Hispanic women sometimes experience *ataques de nervios* ("attacks of nerves"), a unique way of reacting to stress that includes heart palpitations, shaking, shouting, nervousness, depression, and possibly fainting or seizure-like episodes (Spiegel, 1994). In Asia, Khmer refugees sometimes suffer from panic-related fainting spells known as *kyol goeu* (Hinton, Um, & Ba, 2001). And in Southeast Asia, southern China, and Malaysia, a condition called *koro* is occasionally observed. Victims of this disorder, usually men, fear that their penis will shrivel, retract into the body, and cause death. In females, the fear relates to shriveling of the breasts. *Koro* appears only in cultures holding the specific supernatural beliefs that explain it (Tseng et al., 1992).

In short, sociocultural factors create differing social roles, stressors, opportunities, and experiences for people who differ in age, gender, and cultural traditions. They also help shape the disorders and symptoms to which certain categories of people are prone. Any attempt to fully explain psychological disorders must take these sociocultural factors into account.

sociocultural model   An approach to explaining mental disorder that emphasizes the role of factors such as gender and age, physical situations, cultural values and expectations, and historical era.

Diathesis-Stress as an Integrative Explanation

The biopsychosocial model is currently the most comprehensive and influential approach to explaining psychological disorders. It is prominent partly because it encompasses so many important causal factors, including biological imbalances, genetically inherited characteristics, brain damage, enduring psychological traits, socioculturally influenced learning experiences, stressful life events, and many more.

But how do all these factors actually interact to create disorder? Most researchers who study psychopathology believe that inherited characteristics, biological processes, learning experiences, and sociocultural forces combine to create a predisposition, or *diathesis* (pronounced "dye-A-thuh-sis"), for psychological disorders. Whether or not a person eventually develops symptoms of disorder, they say, depends on the nature and amount of stress the person encounters (National Advisory Mental Health Council, 1996; U.S. Surgeon General, 1999; Zuckerman, 1999). For example, a person may have inherited a biological tendency toward depression or may have learned depressing patterns of thinking, but these predispositions might result in a depressive disorder only after the person is faced with a severe financial crisis or suffers the loss of a loved one. If those stressful circumstances do not occur, or if the person has adequate skills for coping with them, depressive symptoms may never appear, or they may be quite mild.

So according to the **diathesis-stress** explanation of psychological disorder, biological, psychological, and sociocultural factors can predispose us toward disorder, but it takes a certain amount of stress to actually trigger it. For those with a strong diathesis, relatively mild stress might be enough to create a problem. Those whose predisposition is weaker might not show signs of disorder until stress becomes extreme or prolonged. Another way to think about the notion of diathesis-stress is in terms of *risk:* The more risk factors for a disorder a person has—whether they take the form of genetic tendencies, personality traits, cultural traditions, or stressful life events—the more likely it is that the person will display a form of psychological disorder associated with those risk factors.

Table 12.1 provides an example of how the diathesis-stress concept combines the three factors highlighted by the biopsychosocial model to explain a particular case of psychopathology. Later, you will see how these biopsychosocial factors are combined to create diathesis-stress explanations of a number of other psychological disorders.

table 12.1

Explaining Psychopathology

Here are the factors that would be highlighted by the biopsychosocial model and summarized in a diathesis-stress explanation in the case of José, the man described at the beginning of this chapter.

Explanatory Domain	Possible Contributing Factors
Neurobiological/medical	José may have organic disorders (e.g., genetic tendency toward anxiety; brain tumor, endocrine dysfunction; neurotransmitter imbalance).
Psychological: psychodynamic	José has unconscious conflicts and desires. Instinctual impulses are breaking through ego defenses into consciousness, causing panic.
Psychological: social-cognitive	Physical stress symptoms are interpreted as signs of serious illness or impending death. Panic is rewarded by avoidance of work stress and the opportunity to stay home.
Psychological: humanistic	José fails to recognize his genuine feelings about work and his place in life, and he fears expressing himself.
Sociocultural	A culturally based belief that "a man should not show weakness" amplifies the intensity of stress reactions and delays José's decision to seek help.
Diathesis-stress summary	José has a biological (possibly genetic) predisposition to be overly responsive to stressors. The stress of work and extra activity exceeds his capacity to cope and triggers panic as a stress response.

diathesis-stress An approach that recognizes the roles of both predispositions and situational factors in the appearance of psychological disorders.

Classifying Psychological Disorders

▶ **How many psychological disorders have been identified?**

Although definitions of abnormality differ within and across cultures, there does seem to be a set of behavior patterns that roughly defines the range of most abnormality in most cultures. It has long been the goal of those who study abnormal behavior to classify these patterns into a set of diagnostic categories.

The purpose of diagnosis is to determine the nature of people's psychological problems. Once the characteristics of these problems are understood, their probable course can be predicted, and the most appropriate method of treatment can be administered. Diagnoses are also important for understanding the causes of psychopathology. If researchers can accurately label the disorder displayed by each troubled person, they will have a better chance of spotting genetic features, biological abnormalities, cognitive processes, and environmental experiences that people in the same diagnostic category might share. Finding that people in one category share a set of features that differs from the sets shared by people in other categories could provide clues to which features are important to the development of each disorder.

In 1952 the American Psychiatric Association published the first edition of what has become the "official" North American diagnostic classification system, the *Diagnostic and Statistical Manual of Mental Disorders (DSM)*. Each edition of the *DSM* has included more categories. The latest editions, *DSM-IV* and *DSM-IV-TR* (which contains some text revisions), include more than 300 specific diagnostic labels (American Psychiatric Association, 1994, 2000). Mental health professionals outside North America diagnose mental disorders using the World Health Organization's *International Classification of Diseases,* now in its tenth edition *(ICD-10),* and its companion volume, the second edition of the *International Classification of Impairments, Disabilities and Handicaps (ICIDH-2)*. To facilitate international communication about—and cross-cultural research on—psychopathology, *DSM-IV* was designed to be compatible with these manuals, and efforts are under way to remove inconsistencies existing between the systems (DeAngelis, 2001; Ottosson et al., 2002).

A Classification System: *DSM-IV*

DSM-IV describes the abnormal patterns of thinking, emotion, and behavior that define various mental disorders. For each disorder, *DSM-IV* provides specific criteria outlining the conditions that must be present before a person is given that diagnostic label. In keeping with the biopsychosocial model, diagnosticians using *DSM-IV* can evaluate troubled people on five dimensions, or *axes* (the plural of *axis*). Together, these axes provide a broad picture of each person's biological and psychological problems, as well as of any sociocultural context factors that might contribute to them. As shown in Table 12.2, mental disorders such as schizophrenia or major depressive disorder are recorded on Axis I, whereas evidence of personality disorders or mental retardation is noted on Axis II. Any medical conditions that might be important in understanding the person's cognitive, emotional, or behavioral problems are listed on Axis III. On Axis IV, the diagnostician notes any psychosocial or environmental problems (such as the loss of a loved one, physical or sexual abuse, discrimination, unemployment, poverty, homelessness, inadequate health care, or conflict with religious or cultural traditions) that are important for understanding the person's psychological problems. Finally, a rating (from 100 down to 1) of the person's current level of psychological, social, and occupational functioning appears on Axis V. Here is a sample *DSM-IV* diagnosis for someone who received labels on all five axes:

Axis I: Major depressive disorder, single episode; alcohol abuse.

Axis II: Dependent personality disorder.

Axis III: Alcoholic cirrhosis of the liver.

table 12.2

The *Diagnostic and Statistical Manual of Mental Disorders (DSM)* of the American Psychiatric Association

Axis I of the fourth edition *(DSM-IV)* lists the major categories of mental disorders. Personality disorders and mental retardation are listed on Axis *II.*

Axis I (Clinical Syndromes)

1. ***Disorders usually first diagnosed in infancy, childhood, or adolescence.*** Problems such as hyperactivity, childhood fears, conduct disorders, frequent bed-wetting or soiling, and other problems in normal social and behavioral development. Autistic spectrum disorders (severe impairment in social, behavioral, and language development), as well as learning disorders.

2. ***Delirium, dementia, and amnesic and other cognitive disorders.*** Problems caused by physical deterioration of the brain due to aging, disease, drugs or other chemicals, or other possible unknown causes. These problems can appear as an inability to "think straight" (delirium) or as loss of memory and other intellectual functions (dementia).

3. ***Substance-related disorders.*** Psychological, behavioral, physical, social, or legal problems caused by dependence on, or abuse of, a variety of chemical substances, including alcohol, heroin, cocaine, amphetamines, hallucinogens, marijuana, and tobacco.

4. ***Schizophrenia and other psychotic disorders.*** Severe conditions characterized by abnormalities in thinking, perception, emotion, movement, and motivation that greatly interfere with daily functioning. Problems involving false beliefs (delusions).

5. ***Mood disorders* (also called *affective disorders*).** Severe disturbances of mood, especially depression, overexcitement (mania), or alternating episodes of each extreme (as in bipolar disorder).

6. ***Anxiety disorders.*** Specific fears (phobias); panic attacks; generalized feelings of dread; rituals of thought and action (obsessive-compulsive disorder) aimed at controlling anxiety; and problems caused by traumatic events, such as rape or military combat (see the chapter on health, stress, and coping for more on posttraumatic stress disorder).

7. ***Somatoform disorders.*** Physical symptoms, such as paralysis and blindness, that have no physical cause. Unusual preoccupation with physical health or with nonexistent physical problems (hypochondriasis, somatization disorder, pain disorder).

8. ***Factitious disorders.*** False mental disorders that are intentionally produced to satisfy some psychological need.

9. ***Dissociative disorders.*** Psychologically caused problems of consciousness and self-identification—e.g., loss of memory (amnesia) or the development of more than one identity (multiple personality).

10. ***Sexual and gender identity disorders.*** Problems of (a) finding sexual arousal through unusual objects or situations (like shoes or exposing oneself), (b) unsatisfactory sexual activity (sexual dysfunction; see the chapter on motivation and emotion), or (c) identifying with the opposite gender.

11. ***Eating disorders.*** Problems associated with eating too little (anorexia nervosa) or binge eating followed by self-induced vomiting (bulimia nervosa). (See the chapter on motivation and emotion.)

12. ***Sleep disorders.*** Severe problems involving the sleep-wake cycle, especially an inability to sleep well at night or to stay awake during the day. (See the chapter on consciousness.)

13. ***Impulse control disorders.*** Compulsive gambling, stealing, or fire setting.

14. ***Adjustment disorders.*** Failure to adjust to, or deal well with, such stressors as divorce, financial problems, family discord, or other unhappy life events.

Axis II (Personality Disorders and Mental Retardation)

1. ***Personality disorders.*** Diagnostic labels given to individuals who may or may not receive an Axis I diagnosis but who show lifelong behavior patterns that are unsatisfactory to them or that disturb other people. These patterns may involve unusual suspiciousness, unusual ways of thinking, self-centeredness, shyness, overdependency, excessive concern with neatness and detail, or overemotionality, among others.

2. ***Mental retardation.*** As described in the chapter on thought, language, and intelligence, the label of "mental retardation" is applied to individuals whose measured IQ is less than about 70 *and* who fail to display the skills at daily living, communication, and other tasks expected of people their age.

Axis IV: Problems with primary support group (death of spouse).

Axis V: Global assessment of functioning = 50.

The terms *neurosis* and *psychosis* are no longer major categories in the *DSM,* because they are not specific enough; however, some mental health professionals still sometimes use them as shorthand descriptions. *Neurosis* refers to conditions in which some form of anxiety is the major characteristic. *Psychosis* refers to conditions involving more extreme problems that leave people "out of touch with reality" or unable to function on a daily basis. The disorders once listed under these headings now appear in various Axis I categories in *DSM-IV.*

Further changes in the diagnostic system will surely appear in *DSM-V,* a new edition of the *DSM* currently under discussion and development (Beutler & Malik, 2002; Helzer & Hudziak, 2002; Maj et al., 2002). For example, some experts are proposing that diagnoses should consist not just of specific labels, such as "major depression," but also of symptom clusters or dimensions that would be rated in terms of severity (Vollebergh et al., 2001; Widiger & Clark, 2000). This *dimensional approach* would allow each symptom a person displays to be recognized and described, whether or not it is normally associated with a particular diagnostic category.

Evaluating the Diagnostic System

How good is the diagnostic system now in use? One way to evaluate *DSM-IV* is to consider *interrater reliability,* the degree to which different mental health professionals give the same person the same diagnostic label. Some studies indicate that interrater agreement is as high as 83 percent for schizophrenia and mood disorders; agreement on many other Axis I categories—such as anxiety disorders—is also high (e.g., Brown et al., 2001; Nathan & Langenbucher, 1999; Simpson et al., 2002). Still other categories, such as Axis II personality disorders, remain more difficult to diagnose reliably (Zanarini et al., 2000). Overall, interrater agreement appears highest when diagnosis is based on structured interviews that systematically address each area of functioning and provide guidelines for interpreting people's responses (Rogers, 2001; Widiger & Sanderson, 1995).

Do diagnostic labels give accurate information that guides correct inferences about people? This *validity* question is difficult to answer, because it is hard to find a fully acceptable standard for accuracy. Still, evidence does support the validity of most *DSM* criteria (Clark, Watson, & Reynolds, 1995). And validity is likely to improve even more as diagnostic labels—and the diagnostic system—are refined in *DSM-V* to reflect what researchers are learning about the characteristics, causes, courses, and cultural factors involved in various disorders.

The diagnostic system is far from perfect, however (Beutler & Malik, 2002; Kendell & Jablensky, 2003; Widiger & Sankis, 2000). First, people's problems often do not fit neatly into a single category. For example, a person may suffer both anxiety and depression. Second, the same symptom (such as difficulty sleeping) can appear as part of more than one disorder. Third, although *DSM-IV* provides many useful diagnostic criteria, some of them—such as "clinically significant impairment"—are open to a certain amount of interpretation. When mental health professionals must decide for themselves whether a particular person's symptoms are severe enough to warrant a particular diagnosis, personal bias can creep into the system (Kim & Ahn, 2002; Widiger & Clark, 2000). All of these factors may lead to misdiagnosis in some cases. Concern over this possibility has grown as the nations of North America and Western Europe become increasingly multicultural, and as diagnosticians encounter more and more people whose cultural backgrounds they may not fully understand or appreciate.

Psychiatrist Thomas Szasz (pronounced "zaws") and other critics also argue that the entire process of labeling people instead of describing problems is dehumanizing, because it ignores features that make each person's case unique (Kutchins & Kirk, 1997; Szasz, 1987, 2002; Wampold, Ahn, & Coleman, 2001). Calling people "schizophrenics" or "alcoholics," he says, actually encourages the behaviors associated with these labels and undermines the confidence of clients and therapists about the chances of improvement.

In summary, it is unlikely that any diagnostic system will ever satisfy everyone. No shorthand label can fully describe a person's problems or predict exactly how that person will behave in the future. All that can be reasonably expected of a diagnostic system is that it allows informative, general descriptions of the types of problems displayed by people who have been placed in various categories.

Some researchers and clinicians worry that problems with the reliability and validity of the diagnostic system are due partly to bias in its construction and use. They point out, for example, that if research that established the criteria for diagnosing a certain disorder focused on only one gender, one ethnic group, or one age group, those criteria might not apply widely enough. Moreover, because diagnosticians, like other people, hold expectations and make assumptions about males versus females, and about individuals from differing cultures or ethnic groups, these cognitive biases could color their judgments. This "pre-judging" process might lead them to apply diagnostic criteria in ways that are subtly, but significantly, different from one case to the next (Garb, 1997; Hartung & Widiger, 1998).

■ What am I being asked to believe or accept?

Here, we focus on ethnicity as a possible source of bias in diagnosing psychopathology. It is of special interest because there is evidence that, like social class and gender, ethnicity is an important sociocultural factor in the development of mental disorder. The assertion to be considered is that clinicians in the United States base their diagnoses partly on clients' ethnic background and, more specifically, that there is bias in diagnosing African Americans.

■ What evidence is available to support the claim?

Several facts suggest the possibility of ethnic bias in psychological diagnosis. For example, African Americans receive the diagnosis of schizophrenia more frequently than European Americans do (Manderscheid & Barrett, 1987; Minsky et al., 2003; Pavkov, Lewis, & Lyons, 1989). Further, relative to their presence in the general population, African Americans are overrepresented in public mental hospitals, where the most serious forms of disorder are seen, and they are underrepresented in private hospitals and outpatient clinics, where less severe problems are treated (Lindsey & Paul, 1989; Snowden & Cheung, 1990; U.S. Surgeon General, 1999).

A more subtle problem is that members of ethnic minorities, including African Americans, are underrepresented in research on psychopathology (Iwamasa, Sorocco, & Koonce, 2002). This lack of minority representation may leave clinicians less aware of sociocultural factors that could influence diagnosis. For example, they might more easily misinterpret an African American's unwillingness to trust a European American diagnostician as evidence of paranoid symptoms (Whaley, 2001).

■ Can that evidence be interpreted another way?

Differences among ethnic groups in diagnosis or treatment do not automatically indicate bias based on ethnicity. Perhaps real differences in psychological functioning are associated with different ethnic groups. If, relative to other groups, African Americans are exposed to more risk factors for disorder, including poverty, violence, and other major stressors, they could be especially vulnerable to more serious forms of mental disorder. And poverty, not diagnostic bias, could be responsible for the fact that African Americans more often seek help at less expensive public hospitals than at more expensive private ones. Finally, there is no guarantee that diagnostic criteria would be significantly different if more African Americans had been included in psychopathology research samples.

■ What evidence would help to evaluate the alternatives?

So do African Americans actually display more signs of mental disorder, or do diagnosticians just perceive them as more disordered? One way of approaching this question is to conduct experiments in which diagnosticians assign labels to clients on the basis of case histories, test scores, and the like. In some studies, the cases are selected so that pairs of clients show about the same amount of disorder, but one member of the pair is identified as European American and the other, as African American. In other studies, the same case materials, identified as representing either African American or European American clients, are presented to different diagnosticians. Bias in diagnosis would be suggested if, for example, patients identified as African American were seen as more seriously disordered than others.

Most studies of this type have actually found little or no ethnic bias (e.g., Angold et al., 2002; Garb, 1997; Littlewood, 1992). These results are difficult to interpret, however, because the diagnosticians may be aware of the purpose of the study, and so may go out of their way to be unbiased (Abreu, 1999). In fact, researchers *have* found evidence of some diagnostic bias against African Americans when clinicians were unaware of the purpose of the research (e.g., Baskin, Bluestone, & Nelson, 1981; Jones, 1982).

Bias has also appeared in studies aimed at identifying the factors influencing clinicians' diagnostic judgments following extensive interviews with patients. For example, one hospital study found that, in arriving at their diagnoses, psychiatrists were more likely to attribute hallucinations and paranoid thinking to African American patients than to non–African American patients. Symptoms of mood disorders were more likely to be attributed to non–African Americans (Trierweiler et al., 2000). As noted earlier, these differences could reflect ethnic differences in the rate of disorder in the population, but when people were interviewed in their own homes as part of large-scale mental health surveys, the diagnosis of schizophrenia was given only slightly more often to African Americans than to European Americans (Robins & Regier, 1991; Snowden & Cheung, 1990). So the presence of ethnic bias is suggested, at least for some diagnoses, for patients who are evaluated in mental hospitals (Trierweiler et al., 2000).

■ What conclusions are most reasonable?

Just as *DSM-IV* is imperfect, so are the people who use it. As described in the chapters on social psychology and on thought, language, and intelligence, cognitive biases and stereotypes affect human thinking to some extent in virtually every social situation. It is not surprising, then, that they operate in diagnosis as well. Diagnostic bias does not necessarily reflect deliberate discrimination, however. At least one study has shown that, like the processes of prejudice discussed in the social psychology chapter, diagnostic bias based on ethnicity can operate unconsciously, without the diagnostician's being aware of it (Abreu, 1999). So no matter how precisely researchers specify the criteria for assigning diagnostic labels, biases and stereotypes are likely to threaten the objectivity of the diagnostic process (Funtowicz & Widiger, 1999; Trierweiler et al., 2000).

Minimizing diagnostic bias requires a better understanding of it. Hope Landrine (1991) suggests that diagnosticians should focus more intently than ever on the fact that their concepts of "normality" and "abnormality" are affected by sociocultural values that they may or may not share with a given client. And Steven Lopez (1989) argues that mental health professionals must become more aware that the same cognitive shortcuts and biases that affect everyone else's thinking and decision making can impair their own clinical judgments. In fact, future research on memory, problem solving, decision making, social attributions, and other aspects of culture and cognition may turn out to be crucial in reducing bias in the diagnosis of psychological disorders. Meanwhile, perhaps the best way to counteract clinicians' cognitive shortcomings is to teach them to base their diag-

anxiety disorder   A condition in which intense feelings of fear and dread are long-standing or disruptive.

phobia   An anxiety disorder that involves strong, irrational fear of an object or situation that does not objectively justify such a reaction.

specific phobias   Phobias that involve fear and avoidance of heights, blood, animals, and other specific stimuli and situations.

social phobias   Strong, irrational fears relating to social situations.

noses solely on standard diagnostic criteria and decision rules rather than relying on their (potentially biased) clinical impressions (Garb, 1997; Nietzel et al., 2003).

We do not have space to cover all the *DSM-IV* categories, so we will sample several of the most prevalent and socially significant examples. As you read, try not to catch "medical student's disease." Just as medical students often think they have the symptoms of every illness they read about, some psychology students worry that certain aspects of their behavior (or that of a relative or friend) might reflect a mental disorder. Remember that everyone has problems sometimes. Before deciding that you or someone you know needs psychological help, consider whether the content, context, and functional impairment associated with the behavior would qualify it as abnormal according to the criteria of the practical approach.

Anxiety Disorders

▶ **What is a phobia?**

If you have ever been tense before an exam, a date, or a job interview, you have a good idea of what anxiety feels like. Common components of anxiety include increased heart rate, sweating, rapid breathing, dry mouth, and a sense of dread. Brief episodes of moderate anxiety are a normal part of life for most people. For others, anxiety is so intense and long-standing that it disrupts their daily functioning; in such cases it is called an **anxiety disorder.**

Types of Anxiety Disorders

Here, we discuss four types of anxiety disorders: *phobia, generalized anxiety disorder, panic disorder,* and *obsessive-compulsive disorder.* Another type, called *posttraumatic stress disorder,* is described in the chapter on health, stress, and coping. Together, these are the most common psychological disorders in North America.

Phobia   An intense, irrational fear of an object or situation that is not likely to be dangerous is called a **phobia.** People who experience phobias usually realize that their fears are groundless, but their discomfort and avoidance of some object or event greatly interfere with daily life. Thousands of phobias have been described; some of them are listed in Table 12.3.

DSM-IV classifies phobias into three subtypes: specific phobia, social phobia, and agoraphobia. **Specific phobias** involve fear and avoidance of heights, blood, animals, automobile or air travel, and other specific stimuli and situations. They are the most prevalent of the anxiety disorders, affecting 7 to 11 percent of U.S. adults and children (American Psychiatric Association, 2000; Kessler et al., 1994; Lichtenstein & Annas, 2000; U.S. Surgeon General, 1999). Here is an example:

> *Mr. L., a fifty-year-old office worker, became terrified whenever he had to drive over a bridge. For years, he avoided bridges by taking roundabout ways to and from work, and he refused to be a passenger in anyone else's car, in case they used a bridge. Even these inconvenient strategies failed when Mr. L. was transferred to a job requiring frequent automobile trips, many of which were over bridges. He refused the transfer and lost his job.*

Social phobias involve anxiety about being negatively evaluated by others or acting in a way that is embarrassing or humiliating. The anxiety is so intense and persistent that it impairs the person's normal functioning. In the United States, social phobia affects about

table 12.3

Some Phobias

Phobia is the Greek word for "morbid fear," after the lesser Greek god Phobos. Phobias are usually named using the Greek word for the feared object or situation, followed by the suffix *-phobia.*

Name	Feared Stimulus
Acrophobia	Heights
Aerophobia	Flying
Claustrophobia	Enclosed places
Cynophobia	Dogs
Entomophobia	Insects
Gamophobia	Marriage
Gephyrophobia	Crossing a bridge
Hematophobia	Blood
Kenophobia	Empty rooms
Melissophobia	Bees
Ophidiphobia	Snakes
Xenophobia	Strangers

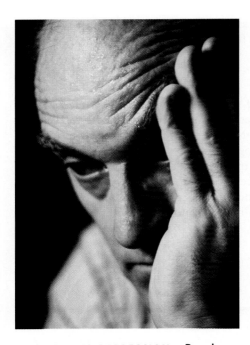

ANXIETY AND DEPRESSION People who experience anxiety disorders—particularly panic disorder, generalized anxiety disorder, or posttraumatic stress disorder—are likely to display some other mental disorder as well, most often depression (Kaufman & Charney, 2000; Roy-Byrne et al., 2000). Accordingly, the next edition of the *DSM* may include *mixed anxiety-depression disorder*, a new category describing people whose symptoms of anxiety and depression combine to impair their daily functioning (Barlow & Campbell, 2000; Widiger & Clark, 2000).

agoraphobia A strong fear of being alone or away from the safety of home.

generalized anxiety disorder A condition that involves long-lasting anxiety that is not focused on any particular object or situation.

panic disorder Anxiety in the form of severe panic attacks that come without warning or obvious cause.

obsessive-compulsive disorder (OCD) An anxiety disorder in which a person becomes obsessed with certain thoughts or feels a compulsion to do certain things.

2 percent of the adult population (U.S. Surgeon General, 1999). Common social phobias include fear of public speaking or performance ("stage fright"), fear of eating in front of others, and fear of using public restrooms (Kleinknecht, 2000). *Generalized social phobia* is a more severe form of social phobia in which fear occurs in virtually all social situations (Mannuzza et al., 1995). Sociocultural factors can alter the form of social phobias. For example, in Japan, where cultural training emphasizes group-oriented values and goals, a common social phobia is *tai-jin kyofu sho*, fear of embarrassing those around you (Kleinknecht, 1994).

Agoraphobia is a strong fear of being away from a safe place, such as home; of being away from a familiar person, such as a spouse or close friend; or of being in situations (such as crowds) that are difficult to leave or where help may be unavailable. Attempts to leave home lead to intense anxiety. In Western cultures, agoraphobia is more often reported by women, many of whom are totally homebound by the time they seek help. In other cultures, such as India, where homebound women are considered less unusual than in the United States, those diagnosed as agoraphobic tend to be male (Raguram & Bhide, 1985). Although agoraphobia occurs less frequently than specific phobias (affecting about 5 percent of the U.S. population), it is the phobia that most often leads people to seek treatment—mainly because it so severely disrupts everyday life (U.S. Surgeon General, 1999).

Generalized Anxiety Disorder Excessive and long-lasting anxiety that is not focused on any particular object or situation marks **generalized anxiety disorder.** Because the problem occurs in virtually all situations and because the person cannot pinpoint its source, this type of anxiety is sometimes called *free-floating anxiety*. For weeks at a time, the person feels anxious and worried, sure that some disaster is imminent. The person becomes jumpy and irritable, and cannot sleep soundly. Fatigue, inability to concentrate, and physiological signs of anxiety are also common. Generalized anxiety disorder affects about 3.4 percent of the U.S. population in any given year, and about 5 percent of the population at some point in their lives (Kessler, Keller, & Wittchen, 2001; U.S. Surgeon General, 1999). It is more common in women, often accompanying other problems such as depression or substance abuse (Wittchen & Hoyer, 2001).

Panic Disorder For some people, anxiety takes the form of **panic disorder.** Like José, whom we met at the beginning of this chapter, people suffering from panic disorder experience recurrent, terrifying *panic attacks* that seem to come without warning or obvious cause. These attacks are marked by intense heart palpitations, pressure or pain in the chest, sweating, dizziness, and feeling faint. Often, victims believe they are having a heart attack. They may worry constantly about suffering further panic episodes, so they limit their activities to avoid possible embarrassment. In fact, it is the fear of experiencing panic attacks that may lead to agoraphobia as the person begins to fear and avoid places where help won't be available should panic recur (Carter & Barlow, 1995). Panic disorder may last for many years, with periods of improvement followed by recurrence (Ehlers, 1995). As many as 30 percent of the U.S. population have experienced at least one panic attack within the past year; full-blown panic disorder is seen in only about 1 to 2 percent of the population in any given year (American Psychiatric Association, 2000; U.S. Surgeon General, 1999). Here is one example:

> *Geri, a thirty-two-year-old nurse, had her first panic attack while driving on a freeway. Afterward, she would not drive on freeways. Her next attack occurred while with a patient and a doctor in a small examining room. A sense of impending doom flooded over her, and she burst out of the office and into the parking lot, where she felt immediate relief. From then on, fear of another attack made it impossible for her to tolerate any close quarters, including crowded shopping malls. She eventually quit her job because of terror of the examining rooms.*

Obsessive-Compulsive Disorder Anxiety is also at the root of **obsessive-compulsive disorder (OCD),** which affects about 2.4 percent of the U.S. population in any given year (American Psychiatric Association, 2000; Howarth & Weissman, 2000; U.S. Surgeon

General, 1999). People displaying this disorder are plagued by persistent, upsetting, and unwanted thoughts—called *obsessions*—that often focus on the possibility of infection, contamination, or doing harm to themselves or others. These obsessive thoughts may then motivate repetitive behaviors—called *compulsions*—that the person believes will prevent infection, aggressive acts, or other events associated with the obsessions (Foa & Kozak, 1995). Common compulsions include rituals such as checking locks; repeating words, images, or numbers; counting things; or arranging objects "just so." Obsessions and compulsions are much more intense than the familiar experience of having a repetitive thought or tune "in the back of your mind" or rechecking a door to see that it is locked. In OCD, the obsessions and compulsions are intense, disturbing, and often strange intrusions that can severely impair daily activities. (*DSM-IV* defines compulsions as taking up more than one hour a day.) Many of those who display OCD recognize that their thoughts and actions are irrational, but they still experience severe anxiety if they try to interrupt their obsessions or give up their compulsive behaviors.

Causes of Anxiety Disorders

As with all the forms of psychopathology we will consider, the exact causes of anxiety disorders are a matter of debate. However, there is good evidence that biological, psychological, and social factors all contribute. Biological predispositions, distortions in thinking, and learning experiences appear to be particularly important causal factors (U.S. Surgeon General, 1999).

Biological Factors   Most anxiety disorders appear to run in families (Kendler et al., 1995, 2001; Pauls et al., 1995; Skre et al., 2000; Wittchen et al., 1994), suggesting that these disorders are influenced by a genetic predisposition (Hettema et al., 2003). For example, if one identical twin suffers an anxiety disorder, the other is more likely to share that disorder than is the case in nonidentical twin pairs (e.g., Hettema, Neale, & Kendler, 2001; Kendler et al., 1992, 2002). What is actually inherited? Anxiety disorders might stem from a tendency to react with anxiety to a wide range of situations, and this tendency, in turn, might result partly from inheriting an autonomic nervous system that is oversensitive to stress (Ahmad et al., 2002; Hamilton et al., 2003; Zinbarg & Barlow, 1996). There may be more specific predispositions as well. One study found that identical twins were more likely than other siblings to share phobias of small animals and social situations, but not of heights or enclosed spaces (Skre et al., 2000).

A predisposition to develop anxiety disorders may also stem from abnormalities in the brain's neurotransmitter systems, which are discussed in the chapter on biology and behavior. Excessive activity of norepinephrine in certain parts of the brain has been linked with panic disorder, and dysregulation of serotonin has been associated with obsessive-compulsive disorder. There is also evidence that anxiety-generating nerve impulses may run unchecked when the neurotransmitter GABA is prevented from exerting its normal inhibitory influence in certain brain pathways (Friedman, Clark, & Gershon, 1992; Zorumski & Isenberg, 1991).

Psychological Factors   Although biological predispositions may set the stage for anxiety disorders, most researchers agree that environmental stressors and psychological factors—especially cognitive processes and learning—are also involved in bringing about most anxiety disorders (Ley, 1994; Schmidt et al., 2000; Stein, Chavira, & Jang, 2001). To see the effects of environmental stressors, one need only look at the dramatic rise in cases of posttraumatic stress disorder following natural disasters or terrorist attacks (Galea et al., 2002). The impact of learning can be seen, for example, in families where parents don't socialize much, tend to be suspicious of others, and constantly exaggerate life's everyday dangers. Such parents might unwittingly promote social anxiety in their children, especially in those born with a tendency toward shyness, by influencing them to interpret social situations as threatening. Abuse or other traumatic childhood experiences also increase the risk of developing an anxiety disorder, particularly panic disorder (Safren et al., 2002).

A CLEANING COMPULSION   Obsessive-compulsive disorder is diagnosed when a culturally expected degree of cleanliness evolves into an obsessive preoccupation with germs and a life-disrupting compulsion to clean things. Learning and stress appear to play the major role in shaping and triggering this and other anxiety disorders, but biological factors, including genetically inherited characteristics and problems in certain neurotransmitter systems, may result in an oversensitive nervous system and a predisposition toward anxiety.

Learned ways of thinking play their part, too. Many people suffering from anxiety disorders exaggerate dangers in their environment, thereby creating an unrealistic expectation that bad things are going to happen (Foa et al., 1996). In addition, they tend to underestimate their own capacity for dealing with threatening events, thus triggering anxiety and desperation when feared events do occur (Beck & Emery, 1985). Consider the development of a panic attack. Whereas the appearance of unexplained symptoms of physical arousal may set the stage for a panic attack, it is the person's sensitivity to, and cognitive interpretation of, those symptoms that can determine whether or not the attack actually develops (Clark et al., 1997; Schmidt, Lerew, & Jackson, 1999). As described the chapter on health, stress, and coping, panic-disorder patients in one study breathed air rich in carbon dioxide. Some were told that they could control the amount of carbon dioxide they were inhaling by turning a dial on a control panel. Others were told they could not control it. In fact, the dial had no effect for either group, but the patients who believed they had control were far less likely to have a full-blown panic attack (Rapee et al., 1992; Sanderson, Rapee, & Barlow, 1989). In another study, panic-disorder patients who inhaled carbon dioxide in the presence of a person they associated with safety were significantly less fearful than patients whose "safe person" was not present (Carter et al., 1995). Results like these suggest that cognitive factors play a role in panic disorder.

LINKAGES
Can we learn to become "abnormal"?
(a link to Learning)

LINKAGES

Anxiety Disorders and Learning

Problems in life such as money troubles, illness, final exams, or unhappy relationships often create upsetting thoughts and worry. And upsetting thoughts create anxiety. These thoughts become particularly difficult to dismiss when you are under stress or feel incapable of dealing effectively with the problems you are worried about. As the thoughts become more persistent, anxiety increases. If an action such as cleaning temporarily relieves the anxiety, that action may be strengthened through the process of negative reinforcement (see the learning chapter). But such actions do nothing to eliminate the obsessive thoughts, so they return and become compulsive, endlessly repeated rituals that keep the person trapped in a vicious circle of anxiety (Barlow, 1988). This kind of analysis has led social-cognitive theorists to see obsessive-compulsive disorder as a learned pattern sparked by distressing thoughts and maintained by operant conditioning.

They also see phobias as based in part on the principles of learning, especially classical conditioning and observational learning. The object of the phobia becomes a conditioned aversive stimulus through association with a traumatic event that acts as an unconditioned stimulus (Öst, 1992). Fear of dogs, for example, may result from a dog attack. Observing or hearing about other people's bad experiences can produce the same result: Most people who fear flying have never been in a plane crash. Once the fear is learned, avoidance of the feared object or situation prevents the person from finding out that there is no need to be afraid. This cycle of avoidance helps explain why many fears do not simply disappear on their own.

Why are phobias involving snakes and spiders so common, even though people are seldom harmed by them? And why are there so few cases of electrical-shock phobia, even though lots of people receive accidental shocks? The answer may be that people are *biologically prepared* to learn to fear and avoid stimuli that had the potential to harm their evolutionary ancestors (Skre et al., 2000; Staddon & Ettinger, 1989). Laboratory research supports the idea that people are biologically prepared to learn certain phobias (Hamm, Vaitl, & Lang, 1989). In one study, a group of Swedish psychologists created conditioned fear reactions to certain stimuli by associating photographs of those stimuli with electrical shocks (Öhman, Dimberg, & Öst, 1985). Their volunteer participants developed approximately equal conditioned anxiety reactions to photos of houses, human faces,

learn by **doing** **BIOLOGICAL PREPAREDNESS** Having a predisposition to learn fear of snakes and other potentially dangerous stimuli makes evolutionary sense. Animals (and humans) who rapidly learn a fear response to objects or situations that they see frightening their parents or peers are more likely to survive to pass on their genes to the next generation. Make a list of the things that you are especially afraid of. How did these fears develop? And how many of them appear to have "survival value"?

and snakes. Later, however, when the participants were shown the photos alone, their conditioned reaction to snakes remained long after the houses and faces had lost their ability to cause a fear response. These results suggest that anxiety disorders probably arise through the combined effects of genetic predispositions and learning.

Somatoform Disorders

▶ Can mental disorder cause blindness?

An athlete's fainting spells prevented her from competing in track and field events, but doctors could find nothing physically wrong. After a program of stress management, however, her symptoms disappeared, and she was able to rejoin her team (Lively, 2001). Sometimes people show symptoms of a *somatic*, or bodily, disorder even though there is no physical cause. Because these are psychological problems that take somatic form, they are called **somatoform disorders.** The classic example is **conversion disorder,** a condition in which a person appears to be, but is not, blind, deaf, paralyzed, or insensitive to pain in various parts of the body. (An earlier term for this disorder was *hysteria.*) Conversion disorders are rare, accounting for only about 2 percent of diagnoses (American Psychiatric Association, 1994, 2000). Although they can occur at any point in life, they usually appear in adolescence or early adulthood.

Conversion disorders differ from true physical disabilities in several ways. First, they tend to appear when a person is under severe stress. Second, they often help reduce that stress by enabling the person to avoid unpleasant situations. Third, the symptoms may be physiologically impossible or improbable, as Figure 12.2 illustrates. Finally, the person may show remarkably little concern about what most people would think was a rather serious problem. One college student, for example, experienced visual impairment that began each Sunday evening and became total blindness by Monday morning. Her vision would begin to return on Friday evenings and was fully restored in time for weekend football games and other social activities. She expressed no undue concern over her

somatoform disorders　Psychological problems in which a person shows the symptoms of some physical (somatic) disorder for which there is no physical cause.

conversion disorder　A somatoform disorder in which a person appears to be, but actually is not, blind, deaf, paralyzed, or insensitive to pain in various parts of the body.

figure 12.2

Glove Anesthesia

In a form of conversion disorder called *glove anesthesia,* lack of feeling stops abruptly at the wrist (Part B). But as shown in Part A, the nerves of the hand and arm blend, so if they were actually impaired, part of the arm would also lose sensitivity. Other neurologically impossible symptoms of conversion disorder include sleepwalking at night on legs that are "paralyzed" during the day.

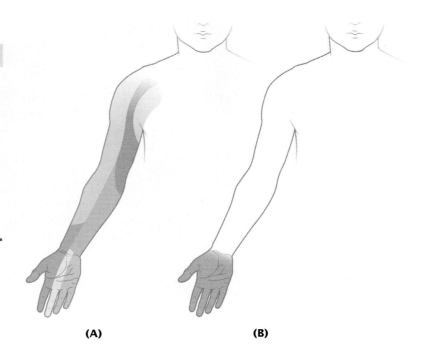

(A)   (B)

condition (Holmes, 1991). In such cases, the visual system remains intact, but the person appears to be unaware of the sensory information that the brain is still processing (Blake, 1998; Halligan & David, 1999).

Another type of somatoform disorder is **hypochondriasis** (pronounced "hye-poh-kon-DRY-a-sis"), a strong, unjustified fear that one has, or might get, cancer, heart disease, AIDS, or some other serious medical problem. The fear prompts frequent visits to doctors and reports of numerous symptoms. Their preoccupation with illness often leads hypochondriacs to become "experts" on their most feared diseases. In a related condition called **somatization disorder,** individuals make dramatic, but vague, reports about a multitude of physical problems rather than any specific illness. **Pain disorder** is marked by complaints of severe, often constant pain (typically in the neck, chest, or back) with no physical cause.

Some cases of somatoform disorder may be related to childhood experiences in which a person learns that symptoms of physical illness bring special attention, care, and nurturance (Barsky et al., 1994). Others, including conversion disorder, may be triggered by severe stressors (Spiegel, 1994). Cognitive factors also come into play. When given information about their health, persons displaying hypochondriasis are strongly biased to focus on threat-confirming information but to ignore reassuring information (Smeets, de Jong, & Mayer, 2000).

Based on such findings, many researchers have adopted a diathesis-stress approach to explaining somatoform disorders. The results of their work suggest that certain people may have biological and psychological traits that make them especially vulnerable to somatoform disorders, particularly when combined with a history of physical illness. Among these traits are self-consciousness and oversensitivity to physical sensations. If such people experience a number of long-lasting stressors, intense emotional conflicts, or severe traumas, they are more likely than others to display physical symptoms in association with emotional arousal (Nietzel et al., 1998).

Sociocultural factors may also shape somatoform disorders. In many Asian, Latin American, and African cultures, people commonly channel psychological or interpersonal conflicts into headaches and other physical symptoms, whereas in North America such conflicts are more likely to result in anxiety or depression (Brislin, 1993). Genetic factors appear to play only a minor role in somatoform disorders.

hypochondriasis   A strong, unjustified fear of physical illness.

somatization disorder   A psychological problem in which a person has numerous physical complaints without verifiable physical illness.

pain disorder   A somatoform disorder marked by complaints of severe, often constant pain with no physical cause.

Dissociative Disorders

▶ What disorders create sudden memory loss?

Have you ever spent hours driving on a boring highway and suddenly realized that you had little or no recollection of what happened during the last half-hour? This common experience does not signal a mental disorder, but when disruptions in a person's memory, consciousness, or identity are more intense and long-lasting, they are known as **dissociative disorders.** These disruptions can come on gradually, but they usually occur suddenly and last from a few hours to many years. Consider the case of John, a thirty-year-old computer executive. When his wife announced that she was leaving him to live with his younger brother, John did not go to work the next day. In fact, nothing was heard from him for two weeks. Then he was arrested for public drunkenness and assault in a city more than 300 miles from his home. The police discovered that during those two weeks, John lived under a different name at a cheap hotel and worked selling tickets at a pornographic movie theater. He did not know his real name or his home address, could not explain how he had reached his new location, and could not remember much about the previous two weeks.

John' displayed a disorder known as **dissociative fugue** (pronounced "fewg"), a sudden loss of personal memory and the adoption of a new identity in a new locale. Another dissociative disorder, **dissociative amnesia,** also involves sudden memory loss. As in fugue, all personal identifying information may be forgotten, but the person does not leave home or create a new identity. These conditions are rare, but they tend to attract intense publicity because they are so dramatic.

The most famous dissociative disorder is **dissociative identity disorder (DID),** formerly known as—and still commonly called—*multiple personality disorder (MPD).* A person with DID appears to have more than one identity, each of which speaks and acts in a different way. Each personality seems to have its own memories, wishes, and (often conflicting) impulses. Here is a case example:

> *Mary, a pleasant and introverted thirty-five-year-old social worker, was referred to a psychiatrist for hypnotic treatment of chronic pain. At an early interview she mentioned the odd fact that though she had no memory of using her car after coming home from work, she often found that it had been driven 50 to 100 miles overnight. It turned out that she also had no memory of large parts of her childhood. Mary rapidly learned self-hypnosis for pain control, but during one hypnotic session, she suddenly began speaking in a hostile manner. She told the doctor her name was Marian, and that it was "she" who had been taking long evening drives. She also called Mary "pathetic" for "wasting time" trying to please other people. Eventually, six other identities emerged, some of whom told of having experienced parental abuse in childhood.* (Spitzer et al., 1994)

How do dissociative disorders develop? Psychodynamic theorists see massive repression of unwanted impulses or memories as the basis for creating a "new person" who acts out otherwise unacceptable impulses or recalls otherwise unbearable memories (e.g., Ross, 1997). Social-cognitive theorists focus on the fact that everyone is capable of behaving in different ways depending on circumstances (e.g., rowdy in a bar, quiet in a museum) and that, in rare cases, this variation can become so extreme that a person feels, and is perceived by others as, a "different person." Further, sudden memory loss or unusual behavior may be rewarded by providing escape from unpleasant situations, responsibilities, or punishment for misbehavior (Lilienfeld et al., 1999).

Evaluating these hypotheses has been difficult, partly because dissociative disorders have been so rare. Recently, however, DID has been diagnosed more frequently, either because clinicians are looking for it more carefully or because the conditions leading to it are more widespread. Research available so far suggests three conclusions. First, many people displaying DID have experienced events they would like to forget or

dissociative disorders Conditions involving sudden and usually temporary disruptions in a person's memory, consciousness, or identity.

dissociative fugue A psychological disorder involving sudden loss of memory and the assumption of a new identity in a new locale.

dissociative amnesia A psychological disorder marked by a sudden loss of memory for one's own name, occupation, or other identifying information.

dissociative identity disorder (DID) A dissociative disorder in which a person appears to have more than one identity, each of which speaks and acts in a different way.

"Would it be possible to speak with the personality that pays the bills?"

Debate and skepticism about the nature and origins of dissociative identity disorder are not confined to professional journals. This drawing appeared in *The New Yorker*.

avoid. The majority (some clinicians believe all) have suffered severe, unavoidable, persistent abuse in childhood (Ross et al., 1991). Second, like Mary, most of these people appear to be skilled at self-hypnosis, through which they can induce a trance-like state. Third, most found that they could escape the trauma of abuse, at least temporarily, by creating "new personalities" to deal with stress (Spiegel, 1994). However, not all abused children display DID, and there is evidence that some cases of DID may be triggered by media stories or by suggestions made to clients by their therapists (Spanos, 1996).

This evidence has led some skeptics to question the existence of multiple personalities (Acocella, 1998; Merckelbach, Devilly, & Rassin, 2002). Others suggest that the increased incidence of dissociative identity disorder may simply reflect its status as a socioculturally approved method of expressing distress (Hacking, 1995; Spanos, 1994). In fact, concerns like these were partly responsible for the change in designation from *multiple personality disorder* to *dissociative identity disorder*. The authors of *DSM-IV* wanted to downplay the idea that people harbor multiple personalities that can easily be "contacted" through hypnosis or related techniques. The new name was chosen to suggest, instead, that dissociation, or separation, between one's memories and other aspects of identity can be so dramatic that people experiencing it may come to believe that they have more than one personality (Gleaves, May, & Cardena, 2001; Spiegel, 1994). Research on the existence and effects of repressed memories (discussed in the memory chapter) is sure to have an impact on our understanding of, and the controversy over, the causes of dissociative identity disorder. ("In Review: Anxiety, Somatoform, and Dissociative Disorders" presents a summary of our discussion of these topics.)

in review

ANXIETY, SOMATOFORM, AND DISSOCIATIVE DISORDERS

Disorder	Subtypes	Major Symptoms
Anxiety disorders	Phobias	Intense, irrational fear of objectively nondangerous situations or things, leading to disruptions of behavior.
	Generalized anxiety disorder	Excessive anxiety not focused on a specific situation or object; free-floating anxiety.
	Panic disorder	Repeated attacks of intense fear involving physical symptoms such as faintness, dizziness, and nausea.
	Obsessive-compulsive disorder	Persistent ideas or worries accompanied by ritualistic behaviors performed to neutralize the anxiety-driven thoughts.
Somatoform disorders	Conversion disorder	A loss of physical ability (e.g., sight, hearing) that is related to psychological factors.
	Hypochondriasis	Preoccupation with, or belief that one has, serious illness in the absence of any physical evidence.
	Somatization disorder	Wide variety of somatic complaints that occur over several years and are not the result of a known physical disorder.
	Pain disorder	Preoccupation with pain in the absence of physical reasons for the pain.
Dissociative disorders	Dissociative amnesia/fugue	Sudden, unexpected loss of memory, which may result in relocation and the assumption of a new identity.
	Dissociative identity disorder (multiple personality disorder)	Appearance within the same person for two or more distinct identities, each with a unique way of thinking and behaving.

? *Concern that some of its symptoms may actually be triggered by media stories or therapists' suggestions has made _____ the most controversial of the dissociative disorders.*

Mood Disorders

▶ **How common is depression?**

Everyone's mood, or *affect,* tends to rise and fall from time to time. However, when people experience long periods of extreme moods such as wild elation or deep depression, when they shift from one extreme to another, and especially when their moods are not consistent with the events around them, they are said to show a **mood disorder,** also known as *affective disorder*. We will describe two main types: depressive disorders and bipolar disorder.

Depressive Disorders

Depression can range from occasional, normal "down" periods to episodes severe enough to require hospitalization. A person suffering **major depressive disorder** feels sad and overwhelmed for weeks or months, typically losing interest in activities and relationships and taking pleasure in nothing (Coryell et al., 1993; Sloan, Strauss, & Wisner, 2001). Exaggerated feelings of inadequacy, worthlessness, hopelessness, or guilt are common. Despite the person's best efforts, anything from conversation to bathing can become an unbearable, exhausting task (Solomon, 1998). Changes in eating habits resulting in weight loss or weight gain often accompany major depressive disorder. So does disturbed sleeping or, sometimes, excessive sleeping. Problems in working, concentrating, making decisions, and thinking clearly are also common, as are symptoms of an accompanying anxiety disorder (Zimmerman, McDermut, & Mattia, 2000). In extreme cases, depressed people may express false beliefs, or **delusions**—worrying, for example, that government agents are planning to punish them. Major depressive disorder may come on suddenly or gradually. It may consist of a single episode or, more commonly, repeated depressive periods. Here is a case example:

> *Mr. J. was a fifty-one-year-old industrial engineer.... Since the death of his wife five years earlier, he had been suffering from continuing episodes of depression marked by extreme social withdrawal and occasional thoughts of suicide.... He drank, and when thoroughly intoxicated would plead to his deceased wife for forgiveness. He lost all capacity for joy.... Once a gourmet, he now had no interest in food and good wine ... and could barely manage to engage in small talk. As might be expected, his work record deteriorated markedly. Appointments were missed and projects haphazardly started and left unfinished.* (Davison & Neale, 1990, p. 221)

Depression is not always so extreme. In a less severe pattern of depression, called **dysthymic disorder,** the person shows the sad mood, lack of interest, and loss of pleasure associated with major depression, but less intensely and for a longer period. (The duration must be at least two years to qualify as dysthymic disorder.) Mental and behavioral disruptions are also less severe. People exhibiting dysthymic disorder rarely require hospitalization.

Major depressive disorder occurs sometime in the lives of about 17 percent of people in North America and Europe (Kessler et al., 1994, 2003; U.S. Surgeon General, 1999). The incidence of the disorder varies considerably across cultures and subcultures, however. For example, it occurs at much higher rates in urban Ireland than in urban Spain (Judd et al., 2002). There are gender differences in some cultures, too. North American and European women are two to three times more likely than men to experience major depressive disorder (American Psychiatric Association, 2000; Weissman et al., 1993), but this difference does not appear in the less economically developed countries of the Middle East, Africa, and Asia (Ayuso-Mateos et al., 2001; Culbertson, 1997). Depression can occur at any age, but it frequently first appears in late adolescence or young adulthood. Increased rates of depression are also found among the elderly (Cross-National Collaborative Group, 1992; Fassler & Dumas, 1997; Sowdon, 2001).

Suicide and Depression Suicide is associated with a variety of psychological disorders, but it is most closely tied to depression. Some form of depression has been implicated in 40 to 60 percent of all suicides (Angst, Angst, & Stassen, 1999; Oquendo & Mann, 2001;

mood disorder A condition in which a person experiences extremes of mood for long periods, shifts from one extreme mood to another, and experiences moods that are inconsistent with events.

major depressive disorder A condition in which a person feels sad and hopeless for weeks or months, often losing interest in all activities and taking pleasure in nothing.

delusions False beliefs, such as those experienced by people suffering from schizophrenia or severe depression.

dysthymic disorder A pattern of depression in which the person shows the sad mood, lack of interest, and loss of pleasure associated with major depressive disorder, but to a lesser degree and for a longer period.

Rihmer, 2001). In fact, thinking about suicide is a symptom of depressive disorders. Hopelessness about the future—another depressive symptom—and a desire to seek instant escape from problems are also related to suicide attempts (Beck et al., 1990; Brown et al., 2000).

About 28,000 people in the United States commit suicide each year, and 10 to 20 times that many people attempt it (Centers for Disease Control and Prevention, 2002c; U.S. Surgeon General, 1999). This puts the U.S. suicide rate at about 10 per 100,000 individuals, making suicide the 11th leading cause of death. Worldwide, the suicide rate is as high as 25 per 100,000 in some northern European countries and Japan (Lamar, 2000), and as low as 6 per 100,000 in countries with stronger religious prohibitions against suicide, such as Greece, Italy, Ireland, and the nations of the Middle East.

Suicide rates differ considerably depending on sociocultural factors such as age, gender, and ethnicity (Centers for Disease Control and Prevention, 2002d; Oquendo et al., 2001). In the United States, suicide is most common among people 65 and older, especially males (Centers for Disease Control and Prevention, 2002d). However, since 1950, suicide among adolescents has tripled, making it the third leading cause of death, after accidents and homicides, among 15- to 24-year-olds (Centers for Disease Control and Prevention, 2002c). Suicide is the second leading cause of death among college students; about 10,000 try to kill themselves each year, and about 1,000 succeed. These figures are much higher than for young people in general, but much lower than for the elderly (U.S. Surgeon General, 1999). Women attempt suicide 3 times as often as men, but men are 4 times as likely to actually kill themselves (Centers for Disease Control and Prevention, 2002d). Suicide rates also differ across ethnic groups in the United States (see Figure 12.3). The suicide rate among adolescent European American males has stabilized since 1986, but it has continued to increase among African American male teens (Centers for Disease Control and Prevention, 1998; Hoyert, Kochanek, & Murphy, 1999).

Predicting who will commit suicide is difficult. For one thing, suicidal thoughts are not uncommon; in surveys, 5.6 percent of all adults and as many as 10 percent of college students report having had such thoughts in the previous year (Brener, Hassan, & Barrios, 1999; Crosby, Cheltenham, & Sacks, 1999). Still, the results of hundreds of research studies provide some predictive guidelines. In the United States, at least, suicide is most likely among European American males, especially those older than forty-five, single or divorced, and living alone. The risk of suicide is also heightened among people diagnosed with a mood disorder, anxiety disorder, or schizophrenia (Boardman & Healy, 2001; Khan et al., 2002; Rihmer, 2001). Among the elderly, suicide is most common in males who suffer depression over health problems (U.S. Surgeon General, 1999). The risk

figure 12.3

Suicide Rates by Gender and Ethnicity

The suicide rates among ethnic groups in the United States vary widely. For example, the rate among American Indians is almost twice that of African Americans. In 2001, more teenagers and young adults died from suicide than from cancer, heart disease, AIDS, birth defects, stroke, pneumonia and influenza, and chronic lung disease *combined* (Centers for Disease Control and Prevention, 2002d).

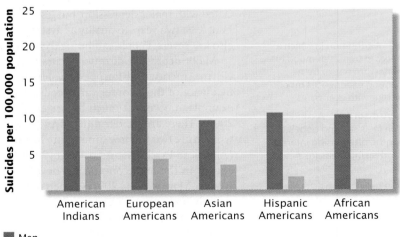

Source: Centers for Disease Control and Prevention (2002d).

is higher, too, in people who have made a specific plan, given away possessions, and are impulsive (Corruble, Damy, & Guelfi, 1999). A previous suicide attempt may not always be a good predictor of eventual suicide, because such attempts may have been help-seeking gestures, not failed efforts to die. In fact, although about 10 percent of unsuccessful attempters try again and succeed, most people who commit suicide had made no prior attempts (Clark & Fawcett, 1992).

One myth about suicide is that people who talk about it will never try it. On the contrary, those who say they are thinking of suicide are much more likely to try suicide than people from the general population. In fact, according to Edwin Shneidman (1987), 80 percent of suicides are preceded by some kind of warning, whether direct ("I think I'm going to kill myself") or vague ("Sometimes I wonder if life is worth living"). Although not everyone who threatens suicide follows through, if you suspect that someone you know is thinking about suicide, encourage the person to contact a mental health professional or a crisis hotline. If the danger is immediate, make the contact yourself, and ask for advice about how to respond. For more information, visit suicide-related web sites, such as that of the American Association of Suicidology (www.suicidology.org).

Bipolar Disorder

The alternating appearance of two emotional extremes, or poles, characterizes **bipolar disorder.** We have already described one emotional pole: depression. The other is **mania,** which is a very agitated, usually elated, emotional state. During periods of mania, people tend to be utterly optimistic, boundlessly energetic, certain of having extraordinary powers and abilities, and bursting with all sorts of ideas. They become irritated with anyone who tries to reason with them or "slow them down," and they may make impulsive and unwise decisions, including spending their life savings on foolish schemes.

In bipolar disorder, episodes of mania may alternate with periods of deep depression. (Sometimes, periods of relatively normal mood separate these extremes.) This pattern has also been called *manic depression.* Compared with major depressive disorder, bipolar disorder is rare. It occurs in only about 1 percent of adults, and it affects men and women about equally. Slightly more common is a pattern of less extreme mood swings known as **cyclothymic disorder,** the bipolar equivalent of dysthymic disorder. Like major depressive disorder, bipolar disorder is extremely disruptive to a person's ability to work or maintain social relationships (Goldberg, Harrow, & Grossman, 1995), and it is often accompanied by anxiety disorders (Freeman, Freeman, & McElroy, 2002). "In Review: Mood Disorders" summarizes the main types of mood disorders.

Causes of Mood Disorders

Research on the causes of mood disorders has focused on biological, psychological, and sociocultural risk factors. The more of these risk factors people have, the more likely they are to experience a mood disorder.

Biological Factors The role of genetics is suggested by twin studies and family studies showing that mood disorders, especially bipolar disorder, tend to run in families (Kelsoe et al., 2001). For example, bipolar disorder is much more likely to be seen in both members of genetically identical twin pairs than in fraternal, or genetically nonidentical, twins (Bowman & Nurnberger, 1993; Egeland et al., 1987; McGuffin et al., 2003). Family studies also show that those who are closely related to people with bipolar disorder are more likely than others to develop the disorder themselves (Blackwood, Visscher, & Muir, 2001). Major depressive disorder, too, is more likely to occur in both members of identical, compared with nonidentical, twins (Kendler et al., 1995; Klein et al., 2001). This genetic influence is especially strong in female twins (Bierut et al., 1999). Researchers continue to look for the specific genes that might be involved in the transmission of elevated risk for mood disorders (Blackwood et al., 2001; Caspi et al., 2003).

LINKAGES
Are some psychological disorders inherited?
(a link to Biology and Behavior)

bipolar disorder A condition in which a person alternates between the two emotional extremes of depression and mania.

mania An elated, active emotional state.

cyclothymic disorder A mood disorder characterized by an alternating pattern of mood swings that are less extreme than those seen in bipolar disorder.

in review

MOOD DISORDERS

Type	Typical Symptoms	Related Features
Major depressive disorder	Deep sadness, feelings of worthlessness, changes in eating and sleeping habits, loss of interest and pleasure	Lasts weeks or months; may occur in repeating episodes; severe cases may include delusions
Dysthymic disorder	Similar to major depressive disorder, but less severe and longer lasting	Hospitalization usually not necessary
Bipolar disorder	Alternating extremes of mood, from deep depression to mania, and back	Manic episodes include impulsivity, unrealistic optimism, high energy, severe agitation
Cyclothymic disorder	Similar to bipolar disorder, but less severe	Hospitalization usually not necessary

? *The risk of suicide is associated with_____ more than with any other symptom of disorder.*

Neuroscientists have discovered other possible biological causes of mood disorders, including problems in the prefrontal cortex, the hippocampus, the amygdala, and other brain regions involved in mood (Blumberg et al., 2003; Cotter et al., 2001; Davidson et al., 2002; Elliot et al., 2002; MacQueen et al., 2003). Imbalances in the brain's neurotransmitters, malfunctioning of the endocrine system, and disruption of biological rhythms have also been suggested as causal factors, and all of these may themselves be influenced by genetics.

As for the role of neurotransmitters, norepinephrine, serotonin, and dopamine were implicated decades ago when scientists discovered that drugs capable of altering these substances also relieved mood disorders. However, the precise nature of the relationship between neurotransmitters and mood disorders is still not fully understood (Martinot et al., 2001; Schloss & Williams, 1998; U.S. Surgeon General, 1999).

Mood disorders have also been related to malfunctions of the endocrine system, especially the subsystem involved in the body's responses to stress (see the chapter on health, stress, and coping). For example, research shows that as many as 70 percent of depressed people secrete abnormally high levels of the stress hormone cortisol (Dinan, 2001; Nemeroff, 1998; Posener et al., 2000).

The cycles of mood swings seen in bipolar disorder and in recurring episodes of major depressive disorder suggest that mood disorders may be related to stressful triggering events (Miklowitz & Alloy, 1999). They may also be related to disturbances in the body's biological clock, which is described in the chapter on biology and behavior (Goodwin & Jamison, 1990). This second possibility seems especially likely to apply to the 15 percent of depressed people who consistently experience a calendar-linked pattern of depressive episodes known as *seasonal affective disorder (SAD)*. During months of shorter daylight, these people slip into severe depression, accompanied by irritability and excessive sleeping. Their depression tends to lift as daylight hours increase (Faedda et al., 1993). Disruption of biological rhythms is also suggested by the fact that many depressed people tend to have trouble sleeping—perhaps partly because during the day, their biological clocks are telling them it is the middle of the night. Resetting the biological clock through methods such as sleep deprivation or light stimulation has relieved depression in many cases (Kuhs & Tolle, 1991; Terman et al., 2001).

TREATING SAD Seasonal affective disorder (SAD) can often be relieved by exposure to full-spectrum light for as little as a couple of hours a day (Campbell & Murphy, 1998; Sato, 1997).

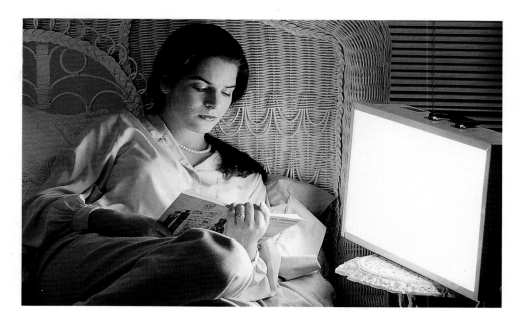

Psychological and Social Factors Researchers have come to recognize that whatever biological causes are involved in mood disorders, their effects are always combined with those of psychological and social causes (U.S. Surgeon General, 1999). As mentioned earlier, the very nature of depressive symptoms can depend on the culture in which a person lives. Biopsychosocial explanations of mood disorders also emphasize the impact of anxiety, negative thinking, and the other psychological and emotional responses triggered by trauma, losses, and other stressful events (Kendler et al., 2003a; Monroe et al., 1999). For example, the higher rate of depression among females—and especially among poor, ethnic minority, single mothers—has been attributed to their greater exposure to stressors of all kinds (Brown & Moran, 1997; Miranda & Green, 1999). Environmental stressors affect men, too (Bierut et al., 1999), which may be one reason why gender differences are smaller in countries where men and women face equally stressful lives. Still, differing stressors may not be the only source of these gender differences (Kendler, Thornton, & Prescott, 2001).

A number of social-cognitive theories suggest that the way people think about their stressors can increase or decrease the likelihood of mood disorders. One of these theories is based on the *learned helplessness* research described in the chapter on learning. Just as animals become inactive and appear depressed when they have no control over negative events (El Yacoubi et al., 2003), humans may experience depression as a result of feeling incapable of controlling their lives, especially the stressors confronting them (Klein & Seligman, 1976; Seligman, 1991). But most of us have limited control; why aren't we all depressed? The ways in which people learn to think about events in their lives may hold the key. For example, Aaron Beck's (1967, 1976) cognitive theory of depression suggests that depressed people develop mental habits of (1) blaming themselves when things go wrong, (2) focusing on and exaggerating the negative side of events, and (3) jumping to overly generalized, pessimistic conclusions. Such cognitive habits, says Beck, are errors that lead to depressing thoughts and other symptoms of depression (Beck & Beck, 1995). Depressed people, in fact, do tend to think about significant negative events in ways that are likely to increase or prolong their depression (Gotlib & Hammen, 1992).

Severe, long-lasting depression is especially likely among people who blame their lack of control or other problems on a permanent, generalized lack of personal competence rather than on a temporary mistake or some external cause (Seligman et al., 1988). This *negative attributional style* may be another important cognitive factor in depression (Alloy, Abramson, & Francis, 1999; Ingram, Miranda, & Segal, 1998). Are depressed people's unusually negative beliefs about themselves actually helping to cause their depression, or are they merely symptoms of it? A number of studies have assessed the attributional styles of large samples of nondepressed people and then kept in touch with them to see if, in the face of equivalent stressors, individuals with negative self-beliefs are more likely to become depressed. These longitudinal studies suggest that a negative attributional style is, in fact, a risk factor for depression, not just a result of being depressed (Garber, Keiley, & Martin, 2002; Runyon & Kenny, 2002; Satterfield, Folkman, & Acree, 2002). In one study, for example, adolescents who held strong negative self-beliefs were more likely than other youngsters to develop depression when faced with stress later in life (Lewinsohn, Joiner, & Rohde, 2001).

Social-cognitive theorists also suggest that whether depression continues or worsens depends in part on how people respond once they start to feel depressed. Those who continuously think about negative events, about why they occur, and even about being depressed are likely to feel more and more depressed (Just & Alloy, 1997). According to Susan Nolen-Hoeksema (1990, 2001), this *ruminative style* is especially characteristic of women and may help explain gender differences in the frequency of depression. When men start to feel sad, she says, they tend to use a *distracting style*. In other words, they engage in activity that distracts them from their concerns and helps bring them out of their depressed mood (Hankin & Abramson, 2001; Just & Alloy, 1997; Nolen-Hoeksema, Morrow, & Fredrickson, 1993).

Notice that social-cognitive explanations of depression are consistent with the diathesis-stress explanation of disorder (Hankin & Abramson, 2001). These explanations suggest that certain cognitive styles serve as a predisposition (or diathesis) that makes a person vulnerable to depression, the occurrence of which is made more likely by stressors. As suggested in the chapter on health, stress, and coping, the depressing effects of these stressors are likely to be magnified by lack of social support, inadequate coping skills, and the presence of other stressful conditions, such as poverty.

Given the number and complexity of biological, psychological, social, and situational factors potentially involved in causing mood disorders, the diathesis-stress approach appears to be an especially appropriate guide to future research. One study based on this approach looked at the role of genetics and stressful events in shaping mood disorders in a large group of female twin pairs. Both factors were associated with major depression; the women at highest genetic risk were the most likely to become depressed following a significant stressor (Kendler, Thorton, & Gardner, 2000, 2001). Another study found that people with a particular version of a single gene were more likely than others to experience depressive symptoms in relation to stressful events (Caspi et al., 2003b). Further, different biological and psychological risk factors may be of particular importance at different stages in life (Kendler, Gardner, & Prescott, 2002). In the final analysis, it may turn out that each subtype of mood disorder is caused by a unique combination of factors. The challenge for researchers is to identify these subtypes and link them to their causes.

Schizophrenia

▶ **Is schizophrenia the same as "split personality"?**

Here is part of a letter that arrived in the mail several years ago:

Dear Sirs:
Pertaining to our continuing failure to prosecute violations of minor's rights to sovereign equality which are occurring in gestations being compromised by the ingestation of controlled substances, . . . the skewing of androgyny which continues in female juveniles even after separation from their mother's has occurred, and as a means of promulflagitating my paying Governor Hickel of Alaska for my employees to have personal services endorsements and controlled substance endorsements, . . . the Iraqi oil being released by the United Nations being identified as Kurdistanian oil, and the July, 1991 issue of the Siberian Review spells President Eltsin's name without a letter y.

The disorganization and strange content of this letter suggest that its writer might be displaying **schizophrenia** (pronounced "skit-so-FREE-nee-uh"), a pattern of severely disturbed thinking, emotion, perception, and behavior that seriously impairs the ability to communicate and relate to others and disrupts most other aspects of daily functioning. Schizophrenia is one of the most severe and disabling of all mental disorders. Its core symptoms are seen virtually everywhere in the world, occurring in about 1 to 2 percent of the population (American Psychiatric Association, 1994, 2000). In the United States, it appears about equally in various ethnic groups, but like most disorders, it tends to be diagnosed more frequently in economically disadvantaged populations. Schizophrenia is seen about equally in men and women, although in women it may appear later in life, be less severe, and respond better to treatment (Aleman, Kahn, & Selten, 2003; American Psychiatric Association, 2000; U.S. Surgeon General, 1999).

Schizophrenia tends to develop in adolescence or early adulthood. In about three out of four cases, symptoms appear gradually over a period of years; in other cases, the onset is more rapid. About 40 percent of schizophrenics improve with treatment and are able to function reasonably well; the rest show continuous or intermittent symptoms that permanently impair their functioning (an der Heiden & Haefner, 2000; Hegarty et al., 1994). It has been estimated that 10 to 13 percent of homeless individuals suffer from schizophrenia (Fischer & Breakey, 1991; Olfson et al., 1999).

One of the best predictors of the outcome of schizophrenia is *premorbid adjustment,* the level of functioning a person had achieved before schizophrenia symptoms first appeared. Improvement is more likely in those who had attained higher levels of education and occupation, and who had established supportive relationships with family and friends (Rabinowitz et al., 2002; Watt & Saiz, 1991).

Symptoms of Schizophrenia

People displaying schizophrenia have problems in how they think and what they think. In fact, the nineteenth-century psychiatrist Eugen Bleuler coined the word *schizophrenia,* or "split mind," to refer to the oddities of schizophrenic thinking. However, schizophrenia does not mean "split personality," as in dissociative identity disorder (multiple personality disorder). It refers instead to a splitting of normally integrated mental processes such as thoughts and feelings. For instance, some schizophrenics may giggle while claiming to feel sad.

Schizophrenic thought and language are often disorganized. Words that have meaning only to the person speaking them (called *neologisms*) are common; "promulflagitating" in the letter above is one example. That letter also illustrates *loose associations,* the tendency for one thought to be logically unconnected or only loosely connected to the next. In the most severe cases, thought becomes just a jumble known as *word salad.* For example, one patient was heard to say, "Upon the advisability of held keeping, environment of the seabeach gathering, to the forest stream, reinstatement to be placed, poling the paddleboat, of the swamp morass, to the forest compensation of the dunce" (Lehman, 1967, p. 627).

The content of schizophrenic thinking is also disturbed. Often it includes a bewildering assortment of delusions (false beliefs), especially delusions of persecution. Some patients believe that space aliens or government agents are trying to steal their internal organs, and they may interpret everything from TV commercials to casual hand gestures as part of the plot. Delusions that such common events are somehow related to oneself are called *ideas of reference. Delusions of grandeur* may also be present; one young man was convinced that the president of the United States was trying to contact him for advice. Other types of delusions include (1) *thought broadcasting,* in which patients believe that their thoughts can be heard by others; (2) *thought blocking* or *thought withdrawal,* the belief that someone is either preventing thoughts or "stealing" them as they appear; and (3) *thought insertion,* the belief that other people's thoughts are appearing in one's own mind. Some patients believe that their behavior is being controlled by others; in one case, a man claimed that the CIA had placed a control device in his brain.

schizophrenia A pattern of severely disturbed thinking, emotion, perception, and behavior that constitutes one of the most serious and disabling of all mental disorders.

People with schizophrenia often report that they cannot focus their attention, and they may feel overwhelmed as they try to attend to everything at once. Various perceptual disorders may also appear. The person may feel detached from the world and see other people as flat cutouts. The body may feel like a machine, or parts of it may seem to be dead or rotting. **Hallucinations,** or false perceptions, are common, often emerging as voices. These voices may sound like an overheard conversation, or they may urge the person to do or not to do things; sometimes they comment on, narrate, or criticize the person's actions. Hallucinations can also involve the experience of nonexistent sights, smells, tastes, and touch sensations. Emotional expression is often muted—a pattern called *flat affect*. But when schizophrenics do display emotion, it is often exaggerated or inappropriate. For example, they may cry for no apparent reason or fly into a rage in response to a simple question.

Some schizophrenics are quite agitated, constantly fidgeting, grimacing, or pacing the floor in ritualized patterns. Others become so withdrawn that they move very little. Lack of motivation and poor social skills, deteriorating personal hygiene, and an inability to function day to day are other common characteristics of schizophrenia.

LINKAGES
Do people perceive hallucinations as real sensory events?
(a link to Sensation and Perception)

Categorizing Schizophrenia

DSM-IV lists five major subtypes of schizophrenia: paranoid, disorganized, catatonic, undifferentiated, and residual. These subtypes are summarized in Table 12.4.

Researchers have also made other useful distinctions among various forms of schizophrenia. One of these distinctions involves the positive-negative symptom dimension. Disorganized thoughts, delusions, and hallucinations are sometimes called *positive symptoms* of schizophrenia, because they appear as undesirable *additions* to a person's mental life (Andreasen et al., 1995; Racenstein et al., 2002). In contrast, the absence of pleasure and motivation, lack of emotional reactivity, social withdrawal, reduced speech, and other deficits seen in schizophrenia are sometimes called *negative symptoms,* because they appear to *subtract* elements from normal mental life (Nicholson & Neufeld, 1993). Many patients exhibit both positive and negative symptoms, but when the negative symptoms are stronger, schizophrenia generally has a more severe course, including long-term disability and relative lack of response to treatment (e.g., Fenton & McGlashan, 1994; Racenstein et al., 2002). Yet another way of categorizing schizophrenic symptoms focuses on whether they are *psychotic* (e.g., hallucinations, delusions), *disorganized* (e.g., incoherent speech, chaotic behavior, inappropriate affect), or *negative* (e.g., lack of speech or motivation). Some researchers believe that each symptom cluster or dimension may ultimately be traceable to different causes. For this reason, schizophrenia is often referred to as the *schizophrenia spectrum* (Tsuang, Stone, & Faraone, 2000).

Causes of Schizophrenia

The search for causes of schizophrenia has been more intense than for any other psychological disorder. The findings so far confirm one thing for certain: As with other disorders, there are biological, psychological, and sociocultural factors at work in causing or worsening all forms of schizophrenia (U.S. Surgeon General, 1999).

Biological Factors   Research in behavioral genetics shows that schizophrenia runs in families (Asarnow et al., 2001; Gottesman, 1991). One family study found that 16 percent of the children of schizophrenic mothers—compared with 2 percent of those of nonschizophrenic mothers—developed schizophrenia themselves over a twenty-five-year period (Parnas et al., 1993). Even if they are adopted by nonschizophrenic families, the children of schizophrenic parents are ten times more likely to develop schizophrenia than adopted children whose biological parents are not schizophrenic (Kety et al., 1994). Still, it is unlikely that a single gene transmits schizophrenia (Chumakov et al., 2002; Kendler & Diehl, 1993). Among identical-twin pairs in which one of the members dis-

hallucinations False or distorted perceptions of objects or events.

table 12.4

Subtypes of Schizophrenia

These traditional categories of schizophrenia convey some useful information. For example, the prognosis for paranoid schizophrenia is somewhat better than for the other subtypes (Fenton & McGlashan, 1991). However, subtype labels are not always accurate, because some symptoms of schizophrenia appear in more than one subtype, and people first placed in one subtype might later display characteristics of another. These concerns, plus the fact that *DSM-IV* subtypes may not be linked to different causal factors, have led researchers to develop additional ways of categorizing schizophrenia (e.g., Haefner & Maurer, 2000).

Type	Frequency	Prominent Features
Paranoid schizophrenia	40 percent of schizophrenics; appears late in life (after age 25–30)	Delusions of grandeur or persecution; anger; anxiety; argumentativeness; extreme jealousy; onset often sudden; signs of impairment may be subtle.
Disorganized schizophrenia	5 percent of all schizophrenics; high prevalance in homeless population	Delusions; hallucinations; incoherent speech; facial grimaces; inappropriate laughter/giggling; neglected personal hygiene; loss of bladder/bowel control.
Catatonic schizophrenia	8 percent of all schizophrenics	Disordered movement, alternating between total immobility (stupor) and wild excitement. In stupor, the person does not speak or attend to communication; also, the body is rigid or can be posed in virtually any posture (a condition called "waxy flexibility").
Undifferentiated schizophrenia	40 percent of all schizophrenics	Patterns of disordered behavior, thought, and emotion that do not fall easily into any other subtype.
Residual schizophrenia	Varies	Applies to people who have had prior episodes of schizophrenia but are not currently displaying symptoms.

CATATONIC STUPOR The symptoms of schizophrenia often occur in characteristic patterns. This woman displays the inactivity and odd posturing associated with catatonic schizophrenia.

plays schizophrenia, 40 percent of the other members display it, too; but 60 percent of them do not (McGue, 1992). It is more likely that some people inherit a predisposition, or diathesis, for schizophrenia that involves many genes and that then combines with other genetic and nongenetic factors to cause the disorder (Moldin & Gottesman, 1997).

The search for biological causes of schizophrenia also focuses on a number of abnormalities in the structure, functioning, and chemistry of the brain that tend to appear in schizophrenics (e.g., Davis et al., 2003). For example, brain imaging studies have compared schizophrenia patients with other mental patients. Many schizophrenia patients (especially those who display mostly negative symptoms) have less tissue in areas of the brain that are involved in emotional expression, thinking, and information processing—functions that are disordered in schizophrenia (Conklin & Iacono, 2002; Gilbert et al., 2001; Highley et al., 2003; Pol et al., 2002; Selemon et al., 2003; Sigmundsson et al., 2001). There is also evidence that worsening symptoms are associated with continued tissue loss in these areas (Ho et al., 2003). Patients with mainly positive symptoms tend to have essentially normal-looking brains (Andreasen, 1997).

Researchers are also investigating the possibility that abnormalities in brain chemistry—especially in neurotransmitter systems that use dopamine—play a role in causing or intensifying the symptoms of schizophrenia. Because drugs that block the brain's dopamine receptors often reduce schizophrenics' hallucinations, disordered thinking, and other positive symptoms, some investigators speculate that schizophrenia results from excess dopamine. However, the relationship between dopamine and schizophrenia is a complex one (Albert et al., 2002; Koh et al., 2002). Some research suggests, for example, that excessive activity in dopamine systems may be related to the appearance of hallucinations, delusions, and other positive symptoms of schizophrenia. Abnormally low dopamine system activity, especially in prefrontal brain areas, has been associated with negative symptoms such as withdrawal (e.g., Cohen & Servan-Schreiber, 1992).

Some researchers are integrating genetic and environmental explanations of schizophrenia by looking for *neurodevelopmental* abnormalities (Cannon et al., 2002; Conklin & Iacono, 2002; Gur et al., 2000; Loeber, Cintron, & Yurgelun-Todd, 2001; McGlashan & Hoffman, 2000; Walbeck et al., 2001). Perhaps, they say, some forms of schizophrenia arise from disruptions in brain development from before birth through childhood, when the brain is growing and its various functions are maturing. For instance, prenatal exposure to viral infections or other physical traumas are associated with increased risk for developing schizophrenia (AbdelMalik et al., 2003; Malaspina et al., 2001; Takei et al., 1994). It may be that the expression of a genetically transmitted predisposition for brain abnormality is enhanced by environmental stressors such as maternal drug use during pregnancy, complications during birth, and childhood malnutrition (Sørenson et al., 2003). Neurodevelopmental factors may help explain why children of schizophrenic parents tend to show cognitive and intellectual problems associated with brain abnormalities (Ashe, Berry, & Boulton; 2001; Cannon et al., 1994; McGlashan & Hoffman, 2000; Neumann et al., 1995).

Psychological and Sociocultural Factors   Psychological factors are no longer considered as primary causes of schizophrenia (Bassett et al., 2001), but psychological processes and sociocultural influences can contribute to the appearance of schizophrenia and influence its course (Blackwood et al., 2001; Pitschel-Walz et al., 2001). These influences include maladaptive learning experiences, dysfunctional cognitive habits, and stressful family communication patterns. For example, schizophrenic individuals who live with relatives who are critical, unsupportive, or emotionally overinvolved are especially likely to relapse following improvement (Rosenfarb et al., 2000; Wearden et al., 2000). Family members' negative attitudes may be a source of stress that actually increases the chances that disruptive or odd behaviors will persist or worsen (Rosenfarb et al., 1995). In contrast, helping schizophrenia patients to develop cognitive stress-coping skills can improve their long-term adjustment (Bustillo et al., 2001; Velligan et al., 2000).

Vulnerability Theory   The causal theories of schizophrenia we have outlined are consistent with more general diathesis-stress explanations, which assume that stress may activate a person's predisposition for disorder (Fowles, 1992). In fact, the diathesis-stress concept forms the basis for the *vulnerability theory* of schizophrenia (Cornblatt & Erlenmeyer-Kimling, 1985; Zubin & Spring, 1977). This theory suggests that (1) vulnerability to schizophrenia is mainly biological; (2) different people have differing degrees of vulnerability; (3) vulnerability is influenced partly by genetic influences on development and partly by abnormalities that arise from environmental risk factors; and (4) psychological components, such as exposure to poor parenting, a high-stress environment, or inadequate coping skills, may help determine whether schizophrenia actually appears, and also influence the course of the disorder (Walker & Diforio, 1998; Wearden et al., 2000).

Many different blends of vulnerability and stress can lead to schizophrenia. People whose genetic characteristics or prenatal experiences leave them vulnerable to develop schizophrenia may be especially likely to do so if they are later exposed to learning experiences, family conflicts, or other stressors that trigger and maintain schizophrenic patterns of thought and action. Those same experiences and stressors would not be expected to lead to schizophrenia in people who are less vulnerable to developing the disorder.

SCHIZOPHRENIA	
Aspect	**Key Features**
Common Symptoms	
Disorders of thought	Disturbed *content,* including delusions; disorganization, including loose associations, neologisms, and word salad
Disorders of perception	Hallucinations or false perceptions; poorly focused attention
Disorders of emotion	Flat affect; inappropriate tears, laughter, or anger
Possible Causes	
Biological	Genetics; abnormalities in brain structure; abnormalities in dopamine systems; neurodevelopmental problems
Psychological and sociocultural	Learned maladaptive behavior; disturbed patterns of family communication

? *The _____ concept forms the basis of the vulnerability theory of schizophrenia.*

In other words, schizophrenia is a highly complex disorder—probably more than one disorder (Kirkpatrick et al., 2001; Tsuang, Stone, & Faraone, 2000)—whose origins appear to lie in numerous biological, psychological, and sociocultural domains, some of which are yet to be discovered (Kapur, 2003; Thaker & Carpenter, 2001). "In Review: Schizophrenia" summarizes what we know about this disorder.

Personality Disorders

▶ **Which personality disorder often leads to crime?**

Personality disorders are long-standing, inflexible ways of behaving that are not so much severe mental disorders as dysfunctional styles of living (Shea et al., 2002). These disorders affect all areas of functioning and, from childhood or adolescence on, create problems for those who display them and for others (Millon & Davis, 1996). Some psychologists view personality disorders as interpersonal strategies (Kiesler, 1996) or as extreme, rigid, and maladaptive expressions of personality traits (Widiger, 1997).

The ten personality disorders found on Axis II of *DSM-IV* are grouped into three clusters that share certain features (see Table 12.5). The *odd-eccentric* cluster includes paranoid, schizoid, and schizotypal personality disorders. People diagnosed as having *schizotypal personality disorder,* for example, display some of the peculiarities seen in schizophrenia but are not disturbed enough to be labeled as schizophrenic. The *anxious-fearful* cluster includes dependent, obsessive-compulsive, and avoidant personality disorders. The *avoidant personality disorder,* for example, is similar to social phobia in the sense that persons labeled with this disorder tend to be "loners" with a long-standing pattern of avoiding social situations and of being particularly sensitive to criticism or rejection. Finally, the *dramatic-erratic* cluster includes the histrionic, narcissistic, borderline, and antisocial personality disorders. The main characteristics of *narcissistic personality disorder,* for example, are an exaggerated sense of self-importance, extreme sensitivity to criticism, a constant need for attention, and a tendency to arrogantly overestimate personal abilities and achievements.

personality disorders Long-standing, inflexible ways of behaving that become styles of life that create problems, usually for others.

table 12.5

Personality Disorders

Here are brief descriptions of the ten personality disorders listed on Axis II of *DSM-IV*.

Type	Typical Features
Paranoid	Suspiciousness and distrust of others, all of whom are assumed to be hostile
Schizoid	Detachment from social relationships; restricted range of emotion
Schizotypal	Detachment from, and great discomfort in, social relationships; odd perceptions, thoughts, beliefs, and behaviors
Dependent	Helplessness; excessive need to be taken care of; submissive and clinging behavior; difficulty in making decisions
Obsessive-compulsive	Preoccupation with orderliness, perfection, and control
Avoidant	Inhibition in social situations; feelings of inadequacy; oversensitivity to criticism
Histrionic	Excessive emotionality and preoccupation with being the center of attention; emotional shallowness; overly dramatic behavior
Narcissistic	Exaggerated ideas of self-importance and achievements; preoccupation with fantasies of success; arrogance
Borderline	Lack of stability in interpersonal relationships, self-image, and emotion; impulsivity; angry outbursts; intense fear of abandonment; recurring suicidal gestures
Antisocial	Shameless disregard for, and violation of, other people's rights

99065636

A CLASSIC CASE OF ANTISOCIAL PERSONALITY DISORDER Alfred Jack Oakley meets women through personals ads, claiming to be a millionaire movie producer, pilot, and novelist. In reality, he is a penniless con artist who uses his smooth-talking charm to gain the women's trust so he can steal from them. In January 2000, on being convicted of stealing a Florida woman's Mercedes, Oakley complimented the prosecutor's skills and the jury's wisdom, and claimed remorse. The judge appeared to see through this ploy ("I don't believe there is a sincere word that ever comes out of your mouth"), but it was still effective enough to get Oakley probation instead of jail time!

Because of its threat to public welfare and safety, the most serious, costly, and intensively studied personality disorder is **antisocial personality disorder** (e.g., Scott, 2001). It is marked by a long-term pattern of irresponsible, impulsive, unscrupulous, and sometimes criminal behavior, beginning in childhood or early adolescence. In the nineteenth century, the pattern was called *moral insanity* because the people displaying it appear to have no morals or common decency. Later, people in this category were called *psychopaths* or *sociopaths*. The current "antisocial personality" label more accurately portrays them as troublesome, but not "insane" by the legal standards we discuss later. About 3 percent of men and about 1 percent of women in the United States fall into this diagnostic category (American Psychiatric Association, 1994, 2000).

At their least troublesome, these people are a nuisance. They are often charming, intelligent "fast talkers" who borrow money and fail to return it; they are arrogant, selfish manipulators who "con" people into doing things for them, usually by lying and taking advantage of the decency and trust of others. A hallmark of those displaying antisocial personality is a lack of anxiety, remorse, or guilt, whether they have wrecked a borrowed car or killed an innocent person (Gray et al., 2003; Hare, 1993). No method has yet been found for permanently altering the behavior of these people (Rice, 1997). Research suggests that the best hope for dealing with them is to identify antisocial personalities early, before the most treatment-resistant traits are fully developed (Crawford, Cohen, & Brooks, 2001; Lynam, 1996; Stoff, Breiling, & Maser, 1997).

There are numerous theories about the causes of antisocial personality. Some research suggests a genetic predisposition (Slutske et al., 2001), possibly in the form of abnormal brain development, impaired neurological functioning, or chronic underarousal of both the autonomic and central nervous systems (Dolan & Park, 2002; Patrick, Cuthbert, & Lang, 1994; Raine et al., 2000). This underarousal may render people less sensitive to punishment, and more likely to seek excitement, than is normally the case (Stoff, Breiling, & Maser, 1997). Broken homes, rejection by parents, poor discipline, lack of good parental models, lack of attachment to early caregivers, impulsivity, conflict-filled childhoods, and poverty have all been suggested as psychological and sociocultural factors contributing to the development of antisocial personality disorder (Lahey et al., 1995; Raine, Brennan, & Mednick, 1994; Tremblay et al., 1994). The biopsychosocial model suggests that antisocial personality disorder results when these psychosocial and environmental conditions combine with genetic predispositions to low arousal and the sensation seeking and impulsivity associated with it (Gray et al., 2003).

FOCUS ON RESEARCH

Exploring Links Between Child Abuse and Antisocial Personality Disorder

One of the most prominent environmental factors associated with the more violent forms of antisocial personality disorder is the experience of abuse in childhood (MacMillan et al., 2001). However, most of the studies that have found a relationship between childhood abuse and antisocial personality disorder were based on potentially biased reports (Monane, Leichter, & Lewis, 1984; Rosenbaum & Bennett, 1986). People with antisocial personalities—especially those with criminal records—are likely to make up stories of abuse in order to shift blame for their behavior onto others. Even if their reports were accurate, however, most of these studies lacked a control group of non-antisocial people from similar backgrounds. Because of this research design flaw, it is virtually impossible to separate the effects of reported child abuse from the effects of poverty or other factors that might also have contributed to the development of antisocial personality disorder.

■ What was the researcher's question?

Can childhood abuse cause antisocial personality disorder? To help answer this question and to correct some of the flaws in earlier studies, Cathy Widom (1989a) used a *prospective* research design, first finding cases of childhood abuse and then looking for the effects of that abuse on adult behavior.

■ How did the researcher answer the question?

Widom began by identifying 416 adults whose backgrounds included official records of their having been physically or sexually abused before the age of eleven. She then explored the stories of these people's lives, as told in police and school records, as well as in a two-hour diagnostic interview. To reduce experimenter bias and distorted reporting, Widom ensured that the interviewers remained "blind" to the purpose of the study and that the respondents were told only that the study's purpose was to talk to people who had grown up in an urban area of the midwestern United States in the late 1960s and early 1970s. Widom also selected a comparison group of 283 people who had no history of abuse, but who were similar to the abused sample in terms of age, gender, ethnicity, hospital of birth, schools attended, and area of residence. Her goal was to obtain a nonabused control group that had been exposed to approximately the same environmental risk factors and socioeconomic conditions as the abused children.

■ What did the researcher find?

First, Widom (1989a) tested the hypothesis that exposure to abuse in childhood is associated with criminality and/or violence in later life. She found that 26 percent of the abused youngsters went on to commit juvenile crimes, 29 percent were arrested as adults, and 11 percent committed violent crimes. These percentages were significantly higher than the figures for the nonabused group. The correlations between criminality and abuse were higher for males than for females, and higher for African Americans than for

antisocial personality disorder
A long-term, persistent pattern of impulsive, selfish, unscrupulous, even criminal behavior.

European Americans. And overall, victims of physical abuse were more likely to commit violent crimes as adults than were victims of sexual abuse.

Next, Widom tested the hypothesis that childhood abuse is associated with the development of antisocial personality disorder (Luntz & Widom, 1994). She found that the abused group did show a significantly higher rate of antisocial personality disorder (13.5 percent) than did the comparison group (7.1 percent). The apparent role of abuse in antisocial personality disorder was particularly pronounced in men, and it remained strong even when other factors—such as age, ethnicity, and socioeconomic status—were accounted for in the statistical analyses. One other factor—failure to graduate from high school—was also strongly associated with the appearance of antisocial personality, whether or not childhood abuse had occurred.

■ What do the results mean?

Widom's research supported earlier studies in finding an association between childhood abuse and criminality, violence, and antisocial personality disorder. Further, although her study did not permit a firm conclusion that abuse alone causes antisocial personality disorder, the data from its prospective design added strength to the argument that abuse may be an important causal factor (Widom, 2000). Finally, Widom's work offers yet another reason—as if more reasons were needed—why it is so important to prevent the physical and sexual abuse of children. The long-term consequences of such abuse can be tragic not only for its immediate victims but also for those victimized by the violence, criminal actions, and antisocial behavior perpetrated by some abused children as they grow up (Weiler & Widom, 1996).

■ What do we still need to know?

Widom's results suggest that one or more of the factors leading teenagers to drop out (or be thrown out) of high school might help create antisocial personality disorder even in children who were not abused. Some of her more recent work suggests, too, that exposure to poverty and other stressors can be as important as abuse in promoting antisocial personality disorder (Horwitz et al., 2001). More research is obviously needed to discover whether antisocial personality disorder stems from abuse itself, from one of the factors accompanying it, or from some specific combination of known and still-unknown risk factors. The importance of combined and interacting risk factors is suggested by the fact that abuse is often part of a larger pool of experiences such as exposure to deviant models, social rejection, poor supervision, and various stressful events. Until we understand how all these potentially causal pieces fit together, we will not fully understand the role played by childhood abuse in the chain of events leading to antisocial personality disorder.

We need to know more, too, about why such a small percentage of the abused children in Widom's sample displayed violence, criminal behavior, and antisocial personality disorder. These results raise the question of what genetic characteristics or environmental experiences serve to protect children from at least some of the devastating effects of abuse (Rind & Tromovitch, 1997; Rind, Tromovitch, & Bauserman, 1998). An understanding of what these protective elements are might go a long way toward the development of programs for the prevention of antisocial personality disorder.

A Sampling of Other Psychological Disorders

▶ How do children's disorders differ from adults' disorders?

The disorders described so far represent some of the most prevalent and socially disruptive psychological problems encountered in cultures around the world. Several others are mentioned in other chapters. In the chapter on consciousness, for example, we discuss insomnia, night terrors, and other sleep disorders; mental retardation is covered in the chapter on thought, language, and intelligence; sexual dysfunctions are mentioned in the chapter on motivation and emotion; and posttraumatic stress disorder is described in the chapter on health, stress, and coping. Here we consider two other significant psychological problems: disorders of childhood and substance-related disorders.

Psychological Disorders of Childhood

The physical, cognitive, emotional, and social changes seen in childhood—and the stress associated with them—can create or worsen psychological disorders in children. Stress can do the same in adults, but childhood disorders are not just miniature versions of adult psychopathology. Because children's development is still incomplete, and because their capacity to cope with stress is limited, children are often vulnerable to special types of disorders. The majority of childhood behavior problems can be placed in two broad categories: externalizing disorders and internalizing disorders (Achenbach, 1997; Nigg, 2000).

The *externalizing*, or *undercontrolled*, category includes behaviors that disturb people in the child's environment. Lack of control shows up as *conduct disorders* in from 1 to 10 percent of children and adolescents, mostly boys (American Psychiatric Association, 2000; Martin & Hoffman, 1990). Conduct disorders are characterized by a relatively stable pattern of aggression, disobedience, destructiveness, and other obnoxious behaviors (Kalb & Loeber, 2003; Lahey et al., 1995). Often these behaviors involve criminal activity, and they may signal the development of antisocial personality disorder (Loeber & Stouthamer-Loeber, 1998). A genetic predisposition toward conduct disorders is suggested by the fact that many such children have parents who display antisocial personality disorder. Children who are temperamentally inclined toward high activity levels are at greater risk for externalizing disorders (Mesman & Koot, 2000). There is no doubt, though, that parental and peer influences, as well as academic problems at school, also help to shape these children's antisocial behavior (Laird et al., 2001; Shaw et al., 2001; U.S. Surgeon General, 1999).

Another kind of externalizing problem, *attention deficit hyperactivity disorder (ADHD),* is seen in 3 to 7 percent of children, mainly boys. An ADHD diagnosis is given to children who, compared with other children their age, are impulsive, inattentive, or both (American Psychiatric Association, 2000; Nigg, 2001). Many of these children also have great difficulty sitting still or otherwise controlling their physical activity. Their impulsiveness and lack of self-control contribute to significant impairments in learning, and to an astonishing ability to annoy and exhaust those around them (Henker & Whalen, 1989). Genetic predisposition, brain damage, poisoning from lead or other household substances, low birth weight, and ineffective parenting have all been proposed as possible causes of ADHD (Clarke et al., 2002; Linnet et al., 2003; Mick et al., 2002; Sergeant, Geurts, & Oosterlaan, 2002; Spencer, 2002). Also uncertain is exactly what constitutes hyperactivity. Cultural standards about acceptable activity levels in children vary, so a "hyperactive" child in one culture might be considered merely "active" in another. In fact, when mental health professionals from four cultures used the same rating scale to judge the presence and severity of hyperactivity in a videotaped sample of children's behavior, the Chinese and Indonesians rated the children as significantly more hyperactive than did their U.S. and Japanese colleagues (Jacobson, 2002; Mann et al., 1992). Such findings remind us that sociocultural factors can be important determinants of what is acceptable, and thus what is abnormal, in various parts of the world.

The second broad category of child behavior problems involves *internalizing*, or *overcontrol*. Children in this category experience significant distress, especially depression and anxiety, and may be socially withdrawn. Those displaying *separation anxiety disorder,* for example, constantly worry that they will be lost, kidnapped, or injured or that some harm may come to a parent (usually the mother). The child clings desperately to the

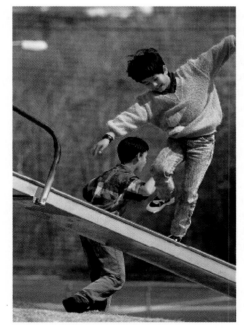

learn **by doing**

ACTIVE OR HYPERACTIVE? Normal behavior for children in one culture might be considered hyperactive in other cultures. Do people in the same culture disagree on this point? To find out, ask two or three friends to join you in observing a group of children at a playground, a schoolyard, a park, or some other public place. Ask your friends to privately identify which children they would label as "hyperactive," and then count how many of their choices agree with yours and with one another's.

parent and becomes upset or sick at the prospect of any separation. Refusal to go to school (sometimes called "school phobia") is often the result. Children who are temperamentally shy or withdrawn are at higher risk for internalizing disorders, but environmental factors such as peer rejection may also be involved (Mesman & Koot, 2000; Prinstein & La Greca, 2002).

A few childhood disorders, such as *pervasive developmental disorders,* do not fall into either the externalizing or internalizing category. Children diagnosed with these disorders show severe deficits in communication and impaired social relationships. They also often show repetitive, stereotyped behaviors and unusual preoccupations and interests (American Psychiatric Association, 2000; Filipek et al., 1999). The disorders in this group, also known as *autistic spectrum disorders* (Filipek et al., 1999; Rutter & Schopler, 1992; U.S. Surgeon General, 1999), share many of these core symptoms, although the severity of the symptoms may vary (Çeponien et al., 2003; Constantino & Todd, 2003). Estimates of the prevalence of autistic spectrum disorders range from 10 to 20 children per 10,000 births (Bryson & Smith, 1998; Filipek et al., 1999) to as high as 62 per 10,000 (Chakrabarti & Fombonne, 2001). About half of these children suffer *autistic disorder,* which can be the most severe disorder of the group. The earliest signs of autistic disorder usually occur within the first thirty months after birth, as these babies show little or no evidence of forming an attachment to their caregivers. Language development is seriously disrupted in most of these children; half of them never learn to speak at all. However, those who display "high functioning autism" or a less severe autistic spectrum disorder called *Asperger's disorder* are able to function adaptively and, in some cases, independently as adults (e.g., Grandin, 1996).

Possible biological roots of autistic disorder include genetic factors (Burac, 2001; Vastag, 2001) or neurodevelopmental abnormalities affecting language and communication (Courchesne et al., 2001; U.S. Surgeon General, 1999). The more specific causes of autistic disorder remain unknown, but it is likely that genetic influences, along with prenatal damage leading to structural brain abnormalities, are involved (Carper & Courchesne, 2000; Juul-Dam, Townsend, & Courchesne, 2001; Rodier, 2000; Szatmari et al., 1998; U.S. Surgeon General, 1999). Researchers today have rejected the once-popular hypothesis that the profound problems in autistic disorder are caused by cold and unresponsive parents.

Disorders of childhood differ from adult disorders not only because the patterns of behavior are distinct but also because their early onset disrupts development. To take one example, children whose separation anxiety causes spotty school attendance may not only fall behind academically but also may fail to form the relationships with other children that promote normal social development. Some children never make up for this deficit. They may drop out of school and risk a life of poverty, crime, and violence. Moreover, children depend on others to get help for their psychological problems, but all too often those problems may go unrecognized or untreated. For some, the long-term result may be adult forms of mental disorder.

Substance-Related Disorders

Childhood disorders, especially externalizing disorders, often lead to substance-related disorders in adolescence and adulthood. *DSM-IV* defines **substance-related disorders** as the use of psychoactive drugs for months or years in ways that harm the user or others. These disorders create major political, economic, social, and health problems worldwide. The substances involved most often are alcohol and other depressants (such as barbiturates), opiates (such as heroin), stimulants (such as cocaine or amphetamines), and hallucinogens (such as LSD).

One effect of using some substances (including alcohol, heroin, and amphetamines) is **addiction,** a physical need for the substance. *DSM-IV* calls addiction *physiological dependence.* Even when the use of a drug does not create physical addiction, some people may overuse, or *abuse,* it because the drug gives them temporary self-confidence, enjoyment,

substance-related disorders Problems involving the use of psychoactive drugs for months or years in ways that harm the user or others.

addiction Development of a physical need for a psychoactive drug.

469

or relief from tension. *DSM-IV* defines *substance abuse* as a pattern of use that causes serious social, legal, or interpersonal problems. In other words, people can become psychologically dependent on psychoactive drugs without becoming physiologically addicted to them. People who are psychologically dependent on a drug often display problems that are at least as serious as, and sometimes more difficult to treat than, those exhibited by people who are addicted. In the consciousness chapter, we describe a wide range of psychoactive drugs and their impact on the brain and behavior. Here, we focus on some of the problems associated with the use and abuse of alcohol, heroin, and cocaine.

Alcohol Use Disorders   About 7.4 percent of U.S. adults—about 14 million people—display *alcohol dependence* or *alcohol abuse,* a pattern of continuous or off-and-on drinking that may lead to addiction and almost always causes severe social, physical, and other problems (NIAAA, 2001). Males outnumber females in this category by a ratio of about three to one, although the problem is on the rise among women and among teenagers of both genders (Chassin, Pitts, & Prost, 2002; U.S. Surgeon General, 1999). Prolonged overuse of alcohol can result in life-threatening liver damage, reduced cognitive abilities, vitamin deficiencies that can lead to severe and permanent memory loss, and a host of other physical ailments (Hommer et al., 2001; Pfefferbaum et al., 2001). Alcohol dependence or abuse, commonly referred to as **alcoholism,** has been implicated in half of all the traffic fatalities, homicides, and suicides that occur each year (NIAAA, 2001). Alcoholism also figures prominently in rape and child abuse, as well as in elevated rates of hospitalization and absenteeism from work, resulting in total costs to society of over $180 billion each year (Harwood, Fountain, & Livermore, 1998; NIAAA, 2001; U.S. Department of Justice, 1998). It is estimated that about half of U.S. adults have a close relative who is or was an alcoholic, and that about 25 percent of children are exposed to adults who display alcohol abuse or dependence (NIAAA, 2001). Children growing up in families in which one or both parents abuse alcohol are at increased risk for developing a host of mental disorders, including substance-related disorders (Hofmann & Cerbone, 2002). And as described in the chapter on human development, children of mothers who abused alcohol during pregnancy may be born with fetal alcohol syndrome.

The biopsychosocial model suggests that alcohol abuse stems from a combination of genetic characteristics (including inherited aspects of temperament such as impulsivity and emotionality) and what people learn in their social and cultural environment (Kendler et al., 2003b; Petry, 2001; Sher et al., 1991; Wall et al., 2001). For example, the children of alcoholics are more likely than others to become alcoholics themselves; and if the children are identical twins, both are at increased risk for alcoholism, even when raised apart (Kendler et al., 1992; McGue, 1999; Slutske et al., 1998). It is still unclear just what might be inherited or which genes are involved. One possibility involves inherited abnormalities in the brain's neurotransmitter systems or in the body's metabolism of alcohol (Devor, 1994; Kranzler & Anton, 1994; Nurnberger et al., 2001). Male alcoholics do tend to be less sensitive than other people to the effects of alcohol—a factor that may contribute to greater consumption (Pollack, 1992; Schuckit, 1998). Recent progress in decoding the human genome has guided researchers to focus on a few specific chromosomes as the possible location of genes that predispose people to—or protect them from—the development of alcoholism (Foroud et al., 2000; NIAAA, 2000, 2001; Reich et al., 1998). However, the genetics of addiction is highly complex; there is probably not a single gene for alcoholism (Crabbe, 2002). As with other disorders, many genes interact with each other and with environmental events, including what people learn about drinking from others.

For example, youngsters typically learn to drink by watching others (especially their friends), and by developing expectations that alcohol will make them feel good and help them cope with stressors (Chassin, Pitts, & Prost , 2002; Koopmans & Boomsma, 1996). But alcohol use can become abuse, and often addiction, if drinking is a person's main

alcoholism   A pattern of continuous or intermittent drinking that may lead to addiction and almost always causes severe social, physical, and other problems.

coping strategy (NIAAA, 2001; see Table 12.6). The importance of learning is supported by evidence that alcoholism is more common among ethnic and cultural groups (such as the Irish and English) in which frequent drinking tends to be socially reinforced than among groups (such as Jews, Italians, and Chinese) in which all but moderate drinking tends to be discouraged (Gray & Nye, 2001; Wilson et al., 1996). Moreover, different forms of social support for drinking can result in different consumption patterns within a cultural group. For example, one study found significantly more drinking among Japanese men living in Japan (where social norms for males' drinking are most permissive) compared with Japanese men living in Hawaii or California, where excessive drinking is less strongly supported (Kitano et al., 1992).

Heroin and Cocaine Dependence   Like alcoholics, heroin and cocaine addicts suffer many serious health problems, as a result of both the drugs themselves and the poor eating and health habits related to use of those drugs. The risk of death from overdose, contaminated drugs, or AIDS (contracted through blood in shared needles), as well as from suicide, is also always present. Drug dependence tends to be more prevalent among males, especially young males (Warner et al., 1995).

Addiction to substances like heroin and cocaine is largely seen as a biological process brought about by the physical effects of the drugs (Phillips et al., 2003), but explaining why people first use them is more complicated. The causes of initial drug use are even less well established than the reasons for alcohol abuse. One line of theorizing suggests that there might be a genetic tendency toward behavioral compulsions that predisposes some people to abuse many kinds of drugs (Crabbe, 2002; NIAAA, 2000). One study supporting this idea found a link between alcoholism in biological parents and drug abuse in the sons they had given up for adoption (Cadoret et al., 1995). The same study also found a link between antisocial personality traits in biological parents and antisocial acts—including drug abuse—in the sons they had put up for adoption.

A number of psychological and environmental factors have been proposed as promoting initial drug use (Alessi et al., 2002; Brems & Namyniuk, 2002; Hoffman & Cerbone, 2002). These include seeing parental drug use, being abused in childhood, efforts to cope with stressors or to ease anxiety or depression, associating drug use with pleasant experiences, peer pressure, thrill seeking, and poor social adjustment

table 12.6

Social Drinking Versus Alcoholism

Social drinking differs markedly from alcoholism, but it is all too easy for people to drift from social to alcoholic drinking patterns. Alcoholism can include heavy drinking on a daily basis, on weekends only, or in isolated binges lasting weeks or months (NIAAA, 2001).

Social Drinkers	Alcoholics
Sip drinks.	Gulp drinks.
Usually drink in moderation and can control the amount consumed.	Drink increasing quantities (develop tolerance). Sometimes drink until blacking out. May not recall events that occur while drinking.
Usually drink to enhance the pleasure of social situations.	Drink for the chemical effect, often to relieve tension or face problems. Often drink alone, including in the morning to reduce hangover or to face the day.
Do not usually think about or talk about drinking in nondrinking situations.	Become preoccupied with getting the next drink, often sneaking drinks during working hours or at home.
Do not experience physical, social, or occupational problems caused by drinking.	Suffer physical disorders, damaged social relationships, and impaired capacity to work because of drinking.

(Dube et al., 2003; Putnam, 2003). Research has not yet established why continued drug use occurs in some people and not in others, but again, it is likely that a biological predisposition sets the stage on which specific psychological processes and stressors play out their roles in specific social and cultural contexts (Kendler et al., 2003b).

Mental Illness and the Law

▶ Can insanity protect criminals from punishment?

Have you wondered why the word *insanity* did not appear in our definition of *mental disorder* or in the *DSM-IV* categories we have described? The reason is that *insanity* is a legal term, not a psychiatric diagnosis (Cassel & Bernstein, 2001). For example, in 1984 John Hinckley Jr. was found "not guilty by reason of insanity" for his attempted assassination of President Ronald Reagan. This verdict reflected U.S. laws and rules that protect people with severe psychological disorders when they are accused of crimes.

This protection takes two forms. First, under certain conditions, people designated as mentally ill may be protected from prosecution. If, at the time of their trial, individuals accused of a crime are unable to understand the proceedings and charges against them or to help in their own defense, they are declared *mentally incompetent* to stand trial. Second, the mentally ill may be protected from punishment. In most U.S. states, defendants may be judged *not guilty by reason of insanity* if, at the time of the crime, mental illness prevented them from (1) understanding what they were doing, (2) knowing that what they were doing was wrong, and (3) resisting the impulse to do wrong. The first two of these criteria relate to a person's ability to think clearly and are called the *M'Naughton rule,* for the defendant in the 1843 case that established it. The third criterion, which relates to the defendant's emotional state during a crime, is known as the *irresistible impulse test.* All three criteria were combined in a rule proposed by the American Law Institute in 1962—a rule that is now followed in about half of the U.S. states.

After the Hinckley verdict, the U.S. Congress passed the Insanity Defense Reform Act, which eliminated the irresistible impulse criterion from the definition of insanity in federal cases. In both federal and state courts, however, the responsibility falls on judges and juries to weigh evidence and testimony and to decide whether or not a defendant should be held responsible for criminal acts. Defendants who are judged not guilty by reason of insanity and who still display a psychological disorder are usually required to receive treatment, typically through commitment to a hospital, until judged to be cured or no longer dangerous. Twelve U.S. states have laws allowing jurors to find defendants "guilty but mentally ill." These defendants are to receive treatment while in prison, though they seldom do (Cassel & Bernstein, 2001).

Critics of insanity rules complain that these rules allow criminals to "get away with murder." Actually, such outcomes are rare. Insanity pleas occur in only 1 out of every 200 felony cases in the United States, and they are successful in only 2 of every 1,000 attempts (Silver, Cirincione, & Steadman, 1994). Even the few defendants found not guilty by reason of insanity are usually hospitalized for two to nine times as long as they would have spent in prison had they been convicted (Silver, 1995; Steadman, 1993). John Hinckley Jr. has been in Saint Elizabeth's hospital in Washington, D.C., since 1982, and in spite of his annual efforts to be released, he is unlikely to get out anytime soon.

In summary, society is constantly seeking the proper balance between protecting the rights of defendants and protecting society from dangerous criminals. In doing so, the sociocultural values that shape our views about what is abnormal also influence judgments about the extent to which abnormality should relieve people of responsibility for criminal behavior.

applying psychology

ASSESSMENT OF MENTAL COMPETENCE Andrea Yates admitted to drowning all five of her children in the bathtub of her Houston, Texas, home in 2001. She had twice tried to kill herself in previous years, and she was reportedly depressed at the time of the murders. Accordingly, she pleaded not guilty by reason of insanity. The first legal step in deciding her fate was to confine her in a mental institution for assessment of her mental competency to stand trial. Following testimony of psychologists who examined her, she was found competent, and ultimately sentenced to life in prison.

Linkages

As noted in the introductory chapter, all of psychology's subfields are related to one another. Our discussion of how mental disorders might be learned illustrates just one way in which the topic of this chapter, psychological disorders, is linked to the subfield of learning, which is discussed in the chapter by that name. The Linkages diagram shows ties to two other subfields as well, and there are many more ties throughout the book. Looking for linkages among subfields will help you see how they all fit together and help you better appreciate the big picture that is psychology.

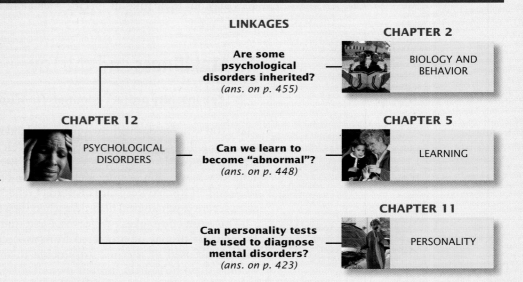

LINKAGES

Are some psychological disorders inherited?
(ans. on p. 455)

CHAPTER 2
BIOLOGY AND BEHAVIOR

CHAPTER 12
PSYCHOLOGICAL DISORDERS

Can we learn to become "abnormal"?
(ans. on p. 448)

CHAPTER 5
LEARNING

Can personality tests be used to diagnose mental disorders?
(ans. on p. 423)

CHAPTER 11
PERSONALITY

Summary

Psychopathology involves patterns of thinking, feeling, and behaving that are maladaptive, disruptive, or distressing—either for the person affected or for others.

DEFINING PSYCHOLOGICAL DISORDERS

▶ **How do psychologists define abnormal behavior?**

Some psychological disorders show considerable similarity across cultures, but the definition of *abnormality* is largely determined by social and cultural factors. The criteria for judging abnormality include statistical infrequency (a comparison with what most people do), norm violations, and personal suffering. Each of these criteria is flawed to some extent. The practical approach, which considers the content, context, and consequences of behavior, emphasizes the question of whether people show **impaired functioning** in fulfilling the roles appropriate for particular people in particular settings, cultures, and historical eras.

EXPLAINING PSYCHOLOGICAL DISORDERS

▶ **What causes abnormality?**

At various times and places, abnormal behavior has been attributed to the action of gods or the devil. Mental health professionals in Western cultures rely on a **biopsychosocial model,** which attributes mental disorders to a combination of biological, psychological, and sociocultural factors. Biological factors, such as brain chemistry, are emphasized in the medical or **neurobiological model** of disorder. The **psychological model** focuses on processes such as inner turmoil, maladaptive learning experiences, or blocked actualization. The **sociocultural model** helps to explain disorder by highlighting gender, ethnicity, and other social and cultural factors that form the context of abnormality. **Diathesis-stress** explana-

tions suggest that biological, psychological, and sociocultural characteristics create predispositions for disorder that are translated into symptoms in the face of sufficient amounts of stress.

CLASSIFYING PSYCHOLOGICAL DISORDERS

▶ **How many psychological disorders have been identified?**

The dominant system for classifying abnormal behavior in North America is the fourth edition of the *Diagnostic and Statistical Manual of Mental Disorders (DSM-IV* and *DSM-IV-TR)* of the American Psychiatric Association. It includes more than 300 specific categories of mental disorder that can be described using five dimensions, or axes. Diagnosis helps to identify the features, causes, and most effective methods of treating various psychological disorders. Research on the reliability and validity of *DSM-IV* shows that it is a useful, but not perfect, classification system.

ANXIETY DISORDERS

▶ **What is a phobia?**

Long-standing and disruptive patterns of anxiety characterize **anxiety disorders.** The most prevalent type of anxiety disorder is **phobia,** a category that includes **specific phobias, social phobias,** and **agoraphobia.** Other anxiety disorders are **generalized anxiety disorder,** which involves nonspecific anxiety; **panic disorder,** which brings unpredictable attacks of intense anxiety; and **obsessive-compulsive disorder (OCD),** which is characterized by uncontrollable repetitive thoughts and ritualistic actions.

The most influential explanations of anxiety disorders suggest that they may develop as a result of a combination of a biological predisposition for strong anxiety reactions and the impact of fear-enhancing thought patterns and learned anxiety responses. Many anxiety disorders appear to develop in accordance with the principles of classical and operant conditioning, as well as with those of observational learning. People may be biologically prepared to learn fear of certain objects and situations.

SOMATOFORM DISORDERS

▶ **Can mental disorder cause blindness?**

Somatoform disorders include *conversion disorder,* which involves physical problems, such as blindness, deafness, and paralysis, that have no apparent physical cause; *hypochondriasis,* an unjustified concern over being or becoming ill; *somatization disorder,* in which the person complains of numerous unconfirmed physical complaints; and *pain disorder,* in which pain is felt in the absence of a physical cause.

DISSOCIATIVE DISORDERS

▶ **What disorders create sudden memory loss?**

Dissociative disorders involve such rare conditions as *dissociative fugue* and *dissociative amnesia,* both of which involve sudden and severe memory loss, and *dissociative identity disorder (DID),* or multiple personality disorder, in which a person appears to develop two or more identities. There is considerable controversy about the origins of dissociative identity disorder.

MOOD DISORDERS

▶ **How common is depression?**

Mood disorders, also known as *affective disorders,* are quite common and involve extreme moods that may be inconsistent with events. *Major depressive disorder* is marked by feelings of inadequacy, worthlessness, and guilt; in extreme cases, *delusions* may also occur. Also seen is *dysthymic disorder,* which includes similar but less severe symptoms persisting for a long period. Suicide is often related to these disorders. Alternating periods of depression and *mania* characterize *bipolar disorder,* which is also known as manic depression. *Cyclothymic disorder,* an alternating pattern of less extreme mood swings, is more common.

Mood disorders have been attributed to biological causes such as genetic inheritance, disruptions in neurotransmitter and endocrine systems, and irregularities in biological rhythms. Significant stressors, and maladaptive patterns of thinking about them, are among the psychological causes proposed. A predisposition toward some of these disorders may be inherited, although their appearance is probably determined by a diathesis-stress process.

SCHIZOPHRENIA

▶ **Is schizophrenia the same as "split personality"?**

Schizophrenia is perhaps the most severe and puzzling disorder of all. Among its symptoms are problems in thinking, perception (often including *hallucinations*), attention, emotion, movement, motivation, and daily functioning. Positive symptoms of schizophrenia include the presence of such features as hallucinations or disordered speech; negative symptoms can include withdrawal, immobility, and the absence of affect.

Genetic influences, neurotransmitter problems, abnormalities in brain structure and functioning, and neurodevelopmental abnormalities are biological factors implicated in schizophrenia. Psychological explanations have pointed to maladaptive learning experiences and disturbed family interactions. Diathesis-stress explanations, including vulnerability theory, provide a promising framework for research into the multiple causes of schizophrenia.

PERSONALITY DISORDERS

▶ **Which personality disorder often leads to crime?**

Personality disorders are long-term patterns of maladaptive behavior that, although not always associated with personal discomfort, may be disturbing to others. These include odd-eccentric types (paranoid, schizoid, and schizotypal personality disorders), anxious-fearful types (dependent, obsessive-compulsive, and avoidant personality disorders), and dramatic-erratic types (histrionic, narcissistic, borderline, and antisocial personality disorders). *Antisocial personality disorder* is marked by impulsive, irresponsible, unscrupulous behavior patterns that often begin in childhood. Childhood abuse appears to be related to the appearance of this potentially dangerous personality disorder.

A SAMPLING OF OTHER PSYCHOLOGICAL DISORDERS

▶ **How do children's disorders differ from adults' disorders?**

Childhood psychological disorders can be categorized as externalizing conditions (such as conduct disorders or attention deficit hyperactivity disorder) and internalizing disorders, in which children show overcontrol, experiencing internal distress (as in separation anxiety disorder). The most severe childhood psychological disorder is autistic disorder, in which the child may show no interest in, or attachment to, others.

Substance-related disorders involving alcohol and other drugs affect millions of people. *Addiction* to, and psychological dependence on, these substances contributes to disastrous personal and social problems, including physical illnesses, accidents, and crime. Genetic factors probably create a predisposition for *alcoholism,* but learning, cultural traditions, and other nonbiological processes are also important. Stress reduction, imitation, thrill seeking, and social maladjustment have been proposed as important factors in drug addiction, along with genetic predisposition; but the exact causes of initial use of these drugs are unknown.

MENTAL ILLNESS AND THE LAW

▶ **Can insanity protect criminals from punishment?**

"Insanity" is a legal term, not a psychiatric diagnosis. Current rules protect people accused of crimes from prosecution or punishment if they are declared mentally incompetent at the time of their trial or if they were legally insane at the time of their crime. Defendants judged not guilty by reason of insanity and who still display a psychological disorder are usually required to receive treatment until judged to be cured or no longer dangerous. Those found guilty but mentally ill are to receive treatment in prison.

Learn by Doing

Put It in Writing

Think about something you have seen someone do recently that you considered truly abnormal. Now write a page describing what happened, and the specific rules or criteria—such as statistical infrequency, norm violation, personal suffering, or impaired functioning—that you used in deciding that this person's behavior qualifies as abnormal. Include a statement about whether you think this person should be treated for his or her behavior problem. Mention also why you think this behavior would be considered abnormal by other people in your culture, and whether you think people in other cultures would agree.

Personal Learning Activity

To what extent do people agree on what is abnormal? To find out, ask at least twenty friends, family members, teachers, classmates in other courses, casual acquaintances, and maybe even some strangers, to read your description of the behavior you diagnosed as abnormal in the Put It in Writing exercise. (Show them only the description, not your comments.) Ask these people to tell you if they think the behavior is normal, merely odd, or seriously abnormal, and if they think the person is in need of treatment. Analyze the results in terms of how many of these people agreed with your diagnosis, and with one another. Did you notice any trends in their responses based on age, gender, educational status, or cultural background? What do your results say about how easy or difficult it is to precisely define abnormality? *For additional projects, see the Personal Learning Activities in the corresponding chapter of the study guide that accompanies this text.*

Step into Action

Courses

Abnormal Psychology
Child Psychopathology
Psychology and the Law

Movies

A Beautiful Mind (schizophrenia)
Boys Don't Cry (gender identity disorder)
The Fisher King (psychosis, depression, substance abuse, avoidant personality disorder)
Mercury Rising (autism)
The Hours (depression and suicidality)
The Silence of the Lambs; The Talented Mr. Ripley; In Cold Blood; Natural Born Killers (antisocial personality disorder)
Ordinary People (depression)
Copycat (agoraphobia)
Blue Sky (borderline personality disorder, substance abuse)
One Flew over the Cuckoo's Nest (life in a state mental hospital of the 1960s)
The Three Faces of Eve; Sybil (dissociative identity disorder)
Vertigo (anxiety disorders)
As Good as It Gets (obsessive-compulsive disorder)
Days of Wine and Roses; Leaving Las Vegas (alcoholism)
Trainspotting (heroin addiction)
Man on the Moon (defining abnormality)
Anatomy of a Murder (use of the insanity defense in a murder case)

Books

William Styron, *Darkness Visible* (Vintage, 1992) (depression and suicidality)
Sally Bedell Smith, *Diana: In Search of Herself—Portrait of a Troubled Princess* (Signet, 2000) (eating disorders, depression, borderline personality disorder)
Vaslav Nijinsky, *The Diary of Vaslav Nijinsky* (Farrar,

Straus and Giroux, 1999) (insight into schizophrenia from one of Eugen Bleuler's most famous patients, the Russian ballet dancer)
Jerald J. Kriesman and Hal Straus, *I Hate You—Don't Leave Me: Understanding the Borderline Personality* (Avon, 1991) (descriptions and explanations of borderline behaviors, focusing on conflicted relationships)
Sylvia Plath, *The Bell Jar* (Harper & Row, 1971) (major depression, suicidality)
Lewis B. Pullen, *Fortunate Son* (Bantam, 1996) (posttraumatic stress disorder)
Kay Redfield Jamison, *An Unquiet Mind* (Random House, 1997) (a psychiatrist writes about her own depression)
Patty Duke, *A Brilliant Madness* (Bantam, 1993) (bipolar disorder)
Judith Rapoport, *The Boy Who Couldn't Stop Washing* (New American Library, 1997) (obsessive-compulsive disorder)
Karlene K. Hale, *Being There: Profiles of Mental Illness* (Dilligaf, 1997) (case studies of mental disorder)
Clark R. Clipson and Jocelyn M. Steer, *Case Studies in Abnormal Psychology* (Houghton Mifflin, 1998) (more case studies)
Joan Acocella, *Creating Hysteria: Women and Multiple Personality Disorder* (Jossey-Bass, 1999) (a description of the influence of culture and other social forces in shaping dissociative identity disorder)
Robert Spitzer et al., *DSM-IV Casebook: A Learning Companion to the Diagnostic and Statistical Manual of Mental Disorders* (American Psychiatric Press, 1994) (a casebook illustrating the disorders listed in *DSM-IV*)
Meyer Glantz and Christine Hartel (Eds.), *Drug Abuse: Origins and Interventions* (American Psychological Association, 2000) (information that challenges various myths about drug abuse)

The Web

The World Wide Web is a good source of additional information about the science of psychology, provided you use it carefully and think critically about the information you find. The web site that accompanies this text offers many resources relevant to this chapter. These resources include interactive NetLab exercises; Thinking Critically and Eval- uating Research exercises; ACE chapter quizzes; recom- mended web links; and articles on current events, books, and movies. At http://college.hmco.com, select *Psychology* and then this textbook.

Review of Key Terms

Can you define each of the key terms in the chapter? Check your definitions against those on the pages listed in parentheses below or in the Glossary/Index at the end of the text.

addiction *(p. 468)*

agoraphobia *(p. 446)*

alcoholism *(p. 469)*

antisocial personality disorder *(p. 464)*

anxiety disorder *(p. 445)*

biopsychosocial model *(p. 436)*

bipolar disorder *(p. 455)*

conversion disorder *(p. 449)*

cyclothymic disorder *(p. 455)*

delusions *(p. 453)*

diathesis-stress *(p. 439)*

dissociative amnesia *(p. 451)*

dissociative disorders *(p. 451)*

dissociative fugue *(p. 451)*

dissociative identity disorder (DID) *(p. 451)*

dysthymic disorder *(p. 453)*

generalized anxiety disorder *(p. 446)*

hallucinations *(p. 460)*

hypochondriasis *(p. 450)*

impaired functioning *(p. 435)*

major depressive disorder *(p. 453)*

mania *(p. 455)*

mood disorder *(p. 453)*

neurobiological model *(p. 437)*

obsessive-compulsive disorder (OCD) *(p. 446)*

pain disorder *(p. 450)*

panic disorder *(p. 446)*

personality disorders *(p. 463)*

phobia *(p. 445)*

psychological model *(p. 437)*

psychopathology *(p. 433)*

schizophrenia *(p. 459)*

social phobias *(p. 445)*

sociocultural model *(p. 438)*

somatization disorder *(p. 450)*

somatoform disorders *(p. 449)*

specific phobias *(p. 445)*

substance-related disorders *(p. 468)*

Multiple-Choice Self-Test

Select the best answer for each of the questions below. Then check your responses against the Answer Key at the end of the text.

1. According to the statistics on psychopathology, _____ percent of people in the United States experience a mental disorder in their lifetime.

   a. less than 5%
   b. approximately 25%
   c. almost 50%
   d. over 75%

2. Babette, a successful opera singer, believes that aliens could snatch her at any time if she isn't wearing her lucky charm. She is constantly worried and insists that the stage be rimmed with foil to ward off evil spirits. According to which criterion of abnormality would Babette **not** be considered abnormal?

   a. statistical
   b. norm violation
   c. practical approach
   d. personal suffering

3. Hippocrates believed that psychological disorders result from imbalances of the four humors: blood, phlegm, black bile, and yellow bile. This suggests that Hippocrates attributed psychological disorders to _____ factors.

   a. biological
   b. psychological
   c. social
   d. biopsychosocial

4. Roberta and Rhonda are identical twins who inherited identical predispositions for depression. Roberta has lived an easy life and has not developed any depressive symptoms. Rhonda, who has been divorced and lost several jobs over the years, has been diagnosed with major depressive disorder. The difference between these twins is most consistent with the _____ approach to abnormality.

   a. neurobiological
   b. psychological
   c. sociocultural
   d. diathesis-stress

5. Dr. Kramer is evaluating a patient brought in for psychiatric treatment. In his report he indicates that his global assessment of the patient's functioning is about 30 on a 100-point scale. Dr. Kramer is using _____ to evaluate the patient.

   a. the M'Naughton rule
   b. norm violation criteria
   c. insanity criteria
   d. DSM-IV

6. Kat dropped out of school because just the thought of leaving her apartment makes her feel nauseated, anxious, and faint. She can't even go out to the mailbox without suffering anxiety. Kat most likely would be diagnosed with

   a. agoraphobia.
   b. simple phobia.
   c. generalized anxiety disorder.
   d. social phobia.

7. Terraba had a difficult time driving to work. Every time she went over a bump she had to drive back around to make sure that she had not run over anything. This occurred ten or twelve times each day, so Terraba was always late for everything. Terraba appears to be suffering from

   a. specific phobia.
   b. panic attacks.
   c. obsessive-compulsive disorder
   d. generalized anxiety disorder.

8. Conversion disorder is characterized by

   a. impairment of movement or sensory ability with no apparent physical cause.
   b. severe pain with no apparent physical cause.
   c. fear of becoming seriously ill.
   d. frequent, vague complaints of physical symptoms.

9. Tomas has been suffering severe back pain for several weeks, but extensive medical tests reveal no physical problem. Tomas appears to be displaying

    a. pain disorder.
    b. hypochondriasis.
    c. paranoid schizophrenia.
    d. somatization disorder.

10. Einer displays many different personalities. One is a young girl named Lili. Another is a five- year old boy. Each personality is unaware of the others. Einer is displaying symptoms of

    a. dissociative fugue.
    b. dissociative identity disorder.
    c. obsessive-compulsive disorder.
    d. schizophrenia.

11. Over the past three months, Barb has been feeling very sad; she has been sleeping as much as fifteen hours a day and has gained thirty pounds. Debbie, too, feels very low, but she can barely sleep and has lost both her appetite and fifteen pounds. Both Barb and Debbie have symptoms of

    a. obsessive-compulsive disorder.
    b. major depressive disorder.
    c. bipolar disorder.
    d. hypochondriasis.

12. Suicide is closely tied to depression. Studies of suicide in the United States have found that

    a. people who talk about suicide typically do not commit suicide.
    b. males over the age of forty-five who are living alone are the most likely to commit suicide.
    c. suicide rates do not vary much across ethnic groups or between genders.
    d. depressed women almost never commit suicide.

13. Carlisle has been very depressed. He can't face his responsibilities and often spends days at a time in bed. A psychologist who adopts the social-cognitive approach would be most likely to see this depression as caused by Carlisle's

    a. attributional style.
    b. brain chemicals.
    c. unconscious conflicts.
    d. blocked actualization.

14. As you sit down next to a disheveled person on a bus, the person says, "Ohms vibrate orange and dishwrings obvious dictionary." The person continues to talk in this manner, so based on your reading of this chapter, you decide that this person is displaying symptoms of

    a. anxiety disorder.
    b. dissociative identity disorder.
    c. schizophrenia.
    d. somatoform disorder.

15. Juan has been diagnosed with schizophrenia. He says he is certain that all the students sitting around him during a test are cheating by reading his thoughts. Juan is displaying a symptom known as thought

    a. blocking.
    b. insertion.
    c. withdrawal.
    d. broadcasting.

16. Forty-year-old Richard believes that he was ordered by God to save the world. He is suspicious of other people because he thinks they want to prevent him from fulfilling his mission. He is unable to keep a job because he is angry and argumentative most of the time. Richard would most likely be diagnosed as displaying

    a. mood disorder.
    b. dissociative identity disorder
    c. paranoid schizophrenia.
    d. catatonic schizophrenia.

17. Al is charming and intelligent, but he has always been irresponsible, impulsive, and unscrupulous. None of his girlfriends knows he is dating other women. He borrows money from friends and doesn't pay it back. He doesn't care about anyone else, including his family. Al would probably be diagnosed as displaying _____ personality disorder.

    a. antisocial
    b. narcissistic
    c. passive-aggressive
    d. inadequate

18. Cathy Widom's research study, discussed in the Focus on Research section of this chapter, found that there was a relationship between antisocial personality disorder and

    a. narcissistic personality disorder.
    b. schizophrenia.
    c. high intelligence.
    d. being abused as a child.

19. Angelo drinks alcohol until he passes out. He is unable to hold a job or take care of himself. Angelo would most likely be diagnosed with

    a. a substance-related disorder.
    b. undercontrolled disorder.
    c. schizophrenia.
    d. a personality disorder.

20. Aaron is an infant who shows no signs of attachment to his parents. He dislikes being held and doesn't smile or laugh. Aaron's symptoms are most consistent with

    a. infantile schizophrenia.
    b. autistic disorder.
    c. antisocial personality disorder.
    d. an externalizing disorder of childhood.

13

Treatment of Psychological Disorders

In old Hollywood movies, such as *The Dark Past* or *The Three Faces of Eve*, troubled people

find instant cures when a psychotherapist helps them discover an unconscious memory that holds the key to their psychological disorder. Somewhat more realistic versions of psychotherapy have been presented in contemporary movies and television shows, such as *Good Will Hunting* and *The Sopranos*. Unfortunately, even these portrayals do not convey what psychotherapy is really like, and even the best of them tell only part of the story of how psychological disorders can be treated. In this chapter we describe a wide range of treatment options, including methods based on psychodynamic, humanistic, behavioral, and biological theories of psychological disorders. We also consider research on the effectiveness of treatment and methods for preventing disorders.

Reading this chapter will help you to answer the following questions:

▶ **What features do all treatment techniques have in common?**

▶ **How did Freud get started as a therapist?**

▶ **Why won't some therapists give advice?**

▶ **Can we learn to conquer fears?**

▶ **How does group therapy differ from individual therapy?**

▶ **How effective is psychotherapy?**

▶ **Is electric shock still used to treat disorders?**

▶ **How can we prevent psychological disorders?**

I n the chapter on psychological disorders, we described José, an electronics technician who had to take medical leave from his job after experiencing panic attacks. After four months of diagnostic testing turned up no physical problems, José's physician suggested that he see a psychologist. José resisted at first, insisting that his condition was not "just in his head," but he eventually began psychological treatment. Within a few months, his panic attacks had ceased, and José had returned to all his old activities. After the psychologist helped him to reconsider his workload, José decided to take early retirement from his job in order to pursue more satisfying work at his home-based computer business.

José's case is by no means unique. During any given year in the United States alone, about 15 percent of adults and about 21 percent of children and adolescents are receiving some form of treatment for a psychological disorder, including substance abuse problems (U.S. Surgeon General, 1999). The economic impact of mental disorders—in treatment costs, disability payments, and lost productivity—is staggering, reaching $150 billion per year in the United States alone. Fortunately, the cost of treating these disorders is more than made up for by the savings it creates; compared with untreated patients, those who receive treatment typically need fewer mental and physical health services later on (American Psychological Association, 2002; Chiles, Lambert, & Hatch, 1999; Clay, 2002b).

In this chapter, we describe a variety of treatment methods, most of which are based on the theories of stress and coping, personality, and psychological disorders reviewed in the chapters on those topics. First, we examine the basic features common to all forms of treatment. Then we discuss approaches that rely on **psychotherapy,** the treatment of psychological disorders through psychological methods, such as talking about problems and exploring new ways of thinking and acting. Next, we consider biological approaches to treatment, which depend mainly on drugs and other physical therapies. (Many clients receive psychoactive drugs in addition to psychotherapy during the course of psychological treatment.)

Basic Features of Treatment

▶ **What features do all treatment techniques have in common?**

All treatments for psychological disorders share certain basic features—not only with one another but also with efforts to help the physically ill (Frank, 1978). These common features include a *client* or *patient,* a *therapist* or helper who is accepted as capable of helping the client, and a *special relationship* between the client and therapist. In addition, all forms of treatment are based on some *theory* about the causes of the client's problems (Dumont & Corsini, 2000). The presumed causes can range from magic spells to infections and everything in between (Frank & Frank, 1991). These theories form the basis of *treatment procedures* for dealing with the client's problems. Traditional healers combat supernatural forces with ceremonies and prayers, medical doctors treat chemical imbalances with drugs, and psychologists focus on altering psychological processes through psychotherapy.

People receiving treatment can be classified into two general categories: inpatients and outpatients. *Inpatients* are treated in a hospital or other residential institution. They are hospitalized because their impairments are severe enough to create a threat to their

MEDIEVAL TREATMENT METHODS Methods used to treat psychological disorders have always been related to the presumed causes of those disorders. In medieval times, when demons were widely blamed for abnormal behavior, physician-priests tried to make the victim's body inhospitable to evil spirits. Here, we see a depiction of such spirits leaving an afflicted person's head as it is placed in an oven.

psychotherapy The treatment of psychological disorders through psychological methods, such as analyzing problems, talking about possible solutions, and encouraging more adaptive ways of thinking and acting.

own well-being or that of others. Depending on their level of functioning, inpatients may stay in the hospital for a few days or weeks or—in rare cases—several years. Their treatment almost always includes psychoactive drugs. *Outpatients* receive psychotherapy and/or psychoactive drugs while living in the community.

Those who provide psychological treatment are a diverse group. **Psychiatrists** are medical doctors who complete specialty training in the treatment of mental disorders. Like other physicians, they are authorized to prescribe drugs for the relief of psychological problems. **Psychologists** who offer psychotherapy have usually completed a doctoral degree in clinical or counseling psychology, often followed by additional specialized training. Except in New Mexico, psychologists in the United States are not authorized to prescribe drugs, though this privilege may eventually be granted to specially trained psychologists elsewhere (Dittmann, 2003; Heiby, 2002; Sammons, Paige, & Levant, 2003). Other therapy providers include *clinical social workers, marriage and family therapists,* and *licensed professional counselors,* all of whom typically hold a master's degree from a graduate program in their respective fields. They provide treatment in many settings, including hospitals, clinics, and private practice. *Psychiatric nurses, substance abuse counselors,* members of the clergy working as *pastoral counselors,* and a host of *paraprofessionals* also provide therapy services, often as part of a hospital or outpatient treatment team (Nietzel et al., 2003; U.S. Surgeon General, 1999).

The general goal of treatment providers is to help troubled people change their thinking, feelings, and behavior in ways that relieve discomfort; promote happiness; and improve functioning as parents, students, employees, and the like. The particular methods used in each case—whether some form of psychotherapy, a drug treatment, or both—depend on the problems, preferences, and financial circumstances of the client; the time available for treatment; and the therapist's theoretical leanings, methodological preferences, and professional qualifications. Later, we will discuss drugs and other biological treatments; for now, however, let's consider several forms of psychotherapy, each of which is based on psychodynamic, humanistic, or behavioral explanations of mental disorder.

Although we describe different approaches in separate sections, keep in mind that the majority of mental health professionals see themselves as *eclectic* therapists. In other words, they might lean toward one set of treatment methods, but when working with particular clients or particular problems, they may employ other methods as well (Hayes & Harris, 2000; Jensen, Bergin, & Greaves, 1990; Slife & Reber, 2001).

Psychodynamic Psychotherapy

► **How did Freud get started as a therapist?**

The field of formal psychotherapy began in the late 1800s when Sigmund Freud established the psychodynamic approach to personality and mental disorders (see the chapter on personality). Freud's method of treatment, **psychoanalysis,** was aimed at understanding unconscious conflicts and how they affect clients. Almost all forms of psychotherapy reflect some of Freud's ideas, including (1) his one-to-one method of treating people; (2) his systematic search for relationships between an individual's life history and current problems; (3) his emphasis on thoughts, emotions, and motivations in treatment; and (4) his focus on the client-therapist relationship. We will describe Freud's original methods first and then consider some more recent treatments that are rooted in his psychodynamic approach.

Classical Psychoanalysis

Classical psychoanalysis developed mainly out of Freud's medical practice. He was puzzled by patients who suffered from "hysterical" ailments—blindness, paralysis, or other symptoms that had no physical cause. (As noted in the chapter on psychological disorders, these are now called *conversion disorders.*) Freud tried to cure these patients with

psychiatrists Medical doctors who have completed special training in the treatment of mental disorders.

psychologists In the area of treatment, therapists with advanced training in clinical or counseling psychology.

psychoanalysis A method of psychotherapy that seeks to help clients gain insight into, and work through, unconscious thoughts and emotions presumed to cause psychological problems.

FREUD'S CONSULTING ROOM During psychoanalytic sessions, Freud's patients lay on this couch, free-associating or describing dreams and events in their lives, while he sat in the chair behind them. According to Freud, even apparently trivial or accidental behavior may hold important messages from the unconscious. Forgetting a dream or missing a therapy appointment might reflect a client's unconscious resistance to treatment. Even accidents may be meaningful. The waiter who spills hot soup on an older male customer might be seen as acting out unconscious aggressive impulses against a father figure.

hypnotic suggestions, but he found this method to be only partially and temporarily successful. Later, he asked hypnotized patients to recall events that might have caused their symptoms. Eventually, however, he stopped using hypnosis and merely had patients lie on a couch and report whatever thoughts, memories, or images came to mind. Freud called this process *free association*.

Freud's "talking cure" produced surprising results. He was struck by how many patients reported childhood memories of sexual abuse, usually by a parent or other close relative (Esterson, 2001). Either child abuse was rampant in Vienna or his patients' reports were distorted by psychological factors. Freud ultimately concluded that his patients' memories of childhood seduction probably reflected fantasies—a conclusion that, as described in the personality chapter, has become quite controversial. Psychoanalysis came to focus on exploring unconscious impulses and fantasies. His patients' hysterical symptoms, Freud concluded, developed out of conflicts involving those impulses and fantasies.

Classical psychoanalytic treatment involves the use of free association, dream analysis, and analysis of the client's reactions to the therapist (called *transference*) to help the client gain insight into problems. Clients are encouraged, first, to recognize unconscious thoughts and emotions. Then they are encouraged to discover, or *work through*, the many ways in which those unconscious elements continue to motivate maladaptive thinking and behavior in everyday life. The treatment may require as many as three to five sessions per week, usually over several years. Generally, the psychoanalyst remains compassionate but neutral as the client slowly develops insight into how past conflicts have shaped current problems (Gabbard, 2000).

Contemporary Variations on Psychoanalysis

Classical psychoanalysis is still practiced, but not as much as it was several decades ago (Gabbard, 2000; Horgan, 1996). The decline is due in part to the growth of several alternative forms of treatment, including variations on classical psychoanalysis. Many of these variations were developed by neo-Freudian theorists. As noted in the personality chapter, these theorists placed less emphasis than Freud did on biologically based drives coming from the id and the unconscious. They focused instead on the role played by social relationships in clients' problems and on how the power of the ego can be harnessed to solve them. Psychotherapists who adopt various neo-Freudian treatment methods tend to take a much more active role than classical analysts do—in particular, by directing the client's attention to evidence of certain conflicts in social relationships.

applying psychology **A PLAY THERAPY SESSION** Modern versions of psychoanalytic treatment include fantasy play and other techniques that make the approach more useful with children. A child's behavior and comments while playing with puppets representing family members, for example, are seen as a form of free association that the therapist hopes will reveal important unconscious material, such as fear of abandonment (Booth & Lindaman, 2000).

Many of these methods have come to be known as *short-term dynamic psychotherapy* because they aim to provide benefits in far less time than is required in classical psycho-analysis (Davanloo, 1999; Levenson, 2003). In one short-term psychodynamic treatment called *supportive-expressive therapy*, the therapist helps the client recognize a "core conflict" that appears repeatedly across a variety of relationships, including the therapy relationship (Luborsky, 1997). In another popular contemporary psychodynamic approach, called *object relations therapy* (Scharff & Scharff, 1998; St. Clair, 1999), the powerful need for human contact and support takes center stage. Object relations therapists believe that most of the problems that bring clients to treatment ultimately stem from their relationships with others, especially their earliest caregivers. (The term *object* usually refers to a person who has emotional significance for the client.) Accordingly, these therapists work to create a nurturing relationship in which the client's problems can be understood and corrected (Kahn & Rachman, 2000; Lieberman & Pawl, 1988; Wallerstein, 2002). This relationship provides a "second chance" for the client to receive the support that might have been absent in infancy and to counteract some of the consequences of maladaptive early attachment patterns. For example, object relations therapists take pains to show that they will not abandon their clients, as might have happened to these people in the past. *Interpersonal therapy,* too, is rooted partly in neo-Freudian theory (Sullivan, 1954), but it focuses on helping clients explore and overcome the problematic effects of interpersonal events that occur *after* early childhood—events such as the loss of a loved one, conflicts with a parent or a spouse, job loss, or social isolation (Weissman, Markowitz, & Klerman, 2000).

With their focus on interpersonal relationships rather than instincts, their emphasis on clients' potential for self-directed problem solving, and their reassurance and emotional supportiveness, contemporary variants on classical psychoanalysis have helped the psychodynamic approach to retain its influence among mental health professionals (Westen & Gabbard, 1999).

Humanistic Psychotherapy

▶ **Why won't some therapists give advice?**

Whereas some therapists revised Freud's ideas, others developed radical new therapies based on a humanistic approach to personality (see the chapter on personality). *Humanistic psychologists,* sometimes called *phenomenologists,* emphasize the ways in which people interpret the events in their lives. They view people as capable of consciously controlling their own actions and taking responsibility for their decisions. Many humanistic therapists believe that human behavior is motivated not by sexual or aggressive impulses but by an innate drive toward growth that is guided from moment to moment by the way people perceive their world. Disordered behavior, they say, reflects a blockage in natural growth brought on by distorted perceptions or lack of awareness about feelings. Accordingly, humanistic (or phenomenological) therapists operate on the following assumptions:

1. Treatment is an encounter between equals, not a "cure" given by an expert. It is a way to help clients restart their natural growth and to feel and behave in a more genuine way.

2. Clients will improve on their own, given the right conditions. These ideal conditions promote clients' awareness, acceptance, and expression of their feelings and perceptions.

3. Ideal conditions in therapy can best be established through a therapeutic relationship in which clients are made to feel accepted and supported as human beings, no matter how problematic or undesirable their behavior may be. It is the client's experience of this relationship that brings beneficial changes. (Notice that this assumption is shared with object relations therapy.)

4. Clients must remain responsible for choosing how they will think and behave.

client-centered therapy   A type of therapy in which the client decides what to talk about and when, without direction, judgment, or interpretation from the therapist. Also called *person-centered therapy.*

unconditional positive regard   In client-centered therapy, the therapist's attitude that expresses caring for, and acceptance of, the client as a valued person.

empathy   In client-centered therapy, the therapist's attempt to appreciate how the world looks from the client's point of view.

reflection   Restating or paraphrasing what the client has said.

Of the many humanistically oriented treatments in use today, the most influential are client-centered therapy, developed by Carl Rogers, and Gestalt therapy, developed by Frederick and Laura Perls (Cain & Seeman, 2002).

Client-Centered Therapy

Carl Rogers was trained in psychodynamic therapy methods during the 1930s, but he soon began to question their value. He especially disliked being a detached expert whose task is to "figure out" the client. Eventually convinced that a less formal approach would be more effective, Rogers allowed his clients to decide what to talk about and when, without direction, judgment, or interpretation by the therapist. This approach, now called **client-centered**—or **person-centered—therapy,** relies on the creation of a relationship that reflects three intertwined therapist attitudes: unconditional positive regard, empathy, and congruence.

Unconditional Positive Regard   The attitude Rogers called **unconditional positive regard** consists of treating the client as a valued person, no matter what. This attitude is communicated through the therapist's willingness to listen, without interrupting, and to accept what is said without evaluating it. The therapist doesn't have to approve of everything the client says, but must accept it as reflecting that client's view of the world. Because Rogerian therapists trust clients to solve their own problems, they rarely give advice. Doing so, said Rogers, would send clients an unspoken message that they are incompetent, making them less confident and more dependent on help.

Empathy   In addition, the client-centered therapist tries to see the world as the client sees it, and not to look at clients from the outside. In other words, the therapist tries to develop **empathy,** an emotional understanding of what the client might be thinking and feeling. Client-centered therapists convey empathy by showing that they are actively listening to the client. Like other skillful interviewers, they make eye contact with the client, nod in recognition as the client speaks, and give other signs of careful attention. They also use **reflection,** a paraphrased summary of the client's words that emphasizes the feelings and meanings that appear to go along with them. Reflection confirms what the client has said while also expressing the therapist's interest and helping the client to be aware of the thoughts and feelings expressed. Here is an example:

> *Client:* This has been such a bad day. I've felt ready to cry any minute, and I'm not even sure what's wrong!
>
> *Therapist:* You really do feel so bad. The tears just seem to well up inside, and I wonder if it is a little scary to not even know why you feel this way.

applying psychology   **A CLIENT-CENTERED THERAPY GROUP** Carl Rogers (shown here in shirtsleeves) believed that people in successful client-centered therapy become more self-confident, more aware of their feelings, more accepting of themselves, more comfortable and genuine with other people, more reliant on self-evaluation than on the judgments of others, and more effective and relaxed.

Notice that in rephrasing the client's statements, the therapist reflected back not only the obvious feelings of sadness but also the fear in the client's voice. Most clients respond to empathic reflection by giving more details about their feelings. In this example, the client went on to say, "It is scary, because I don't like to feel in the dark about myself. I have always prided myself on being in control."

Empathic listening tends to be so effective in promoting self-understanding and awareness that it is used across a wide range of therapies (Corsini & Wedding, 2001). Even beyond the realm of therapy, people who are thought of as easy to talk to are usually "good listeners" who reflect back the important messages they hear from others.

Congruence   Rogerian therapists also try to convey **congruence** (sometimes called *genuineness*) by acting in ways that are consistent with their feelings during therapy. For example, if confused by what a client has said, they would say so rather than trying to pretend that they always understand everything. When the therapist's unconditional positive regard and empathy are genuine, the client is able to see that relationships can be built on openness and honesty. Ideally, this experience will help the client become more congruent in other relationships.

Gestalt Therapy

Another form of humanistic treatment was developed by Frederick S. (Fritz) Perls, along with his wife, Laura Perls. A European psychoanalyst, Frederick Perls was greatly influenced by Gestalt psychology. (As noted in the chapter on sensation and perception, Gestalt psychologists emphasized the idea that people actively organize their perceptions of the world.) As a result, he believed that (1) people create their own versions of reality and (2) people's natural psychological growth continues only as long as they perceive, remain aware of, and act on their true feelings. Growth stops and symptoms of mental disorder appear, said Perls, when people are not aware of all aspects of themselves (Perls, 1969; Perls, Hefferline, & Goodman, 1951).

Like client-centered therapy, **Gestalt therapy** seeks to create conditions in which clients can become more unified, self-aware, and self-accepting, and thus ready to grow again. However, Gestalt therapists use more direct and dramatic methods than do Rogerians. Often working with groups, Gestalt therapists prod clients to become aware of feelings and impulses that they have disowned and to discard feelings, ideas, and values that are not really their own. For example, the therapist or other group members might point out inconsistencies between what clients say and how they behave. Gestalt therapists pay particular attention to clients' gestures and other kinds of "body language" that appear to conflict with what the clients are saying (Kepner, 2001). The therapist may also ask clients to engage in imaginary dialogues with other people, with parts of their own personalities, and even with objects. Like a shy person who can be socially outgoing only while at a costume party, clients often find that these dialogues help to get them in touch with, and express, their feelings (Paivio & Greenberg, 1995).

Behavior Therapy

▶ **Can we learn to conquer fears?**

Behavior therapists emphasize a different kind of self-awareness: They try to help clients view psychological problems as *learned behaviors* that can be changed without first searching for hidden meanings or unconscious causes (Miltenberger, 2001). For example, suppose you have a panic attack every time you leave home and find relief only when you return. Making excuses when friends invite you out temporarily eases your anxiety but does nothing to solve the problem. Could you reduce your fear without looking for its "underlying meaning"? Behavior therapy would offer just such an alternative by first

congruence   In client-centered therapy, a consistency between the way therapists feel and the way they act toward the client.

Gestalt therapy   A form of treatment that seeks to create conditions in which clients can become more unified, more self-aware, and more self-accepting.

behavior therapy   Treatments that use classical conditioning principles to change behavior.

behavior modification   Treatments that use operant conditioning methods to change behavior.

cognitive-behavior therapy   Behavioral treatment methods that help clients change the way they think, as well as the way they behave.

systematic desensitization   A behavioral method for treating anxiety in which clients visualize a graduated series of anxiety-provoking stimuli while maintaining a state of relaxation.

helping you to understand the learning principles that maintain your fear and then helping you to learn new responses in feared situations.

These goals are based on the behavioral approach to psychology in general and, in particular, on the social-cognitive approach to personality and disorder. As described in the personality chapter, social-cognitive theorists see learning as the basis of normal personality, and of most behavior disorders. According to this perspective, disordered behavior and thinking are examples of the maladaptive thoughts and actions that the client has learned. So a fear of leaving home (called *agoraphobia*) would be seen by behavior therapists as stemming from classically conditioned associations between being away from home and having panic attacks. The problem is partly maintained, they say, through operant conditioning: Staying home, and making excuses for doing so, is rewarded by reduced anxiety. Therapists who adopt a behavioral approach argue that if problems can be created through learning, they can also be eliminated through learning. Even if the learning that led to phobias and other problems began in childhood, behavior therapists seek to solve those problems by creating beneficial new experiences based on the principles discussed in the chapter on learning.

Behavioral approaches to treatment have their roots in the work of John B. Watson, Ivan Pavlov, and others who studied the learned nature of fear in the 1920s, as well as in B. F. Skinner's research on the impact of reward and punishment on behavior. In the late 1950s and early 1960s, researchers began using classical and operant conditioning principles to alter disordered human behavior (Thorpe & Olson, 1997). By 1970, behavioral treatment had become a popular alternative to psychodynamic and humanistic methods. The most notable features of behavioral treatment include the following:

1. Development of a productive therapist-client relationship. As in other therapies, this relationship enhances clients' confidence that change is possible and makes it easier for them to speak openly and to cooperate in, and benefit from, treatment (Cahill, Carrigan, & Evans, 1998; Wilson, 1995).

2. A careful listing of the behaviors and thoughts to be changed. This assessment and the establishment of specific treatment goals sometimes replace the formal diagnosis used in some other therapy approaches. So instead of treating "depression" or "obsessive-compulsive disorder," behavior therapists work to change the specific thoughts, behaviors, and emotional reactions that cause people to receive these diagnostic labels.

3. A therapist who acts as a kind of teacher/assistant by providing learning-based treatments, giving "homework" assignments, and helping the client make specific plans for dealing with problems.

4. Continuous monitoring and evaluation of treatment, along with constant adjustments to any procedures that do not seem to be effective.

Behavioral treatment can take many forms. By tradition, those that rely mainly on classical conditioning principles are referred to as **behavior therapy.** Those that focus on operant conditioning methods are usually called **behavior modification.** And behavioral treatment that focuses on changing thoughts as well as overt behaviors is called **cognitive-behavior therapy**.

LINKAGES
Can people learn their way out of a disorder?
(a link to Learning)

Techniques for Modifying Behavior

Some of the most important and commonly used behavioral treatment techniques are systematic desensitization, modeling, positive reinforcement, extinction, aversive conditioning, and punishment.

Systematic Desensitization   Joseph Wolpe (1958) developed one of the first behavioral methods for helping clients overcome phobias and other forms of anxiety. Called **systematic desensitization,** it is a treatment in which the client visualizes a series of

table 13.1

A Desensitization Hierarchy

Desensitization hierarchies are lists of increasingly fear-provoking situations that clients visualize while using relaxation methods to remain calm. Here are a few items from the beginning and the end of a hierarchy that was used to help a client overcome fear of flying.

1. You are reading a newspaper and notice an ad for an airline.
2. You are watching a television program that shows a group of people boarding a plane.
3. Your boss tells you that you need to take a business trip by air.
4. You are in your bedroom packing your suitcase for your trip.
.
.
.
12. Your plane begins to move as you hear the flight attendant say, "Be sure your seat belt is securely fastened."
13. You look at the runway as the plane is readied for takeoff.
14. You look out the window as the plane rolls down the runway.
15. You look out the window as the plane leaves the ground.

anxiety-provoking stimuli while remaining relaxed. Wolpe believed that this process gradually weakens the learned association between anxiety and the feared object until the fear disappears.

Wolpe first helped his clients learn to relax, often using *progressive relaxation training* (described in the chapter on health, stress, and coping) to prevent anxiety. Then, while relaxing, clients would be asked to imagine an item from a *desensitization hierarchy,* a list of increasingly fear-provoking situations (see Table 13.1). The client would imagine each item in the hierarchy, one at a time, moving to a more difficult item only after learning to imagine the previous one without distress. Wolpe found that once clients can calmly imagine being in feared situations, they are better able to deal with them in reality later on.

Desensitization appears especially effective if it slowly and carefully presents clients with real, rather than imagined, hierarchy items (Chambless, 1990; McGlynn et al., 1999). This *in vivo,* or "real life," desensitization was once difficult to arrange or control, especially in cases involving fear of flying, heights, or highway driving, for example. Recently, however, a technique known as *virtual reality graded exposure* has made it possible for clients to "experience" vivid and precisely graduated versions of feared situations without actually being exposed to them. In one study, clients who feared heights wore a head-mounted virtual reality helmet that gave the impression of standing on bridges of gradually increasing heights, on outdoor balconies at higher and higher floors, and in a glass elevator as it slowly rose forty-nine stories (Rothbaum et al., 1995). The same technology has been used successfully in the treatment of many other anxiety disorders, ranging from fear of spiders and flying to posttraumatic stress disorder (Choi et al., 2001; Gershon et al., 2002; Glantz, Rizzo, & Graap, 2003; Robbins, 2000; Rothbaum et al., 1999, 2000, 2002).

Modeling	Therapists often teach clients desirable behaviors by demonstrating those behaviors. In **modeling** treatments, the client learns important skills by watching other people perform desired behaviors. For example, modeling can teach fearful clients how to respond fearlessly and confidently. In one case, a therapist first showed a spider-phobic client how to calmly kill spiders with a fly swatter and then assigned her to practice this skill at home with rubber spiders (MacDonald & Bernstein, 1974). The combination of fearless demonstrations and then first-hand practice is called *participant modeling;* it is one of the most powerful treatments for fear (e.g., Bandura, Blanchard, & Ritter, 1969; Faust, Olson, & Rodriguez, 1991).

modeling	A method of therapy in which desirable behaviors are demonstrated as a way of teaching them to clients.

assertiveness training	A set of methods for helping clients learn to express their feelings and stand up for their rights in social situations.

positive reinforcement	Presenting a positive reinforcer (reward) after a desired response.

token economy	A system for improving the behavior of severely disturbed or mentally retarded clients in institutions by rewarding desirable behaviors with tokens that can be exchanged for various rewards.

applying psychology   **VIRTUAL DESENSITIZA-TION**   A client who fears heights wears a virtual reality display that allows him to "experience" what he would see as a glass elevator gradually rises higher and higher. After learning to tolerate these realistic images without anxiety, clients are better able to fearlessly face the situations they once avoided.

Modeling is also a major part of assertiveness training and social skills training, which help clients learn how to deal with people more comfortably and effectively. The goals of social skills training range from helping social-phobic college students make conversation on dates to rebuilding mental patients' ability to interact normally with people outside the hospital (McQuaid et al., 2000; Spence, Donovan, & Brechman-Toussaint, 2000; Trower, 1995). In **assertiveness training,** the therapist helps clients learn to express their feelings and stand up for their rights in social situations (Alberti & Emmons, 1986; Ballou, 1995). Assertiveness training is often done in groups and involves both modeling and role playing of specific situations. For example, group assertiveness training helped wheelchair-bound adults and learning-disabled students more comfortably handle the socially awkward situations in which they sometimes find themselves (Gleuckauf & Quittner, 1992; Weston & Went, 1999).

Positive Reinforcement   Behavior therapists also use **positive reinforcement** to alter problematic behaviors and to teach new skills in cases ranging from childhood tantrums and juvenile delinquency to schizophrenia and self-starvation. Employing operant conditioning principles, they set up *contingencies,* or rules, that specify the behaviors to be strengthened through reinforcement. In one study, children with autistic disorder, who typically speak very little, were given grapes, popcorn, or other items they liked in return for saying "please," "thank you," and "you're welcome" while exchanging crayons and blocks with a therapist. After the therapist modeled the desired behavior by saying the appropriate words at the appropriate times, the children began to say these words on their own. Their use of language also began to appear in other situations, and as shown in Figure 13.1, the new skills were still evident six months later (Matson et al., 1990).

For severely retarded or disturbed clients in institutions, behavior therapists sometimes establish a **token economy,** which is a system for reinforcing desirable behaviors with poker chips or other tokens that can be exchanged later for snacks, access to television, or other desired rewards (Ayllon, 1999; Ayllon & Azrin, 1968; Paul & Lentz, 1977). The goal is to shape behavior patterns that will persist outside the institution (Moore et al., 2001; Paul, 2000; Paul, Stuve, & Cross, 1997).

figure 13.1

Positive Reinforcement for an Autistic Child

applying psychology   During each pretreatment baseline period, the child rarely said "please," "thank you," or "you're welcome," but these statements began to occur once they were modeled, then reinforced. Did modeling and reinforcement actually cause the change? Probably, because each type of response did not start to increase until the therapist began demonstrating and reinforcing it.

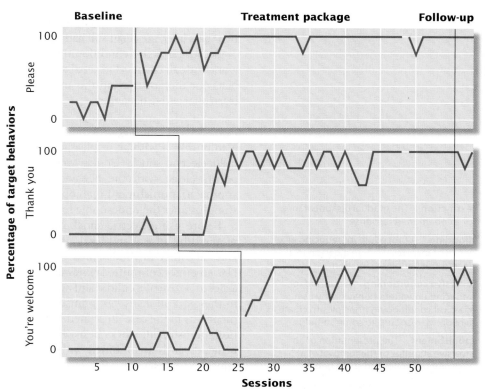

Source: Matson et al. (1990).

applying psychology

TREATING FEAR THROUGH FLOODING Flooding is designed to extinguish anxiety by allowing it to occur without the harmful consequences the person dreads. This man's fear of flying is obvious here, on takeoff, but is likely to diminish during and after uneventful flight. Like other behavioral treatments, flooding is based on the idea that phobias and other psychological disorders are learned and can thus be "unlearned." Some therapists prefer more gradual exposure methods similar to those of in vivo desensitization, which start with situations that are lower on the client's fear hierarchy (Back et al., 2001; Fava et al., 2001; Fritzler, Hecker, & Losee, 1997).

extinction The gradual disappearance of a conditioned response.

flooding A procedure for reducing anxiety that involves keeping a person in a feared, but harmless, situation.

aversive conditioning A method for reducing unwanted behaviors by using classical conditioning principles to create a negative response to some stimulus.

punishment The presentation of an aversive stimulus or the removal of a pleasant one following some behavior.

Extinction   Just as reinforcing desirable behaviors can make them more likely to occur, failing to reinforce undesirable behaviors can make them less likely to occur, a process known as **extinction.** Treatment methods that use extinction change behavior rather slowly, but offer a valuable way of reducing inappropriate behavior in children and in retarded or seriously disturbed adults. For example, a client who gets attention by disrupting a classroom, damaging property, or violating hospital rules might be placed in a quiet, boring "time out" room for a few minutes to eliminate reinforcement for misbehavior (e.g., Kee, Hill, & Weist, 1999; Reitman & Drabman, 1999).

Extinction is also the basis of a fear-reduction treatment called **flooding,** which puts clients into the very situation they fear the most. The client is flooded with fear at first, but after an extended period of exposure to the conditioned fear stimulus (a frog, say) without experiencing pain, injury, or any other dreaded result, the association between the feared stimulus and the fear response gradually weakens, and the conditioned fear response is extinguished (Basoglu, Livanou, & Salcioglu, 2003; Harris & Goetsch, 1990; Öst et al., 2001). In one study, twenty clients who feared needles were exposed for two hours to the sight and feel of needles, including mild finger pricks, harmless injections, and blood samplings (Öst, Hellström, & Kåver, 1992). Afterward, all but one client were able to have a blood sample drawn without experiencing significant anxiety.

Aversive Conditioning   Some unwanted behaviors, such as eating junk food, can become so habitual and rewarding that they must be made less attractive if a client is to have any chance of giving them up in favor of a more desirable alternative. Methods for lessening the appeal of certain stimuli are known as **aversive conditioning,** because they employ classical conditioning principles to associate physical or psychological discomfort with stimuli or actions the client wishes to avoid (e.g., Clapham & Abramson, 1985).

One form of aversive conditioning, called *covert sensitization,* operates in a way that is the reverse of systematic desensitization. The client first visualizes the stimulus or situation that is to be made less attractive and is then exposed to frightening or disgusting stimuli. For example, a man who had been repeatedly arrested for making obscene phone calls was asked to imagine making such a call. As he did so, the therapist presented vivid descriptions of things the client feared the most: snakes, vomiting, and choking. He was also instructed to imagine his mother walking in on him during an obscene call. After a month of covert sensitization, the thought of making obscene calls no longer created sexual arousal, and even two years later, the client still had not made any (Moergen, Merkel, & Brown, 1990).

Because aversive conditioning is unpleasant and uncomfortable, because it may not work with all clients (Flor et al., 2002), and because its effects are often temporary, most behavior therapists avoid this method or use it only long enough to allow the client to learn alternative behaviors.

Punishment   Sometimes the only way to eliminate a dangerous or disruptive behavior is to punish it with an unpleasant, but harmless, stimulus, such as a shouted "No!" or a mild electric shock. Unlike aversive conditioning, in which the unpleasant stimulus occurs along with the behavior that is to be eliminated (a classical conditioning approach), **punishment** is an operant conditioning technique; it presents the unpleasant stimulus *after* the undesirable response occurs.

Before using electric shock or other forms of punishment, behavior therapists are required by ethical and legal guidelines to ask themselves several important questions: Have all other methods failed? Would the client's life be in danger without treatment? Has an ethics committee reviewed and approved the procedures? Has the adult client or a close relative of a child client agreed to the treatment? (Kazdin, 1994). When the answer to these questions is yes, punishment can be an effective, sometimes life-saving, treatment—as in the case illustrated in Figure 5.12 in the chapter on learning. As with extinction, punishment works best when it is used just long enough to eliminate undesirable behavior and is combined with other behavioral methods designed to reward more appropriate behavior.

ALBERT ELLIS Rational-emotive behavior therapy (REBT) focuses on altering the self-defeating thoughts that Ellis believes underlie people's behavior disorders. Ellis argues, for example, that students do not get upset because they fail a test but because they have learned to believe that failure is a disaster that indicates they are worthless. Many of Ellis's ideas have been incorporated into various forms of cognitive-behavior therapy.

rational-emotive behavior therapy (REBT) A treatment that involves identifying illogical, self-defeating thoughts that clients have learned, then helping clients replace these maladaptive thoughts with more realistic and beneficial ones.

Cognitive-Behavior Therapy

Like psychodynamic and humanistic therapists, most behavior therapists recognize that depression, anxiety, and many other behavior disorders can stem from how clients think about themselves and the world. And like other therapists, most behavior therapists try to change clients' troublesome ways of thinking, not just their overt behavior. Unlike other therapists, however, behavior therapists rely on learning principles to help clients change the way they think. Their methods are known collectively as *cognitive-behavior therapy* (Dobson, 2001; Goldfried et al., 1997; McMullin, 2000; Sperry, 1999). For example, some clients already know how to stand up for themselves at work or in social situations, but they have not learned to recognize the habitual thoughts (such as "I shouldn't make a fuss") that get in the way of self-expression and help to create anxiety and depression. Cognitive-behavior therapists help clients learn to identify these cognitive obstacles, and then encourage them to try new ways of thinking that promote more desirable behavior and less distress (Meichenbaum, 1995).

Rational-Emotive Behavior Therapy One prominent form of cognitive-behavior therapy is **rational-emotive behavior therapy (REBT),** which was developed by Albert Ellis (1962, 1993, 1995). REBT aims first at identifying self-defeating thoughts, such as "I must be loved or approved by everyone" or "I must always be competent, adequate, and achieving to be worthwhile." After the client learns to recognize thoughts like these and to see how they can cause problems, the therapist uses suggestions, encouragement, and logic to help the client replace such thoughts with more realistic and beneficial ones. The client is then given "homework" assignments to try out these new ways of thinking in everyday situations. Here is part of an REBT session with a woman who suffered from panic attacks. She has just said that it would be "terrible" if she had an attack in a restaurant and that people "should be able to handle themselves!"

Therapist: . . . *The reality is that . . . "shoulds" and "musts" are the rules that other people hand down to us, and we grow up accepting them as if they are the absolute truth, which they most assuredly aren't.*

Client: *You mean it is perfectly okay to, you know, pass out in a restaurant?*

Therapist: *Sure!*

Client: *But . . . I know I wouldn't like it to happen.*

Therapist: *I can certainly understand that. It would be unpleasant, awkward, inconvenient. But it is illogical to think that it would be terrible, or . . . that it somehow bears on your worth as a person.*

Client: *What do you mean?*

Therapist: *Well, suppose one of your friends calls you up and invites you back to that restaurant. If you start telling yourself, "I might panic and pass out and people might make fun of me and that would be terrible," . . . you might find you are dreading going to the restaurant, and you probably won't enjoy the meal very much.*

Client: *Well, that is what usually happens.*

Therapist: *But it doesn't have to be that way. . . . The way you feel, your reaction . . . depends on what you choose to believe or think, or say to yourself.* (Masters et al., 1987)

Cognitive-behavior therapists use many techniques related to REBT to help clients learn to think in more adaptive ways. Techniques aimed at replacing upsetting thoughts with alternative thinking patterns were originally described by behaviorists as *cognitive restructuring* (Lazarus, 1971). They help clients plan calming thoughts to use during exams, tense conversations, and other anxiety-provoking situations. These thoughts may include "OK, stay calm, you can handle this. Just focus on the task, and don't worry about being perfect." Sometimes, these techniques are expanded to include *stress inoculation training,* in which clients imagine being in a stressful situation and then practice newly learned cognitive skills to remain calm (Meichenbaum, 1995).

table 13.2

Some Examples of Negative Thinking

learn **by** **doing** Here are just a few examples of the kinds of thoughts that cognitive-behavior therapists see as underlying anxiety, depression, and other behavior problems. After reading this list, try writing an alternative thought that clients could use to replace each of these ingrained cognitive habits. Then jot down a "homework assignment" that you would recommend to help clients challenge each maladaptive statement, and thus develop new ways of thinking about themselves.

"I shouldn't draw attention to myself."

"I will never be any good at this."

"It would be so awful if I don't know the answer."

"Everyone is smarter than I am."

"Nobody likes me."

"I should be able to do this job perfectly."

"What if I panic?"

"I'll never be happy."

"I should have accomplished more by this point in my life."

Beck's Cognitive Therapy　Many behavior therapists seek a different kind of cognitive restructuring using Aaron Beck's **cognitive therapy** (Beck, 1976, 1995; Beck & Beck, 1995). Beck's treatment approach is based on the idea that certain mental disorders—especially those involving depression and anxiety—can often be traced to errors in logic (e.g., "If I fail my driver's test the first time, I will never pass it") and false beliefs (e.g., "Everyone ignores me"). Beck says that over time, these learned *cognitive distortions* occur so quickly and automatically that the client never stops to consider that they might not be true.

Cognitive therapy is an organized problem-solving approach in which the therapist first helps clients learn to identify the errors in logic, false beliefs, and other cognitive distortions that precede anxiety, depression, and other psychological problems (see Table 13.2). Then, much as in the five-step critical thinking system illustrated throughout this book, these thoughts and beliefs are considered as hypotheses to be tested, not as "facts" to be uncritically accepted (Hatcher, Brown, & Gariglietti, 2001). In other words, the therapist and client become a team of "investigators" as they plan ways to test beliefs such as "I'm no good around the house." For example, they might agree on tasks that the client will attempt as "homework"—such as cleaning out the basement, getting advice on hanging a picture, or just cutting the grass. Success at accomplishing even one of these tasks provides concrete evidence to challenge a false belief that has supported depression, thus helping to reduce it (Beck et al., 1992).

As described in the chapter on psychological disorders, however, depression and anxiety may not be due entirely to specific thoughts or beliefs about specific situations. Sometimes they stem from a more general cognitive style that leads people to expect that the worst will always happen to them and to assume that negative events occur because they are completely and permanently incompetent and worthless (Peterson, 1995; Peterson & Seligman, 1984). Accordingly, cognitive-behavior therapists also help depressed clients to develop more optimistic ways of thinking and to reduce their tendency to blame themselves for negative outcomes (Persons, Davidson, & Tompkins, 2001). In some cases, cognitive restructuring is combined with practice at using logical thinking, anxiety management techniques, and skill training—all designed to help clients experience success and develop confidence in situations where they had previously expected to fail (Beck & Beck, 1995).

Group, Family, and Couples Therapy

▶ **How does group therapy differ from individual therapy?**

The one-to-one methods of psychodynamic, humanistic, and behavioral treatment we have described are often adapted for use with groups of clients or family units (Petrocelli, 2002; Rosen, Stukenbert, & Saeks, 2001; Thorngren & Kleist, 2002).

cognitive therapy　An organized problem-solving approach in which the therapist actively collaborates with clients to help them notice how certain negative thoughts precede anxiety and depression.

group therapy　Psychotherapy involving six to twelve unrelated individuals.

family therapy　A type of treatment involving two or more clients from the same family.

Group Therapy

Group therapy refers to the treatment of several clients under the guidance of a therapist who encourages helpful interactions among group members. Many groups are organized around one type of problem (such as alcoholism) or one type of client (such as adolescents). In most cases, six to twelve clients meet with their therapist at least once a week for about two hours. All group members agree to hold confidential everything that occurs within group sessions.

Group therapy offers features not found in individual treatment (Yalom, 1995). First, group therapy allows the therapist to observe clients interacting with one another. Second, clients often feel less alone as they listen to others and realize that many people struggle with difficulties as least as severe as their own. This realization tends to raise each client's expectations for improvement, a factor important in all forms of treatment. Third, group members can boost one another's self-confidence and self-acceptance as they come to trust and value one another. Fourth, clients learn from one another. They share ideas for solving problems and give one another honest feedback about their attitudes and behavior. Fifth, perhaps through mutual modeling, the group experience makes clients more willing to share their feelings and more sensitive to other people's needs, motives, and messages. Finally, group therapy allows clients to try out new skills in a supportive environment.

Family and Couples Therapy

As its name implies, **family therapy** involves treatment of two or more individuals from the same family. One of these, often a troubled adolescent or child, is the initially identified client. However, family therapists believe that the problems displayed by one family member often reflect problems in the functioning of the entire *family system* (Beels, 2002; Clarkin & Carpenter, 1995; Pilling et al., 2002). Ultimately, then, the family becomes the client, and treatment involves as many members as possible. In fact, the goal of family therapy is not just to ease the identified client's problems but also to create greater harmony and balance within the family by helping each member

table 13.3

Some "Rules for Talking" in Couples Therapy

learn by **doing** Many forms of couples therapy help partners improve communication through establishing rules such as these. Think about your own experience in relationships or your observations of couples as they interact, and then write down some rules you would add to this list. Why do you think it would be important for couples to follow the rules on your list?

1. Always begin with something positive when stating a problem.

2. Use specific behaviors rather than derogatory labels or overgeneralizations to describe what is bothersome about the other person.

3. Make connections between those specific behaviors and feelings that arise in response to them (e.g., "It makes me sad when you . . .").

4. Admit your own role in the development of the problem.

5. Be brief; don't lecture or harangue.

6. Maintain a focus on the present or the future; don't review all previous examples of the problem or ask "why" questions such as "Why do you always . . .?"

7. Talk about observable events; don't make inferences about them (e.g., say "I get angry when you interrupt me" rather than "Stop trying to make me feel stupid").

8. Paraphrase what your partner has said, and check out your own perceptions of what was said before responding. (Note that this suggestion is based on the same principle as Rogers's empathic listening.)

understand family interaction patterns and the problems they create (Blow & Timm, 2002; Goldenberg & Goldenberg, 1995). As with group therapy, the family therapy format gives the therapist an excellent view of how the initially identified client interacts with others, thus providing a basis for discussion of topics important to each family member.

In **couples therapy,** improving communication between partners is one of the most important targets of treatment (Cordova & Jacobson, 1993; Gruman & Fraenkel, 2002). Discussion in couples therapy sessions typically focuses on identifying and improving the miscommunication or lack of communication that is interfering with the couples' happiness and intimacy. Often, the sessions revolve around learning to abide by certain "rules for talking," such as those listed in Table 13.3. Some therapists also focus on helping couples to accept one another as a way of becoming closer; they even offer preventive treatment to couples who are at risk for relationship problems (Berger & Hannah, 1999;

in review

APPROACHES TO PSYCHOLOGICAL TREATMENT

Dimension	Classical Psychoanalytic	Contemporary Psychodynamic	Humanistic	Behavioral/ Cognitive-Behavioral
Nature of the human being	Driven by sexual and aggressive urges	Driven by the need for human relationships	Has free will, choice, and capacity for self-actualization	Is a product of social learning and conditioning; behaves on the basis of past experience
Therapist's role	Neutral; helps client explore meaning of free associations and other material from the unconscious	Active; develops relationship with client as a model for other relationships	Facilitates client's growth; some therapists are active, some are nondirective	Teacher/trainer who helps client replace undesirable thoughts and behaviors; active, action oriented
Focus	Unresolved unconscious conflicts from the distant past	Understanding the past, but focusing on current relationships	Here and now; focus on immediate experience	Current behavior and thoughts; may not need to know original causes to create change
Goals	Psychosexual maturity through insight; strengthening of ego functions	Correction of effects of failures of early attachment; development of satisfying intimate relationships	Expanded awareness; fulfillment of potential; self-acceptance	Changes in thinking and behaving in particular classes of situations; better self-management
Typical methods	Free association; dream analysis, analysis of transference	Analysis of interpersonal relationships, including the client-therapist relationship	Reflection-oriented interviews designed to convey unconditional positive regard, empathy, and congruence; exercises to promote self-awareness	Systematic desensitization, modeling, assertiveness and social skills training, positive reinforcement, extinction, aversive conditioning, punishment, cognitive restructuring

? *Object relations therapy and interpersonal therapy are both contemporary examples of the _____ approach to psychological treatment.*

Jacobson et al., 2000). ("In Review: Approaches to Psychological Treatment" summarizes key features of the main approaches to treatment that we have discussed so far.)

Evaluating Psychotherapy

▶ **How effective is psychotherapy?**

Psychotherapy has been available for over a hundred years, and people are still asking if it works. The question persists because although most psychotherapists and their clients find psychotherapy effective (*Consumer Reports,* 1995), confirming that effectiveness through experimental research has proven to be challenging and controversial (Beutler, 2002; DeRubeis & Crits-Christoph, 1998; Lambert & Barley, 2001; Nathan, Stuart, & Dolan, 2000; Seligman, 1995, 1996).

The value of psychotherapy was first widely questioned in 1952, when British psychologist Hans Eysenck reviewed studies in which thousands of clients had received either traditional psychodynamic therapy, various other therapies, or no treatment. To the surprise and dismay of many therapists, Eysenck (1952) found that the percentage of clients who improved following any kind of psychotherapy was actually lower than among people who received no treatment. Eysenck (1961, 1966) later supported his conclusions with additional evidence.

Critics argued that Eysenck was wrong (e.g., Bergin, 1971; de Charms, Levy, & Wertheimer, 1954; Luborsky, 1972). They claimed that he ignored studies supporting the value of psychotherapy and misinterpreted his data. They pointed out, for example, that untreated clients may have been less disturbed than those in treatment, that so-called untreated clients may have received informal treatment from their medical doctors, and that physicians who judged untreated clients' progress might have used less demanding criteria than the psychotherapists who rated their own clients. In fact, when some of these critics reviewed treatment successes and failures themselves, they concluded that psychotherapy tends to be more helpful than no treatment (e.g., Bergin, 1971).

Debate over Eysenck's findings—and the contradictory reports that followed them—highlight several reasons why it is so difficult to answer the apparently simple question, Does psychotherapy work? For one thing, there is the problem of how to measure improvement in psychotherapy. Should the yardstick be psychological test results, behavioral observations, interviews, or a combination of all three? What kinds of tests should be used; where should clients be observed (and by whom); and should equal weight be given to interviews with clients, friends, relatives, therapists, and teachers? Further, different measurements may tell somewhat different stories about improvement, making it difficult for researchers to compare or combine the results of different studies and draw conclusions about the overall effectiveness of treatment (Lambert & Hill, 1994).

The problem of evaluating psychotherapy is also complicated by the broad range of clients, therapists, and treatments involved. Clients differ in the problems they present, in their motivation to solve those problems, and in the amount of stress and social support present in their environments. Therapists differ, too, not only in skill, experience, and personality but also in which of the hundreds of available treatment procedures they choose to employ (Feltham, 2000). Further, differences in the nature and quality of the client-therapist relationship from one case to another can significantly alter the course of treatment, the clients' faith in the procedures, and their willingness to cooperate (Lambert & Barley, 2001). Because clients' responses to psychotherapy can be influenced by all these factors, results from any particular treatment evaluation study might not tell us much about how well different therapists, using different methods, would do with other kinds of clients and problems (Kazdin, 1994).

In short, the question of whether psychotherapy "works" is difficult or impossible to answer scientifically in a way that applies to all therapies for all disorders. However,

LINKAGES
Can therapy change personality?
(a link to Personality)

couples therapy   A form of therapy that focuses on improving communication between partners.

figure 13.2

An Analysis of Psychotherapy's Effects

These curves show the results of one large-scale analysis of the effects of psychotherapy. Notice that on average, people who received therapy were better off than 80 percent of troubled people who did not. The overall effectiveness of psychotherapy has also been confirmed in a more recent analysis of ninety treatment outcome studies (Shadish et al., 2000).

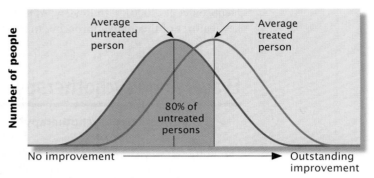

Source: Data from Smith, Glass, & Miller (1980).

several research reviews (Galatzer-Levy et al., 2000; Shadish et al., 2000; Smith, Glass, & Miller, 1980; Weisz & Jensen, 1999) leave psychotherapists convinced that it does work (see Figure 13.2).

LINKAGES
Does psychotherapy work?
(a link to Introduction to the Science of Psychology)

Most therapists believe that the theoretical approach and treatment methods *they* use are superior to those of other therapists (e.g., Giles, 1990). They can't all be right, of course, so what is going on?

Are All Forms of Therapy Equally Effective?

■ What am I being asked to believe or accept?

Some researchers argue that theories of behavior disorder and the specific treatment methods based on them don't have much to do with the success of psychotherapy. All approaches, they say, are equally effective. This has been called the "Dodo Bird Verdict," after the *Alice in Wonderland* creature who, when called on to judge who had won a race, answered, "Everybody has won and all must have prizes" (Luborsky, Singer, & Luborsky, 1975).

■ Is there evidence available to support the claim?

Some evidence does suggest that there are no significant differences in the overall effectiveness of the psychodynamic, humanistic, and behavioral approaches to therapy. Statistical analyses that combine the results of a large number of therapy studies show that the three approaches are associated with about the same degree of success (Lambert & Bergin, 1994; Luborsky et al., 2002; Shadish et al., 2000; Smith, Glass, & Miller, 1980).

■ Can that evidence be interpreted another way?

It is possible, however, that the evidence for the Dodo Bird Verdict is based on methods that cannot detect genuine differences among treatments. For example, a statistical analysis that averages the results of many different studies might not reveal important differences in the impact of particular treatments for particular problems (Beutler, 2002; Eysenck, 1978; Wilson, 1985). It may also be that some specific techniques are more successful than others, but because the therapies have been grouped in terms of their broad theoretical approach (psychodynamic, humanistic, or behavioral) rather than by specific procedures, the impact of those procedures might not be noticed (Giles, 1990; Marmar, 1990). For example, certain cognitive-behavioral techniques not used in other psychotherapy methods have been shown to be especially successful in the treatment of anxiety (Chambless & Ollendick, 2001).

Further, differences among the effects of specific procedures might be overshadowed by the beneficial features shared by almost all forms of therapy—such as the support of the therapist, the hope and expectancy for improvement that therapy creates, and the trust that develops between client and therapist (Barber et al., 2000; Martin, Garske, & Davis, 2000). In other words, a therapist whose personal characteristics motivate a client to change might promote that change regardless of the therapeutic methods being used (Elkin, 1999; Hubble, Duncan, & Miller, 1999).

■ What evidence would help to evaluate the alternatives?

The debate about whether all forms of psychotherapy are about equally effective on the average is likely to continue, but many researchers believe that it focuses on the wrong question. They believe that it is pointless to compare the effects of psychodynamic, humanistic, and behavioral methods in general. It is more important, they say, to address what Gordon Paul called the "ultimate question" about psychotherapy: "What treatment, by whom, is most effective for this individual with that specific problem, under what set of circumstances?" (Paul, 1969, p. 44).

■ What conclusions are most reasonable?

Statistical analyses show that various treatment approaches appear about equally effective overall. But this does not mean that every psychotherapy experience will be equally helpful. Potential clients must realize that the success of their treatment can still be affected by how severe their problems are, by the quality of the relationship they form with a therapist, by their motivation to change, and by the appropriateness of the therapy methods chosen for their problems.

Like those seeking treatment, many clinical psychologists, too, are eager for more specific scientific evidence about the effectiveness of particular therapies for particular kinds of clients and disorders. Empirically oriented clinicians and others are concerned that all too often, therapists' choice of therapy methods depends too much on personal preferences or current trends and not enough on scientific evidence of effectiveness (Davison, 1998; Lynn, Lilienfeld, & Lohr, 2003; Nathan, Stuart, & Dolan, 2000; Tavris, 2003). They believe that advocates of any treatment—whether it is object relations therapy or systematic desensitization—must demonstrate that its benefits are the result of the treatment itself and not just of the passage of time, the effects of repeated assessment, the client's motivation and personal characteristics, or other confounding factors (Chambless & Hollon, 1998).

They also want to see evidence that the benefits of treatment are clinically significant. To be *clinically significant,* therapeutic changes must be great enough to make treated clients' feelings and actions similar to those of people who have not experienced these clients' disorders (Kendall, 1999; Kendall & Sheldrick, 2000). The need to demonstrate clinical significance has become more important than ever as increasingly cost-conscious clients—and their health insurance companies—decide whether, and how much, to pay for various psychotherapy services (Dawes, 1994; Farberman, 1999; Roberts, 2002). The ideal way to evaluate treatment effects is through experiments in which clients are randomly assigned to various treatments or control conditions and their progress is objectively measured.

To help clinicians select treatment methods on the basis of empirical evidence, the American Psychological Association's Division of Clinical Psychology created a task force on effective psychotherapies (Task Force on Promotion and Dissemination of Psychological Procedures, 1995).

FOCUS ON RESEARCH

Which Therapies Work Best for Which Problems?

■ What was the researchers' question?

The question addressed by this task force was "What therapies have proven themselves most effective in treating various kinds of psychological disorders?"

■ How did the researchers answer the question?

Working with other empirically oriented clinical psychologists, members of this task force examined the outcomes of thousands of well-controlled experiments that evaluated psychotherapy methods used to treat mental disorder, marital distress, and health-related behavior problems in adults, children, and adolescents (Baucom et al., 1998; Chambless & Ollendick, 2001; Compas et al., 1998; DeRubeis & Crits-Christoph, 1998; Kazdin & Weisz, 1998; Kendall & Chambless, 1998).

■ What did the researchers find?

The task force found that a number of treatments—known as **empirically supported therapies,** or **ESTs**—have been validated by controlled experimental research (Chambless & Ollendick, 2001; DeRubeis & Crits-Christoph, 1998; Kendall & Chambless, 1998). Table 13.4 contains some examples of these therapies. Notice that the treatments identified as effective for particular problems in adult clients are mainly behavioral, cognitive, and cognitive-behavioral methods, but that certain psychodynamic therapies (e.g., interpersonal therapy and brief dynamic therapy) also made the list (Chambless & Ollendick, 2001).

■ What do the results mean?

The authors of the report on empirically supported therapies, and those who support their efforts, claim that relying on analysis of experimental research has allowed a scientific evaluation of various treatments and generated a list of methods from which clinicians and consumers can choose with confidence when facing specific disorders (e.g., Hunsley & Rumstein-McKean, 1999; Kendall & Chambless, 1998). Therapists are even being urged to follow *treatment manuals* stemming from this research to help them deliver empirically supported therapies exactly as they were intended (Addis, 1997; Wade, Treat, & Stuart, 1998). The state of Kansas has been the first in the United States to formally encourage the use of empirically supported treatments for children (Roberts, 2002).

Not everyone agrees with this interpretation or these recommendations. Critics note, first, that treatment methods are not necessarily discredited just because they aren't on the latest list of empirically supported therapies; they have simply not been validated according to the efficacy criteria selected by the task force. Further, these critics take issue with some of those criteria. They argue that the list of empirically supported therapies is based on research that may not be relevant to clinicians practicing in the real world. They point out that experimental studies of psychotherapy have focused mainly on the therapeutic procedures used rather than on the characteristics and interactions of therapists and clients (Garfield, 1998; Hilliard, Henry, & Strupp, 2000). This emphasis on procedure is a problem, they say, because the outcome of therapy in these experiments might have been affected by whether the random assignment of clients to therapists resulted in a match or a mismatch on certain personal characteristics. These critics say that in real clinical situations, clients and therapists are not paired up at random (Hohmann & Shear, 2002; Persons & Silberschatz, 1998). Finally, because therapists participating in experimental research were required to follow standard treatment manuals, they were not free to adapt treatment methods, as they normally would, to the needs of particular clients (Garfield, 1998). Perhaps, say these critics, when there is less experimental control over the treatment situation, all therapies are about equally effective, as suggested by the statistical analyses of outcome research we mentioned earlier (Shadish et al., 2000; Smith, Glass, & Miller, 1980).

In short, critics reject the empirically supported therapies list as a useful guide. In fact, some see it as an incomplete, irrelevant, and ultimately misleading document. They worry that it is based on research designed to evaluate treatment effects without

empirically supported therapies (ESTs) Treatments for psychological disorders whose effectiveness has been validated by controlled experimental research.

table 13.4

Examples of Empirically Supported Therapies for Selected Disorders

Treatments listed as "efficacious and specific" (pronounced "eff-eh-KAY-shus") were shown to be superior to no treatment, or to some alternative treatment, in at least two experiments in which clients were randomly assigned to various treatment conditions. These experiments are called *randomized clinical trials,* or *RCTs.* Also included in this category are treatments supported by scientific outcome measures from a large number of carefully conducted case studies. Treatments listed as "probably efficacious" are supported by at least one RCT or by a smaller number of rigorously evaluated case studies. Those listed as "possibly efficacious" are supported by a mixture of data, generally from single-case studies or other nonexperimental studies (Chambless & Ollendick, 2001).

Problem	Efficacious and Specific	Probably Efficacious	Possibly Efficacious
Major depressive disorder	Behavior therapy Cognitive-behavior therapy Interpersonal therapy	Brief dynamic therapy Social problem solving Self-control therapy	
Specific phobia	Exposure therapy	Systematic desensitization	
Agoraphobia/panic disorder	Cognitive-behavioral therapy	Couples training + exposure therapy	
Generalized anxiety disorder	Cognitive-behavior therapy	Applied relaxation therapy	
Obsessive-compulsive disorder	Exposure therapy +response prevention	Cognitive therapy Family-assisted exposure therapy + response prevention + relaxation	Rational emotive behavior therapy+ exposure therapy
Posttraumatic stress disorder		Exposure Stress inoculation Cognitive therapy + stress inoculation + exposure	Structured psychodynamic treatment
Schizophrenia	Behavioral family therapy	Family systems therapy Social skills training Supportive group therapy	Cognitive therapy (for delusions)
Alcohol abuse and dependence	Community reinforcement	Cue exposure therapy Behavioral marital therapy + anti-alcohol drug, disulfiram Social skills training (with inpatients)	
Opiate abuse and dependence		Behavior therapy Brief dynamic therapy Cognitive therapy	
Marital discord	Behavioral marital therapy	Insight-oriented marital therapy	

Source: Chambless & Ollendick (2001).

adequately taking into account either the personal qualities and theoretical biases of those who offer therapy, or how those factors might interact with the characteristics of the clients who receive therapy (e.g., Henry, 1998). There is worry, too, that widespread use of treatment manuals would make psychotherapy too mechanical and less effective, and that it might suppress therapists' creativity in developing new treatment methods (Addis & Krasnow, 2000; Beutler, 2000; Garfield, 1998).

■ **What do we still need to know?**

The efforts of the APA task force represent an important step in responding to Paul's (1969) "ultimate question" about psychotherapy: "What treatment, by whom, is most effective for this individual with that specific problem, under what set of circumstances?" As a result of their work, we know a lot more than ever before about the answer to the question "What treatment is most effective for this specific problem?" We still have a long way to go to answer the rest of Paul's complex question, but empirically oriented clinical psychologists are determined to do so (Foxhall, 2000a). The work of at least three APA task forces will focus not only on the long-term efficacy of psychotherapy—in naturalistic as well as laboratory settings—but also on the role of the therapeutic relationship in promoting that efficacy (Nathan, Stuart, & Dolan, 2000; Norcross, 2001; Wampold, Lichtenberg, & Waehler, 2002; Westen & Morrison, 2001).

What we know so far is that when differences do show up in comparative studies of adult psychotherapy, they tend to reveal a small to moderate advantage for behavioral and cognitive-behavioral methods, especially in the treatment of phobias and certain other anxiety disorders (Barrowclough et al., 2001; Borkovec & Costello, 1993; DeRubeis & Crits-Christoph, 1998; Lambert & Bergin, 1994; Weisz et al., 1995), as well as bulimia nervosa, an eating disorder (Wilson, 1997). The same tends to be true for child and adolescent clients (Epstein et al., 1994; Weiss & Weisz, 1995; Weisz et al., 1995).

Further, the client-therapist relationship seems to play a significant role in the success of many forms of treatment (Barber et al., 2000; Beutler, 2000; Brown & O'Leary, 2000; Elkin et al., 1999; Martin, Garske, & Davis, 2000; Messer & Wampold, 2002). Certain people seem to be particularly effective in forming productive human relationships. Even without formal training, these people can sometimes be as helpful as professional therapists because of personal qualities that are inspiring, healing, and soothing to others (Stein & Lambert, 1995). These qualities may help account for the success of many kinds of therapy. (It would be ideal if we could learn more about these people's qualities and, if possible, train others to develop them, too.)

Before choosing a therapist and treatment approach, then, a potential client must carefully consider (1) what treatment approach, methods, and goals the person finds comfortable and appealing; (2) information about the potential therapist's "track record" with a particular method for treating problems similar to those the person faces; and (3) the likelihood of forming a productive relationship with the therapist. This last consideration assumes special importance when client and therapist do not share similar cultural backgrounds.

Cultural Factors in Therapy

If cultural differences, including religious differences, create miscommunication or a lack of trust, the potential for a good client-therapist relationship can be threatened. Accordingly, major efforts are under way to ensure that such differences do not impede the delivery of treatment to anyone who wants or needs it (Richards & Bergin, 2000; Sue et al., 1999). Virtually every mental health training program in North America is seeking to recruit more students from traditionally underserved minority groups to eventually make it easier to match clients with therapists from similar cultural backgrounds (e.g., Norcross, Hedges, & Prochaska, 2002; Sleek, 1999). In the meantime, many minority clients are likely to encounter a therapist from a differing background, so researchers have also examined the value of matching therapeutic techniques with clients' culturally based expectations and preferences (Hays, 1995; Preciado, 1994; Sue, 1998; Tanaka-Matsumi & Higginbotham, 1994).

Today, psychotherapists are more sensitive than ever to the cultural values of particular groups and the difficulties that can impair intercultural communication (Carrillo &

PREPARING FOR THERAPY   Special pretreatment orientation programs may be offered to clients who, because of cultural or subcultural factors, are unfamiliar with the rules and procedures of psychotherapy. These programs provide a preview of what psychotherapy is, how it can help, and what the client is expected to do to make it more effective (Sue, Zane, & Young, 1994).

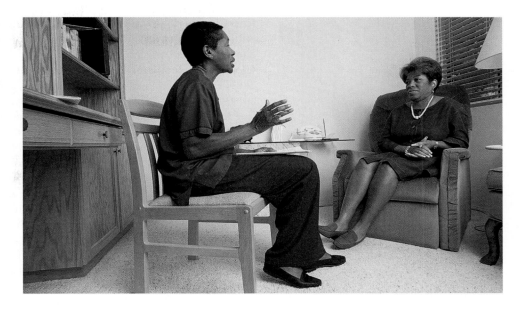

Lopez, 2001; Hall, 2001; Knox, et al., 2003). Some U.S. states now require psychologists to complete courses on the role of cultural factors in therapy before being licensed. This cultural sensitivity training helps clinicians appreciate, for example, that it is considered impolite in some cultures to make eye contact with a stranger. Armed with this information, a therapist is more likely to realize that clients from those cultures are not necessarily depressed, lacking in self-esteem, or overly submissive just because they look at the floor during an interview. More and more graduate students in clinical and counseling psychology are receiving this training, too (Clay, 2001; Norcross, Hedges, & Prochaska, 2002).

There is no guarantee that cultural sensitivity training will improve treatment results (Pope-Davis et al., 1995; Quintana & Bernal, 1995; Ramirez et al., 1996), but there is some evidence that it can help (e.g., Razali, Aminah, & Umeed, 2002). And although it is unrealistic to expect all therapists to be equally effective with clients of every ethnic or religious background, cultural sensitivity training offers a way to improve their *cultural competence,* an extension of Carl Rogers's concept of "empathy." When therapists appreciate the client's view of the world, it is easier for them to set goals that are in harmony with that view (Dyche & Zayas, 2001; Pedersen & Draguns, 2002; Ulrich, Richards, & Bergin, 2000). Minimizing cultural misunderstanding and miscommunication is one of the many ethical obligations that therapists assume when working with clients (Tomes, 1999). Let's consider some others.

Rules and Rights in the Therapeutic Relationship

Treatment can be an intensely emotional experience, and the relationship established with a therapist can profoundly affect a client's life. Professional ethics and common sense require the therapist to ensure that this relationship does not harm the client. For example, the American Psychological Association's *Ethical Principles of Psychologists and Code of Conduct* forbids a sexual relationship between therapist and client—during treatment and for at least two years afterward—because of the severe harm it can cause the client (American Psychological Association, 2002).

These ethical standards also require therapists, with a few exceptions, to keep strictly confidential everything a client says in therapy. Confidentiality is one of the most important features of a successful therapeutic relationship. It allows the client to reveal unpleasant or embarrassing impulses, behaviors, or events without fear that this information will be repeated to anyone else. Professionals do sometimes consult with one another about a client, but each is required not to reveal information to outsiders

Source: The Museum of the History of Medicine of the University of Zurich, accessed on-line at http://www.nobel.se/medicine/articles/moniz/.

HOSPITAL RESTRAINTS Here are examples of the chains, straitjackets, belts, and covered bathtubs that were used to restrain disruptive patients in North American and European mental hospitals in the 1800s and well into the 1900s. These devices were gentle compared with some of the methods endorsed in the late 1700s by Benjamin Rush. Known as the "father of American psychiatry," Rush advocated curing patients by frightening or disorienting them—for example, by placing them in a coffin-like box that was then briefly immersed in water.

(including members of the client's family) without the client's consent. The APA's code of ethics even includes standards for protecting confidentiality for the growing number of clients who seek psychological services via *telehealth* or *e-health* channels, which include telephone, videophone, e-mail, or other Internet links (APA, 2002; Barnett & Scheeetz, 2003; Fisher & Fried, 2003; Krupinski et al., 2002). One of these standards requires therapists to inform clients that others might be able to gain access to their e-mail messages.

Professional rules about confidentiality are backed up in most U.S. states, and in federal courts, by laws recognizing that information revealed in therapy (like information given to a priest, a lawyer, or a physician) is privileged communication. This means that a therapist can refuse, even in court, to answer questions about a client or to provide personal notes or tape recordings from therapy sessions. Only under special circumstances can therapists be legally required to violate confidentiality. These circumstances include those in which (1) a client is so severely disturbed or suicidal that hospitalization is needed, (2) a client uses his or her mental condition and history of therapy as part of his or her defense in a civil or criminal trial, (3) the therapist must defend against a client's charge of malpractice, (4) a client reveals information about sexual or physical abuse of a child, and (5) the therapist believes a client may commit a violent act against a specific person.

Biological Treatments

▶ **Is electric shock still used to treat disorders?**

So far, we have described psychological approaches to the treatment of mental disorders. But biological treatments are also available—primarily through psychiatrists and other medical doctors, who often work in cooperation with psychologists. Today, biological treatments for psychological problems mainly involve the prescribing of psychoactive drugs. In the mid 1900s, however, the most common biological treatment was inducement of seizures using electric shock.

Electroconvulsive Therapy

In the 1930s, a Hungarian physician named Ladislaus Von Meduna used a drug to induce convulsions in schizophrenics. He believed—incorrectly—that because schizophrenia and epilepsy rarely occur in the same person, epileptic-like seizures might combat schizophrenia. In 1938, Italian physicians Ugo Cerletti and Lucio Bini created seizures by passing an electric current through schizophrenics' brains. During the next twenty years or so, this procedure, called **electroconvulsive therapy (ECT),** became a routine treatment for schizophrenia, depression, and sometimes mania. Although many patients improved, they often relapsed. The benefits of ECT also had to be weighed against such side effects as memory loss, confusion, speech disorders, and in some cases, death due to cardiac arrest (Lickey & Gordon, 1991; Shiwach, Reid, & Carmody, 2001).

To make ECT safer, patients are now given an anesthetic so that they are unconscious before the shock is delivered, along with a muscle relaxant to prevent bone fractures during convulsions. Also, the shock now lasts only about half a second and is usually delivered to only one side of the brain (Sackeim et al., 2000). Finally, in contrast to the dozens of treatments administered decades ago, patients now receive only about six to twelve shocks, one approximately every two days (Fink, 1999). Researchers have also begun experimenting with a procedure called *repetitive transcranial magnetic stimulation (rTMS)* to cause seizures without electric shock (Fitzgerald et al., 2003; Gershon, Dannon, & Grunhaus, 2003; Hoffman et al., 2003; Lisanby et al., 2001; Wasserman & Lisanby, 2001).

Today, ECT is used mainly with patients suffering severe depression (and occasionally with manic patients) who do not respond to less drastic treatments (Ciapparelli et al., 2001; Daly et al., 2001). ECT can be effective in such cases—especially when followed up

electroconvulsive therapy (ECT) A brief electric shock administered to the brain, usually to reduce severe depression that does not respond to drug treatments.

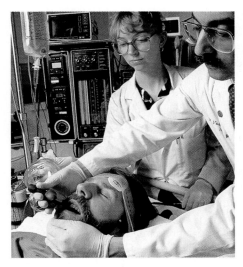

ELECTROCONVULSIVE THERAPY
There are no national statistics on the use of ECT in the United States; estimates of the number of people receiving this treatment each year range from 30,000 to over 100,000 (Hermann et al., 1995). A survey in the United Kingdom suggests that about 12,000 patients a year are receiving ECT (U.K. Statistical Bulletin, 1999). Because of its dramatic and potentially dangerous nature, ECT remains a controversial method of treatment. Critics want it outlawed, but proponents say the benefits of ECT for certain patients outweigh its potential costs (Breggin, 1997; Fink, 1999).

with medication—and it does not appear to cause brain damage, even when administered repeatedly (e.g., Anghelescu et al., 2001; Ende et al., 2000; Sackeim et al., 2001; U.S. Surgeon General, 1999). However, no one knows for sure how ECT works (Rudorfer, Henry, & Sackheim, 1997; Sackeim, 1994).

Psychoactive Drugs

The use of ECT declined after the 1950s, in part because psychoactive drugs had begun to emerge as more convenient and effective treatment alternatives. In the chapters on biology and behavior and on consciousness, we discuss the effects of psychoactive drugs on neurotransmitter systems, autonomic activity, emotions, thinking, and behavior. Here, we describe their role in combating schizophrenia, depression, mania, and anxiety.

Neuroleptics   One group of drugs, called **neuroleptics** or *antipsychotics,* dramatically reduces the intensity of psychotic symptoms such as hallucinations, delusions, paranoid suspiciousness, disordered thinking, and confused speech in many mental patients, especially schizophrenics. The most widely used antipsychotic drugs are the *phenothiazines* (pronounced "fee-noh-THIGH-uh-zeens"), of which the first, chlorpromazine (marketed as Thorazine in the United States and as Largactil in Canada and the United Kingdom), has been especially popular. Another neuroleptic, haloperidol (Haldol), is about as effective as the phenothiazines, but it creates less sedation (Julien, 2001). Patients who do not respond to one type of neuroleptic may respond to the other (Davis, Chen, & Glick, 2003). Between 60 and 70 percent of patients receiving these drugs show improvement, though fewer than 30 percent respond well enough to live successfully on their own.

Neuroleptics have side effects ranging from dry mouth and dizziness to symptoms similar to those of Parkinson's disease, including muscle rigidity, restlessness, tremors, and slowed movement. Some of these side effects can be treated with medication, but at least 25 percent of patients who take chlorpromazine or haloperidol for several years develop an irreversible disorder of the motor system. This disorder, called *tardive dyskinesia (TD),* causes uncontrollable, repetitive movements of the body, often including twitching of the face and body and thrusting of the tongue.

Among a newer generation of antipsychotic drugs (also called *atypical neuroleptics*) is clozapine (Clozaril), which has effects like those of the phenothiazines but does not cause movement disorders. Although no more effective overall than the phenothiazines, clozapine has helped many patients who did not respond to the phenothiazines or haloperidol (Green & Patel, 1996; Rabinowitz et al., 2001). Unfortunately, taking clozapine carries the risk of developing a fatal blood disease called *agranulocytosis* (Alvir et al., 1993). Weekly blood tests to detect early signs of this disease greatly increase the cost of using this drug (Meltzer, 1997).

Several other atypical neuroleptics have been introduced recently, including risperidone (Risperdal), olanzapine (Zyprexa), quetiapine (Seroquel), ziprasidone (Geodon), and most recently, aripiprazole (Abilify). These medications are expensive, but they have even fewer side effects than clozapine, and they do not cause agranulocytosis. Like clozapine, they also appear to reduce the "negative" symptoms of schizophrenia, such as lack of emotion, social withdrawal, and reduced speech (Azorin et al., 2001; Bailey, 2002; Conley & Mahmoud, 2001; Davis, Chen, & Glick, 2003; Kane et al., 2003; Lieberman et al., 2003; Potkin et al., 2003; Volavka et al., 2002).

Antidepressants   Soon after antipsychotic drugs appeared, they were joined by **antidepressants,** a class of drugs that is now widely prescribed for relieving the symptoms of depression (Olfson et al., 2002). These drugs have almost immediate effects on neurotransmitters (usually increasing the availability of serotonin or norepinephrine), but it usually takes a week or two before reduction in depressive symptoms begins, and maximum benefits take even longer (Quitkin et al., 2003).

There are several classes of antidepressant drugs. The *monoamine oxidase inhibitors (MAOIs)* are used to treat many cases of depression, especially clients who also

neuroleptics   Drugs that relieve the symptoms of schizophrenia or other severe forms of psychological disorder. Also called *antipsychotics.*

antidepressants   Drugs that reduce depression.

A NATURAL CURE?   An herbal remedy from a plant called *Saint John's wort* has recently become popular in the treatment of depression. One of its active ingredients is *hypericin,* a substance that, like Prozac, is thought to affect the neurotransmitter serotonin. Double-blind, placebo-controlled studies have shown Saint John's wort to be as effective as Prozac, but only for the mildest forms of depression (Brenner et al., 2000; Gaster & Holroyd, 2000; Hypericum Depression Trial Study Group, 2002; Lecrubier et al., 2002; Volz & Laux, 2000; Woelk, 2000). The design of some of these studies has been questioned, however (e.g., Spira, 2001), so final conclusions about the safety and effectiveness of Saint John's wort for even mild depression must await the results of further research (Ernst, 2000; Josefson, 2002; Shelton et al., 2001).

experience anxiety and panic (Julien, 2001). The *tricyclic antidepressants (TCAs)* are another popular class of antidepressants. The TCAs have been prescribed more frequently than MAOI drugs because they seem to work somewhat better and have fewer side effects. However, taking TCAs and drinking alcohol can increase the effects of both, with potentially fatal results.

The most prominent of several newer antidepressants is fluoxetine (Prozac). Introduced in 1986, fluoxetine quickly became the most widely used antidepressant in the United States. Its popularity is due to the fact that it is about as effective as older drugs and, in most cases, has milder side effects (Cookson & Duffett, 1998; *Harvard Mental Health Letter,* 1998a, 1998b; Stokes, 1998). An improved version of Prozac, containing a purer active ingredient called *R-fluoxetine,* is currently being developed. Other, even newer antidepressants, including venlafaxine (Effexor), nefazodone (Serzone), and bupropion (Wellbutrin), are also being used (Appleton, 2000; Croft et al., 1999; Quitkin et al., 2000).

About 50 to 60 percent of patients who take antidepressant drugs show improved mood, greater physical activity, increased appetite, and better sleep (Hollon, Thase, & Markowitz, 2002). This degree of improvement is seen in only 10 to 20 percent of the most severe cases of psychotic depression (Agency for Healthcare Research and Quality, 1999; U.S. Surgeon General, 1999). It has long been assumed that these results were due to the drugs' active ingredients, but some critics have cast some doubt on this assumption. A recent analysis of clinical trial data submitted to the U.S. Food and Drug Administration by the makers of six widely prescribed antidepressant drugs showed that in 57 percent of the trials, antidepressant drugs did only a little better than placebo medications ("sugar pills") at relieving depression (Kirsch, Scoboria, & Moore, 2002; Kirsch et al., 2002). Defenders of antidepressant medications argue that even relatively small effects are better than none (e.g., Thase, 2002), whereas critics contend that those effects are too small to matter.

Lithium and Anticonvulsants   The mineral salt lithium carbonate, when taken regularly, prevents both the depression and the mania associated with bipolar disorder in some patients (Baldessarini & Tondo, 2000; Manji, Bowden, & Belmaker, 2000). Without lithium, the typical bipolar patient has a manic episode about every fourteen months and a depressive episode about every seventeen months; with lithium, attacks of mania occur as rarely as every nine years (Bowden, 2000). The lithium dosage must be exact and carefully controlled, however, because taking too much can cause vomiting, nausea, tremor, fatigue, slurred speech, and with severe overdoses, coma or death. In recent years, anticonvulsant drugs such as divalproex and lamotrigine (Epival/Depakote; Lamictal) have been used as an alternative to lithium in treating mania. Compared with lithium, these drugs cause fewer side effects, are less dangerous at higher doses, and are easier to regulate (Bowden et al., 2000, 2003; Hirschfeld et al., 1999). However, their long-term benefits in reducing mania and the risk of suicide are not as well established, so lithium is still considered the treatment of choice against which others are measured (Baldessarini et al., 2002; Dinan, 2002; Goodwin et al., 2003;).

Anxiolytics   During the 1950s, a new class of drugs called *tranquilizers* was shown to reduce mental and physical tension and the symptoms of anxiety. The first of these drugs, meprobamate (Miltown or Equanil), acts somewhat like barbiturate sleeping pills, meaning that overdoses can cause sleep and even death. Because they do not pose this danger, the *benzodiazepines*—particularly chlordiazepoxide (Librium) and diazepam (Valium)—became the worldwide drug treatment of choice for anxiety (Blackwell, 1973). Today, these and other anti-anxiety drugs, now called **anxiolytics** (pronounced "ang-zee-oh-LIT-ix), continue to be the most widely prescribed and used of all legal drugs. They have an immediate calming effect and are quite useful in treating the symptoms of generalized anxiety and posttraumatic stress disorder. One of the benzodiazepines, alprazolam (Xanax), has become especially popular for the treatment of panic disorder and agoraphobia (Greenblatt, Harmatz, & Shader, 1993). Another

anxiolytics Drugs that reduce tension and symptoms of anxiety.

benzodiazepine, clonazepam (Klonopin), is also being used, alone or in combination with other anxiolytics, in the treatment of anxiety ranging from phobias to panic disorder (Worthington et al., 1998).

Benzodiazepines can have bothersome side effects, such as sleepiness, lightheadedness, and impaired memory and thinking. Combining these drugs with alcohol can be fatal, and continued use of anxiolytics can lead to tolerance and physical dependence. After heavy or long-term use, attempts to stop taking these drugs can result in severe withdrawal symptoms, including seizures and anxiety attacks (Rickels et al., 1993). The anxiolytic called *buspirone (BuSpar)* provides an alternative anxiety treatment that eliminates some of these problems (Lickey & Gordon, 1991; Stahl, 2002; Wagner et al., 2003). Its effects do not occur for days or weeks after treatment begins, but buspirone can ultimately equal diazepam in reducing generalized anxiety (Schnabel, 1987; U.S. Surgeon General, 1999). Further, it does not seem to promote dependence, it causes less interference with thinking, and it does not interact dangerously with alcohol.

A number of antidepressant drugs—including fluoxetine (Prozac), paroxetine (Paxil), clomipramine (Anafranil), fluvoxamine (Luvox), and sertraline (Zoloft)—have also been used in treating anxiety-related problems such as panic disorder, social phobia, obsessive-compulsive disorder, and posttraumatic stress disorder (Davidson et al., 2001; Gorman, 2002; Rickels et al., 2003; Stein et al., 2002; Todorov, Freeston, & Borgeat, 2000; Van Ameringen et al., 2001; Walkup et al., 2001). Table 13.5 lists the effects and side effects of some of the psychoactive drugs we have described.

Drugs and Psychotherapy

We have seen that both drugs and psychotherapy can be effective in treating psychological disorders. Which is better? Can they be effectively combined? A considerable amount of research is being conducted to address these questions.

Although occasionally a study does show that one form of treatment or the other is more effective, neither form of therapy is clearly superior overall for treating problems such as anxiety disorders and major depressive disorder (Antonuccio, Danton, & DeNelsky, 1995). For example, several studies of treatment for severe depression have found that cognitive-behavior therapy and interpersonal psychotherapy can be as effective as an antidepressant drug (DeRubeis et al., 1999; Hollon, Thase, & Markowitz, 2002; Spanier et al., 1996). Cognitive-behavior therapy has also equaled drug effects in the initial treatment of phobias (Otto et al., 2000; Thom, Sartory, & Jöhren, 2000), panic disorder (Klosko et al., 1990), generalized anxiety disorder (Gould et al., 1997), and obsessive-compulsive disorder (Abramowitz, 1997; Kozak, Liebowitz, & Foa, 2000). Further, the dropout rate from psychotherapy may be lower than from drug therapies (Casacalenda, Perry, & Looper, 2002), and the benefits of many kinds of psychotherapy may last longer than those of drug therapies (e.g., Hollon, Thase, & Markowitz, 2002; Segal, Gemar, & Williams, 2000; Thom, Sartory, & Jöhren, 2000).

What about combining drugs and psychotherapy? One research team compared the effects of a form of *in vivo* desensitization called *gradual exposure* and an anti-anxiety drug (Xanax) in the treatment of agoraphobia. Clients receiving gradual exposure alone showed better short- and long-term benefits than those getting either the drug alone or a combination of the drug and gradual exposure (Echeburua et al., 1993). Other studies, too, have found that combining drugs and psychotherapy may produce surprisingly little advantage (e.g., Elkin, 1994; Spiegel & Bruce, 1997). However, the combination of drugs and psychotherapy has been shown to be more effective than either method alone in treating certain disorders, including attention deficit hyperactivity disorder, obsessive-compulsive disorder, alcoholism, stammering, compulsive sexual behavior, and chronic depression (e.g., Barlow et al., 2000; deBeurs et al., 1995; Engeland, 1993; Keller et al., 2000; Reynolds et al., 1999). This combined approach may be especially helpful for clients who are initially too distressed to cooperate in psychotherapy (Kahn, 1995). Another approach, already found successful with clients who have been taking drugs for

table 13.5

A Sampling of Psychoactive Drugs Used for Treating Psychological Disorders

Psychoactive drugs have been successful in dramatically reducing the symptoms of many psychological disorders. Critics point out that drugs can have troublesome side effects, however, and they may create dependence, especially after years of use (e.g., Breggin, 1997). They note, too, that drugs do not "cure" mental disorders (NIMH, 1995), that their effects are not always strong (Kirsch et al., 2002), and that temporary symptom relief may make some patients less likely to seek a permanent solution to their psychological problems.

For Schizophrenia: Neuroleptics (Antipsychotics)

Chemical Name	Trade Name	Effects and Side Effects
Chlorpromazine	Thorazine	Reduce hallucinations, delusions, incoherence, jumbled thought processes; cause movement-disorder side effects, including tardive dyskinesia
Haloperidol	Haldol	
Clozapine	Clozaril	Reduces psychotic symptoms; causes no movement disorders, but raises risk of serious blood disease
Risperidone	Risperdal	Reduces positive and negative psychotic symptoms without risk of blood disease
Ziprasidone	Geodon	Reduces positive and negative psychotic symptoms without causing weight gain
Aripiprazole	Abilify	Reduces positive and negative psychotic symptoms without weight gain, and with few side effects

For Mood Disorders: Antidepressants and Mood Elevators

Tricyclics

Imipramine	Tofranil	Act as antidepressants, but also have antipanic action; cause sleepiness andother moderate side effects; potentially dangerous if taken with alcohol
Amitriptyline	Elavil, Amitid	

Other Antidepressants

Fluoxetine	Prozac	Have antidepressant, antipanic, and anti-obsessive action
Clomipramine	Anafranil	
Fluvoxamine	Luvox	
Sertraline	Zoloft	

Other Drugs

Lithium carbonate	Carbolith, Lithizine	Calms mania; reduces mood swings of bipolar disorder; overdose harmful, potentially deadly
Divalproex	Depakote	Are effective against mania, with fewer side effects
Lamotrigine	Lamictal	

For Anxiety Disorders: Anxiolytics

Benzodiazepines

Chlordiazepoxide	Librium	Act as potent anxiolytics for generalized anxiety, panic, stress; extended use may cause physical dependence and withdrawal syndrome if abruptly discontinued
Diazepam	Valium	
Alprazolam	Xanax	Also has antidepressant effects; often used in agoraphobia (has high dependence potential)
Clonazepam	Klonopin	Is often used in combination with other anxiolytics for panic disorder

Other Anti-anxiety Agents

Buspirone	BuSpar	Has slow-acting anti-anxiety action; no known dependence problems

There is widespread concern that psychiatrists, and especially general practitioners, rely too heavily on drugs to deal with psychological problems (Glenmullen, 2000). In one case, dramatically increased medication failed to stop a paranoid schizophrenia patient from repeatedly running away from a mental hospital. But allowing him to use a telephone at a nearby shopping mall eliminated the problem. A psychologist discovered that the man had been afraid to use "bugged" hospital phones and kept escaping to call his mother (Rabasca, 1999b).

"I medicate first and ask questions later."

panic disorder, is to use psychotherapy to prevent relapse and make further progress as drug treatment is discontinued (e.g., Bruce, Spiegel, & Hegel, 1999; Lam et al., 2003).

It has been suggested that the most conservative strategy for treating most cases of anxiety and depression is to begin with cognitive or interpersonal psychotherapy (which have no major negative side effects) and then to add or switch to drug treatment if psychotherapy alone is ineffective.

LINKAGES

How do psychoactive drugs work?
(a link to Treatment of Psychological Disorders)

As noted in the chapter on biology and behavior, human feelings, thoughts, and actions—whether normal or abnormal—are ultimately the result of biological processes, especially those involving neurotransmitters and their receptors in the brain. Because different neurotransmitters are especially prominent in particular brain regions or circuits, altering the functioning of particular neurotransmitter systems will have relatively specific psychological and behavioral effects.

Let's consider some of the ways in which therapeutic psychoactive drugs affect neurotransmitters and their receptors. Some therapeutic drugs cause neurons to fire, whereas others inhibit neuron firing. For example, benzodiazepines (e.g., Valium and Xanax) exert their anti-anxiety effects by helping the inhibitory neurotransmitter GABA bind to receptors and thus suppress neuron firing. This increased inhibitory effect acts as a sort of braking system that slows the activity of GABA-sensitive neurons involved in the experience of anxiety. However, benzodiazepines also slow the action of all neural systems that use GABA, including those associated with motor activity and mental processing, which are spread throughout the brain. The result is the decreased motor coordination and clouded thinking that appear as benzodiazepines' side effects. Research suggests that it might soon be possible to develop drugs that will bind only to certain kinds of GABA receptors and thus greatly reduce these side effects (Löw et al., 2000; Stahl, 2002).

LINKAGES

Biology, Behavior, and the Treatment of Psychological Disorders

LINKAGES
How do drugs help people who suffer from schizophrenia?
(a link to Biology and Behavior)

applying psychology

COMMUNITY MENTAL HEALTH EFFORTS Professional and nonprofessional staff members at community mental health centers provide traditional therapy and mental health education, as well as walk-in facilities and hotlines for people who are suicidal or in crisis because of rape or domestic violence. They also offer day treatment to former mental patients, many of whom are homeless.

community psychology A mental health approach whose goal is to minimize or prevent psychological disorders by promoting social change and making treatment methods more accessible to those who normally have little or no access to psychological services.

Other therapeutic drugs serve as receptor antagonists (see Figure 4.8 in the consciousness chapter), acting to block the receptor site normally used by a particular neurotransmitter. The phenothiazines and haloperidol, for example, exert their antipsychotic effects by blocking receptors for dopamine, a neurotransmitter that is important for movement, as described in the chapter on biology and behavior. Blocking dopamine seems to normalize the jumbled thinking of many schizophrenia patients, but it can create severe disorders—including tardive dyskinesia—in the movement systems that are also controlled by dopamine.

Some psychoactive drugs exert their therapeutic influence by increasing the amount of a neurotransmitter available to act on receptors. This effect usually occurs because the drug slows a process called *reuptake,* by which the neurotransmitter would normally return to the brain cell from which it was released. The tricyclic antidepressants, for example, operate by slowing the reuptake of norepinephrine. Prozac, Anafranil, and some other antidepressants are called *selective serotonin reuptake inhibitors (SSRIs)* because they slow the reuptake of serotonin. Others, such as Effexor, slow the reuptake of both serotonin and norepinephrine.

Community Psychology

▶ **How can we prevent psychological disorders?**

It has long been argued that even if psychologists and psychiatrists knew exactly how to treat every psychological problem, there would never be enough mental health professionals to help everyone who needs it (Albee, 1968). This view fostered the rise of **community psychology,** an approach whose goals are to treat people in their home communities and to work for social changes that can prevent psychological disorders.

One aspect of community psychology, the *community mental health movement,* arose during the 1960s as an attempt to make treatment available to people in their own communities. As antipsychotic drugs became available, and as concern grew that patients were not improving—and might be getting worse—after years of confinement in mental hospitals, thousands of these patients were released. The plan was for them to receive drugs and other mental health services in newly funded community mental health centers. This *deinstitutionalization* process did spare patients the boredom and isolation of the hospital environment, but the mental health services available in the community never matched the need for them. Some former hospital patients and many people whose disorders might once have sent them to mental hospitals are now living in halfway houses and other community-based facilities where they receive *psychosocial rehabilitation.* These community support services are not designed to "cure" them but to help them cope with their problems and develop the social and occupational skills necessary for semi-independent living (Hunter, 1995; Liberman et al., 1998). All too many others with severe psychological disorders are to be found enduring the dangers of homelessness on city streets or of confinement in jails and prisons (Ditton, 1999; U.S. Department of Health and Human Services, 2001b).

Community psychology also attempts to prevent psychopathology by addressing unemployment, poverty, overcrowded substandard housing, and other stressful social problems that may underlie some disorders (Albee, 1985; Tucker & Herman, 2002; Weissberg, Kumpfer, & Seligman et al., 2003). Less ambitious, but perhaps even more significant, are efforts to detect psychological problems in their earliest stages and keep them from becoming worse (e.g., President's New Freedom Commission on Mental Health, 2003; Sanders et al., 2000). Examples include prevention of depression and suicide (Beardslee et al., 2003; Freres et al., 2002); programs, including Project Head Start, that help preschoolers whose backgrounds hurt their chances of doing well in school and put them at risk for delinquency

(Tremblay et al., 1995; Zigler, Taussig, & Black, 1992); identification of children who are at risk for disorder because of parental divorce or being rejected or victimized at school (e.g., Greenberg et al., 1999; Martinez & Forgatch, 2001); interventions to head off anxiety disorders or schizophrenia in children and adults (Dadds et al., 1999; McGorry et al., 2002); and programs designed to promote health consciousness in ethnic minority communities (Borg, 2002).

Further, community psychology supports the notion that nonprofessionals—including the relatives and friends of troubled clients—can be enlisted in efforts to combat psychological disorders (e.g., Bright, Baker, & Neimeyer, 1999). This idea is compatible with, and has encouraged the development of, *self-help* or *mutual-help* organizations. Self-help groups, such as Alcoholics Anonymous (AA), are made up of people who share some problematic experience and want to help one another. Millions of people in the United States and Canada take part each year in self-help groups for alcohol and drug addiction, childhood sexual abuse, cancer, overeating, overspending, bereavement, compulsive gambling, schizophrenia, and many other problems (Barlow et al., 2000; Nietzel et al., 2003; Norcross et al., 2000; Swindle et al., 2000).

Lack of reliable data makes it difficult to assess the value of many self-help groups, but available information suggests that active members may obtain some moderate improvement in their lives (Moos et al., 2001; Morganstern et al., 1997). Some professional therapists view these groups with suspicion; others encourage clients to participate in them as part of their treatment or as a first step that might lead to more formal treatment (Haaga, 2000; Salzer, Rappaport, & Segre, 1999). This recommendation is especially likely for clients with problems such as eating disorders, alcoholism, and other substance-related disorders (Dunne & Fitzpatrick, 1999).

active review   Treatment of Psychological Disorders

Linkages

As noted in the introductory chapter, all of psychology's subfields are related to one another. Our discussion of the psychopharmacology of drug treatment illustrates just one way in which the topic of this chapter, treatment of psychological disorders, is linked to the subfield of biological psychology, which is described in the chapter on biology and behavior. The Linkages diagram shows ties to two other subfields as well, and there are many more ties throughout the book. Looking for linkages among subfields will help you see how they all fit together and help you better appreciate the big picture that is psychology.

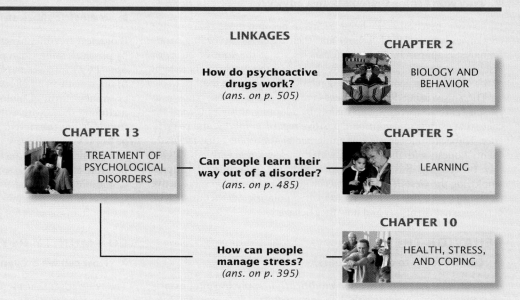

LINKAGES

CHAPTER 13
TREATMENT OF PSYCHOLOGICAL DISORDERS

How do psychoactive drugs work?
(ans. on p. 505)

CHAPTER 2
BIOLOGY AND BEHAVIOR

Can people learn their way out of a disorder?
(ans. on p. 485)

CHAPTER 5
LEARNING

How can people manage stress?
(ans. on p. 395)

CHAPTER 10
HEALTH, STRESS, AND COPING

Summary

BASIC FEATURES OF TREATMENT

▶ **What features do all treatment techniques have in common?**

Psychotherapy for psychological disorders is usually based on psychodynamic, humanistic, or behavioral theories of personality and behavior disorder. Many therapists employ elements of more than one approach. The biological approach is reflected in the use of drugs and other physical treatment methods.

All forms of treatment include a client, a therapist, a theory of behavior disorder, a set of treatment procedures suggested by the theory, and a special relationship between the client and therapist. Therapy may be offered to inpatients and outpatients in many different settings by *psychologists, psychiatrists,* and other helpers. The goal of treatment is to help people change their thinking, feelings, and behavior so that they will be happier and function better.

PSYCHODYNAMIC PSYCHOTHERAPY

▶ **How did Freud get started as a therapist?**

Psychodynamic psychotherapy began with Freud's *psychoanalysis,* which seeks to help clients gain insight into unconscious conflicts and impulses and then to explore how those factors have created disorders. Exploration of the unconscious is aided by the use of free association, dream interpretation, and related methods. Some variations on psychoanalysis retain most of Freud's principles but use a more flexible format. Others, such as object relations therapy and interpersonal therapy, focus less on the id and the unconscious and more on helping clients to understand the role of early relationships with caregivers, as well as postchildhood events, in creating current problems.

HUMANISTIC PSYCHOTHERAPY

▶ **Why won't some therapists give advice?**

Humanistic psychotherapy helps clients to become more aware of discrepancies between their feelings and their behavior. According to the humanistic approach, these discrepancies are at the root of behavior disorders and can be resolved by the client once they are brought to light in the context of a genuine, trusting relationship with the therapist. Therapists using Rogers's *client-centered therapy,* also known as *person-centered therapy,* help mainly by adopting attitudes toward the client that express *unconditional positive regard, empathy,* and *congruence.* These attitudes create a nonjudgmental atmosphere that facilitates clients' honesty with the therapist, with themselves, and with others. One way of creating this atmosphere is through *reflection.* Therapists employing the *Gestalt therapy* of Fritz and Laura Perls use more active techniques than Rogerian therapists, often pointing out inconsistencies between what clients say and how they behave.

BEHAVIOR THERAPY

▶ **Can we learn to conquer fears?**

Behavior therapy and *behavior modification* apply learning principles to eliminate undesirable behavior patterns and to strengthen more desirable alternatives. The methods they employ include *systematic desensitization, modeling, assertiveness training* and social skills training, *positive reinforcement* (sometimes within a *token economy*), *extinction* techniques (such as *flooding*), *aversive conditioning,* and *punishment.*

Many behavior therapists also employ *cognitive-behavior therapy* to help clients alter the way they think, as well as the way they behave. Among the specific cognitive-behavioral methods are *rational-emotive behavior therapy (REBT),* cognitive restructuring, stress inoculation training, and *cognitive therapy.*

GROUP, FAMILY, AND COUPLES THERAPY

▶ **How does group therapy differ from individual therapy?**

Therapists of all theoretical persuasions offer *group therapy, family therapy,* and *couples therapy.* These forms of treatment take advantage of relationships in the group, family, or couple to enhance the effects of treatment.

EVALUATING PSYCHOTHERAPY

▶ **How effective is psychotherapy?**

Research has found that clients who receive psychotherapy are better off than most clients who receive no treatment, but that no single approach is uniformly better than all others for all clients and problems. Still, some methods appear effective enough in the treatment of particular disorders to have been listed by an American Psychological Association task force as *empirically supported therapies (ESTs).* Further research is needed to discover all the combinations of therapists, clients, and treatments ideally suited to treating particular psychological problems. Several factors, including personal preferences, must be considered when choosing a form of treatment and a therapist. The effects of cultural differences in the values and goals of therapist and client have also attracted increasing attention. Whatever the specific form of treatment, the client's rights include the right to confidentiality.

BIOLOGICAL TREATMENTS

▶ **Is electric shock still used to treat disorders?**

Biological treatment methods seek to relieve psychological disorders by physical, rather than psychological, means. *Electroconvulsive therapy (ECT)* involves passing an electric current through the patient's brain, usually in an effort to relieve severe depression. Today, the most prominent form of biological treatment involves psychoactive drugs, including those with antipsychotic *(neuroleptic), antidepressant,* or tranquilizing *(anxiolytic)* effects. Psychoactive drugs have proven to be impressively effective in many cases, but critics point out a number of undesirable side effects associated with these drugs. Drugs may be no more effective than some forms of psychotherapy for many people. Combining drugs and psychotherapy may help in some cases and in the treatment of certain disorders, but their joint effect may be no greater than the effect of either one alone.

COMMUNITY PSYCHOLOGY

▶ **How can we prevent psychological disorders?**

The realization that there will never be enough therapists to treat all who need help prompted the development of *community psychology.* Community mental health programs and efforts to prevent mental disorders are the two main elements of community psychology. The growth of self-help or mutual-help organizations is compatible with the goals of community psychology.

Learn by Doing

Put It in Writing

Imagine that you have decided to get help for depression, anxiety, or some other psychological problem. Using what you have learned in this chapter, write a page describing what approach to treatment you would prefer, and why. Tell whether you would choose that approach for all kinds of problems, or whether your choice would depend on the nature of the problem. Finally, list the characteristics of your ideal therapist, and say why you think those characteristics might lead to successful treatment.

Personal Learning Activity

To get a better idea of how practicing therapists choose their treatment methods, ask a local psychologist, psychiatrist, or counselor (at the student counseling center on campus, perhaps) to meet with you for a short research interview. Ask this person what treatment approach and methods he or she prefers, how this preference developed, and what convinces him or her to continue using these methods. Write a summary of what you learned in this interview, and don't forget to include your impressions of whether this therapist's choice of treatment methods depends mainly on personal experience, empirical research evidence, or a combination of both. *For additional projects, see the Personal Learning Activities in the corresponding chapter of the study guide that accompanies this text.*

Step into Action

Courses

Clinical Psychology
Methods of Psychotherapy
Psychopharmacology
Behavior Modification
Community Psychology

Movies

Good Will Hunting; Analyze This; Vertigo (Hollywood portrayals of psychotherapy)
One Flew over the Cuckoo's Nest; Girl, Interrupted (institutional treatment)
A Beautiful Mind (biological treatment of schizophrenia)
I Never Promised You a Rose Garden (psychodynamic treatment for schizophrenia)
Antwone Fisher (psychotherapy)

Books

Peter Wyden, *Conquering Schizophrenia: A Father, His Son, and a Medical Breakthrough* (Knopf, 1998) (a father searches for a cure for his schizophrenic son)
Ken Kesey, *One Flew over the Cuckoo's Nest* (New American Library, 1989) (the book from which the award-winning movie was adapted)
Michael Winerip, *9 Highland Road* (Vintage, 1995) (the aftermath of deinstitutionalization)
Peter Kramer, *Listening to Prozac* (Penguin, 1997) (psychotropic antidepressant medications)
Susan Sheehan, *Is There No Place on Earth for Me?* (Vintage, 1983) (inadequate treatment for a woman with schizophrenia)

Raymond J. Corsini and Danny Wedding, *Current Psychotherapies* (6th ed.) (Peacock, 2001) (a comparison of numerous approaches to psychotherapy)
Frank Dumont and Raymond J. Corsini (Eds.), *Six Therapists and One Client* (Springer, 2000) (therapists representing six different treatment methods describe how they would help the same client)
W. S. Appleton, *Prozac and the New Antidepressants: What You Need to Know About Prozac, Zoloft, Paxil, Luvox, Wellbutrin, Effexor, Serzone, Vestra, Celexa, St. John's Wort, and Others* (Rev. ed.) (Plume Books, 2000) (a summary of modern drug treatment alternatives for depression)
T. M. Luhrmann, *Of Two Minds: The Growing Disorder in American Psychiatry* (Knopf, 2000) (summary of the conflict between biological and psychological approaches to treatment)

The Web

The World Wide Web is a good source of additional information about the science of psychology, provided you use it carefully and think critically about the information you find. The web site that accompanies this text offers many resources relevant to this chapter. These resources include interactive NetLab exercises; Thinking Critically and Evaluating Research exercises; ACE chapter quizzes; recommended web links; and articles on current events, books, and movies. At http://college.hmco.com, select *Psychology* and then this textbook.

Review of Key Terms

Can you define each of the key terms in the chapter? Check your definitions against those on the pages listed in parentheses below or in the Glossary/Index at the end of the text.

antidepressants *(p. 501)*

anxiolytics *(p. 502)*

assertiveness training *(p. 487)*

aversive conditioning *(p. 488)*

behavior modification *(p. 485)*

behavior therapy *(p. 485)*

client-centered therapy *(p. 483)*

cognitive-behavior therapy *(p. 485)*

cognitive therapy *(p. 490)*

community psychology *(p. 506)*

congruence *(p. 484)*

couples therapy *(p. 492)*

electroconvulsive therapy (ECT) *(p. 500)*

empathy *(p. 483)*

empirically supported therapies (ESTs) *(p. 496)*

extinction *(p. 488)*

family therapy *(p. 491)*

flooding *(p. 488)*

Gestalt therapy *(p. 484)*

group therapy *(p. 491)*

modeling *(p. 486)*

neuroleptics *(p. 501)*

person-centered therapy *(p. 483)*

positive reinforcement *(p. 487)*

psychiatrists *(p. 480)*

psychoanalysis *(p. 480)*

psychologists *(p. 480)*

psychotherapy *(p. 479)*

punishment *(p. 488)*

rational-emotive behavior therapy (REBT) *(p. 489)*

reflection *(p. 483)*

systematic desensitization *(p. 485)*

token economy *(p. 487)*

unconditional positive regard *(p. 483)*

Multiple-Choice Self-Test

Select the best answer for each of the questions below. Then check your responses against the Answer Key at the end of the text.

1. Claudia's therapist asks her to talk about whatever thoughts, memories, or ideas come into her mind. He asks her not to "edit" any of her thoughts. This technique is called _____ and is part of _____ therapy.

   a. reflection; psychodynamic
   b. reflection; humanistic
   c. free association; psychodynamic
   d. free association; humanistic

2. Vernon tells his therapist about a dream in which a fish got stuck between his toes. The therapist says to Vernon, "Be the fish. What is that fish saying?" Vernon's therapist is using _____ therapy methods.

   a. Gestalt   c. behavior
   b. psychodynamic d. cognitive

3. Melinda is a licensed clinical psychologist, which means she probably has

   a. a doctoral degree in psychology.
   b. a psychodynamic approach to therapy.
   c. the right to prescribe drugs in any U.S. state.
   d. a medical degree.

4. A primary aim of classical psychoanalysis is to

   a. help clients get in touch with their current feelings.
   b. help clients gain insight into their unconscious conflicts.
   c. replace clients' problematic behaviors with more desirable behaviors.
   d. teach clients new ways of thinking.

5. Client-centered therapists convey empathy by

   a. trying to see the world from the client's point of view.
   b. being actualized.
   c. exhibiting unconditional positive regard.
   d. being congruent.

6. Carl Rogers developed

   a. client-centered therapy.
   b. rational-emotive behavior therapy.
   c. cognitive-behavior therapy.
   d. object relations therapy.

7. Shanobi is tearfully telling a friend that she is depressed and does not know why. Her friend says, "You seem so unhappy, and maybe a bit scared, too." The friend's response is most like which method used in client-centered therapy?

   a. sympathy   c. reflection
   b. empathy   d. actualization

8. In psychoanalysis, insight begins when

   a. unconscious thoughts and impulses become conscious.
   b. clients shift feelings about a significant person onto the therapist.
   c. the manifest content of a dream is translated into latent content.
   d. free association reveals conscious processes.

9. Brandon complains that he has an intense need to touch all four walls of any room he enters for the first time. His therapist suggests that Brandon might have learned this compulsive behavior because it helped him avoid anxiety. The therapist appears to favor the _____ approach to treatment.

   a. psychodynamic   c. behavioral
   b. humanistic   d. neurobiological

10. Compared with classical psychoanalysis, contemporary variations on psychoanalysis

   a. use group rather than individual treatment.
   b. emphasize behaviors, not feelings.
   c. focus on interpersonal relationships rather than id impulses.
   d. focus less on the client-patient relationship.

11. According to the American Psychological Association's *Ethical Principles of Psychologists and Code of Conduct*, a therapist may reveal information learned about a client during therapy if

    a. the client is applying for a job and the employer requests this information.
    b. the client drops out of therapy.
    c. the client is suicidal and needs immediate hospitalization.
    d. the therapist feels it will do no harm.

12. Juanita is trying to influence lawmakers to pass laws that will help prevent psychological problems caused by malnutrition, overcrowding, and homelessness. She is most likely a _____ psychologist.

    a. behavioral   c. humanistic
    b. community   d. psychodynamic

13. Rafer's intense fear of spiders greatly interferes with his job as a forest ranger. His therapist suggests that he stay in a room full of harmless spiders until he feels no further anxiety. This therapy technique is known as

    a. flooding.   c. systematic desensitization.
    b. punishment.   d. aversive conditioning.

14. Sally constantly tells herself that she is "worthless" and "will never succeed at anything." Her therapist helps her practice new thoughts such as "I'm as good as the next person" and "I am going to try my best." Her therapist is using the technique of _____, which is part of _____ therapy.

    a. free association; psychodynamic
    b. reflection; humanistic
    c. stress inoculation; behavioral
    d. cognitive restructuring; cognitive-behavior

15. Lucinda is experiencing severe depression that leaves her unable to enjoy life. She has not responded to psychotherapies or medication. Lucinda would be a candidate for

    a. neuroleptics.   c. aversive conditioning.
    b. ECT.   d. cognitive restructuring.

16. The "Dodo Bird Verdict" about psychotherapy is that

    a. all treatments are equally effective.
    b. some treatments are better for some disorders.
    c. people receiving treatment get better at the same rate as people not receiving treatment.
    d. bartenders and hair stylists are as effective as professional therapists.

17. An important element in the success of many forms of psychotherapy is

    a. the client-therapist relationship.
    b. randomly assigning therapists to clients.
    c. having a therapist trained in a variety of therapeutic methods.
    d. having appropriate assessment methods to measure outcomes.

18. When prescribing neuroleptics for schizophrenics, psychiatrists must consider that patients may

    a. become addicted to them.
    b. become insensitive to them after an extended period of time.
    c. develop problematic side effects such as tardive dyskinesia.
    d. experience hallucinations after extensive use.

19. Jon's therapist has prescribed anxiolytics for him. Jon is probably being treated for

    a. depression.   c. schizophrenia.
    b. an anxiety disorder. d. somatoform disorder.

20. Which of the following is not an advantage of group therapy?

    a. It allows the therapist to observe clients interacting with one another.
    b. Clients learn from one another.
    c. Clients improve more quickly.
    d. Clients feel less alone.

14

Social Psychology

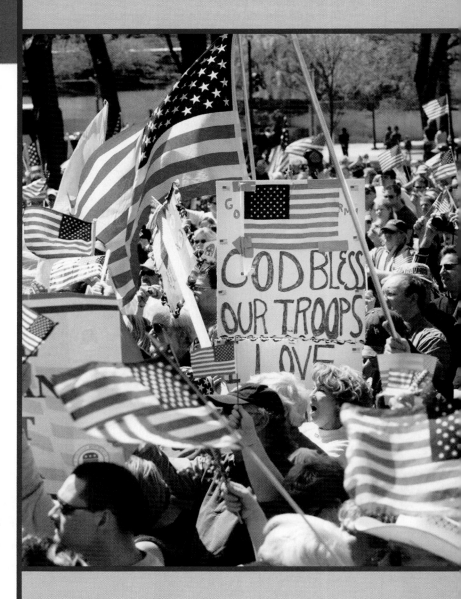

If you are like most people, there is probably at least one thing you do in private that you would never do when someone else is around. The tendency to behave differently when others are present is just one aspect of social psychology. This chapter describes many other ways in which the presence and behavior of other people affect our thoughts and behaviors, and how we, in turn, affect the thoughts and behaviors of others. It explores how perception, learning, memory, thinking, and emotion occur in relation to other people; how people think about themselves and others; why we may like one person but dislike another; how people form and change attitudes; and why and how we judge other people, sometimes in biased ways. Social pressure, ranging from unspoken social rules to commands for obedience, is another concern of social psychologists. The chapter also reviews some of the helpful, cooperative, competitive, and aggressive ways in which people behave toward one another in the workplace and in other social situations. Finally, it considers group decision making and other group processes.

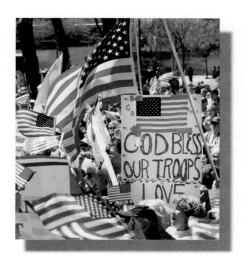

Reading this chapter will help you to answer the following questions:

► **How do we compare ourselves with others?**

► **Do we perceive people and objects in similar ways?**

► **Do attitudes always determine behavior?**

► **How does prejudice develop?**

► **What factors affect who likes whom?**

► **What social rules shape our behavior?**

► **How far will people go in obeying authority?**

► **Are people born aggressive?**

► **What motivates people to help one another?**

► **What makes a good leader?**

On September 11, 2001, terrorists who had hijacked American Airlines Flight 11 crashed the plane into the north tower of New York City's World Trade Center. Another group of hijackers flew United Airlines Flight 175 into the Trade Center's south tower. Less than an hour later, a third team of terrorists flew American Airlines Flight 77 into the Pentagon building, in Washington, D.C. Hijackers of a fourth plane were prevented from striking another target in Washington by courageous passengers who attacked the hijackers. That plane, United Flight 93, crashed in a Pennsylvania field, killing everyone aboard. The death toll in these attacks exceeded 3,000, the largest number of people to die violently on American soil in a single day since 1862, during the U.S. Civil War.

Almost all of the questions that can be asked about this horrendous tragedy, and about terrorism in general, relate to human behavior. For example, what could lead people to kill themselves, along with thousands of innocent people, in the name of political or religious beliefs? Why did hundreds of firefighters, police officers, emergency medical workers, and others enter the World Trade Center's burning towers to save the lives of others while risking, and ultimately losing, their own? Why did some of the people who were fleeing the damaged buildings return to their offices after hearing an announcement telling them to do so? Is there any reason to hope that the hatred and distrust that brought about this disaster can someday be reduced or eliminated?

We may never have final answers to questions like these, but some partial answers may lie in the study of **social psychology,** the scientific study of how people's thoughts and feelings influence their behavior toward others, and how the behavior of others influences people's own thoughts, feelings, and behavior. In this chapter, we focus on several topics in social psychology, including **social cognition** (the mental processes associated with how people perceive and react to other individuals and groups) and group and interpersonal behaviors such as conformity, aggression, and helping. One important aspect of social cognition is how it affects the way we see ourselves.

Social Influences on the Self

▶ **How do we compare ourselves with others?**

Each of us lives in both a personal and a social world. This means that although you experience your thoughts and feelings as your own, they have been strongly influenced by other people.

The thoughts, feelings, and beliefs about what characteristics you have and who you are make up your **self-concept.** Although your self-concept is unique to you, it is a product of your social and cultural environment. In the chapters on human development and personality, we describe how each individual develops within a cultural context, and how collectivist and individualist cultures emphasize different core values and encourage contrasting definitions of the self. As you will see in this chapter, culture also provides the context for **self-esteem,** the evaluations you make of your worth as a human being. Let's look at how self-esteem develops.

Social Comparison

People spend a lot of time thinking about themselves, trying to evaluate their own perceptions, opinions, values, abilities, and so on (Buunk & Oldersma, 2001). Decades ago, Leon Festinger (1954) noted that self-evaluation involves two distinct types of questions: those that can be answered by taking objective measurements and those that cannot. You can determine your height or weight by measuring it, but for other types of questions—about your creativity or attractiveness, for example—there are no objective criteria, no obvious yardsticks. In these cases, according to Festinger's theory of **social comparison,** people evaluate themselves in relation to others. When you wonder how creative, interesting, or attractive you are, you use social rather than objective criteria (Oyserman, 2001).

Who serves as your basis of comparison? Festinger said that people usually look to others who are similar to themselves. For example, if you are curious about how good you are at swimming or science, you will probably compare yourself with people who are at about your own level of experience and ability, not with Olympic champions or Nobel Prize winners (Major, Sciacchtinano, & Crocker, 1993). The categories of people you feel you belong to, and usually compare yourself with, are called your **reference groups.**

social psychology   The subfield of psychology that explores the effects of the social world on the behavior and mental processes of individuals and groups.

social cognition   Mental processes associated with people's perceptions of, and reactions to, other people.

self-concept   The way one thinks of oneself.

self-esteem   The evaluations people make about their worth as human beings.

social comparison   Using other people as a basis of comparison for evaluating oneself.

reference groups   Categories of people with whom individuals compare themselves.

The performance of individuals in your reference groups can affect your self-esteem (Baumeister, 1998). For example, if being good at science is important to you, knowing that someone in your reference group always scores much higher than you on science tests can lower your self-esteem. To protect their self-esteem and make themselves feel better, people sometimes compare themselves with those who are not as good, a strategy called *downward social comparison*. They may also sometimes engage in *upward social comparison*, comparing themselves with people who are doing much better than they are (Wood, Michele, & Giordano, 2000). They do this because the upward comparison can make them optimistic about improving their performance in the future. As another way of protecting self-esteem, people might tell themselves that the superior performer is not really similar enough to be in their reference group, or even that the ability in question is not that important to them (Alicke et al., 1997).

An unfavorable comparison of your own status with that of others can produce **relative deprivation**—the belief that whatever you are getting, it is less than what you deserve (Corning, 2000). If a person with an average income constantly identifies very wealthy people as a reference group, the resulting relative deprivation can create depression and anxiety (Taylor & Lobel, 1989). And if a large group experiences relative deprivation, political unrest may follow. The turmoil usually starts after the members of an oppressed group experience some improvement in their lives and begin to compare their circumstances with those in other groups (Worchel et al., 2000). This improvement brings higher expectations about what they deserve. It is likely, for example, that resentment over U.S. prosperity and global influence plays a role in creating the hatred that leads some people to engage in terrorist attacks against the United States.

FOCUS ON RESEARCH

Self-Esteem and the Ultimate Terror

Why is self-esteem so important to so many people? An intriguing answer to this question comes from the *terror management theory* proposed by Jeff Greenberg, Tom Pyszczynski, and Sheldon Solomon. This theory is based on the notion that humans are the only creatures capable of thinking about the future and realizing that we will all eventually die. Terror management theory suggests that humans cope with anxiety, including the terror that thoughts about death might bring, by developing a variety of self-protective psychological strategies. One of these is the effort to establish and maintain high self-esteem (Greenberg, Pyszczynski, & Solomon, 2003; Pyszczynski, Greenberg, & Solomon, 2001).

■ **What was the researchers' question?**

In one series of experiments, Greenberg and his colleagues (1992) asked whether high self-esteem would, in fact, serve as a buffer against anxiety—specifically, the anxiety brought on by thoughts about death and pain.

■ **How did the researchers answer the question?**

About 150 students at several North American universities participated in one of three studies, each of which followed a similar format. The first step was to temporarily alter the participants' self-esteem. To do so, the researchers gave the students feedback on a personality or intelligence test they had taken earlier in the semester. Half the participants received positive feedback designed to increase their self-esteem. The other half received feedback that was neutral—it was neither flattering nor depressing. (Measurement of the students' self-esteem showed that the positive feedback actually did create higher self-esteem than the neutral feedback.) In the next phase of each experiment, the researchers used a film about death, or the (false) threat of a mild electric shock, to provoke some anxiety in half the participants in the positive feedback group and half the participants in the neutral feedback group. The amount of anxiety created was measured

relative deprivation The sense that one is not getting all that one deserves.

by the participants' self-reports or by monitoring galvanic skin resistance (GSR), a measure of perspiration in their skin that reflects anxiety-related physiological arousal (Dawson, Scheel, & Fillon, 2000).

■ What did the researchers find?

Self-reports and GSR measures revealed that participants in all three experiments were significantly less upset by an anxiety-provoking experience (the death film or the threat of shock) if they had first received esteem-building feedback about their previous test performance.

■ What do the results mean?

The researchers concluded that their results support the notion that self-esteem can act as a buffer against anxiety and other negative feelings. This conclusion would help explain why people are so eager to maintain or enhance their self-esteem (Tesser, 2001): We don't like to feel anxious, and increased self-esteem reduces most people's anxiety.

■ What do we still need to know?

These results certainly support terror management theory, but by themselves, they are not broad enough to confirm all of its assumptions. For example, the theory also predicts that when people are sensitized to the threat of death, they will seek to protect themselves by avoiding thoughts of death, denying personal vulnerability to death, and doing things to increase social support from those around them. Other studies by Greenberg and his colleagues show that people do, indeed, use these strategies (e.g., Greenberg et al., 2003; Jonas et al., 2002; Pyszczynski, Greenberg, & Solomon, 2003). For example, increased patriotism, a common response in people concerned about death, has been evident in the United States since the September 11, 2001, terrorist attacks. Reliance on religious faith is another widespread response.

But which strategies are people most likely to use, and why? Are some strategies more or less likely to be adopted at different times in a person's life or among people in certain cultures? And what forms of self-esteem are most important in different cultures? So far, most of the research on terror management theory has been done in individualistic cultures such as North America, where self-esteem is largely based on personal accomplishments. However, terror management theory has also been supported by preliminary studies in Japan, aboriginal Australia, and other collectivist cultures where feelings of self-worth tend to be more closely tied to the performance and status of the groups to which people belong (Halloran & Kashima, in press; Heine, Harihara, & Niiya, 2002). It will take many more experiments to test all the predictions derived from the theory.

Social Identity Theory

Stop reading for a moment, and complete the following sentence: I am a(n) _____. Some people fill in the blank using characteristics such as "hard worker," "good sport," or some other aspect of their *personal* identity. However, many others identify themselves using a word or phrase that refers to their nationality, gender, or religion. These latter responses reflect **social identity,** our beliefs about the groups to which we belong. Our social identity is therefore a part of our self-concept (Ellemers, Spears, & Doojse, 2002).

Our social or group identity permits us to feel part of a larger whole (Arnett, 2002; Deaux & Martin, 2003). Its importance is seen in the pride that people feel when a member of their family graduates from college or when a local team wins a big game (Burris,

learn by**doing**

social identity   The beliefs we hold about the groups to which we belong.

social perception   The processes through which people interpret information about others, draw inferences about them, and develop mental representations of them.

schemas   Mental representations about people and social situations.

Branscombe, & Klar, 1997). In wars between national, ethnic, or religious groups, individuals sacrifice and sometimes die for the sake of their group identity. A group identity is also one reason people donate money to those in need, support friends in a crisis, and display other helping behaviors. As we shall see later, however, defining ourselves in terms of a group identity can foster an "us versus them" mentality that sets the stage for prejudice, discrimination, and intergroup conflict (Brewer, 2001).

Social Perception

▶ **Do we perceive people and objects in similar ways?**

There is a story about a company president who was having lunch with a man being considered for an executive position. When the man salted his food without first tasting it, the president decided not to hire him. The reason, she explained, was that the company had no room for a person who acted before collecting all relevant information. The candidate lost his chance because of the president's **social perception,** the processes through which people interpret information about others, form impressions of them, and draw conclusions about the reasons for their behavior. In this section we will examine how and why social perception influences our thoughts, feelings, and actions.

The Role of Schemas

The perception of people follows many of the same laws that govern the perception of objects, including the Gestalt principles discussed in the chapter on sensation and perception. Consider Figure 14.1. Consistent with Gestalt principles, most people would describe it as "a square with a notch in one side," not as eight straight lines (Woodworth & Schlosberg, 1954). The reason is that they interpret new information using the mental representations, or **schemas,** that they already have about squares. In other words, they interpret this diagram as a square with a slight modification.

Schemas about people, too, can affect our perception of them. For one thing, schemas influence what we pay attention to and what we ignore. We tend to process information about the other person more quickly if it confirms our beliefs about that person's gender or ethnic group, for example, than if it violates those beliefs (Smith & Quellar, 2001). Second, schemas influence what we remember about others. In one study, if people thought a woman they saw in a videotape was a waitress, they recalled that she had a beer with dinner and owned a TV set. Those who thought she was a librarian remembered that she was wearing glasses and liked classical music (Cohen, 1981). Finally, schemas affect our judgment about the behavior of others (Fiske, 1995). Thomas Hill and his colleagues (1989) found that participants' ratings of male and female friends' sadness were influenced not only by the friends' actual behavior but also by the participants' general schemas about how much sadness men versus women experience.

In other words, through top-down processing (discussed in the sensation and perception chapter), our schemas about people influence our perceptions of them. And just as schemas help us read sentences whose words have missing letters, they also allow us to efficiently "fill in the blanks" about people. Our schemas tell us, for example, that someone wearing a store uniform or name tag is likely to know where merchandise is located, so we usually approach that person for help. Accurate schemas help us to categorize people quickly and respond appropriately in social situations, but if schemas are incorrect they can create false expectations and errors in judgment about people that can lead to narrow-mindedness and even prejudice.

LINKAGES
Do we sometimes perceive people the same way we perceive objects? (a link to Sensation and Perception)

figure 14.1

A Schema-Plus-Correction

People who see an object like this tend to use a pre-existing mental representation (their schema of a square) and then correct or modify it in some way (here, with a notch).

MAY I HELP YOU? Schemas help us to quickly categorize people and respond appropriately to them, but they can also create narrow-mindedness and, as we shall see later, prejudice. If this woman does not fulfill your schema—your mental representation—of how carpenters are supposed to look, you might be less likely to ask her advice on your home improvement project. One expert carpenter who manages the hardware department of a large home improvement store told us that most customers walk right past her in order to ask the advice of one of her less-experienced male clerks.

First Impressions

Our schemas about people shape our first impression of them. That impression, in turn, influences both our later perceptions of their behavior and our reactions to it. First impressions are formed quickly, usually change slowly, and typically have a long-lasting influence. No wonder they are so important in the development of social relations (Brehm, Kassin, & Fein, 2002). How do people form impressions of other people? And why are these impressions so resistant to change?

Forming Impressions   Think about your first impression of a close friend. It probably formed rapidly, because existing schemas create a tendency to automatically infer a great deal about a person on the basis of limited information (Smith & Quellar, 2001). An ethnic name, for example, might have caused you to draw inferences about your friend's religion, food preferences, or temperament. Clothing or hairstyle might have led you to make assumptions about her political views or taste in music. These inferences and assumptions may or may not be accurate. How many turned out to be true in your friend's case?

One type of schema has a particularly strong influence on first impressions: We tend to assume that the people we meet hold attitudes and values similar to our own (Hoyle, 1993). So, all else being equal, we are inclined to like other people. However, even a small amount of negative information can change our minds. Why? The main reason is that most of us don't expect other people to act negatively toward us. When unexpectedly negative behaviors do occur, they capture our attention and lead us to believe that these behaviors reflect something negative about the other person (Taylor, Peplau, & Sears,

Noticeable features or actions help shape our impressions of others. Those impressions may or may not be correct.

2003). Accordingly, negative information attracts more attention and carries more weight than positive information in shaping first impressions (Smith & Mackie, 2000).

Lasting Impressions   Does your friend seem the same today as when you first met? First impressions can change, but the process is usually very slow. One reason is that humans tend to be "cognitive misers" (Fiske, 1995). We like to hold on to our beliefs about the world, often using our schemas to preserve a reality that fits our expectations. Clinging to existing impressions appears to be part of this effort. If your friend recently violated your expectations by being impatient, your view of her probably did not change much, if at all. In fact, you may have acted to preserve your impression of her by thinking something like, "She is not herself today." In other words, impressions change slowly because the meaning we give to new information about people is shaped by what we already know or believe about them (Sherman & Klein, 1994).

Self-Fulfilling Prophecies   Another reason first impressions tend to be stable is that we often do things that cause others to confirm our impressions (Franzoi, 2003). For example, counselors can draw extraverted behavior from clients whom they *believe* to be extraverted, whether or not the clients actually are extraverted (Copeland & Snyder, 1995). When, without our awareness, schemas cause us to subtly lead people to behave in line with our expectations, a **self-fulfilling prophecy** is at work.

Self-fulfilling prophecies also help maintain judgments about groups. If you assume that members of a certain ethnic group are pushy or aggressive, for example, you might be defensive or even hostile toward someone in that group. That person might react to your behavior with frustration and anger. These reactions fulfill your prophecy and strengthen the impressions that created it (Ross & Jackson, 1991).

Explaining Behavior: Attribution

So far, we have examined how people form impressions about other people's characteristics. But our perceptions of others also include our explanations of their behavior. People tend to form ideas about why people (including themselves) behave as they do and about

SELF-FULFILLING PROPHECIES IN THE CLASSROOM   If teachers inadvertently spend less time helping children who initially impressed them as "dull," those children may not learn as much, thus fulfilling the teachers' expectations. If the girl in the back row has not impressed this teacher as being bright, how likely do you think it is that she will be called on?

self-fulfilling prophecy   A process in which an initial impression causes us to bring out behavior in another that confirms the impression.

what behavior to expect in the future (Brehm, Kassin, & Fein, 2002). Psychologists use the term **attribution** to describe the process we go through to explain the causes of behavior (including our own).

As an example, suppose a classmate fails to return borrowed notes on time. You could attribute this behavior to many causes, from an emergency situation to selfishness. Which of these explanations you choose is important, because it will help you *understand* your classmate's behavior, *predict* what will happen if this person asks to borrow something in the future, and decide how to *control* the situation should it arise again. Similarly, whether a person attributes a partner's nagging to temporary stress or to loss of affection can influence whether that person will work on the relationship or get out of it.

People usually attribute behavior in a particular situation to either internal causes (characteristics of the person) or external causes (aspects of the situation). For example, if you thought your classmate's failure to return your notes was due mainly to lack of consideration or laziness, you would be making an *internal attribution*. If you thought that the oversight was due mainly to time pressure caused by an upcoming exam or a family crisis, you would be making an *external attribution*. Similarly, if you failed an exam, you could explain it by concluding that you're not very smart (internal attribution) or that your work schedule left you too little time to study (external attribution). The attribution that you make, in turn, might determine how much you study for the next exam or even whether you decide to stay in school.

Biases in Attribution

Most people are usually logical in their attempts to explain behavior (Trope, Cohen, & Alfieri, 1991). However, they are also prone to *attributional biases,* or errors, that can distort their view of behavior (Gilbert, 1998).

North American psychologists have paid special attention to the **fundamental attribution error,** a tendency to overattribute the behavior of others to internal factors (Gilbert & Malone, 1995). Imagine that you hear a student give an incorrect answer in class. You will probably attribute this behavior to an internal cause and infer that the person is not very smart. In doing so, however, you might be ignoring possible external factors (such as lack of study time).

A related form of attributional bias is called the *ultimate attribution error*. Through this error, the positive actions of people from a different ethnic or social group are attributed to external causes, such as luck, whereas their negative actions are attributed to internal causes, such as dishonesty (Pettigrew, 1979). The ultimate attribution error causes people to see good deeds done by those in their own group as being due to internal factors and bad deeds as stemming from external causes. In this way, the ultimate attribution error helps to create and maintain people's negative views of other groups and positive views of their own group (Fiske, 1998).

Like other aspects of social cognition, these attributional biases may not be universal (Sabini, Siepmann, & Stein, 2001). For example, research suggests that the fundamental attribution error and the ultimate attribution error are less likely to appear among people in collectivist cultures such as India, China, Japan, and Korea compared with people in the individualist cultures of North America and Europe (Morris & Peng, 1994). Even within individualistic cultures, some people are probably more likely than others to commit these errors (Miller, 2001; Vandello & Cohen, 1999).

The inclination toward internal attributions is much less pronounced when people explain their own behavior. In fact, there tends to be an **actor-observer bias:** Whereas people often attribute other people's behavior to internal causes, they tend to attribute their own behavior to external factors, especially when that behavior is inappropriate or inadequate (Baumeister, 1998). For example, when you drive slowly, it is because you are looking for an address, not because you are a big loser like that jerk who crawled along in front of you yesterday.

attribution   The process of explaining the causes of people's behavior, including our own.

fundamental attribution error   A bias toward overattributing the behavior of others to internal factors.

actor-observer bias   The tendency to attribute other people's behavior to internal causes while attributing one's own behavior to external causes.

WHY ARE THEY HELPING? Attributional biases are more common in some cultures than others. In one study, students in an individualist culture were more likely than those in a collectivist culture to explain acts of helping as being due to internal causes such as kindness or enjoyment of helping (Miller & Bersoff, 1994).

The actor-observer bias occurs mainly because people have different kinds of information about their own behavior and the behavior of others (Krueger, Ham, & Linford, 1996). When *you* are behaving in some situation—giving a speech, perhaps—the information most available to you is likely to be external and situational, such as the temperature of the room and the size of the audience. You also have a lot of information about other external factors, such as the amount of time you had to prepare your talk or the upsetting conversation that occurred this morning. Whatever the outcome of your efforts, you can easily attribute it to one or all of these external causes. But when you observe someone else, the most obvious information in the situation is *that person*. You do not know what happened to the person last night or this morning, so you are likely to attribute whatever he or she does to stable, internal characteristics (Gilbert, 1998).

Of course, people do not always attribute their own behavior to external forces. In fact, whether they do so often depends on whether the outcome is positive or negative. One group of researchers assigned pairs of students to work together on a task and then, no matter how well the teams actually did, told them that they had either succeeded or failed on the task. If told the team was successful, the students took personal credit for the success; but if they failed, they blamed their partner (Sedikides et al., 1998). These students showed a **self-serving bias**, the tendency to take personal credit for success but to blame external causes for failure.

The self-serving bias occurs, in part, because people are motivated to maintain their self-esteem—and ignoring negative information about themselves is one way to do so. If you just failed an exam, it is painful to admit that it was fair. In short, people think about their failures and shortcomings in ways that protect their self-esteem (Tesser, 2001).

Self-protective cognitive biases help us temporarily escape from painful situations, but they also set the stage for a distorted view of reality and create problems in the long run (Kruger & Dunning, 1999). One such problem is *unrealistic optimism,* the tendency to believe that good things (e.g., financial success) are likely to happen to you, but that bad things (e.g., accidents or illness) are not (Radcliffe & Klein, 2002). Unrealistic optimism tends to persist even when there is strong evidence against it, and it can lead to potentially harmful behaviors. For example, people who are unrealistically optimistic about their health may not bother to exercise and may ignore information about how to prevent heart disease (Davidson & Prkachin, 1997). ("In Review: Some Biases in Social Perception" summarizes the common cognitive biases discussed here.)

self-serving bias The cognitive tendency to attribute one's successes to internal characteristics while blaming one's failures on external causes.

in review

SOME BIASES IN SOCIAL PERCEPTION

Bias	Description
Importance of first impression	Ambiguous information is interpreted in line with a first impression, and the initial schema is recalled better and more vividly than any later correction to it. Actions based on this impression may elicit behavior that confirms it.
Fundamental attribution error	The tendency to overattribute the behavior of others to internal factors.
Actor-observer bias	The tendency for actors to attribute their own behavior to external causes and for observers to attribute the behavior of others to internal factors.
Self-serving bias	The tendency to attribute one's successes to internal factors and one's failures to external factors.
Unrealistic optimism	The tendency of people to believe that good things will happen to them but that bad things will not.

? *The fundamental attribution error appears to be somewhat less likely to occur among people in _____ cultures.*

Attitudes

▶ **Do attitudes always determine behavior?**

Our views about health, safety, or any other topic reflect our attitudes. Social psychologists have studied this aspect of social cognition longer and more intensely than any other. An **attitude** is the tendency to think, feel, or act positively or negatively toward objects in our environment (Ajzen, 2001). Attitudes play an important role in guiding how we react to other people, what causes and politicians we support, which products we buy, and countless other daily decisions.

The Structure of Attitudes

Social psychologists have long viewed attitudes as having three components (Bohner & Schwarz, 2001). The *cognitive* component is a set of beliefs about the attitude object. The emotional, or *affective,* component includes feelings about the object. And the *behavioral* component is the way people act toward the object. If these three components were always in harmony, we would be able to predict people's behavior toward the homeless, for example, on the basis of the thoughts or feelings they express, and vice versa. This is often not the case, however (Schwarz & Bohner, 2001). Many people's charitable thoughts and sympathetic emotions regarding the homeless are never translated into actions aimed at helping them.

   What determines whether people's behavior will be consistent with the cognitive and affective components of their attitudes? Several factors are important. For one thing, consistency is most likely when the person's thoughts and feelings are in agreement (Taylor, Peplau, & Sears, 2003). Second, consistency is more likely when the behavioral component of the attitude is in line with a *subjective norm,* our view of how the important

attitude A tendency toward a particular cognitive, emotional, or behavioral reaction to objects in one's environment.

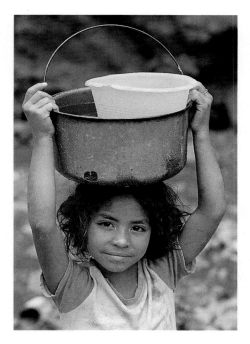

A REMINDER ABOUT POVERTY   Fundraisers use photographs like this one to remind people of the kind thoughts and charitable feelings they have toward needy people and other worthy causes. As a result, people may be more likely to behave in accordance with the cognitive and affective components of their attitudes and make a donation to these causes. Browse through several popular magazines, and calculate the percentage of such photos you find in ads for charitable organizations. While you are at it, make a note of other stimuli in these organizations' appeals that remind us of our concern for the less fortunate.

learn ^{by}doing

elaboration likelihood model   A model of attitude change suggesting that people can change their attitudes through a central route (by considering an argument's content) or through a peripheral route (in which they rely on irrelevant persuasion cues).

people in our lives want us to act. If there is a conflict between what we want to do and what a subjective norm tells us we should do, we may end up behaving in ways that are inconsistent with our attitudes (Ajzen, 2001). For example, someone who believes that the rights of gay men and lesbians should be protected might not go out and campaign for this cause, because doing so would upset valued family members or co-workers who are strongly against it. Third, attitude-consistent behavior is more likely when people have *perceived control,* a belief that they can actually perform the behavior (Ajzen & Fishbein, 2002). The cognitive and emotional components of your attitude toward protecting an endangered species might be positive, but if you don't believe you can do anything about it, you are not likely to even try. Finally, *direct experience* with the object of an attitude increases the likelihood of attitude-consistent behavior (Bohner & Schwarz, 2001). If your positive attitude toward dogs is based on having had a dog yourself, you are more likely to donate time or money to shelters for homeless dogs than if you had only heard about the joys a dog can bring.

Forming Attitudes

People's attitudes about objects begin to appear in early childhood and continue to emerge throughout life. How do these attitudes form? Genetics may have a certain amount of influence on some attitudes (Abrahamson, Baker, & Caspi, 2002), but the formation of attitudes is primarily explained by the principles discussed in the chapter on learning. In childhood, modeling and other forms of social learning play a major role. Children learn not only the names of objects but also what they should believe and feel about them and how they should act toward them. For example, a parent's words may teach a child not only that snakes are reptiles but also that they should be feared and avoided. So as children learn concepts such as "reptile" or "work," they learn attitudes about those concepts, too (Bohner & Schwarz, 2001).

Classical and operant conditioning can also shape positive or negative attitudes (Baron & Byrne, 2003). Advertisers pair up enjoyable music or soothing colors with the products they try to sell (Pratkanis & Aronson, 2001), and parents, teachers, and peers reward children for stating particular views. The *mere-exposure effect* described in the consciousness chapter is influential as well. All else being equal, attitudes toward an object will become more positive the more frequently people are exposed to the object (Zajonc, 2001b). One study even found that newborns preferred to listen to stories that had been read aloud while they were still in the womb (Cacioppo, Berntson, & Petty, 1997). This exposure effect helps explain why commercials and political ads are aired over and over, and why some rock bands won't include new songs in a live concert until their fans have repeatedly heard, and come to like, the recorded version.

Changing Attitudes

The nearly $100 billion a year spent on advertising in the United States alone provides but one example of how people constantly try to change our attitudes (Clay, 2002a). Stop for a moment and make a list of other examples, starting, perhaps, with the persuasive messages of groups concerned with abortion or gun control or recycling—and don't forget your friends who want you to do something that you think is a waste of time.

Two Routes to Attitude Change   Whether a persuasive message succeeds in changing attitudes depends mainly on three factors: (1) the person communicating the message, (2) the content of the message, and (3) the audience who receives it (Bohner & Schwarz, 2001). The **elaboration likelihood model** of attitude change—illustrated in Figure 14.2—provides a framework for understanding when and how these factors affect

Central route

Persuasive message → High elaboration → Careful processing of information → Degree of attitude change depends on quality of arguments

Peripheral route

Low elaboration → Careful processing does not occur → Attitude change depends on presence of persuasion cues

figure 14.2

The Elaboration Likelihood Model of Attitude Change

The central route to attitude change involves carefully processing and evaluating a message's content (high elaboration). The peripheral route involves low elaboration, or processing, of the message and reliance on persuasion cues such as the attractiveness of the person making the argument (Cacioppo, Petty, & Crites, 1993).

attitude change. The model is based on the idea that persuasive messages can change people's attitudes through one of two main routes. The first is called the *peripheral route* because when it is activated, we devote little attention to the central content of the persuasive message. We tend to be affected instead by peripheral, or surrounding, persuasion cues, such as the confidence, attractiveness, or other characteristics of the person who delivers the message. These persuasion cues influence attitude change even though they may have nothing to do with the logic or validity of the message itself. Commercials in which movie stars or other attractive nonexperts endorse pain relievers or denture cleaners are designed to encourage the peripheral route to attitude change. By contrast, when the *central route* to attitude change is activated, the core content of the message becomes more important than the communicator's characteristics in determining attitude change. A person following the central route uses logical steps—like those outlined in the Thinking Critically sections of this book—to analyze the content of the persuasive message, including the validity of its claims, whether it leaves out pertinent information, alternative interpretations of evidence, and so on.

What determines which route people will follow? Personal involvement with message content is an important factor. The elaboration likelihood model predicts that the more personally involving a topic is, the more likely it is that the central route will be activated (Petty & Wegener, 1998; Wood, 2000). Suppose, for example, that you hear someone arguing for the cancellation of student loans in Chile. This message might persuade you through the peripheral route if it comes from someone who looks attractive and sounds intelligent. However, you are more likely to follow the central route if the message proposes terminating student loans at your own school. You might still be persuaded, but only if the logic of the message is clear and convincing. This is why celebrity endorsements tend to be more effective when the products being advertised are relatively unimportant to the audience.

Persuasive messages are not the only means of changing attitudes. Another approach is to get people to act in ways that are inconsistent with their attitudes, in the hope that they will adjust those attitudes to match their behavior. Often, such adjustments do occur. Cognitive dissonance theory attempts to explain why.

cognitive dissonance theory   A theory stating that uneasiness results when people's thoughts, beliefs, and attitudes are inconsistent with one another and with their behavior, and that such uneasiness motivates people to try to restore consistency.

Cognitive Dissonance Theory   Leon Festinger's (1957) classic **cognitive dissonance theory** holds that people want their thoughts, beliefs, and attitudes to be in harmony with one another and with their behavior. When these various elements are inconsistent, or *dissonant*, people become anxious and motivated to make them more consistent (Harmon-Jones et al., 1996). For example, someone who believes that "smoking is dangerous" but who must also

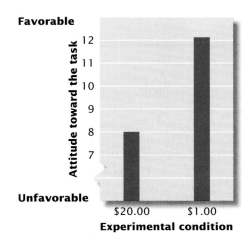

Favorable

Unfavorable

Experimental condition

■ High justification (low dissonance)
■ Low justification (high dissonance)

Source: Festinger & Carlsmith (1959).

figure 14.3

Cognitive Dissonance and Attitude Change

According to cognitive dissonance theory, people given $20 to say that a boring task was enjoyable had clear justification for lying and should experience little dissonance between what they said and what they felt about the task. In fact, their attitude toward the task did not change much. However, people who received only $1 had little justification to lie and reduced their dissonance mainly by displaying a more positive attitude toward the task.

acknowledge that "I smoke" would be motivated to reduce the resulting dissonance. Because it is often difficult to change behavior, people usually reduce cognitive dissonance by changing attitudes that are inconsistent with the behavior. So rather than quit smoking, the smoker might decide that smoking is not so dangerous after all.

In one of the first studies of cognitive dissonance, Festinger and his colleague Merrill Carlsmith (1959) asked people to turn pegs in a pegboard, a very dull task. Later, some of these people were asked to persuade a person waiting to participate in the study that the task was "exciting and fun." Some were told that they would be paid $1 to tell this lie. Others were promised $20. After they had talked to the waiting person, their attitudes toward the dull task were measured. Figure 14.3 shows and explains the surprising results. The people who were paid just $1 to lie liked the dull task more than those who were paid $20 (Festinger & Carlsmith, 1959).

Hundreds of other experiments have also found that when people publicly engage in behaviors that are inconsistent with their privately held attitudes, they are likely to change their attitudes to be consistent with their behavior (Stone & Cooper, 2001). These experiments have found that attitude-behavior inconsistency is likely to change attitudes when (1) the inconsistency causes some distress or discomfort in a person and (2) changing attitudes will reduce that discomfort. But why should attitude-behavior inconsistency cause discomfort in the first place? There is considerable debate among attitude researchers about this question (Wood, 2000).

One of the most popular of several proposed answers is that the discomfort is caused when people's positive self-concept (e.g., "I am honest") is threatened by the fact that they have, say, encouraged others to do something that they don't actually believe in or wouldn't do themselves. When their behavior is inconsistent with their self-concept, most people feel dishonest, so they change their attitudes to reduce or eliminate this unpleasant feeling (Stone & Cooper, 2001). In other words, if people can persuade themselves that they really believe in what they have said or done, the inconsistency disappears, their positive self-concept is restored, and they can feel good about themselves again.

The power of cognitive dissonance to change attitudes may be greater in the individualist cultures of Europe and North America than in collectivist cultures such as Japan and China. What is behind these cultural differences? Where group rather than individual values and goals are emphasized, behaving at odds with one's personal beliefs may create less discomfort—and less motivation for attitude change—because holding to those beliefs tends to be less important for self-esteem. ("In Review: Forming and Changing Attitudes" summarizes some of the main processes through which attitudes are formed and changed.)

in review

FORMING AND CHANGING ATTITUDES

Type of Influence	Description
Modeling and conditioning	Attitudes are usually formed through observation of how others behave and speak about an attitude object, as well as through classical and operant conditioning.
Elaboration likelihood model	People change attitudes through either a central or peripheral route, depending on factors such as personal involvement.
Cognitive dissonance	Holding inconsistent cognitions can motivate attitude change.

? *According to the elaboration likelihood model, people are more likely to pay close attention to the content and logic of a persuasive message if the _____ route to attitude change has been activated.*

LINKAGES
Can subconscious processes alter our responses to people?
(a link to Consciousness)

Prejudice and Stereotypes

▶ How does prejudice develop?

All of the principles that underlie impression formation, attribution, and attitudes come together in prejudice and stereotypes. **Stereotypes** are the perceptions, beliefs, and expectations a person has about members of some group. They are schemas about entire groups of people (Dion, 2003). Usually, they involve the false assumption that all members of a group share the same characteristics. The characteristics that make up the stereotype may be positive, but more often they are negative. The most prevalent and powerful stereotypes focus on observable personal attributes, particularly ethnicity, gender, and age (Operario & Fiske, 2001).

The stereotypes people hold can be so ingrained that their effects on behavior can be automatic and unconscious (Banaji, Lemm, & Carpenter, 2001). In one study, for example, European American and African American participants played a video game in which white or black men suddenly appeared on a screen, holding an object that might be a weapon (Correll et al., 2002; see Figure 14.4). The participants had to immediately "shoot" armed men, but not unarmed ones. Under this time pressure, participants' errors were not random. If they "shot" an unarmed man, he was more likely to be black than white; when they failed to "shoot" an armed man, he was more likely to be white than black. These differences appeared in both European American and African American participants, but was most pronounced among those who held the strongest cultural stereotypes about blacks.

Stereotyping often leads to **prejudice,** which is a positive or negative attitude toward an individual based simply on that individual's membership in some group (Dion, 2003). The word *prejudice* means "to prejudge." Many theorists believe that prejudice, like other attitudes, has cognitive, affective, and behavioral components. Stereotyped thinking is the cognitive component of prejudicial attitudes. The hatred, admiration, anger, and other feelings people have about stereotyped groups constitute the affective component. The behavioral component of prejudice involves **discrimination,** which is differential treatment of individuals who belong to different groups.

Theories of Prejudice and Stereotyping

Prejudice and stereotyping may occur for several reasons. Let's consider three explanatory theories, each of which has empirical support and accounts for many instances of stereotyping and prejudice.

Motivational Theories   For some people, prejudice against certain groups serves to meet certain needs and increases their sense of security. This idea was first proposed by Theodor W. Adorno and his associates more than fifty years ago (Adorno et al., 1950) and was elaborated more recently by Bob Altemeyer (1996). These researchers suggest that prejudice is especially likely among people who display a personality trait called *authoritarianism.* According to Altemeyer, authoritarianism is composed of three main elements: (1) acceptance of very conventional or traditional values, (2) willingness to unquestioningly follow the orders of authority figures, and (3) an inclination to act aggressively toward individuals or groups identified by these authority figures as threats to the person's values or well-being. In fact, people with an authoritarian orientation tend to view the world as a threatening place (Winter, 1996). One way to protect themselves from the threats they perceive all around them is to strongly identify with people like themselves—their *in-group*—and to reject, dislike, and perhaps even punish people from groups that are different from their own. Looking down on, and discriminating against, members of these *out-groups*—such as gay men and lesbians, African Americans, European Americans, or Muslims, for example—may help authoritarian people feel safer and better about themselves (Haddock & Zanna, 1998b).

Another motivational explanation of prejudice involves the concept of social identity discussed earlier. Recall that whether or not they display authoritarianism, most people

figure 14.4

The Impact of Stereotypes on Behavior

learn by doing

When these characters suddenly appeared on a video screen, participants were supposed to "shoot" them, but only if they appeared to be armed (Correll et al., 2002). Stereotypes about whether white men or black men are more likely to be armed significantly affected the errors made by participants in firing their video game "weapons." Cover each of these characters with an index card; then ask a few friends to watch as you reveal each character for an instant before covering it again. Then ask your friends to say whether either character appeared to be armed. Was one character more often seen as armed? If so, which one?

are motivated to identify with their in-group and tend to see it as better than other groups (Brewer & Brown, 1998; Prentice & Miller, 2002). As a result, members of an in-group often see all members of out-groups as less attractive and less socially appropriate than members of the in-group and may thus treat them badly (Jackson, 2002). In other words, prejudice may result when people's motivation to enhance their own self-esteem causes them to disrespect other people.

Cognitive Theories   Stereotyping and prejudice may also result from the social-cognitive processes that people use in dealing with the world. There are so many other people, so many situations in which one meets them, and so many behaviors that others might display that we cannot possibly attend to and remember them all. Therefore, people must use schemas and other cognitive shortcuts to organize and make sense of their social world (Kunda & Spencer, 2003). Often these cognitive processes provide accurate and useful summaries of other people, but sometimes they lead to inaccurate stereotypes. Instead of remembering every single detail about every person we meet, we often group people into *social categories,* such as doctor, senior citizen, Republican, student, Italian, and the like (Dovidio, Kawakami, & Gaertner, 2000). To further simplify perception of these categories, we tend to see group members as being quite similar to one another. Members of one ethnic group may even find it harder to distinguish among specific faces in other ethnic groups than in their own (Anthony, Cooper, & Mullen, 1992). People also tend to assume that all members of a different group hold the same beliefs and values, and that those beliefs and values differ from their own (Dion, 2003). Finally, because particularly noticeable stimuli tend to draw a lot of attention, noticeably rude behavior by even a few members of an easily identified ethnic group may lead people to see an *illusory correlation* between rudeness and ethnicity (Hamilton & Sherman, 1994). As a result, they may incorrectly believe that all or most members of that group are rude.

Learning Theories   Like other attitudes, prejudice can be learned. Some prejudice is learned as a result of conflicts between members of different groups, but people also develop negative attitudes toward groups with whom they have had little or no contact. Learning theories suggest that children can acquire prejudices just by watching and listening to parents, peers, and others (Rohan & Zanna, 1996). Movies and television also portray ethnic or other groups in ways that teach stereotypes and prejudice (Smith & Mackie, 2000). And as mentioned earlier, children may be directly reinforced for expressing prejudice. In fact, small children often know about the supposed negative characteristics of many groups long before they ever meet people in those groups (Quintana, 1998).

Reducing Prejudice

One clear implication of the cognitive and learning theories of prejudice and stereotyping is that members of one group are often ignorant or misinformed about the characteristics of people in other groups. Before 1954, for example, most black and white schoolchildren in the United States knew very little about one another because they went to separate schools. Then the Supreme Court declared that segregated public schools should be prohibited. In doing so, the court created a real-life test of the **contact hypothesis,** which states that stereotypes and prejudice toward a group will diminish as contact with that group increases (Hewstone, 2003).

Did the desegregation of U.S. schools in the 1960s and 1970s confirm the contact hypothesis? In a few schools, integration was followed by a decrease in prejudice, but in most places, either no change occurred or prejudice actually increased (Oskamp & Schultz, 1998). However, these results did not necessarily disprove the contact hypothesis. In-depth studies of schools with successful desegregation suggested that contact alone was not enough; integration reduced prejudice only when certain social conditions were created (Pettigrew & Tropp, 2000). First, members of the two groups had to be of roughly equal social and economic status. Second, school authorities had to promote cooperation and interdependence between ethnic groups by having members of the two

stereotypes   Impressions or schemas of an entire group of people that involve the false assumption that all members of the group share the same characteristics.

prejudice   A positive or negative attitude toward people in certain groups.

discrimination   Differential treatment of people in certain groups; the behavioral component of prejudice.

contact hypothesis   The idea that stereotypes and prejudice toward a group will diminish as contact with the group increases.

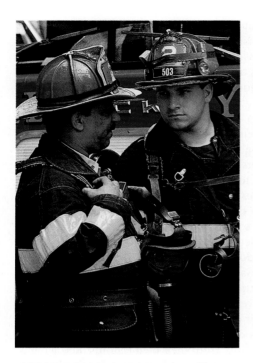

FIGHTING ETHNIC PREJUDICE   Negative attitudes about members of ethnic groups are often based on negative personal experiences or the negative experiences and attitudes people hear about from others. Cooperative contact between equals can help promote mutual respect and reduce ethnic prejudice.

groups work together on projects that required reliance on one another to achieve success. Third, the contact between group members had to occur on a one-to-one basis. It was only when *individuals* got to know each other that the errors contained in stereotypes became apparent. Finally, the members of each group had to be seen as typical and not unusual in any significant way. When these four conditions were met, the children's attitudes toward one another became more positive.

Elliot Aronson (1995) describes a teaching strategy, called the *jigsaw technique,* that helps create these conditions. Children from several ethnic groups must work together on a team to complete a task, such as writing a report about a famous person in history. Each child learns, and provides the team with, a separate piece of information about this person, such as place of birth or greatest achievement (Aronson, 1990). Studies show that children from various ethnic groups who take part in the jigsaw technique and other cooperative learning experiences display substantial reductions in prejudice toward other groups (e.g., Aronson, 1997). The success reported in these studies has greatly increased the popularity of cooperative learning exercises in U.S. classrooms. Such exercises may not eliminate all aspects of ethnic prejudice in children, but they seem to be a step in the right direction.

Can friendly, cooperative, interdependent contact reduce the more entrenched forms of prejudice seen in adults? It may. When equal-status adults from different ethnic groups work jointly toward a common goal, bias and distrust can be reduced. This is especially true if they come to see themselves as members of the same group rather than as belonging to opposing groups (Dovidio, Kawakami, & Gaertner, 2000; Fiske, 2000). The challenge to be met in creating such cooperative experiences in the real world is that the participants must be of equal status—a challenge made more difficult in many countries by the sizable status differences that still exist between ethnic groups (Pettigrew & Tropp, 2000).

In the final analysis, contact can provide only part of the solution to the problems of stereotyping, prejudice, and discrimination. To reduce ethnic prejudice, we must develop additional techniques to address the social cognitions and perceptions that lie at the core of bigotry and hatred toward people who are different from ourselves (Monteith, Zuwerink, & Devine, 1994). Altering these mental processes will be difficult because, as we saw earlier, they can operate both consciously and unconsciously, causing even those who do not see themselves as prejudiced to discriminate against individuals who are different (Blair & Banaji, 1996; McPhail & Penner, 1995; Phelps et al., 2000). However, recent research suggests that it may be possible to change even unconscious forms of stereotyping and prejudice (Blair, 2002).

Interpersonal Attraction

▶ **What factors affect who likes whom?**

Research on prejudice suggests some of the reasons why people, from childhood on, may come to dislike or even hate other people. An equally fascinating aspect of social cognition is why people like or love other people. Folklore tells us that "opposites attract," but also that "birds of a feather flock together." Although valid to some degree, each of these statements needs to be qualified. We begin our coverage of interpersonal attraction by discussing the factors that lead to initial attraction; we then examine how liking sometimes develops into more intimate relationships.

Keys to Attraction

Whether you like someone or not depends partly on situational factors and partly on personal characteristics.

The Environment   One of the most important determinants of attraction is simple physical proximity (Berscheid & Reis, 1998). As long as you do not initially dislike a per-

PROXIMITY AND LIKING Research on environmental factors in attraction suggests that, barring bad first impressions, the more often we make contact with someone—as neighbors, classmates, or co-workers, for example—the more we tend to like that person. Does this principle apply in your life? To find out, think about how and where you met each of your closest friends. If you can think of cases in which proximity did not lead to liking, what do you think interfered with the formation of friendship?

son, your liking for that person will increase with additional contact (Bornstein, 1992). This proximity phenomenon—another example of the *mere-exposure effect* mentioned earlier—helps account for why next-door neighbors are usually more likely to become friends than people who live farther from one another. Chances are, most of your friends are people you met as neighbors, co-workers, or classmates.

The circumstances under which people first meet also influence attraction. You are much more likely to be attracted to a stranger you meet in comfortable, as opposed to uncomfortable, physical conditions. Similarly, if you receive a reward in the presence of a stranger, the chances are greater that you will like that stranger, even if the stranger is not the one giving the reward (Clark & Pataki, 1995). In one study, for example, an experimenter judged one person's creativity while another person watched. Compared with those who received a negative evaluation, participants who were evaluated positively tended to like the observer more (Griffitt & Guay, 1969). At least among strangers, then, liking can occur through associating someone with something pleasant.

Similarity People also tend to like those they perceive as similar to themselves on variables such as age, religion, smoking or drinking habits, or being a "morning" or "evening" person (Buston & Emlen, 2003). Similarity in attitudes is another important influence on attraction (Brehm, Kassin, & Fein, 2002).

An especially good predictor of liking is similarity in attitudes about mutual acquaintances, because in general, people prefer relationships that are *balanced*. As illustrated in Figure 14.5, if Meagan likes Abigail, the relationship is balanced as long as they agree on their evaluation of a third person, regardless of whether they like or dislike that person. However, the relationship will be imbalanced if Meagan and Abigail disagree on their evaluation of a third person.

One reason why we like people whose attitudes are similar to our own is that we expect such people to think highly of us (Condon & Crano, 1988). It's hard to say, though, whether attraction is a cause or an effect of similarity. For example, you might like someone because his attitudes are similar to yours, but it is also possible that as a result of liking him, your attitudes will become more similar to his (Davis & Rusbult, 2001). Even if your own attitudes do not change, you may change your perceptions of the liked person's attitudes such that those attitudes now seem more similar to yours (Brehm, 1992).

Physical Attractiveness Physical characteristics are another important factor in attraction, particularly in the early stages of a relationship (Buston & Emlen, 2003; Franzoi, 2003). From preschool through adulthood, physical attractiveness is a key to

figure 14.5

Balanced and Imbalanced Relationships

Here are some common examples of balanced and imbalanced patterns of relationships among three people. The plus and minus signs refer to liking and disliking, respectively. Balanced relationships are comfortable and harmonious; imbalanced ones often bring conflict.

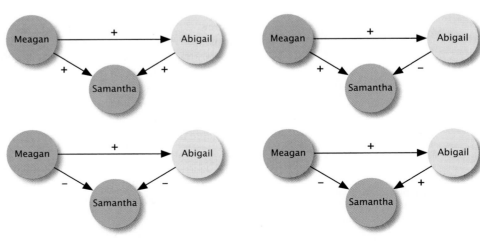

Balanced relationships   **Imbalanced relationships**

figure 14.6

Sex Differences in Date and Mate Preferences

According to evolutionary psychologists, men and women have developed different strategies for selecting sexual partners. These psychologists say that women became more selective than men because they can have relatively few children and want a partner who can help care for those children. Here are some data that support this idea. When asked about the intelligence of people they would choose for one-night stands, dating, and sexual relationships, women preferred much smarter partners than men did. Only when the choices concerned steady dating and marriage did the men's preference for bright partners equal that of the women. Critics of the evolutionary approach explain such sex differences as reflecting learned social norms and expectations of the way men and women should behave (Eagly & Wood, 1999; Miller, Putcha-Bhagavatula, & Pedersen, 2002).

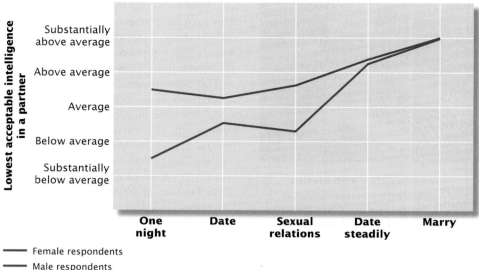

Source: Kenrick et al. (1993).

popularity with members of both sexes (Langlois et al., 2000; Lemly, 2000). Consistent with the **matching hypothesis** of interpersonal attraction, however, people tend to date, marry, or form other committed relationships with those who are similar to themselves in physical attractiveness (Yela & Sangrador, 2001). One possible reason for this outcome is that although people tend to be most attracted to those with the greatest physical appeal, they also want to avoid being rejected by such individuals. In short, it may be compromise, not preference, that leads people to pair off with those who are roughly equivalent to themselves in physical attractiveness (Carli, Ganley, & Pierce-Otay, 1991).

Intimate Relationships and Love

There is much about intimate relationships that psychologists do not, and may never, understand, but they are learning all the time. For example, they know that the physical appearance of a partner tends to be more important to men than to women, whereas the partner's intelligence tends to be more important to women than to men (Buss, 1999; see Figure 14.6).

Intimate Relationships   Eventually, people who are attracted to each other usually become *interdependent,* which means that the thoughts, emotions, and behaviors of one person affect the thoughts, emotions, and behaviors of the other (Rusbult, Arriga, & Agnew, 2001). Interdependence is one of the defining characteristics of intimate relationships (Agnew et al., 1998).

Another key component of successful intimate relationships is *commitment,* which is the extent to which each person is psychologically attached to the relationship and wants to remain in it (Rusbult & Van Lange, 1996). People feel committed to a relationship when they are satisfied with the rewards they receive from it, have invested significant tangible and intangible resources in it, and have few attractive alternative relationships available to them (Bui, Peplau, & Hill, 1996).

Analyzing Love   Affection, emotional expressiveness, social support, cohesiveness, sexuality—these characteristics of intimate relationships bring something else to mind: love. Yet *intimacy* and *love* are not the same. Most theorists agree that there are several different types of love (Brehm, Kassin, & Fein, 2002). One widely accepted view distinguishes between passionate love and companionate love (Hatfield & Rapson, 1995). *Passionate love* is intense, arousing, and marked by both strong physical attraction and deep

matching hypothesis   A proposition stating that people are most likely to date, marry, or form committed relationships with others who are similar to themselves in physical attractiveness.

learn ^{by}**doing** **HAPPY AND HEALTHY** People in satisfying marriages and other long-term relationships tend to enjoy better physical and psychological health than those in unsatisfying relationships. In light of research in the chapter on health, stress, and coping, make a list of the reasons why this might be the case.

emotional attachment. Sexual feelings are very strong, and thoughts of the other intrude on each person's awareness frequently. *Companionate love* is less arousing but psychologically more intimate. It is marked by mutual concern for the welfare of the other (Hendrick & Hendrick, 1986).

Robert Sternberg (1988a, 1997a) has offered a more detailed analysis of love. According to his *triangular theory,* the three basic components of love are passion, intimacy, and commitment. Various combinations of these components result in various types of love. For example, Sternberg suggests that *romantic love* involves a high degree of passion and intimacy, yet lacks substantial commitment to the other person. *Companionate love* is marked by a great deal of intimacy and commitment but little passion. *Consummate love* is the most complete and satisfying. It is the most complete because it includes a high level of all three components. It is the most satisfying because the relationship is likely to fulfill many of the needs of each partner.

Cultural factors have a strong influence on the way people think about love and marriage. For example, in individualistic cultures such as the United States and Australia, people believe that they must love the person they marry, but in collectivist cultures such as India, Pakistan, and Thailand, love is not the major reason why people marry. In these countries, the decision to marry is more likely to be influenced by the wishes of the couple's family (Aronson, Wilson, & Akert, 2002).

Strong and Weak Marriages Long-term studies of successful and unsuccessful marriages suggest that premarital attitudes and feelings are predictive of marital success. In one study, couples who had a close, intimate relationship and similar attitudes when they were dating were more likely to still be married fifteen years later (Hill & Peplau, 1998).

Among married couples, women—but not men—generally tend to be more satisfied with their marriage when the partners talk a lot about the relationship (Acitelli, 1992). Partners in successful marriages also tend to share each other's view of themselves and the other, even if that view is a negative one (Swann, De La Ronde, & Hixon, 1994). The perception that the relationship is fair and equitable also increases marital satisfaction (Grote & Clark, 2001). After the birth of a first child, for example, many wives find that they have much more work than they had anticipated. If their husbands do not share this work to the degree they had expected, wives' marital satisfaction tends to decrease (Hackel & Ruble, 1992).

Long-term studies of marriage have identified some of the factors leading to divorce (Fincham, 2003). Frequent conflicts and negative feelings toward one another are associated with divorces that occur shortly after marriage. The husband and wife trade increasingly nasty and hurtful remarks until communication breaks down (Gottman et al., 1998). A different picture emerges, however, in couples whose divorce occurs after many years of marriage. These people do not necessarily display negative emotions toward one another, but they are unlikely to express positive feelings and love toward one another. In other words, these later-divorcing couples may not dislike one another; they just don't love one another (Gottman & Levenson, 2000; Huston et al., 2001). These findings help explain why people in an apparently strong marriage suddenly announce that they are divorcing, and why they may remain friends afterward.

Social Influence

► **What social rules shape our behavior?**

So far, we have considered social cognition, the mental processes associated with people's perceptions of, and reactions to, other people. Let's now explore *social influence,* the process through which individuals and groups directly and indirectly influence a person's thoughts, feelings, and behavior. Research has shown, for example, that suicide rates

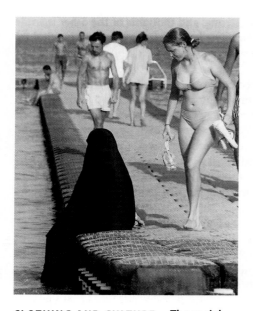

CLOTHING AND CULTURE   The social norms that guide how people dress and behave in various situations are part of the culturally determined socialization process described in the chapter on human development. The process is the same worldwide, but differences in those norms result in quite different behaviors from culture to culture.

increase following well-publicized suicides and that murder rates increase after well-publicized homicides (Garland & Zigler, 1993; Phillips & Cartensen, 1986). Do these correlations mean that media coverage of violence triggers similar violence? As described in the chapter on learning, televised violence can play a causal role in aggressive behavior, but there are other reasons to believe that when murders or suicides become media events, they stimulate imitators. For one thing, many of the people who kill themselves after a widely reported suicide are similar to the original victim in some respect (Cialdini, 2001). For example, after German television reported a story about a young man who committed suicide by jumping in front of a train, there was a dramatic increase in the number of young German men who committed suicide in the same way (Schmidtke & Hafner, 1988). This phenomenon—known as "copycat" violence—illustrates the effects of social influence.

Social Norms

The most pervasive, yet subtle, form of social influence is communicated through social norms. **Norms** are learned, socially based rules that prescribe what people should or should not do in various situations (Cialdini, 2003). Parents, teachers, members of the clergy, peers, and other agents of culture transmit these norms. Because of the power of norms, people often follow them automatically. In North America and Britain, for example, norms tell us that we should get in line to buy a movie ticket rather than crowd around the box office window. They also lead us to expect that others will do the same. By informing people of what is expected of them and others, norms make social situations clearer, more predictable, and more comfortable.

One particularly powerful norm is *reciprocity,* the tendency to respond to others as they have acted toward you (Cialdini & Trost, 1998). To explore the nature of reciprocity, a researcher sent Christmas cards to strangers, most of whom responded with a card of their own. Some even added a personal note of good cheer (Kunz & Woolcott, 1976). The reciprocity norm probably exists in every culture, but other norms are neither universal nor unchanging (Miller, 2001). For instance, people around the world differ greatly in terms of the physical distance they keep between themselves and others while talking. People from South America usually stand much closer to each other than do people from North America. And as suggested in the chapter on psychological disorders, behavior considered normal and friendly in one culture may be seen as offensive, or even abnormal, in another.

The social influence exerted by norms creates orderly social behavior. But social influence can also lead to a breakdown in order. For example, **deindividuation** is a psychological state in which a person becomes "submerged in the group" and loses the sense of individuality (Postmes et al., 2001). When people experience deindividuation, they become emotionally aroused and feel intense closeness with the group. In fact, they appear to become part of the "herd," and they may perform acts that they would not do otherwise. Deindividuation appears to occur when two factors are present. The first is believing that, as part of a group, one cannot be held personally accountable for one's actions. The second is a shift in what influences those actions; the group's norms become more important than one's own thoughts and standards (Postmes & Spears, 1998). Creating a group identity by having members of a group all wear unusual uniforms (such as Ku Klux Klan robes) creates the conditions for deindividuation.

Deindividuation usually results in antisocial acts, and the emotional arousal associated with it makes these acts difficult to stop (Taylor, Peplau, & Sears, 2003). Fans at rock concerts and athletic events have trampled one another to death in their frenzy to get the best seats; normally mild-mannered adults have thrown rocks or fire bombs at police during political protests. Such behavior becomes more extreme as people feel less identifiable. An analysis of newspaper accounts of lynchings in the United States over a fifty-year period showed that larger lynch mobs were more savage and vicious than smaller ones (Mullen, 1986). Deindividuation provides an example of how, given the right circumstances, quite normal people can engage in destructive, even violent, behavior.

norms   Learned, socially based rules that prescribe what people should or should not do in various situations.

deindividuation   A psychological state occurring in group members that results in loss of individuality and a tendency to do things not normally done when alone.

conformity   The changing of one's behavior or beliefs to match those of others, generally as a result of real or imagined, though unspoken, group pressure.

Standard line

(A)

Test lines

(B)

figure 14.7

Types of Stimulus Lines Used in Experiments by Asch

learn by doing Participants in Asch's experiments saw a new set of lines like these on each trial. The middle line in Part B matches the one in Part A, but when several of Asch's assistants claimed that a different line matched, so did many of the participants. Try re-creating this experiment with four friends. Secretly ask three of them to say that the test line on the left matches the standard line; then show this drawing to all four. Did the fourth person conform to the group norm? If not, do you think it was something about the person, the length of the incorrect line chosen, or both that led to nonconformity? Would conformity be more likely if the first three people had chosen the line on the right? (Read on for more about this possibility.)

compliance The adjustment of one's behavior because of a direct request.

Conformity and Compliance

When people change their behavior or beliefs to match those of other members of a group, they are said to conform. **Conformity** occurs as a result of unspoken group pressure, real or imagined (Cialdini & Trost, 1998). You probably have experienced group pressure when everyone around you stands to applaud a performance you thought was not that great. You may conform by standing as well, though no one told you to do so; the group's behavior creates a silent, but influential, pressure to follow suit. **Compliance,** in contrast, occurs when people adjust their behavior because of a request. The request can be clear and direct, such as "Please do me favor," or it can be more subtle—as when someone simply looks at you in a way that lets you know the person needs a favor.

Conformity and compliance are usually generated by spoken or unspoken norms. In a classic experiment, Muzafer Sherif (1937) charted the formation of a group norm by taking advantage of the perceptual illusion whereby a fixed point of light in a completely dark room appears to move. A person's estimates of how far the light seems to move tend to stay the same over time if the person is alone in the room. But when Sherif tested several people at once, asking each person to say aloud how far the light moved on repeated trials, their estimates tended to converge; they had established a group norm. Even more important, when individuals who had been in the group were later tested alone, they continued to be influenced by this norm.

In another classic experiment, Solomon Asch (1956) explored what people do when faced with a norm that is obviously wrong. The participants in this experiment saw a standard line like the one in Figure 14.7(A); then they saw a display like that in Figure 14.7(B). Their task was to pick out the line in the display that was the same length as the one they had first been shown.

Each participant performed this task in a small group of people who posed as fellow participants, but who were actually the experimenter's assistants. There were two conditions. In the control condition, the real participant responded first. In the experimental condition, the participant did not respond until after the other people did. The experimenter's assistants chose the correct response on 6 trials, but on the other 12 trials they all gave the same, obviously incorrect, response. So, on 12 trials, each participant was confronted with a "social reality" created by a group norm that conflicted with the physical reality created by what the person could clearly see. Only 5 percent of the participants in the control condition ever made a mistake on this easy perceptual task. However, among participants who heard the assistants' incorrect responses before giving their own, about 70 percent made at least one error by conforming to the group norm. An analysis of 133 studies conducted in 17 countries reveals that conformity in Asch-type situations has declined somewhat in the United States since the 1950s, but that it still occurs. It is especially likely in collectivist cultures, where conformity to group norms is emphasized (Cialdini et al., 2001).

Why Do People Conform? Why did so many people in Asch's experiment give incorrect responses when they were capable of near-perfect performance? One possibility, called *public conformity,* is that they gave an answer they did not believe in simply because it was the socially desirable thing to do. Another possibility is that they experienced *private acceptance,* meaning that the participants used the other people's responses as legitimate evidence about reality, were convinced that their own perceptions were wrong, and actually changed their minds. Morton Deutsch and Harold Gerard (1955) reasoned that if conformity disappeared when people gave their responses without identifying themselves, then Asch's findings must reflect public conformity, not private acceptance. In fact, conformity does decrease when people respond privately instead of publicly, but it is not eliminated (Deutsch & Gerard, 1955). People sometimes publicly produce responses that they do not believe in, but hearing other people's responses also influences their private beliefs (Moscovici, 1985).

Why are group norms so powerful? Research suggests three influential factors (Cialdini & Trost, 1998). First, people are motivated to be correct, and norms provide information about what is right and wrong. This factor may help explain why some extremely disturbed or distressed people consider stories about suicide to be "social proof" that self-destruction is a reasonable way out of their problems (Cialdini, 2001). Second, people want to be liked by others, and we generally like those who agree with us. Finally, norms affect the distribution of social reward and punishment (Cialdini, 1995). From childhood on, people in many cultures learn that going along with group norms is good and earns rewards. (These positive outcomes presumably help compensate for not always saying or doing exactly what we please.) People also learn that breaking a norm may bring punishments ranging from scoldings for small transgressions to imprisonment for violation of norms that have been translated into laws.

When Do People Conform?   People do not always conform to group influence. In the Asch studies, for example, nearly 30 percent of the participants did not go along with the assistants' obviously wrong judgments. Countless experiments have probed the question of what combinations of people and circumstances do and do not lead to conformity.

learn
by doing

For example, *ambiguity,* or uncertainty, is important in determining how much conformity will occur. As the features of a situation become less clear, people rely more and more on others' opinions, and conformity to a group norm becomes increasingly likely (Aronson, Wilson, & Akert, 2002). You can demonstrate this aspect of conformity on any street corner. First, create an ambiguous situation by having several people look at the sky or the top of a building. When passersby ask what is going on, be sure everyone excitedly reports seeing something interesting, but fleeting—perhaps a faint light or a tiny, shiny object. If you are especially successful, conforming newcomers will begin persuading other passersby that there is something fascinating to be seen.

If ambiguity contributes so much to conformity, though, why did so many of Asch's participants conform to a judgment that was clearly wrong? The answer has to do with the fact that the group was *unanimous* in giving the same incorrect answer, as well as with the number of people who express this unanimous majority judgment. Specifically, people experience intense pressure to conform as long as the majority is unanimous. If even one other person in the group disagrees with the majority view, conformity drops greatly. When Asch (1951) arranged for just one assistant to disagree with the others, fewer than 10 percent of the real participants conformed. Once unanimity is broken, it becomes much easier to disagree with the majority, even if the other nonconformist does not agree with the person's own view (Turner, 1991).

Conformity also depends on the *size of the majority*. Asch (1955) demonstrated this phenomenon by varying the number of assistants in the group from one to fifteen. Conformity to incorrect norms grew as the number of people in the group increased. However, most of the growth in conformity occurred as the size of the majority rose from one to about three or four members. Psychologists believe that this effect occurs because pressure to conform has already reached a peak after someone has heard three or four people agree. Hearing more people confirm the majority view thus has little additional social impact (Latané, 1981).

Conformity can also occur through *minority influence,* by which a minority of group members influence the behavior or beliefs of the majority (Gordijn, De Vries, & De Dreu, 2002). This phenomenon is less common than majority influence, but when members of a minority persist in their views and show agreement with one another, they can be influential (Martin, Gardikotis, & Hewstone, 2002). However, minority-influenced change often takes a while to occur and may involve only a moderate adjustment of the majority view in the direction favored by the minority (Alvaro & Crano, 1997; Crano & Chen, 1998).

Does gender affect conformity? Early research suggested that women conform more than men, but the gender difference stemmed mainly from the fact that the tasks used in those studies were often more familiar to men than to women. This fact is important because people are especially likely to conform when they are faced with an unfamiliar situation (Cialdini & Trost, 1998). No male-female differences in conformity have been found in subsequent research using materials that are equally familiar to both genders (Maupin & Fisher, 1989).

So why do some people still perceive women as more conforming than men, despite evidence to the contrary? Part of the answer may lie in their perception of the relative social status of men and women. People who think of women as having lower social status than men in most social situations are likely to see women as easier to influence, even though men and women conform equally often (Eagly, 1987).

Creating Compliance   In the experiments just described, the participants experienced psychological pressure to conform to the views or actions of others, even though no one specifically asked them to do so. In contrast, *compliance* involves changing what you say or do because of a direct request.

How is compliance brought about? Many people believe that the direct approach is always best: If you want something, ask for it. But salespeople, political strategists, social psychologists, and other experts have learned that often the best way to get something is to ask for something else. Three examples of this strategy are the foot-in-the-door technique, the door-in-the-face procedure, and the low-ball approach.

The *foot-in-the-door technique* consists of getting a person to agree to small requests and then working up to larger ones. In the original experiment on this strategy, homeowners were asked to do one of two things. Some were asked to allow a large, unattractive "Drive Carefully" sign to be placed on their front lawn. About 17 percent of the people approached in this way complied with the request. In the foot-in-the-door condition, however, homeowners were first asked only to sign a petition supporting laws aimed at reducing traffic accidents. Several weeks later, when a different person asked these same homeowners to put the "Drive Carefully" sign on their lawns, 55 percent of them complied (Freedman & Fraser, 1966).

Why should the granting of small favors lead to granting larger ones? First, people are usually far more likely to comply with a request that costs little in time, money, effort, or inconvenience. Second, complying with a small request makes people think of themselves as being committed to the cause or issue involved (Cialdini & Trost, 1998). In the study just described, participants who signed the petition might have thought, "I must care enough about traffic safety to do something about it." Compliance with the higher-cost request (displaying the sign) increased because it was consistent with these people's self-perceptions and past actions (Eisenberg et al., 1987).

The foot-in-the-door technique can be very effective. Steven Sherman (1980) created a 700 percent increase in the rate at which people volunteered to work for a charity simply by first getting them to say that in a hypothetical situation, they would volunteer if asked. For some companies, the foot in the door is a request that potential customers merely answer a few questions; the request to buy something comes later. Others offer a small gift, or "door opener," as salespeople call it. Acceptance of the gift not only gives the salesperson a foot in the door but also may invoke the reciprocity norm: Many people who get something for free today feel obligated to reciprocate by buying something later (Cialdini, 2001).

The *door-in-the-face procedure* offers a second effective way of obtaining compliance (Cialdini, 2001). This strategy begins with a request for a favor that is likely to be denied. The person making the request then concedes that this favor was too much to ask and substitutes a lesser alternative—which is what the person really wanted in the first place! Because the person appears willing to compromise, and because the second request seems small in comparison with the first one, it is more likely to be granted than if it had been made at the outset. The door-in-the-face strategy is at the heart of bargaining among political groups and between labor and management.

The third technique, called the *low-ball approach,* is commonly used by car dealers and other businesses (Cialdini, 2001). The first step in this strategy is to get a person's oral commitment to do something, such as to purchase a car. Once this commitment is made, the cost of fulfilling it is increased, often because of an "error" in computing the car's price. Why do buyers end up paying much more than originally planned for "low-balled" items? Apparently, once people commit themselves to do something, they feel obligated to follow through, especially when the person who obtains the initial commitment also makes the higher-cost request (Burger & Petty, 1981).

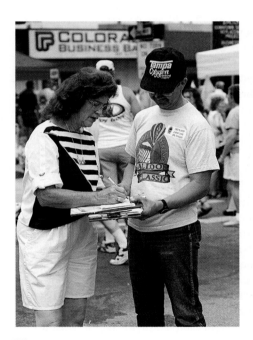

applying psychology   **PROMOTING COMPLIANCE**   Have you ever been asked to sign a petition favoring some political, social, or economic cause? Supporters of these causes know that people who comply with this small request are the best people to contact later with requests to do more. Complying with larger requests is made more likely because it is consistent with the signer's initial commitment to the cause. If you were contacted after signing a petition, did you agree to donate money or become a volunteer?

figure 14.8

Studying Obedience in the Laboratory

In this photograph from Milgram's original experiment, a man is being strapped into a chair with electrodes on his arm. Although participants in the experiment do not know it, the man is actually the experimenter's research assistant and receives no shock.

Obedience

▶ **How far will people go in obeying authority?**

Compliance involves a change in behavior in response to a request. In the case of **obedience,** the behavior change comes in response to a *demand* from an authority figure (Lutsky, 1995). In the 1960s, Stanley Milgram developed a laboratory procedure at Yale University to study obedience. In his first experiment he used newspaper ads to recruit forty male volunteers between the ages of twenty and fifty from the local community. Among the participants were professionals, white-collar businessmen, and unskilled workers (Milgram, 1963).

Imagine you are one of the people who answered the ad. When you arrive for the experiment, you join a fifty-year-old gentleman who has also volunteered and has been scheduled for the same session. The experimenter explains that the purpose of the experiment is to examine the effects of punishment on learning. One of you—the "teacher"—will help the "learner" remember a list of words by administering electric shock whenever the learner makes a mistake. Then the experimenter turns to you and asks you to draw one of two cards out of a hat. Your card says, "TEACHER." You think to yourself that this must be your lucky day.

Now the learner is taken into another room and strapped into a chair, as illustrated in Figure 14.8. Electrodes are attached to his arm. You are shown a shock generator with 30 switches. The experimenter explains that the switch on the far left administers a mild, 15-volt shock and that each succeeding switch increases the shock by 15 volts. The one on the far right delivers 450 volts. The far left section of the shock generator is labeled "Slight shock." Looking across the panel, you see "Moderate shock," "Very strong shock," and at the far right, "Danger—severe shock." The last 2 switches are ominously labeled "XXX." The experimenter explains that you, the teacher, will begin by reading a list of word pairs to the learner. Then you will go through the list again, presenting just 1 word of each pair. The learner will have to say which word went with it. After the first mistake, you are to throw the switch to deliver 15 volts of shock. Each time the learner makes another mistake, you are to increase the shock by 15 volts.

You begin, following the experimenter's instructions. But after the learner makes his 5th mistake and you throw the switch to give him 75 volts, you hear a loud moan. At 90 volts, the learner cries out in pain. At 150 volts, he screams and asks to be let out of the experiment. You look to the experimenter, who says, "Proceed with the next word."

No shock was actually delivered in Milgram's experiments. The learner was always an employee of the experimenter, and the moans and other sounds of pain came from a prerecorded tape. But you do not know that. What would you do in this situation? Suppose you continue and eventually deliver 180 volts. The learner screams that he cannot stand the pain any longer and starts banging on the wall. The experimenter says, "You have no other choice; you must go on." Would you continue? Would you keep going even when the learner begged to be let out of the experiment and then fell silent? Would you administer 450 volts of potentially deadly shock to an innocent stranger just because an experimenter demanded that you do so?

Figure 14.9 shows that only 5 participants in Milgram's experiment stopped before 300 volts, and 26 out of 40 (65 percent) went all the way to the 450-volt level. The decision to continue was difficult and stressful for the participants. Many protested repeatedly. But each time the experimenter told them to continue, they did so. Here is a partial transcript of what a typical participant said:

> [After throwing the 180-volt switch]: He can't stand it. I'm not going to kill that man in there. Do you hear him hollering? He's hollering. He can't stand it. What if something happens to him? I'm not going to get that man sick in there. He's hollering in there. Do you know what I mean? I mean, I refuse to take responsibility. He's getting hurt in there. . . . Too many left here. Geez, if he gets them wrong. There are too many of them left. I mean, who is going to take responsibility if anything happens to that gentleman?

obedience   A form of compliance in which people comply with a demand from an authority figure.

figure 14.9

Results of Milgram's Obedience Experiment

When Milgram asked a group of under-graduates and a group of psychiatrists to predict how participants in his experiment would respond, they estimated that fewer than 2 percent would go all the way to 450 volts. In fact, 65 percent of the participants did so. What do you think you would have done in this situation?

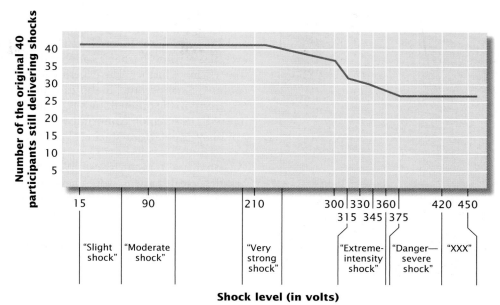

Source: Milgram (1963).

[After the experimenter accepts responsibility]: All right. . . .
[After administering 240 volts]: Oh, no, you mean I've got to keep going up the scale? No sir, I'm not going to kill that man. I'm not going to give him 450 volts.
[After the experimenter says, "The experiment requires that you go on"]: I know it does, but that man is hollering in there, sir.

This participant administered shock up to 450 volts (Milgram, 1974).

Factors Affecting Obedience

Milgram had not expected so many people to deliver such apparently intense shocks. Was there something about his procedure that produced this high level of obedience? To find out, Milgram and other researchers varied the original procedure in numerous ways. The overall level of obedience to an authority figure was usually quite high, but the degree of obedience was affected by several aspects of the situation and procedure.

Experimenter Status and Prestige   One possibility is that the experimenter's status as a Yale University professor helped produce high levels of obedience in Milgram's original experiment (Blass & Schmitt, 2001). To test the effects of status and prestige, Milgram rented an office in a run-down building in Bridgeport, Connecticut. He then placed a newspaper ad for research sponsored by a private firm. There was no mention of Yale. In all other ways, the experimental procedure was identical to the original.

Under these less prestigious circumstances, the level of obedience dropped, but not as much as Milgram expected: 48 percent of the participants continued to the maximum level of shock, compared with 65 percent in the original study. Milgram concluded that people are willing to obey orders to do great harm to another person even when the authority making the demand is not especially reputable or prestigious.

The Behavior of Other People   To study how the behavior of fellow participants might affect obedience, Milgram (1965) created a situation in which there appeared to be three teachers. Teacher 1 (in reality, a research assistant) read the words to the learner. Teacher 2 (another research assistant) stated whether or not the learner's response was correct. Teacher 3 (the actual participant) was to deliver shock when the learner made mistakes. At 150 volts, when the learner began to complain that the shock was too

PROXIMITY AND OBEDIENCE
Milgram's research showed that close physical proximity to an authority figure is one of several factors that can enhance obedience to authority (Rada & Rogers, 1973). This proximity principle is used in the military, where no one is ever far away from the authority of a higher-ranking person.

painful, Teacher 1 refused to participate any longer and left the room. The experimenter asked him to come back, but he refused. The experimenter then instructed Teachers 2 and 3 to continue by themselves. The experiment continued for several more trials. However, at 210 volts, Teacher 2 said that the learner was suffering too much and also refused to participate further. The experimenter then told Teacher 3 (the actual participant) to continue the procedure. In this case, only 10 percent of the participants (compared with 65 percent in the original study) continued to deliver shock all the way up to 450 volts. In line with research on conformity, the presence of others who disobey appears to be the most powerful factor reducing obedience.

Personality Characteristics   Were the participants in Milgram's original experiment heartless creatures who would have given strong shocks even if there had been no pressure on them to do so? Quite the opposite; most of them were nice people who were influenced by experimental situations to behave in apparently antisocial ways. In a later demonstration of the same phenomenon, college students playing the role of prison guards behaved with aggressive heartlessness toward other students who were playing the role of prisoners (Zimbardo, 1973).

Still, not everyone is equally obedient to authority. For example, people who display what we described earlier as *authoritarianism* are more likely than others to comply with an experimenter's request to shock the learner (Blass, 2000). Real-world support for this idea comes from recent findings that German soldiers who may have obeyed orders to kill Jews during World War II were higher on authoritarianism than other German men of the same age and background (Steiner & Fahrenberg, 2000).

Evaluating Obedience Research

Milgram's obedience studies were conducted forty years ago. How relevant are they today? Consider this fact: The U.S. Federal Aviation Authority attributes many commercial airplane accidents to "Captainitis," where the pilot of an airliner makes an obvious error, but none of the other crew members are willing to challenge the captain's authority by pointing out the error. As a result, planes have crashed and people have died (Kanki & Foushee, 1990). Captainitis might have been operating aboard the nuclear submarine USS *Greeneville* on February 9, 2001, when, as it surfaced off the coast of Hawaii, it struck and sank a Japanese fishing boat, killing nine people. A navy board of inquiry found that crew members had been reluctant to challenge their captain's order to surface, even though they felt he had not checked carefully enough for other vessels in the area (Myers, 2001). Obedience to authority may also have operated during the World Trade Center attack on September 11, 2001, when some people returned to their offices after hearing an ill-advised public address announcement telling them to do so. Most of these people died as a result.

These tragic events suggest that Milgram's findings are still relevant and important (Saks, 1992). In fact, the results of his experiments have been confirmed in recent years in several Western countries, with female, as well as male, participants (Blass, 2000; Smith & Bond, 1999). Nevertheless, there is still debate over the ethics and meaning of Milgram's work. (For a summary of Milgram's results, plus those of studies on conformity and compliance, see "In Review: Types of Social Influence.")

Questions About Ethics   Although the "learners" in Milgram's experiment suffered no discomfort, the participants did. Milgram (1963) observed participants "sweat, stutter, tremble, groan, bite their lips, and dig their fingernails into their flesh" (p. 375). Against the potential harm inflicted by Milgram's experiments stand the potential gains. For example, people who learn about Milgram's work often take his findings into account when deciding how to act in social situations (Sherman, 1980). But even if social value has come from Milgram's studies, a question remains: Was it ethical for Milgram to treat his participants as he did?

LINKAGES
Is it ethical to deceive people to learn about their social behavior?
(a link to Introduction to the Science of Psychology)

in review

TYPES OF SOCIAL INFLUENCE

Type	Definition	Key Findings
Conformity	A change in behavior or beliefs to match those of others	In cases of ambiguity, people develop a group norm and then adhere to it. Conformity occurs because people want to be right, because they want to be liked by others, and because conformity to group norms is usually reinforced. Conformity usually increases with the ambiguity of the situation, as well as with the unanimity and size of the majority.
Compliance	A change in behavior because of a request	Compliance increases with the foot-in-the-door technique, which begins with a small request and works up to a larger one. The door-in-the-face procedure can also be used. After making a large request that is denied, the person substitutes a less extreme alternative that was desired all along. The low-ball approach also elicits compliance. An oral commitment for something is first obtained; then the person claims that only a higher-cost version of the original request will suffice.
Obedience	A change in behavior in response to an explicit demand, typically from an acknowledged authority figure	People may inflict great harm on others when an authority demands that they do so. Even when people obey orders to harm another person, they often agonize over the decision. People are most likely to disobey orders to harm someone else when they see another person disobey.

? *Going to the end of a ticket line is an example of _____, whereas forming two lines when a theater employee requests it is an example of _____.*

In the years before his death in 1984, Milgram defended his experiments (e.g., Milgram, 1977). He argued that the way he dealt with his participants after the experiment prevented any lasting harm. For example, he explained to them that the learner did not experience any shock; in fact, the learner came in and chatted with each participant. On a later questionnaire, 84 percent of the participants said that they had learned something important about themselves and that the experience had been worthwhile. Milgram argued, therefore, that the experience was actually a positive one. Still, the committees charged with protecting human participants in research today would be unlikely to approve Milgram's experiments, and less controversial ways to study obedience have now been developed (Meeus & Raaijmakers, 1995).

Questions About Meaning Do Milgram's dramatic results mean that most people are putty in the hands of authority figures and that most of us would blindly follow inhumane orders from our leaders? Some critics have argued that Milgram's results cannot be interpreted in this way because his participants knew they were in an experiment and may simply have been playing a cooperative role. If so, the social influence processes identified in his studies may not explain obedience in the real world today (Berkowitz, 1999).

Most psychologists believe, however, that Milgram demonstrated a basic truth about human behavior—namely, that under certain circumstances people are capable of unspeakable acts of brutality toward other people. Sadly, examples abound. And one of the most horrifying aspects of human inhumanity—whether it is the Nazis' campaign of genocide against Jews sixty years ago or the campaigns of terror under way today—is that the perpetrators are not necessarily demented, sadistic fiends. Most of them are normal people who, because of the situations they face, are influenced to behave in a demented and fiendish manner.

Worse, inhumanity can occur even without pressure to obey. For example, a good deal of people's aggressiveness toward other people appears to come from within. In the next section, we consider human aggressiveness and some of the circumstances that influence its expression.

Aggression

▶ **Are people born aggressive?**

Aggression is an action intended to harm another person. It is all too common. More than 1.6 million violent crimes are committed each year in the United States alone, including over 91,000 rapes and 16,000 murders (Federal Bureau of Investigation, 2002). In fact, homicide is the second leading cause of death for people in the United States between the ages of 15 and 24 (National Center for Injury Prevention and Control, 2002). One of the most disturbing aspects of these figures is that about 45 percent of all murder victims knew their assailants, and over 60 percent of rapists were romantic partners, friends, relatives, or acquaintances of their victims (U.S. Department of Justice, 2002a). Further, as many as one-third of married and unmarried couples in the United States have engaged in aggressive acts toward each other that range from pushing, shoving, and slapping to beatings and the threatened or actual use of weapons (Archer, 2000; Heyman & Neidig, 1999).

Why Are People Aggressive?

Sigmund Freud suggested that people have death instincts that account for aggression. Evolutionary psychologists believe that aggression helped prehistoric people compete for mates, thus ensuring the survival of their genes in the next generation (Malamuth & Addison, 2001). Through natural selection, they say, aggressive tendencies are passed on through successive generations.

Freudian and evolutionary theories seem too simplistic to fully account for human aggressiveness, however. For one thing, there are large differences in aggression from culture to culture. The murder rate in the Philippines, for example, is forty-six times higher than in China or Finland; and the U.S. murder rate is almost nine times higher than in those latter two countries (Geen, 1998a; Triandis, 1994). These data suggest that even if aggressive *impulses* are universal, the appearance of aggressive *behavior* reflects an interplay of nature and nurture (Malamuth & Addison, 2001). No equation can predict when people will be aggressive, but years of research have revealed a number of important biological, learning, and environmental factors that combine in various ways to produce aggression in various situations.

Genetic and Biological Mechanisms   The evidence for hereditary influences on aggression is strong, especially in animals (Cairns, Gariepy, & Hood, 1990). In one study, the most aggressive members of a large group of mice were interbred; then the most aggressive of their offspring were also interbred. After this procedure was followed for twenty-five generations, the resulting animals would immediately attack any mouse put in their cage. Continuous inbreeding of the least aggressive members of the original

aggression   An act that is intended to harm another person.

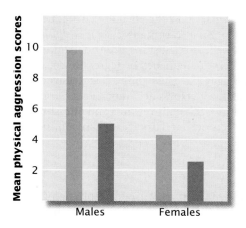

figure 14.10

Testosterone and Aggression

In the study illustrated here, the children of women who had taken testosterone during pregnancy to prevent miscarriage became more aggressive than the mothers' other children of the same sex who had not been exposed to testosterone during prenatal development. This outcome appeared in both males and females.

group produced animals that were so nonaggressive that they would refuse to fight even when attacked (Lagerspetz & Lagerspetz, 1983). Research on human twins reared together or apart suggests that there is a genetic component to aggression in people as well (Tellegen et al., 1988). However, other research suggests that people do not necessarily inherit the tendency to be aggressive. Instead, they may inherit certain temperaments, such as impulsiveness, that in turn make aggression more likely (Rowe, Almeida, & Jacobson, 1999).

Several parts of the brain influence aggression (Anderson & Bushman, 2002). One of these is the limbic system, which includes the amygdala, the hypothalamus, and related areas. Damage to these structures may produce *defensive aggression,* which includes heightened aggressiveness to stimuli that are not usually threatening or a decrease in the responses that normally inhibit aggression (Coccaro, 1989; Eichelman, 1983). The cerebral cortex may also be involved in aggression (Pietro et al., 2000).

Hormones, too, may play an important role in aggression. One possibility is that aggression is related to a person's level of *testosterone,* the masculine hormone that is present in both sexes (Dabbs & Dabbs, 2001). Experiments have shown that aggressive behavior increases or decreases dramatically with the amount of testosterone in an animal's body (Pope, Kouri, & Hudson, 2000; Yates, 2000). Among criminals, those who commit violent crimes have higher levels of testosterone than those whose crimes are nonviolent. And among murderers, those with higher levels of testosterone are more likely than others to have known their victims and to have planned their crimes before committing them (Dabbs, Riad, & Chance, 2001)

Testosterone may have its most significant and durable influence through its impact on early brain development. One natural test of this hypothesis occurred when pregnant women were given testosterone in an attempt to prevent miscarriage. As a result, their children were exposed to high doses of testosterone during prenatal development. Figure 14.10 shows that these children grew up to be more aggressive than their same-sex siblings who were not exposed to testosterone during prenatal development (Reinisch, Ziemba-Davis, & Sanders, 1991).

Drugs that affect the central nervous system also affect the likelihood that a person will act aggressively. Even relatively small amounts of alcohol, for example, can substantially increase some people's aggressiveness. Canadian researchers have found that in almost 70 percent of the acts of aggression they studied, the aggressors had been drinking alcohol. And the more alcohol the aggressors consumed, the more aggressive they were (Wells, Graham, & West, 2000). No one knows exactly why alcohol increases aggression, but research suggests that the drug may affect areas of the brain that normally inhibit aggressive responses (Lau, Pihl, & Peterson, 1995).

Learning and Cultural Mechanisms Biological factors may increase or decrease the likelihood of aggression, but cross-cultural research makes it clear that learning also plays a role. Aggressive behavior is much more common in individualist than in collectivist cultures, for example (Oatley, 1993). Cultural differences in the expression of aggression appear to stem in part from differing cultural values (Cohen, 1998). For example, the Utku (an Inuit culture) view aggression in any form as a sign of social incompetence. In fact, the Utku word for "aggressive" also means "childish" (Oatley, 1993). The effects of culture on aggression can also be seen in the fact that the amount of aggression in a given culture changes over time as cultural values change (Matsumoto, 2000).

In addition, people learn many aggressive responses by watching others (Bushman & Anderson, 2001). Children, in particular, learn and perform many of the aggressive responses that they see modeled by others. Bandura's "Bobo" doll experiments, which are described in the chapter on learning, provide impressive demonstrations of the power of observational learning. The significance of observational learning is highlighted, too, by studies described in that chapter on the effects of televised violence. For example, the amount of violent content eight-year-olds watch on television predicts aggressiveness in these children even fifteen years later (Huesmann et al., 1997, 2003). Fortunately, not everyone who sees aggression becomes aggressive; individual differences in temperament, the modeling of nonaggressive behavior by parents, and other factors can reduce the effects of violent television. Nevertheless, observational learning does play a significant role in the development and display of aggressive behavior (Bushman & Anderson, 2001).

Immediate reward or punishment can also alter the frequency of aggressive acts. People become more aggressive when rewarded for aggressiveness and less aggressive when punished for aggression (Geen, 1998a). In short, a person's accumulated experiences, including culturally transmitted teachings, combine with daily rewards and punishments to influence whether, when, and how aggressive acts occur (Baron & Richardson, 1994).

When Are People Aggressive?

In general, people are more likely to be aggressive when they are both physiologically aroused and experiencing a strong emotion such as anger (Anderson & Bushman, 2002). People tend either to lash out at those who make them angry or to displace their anger onto children, pets, or other defenseless targets. However, aggression can also be made more likely by other forms of emotional arousal, especially *frustration,* which occurs when we are prevented from reaching some goal.

Frustration and Aggression   Suppose that a friend interrupts your studying for an exam by asking to borrow a book. If things have been going well that day and you are feeling confident about the exam, you are likely to be friendly and accommodating. But what if you are feeling frustrated because your friend's visit was the fifth interruption in the last hour? Under these emotional circumstances, you may react aggressively, perhaps snapping at your startled visitor for not calling ahead.

Your aggressiveness in this situation would be predicted by the **frustration-aggression hypothesis,** which suggests that frustration leads to aggression (Dollard et al., 1939). Research on this hypothesis has shown that it is too simple and too general, however. For one thing, frustration sometimes produces depression and withdrawal, not aggression (Berkowitz, 1998). In addition, not all aggression is preceded by frustration (Berkowitz, 1994).

After many years of research, Leonard Berkowitz suggested that the frustration-aggression hypothesis be modified in two ways. First, he proposed that it may be stress in general, not just frustration, that is involved in aggression. Stress, he said, produces a readiness for aggression that may or may not be translated into aggressive behavior

FOLLOWING ADULT EXAMPLES   Learning to express aggression is especially easy for children who, like these young Palestinians in the West Bank city of Nablus, see aggressive acts modeled for them all too often.

frustration-aggression hypothesis   A proposition stating that the existence of frustration always leads to some form of aggressive behavior.

(Berkowitz, 1998). Once this readiness exists, however, aggression can be more easily triggered by stimuli in the environment. The triggering stimuli might be guns or knives, televised scenes of people arguing, or other cues associated with aggression. In other words, neither stress alone nor environmental cues alone are sufficient to set off aggression. When combined, however, they often do. Support for this aspect of Berkowitz's theory has been quite strong (Malamuth & Anderson, 2001).

Second, Berkowitz argues that the direct cause of most kinds of aggression is negative feelings, or *negative affect* (Berkowitz, 1998). Research suggests that the more negative affect people experience, regardless of what caused it, the stronger is their readiness to be aggressive. Participants in one study experienced negative affect caused by the pain of immersing their hands in ice water. They became more aggressive than participants in a control group whose hands were in water of room temperature (Berkowitz, 1998).

Generalized Arousal   Imagine that you've just jogged three miles. You are hot, sweaty, and out of breath, but you are not angry. Still, the physiological arousal caused by jogging may increase the probability that you will become aggressive if, say, a passerby shouts an insult (Zillmann, 1988). Why? The answer lies in a phenomenon described in the chapter on motivation and emotion: Arousal from one experience may carry over to a new situation, producing what is called *excitation transfer*. So the physiological arousal caused by jogging may intensify your reaction to an insult (Geen, 1998b).

By itself, however, arousal does not lead to aggression. It is most likely to produce aggression when a situation presents some reason, opportunity, or target for aggression (Zillmann, 1988). In one study, for example, people engaged in two minutes of vigorous exercise. Then they had the opportunity to deliver electric shock to another person. The participants chose to give high levels of shock only if they had first been insulted (Zillmann, Katcher, & Milavsky, 1972). Apparently, the arousal resulting from the exercise made aggression more likely; the insult "released" it. These findings are in keeping with the notion that aggression is caused not by internal impulses alone or by particular situations alone, but by the interaction of the two.

THINKING CRITICALLY

Does Pornography Cause Aggression?

In both men and women, sexual stimulation produces strong, generalized physiological arousal, especially in the sympathetic nervous system. If arousal in general can make a person more likely to be aggressive (given a reason, opportunity, and target), could stimuli that create sexual arousal be dangerous? In particular, does viewing pornographic material make people more likely to be aggressive? Prior to the mid-1980s, numerous scholars had concluded that there was no evidence for an overall relationship between any type of antisocial behavior and mere exposure to pornographic material (Donnerstein, 1984b). However, in 1986 the U.S. Attorney General's Commission on Pornography re-examined the question and concluded that pornography is dangerous.

■ **What am I being asked to believe or accept?**

Specifically, the commission proposed that there is a cause-effect link between viewing erotic material and several forms of antisocial behavior, including sexually related violent crimes.

■ **Is there evidence available to support the claim?**

The commission cited several types of evidence in support of its conclusion. First, there was the testimony of men convicted of sex crimes. Rapists, for example, are unusually heavy consumers of pornography, and they often say that they were aroused by erotic material immediately before committing a rape (Silbert & Pines, 1984). Similarly, child molesters often view child pornography immediately before committing their crimes (Marshall, 1989).

In addition, the commission cited experimental evidence that men who are most aroused by aggressive themes in pornography are also the most potentially sexually aggressive. One study, for example, showed that men who said they could commit a rape became sexually aroused by scenes of rape and less aroused by scenes of mutually consenting sex; this was not true for men who said they could never commit a rape (Malamuth & Check, 1983).

Perhaps the strongest evidence cited by the commission, however, came from excitation transfer studies. In one experiment, male participants were told that a person in another room (actually an employee of the experimenter) would be performing a learning task and that they were to administer an electric shock every time the person made a mistake. The intensity of shock could be varied (as in the Milgram studies, no shock actually reached the employee), but participants were told that changing the intensity would not affect the speed of learning. So the shock intensity (and presumed pain) that they chose to administer was considered to be a measure of aggressive behavior. Before the learning trials began, some participants watched a sexually explicit film in which several men had sex with the same woman. The arousal created by the film appeared to translate into greater aggression, especially among participants who found the arousal unpleasant (Donnerstein, 1984b).

■ Can that evidence be interpreted another way?

The commission's interpretation of all this evidence was questioned for several reasons. First, critics argued that some of the evidence should be given little weight. In particular, how much should we rely on what convicted sex offenders say? Their testimony may reflect self-serving attempts to lay the blame for their crimes on pornography. These reports cannot establish that exposure to pornography causes aggression. In fact, it may be that pornography partially *satisfies* sex offenders' aggressive impulses rather than creating them. Similarly, the fact that potential rapists are most aroused by rape-oriented material may show only that they prefer violence-oriented pornography, not that such materials created their impulse to rape.

What about the evidence from excitation transfer studies? To interpret these studies, you need to know that the pornography that led to increased aggression contained violence, as well as sex. The sexual activity depicted was painful for, or unwanted by, the woman. So the higher levels of aggression that followed viewing these films could have been due to the transfer of sexual arousal, the effects of observing violent behavior, or the effects of seeing sex combined with violence (Donnerstein, Slaby, & Eron, 1995).

Several careful experiments have found that highly arousing sexual themes, in and of themselves, do not produce aggression. When men in excitation transfer studies experience pleasant arousal by viewing a film depicting nudity or mutually consenting sexual activity, their subsequent aggression is actually less than when they viewed no film or a neutral film (Linz, Donnerstein, & Penrod, 1987). In short, excitation transfer studies might be interpreted as showing that aggressiveness is influenced by portrayals of sexual violence, but not by watching other kinds of sexually arousing material.

■ What evidence would help to evaluate the alternatives?

Two types of evidence are needed to better understand the effects of pornography on aggression. First, because pornography can include sexual acts, aggressive acts, or both, the effects of each of these components must be more carefully examined. Second, factors affecting mens' reactions to pornography, particularly pornography that involves violence, must be more clearly understood. Work has already begun on each of these fronts.

Whether specifically paired with sexual activity or not, aggressive themes do appear to increase subsequent aggression (Bushman & Anderson, 2001). Research has focused on *aggressive pornography,* which contains sexual themes but also scenes of violence against

Small amount of pornography watched
Large amount of pornography watched

figure 14.11

Pornography and Sexual Aggression

Extensive exposure to pornography does not, by itself, increase most men's sexual aggressiveness. Such aggressiveness is much more likely, however, among men who not only watch a lot of pornography but also are hostile toward women and are sexually promiscuous.

women. In laboratory experiments, males often administer stronger electric shocks to females after viewing aggressive pornographic films as compared with neutral films. Yet there is no parallel increase in aggression against other men, suggesting that aggressive pornography creates an increase in aggressiveness that is specifically directed toward women (Aronson, Wilson, & Akert, 2002). Similarly, viewing aggressive pornography in which a rape victim appears aroused by the aggression usually leads males to become less sympathetic toward the victim and more tolerant of aggressive acts toward women (Donnerstein & Linz, 1995). Sexually explicit films that do not contain violence have no effects on attitudes toward rape (Linz, Donnerstein, & Penrod, 1987).

Are all men who are exposed to aggressive pornography equally likely to become rapists? The evidence available so far suggests that the answer is no. Whether aggressive pornography alters men's behavior and attitudes toward women depends to some extent on the men. For example, one study of about 2,700 men in the United States collected data on their sexual aggressiveness, their consumption of pornography, their history of sexual promiscuity, and their feelings of hostility toward women (Malamuth, 1998). Among men low in promiscuity and hostility, viewing pornography had little, if any, impact on sexual aggression; but among men who were high in promiscuity and hostility, pornography dramatically increased the chances that these men would engage in sexual aggression. In fact, 72 percent of the men who were high in all three factors had done so (see Figure 14.11).

■ What conclusions are most reasonable?

The attorney general's commission appeared to ignore numerous studies showing that the relationship between sexual arousal and aggression is neither consistent nor simple (Seto, Maric, & Barabee, 2001). Analysis of this relationship reveals the importance of distinguishing between pornography in general and aggressive pornography in particular. Aggressive pornography can lead to violence against women, especially in men who are already inclined to abuse and exploit women. So there is reason for concern over the impact of sexual violence commonly seen on television and in movies—especially in "slasher" films. Remarkably, such films are sometimes given less-restrictive ratings ("R" or even "PG-13") than films that are nonviolent but erotic.

The effects of nonaggressive pornography are more complicated. For most men, it has little or no impact on their behavior toward women. But among men who are inclined to abuse and exploit women, watching a lot of pornography might increase the chances that they would act on their abusive impulses (Malamuth, Addison, & Koss, 2000; Seto, Maric, & Barabaree, 2001). In summary, pornography is probably not, by itself, a major cause of violence against women. In combination with other factors, however, pornography—and especially aggressive pornography—can play a role in sexual aggression.

Murder
Rape
Violent crime

Source: Anderson & Anderson (1998).

figure 14.12

Temperature and Aggression

Studies from around the world indicate that aggressive behaviors are most likely to occur during the hottest months of the year. These studies support the hypothesis that environmental factors can affect aggression.

environmental psychology The study of the effects of the physical environment on people's behavior and mental processes.

Environmental Influences on Aggression   The link between stress, arousal, and the likelihood of aggressive behavior suggests that stressful environmental conditions can create enough arousal to make aggressive behavior more likely (Anderson, 2001). This possibility is one of the research topics in **environmental psychology,** the study of the relationship between people's physical environment and their behavior (Sommer, 1999). One aspect of the environment that clearly affects social behavior is the weather, especially temperature. High temperatures are a source of stress; as Figure 14.12 indicates, murder and other violent crimes are most likely to occur during the hottest months of the year (Anderson et al., 2000).

Living arrangements also influence aggressiveness. Compared with the tenants of crowded apartment buildings, those in buildings with relatively few residents are less likely to behave aggressively (Bell et al., 1996). This difference appears to be due in part to how people feel when they are crowded. Crowding tends to create physiological arousal and to make people tense, uncomfortable, and more likely to report negative feelings

(Oskamp & Schultz, 1998). This arousal and tension can influence people to like one another less and to be more aggressive (Ray et al., 1982).

Altruism and Helping Behavior

▶ **What motivates people to help one another?**

Like all acts of terrorism, the attacks on the World Trade Center and the Pentagon in September 2001 were horrifying examples of human behavior at its worst. But like all tragedies, they drew responses that provide inspiring examples of human behavior at its best. For example, Michael Benfante and John Cerqueira were working in the World Trade Center when one of the hijacked planes struck their building. They headed for a stairwell, but they did not just save themselves. Although it slowed their own escape, they chose to carry Tina Hansen, a wheelchair-bound co-worker, down sixty-eight flights of stairs to safety. Acts of selflessness and sacrifice were common that day, and in the days and weeks and months that followed. Police officers, medical personnel, search-and-rescue specialists, and just ordinary people came to New York from all over the United States to help clear wreckage, look for survivors, and recover bodies. More than $1 billion in donations to the Red Cross and other charity organizations poured in to help victims, and volunteering in general more than tripled in the weeks following the attacks (Penner, 2002).

All of these actions are examples of **helping behavior,** which is defined as any act that is intended to benefit another person. Helping can range from picking up dropped packages to donating a kidney. Closely related to helping is **altruism,** an unselfish concern for another's welfare (Penner, in press). In the following sections we examine some of the reasons for helping and altruism, along with some of the conditions under which people are most likely to help others.

Why Do People Help?

The tendency to help others begins early, although at first it is not spontaneous; children have to learn to be helpful (Eisenberg & Fabes, 1998). In most cultures, very young children usually help others only when they are asked to do so or are offered a reward (Grusec, 1991). Still, Carolyn Zahn-Waxler and her associates (1992) found that almost half of the two-year-olds they observed acted helpfully toward a friend or family member. As they grow older, children use helping behavior to gain social approval, and their efforts at helping become more elaborate. The role of social influence in the development of helping is seen as children follow examples set by people around them. Their helping behaviors are shaped by the norms established by their families and the broader culture (Grusec & Goodnow, 1994). In addition, children are usually praised and given other rewards for helpfulness, but scolded for selfishness. Eventually most children come to believe that being helpful is good and that they are good when they are helpful. By the late teens, people often help others even when no one is watching and no one will know that they did so (Cialdini, Baumann, & Kenrick, 1981). There are three major theories about why people help even when they cannot expect any external rewards for doing so.

Arousal:Cost-Reward Theory   One approach to explaining why people help is called the **arousal:cost-reward theory** (Piliavin et al., 1981). This theory proposes that people find the sight of a victim distressing and anxiety-provoking and that this experience motivates them to do something to reduce the unpleasant arousal. Before rushing to a victim's aid, however, the bystander will first evaluate two aspects of the situation: the costs associated with helping and the costs (to the bystander and the other person) of not helping. Whether or not the bystander actually helps depends on the outcome of this

A YOUNG HELPER   Even before their second birthday, some children offer help to those who are hurt or crying by snuggling, patting, or offering food or even their own teddy bears.

evaluation (Dovidio et al., 1991). If the costs of helping are low (as when helping someone pick up a dropped grocery bag) and the costs of not helping are high (as when the other person is physically unable to do this alone), the bystander will almost certainly help. However, if the costs of helping are high (as when helping someone lift a heavy box into a car) and the costs of not helping are low (as when the other person is obviously strong enough to do the job alone), the bystander is unlikely to offer help (Fritzsche, Finkelstein, & Penner, 2000). One of the strengths of the arousal:cost-reward theory is that it is comprehensive enough to explain several factors that affect helping. Let's consider some of these factors now.

In March 2000, a sixty-two-year-old woman in Darby, Pennsylvania, was walking to the grocery store when she was pushed from behind by an attacker. She fended him off and then did her shopping as usual. It was only when she got home and her daughter saw the handle of a knife protruding from her back that she realized that the assailant had stabbed her! No one in the grocery store said anything to her about the knife, let alone offered to help. Why? Mainly because the woman did nothing to suggest that help was necessary. This bizarre case illustrates that the first major factor affecting whether people offer help is the *clarity of the need for help* (Dovidio et al., 1991). In one study of this factor, undergraduate students waiting alone in a campus building observed what appeared to be an accident involving a window washer. The man screamed as he and his ladder fell to the ground; then he clutched his ankle and groaned in pain. All of the students looked out of the window to see what had happened, but only 29 percent of them did anything to help. Other students witnessed the same "accident," but with one important added element: The man said he was hurt and needed help. In this case, more than 80 percent of the participants came to his aid (Yakimovich & Saltz, 1971). Why so many? Apparently, this one additional cue eliminated any uncertainty about whether help was needed. The man's more obvious need for help served to raise the perceived costs of not helping him, thus making helping more likely.

The *presence of others* also has a strong influence on the tendency to help. Somewhat surprisingly, however, their presence actually tends to inhibit helping behavior (Garcia et al., 2002). One of the most highly publicized examples of this phenomenon occurred on a New York City street in 1964. During a thirty-minute struggle, a man repeatedly stabbed a woman named Kitty Genovese, but none of the dozens of neighbors who witnessed the attack intervened or even called the police until it was too late to save her life. Public dismay and disbelief followed. Psychologists wondered whether something about the situation that night had prevented people from helping.

The numerous studies of helping behavior stimulated by this tragedy, and others like it, revealed a social phenomenon that may explain why Genovese's neighbors did nothing to help her. This phenomenon, called the **bystander effect,** can be described as follows: The chance that someone will help in an emergency usually decreases as the number of people present increases (Dovidio & Penner, 2001). Why does the bystander effect occur? One explanation is that each witness assumes someone else will take responsibility for helping the victim. This *diffusion of responsibility* among all the witnesses leaves each witness feeling less obligated to help and thus lowers the perceived cost of not helping (Schroeder et al., 1995).

The degree to which the presence of other people will inhibit helping may depend on who those other people are. When they are strangers, perhaps poor communication interferes with helping. Many people have difficulty speaking to strangers, particularly in an emergency; and without speaking, they have difficulty knowing what the others intend to do. According to this logic, if people are with friends rather than strangers, they should be less embarrassed, more willing to discuss the problem, and more likely to help.

In an experiment designed to test this idea, a female experimenter left a research participant in a waiting room, either alone, with a friend, with a stranger, or with a stranger who was an assistant to the experimenter (Latané & Rodin, 1969). The experimenter then stepped behind a curtain into an office. For nearly five minutes, she could be heard opening and closing the drawers of her desk, shuffling papers, and so on. Then

helping behavior Any act that is intended to benefit another person.

altruism An unselfish concern with another's welfare.

arousal:cost-reward theory A theory that attributes helping behavior to people's efforts to reduce the unpleasant arousal they feel when confronted with a suffering victim, while also considering the costs involved.

bystander effect A phenomenon in which the chances that someone will help in an emergency decrease as the number of people present increases.

DIFFUSION OF RESPONSIBILITY Does the man on the sidewalk need help? The people walking by him are probably not sure, and they might assume that if he does need help, someone else will assist him. Research on factors affecting helping suggests that if you are ever in need of help, especially in a crowd, it is important not only to clearly ask for help but also to tell a specific onlooker to take specific action (e.g., "You, in the yellow shirt, please call an ambulance!").

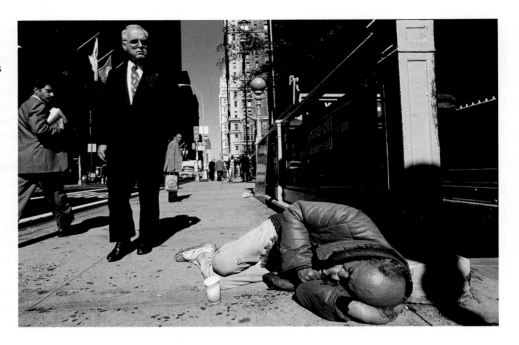

there was a loud crash, and she screamed, "Oh, my god—my foot, I—I can't move it. Oh, my ankle—I can't get this—thing off me." Then the participant heard her groan and cry.

Would the participant go behind the curtain to help? Once again, people were most likely to help if they were alone. When one other person was present, participants were more likely to communicate with one another, and to offer help, if they were friends than if they were strangers. When the stranger was the experimenter's assistant—who had been instructed not to help—very few participants offered to help. Other studies have confirmed that bystanders' tendency to help increases when they know one another (Rutkowski, Gruder, & Romer, 1983).

Research suggests that the *personality of the helper* also plays a role in helping. Some people are simply more likely to help than others. Consider, for example, the Christians who risked their lives to save Jews from the Nazi Holocaust. Samuel and Pearl Oliner (1988) interviewed more than 200 of these rescuers and compared their personalities with those of people who had a chance to save Jews but did not do so. The rescuers were found to have more *empathy* (the ability to understand or experience another's emotional state) (Davis, 1994), more concern about others, a greater sense of responsibility for their own actions, and greater confidence that their efforts would succeed. Louis Penner and his associates (Penner, 2002; Penner & Finkelstein, 1998) have found that these kinds of personality traits predict a broad spectrum of helping behaviors, ranging from willingness to help a co-worker to how much time volunteers spend helping AIDS patients (Penner & Finkelstein, 1998; Rioux & Penner, 2001). Consistent with the arousal:cost-reward theory, these personality characteristics are correlated with people's estimates of the costs of helping and not helping. For example, empathic individuals usually estimate the costs of not helping as high, and people who are confident about their ability to help usually rate the costs of helping as low (Penner et al., 1995).

Valuable as it is, the arousal:cost-reward theory cannot account for all aspects of helping. For instance, it cannot easily explain why environmental factors affect helping. Research conducted in several countries has shown that people in urban areas are generally less helpful than those in rural areas (Aronson, Wilson, & Akert, 2002). Why? It is probably not the simple fact of living in a city but rather the stressors one finds there that tend to make some urban people less helpful. Studies of cities in the United States, the United Kingdom, the Middle East, and Africa found that people's tendency to help was more strongly related to the population density (the number of people per square mile) where they lived than to the overall size of their city (Hedge & Yousif, 1992; Levine et al., 1994; Yousif & Korte, 1995). The higher the density, the less likely people were to help others. Why should stress make people less helpful? Two explanations have been suggested. The first is that stressful environments create bad moods—and generally speaking, people in a bad mood are less likely to help (Salovey, Mayer, & Rosenhan, 1991). A second possibility is that noise, crowding, and other urban stressors create too much stimulation. To reduce this stimulation, people may pay less attention to their surroundings, including less attention to individuals who need help.

Empathy-Altruism Theory The second major approach to explaining helping is embodied in the **empathy-altruism theory,** which asserts that people are more likely to engage in altruistic, or unselfish, helping—even at a high cost—if they feel empathy toward the person in need (Batson, 1998). In one experiment illustrating this phenomenon, students listened to a tape-recorded interview in which a young woman told how her parents had died in an automobile accident, leaving no life insurance (Batson et al., 1997). She said that she was trying to take care of her younger brother and sister while going to college, but that time and money were so tight that she might have to quit school or give up her siblings for adoption. Actually, the woman was an actress telling a story written by the researchers, but the participants thought it was real. Before hearing the tape, half the participants were given information about the woman that would increase their empathy for her; the other half were not. After listening to the tape, all participants were asked to help the woman raise money for herself and her siblings. Consistent with the empathy-altruism theory, more participants in the empathy group offered to help than did those in the control group.

Were the students who offered help in this experiment being utterly unselfish, or could there have been other reasons for their apparent altruism? This is a hotly debated question. Some researchers see the results as supporting the contention that empathizing with another person can sometimes lead to unselfish helping (Dovidio & Penner, 2001). Others have their doubts. They suggest instead that people help in such situations for more selfish reasons, such as relieving the distress they experienced after hearing of the woman's problems (Maner et al., 2002). The final verdict on this question is not yet in.

Evolutionary Theory The evolutionary approach to social psychology offers a third way to explain helping. This approach sees many human social behaviors as echoes of actions that contributed to the survival of our prehistoric ancestors (Burnstein & Brannigan, 2001). At first glance, it might not seem reasonable to apply evolutionary theory to helping and altruism, because helping others at the risk of our own well-being does not appear adaptive. If we die while trying to save others, it will be their genes, not ours, that will survive. In fact, according to Darwin's concept of the "survival of the fittest," helpers—and their genes—should have disappeared long ago. Contemporary evolutionary theorists suggest, however, that Darwin's thinking about natural selection focused too much on the survival of the fittest *individuals* and not enough on the survival of their genes in *others*. Accordingly, the concept of survival of the fittest has been replaced by the concept of *inclusive fitness,* the survival of one's genes in future generations (Kruger, 2003). Because we share genes with our relatives, helping—or even dying for—a cousin, a sibling, or above all, our own child potentially increases the likelihood that at least some of our genetic characteristics will be passed on to the next generation through the beneficiary's future reproduction. So *kin selection,* or helping a relative to survive, may produce genetic benefits for the helper even if it provides no personal benefits (McAndrew, 2002).

There is considerable evidence that kin selection occurs among birds, squirrels, and other animals. The more closely the animals are related, the more likely they are to risk their lives for one another. Studies in a wide variety of cultures show the same pattern of helping among humans (Buss, 1999; Clutton-Brock, 2002). For example, people in the United States are three times as likely to donate a kidney to a relative as to a nonrelative

empathy-altruism theory A theory suggesting that people help others because they feel empathy toward them.

in review

HELPING BEHAVIOR		
Theory	**Basic Premise**	**Important Variables**
Arousal: cost-reward	People help in order to reduce the unpleasant arousal caused by another person's distress. They attempt to minimize the costs of doing this.	Factors that affect the costs of helping and of not helping
Empathy-altruism	People sometimes help for unselfish reasons if they feel empathy for a person in need. They are motivated by a desire to increase another person's well-being.	The amount of empathy that one person feels for another
Evolutionary	People help relatives because it increases the chances that the helper's genes will survive in future generations.	The biological relationship between the helper and the recipient of help

? *If you could save only one person from a burning house, the _____ theory of helping would predict that it would be your own child rather than, say, a grandparent.*

(Borgida, Conner, & Monteufel, 1992). (See "In Review: Helping Behavior" for a summary of the major reasons why people help and the conditions under which they are most likely to do so.)

Cooperation, Competition, and Conflict

cooperation   Any type of behavior in which several people work together to attain a goal.

competition   Any type of behavior in which individuals try to attain a goal for themselves while denying that goal to others.

conflict   What occurs when a person or group believes that another person or group interferes with the attainment of a goal.

social dilemmas   Situations in which actions that produce rewards for one individual will produce negative consequences if they are adopted by everyone.

social facilitation   A phenomenon in which the mere presence of other people improves a person's performance on a given task.

social impairment   A reduction in performance due to the presence of other people.

social loafing   Exerting less effort when performing a group task because one's contribution cannot be identified.

Helping is one of several ways in which people *cooperate* with one another. **Cooperation** is any type of behavior in which people work together to attain a goal. For example, several law students might form a study group to help one another pass the bar exam. But people also compete with others for limited resources. Those same students might later try to outdo one another to be chosen for a single job opening at a top law firm. **Competition** exists whenever individuals try to attain a goal for themselves while denying that goal to others. Finally, there is **conflict,** which occurs when a person or group believes that another person or group interferes with the attainment of a goal. When the law students become attorneys and represent opposing parties in a trial, they will be in conflict with one another. One way in which psychologists have learned about all three of these phenomena is by studying social dilemmas (Gifford & Hine, 1997).

Social dilemmas are situations in which an action that is most rewarding for each individual will, if adopted by all others in the situation, create problems for everyone. For instance, it might benefit a factory owner's immediate profit picture to dump toxic waste into a river; but if all factories do the same, the environment will eventually become uninhabitable for everyone. Similarly, during a drought, each homeowner is better off in the short run by watering the lawn as often as necessary to keep it from dying; but if everyone ignores local water restrictions, there will be no drinking water for anyone in the long run. Social dilemmas reflect conflicts between the interests of the individual and those of the group, and between short-term and long-term interests (Schroeder, 1995). Are people from collectivist cultures (which emphasize cooperation) less likely to act competitively or selfishly in social dilemma situations? This may be true in general, but interpersonal conflict in such situations still appears to some extent in all cultures (Smith & Bond, 1999).

Group Processes

► **What makes a good leader?**

Although Western industrialized cultures tend to emphasize individuals over groups, the fact remains that most important decisions and efforts by governments and businesses in those cultures and elsewhere are made by groups, not individuals. Sometimes groups function very well. Perhaps you recall the extraordinary teamwork by engineers, emergency workers, and volunteers that led to the dramatic rescue of nine men trapped in a flooded Pennsylvania coal mine in July 2002. At other times, though, groups have been known to make bad, or even disastrous, decisions. To begin to understand why, let's consider some of the social psychological processes that often occur in groups to alter the behavior of individuals and the quality of their collective efforts.

The Presence of Others

In 1897, in what was probably the first social psychological experiment ever conducted, Norman Triplett demonstrated that an individual's behavior is affected by the mere presence of other people. Triplett found that bicycle racers went much faster when another racer was nearby than when they were simply racing against time. This effect occurred even when the cyclists were not competing against each other. There was something about the presence of another person, not just competition, that made riders go faster.

The term **social facilitation** describes circumstances in which the presence of other people can improve performance (Aiello & Douthitt, 2001). This improvement does not always occur, however. In fact, having other people present sometimes hurts performance, a process known as **social impairment.** For decades, these results seemed contradictory; then Robert Zajonc (pronounced "ZYE-onze") suggested that both effects could be explained by one process: arousal.

The presence of other people, said Zajonc, increases a person's general level of arousal or motivation (Zajonc, 1965). Arousal increases the tendency to perform those behaviors that are most *dominant*—the ones you know best. This tendency can either help or hinder performance. When you are performing an easy, familiar task, such as riding a bike, increased arousal due to the presence of others should allow you to ride even faster than normal. But when a task is hard or unfamiliar—such as trying to perform a complex new dance routine in front of an audience—the most dominant responses may be incorrect and cause performance to suffer. In other words, the impact of other people on performance depends on whether the task is easy or difficult.

What if a person is not merely in the presence of others, but is working with them on some task? In these situations, people often exert less effort than when performing alone, a phenomenon called **social loafing** (Karau & Williams, 1997). Whether the task is pulling on a rope, clapping as loudly as possible, or trying to solve mental puzzles, people tend to work harder when alone than with others (Baron, Kerr, & Miller, 1992). Steven Karau and Kipling Williams (2001) have proposed that social loafing is most likely to occur when people do not see a direct connection between the amount of effort they exert and the amount of reward they receive.

In Western cultures, social loafing occurs more often among men than women, and it appears in groups of all sorts, from volunteer committees to search parties. It is much less likely among people of either gender in cultures such as those in China and Japan (Smith & Bond, 1999). These differences probably reflect the fact that women, and people from Eastern cultures, tend to have a collectivist orientation. This orientation emphasizes the

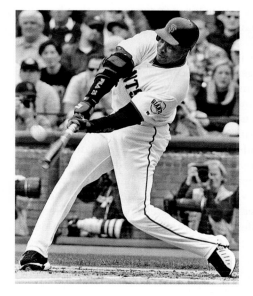

SOCIAL FACILITATION On his way to a new home run record during the 2001 baseball season, Barry Bonds, shown here adding to his total, was able to perform at his best even though large crowds were present. In fact, the crowds probably helped him hit well, because the presence of others tends to increase arousal, which enhances the performance of familiar and well-learned skills, such as a batting swing. However, arousal created by an audience tends to interfere with the performance of unfamiliar and poorly developed skills. This is one reason why professional athletes who show flawless grace in front of thousands of fans are likely to freeze up or blow their lines in front of a small production crew when trying for the first time to tape a TV ad or a public service announcement.

importance of group performance and discourages social loafing. The role of group leaders becomes especially important when social loafing and other obstacles threaten to impair the effectiveness of group efforts.

Group Leadership

A good leader can help a group pursue its goals, but a bad one can get in the way of a group's functioning. What makes a good leader? Early research suggested that the personalities of good and bad leaders were about the same, but we now know that certain personality traits often distinguish effective from ineffective leaders. For example, using tests similar to those that measure the big-five traits described in the personality chapter, Colin Silverthorne (2001) examined the characteristics of leaders in the United States, Thailand, and China. He found that effective leaders in all three countries tended to score high on agreeableness, emotional stability, extraversion, and conscientiousness. Other researchers have found that in general, effective leaders are intelligent, success oriented, and flexible (Levine & Moreland, 1998).

Having particular personality traits does not guarantee good leadership ability, however. People who are effective leaders in one situation may be ineffective in another (Yukl & Van Fleet, 1992). The reason is that effective leadership also depends on the characteristics of the group members; the task at hand; and most important, the interaction between these factors and the leader's style.

Two main styles of leadership have been identified. **Task-oriented leaders** provide close supervision, lead by giving orders, and generally discourage group discussion (Yukl & Van Fleet, 1992). Their style may make them unpopular. In contrast, **person-oriented leaders** provide loose supervision, ask for group members' ideas, and are generally concerned with subordinates' feelings. They are usually well liked by the group, even when they must reprimand someone (Taylor, Peplau, & Sears, 2003).

Research on leadership effectiveness and gender provides one explanation as to why one leadership style is not always better than another. According to Alice Eagly and her associates, men and women in Western cultures tend to have different leadership styles (Eagly, Johannesen-Schmidt, & van Engen, 2003). Men tend to be more task oriented; women, more person oriented. One interpretation of these differences is that the gender-role learning processes described in the chapter on human development influence men and women to "specialize" in different leadership behaviors. Overall, men and women are equally capable leaders, but men tend to be more effective when success requires a more task-oriented leader, and women tend to be more effective when success requires a more person-oriented leader. In other words, people of each gender tend to be most effective when they are acting in a manner consistent with gender-role traditions (Eagly & Karau, 1991; Eagly, Karau, & Makhijani, 1995). This may be one reason why some people do not like female leaders who act in a "masculine" manner or occupy leadership positions traditionally held by men. In certain circumstances, these negative responses create bias against female leaders, particularly among male members of the groups they lead (Eagly, Makhijani, & Klonsky, 1992).

Most contemporary theories of leadership are known as *contingency* theories (Levine & Moreland, 1998), because they suggest that leadership effectiveness is contingent, or depends, on factors such as the leader's relations with group members and the nature of the group's task. According to these theories, for example, task-oriented leaders tend to be most effective when the group is working under time pressure, when the task is unstructured, and when circumstances do not make it clear what needs to be done first and how duties should be divided. People stranded in a burning building, for example, need a task-oriented leader. Conversely, person-oriented leaders tend to be most effective when the task is structured and there are no severe time limits (Chemers, 1987). These people would be particularly successful, for example, in managing an office in which the workers knew their jobs well.

task-oriented leaders Leaders who provide close supervision, lead by giving directions, and generally discourage group discussion.

person-oriented leaders Leaders who provide loose supervision, ask for group members' ideas, and are generally concerned with subordinates' feelings.

Groupthink

The emphasis on group decisions in most large organizations is based on the belief that several people working together will make better decisions than will individuals working alone. As noted in the chapter on thought, language, and intelligence, this belief is generally correct; yet under certain circumstances, groups have been known to make amazingly bad decisions (Brownstein, 2003). Consider two examples. First, in the late 1930s, U.S. government leaders decided not to take special precautions to defend Hawaii's Pearl Harbor. The Japanese attack there on December 7, 1941, killed 2,500 people. Second, in 1986, administrators at the National Aeronautics and Space Administration (NASA) ignored engineers' warnings about the effects of cold weather and decided to launch the space shuttle *Challenger*. The spacecraft exploded seventy-three seconds after liftoff, killing all aboard. After analyzing these and other disastrous decisions, Irving Janis (1989) proposed that they can be attributed to a phenomenon called *groupthink*. **Groupthink** occurs, he said, when group members are unable to realistically evaluate the options available to them or to fully consider the potential negative consequences of the option they are about to choose.

Groupthink is particularly likely when four conditions exist: (1) the group is isolated from outside influences, (2) the group is working under time pressure or other intense stressors, (3) the group does not carefully evaluate alternative ways of solving the problem, and (4) there is a strong leader who obviously favors a particular solution (Brehm, Kassin, & Fein, 2002). This last condition appeared to play a crucial role in President John F. Kennedy's decision to support what turned out to be an unsuccessful invasion of Cuba by anti-Castro Cubans in 1961. Before the final decision was made, several advisers were told that Kennedy had made up his mind and it was time to "close ranks with the president." This situation created enormous pressure for conformity (May & Zelikow, 1997).

When these conditions exist, groups tend to become close-minded and to think of the favored option as the only reasonable one. They dismiss other options and quickly suppress any dissenting voices. As a result, the group becomes more and more certain that its decision cannot possibly be wrong. Some researchers have questioned the prevalence and dangers of groupthink (e.g., Park, 2000; Paulus, 1998). Most researchers agree that it does occur, though, and many of them have worked on developing techniques to help groups avoid it.

One way to avoid groupthink is to designate someone to play the "devil's advocate," a person who constantly challenges the group's emerging decisions and offers alternatives (Janis, 1989; Risen, 1998). Another is to encourage diverse opinions by allowing people to express them anonymously. For example, group members might communicate by e-mail on networked computers that hide the sender's identity. Research suggests that allowing groups to discuss decision options without knowing who is saying what stimulates logical debate and makes it easier for people to disagree with the group ('t Hart, 1998).

LINKAGES
How does stress affect group decision making?
(a link to Health, Stress, and Coping)

LINKAGES
Can we "see" prejudice in the brain?
(a link to Biology and Behavior)

groupthink   A pattern of thinking that renders group members unable to evaluate realistically the wisdom of various options and decisions.

social neuroscience   A specialty that focuses on the influence of social processes on biological processes and on the influence of biological processes on social psychological phenomena.

LINKAGES

Biological and Social Psychology

Research in social psychology was once thought to be entirely separate from research on the biological processes that underlie social behavior (Winkielman, Berntson, & Cacioppo, 2001). Social psychologists believed it was impossible to reduce complex social psychological processes to the firing of neurons or the secretion of hormones. For their part, biological psychologists, more commonly known as *neuroscientists,* viewed the study of social psychology as having little, if any, relevance to the understanding of, say, behavioral genetics or the functioning of the nervous system. Recently, however, scientists in both subfields have begun to take a closer look at each other's research and at how that research is linked. The result has been the emergence of a new specialty called **social neuroscience** or *social cognitive neuroscience* (Harmon-Jones & Devine, 2003; Ochsner & Lieberman, 2001; Tryon, 2002). This new specialty focuses on the influence of social processes on biological processes and on the influence of biological processes on social psychological phenomena (e.g., Curtis & Wang, 2003).

There are many reasons to believe that this approach will be valuable. For example, the chapter on health, stress, and coping contains numerous examples of how social stressors can have health-related biological consequences. Health psychologists have also found that the availability and quality of a person's social support network can affect biological processes ranging from blood pressure to the healing of wounds (Kiecolt-Glaser et al., 1998; Uchino, Cacioppo, & Kiecolt-Glaser, 1996). In addition, as discussed in the chapter on psychological disorders, some problems in social behavior can result from the interaction of environmental stressors with genetic influences. One recent study compared the amount of antisocial behavior displayed by men who had, or had not, suffered the stress of parental abuse in childhood. Antisocial behavior was much more common among men who had been abused, but this behavior was most common among abused men who also had inherited characteristics associated with antisocial behaviors (Caspi et al., 2002).

Researchers are beginning to identify the biological underpinnings of many social processes. One example can be seen in studies of how the amygdala—a brain structure involved in emotion—is related to the stereotyping and prejudice discussed earlier in this chapter. Researchers found that European Americans who were prejudiced against African Americans showed significantly more amygdala activity when looking at pictures of black people than when looking at pictures of white people (Hart et al., 2000; Phelps et al., 2000).

In short, social cognitive neuroscience shows great promise for creating a better understanding of the linkages among social, cognitive, and biological phenomena, as well as a better understanding of complex social and physiological processes (Ochsner & Lieberman, 2001).

active review   Social Psychology

Linkages

As noted in the introductory chapter, all of psychology's subfields are related to one another. Our discussion of social neuroscience illustrates just one way in which the topic of this chapter, social psychology, is linked to the subfield of biological psychology, which is discussed in the chapter on biology and behavior. The Linkages diagram also shows ties to two other subfields as well, and there are many more ties throughout the book. Looking for linkages among subfields will help you see how they all fit together and help you better appreciate the big picture that is psychology.

Summary

Social cognition, the mental processes through which people perceive and react to others, is one aspect of social psychology, the study of how people influence and are influenced by other people. Through social cognition, each person creates a unique perception of reality.

SOCIAL INFLUENCES ON THE SELF

▶ **How do we compare ourselves with others?**

People's social and cultural environments affect their thoughts and feelings about themselves, including their self-concept and their self-esteem. When people have no objective criteria by which to judge themselves, they look to others as the basis for social comparison. Such comparison can affect self-evaluation or self-esteem. Categories of people that are habitually used for social comparison are known as reference groups. Comparison with reference groups sometimes produces relative deprivation, which in turn can cause personal and social turmoil.

A person's social identity is formed from beliefs about the groups to which the person belongs. Social identity affects the beliefs we hold about ourselves, our self-concept. Social identity permits people to feel part of a larger group, engendering loyalty and sacrifice from group members, but also potentially creating bias and discrimination toward people who are not members of the group.

SOCIAL PERCEPTION

▶ **Do we perceive people and objects in similar ways?**

Social perception concerns the processes by which people interpret information about others, form impressions of them, and draw conclusions about the reasons for their behavior. Schemas, the mental representations about people and social situations that we carry into social interactions, affect what we pay attention to, what we remember, and how we judge people and events.

First impressions are formed easily and quickly, in part because people apply existing schemas to their perceptions of others. First impressions change slowly, because people are "cognitive misers"; once we form an impression about another person, we try to maintain it, because doing so simplifies the world. Schemas, however, can create self-fulfilling prophecies, leading us to act in ways that bring out behavior in others that is consistent with our expectations of them.

Attribution is the process of explaining the causes of people's behavior, including our own. Observers tend to attribute behavior to causes that are either internal or external to the actor. Attributions are also affected by biases that systematically distort one's view of behavior. The most common attributional biases are the fundamental attribution error (and its cousin, the ultimate attribution error), the actor-observer bias, and the self-serving bias. Personal and cultural factors can affect the extent to which people exhibit attributional biases.

ATTITUDES

▶ **Do attitudes always determine behavior?**

An attitude is the tendency to respond positively or negatively to a particular object. Attitudes affect a wide range of behaviors. Most social psychologists see attitudes as composed of three components: cognitive (beliefs), affective (feelings), and behavioral (actions). However, it is often difficult to predict a specific behavior from a person's beliefs or feelings about an object. Cognitive theories suggest that the likelihood of attitude-behavior consistency depends on agreement of the person's thoughts and feelings, subjective norms, perceived control over the behavior, and prior direct experience with the attitude object.

Attitudes can be learned through modeling, as well as through classical or operant conditioning. They are also subject to the mere-exposure effect: All else being equal, people develop greater liking for a new object the more often they are exposed to it.

The effectiveness of a persuasive message in changing attitudes is influenced by the characteristics of the person who communicates the message, by its content, and by the audience receiving it. The elaboration likelihood model suggests that attitude change can occur via either the peripheral or the central route, depending on a person's ability and motivation to carefully consider an argument. Accordingly, different messages will produce attitude change under different circumstances. Another approach is to change a person's behavior, in the hope that attitudes will be adjusted to match the behavior. Cognitive dissonance theory holds that if inconsistency between attitude and behavior creates discomfort related to a person's self-concept, the attitude may change in order to reduce the conflict.

PREJUDICE AND STEREOTYPES

▶ **How does prejudice develop?**

Stereotypes often lead to prejudice and discrimination. Motivational theories of prejudice suggest that some people have a need to dislike people who differ from themselves. This need may stem from the trait of authoritarianism, as well as from a strong social identity with one's in-group. In either case, feeling superior to members of out-groups helps these people to feel better about themselves. As a result, in-group members tend to discriminate against out-groups. Cognitive theories suggest that people categorize others into groups in order to reduce social complexity. Learning theories maintain that stereotypes, prejudice, and discriminatory behaviors can be learned from parents, peers, and the media. The contact hypothesis proposes that intergroup contact can reduce prejudice and lead to more favorable attitudes toward the stereotyped group—but only if the contact occurs under specific conditions, such as equal status between groups. Even under these conditions, it is not easy to change unconscious aspects of prejudice and stereotyping.

INTERPERSONAL ATTRACTION

▶ **What factors affect who likes whom?**

Interpersonal attraction is affected by many variables. Physical proximity is important because it allows people to meet. The situation in which they meet is important because positive or negative aspects of the situation tend to be associated with the other person. Characteristics of the other person are also important. Attraction tends to be greater when two people share similar attitudes and personal characteristics. Physical appearance plays a role in attraction; initially, attraction is strongest to those who are most physically attractive. But for long-term relationships, the matching hypothesis applies: People tend to choose others whose physical attractiveness is about the same as theirs.

Two key components of successful intimate relationships are interdependence and mutual commitment. Sternberg's triangular theory suggests that love is a function of three components: passion, intimacy, and commitment. Varying combinations of these three components create qualitatively different types of love. Marital satisfaction depends on communication, the perception that the relationship is equitable, the couple's ability to deal effectively with conflict and anger, and agreement on important issues in the marriage.

SOCIAL INFLUENCE

▶ What social rules shape our behavior?

Norms establish the rules for what should and should not be done in a particular situation. One particularly powerful norm is reciprocity, the tendency to respond to others as they have acted toward you. *Deindividuation* is a psychological state in which people temporarily lose their individuality, their normal inhibitions are relaxed, and they may perform aggressive or illegal acts that they would not do otherwise.

When behavior or beliefs change as the result of unspoken or implicit group pressure, *conformity* has occurred; when the change is the result of a request, *compliance* has occurred. People tend to follow the normative responses of others, and groups create norms when none already exist. People sometimes exhibit public conformity without private acceptance; at other times, the responses of others have an impact on private beliefs. People conform because they want to be right, because they want to be liked, and because they tend to be rewarded for doing so. People are most likely to conform when the situation is unclear, as well as when others in the group are in unanimous agreement. Up to a point, conformity usually increases as the number of people holding the majority view grows larger. Effective strategies for inducing compliance include the foot-in-the-door technique, the door-in-the-face procedure, and the low-ball approach.

OBEDIENCE

▶ How far will people go in obeying authority?

Obedience involves complying with an explicit demand from an authority figure. Research by Milgram indicates that obedience is likely even when obeying an authority appears to result in pain and suffering for another person. Obedience declines when the status of the authority figure declines, as well as when others are observed to disobey. Some people are more likely to obey orders than others. Because participants in Milgram's studies experienced considerable stress, the experiments have been questioned on ethical grounds. Nevertheless, his research showed that people do not have to be psychologically disordered to inflict pain on others.

AGGRESSION

▶ Are people born aggressive?

Aggression is an act intended to harm another person. Freud saw aggression as due partly to death instincts. More recent theories attribute aggressive tendencies to genetic and evolutionary factors, brain dysfunctions, and hormonal influences. Learning is also important; people learn to display aggression by watching others and by being rewarded for aggressive behavior. There are wide cultural differences in the occurrence of aggression.

A variety of emotional factors play a role in aggression. The *frustration-aggression hypothesis* suggests that frustration can lead to aggression, particularly in the presence of cues that invite or promote aggression. Arousal from sources unrelated to aggression, such as exercise, can also make aggressive responses more likely, especially if aggression is already a dominant response in that situation. Research in *environmental psychology* suggests that factors such as high temperature and crowding increase the likelihood of aggressive behavior, particularly among people who are already angry.

ALTRUISM AND HELPING BEHAVIOR

▶ What motivates people to help one another?

Humans often display *helping behavior* and *altruism.* There are three major theories of why people help others. According to the *arousal:cost-reward theory,* people help in order to reduce the unpleasant arousal they experience when others are in distress. Their specific reaction to a suffering person depends on the costs associated with helping or not helping. Helping behavior is most likely when the need for help is clear and when diffusion of responsibility is not created by the presence of other people—a phenomenon called the *bystander effect.* Environmental and personality factors also affect willingness to help. The *empathy-altruism theory* suggests that helping can be truly unselfish if the helper feels empathy for the person in need. Finally, evolutionary theory suggests that humans have an innate tendency to help others, especially relatives, because doing so increases the likelihood that family genes will survive.

Cooperation is any type of behavior in which people work together to attain a goal; *competition* exists whenever individuals try to attain a goal for themselves while denying that goal to others. Interpersonal or intergroup *conflict* occurs when one person or group believes that another stands in the way of reaching some goal. Psychologists study conflict by observing behavior in *social dilemmas,* situations in which behavior that benefits individuals in the short run may spell disaster for an entire group in the long run.

GROUP PROCESSES

▶ What makes a good leader?

People's behavior is affected by the mere presence of other people. By enhancing one's most likely behavior in a situation, the presence of others sometimes creates *social facilitation* (which improves performance) and sometimes creates *social impairment* (which interferes with performance). When people work in groups, they often exert less effort than when alone, a phenomenon called *social loafing.* Effective group leaders tend to score high on emotional stability, agreeableness, and conscientiousness. In general, they are also intelligent, success oriented, and flexible. *Task-oriented leaders* provide close supervision, lead by giving orders, and generally discourage group discussion. *Person-oriented leaders* provide loose supervision, ask for group members' ideas, and are generally concerned with subordinates' feelings. Overall, men and women are equally capable leaders, but men tend to be more effective when success requires a more task-oriented leader, and women tend to be more effective when success requires a more person-oriented leader.

When *groupthink* occurs, group members fail to realistically evaluate the options available to them, leading to poor decisions. Groupthink is most likely to occur in groups that are isolated from outside influence; do not carefully consider alternative solutions; work under time pressure or other stressors; and have a strong, opinionated leader.

A new specialty called *social neuroscience* focuses on the influence of social processes on biological processes and on the influence of biological processes on social psychological phenomena.

Learn by Doing

Put It in Writing

A survey reveals that first-graders from various ethnic groups in a local school hold prejudiced attitudes toward one another. Imagine that you have been hired to develop a program to help these children become less prejudiced and more accepting of members of other ethnic groups. Write a one-page description of two or three classroom activities that would help you to accomplish this goal, and tell why you think they would do so. Do you think these activities could be successful in eliminating all prejudiced thinking in the children? Why or why not?

Personal Learning Activity

Research cited in this chapter suggests that the physical appearance of a partner tends to be more important to men, whereas a partner's intelligence tends to be more important to women. If that is true, what would you hypothesize about the qualities men versus women say they are looking for when they place ads for a partner in a personals column or web site? Develop a research plan to test your hypothesis, and then collect some data by reading and analyzing personals ads in your local newspaper or on a web site for singles. Was your hypothesis supported? Did gender differences in the content of the ads hold true for homosexuals as well as heterosexuals? Write a brief report of your findings, and summarize what you think they can and cannot say about the factors that attract people to each other. *For additional projects, see the Personal Learning Activities in the corresponding chapter of the study guide that accompanies this text.*

Step into Action

Courses

Social Psychology
Social Conflict
Marriage and Family
Social Cognition
Interpersonal Processes
Prejudice and Discrimination

Movies

The Last of the Mohicans (reference groups)
Rosewood; A Patch of Blue (prejudice and discrimination)
Higher Learning; Revenge of the Nerds; Legally Blonde (cultural diversity and stereotypes)
Snow Falling on Cedars (stereotypes, prejudice)
Schindler's List (obedience, compliance)

Books

Henry Louis Gates, Jr., *Colored People: A Memoir* (Vintage, 1994) (growing up black in segregated West Virginia)
James Goodman, *Stories of Scottsboro* (Vintage, 1994) (prejudice and discrimination lead to wrongful rape convictions of young black men in Alabama in 1931)
Elliot Aronson, *Nobody Left to Hate* (W.H. Freeman, 2000) (a social psychologist explores the social roots of the Columbine school massacre).
Alex Kotlowitz, *The Other Side of the River: A Story of Two Towns, a Death, and America's Dilemma* (Doubleday, 1998) (a story of discrimination in law enforcement and prejudice in a town that is racially and geographically divided)

John Gray, *Men Are from Mars, Women Are from Venus* (HarperCollins, 1993) (interpersonal relationships)
Hans-Werner Bierhoff, *Prosocial Behaviour* (Psychology Press, 2002) (an introductory overview of research on helping and altruism)
Charles Stangor (Ed.), *Stereotypes and Prejudice: Essential Readings* (Psychology Press, 2000) (a collection of research articles on prejudice)
Robert Cialdini, *Influence: Science and Practice* (Addison-Wesley, 2001) (summary of research on influence and how it is applied in everyday life)
Russell Geen and Edward Donnerstein (Eds.), *Human Aggression: Theory, Research, and Implications for Social Policy* (Academic Press, 1998) (readings on the origins of, and factors in, aggression)
Malcom Gladwell, *The Tipping Point: How Little Things Can Make a Big Difference* (Back Bay Books, 2002) (describes how concepts from social psychology can help explain the development of popular fads and trends)

The Web

The World Wide Web is a good source of additional information about the science of psychology, provided you use it carefully and think critically about the information you find. The web site that accompanies this text offers many resources relevant to this chapter. These resources include interactive NetLab exercises; Thinking Critically and Evaluating Research exercises; ACE chapter quizzes; recommended web links; and articles on current events, books, and movies. At http://college.hmco.com, select *Psychology* and then this textbook.

Review of Key Terms

Can you define each of the key terms in the chapter? Check your definitions against those on the pages listed in parentheses below or in the Glossary/Index at the end of the text.

actor-observer bias *(p. 520)*

aggression *(p. 540)*

altruism *(p. 546)*

arousal:cost-reward theory *(p. 546)*

attitude *(p. 522)*

attribution *(p. 520)*

bystander effect *(p. 547)*

cognitive dissonance theory *(p. 524)*

competition *(p. 550)*

compliance *(p. 533)*

conflict *(p. 550)*

conformity *(p. 533)*

contact hypothesis *(p. 527)*

cooperation *(p. 550)*

deindividuation *(p. 532)*

discrimination *(p. 526)*

elaboration likelihood model *(p. 523)*

empathy-altruism theory *(p. 549)*

environmental psychology *(p. 545)*

frustration-aggression hypothesis *(p. 542)*

fundamental attribution error *(p. 520)*

groupthink *(p. 553)*

helping behavior *(p. 546)*

matching hypothesis *(p. 530)*

norms *(p. 532)*

obedience *(p. 536)*

person-oriented leaders *(p. 552)*

prejudice *(p. 526)*

reference groups *(p. 514)*

relative deprivation *(p. 515)*

schemas *(p. 517)*

self-concept *(p. 514)*

self-esteem *(p. 514)*

self-fulfilling prophecy *(p. 519)*

self-serving bias *(p. 521)*

social cognition *(p. 514)*

social comparison *(p. 514)*

social dilemmas *(p. 550)*

social facilitation *(p. 551)*

social identity *(p. 516)*

social impairment *(p. 551)*

social loafing *(p. 551)*

social neuroscience *(p. 553)*

social perception *(p. 517)*

social psychology *(p. 514)*

stereotypes *(p. 526)*

task-oriented leaders *(p. 552)*

Multiple-Choice Self-Test

Select the best answer for each of the questions below. Then check your responses against the Answer Key at the end of the text.

1. Jack took an entry-level job after completing college with honors and having one of his term papers published. Now Jack is depressed because the older people around him make more money than he does and are more advanced in their careers. Jack is experiencing

   a. cognitive dissonance.   c. social facilitation.
   b. relative deprivation.   d. a self-fulfilling prophecy.

2. When Alaa says, "I am a Muslim," he is describing his

   a. self-esteem.   c. social identity.
   b. self-schema.   d. social perception.

3. When Rowland first met Jacob, Jacob wasn't feeling well and threw up on Rowland's shoes. According to research on first impressions, we would expect Rowland to

   a. feel sorry for Jacob and thus have a positive first impression of him.
   b. develop a negative impression of Jacob because of the negative first experience with him.
   c. have an initial negative impression that will become positive later, no matter what Jacob does.
   d. have a positive first impression of Jacob because he is a male.

4. Gena is in a bad mood because she is convinced that she won't like her blind date, Pat. When Pat arrives, he is outgoing and considerate, but Gena is short-tempered and rude to him. Soon Pat becomes irritable and ends the date early. Gina's prediction that she wouldn't have a good time came true mainly because of

   a. cognitive dissonance.
   b. prejudice.
   c. a self-fulfilling prophecy.
   d. the fundamental attribution error.

5. "I earned an A on my history test because I studied hard and I'm smart, but I failed my philosophy test because the test was poorly worded and the teacher doesn't like me." This statement is an example of

   a. actor-observer bias.
   b. the fundamental attribution error.
   c. a self-fulfilling prophecy.
   d. a self-serving bias.

6. Richard markets a new toothpaste by including a picture of an attractive celebrity in his ads. He is using the _____ route to try to achieve attitude change among consumers.

   a. central   c. direct
   b. peripheral   d. persuasive

7. Rachel and Matteus listen to a boring lecture. Afterward, Rachel is offered $100 and Matteus is offered $1 to tell the lecturer's next class that the lecture was interesting and fun. Both agree to do so. According to cognitive dissonance theory, we would expect real attitude change about the lecture to occur in

   a. Rachel, but not Matteus.
   b. Matteus, but not Rachel.
   c. both Rachel and Matteus.
   d. neither Rachel nor Matteus.

8. Lila doesn't like people with red hair because she believes that they are impulsive and not very bright. The best way to reduce Lila's prejudice against red-haired people would be to

   a. tell her about research showing that red-haired people do not differ from other people.
   b. arrange for Lila to supervise a group of red-haired people as they solve a problem.
   c. assign Lila to work with a group, which includes red-heads, to build a playground.
   d. put Lila on a committee led by a red-haired person.

9. According to research on interpersonal attraction, a good predictor of whether one person will like another person is

   a. similar attitudes.
   b. similar age.
   c. similar ways of dealing with anger.
   d. similar height and weight.

10. Giorgio and Louisa share their thoughts, hopes, and daily worries. They plan to stay married throughout their lifetime, and they enjoy an active and satisfying sex life. According to Sternberg's theory, Giorgio and Louisa are experiencing _____ love.

    a. consummate
    b. companionate
    c. temporary
    d. romantic

11. When Ashley laughed during her uncle's funeral, the other members of her family felt very uncomfortable. Ashley's laughter was an example of

    a. deindividuation.
    b. social loafing.
    c. social inhibition.
    d. a norm violation.

12. In Harper Lee's novel *To Kill a Mockingbird*, an angry mob tries to lynch a prisoner. The prisoner's attorney, Atticus Finch, and his young daughter, talk to the crowd, calling people by name, and reminding them of their families. Soon the mob disperses, no longer a faceless crowd but a group of identifiable individuals. Atticus and his daughter disrupted the phenomenon of

    a. diffusion of responsibility.
    b. deindividuation.
    c. situational ambiguity.
    d. social facilitation.

13. Shawn's teacher doesn't keep track of her students' performance in groups, so Shawn does not put as much effort into his group project as he does into his individual project. Shawn is exhibiting

    a. a self-serving bias.
    b. social facilitation.
    c. social loafing.
    d. diffusion of responsibility.

14. Keyonna thought that the play she had just seen was boring, but everyone else seemed to like it. At the closing curtain, the audience gave the actors a standing ovation. Keyonna stood up and applauded, too, even though she didn't believe the actors deserved it. Keyonna's behavior in this situation is an example of

    a. conformity.
    b. compliance.
    c. obedience.
    d. a self-fulfilling prophecy.

15. Colleen knows she should take a day off from work to study for a big exam, but she also knows her boss won't like it. So she first asks for the entire week off. When the boss refuses, she asks for the one day off instead, and he agrees. Colleen used the _____ approach to gain her boss's compliance.

    a. foot-in-the-door
    b. door-in-the-face
    c. low-ball
    d. peripheral

16. Which of the following is not a major factor in determining whether or not a person will obey an order?

    a. the status of the authority figure giving the order
    b. the personality characteristics of the person receiving the order
    c. the presence of another person who disobeys the order
    d. the gender of the person given the order

17. Leonard is upset because he just learned that he failed his physics final exam and will not be able to graduate on time. When his roommate comes home and accidentally knocks over Leonard's glass of lemonade, Leonard becomes abusive, screaming at his roommate and throwing books and pillows at him. This is an example of the _____ theory of aggression.

    a. frustration-aggression
    b. generalized arousal
    c. authoritarian
    d. biological

18. According to the arousal: cost-reward theory, Ruth will be most likely to help a lost child she finds crying in the mall if she

    a. works with children every day.
    b. is upset by the crying and has the time to help.
    c. never shopped in that mall before.
    d. was lost in a mall as a small child herself.

19. Which of the following summarizes the evolutionary view of helping behavior?

    a. People feel good when they help others.
    b. People help others in order to improve the chance that some of their genes will survive in future generations.
    c. People are motivated to protect others if the costs of helping are outweighed by the benefits.
    d. People learn to be helpful.

20. When groups are isolated from outside influence, work under time pressure, don't consider all their options, and are headed by biased leaders, they often make poor decisions because of a phenomenon called

    a. deindividuation.
    b. groupthink.
    c. social facilitation.
    d. social impairment.

STATISTICS IN PSYCHOLOGICAL RESEARCH

Understanding and interpreting the results of psychological research depend on *statistical analyses,* the methods for describing and drawing conclusions from data. The introductory chapter introduced some terms and concepts associated with these analyses. *Descriptive statistics* are the numbers that psychologists use to describe and present their data. *Inferential statistics* are the mathematical procedures they use to draw conclusions from data and to make inferences about what the data mean. Here, we present more details about these statistical analyses that will help you to evaluate research results.

DESCRIBING DATA

To illustrate our discussion, let's imagine a hypothetical experiment on the effects of rewards on performance. The experimenter presents a set of mathematics problems to two groups of people. Each group must solve the problems within a fixed time. For each correct answer, the low-reward group is paid ten cents. The high-reward group gets one dollar. The hypothesis to be tested is the **null hypothesis,** the assertion that the independent variable manipulated by the experimenter will have no effect on the dependent variable measured by the experimenter. In this case, the null hypothesis is that the size of the reward (the independent variable) will not affect performance on the mathematics task (the dependent variable).

Assume that the experimenter has obtained a sample of participants, assigned them randomly to the two groups, and done everything possible to avoid the influence of confounding variables and other research problems discussed in the introductory chapter. The experiment has been run, and the researcher now has the data, a list of the number of correct answers given by each participant in each group. Now comes the first task of statistical analysis. We must describe the data in a way that makes them easy to understand.

The Frequency Histogram

The simplest way to describe the data is to draw up something like Table 1, in which all the numbers are simply listed. After examining the table, you might notice that the high-reward group seems to have done better than the low-reward group. But the difference is not immediately obvious. It might be even harder to see if more participants had been involved or if the scores included three-digit numbers. A more satisfactory way of presenting the same data is in a picture-like graphic known as a **frequency histogram** (see Figure 1).

Construction of a histogram is simple. First, divide the scale for measuring the dependent variable (in this case, the number of correct solutions) into a number of categories, or "bins." The bins in our example are 1–2, 3–4, 5–6, 7–8, and 9–10. Next, sort the raw data into the appropriate bin. (For example, the score of a participant who had 5 correct answers would go into the 5–6 bin, a score of 8 would go into the 7–8 bin, and so on.) Finally, for each bin, count the number of scores in that bin, and draw a bar up to the height of that number on the vertical axis of the graph. The set of bars makes up the frequency histogram. Figure 1 shows a histogram comparing the scores of the high-reward group and the low-reward group. Now the difference between groups that was difficult to see in Table 1 becomes clearly visible. More high scores appeared in the high-reward group than in the low-reward group.

null hypothesis A testable statement that the independent variable manipulated by an experimenter will have no effect on the dependent variable being measured by the experimenter.

frequency histogram A pictorial presentation of how often each possible score on a dependent variable occurs in a set of research data.

table 1

A Simple Data Set

Here are the test scores obtained by thirteen participants performing under low-reward conditions and thirteen participants performing under high-reward conditions.

Low Reward	High Reward
4	6
6	4
2	10
7	10
6	7
8	10
3	6
5	7
2	5
3	9
5	9
9	3
5	8

Test score categories
Low reward

Test score categories
High reward

1–2   5–6   9–10
3–4   7–8

figure 1

A Frequency Histogram

The height of each bar of a histogram represents the number of scores falling within each range of score values. The pattern formed by these bars gives a visual image of how research results are distributed.

Histograms and other "pictures" of data are useful for visualizing and better understanding the "shape" of research data. But in order to analyze data statistically, we need to use other ways of handling the numbers that make up these graphic presentations. For example, before we can tell whether two histograms are different statistically or just visually, the data they represent must be summarized using descriptive statistics.

Descriptive Statistics

The four basic categories of descriptive statistics do the following: (1) count the number of observations made; (2) summarize the typical value of a set of data; (3) summarize the spread, or variability, in a set of data; and (4) express the correlation between two sets of data, using the correlation coefficient described in the introductory chapter.

N   The easiest statistic to compute, abbreviated as N, simply describes the number of observations that make up the data set. In Table 1, for example, $N = 13$ for each group, or 26 for the entire data set. Simple as it is, N plays a very important role in more sophisticated statistical analyses.

Measures of Central Tendency   It is apparent in Figure 1 that there is a difference in the pattern of scores between the two groups. But how much of a difference? What is the typical value, the *central tendency,* that represents each group's performance? There are three measures that capture this typical value: the mode, the median, and the mean. The *mode* is the value or score that occurs most frequently in the data set. The *median* is the halfway point in a set of data; half the scores fall above the median, and half fall below it. The *mean* is the arithmetic average. To find the mean, add the values of all the scores and divide by the number of scores *(N)*.

Measures of Variability   The variability (or spread or dispersion) of a set of data is often just as important as its central tendency. This variability can be described by measures known as the *range* and the *standard deviation.* The range is simply the difference between the highest and the lowest values in a data set. For the data in Table 1, the range for the low-reward group is $9 - 2 = 7$; for the high-reward group, the range is $10 - 3 = 7$. The standard deviation, or SD, describes the average difference between each score and the mean of the data set.

The Normal Distribution   In most subfields in psychology, when researchers collect many measurements and plot their data in histograms, the pattern that results often resembles that shown for the low-reward group in Figure 1. That is, the majority of

Statistics can be valuable for describing research results, but critical thinking demands that we evaluate them carefully before drawing conclusions about what they mean. Knowing this pointy-haired executive's tendency toward uncritical thinking, you can bet that Dogbert's impressive-sounding restatement of the definition of *median* will win him an extension of his pricey consulting contract.

DILBERT reprinted by permission of United Feature Syndicate, Inc.

scores tend to fall in the middle of the distribution, whereas fewer and fewer scores occur as one moves toward the extremes. As more and more data are collected, and as smaller and smaller bins are used (perhaps containing only one value each), the histogram tends to smooth out until it resembles the bell-shaped curve known as the **normal distribution,** or normal curve, which is shown in Figure 2. When a distribution of scores follows a truly normal curve, its mean, median, and mode all have the same value. Furthermore, if the curve is normal, we can use its standard deviation to describe how any particular score stands in relation to the rest of the distribution.

The distribution of IQ scores shown in Figure 2 provides an example. They are distributed in a normal curve, with a mean, median, and mode of 100 and a standard deviation (SD) of 16. In such a distribution, half of the population will have an IQ above 100, and half will have an IQ below 100. The shape of the true normal curve is such that 68 percent of the area under it lies within 1 standard deviation above and below the mean. In terms of IQ, this means that 68 percent of the population has an IQ somewhere between 84 (100 minus 16) and 116 (100 plus 16). Of the remaining 32 percent of the population, half falls more than 1 SD above the mean, and half falls more than 1 SD below the mean. So, 16 percent of the population has an IQ above 116, and 16 percent scores below 84.

The normal curve is also the basis for percentiles. A **percentile score** indicates the percentage of people or observations that fall at or below a given score in a normal distribution. In Figure 2, for example, the mean score (which is also the median) lies at a point below which 50 percent of the scores fall. Thus, the mean of a normal distribution is at the 50th percentile. What does this mean for IQ? If you score 1 SD above the mean, your score is at a point above which only 16 percent of the population falls. This means that

figure 2

The Normal Distribution

Many kinds of research data approximate the shape of the normal curve, in which most scores fall toward the center of the range.

normal distribution   A smooth, bell-shaped curve representing a set of data in which most scores occur in the middle of the possible range, with fewer and fewer scores occurring toward the extremes of the range.

percentile score   A way of stating what percentage of scores in a data set fall at or below a certain score.

The normal distribution of IQ

84 percent of the population (100 percent minus 16 percent) must be below that score. So this IQ score is at the 84th percentile. A score at 2 SDs above the mean is at the 97.5 percentile, because 97.5 percent of the scores are below it in a normal distribution.

Scores may also be expressed in terms of their distance in standard deviations from the mean, producing what are called **standard scores.** A standard score of 1.5, for example, is 1.5 standard deviations from the mean.

INFERENTIAL STATISTICS

It can be hard to understand the meaning of research results that are summarized by descriptive statistics alone. Is a correlation between college grade-point averages and the eating of certain foods large enough to support the hypothesis that diet is important for mental functioning? Is the difference in the effects of two different kinds of psychotherapy large enough to recommend one over the other? The answers to questions such as these are based largely on the results of analyses that use inferential statistics.

Consider again the descriptive statistics from our rewards experiment. They tell us that the performances of the high- and low-reward groups differ, but there is some uncertainty. Is the difference large enough to be important? Does it represent a real effect or a fluke? The researcher would like to have some measure of confidence that the difference between groups did not occur by chance alone. **Inferential statistics** use certain rules to estimate the likelihood that a particular correlation or a particular difference between groups was due to chance. If that likelihood is small enough, the researcher can usually conclude that the correlation or difference is *statistically significant.*

Differences Between Means: The *t* Test

One of the most important tools of inferential statistics is the *t* test. It allows the researcher to ask how likely it is that the difference between two means occurred by chance rather than because of the independent variable. When the *t* test or another inferential statistic says that the probability of chance effects is small enough (usually less than 5 percent), the results are said to be *statistically significant.* Conducting a *t* test of statistical significance requires the use of three descriptive statistics.

The first component of the *t* test is the size of the observed effect, the difference between the means. Recall that the mean is calculated by summing a group's scores and dividing by the number of scores. In the example shown in Table 1, the mean of the high-reward group is 94/13, or 7.23, and the mean of the low-reward group is 65/13, or 5. Thus the difference between the means for the high- and low-reward groups is $7.23 - 5 = 2.23$.

Second, the standard deviation of scores in each group must be known. If the scores in the groups are quite variable, their standard deviations will be large, indicating that chance may have played a large role in producing the results. If the scores within each group are all very similar, however, their standard deviations will be small, which suggests that the participants in each group reacted in about the same way to the rewards they were given. So, the difference between groups is more likely to be significant when each group's standard deviation is small. In Table 1, some people in the low-reward group actually did better on the math test than some in the high-reward group. If variability is high enough that the scores of two groups overlap, the difference between group means, though large, may not be statistically significant.

Third, we need to take the sample size, *N,* into account. The larger the number of participants or observations, the more likely it is that a given difference between means is significant. This is so because with larger samples, random factors within a group will have less impact on the group's mean. The unusual performance of a few people who were sleepy or anxious or hostile, for example, will likely be canceled out by the scores of the more representative majority of people. The same effect of sample size can be seen in coin tossing. If you toss a quarter 5 times, you might not be too surprised if heads come up 80 percent of the time. But if you get 80 percent heads after 100 tosses, you might begin to suspect that this is probably not due to chance alone. Some other effect, perhaps

standard score A way of stating how many standard deviations separate a particular score from the mean of all the scores in a data set.

inferential statistics A form of statistical analysis designed to provide a measure of confidence about how likely it is that a certain result appeared by chance.

some bias in the coin, is probably producing the results. For the same reason, a relatively small correlation coefficient—between diet and grades, say—might be statistically significant if it was based on 50,000 students. As the number of participants increases, it becomes less likely that the correlation reflects the influence of a few oddball cases.

To summarize, as the difference between the means gets larger, as N increases, and as standard deviations get smaller, t increases. This increase in t raises the researcher's confidence in the significance of the difference between means.

Beyond the *t* Test

Many experiments in psychology are considerably more complex than simple comparisons between two groups. They often involve three or more experimental and control groups. Some experiments also include more than one independent variable. For example, suppose we were interested not only in the effect of reward size on performance but also in the effect of problem difficulty. We might then create six groups whose members would perform easy, moderate, or difficult problems under low- or high-reward conditions.

In an experiment like this, the results might be due to the size of the reward, the difficulty of the problem, or the combined effects (known as the *interaction*) of the two. Analyzing the size and source of these effects is typically accomplished through procedures known as *analysis of variance*. The details of analysis of variance are beyond the scope of this book, but note that, as in the t test, the statistical significance of each effect is influenced by differences between means, by standard deviation, and by sample size.

For more detailed information about how analysis of variance and other inferential statistics are used to understand and interpret the results of psychological research, consider taking courses in research methods and statistical or quantitative methods.

Chapter 1   Introduction to the Science of Psychology

1A Scientific psychology has its roots in philosophy and especially in a philosophical view called empiricism *(p. 9)*.   **2B** A behaviorist uses functional analysis of behavior to see what benefits certain actions have *(p. 12)*.   **3B** Someone who believes that human behavior is influenced by genetic inheritance, unconscious motivations, and environmental influences exemplifies the multiple perspectives of the eclectic approach *(p. 14)*.   **4C** The psychodynamic approach, developed by Freud, emphasizes unconscious mental processes in explaining human thought, feelings, and behavior *(p. 15)*.   **5A** Behaviorists say that people think and behave in ways that have previously been rewarded *(p. 16)*.   **6C** Cognitive psychologists study basic mental processes such as sensation and perception, learning and memory, judgment, decision-making and problem-solving *(p. 4)*.   **7D** Recognition of a smile is a behavior that cross-cultural psychologists find to be similar around the world *(p. 19)*.   **8D** Critical thinkers are least likely to ask, "Which celebrities have gone on record as endorsing this form of therapy?" All of the other responses are part of the critical thinking process *(p. 23)*.   **9D** The correct list of scientific research goals is description, prediction, control, and explanation *(p. 25)*.   **10C** Case Studies are used to collect descriptive data *(pp. 25–26)*.   **11D** Before using survey results to support a hypothesis, we must be sure that the questions are properly worded, the sample used is representative of the population of interest, and the responses are not biased by efforts to appear "socially acceptable" *(pp. 26–27)*.   **12A** Room temperature, time of day, and participants' personalities are all possible random variable *(p. 30)*.   **13D** To avoid the possibility that experimenter bias may confound the results of an experiment aimed at testing an hypothesis, a researcher should use a double-blind study *(p. 31)*.   **14A** In an experiment, the outcome behavior being measured (such as memory) is the dependent variable *(p. 28)*.   **15B** In an experiment, the group that receives the "treatment" or intervention is the experimental group *(p. 28)*.   **16B** Using a true experiment to try to scientifically study this problem would pose the greatest ethical problems for Jose because it is not ethical to purposely create abusive conditions for children *(pp. 35–36)*.   **17B** The number closest to ±1.00 is the strongest correlation coefficient *(p. 34)*.   **18D** A correlation coefficient can tell us the strength, direction, and existence of a relationship between two variables, but not its cause *(pp. 34–35)*.   **19C** To select participants for study such as smoking habits of a group of students, you would use a representative sample *(pp. 32–33)*.   **20D** All are good reasons for ethical behavior *(pp. 35–36)*.

Chapter 2   Biology and Behavior

1D The genetic information that tells cells what to do is found in the nucleus of each cell *(p. 48)*.   **2C** Malfunctions of serotonin systems contribute to depression, and malfunctions in dopamine systems contribute to Parkinson's disease *(p. 51)*.   **3A** Overactivity of glutamate, which occurs when oxygen is cut off from neurons in the brain, can result in a stroke *(p. 52)*.   **4D** Research on nootropics, or "smart drugs," suggests that the best benefits for memory and brain function would result from exercising your brain *(p. 54)*.   **5C** The somatic system carries information to and from the central nervous system *(p. 56)*.   **6D** The sympathetic nervous system is less active, and the parasympathetic system is more active, now that Kalli is relaxing *(pp. 56–57)*.   **7A** Some simple behaviors like reflexes occur automatically via the spinal cord and without instructions from the other portion of the central nervous system, the brain *(p. 58)*.   **8C** The procedure that provides a "moving picture" of the brain is an fMRI *(p. 60)*.   **9A** The medulla, located in the hindbrain, helps to regulate heart rate, blood pressure, and breathing *(p. 60)*.   **10D** If the reticular formation fibers in Lily's hindbrain were damaged, she would go into a coma *(p. 60)*.   **11A** The cerebellum is that part of the hindbrain that controls finely coordinated movements *(p. 59)*.   **12B** Defects in the hippocampus have been found in people with Alzheimer's disease *(p. 63)*.   **13A** The sensory system provides information about the environment *(pp. 64–65)*.   **14C** The sensory cortex in the occipital lobe receives information concerning vision *(p. 64)*.

15A Voluntary movements are controlled by neurons in the motor cortex, located in the frontal lobe *(p. 65)*.   **16A** Damage to Broca's area creates difficulties in speaking *(p. 67)*.   **17B** Broca's area and Wernicke's area, both located in the left cerebral hemisphere, are responsible for comprehension and production of language *(p. 67)*.   **18B** Scientists did initially have some success in treating Parkinsonism with transplanted tissue from a fetal brain, but improvement faded over time, some patients had serious side effects, and the procedure in humans is highly controversial *(p. 71)*.   **19A** Neurons secrete neurotransmitters across synapses and endocrine organs release hormones into the blood stream *(p. 72)*.   **20A** Glands release hormones such as cortisol into the bloodstream *(p. 73)*.

Chapter 3   Sensation and Perception

1A Perception is the process of using information and your understanding of the world so that messages from the senses become meaningful experiences *(p. 80)*.   **2B** Transduction is the process of converting incoming energy into neural activities *(p. 81)*.   **3A** The described procedure defines absolute threshold *(pp. 81–82)*.   **4B** Expecting a stimulus to occur lowers the response criterion *(p. 82)*.   **5C** According to Weber's law, the lighter the objects being compared, the smaller the weight difference needed to detect a change in weight *(p. 83)*.   **6B** When a star is faint, it is more easily seen by looking slightly away from where the star is expected to be *(p. 87)*.   **7D** The trichromatic theory proposes that combining three primary colors can produce any other color *(p. 88)*.   **8A** According to the opponent-processing theory, when one member of an opponent color pair (red/green, blue/yellow, black/white) is no longer stimulated, the other is activated *(p. 90)*.   **9C** Constant loud noise causes hair cell damage, literally ripping off hair cells form his inner ear, resulting in nerve deafness *(p. 94)*.   **10A** The frequency of a sound wave determines pitch *(p. 93)*.   **11B** Gustation is the sense of taste *(p. 96)*.   **12D** Nutritional state and temperature can both contribute to food's flavor *(p. 96)*.   **13B** There is no solid evidence that humans give off or can detect pheromones that act as sexual attractants *(p. 98)*.   **14A** Kinesthesia gives us knowledge of the position of our body parts *(pp. 99, 103)*.   **15A** Shanelle wants to be sure the children are dressed alike (similarity) so they will be perceived as a group *(p. 106)*.   **16B** People moving at the same speed, in a sense having a "common fate," are perceived as a group *(p. 107)*.   **17C** Interposition is the depth perception cue that operates on this basis *(p. 108)*.   **18B** Looming is a motion cue such that objects increasingly fill the retinal space as they get closer *(p. 109)*.   **19A** Redundancy allows us to fill in gaps when information, such as letters in the given example, are missing *(p. 116)*.   **20A** Covert orienting involves a shift of attention that isn't easily observed *(p. 119)*.

Chapter 4   Consciousness

1A Mental processing of bodily processes, such as the brain regulating blood pressure, occur at the nonconscious level, and some people are able to learn to control these processes through biofeedback *(p. 130)*.   **2B** According to Freud, unacceptable thoughts, feeling, and memories are kept in the unconscious to protect a person from anxiety *(p. 117)*.   **3B** Zandra's exposure to Rembrandt's paintings caused her to like them more *(p. 132)*.   **4B** Edie's success depends on her expectation that the messages will help her *(pp. 132–134)*.   **5A** In an altered state of consciousness, changes in mental processing are great enough to produce differences in functioning that are noticed by the person or others *(p. 135)*.   **6D** During REM sleep, mental activity, heart rate, and blood pressure increase while muscle tension decreases *(p. 137)*.   **7B** People with narcolepsy abruptly enter REM sleep directly from the waking state, usually as they are experiencing an emotional state *(p. 139)*.   **8A** SIDS (sudden infant death syndrome) has been greatly reduced in the United States by the "back to sleep" program, which advises parents to have their babies sleep face up *(p. 140)*.   **9A** Disruptions of your circadian rhythm can make you grouchy and less productive *(pp. 140–141)*.   **10C** It is non-REM sleep that researchers believe is important for restoring the body and brain's energy stores for the next day's activity, the other three responses are functions of REM sleep *(pp. 141–142)*. **11D** According to the activation-synthesis theory, dreams are meaningless, random byproducts of REM sleep *(p. 143)*. **12C** Dissociation means a split in consciousness that allows the hypnotized person and hypnotist to share control *(p. 145)*. **13C** Hypnosis has been used to help people reduce nausea from chemotherapy, surgical bleeding, and pain *(p. 145)*. **14A** Norman is about to meditate *(p. 146)*. **15B** An antagonist is a molecule that fits into a receptor and blocks other neurotransmitters from binding *(pp. 146–147)*. **16A** Tolerance is a condition in which increasingly larger drug doses are required to produce the same effect *(p. 148)*. **17D** Since alcohol's physiological effects involve dopamine, dopamine agonists can reduce cravings and withdrawal effects *(p. 149)*. **18C** Caffeine is a stimulant which does not cause hallucinations *(pp. 151, 154)*. **19B** Opiates relieve pain and cause sleep *(p. 152)*. **20B** Marijuana disrupts memory function and reduces creativity *(pp. 153–154)*.

Chapter 5   Learning

1C The expression "Once burned, twice shy" reflects a change in knowledge (or behavior) due to experience *(p. 162)*. **2B** After repeated pairings with a stimulus that already triggers a reflexive response, the conditioned stimulus alone elicits the reflexive-like response *(pp. 164–165)*. **3A** The green light should predict the presentation of the puff of air *(pp. 163–165)*. **4B** Extinction is the gradual disappearance of a conditioned response when the UCS is eliminated *(p. 165)*. **5D** Seeing a dog is enough to make Najla fearful *(pp. 164–165)*. **6B** Spontaneous recovery is the reappearance of a conditioned response after extinction *(p. 164)*. **7A** Having been classically conditioned to a white lab rat, Albert now generalizes to other white, furry animals *(pp. 165–166)*. **8C** For survival reasons, people are biologically prepared to link taste signals with illness *(p. 167)*. **9A** When an organism stops responding to a repeated stimulus, habituation has occurred *(p. 169)*. **10C** Operant conditioning involves learning that behaviors have consequences *(p. 171)*. **11B** Negative reinforcement strengthens behavior that is followed by the removal of an unpleasant event or stimulus *(p. 171)*. **12B** Once avoidance conditioning is learned, avoidance can be a difficult habit to break *(pp. 171–172)*. **13D** A discriminative stimulus signals that a reward will occur if a certain response is given *(p. 172)*. **14D** Shaping is the process of reinforcing successive approximations to the target behavior *(pp. 173–174)*. **15B** Jamey must exhibit a fixed number of behaviors while Susan must work a variable amount of time *(p. 175)*. **16D** They are all problems with using punishment *(pp. 177–179)*. **17B** Learned helplessness occurs when people learn they are unable to control circumstances or outcomes *(p. 181)*. **18C** Latent learning is learning that is not demonstrated when it is first learned *(pp. 182–183)*. **19D** Najla has learned from the experience of watching others pet a dog *(pp. 185–186)*. **20D** Working in groups is an active learning method that improves students' recall of information *(p. 190)*.

Chapter 6   Memory

1A Acoustic codes represent information as sequences of sounds, such as a tune or a rhyme *(p. 199)*. **2C** Episodic memory is a person's recall of a specific event that happened while that person was present; procedural memory involves knowledge of how to do things *(p. 200)*. **3C** Implicit memories are not purposefully recalled but do influence behavior *(pp. 200–201)*. **4B** Maintenance rehearsal is a method of keeping information in short-term memory by repeating it *(p. 201)*. **5B** The transfer-appropriate processing model of memory suggests that a critical factor in memory is how the encoding process matches up with what is later retrieved *(p. 201)*. **6C** Selective attention allows Reepal to focus on the most important information *(pp. 204–205)*. **7B** Unrehearsed information stays in short-term memory for about eighteen seconds *(p. 206)*. **8A** Chunking involves grouping information into meaningful units that can be stored *(p. 205)*. **9C** Semantic memory contains general knowledge not linked to a specific event *(p. 206)*. **10D** Research on long term memory found, for example, that 32 months after the O. J. Simpson murder trial, 71% of study participants' recollections were inaccurate *(p. 207)*. **11A** Due to the primacy effect, items at the beginning of a list are well-remembered *(pp. 208–209)*. **12B** People sometimes remember material better when they are in the same place as when they learned it *(p. 210)*. **13C** Semantic networks are links of related information. When a person recalls information from one node of the network, it can feel as if the person is very close to accessing the information needed in the next node *(pp. 210–211)*. **14C** Constructive memory is a fabricated, but seemingly real, recollection *(pp. 211–212)*. **15C** Recent use of DNA evidence has revealed that many people in prison for serious crimes did not commit those crimes *(pp. 215–216)*. **16C** As Ebbinghaus discovered, relearning

takes much less time than original learning. This difference represents the savings from one learning to the next learning *(p. 217)*. **17C** Proactive interference occurs when old information disrupts the learning of new information *(pp. 218–219)*. **18A** The hippocampus is crucial for episodic memory *(p. 224)*. **19B** Anterograde amnesia is the inability to form new long-term memories following a brain injury *(p. 224)*. **20A** The method of loci involves mentally placing objects in various spots in a familiar location (loci) *(p. 226)*.

Chapter 7   Thought, Language, and Intelligence

1D Thinking is part of an information processing system that manipulates mental representations *(p. 236)*. **2B** Cognitive maps are mental representations of familiar parts of your world *(p. 240)*. **3B** Basing his strategy on an algorithm would require Clint to evaluate every possible move and countermove *(pp. 240–242)*. **4B** Mental models are clusters of propositions that represent people's understanding of how things work *(pp. 238–239)*. **5B** Setting aside a difficult problem, hoping for a solution to occur while working on something else, is called incubation *(p. 222)*. **6D** Functional fixedness occurs when a person fails to use a familiar object in a novel way to solve a problem *(p. 248)*. **7C** Confirmation bias is a strong tendency to confirm rather than refute the preferred hypothesis, even in the face of strong evidence against the hypothesis *(p. 248)*. **8A** The gambler's fallacy has led Richard to believe that the probability of a random event will change over time *(p. 253)*. **9C** Incorrect words or word endings are not likely to have been reinforced. They are overgeneralizations of a language rule the child has learned *(pp. 257–258)*. **10A** A critical period is a limited window of opportunity for language learning. If the critical period is missed, normal language development will not occur *(p. 259)*. **11A** Alfred Binet designed the first IQ test to identify children with special educational needs *(p. 260)*. **12D** Formal reasoning is based on the rules of logic *(pp. 240–241)*. **13C** As a result of current scoring methods, an IQ score reflects how well a person performs relative to other people of the same age *(pp. 260–261)*. **14C** If the scores from this preemployment test predict future performance on the job, the test is valid for the purpose of employee selection *(p. 264)*. **15A** A reliable test yields consistent and stable scores over time *(pp. 263–264)*. **16A** IQ tests appear to be most valid for assessing aspects of intelligence that are related to school work *(p. 265)*. **17D** The highest correlation is likely to be found between the identical twins' scores *(pp. 265–266)*. **18C** An IQ score between 50 and 70 reflects mild mental retardation. This individual will have difficulty with academic material and abstract reasoning *(p. 272)*. **19B** The multiple intelligences approach focuses on abilities not measured by IQ tests *(pp. 270–271)*. **20A** Creative people are internally motivated, have a set of creative skills, use divergent thinking, and have expertise in the field of pursuit *(pp. 251–252)*.

Chapter 8   Motivation and Emotion

1B The evolutionary approach suggests that adaptive behaviors that promote the survival of the species reflect inborn motivations to pass on genes *(p. 283)*. **2A** Homeostasis is the tendency to maintain physiological systems at a steady, stable level by adjusting to changes *(p. 283)*. **3D** Arousal theory states that people are motivated to behave in ways that maintain an individual, optimal level of arousal *(p. 284)*. **4B** Incentive theory states that behavior is goal directed to obtain positive stimuli and avoid negative stimuli *(p. 285)*. **5A** When stimulated, the ventromedial nucleus tells Ahmed that there is no need to eat *(p. 287)*. **6A** The mere presence of others tends to increase food consumption *(p. 288)*. **7B** Although bulimics can maintain normal weight, they may experience dehydration and other symptoms *(p. 290)*. **8C** The Chicago survey found that people in the United States have sex less frequently and with fewer partners than was earlier believed *(p. 292)*. **9C** Only men experience the refractory period *(p. 293)*. **10B** Edwina will encourage her son to try difficult tasks, praise his efforts, and help him learn from his mistakes *(p. 300)*. **11A** People with high achievement needs set realistic but not impossible goals, actively seek success, and take risks *(p. 299)*. **12A** Physiological needs, including those for food and water, come first in Maslow's hierarchy *(pp. 303–304)*. **13C** Jill's situation has both positive and negative features, so she is faced with an approach-avoidance conflict *(p. 304)*. **14B** The sympathetic nervous system is involved in the fight-or-flight syndrome *(pp. 306–307)*. **15A** James's theory states that we experience emotions only by perceiving our physiological response to an event *(pp. 208–309)*. **16D** Excitation transfer occurs when arousal from an experience carries over to a different situation. This is consistent with Schachter's theory of emotion *(pp. 312–313)*. **17B** Cannon's theory maintains that emotional experience originates in the thalamus and simultaneously triggers physiological arousal and cognitive awareness (p. 312). **18D** As children grow up, they learn an emotional culture, which are rules that govern what emotions are appropriate, in what situations, and what expressions are allowed (p. 317). **19B** Human emotions are communicated mainly through facial movements and expressions (pp. 315–317). **20B** In allowing Diane's emotional state to guide his behavior, Sam is using social referencing (pp. 317–318).

Chapter 9   Human Development

1C Behavioral genetics researches nature vs. nurture, heredity, and differences among individuals or groups characteristics (pp. 326–327). **2D** Alcohol, drugs, and smoking are teratogens and potentially dangerous to the developing baby during pregnancy (pp. 328–329). **3C** Maturation refers to the natural growth or change triggered by biological factors that are relatively independent of the environment (p. 325). **4D** Newborns visually prefer novelty and shapes that resemble human faces (p. 330). **5C** With normal brain development, grasping and rooting reflexes should have disappeared by 6 months of age (p. 330). **6A** Assimilation is the process of taking in information that adds to an existing schema (pp. 332–333). **7B** Adriana is probably four to six years old; she is in the preoperational stage (p. 336). **8B** Babies stare longer when natural physical laws are defied (pp. 334–336). **9B** We are unlikely to recall anything about our first year due to infantile amnesia. (pp. 338–340). **10A** The easy baby adapts easily, fusses little, and calms quickly (p. 343). **11B** Harlow's attachment studies demonstrate that infant monkeys form attachments based on contact comfort needs (pp. 344–345). **12D** With ambivalent insecure attachment, the child sometimes prefers and sometimes rejects the primary caregiver (p. 345). **13C** Authoritative parents are sympathetic but firm; permissive parents give lots of freedom (p. 349). **14B** In North American cultures, males are usually encouraged to achieve, act independently, explore, and assume responsibility (p. 351). **15C** Ludmilla is still confused about her identity (pp. 348, 355). **16C** Asian American adolescents are less likely to engage in sexual activity (p. 354). **17A** People at the Stage 1 (preconventional) level of moral reasoning are concerned with avoiding punishment (p. 356). **18C** These changes occur mainly in middle adulthood (pp. 358–359). **19A** Adults over sixty-five years of age are generally slower and less effective than younger ones at solving complex problems they have not seen before (pp. 363–364). **20B** Terminal drop is the decline in mental functioning that occurs in the months or years preceding death (p. 364).

Chapter 10   Health, Stress, and Coping

1D Stressors include physical and psychological components that affect health (pp. 373–374). **2A** The more stressors Lila has, the more physical, psychological, and behavioral responses she will probably experience (p. 373–374). **3D** Psychological stressors are events and situations to which people must adjust or adapt (p. 374). **4A** The first stage of the GAS, the alarm reaction, involves some version of the fight-or-flight syndrome (p. 376). **5C** Exhaustion is the last stage of the GAS and represents a serious, progressive depletion of resources (p. 377). **6B** Rumination is continuously thinking about negative events and it tends to intensify negative emotional states (p. 378). **7B** Catastrophizing involves the exaggeration of negative consequences (p. 378). **8D** Behavioral stress responses are changes in the way people look, act, or talk (pp. 378). **9B** Flashbacks are associated with posttraumatic stress disorder (pp. 379–380). **10C** Stressors that are predictable have less impact than those that are unpredictable (p. 381). **11C** Perceived control over stressful events helps reduce their negative effects (p. 382). **12B** Laton is trying to improve the employees' social support networks (pp. 383–384). **13B** People who are impulsive or low on conscientiousness are more likely to die from accidents or violence (pp. 385–386). **14C** Natural killer cells of the immune system have antiviral properties and help prevent tumors (p. 388). **15B** Hostility is a risk factor in heart disease (pp. 389–390). **16A** Smoking is not only related to cancer, it also aggravates many other dangerous illnesses (p. 391). **17A** Personalizing the risk of danger to the individual should increase the likelihood of behavioral change (p. 392). **18B** Being aware of a problem behavior and thinking about changing it occur during the contemplation stage of readiness to alter a health-related behavior (p. 393). **19A** Sayumi is using the coping strategy of cognitive restructuring, or changing her thinking about an event or person (p. 395). **20C** Progressive relaxation trains a person to physically relax muscles, thus reducing heart rate and blood pressure (p. 395).

Chapter 11   Personality

1B Personality is defined as a person's unique pattern of enduring psychological and behavioral characteristics (p. 401). **2A** The id contains the life and death instincts, is impulsive and pleasure seeking (p. 402). **3D** During the latency period, which lasts from about age five until puberty, an individual's focus is on education and social development (p. 404). **4B** Displacement is deflecting an impulse from its original target to a less threatening one (p. 403). **5A** Overly strict toilet training can lead to an anal fixation that appears as sloppy, disorganized, and impulsive behavior in adulthood (p. 404). **6D** Although based on a small, culturally biased sample and not scientifically derived, Freud's theory is comprehensive and has profoundly affected psychology (p. 406). **7B** Trait theory assumes that personality traits are relatively stable, consistent, and predictable (p. 407). **8C** Allport believed that personality can be described using about seven central traits (p. 407). **9D** Trait theorists have identified five (called "the big-five") main factors that make up personality (pp. 408–409). **10C** Trait theories describe personality but do not explain how personality develops (p. 413). **11B** Twin studies suggest that there are genetic predispositions toward particular personality traits and temperament (p. 413). **12A** Internals expect outcomes and events to be controlled mainly by their own efforts (p. 414). **13C** Reciprocal determinism is a mutually influential interaction among cognitive patterns, the environment, and behavior (p. 414). **14D** According to Mischel, Person variables and situation variables are important in explaining particular behaviors (p. 415). **15C** Social-cognitive theories describe personality as 1 patterns of thought and behavior that are learned though experience in social situations (pp. 413–414). **16C** Conditions of worth are created when "people" are evaluated instead of their behavior (pp. 416–417). **17B** A preoccupation with perceived need for material things and a devaluation of what one does have, reflects a deficiency orientation (p. 418). **18D** Unconscious needs, motives, and conflicts supposedly guide responses to the relatively unstructured stimuli of projective tests (p. 425). **19C** Research has found that those rated as ill-tempered as children are more likely to be aggressive in adulthood (pp. 421–422). **20B** An objective test contains clear, specific questions or statements; responses can be scored and evaluated mathematically (p. 423).

Chapter 12   Psychological Disorders

1C Approximately 48 percent of the population in the United States have experienced a mental disorder at some point in their lives (p. 433). **2C** The practical approach defines abnormality based on the content, context, and consequence of behavior (p. 435). **3A** Hippocrates attributed psychological disorders to biological factors, which included the four humors (pp. 436–437). **4D** Diathesis-stress approach attributes abnormal behavior to the interaction of stress with biological, environmental, and psychological predispositions (pp. 438–439). **5D** The global assessment of functioning is one evaluation axis of the DSM IV (pp. 440–442). **6A** Agoraphobia is the fear of being alone or away from the security of home (pp. 446–447). **7C** OCD involves an obsession with particular thoughts or images, which motivates repetitive, uncontrollable behaviors called compulsions (pp. 446–447). **8A** Conversion disorder involves functional impairment with no physical cause (p. 449). **9A** Severe pain in the absence of any physical problem is symptomatic of pain disorder (p. 450). **10B** Dissociative identity disorder is a condition in which a person appears to have more than one identity (p. 451). **11B** Sleep changes and weight gain or loss are typical of major depressive disorder (p. 453). **12B** Depressed women, certain ethnic groups, males over forty-five and living alone, and those who talk about suicide do tend to be at elevated risk for committing suicide (pp. 453–455). **13A** Attribution is the process of explaining the causes of one's own and other's behavior; social-cognitive theorists see a depressive attributional style as partly responsible for depression (pp. 457–458). **14C** Schizophrenia is characterized by abnormality in thinking, writing, speaking, affect, perception and attention, and personal identity (p. 459). **15D** Thought broadcasting is a delusion in which patients believe that their thoughts can be heard by others (p. 459). **16C** The most common symptoms of paranoid schizophrenia include delusions of grandeur or persecution, which are often accompanied by anger, anxiety, or jealousy (p. 461). **17A** People diagnosed with antisocial personality disorder display impulsive, selfish, unscrupulous behavior and have few morals or deep feelings for others (p. 464). **18D** The more violent forms of antisocial personality disorder are associated with the experience of abuse in childhood (pp. 465–466). **19A** A substance-related disorder is characterized by long-term drug/alcohol use that causes physical or psychological harm to the user or others (pp. 468–469). **20B** Children with autistic disorder usually show little attachment, poor eye contact, and asocial behavior (p. 468).

Chapter 13   Treatment of Psychological Disorders

1C As a part of psychodynamic therapy, the client reports all feelings, thoughts, memories, and images that come to mind in free association (*pp. 480–481*). **2A** Gestalt therapy uses role playing, among other techniques, to help clients become more self-aware and self-accepting (*p. 484*). **3A** Licensed clinical psychologists generally hold a doctoral degree in clinical or counseling psychology (*p. 480*). **4B** Psychoanalysis focuses on revealing and working through unconscious conflicts (*p. 480*). **5A** Empathy involves an effort to perceive the client's view of reality (*pp. 482–483*). **6A** Carl Rogers developed client-centered therapy (*p. 483*). **7C** By paraphrasing what Shanobi has said, her friend is responding in a manner consistent with reflection (*p. 483*). **8A** Insight involves becoming aware of previously unconscious material (*p. 481*). **9C** Behavioral therapists see compulsive behaviors as learned habits (*pp. 484–485*). **10C** Psychoanalysts today focus less on instincts and more on interpersonal relationships (*p. 481*). **11C** Confidentiality is a critical aspect of therapy than can be violated only under special circumstances, as when the therapist believes the client's life is in danger (*pp. 499–500*). **12B** Community psychologists are concerned with promoting social changes that prevent psychological problems (*pp. 406–407*). **13A** Flooding is a behavior therapy technique that places a client in a feared but harmless situation to extinguish the fear (*p. 488*). **14D** Cognitive restructuring replaces stress-provoking thoughts with more constructive thoughts thereby using thoughts to change behavior (*p. 490*). **15B** ECT involves passing electric current through the brain to treat depression when other treatments have failed (*p. 500*). **16A** The Dodo Bird Verdict suggests that specific methods of treatment are irrelevant to the success of psychotherapy (*pp. 494–495*). **17A** One of the most important elements of success with any therapy is the client-therapist relationship, which involves trust, disclosure, and empathy (*p. 498*). **18C** Neuroleptics are drugs that can reduce psychotic symptoms but some of these drugs can cause severe side effects (*p. 501*). **19B** Anxiolytics are drugs that reduce anxiety and tension (*p. 502*). **20C** Simultaneous treatment of several clients has many positive features, but client improvement is not more rapid with this technique than with others (*p. 491*).

Chapter 14   Social Psychology

1B Jack is experiencing relative deprivation, comparing himself to others around him (*p. 515*). **2C** Alaa is describing his social identity as a Muslim (*p. 516*). **3B** The first impression is formed quickly and is difficult to change (*pp. 518–519*). **4C** The change in her date's behavior was probably due to a self-fulfilling prophecy (*p. 519*). **5D** A self-serving bias is the tendency to take credit for success and blame external causes for failures (*p. 519*). **6B** In utilizing a celebrity to sell this product, Richard is taking the peripheral route to attitude change (*pp. 523–524*). **7B** The amount of money Matteus received was too small to justify lying about what he thought about the lecture, so he changed his attitude toward the lecture, thus making his attitude consistent with his behavior (*pp. 523–524*). **8C** The contact hypothesis suggests that stereotypes and prejudices can be reduced through cooperation and interdependence (*pp. 527–528*). **9A** People tend to like others who have attitudes similar to their own, especially attitudes about other people (*pp. 528–529*). **10A** Intimacy, commitment, and passion are characteristic of consummate love (*p. 531*). **11D** Laughing during a funeral is an example of norm violation (*pp. 532–533*). **12B** Deindividuation occurs when people in a group temporarily lose their individuality and behave in ways they otherwise would not (*pp. 532–533*). **13C** Shawn is exhibiting social loafing by not putting in as much effort as other group members (*p. 550*). **14A** Conformity results from unspoken group pressure (*pp. 532–533*). **15B** Colleen used the door-in-the-face approach, first asking for an unrealistic favor, then a smaller one (*p. 535*). **16D** The gender of the person giving the order is not a major factor determining whether someone will obey the order (*pp. 537–539*). **17A** According to frustration-aggression theory, frustration produces a readiness to respond aggressively, which can later be environmentally triggered (*p. 542*). **18B** Ruth will be most likely to help if she is upset by the child's situation and the cost of helping is not very high (*p. 546*). **19B** According to the evolutionary view, people display helping behaviors to improve the chances that some of their genes will survive in future generations (*p. 549*). **20B** Groupthink impairs a group's ability to realistically evaluate options and their own decisions (*p. 553*).

Chapter 15   Industrial/Organizational Psychology

1C I/O psychologists conduct scientific research on workplace-related topics *and* are hands-on practitioners applying the findings of that research to workplace-related problems (*p. 562*). **2C** The information from a job analysis of the position is used to guide decisions about whom to hire (*p. 563*). **3A** A job-oriented approach describes the tasks involved in doing a job (*p. 563*). **4B** A job analysis identifies the KSAOs required for a specific position (*pp. 563–564*). **5C** KSAOs are attributes or characteristics necessary to successfully perform a job (*p. 564*). **6A** In an unstructured interview the course of the conversation is spontaneous and variable (*p. 565*). **7A** Assessment centers are used primarily to determine an individual's suitability for a position and are often used to hire or promote managers (*p. 565*). **8D** Performance appraisals are used for all of these purposes (*pp. 566–567*). **9C** A theoretical criterion is a general statement of what we mean by good or poor performance (*p. 566*). **10A** Subjective measures of job performance take the form of judgments about various aspects of an employee's work (*p. 567*). **11B** A critical incident provides an example of what is considered to be effective or ineffective behavior by an employee (*p. 569*). **12B** The most valuable training programs are those that teach knowledge or skills that can be applied or transferred to the workplace (*p. 573*). **13C** Massed training is less expensive and disruptive to employees' work schedules but people do not retain as much after mass training as they do after distributed or spaced training (*p. 573*). **14B** I/O psychologists usually conduct a training needs assessment; design the training; and evaluate the training but do not usually deliver the training (*pp. 572–574*). **15D** In Maslow's theory the need for water is a physiological need; in Alderfer's theory it is an existence need (*pp. 575–576*). **16B** The facet approach to job satisfaction presumes that employees can be satisfied with some aspects of their jobs, but dissatisfied with others (*p. 576*). **17A** Knowing that salary and pay raise decisions are made in a fair way can be more important to job satisfaction than to the amount of money employees receive (*p. 578*). **18B** I/O psychologists suggest that when workplace stress creates negative emotions, those emotions can motivate CWB (*p. 582*). **19B** A work team is a special kind of workgroup in which the members' activities depend on one another; each person has a specialized task, and everyone is working toward a common goal (*p. 586*). **20A** Leader-member exchange theory suggests that most leaders tend to adopt different styles with different kinds of subordinates (*p. 588*).

The questions at the bottom of each chapter's In Review charts are listed here, followed in parentheses by the correct answers. The questions are grouped under each chapter's title and by the name and page number of the In Review chart in which they appear. The answer key for the optional Industrial/Organizational Psychology chapter appears in blue.

Chapter 1   Introduction to the Science of Psychology

The Development of Psychology (p. 13)
In the history of psychology, _____ was the first school of thought to appear. (*structuralism*)

Approaches to Psychology (p. 17)
Charles Darwin was not a psychologist, but his work influenced the _____ approach to psychology. (*evolutionary*)

Methods of Psychology (p. 33)
The _____ method is most likely to use a double-blind design. (*experimental*)

Chapter 2   Biology and Behavior

Neurons, Neurotransmitters, and Receptors (p. 49)
For one neuron to communicate with another, a _____ has to cross the _____ between them. (*neurotransmitter; synapse*)

Classes of Neurotransmitters (p. 52)
The main neurotransmitter for slowing, or inhibiting, brain activity is _____. (*GABA*)

Organization of the Brain (p. 64)
The oldest part of the brain is the _____. (*hindbrain*)

Chapter 3   Sensation and Perception

Seeing (p. 90)
When you are able to see in very dim light, it is because of photoreceptors called _____. (*rods*)

Hearing (p. 95)
The basilar membrane can be found inside a fluid-filled tube in the _____ where sound energy is converted into neural activity. (*cochlea*)

Smell and Taste (p. 98)
The flavor of food arises from a combination of _____ and _____. (*smell; taste*)

Body Senses (p. 104)
Gate control theory offers an explanation of why we sometimes do not feel _____. (*pain*)

Principles of Perceptual Organization and Constancy (p. 113)
The movement we see in movies, videos, and DVDs is due to a perceptual illusion called _____. (*stroboscopic motion*)

Mechanisms of Pattern Recognition (p. 116)
Your ability to read a battered old sign that has some letters missing is a result of _____ processing. (*top-down*)

Chapter 4   Consciousness

Major Classes of Psychoactive Drugs (p. 154)
Physical dependence on a drug is a condition more commonly known as _____. (*addiction*)

Chapter 5   Learning

Basic Processes of Classical Conditioning (p. 168)
If your conditioned fear of spiders is triggered by the sight of other creatures that look like spiders, you are demonstrating stimulus _____. (*generalization*)

Reinforcement and Punishment (p. 179)
Taking an aspirin can relieve headache pain, so people learn to do so through the process of _____ reinforcement. (*negative*)

Chapter 6   Memory

Models of Memory (p. 202)
The value of elaborative rehearsal over maintenance rehearsal has been cited as evidence for the _____ model of memory. (*levels of processing*)

Storing New Memories (p. 208)
If you looked up a phone number, but forgot it before you could call it, the information was probably lost from _____ memory. (*short-term*)

Factors Affecting Retrieval from Long-Term Memory (p. 210)
Stimuli called _____ help you recall information stored in long-term memory. They are more plentiful on _____ tests than on _____ tests. (*retrieval cues; multiple-choice; essay*)

Improving Your Memory (p. 228)
Using mnemonics and the PQ4R system to better remember course material are examples of the value of _____ rehearsal. (*elaborative*)

Chapter 7   Thought, Language, and Intelligence

Ingredients of Thought (p. 241)
Thinking is the manipulation of _____. (*mental representations*)

Solving Problems (p. 250)
If you were lost and thirsty on a barren plain, but it doesn't occur to you to use your shoes to collect water during a sudden shower, you would be the victim of an obstacle to problem solving called _____. (*functional fixedness*)

Influences on IQ Scores (p. 270)
Intelligence is determined by both _____ and _____. (*heredity; environment*)

Chapter 8   Motivation and Emotion

Theories of Motivation (p. 285)
The fact that some people like roller coasters and other scary amusement park rides has been cited as evidence for the _____ theory of motivation. (*arousal*)

Major Factors Controlling Hunger and Eating (p. 291)
Many people eat dessert after dinner even when they are already "full," suggesting that eating is controlled not only by hunger but by _____. (*appetite,* or *the pleasures of food*)

Theories of Emotion *(p. 314)*
Research showing that there are pleasure centers in the brain has been cited in support of the _____ theory of emotion. *(Cannon-Bard, or central)*

Chapter 9   Human Development

Milestones of Cognitive Development in Infancy and Childhood *(p. 339)*
Research in cognitive development suggests that children form mental representations _____ than Piaget thought they did. *(sooner, or at a younger age)*

Social and Emotional Development During Infancy and Childhood *(p. 352)*
As part of their social development, children learn _____, which tell them what patterns of appearance and behavior are associated with being male or female. *(gender roles)*

Milestones of Adolescence and Adulthood *(p. 364)*
The greatest threat to cognitive abilities in late adulthood is _____ disease. *(Alzheimer's)*

Chapter 10   Health, Stress, and Coping

Stress Responses and Stress Mediators *(p. 386)*
The friends and family we can depend on to help us deal with stressors are called our _____ system. *(social support)*

Methods for Coping with Stress *(p. 395)*
Reminding yourself that you have prepared for the exam you are about to take, that everyone makes mistakes now and then, and that you will do better if you remain calm are all examples of _____ stress coping strategies. *(cognitive)*

Chapter 11   Personality

Major Approaches to Personality *(p. 419)*
Tests that measure the big-five dimensions of personality are based on the _____ approach to personality. *(trait)*

Personality Tests *(p. 426)*
Projective personality tests are based on the _____ approach to personality. *(psychodynamic)*

Chapter 12   Psychological Disorders

Anxiety, Somatoform, and Dissociative Disorders *(p. 452)*
Concern that some of its symptoms may actually be triggered by media stories or therapists' suggestions has made _____ the most controversial of the dissociative disorders. *(dissociative identity disorder, or multiple personality disorder)*

Mood Disorders *(p. 456)*
The risk of suicide is associated with _____ more than with any other symptom of disorder. *(depression)*

Schizophrenia *(p. 462)*
The _____ concept forms the basis for the vulnerability theory of schizophrenia. *(diathesis-stress)*

Chapter 13   Treatment of Psychological Disorders

Approaches to Psychological Treatment *(p. 492)*
Object relations therapy and interpersonal therapy are both contemporary examples of the _____ approach to psychological treatment. *(psychodynamic)*

Chapter 14   Social Psychology

Some Biases in Social Perception *(p. 522)*
The fundamental attribution error appears to be somewhat less likely to occur among people in _____ cultures. *(collectivist)*

Forming and Changing Attitudes *(p. 525)*
According to the elaboration likelihood model, people are more likely to pay close attention to the content and logic of a persuasive message if the _____ route to attitude change has been activated. *(central)*

Types of Social Influence *(p. 539)*
Going to the end of a ticket line is an example of _____, whereas forming two lines when a theater employee requests it is an example of _____. *(conformity; compliance)*

Helping Behavior *(p. 550)*
If you could save only one person from a burning house, the _____ theory of helping would predict that it would be your own child rather than, say, a grandparent. *(evolutionary)*

Chapter 15   Industrial/Organizational Psychology

Assessing People, Jobs, and Job Performance *(p. 568)*
Lists of critical incidents are contained in _____-focused employee rating forms. *(behavior)*

Recruiting, Selecting, and Training Employees *(p. 575)*
Employees tend to remember more from a training program when it is set up on a _____ rather than a _____ schedule. *(distributed; massed)*

REFERENCES

Aaron, D. J., Chang, Y.-F., Markovic, N., & LaPorte, R. E. (2003). Estimating the lesbian population: A capture-recapture approach. *Journal of Epidemiology and Community Health, 57,* 207–209.

Abbott, B. B., Schoen, L. S., & Badia, P. (1984). Predictable and unpredictable shock: Behavioral measures of aversion and physiological measures of stress. *Psychological Bulletin, 96,* 45–71.

AbdelMalik, P., Husted, J., Chow, E. W., & Bassett, A. S. (2003). Childhood head injury and expression of schizophrenia in multiply affected families. *Archives of General Psychiatry, 60,* 231–236.

Abi-Hashem, N. (2000). Psychology, time, and culture. *American Psychologist, 55,* 342–343.

Abrahamson, A. C., Baker, L. A., & Caspi, A. (2002). Rebellious teens? Genetic and environmental influences on the social attitudes of adolescents. *Journal of Personality and Social Psychology, 83,* 1392–1408.

Abramis, D. J. (1994). Work role ambiguity, job satisfaction, and job performance: Meta-analyses and review. *Psychological Reports, 75,* 1411–1433.

Abramowitz, J. S. (1997). Effectiveness of psychological and pharmacological treatments for obsessive-compulsive disorder: A quantitative review. *Journal of Consulting and Clinical Psychology, 65,* 44–52.

Abrams, R. L., & Greenwald, A. G. (2000). Parts outweigh the whole (word) in unconscious analysis of meaning. *Psychological Science, 11,* 118–124.

Abreu, J. M. (1999). Conscious and unconscious African American stereotypes: Impact on first impression and diagnostic ratings by therapists. *Journal of Consulting and Clinical Psychology, 67,* 387–393.

Abu-Elheiga, L., Matzuk, M. M., Abo-Hashema, K. A., & Wakil, S. J. (2001). Continuous fatty acid oxidation and reduced fat storage in mice lacking acetyl-CoA carboxylase 2. *Science, 291,* 2558–2559.

Achenbach, T. M. (1997). *Empirically based assessment of child and adolescent psychopathology.* Thousand Oaks, CA: Sage.

Acitelli, L. K. (1992). Gender differences in relationship awareness and marital satisfaction among young married couples. *Personality and Social Psychology Bulletin, 18,* 102–110.

Ackerman, M. J., Siu, B. L., Sturner, W. Q., Tester, D. J., Valdivia, C. R., Makielski, J. C., & Towbin, J. A. (2001). Postmortem molecular analysis of SCN5A defects in sudden infant death syndrome. *Journal of the American Medical Association, 286,* 2264–2269.

Acocella, J. (1998, April 6). The politics of hysteria. *New Yorker,* pp. 64–79.

Addis, M. E. (1997). Evaluating the treatment manual as a means of disseminating empirically validated psychotherapies. *Clinical Psychology: Science and Practice, 4,* 1–11.

Addis, M. E., & Krasnow, A. D. (2000) A national survey of practicing psychologists' attitudes toward psychotherapy treatment manuals. *Journal of Consulting and Clinical Psychology, 68,* 331–339.

Ader, R. (2001). Psychoneuroimmunology. *Current Directions in Psychological Science, 10,* 94–98.

Adler, T. (1993, March). Bad mix: Combat stress, decisions. *APA Monitor,* p. 1.

Adolphs, R., Tranel, D., & Damasio, A. R. (1998). The human amygdala in social judgment. *Nature, 393*(6684), 470–474.

Adorno, T. W., Frenkel-Brunswik, E., Levinson, D. J., & Sanford, R. N. (1950). *The authoritarian personality.* New York: Harper & Row.

Agarwal, D. P. (1997). Molecular genetic aspects of alcohol metabolism and alcoholism. *Pharmacopsychiatry, 30*(3), 79–84.

Agency for Healthcare Research and Quality (AHRQ). (1999). *Treatment of depression–newer pharmacotherapies* (Evidence Report/Technology Assessment, Number 7, Pub. No. 99–E014). Rockville, MD: Author.

Aggleton, J. F. (1993). The contribution of the amygdala to normal and abnormal emotional states. *Trends in Neuroscience, 16*(8), 328–333.

Agnew, C. R., Van Lange, P. A. M., Rusbult, C. E., & Langston, C. A. (1998). Cognitive interdependence: Commitment and the mental representation of close relationships. *Journal of Personality and Social Psychology, 74,* 939–954.

Ahima, R. S., & Flier, J. S. (2000). Leptin. *Annual Review of Physiology, 62,* 413–437.

Ahmad, R. H., Venkata, S. M., Alessandro, T., Bhaskar, K., Francesco, F., Goldman, D., et al. (2002). Serotonin transporter genetic variation and the response of the human amygdala. *Science, 297,* 400–403.

Ahmed, A., & Ruffman, T. (1998). Why do infants make A not B errors in a search task, yet show memory for the location of hidden objects in a nonsearch task? *Developmental Psychology, 34,* 441–453.

Aiello, J. R., & Douthitt, E. A. (2001). Social facilitation from Triplett to electronic performance monitoring. *Group Dynamics, 5,* 163–180.

Aiken, L. R. (1994). *Psychological testing and assessment* (8th ed.). Boston: Allyn & Bacon.

Ainsworth, M. D. S., Blehar, M. D., Waters, E., & Wall, S. (1978). *Patterns of attachment: A psychological study of the Strange Situation.* Hillsdale, NJ: Erlbaum.

Ainsworth, M. D. S., & Bowlby, J. (1991). An ethological approach to personality development. *American Psychologist, 46,* 333–341.

Ainsworth, M. D. S., & Marvin, R. S. (1995). On the shaping of attachment theory and research: An interview with Mary D. S. Ainsworth (Fall 1994). *Monographs of the Society for Research in Child Development, 60,* 3–21.

Aizawa, N. (2002). Grandiose traits and hypersensitive traits of the narcissistic personality. *Japanese Journal of Educational Psychology, 50,* 215–224.

Ajzen, I. (2001). Nature and operation of attitudes. *Annual Review of Psychology, 52,* 27–58.

Ajzen, I., & Fishbein, M. (2002). Attitudes and the attitude behavior relation: Reasoned and automatic processes. In W. Stroebe & M. Hewstone (Eds.), *European review of social psychology* (pp. 1–33). New York: Wiley.

Albarracin, D., Johnson, B. T., Fishbein, M., & Muellerleile, P. A. (2001). Theories of reasoned action and planned behavior as models of condom use: A meta-analysis. *Psychological Bulletin, 127,* 142–161.

Albee, G. (1968). Conceptual models and manpower requirements in psychology. *American Psychologist, 23,* 317–320.

Albee, G. W. (1985, February). The answer is prevention. *Psychology Today, 19,* 60–62.

Albert, K. A., Hemmings, H. C., Adamo, A. I. B., Potkin, S. G., Akbarian, S., Sandman, C. A. (2002). Evidence for decreased DARPP-32 in the prefrontal cortex of patients with schizophrenia. *Archives of General Psychiatry, 59,* 705–712.

Albert, M. S., Savage, C. R., Blazer, D., Jones, K., Berkman, L., & Seeman, T. (1995). Predictors of cognitive change in older persons: MacArthur studies of successful aging. *Psychology and Aging, 10,* 578–589.

Alberti, R. E., & Emmons, M. L. (1986). *Your perfect right: A guide to assertive living* (5th ed.). San Luis Obispo, CA: Impact Publishers.

Alberto, P. A., Troutman, A. C., & Feagin, J. R. (2002). *Applied behavior analysis for teachers* (6th ed.). Englewood Cliffs, NJ: Prentice Hall.

Alcock, J. (2001). *Animal behavior: An evolutionary approach* (7th ed.). Sunderland, MA: Sinauer.

Alderete, E., Eskenazi, B., & Sholtz, R. (1995). Effect of cigarette smoking and coffee drinking on time to conception. Epidemiology, 6(4), 403–408.

Alderfer, C. P. (1969). An empirical test of a new theory of human needs. *Organizational Behavior and Human Performance, 4,* 142–175.

Aleman, A., Kahn, R. S., & Selten, J.-P. (2003). Sex differences in the risk of schizophrenia: Evidence from meta-analysis. *Archives of General Psychiatry, 60,* 565–571.

Alessi, S. M., Roll, J. M., Reilly, M. P., & Johanson, C.-E. (2002). Establishment of a diazepam preference in human volunteers following a differential-conditioning history of placebo versus diazepam choice. *Experimental & Clinical Psychopharmacology, 10,* 77–83.

Alicke, M., LoSchiavo, F. M., Zerbst, J., & Zhang, S. (1997). The person who outperforms me is a genius: Maintaining perceived competence in upward social comparisons. *Journal of Personality and Social Psychology, 73,* 781–789.

Allen, B. P. (2003). *Personality theories: Development, growth, and diversity* (4th ed). Boston: Pearson Allyn & Bacon.

Allen, J. B., Kenrick, D. T., Linder, D. E., & McCall, M. A. (1989). Arousal and attraction: A response-facilitation alternative to misattribution and negative-reinforcement models. *Journal of Personality and Social Psychology, 57,* 261–270.

Allen, T. D., Herst, D. E. L., Bruck, C. S., & Sutton, M. (2000). Consequences associated with work-to-family conflict: A review and agenda for future research. *Journal of Occupational Health Psychology, 5,* 278–308.

Alliger, G. M., & Dwight, S. A. (2000). A meta-analytic investigation of the susceptibility of integrity tests to faking and coaching. *Educational & Psychological Measurement, 60,* 59–72.

Alliger, G. M., Tannenbaum, S. I., Bennett, W., Jr., Traver, H., & Shotland, A. (1997). A meta-analysis of the relations among training criteria. *Personnel Psychology, 50,* 341–358.

Alloy, L. B., Abramson, L. Y., & Francis, E. L. (1999). Do negative cognitive styles confer vulnerability to depression? *Current Directions in Psychological Science, 8,* 128–132.

Allport, G. W. (1961). *Pattern and growth in personality.* New York: Holt, Rinehart & Winston.

Alston, J. H. (1920). Spatial condition of the fusion of warmth and cold in heat. *American Journal of Psychology, 31,* 303–312.

Altemeyer, B. (1996). *The authoritarian specter.* Cambridge: Harvard University Press.

Altman, L. K. (2000, April 10). Company developing marijuana for medical uses. *New York Times.* Retrieved July 23, 2003, from http://www.mapinc.org/drugnews/v00/n474/a01.html

Aluja-Fabregat, A., & Torrubia-Beltri, R. (1998). Viewing of mass media violence, perception of violence, personality and academic achievement. *Personality and Individual Differences, 25,* 973–989.

Alvarez, F. J., Delrio, M. C., & Prada, R. (1995). Drinking and driving in Spain. *Journal of Studies on Alcohol, 56*(4), 403–407.

Alvarez-Buylla, A., Garcia-Verdugo, J. M., & Tramontin, A. D. (2001). A unified hypothesis on the lineage of neural stem cells. *National Review of Neuroscience, 2,* 287–293.

Alvaro, E. M., & Crano, W. D. (1997). Indirect minority influence: Evidence for leniency in source evaluation and counterargumentation. *Journal of Personality and Social Psychology, 72,* 949–964.

Alvir, J. M., Lieberman, J. A., Safferman, A. Z., Schwimmer, J. L., & Schaaf, J. A. (1993). Clozapine-induced agranulocytosis. Incidence and risk factors in the United States. *New England Journal of Medicine, 329,* 162–167.

Amabile, T. M. (1996). *Creativity in context: Update to "The Social Psychology of Creativity."* Boulder, CO: Westview.

Amabile, T. M. (2001). Beyond talent: John Irving and the passionate craft of creativity. *American Psychologist, 56,* 333–336.

Amabile, T. M., Hennessey, B. A., & Grossman, B. S. (1986). Social influences on creativity: The effects of contracted-for reward. *Journal of Personality & Social Psychology, 50,* 14–23.

Amabile, T. M., Hill, K. G., Hennessey, B. A., & Tighe, E. M. (1994). The Work Preference Inventory: Assessing intrinsic and extrinsic motivational orientations. *Journal of Personality and Social Psychology, 66*(5), 950–967.

American Academy of Pediatrics. (2001). Condom use by adolescents. *Pediatrics, 107,* 1463–1469.

American Educational Research Association, American Psychological Association, & National Council on Measurement in Education. (1999). *Standards for educational and psychological testing.* Washington, DC: American Educational Research Association.

American Lung Association. (2002). *Trends in tobacco use.* Retrieved July 23, 2003, from http//www/lungusa.org/data/smoke/SMK1.pdf

American Psychiatric Association. (1994). *Diagnostic and statistical manual of mental disorders* (4th ed.). Washington, DC: Author.

American Psychiatric Association. (1999). Position statement on psychiatric treatment and sexual orientation. *American Journal of Psychiatry, 156,* 1131.

American Psychiatric Association. (2000). *Diagnostic and statistical manual of mental disorders* (4th ed., rev.). Washington DC: Author.

American Psychiatric Association Work Group on Eating Disorders. (2000). Practice guidelines for the treatment of patients with eating disorders (revision). *American Journal of Psychiatry, 157,* 1–39.

American Psychological Association. (1993). *Violence and youth: Psychology's response.* Washington: DC: Author.

American Psychological Association. (2000). *1998–1999 Survey of undergraduate departments of psychology.* Washington, DC: Author.

American Psychological Association. (2002a). *Answers to your questions about sexual orientation and homosexuality.* Retrieved July 28, 2003, from http://www.apa.org/pubinfo/answers.html#whatis

American Psychological Association. (2002b). Ethical standards of psychologists and code of conduct. *American Psychologist, 57,* 1060–1073.

American Psychological Association. (2002c). *Medical cost offset.* Retrieved July 28, 2003, from http://www.apa.org/practice/offset3.html

American Society for Microbiology. (2000, September 18). *America's dirty little secret—our hands.* Washington, DC: Author.

an der Heiden, W., & Haefner, H. (2000). The epidemiology of onset and course of schizophrenia. *European Archives of Psychiatry and Clinical Neuroscience, 250,* 292–303.

Anastasi, A. (1997). *Psychological testing* (7th ed.). Upper Saddle River, NJ: Prentice-Hall.

Anastasiadis, A.G., Davis, A. R., Salomon, L., Burchardt, M., & Shabsigh, R. (2002). Hormonal factors in female sexual dysfunction. *Current Opinion in Urology, 12,* 503–507.

Andersen, S. M., & Chen, S. (2002). The relational self: An interpersonal social-cognitive theory. *Psychological Review, 109,* 619–645.

Andersen, S. M., & Miranda, R. (2000). Transference: How past relationships emerge in the present. *Psychologist, 13,* 608–609.

Anderson, A., & Conwell, Y. (2002). Doctors study why elderly so prone to suicide. *American Journal of Geriatric Psychiatry,* from CNN.com/Health.

Anderson, A. K., & Phelps, E. A. (2001). Lesions of the human amygdala impair enhanced perception of emotionally salient events. *Nature, 411,* 305–309.

Anderson, C., John, O. P., Keltner, D., & Kring, A. M. (2001). Who attains social status? Effects of personality and physical attractiveness in social groups. *Journal of Personality and Social Psychology, 81,* 116–132.

Anderson, C. A. (2001). Heat and violence. *Current Directions in Psychological Science, 10,* 33–38.

Anderson, C. A., & Anderson, K. B. (1998). Temperature and aggression: Paradox, controversy, and a (fairly) clear picture. In R. G. Geen & E. Donnerstein (Eds.), *Human aggression* (pp. 248–298). San Diego: Academic Press.

Anderson, C. A., Anderson, K. B., Dorr, N., DeNeve, K. M., & Flanagan, M. (2000). Temperature and aggression. In M. Zanna (Ed.), *Advances in experimental social psychology* (Vol. 32, pp. 63–133). New York: Academic Press.

Anderson, C. A., & Bushman, B. J. (2001). Effects of violent video games on aggressive behavior, aggressive cognition, aggressive affect, physiological arousal, and prosocial behavior: A meta-analytic review of the scientific literature. *Psychological Science, 12,* 353–359.

Anderson, C. A., & Bushman, B. J. (2002a). Human aggression. *Annual Review of Psychology, 53,* 27–51.

Anderson, C. A., & Bushman, B. J. (2002b). Media violence and the American public revisited. *American Psychologist, 57,* 448–450.

Anderson, C. A., & Dill, K. E. (2000). Video games and aggressive thoughts, feelings, and behavior in the laboratory and in life. *Journal of Personality and Social Psychology, 78,* 772–790.

Anderson, C. A., Lindsay, J. J., & Bushman, B. J. (1999). Research in the psychological laboratory: Truth or triviality? *Current Directions in Psychological Science, 8,* 3–9.

Anderson, J. R. (1990). *Cognitive psychology and its implications* (3rd ed.). New York: Freeman.

Anderson, J. R. (1995). *Learning and memory: An integrated approach.* New York: Wiley.

Anderson, J. R. (2000). *Cognitive psychology and its implications* (5th ed). New York: Worth.

Anderson, M. C., & Green, C. (2001). Suppressing unwanted memories by executive control. *Nature, 410,* 366–369.

Anderssen, N., Amlie, C., & Ytteroy, E. A. (2002). Outcomes for children with lesbian or gay parents: A review of studies from 1978 to 2000. *Scandinavian Journal of Psychology, 43,* 335–351.

Andrade, L., Walters, E. E., Gentil, V., & Laurenti, R. (2002). Prevalence of ICD-10 mental disorders in a catchment area in the city of San Paolo, Brazil. *Social Psychiatry and Psychiatric Epidemiology, 37,* 316–325.

Andreasen, N. C. (1997). Linking mind and brain in the study of mental illnesses: A project for a scientific psychopathology. *Science, 275,* 1586–1593.

Andreasen, N. C., Arndt, S., Alliger, R., Miller, D., & Flaum, M. (1995). Symptoms of schizophrenia. *Archives of General Psychiatry, 52,* 341–351.

Andre-Petersson, L., Engstrom, G., Hagberg, B., Janzon, L., Steen, G., Lane, D. A., et al. (2001). Adaptive behavior in stressful situations and stroke incidence in hypertensive men: Results from prospective cohort study "Men Born in 1914" in Malmo, Sweden. *Stroke, 32,* 1712–1720.

Andrew, D., & Craig, A. D. (2001). Spinothalamic lamina I neurons selectively sensitive to histamine: A central neural pathway for itch. *Nature Neuroscience, 4,* 72–77.

Andrews, B., Brewin, C., Ochera, J., Morton, J., Bekerian, D. A., Davies, G. M., & Mollon, P. (2000). The timing, triggers, and quality of recovered memories in therapy. *British Journal of Clinical Psychology, 39,* 11–26.

Anghelescu, I., Klawe, C. J., Bartenstein, P., & Szegedi, A. (2001). Normal PET after long-term ETC. *American Journal of Psychiatry, 158,* 1527.

Angold, A., Erkanli, A., Farmer, E. M. Z., Fairbank, J. A., Burns, B. J., Keeler, G., & Costello, E. J. (2002). Psychiatric disorder, impairment, and service use in rural African American and white youth. *Archives of General Psychiatry, 59,* 893–901.

Angst, J., Angst, F., & Stassen, H. H. (1999). Suicide risks inpatients with major depressive disorder. *Journal of Clinical Psychiatry, 60*(Suppl. 2), 57–62.

Annenberg Public Policy Center. (1999). *The 1999 state of children's television report: Programming for children over broadcast and cable television.* Washington, DC: Author.

Annenberg Public Policy Center. (2000). *Media in the home: The fifth annual survey of parents and children 2000.* Washington, DC: Author.

Anrep, G. V. (1920). Pitch discrimination in the dog. *Journal of Physiology, 53,* 367–385.

Anshel, M. (1996). Coping styles among adolescent competitive athletes. *Journal of Social Psychology, 136,* 311–323.

Anthony, T., Cooper, C., & Mullen, B. (1992). Cross-racial facial identification: Five studies of sex differences in facial prominence. *Personality and Social Psychology Bulletin, 18,* 296–301.

Antoni, M. H., Cruess, D. G., Cruess, S., Lutgendorf, S., Kumar, M., Ironson, G., et al. (2000). Cognitive-behavioral stress management intervention effects on anxiety, 24-hr urinary norepinephrine output, and t-cytotoxic/suppressor cells over time among symptomatic HIV-infected gay men. *Journal of Consulting and Clinical Psychology, 68,* 31–45.

Antonuccio, D. O., Danton, W. G., & DeNelsky, G. Y. (1995). Psychotherapy versus medication for depression: Challenging the conventional wisdom with data. *Professional Psychology: Research and Practice, 26,* 574–585.

Antrobus, J. (2001). Rethinking the fundamental process of dream and sleep mentation production: Defining new questions that avoid the distraction of REM versus NREM comparisons. *Sleep and Hypnosis, 3,* 1–8.

APA Office of Ethnic Minority Affairs. (2000). *Guidelines for research in ethnic minority communities.* Washington, DC: American Psychological Association.

Appelle, S., Lynn, S. J., & Newman, L. (2000). Alien abduction experiences. In E. Cardena, S. J. Lynn, & S. Krippner (Eds.), *Varieties of anomalous experience: Examining the scientific evidence* (pp. 253–282). Washington, DC: American Psychological Association.

Appleton, W. S. (2000). *Prozac and the new antidepressants: What you need to know about Prozac, Zoloft, Paxil, Luvox, Wellbutrin, Effexor, Serzone, Vestra, Celexa, St. John's Wort, and others* (Rev. ed.). New York: Plume Books.

Arbelle, S., Benjamin, J., Golin, M., Kremer, I., Belmaker, R. H., & Ebstein, R. P. (2003). Relation of shyness in grade school children to the genotype for the long form of the serotonin transporter promoter region polymorphism. *American Journal of Psychiatry, 160,* 671–676.

Archer, J. (2000). Sex differences between heterosexual partners: A meta-analytic review. *Psychological Bulletin, 126,* 651–680.

Arenberg, D. (1982). Changes with age in problem solving. In F. I. M. Craik & S. Trehub (Eds.), *Aging and cognitive processes* (pp. 221–236). New York: Plenum.

Arkes, H. R., & Ayton, P. (1999). The sunk cost and Concorde effects: Are humans less rational than lower animals? *Psychological Bulletin, 125,* 591–600.

Arndt, J., Goldenberg, J., Greenberg, J., Pyszcynski, T., & Solomon, S. (2000). Death can be hazardous to your health: Adaptive and ironic consequences of defenses against the terror of death. In. R. P. Duberstein & J. Masling (Eds.), *Psychodynamic perspectives on sickness and health* (pp. 201–257). Washington, DC: American Psychological Association.

Arndt, J., Greenberg, J., Pyszczynski, T., & Solomon, S. (1997). Subliminal exposure to death-related stimuli increases defense of the cultural worldview. *Psychological Science, 8,* 379–385.

Arner, P. (2000). Obesity: A genetic disease of adipose tissue? *British Journal of Nutrition, 83,* S9–S16.

Arnett, J. J. (1999). Adolescent storm and stress, reconsidered. *American Psychologist, 54,* 317–326.

Arnett, J. J. (2000). Emerging adulthood: A theory of development from the late teens through the twenties. *American Psychologist, 55,* 469–480.

Arnett, J. J. (2002). The psychology of globalization. *American Psychologist, 57,* 774–783.

Aronoff, J., Barclay, A. M., & Stevenson, L. A. (1988). The recognition of threatening stimuli. *Journal of Personality and Social Psychology, 54,* 647–655.

Aronson, E. (1990). Applying social psychology to desegregation and energy conservation. *Personality and Social Psychology Bulletin, 16,* 118–132.

Aronson, E. (1999). *The social animal* (8th ed.). New York: Worth Publishers/Freeman.

Aronson, E. (1997). *The jigsaw classroom.* New York: Longman.

Aronson, E., Wilson, T. D., & Akert, R. M. (2002). *Social psychology* (4th ed.). New York: Longman.

Arterberry, M. E., Craton, L. G., & Yonas, A. (1993). Infants' sensitivity to motion-carried information for depth and object properties. In C. Granrud (Ed.), *Visual perception and cognition in infancy. Carnegie Mellon symposia on cognition* (pp. 215–234). Hillsdale, NJ: Erlbaum.

Arterburn, D., & Noel, P. H. (2001). Obesity: Clinical review. *British Medical Journal, 322,* 1406–1409.

Arthur, W. Jr., Day, E. A., McNelly, T. L., & Edens, P. S. (2003). A meta-analysis of the criterion-related validity of assessment center dimensions. *Personnel Psychology, 56,* 125–154.

Arvey, R. D., Bouchard, T. J., Segal, N. L., & Abraham, L. M. (1989). Job satisfaction: Environmental and genetic components. *Journal of Applied Psychology, 74,* 187–192.

Asarnow, R. F., Nuechterlein, K. H., Fogelson, D., Subotnik, K. L., Payne, D. A., Russell, A. T., et al. (2001). Schizophrenia and schizophrenia-spectrum personality disorders in the first-degree relatives of children with schizophrenia: The UCLA family study. *Archives of General Psychiatry, 58,* 581–588.

Asch, S. E. (1951). Effects of group pressure upon the modification and distortion of judgments. In H. Guetzkow (Ed.), *Groups, leadership, and men* (pp. 177–190). Pittsburgh: Carnegie Press.

Asch, S. E. (1955). Opinions and social pressure. *Scientific American, 193,* 31–35.

Asch, S. E. (1956). Studies of independence and conformity: A minority of one against a unanimous majority. *Psychological Monographs, 70,* 1–70.

Ash, R. A., & Levine, E. L. (1980). A framework for evaluating job analysis methods. *Personnel, 57,* 53–59.

Ashcraft, M. H. (1989). *Human memory and cognition.* Glenview, IL: Scott, Foresman.

Ashe, P. C., Berry, M. D., & Boulton, A. A. (2001). Schizophrenia, a neurodegenerative disorder with neurodevelopmental antecedents. *Progress in Neuro-Psychopharmacology and Biological Psychiatry, 25,* 691–707.

Ashton, H. (1995). Protracted withdrawal from benzodiazepines: The post-withdrawal syndrome. *Psychiatric Annals, 25*(3), 174–179.

Aslin, R. N., Jusczyk, P. W., & Pisoni, D. B. (1998). Speech and auditory processing during infancy: Constraints on and precursors to language. In W. Damon (Ed.), *Handbook of child psychology* (5th ed., pp. 147–198). New York: Wiley.

Aspinwall, L. G., & Duran, R. E. F. (1999). Psychology applied to health. In A. M. Stec & D. A. Bernstein (Eds.), *Psychology: Fields of application* (pp. 17–38). Boston: Houghton Mifflin.

Aspinwall, L. G., & Taylor, S. E. (1992). Modeling cognition adaptation: A longitudinal investigation of the impact of individual differences and coping on college adjustment and performance. *Journal of Personality and Social Psychology, 63,* 989–1003.

Assefi, S. L., & Garry, M. (2003). Absolut® memory distortions: Alcohol placebos influence misinformation effect. *Psychological Science, 14,* 77–80.

Associated Press. (1997, October 22). Forty percent in senior classes fail at science. *Chicago Tribune.*

Associated Press. (1999, November 17). Stripes near Waldo mean slow down. *St. Petersburg Times.*

Associated Press. (2002, March 9). Odds and ends. *Naples Daily News.* Retrieved August 27, 2003, from http://www.nctimes.net/news/2002/20020313/wwww.html

Associated Press. (2003, January 10). Man to get $900,000 for 20 years spent in prison for rape he did not commit. *Naples Daily News.*

Atkinson, J. W., & Raynor, J. O. (1974). *Personality, motivation, and achievement.* Washington, DC: Hemisphere.

Aviezer, O., Sagi, A., Joels, T., & Ziv, Y. (1999). Emotional availability and attachment representations in kibbutz infants and their mothers. *Developmental Psychology, 35,* 811–821.

Ayllon, T. (1999). *How to use token economy and point systems* (2nd ed.). Austin, TX: Pro-Ed.

Ayllon, T., & Azrin, N. H. (1968). *The token economy: A motivational system for therapy and rehabilitation.* New York: Appleton-Century-Crofts.

Ayuso-Mmateos, J. L., Vazquez-Barquero, J. L., Dowrick, C., Lehtinen, V., Dalgard, O. S., Casey, P., et al. (2001). Depressive disorders in Europe: Prevalence figures fromt he ODIN study. *British Journal of Psychiatry, 179,* 308–316.

Azar, B. (1996, November). Project explores landscape of midlife. *APA Monitor,* p. 26.

Azar, B. (2002). The "science of learning" moves mainstream. *Monitor on Psychology, 33,* 60–62.

Azorin, J.-M., Spiegel, R., Remington, G., Vanelle, J.-M., Pere, J.-J., Giguere, M., & Bourdeix, I. (2001). A double-blind comparative study of clozapine and risperidone in the management of severe chronic schizophrenia. *American Journal of Psychiatry, 158,* 1305–1313.

Baare, W. F. C., van Oel, C. J., Hushoff, H. E., Schnack, H. G., Durston, S., Sitskoorn, M. M., & Kahn, R. S. (2001). Volumes of brain structures in twins discordant for schizophrenia. *Archives of General Psychiatry, 58,* 33–40.

Bacharach, V. R., & Baumeister, A. A. (1998). Direct and indirect effects of maternal intelligence, maternal age, income, and home environment on intelligence of preterm, low-birth-weight children. *Journal of Applied Developmental Psychology, 19,* 361–375.

Back, S. E., Dansky, B. S., Carroll, K. M., Foa, E. B., & Brady, K. T. (2001). Exposure therapy in the treatment of PTSD among cocaine-dependent individuals: Description of procedures. *Journal of Substance Abuse Treatment, 21,* 35–45.

Backman, L., & Nilsson, L. (1991). Effects of divided attention on free and cued recall of verbal events and action events. *Bulletin of the Psychonomic Society, 29,* 51–54.

Baddeley, A. (1982). *Your memory: A user's guide.* New York: Macmillan.

Baddeley, A. (1992). Working memory. *Science, 255,* 556–559.

Baddeley, A. (1998). *Human memory: Theory and practice.* Boston: Allyn & Bacon.

Baddeley, A. (2000). The episodic buffer: An new component for working memory? *Trends in Cognitive Sciences, 4,* 417–423.

Bagley, C., & Tremblay, P. (1998). On the prevalence of homosexuality and bisexuality, in a random survey of 750 men aged 18–27. *Journal of Homosexuality, 36,* 1–18.

Bahrick, H. P., Bahrick, P. O., & Wittlinger, R. P. (1975). Fifty years of memory for names and faces: A cross-cultural approach. *Journal of Experimental Psychology: General, 104,* 54–75.

Bahrick, H. P., & Hall, L. K. (1991). Lifetime maintenance of high school mathematics content. *Journal of Experimental Psychology: General, 120,* 20–33.

Bahrick, H. P., Hall, L. K., & Berger, S. A. (1996). Accuracy and distortion in memory for high school grades. *Psychological Science, 7,* 265–271.

Bahrick, H. P., Hall, L. K., Noggin, J. P., & Bahrick, L. E. (1994). Fifty years of language maintenance and language dominance in bilingual Hispanic immigrants. *Journal of Experimental Psychology: General, 123,* 264–283.

Bailey, J. M., & Benishay, D. S. (1993). Familial aggregation of female sexual orientation. *American Journal of Psychiatry, 150,* 272–277.

Bailey, J. M., Bobrow, D., Wolfe, M., & Mikach, S. (1995). Sexual orientation of adult sons of gay fathers. *Developmental Psychology, 31*(1), 124–129.

Bailey, J. M., Dunne, M. P., & Martin, N. G. (2000). Genetic and environmental influences on sexual orientation and its correlates in an Australian twin sample. *Journal of Personality and Social Psychology, 78,* 524–536.

Bailey, J. M., Dunne, M. P., & Nicholas, G. (2000). Genetic and environmental influences on sexual orientation and its correlates in an Australian twin sample. *Journal of Personality and Social Psychology, 78,* 524–536.

Bailey, J. M., & Pillard, R. C. (1991). A genetic study of male sexual orientation. *Archives of General Psychiatry, 48,* 1086–1096.

Bailey, J. M., Pillard, R. C., Neale, M. C., & Agyei, Y. (1993). Heritable factors influence sexual orientation in women. *Archives of General Psychiatry, 50,* 217–223.

Bailey, K. P. (2002). Choosing between atypical antipsychotics: Weighing the risks and benefits. *Archives of Psychiatric Nursing, 16,* S2–S11A.

Baillargeon, R. (1992). A model of physical reasoning in infancy. In C. Rovee-Collier & L. P. Lipsett (Eds.), *Advances in infancy research.* Norwood, NJ: Ablex.

Baillargeon, R. (1994a). How do infants learn about the physical world? *Current Directions in Psychological Science, 3,* 133–139.

Baillargeon, R. (1994b). Physical reasoning in young infants: Seeking explanations for impossible events. *Journal of Development Psychology, 12,* 9–33.

Baillargeon, R. (1995). Physical reasoning in infancy. In M. S. Gazzaniga (Ed.), *The cognitive neurosciences* (pp. 181–204). Cambridge, MA: MIT Press.

Baker, M. C. (2002). *The atoms of language: The mind's hidden rules of grammar.* New York: Basic Books.

Balaban, M. T. (1995). Affective influences on startle in five-month-old infants: Reactions to facial expressions of emotion. *Child Development, 66*(1), 28–36.

Baldessarini, R. J., & Tondo, L. (2000). Does lithium treatment still work? Evidence of stable responses over three decades. *Archives of General Psychiatry, 57,* 187–190.

Baldessarini, R. J., Tondo, L., Hennen, J., Viguera, A. C. (2002). Is lithium still worth using? An update of selected research. *Harvard Review of Psychiatry, 10,* 59–75.

Baldwin, T. T., & Ford, J. K. (1988). Transfer of training: A review and directions for future research. *Personnel Psychology, 41,* 63–105.

Balfour, D. J. (2002). The neurobiology of tobacco dependence: A commentary. *Respiration, 69,* 7–11.

Balleine, B., & Dickinson, A. (1994). Role of cholecystokinin in the motivational control of instrumental action in rats. *Behavioral Neuroscience, 108*(3), 590–605.

Ballou, M. (1995). Assertiveness training. In M. Ballou (Ed.), *Psychological interventions: A guide to strategies* (pp. 125–136). Westport, CT: Praeger.

Baltes, B. B., Briggs, T. E., Huff, J. W., Wright, J. A., & Neumann, G. A. (1999). Flexible and compressed workweek schedules: A meta-analysis of their effects on work-related criteria. *Journal of Applied Psychology, 84,* 496–513.

Baltes, P. B. (1993). The aging mind: Potential and limits. *The Gerontologist, 33,* 580–594.

Baltes, P. B. (1994, August). *Life-span developmental psychology: On the overall landscape of human development.* Invited address presented at the annual meeting of the American Psychological Association, Los Angeles.

Balzer, W. K., & Sulsky, L. M. (1992). Halo and performance appraisal research: A critical examination. *Journal of Applied Psychology, 77,* 975–985.

Banaji, M., Lemm, K. M., & Carpenter, S. J. (2001). The social unconscious. In A. Tesser & N. Schwarz (Eds.), *Blackwell handbook of social psychology: Intraindividual processes* (pp. 134–158). Oxford, England: Blackwell.

Bancroft, J. (1994). Homosexual orientation: The search for a biological basis. *British Journal of Psychiatry, 164,* 437–440.

Bancroft, J. (1997). *Researching sexual behavior: Methodological issues.* Bloomington, IN: Indiana University Press.

Bandura, A. (1965). Influence of a model's reinforcement contingencies on the acquisition of imitative responses. *Journal of Personality and Social Psychology, 1,* 589–595.

Bandura, A. (1983). Psychological mechanisms of aggression. In R. G. Geen & C. I. Donnerstein (Eds.), *Aggression: Theoretical and empirical reviews* (Vol. 1, pp. 1–40). New York: Academic Press.

Bandura, A. (1992). Self-efficacy mechanism in psychobiologic functioning. In R. Schwarzer (Ed.), *Self-efficacy: Thought control of action* (pp. 355–394). Washington, DC: Hemisphere.

Bandura, A. (1997). *Self-efficacy: The exercise of control.* New York: Freeman.

Bandura, A. (1999). Social cognitive theory of personality. In L. Pervin & O. John (Eds.), *Handbook of personality research* (2nd ed., pp. 154–196). New York: Guilford.

Bandura, A. (2000). Exercise of human agency through collective efficacy. *Current Directions in Psychological Science, 9,* 75–78.

Bandura, A. (2002). Growing primacy of human agency in adaptation and change in the electronic era. *European Psychologist, 7,* 2–16.

Bandura, A., Blanchard, E. B., & Ritter, B. (1969). The relative efficacy of desensitization and modeling approaches for inducing behavioral, affective, and attitudinal changes. *Journal of Personality and Social Psychology, 13,* 173–199.

Bandura, A., Ross, D., & Ross, S. A. (1963). Imitation of film-mediated aggressive models. *Journal of Abnormal and Social Psychology, 66,* 3–11.

Bandura, A., & Walters, R. H. (1963). *Social learning and personality development.* New York: Holt, Rinehart & Winston.

Banich, M. (2003). *Neuropsychology: The neural bases of mental function.* Boston: Houghton Mifflin.

Banich, M. T., & Heller, W. (1998). Evolving perspectives on lateralization of function. Evolving perspectives on lateralization of function. *Current Directions in Psychological Science, 7,* 1–2.

Banich, M. T., Stolar, N., Heller, W., & Goldman, R. B. (1992). A deficit in right-hemisphere performance after induction of a depressed mood. *Neuropsychiatry, Neuropsychology, and Behavioral Neurology, 5*(1), 20–27.

Banker, R. D., Field, J. M., Schroeder, R. G., & Sinha, K. K. (1996). Impact of work teams on manufacturing performance: A longitudinal field study. *Academy of Management Journal, 39,* 867–890.

Banks, M. S., & Salapatek, P. (1983). Infant visual perception. In P. H. Mussen (Ed.), *Handbook of child psychology: Vol. 2. Infancy and developmental psychobiology* (pp. 435–571). New York: Wiley.

Banta, B. D. (1997). Cooperation and competition in peaceful societies. *Psychological Bulletin, 121,* 299–320.

Bar, M., & Biederman, I. (1998). Subliminal visual priming. *Psychological Science, 9,* 464–469.

Baranano, D. E., Ferris, C. D., & Snyder, S. H. (2001). Atypical neural messengers. *Trends Neuroscience, 24,* 99–106.

Barber, J. P., Connolly, M. B., Crits-Christoph, P., Gladis, L., & Siqueland, L. (2000). Alliance predicts patients' outcome beyond in-treatment change in symptoms. *Journal of Consulting & Clinical Psychology, 68,* 1027–1032.

Barclay, J. R., Bransford, J. D., Franks, J. J., McCarrell, N. S., & Nitsch, K. (1974). Comprehension and semantic flexibility. *Journal of Verbal Learning and Verbal Behavior, 13,* 471–481.

Bardo, M. T. (1998). Neuropharmacological mechanisms of drug reward: Beyond dopamine in the nucleus accumbens. *Critical Reviews of Neurobiology, 12*(1–2), 37–67.

Bargones, J. Y., & Werner, L. A. (1994). Adults listen selectively; infants do not. *Psychological Science, 5,* 170–174.

Barling, J., & Frone, M. R. (Eds.). (2004). *The psychology of workplace safety.* Washington, DC: APA Books.

Barling, J., Weber, T., & Kelloway, E. K. (1996). Effects of transformational leadership training on attitudinal and financial outcomes: A field experiment. *Journal of Applied Psychology, 81,* 827–832.

Barlow, D. H. (1988). *Anxiety and its disorders: The nature and treatment of panic and anxiety.* New York: Guilford.

Barlow, D. H., & Campbell, L. A. (2000). Mixed anxiety-depression and its implications for models of mood and anxiety disorders. *Comprehensive Psychiatry, 41,* 55–60.

Barlow, D. H., Gorman, J. M., Shear, M. K., & Woods, S. W. (2000). Cognitive-behavioral therapy, imipramine, or their combination for panic disorder: A randomized controlled trial. *Journal of the American Medical Association, 283,* 2529–2536.

Barnett, J. E., & Scheetz, K. (2003). Technological advances and telehealth: Ethics, law, and the practice of psychotherapy. *Psychotherapy: Theory, Research, Practice, and Training, 40,* 86–93.

Barnett, W. S. (1998). Long-term cognitive and academic effects of early childhood education of children in poverty. *Preventive Medicine: An International Devoted Practice & Theory, 27,* 204–207.

Barnier, A. J. (2002). Posthypnotic amnesia for autobiographical episodes: A laboratory model of functional amnesia? *Psychological Science, 13,* 232–237.

Barnier, A. J., & McConkey, K. M. (1998). Posthypnotic responding away from the hypnotic setting. *Psychological Science, 9,* 256–262.

Baron, R., & Byrne, D. (2003). *Social pychology* (10th ed.). Boston: Allyn Bacon.

Baron, R. A., & Richardson, D. C. (1994). *Human aggression* (2nd ed.). New York: Plenum.

Baron, R. S., Kerr, N. L., & Miller, N. (1992). *Group process, group decision, group action.* Pacific Grove, CA: Brooks/Cole.

Barrett, L. F. (1995). Valence focus and arousal focus: Individual differences in the structure of affective experience. *Journal of Personality and Social Psychology, 69,* 153–166.

Barrett, L. F., Gross, J., Christensen, T. C., & Benvenuto, M. (2001). Knowing what you're feeling and knowing what to do about it: Mapping the relation between emotion differentiation and emotion regulation. *Cognition and Emotion, 15,* 713–724.

Barrett, L. F., Lane, R. D., Sechrest, L., & Schwartz, G. E. (2000). Sex differences in emotional awareness. *Personality and Social Psychology Bulletin, 26,* 1027–1035.

Barrick, M. R., & Mount, M. K. (1991). The Big Five personality dimensions and job performance: A meta-analysis. *Personnel Psychology, 44,* 1–26.

Barron, K. E., & Harackiewicz, J. M. (2001). Achievement goals and optimal motivation: Testing multiple goal models. *Journal of Personality and Social Psychology, 80,* 706–722.

Barrowclough, C., King, P., Colville, J., Russell, E., Burns, A., & Tarrier, N. (2001). A randomized trial of the effectiveness of cognitive-behavioral therapy and supportive counseling for anxiety symptoms in older adults. *Journal of Consulting and Clinical Psychology, 69,* 756–762.

Barsalou, L. W. (1993). Flexibility, structure, and linguistic vagary in concepts: Manifestations of a compositional system of perceptual symbols. In A. F. Collins, S. E. Gathercole, M. A. Conway, & P. E. Morris (Eds.), *Theories of memory* (pp. 29–102). Hillsdale, NJ: Erlbaum.

Barsky, A. J., Wool, C., Barnett, M. C., & Cleary, P. D. (1994). Histories of childhood trauma in adult hypochondriacal patients. *American Journal of Psychiatry, 151,* 397–401.

Barton, J., & Folkard, S. (1991). The response of day and night nurses to their work schedules. *Journal of Occupational Psychology, 64,* 207–218.

Bartoshuk, L. M. (1991). Taste, smell, and pleasure. In R. C. Bollef (Ed.), *The hedonics of taste* (pp. 15–28). Hillsdale, NJ: Erlbaum.

Bartoshuk, L. M. (2000). Comparing sensory experiences across individuals: Recent psychophysical advances illuminate genetic variation in taste perception. *Chemical Senses, 25,* 447–460.

Bartoshuk, L. M., & Wolfe, J. M. (1990). Conditioned taste aversion in humans: Are there olfactory versions? *Chemical Senses, 15,* 551.

Bashore, T. R., & Ridderinkhof, K. R. (2002). Older age, traumatic brain injury, and cognitive slowing: Some convergent and divergent findings. *Psychological Bulletin, 128,* 151–198.

Baskin, D., Bluestone, H., & Nelson, M. (1981). Ethnicity and psychiatric diagnosis. *Journal of Clinical Psychology, 37,* 529–537.

Basoglu, M., Livanou, M., & Salcioglu, E. (2003). A single session with an earthquake simulator for traumatic stress in earthquake survivors. *American Journal of Psychiatry, 160,* 788–790.

Bass, B. M., Avolio, B. J., Jung, D. I., & Berson, Y. (2003). Predicting unit performance by assessing transformational and transactional leadership. *Journal of Applied Psychology, 88,* 207–218.

Bass, E., & Davis, L. (1994). *The courage to heal* (3rd ed.). New York: Harper Perennial Library.

Bassett, A. S., Chow, E. W. C., O'Neill, S., & Brzustowicz, L. M. (2001). Genetic insights into the neurodevelopmental hypothesis of schizophrenia. *Schizophrenia Bulletin, 27,* 417–430.

Bates, E. (1993, March). *Nature, nurture, and language development.* Paper presented at the biennial meeting of the Society for Research in Child Development, New Orleans.

Batson, C. D. (1998). Altruism and prosocial behavior. In D. Gilbert, S. T. Fiske, & G. Lindzey (Eds.), *Handbook of social psychology* (Vol. 2, 4th ed., pp. 282–316). Boston: McGraw-Hill.

Batson, C. D., Sager, K., Garst, E., & Kang, M. (1997). Is empathy-induced helping due to self-other merging? *Journal of Personality and Social Psychology, 73,* 495–509.

Battaglia, G., Yeh, S. Y., & De Souza, E. B. (1988). MDMA-induced neurotoxicity: Parameters of degeneration and recovery of brain serotonin neurons. *Pharmacology, Biochemistry and Behavior, 29,* 269–274.

Batterham, R. L., Cohen, M. A., Ellis, S. M., Le Roux, C. W., Withers, D. J., Frost, G. S., et al. (2003). Inhibition of food intake in obese subjects by peptide YY3–36. The *New England Journal of Medicine, 349,* 941–948.

Batterham, R. L., Cowley, M. A., Small, C. J., Herzog, H., Cohen, M. A., Dakin, C. L., et al. (2002). Gut hormone PYY3–36 physiologically inhibits food intake. *Nature, 418,* 650–654.

Baucom, D. H., Shoham, V., Mueser, K. T., Daiuto, A. D., & Stickle, T. R. (1998). Empirically supported couple and family interventions for marital distress and adult mental health problems. *Journal of Consulting and Clinical Psychology, 66,* 53–88.

Bauer, P. J. (1996). What do infants recall of their lives?: Memory for specific events by one- to two-year-olds. *American Psychologist, 51,* 29–41.

Bauer, P. J. (2002). Long-term recall memory: Behavioral and neuro-developmental changes in the first 2 years of life. *Current Directions in Psychological Science, 11,* 137–141.

Bauer, T. N., & Green, S. G. (1996). Development of leader-member exchange: A longitudinal test. *Academy of Management Journal, 39,* 1538–1567.

Baum, A., Gatchel, R. J., & Krantz, D. S. (1997). *Introduction to health psychology* (3rd ed.). New York: McGraw-Hill.

Baum, A., Revenson, T. A., & Singer, J. E. (Eds.). (2001). *Handbook of health psychology.* Mahwah, NJ: Erlbaum.

Baumeister, R. F. (1998). The self. In D. Gilbert, S. T. Fiske, & G. Lindzey (Eds.), *Handbook of social psychology* (Vol. 1, 4th ed., pp. 680–740). Boston: McGraw-Hill.

Baumeister, R. F. (2000). Gender differences in erotic plasticity: The female sex drive as socially flexible and responsive. *Psychological Bulletin, 126,* 347–374.

Baumeister, R. F., Campbell, J. D., Krueger, J. I., & Vohs, K. D. (2003). Does high self-esteem cause better performance, interpersonal success, happiness, or healthier lifestyles? *Psychological Science in the Public Interest, 4,* 1–44.

Baumeister, R. F., Catanese, K. R., & Vohs, K. D. (2001). Is there a gender difference in strength of sex drive? *Personality and Social Psychology Review, 5,* 242–273.

Baumeister, R. F., & Leary, M. R. (1995). The need to belong: Desire for interpersonal attachments as a fundamental human motivation. *Psychological Bulletin, 117*(3), 497–529.

Baumrind, D. (1971). Current patterns of parental authority. *Developmental Psychology Monographs, 4*(1, part 2).

Baumrind, D. (1986). *Familial antecedents of social competence in middle childhood.* Unpublished monograph, Institute of Human Development, University of California, Berkeley.

Baumrind, D. (1991). Effective parenting during the early adolescent transition. In P. A. Cowan & E. M. Hetherington (Eds.), *Family transition* (pp. 111–163). Hillsdale, NJ: Erlbaum.

Baumrind, D., Larzelere, R. E., & Cowan, P. A. (2002). Ordinary physical punishment: Is it harmful? Comment on Gershoff. *Psychological Bulletin, 128,* 580–589.

Bayley, P. J., Hopkins, R. O., & Squire, L. R. (2003). Successful recollection of remote autobiographical memories by amnesic patients with medial temporal lobe lesions. *Neuron, 38,* 135–144.

Bazzano, L. A., He, J., Ogden, L. G., Loria, C. M., & Whelton, P. K. (2003). Dietary fiber intake and reduced risk of coronary heart disease in US men and women. *Archives of Internal Medicine, 163,* 1897–1904.

Beardslee, W. R., Gladstone, T. R. G., Wright, E. J., & Cooper, A. B. (2003). A family-based approach to the prevention of depressive symptoms in children at risk: Evidence of parental and child change. *Pediatrics, 112,* 119–131.

Beatty, J. (1995). *Principles of behavioral neuroscience.* Dubuque: Brown and Benchmark.

Beauchamp-Turner, D. L., & Levinson, D. M. (1992). Effects of meditation on stress, health, and affect. *Medical Psychotherapy: An International Journal, 5,* 123–131.

Beaumont, M., Batejat, D., Pierard, C., Coste, O., Doireau, P., Van Beers, P., et al. (2001). Slow release caffeine and prolonged (64-h) continuous wakefulness: effects on vigilance and cognitive performance. *Journal of Sleep Research, 10*(4), 265.

Beck, A. T. (1967). *Depression: Clinical, experimental and theoretical aspects.* New York: Harper & Row.

Beck, A. T. (1976). *Cognitive therapy and the emotional disorders.* New York: International Universities Press.

Beck, A. T. (1995). Cognitive therapy: A 30-year retrospective. In S. O. Lilienfeld (Ed.), *Seeing both sides: Classic controversies in abnormal psychology* (pp. 303–311). Pacific Grove, CA: Brooks/Cole. (Original work published 1991)

Beck, A. T., Brown, G., Berchick, R. J., Stewart, B. L., & Steer, R. A. (1990). Relationship between hopelessness and ultimate suicide: A replication with psychiatric outpatients. *American Journal of Psychiatry, 147,* 190–195.

Beck, A. T., & Emery, G. (1985). *Anxiety disorders and phobias: A cognitive perspective.* New York: Basic Books.

Beck, A. T., Sokol, L., Clark, D., Berchick, R., & Wright, F. (1992). A crossover study of focused cognitive therapy for panic disorder. *American Journal of Psychiatry, 149,* 778–783.

Beck, M. (1992, December 7). The new middle age. *Newsweek,* pp. 50–56.

Beck, J. S., & Beck, A. T. (1995). *Cognitive therapy: Basics and beyond.* New York: Guilford.

Beels, C. C. (2002). Notes for a cultural history of family therapy. *Family Process, 41,* 67–82.

Begley, S. (1997, September 29). Hope for "snow babies." *Newsweek,* pp. 62–63.

Belin, P., Zatorre, R. J., & Ahad, P. (2002). Human temporal-lobe response to vocal sounds. *Brain Research and Cognitive Brain Research, 13,* 17–26.

Belin, P., Zatorre, R. J., Lafaille, P., Ahad, P., & Pike, B. (2000). Voice-selective areas in human auditory cortex. *Nature, 403,* 309–312.

Bell, B. E., & Loftus, E. F. (1989). Trivial persuasion in the courtroom: The power of (a few) minor details. *Journal of Personality and Social Psychology, 56,* 669–679.

Bell, P. A., Fisher, J. D., Baum, A., & Greene, T. (1996). *Environmental psychology* (4th ed.). Fort Worth, TX: Holt, Rinehart & Winston.

Bellaby, P. (2003). Communication and miscommunication of risk: Understanding UK parents' attitudes to combined MMR vaccination. *British Medical Journal, 327,* 725–728.

Belli, R. F., & Loftus, E. F. (1996). The pliability of autobiographical memory: Misinformation and the false memory problem. In D. C. Rubin (Ed.), *Remembering our past: Studies in autobiographical memory* (pp. 157–179). New York: Cambridge University Press.

Belsky, J., & Kelly, J. (1994). *The transition to parenthood.* New York: Dell.

Ben-Ari, A., & Gil, S. (2002). Traditional support systems: Are they sufficient in a culturally diverse academic environment? *British Journal of Social Work, 32,* 629–638.

Benecke, M. (1999). Spontaneous human combustion: Thoughts of a forensic biologist. *Skeptical Inquirer, 22,* 47–51.

Benedetti, F., & Amanzio, M. (1997). The neurobiology of placebo analgesia: From endogenous opioids to cholecystokinin. *Progress in Neurobiology, 52,* 109–125.

Benedetti, F., Arduino, C., & Amanzio, M. (1999). Somatotopic activation of opioid systems by target-directed expectations of analgesia. *Journal of Neuroscience, 19,* 3639–3648.

Benight, C. C., Swift, E., Sanger, J., Smith, A., & Zeppelin, D. (1999). Coping self-efficacy as a mediator of distress following a natural disaster. *Journal of Applied Social Psychology, 29,* 2443–2464.

Bennett, H. L., Giannini, J. A., & Davis, H. S. (1985). Nonverbal response to intra-operational conversation. *British Journal of Anaesthesia, 57,* 174–179.

Bennett, K. K., & Elliott, M. (2002). Explanatory style and health: Mechanisms linking pessimism to illness. *Journal of Applied Social Psychology, 32,* 1508–1526.

Bennett, R. J., & Robinson, S. L. (2000). Development of a measure of workplace deviance. *Journal of Applied Psychology, 85,* 349–360.

Ben-Shakhar, G., Bar-Hillel, M., & Kremnitzer, M. (2002). Trial by polygraph: Reconsidering the use of the guilty knowledge technique in court. *Law & Human Behavior, 26,* 527–541.

Ben-Shakhar, G., & Furedy, J. J. (1990). *Theories and applications in the detection of deception: A psychophysiological and international perspective.* New York: Springer-Verlag.

Benson, E. (2003). Sex: The science of sexual arousal. *Monitor on Psychology, 34,* 50.

Benson, H. (1975). *The relaxation response.* New York: Morrow.

Ben-Zur, H. (2002a). Associations of type A behavior with the emotional traits of anger and curiosity. *Anxiety, Stress, & Coping, 15,* 95–104.

Ben-Zur, H. (2002b). Coping, affect and aging: The roles of mastery and self-esteem. *Personality & Individual Differences, 32*(2), 357–372.

Berger, R., & Hannah, M. T. (Eds.). (1999). *Preventative approaches in couples therapy.* Bristol, PA: Brunner/Mazel.

Bergin, A. E. (1971). The evaluation of therapeutic outcomes. In A. E. Bergin & S. L. Garfield (Eds.), *Handbook of psychotherapy and behavior change: An empirical analysis* (pp. 217–270). New York: Wiley.

Berkowitz, L. (1994). Is something missing? Some observations prompted by the Cognitive-neoassociationist view of anger and emotional aggression. In L. R. Huesmann (Ed.), *Human aggression: Current perspectives* (pp. 35–60). New York: Plenum.

Berkowitz, L. (1998). Affective aggression: The role of stress, pain, and negative affect. In R. G. Geen & E. Donnerstein (Eds.), *Human aggression* (pp. 49–72). San Diego: Academic Press.

Berkowitz, L. (1999). Evil is more than banal: Situationism and the concept of evil. *Personality and Social Psychology Review, 3,* 246–253.

Berlin, L. J., Cassidy, J., & Belsky, J. (1995). Loneliness in young children and infant-mother attachment: A longitudinal study. *Merrill-Palmer Quarterly, 41,* 91–103.

Bernard, L. L. (1924). *Instinct.* New York: Holt, Rinehart & Winston.

Bernardin, H. J., & Beatty, R. W. (1984). *Performance appraisal: Assessing human behavior at work.* Boston: Kent.

Bernat, J. A., Calhoun, K. S., Adams, H. E., & Zeichner, A. (2001). Homophobia and physical aggression toward homosexual and heterosexual individuals. *Journal of Abnormal Psychology, 110,* 179–187.

Berns, G. S., McClure, S. M., Pagnoni, G., & Montague, P. R. (2001). Predictability modulates human brain response to reward. *The Journal of Neuroscience, 21,* 2793–2798.

Bernstein, D. A. (1970). The modification of smoking behavior: A search for effective variables. *Behaviour Research and Therapy, 8,* 133–146.

Bernstein, D. A., Borkovec, T. D., & Hazlette-Stevens, H. (2000). *Progressive relaxation training: A manual for the helping professions* (2nd ed.) New York: Praeger.

Bernstein, D. M., & Roberts, B. (1995). Assessing dreams through self-report questionnaires: Relation with past research and personality. *Dreaming: Journal of the Association for the Study of Dreams, 5,* 13–27.

Bernstein, I. L. (1978). Learned taste aversions in children receiving chemotherapy. *Science, 200,* 1302–1303.

Berry, J. W., & Bennett, J. A. (1992). Cree conceptions of cognitive competence. *International Journal of Psychology, 27,* 73–88.

Berscheid, E., & Reis, H. T. (1998). Attraction and close relationships. In D. Gilbert, S. T. Fiske, & G. Lindzey (Eds.), *Handbook of social psychology* (Vol. 2, 4th ed., pp. 193–281). Boston: McGraw-Hill.

Bersoff, D. M. (1999). Why good people sometimes do bad things: Motivated reasoning and unethical behavior. *Personality & Social Psychology Bulletin, 25,* 28–39.

Berson, D. M., Dunn, F. A., & Takao, M. (2002). Phototransduction by retinal ganglion cells that set the circadian clock. *Science, 295,* 1070–1073.

Berthoud, H. R., & Neuhuber, W. L. (2000). Functional and chemical anatomy of the afferent vagal system. *Autonomic Neuroscience, 85,* 1–17.

Besson, M., Faita, F., Peretz, I., Bonnel, A.-M., & Requin, J. (1998). Singing in the brain: Independence of lyrics and tunes. *Psychological Science, 9,* 494–498.

Best, D. (1992, June). *Cross-cultural themes in developmental psychology.* Paper presented at workshop on cross-cultural aspects of psychology. Western Washington University, Bellingham.

Best, J. B. (1999). *Cognitive psychology* (5th ed.). Belmont, CA: Brooks/Cole.

Beuckmann, C. T., & Yanagisawa, M. (2002). Orexins: From neuropeptide to energy homeostasis and sleep/wake regulation. *Journal of Molecular Medicine, 80,* 329–342.

Beutler, L. E. (2000). David and Goliath: When empirical and clinical standards of practice meet. *Trends in Neuroscience, 17,* 509–512.

Beutler, L. E. (2002). The dodo bird is extinct. *Clinical Psychology: Science and Practice, 9,* 30–34.

Beutler, L. E., & Malik, M. L. (Eds.). (2002). *Rethinking DSM: A psychological perspective.* Washington DC: American Psychological Association.

Beyerstein, B. L. (1999). Pseudoscience and the brain: Tuners and tonics for aspiring superhumans. In S. Della Sala (Ed.), *Mind myths: Exploring popular assumptions about the mind and brain* (pp. 59–82). Chichester, England: Wiley.

Bhagat, R. S., Kedia, B. L., Harveston, P. D., & Triandis, H. C. (2002). Cultural variations in the cross-border transfer of organizational knowledge: An integrative framework. *Academy of Management Review, 27,* 204–221.

Bhutta, A. T., Cleves, M. A., Casey, P. H., Cradock, M. M., & Anand, K. J. S. (2002). Cognitive and behavioral outcomes of school-aged children who were born preterm. *JAMA, 288,* 728–737.

Bickis, M., Kelly, I. W., & Byrnes, G. (1995). Crisis calls and temporal and lunar variables: A comprehensive study. *The Journal of Psychology, 129,* 701–711.

Bierhaus, A., Wolf, J., Andrassy, M., Rohleder, N., Humpert, P. M., Petrov, D., et al. (2003). A mechanism converting psychosocial stress into mononuclear cell activation. *Proceedings of the National Academy of Sciences, 100,* 1920–1925.

Bierut, L. J., Heath, A. C., Bucholz, K. K., Dinwiddie, S. H., Madden, P. A., Statham, D. J., et al. (1999). Major depressive disorder in a community-based twin sample: Are there different genetic and environmental contributions for men and women? *Archives of General Psychiatry, 56,* 557–563.

Bies, R. J., Tripp, T. M., & Kramer, R. M. (1997). At the breaking point: Cognitive and social dynamics of revenge in organizations. In R. A. Giacalone & J. Greenberg (Eds.), *Antisocial behavior in organizations* (pp. 18–36). Thousand Oaks, CA: Sage.

Binet, A., & Simon, T. (1905). Methodes nouvelles pour le diagnostic du niveau intellectuel des anormaux. *L'Annee Psychologique, 11,* 191–244.

Binson, D., Michaels, S., Stall, R., Coates, T. J., Gagnon, J. H., & Catania, J. A. (1995). Prevalence and social distribution of men who have sex with men: United States and its urban centers. *Journal of Sex Research, 32*(3), 245–254.

Binzen, C. A., Swan, P. D., & Manore, M. M. (2001). Postexercise oxygen consumption and substrate use after resistance exercise in women. *Medicine and Science in Sports and Exercise, 33,* 932–938.

Bjil, R. V., de Graaf , R., Hiripi , E., Kessler, R. C., Kohn , R., Offord , D. R., et al. (2003). The prevalence of treated and untreated mental disorders in five countries. *Health Affairs, 22,* 122–133.

Bjork, R. A. (1979). An information-processing analysis of college teaching. *Educational Psychologist, 14,* 15–23.

Bjork, R. A. (1998). Assessing our own competence: Heuristics and biases. In D. Gopher & A. Koriat (Eds.), *Attention and performance* (Vol. 17). Orlando: Academic Press.

Bjork, R. A. (1999). Assessing our own competence: Heuristics and illusions. In D. Gopher & A. Koriat (Eds.), *Attention and performance XVII. Cognitive regulation of performance: Interaction of theory and application* (pp. 435–459). Cambridge: MIT Press.

Bjork, R. A., & Vanhuele, M. (1992). Retrieval inhibition and related adaptive peculiarities of human memory. *Advances in Consumer Research, 19,* 155–160.

Bjorklund, D. F., & Green, B. L. (1992). The adaptive nature of cognitive immaturity. *American Psychologist, 47,* 46–54.

Blackwell, B. (1973). Psychotropic drugs in use today. *Journal of the American Medical Association, 225,* 1637–1641.

Blackwood, D. H. R., Visscher, P. M., & Muir, W. J. (2001). Genetic studies of bipolar affective disorder in large families. *British Journal of Psychiatry, 178*(Suppl. 14), 134–136.

Blackwood, N. J., Howard, R. H., Bentall, R. P., & Murray, R. M. (2001). Cognitive neuropsychiatric models of persecutory delusions. *American Journal of Psychiatry, 158,* 527–539.

Blagrove, M. (1996). Problems with the cognitive psychological modeling of dreaming. *Journal of Mind and Behavior, 17,* 99–134.

Blair, I. V. (2002). The malleability of automatic stereotypes and prejudice. *Personality and Social Psychology Review, 6,* 242–261.

Blair, I. V., & Banaji, M. (1996) Automatic and controlled processes in stereotype priming. *Journal of Personality and Social Psychology, 70,* 1142–1163.

Blake, J., & de Boysson-Bardies, B. (1992). Patterns in babbling: A cross-linguistic study. *Journal of Child Language, 19,* 51–74.

Blake, R. (1998). What can be "perceived" in the absence of visual awareness? *Current Directions in Psychological Science, 6,* 157–162.

Blakeslee, S. (2000, January 4). A decade of discovery yields a shock about the brain. *New York Times.*

Blakeslee, S. (2001, August 28). Therapies push injured brains and spinal cords into new paths. *New York Times.* Retrieved July 28, 2003, from http://www.nytimes.com/2001./08/28/health/anatomy/28REHA.html

Blass, T. (2000). The Milgram paradigm 35 years later: Some things we now know about obedience to authority. In T. Blass (Ed.), *Current perspectives on the Milgram paradigm.* Mahwah, N.J: Erlbaum.

Blass, T., & Schmitt, C. (2001). The nature of perceived authority in the Milgram paradigm: Two replications. *Current Psychology: Developmental, Learning, Personality, Social, 20,* 115–121.

Block, J. (2001). Millennial contrarianism: The Five-Factor approach to personality description 5 years later. *Journal of Research in Personality, 35,* 98–107.

Block, J. A. (1971). *Lives through time.* Berkeley: Bancroft Books.

Block, R. I., & Ghoneim, M. M. (1993). Effects of chronic marijuana use on human cognition. *Psychopharmacology, 110*(1–2), 219–228.

Blood, A. J., & Zatorre, R. J. (2001). Intensely pleasurable responses to music correlate with activity in brain regions implicated in reward and emotion. *Proceedings of the National Academy of Science, 98,* 11818–11823.

Bloom, L. (1995). *The transition from infancy to language: Acquiring the power of expression.* New York: Cambridge University Press.

Blow, A. J., & Timm, T. M. (2002). Promoting community through family therapy: Helping clients develop a network of significant social relationships. *Journal of Systematic Therapies, 21,* 67–89.

Blum, R. W., Beuhring, T., & Rinehart, P. M. (2000). *Protecting teens: Beyond race, income and family structure.* Minneapolis, MN: Center for Adolescent Health, University of Minnesota.

Blumberg, H. P., Leung, H.-C., Skudlarski, P., Lacadie, C. M., Fredericks, C. A., Harris, B. C., et al. (2003). A functional magnetic resonance imaging study of bipolar disorder: State- and trait-related dysfunction in ventral prefrontal cortices. *Archives of General Psychiatry, 60,* 601–609.

Blumberg, M. S., & Lucas, D. E. (1994). Dual mechanisms of twitching during sleep in neonatal rats. *Behavioral Neuroscience, 108*(6), 1196–1202.

Blume, E. S. (1998). *Secret survivors: Uncovering incest and its aftereffects in women.* New York: Ballantine.

Blundell, J. E., & Cooling, J. (2000). Routes to obesity: Phenotypes, food choices, and activity. *British Journal of Nutrition, 83,* S33–S38.

Boardman, A. P., & Healy, D. (2001). Modeling suicide risk in affective disorders. *European Psychiatry, 16,* 400–405.

Bodian, S. (1999). *Meditation for dummies.* Indianapolis: IDG Books Worldwide.

Boehning, D., & Snyder, S. H. (2002). Circadian rhythms: Carbon monoxide and clocks. *Science, 298,* 2339–2340.

Bogartz, R. S., Shinskey, J. L., & Speaker, C. J. (1997). Interpreting infant looking: The event set x event set design. *Developmental Psychology, 33,* 408–422.

Bohner, G., & Schwarz, N. (2001). Attitudes persuasion and behavior. In A. Tesser & N. Schwarz (Eds.), *Blackwell handbook of social psychology: Intraindividual processes* (pp. 413–435). Oxford, England: Blackwell.

Bolla, K. I., Brown, K., Eldreth, D., Tate, K. & Cadet, J. L. (2002). Dose-related neurocognitive effects of marijuana use. *Neurology, 59,* 1337–1343.

Bomze, H. M., Bulsara, K. R., Iskandar, B. J., Caroni, P., & Skene, J. H. (2001). Spinal axon regeneration evoked by replacing two growth cone proteins in adult neurons. *Nature Neuroscience, 4,* 38–43.

Bond, G., Aiken, L., & Somerville, S. (1992). The Health Beliefs Model and adolescents with insulin-dependent diabetes mellitus. *Health Psychology, 11,* 190–198.

Bonner, R. (2001, August 24). Death row inmate is freed after DNA test clears him. T*he New York Times.*

Bonwell, C. C., & Eison, J. A. (1991). *Active learning: Creating excitement in the classroom.* Washington, DC: George Washington University.

Booth, C. B., Clarke-Stewart, K. A., Vandell, D. L., McCartney, K., & Owen, M. T. (2002). Child-care usage and mother-infant "quality time." *Journal of Marriage and the Family, 64,* 16–26.

Booth, P. B., & Lindaman, S. (2000). Theraplay for enhancing attachment in adopted children. In H. G. Kaduson & C. Schaefer (Eds.), *Short-term play therapy for children.* New York: Guilford.

Booth, R. J., Cohen, S., Cunningham, A., Dossey, L., Dreher, H., Kiecolt-Glaser, J. K., et al. (2001). The state of the science: The best evidence for the involvement of thoughts and feelings in physical health. *Advances, 17,* 2–59.

Borg, M. B., Jr. (2002). The Avalon Garden men's association: A community health psychology case study. *Journal of Health Psychology, 7,* 345–357.

Borgida, E., Conner, C., & Monteufel, L. (1992). Understanding living kidney donors: A behavioral decision-making perspective. In S. Spacapan & S. Oskamp (Eds.), *Helping and being helped* (pp. 183–212). Newbury Park, CA: Sage.

Borkenau, P., Riemann, R., Angleitner, A., & Spinath, F. M. (2001). *Journal of Personality and Social Psychology, 80,* 655–668.

Borkenau, P., Riemann, R., Angleitner, A., & Spinath, F. M. (2002). Similarity of childhood experiences and personality resemblance in monozygotic and dizygotic twins: A test of the equal environments assumption. *Personality & Individual Differences, 33,* 261–269.

Borkovec, T. C., & Costello, E. (1993). Efficacy of applied relaxation and cognitive behavioral therapy in the treatment of generalized anxiety disorder. *Journal of Consulting and Clinical Psychology, 61,* 611–619.

Borman, W. C., Hanson, M. A., & Hedge, J. W. (1997). Personnel selection. *Annual Review of Psychology, 48,* 299–337.

Borman, W. C., Penner, L. A., Allen T. D. & Motowidlo, S. (2001). Personality predictors of citizenship performance. *International Journal of Selection and Assessment, 9,* 52–69.

Bornstein, R. F. (1992). Subliminal mere exposure effects. In R. F. Bornstein & T. S. Pittman (Eds.), *Perception without awareness: Cognitive, clinical, and social perspectives* (pp. 191–210). New York: Guilford.

Bosma, H., Marmot, M. G., Hemingway, H., Nicholson, A. C., Brunner, E., & Stansfeld, S. A. (1997). Low job control and risk of coronary heart disease in Whitehall II (prospective cohort) study. *British Medical Journal, 314,* 558–565.

Bosompra, K., Ashikaga, T., Worden, J. K., & Flynn, B. S. (2001). Is more optimism associated with better health? Findings from a population-based survey. *International Quarterly of Community Health Education, 20,* 29–58.

Boss, P. (1999). *Ambiguous loss: Learning to live with unresolved grief.* Cambridge, MA: Harvard University Press.

Botwinick, J. (1961). Husband and father-in-law: A reversible figure. *American Journal of Psychology, 74,* 312–313.

Bouchard, T. J. (1999). Genes, environment, and personality. In S. J. Ceci & W. M. Williams (Eds.), *The nature-nurture debate: The essential readings* (pp.97–103). Malden, MA: Blackwell.

Bouchard, T., & McGue, M. (1981). Familial studies of intelligence: A review. *Science, 212*(4498), 1055–1059.

Bourassa, M., & Vaugeois, P. (2001). Effects of marijuana use on divergent thinking. *Creativity Research Journal, 13,* 411–416.

Bouton, M., Mineka, S., & Barlow, D. (2001). A modern learning theory perspective on the etiology of panic disorder. *Psychological Review, 107,* 4–32.

Bowden, C. L. (2000). Efficacy of lithium in mania and maintenance therapy of bipolar disorder. *Journal of Clinical Psychiatry, 61,* 35–40.

Bowden, C. L., Calabrese, J. R., McElroy, S. L., Gyulai, L., Wassef, A., Petty, F., et al. (2000). A randomized, placebo-controlled 12-month trial of divalproex and lithium in treatment of outpatients with bipolar I disorder. *Archives of General Psychiatry, 57,* 481–489.

Bowden, C. L., Calabrese, J. R., Sachs, G., Yatham, L. N., Asghar, S. A., Hompland, M., et al. (2003). A placebo-controlled 18-month trial of lamotrigine and lithium maintenance treatment in recently manic or hypomanic patients with bipolar I disorder. *Archives of General Psychiatry, 60,* 392–400.

Bower, G. H. (1981). Mood and memory. *American Psychologist, 36,* 129–148.

Bower, J. E., Kemeny, M. E., Taylor, S. E., & Fahey, J. L. (1999). Cognitive processing, discovery of meaning, CD4 decline, and AIDS-related mortality among bereaved HIV-seropositive men. *Journal of Consulting and Clinical Psychology, 66,* 979–986.

Bowlby, J. (1951). *Maternal care and mental health. World Health Organization Monograph 2.* Geneva: World Health Organization.

Bowlby, J. (1973). *Attachment and loss: Vol. 2. Separation.* New York: Basic Books.

Bowman, E. S., & Nurnberger, J. I. (1993). Genetics of psychiatry diagnosis and treatment. In D. L. Dummer (Ed.), *Current psychiatric therapy* (pp. 46–56). Philadelphia: Saunders.

Bozarth, M. A., & Wise, R. A. (1984). Anatomically distinct opiate receptor fields mediate reward and physical dependence. *Science, 224,* 516–518.

Bracken, B. A., & McCallum, R. S. (1998). *Universal Nonverbal Intelligence Test (UNIT).* Boston: Riverside.

Bracken, P., & Thomas, P. (2001). Postpsychiatry: A new direction for mental health. *British Journal of Psychiatry, 322,* 724–727.

Bradley-Johnson, S., Graham, D. P., & Johnson, C. M. (1986). Token reinforcement on WISC-R performance for white, low-socioeconomic, upper and lower elementary-school-age students. *Journal of School Psychology, 24,* 73–79.

Bradshaw, G. L. (1993a). Why did the Wright brothers get there first? Part 1. *Chemtech, 23*(6), 8–13.

Bradshaw, G. L. (1993b). Why did the Wright brothers get there first? Part 2. *Chemtech, 23*(7), 16–22.

Brainerd, C. J., & Reyna, V. F. (1998). When things that were never experienced are easier to "remember" than things that were. *Psychological Science, 9,* 484–489.

Brainerd, C. J., & Reyna, V. F. (2002). Fuzzy-trace theory and false memory. *Current Directions in Psychological Science, 11,* 164–169.

Brandimonte, M. A., Hitch, G. J., & Bishop, D. V. M. (1992). Influence of short-term memory codes on visual image processing: Evidence from image transformation tasks. *Journal of Experimental Psychology: Learning, Memory, and Cognition, 18,* 157–165.

Brandtstadter, J., & Renner, G. (1990). Tenacious goal pursuit and flexible goal adjustment: Explication and age-related analysis of assimilative and accommodative strategies of coping. *Psychology and Aging, 5,* 58–67.

Brannick, M., & Levine. E. (2002). *Job analysis.* Thousand Oaks: CA: Sage.

Bransford, J. D., & Stein, B. S. (1993). *The ideal problem solver* (2nd ed.). New York: Freeman.

Branson, R., Potoczna, N., Kral, J. G., Lentes, K.-U., Hoehe, M. R., & Horber, F. F. (2003). Binge eating as a major phenotype of melanocortin 4 receptor gene mutations. *The New England Journal of Medicine, 348,* 1096–1103.

Brasher, E. E., & Chen, P. Y. (1999). Evaluation of success criteria in job search: A process perspective. *Journal of Occupational and Organizational Psychology, 72,* 57–70.

Braun, A. E., Balkin, T. J., & Wesensten, N. J. (1998). Dissociated pattern of activity in visual cortices and their projections during human rapid eye movement sleep. *Science, 279,* 91–95.

Braver, T. S., Reynolds, J. R., & Donaldson, D. I. (2003). Neural mechanisms of transient and sustained cognitive control during task switching. *Neuron, 39,* 713–726.

Bray, G. A., & Tartaglia, L. A. (2000). Medicinal strategies in the treatment of obesity. *Nature, 404,* 672–677.

Breggin, P. R. (1997). *Brain-disabling treatments in psychiatry: Drugs, electroshock, and the role of the FDA.* New York: Springer.

Brehm, S. (1992). *Intimate relationships.* New York: McGraw-Hill.

Brehm, S., Kassin, S., & Fein, S. (1999). *Social psychology* (4th ed., Table 6.4). Boston: Houghton Mifflin.

Brehm, S., Kassin, S., & Fein, S. (2002). *Social pychology* (5th ed.). Boston: Houghton Mifflin.

Breiter, H. C., Aharon, I., Kahneman, D., Dale, A., & Shizgal, P. (2001). Functional imaging of neural responses to expectancy and experience of monetary gains and losses. *Neuron, 30,* 619–639.

Brelsford, J. W. (1993). Physics education in a virtual environment. In *Proceedings of the 37th Annual Meeting of the Human Factors and Ergonomics Society.* Santa Monica, CA: Human Factors.

Bremner, J. D., Shobe, K. K., & Kihlstrom, J. F. (2000). False memories in women with self-reported childhood sexual abuse. *Psychological Science, 11,* 333–337.

Brems, C., & Namyniuk, L. (2002). The relationship of childhood abuse history and substance use in an Alaska Sample. *Substance Use and Misuse, 37,* 473–494.

Brener, N. D., Hassan, S. S., & Barrios, L. C. (1999). Suicidal ideation among college students in the United States. *Journal of Consulting and Clinical Psychology, 67,* 1004–1008.

Brenes, G. A., Rapp, S. R., Rejeski, W. J., & Miller, M. E. (2002). Do optimism and pessimism predict physical functioning? *Journal of Behavioral Medicine, 25,* 219–231.

Brennan, F. X. & Charnetski, C. J. (2000). Explanatory style and Immunoglobulin A (IgA). *Integrative Physiological & Behavioral Science, 35,* 251–255.

Brennen, T., Baguley, T., Bright, J., & Bruce, V. (1990). Resolving semantically induced tip-of-the-tongue states for proper nouns. *Memory & Cognition, 18,* 339–347.

Brenner, R., Azbel, V., Madhusoodanan, S., & Pawlowska, M. (2000). *Clinical Therapeutics, 22,* 411–419.

Brenner, R. A., Trumble, A. C., Smith, G. S., Kessler, E. P., & Overpeck, M. D. (2001). Where children drown, United States, 1995. *Pediatrics, 108,* 85–89.

Brewer, M. B. (2001). The many faces of social identity: Implications for political psychology. *Political Psychology, 22,* 115–125.

Brewer, M. B., & Brown, R. J. (1998). Intergroup relations. In D. Gilbert, S. T. Fiske, & G. Lindzey (Eds.), *Handbook of social psychology* (Vol. 2, 4th ed., pp. 554–594). Boston: McGraw-Hill.

Brewer, W. F. (1977). Memory for the pragmatic implications of sentences. *Memory & Cognition, 5,* 673–678.

Brewer, W. F., & Treyens, J. C. (1981). Role of schemata in memory for places. *Cognitive Psychology, 13,* 207–230.

Brigham, C. C. (1923). *A study of American intelligence.* Princeton, NJ: Princeton University Press.

Bright, J. I., Baker, K. D., & Neimeyer, R. A. (1999). Professional and paraprofessional group treatments for depression: A comparison of cognitive-behavioral and mutual support interventions. *Journal of Consulting and Clinical Psychology, 67,* 491–501.

Brim, O. G., Baltes, P. B., Bumpass, L. L., Cleary, P. D., Featherman, D. L., Hazzard, W. R., et al. (2000). *National Survey of MidlifeDevelopment in the United States (MIDUS), 1995–1996.* Ann Arbor, MI: Interuniversity Consortium for Political and Social Research.

Brislin, R. (1993). *Understanding culture's influence on behavior.* Fort Worth: Harcourt, Brace, Jovanovich.

British Medical Association. (2000). *Acupuncture: Efficacy, safety, and practice.* London: Harwood Academic Publishers.

Broad, W. J., & Revkin, A. C. (2003, February 6). Engineers list all the ideas, striking them one by one. *New York Times.*Retrieved August 18, 2003, from http://www.khbo.be/~lodew/Engineers%20List%20All%20the%20Ideas,%20Striking%20Them%20One%20by%20One.htm

Broadbent, E., Petrie, K. J., Alley, P. G., & Booth, R. J. (2003). Psychological stress impairs early wound repair following surgery. *Psychosomatic Medicine, 65,* 865–869.

Brock, J. W., Farooqui, S. M., Ross, K. D., & Payne, S. (1994). Stress-related behavior and central norepinephrine concentrations in the REM sleep-deprived rat. *Physiology and Behavior, 55*(6), 997–1003.

Brody, N., & Ehrlichman, H. (1998). *Personality psychology: The science of individuality.* Upper Saddle River, NJ: Prentice-Hall.

Bronstein, P., Duncan, P., Clauson, J., Abrams, C. L., Yannett, N., Ginsburg, G., & Milne, M. (1998). Preventing middle school adjustment problems for children from lower-income families: A program for aware parenting. *Journal of Applied Developmental Psychology, 19,* 129–152.

Brooks-Gunn, J., & Chase-Lansdale, P. L. (2002). Adolescent parenthood. In M. H. Bornstein (Ed.), *Handbook of parenting* (2nd ed). Mahwah, NJ: Erlbaum.

Brooks-Gunn, J., Klebanov, P. K., & Duncan, G. J. (1996). Ethnic differences in children's intelligence test scores: Role of economic deprivation, home environment, and maternal characteristics. *Child Development, 67,* 396–408.

Brown, A. L., Campione, J. C., Webber, L. S., & McGilly, K. (1992). Interactive learning environments: A new look at assessment and instruction. In B. Gifford & M. C. O'Connor (Eds.), *Changing assessments: Alternative views of aptitude, achievement, and instruction* (pp. 121–212). Boston: Kluever.

Brown, A. S. (1991). A review of the tip-of-the-tongue experience. *Psychological Bulletin, 109,* 204–233.

Brown, A. S., & Nix, L. A. (1996). Age-related changes in the tip-of-the-tongue experience. *American Journal of Psychology, 109,* 79–91.

Brown, C. (2003, January 31). The man who mistook his wife for a deer. *The New York Times Magazine.* Retrieved August 18, 2003, from http://query.nytimes.com/gst/abstract.html?res=F10614FB395D0C718CDDAB0894DB404482

Brown, G. K., Beck, A. T., Steer, R. A., & Grisham, J. R. (2000). Risk factors for suicide in psychiatric outpatients: A 20-year prospective study. *Journal of Consulting and Clinical Psychology, 68,* 371–377.

Brown, G. W., & Moran, P. M. (1997). Single mothers, poverty and depression. *Psychological Medicine, 27,* 21–33.

Brown, J. (1958). Some tests of the decay theory of immediate memory. *Quarterly Journal of Experimental Psychology, 10,* 12–21.

Brown, J. R., & Dunn, J. (1996). Continuities in emotion understanding from three to six years. *Child Development, 67,* 789–802.

Brown, P. D., & O'Leary, K. D. (2000). Therapeutic alliance: Predicting continuance and success in group treatment for spouse abuse. *Journal of Consulting and Clinical Psychology, 68,* 340–345.

Brown, R. A. (1973). *First language.* Cambridge: Harvard University Press.

Brown, R., & Kulik, J. (1977). Flashbulb memories. *Cognition, 5,* 73–99.

Brown, R., & McNeill, D. (1966). The "tip-of-the-tongue" phenomenon. *Journal of Verbal Learning and Verbal Behavior, 5,* 325–337.

Brown, T. A., NiNardo, P. A., Lehman, C. L., & Campbell, L. A. (2001). Reliability of DSM-IV anxiety and mood disorders: Implications for the classification of emotional disorders. *Journal of Abnormal Psychology, 110,* 49–58.

Brownell, K. D., & Rodin, J. (1994). The dieting maelstrom: Is it possible and advisable to lose weight? *American Psychologist, 49*(9), 781–791.

Brownstein, A. L. (2003). Biased predecision processing. *Psychological Bulletin, 129,* 545–568.

Bruce, D., Dolan, A., & Phillips-Grant, K. (2000). On the transition from childhood amnesia to the recall of personal memories. *Psychological Science, 11,* 360–364.

Bruce, T. J., Spiegel, D. A., & Hegel, M. T. (1999). Cognitive-behavioral therapy helps prevent relapse and recurrence of panic disorder following Alpazolam discontinuation: A long-term follow-up of the Peoria and Dartmouth studies. *Journal of Consulting and Clinical Psychology, 67,* 151–156.

Bruck, M., Cavanagh, P., & Ceci, S. J. (1991). Fortysomething: Recognizing faces at one's 25th reunion. *Memory & Cognition, 19,* 221–228.

Brüning, J. C., Gautam, D., Burks, D. J., Gillette, J., Schubert, M., Orban, P. C., et al. (2000). Role of brain insulin receptor in control of body weight and reproduction. *Science, 289,* 2122–2125.

Brunvald, J. H. (1989). *Curses! Broiled again! The hottest urban legends going.* New York: Norton.

Brush, D. H., Moch, M. K., & Pooyan, A. (1987). Individual demographic differences and job satisfaction. *Journal of Occupational Behaviour, 8,* 139–155.

Bryant, R. A., & McConkey, K. M. (1989). Hypnotic blindness: A behavioral and experiential analysis. *Journal of Abnormal Psychology, 98,* 71–77.

Bryson, S. E., & Smith, I. M. (1998). Autism. *Mental Retardation & Developmental Disabilities Research Reviews, 4,* 97–103.

Buckner, R. L., & Wheeler, M. E. (2001). The cognitive neuroscience of remembering. *Nature Reviews Neuroscience, 2,* 1–12.

Budney, A. J., Hughes, J. R., Moore, B. A., & Novy, P. L. (2001). Marijuana abstinence effects in marijuana smokers maintained in their home environment. *Archives of General Psychiatry, 58,* 917–924.

Budney, A. J., Moore, B. A., Vandrey, R. G., & Hughes, J. R. (2003). The time course and significance of cannabis withdrawal. *Journal of Abnormal Psychology, 112,* 393–402.

Bugental, D. B., & Johnstone, C. (2002). Parental and child cognitions in the context of the family. *Annual Review of Psychology, 51,* 315–44.

Bui, K.-V. T., Peplau, L. A., & Hill, C. T. (1996). Testing the Rusbult model of relationship commitment and stability in a 15-year study of heterosexual couples. *Personality and Social Psychology Bulletin, 22,* 1244–1257.

Bulik, C. M., Sullivan, P. F., Wade, T. D., & Kendler, K. S. (2000). Twin studies of eating disorders: A review. *International Journal of Eating Disorders, 27,* 1–20.

Bulik, C. M., Tozzi, F., Anderson, C., Mazzeo, S. E., Aggen, S., & Sullivan, P. F. (2003). The relation between eating disorders and components of perfectionism. *American Journal of Psychiatry, 160,* 366–368.

Bullough, V. L. (1995, August). Sex matters. *Scientific American,* pp. 105–106.

Burac, J. A. (2001). *Development of autism: Perspectives from theory and research.* Hillsdale, NJ: Erlbaum.

Burchard, R. E. (1992). Coca chewing and diet. *Current Anthropology, 33*(1), 1–24.

Burger, J. M., & Petty, R. E. (1981). The low-ball compliance technique: Task or person commitment? *Journal of Personality and Social Psychology, 40,* 492–500.

Burleson, B. R., Albrecht, T. L., & Sarason, I. G. (Eds.). (1994). *Communication of social support: Messages, interactions, relationships, and community.* Thousand Oaks, CA: Sage.

Burleson, M. H., Gregory, W. L., & Trevarthen, W. R. (1995). Heterosexual activity: Relationship with ovarian function. *Psychoneuroendocrinology, 20*(4), 405–421.

Burnstein, E., & Branigan, C. (2001). Evolutionary analyses in social-psychology. In A. Tesser & N. Schwarz (Eds.), *Blackwell handbook of social psychology: Intraindividual processes* (pp. 3–21). Oxford, England: Blackwell.

Burr, D. C., Morrone, C., & Fiorentini, A. (1996). Spatial and temporal properties of infant colour vision. In F. Vital-Durand, J. Atkinson, & O. J. Braddick (Eds.), *Infant vision* (pp. 63–77). Oxford: Oxford University Press.

Burris, C. T., Branscombe, N. R., & Klar, Y. (1997). Maladjustment implications of self and group gender-role discrepancies: An ordered-discrepancy model. *European Journal of Social Psychology, 27,* 75–95.

Burton, A. M., Wilson, S., Cowan, M., & Bruce, V. (1999). Face recognition in poor-quality video: Evidence from security surveillance. *Psychological Science, 10,* 243–248.

Bushman, B. J. (1998). Priming effects of media violence on the accessibility of aggressive constructs in memory. *Personality and Social Psychology Bulletin, 24,* 537–545.

Bushman, B. J., & Anderson, C. A. (2001). Media violence and the American public: Scientific facts versus media misinformation. *American Psychologist, 56,* 477–489.

Buss, A. H. (1997). Evolutionary perspectives on personality traits. In R. Hogan, J. Johnson, & S. Briggs (Eds.), *Handbook of personality psychology* (pp. 345–366). San Diego: Academic Press.

Buss, D. M. (1999). *Evolutionary psychology: The new science of the mind.* Boston: Allyn & Bacon.

Buston, P. M., & Emlen, S. T. (2003). Cognitive processes underlying human mate choice: The relationship between self-perception and mate preference in Western society. *Proceedings of the National Academy of Sciences, 100,* 8805–8810.

Bustillo, J. R., Lauriello, J., Horan, W. P., & Keith, S. J. (2001) The psychosocial treatment of schizophrenia: An update. *American Journal of Psychiatry, 158,* 163–175.

Butcher, J. N., & Rouse, S. V. (1996). Personality: Individual differences and clinical assessment. *Annual Review of Psychology, 47,* 87–111.

Butler, R. (1998). Information seeking and achievement motivation in middle childhood and adolescence: The role of conceptions of ability. *Developmental Psychology, 35,* 146–163.

Buunk, B., & Oldersma, F. L. (2001). Social comparisons and close relationships. In G. Fletcher & M. Clark (Eds.), *Blackwell handbook of social psychology: Interpersonal processes* (pp. 388–408). Oxford, England: Blackwell.

Buxhoeveden, D. P., Switala, A. E., Roy, E., Litaker, M., & Casanova, M. F. (2001). Morphological differences between minicolumns in human and nonhuman primate cortex. *American Journal of Physical Anthropology, 115,* 361–371.

Byne, W., Buchsbaum, M. S., Kemether, E., Hazlett, E. A., Shinwari, A., Mitropoulou, V., & Siever, L. J. (2001). Magnetic resonance imaging of the thalamic mediodorsal nucleus and pulvinar in schizophrenia and schizotypal personality disorder. *Archives of General Psychiatry, 58,* 133–140.

Cabanac, M., & Morrissette, J. (1992). Acute, but not chronic, exercise lowers the body weight set-point in male rats. *Physiology and Behavior, 52*(6) 1173–1177.

Cabeza, R., & Nyberg, L. (2000). Imaging cognition II: An empirical review of 275 PET and MRI studies. *Journal of Cognitive Neuroscience, 12,* 1–47.

Cabeza, R., Rao, S. M., Wagner, A. D., Mayer, A. R., & Schacter, D. L. (2001). Can medial temporal lobe regions distinguish true from false? An event-related functional MRI study of veridical and illusory recognition memory. *Proceedings of the National Academy of Science, 98,* 4805–4810.

Cabot, P. J. (2001). Immune-derived opioids and peripheral antinociception. *Clinical and Experimental Pharmacology and Physiology, 28,* 230–232.

Cacioppo, J. T., Berntson, G. G., & Petty, R. E. (1997). *Persuasion. Encyclopedia of human biology* (Vol. 6, pp. 679–690). San Diego: Academic Press.

Cacioppo, J. T., Berntson, G. G., Sheridan, J. F., & McClintock, M. K. (2000). Multilevel integrative analyses of human behavior: Social neuroscience and the complementing nature of social and biological approaches. *Psychological Bulletin, 126,* 829–843.

Cacioppo, J. T., Malarkey, W. B., Kiecolt-Glaser, J. K., Uchino, B. N., Sgoutas-Emch, S. A., Sheridan, J. F., et al. (1995). Heterogeneity in neuroendocrine and immune responses to brief psychological stressors as a function of autonomic cardiac activation. *Psychosomatic Medicine, 57,* 154–164.

Cacioppo, J. T., Petty, R. E., & Crites, S. L. (1993). Attitude change. In V. S. Ramachandran (Ed.), *Encyclopedia of human behavior* (pp. 261–270). San Diego: Academic Press.

Cacioppo, J. T., Poehlmann, K. M., Kiecolt-Glaser, J. K., Malarkey, W. B., Burleson, M. H., Berntson, G. G., & Glaser, R. (1998). Cellular immune responses to acute stress in female caregivers of dementia patients and matched controls. *Health Psychology, 17,* 182–189.

Cadoret, R. J., Yates, W. R., Troughton, E., Woodworth, G., & Stewart, M. A. (1995). Adoption study demonstrating two genetic pathways to drug abuse. *Archives of General Psychiatry, 52,* 42–52.

Cahill, L., & McGaugh, J. L. (1998). Mechanisms of emotional arousal and lasting declarative memory. *Trends in Neuroscience, 21,* 294–299.

Cahill, S. P., Carrigan, M. H., & Evans, I. M. (1998). The relationship between behavior theory and behavior therapy: Challenges and promises. In J. J. Plaud & G. H. Eifert (Eds.), *From behavior theory to behavior therapy* (pp. 294–319). Boston: Allyn & Bacon.

Cahill, S. P., Carrigan, M. H., & Frueh, B. C. (1999). Does EMDR work? And if so, why?: A critical review of controlled outcome and dismantling research. *Journal of Anxiety Disorders, 13,* 5–33.

Cain, D. J., & Seeman, J. (Eds.). (2002). *Humanistic psychotherapies: Handbook of research and practice.* Washington, DC: APA Books.

Cairns, R. B., Gariepy, J., & Hood, K. E. (1990). Development, microevolution, and social behavior. *Psychological Review, 97,* 49–65.

Calle, E. E., Rodriguez, C., Walker-Thurmond, K., & Thun, M. J. (2003). Overweight, obesity, and mortality from cancer in a prospectively studied cohort of U.S. adults. *The New England Journal of Medicine, 348,* 1625–1638.

Calvert, G. A., Bullmore, E. T., Brammer, M. J., Campbell, R., Williams, S. C., McGuire, P. K., et al. (1997). Activation of auditory cortex during silent lipreading. *Science, 276*(5312), 593–596.

Campbell, F. A., Pungello, E. P., Miller-Johnson, S., Burchinal, M., & Ramey, C. T. (2001). The development of cognitive and academic abilities: Growth curves

from an early childhood educational experiment. *Developmental Psychology, 37,* 231–242.

Campbell, R. S., & Pennebaker, J. W. (2003). The secret life of pronouns: Flexibility in writing style and physical health. *Psychological Science, 14,* 60–65.

Campbell, S. S., & Murphy, P. J. (1998). Extraocular circadian phototransduction in humans. *Science, 279,* 396–399.

Campion, M. A., & Campion, J. E. (1987). Evaluation of an interviewee skills training program in a natural field experiment. *Personnel Psychology, 40,* 676–691.

Campion, M. A., Palmer, D. K., & Campion, J. E. (1997). A review of structure in the selection interview. *Personnel Psychology, 50,* 655–702.

Campione, J. C., Brown, A. L., & Ferrara, R. A. (1982). Mental retardation and intelligence. In R. J. Sternberg (Ed.), *Handbook of human intelligence* (pp. 392–490). Cambridge: Cambridge University Press.

Campos, J. J. (1980). Human emotions: Their new importance and their role in social referencing. *Research and Clinical Center for Child Development, 1980–81 Annual Report, 1*–7.

Candia, V., Weinbruch, C., Elbert, T., Rockstroh, B., & Ray, W. (2003). Effective behavioral treatment of focal hand dystonia in musicians alters somatosensory cortical organization. *Proceedings of the National Academy of Sciences, 100,* 7942–7946.

Cann, A., & Ross, D. A. (1989). Olfactory stimuli as context cues in human memory. *American Journal of Psychology, 102,* 91–102.

Cannon, T. D., van Erp, T. G. M., Rosso, I. M., Huttunen, M., Lonnqvist, J., Pirkola, T., et al. (2002). Fetal hypoxia and structural brain abnormalities in schizophrenic patients, their siblings, and controls. *Archives of General Psychiatry, 59,* 35–41.

Cannon, T. D., Zorrilla, L. E., Shtasel, D., Gur, R. E., Gur, R. C., Marco, E. J., Moberg, P., & Price, A. (1994). Neuropsychological functioning in siblings discordant for schizophrenia and healthy volunteers. *Archives of General Psychiatry, 51,* 651–661.

Cannon, W. B. (1987). The James-Lange theory of emotions: A critical examination and an alternative theory. Special issue: 100 years of the American Journal of Psychology. *American Journal of Psychology, 100*(3–4), 567–586. (Original work published 1927)

Cannon, W. B., & Washburn, A. L. (1912). An explanation of hunger. *American Journal of Physiology, 29,* 444–454.

Canter, P. H. (2003). The therapeutic effects of meditation. *British Medical Journal, 326,* 1049–1050.

Capron, C., & Duyme, M. (1996). Effect of socioeconomic status of biological and adpotive parents on WISC-R subtest scores of their French adopted children. *Intelligence, 22,* 259–276.

Caramazza, A., & Hillis, A. E. (1991). Lexical organization of nouns and verbs in the brain. *Nature, 349,* 788–790.

Cardinal, R. N., Pennicott, D. R., Sugathapala, C. L., Robbins, T. W., & Everitt, B. J. (2001, May 24). Impulsive choice induced in rats by lesions of the nucleus accumbens core. *Science* [Online]. Retrieved August 18, 2003, from www.sciencemag.org

Cardon, L. R., & Fulker, D. W. (1993). Genetics of specific cognitive abilities. In R. Plomin, & G. McClearn (Eds.), *Nature, nurture, and psychology* (pp. 99–120). Washington, DC: American Psychological Association.

Cardon, L. R., Fulker, D. W., DeFries, J. C., & Plomin, R. (1992). Multivariate genetic analysis of specific cognitive abilities in the Colorado Adoption Project at age 7. *Intelligence, 16,* 383–400.

Carli, L. L., Ganley, R., & Pierce-Otay, A. (1991). Similarity and satisfaction in romantic relationships. *Personality and Social Psychology Bulletin, 17,* 419–426.

Carlo, G. L., & Thibodeau, P. M. (Eds.). (2001). *Wireless phones and health II: State of the science.* Boston: Kluwer Academic.

Carlson, N. R. (1998). *Physiology of behavior.* Boston: Allyn & Bacon.

Carlson, N. R. (2001). *Physiology of behavior* (7th ed.). Boston: Allyn & Bacon.

Carmichael, L. L., Hogan, H. P., & Walter, A. A. (1932). An experimental study of the effect of language on the reproduction of visually perceived form. *Journal of Experimental Psychology, 15,* 73–86.

Carnegie Task Force on Learning in the Primary Grades. (1996). *Years of promise: A comprehensive learning strategy for America's children.* New York: Carnegie Corporation.

Carney, R. M., McMahon, P., Freedland, K. E., Becker, L., Krantz, D. S., Proschan, M. A., et al. (1998). Reproducibility of mental stress-induced myocardial ischemia in the psychophysiological investigations of myocardial ischemia (PIMI). *Psychosomatic Medicine, 60,* 64–70.

Carper, R. A., & Courchesne, E. (2002). Inverse correlation between frontal lobe and cerebellum sizes in children with autism. *Brain, 123,* 836–844.

Carraher, T. N., Carraher, D., & Schliemann, A. D. (1985). Mathematics in the streets and in the schools. *British Journal of Developmental Psychology, 3,* 21–29.

Carrillo, E., & Lopez, A. (Eds.). (2001). *The Latino psychiatric patient: Assessment and treatment.* Washington, DC: American Psychiatric Press.

Carstensen, L. (1997, August). *Psychology and the aging revolution: Changes in social needs and social goals across the lifespan.* Paper presented at the annual convention of the American Psychological Association.

Carter, M. M., & Barlow, D. H. (1995). Learned alarms: The origins of panic. In W. T. O'Donohue & L. Krasner (Eds.), *Theories of behavior therapy: Exploring behavior change* (pp. 209–228). Washington, DC: American Psychological Association.

Carter, M. M., Hollon, S. D., Carson, R., & Shelton, R. C. (1995). Effects of a safe person on induced distress following a biological challenge in panic disorder with agoraphobia. *Journal of Abnormal Psychology, 104,* 156–163.

Cartwright, R. D. (1978). *A primer on sleep and dreaming.* Reading, MA: Addison-Wesley.

Casacalenda, N., Perry, J. C., & Looper, K. (2002). Remission in major depressive disorder: A comparison of pharmacotherapy, psychotherapy, and control conditions. *American Journal of Psychiatry, 159,* 1354–1360.

Casagrande, M., Violani, C., Lucidi, F., Buttinelli, E., & Bertini, M. (1996). Variations in sleep mentation as a function of time of night. *International Journal of Neuroscience, 85,* 19–30.

Casbon, T. S., Curtin, J. J., Lang, A. R., & Patrick, C. J. (2003). Deleterious effects of alcohol intoxication: Diminished cognitive control and its behavioral consequences. *Journal of Abnormal Psychology, 112,* 476–487.

Case, L., & Smith, T. B. (2000). Ethnic representation in a sample of the literature of applied psychology. *Journal of Consulting and Clinical Psychology, 68,* 1107–1110.

Caspi, A. (1998). Personality development across the life course. In W. Damon & N. Eisenberg (Eds.), *Handbook of child psychology: Vol. 3. Social, emotional, and personality development* (5th ed., pp. 311–388). New York: Wiley.

Caspi, A. (2000). The child is the father of man: Personality continuities from childhood to adulthood. *Journal of Personality and Social Psychology, 78,* 158–172.

Caspi, A., Begg, D., Dickson, N., Harrington, H., Langley, J., Moffitt, T. E., & Silva, P. A. (1997). Personality differences predict health-risk behaviors in young adulthood: Evidence from a longitudinal study. *Journal of Personality and Social Psychology, 73,* 1052–1063.

Caspi, A., Bem, D. J., & Elder, G. H., Jr. (1989). Continuities and consequences of interactional styles across the life course. *Journal of Personality, 57,* 375–406.

Caspi, A., Harrington, H., Milne, B., Amell, J. W., Theodore, R. F., & Moffitt, T. E. (2003). Children's behavioral styles at age 3 are linked to their adult personality traits at age 26. *Journal of Personality, 71,* 495–513.

Caspi, A., Henry, B., McGee, R. O., Moffitt, T. E., & Silva, P. A. (1995). Temperamental origins of child and adolescent behavior problems: From age 3 to Age 15. *Child Development, 66,* 55–68.

Caspi, A., McClay, J., Moffitt, T., Mill, J., Martin, J., Craig, I. W., et al. (2002). Role of genotype in the cycle of violence in maltreated children. *Science, 297,* 851–854.

Caspi, A., & Roberts, B. (1999). Personality continuity and change. In L. Pervin & O. John (Eds.), *Handbook of personality: Theory and research* (2nd ed., pp. 300–326). New York: Guilford.

Caspi, A., & Roberts, B. W. (2001). Target article: Personality development across the life course: The argument for change and continuity. *Psychological Inquiry, 12,* 49–66.

Caspi, A., & Silva, P. A. (1995). Temperamental qualities at age 3 predict personality traits in young adulthood: Longitudinal evidence from a birth cohort. *Child Development, 66,* 468–498.

Caspi, A., Sugden, K., Moffitt, T. E., Taylor, A., Craig, I.W., Harrington, H., et al. (2003). Influence of life stress on depression: Moderation by a polymorphism in the 5-HTT gene. *Science, 301,* 386–389.

Cassel, E., & Bernstein, D. A. (2001). *Criminal behavior.* Boston: Allyn & Bacon.

Catalano, M. C., Glass, J. M., Catalano, G., Burrows, S. L., Lynn, W. A., & Weitzner, B. S. (2001). Gabba butyrolactone (GBL) withdrawal syndrome. *Psychosomatics, 42,* 83–88.

Cavaiola, A. A., & Desordi, E. G. (2000). Locus of control in drinking driving offenders and nonoffenders. *Alcoholism Treatment Quarterly, 18,* 63–73.

Cavallaro, S., D'Agata, V., Manickam, P., Dufour, F., & Alkon, D.L. (2002). Memory-specific temporal profiles of gene expression in the hippocampus. *Proceedings of the National Academy of Sciences, 99,* 16279–16284.

Ceci, S. J., Huffman, M. L. C., Smith, E., & Loftus, E. F. (1994). Repeatedly thinking about a non-event: Source misattributions among preschoolers. *Consciousness and Cognition, 3,* 388–407.

Centers for Disease Control and Prevention. (1998). *Trends in the HIV & AIDS epidemic.* Washington, DC: U.S. Government Printing Office.

Centers for Disease Control and Prevention. (1999a). *Centers for Disease Control and Prevention HIV/AIDS surveillance report.* Atlanta, Georgia: National Center for HIV, STD, and TB Prevention.

Centers for Disease Control and Prevention. (1999b). *Chronic diseases and their risk factors.* Washington, DC: U.S. Government Printing Office.

Centers for Disease Control and Prevention. (2001). Deaths: Preliminary data for 2000. *National Vital Statistics Reports, 49,* 1–40.

Centers for Disease Control and Prevention. (2002a). Cigarette Smoking Among Adults–United States, 2000. *Morbidity and Mortality Weekly Report,* July 26.

Centers for Disease Control and Prevention. (2002b). *A glance at the HIV epidemic.* Retrieved December 26, 2002, from http://www.cdc.gov/nchstp/od/news/At-a-Glance.pdf

Centers for Disease Control and Prevention. (2002c). *National Center for Health Statistics faststats, A to Z: Suicide.*

Centers for Disease Control and Prevention. (2002d). *Table 47: Death rates for suicide, according to sex, race, Hispanic origin, and age: United States, selected years 1950–1999.* Retrieved September 25, 2002 from http://www/cdc.gov/nchs/faststats/pdf/nvsr49_11tb1/pds.

Centerwall, L. (1990). Controlled TV viewing and suicide in countries: Young adult suicide and exposure to television. *Social Psychiatry and Social Epidemiology, 25,* 149–153.

Centonze, D., Picconi, B., Baunez, C., Borrelli, E., Pisani, A., Bernardi, G., & Calabresi, P. (2002). Cocaine and amphetamine depress striatal GABAergic synaptic transmission through D2 dopamine receptors. *Neuropsychopharmacology, 26,* 164–175.

Çeponien, R., Lepisto, T., Shesakova, A., Vanhala, R., Alku, P., Naatanen, R., & Yaguchi, K. (2003). Speech-sound-selective auditory impairment in children with autism: They can perceive but do not attend. *Proceedings of the National Academy of Sciences, 100,* 5567–5572.

Cervone, D., & Shoda, Y. (1999). *The coherence of personality: social cognitive bases of consistency, variability, and organization.* New York: Guilford.

Cha, J. H., Farrell, L. A., Ahmed, S. F., Frey, A., Hsiao-Ashe, K. K., Young, A. B., et al. (2001). Glutamate receptor dysregulation in the hippocampus of transgenic mice carrying mutated human amyloid precursor protein. *Neurobiological Disorders, 8,* 90–102.

Chakrabarti, S., & Fombonne, E. (2001). Pervasive developmental disorders in preschool children. *Journal of the American Medical Association, 285,* 3093–3099.

Chamberlin, J. (2000). Easing children's psychological distress in the emergency room. *Monitor on Psychology, 31,* 40–42.

Chambless, D. L. (1990). Spacing of exposure sessions in the treatment of agoraphobia and simple phobia. *Behavior Therapy, 21,* 217–229.

Chambless, D. L., & Ollendick, T. H. (2001). Empirically supported psychological treatments. *Annual Review of Psychology, 52,* 685–716.

Chambless, D. L., & Hollon, S. D. (1998). Defining empirically supported therapies. *Journal of Consulting and Clinical Psychology, 66,* 7–18.

Champion, V., & Huster, G. (1995). Effect of interventions on stage of mammography adoption. *Journal of Behavioral Medicine, 18,* 159–188.

Chao, R. K. (1994). Beyond parental control and authoritarian parenting style: Understanding Chinese parenting through the cultural notion of training. *Child Development, 65,* 1111–1119.

Chapman, S., & Morrell, S. (2000). Barking mad? Another lunatic hypothesis bites the dust. *British Medical Journal, 321,* 1561–1563.

Charles, S. T., Mather, M., & Carstensen, L. L. (2003). Aging and emotional memory: The forgettable nature of negative images for older adults. *Journal of Experimental Psychology: General, 132,* 310–324.

Charleton, T., Gunter, B., & Coles, D. (1998). Broadcast television as a cause of aggression? Recent findings from a naturalistic study. *Emotional and Behavioral Difficulties, 3,* 5–13.

Chase, T. N. (1998). The significance of continuous dopaminergic stimulation in the treatment of Parkinson's disease. *Drugs, 55*(Suppl. 1), 1–9.

Chassin, L., Pitts, S. C., & Prost, J. (2002). Binge drinking trajectories from adolescence to emerging adulthood in a high-risk sample: Predictors and substance abuse outcomes. *Journal of Consulting and Clinical Psychology, 70,* 67–78.

Chastain, G., & Thurber, S. (1989). The SQ3R study technique enhances comprehension of an introductory psychology textbook. *Reading Improvement, 26,* 94–96.

Chemers, M. M. (1987). Leadership processes: Intrapersonal, interpersonal, and societal influences. In C. Hendrick (Ed.), *Group processes.* Newbury Park, CA: Sage.

Chen, Z., & Siegler, R. S. (2000). Intellectual development in childhood. In R.J. Sternberg (Ed.), *Handbook of intelligence* (pp. 92–116). New York: Cambridge University Press.

Cheng, Y., Kawachi, I., Coakley, E. H., Schwartz, J., & Colditz, G. (2000). Association between psychosocial work characteristics and health functioning in American women: Prospective study. *British Medical Journal, 320,* 1432–1436.

Cherkin, D. C., Eisenberg, D., Sherman, K. J., Barlow, W., Kaptchuk, T. J., Street, J., & Deyo, R. A. (2001). Randomized trial comparing traditional Chinese medical acupuncture, therapeutic massage, and self-care education for chronic low back pain. *Archives of Internal Medicine, 161,* 1081–1088.

Chiles, J. A., Lambert, M. J., & Hatch, A. L. (1999). The impact of psychological interventions on medical cost offset: A meta-analytic review. *Clinical Psychology: Science and Practice, 6,* 204–220.

Chisholm, K. (1997, June). Trauma at an early age inhibits ability to bond. *APA Monitor,* p. 11.

Cho, Z. H., Chung, S. C., Jones, J. P., Park, J. B., Park, H. J., Lee, H. J., et al. (1998). New findings of the correlation between acupoints and corresponding brain cortices using functional MRI. *Proceedings of the National Academy of Sciences, 95,* 2670–2673.

Cho, Z. H., Wong, E. K., & Fallon, J. D. (2001). *Neuroacupuncture.* Los Angeles: Q-puncture, Inc.

Chodosh, J., Reuben, D. B., Albert, M. S., & Seeman, T. E. (2002). Predicting cognitive impairment in high-functioning community-dwelling older persons: MacArthur studies of successful aging. *Journal of the American Geriatrics Society, 50*(6), 1051–1060.

Choi, Y. H., Jang, D. P., Ku, J. H., Shin, M. B., Kim, S. I. (2001). Short-term treatment of acrophobia with virtual reality therapy (VRT): A case report. *CyberPsychology and Behavior, 4,* 349–354.

Chomsky, N. (1965). *Aspects of the theory of syntax.* Cambridge, MA: MIT Press.

Chomsky, N. (1986). *Knowledge of language: Its nature, origin, and use.* New York: Praeger.

Choo, K. L., & Guilleminault, C. (1998). Narcolepsy and idiopathic hypersomnolence. *Clinical Chest Medicine, 19*(1), 169–181.

Chorney, M. L., Chorney, K., Sense, N., Owen, M. J., Daniels, J., McGuffin, P., et al. (1998). A quantitative trait locus (QTL) associated with cognitive ability in children. *Psychological Science, 9,* 159–166.

Christensen, K. A., Stephens, M. A. P., & Townsend, A. L. (1998). Mastery in women's multiple roles and well-being: Adult daughters providing care to impaired parents. *Health Psychology, 17,* 163–171.

Chu, J. (1994). Active learning in epidemiology and biostatistics. *Teaching and Learning in Medicine, 6,* 191–193.

Chugani, H. T., & Phelps, M. E. (1986). Maturational changes in cerebral function in infants determined by 18FDG positron emission tomography. *Science, 231,* 840–843.

Chumakov, I., Blumenfeld, M., Guerassimenko, O., Cavarec, L., Palicio, M., Abderrahim, H., et al. (2002). Genetic and physiological data implicating the new human gene G72 and the gene for D-amino acid oxidase in schizophrenia. *Proceedings of the National Academies of Science, 99,* 13675–13680.

Churchland, P. M. (1989). *A neurocomputational perspective: The nature of mind and the structure of science.* Cambridge, MA: MIT Press.

Cialdini, R. B. (1995). Principles and techniques of social influence. In A. Tesser (Ed.), *Advanced social psychology* (pp. 257–282). New York: McGraw-Hill.

Cialdini, R. B. (2001). *Influence: Science and practice* (4th ed.). Boston: Allyn & Bacon.

Cialdini, R. B. (2003). Crafting normative messages to protect the environment. *Current Directions in Psychological Science, 12,* 105–109.

Cialdini, R. B., & Trost, M. (1998). Social influence: Social norms, conformity, and compliance. In D. Gilbert, S. T. Fiske, & G. Lindzey (Eds.), *Handbook of social psychology* (Vol. 2, 4th ed., pp. 151–192). Boston: McGraw-Hill.

Cialdini, R. B., Baumann, D. J., & Kenrick, D. T. (1981). Insights from sadness: A three-step model of the development of altruism as hedonism. *Developmental Review, 1,* 207–223.

Cialdini, R. B., Wosinska, W. B., Barrett, D. W., Butner, J., & Gornik-Durose, M. (2001). The differential impact of two social influence principles on individualists and collectivists in Poland and the United States. In W. Wosinska, R. B. Cialdini, D.W. Barrett, & J. Reykowski (Eds.), *The practice of social influence in multiple cultures: Applied social research* (pp. 33–50). Mahwah, NJ: Erlbaum.

Ciapparelli, A., Dell'Osso, L., Tundo, A., Pini, S., Chiavacci, M. C., Di Sacco, I., & Cassano, G. B. (2001). Electroconvulsive therapy in -medication-nonresponsive patients with mixed mania and bipolar depression. *Journal of Clinical Psychiatry, 62,* 552–555.

Ciccocioppo, R., Sanna, P. P., & Weiss, F. (2001). Cocaine-predictive stimulus induces drug-seeking behavior and neural activation in limbic brain regions after multiple months of abstinence: Reversal by D1 antagonists. *Proceedings of the National Academy of Sciences, 98,* 1976–1981.

Clancy, S. A., Schacter, D. L., McNally, R. J., & Pittman, R. K. (2000). False recognition in women reporting recovered memories of sexual abuse. *Psychological Science, 11,* 26–31.

Clancy, S. A., McNally, R. J., Schacter, D. L., Lenzenweger, M. F., & Pitman, R. K. (2002). Memory distortion in people reporting abduction by aliens. *Journal of Abnormal Psychology, 111,* 455–461.

Clapham, K., & Abramson, E. E. (1985). Aversive conditioning of junk food consumption: A multiple baseline study. *Addictive Behaviors, 10,* 437–440.

Clark, A., Oswald, A., & Warr, P. (1996). Is job satisfaction U-shaped in age? *Journal of Occupational and Organizational Psychology, 69,* 57–81.

Clark, D. C., & Fawcett, J. (1992). Review of empirical risk factors for evaluation of the suicidal patient. In B. Bongar (Ed.), *Suicide: Guidelines for assessment, management, and treatment* (pp. 16–48). New York: Oxford University Press.

Clark, D. M., Salkovskis, P. M., Ost, L.-G., Breitholtz, E., Koehler, K. A., Westling, B. E., Jeavons, A., & Gelder, M. (1997). Misinterpretation of body sensations in panic disorder. *Journal of Consulting and Clinical Psychology, 65,* 203–213.

Clark, E. V. (1983). Meanings and concepts. In P. H. Mussen, J. H. Flavell, & E. M. Markman (Eds.), *Handbook of child psychology: Vol. 3. Cognitive development* (4th ed., pp. 787–840). New York: Wiley.

Clark, E. V. (1993). *The lexicon in acquisition.* Cambridge: Cambridge University Press.

Clark, L. A., Watson, D., & Reynolds, S. (1995). Diagnosis and classification of psychopathology: Challenges to the current system and future directions. *Annual Review of Psychology, 46,* 121–153.

Clark, M. S., & Pataki, S. P. (1995). Interpersonal processes influencing attraction and relationships. In A. Tesser (Ed.), *Advanced social psychology* (pp. 283–332). New York: McGraw-Hill.

Clarke, L., Ungerer, J., Chahoud, K., Johnson, S., Stiefel, I. (2002). Attention deficit hyperactivity disorder is associated with attachment insecurity. *Clinical Child Psychology and Psychiatry, 7,* 179–198.

Clarke-Stewart, K. A. (1989). Infant day care: Maligned or malignant? *American Psychologist, 44,* 266–273.

Clarke-Stewart, K. A., & Fein, G. G. (1983). Early childhood programs. In P. H. Mussen (Ed.), *Handbook of child psychology: Vol. 2. Infancy and developmental psychobiology.* New York: Wiley.

Clarkin, J. F., & Carpenter, D. (1995). Family therapy in historical perspective. In B. Bongar & L. E. Beutler (Eds.), *Comprehensive textbook of psychotherapy: Theory and practice* (pp. 205–227). New York: Oxford University Press.

Clausen, J., Sersen, E., & Lidsky, A. (1974). Variability of sleep measures in normal subjects. *Psychophysiology, 11,* 509–516.

Clay, R. A. (2000). Often, the bells and whistles backfire. *Monitor on Psychology, 31,* 64–65.

Clay, R. A. (2001). Training that's more than bilingual. *Monitor on Psychology, 32,* 70–72.

Clay, R. A. (2002a). Advertising as science. *Monitor on Psychology, 33,* 38–41.

Clay, R. A. (2002b). Psychotherapy *is* cost-effective. *Monitor on Psychology, 31,* Retrieved October 3, 2002 from http://www.apa.org/monitor/jan00/pr2.html

Clendenen, V. I., Herman, C. P., & Polivy, J. (1995). Social facilitation of eating among friends and strangers. *Appetite, 23,* 1–13.

Clifton, R. K. (1992). The development of spatial hearing in human infants. In L. A. Werner & E. W. Rubel (Eds.), *Developmental psychoacoustics* (pp. 135–157). Washington, DC: American Psychological Association.

Clifton, R. K., Rochat, P., Litovsky, R., & Perris, E. (1991). Object representation guides infants' reaching in the dark. *Journal of Experimental Psychology: Human Perception and Performance, 17,* 323–329.

Clower, C. E., & Bothwell, R. K. (2001). An exploratory study of the relationship between the Big Five and inmate recidivism. *Journal of Research in Personality, 35,* 231–237.

Clutton-Brock, T. (2002). Breeding together: Kin selection and mutualism in cooperative vertebrates. *Science, 296,* 69–72.

Cnattingius, S., Signorello, L. B., Anneren, G., Clausson, B., Ekbom, A., Ljunger, E., et al. (2000). Caffeine intake and the risk of first-trimester spontaneous abortion. *New England Journal of Medicine, 343,* 1839–1845.

CNN/Time. (1997). Poll: U.S. hiding knowledge of aliens. *CNN/Time* [On-line]. Retrieved August 20, 2003, from http://www-cgi.cnn.com/US/9706/15/ufo.poll/index.html

Coccaro, E. F. (1989). Central serotonin and impulsive aggression. *British Journal of Psychiatry, 155,* 52–62.

Cofer, L. F., Grice, J., Palmer, D., Sethre-Hofstad, L., & Zimmermann, K. (1992, June 20–22). *Evidence for developmental continuity of individual differences in morningness-eveningness.* Paper presented at the annual meeting of the American Psychological Society, San Diego, CA.

Cohan, C., & Cole, S. (2002). Life course transitions and natural disaster: Marriage, birth, and divorce following Hurricane Hugo. *Journal of Family Psychology, 16,* 14–25.

Cohen, C. E. (1981). Person categories and social perception: Testing some boundaries of the processing effects of prior knowledge. *Journal of Personality and Social Psychology, 40,* 441–452.

Cohen, D. (1998). Culture, social organization, and patterns of violence. *Journal of Personality and Social Psychology, 75,* 408–419.

Cohen, J., & Servan-Schreiber, D. (1992). Context, cortex, and dopamine: A connectionist approach to behavior and biology in schizophrenia. *Psychological Review, 99,* 45–77.

Cohen, N. J., & Corkin, S. (1981). The amnesic patient H. M.: Learning and retention of a cognitive skill. *Neuroscience Abstracts, 7,* 235.

Cohen, S., & Herbert, T. B. (1996). Health psychology: Psychological factors and physical disease from the perspective of human psychoneuroimmunology. In J. Spence, D. Foss, & J. Darley (Eds.), *Annual review of psychology* (Vol. 42). El Camino, CA: Annual Review, Inc.

Cohen-Cory, S. (2002). The developing synapse: Construction and modulation of synaptic structures and circuits. *Science, 298,* 789–791.

Cohn, J. F., & Tronick, E. Z. (1983). Three-month-old infants' reaction to simulated maternal depression. *Child Development, 54,* 185–193.

Colcombe, S., & Kramer, A. F. (2003). Fitness effects on the cognitive function of older adults: A meta-analytic study. *Psychological Science, 14,* 125–130.

Cole, K. N., Mills, P. E., Dale, P. S., & Jenkins, J. R. (1991). Effects of preschool integration for children with disabilities. *Exceptional Children, 58,* 36–45.

Coleman, D. (1992). Why do I feel so tired? Too little, too late. *American Health, 11*(4), 43–46.

Coley, R. L., & Chase-Lansdale, P. L. (1998). Adolescent pregnancy and parenthood: Recent evidence and future directions. *American Psychologist, 53,* 152–166.

Collacott, E. A., Zimmerman, J. T., White, D. W., & Rindone, J. P. (2000). Bipolar permanent magnets for the treatment of chronic low back pain: a pilot study. *Journal of the American Medical Association, 283,* 1322–1325.

Collins, W. A., Maccoby, E. E., Steinberg, L., Hetherington, E. M., & Bornstein, M. H. (2000). Contemporary research on parenting: The case for nature and nurture. *American Psychologist, 55,* 218–232.

Colombo, M., D'Amato, M. R., Rodman, H. R., & Gross, C. G. (1990). Auditory association cortex lesions impair auditory short-term memory in monkeys. *Science, 247,* 336–338.

Committee to Review the Scientific Evidence on the Polygraph. (2002). *The polygraph and lie detection.* Washington, DC: National Academies Press.

Compagnone, N. A., & Mellon, S. H. (2000). Neurosteroids: Biosynthesis and function of these novel neuromodulators. *Frontiers of Neuroendocrinology, 21,* 1–56.

Compas, B. E., Haaga, D. A. F., Keefe, F. J., Leitenberg, H., & Williams, D. A. (1998). Sampling of empirically supported psychological treatments from health psychology: Smoking, chronic pain, cancer, and bulimia nervosa. *Journal of Consulting and Clinical Psychology, 66,* 89–112.

Conel, J. L. (1939/1967). *The postnatal development of the human cerebral cortex* (Vols. 1, 8). Cambridge, MA: Harvard University Press.

Condic, M. L. (2001). Adult neuronal regeneration induced by transgenic integrin expression. *Journal of Neuroscience, 21,* 4782–4788.

Condon, J. W., & Crano, W. D. (1988). Inferred evaluation and the relationship between attitude similarity and interpersonal attraction. *Journal of Personality and Social Psychology, 54,* 789–797.

Conger, R. D., Cui, M., Bryant, C. M., & Elder, G. H. (2000). Competence in early adult romantic relationships: A developmental perspective on family influences. *Journal of Personality and Social Psychology, 79*(2), 224–237.

Conklin, H. M., & Iacono, W. G. (2002). Schizophrenia: A neurodevelopmental perspective. *Current Directions in Psychological Science, 11,* 33–37.

Conley, R. R., & Mahmoud, R. (2001). A randomized double-blind study of risperidone and olanzapine in the treatment of schizophrenia or schizoaffective disorder. *The American Journal of Psychiatry, 158,* 765–774.

Conner, A. (2001). They all answer to "psychologist." *APS Observer, 14,* 1, 8–9, 11.

Connor, L. T., Balota, D. A., & Neely, J. H. (1992). On the relation between feeling of knowing and lexical decision: Persistent subthreshold activation of topic familiarity? *Journal of Experimental Psychology: Learning, Memory, and Cognition, 18,* 544–554.

Conrad, R. (1964). Acoustic confusions in immediate memory. *British Journal of Psychology, 55,* 75–84.

Constantino, J. N., & Todd, R. D. (2003). Autistic traits in the general population: A twin study. *Archives General Psychiatry, 60,* 524–530.

Contrada, R. J., Ashmore, R. D., Gary, M. L., Coups, E., Egeth, J. D., Sewell, A., et al. (2000). Ethnicity-related sources of stress and their effects on well-being. *Current Directions in Psychological Science, 9,* 136–139.

Consumer Reports. (1995, November). Mental health: Does therapy help? *Consumer Reports,* pp. 734–739.

Cookson, J., & Duffett, R. (1998). Fluoxetine: therapeutic and undesirable effects. *Hospital Medicine, 59,* 622–626.

Cooper, M. L., Russell, M., Skinner, J. B., Frone, M. R., & Mudar, P. (1992). Stress and alcohol use: The moderating effects of gender, coping, and alcohol expectancies. *Journal of Abnormal Psychology, 101,* 139–152.

Copeland, J., & Snyder, M. (1995). When counselors confirm: A functional analysis. *Personality and Social Psychology Bulletin, 21,* 1210–1220.

Corbetta, M., Miezin, F. M., Dobmeyer, S., Shulman, G. L., & Petersen, S. E. (1991). Selective and divided attention during visual discriminations of shape, color, and speed: Functional anatomy by positron emission tomography. *Journal of Neuroscience, 11,* 2383–2402.

Cordery, J. L., Mueller, W. S., & Smith, L. M. (1991). Attitudinal and behavioral effects of autonomous group working: A longitudinal field study. *Academy of Management Journal, 34,* 464–476.

Cordova, J. V., & Jacobson, N. S. (1993). Couple distress. In D. H. Barlow (Ed.), *Clinical handbook of psychological disorders: A step-by-step treatment manual* (2nd ed., pp. 481–512). New York: Guilford.

Coren, S. (1999). Psychology applied to animal training. In A. Stec & D. Bernstein (Eds.), *Psychology: Fields of application.* Boston: Houghton Mifflin.

Cork, R. C., Kihlstrom, J. F., & Hameroff, S. R. (1992). Explicit and implicit memory dissociated by anesthetic technique. *Society for Neuroscience Abstracts, 22,* 523.

Cornblatt, B., & Erlenmeyer-Kimling, L. E. (1985). Global attentional deviance in children at risk for schizophrenia: Specificity and predictive validity. *Journal of Abnormal Psychology, 94,* 470–486.

Cornelius, R. R. (1996). *The science of emotion.* Upper Saddle River, NJ: Prentice-Hall.

Corning, A. F. (2000). Assessing perceived social inequity: A relative deprivation framework. *Journal of Personality and Social Psychology, 78,* 463–477.

Correll, J., Park, B., Judd, C. M., & Wittenbrink, B. (2002). The police officer's dilemma: Using ethnicity to disambiguate potentially threatening individuals. *Journal of Personality and Social Psychology, 83,* 1314–1329.

Corruble, E., Damy, C., & Guelfi, J. D. (1999). Impulsivity: A relevant dimension in depression regarding suicide attempts. *Journal of Affective Disorders, 53,* 211–215.

Corsini, R. J., & Wedding, D. (2001). *Current psychotherapies* (6th ed.). Itasca, IL: Peacock.

Corwin, M. J., Lesko, S. M., Heeren, T., Vezina, R. M., Hunt, C. E., Mandell, F., et al. (2003). Secular changes in sleep position during infancy: 1995–1998. *Pediatrics, 111,* 52–60.

Coryell, W., Scheftner, W., Keller, M., Endicott, J., Maser, J., & Klerman, G. (1993). The enduring consequences of mania and depression. *American Journal of Psychiatry, 150,* 720–727.

Costa, P. (2001, June). *New insights on personality and leadership provided by the five-factor model.* Paper presented at Annual Convention of American Psychological Society, Toronto, Canada.

Costa, P. T., Jr., & McCrae, R. (1992). *Revised NEO Personality Inventory: NEO PI and NEO Five-Factor Inventory (NEO FFI: Professional Manual).* Odessa, FL: Psychological Assessment Resources.

Costa, P. T., Jr., & McCrae, R. R. (1995). Primary traits of Eysenck's P-E-N system: Three- and five-factor solutions. *Journal of Personality and Social Psychology, 69,* 308–317.

Costa, P. T., & McCrae, R. R. (2002). Looking backwards: Changes in mean levels of personality traits from 80 to 12. In D. Cervone, & W. Mischel (Eds.), *Advances in personality science* (pp. 196–217). New York: Guilford Press.

Costello, E. J., Mustillo, S., Erkanli, A., Keeler, G., & Angold, A. (2003). Prevalence and development of psychiatric disorders in childhood and adolescence. *Archives of General Psychiatry, 60,* 837–844.

Cota, D., Marsicano, G., Lutz, B., Vicennati, V., Stalla, G.K., Pasquali, R., & Pagotto, U. (2003). Endogenous cannabinoid system as a modulator of food intake. *International Journal of Obesity, 27,* 289–301.

Cotanche, D. A. (1997). Hair cell regeneration in the avian cochlea. *Ann Otol Rhinol Laryngol Supplement, 168,* 9–15.

Cote, J. K., & Pepler, C. (2002). A randomized trial of a cognitive coping intervention for acutely ill HIV-positive men. *Nursing Research, 51,* 237–244.

Cotter, D., Mackay, D., Landau, S., Kerwin, R., & Everall, I. (2001). Reduced glial cell density and neuronal size in the anterior cingulate cortex in major depressive disorder. *Archives of General Psychiatry, 58,* 545–553.

Courchesne, E., Karns, C. M., Davis, H. R., Ziccardi, R., Carper, R. A., Tigue, Z. D., et al. (2001). Unusual brain growth patterns in early life in patients with autistic disorder: An MRI study. *Neurology, 57,* 245–254.

Cowan, D. T., Allan, L. G., Libretto, S. E., & Griffiths, P. (2001). Opiod drugs: A comparative survey of therapeutic and "street" use. *Pain, 2,* 193–203.

Cowan, N. (1988). Evolving concepts of memory storage, selective attention, and their mutual constraints within the human information-processing system. *Psychological Bulletin, 104,* 163–191.

Cowey, A. (1994). Cortical visual areas and the neurobiology of higher visual processes. In M. J. Farah & G. Ratcliff (Eds.), *The neurophysiology of high-level vision: Collected tutorial essays* (pp. 3–31). Hillsdale, NJ: Erlbaum.

Crabbe, J. C. (2002). Alcohol and genetics: new models. *American Journal of Medical Genetics, 114,* 969–974.

Craig, A. D., & Bushnell, M. C. (1994). The thermal grill illusion: Unmasking the burn of cold pain. *Science, 265,* 252–254.

Craik, F. I. M. (1994). Memory changes in normal aging. *Current Directions in Psychological Science, 3,* 155–158.

Craik, F. I. M., Moroz, T. M., Moscovitch, M., Stuss, D. T., Winocur, G., Tulving, E., & Kapur, S. (1999). In search of the self: A positron emission topography study. *Psychological Science, 10,* 26–34.

Craik, F. I. M., & Rabinowitz, J. C. (1984). Age differences in the acquisition and use of verbal information. In H. Bouma & D. G. Bouwhuis (Eds.), *Attention and performance* (Vol. 10, pp. 471–499). Hillsdale, NJ: Erlbaum.

Crandall, C. S., Preisler, J. J., & Aussprung, J. (1992). Measuring life event stress in the lives of college students: The Undergraduate Stress Questionnaire (USQ). *Journal of Behavioral Medicine, 15,* 627–662.

Crano, W. D., & Chen, X. (1998). The leniency contract and persistence of majority and minority influence. *Journal of Personality and Social Psychology, 74,* 1437–1450.

Craske, M. G. (1999). *Anxiety disorders: Psychological approaches to theory and treatment.* Boulder, CO: Westview Press.

Crawford, H. J., Brown, A. M., & Moon, C. E. (1993). Sustained attentional and disattentional abilities: Differences between low and highly hypnotizable persons. *Journal of Abnormal Psychology, 102*(4), 534–543.

Crawford, J. G. (1998). Alzheimer's disease risk factors as related to cerebral blood flow: Additional evidence. *Medical Hypotheses, 50,* 25–36.

Crawford, T. N., Cohen, P., & Brooks, J. S. (2001). Dramatic-erratic personality disorder symptoms: II. Developmental pathways from early adolescence to adulthood. *Journal of Personality Disorders, 15,* 336–350.

Crews, F. (1996). The verdict on Freud. *Psychological Science, 7,* 63–67.

Crick, F., & Koch, C. (1998). Consciousness and neuroscience. *Cerebral Cortex, 8,* 97–107.

Crick, N. R., Werner, N. E., Casas, J. F., O'Brien, K. M., Nelson, D. A., Grotpeter, J. K., et al. (1999). Childhood aggression and gender: A new look at an old problem. In D. Bernstein (Ed.), *Nebraska Symposium on Motivation* (Vol. 44, pp. 75–141). Lincoln: University of Nebraska Press.

Critchley, E. M. (1991). Speech and the right hemisphere. *Behavioural Neurology, 4*(3), 143–151.

Crocker, J., & Wolfe, T. (2001). Contingencies of self-worth. *Psychological Review, 108,* 593–623.

Croen, L. A., Grether, J. K., & Selvin, S. (2001). The epidemiology of mental retardation of unknown cause. *Pediatrics, 107,* 86.

Croft, H., Settle, E., Jr., Houser, T., Batey, S. R., Donahue, R. M., & Ascher, J. A. (1999). A placebo-controlled comparison of the antidepressant efficacy and effects on sexual functioning of sustained-release bupropion and sertraline. *Clinical Therapeutics, 21,* 643–658.

Cronbach, L. J. (1990). *Essentials of psychological testing* (5th ed.). New York: Harper & Row.

Cronbach, L. J. (1996). Acceleration among the Terman males: Correlates in midlife and after. In C. P. Benbow & D. J. Lubinski (Eds.), *Intellectual talent: Psychometric and social issues* (pp. 179–191). Baltimore: Johns-Hopkins University Press.

Crosby, A. E., Cheltenham, M. P., & Sacks, J. J. (1999). Incidence of suicidal ideation and behavior in the United States, 1994. *Suicide & Life Threatening Behavior, 29,* 131–140.

Cross, S. E., & Madson, L. (1997). Models of the self: Self-construals and gender. *Psychological Bulletin, 122,* 5–37.

Cross, S. E., & Markus, H. R. (1999). The cultural constitution of personality. In L. Pervin & O. John (Eds.), *Handbook of personality research* (2nd ed., pp. 378–398). New York: Guilford.

Cross-National Collaborative Group. (2002). The changing rate of major depression: Cross-national comparisons. *Journal of the American Medical Association, 268,* 3098–3105.

Crowther, J. H., Sanftner, J., Bonifazi, D. Z., & Shepherd, K. L. (2001). The role of daily hassles in binge eating. *International Journal of Eating Disorders, 29,* 449–454.

Cruz, A., & Green, B. (2000). Thermal stimulation of taste. *Nature, 403,* 889–892.

Csikszentmihalyi, M. (1999). If we are so rich, why aren't we happy? *American Psychologist, 54,* 821–827.

Culbertson, F. M. (1997). Depression and gender: An international review. *American Psychologist, 52,* 25–31.

Culp, R. E., Cook, A. S., & Housley, P. C. (1983). A comparison of observed and reported adult-infant interactions: Effects of perceived sex. *Sex Roles, 9,* 475–479.

Cumsille, P. E., Sayer, A. G., & Graham, J. W. (2000). Perceived exposure to peer and adult drinking as predictors of growth in positive alcohol expectancies during adolescence. *Journal of Consulting and Clinical Psychology, 68,* 531–536.

Curran, H. V., & Monaghan, L. (2001). In and out of the K-hole: A comparison of the acute and residual effects of ketamine in frequent and infrequent ketamine users. *Addiction, 96,* 749–760.

Curtis, J. T., & Wang, Z. (2003). The neurochemistry of pair bonding. *Current Directions in Psychological Science, 12,* 49–52.

Curtis, T., Miller, B. C., & Berry, E. H. (2000). Changes in reports and incidence of child abuse following natural disasters. *Child Abuse & Neglect, 24,* 1151–1162.

Cusack, K., & Spates, C. R. (1999). The cognitive dismantling of eye movement desensitization and reprocessing (EMDR) treatment of posttraumatic stress disorder (PTSD). *Journal of Anxiety Disorders, 13,* 87–99.

Czeisler, C. A., Duffy, J. F., Shanahan, T. L., Brown, E. N., Mitchell, J. F., Rimmer, D. W., et al. (1999). Stability, precision, and near 24-hour period of the human circadian pacemaker. *Science, 284,* 2177–2181.

Dabbs, J., & Dabbs, M. G. (2001). *Heroes, rogues, and lovers: Testosterone and behavior.* New York: McGraw-Hill.

Dabbs, J. M., Jr., Riad, J. K., & Chance, S. E. (2001). Testosterone and ruthless homicide. *Personality and Individual Differences, 31,* 599–603.

Dadds, M. R., Holland, D. E., Laurens, K. R., Mullins, M., Barrett, P. M., & Spence, S. H. (1999). Early intervention and prevention of anxiety disorders in children: Results at 2-year follow-up. *Journal of Consulting & Clinical Psychology, 67,* 145–150.

D'Agostino, R. B., Sr., Grundy, S., Sullivan, L. M., & Wilson, P. (2001). Validation of the Framingham coronary heart disease prediction scores: Results of a multiple ethnic groups investigation. *Journal of the American Medical Association, 286,* 180–187.

Dale, P. S. (1976). *Language and the development of structure and function.* New York: Holt, Rinehart & Winston.

Dalton, D. R., & Mesch, D. J. (1991). On the extent and reduction of avoidable absenteeism: An assessment of absence policy provisions. *Journal of Applied Psychology, 76,* 810–817.

Daly, J. J., Prudic, J., Devanand, D. P., Nobler, M. S., Mitchell, S., Lisanby, S. H., et al. (2001). ECT in bipolar and unipolar depression: Differences in speed of response. *Bipolar Disorders, 3,* 95–104.

Damasio, A. R., Grabowski, T. J., Bechara, A., Damasio, H., Ponto, L. L. B., Parvizi, J., & Hichwa, R. D. (2000). Subcortical and cortical brain activity during the feeling of self-generated emotions. *Nature Neuroscience, 3,* 1049–1056.

Damos, D. (1992). *Multiple task performance.* London: Taylor & Francis.

Dansereau, F., Jr., Graen, G., & Haga, W. J. (1975). A vertical dyad linkage approach to leadership with formal organizations. *Organizational Behavior and Human Performance, 13,* 46–78.

Dark, V. J., & Benbow, C. P. (1993). Cognitive differences among the gifted: A review and new data. In D. K. Detterman (Ed.), *Current topics in human intelligence* (Vol. 3, pp. 85–120). Norwood, NJ: Ablex.

Darkes, J., & Goldman, M. S. (1993). Expectancy challenge and drinking reduction. *Journal of Clinical and Consulting Psychology, 61,* 344–353.

Darwin, C. E. (1965). *The expression of emotions in man and animals.* Chicago: University of Chicago Press. (Original work published 1872)

Dasgupta, A. M., Juza, D. M., White, G. M., & Maloney, J. F. (1995). Memory and hypnosis: A comparative analysis of guided memory, cognitive interview, and hypnotic hypermnesia. *Imagination, Cognition, and Personality, 14*(2), 117–130.

Daus, C. S., Sanders, D. N., & Campbell, D. P. (1998). Consequences of alternative work schedules. In C. L. Cooper & I. T. Robertson (Eds.), *International review of industrial and organizational psychology 1998* (pp. 185–223). Chichester, UK: Wiley.

Davachi, L., Mitchell, J. P., & Wagner, A. D. (2003). Multiple routes to memory: Distinct medial temporal lobe processes build item and source memories. *Proceedings of the National Academy of Sciences,100,* 2157–2162.

Davanloo, H. (1999). Intensive short-term dynamic psychotherapy-central dynamic sequence: Phase of challenge. *International Journal of Short-Term Dynamic Psychotherapy, 13,* 237–262.

Davidson, J. K., & Moore, N. B. (1994). Guilt and lack of orgasm during sexual intercourse: Myth versus reality in college women. *Journal of Sex Education and Therapy, 20*(3), 153–174.

Davidson, J. M., Camargo, C. A., & Smith, E. R. (1979). Effects of androgen on sexual behavior in hypogonadal men. *Journal of Clinical Endocrinological Metabolism, 48,* 955–958.

Davidson, J. R. T., Rothbaum, B. O., van der Kolk, B. A., Sikes, C. R., & Farfel, G. M. (2001). Multicenter, double-blind comparison of sertraline and placebo in the treatment of posttraumatic stress disorder. *Archives of General Psychiatry, 58,* 485–492.

Davidson, K., Hall, P., & MacGregor, M. (1996). Gender differences in the relation between interview-derived hostility scores and resting blood pressure. *Journal of Behavioral Medicine, 19,* 185–201.

Davidson, K., & Prkachin, K. (1997). Optimism and unrealistic optimism have an interacting impact on health-promoting behavior and knowledge changes. *Personality and Social Psychology Bulletin, 23,* 617–625.

Davidson, P. R., & Parker, K. C. (2001). Eye movement desensitization and reprocessing (EMDR): A meta-analysis. *Journal of Consulting and Clinical Psychology, 69,* 305–316.

Davidson, R. J. (2000). Affective style, psychopathology, and resilience: Brain mechanisms and plasticity. *American Psychologist, 55,* 1196–1214.

Davidson, R. J., Kabat-Zinn, J., Schumacher, J., Rosenkranz, M., Muller, D., Santorelli, S. F., et al. (2003). Alterations in brain and immune function produced by mindfulness meditation. *Psychosomatic Medicine, 65,* 564–570.

Davidson, R. J., Pizzagalli, D., Nitschke, J. B., & Putnam, K. (2002). Depression: Perspectives from affective neuroscience. *Annual Review of Psychology, 53,* 545–574.

Davies, C. (1999, April 21). Junior doctor is cleared in baby overdose death. *London Daily Telegraph,* p. 2.

Davies, R. J., & Stradling, J. R. (2000). The efficacy of nasal continuous positive airway pressure in the treatment of obstructive sleep apnea syndrome is proven. *American Journal of Respiratory Critical Care Medicine, 161,* 1775–1776.

Davis, J. D., Gallagher, R. J., Ladove, R. F., & Turansky, A. J. (1969). Inhibition of food intake by a humoral factor. *Journal of Comparative and Physiological Psychology, 67,* 407–414.

Davis, J. L., & Rusbult, C. (2001). Attitude alignment in close relationships. *Journal of Personality and Social Psychology, 81,* 65–84.

Davis, J. M., Chen, N., & Glick, I. D. (2003). A meta-analysis of the efficacy of second-generation antipsychotics. *Archives of General Psychiatry, 60,* 553–564.

Davis, K. L., Stewart, D. G., Friedman, J. I., Buchsbaum, M., Harvey, P. D., Hof, P. R., et al. (2003). White matter changes in schizophrenia: Evidence for myelin-related dysfunction. *Archives of General Psychiatry, 60,* 443–456.

Davis, M. H. (1994). *Empathy: A social psychological approach.* Madison, WI: Brown and Benchmark.

Davis, M. H., Luce, C., & Kraus, S. J. (1994). The heritability of characteristics associated with dispositional empathy. *Journal of Personality, 60,* 369–391.

Davis, R. A., & Moore, C. C. (1935). Methods of measuring retention. *Journal of General Psychology, 12,* 144–155.

Davison, G. C. (1998). Being bolder with the Boulder Model: The challenge of education and training in empirically supported treatments. *Journal of Consulting and Clinical Psychology, 66,* 163–167.

Davison, G. C., & Neale, J. M. (1990). *Abnormal psychology* (5th ed.). New York: Wiley.

Dawes, R. M. (1994). *House of cards: Psychology and psychotherapy built on myth.* New York: Free Press.

Dawes, R. M. (1998). Behavioral decision making and judgment. In D. Gilbert, S. T. Fiske, & G. Lindzey (Eds.), *Handbook of social psychology* (Vol. 1, 4th ed., pp. 497–549). Boston: McGraw-Hill.

Dawson, D., & Reid, K. (1997). Fatigue, alcohol and performance impairment. *Nature, 388,* 235.

Dawson, D. A., Wadsworth, G., & Palmer, A. M. (2001). A comparative assessment of the efficacy and side-effect liability of neuroprotective compounds in experimental stroke. *Brain Research, 892,* 344–350.

Dawson, M., Schell, A. M., & Fillion, D. L. (2000). The electodermal system. In J. Cacioppo, L. Tassinary, & G. Bernston (Eds.), *Handbook of psychophysiology* (2nd ed., pp. 200–222). New York: Cambridge University Press.

Dawson-Basoa, M., & Gintzler, A. R. (1997). Involvement of spinal cord delta opiate receptors in the antinociception of gestation and its hormonal simulation. *Brain Research, 757,* 37–42.

Day, A. L., & Jreige, S. (2002). Examining Type A behavior pattern to explain the relationship between job stressors and psychosocial outcomes. *Journal of Occupational Health Psychology, 7,* 109–120.

Dayan, K., Kasten, R., & Fox, S. (2002). Entry-level police candidate assessment center: An efficient tool or a hammer to kill a fly? *Personnel Psychology, 55,* 827–849.

De Benedittis, G., Lornenzetti, A., & Pieri, A. (1990). The role of stressful life events in the onset of chronic primary headache. *Pain, 40,* 65–75.

de Castro, J. M., & Goldstein, S. J. (1995). Eating attitudes and behaviors pre- and postpubertal females: Clues to the etiology of eating disorders. *Physiology and Behavior, 58*(1), 15–23.

de Charms, R., Levy, J., & Wertheimer, M. (1954). A note on attempted evaluations of psychotherapy. *Journal of Clinical Psychology, 10,* 233–235.

De Houwer, A. (1995). Bilingual language acquisition. In P. Fletcher & B. MacWhinney (Eds.), *The handbook of child language* (pp. 219–250). Cambridge, MA: Blackwell.

de Rios, M. D. (1989). Power and hallucinogenic states of consciousness among the Moche: An ancient Peruvian society. In C. A. Ward (Ed.), *Altered states of consciousness and mental health: A cross-cultural perspective* (pp. 285–299). Newbury Park, CA: Sage.

de Silva, P. (1994). Psychological treatment of sexual problems. *International Review of Psychiatry, 6*(2–3), 163–173.

De Vaus, D. (2002). Marriage and mental health. *Family Matters, 62.*

de Waal, F. B. M. (2002). Evolutionary psychology: The wheat and the chaff. *Current Directions in Psychological Science, 11,* 187–191.

DeAngelis, T. (2000). School psychologists: In demand and expanding their reach. *Monitor on Psychology, 31,* 30–32.

DeAngelis, T. (2001). APA has lead role in revising classification system. *Monitor on Psychology, 32,* 54–56.

Death Penalty Information Center. (2002). *The death penalty in 2002: Year end report.* Washington, DC: Death Penalty Information Center.

Deaux, K., & Martin, D. (2003). Interpersonal networks and social categories: Specifying levels of context in identity processes. *Social Psychology Quarterly, 66,* 101–117.

DeBeurs, E., van Balkom, A. J. L. M., Lange, A., Koele, P., & van Dyck, R. (1995). Treatment of panic disorder with agoraphobia: Comparison of fluvoxamine, placebo, and psychological panic management combined with exposure and of exposure in vivo alone. *American Journal of Psychiatry, 152*(5), 683–691.

Deci, E., Koestner, R., & Ryan, R. M. (1999). The undermining effect is a reality after all—Extrinsic rewards, task interest, and self-determination: Reply to Eisenberger, Pierce, and Cameron (1999) and Lepper, Henderlong, and Gringras (1999). *Psychological Bulletin, 125,* 692–700.

Deci, E., Koestner, R., & Ryan, R. M. (2001). A meta-analytic review of experiments examining the effects of extrinsic rewards on intrinsic motivation. *Psychological Bulletin, 125,* 627–668.

Dehaene-Lambertz, G., Dehaene, S., & Hertz-Pannier, L. (2002). Functional neuroimaging of speech perception in infants. *Science, 298,* 2013–2015.

DeJoy, D. M., Searcy, C. A., Murphy, L. R., & Gershon, R. R. M. (2000). Behavioral-diagnostic analysis of compliance with universal precautions among nurses. *Journal of Occupational Health Psychology, 5,* 127–141.

DeLisi, L. E., Maurizio, A., Yost, M., Papparozzi, C. F., Fulchino, C., Katz, C. L., et al. (2003). A survey of New Yorkers after the Sept. 11, 2001, terrorist attacks. *American Journal of Psychiatry, 160,* 780–783.

Demaray, M. K., & Malecki, C. K. (2002). Critical levels of perceived social support associated with student adjustment. *School Psychology Quarterly, 17,* 213–241.

Dement, W. (1960). The effect of dream deprivation. *Science, 131,* 1705–1707.

Dement, W., & Kleitman, N. (1957). Cyclic variations in EEG during sleep and their relation to eye movements, body motility and dreaming. *Electroencephalography and Clinical Neurophysiology, 9,* 673–690.

Demo, D. H., Allen, K. R., & Fine, M. A. (Eds.). (2000). *Handbook of family diversity.* New York: Oxford University Press.

DePaulo, B. M. (1994). Spotting lies: Can humans learn to do better? *Current Directions in Psychological Science, 3,* 83–86.

Derogowski, J. B. (1989). Real space and represented space: Cross-cultural perspectives. *Behavior and Brain Sciences, 12,* 51–73.

Derryberry, D., & Tucker, D. M. (1992). Neural mechanisms of emotion. *Journal of Consulting and Clinical Psychology, 60,* 329–338.

DeRubeis, R. J., & Crits-Christoph, P. (1998). Empirically supported individual and group psychological treatments for adult mental disorders. *Journal of Consulting and Clinical Psychology, 66,* 37–52.

DeRubeis, R. J., Gelfand, L. A., Tang, T. Z., & Simons, A. D. (1999). Medications versus cognitive behavior therapy for severely depressed outpatients: Mega-analysis of four randomized comparisons. *American Journal of Psychiatry, 156,* 1007–1013.

Deschaumes, M. C., Dittmar, A., Sicard, G., & Vernet, M. E. (1991). Results from six autonomic nervous system responses confirm "autonomic response specificity" hypothesis. *Homeostasis in Health and Disease, 33*(5–6), 225–234.

Deutsch, M., & Gerard, H. B. (1955). A study of normative and informative social influences on individual judgments. *Journal of Abnormal and Social Psychology, 51,* 629–636.

Devor, E. J. (1994). A developmental-genetic model of alcoholism: Implications for genetic research. *Journal of Consulting and Clinical Psychology, 62,* 1108–1115.

DeVries, R. (1969). Constancy of generic identity in the years three to six. *Monographs of the Society for Research in Child Development, 34*(3, Serial No. 127).

DeWitt, L. A., & Samuel, A. G. (1990). The role of knowledge-based function in music perception. *Journal of Experimental Psychology: General, 119,* 123–144.

DeWolff, M. S., & van IJzendoorn, M. H. (1997). Sensitivity and attachment: A meta-analysis on parental antecedents of infant attachment. *Child Development, 68,* 571–591.

Dhurandhar, N. V., Israel, B. A., Kolesar, J. M., Mayhew, G. F., Cook, M. E., & Atkinson, R. L. (2000). Increased adiposity in animals due to a human virus. *International Journal of Obesity, 24,* 989–996.

Di Marzo, V., Goparaju, S. K., Wang, L., Liu, J., Batkai, S., Jarai, Z., et al. (2001). Leptin-regulated endocannabinoids are involved in maintaining food intake. *Nature, 410,* 822–825.

Diakidoy, I. N., & Spanoudis, G. (2002). Domain specificity in creativity testing: A comparison of performance on a general divergent-thinking test and a parallel, content-specific test. *Journal of Creative Behavior, 36,* 41–61.

Dickinson, A. (2001). Causal learning: Association versus computation. *Current Directions in Psychological Science, 10,* 127–132.

Diener, E. (2000). Subjective well-being: The science of happiness and a proposal for a national index. *American Psychologist, 55,* 34–43.

Diener, E., & Biswas-Diener, R. (2002). Will money increase subjective well-being? *Social Indicators Research, 57,* 119–169.

Diener, E., & Diener, C. (1995). Most people are happy. *Psychological Science, 7,* 181–185.

Dijkstra, A., DeVries, H., & Bakker, M. (1996). Pros and cons of quitting, self-efficacy, and the stages of change in smoking cessation. *Journal of Consulting and Clinical Psychology, 64,* 758–763.

Dinan, T. G. (2001). Novel approaches to the treatment of depression by modulating the hypothalamic-pituitary-adrenal axis. *Human Psychopharmacology: Clinical and Experimental, 16,* 89–93.

Dinan, T. G. (2002). Lithuim in bipolar mood disorder. *British Medical Journal, 324,* 989–990.

Dion, K. (2003). Prejudice, racism and discrimination. In T. Millon & M. Lerner (Eds.) *Handbook of psychology: Volume 5: Personality and social psychology* (pp. 507–536). Hoboken, NJ: Wiley.

Dionne, V. E., & Dubin, A. E. (1994). Transduction diversity in olfaction. *Journal of Experimental Biology, 194,* 1–21.

Dittmann, M. (2003). Psychology's first prescribers. *Monitor on Psychology, 34,* 36–39.

Ditton, P. M. (1999). *Mental health and treatment of inmates and probationers* (Special Report NCJ 174463). Washington, DC: U.S. Department of Justice.

Dixon, J. B., Schachter, L. M., & O'Brien, P. E. (2001). Sleep disturbance and obesity: Changes following surgically induced weight loss. *Archives of Internal Medicine, 161,* 102–106.

Dixon, M., Brunet, A., & Laurence, J.-R. (1990). Hypnotizability and automaticity: Toward a parallel distributed processing model of hypnotic responding. *Journal of Abnormal Psychology, 99,* 336–343.

Dobson, K. S. (Ed.). (2001). *Handbook of cognitive-behavioral therapies* (2nd ed.). New York: The Guilford Press.

Dodds, J. P., Nardone, A., Mercey, D. E., & Johnson, A. M. (2000). Increase in high risk sexual behaviour among homosexual men, London 1996–98: Cross sectional, questionnaire study. *British Medical Journal, 320,* 1510–1511.

Dodson, C., & Reisberg, D. (1991). Indirect testing of eyewitness memory: The (non)effect of misinformation. *Bulletin of the Psychonomic Society, 29,* 333–336.

Dohrenwend, B. P., Raphael, K. G., Schwartz, S., Stueve, A., & Skodol, A. (1993). The structured event probe and narrative rating method for measuring stressful life events. In L. Goldenberger & S. Breznitz (Eds.), *Handbook of stress: Theoretical and clinical aspects* (2nd ed.). New York: The Free Press.

Dolan, M., & Park, I. (2002). The neuropsychology of antisocial personality disorder. *Psychological Medicine, 32,* 417–427.

Dollard, J., Doob, L., Miller, N., Mowrer, O. H., & Sears, R. R. (1939). *Frustration and aggression.* New Haven, CT: Yale University Press.

Dollinger, S. J. (2000). Locus of control and incidental learning: An application to college students. *College Student Journal, 34,* 537–540.

Domhoff, G. W. (1996). *Finding meaning in dreams: A quantitative approach.* New York: Plenum.

Domhoff, G. W. (1999). Drawing theoretical implications from descriptive empirical findings on dream content. *Dreaming, 9,* 201–210.

Domhoff, G. W. (2001). A new neurocognitive theory of dreams. *Dreaming: Journal of the Association for the Study of Dreams, 11,* 13–33.

Donnerstein, E. (1984). Pornography: Its effects on violence against women. In N. M. Malamuth & E. Donnerstein (Eds.), *Pornography and sexual aggression.* New York: Academic Press.

Donnerstein, E., & Linz, D. (1995). The mass media: A role in injury causation and prevention. *Adolescent Medicine: State of the Art Reviews, 6,* 271–284.

Donnerstein, E., Slaby, R. G., & Eron, L. D. (1995). The mass media and youth aggression. In L. Eron, J. Gentry, & P. Schlegel (Eds.), *Reason to hope: A psychosocial perspective on violence and youth* (pp. 219–250). Washington, DC: American Psychological Association.

Donovan, J. J., & Radosevich, D. J. (1999). A meta-analytic review of the distribution of practice effect: Now you see it, now you don't. *Journal of Applied Psychology, 84,* 795–805.

Dooley, D. (2001). *Social research methods* (4th ed.). Upper Saddle River, NJ: Prentice Hall.

Dordain, G., & Deffond, D. (1994). Pyridoxine neuropathies: Review of the literature. *Therapie, 49*(4), 333–337.

Dovidio, J. F., Kawakami, K., & Gaertner, S. L. (2000). Reducing contemporary prejudice: Combating explicit and implicit bias at the individual and intergroup level. In S. Oskamp (Ed.), *Reducing prejudice and discrimination* (pp. 137–163). Hillsdale, NJ: Erlbaum.

Dovidio, J. F., & Penner, L. A. (2001). Helping and altruism. In G. Fletcher & M. Clark (Eds.), *Blackwell handbook of social psychology: Interpersonal processes* (pp. 162–195). Boston: Blackwell.

Dovidio, J. F., Piliavin, J. A., Gaertner, S. L., Schroeder, D. A., & Clark, R. D., III. (1991). The arousal: cost-reward model and the process of intervention: A review of the evidence. In M. Clark (Ed.), *Review of personality and social psychology: Vol. 12. Prosocial behavior* (pp. 86–118). Newbury Park, CA: Sage.

Downey-Lamb, M. M., & Woodruff-Pak, D. S. (1999). Early detection of cognitive deficits using eyeblink classical conditioning. *Alzheimer's Reports, 2,* 37–44.

Dowson, D. I., Lewith, G. T., & Machin, D. (1985). The effects of acupuncture versus placebo in the treatment of headache. *Pain, 21,* 35–42.

Dreyfus, H. L., & Dreyfus, S. E. (1988). Making a mind versus modeling the brain: Intelligence back at a branchpoint. In S. R. Graubard (Ed.), *The artificial intelligence debate.* Cambridge: MIT Press.

Driskell, J. E., Willis, R., & Copper, C. (1992). Effect of overlearning on retention. *Journal of Applied Psychology, 77,* 615–622.

Druckman, D., & Bjork, R. A. (1994). *Learning, remembering, believing: Enhancing human performance.* Washington, DC: National Academy Press.

Drummond, S. P., Brown, G. G., Gillin, J. C., Stricker, J. L., Wong, E. C., & Buxton, R. B. (2000). Altered brain response to verbal learning following sleep deprivation. *Nature, 403,* 655–657.

Druss, B. G., Rosenheck, R. A., & Sledge, W. H. (2000). Health and disability costs of depressive illness in a major U.S. Corporation. *American Journal of Psychiatry, 157,* 1274–1278.

Dube, S. R., Felitti, V. J., Dong, M., Chapman, D. P., Giles, W. H., & Anda, R. F. (2003). Childhood abuse, neglect, and household dysfunction and the risk of illicit drug use: the adverse childhood experiences study. *Pediatrics, 111,* 564–572.

DuBreuil, S. C., Garry, M., & Loftus, E. F. (1998). Tales from the crib: Memories of infancy. In S. J. Lynn, & K. M. McConkey (Eds.), *Truth in memory* (pp. 137–160). New York: Guilford.

Duchamp-Viret, P., Chaput, M. A., & Duchamp, A. (1999). Odor response properties of rat olfactory receptor neurons. *Science, 284,* 2171–2174.

Duclos, S. E., & Laird, J. D. (2001). The deliberate control of emotional experience through control of expressions. *Cognition and Emotion, 15,* 27–56.

Dujovne, V., & Houston, B. (1991). Hostility-related variables and plasma lipid levels. *Journal of Behavioral Medicine, 14,* 555–564.

Dumont, F., & Corsini, R. J. (2000). *Six therapists and one client.* New York: Springer.

Duncan, G. J., Brooks-Gunn, J., & Klebanov, P. K. (1994). Economic deprivation and early childhood development. *Child Development, 65,* 296–318.

Dunn, J., Brown, H., Slomkowski, C., Tesla, C., & Youngblade, L. (1991). Young children's understanding of other people's feelings and beliefs: Individual differences and their antecedents. *Child Development, 62,* 1352–1366.

Dunn, J., & Hughes, C. (2001). "I got some swords and you're dead!": Violent fantasy, antisocial behavior, friendship, and moral sensibility in young children. *Child Development, 72,* 491–505.

Dunne, E., & Fitzpatrick, A. C. (1999). The views of professionals on the role of self-help groups in the mental health area. *Irish Journal of Psychological Medicine, 16,* 84–89.

Dutton, D. G., & Aron, A. P. (1974). Some evidence for heightened sexual attraction under conditions of high anxiety. *Journal of Personality and Social Psychology, 30,* 510–517.

Dweck, C. S. (1998). The development of early self-conceptions: Their relevance for motivational processes. In J. Heckhausen & C. S. Dweck (Eds.), *Motivation and self-regulation across the life span.* New York: Cambridge University Press.

Dyche, L., & Zayas, L. H. (2001). Cross-cultural empathy and training the contemporary psychotherapist. *Clinical Social Work Journal, 29,* 245–258.

d'Ydewalle, G., & Rosselle, H. (1978). Text expectations in text learning. In M. M. Gruneberg, P. E. Morris, & R. N. Sykes (Eds.), *Practical aspects of memory.* Orlando, FL: Academic Press.

Eagly, A. H. (1987). *Sex differences in social behavior: A social-role interpretation.* Hillsdale, NJ: Erlbaum.

Eagly, A. H., Johannesen-Schmidt, M. C., & van Engen, M. L. (2003). Transformational, transactional, and laissez-faire leadership styles: A meta-analysis comparing women and men. *Psychological Bulletin, 129,* 569–591.

Eagly, A. H., & Karau, S. J. (1991). Gender and the emergence of leaders: A meta-analysis. *Journal of Personality and Social Psychology, 60,* 685–710.

Eagly, A. H., Karau, S. J., & Makhijani, M. G. (1995). Gender and the effectiveness of leaders: A meta-analysis. *Psychological Bulletin, 117,* 125–145.

Eagly, A. H., Makhijani, M. G., & Klonsky, B. G. (1992). Gender and evaluation of leaders: A meta-analysis. *Psychological Bulletin, 111,* 3–22.

Eagly, A. H., & Wood, W. (1999). The origins of sex differences in human behavior: Evolved dispositions versus social roles. *American Psychologist, 54,* 408–423.

Ebert, S. A., Tucker, D. C., & Roth, D. L. (2002). Psychological resistance factors as predictors of general health status and physical symptom reporting. *Psychology Health & Medicine, 7,* 363–375.

Eccleston, C., & Crombez, G. (1999). Pain demands attention: A cognitive-affective model of the interruptive function of pain. *Psychological Bulletin, 125,* 356–366.

Echeburua, E., de Corral, P., Garcia Bajos, E., & Borda, M. (1993). Interactions between self-exposure and alprazolam in the treatment of agoraphobia without current panic: An exploratory study. *Behavioural and Cognitive Psychotherapy, 21,* 219–238.

Edelman, G. M. (2003). Naturalizing consciousness: A theoretical framework. *Proceedings of the National Academy of Sciences, 100,* 5520–5524.

Edinger, J. D., Wohlgemuth, W. K., Radtke, R. A., Marsh, G. R., & Quillian, R. E. (2001). Cognitive behavioral therapy for treatment of chronic primary insomnia. *American Medical Association, 285,* 1865–1864.

Egeland, J. A., Gerhard, D. S., Pauls, D. L., Sussex, J. N., Kidd, K. K., Allen, C. R., et al. (1987). Bipolar affective disorders linked to DNA markers on chromosome 11. *Nature, 325,* 783–787.

Ehlers, A. (1995). A 1-year prospective study of panic attacks: Clinical course and factors associated with maintenance. *Journal of Abnormal Psychology, 104,* 164–172.

Ehrlichman, H., & Halpern, J. N. (1988). Affect and memory: Effects of pleasant and unpleasant odors on retrieval of happy and unhappy memories. *Journal of Personality and Social Psychology, 55,* 769–779.

Eich, E. (1989). Theoretical issues in state dependent memory. In H. L. Roediger & F. I. M. Craik (Eds.), *Varieties of memory and consciousness.* Hillsdale, NJ: Erlbaum.

Eich, E., & Macaulay, D. (2000). Are real moods required to reveal mood-congruent and mood-dependent memory? *Psychological Science, 11,* 244–248.

Eich, E., & Metcalfe, J. (1989). Mood dependent memory for internal versus external events. *Experimental Psychology: Learning, Memory, and Cognition, 15,* 443–455.

Eich, J. E., Weingartner, H., Stillman, R. C., & Gillin, J. C. (1975). State dependent accessibility of retrieval cues in the retention of a categorized list. *Journal of Verbal Learning and Verbal Behavior, 14,* 408–417.

Eichelman, B. (1983). The limbic system and aggression in humans. *Neuroscience and Biobehavioral Reviews, 7,* 391–394.

Einhorn, H., & Hogarth, R. (1982). Prediction, diagnosis and causal thinking in forecasting. *Journal of Forecasting, 1,* 23–36.

Eisenberg, M., Kobilo, T., Berman, D. E., & Dudai, Y. (2003). Stability of retrieved memory: Inverse correlation with trace dominance. *Science, 301,* 1102–1104.

Eisenberg, N. (1998). Introduction. In W. Damon & N. Eisenberg (Eds.), *Handbook of child psychology: Vol. 3. Social, emotional, and personality development* (5th ed., pp. 1–24). New York: Wiley.

Eisenberg, N., Cialdini, R. B., McCreath, H., & Shell, R. (1987). Consistency-based compliance: When and why do children become vulnerable? *Journal of Personality and Social Psychology, 52,* 1174–1181.

Eisenberg, N., & Fabes, R. A. (1998). Prosocial development. In W. Damon & N. Eisenberg (Eds.), *Handbook of child psychology: Vol. 3. Social, emotional, and personality development* (5th ed., pp. 701–778). New York: Wiley.

Eisenberg, N., Fabes, R. A., & Murphy, B. C. (1995). Relations of shyness and low sociability to regulation and emotionality. *Journal of Personality and Social Psychology, 68,* 505–518.

Eisenman, R. (1994). Conservative sexual values: Effects of an abstinence program on student attitudes. *Journal of Sex Education and Therapy, 20*(2), 75–78.

Ekman, P. (1993). Facial expression and emotion. *American Psychologist, 48,* 384–392.

Ekman, P. (1994). Strong evidence for universals in facial expressions: A reply to Russell's mistaken critique. *Psychological Bulletin, 115*(2), 268–287.

Ekman, P., & Davidson, R. J. (1993). Voluntary smiling changes regional brain activity. *Psychological Science, 4*(5), 342–345.

Ekman, P., Davidson, R. J., & Friesen, W. V. (1990). The Duchenne smile: Emotional expression and brain physiology II. *Journal of Personality and Social Psychology, 58,* 342–353.

Ekman, P., Friesen, W. V., & Ellsworth, P. (1972). *Emotion in the human face: Guidelines for research and a review of findings.* New York: Pergamon Press.

Ekman, P., Levenson, R. W., & Friesen, W. V. (1983). Autonomic nervous system activity distinguishes among emotions. *Science, 221,* 1208–1210.

Elkin, I. (1994). The NIMH treatment of depression collaborative research program: Where we began and where we are. In A. E. Bergin & S. L. Garfield (Eds.), *Handbook of psychotherapy and behavior change.* New York: Wiley.

Elkin, I. (1999). A major dilemma in psychotherapy outcome research: Disentangling therapists from therapies. *Clinical Psychology: Science and Practice, 6,* 10–32.

Elkin, I., Yamaguchi, J. L., Arnoff, D. B., Glass, C. R., Sotsky, S. M., & Krupnick, J. L. (1999). "Patient-treatment fit" and early engagement in therapy. *Psychotherapy Research, 9,* 437–451.

Ellemers, N., Spears, R., & Doosje, B. (2002). Self and social identity. *Annual Review of Psychology, 53,* 161–186.

Elliot, A. J., Chirkov, V. I., Kim, Y., & Shelldon, K. M. (2001). A cross-cultural analysis of avoidance (relative to approach) personal goals. *Psychological Science, 12,* 505–510.

Elliott, R., Rubinsztein, J. S., Sahakian, B. J., & Dolan, R. J. (2002). The neural basis of mood-congruent processing biases in depression. *Archives of General Psychiatry, 59,* 597–604.

Ellis, A. (1962). *Reason and emotion in psychotherapy.* New York: Lyle Stuart.

Ellis, A. (1993). Reflections on rational-emotive therapy. *Journal of Consulting and Clinical Psychology, 61,* 199–201.

Ellis, A. (1995). Rational emotive behavior therapy. In R. J. Corsini & D. Wedding (Eds.), *Current psychotherapies* (5th ed., pp. 162–196). Itasca, IL: Peacock.

Ellis, A. L., & Mitchell, R. W. (2000). Sexual orientation. In L. T. Szuchman & F. Muscarella (Eds.), *Psychological perspectives on human sexuality.* New York: Wiley.

Ellis, N. R. (1991). Automatic and effortful processes in memory for spatial location. *Bulletin of the Psychonomic Society, 29,* 28–30.

Elovainio, M., Kivimäki, M., & Vahtera, J. (2002). Organizational justice: Evidence on a new psychosocial predictor of health. *American Journal of Public Health, 92,* 105–108.

El Yacoubi, M., Bouali, S., Popa, D., Naudon, L., Leroux-Nicollet, I., Hamon, M., et al. (2003). Behavioral, neurochemical, and electrophysiological characterization of a genetic mouse model of depression. *Proceedings of the National Academy of Sciences, 100,* 6227–6232.

Emery, C. E. (2002). Death, taxes, and failed psychic predictions: Tabloid psychics fail again in 2002. *Skeptical Inquirer, 27,* 6–7.

Ende, G., Braus, D. F., Walter, S., Weber-Fahr, W., & Henn, F. A. (2000). The hippocampus in patients treated with electroconvulsive therapy. *Archives of General Psychiatry, 57,* 937–943.

Engebretson, T. O., & Stoney, C. M. (1995). Anger expression and lipid concentrations. *International Journal of Behavioral Medicine, 2,* 281–298.

Engeland, H. V. (1993). Pharmacotherapy and behaviour therapy: Competition or cooperation? *Acta Paedopsychiatrica International Journal of Child and Adolescent Psychiatry, 56*(2), 123–127.

Engen, T., Gilmore, M. M., & Mair, R. G. (1991). Odor memory. In T. V. Getchell et al. (Eds.), *Taste and smell in health and disease.* New York: Raven Press.

Engle, R. W., & Oransky, N. (1991). The evolution from short-term to working memory: Multi-store to dynamic models of temporary storage. In R. Sternberg (Ed.), *The nature of human cognition* (pp. 514–555). Cambridge: MIT Press.

Engler, B. (2003). *Personality theories: An introduction* (6th ed.). Boston: Houghton Mifflin.

Epping-Jordan, M. P., Watkins, S. S., Koob, G. F., & Markou, A. (1998). Dramatic decreases in brain reward function during nicotine withdrawal. *Nature, 393,* 76–79.

Epstein, L. H., Valoski, A., Wing, R. R., & McCurley, J. (1994). Ten-year outcomes of behavioral family-based treatment for childhood obesity. *Health Psychology, 13,* 373–383.

Erdelyi, M. H. (1985). *Psychoanalysis: Freud's cognitive psychology.* San Francisco: Freeman.

Erel, O., & Burman, B. (1995). Interrelatedness of marital relations and parent-child relations: A meta-analytic review. *Psychological Bulletin, 118,* 108–132.

Erickson, R. J., Nichols, L., & Ritter, C. (2000). Family influences on absenteeism: Testing an expanded process model. *Journal of Vocational Behavior, 57,* 246–272.

Ericsson, K. A., & Charness, N. (1994). Expert performance: Its structure and acquisition. *American Psychologist, 49,* 725–747.

Ericsson, K. A., & Simon, H. A. (1994). *Protocol analysis: Verbal reports as data* (Rev. ed.). Cambridge, MA: MIT Press.

Ericsson, K. A., & Staszewski, J. (1989). Skilled memory and expertise: Mechanisms of exceptional performance. In D. Klahr & K. Kotovsky (Eds.), *Complex information processing: The impact of Herbert A. Simon.* Hillsdale, NJ: Erlbaum.

Erikson, E. H. (1968). *Identity: Youth and crisis.* New York: Norton.

Eriksson, P. S., Perfilieva, E., Bjork-Eriksson, T., Alborn, A. M., Nordborg, C., Peterson, D. A., et al. (1998). Neurogenesis in the adult human hippocampus. *Nature Medicine, 4,* 1313–1317.

Ernst, E. (2000). Herbal medicines: Where is the evidence? *British Medical Journal, 321,* 395–396.

Ernst, M., Matochik, J. A., Heishman, S. J., Van Horn, J. D., Jons, P. H., Henningfield, J. E., & London, E. D. (2001). Effect of nicotine on brain activation during performance of a working memory task. *Proceedings of the National Academy of Science, 98,* 4728–4733.

Eron, L. D., Huesmann, L. R., Lefkowitz, M. M., & Walder, L. O. (1996). Does television violence cause aggression? In D. F. Greenberg (Ed.), *Criminal careers: Vol. 2. The international library of criminology, criminal justice and penology* (pp. 311–321). Aldershot, England: Dartmouth.

Esterson, A. (2001). The mythologizing of psychoanalytic history: Deception and self-deception in Freud's account of the seduction theory episode. *History of Psychiatry, 12,* 329–352.

Evans, D. A., Hebert, L. E., Beckett, L. A., Scherr, P. A., Albert, M. S., Chown, M. J., et al. (1997). Education and other measures of socioeconomic status and risk of incident Alzheimer's disease in a defined population of older persons. *Archives of Neurology, 54,* 1399–1405.

Evans, G. W., Hygge, S., & Bullinger, M. (1995). Chronic noise and psychological stress. *Psychological Science, 6,* 333–338.

Evans, G. W., & Johnson, D. (2000). Stress and open-office noise. *Journal of Applied Psychology, 85,* 779–783.

Evans, G. W., Wells, N. M., Chan, H.-Y. E., & Saltzman, H. (2000). Housing quality and mental health. *Journal of Consulting and Clinical Psychology, 68,* 526–530.

Everaerd, W., & Laan, E. (1994). Cognitive aspects of sexual functioning and dys-functioning. *Sexual and Marital Therapy, 9,* 225–230.

Everett, S. A., Warren, C. W., Santelli, J. S., Kann, L., Collins, J. L., & Kolbe, L. J. (2000). Use of birth control pills, condoms, and withdrawal among U.S. high school students. *Journal of Adolescent Health, 27,* 112–118.

Eysenck, H. J. (1952). The effects of psychotherapy: An evaluation. *Journal of Consulting Psychology, 16,* 319–324.

Eysenck, H. J. (1961). The effects of psychotherapy. In H. J. Eysenck (Ed.), *Handbook of abnormal psychology.* New York: Basic Books.

Eysenck, H. J. (1966). *The effects of psychotherapy.* New York: International Science Press.

Eysenck, H. J. (1978). An exercise in mega-silliness. *American Psychologist, 33,* 517.

Eysenck, H. J. (1986). What is intelligence? In R. J. Sternberg & D. K. Detterman (Eds.), *What is intelligence? Contemporary viewpoints on its nature and definition.* Norwood, NJ: Ablex.

Eysenck, H. J. (1990). Biological dimensions of personality. In L. A. Pervin (Ed.), *Handbook of personality: Theory and research* (pp. 244–276). New York: Guilford.

Eysenck, H. J. (1994). A biological theory of intelligence. In D. K. Detterman (Ed.), *Current topics in human intelligence* (Vol. 4). Norwood, NJ: Ablex.

Eysenck, H. J., & Rachman, S. (1965). *The causes and cures of neurosis: An introduction to modern behavior therapy based on learning theory and the principle of conditioning.* San Diego: Knapp.

Faedda, G., Tondo, L., Teicher, M., Baldessarini, R., Gelbard, H., & Floris, G. (1993). Seasonal mood disorders: Patterns of seasonal recurrence in mania and depression. *Archives of General Psychiatry, 50,* 17–23.

Fagan, J. F. (2000). A theory of intelligence as processing. *Psychology, Public Policy, and Law, 26,* 168–179.

Farah, M. J. (2000). *The cognitive neuroscience of vision.* Malden, MA: Blackwell.

Farberman, R. (1999, February). As managed care grows, public unhappiness rises. *APA Monitor,* p. 14.

Farley, F. (1986). The big T in personality. *Psychology Today, 20,* 44–52.

Farooqi, I. S., Jebb, S. A., Langmack, G., Lawrence, E., Cheetham, C. H., Prentice, A. M., et al. (1999). Effects of recombinant leptin therapy in a child with congenital leptin deficiency. *The New England Journal of Medicine, 341,* 879–884.

Farooqi, I. S., Keogh, J. M., Kamath, S., Jones, S., Gibson, W. T., Trussel, R., et al. (2001). Metabolism: Partial leptin deficiency and human adiposity. *Nature, 414,* 34–35.

Farrell, D., & Stamm, C. L. (1988). Meta-analysis of the correlates of employee absence. *Human Relations, 41,* 211–227.

Farroni, T., Csibra, G., Simion, F., & Johnson, M. H. (2002). Eye contact detection in humans from birth. *Proceedings of the National Academy of Science, 99,* 9602–9605.

Fassler, D. G., & Dumas, L. S. (1997). *Help me, I'm sad: Recognizing, treating, and preventing childhood depression.* New York: Viking Press.

Faulkner, M. (2001). The onset and alleviation of learned helplessness in older hospitalized people. *Aging & Mental Health, 5,* 379–386.

Faust, J., Olson, R., & Rodriguez, H. (1991). Same-day surgery preparation: Reduction of pediatric patient arousal and distress through participant modeling. *Journal of Consulting and Clinical Psychology, 59,* 475–478.

Fava, G. A., Grandi, S. Rafanelli, C., Ruini, C., Conti, S., & Bellurado, P. (2001). Long-term outcome of social phobia treated by exposure. *Psychological Medicine, 31,* 899–905.

Faymonville, M. E., Laureys, S., Degueldre, C., DelFiore, G., Luxen, A., Franck, G., et al. (2000). Neural mechanisms of antinociceptive effects of hypnosis. *Anesthesiology, 92,* 1257–1267.

Federal Bureau of Investigation. (2002). *Preliminary semiannual uniform crime report.* Washington, DC: U.S. Government.

Feingold, A., & Mazzella, R. (1998). Gender differences in body image are increasing. *Psychological Science, 9,* 190–195.

Feist, J., & Feist, G. J. (2002). *Theories of personality* (5th ed.) New York: McGraw-Hill.

Felder, R. M. & Brent, R. (2001). Effective strategies for cooperative learning. *Journal of Cooperation & Collaboration in College Teaching, 10,* 69–75.

Felten, D. L., Cohen, N., Ader, R., Felten, S. Y., Carlson, S. L., & Roszman, T. L. (1991). Central neural circuits involved in neural-immune interactions. In R. Ader (Ed.), *Psychoneuroimmunology* (2nd ed.). New York: Academic Press.

Feltham, C. (2000). What are counselling and psychotherapy? In C. Feltham and I. Horton (Eds.), *Handbook of counselling and psychotherapy.* London: Sage.

Feng-Chen, K. C., & Wolpaw, J. R. (1996). Operant conditioning of H-reflex changes synaptic terminals on primate motoneurons. *Proceedings of the National Academy of Science USA, 93,* 9206–9211.

Fenson, L., Dale, P. S., Reznick, J. S., & Bates, E. (1994). Variability in early communicative development. *Monographs of the Society for Research in Child Development, 59,* 173.

Fenton, W. S., & McGlashan, T. H. (1991). Natural history of schizophrenia subtypes: 1. Longitudinal study of paranoid, hebephrenic, and undifferentiated schizophrenia. *Archives of General Psychiatry, 48,* 969–977.

Ferguson, C. J. (2002). Media violence: Miscast causality. *American Psychologist, 57,* 446–447.

Fernald, A. (1990, December). Cited by T. Adler, "Melody is the message" of infant-directed speech. *APA Monitor*, p. 9.

Fernández-Dols, J.-M., & Ruiz-Belda, M.-A. (1995). Are smiles a sign of happiness?: Gold medal winners at the Olympic Games. *Journal of Personality and Social Psychology, 69,* 1113–1119.

Ferris, G. R., Judge, T. A., Rowland, K. M., & Fitzgibbons, D. E. (1994). Subordinate influence and the performance evaluation process: Test of a model. *Organizational and Human Decision Processes, 58,* 101–135.

Festinger, L. (1954). A theory of social comparison processes. *Human Relations, 7,* 117–140.

Festinger, L. (1957). *A theory of cognitive dissonance.* Evanston, IL: Row, Petersen.

Festinger, L., & Carlsmith, J. M. (1959). Cognitive consequences of forced compliance. *Journal of Abnormal and Social Psychology, 58,* 203–210.

Fiedler, K., Walther, E., Freytag, P., & Plessner, H. (2002). Judgment biases in a simulated classroom—A cognitive-environmental approach. *Organizational Behavior and Human Decision Processes, 88,* 527–561.

Filipek, P. A., Accardo, P. J., Barancek, G. T., Cook, E. H., Jr., Dawson, G., Gordon, B., et al. (1999). The screening and diagnosis of autistic spectrum disorders. *Journal of Autism and Developmental Disorders, 29,* 439–484.

Fincham, F. A. (2003). Marital conflict: Correlates, structure, and context. *Current Directions in Psychological Science, 12,* 23–26.

Finer, N., James, W. P., Kopelman, P. G., Lean, M. E., & Williams, G. (2000). One-year treatment of obesity: A randomized, double-blind, placebo-controlled, multicentre study of orlistat, a gastrointestinal lipase inhibitor. *International Journal of Obesity and Related Metabolic Disorders, 24,* 306–313.

Fink, M. (1999). *Electroshock: Restoring the mind.* New York: Oxford University Press.

Fischer, K. W., & Bidell, T. (1991). Constraining nativist inferences about cognitive capacities. In S. Carey & R. Gelman (Eds.), *The epigenesis of mind: Essays on biology and cognition* (pp. 199–235). Hillsdale, NJ: Erlbaum.

Fischer, K. W., & Hencke, R. W. (1996). Infants' construction of actions in context: Piaget's contribution to research on early development. *Psychological Science, 7,* 204–209.

Fischer, P. J., & Breakey, W. R. (1991). The epidemiology of alcohol, drug, and mental disorders among homeless persons. *American Psychologist, 46,* 1115–1128.

Fischer, S., Hallschmid, M., Elsner, A. L., & Born, J. (2002). Sleep forms memory for finger skills. *Proceedings of the National Academy of Sciences, 99,* 11987–11991.

Fischoff, B., & MacGregor, D. (1982). Subjective confidence in forecasts. *Journal of Forecasting, 1,* 155–172.

Fisher, C. B., & Fried, A. L. (2003). Internet-mediated psychological services and the American Psychological Association ethics code. *Psychotherapy: Theory, Research, Practice, and Training, 40,* 103–111.

Fisher, C. D. (2000). Mood and emotion while working: Missing pieces of job satisfaction? *Journal of Organizational Behavior, 21,* 185–202.

Fisher, W. A., Fisher, J. D., & Rye, B. J. (1995). Understanding and promoting AIDS-preventive behavior: Insights from the theory of reasoned action. *Health Psychology, 14,* 255–264.

Fiske, A. P., Kitayama, S., Markus, H. R., & Nisbett, R. E. (1998). The cultural matrix of social psychology. In D. T. Gilbert, S. T. Fiske, & G. Lindzey (Eds.), *Handbook of social psychology* (Vol. 2, 4th ed., pp. 915–981). Boston: McGraw-Hill.

Fiske, S. T. (1995). Social cognition. In A. Tesser (Ed.), *Advanced social psychology* (pp. 149–194). New York: McGraw-Hill.

Fiske, S. T. (1998). Stereotyping, prejudice, and discrimination. In D. Gilbert, S. T. Fiske, & G. Lindzey (Eds.), *Handbook of social psychology* (Vol.2, 4th ed., pp. 357–414). Boston: McGraw-Hill.

Fiske, S. T. (2000). Interdependence and the reduction of prejudice. In S. Oskamp (Ed.), *Reducing prejudice and discrimination* (pp. 115–135). Mahwah, NJ: Erlbaum.

Fitzgerald, P. B., Brown, T. L., Marston, N. A. U., de Castella, A., & Kulkarni, J. (2003). Transcranial magnetic stimulation in the treatment of depression. *Archives of General Psychiatry, 60,* 1002–1008.

Fitzgerald, T. E., Tennen, H., Affleck, G. S., & Pransky, G. (1993). The relative importance of dispositional optimism and control appraisals in quality of life after coronary artery bypass surgery. *Journal of Behavioral Medicine, 16,* 25–43.

Flanagan, J. C. (1954). The critical incident technique. *Psychological Bulletin, 51,* 327–358.

Flavell, J. E., Azrin, N., Baumeister, A., Carr, E., Dorsey, M., Forehand, R., et al. (1982). The treatment of self-injurious behavior. *Behavior Therapy, 13,* 529–554.

Flavell, J. H. (1996). Piaget's legacy. *Psychological Science, 7,* 200–203.

Fleeson, W., Malanos, A. B., & Achille, N. M. (2002). An intraindividual process approach to the relationship between extraversion and positive affect: Is acting extraverted as "good" as being extraverted? *Journal of Personality & Social Psychology, 83,* 1409–1422.

Flegal, K. M., Carroll, M. D., Ogden, C. L., & Johnson, C. L. (2002). Prevalence and trends in obesity among US adults, 1999–2000. *Journal of the American Medical Association, 288,* 1723–1727.

Fleishman, E. A., & Harris, E. F. (1962). Patterns of leadership behavior related to employee grievances and turnover. *Personnel Psychology, 15,* 43–56.

Flor, H. (2002). The modification of cortical reorganization and chronic pain by sensory feedback. *Applied Psychophysiological Biofeedback, 27,* 215–227.

Flor, H., Birbaumer, N., Herman, C., Ziegler, S., & Patrick, C. J. (2002). Aversive Pavlovian conditioning in psychopaths: Peripheral and central correlates. *Psychophysiology, 39,* 505–518.

Flynn, J. T. (1999). Searching for justice: The discovery of IQ gains over time. *American Psychologist, 54,* 5–20.

Foa, E. B., Dancu, C. V., Hembree, E. A., Jaycox, L. H., Meadows, E. A., & Street, G. P. (1999). A comparison of exposure therapy, stress-inoculation training, and their combination for reducing posttraumatic stress disorder in female assault victims. *Journal of Consulting and Clinical Psychology, 67,* 194–200.

Foa, E. B., Franklin, M. E., Perry, K. J., & Herbert, J. D. (1996). Cognitive biases in generalized social phobia. *Journal of Abnormal Psychology, 105,* 433–439.

Foa, E. B., & Kozak, M. J. (1995). DSM-IV field trial: Obsessive-compulsive disorder. *American Journal of Psychiatry, 152,* 90–96.

Folk, C. L., Remington, R. W., & Wright, J. H. (1994). The structure of attentional control: Contingent attentional capture by apparent motion, abrupt onset, and color. *Journal of Experimental Psychology: Human Perception and Performance, 20,* 317–329.

Folkman, S., & Lazarus, R. (1988). *Manual for the ways of coping questionnaire.* Palo Alto, CA: Consulting Psychologists Press.

Folkman, S., Lazarus, R. S., Dunkel-Schetter, C., DeLongis, A., & Gruen, R. J. (2000). The dynamics of a stressful encounter. In E. T. Higgins & A. W. Kruglanski (Eds.), *Motivational science: Social and personality perspectives* (pp. 111–127). Hove, UK: Psychology Press.

Folkman, S., Lazarus, R. S., Gruen, R. J., & DeLongis, A. (1986). Appraisal, coping, health status, and psychological symptoms. *Journal of Personality and Social Psychology, 50,* 571–579.

Folkman, S., & Moskowitz, J. T. (2000). Stress, positive emotion, and coping. *Current Directions in Psychological Science, 9,* 115–118.

Fontaine, K. R., Redden, D. T., Wang, C., Westfall, A. O., & Allison, D. B. (2003). Years of life lost due to obesity. *Journal of the American Medical Association, 289,* 187–193.

Forbes, S., Bui, S., Robinson, B. R., Hochgeschwender, U., & Brennan, M. B. (2001). Integrated control of appetite and fat metabolism by the leptin-proopiommelanocortin pathway. *Proceedings of the National Academy of Science, 98,* 4233–4237.

Ford, D. E., & Kamerow, D. B. (1989). Epidemiological study of sleep disturbances and psychiatric disorders: An opportunity for prevention? *Journal of the American Medical Association, 262,* 1479–1484.

Foroud, T., Edenberg, H. J., Goate, A., Rice, J., Flury, L., Koller, D. L., et al. (2000). Alcoholism susceptibility loci: Confirmation studies in a replicate sample and further mapping. *Alcoholism: Clinical and Experimental Research, 24,* 933–945.

Fosse, R., Stickgold, R., & Hobson, J. A. (2001). Brain-mind states: Reciprocal variation in thoughts and hallucinations. *Psychological Science, 12,* 30–36.

Foster, M. D. (2000). Positive and negative responses to personal discrimination: Does coping make a difference? *Journal of Social Psychology, 140,* 93–106.

Foulkes, D. (1985). *Dreaming: A cognitive-psychological analysis.* Hillsdale, NJ: Erlbaum.

Fountain, J. W. (2000, November 28). Exorcists and Exorcisms Proliferate Across U.S. *The New York Times.*

Fowler, R. D. (2000). A lesson in taking our own advice. *Monitor on Psychology, 31,* 9.

Fowles, D. (1992). Schizophrenia: Diathesis-stress revisited. *Annual Review of Psychology, 43,* 303–336.

Fox, A. S., & Olster, D. H. (2000). Effects of intracerebroventricular leptin administration on feeding and sexual behaviors in lean and obese female zucker rats. *Hormones and Behavior, 37,* 377–387.

Fox, S., Spector, P. E., & Miles, D. (2001). Counterproductive work behavior (CWB) in response to job stressors and organizational justice: Some mediator and moderator tests for autonomy and emotions. *Journal of Vocational Behavior, 59,* 291–309.

Foxhall, K. (2000). Research for the real world. *Monitor on Psychology, 31,* 28–36.

Fozard, J., Wolf, E., Bell, B., Farland, R., & Podolsky, S. (1977). Visual perception and communication. In J. Birren & K. Schaie (Eds.), *Handbook of the psychology of aging.* New York: Van Nostrand Reinhold.

Frank, J. D., & Frank, J. B. (1991). *Persuasion and healing: A comparative study of psychotherapy* (3rd ed.). Baltimore, MD: Johns Hopkins University Press.

Frank, J. S. (1978). *Psychotherapy and the human predicament.* New York: Schocken Books.

Frank, M. G., Ekman, P., & Friesen, W. V. (1993). Behavioral markers and recognizability of the smile of enjoyment. *Journal of Personality and Social Psychology, 64*(1), 83–93.

Frankenberg, W. K., & Dodds, J. B. (1967). The Denver developmental screening test. *Journal of Pediatrics, 71,* 181–191.

Franzoi, S. (2003). *Social psychology* (3rd ed.). New York: McGraw-Hill.

Freed, C. R., Greene, P. E., Breeze, R. E., Tsai, W. Y., DuMouchel, W., Kao, R., et al.(2001). Transplantation of embryonic dopamine neurons for severe Parkinson's disease. *New England Journal of Medicine, 344,* 710–719.

Freedland, R. L., & Bertenthal, B. I. (1994). Developmental changes in interlimb coordination: Transition to hands-and-knees crawling. *Psychological Science, 5,* 26–32.

Freedman, J. L. (1992). Television violence and aggression: What psychologists should tell the public. In P. Suedfeld & P. E. Tetlock (Eds.), *Psychology and social policy.* New York: Hemisphere.

Freedman, J. L., & Fraser, S. C. (1966). Compliance without pressure: The foot-in-the-door technique. *Journal of Personality and Social Psychology, 4,* 195–202.

Freedman, V. A., Aykan, H., & Martin, L. G. (2001). Aggregate changes in severe cognitive impairment among older Americans: 1993 and 1998. *Journal of Gerontology, 56B,* S100–S111.

Freeman, M. P., Freeman, S. A., & McElroy, S. L. (2002). The comorbidity of bipolar and anxiety disorders: Prevalence, psychobiology, and treatment issues. *Journal of Affective Disorders, 68,* 1–23.

Fremerman, S. (1998, March–April). Clearing the fog: How to sharpen your mind. *Natural Health.* Retrieved November 11, 2002, from http://www.findarticles.com/cf_0/m0NAH/n2_v27/20353564/p1/article.jhtml?term=%22Clearing+the+fog%22

Fremgen, A., & Fay, D. (1980). Overextensions in production and comprehension: A methodological clarification. *Journal of Child Language, 7,* 205–211.

Freres, D. R., Gillham, J. E., Reivich, K., & Shatte, A. J. (2002). Preventing depressive symptoms in middle school students: The Penn Resiliency Program. *International Journal of Emergency Mental Health, 4,* 31–40.

Frese, M., Beimel, S., & Schoenborn, S. (2003). Action training for charismatic leadership: Two evaluations of studies of a commercial training module on inspirational communication of a vision. *Personnel Psychology, 56,* 671–697.

Freud, S. (1900). The interpretation of dreams. In J. Strachey (Ed.), *The standard edition of the complete psychological works of Sigmund Freud* (Vol. 8). London: Hogarth Press.

Fridlund, A., Sabini, J. P., Hedlund, L. E., Schaut, J. A., Shenker, J. I., & Knauer, M. J. (1990). Audience effects on solitary faces during imagery: Displaying to the people in your head. *Journal of Nonverbal Behavior, 14*(2), 113–137.

Fried, P. A., Watkinson, B., & Gray, R. (1992). A follow-up study of attentional behavior in 6-year-old children exposed prenatally to marijuana, cigarettes, and alcohol. *Neurotoxicity and Teratology, 14*(5), 299–311.

Fried, Y., & Ferris, G. R. (1987). The validity of the job characteristics model: A review and meta-analysis. *Personnel Psychology, 40,* 287–322.

Fried, Y., & Tiegs, R. B. (1995). Supervisors' role conflict and role ambiguity differential relations with performance ratings of subordinates and the moderating effect of screening ability. *Journal of Applied Psychology, 80,* 282–291.

Friedland, R. P., Fritsch, T., Smyth, K. A., Koss, E., Lerner, A. J., Chen, C. H., et al. (2001). Patients with Alzheimer's disease have reduced activities in midlife compared with healthy control-group members. *Proceedings of the National Academy of Science, 98,* 3440–3445.

Friedman, E., Clark, D., & Gershon, S. (1992). Stress, anxiety, and depression: Review of biological, diagnostic, and nosologic issues. *Journal of Anxiety Disorders, 6,* 337–363.

Friedman, H. S., & Schustack, M. W. (2003). *Personality: Classic theories and modern research.* Boston: Allyn & Bacon.

Friedman, H. S., Tucker, J. S., Schwartz, J. E., Martin, L. R., Tomlinson-Keasey, C., Wingard, D. L., & Criqui, M. H. (1995a). Childhood conscientiousness and longevity: Health behaviors and cause of death. *Journal of Personality and Social Psychology, 68,* 696–703.

Friedman, H. S., Tucker, J. S., Schwartz, J. E., Tomlinson-Keasey, C., Martin, L. R., Wingard, D. L., & Criqui, M. H. (1995b). Psychosocial and behavioral predic-

tors of longevity: The aging and death of the "Termites." *American Psychologist, 50,* 69–78.

Friedman, M., & Rosenman, R. H. (1974). *Type A behavior and your heart.* New York: Knopf.

Fritzler, B. K., Hecker, J. E., & Losee, M. C. (1997). Self-directed treatment with minimal therapist contact: Preliminary findings for obsessive-compulsive disorder. *Behaviour Research and Therapy, 35,* 627–631.

Fritzsche, B., Finkelstein, M., & Penner, L. A. (2000). To help or not to help: Capturing individual's decision policies. *Social Behavior and Personality, 28,* 561–578.

Fuligni, A. J., & Pedersen, S. (2002). Family obligation and the transition to young adulthood. *Developmental Psychology, 38*(5), 856–868.

Funder, D. (2001a). Personality. *Annual Review of Psychology, 52,* 197–222.

Funder, D. (2001b). *The personality puzzle* (2nd ed.). New York: Norton.

Funtowicz, M. N., & Widiger, T. A. (1999). Sex bias in the diagnosis of personality disorders: An evaluation of DSM-IV criteria. *Journal of Abnormal Psychology, 108,* 195–201.

Furey, M. L., Pietrini, P., & Haxby, J. V. (2000). Cholinergic enhancement and increased selectivity of perceptual processing during working memory. *Science, 290,* 2315–2319.

Furnham, A. (2001). Personality and individual differences in the workplace: Person-organization-outcome fit. In R. Hogan & B. Roberts (Eds.), *Personality psychology in the workplace* (pp. 223–251). Washington, DC: American Psychological Association.

Gabbard, G. O. (2000). *Psychodymanic psychiatry in clinical practice* (3rd ed.). Washington, DC: American Psychiatric Press, Inc.

Gabrieli, J. D. E. (1998). Cognitive neuroscience of human memory. *Annual Review of Psychology, 49,* 87–115.

Gabryel, B., & Trzeciak, H. I. (1994). Nootropics: pharmacological properties and therapeutic use. *Polish Journal of Pharmacology, 46,* 383–94.

Galanter, E. (1962). Contemporary psychophysics. In R. Brown (Ed.), *New directions in psychology* (Vol. 1). New York: Holt, Rinehart, Winston.

Galatzer-Levy, R. M., Bachrach, H., Skolnikoff, A., & Waldron, S., Jr. (2000). *Does psychoanalysis work?* New Haven, CT: Yale University Press.

Galea, S., Ahern, J., Resnick H., Kilpatrick D., Bucuvalas M., Gold, J., & Vlahov, D. (2002). Psychological sequelae of the September 11 terrorist attacks in New York City. *New England Journal of Medicine, 346,* 982–987.

Galea, S., Resnick, H., Ahern, J., Gold, J., Bucuvalas, M., Kilpatrick, D., et al.. (2002). Posttraumatic stress disorder in Manhattan, New York City, after the September 11th terrorist attacks. *Journal of Urban Health, 79,* 340–353.

Gallagher, M. (1998, January 26). Day careless. *National Review,* pp. 37–41.

Gallagher, M., & Chiba, A. A. (1996). The amygdala and emotion. *Current Opinions in Neurobiology, 6*(2), 221–227.

Gallup. (1999, August 29). *American workers generally satisfied, but indicate their jobs leave much to be desired.* Princeton, NJ: Gallup Organization.

Galotti, K. M. (1999). *Cognitive psychology in and out of the laboratory* (2nd ed.). Belmont, CA: Brooks/Cole.

Ganchrow, J. R., Steiner, J. E., & Daher, M. (1983). Neonatal facial expressions in response to different qualities and intensities of gustatory stimuli. *Infant Behavior and Development, 6,* 189–200.

Garb, H. N. (1997). Race bias, social class bias, and gender bias in clinical judgment. *Clinical Psychology: Science and Practice, 4,* 99–120.

Garb, H. N., Florio, C. M., & Grove, W. M. (1998). The validity of the Rorschach and the Minnesota Multiphasic Personality Inventory: Results from meta-analyses. *Psychological Science, 9,* 402–404.

Garbarino, S., Nobili, L., Beelke, M., De Carli, F., & Ferrillo, F. (2001). The contributing role of sleepiness in highway vehicle accidents. *Sleep: Journal of Sleep Research and Sleep Medicine, 24,* 203–206.

Garber, J., Keiley, M. K., & Martin, N. C. (2002). Developmental trajectories of adolescents' depressive symptoms: Predictors of change. *Journal of Consulting and Clinical Psychology, 70,* 9–95.

Garcia, J., & Koelling, R. A. (1966). Relation of cue to consequences in avoidance learning. *Psychonomic Science, 4,* 123–124.

Garcia, S. M., Weaver, K., Moskowitz, G. B., & Darley, J. M. (2002). Crowded minds: The implicit bystander effect. *Journal of Personality and Social Psychology, 83,* 843–853.

Gardner, H. (1993). *Multiple intelligences: The theory in practice.* New York: Basic Books.

Gardner, H. (1998). Are there additional intelligences? The case for naturalistic, spiritual, and existential intelligence. In J. Kane (Ed.), *Education, information, and transformation.* Englewood Cliffs, NJ: Prentice-Hall.

Gardner, H. (1999). Are there additional intelligences? The case for naturalist, spiritual, and existential intelligences. In J. Kane (Ed.), *Education, information and transformation: Essays on learning and thinking* (pp. 111–131). Englewood Cliffs, NJ: Prentice Hall.

Gardner, H. (2002). *Learning from extraordinary minds.* Mahwah, NJ: Erlbaum.

Gardner, R., Heward, W. L., & Grossi, T. A. (1994). Effects of response cards on student participation and academic achievement: A systematic replication with inner-city students during whole-class science instruction. *Journal of Applied Behavior Analysis, 27,* 63–71.

Garfield, S. L. (1998). Some comments on empirically supported treatments. *Journal of Consulting and Clinical Psychology, 66,* 121–125.

Garland, A. F., & Zigler, E. (1993). Adolescent suicide prevention: Current research and social policy implications. *American Psychologist, 48,* 169–182.

Garry, M., & Loftus, E. (1994). Pseudomemories without hypnosis. *International Journal of Clinical and Experimental Hypnosis, 42*(4), 363–373.

Garry, M., & Polaschek, D. L. L. (2000). Imagination and memory. *Current Directions in Psychological Science, 9,* 6–10.

Gaster, B., & Holroyd, J. (2000). St. John's wort for depression: A systematic review. *Archives of Internal Medicine, 160,* 152–156.

Gates, G. A., & Miyamoto, R. T. (2003). Cochlear implants. *The New England Journal of Medicine, 349,* 421–423.

Gatewood, R. D., & Feild, H. S. (2001). *Human resource selection* (5th ed.). Fort Worth, TX: Harcourt.

Gatz, M., Svedberg, P., Pedersen, N. L., Mortimer, J. A., Berg, S., & Johansson, B. (2001). Education and the risk of Alzheimer's disease: findings from the study of dementia in Swedish twins. *Journals of Gerontology, Series B, Psychological Sciences and Social Sciences, 56,* 292–300.

Gauvain, M. (2001). *The social context of cognitive development.* New York: Guilford.

Gazzaniga, M. S., Fendrich, R., & Wessinger, C. M. (1994). Blindsight reconsidered. *Current Directions in Psychological Science, 3*(3), 93–95.

Gazzaniga, M. S., & LeDoux, J. E. (1978). *The integrated mind.* New York: Plenum.

Ge, X., Conger, R., & Elder, G. H. (2001) Pubertal transition, stressful life events, and the emergence of gender differences in adolescent depressive symptoms. *Developmental Psychology, 37,* 404–417.

Geary, D. C. (1999). Evolution and developmental sex differences. *Current Directions in Psychological Science, 8,* 115–120.

Geary, D. C. (2000). Evolution and proximate expression of human paternal investment. *Psychological Bulletin, 126,* 55–77.

Geen, R. G. (1998a). Aggression and antisocial behavior. In D. Gilbert, S. T. Fiske, & G. Lindzey (Eds.), *Handbook of social psychology* (Vol. 2, 4th ed., pp. 317–356). Boston: McGraw-Hill.

Geen, R. G. (1998b). Process and personal variables in affective aggression. In R. G. Geen & E. Donnerstein (Eds.), *Human aggression* (pp. 2–24). San Diego: Academic Press.

Gelabert-Gonzalez, M., & Fernandez-Villa, J. (2001). Mutism after posterior fossa surgery: Review of the literature. *Clinical Neurology & Neurosurgery, 103,* 111–114.

Gelman, R., & Baillargeon, R. (1983). A review of some Piagetian concepts. In P. H. Mussen (Ed.), *Handbook of child psychology* (Vol. 3, pp. 167–230). New York: Wiley.

George, M. S., Antonm, R. F., Bloomer, C., Teneback, C., Drobes, D. J., Lorberbaum, J. P., et al. (2001). Activation of prefrontal cortex and anterior thalamus in alcoholic subjects on exposure to alcohol-specific cues. *Archives of General Psychiatry, 58,* 345–352.

George, W. H., & Marlatt, G. A. (1986). The effects of alcohol and anger on interest in violence, erotica, and deviance. *Journal of Abnormal Psychology, 95,* 150–158.

Gerbner, G., Morgan, M., & Signorielli, N. (1994). *Television violence profile No. 16: The turning point.* Philadelphia: Annenberg School for Communication.

Gerschman, J. A., Reade, P. C., & Burrows, G. D. (1980). Hypnosis and dentistry. In G. D. Burrows & L. Dennerstein (Eds.), *Handbook of hypnosis and psychosomatic medicine.* Amsterdam: Elsevier.

Gershoff, E. T. (2002). Corporal punishment by parents and associated child behaviors and experiences: A meta-analytic and theoretical review. *Psychological Bulletin, 128,* 539–579.

Gershon, A. A., Dannon, P. N., & Grunhaus, L. (2003). Transcranial magnetic stimulation in the treatment of depression. *American Journal of Psychiatry, 160,* 835–845.

Gershon, J., Anderson, P., Graap, K., Zimand, E., Hodges, L., & Rothbaum, B. O. (2002). Virtual reality exposure therapy in the treatment of anxiety disorders. *The Scientific Review of Mental Health Practice, 1.* Retrieved October 12, 2002 from http://www.scientificmentalhealth.org/SRMHP/current.html

Gerstner, C. R., & Day, D. V. (1997). Meta-analytic review of leader–member exchange theory: Correlates and construct issues. *Journal of Applied Psychology, 82,* 827–844.

Gessner, B. D., Ives, G. C., & Perham-Hester, K. A. (2001). Association between sudden infant death syndrome and prone sleep position, bed sharing, and sleeping outside an infant crib in Alaska. *Pediatrics, 108,* 923–927.

Gfeller, J. D. (1994). Hypnotizability enhancement: Clinical implications of empirical findings. *American Journal of Clinical Hypnosis, 37*(2), 107–116.

Gianakos, I. (2002). Predictors of coping with work stress: The influences of sex, gender role, social desirability, and locus of control. *Sex Roles, 46,* 149–158.

Gibbs, W. W. (1996). Gaining on fat. *Scientific American, 275,* 88–94.

Gibson, E., Dembofsky, C. A., Rubin, S., & Greenspan, J. S. (2000). Infant sleep position practices 2 years into the "back to sleep" campaign. *Clinical Pediatrics, 39,* 285–289.

Gibson, E. J., & Walk, R. D. (1960). The visual cliff. *Scientific American, 202,* 64–71.

Gifford, R., & Hine, D. (1997). Toward cooperation in the commons dilemma. *Canadian Journal of Behavioural Science, 29,* 167–178.

Gilbert, A. R., Rosenberg, D. R., Harenski, K., Spencer, S., Sweeney, J. A., & Keshavan, M. S. (2001). Thalamic volumes in patients with first-episode schizophrenia. *American Journal of Psychiatry, 158,* 618–624.

Gilbert, D. T. (1998). Ordinary personology. In D. Gilbert, S. T. Fiske, & G. Lindzey (Eds.), *Handbook of social psychology* (Vol.2, 4th ed., pp. 89–150). Boston: McGraw-Hill.

Gilbert, D. T., & Malone, P. S. (1995). The correspondence bias. *Psychological Bulletin, 117,* 21–38.

Gilbert, D. T., & Wilson, T. D. (1998). Miswanting: Some problems in the forecasting of future affective states. In J. P. Forgas (Ed.), *Feeling and thinking: The role of affect in social cognition* (pp. 178–197). New York: Cambridge University Press.

Gilbert, S. (1997, August 20). Two spanking studies indicate parents should be cautious. *New York Times Magazine.*

Gilboa-Schechtman, E., & Foa, E. B. (2001). Patterns of recovery from trauma: The use of intraindividual analysis. *Journal of Abnormal Psychology, 110,* 392–400.

Giles, T. R. (1990). Bias against behavior therapy in outcome reviews: Who speaks for the patient? *The Behavior Therapist, 13,* 86–90.

Gilligan, C. (1982). *In a different voice: Psychological theory and women's development.* Cambridge, MA: Harvard University Press.

Gilligan, C. (1993). Adolescent development reconsidered. In A. Garrod (Ed.), *Approaches to moral development: New research and emerging themes.* New York: Teachers College Press.

Gilliland, F. D., Li, Y.-F., & Peters, J. M. (2001). Effects of maternal smoking during pregnancy and environmental tobacco smoke on asthma and wheezing in children. *American Journal of Respiratory and Critical Care Medicine, 163,* 429–436.

Gilman, A. G., Goodman, L. S., Rall, T. W., & Murad, F. (1985). *Goodman and Gilman's the pharmacological basis of therapeutics* (7th ed.). New York: Macmillan.

Gilovich, T. (1997). Some systematic biases of everyday judgment. *Skeptical Inquirer, 21,* 31–35.

Giosan, C., Glovsky, V., & Haslam, N. (2001). The lay conception of "mental disorder": A cross-cultural study. *Transcultural Psychiatry, 38,* 317–332.

Givens, B. (1995). Low doses of ethanol impair spatial working memory and reduce hippocampal theta activity. *Alcoholism Clinical and Experimental Research, 19*(3), 763–767.

Glantz, K., Rizzo, A., & Graap, K. (2003). Virtual reality for psychotherapy: Current reality and future possibilities. *Psychotherapy: Theory, Research, Practice, and Training, 40,* 55–67.

Glanzer, M., & Cunitz, A. (1966). Two storage mechanisms in free recall. *Journal of Verbal Learning and Verbal Behavior, 5,* 351–360.

Glassop, L. I. (2002). The organizational benefits of teams. *Human Relations, 55,* 225–249.

Gleaves, D. H., May, M. C., & Cardena, E. (2001). An examination of the diagnostic validity of dissociative identity disorder. *Clinical Psychology Review, 21,* 577–608.

Gleitman, L., & Landau, B. (1994). *The acquisition of the lexicon.* Cambridge: MIT Press.

Glenmullen, J. (2000). *Prozac backlash: Overcoming the dangers of Prozac, Zoloft, Paxil, and other antidepressants with safe, effective alternatives.* New York: Simon & Schuster.

Gleuckauf, R., & Quittner, A. (1992). Assertiveness training for disabled adults in wheelchairs: Self-report, role-play, and activity pattern outcomes. *Journal of Consulting and Clinical Psychology, 60,* 419–425.

Glover, J. A., Krug, D., Dietzer, M., George, B. W., & Hannon, M. (1990). "Advance" advance organizers. *Bulletin of the Psychonomic Society, 28,* 4–6.

Goenjian, A. K., Molina, L., Steinberg, A. M., Fairbanks, L. A., Alvarez, M. L., Goenjian, H. A., & Pynoos, R. S. (2001). Posttraumatic stress and depressive reactions among Nicaraguan adolescents after hurricane Mitch. *American Journal of Psychiatry, 158,* 788–794.

Gold, M. S. (1994). The epidemiology, attitudes, and pharmacology of LSD use in the 1990s. *Psychiatric Annals, 24*(3), 124–126.

Gold, P. E., Cahill, L., & Wenk, G. L. (2003). The lowdown on Ginkgo biloba. *Scientific American, 288,* 86–91.

Goldberg, J. F., Harrow, M., & Grossman, L. S. (1995). Course and outcome in bipolar affective disorder: A longitudinal follow-up study. *American Journal of Psychiatry, 152,* 379–384.

Goldenberg, I., & Goldenberg, H. (1995). Family therapy. In R. J. Corsini & D. Wedding (Eds.), *Current psychotherapies* (5th ed.). Itasca, IL: Peacock.

Goldfried, M. R., Castonguay, L. G., Hayes, A. M., Drozd, J. F., & Shapiro, D. A. (1997). A comparative analysis of the therapeutic focus in cognitive-behavioral and psychodynamic-interpersonal sessions. *Journal of Consulting and Clinical Psychology, 65,* 720–748.

Goldman, M. S., Darkes, J., & Del Boca, F. K. (1999). Expectancy meditation of biopsychosocial risk for alcohol use and alcoholism. In I. Kirsch (Ed.), *How expectancies shape experience* (pp. 233–262). Washington, DC: American Psychological Association.

Goldstein, A. J., de Beurs, E., Chambless, D. L., & Wilson, K. A. (2000). EMDR for panic disorder with agoraphobia: Comparison with waiting list and credible attention-placebo control conditions. *Journal of Consulting and Clinical Psychology, 68,* 947–956.

Goldstein, E. B. (1999). *Sensation and perception* (5th ed.). Pacific Grove, CA: Brooks/Cole.

Goldstein, I. L. (1993). *Training in organizations: Needs assessment, development, and evaluation* (3rd ed.). Monterey, CA: Brooks/Cole.

Goldstein, I., & Rosen, R. C. (Eds.). (2002). Guest editors' introduction: Female sexuality and sexual dysfunction. *Archives of Sexual Behavior, 31,* 391.

Goldstein, M. H., King, A. P., & West, M. J. (2003). Social interaction shapes babbling: Testing parallels between birdsong and speech. *Proceedings of the National Academy of Sciences, 100,* 8030–8035.

Goldstein, R. Z., & Volkow, N. D. (2002). Drug addiction and its underlying neurobiological basis: Neuroimaging evidence for the involvement of the frontal cortex. *American Journal of Psychiatry,159,* 1642–1652.

Golomb, J., Kluger, A., De Leon, M. J., Ferris, S. H., Convit, A., Mittelman, M. S., et al. (1994). Hippocampal formation size in normal human aging: A correlate of delayed secondary memory performance. *Learning and Memory, 1,* 45–54.

Goltz, H. C., DeSouza, J. F. X., Menon, R. S., Tweed, D. B., & Vilis, T. (2003). Interaction of retinal image and eye velocity in motion perception. *Neuron, 39,* 569–576.

Gonsalves, B., & Paller, K. A. (2000). Neural events that underlie remembering something that never happened. *Nature Neuroscience, 3,* 1316–1321.

Goode, K. T., Haley, W. E., Roth, D. L., & Ford, G. L. (1998). Predicting longitudinal changes in caregiver physical and mental health: A stress process model. *Health Psychology, 17,* 190–198.

Goodenough, F. L. (1932). Expression of the emotions in a blind-deaf child. *Journal of Abnormal and Social Psychology, 27,* 328–333.

Goodman, G. S., Ghetti, S., Quas, J. A., Edelstein, R. S., Alexander, K. W., Redlich, A. D., et al. (2003). A prospective study of memory for child sexual abuse: New findings relevant to the repressed-memory controversy. *Psychological Science, 14,* 113–118.

Goodwin, F. K., Fireman, B., Simon, G. E., Hunkeler, E. M., Lee, J., & Revicki, D. (2003). Suicide risk in bipolar disorder during treatment with lithium and divalproex. *Journal of the American Medical Association, 290,* 1467–1473.

Goodwin, F. K., & Jamison, K. R. (Eds.). (1990). *Manic-depressive illness.* New York: Oxford University Press.

Gordijn, E. H., De Vries, N. K., & De Dreu, C. K. (2002). Minority influence on focal and related attitudes: Change in size, attributions and information processing. *Personality and Social Psychology Bulletin, 28,* 1315–1326.

Gorman, J. M. (2002). Treatment of generalized anxiety disorder. *Journal of Clinical Psychiatry, 63,* 17–23.

Gosling, S. D. (2001). From mice to men: What can we learn about personality from animal research? *Psychological Bulletin, 127,* 45–86.

Gotlib, I. H., & Hammen, C. L. (1992). *Psychological aspects of depression: Toward cognitive interpersonal integration.* Chichester, England: Wiley.

Gottesman, I. I. (1991). *Schizophrenia genesis.* New York: Freeman.

Gottfredson, L. S. (1997). Why g matters: The complexity of everyday life. *Intelligence, 24,* 79–132.

Gottfried, A. W. (1997, June). Parents' role is critical to children's learning. *APA Monitor,* p. 24.

Gottfried, J. A., O'Doherty, J., & Dolan, R. J. (2003). Encoding predictive reward value in human amygdala and orbitofrontal cortex. *Science, 301,* 1104–1107.

Gottman, J. M., Coan, J., Carrere, S., & Swanson, C. (1998). Predicting marital happiness and stability from newlywed interactions. *Journal of Marriage and the Family, 60,* 5–22.

Gottman, J. M., & Levenson, R. W. (2000). The timing of divorce: Predicting when a couple will divorce over a 14-year period. *Journal of Marriage and the Family, 62,* 737–745.

Gould, E., Beylin, A., Tanapat, P., Reeves, A., & Shors, T. J. (1999). Learning enhances adult neurogenesis in the hippocampal formation. *Nature Neuroscience, 2,* 260–265.

Gould, R. A., Otto, M. W., Pollack, M. H., & Yap, L. (1997). Cognitive behavioral and pharmacological treatment of generalized anxiety disorder: A preliminary meta-analysis. *Behavior Therapy, 28,* 285–305.

Grandin, T. (1996). *Thinking in pictures: And other reports from my life with autism.* New York: Vintage Press.

Grant, H., & Dweck, C. S. (2003). Clarifying achievement goals and their impact. *Journal of Personality and Social Psychology, 85,* 541–553.

Grant, J. E., & Kim, S. W. (2002). *Stop me because I can't stop myself: Taking control of impulsive behavior.* New York: McGraw-Hill.

Grassi, L., Rasconi, G., Pedriali, A., Corridoni, A., & Bevilacqua, M. (2000). Social support and psychological distress in primary care attenders. *Psychotherapy and Psychosomatics, 69,* 95–100.

Graves, L., Pack, A., & Abel, T. (2001). Sleep and memory: A molecular perspective. *Trends in Neurosciences, 24,* 237–243.

Gray, N. S., MacCulloch, M. J., Smith, J., Morris, M., & Snowden, R. J. (2003). Forensic psychology: Violence viewed by psychopathic murderers. *Nature, 423,* 497.

Gray, N., & Nye, P. S. (2001). American Indian and Alaska Native substance abuse: Co-morbidity and cultural issues. *American Indian and Alaska Native Mental Health Research, 10,* 67–84.

Gray-Little, B., & Hafdahl, A. R. (2000). Factors influencing racial comparisons of self-esteem: A quantitative review. *Psychological Bulletin, 126,* 26–54.

Graziano, M. S. A., Alisharan, S. E., Hu, X., & Gross, C. G. (2002). The clothing effect: Tactile neurons in the precentral gyrus do not respond to the touch of the familiar primate chair. *Proceedings of the New York Academy of Sciences, 99,* 11930–11933.

Graziano, M. S., Taylor, C. S., & Moore, T. (2002). Complex movements evoked by microstimulation of precentral cortex. *Neuron, 34,* 841–851.

Green, A. I., & Patel, J. K. (1996) The new pharmacology of schizophrenia. *Harvard Mental Health Letter, 13*(6), 5–7.

Green, C. S., & Bavelier, D. (2003). Action video game modifies visual selective attention. *Nature, 423,* 534–537.

Green, D. M., & Swets, J. A. (1966). *Signal detection theory and psychophysics.* New York: Wiley.

Green, J. P., & Lynn, S. J. (1995). Hypnosis, dissociation, and simultaneous task performance. *Journal of Personality and Social Psychology, 69,* 728–735.

Green, J. T., & Woodruff-Pak, D. S. (2000). Eyeblink classical conditioning: Hippocampal formation is for neutral stimulus associations as cerebellum is for association response. *Psychological Bulletin, 126,* 138–158.

Green, R. A., Cross, A. J., & Goodwin, G. M. (1995). Review of the pharmacology and clinical pharmacology of 3,4-methylenedioxymethamphetamine (MDMA or "ecstacy"). *Psychopharmacology, 119,* 247–260.

Greenberg, J., Arndt, J., Schimel, J., Pyszczynski, T., & Solomon, S. (2001). Clarifying the function of mortality salience-induced worldview defense: Renewed suppression or reduced accessibility of death-related thoughts? *Journal of Experimental Social Psychology, 37,* 70–76.

Greenberg, J. R., & Mitchell, S. A. (1983). *Object relations in psychoanalytic theory.* Cambridge, MA: Harvard University Press.

Greenberg, J., Pyszczynski, T., & Solomon, S. (2003). A perilous leap from Becker's theorizing to empirical science: Terror management and research. In D. Leichty (Ed.), *Death and denial: Interdisciplinary essays: The legacy of Ernest Becker.* New York: Praeger.

Greenberg, J., Solomon, S., Pyszczynski, T., & Rosenblatt, A. (1992). Why do people need self-esteem? Converging evidence that self-esteem serves an anxiety-buffering function. *Journal of Personality and Social Psychology, 63,* 913–922.

Greenberg, M. T., Lengua, L. J., Coie, J. D., Pinderhughes, E. E., Bierman, K., Dodge, K. A., et al. (1999). Predicting developmental outcomes at school entry using a multiple-risk model: Four American communities. *Developmental Psychology, 35,* 403–417.

Greenblatt, D., Harmatz, J., & Shader, R. I. (1993). Plasma alprazolam concentrations: Relation to efficacy and side effects in the treatment of panic disorder. *Archives of General Psychiatry, 50,* 715–732.

Greenfield, P. M. (1994). Video games as cultural artifacts. *Journal of Applied Developmental Psychology, 15,* 3–12.

Greenfield, P. M. (1995, Winter). Culture, ethnicity, race, and development: Implications for teaching theory and research. *Society for Research in Child Development Newsletter,* pp. 3, 4, 12.

Greenfield, P. M., Camaioni, L., Ercolani, P., Weiss, L., Lauber, B. A., & Perucchini, P. (1994). Cognitive socialization by computer games in two cultures: Inductive discovery or mastery of an iconic code? *Journal of Applied Developmental Psychology, 15,* 59–86.

Greenfield, P. M., & Childs, C. P. (1991). Developmental continuity in biocultural context. In R. Cohen & A. W. Siegel (Eds.), *Context and development* (pp. 135–159). Hillsdale, NJ: Erlbaum.

Greenhaus, J. H., Parasuraman, S., & Wormley, W. M. (1990). Effects of race on organizational experiences, job performance evaluations, and career outcomes. *Academy of Management Journal, 33,* 64–86.

Greenland, P., Knoll, M. D., Stamler, J., Neaton, J. D., Dyer, A. R., Garside, D. B., & Wilson, P. W. (2003). Major risk factors as antecedents of fatal and nonfatal coronary heart disease events. *Journal of the American Medical Association, 290,* 891–897.

Greenwald, A. G., & Banaji, M. R. (1995). Implicit social cognition: Attitudes, self-esteem, and stereotypes. *Psychological Review, 102,* 4–27.

Greenwald, A. G., Klinger, M. R., & Schuh, E. S. (1995). Activation by marginally perceptible ("subliminal") stimuli: Dissociation of unconscious from conscious cognition. *Experimental Psychology: General, 124*(1), 22–42.

Greer, A. E., & Buss, D. M. (1994). Tactics for promoting sexual encounters. *Journal of Sex Research, 31*(3), 185–201.

Griffeth, R. W., Hom, P. W., & Gaertner, S. (2000). A meta-analysis of antecedents and correlates of employee turnover: Update, moderator tests, and research implications for the next millennium. *Journal of Management, 26,* 463–488.

Griffin, M. A., & Neal, A. (2000). Perceptions of safety at work: A framework for linking safety climate to safety performance, knowledge, and motivation. *Journal of Occupational Health Psychology, 5,* 347–358.

Griffitt, W. B., & Guay, P. (1969) "Object" evaluation and conditioned affect. *Journal of Experimental Research in Personality, 4,* 1–8.

Grigorenko, E. L. (2002). In search of the genetic engram of personality. In D. Cervone & W. Mischel (Eds.), *Advances in personality science* (pp. 29–82). New York: The Guilford Press.

Grinspoon, L. (1999). The future of medical marijuana. *Forsch Komplementarmed, 6,* 40–43.

Grinspoon, S., Thomas, E., Pitts, S., Gross, E., Mickley, D., Killer, K., et al. (2000). Prevalence and predictive factors for regional osteopenia in women with anorexia nervosa. *Annals of Internal Medicine, 133,* 790–794.

Grob, C., & Dobkin-de-Rios, M. (1992). Adolescent drug use in cross-cultural perspective. *Journal of Drug Issues, 22*(1), 121–138.

Groopman, J. (2000, January 24). Second opinion. *The New Yorker,* pp. 40–49.

Groopman, J. (2002, July 29). Hormones for men. *The New Yorker,* pp. 34–38.

Gross, J. J. (2001). Emotion regulation in adulthood: Timing is everything. *Current Directions in Psychological Science, 10,* 214–219.

Grote, N. K., & Clark, M. S. (2001). Perceiving unfairness in the family: Cause or consequence of marital distress? *Journal of Personality and Social Psychology, 80,* 281–293.

Groth-Marnat, G. (1997). *Handbook of psychological assessment* (3rd ed.). New York: Wiley.

Gruman, A. S., & Fraenkel, P. (2002). The history of couple therapy: A millennial review. *Family Process, 41,* 199–260.

Grunberg, N. E. (1994). Overview: Biological processes relevant to drugs of dependence. *Addiction, 89*(11), 1443–1446.

Grusec, J. E. (1991). Socialization of concern for others in the home. *Developmental Psychology, 27,* 338–342.

Grusec, J. E., & Goodnow, J. J. (1994). Impact of parental discipline methods on the child's internalization of values. *Developmental Psychology, 30,* 4–19.

Guerin, D. W., Gottfried, A. W., & Thomas, C. W. (1997). Difficult temperament and behaviour problems: A longitudinal study from 1.5 to 12 years. *International Journal of Behavioral Development, 21,* 71–90.

Guevara, M. A., Lorenzo, I., Ramos, J., & Corsi-Cabrera, M. (1995). Inter- and intra-hemispheric EEG correlation during sleep and wakefulness. *Sleep, 18*(4), 257–265.

Guilford, J. P. (1959). Traits of creativity. In H. H. Anderson (Ed.), *Creativity and its cultivation* (pp. 142–161). New York: Harper & Row.

Guilleminault, C., Palombini, L., Pelayo, R., & Chervin, R. D. (2003). Sleepwalking and sleep terrors in prepubertal children: What triggers them? *Pediatrics, 111,* 17–25.

Guntheroth, W. G., & Spiers, P. S. (1992). Sleeping prone and the risk of sudden infant death syndrome. *Journal of the American Medical Association, 267,* 2359–2362.

Guntheroth, W. G., & Spiers, P. S. (2002). The triple risk hypothesis in sudden infant death syndrome. *Pediatrics, 110,* p. e64.

Gupta, M. A., & Gupta, A. K. (2002, May 13). Use of eye movement desensitization and reprocessing (EMDR) in the treatment of dermatologic disorders. *Journal of Cutaneous Medicine and Surgery.*

Gur, R. E., Cowell, P. E., Latshaw, A., Turetsky, B. I., Grossman, R. I., Arnold, S. E., et al. (2000). Reduced dorsal and orbital prefrontal gray matter volumes in schizophrenia. *Archives of General Psychiatry, 57,* 761–768.

Gura, T. (1999). Leptin not impressive in clinical trial. *Science, 286,* 881–882.

Gustafson, D., Rothenberg, E., Blennow, K., Steen, B., & Skoog, I. (2003). An 18-year follow-up of overweight and risk of Alzheimer disease. *Archives of Internal Medicine, 163,* 1524–1528.

Guyer, B., Freedman, M. A., Strobino, D. M., & Sondik, E. J. (2000). Annual summary of vital statistics: Trends in the health of Americans during the 20th century. *Pediatrics, 106,* 1307–1317.

Guyton, A. C. (1991). *Textbook of medical physiology* (8th ed.). Philadelphia: Saunders.

Ha, H., Tan, E. C., Fukunaga, H., & Aochi, O. (1981). Naloxone reversal of acupuncture analgesia in the monkey. *Experimental Neurology, 73,* 298–303.

Haaga, D. A. (2000). Introduction to the special section on stepped care models in psychotherapy. *Journal of Consulting and Clinical Psychology, 68,* 547–548.

Haber, R. N. (1979). Twenty years of haunting eidetic imagery: Where's the ghost? *The Behavioral and Brain Sciences, 2,* 583–629.

Haberlandt, K. (1999). *Human memory: Exploration and application.* Boston: Allyn & Bacon.

Hackel, L. S., & Ruble, D. N. (1992). Changes in the marital relationship after the first baby is born: Predicting the impact of expectancy-disconfirmation. *Journal of Personality and Social Psychology, 62,* 944–957.

Hacking, I. (1995). *Rewriting the soul: Multiple personality and the sciences of memory.* Princeton, NJ: Princeton University Press.

Hackman, J. R. (1998). Why don't teams work? In R. S. Tindale, J. Edwards, & E. J. Posavac (Eds.), *Applications of theory and research on groups to social issues.* New York: Plenum.

Hackman, J. R., & Oldham, G. R. (1980). *Work redesign.* Reading, MA: Addison-Wesley.

Haddock, G., & Zanna, M. P. (1998). Authoritarianism, values, and the favorability and structure of antigay attitudes. In G. Herek (Ed.), *Stigma and sexual orientation: Understanding prejudice against lesbians, gay men, and bisexuals. Psychological perspectives on lesbian and gay issues.* New York: Sage.

Haefner, H., & Maurer, K. (2000). The early course of schizophrenia: New concepts for early intervention. In G. Andrews & S. Henderson (Eds.), *Unmet need in psychiatry: Problems, resources, responses* (p. 218–232). New York: Cambridge University Press.

Hake, R. R. (1998). Interactive-engagement vs. traditional methods: A six-thousand-student survey of mechanics test data for introductory physics courses. *American Journal of Physics, 66,* 64–74.

Hakuta, K., Bialystok, E., & Wiley, E. (2003). Critical evidence: A test of the critical-period hypothesis for second language acquisition. *Psychological Science, 14,* 31–38.

Haldeman, D. C. (1994). The practice and ethics of sexual orientation-conversion therapy. *Consulting and Clinical Psychology, 62*(2), 221–227.

Hall, C. S., Lindzey, G., & Campbell, J. P. (1998). *Theories of personality* (4th ed.). New York: Wiley.

Hall, G. C. N. (2001). Psychotherapy research with ethnic minorities: Empirical, ethical, and conceptual issues. *Journal of Consulting and Clinical Psychology, 69,* 502–510.

Hall, L. K., & Bahrick, H. P. (1998). The validity of metacognitive predictions of widespread learning and long-term retention. In G. Mazzoni & T. Nelson (Eds.), *Metacognition and cognitive neuropsychology: Monitoring and control processes* (pp. 23–36). Mahwah, NJ: Erlbaum.

Hall, R. C., Hoffman, R. S., Beresford, T. P., Wooley, B., et al. (1989). Physical illness encountered in patients with eating disorders. *Psychosomatics, 30,* 174–191.

Halligan, P. W., & David, A. S. (Eds.). (1999). *Conversion hysteria: Towards a cognitive neuropsychological account.* Hove, England: Psychology Press.

Halloran, M. J., & Kashima, E. S. (in press). Cultural validation in context: The effect of mortality salience on endorsement of cultural values in context defined by social identities. *Personality and Social Psychology Bulletin.*

Halpern, D. F. (1997). Sex differences in intelligence. *American Psychologist, 52,* 1091–1102.

Hamarat, E., Thompson, D., Steele, D., Matheny, K., & Simons, C. (2002). Age differences in coping resources and satisfaction with life among middle-aged, young-old, and oldest-old adults. *Journal of Genetic Psychology, 163*(3), 360–367.

Hamilton, D. L., & Sherman, J. (1994). Social stereotypes. In R. S. Wyer & T. K. Srull (Eds.), *Handbook of social cognition* (2nd ed.). Hillsdale, NJ: Erlbaum.

Hamilton, S. P., Fyer, A. J., Durner, M., Heiman, G. A., Baisre de Leon, A., Hodge, S. E., et al. (2003). Further genetic evidence for a panic disorder syndrome mapping to chromosome 13q. *Proceedings of the National Academy of Sciences, 100,* 2550–2255.

Hamm, A. O., Vaitl, D., & Lang, P. J. (1989). Fear conditioning, meaning, and belongingness: A selective association analysis. *Journal of Abnormal Psychology, 98,* 395–406.

Han, S., & Shavitt, S. (1994). Persuasion and culture: Advertising appeals in individualist and collectivist societies. *Journal of Experimental Social Psychology, 30,* 326–350.

Haney, M., Ward, A. S., Comer, S. D., Foltin, R. W., & Fischman, M. W. (1999). Abstinence symptoms following smoked marijuana in humans. *Psychopharmacology, 141,* 395–404.

Hankin, B. L., & Abramson, L. Y. (2001). Development of gender differences in depression: An elaborated cognitive vulnerability-transactional stress theory. *Psychological Bulletin, 127,* 773–796.

Hannigan, S. L., & Reinitz, M. T. (2001). A demonstration and comparison of two types of inference-based memory errors. *Journal of Experimental Psychology: Learning, Memory, and Cognition, 27,* 931–940.

Hanson, G., & Venturelli, P. J. (1995). *Drugs and society* (4th ed.). Boston: Jones & Bartlett.

Hare, R. D. (1993). *Without conscience: The disturbing world of the psychopaths among us.* New York: Pocket Books.

Harlow, H. F. (1949). The formation of learning sets. *Psychological Review, 56,* 51–65.

Harlow, H. F. (1959, June). Love in infant monkeys. *Scientific American,* pp. 68–74.

Harmon-Jones, E., Brehm, J. W., Greenberg, J., Simon, L., & Nelson, D. E. (1996). Evidence that the production of negative consequences is not necessary to produce cognitive dissonance. *Journal of Personality and Social Psychology, 72,* 515–525.

Harmon-Jones, E., & Devine, P. (2003). Introduction to the special section on social neuroscience: promise and caveats. *Journal of Personality and Social Psychology, 85,* 589–593.

Harper, R. C., Frysinger, J. D., Marks, J. X., & Zhang, R. B. (1988). Cardiorespiratory control during sleep. In P. J. Schwartz (Ed.), *The sudden infant death syndrome: Cardiac and respiratory mechanisms and interventions* (Annals of the New York Academy of Sciences, Vol. 533). New York: New York Academy of Sciences.

Harris, C. V., & Goetsch, V. L. (1990). Multi-component flooding treatment of adolescent phobia. In E. L. Feindler & G. R. Kalfus (Eds.), *Adolescent behavior therapy handbook* (Vol. 22). New York: Springer.

Harris, G. C., & Aston-Jones, G. (1995). Involvement of D2 dopamine receptors in the nucleus accumbens in opiate withdrawal syndrome. *Nature, 371,* 155–157.

Harris, J. R. (1995). Where is the child's environment? A group socialization theory of development. *Psychological Review, 102,* 458–489.

Harris, J. R. (1998). *The nurture assumption.* New York: Free Press.

Harris, J. R. (2000). Context-specific learning, personality, and birth order. *Current Directions in Psychological Science, 9,* 174–177.

Hart, A. J., Whalen, P. J., Shin, L. M., McInerney, S. C., Fischer, H., & Rauch, S. L. (2000). Differential response in the human amygdala to racial outgroup vs. ingroup face stimuli. *Neuroreport, 11,* 2351–2355.

Hartman, E., Baekeland, F., & Zwilling, G. (1972). Psychological differences between long and short sleepers. *Archives of General Psychiatry, 26,* 463–468.

Hartung, C. M., & Widiger, T. A. (1998). Gender differences in the diagnosis of mental disorders: Conclusions and controversies of *DSM-IV. Psychological Bulletin, 123,* 260–278.

Hartup, W. W., & Stevens, N. (1997). Friendships and adaptation in the life course. *Psychological Bulletin, 121,* 355–370.

Harvard Mental Health Letter. (1998a). Mood disorders: An overview—Part II. *Harvard Mental Health Letter, 14*(7), 1–5.

Harvard Mental Health Letter. (1998b). Mood disorders: An overview—Part III. *Harvard Mental Health Letter, 14*(8), 1–5.

Harwood, H., Fountain, D., & Livermore, G. (1998). *The economic costs of alcohol and drug abuse in the United States, 1992* (Publication No. 98–4327). Bethesda, MD: National Institute on Drug Abuse and the National Institute on Alcohol Abuse and Alcoholism.

Hastie, R., Penrod, S. D., & Pennington, N. (1984). *Inside the jury.* Cambridge: Harvard University Press.

Hatcher, D., Brown, T., & Gariglietti, K. P. (2001). Critical thinking and rational emotive behavior therapy. *Inquiry: Critical Thinking Across the Disciplines, 20,* 6–18.

Hatfield, E., & Rapson, R. L. (1995). *Love and sex: Cross-cultural perspectives.* Boston: Allyn & Bacon.

Hatfield, J., Job, R. F. S., Hede, A. J., Carter, N. L., Peploe, P., Taylor, R., & Morrell, S. (2002). Human response to environmental noise: The role of perceived control. *International Journal of Behavioral Medicine, 9,* 341–359.

Hathaway, W. (2002, December 22). Henry M: The day one man's memory died. *Hartford Courant.*

Hattori, M., Fujiyama A., Taylor, T. D., Watanabe, H., Yada, T., Park, H. S., et al. (2000). The DNA sequence of human chromosome 21. *Nature, 405,* 311–319.

Hauck, F. R., Moore, C. M., Herman, S. M., Donovan, M., Kalelkar, M., Christoffel, K. K., et al. (2002). The contributions of prone sleeping to the racial disparity in sudden infant death syndrome: The Chicago Infant Mortality Study. *Pediatrics, 110,* 772–780.

Hauptman, J., Lucas, C., Boldrin, M. N., Collins, H., & Segal, K. R. (2000). Orlistat in the long-term treatment of obesity in primary care settings. *Archives of Family Medicine, 9,* 160–167.

Hawkins, H. L., Kramer, A. R., & Capaldi, D. (1993). Aging, exercise, and attention. *Psychology and Aging, 7,* 643–653.

Hayes, A. M., & Harris, M. S. (2000). The development of an integrative therapy for depression. In S. L. Johnson & A. M. Hayes (Eds.), *Stress, coping, and depression* (pp. 291–306). Mahwah, NJ: Erlbaum.

Hays, P. A. (1995). Multicultural applications of cognitive-behavior therapy. *Professional Psychology: Research and Practice, 26,* 309–315.

Hays, W. L. (1981). *Statistics* (3rd ed.). New York: Holt, Rinehart, Winston.

Hazeltine, E., & Ivry, R. B. (2002). Neuroscience: Can we teach the cerebellum new tricks? *Science, 296,* 1979–1980.

He, L. F. (1987). Involvement of endogenous opioid peptides in acupuncture analgesia. *Pain, 31,* 99–121.

Hebb, D. O. (1955). Drives and the C. N. S. (conceptual nervous system). *Psychological Review, 62,* 243–254.

Hedge, A., & Yousif, Y. H. (1992). Effects of urban size, urgency, and cost of helpfulness: A cross-cultural comparison between the United Kingdom and the Sudan. *Journal of Cross-Cultural Psychology, 23,* 107–115.

Hegarty, J. D., Baldessarini, R. J., Tohen, M., Waternaux, C., & Oepen, G. (1994). One hundred years of schizophrenia: A meta-analysis of the outcome literature. *American Journal of Psychiatry, 151,* 1409–1416.

Heiby, E. M. (2002). Concluding remarks on the debate about prescription privileges for psychologists. *Journal of Clinical Psychology, 58*[Special issue], 709–722.

Heim, C., Newport, J., Heit, S., Graham, Y. P., Wilcox, M., Bonsall, R., et al. (2000). Pituitary-adrenal and autonomic responses to stress in women after sexual and physical abuse in childhood. *Journal of the American Medical Association, 284,* 592–597.

Heiman, J. R. (2002). Sexual dysfunction: Overview of prevalence, etiological factors, and treatments. *Journal of Sex Research, 39,* 73–78.

Heine, S. J. (2003). Self-enhancement in Japan? A reply to Brown & Kobayashi. *Asian Journal of Social Psychology, 6,* 75–84.

Heine, S. J., Harihara, M., & Niiya, Y. (2002). Terror management in Japan. *Asian Journal of Social Psychology, 5,* 187–196.

Heine, S., Lehman, D., Markus, H., & Kitayama, S. (1999). Is there a universal need for positive regard? *Psychological Review, 106,* 766–794.

Hejmadi, A., Davidson, R. J., & Rozin, P. (2000). Exploring Hindu Indian emotion expressions: Evidence for accurate recognition by Americans and Indians. *Psychological Science, 11,* 183–187.

Heller, W., Etienne, M. A., & Miller, G. A. (1995). Patterns of perceptual asymmetry in depression and anxiety: Implications for neuropsychological models of emotion and psychopathology. *Journal of Abnormal Psychology, 104*(2), 327–333.

Heller, W., Nitschke, J. B., & Miller, G. A. (1998). Lateralization in emotion and emotional disorders. *Current Directions in Psychological Science, 7,* 26–32.

Helmers, K. F., & Krantz, D. S. (1996). Defensive hostility, gender and cardiovascular levels and responses to stress. *Annals of Behavioral Medicine, 18,* 246–254.

Helms, J. E. (1992). Why is there no study of cultural equivalence in standardized cognitive ability testing? *American Psychologist, 47,* 1083–1101.

Helms, J. E. (1997). The triple quandary of race, culture, and social class in standardized cognitive ability testing. In D. P. Flanagan, J. L. Genshaft, & P. L. Harrison (Eds.), *Contemporary intellectual assessment: Theories, tests, and issues.* New York: Guilford Press.

Helson, R., & Moane, G. (1987). Personality change in women from college to midlife. *Journal of Personality and Social Psychology, 53,* 176–186.

Helzer, J. E., Canino, G. J., Yeh, E., Bland, R. C., Lee, C. K., Hwu, H., & Newman, S. (1990). Alcoholism—North America and Asia: A comparison of population surveys with the diagnostic interview schedule. *Archives of General Psychiatry, 47,* 313–319.

Helzer, J. E., & Hudziak, J. J. (Eds.). (2002). *Defining psychopathology in the 21st century: DSM-V and beyond.* Washington DC: American Psychiatric Publishing, Inc.

Hemingway, M. A., & Smith, C. S. (1999). Organizational climate and occupational stressors as predictors of withdrawal behaviours and injuries in nurses. *Journal of Occupational and Organizational Psychology, 72,* 285–299.

Hendrick, C., & Hendrick, S. (1986). A theory and method of love. *Journal of Personality and Social Psychology, 50,* 392–402.

Henkel, L. A., Franklin, N., & Johnson, M. K. (2000). Cross-modal source monitoring, confusion between perceived and imagined events. *Journal of Experimental Psychology: Learning, Memory and Cognition, 26,* 321–335.

Henker, B., & Whalen, C. K. (1989). Hyperactivity and attention deficits. *American Psychologist, 44,* 216–223.

Henry, W. P. (1998). Science, politics, and the politics of science: The use and misuse of empirically validated treatment research. *Psychotherapy Research, 8,* 126–140.

Herbert, J. D., Lilienfeld, S. O., Lohr, J. M., Montgomery, R. W., O'Donohue, W. T., Rosen, G. M., & Tolin, D. F. (2000). Science and pseudoscience in the development of eye movement desensitization and reprocessing: Implications for clinical psychology. *Clinical Psychology Review, 20,* 945–971.

Hergenhahn, B. R., & Olson, M. H. (1999). *An introduction to theories of personality* (5th ed.). Upper Saddle River, NJ: Prentice Hall.

Hermann, R. C., Dorwart, R. A., Hoover, C. W., & Brody, J. (1995). Variation in ECT use in the United States. *American Journal of Psychiatry, 152,* 869–875.

Hernandez, D. J. (1997). Child development and the social demography of childhood. *Child Development, 68,* 149–169.

Herness, M. S., & Gilbertson, T. A. (1999). Cellular mechanisms of taste transduction. *Annual Review of Physiology, 61,* 873–900.

Herrmann, D. J., & Searleman, A. (1992). Memory improvement and memory theory in historical perspective. In D. Herrmann, H. Weingartner, A. Searlman, & C. McEvoy (Eds.), *Memory improvement: Implications for memory theory.* New York: Springer-Verlag.

Herrnstein, R. J., & Murray, C. (1994). *The bell curve: Intelligence and class structure in American Life.* New York: Free Press.

Herxheimer, A., & Petrie, K. J. (2002). Melatonin for the prevention and treatment of jet lag. *Cochrane Database Systematic Review, 2,* CD001520.

Herzog, D. B., Dorer, D. J., Keel, P. K., Selwyn, S. E., Ekeblad, E. R., Flores, A. T., et al. (1999). Recovery and relapse in anorexia and bulimia nervosa: A 7.5-year follow-up study. *Journal of the American Academy of Child and Adolescent Psychiatry, 38,* 829–837.

Herzog, D. B., Greenwood, D. N., Dorer, D. J., Flores, A. T., Ekeblad, E. R., Richards, A., et al. (2000). Mortality in eating disorders: A descriptive study. *International Journal of Eating Disorders, 28,* 20–26.

Hespos, S. J., & Baillargeon, R. (2001). Infants' knowledge about occlusion and containment events: A surprising discrepancy. *Psychological Science, 12,* 141–147.

Hesse, J., Mogelvang, B., & Simonsen, H. (1994). Acupuncture versus metropolol in migraine prophylaxis: A randomized trial of trigger point inactivation. *Journal of Internal Medicine, 235,* 451–456.

Hetherington, E. M., & Clingempeel, W. G. (1992). Coping with marital transitions. *Monographs of the Society for Research in Child Development, 57*(2–3, Serial No. 227).

Hetherington, E. M., & Stanley-Hagan, M. (2002). Parenting in divorced, single-parent, and stepfamilies. In M. H. Bornstein (Ed.), *Handbook of parenting* (2nd ed.). Mahwah, NJ: Erlbaum.

Hettema, J. M., Annas, P., Neale, M. C., Kendler, K. S., & Fredrikson, M. (2003). A twin study of the genetics of fear conditioning. *Archives of General Psychiatry, 60,* 702–708.

Hettema, J. M., Neale, M. C., & Kendler, K. S. (2001). A review and meta-analysis of the genetic epidemiology of anxiety disorders. *American Journal of Psychiatry, 158,* 1568–1578.

Heward, W. L. (1997). Four validated instructional strategies. *Behavior and Social Issues, 7,* 43–51.

Hewstone, M. (2003). Intergroup contact: Panacea for prejudice? *Psychologist, 16,* 352–355.

Heyman, R. E., & Neidig, P. H. (1999). A comparison of spousal aggression prevalence rates in the U.S. army and civilian representative samples. *Journal of Consulting and Clinical Psychology, 67,* 239–242.

Heymsfield, S. B., Greenberg, A. S., Fujioa, K., Dixon, R. M., Kushner, R., Hunt, T., et al. (1999). Recombinant leptin for weight loss in obese and lean adults. *Journal of the American Medical Association, 282,* 1568–1575.

Hicks, R. A., Fernandez, C., & Pelligrini, R. J. (2001). The changing pattern of sleep habits of university students: An update. *Perceptual and Motor Skills, 93,* 648.

Highley, J. R., Walker, M. A., Crow, T. J., Esiri, M. M., & Harrison, P. J. (2003). Low medial and lateral right pulvinar volumes in schizophrenia: A postmortem study. *American Journal of Psychiatry, 160,* 1177–1179.

Hilgard, E. R. (1965). *Hypnotic susceptibility.* New York: Harcourt, Brace & World.

Hilgard, E. R. (1977). *Divided consciousness: Multiple controls in human thought and action.* New York: Wiley.

Hilgard, E. R. (1979). *Personality and hypnosis: A study of imaginative involvement.* Chicago: University of Chicago Press.

Hilgard, E. R. (1982). Hypnotic susceptibility and implications for measurement. International *Journal of Clinical and Experimental Hypnosis, 30,* 394–403.

Hilgard, E. R. (1992). Divided consciousness and dissociation. *Consciousness and Cognition, 1,* 16–31.

Hilgard, E. R., Morgan, A. H., & MacDonald, H. (1975). Pain and dissociation in the cold pressor test: A study of "hidden reports" through automatic key-pressing and automatic talking. *Journal of Abnormal Psychology, 84,* 280–289.

Hill, C. T., & Peplau, L. A. (1998). Premarital predictors of relationship outcomes: A 15-year follow-up of the Boston Couples Study. In T. N. Bradbury (Ed.), *The developmental course of marital dysfunction* (pp. 237–278). New York: Cambridge University Press.

Hill, J. O., & Peters, J. C. (1998). Environmental contributions to the obesity epidemic. *Science, 280,* 1371–1374.

Hill, T., Lewicki, P., Czyzewska, M., & Boss, A. (1989). Self-perpetuating biases in person perception. *Journal of Personality and Social Psychology, 57,* 373–386.

Hilliard, R. B., Henry, W. P., & Strupp, H. H. (2000). An interpersonal model of psychotherapy: Linking patient and therapist developmental history, therapeutic process, and types of outcome. *Journal of Consulting and Clinical Psychology, 68,* 125–133.

Hilton, D. (2002). Thinking about causality: Pragmatic, social and scientific rationality. In P. E. Carruthers, S. Stich, & M. Siegal (Eds.), *The cognitive basis of science* (pp. 211–231). New York: Cambridge University Press.

Hilton, H. (1986). *The executive memory guide.* New York: Simon & Schuster.

Hinshaw, S. P., Zupan, B. A., Simmel, C., Nigg, J. T., & Melnick, S. (1997). Peer status in boys with and without attention-deficit hyperactivity disorder: Predictions from overt and covert antisocial behavior, social isolation, and authoritative parenting beliefs. *Child Development, 68,* 880–896.

Hinsz, V. B. (1990). Cognitive and consensus processes in group recognition memory performance. *Journal of Personality and Social Psychology, 59,* 705–718.

Hinton, D., Um, K., & Ba, P. (2001). Kyol goeu ('wind overload') Part I: A cultural syndrome of orthostatic panic among Khmer refugees. *Transcultural Psychiatry, 38,* 403–432.

Hintzman, D. L. (1978). *The psychology of learning and memory.* Freeman: San Francisco.

Hintzman, D. (1991). Human learning and memory. *Annual Review of Psychology, 41,* 109–139.

Hiroto, D. S. (1974). Locus of control and learned helplessness. *Journal of Experimental Psychology, 102,* 187–193.

Hirschfeld, J. A. (1995). The "Back-to-Sleep" campaign against SIDS. *American Family Physician, 51*(3), 611–612.

Hirschfeld, R. M., Allen, M. H., McEvoy, J. P., Keck, P. E., Jr, & Russell, J. M. (1999). Safety and tolerability of oral loading divalproex sodium in acutely manic bipolar patients. *Journal of Clinical Psychiatry, 60,* 815–818.

Hirsch-Pasek, K., Treiman, R., & Schneiderman, M. (1984). Brown and Hanlon revisited: Mothers' sensitivity to ungrammatical forms. *Journal of Child Language, 11,* 81–88.

Ho, B.-C., Andreasen, N. C., Nopoulos, P., Arndt, S., Magnotta, V., & Flaum M. (2003). Progressive structural brain abnormalities and their relationship to clinical outcome: A longitudinal magnetic resonance imaging study early in schizophrenia. *Archives of General Psychiatry, 60,* 585–594.

Ho, D. Y., & Chiu, C. (1998). Component ideas of individual, collectivism, and social organization. In U. Kim, C. Kagitcibasi, & H. C. Triandis (Eds.), *Individualism and collectivism: Theory, method, and applications.* Thousand Oaks, CA: Sage.

Hobson, J. (1997). Dreaming as delirium: A mental status analysis of our nightly madness. *Seminar in Neurology, 17,* 121–128.

Hobson, J. A., Pace-Schott, E. F., Stickgold, R., & Kahn, D. (1998). To dream or not to dream? Relevant data from new neuroimaging and electrophysical studies. *Current Opinions in Neurobiology, 8,* 239–244.

Hobson, J. A., & Stickgold, R. (1994). Dreaming: A neurocognitive approach. *Consciousness and Cognition, 3,* 1–15.

Hoffman, D. (1999, February 11). When the nuclear alarms went off, he guessed right. *International Herald Tribune,* p. 2.

Hoffman, J. P., & Cerbone, F. G. (2002). Parental substance use disorder and the risk of adolescent drug abuse: An event history analysis. *Drug and Alcohol Dependence, 66,* 255–264.

Hoffman, R. E., Hawkins, K. A., Gueorguieva, R., Boutros, N. N., Rachid, F., Carroll, K., & Krystal, J. H. (2003). Transcranial magnetic stimulation of left temporoparietal cortex and medication-resistant auditory hallucinations. *Archives of General Psychiatry, 60,* 49–56.

Hogan, R., Curphy, G. J., & Hogan, J. (1994). What we know about leadership. *American Psychologist, 49,* 493–504.

Hogarth, R. M., & Einhorn, H. J. (1992). Order effects in belief updating: The belief adjustment model. *Cognitive Psychology, 24,* 1–55.

Hoglinger, G. U., Widmer, H. R., Spenger, C., Meyer, M., Seiler, R. W., Oertel, W. H., & Sautter, J. (2001). Influence of time in culture and BDNF pretreatment on survival and function of grafted embryonic rat ventral mesencephalon in the 6-OHDA rat model of Parkinson's disease. *Experimental Neurology, 167,* 148–157.

Hohmann, A. A., & Shear, M. K. (2002). Community-based intervention research: Coping with the "noise" of real life in study design. *American Journal of Psychiatry, 159,* 201–207.

Holden, C. (1996). Small refugees suffer the effects of early neglect. *Science, 274,* 1076–1077.

Holden, C. (1998). New clues to alcoholism risk. *Science, 280,* 1348–1349.

Hollinger, R. C., Dabney, D. A., Lee, G., Hayes, R., Hunter, J., & Cummings, M. (1996). *1996 national retail security survey final report.* Gainesville: University of Florida.

Hollon, S. D., Thase, M. E., & Markowitz, J. C. (2002). Treatment and prevention of depression. *Psychological Science in the Public Interest, 3,* 39–77.

Holman, B. R. (1994). Biological effects of central nervous system stimulants. *Addiction, 89*(11), 1435–1441.

Holmes, D. S. (1991). *Abnormal psychology.* New York: HarperCollins.

Holway, A. H., & Boring, E. G. (1941). Determinants of apparent visual size with distance variant. *American Journal of Psychology, 54,* 21–37.

Hommer, D. W., Momenan, R., Kaiser, E., & Rawlings, R. R. (2001). Evidence for a gender-related effect of alcoholism on brain volumes. *The American Journal of Psychiatry, 158,* 198–204.

Hong, Y., Morris, M. W., Chiu, C., & Benet-Martinez, V. (2000). Multicultural minds: A dynamic constructivist approach to culture and cognition. *American Psychologist, 55,* 709–720.

Honts, C. R., & Quick, B. D. (1995). The polygraph in 1996: Progress in science and the law. *North Dakota Law Review, 71,* 997–1020.

Hood, B. M., Willen, J. D., & Driver, J. (1998). Adult's eyes trigger shifts of visual attention in human infants. *Psychological Science, 9,* 131–134.

Hooker, E. (1993). Reflections of a 40-year exploration: A scientific view on homosexuality. *American Psychologist, 48,* 450–453.

Hopf, H. C., Muller, F. W., & Hopf, N. J. (1992). Localization of emotional and volitional facial paresis. *Neurology, 42*(10), 1918–1923.

Hopper, K., & Wanderling, J. (2000) Revisiting the developed versus developing country distinction in course and outcome in schizophrenia: Results from ISoS, the WHO Collaborative Followup Project. *Schizophrenia Bulletin, 26,* 835–846.

Hoptman, M. J., & Davidson, R. J. (1994). How and why do the two cerebral hemispheres interact? *Psychological Bulletin, 116,* 195–219.

Horgan, J. (1996, December). Why Freud isn't dead. *Scientific American,* pp. 106–111.

Horne, J. A. (1988). *Why we sleep: The functions of sleep in humans.* Oxford: Oxford University Press.

Horner, P. J. & Gage, F. H. (2002). Regeneration in the adult and aging brain. *Archives of Neurology, 59,* 1717–1720.

Horney, K. (1937). *Neurotic personality of our times.* New York: Norton.

Horowitz, L. M., Rosenberg, S. E., & Bartholomew, K. (1993). Interpersonal problems, attachment styles, and outcome in brief dynamic psychotherapy. *Journal of Consulting and Clinical Psychology, 61,* 549–560.

Horwitz, A. V., Widom, C. S., McLaughlin, J., & White, H. R. (2001). The impact of childhood abuse and neglect on adult mental health: A prospective study. *Journal of Health and Social Behavior, 42,* 184–201.

Horwitz, P., & Christie, M. A. (2000). Computer-based manipulatives for teaching scientific reasoning: An example. In M. J. Jacobson & R. B. Kozuma (Eds.), *Innovations in science and mathematics education: Advanced designs for technologies of learning* (pp. 163–191). Mahwah, NJ: Erlbaum.

Houpt, T. R. (1994). Gastric pressure in pigs during eating and drinking. *Physiology and Behavior, 56*(2), 311–317.

House, J. S., Landis, K. R., & Umberson, D. (1988). Structures and processes of social support. *Annual Review of Sociology, 14,* 293–318.

House, R. J., Hanges, P. J., Ruiz-Quintanilla, S. A., Dorfman, P. W., Javidan, M., Dickson, M., et al. (1999). Cultural influences on leadership and organizations: Project GLOBE. In W. H. Mobley, M. J. Gessner, & V. Arnold (Eds.), *Advances in global leadership* (Vol. 1, pp. 171–233). Stamford, CT: JAI.

Howard, D. V. (1983). *Cognitive psychology.* New York: Macmillan.

Howarth, E., & Weissman, M. M. (2000). The epidemiology and cross-national presentation of obsessive-compulsive disorder. *Psychiatric Clinics of North America, 23,* 493–507.

Howe, M. J. A., Davidson, J. W., & Sloboda, J. A. (1998). Innate talent: Reality or myth? *Behavioral and Brain Sciences, 21,* 399–442.

Howe, M. L. (1995, March). *Differentiating cognitive and sociolinguistic factors in the decline of infantile amnesia.* Paper presented at the biennial meeting of the Society for Research in Child Development, Indianapolis.

Howe, M. L. (2003). Memories from the cradle. *Current Directions in Psychological Science, 12,* 62–65.

Hoyert, D. L., Kochanek, K. D., & Murphy, S. L. (1999). *Deaths: Final data for 1997 National Vital Statistics Report* (DHHS Publication No. [PHS] 99–1120). Hyattsville, MD: National Center for Health Statistics.

Hoyle, R. H. (1993). Interpersonal attraction in the absence of explicit attitudinal information. *Social Cognition, 11,* 309–320.

Hoyle, R. H., Harris, M. J., & Judd, C. M. (2002). *Research methods in social relations.* Belmont, CA: Wadsworth.

Hser, Y. I., Hoffman, V., Grella, C. E., & Anglin, M. D. (2001). A 33-year follow-up of narcotics addicts. *Archives of General Psychiatry, 58,* 503–508.

Hu, F. B., Li, T. Y., Colditz, G. A., Willett, W. C., & Manson, J. E. (2003). Television watching and other sedentary behaviors in relation to risk of obesity and Type 2 diabetes mellitus in women. *Journal of the American Medical Association, 289,* 1785–1791.

Hu, F. B., Stampfer, M. J., Manson, J. E., Grodstein, F., Colditz, G. A., Speizer, F. E., Willett, W. C. (2000). Trends in the incidence of coronary heart disease and changes in diet and lifestyle in women. *The New England Journal of Medicine, 343,* 530–537.

Hu, S., Patatucci, A. M. L., Patterson, C., Li, L., Fulker, D. W., Cherny, S. S., et al. (1995). Linkage between sexual orientation and chromosome Xq28 in males but not females. *Nature Genetics, 11,* 248–256.

Huang, L., & Li, C. (2000). Leptin: A multifunctional hormone. *Cell Research, 10,* 81–92.

Hubble, M. A., Duncan, B. L., & Miller, S. D. (Eds.). (1999). *The heart and soul of change: What works in psychotherapy.* Washington, DC: American Psychological Assocation.

Hubel, D. H., & Wiesel, T. N. (1979). Brain mechanisms of vision. *Scientific American, 241,* 150–162.

Hudson, W. (1960). Pictorial depth perception in subcultural groups in Africa. *Journal of Social Psychology, 52,* 183–208.

Huesmann, L. R. (1995). *Screen violence and real violence: Understanding the link.* Auckland, NZ: Media Aware.

Huesmann, L. R. (1998). The role of social information processing and cognitive schema in the acquisition and maintenance of habitual aggressive behavior. In R. G. Geen & E. Donnerstein (Eds.), *Human aggression.* San Diego: Academic Press.

Huesmann, L. R., & Eron, L. D. (1986). *Television and the aggressive child: A cross-national comparison.* Hillsdale, NJ: Erlbaum.

Huesmann, L. R., Moise, J., Podolski, C., & Eron, L. (1997, April). *Longitudinal relations between early exposure to television violence and young adult aggression: 1977–1992.* Paper presented at the annual meeting of the Society for Research in Child Development, Washington, DC.

Huesmann, L. R., Moise-Titus, J., Podolski, C.-L., & Eron, L. D. (2003). Longitudinal relations between children's exposure to TV violence and their aggressive and violent behavior in young adulthood: 1977–1992. *Developmental Psychology, 39,* 201–221.

Huffcutt, A. I., Conway, J. M., Roth, P. L., & Stone, N. J. (2001). Identification and meta-analytic assessment of psychological constructs measured in employment interviews. *Journal of Applied Psychology, 86,* 897–913.

Hughes, J. R., Higgins, S. T., & Bickel, W. K. (1994). Nicotine withdrawal versus other drug withdrawal syndromes: Similarities and dissimilarities. *Addiction, 89*(11), 1461–1470.

Hui, C., Lam, S. S. K., & Law, K. K. S. (2000). Instrumental values of organizational citizenship behavior for promotion: A field quasi-experiment. *Journal of Applied Psychology, 85,* 822–828.

Hull, C. L. (1951). *Essentials of behavior.* New Haven, CT: Yale University Press.

Humphreys, L. G. (1984). General intelligence. In C. R. Reynolds & R. T. Brown (Eds.), *Perspectives on bias in mental testing.* New York: Plenum.

Hunsley, J., & Bailey, J. M. (1999). The clinical utility of the Rorschach: Unfulfilled promises and an uncertain future. *Psychological Assessment, 11,* 266–277.

Hunsley, J., & Rumstein-McKean, O. (1999). Improving psychotherapeutic services via randomized trials, treatment manuals, and component analysis designs. *Journal of Clinical Psychology, 55,* 1507–1517.

Hunt, E. (1983). On the nature of intelligence. *Science, 219,* 141–146.

Hunt, M. (1982). *The universe within.* New York: Simon & Schuster.

Hunt, R., & Rouse, W. B. (1981). Problem solving skills of maintenance trainees in diagnosing faults in simulated power plants. *Human Factors, 23,* 317–328.

Hunter, M. A., & Ames, E. W. (1988). A multifactor model of infants' preferences for novel and familiar stimuli. In C. Rovee-Collier & L. P. Lipsitt (Eds.), *Advances in infancy research* (Vol. 5, pp. 69–91). Norwood, NJ: Ablex.

Hunter, R. H. (1995). Benefits of competency-based treatment programs. *American Psychologist, 50,* 509–513.

Hurt, H., Brodsky, N. L., Betancourt, L., & Braitman, L. E. (1995). Cocaine-exposed children: Follow-up through 30 months. *Journal of Developmental and Behavioral Pediatrics, 16*(1), 29–35.

Huston, A. C., & Wright, J. C. (1989). The forms of television and the child viewer. In G. Comstock (Ed.), *Public communication and behavior* (Vol. 2, pp. 103–159). San Diego: Academic Press.

Huston, T. L., Caughlin, J. P., Houts, R. M., Smith, S. E., & George, L. J. (2001). The connubial crucible: Newlywed years as predictors of marital delight, distress, and divorce. *Journal of Personality and Social Psychology, 80,* 237–252.

Huttenlocher, P. R. (1990). Morphometric study of human cerebral cortex development. *Neuropsychologia, 28,* 517–527.

Hyde, J. S. (1986). Gender differences in aggression. In J. S. Hyde & M. C. Linn (Eds.), *The psychology of gender: Advances through meta-analysis.* Baltimore: Johns Hopkins University Press.

Hyde, J. S., & Durik, A. M. (2000). Gender differences in erotic plasticity—Evolutionary or sociocultural forces? Comment on Baumeister (2000). *Psychological Bulletin, 126,* 375–379.

Hygge, S., Evans, G.W., & Bullinger, M. (2002). A prospective study of some effects of aircraft noise on cognitive performance in schoolchildren. *Psychological Science, 13,* 469–474.

Hyman, I. E., Jr. (2000). The memory wars. In U. Neisser & I. E. Hyman Jr. (Eds.), *Memory observed* (2nd ed., pp. 374–379). New York: Worth.

Hyman, I. E., & Pentland, J. (1996). The role of mental imagery in the creation of false childhood memories. *Journal of Memory and Language, 35,* 101–117.

Hypericum Depression Trial Study Group. (2002). Effect of *Hypericum perforatum* (St. John's wort) in major depressive disorder: A randomized, controlled trial. *Journal of the American Medical Association, 287,* 1807–1814.

Igalens, J., & Roussel, P. (2000). A study of the relationships between compensation package, work motivation, and job satisfaction. *Journal of Organizational Behavior, 20,* 1003–1025.

Ilgen, D. R., & Pulakos, E. D. (Eds.). (1999). *The changing nature of performance: Implications for staffing, motivation, and development.* San Francisco, CA: Jossey-Bass.

Ilies, R., & Judge, T. A. (2003). On the heritability of job satisfaction: The mediating role of personality. *Journal of Applied Psychology, 88,* 750–759.

Inciardi, J. A., Surratt, H. L., & Saum, C. A. (1997). *Cocaine-exposed infants: Social, legal, and public health issues.* Thousand Oaks, CA: Sage.

Indovina, I., & Sanes, J. N. (2001). On somatotopic representation centers for finger movements in human primary motor cortex and supplementary motor area. *Neuroimage, 13,* 1027–1034.

Ingram, R. E., Miranda, J., & Segal, Z. V. (1998). *Cognitive vulnerability to depression.* New York: Guilford.

Inskip, P. D., Tarone, R. E., Hatch, E. E., Wilcosky, T. C., Shapiro, W. R., Selker, R. G., et al. (2001). Cellular-telephone use and brain tumors. *The New England Journal of Medicine, 344,* 79–86.

International Association for the Evaluation of Education Achievement. (1999). *Trends in mathematics and science achievement around the world.* Boston: Lynch School of Education, Boston College.

International Human Genome Sequencing Consortium. (2001). Initial sequencing and analysis of the human genome. *Nature, 409,* 860–921.

Irnich, D., Behrens, N., Molzen, H., Konig, A., Gleditsch, J., Krauss, M., et al. (2001). Randomised trial of acupuncture compared with conventional massage and "sham" laser acupuncture for treatment of chronic neck pain. *British Medical Journal, 322,* 1574–1578.

Ironson, G., Freund, B., Strauss, J. L., & Williams J. (2002). Comparison of two treatments for traumatic stress: A community-based study of EMDR and prolonged exposure. *Journal of Clinical Psychology, 58,* 113–128.

Ironson, G. H., Smith, P. C., Brannick, M. T., Gibson, W. M., & Paul, K. B. (1989). Constitution of a Job in General scale: A comparison of global, composite, and specific measures. *Journal of Applied Psychology, 74,* 193–200.

Ironson, G., Wynings, C., Schneiderman, N., Baum, A., Rodriguez, M., Greenwood, D., et al. (1997). Posttraumatic stress symptoms, intrusive thoughts, loss, and immune function after Hurricane Andrew. *Psychosomatic Medicine, 59,* 128–141.

Irwin, M., Daniels, M., Smith, T., Bloom, E., & Weiner, H. (1987). Impaired natural killer cell activity during bereavement. *Brain, Behavior, and Immunity, 1,* 98–104.

Iversen, L. L., & Snyder, S. H. (2000). *The science of marijuana.* Oxford, England: Oxford University Press.

Iwahashi, K., Matsuo, Y., Suwaki, H., Nakamura, K., & Ichikawa, Y. (1995). CYP2E1 and ALDH2 genotypes and alcohol dependence in Japanese. *Alcoholism Clinical and Experimental Research, 19*(3), 564–566.

Iwamasa, G. Y., Sorocco, K. H., & Koonce, D. A. (2002). Ethnicity and clinical psychology: A content analysis of the literature. *Clinical Psychology Review, 22,* 932–944.

Izard, C. E. (1977). *Human emotions.* New York: Plenum.

Izard, C. E. (1993). Organizational and motivational functions of discrete emotions. In M. Lewis & J. M. Haviland (Eds.), *Handbook of emotions.* New York: Guilford.

Izard, C., Fine, S., Schultz, D., Mostow, A., Ackerman, B., & Youngstrom, E. (2001). Emotion knowledge as a predictor of social behavior and academic competence in children at risk. *Psychological Science, 12,* 18–23.

Jackson, B., Sellers, R. M., & Peterson, C. (2002). Pessimistic explanatory style moderates the effect of stress on physical illness. *Personality & Individual Differences, 32,* 567–573.

Jackson, J. W. (2002). The relationship between group identity and intergroup prejudice is moderated by sociostructural variation. *Journal of Applied Social Psychology, 32,* 908–933.

Jacob, S., Kinnunen, L. H., Metz, J., Cooper, M.., & McClintock, M. K. (2001). Sustained human chemosignal unconsciously alters brain function. *Neuroreport, 12,* 2391–2394.

Jacob, S., & McClintock, M. K. (2000). Psychological state and mood effects of steroidal chemosignals in women and men. *Hormones and Behavior, 37,* 57–78.

Jacobs, R., & Solomon, T. (1977). Strategies for enhancing the prediction of job performance from job satisfaction. *Journal of Applied Psychology, 62,* 417–421.

Jacobson, K. (2002). ADHD in cross-cultural perspective: Some empirical results. *American Anthropologist, 104,* 283–286.

Jacobson, N. S., Christensen, A., Prince, S. E., Cordova, J., & Eldridge, K. (2000). Integrative behavioral couples therapy: An acceptance-based, promising new treatment for couple discord. *Journal of Consulting and Clinical Psychology, 68,* 351–355.

Jaffee, S., & Hyde, J. S. (2000). Gender differences in moral orientation: A meta-analysis. *Psychological Bulletin, 126,* 703–726.

Jagger, C., Clarke, M., & Stone, A. (1995). Predictors of survival with Alzheimer's disease: A community-based study. *Psychological Medicine, 25,* 171–177.

Jahnke, J. C., & Nowaczyk, R. H. (1998). *Cognition.* Upper Saddle River, NJ: Prentice-Hall.

James, W. (1884). Some omissions of introspective psychology. *Mind, 9,* 1–26.

James, W. (1890). *Principles of psychology.* New York: Holt.

James, W. (1892). *Psychology: Briefer course.* New York: Holt.

Jancke, L., & Kaufmann, N. (1994). Facial EMG responses to odors in solitude and with an audience. *Chemical Senses, 19*(2), 99–111.

Janis, I. L. (1989). *Crucial decisions: Leadership in policy making and crisis management.* New York: Free Press.

Janowiak, J. J., & Hackman, R. (1994). Meditation and college students' self-actualization and rated stress. *Psychological Reports, 75*(2), 1007–1010.

Janowitz, H. D. (1967). Role of gastrointestinal tract in the regulation of food intake. In C. F. Code (Ed.), *Handbook of physiology: Alimentary canal 1.* Washington, DC: American Physiological Society.

Jason, L. A., Witter, E., & Torres-Harding, S. (2003). Chronic fatigue syndrome, coping, optimism and social support. *Journal of Mental Health, 12,* 109–118.

Je, J., Vupputuri, S., Allen, K., Prerost, M. R., Hughes, J., Whelton, P. K. (1999). Passive smoking and the risk of coronary heart disease—A meta-analysis of epidemiological studies. *The New England Journal of Medicine, 340,* 920–926.

Jefferis, B. M. J. H., Power, C., & Hertzman, C. (2002). Birth weight, childhood socioeconomic environment, and cognitive development in the 1958 British birth cohort study [Electronic version]. *British Medical Journal, 325,* 305.

Jensen, J. P., Bergin, A. E., & Greaves, D. W. (1990). The meaning of eclecticism: New survey and analysis of components. *Professional Psychology: Research and Practice, 21,* 124–130.

Jevtovic-Todorovic, V., Wozniak, D. F., Benshoff, N. D., & Olney, J. W. (2001). A comparative evaluation of the neurotoxic properties of ketamine and nitrous oxide. *Brain Research, 895,* 264–267.

Jex, S. M., Adams, G. A., Elacqua, T. C., & Bachrach, D. G. (2002). Type A as a moderator of stressors and job complexity: A comparison of achievement strivings and impatience-irritability. *Journal of Applied Social Psychology, 32,* 977–996.

Jhanwar, U. M., Beck, B., Jhanwar, Y. S., & Burlet, C. (1993). Neuropeptide Y projection from the arcuate nucleus to the parvocellular division of the paraventricular nucleus: Specific relation to the ingestion of carbohydrate. *Brain Research, 631*(1), 97–106.

Johansen, J. P., Fields, H. L., & Manning, B. H. (2001). The affective component of pain in rodents: Direct evidence for a contribution of the anterior cingulate cortex. *Proceedings of the National Academy of Sciences, 98,* 8077–8082.

John, O., & Srivastava, S. (1999). The big five taxonomy: History, measurement, and theoretical perspectives. In L. Pervin & O. John (Eds.), *Handbook of personality: Theory and research* (2nd ed., pp. 102–138). New York: Guilford.

Johnson, D. R., Westermeyer, J., Kattar, K., & Thuras, P. (2002). Daily charting of posttraumatic stress symptoms: A pilot study. *Journal of Nervous & Mental Disease, 190,* 683–692.

Johnson, J. G., Cohen, P., Dohrenwend, B. P., Link, B. G., & Brook, J. S. (1999). A longitudinal investigation of social causation and social selection processes involved in the association between socioeconomic status and psychiatric disorders. *Journal of Abnormal Psychology, 108,* 490–499.

Johnson, J. G., Cohen, P., Smailes, E. M., Kasen, S., & Brook, J. S. (2002). Television viewing and aggressive behavior during adolescence and adulthood. *Science, 295,* 2468–2471.

Johnson, J. M., & Endler, N. S. (2002). Coping with human immunodeficiency virus: Do optimists fare better? *Current Psychology: Developmental, Learning, Personality, Social, 21,* 3–16.

Johnson, J. S., & Newport, E. L. (1989). Critical period effects in second language learning. *Cognitive Psychology, 21,* 60–99.

Johnson, J., & Vickers, Z. (1993). Effects of flavor and macronutrient composition of food servings on liking, hunger and subsequent intake. *Appetite, 21*(1), 25–39.

Johnson, M. A., Dziurawiec, S., Ellis, H., & Morton, J. (1991). Newborns' preferential tracking of face-like stimuli and its subsequent decline. *Cognition, 4,* 1–19.

Johnson, M. K., & Raye, C. L. (1998). False memories and confabulation. *Trends in Cognitive Sciences, 2,* 137–145.

Johnson, S. P., Amso, D., & Slemmer, J. A. (2003). Development of object concepts in infancy: Evidence for early learning in an eye-tracking paradigm. *Proceedings of the National Academy of Sciences, 100,* 10568–10573.

Johnson, W. R., & Neal, D. (1998). Basic skills and the black-white earnings gap. In C. Jencks & M. Phillips (Eds.), *The black-white test score gap* (pp. 480–497). Washington, DC: Brookings Institute Press.

Johnson-Laird, P. N. (1983). *Mental models: Toward a cognitive science of language, inference, and consciousness.* Cambridge: Harvard University Press.

Johnston, K. (1988). Adolescents' solutions to dilemmas in fables: Two moral orientations. In C. Gilligan, J. V. Ward, J. M. Taylor, & B. Bardige (Eds.), *Mapping the moral domain: A contribution to psychological theory and education.* Cambridge: Harvard University Press.

Jonas, E., Schimel, J., Greenberg, J., & Pyszczynski, T. (2002). The Scrooge effect: Evidence that mortality salience increases prosocial attitudes and behavior. *Personality and Social Psychology Bulletin, 28,* 1342–1353.

Jones, E. E. (1982). Psychotherapists' impressions of treatment outcome as a function of race. *Journal of Clinical Psychology, 38,* 722–731.

Jones, G. V. (1990). Misremembering a common object: When left is not right. *Memory & Cognition, 18,* 174–182.

Jordan, N. C., Huttenlocher, J., & Levine, S. C. (1992). Differential calculation abilities in young children from middle- and low-income families. *Developmental Psychology, 28,* 644–653.

Josefson, D. (2002, August 31). St. John's wort interferes with chemotherapy, study shows. *British Medical Journal* [online version]. Retrieved August 20, 2003, from http://bmj.com

Josephson, W. L. (1987). Television violence and children's aggression: Testing the priming, social script, and disinhibition predictions. *Journal of Personality and Social Psychology, 53,* 882–890.

Joy, J. E., Watson, S. J., Jr., & Benson, J. A., Jr. (1999). *Marijuana and medicine: Assessing the science base.* Washington, DC: National Academy Press.

Judd, F. K., Jackson, H. J., Komiti, A., Murray, G., Hodgins, G., Fraser, C. (2002). High prevalence disorders in urban and rural communities. *Australian and New Zealand Journal of Psychiatry, 36,* 104–113.

Judge, T. A., Thoresen, C. J., Bono, J. E., & Patton, G. K. (2001). The job satisfaction-job performance relationship: A qualitative and quantitative review. *Psychological Bulletin, 127,* 376–407.

Julien, R. M. (2001). *A primer of drug action* (9th ed.). New York: Freeman.

Jung, C. G. (1916). *Analytical psychology.* New York: Moffat.

Jung, C. G. (1933). *Psychological types.* New York: Harcourt, Brace and World.

Just, M. A., Carpenter, P. A., Keller, T. A., Emery, L., Zajac, H., & Thulborn, K. R. (2001). Interdependence of nonoverlapping cortical systems in dual cognitive tasks. *Neuroimage, 14,* 417–426.

Just, N., & Alloy, L. B. (1997). The response styles theory of depression: Tests and an extension of the theory. *Journal of Abnormal Psychology, 106,* 221–229.

Juul-Dam, N., Townsend, J., & Courchesne, E. (2001). Prenatal, perinatal, and neonatal factors in autism, pervasive developmental disorder–not other-wise specified, and the general population. *Pediatrics, 107,* e63.

Kadotani, H., Kadotani, T., Young, T., Peppard, P. E., Finn, L., Colrain, I. M., et al. (2001). Association between apolipoprotein E epsilon4 and sleep-disordered breathing in adults. *Journal of the American Medical Association, 285,* 2888–2890.

Kagan, J. R., Snidman, N., Arcus, D., & Resnick, J. S. (1994). *Galen's prophecy: Temperament in human nature.* New York: Basic Books.

Kahen, V., Katz, L. F., & Gottman, J. M. (1994). Linkages between parent-child interaction and conversations of friends. *Social Development, 3,* 238–254.

Kahn, D. A. (1995). New strategies in bipolar disorder: Part II. Treatment. *Journal of Practical Psychiatry and Behavioral Health, 3,* 148–157.

Kahn, E., & Rachman, A. W. (2000). Carl Rogers and Heinz Kohut: A historical perspective. *Psychoanalytic Psychology, 17,* 294–312.

Kahneman, D., & Tversky, A. (1973). On the psychology of prediction. *Psychological Review, 80,* 237–251.

Kahneman, D., & Tversky, A. (1984). Choices, values, and frames. *American Psychologist, 29,* 341–356.

Kalb, L. M., & Loeber, R. (2003). Child disobedience and noncompliance: A review. *Pediatrics, 111,* 641–652.

Kales, A., & Kales, J. (1973). Recent advances in the diagnosis and treatment of sleep disorders. In G. Usdin (Ed.), *Sleep research and clinical practice.* New York: Brunner/Mazel.

Kamarck, T. W., Everson, S. A., Kaplan, G. A., Manuck, S. B., Jennings, J. R., Salonen, T., & Salonen, J. T. (1997). Exaggerated blood pressure responses during mental stress are associated with enhanced carotid atherosclerosis in middle-aged Finnish men. *Circulation, 96,* 3842–3848.

Kamphuis, J. H., & Emmelkamp, P. M. (2001). Traumatic distress among support-seeking female victims of stalking. *American Journal of Psychiatry, 158,* 795–798.

Kane, J. M., Eerdekens, M., Lindenmayer, J.-P., Keith, S. J., Lesem, M., & Karcher, K. (2003). Long-acting injectable risperidone: Efficacy and safety of the first long-acting atypical antipsychotic. *American Journal of Psychiatry, 160,* 1125–1132.

Kanfer, R. (1992). Work motivation: New directions in theory and research. In C. L. Cooper & I. T. Robertson (Eds.), *International review of industrial and organizational psychology 1992* (pp. 1–53). Chichester, UK: Wiley.

Kanki, B. J., & Foushee, H. C. (1990). Crew factors in the aerospace workplace. In S. Oskamp & S. Spacepan (Eds.), *People's reactions to technology* (pp. 18–31). Newbury Park, CA: Sage.

Kanner, B. (1995). *Are you normal?* New York: St. Martin's Press.

Kaplan, M. F. (1987). The influencing process in group decision making. In C. Hendrick (Ed.), *Group processes* (pp. 189–212). Newbury Park, CA: Sage.

Kaplan, M. F., & Miller, C. E. (1987). Group decision making and normative vs. informational influence: Effects of type of issue and assigned decision rule. *Journal of Personality and Social Psychology, 53,* 306–313.

Kaptchuk, T. J. (2001). Methodological issues in trials of acupuncture. *Journal of the American Medical Association, 285,* 1015–1016.

Kapur, N. (1999). Syndromes of retrograde amnesia: A conceptual and empirical synthesis. *Psychological Bulletin, 125,* 800–825.

Kapur, S. (2003). Psychosis as a state of aberrant salience: A framework linking biology, phenomenology, and pharmacology in schizophrenia. *American Journal of Psychiatry, 160,* 13–23.

Karau, S. J., & Williams, K. D. (1997). The effects of group cohesiveness on social loafing and social compensation. *Group Dynamics, 1,* 156–168.

Karau, S. J., & Williams, K. D. (2001). Understanding individual motivation in groups: The collective effort model. In M . E. Turner (Ed.), *Groups at work: Theory and research. Applied social research* (pp. 113–141). Mahwah, NJ: Erlbaum.

Karni, A., Meyer, G., Adams, M., Turner, R., & Ungerleider, L. G. (1994). The acquisition and retention of a motor skill: A functional MRI study of long-term motor cortex plasticity. *Abstracts of the Society for Neuroscience, 20,* 1291.

Karon, B. P., & Widener, A. J. (1997). Repressed memories and World War II: Lest we forget. *Professional Psychology: Research and Practice, 28*(4), 338–340.

Kasagi, F., Akahoshi, M., & Shimaoki, K. (1995). Relation between cold pressor test and development of hypertension based on 28-year follow-up. *Hypertension, 25,* 71–76.

Kass, S. (1999). Frequent testing means better grades, studies find. *APA Monitor, 30,* 10.

Kassin, S. M., Rigby, S., & Castillo, S. R. (1991). The accuracy-confidence correlation in eyewitness testimony: Limits and extensions of the retrospective self-awareness effect. *Journal of Personality and Social Psychology, 61,* 698–707.

Kastenbaum, R., Kastenbaum, B. K., & Morris, J. (1989). *Strengths and preferences of the terminally ill: Data from the National Hospice Demonstration Study.*

Katkin, E. S., Wiens, S., & Öhman, A. (2001). Nonconscious fear conditioning, visceral perception, and the development of gut feelings. *Psychological Science, 12,* 366–370.

Kato, S., Wakasa, Y., & Yamagita, T. (1987). Relationship between minimum reinforcing doses and injection speed in cocaine and pentobarbital self-administration in crab-eating monkeys. *Pharmacology, Biochemistry, and Behavior, 28,* 407–410.

Katzell, R. A., & Thompson, D. E. (1990). Work motivation: Theory and practice. *American Psychologist, 45,* 144–153.

Kauffman, N. A., Herman, C. P., & Polivy, J. (1995). Hunger-induced finickiness in humans. *Appetite, 24,* 203–218.

Kaufman, J., & Charney, D. (2000). Comorbidity of mood and anxiety disorders. *Depression and Anxiety, 12*(Suppl. 1), 69–76.

Kawachi, I., Colditz, G. A., & Stone, C. B. (1994). Does drinking coffee increase the risk of coronary heart disease? Results from a meta-analysis. *British Heart Journal, 72*(3), 269–275.

Kawamura, N., Kim, Y., & Asukai, N. (2001). Suppression of cellular immunity in men with a past history of posttraumatic stress disorder. *American Journal of Psychiatry, 158,* 484–486.

Kawasaki, H., Adolphs, R., Kaufman, O., Damasio, H., Damasio, A. R., Granner, M., et al. (2001). Single-neuron responses to emotional visual stimuli recorded in human ventral prefrontal cortex. *Nature Neuroscience, 4,* 15–16.

Kaye, W. H., Klump, K. L., Frank, G. K., & Strober, M. (2000). Anorexia and bulimia nervosa. *Annual Review of Medicine, 51,* 299–313.

Kazarian, S. S., & Evans, D. R. (Eds.). (2001). *Handbook of cultural health psychology.* New York: Academic Press.

Kazdin, A. E. (1994). *Behavior modification in applied settings* (5th ed.). Pacific Grove, CA: Brooks/Cole.

Kazdin, A. E., & Weisz, J. R. (1998). Identifying and developing empirically supported child and adolescent treatments. *Journal of Consulting and Clinical Psychology, 66,* 19–36.

Keating, D. P. (1990). Adolescent thinking. In S. S. Feldman & G. R. Elliott (Eds.), *At the threshold: The developing adolescent* (pp. 4–89). Cambridge, MA: Harvard University Press.

Kee, M., Hill, S. M., & Weist, M. D. (1999). School-based behavior management of cursing, hitting, and spitting in a girl with profound retardation. *Education and Treatment of Children, 22,* 171–178.

Keefe, F. J., & France, C. R. (1999). Pain: Biopsychosocial mechanisms and management. *Current Directions in Psychological Science, 8,* 137–141.

Keel, P. K., & Klump, K. L. (2003). Are eating disorders culture-bound syndromes?: Implications for conceptualizing their etiology. *Psychological Bulletin, 129,* 749–769.

Keeling, P. J., & Roger, A. J. (1995). The selfish pursuit of sex. *Nature, 375,* 283.

Keesey, R. E., & Powley, T. L. (1986). The regulation of body weight. *Annual Review of Psychology, 37,* 109–133.

Kefalov, V., Fu, Y., Marsh-Armstrong, N., & Yau, K.-W. (2003). Role of visual pigment properties in rod and cone phototransduction. *Nature, 425,* 526–531.

Keinan, G., Friedland, N., & Ben-Porath, Y. (1987). Decision making under stress: Scanning of alternatives under physical threat. *Acta Psychologica, 64,* 219–228.

Keller, M. B., McCullough, J. P., Klein, D. N., Arnow, B., Dunner, D. L., Gelenberg, A. J., et al. (2000). A comparison of nefazodone, the cognitive behavioral-analysis system of psychotherapy, and their combination for the treatment of chronic depression. *The New England Journal of Medicine, 342,* 1462–1470.

Kelley, A. E., & Berridge, K. C. (2002). The neuroscience of natural rewards: Relevance to addictive drugs. *Journal of Neuroscience, 22,* 3306–3311.

Kelley, K. W. (1985). Immunological consequences of changing environmental stimuli. In G. P. Moberg (Ed.), *Animal stress.* Bethesda, MD: American Physiological Society.

Kellman, P. J., & Banks, M. S. (1998). Infant visual perception. In W. Damon, D. Kuhn, & R. Siegler (Eds.), *Handbook of child psychology: Vol. 2. Cognition, language and perception* (5th ed., pp. 103–146). New York: Wiley.

Kellum, K. K., Carr, J. E., & Dozier, C. L. (2001). Response-card instruction and student learning in a college classroom. *Teaching of Psychology, 28,* 101–104.

Kelly, G. A. (1980). A psychology of the optimal man. In A. W. Landfield & L. M. Leitner (Eds.), *Personal construct psychology: Psychotherapy and personality.* New York: Wiley.

Kelly, T. H., Foltin, R. W., Emurian, C. S., & Fischman, M. W. (1990). Multidimensional behavioral effects of marijuana. *Progress in Neuro-Psychopharmacology and Biological Psychiatry, 14,* 885–902.

Kelsoe, J. R., Spence, M. A., Loetscher, E., Foguet, M., Sadovnick, A. D., Remick, R. A., et al. (2001). A genome survey indicates a possible susceptibility locus for bipolar disorder on chromosome 22. *Proceedings of the National Academy of Science, 98,* 585–590.

Kelter, D., & Buswell, B. N. (1996). Evidence for the distinctiveness of embarrassment, shame, and guilt: A study of recalled antecedents and facial expressions of emotion. *Cognition and Emotion, 10,* 117–125.

Kemble, E. D., Filipi, T., & Gravlin, L. (1985). Some simple classroom experiments on cerebral lateralization. *Teaching of Psychology, 12,* 81–83.

Kendall, P. C. (1999). Clinical significance. *Journal of Consulting and Clinical Psychology, 67,* 283–284.

Kendall, P. C., & Chambless, D. L. (Eds.). (1998). Special section: Empirically supported psychological therapies. *Journal of Consulting and Clinical Psychology, 66,* 3–167.

Kendall, P. C., & Sheldrick, R. C. (2000). Normative data for normative comparisons *Journal of Consulting and Clinical Psychology, 68,* 767–773.

Kendell, R., & Jablensky, A. (2003). Distinguishing between the validity and utility of psychiatric diagnoses. *American Journal of Psychiatry, 160,* 4–12.

Kendler, K. S., & Diehl, N. S. (1993). The genetics of schizophrenia: A current genetic-epidemiologic perspective. *Schizophrenia Bulletin, 19,* 87–112.

Kendler, K. S., Gardner, C. O., & Prescott, C. A. (2002). Toward a comprehensive developmental model for major depression in women. *American Journal of Psychiatry, 159,* 1133–1145.

Kendler, K. S., Heath, A. C., Neale, M. C., Kessler, R. C., & Eaves, L. J (1992). A population-based twin study of alcoholism in women. *Journal of the American Medical Association, 268,* 1877–1882.

Kendler, K. S., Hettema, J. M., Butera, F., Gardner, C. O., & Prescott, C. A. (2003a). Life event dimensions of loss, humiliation, entrapment, and danger in the prediction of onsets of major depression and generalized anxiety. *Archives of General Psychiatry, 60,* 789–796.

Kendler, K. S., Jacobson, K. C., Myers, J., & Prescott, C. A. (2002). Sex differences in genetic and environmental risk factors for irrational fears and phobias. *Psychological Medicine, 32,* 209–217.

Kendler, K. S., Jacobson, K. C., Prescott, C. A., & Neale, M. C. (2003b). Specificity of genetic and environmental risk factors for use and abuse/dependence of cannabis, cocaine, hallucinogens, sedatives, stimulants, and opiates in male twins. *American Journal of Psychiatry, 160,* 687–695.

Kendler, K. S., Kessler, R. C., Walters, E. E., MacLean, C., Neale, M. C., Heath, A. C., & Eaves, L. J. (1995). Stressful life events, genetic liability, and onset of an episode of major depression in women. *American Journal of Psychiatry, 152,* 833–842.

Kendler, K. S., Meyers, J., Prescott, C. A., & Neale, M. C. (2001). The genetic epidemiology of irrational fears and phobias in men. *Archives of General Psychiatry, 58,* 257–265.

Kendler, K. S., Neale, M. C., Kessler, R. C., Heath, A. C., & Eaves, L. J. (1992). Major depression and generalized anxiety disorder: Same genes, (partly) different environments? *Archives of General Psychiatry, 49,* 716–722.

Kendler, K. S., Prescott, C. A., Myers, J., & Neal, M. C. (2003c). The structure of genetic and environmental risk factors for common psychiatric and substance abuse disorders in men and women. *Archives of General Psychiatry, 60,* 929–937.

Kendler, K. S., Thornton, L. M., & Gardner, C. O. (2000). Stressful life events and previous episodes in the etiology of major depression in women: An evaluation of the "kindling" hypothesis. *American Journal of Psychiatry, 157,* 1243–1251.

Kendler, K. S., Thornton, L. M., & Gardner, C. O. (2001). Genetic risk, number of previous depressive episodes, and stressful life events in predicting onset of major depression. *American Journal of Psychiatry, 158,* 582–586.

Kendler, K. S., Thornton, L. M., Gilman, S. E., & Kessler, R. C. (2000). Sexual orientation in a U.S. national sample of twin and nontwin sibling pairs. *American Journal of Psychiatry, 157,* 1843–1846.

Kendler, K. S., Thornton, L. M., & Prescott, C. A. (2001). Gender differences in the rates of exposure to stressful life events and sensitivity to their depressogenic effects. *American Journal of Psychiatry, 158,* 587–593.

Kenrick, D. T., Groth, G., Trost, M., & Sadalla, E. K. (1993). Integrating evolutionary and social exchange perspectives on relationships: Effects of gender, self-appraisal, and involvement level on mate selection. *Journal of Personality and Social Psychology, 64,* 951–969.

Kent, S., Rodriguez, F., Kelley, K. W., & Dantzer, R. (1994). Reduction in food and water intake induced by microinjection of interleukin-1b in the ventromedial hypothalamus of the rat. *Physiology and Behavior, 56*(5), 1031–1036.

Kepner, J. (2001). Touch in Gestalt body process psychotherapy: Purpose, practice, and ethics. *Gestalt Review, 5,* 97–114.

Kerr, M. P., & Payne, S. J. (1994). Learning to use a spreadsheet by doing and by watching. *Interacting with Computers, 6,* 3–22.

Kessler, R. C. (1997). The effects of stressful life events on depression. *Annual Review of Psychology, 48,* 191–214.

Kessler, R. C., Berglund, P., Demler, O., Jin, R., Koretz, D., Merikangas, K.R., et al. (2003). The epidemiology of major depressive disorder: Results from the national comorbidity survey replication (NCS-R). *Journal of the American Medical Association, 289,* 3095–3105.

Kessler, R. C., Berglund, P. A., Zhao, S., Leaf, P. J., Kouzis, A. C., Bruce, M. L., et al. (1996). The 12-month prevalence and correlates of serious mental illness. In R. W. Manderscheid & M. A. Sonnenschein (Eds.), *Mental health, United States, 1996* (DHHS Publication No. [SMA] 96–3098, pp. 59–70). Washington, DC: U.S. Government Printing Office.

Kessler, R. C., Keller, M. B., & Wittchen, H-U. (2001). The epidemiology of generalized anxiety disorder. *Psychiatric Clinics of North America, 24,* 19–39.

Kessler, R. C., McGonagle, K. A., Zhao, S., Nelson, C. B., Hughes, M., Eshleman, S., et al. (1994). Lifetime and 12-month prevalence of DSM-III-R psychiatric disorders in the United States. *Archives of General Psychiatry, 51,* 8–19.

Kest, B., Wilson, S. G., & Mogil, J. S. (1999). Sex differences in supraspinal morphine analgesia are dependent on genotype. *Journal of Pharmacology & Experimental Therapeutics, 289,* 1370–1375.

Kety, S. S., Wender, P. H., Jacobsen, B., Ingraham, L. J., Jansson, L., Faber, B., & Kinney, D. K. (1994). Mental illness in the biological and adoptive relatives of schizophrenic adoptees. *Archives of General Psychiatry, 51,* 442–455.

Khan, A., Leventhal, R. M., Khan, S., & Brown, W. A. (2002). Suicide risk in patients with anxiety disorders: A meta-analysis of the FDA database. *Journal of Affective Disorders, 69,* 183–190.

Khan, J., Wei, J. S., Ringner, M., Saal, L. H., Ladanyi, M., Westermann, F., et al. (2001). Classification and diagnostic prediction of cancers using gene expression profiling and artificial neural networks. *Nature Medicine, 7,* 673–679.

Khot, U. N., Khot, M. B., Bajzer, C. T., Sapp, S. K., Ohman, E. M., Brener, S. J., et al. (2003). Prevalence of conventional risk factors in patients with coronary heart disease. *Journal of the American Medical Association, 290,* 898–904.

Kiecolt-Glaser, J. K., & Glaser, R. (2001). Stress and immunity: Age enhances the risks. *Current Directions in Psychological Science, 10,* 18–21.

Kiecolt-Glaser, J. K., & Newton, T. L. (2001). Marriage and health: His and hers. *Psychological Bulletin, 127,* 472–503.

Kiecolt-Glaser, J. K., McGuire, L., Robles, T. F., & Glaser, R. (2002). Psychoneuroimmunology: Psychological influences on immune function and health. *Journal of Consulting & Clinical Psychology, 70,* 537–547.

Kiecolt-Glaser, J. K., Page, G. G., Marucha, P. T., MacCallum, R. C., & Glaser, R. (1998). Psychological influences on surgical recovery: Perspectives from psychoneuroimmunology. *American Psychologist, 11,* 1209–1218.

Kiecolt-Glaser, J. K., Preacher, K. J., MacCallum, R. C., Atkinson, C., Malarkey, W. B., & Glaser, R. (2003). Chronic stress and age-related increases in the proinflammatory cytokine IL-6. *Proceedings of the National Academy of Sciences, 100,* 9090–9095.

Kiesler, D. J. (1996). *Contemporary interpersonal theory and research.* New York: Wiley.

Kihlstrom, J. F. (1999). The psychological unconscious. In L. Pervin & O. John (Eds.), *Handbook of personality* (pp. 424–442). New York: Guilford.

Kilgard, M. P., & Merzenich, M. M. (1998). Cortical map reorganization enabled by nucleus basalis activity. *Science, 279,* 1714–1718.

Kim, K. J., Conger, R. D., Lorenz, F. O., & Elder, G. H., Jr. (2001). Parent-adolescent reciprocity in negative affect and its relation to early adult social development. *Developmental Psychology, 37*(6), 775–790.

Kim, N. S., & Ahn, W.-K. (2002). Clinical psychologists' theory-based representations of mental disorders predict their diagnostic reasoning and memory. *Journal of Experimental Psychology: General, 131,* 451–476.

Kimble, G. A. (1999). Functional behaviorism: A plan for unity in psychology. *American Psychologist, 54,* 981–988.

Kimble, G. A. (2000). Behaviorism and unity in psychology. *Current Directions in Psychological Science, 9,* 208–212.

King, J., & Pribram, K. H. (Eds.). (1995). *The scale of conscious experience: Is the brain too important to be left to specialists to study?* Mahwah, NJ: Erlbaum.

Kinsbourne, M., & Cook, J. (1971). Generalized and lateralized effects of concurrent verbalization on a unimanual skill. *Quarterly Journal of Experimental Psychology, 23,* 341–345.

Kinsey, A. C., Pomeroy, W. B., & Martin, C. E. (1948). *Sexual behavior in the human male.* Philadelphia: Saunders.

Kinsey, A. C., Pomeroy, W. B., Martin, C. E., & Gebhard, P. H. (1953). *Sexual behavior in the human female.* Philadelphia: Saunders.

Kircher, J. C., Horowitz, S. W., & Raskin, D. C. (1988). Meta-analysis of mock crime studies of the control question polygraph technique. *Law and Human Behavior, 12,* 79–90.

Kirkpatrick, B., Buchanan, R. W., Ross, D. E., & Carpenter, W. T., Jr. (2001). A separate disease within the syndrome of schizophrenia. *Archives of General Psychiatry, 58,* 165–171.

Kirkpatrick, D. L. (1977). Evaluating training programs: Evidence versus proof. *Training and Development Journal, 31,* 9–12.

Kirsch, I. (1994a). Clinical hypnosis as a nondeceptive placebo: Empirically derived techniques. *American Journal of Clinical Hypnosis, 37*(2), 95–106.

Kirsch, I. (1994b). Defining hypnosis for the public. *Contemporary Hypnosis, 11*(3), 142–143.

Kirsch, I., & Braffman, W. (2001). Imaginative suggestibility and hypnotizability. *Psychological Science, 10,* 57–61.

Kirsch, I., Moore, T. J., Scoboria, A., & Nicholls, S. S. (2002). The emperor's new drugs: An analysis of antidepressant medication data submitted to the U.S. Food and Drug Administration. *Prevention and Treatment, 5,* np.

Kirsch, I., Scoboria, A., & Moore, T. J. (2002). Antidepressants and placebos: Secrets, revelations, and unanswered questions. *Prevention and Treatment, 5,* np.

Kishioka, S., Miyamoto, Y., Fukunaga, Y., Nishida, S., & Yamamoto, H. (1994). Effects of a mixture of peptidase inhibitors (Amastatin, Captopril and Phosphoramidon) on met enkephalin, betaa mixture of peptidase inhibitors (Amastatin, Captopril and Phosphoramidon) on met enkephalin, beta-endorphin, dynorphin (1–13) and electroacupun. *Japanese Journal of Pharmacology, 66,* 337–345.

Kisilevsky, B. S., Hains, S. M. J., Lee, K., Xie, X., Huang, H., Ye, H. H., et al. (2003). Effects of experience on fetal voice recognition. *Psychological Science, 14,* 220–224.

Kitano, H., Chi, I., Rhee, S., Law, C., & Lubben, J. (1992). Norms and alcohol consumption: Japanese in Japan, Hawaii, and California. *Journal of Studies on Alcohol, 53,* 33–39.

Kitayama, S., & Markus, H. R. (1992, May). *Construal of self as cultural frame: Implications for internationalizing psychology.* Paper presented at the Symposium on Internationalization and Higher Education, Ann Arbor.

Kjaer, T. W., Bertelsen, C., Piccini, P., Brooks, D., Alving, J., & Lou, H. C. (2002). Increased dopamine tone during meditation-induced change of consciousness. *Cognitive Brain Research, 13,* 255–259.

Kjellberg, A., Landstrom, U., Tesarz, M., Soderberg, L., & Akerlund, E. (1996). The effects of nonphysical noise characteristics, ongoing task and noise sensitivity on annoyance and distraction due to noise at work. *Journal of Environmental Psychology, 16,* 123–136.

Klahr, D., & Simon, H. (1999). Studies of scientific discovery: Complementary approaches and convergent findings. *Psychological Bulletin, 125,* 524–543.

Klaus, M. H., & Kennell, J. H. (1976). *Maternal infant bonding: The impact of early separation or loss on family development.* St. Louis: Mosby.

Klein, D. C., & Seligman, M. E. P. (1976). Reversal of performance deficits and perceptual deficits in learned helplessness and depression. *Journal of Abnormal Psychology, 85,* 11–26.

Klein, D. N. (1993). False suffocation alarms, spontaneous panics, and related conditions: An integrative hypothesis. *Archives of General Psychiatry, 50,* 306–316.

Klein, D., Lewinsohn,. P. M., Seeley, J. R., & Rohde, P. (2001). A family study of major depressive disorder in a community sample of adolescents. *Archives of General Psychiatry, 58,* 13–20.

Klein, M. (1975). *The writings of Melanie Klein: Vol. 3.* London: Hogarth Press.

Kleinknecht, R. A. (1991). *Mastering anxiety: The nature and treatment of anxious conditions.* New York: Plenum.

Kleinknecht, R. A. (1994). Acquisition of blood, injury, and needle fears and phobias. *Behaviour Research and Therapy, 32,* 817–823.

Kleinknecht, R. A. (2000). Social phobia. In M. Hersen & M. K. Biaggio (Eds.), *Effective brief therapies: A clinician's guide.* New York: Academic Press.

Kleinman, A. (1991, April). *Culture and DSM-IV: Recommendations for the introduction and for the overall structure.* Paper presented at the National Institute of Mental Health-sponsored Conference on Culture and Diagnosis, Pittsburgh, PA.

Klepp, K.-I., Kelder, S. H., & Perry, C. L. (1995). Alcohol and marijuana use among adolescents: Long-term outcomes of the class of 1989 study. *Annals of Behavioral Medicine, 17,* 19–24.

Klerman, L. V. (2002). Adolescent pregnancy in the United States. *International Journal of Adolescent Medicine & Health, 14,* 91–96.

Kline, S., & Groninger, L. D. (1991). The imagery bizarreness effect as a function of sentence complexity and presentation time. *Bulletin of the Psychonomic Society, 29,* 25–27.

Kling, K. C., Hyde, J. S., Showers, C. J., & Buswell, B. N. (1999). Gender differences in self-esteem: A meta-analysis. *Psychological Bulletin, 125,* 470–500.

Klintsova, A. Y., & Greenough, W. T. (1999). Synaptic plasticity in cortical systems. *Current Opinion in Neurobiology, 9,* 203–208.

Klohnen, E., & Bera, S. (1998). Behavioral and experiential patterns of avoidantly and securely attached women across adulthood: A 31-year longitudinal perspective. *Journal of Personality and Social Psychology, 74,* 211–223.

Klonoff-Cohen, H. S., & Edelstein, S. L. (1995). A case-control study of routine death scene sleep position in sudden infant death syndrom in Southern California. *Journal of the American Medical Association, 273*(10), 790–794.

Klosko, J. S., Barlow, D. H., Tassinari, R., & Cerny, J. A. (1990). A comparison of alprazolam and behavior therapy in treatment of panic disorder. *Journal of Consulting and Clinical Psychology, 58,* 77–84.

Kluger, A. N., & DeNisi, A. (1998). Feedback interventions: Toward the understanding of a double-edged sword. *Current Directions in Psychological Science, 7,* 67–72.

Knox, S., Burkard, A. W., Johnson, A. J., Suzuki, L. A., & Ponterotto, J. G. (2003). African American and European American therapists' experiences of addressing race in cross-racial psychotherapy dyads. *Journal of Counseling Psychology, 50,* 466–481.

Koh, P. O., Undie, A. S., Kabbani, N., Levenson, R., Goldman-Rakic, P. S., & Lidow, M. S. (2002). Up-regulation of neuronal calcium sensor-1 (NCS-1) in the prefrontal cortex of schizophrenic and bipolar patients. *Proceedings of the National Academies of Science, 100,* 313–317.

Kohlberg, L., & Gilligan, C. (1971). The adolescent as a philosopher: The discovery of the self in a postconventional world. *Daedalus, 100,* 1051–1086.

Köhler, W. (1924). *The mentality of apes.* New York: Harcourt Brace.

Kohut, H. (1983). Selected problems of self-psychological theory. In J. D. Lichtenberg & S. Kaplan (Eds.), *Reflections on self psychology* (pp. 387–416). Hillsdale, NJ: Erlbaum

Kok, M. R., & Boon, M. E. (1996). Consequences of neural network technology for cervical screening: increase in diagnostic consistency and positive scores. *Cancer, 78,* 112–117.

Kolata, G. (2002, August 19.). Male hormone therapy popular but untested. *The New York Times.*

Kolata, G. (2003, April 22). Hormone studies: What went wrong? *The New York Times.*

Kolata, G., & Markel, H. (2001, April 29). Baby not crawling? Reason seems to be less tummy time. *New York Times.*

Kolb, B., Gibb, R., & Robinson, T. E. (2003). Brain plasticity and behavior. *Current Directions in Psychological Science, 12,* 1–5.

Kolb, B., Gorny, G., Li, Y., Samaha, A.-N., & Robinson, T. E. (2003). Amphetamine or cocaine limits the ability of later experience to promote structural plasticity in the neocortex and nucleus accumbens. *Proceedings of the National Academy of Sciences, 100,* 10523–10528.

Koller, M., Kundi, M., & Cervinka, R. (1978). Field studies of shift work at an Austrian oil refinery: I. Health and psychosocial well-being of workers who drop out of shiftwork. *Ergonomics, 21,* 835–847.

Koob, G. F., & Bloom, F. E. (1988). Cellular and molecular mechanisms of drug dependence. *Science, 242,* 715–723.

Koob, G. F., Roberts, A. J., Schulteis, G., Parsons, L. H., Heyser, C. J., Hyytia, P., Merlo-Pich, E., & Weiss, F. (1998). Neurocircuitry targets in ethanol reward and dependence. *Alcohol: Clinical and Experimental Research, 22*(1), 3–9.

Koopmans, J. R., & Boomsma, D. I. (1996). Familial resemblance in alcohol use: Genetic or cultural transmission? *Journal of Studies in Alcoholism, 57,* 19–28.

Koppenaal, L., & Glanzer, M. (1990). An examination of the continuous distractor task and the "long-term recency effect." *Memory & Cognition, 18,* 183–195.

Kordower, J. H., Emborg, M. E., Bloch, J., Ma, S. Y., Chu, Y., Leventhal, L., et al. (2000). Neurodegeneration prevented by lentiviral vector delivery of GDNF in primate models of Parkinson's disease. *Science, 290,* 767–773.

Korner, J., & Leibel, R. L. (2003). To eat or not to eat—How the gut talks to the brain. *The New England Journal of Medicine, 349,* 926–928.

Kornhaber, M., Krechevsky, M., & Gardner, H. (1990). Engaging intelligence. *Educational Psychologist, 25,* 177–199.

Korochkin, L. I., Aleksandrova, M. A., Bashkirov, V. N., Trukhacheva, A. A., Dzitoyeva, S. G., Pavlova, G. V., et al. (2002). Xenografts of embryonic nerve tissue from Drosophila neuromutants stimulate development of neural homografts in rat brain and block glial scar formation. *Tsitologiia, 44,* 1181–1185.

Korteling, J. (1991). Effects of skill integration and perceptual competition on age-related differences in dual-task performance. *Human Factors, 33,* 35–44.

Kossek, E. E., & Ozeki, C. (1998). Work-family conflict, policies, and the job-life satisfaction relationship: A review and directions for organizational behavior-human resources research. *Journal of Applied Psychology, 83,* 139–149.

Kouri, E. M., Pope, H. G., & Lukas, S. E. (1999). Changes in aggressive behavior during withdrawal from long-term marijuana use. *Psychopharmacology, 143,* 302–308.

Kozak, M. J., Liebowitz, M. R., & Foa, E. B. (2000). Cognitive behavior therapy and pharmacotherapy for obsessive-compulsive disorder: The NIMH-sponsored collaborative study. In W. K. Goodman, M. V. Rudorfer, & J. D. Maser (Eds.), *Obsessive-compulsive disorder: Contemporary issues in treatment* (pp. 501–530). Mahwah, NJ: Erlbaum.

Krakauer, J. (1997). *Into thin air.* New York: Villard.

Kramer, A. F., & Willis, S. (2002). Enhancing the cognitive vitality of older adults. *Current Directions in Psychological Science, 11,* 173–177.

Krantz, D., Contrada, R., Hill, D., & Friedler, E. (1988). Environmental stress and biobehavioral antecedents of coronary heart disease. *Journal of Consulting and Clinical Psychology, 56,* 333–341.

Krantz, D., & Durel, L. (1983). Psychobiological substrates of the Type A behavior pattern. *Health Psychology, 2,* 393–411.

Krantz, D. S., & McCeney, M. K. (2002). Effects of psychological and social factors on organic disease: A critical assessment of research on coronary heart disease. *Annual Review of Psychology, 53,* 341–369.

Kranzler, H. R., & Anton, R. F. (1994). Implications of recent neuropsychopharmacologic research for understanding the etiology and development of alcoholism. *Journal of Consulting and Clinical Psychology, 62,* 1116–1126.

Kraus, W. E., Houmard, J. A., Duscha, B. D., Knetzger, K. J., Wharton, M. B., McCartney, J. S., et al. (2002). Effects of the amount and intensity of exercise on plasma lipoproteins. *The New England Journal of Medicine, 347,* 1483–1492.

Krause, N., & Shaw, B. A. (2000). Role-specific feelings of control and mortality. *Psychology and Aging, 15,* 617–626.

Krauzlis, R. J. (2002). Reaching for answers. *Neuron, 34,* 673–674.

Krauzlis, R. J., & Lisberger, S. G. (1991). Visual motion commands for pursuit eye movements in the cerebellum. *Science, 253,* 568–571.

Kring, A. M., & Gordon, A. H. (1998). Sex differences in emotion: Expression, experience, and physiology. *Journal of Personality & Social Psychology, 74,* 686–703.

Kristof, N. D. (1997, August 17). Where children rule. *New York Times Magazine.*

Krosnick, J. A., Betz, A. L., Jussim, L. J., & Lynn, A. R. (1992). Subliminal conditioning of attitude. *Personality and Social Psychology Bulletin, 18,* 152–162.

Krueger, J., Ham, J. J., & Linford, K. M. (1996). Perceptions of behavioral consistency: Are people aware of the actor-observer effect? *Psychological Science, 7,* 259–264.

Krueger, R. F., Markon, K. E., & Bouchard, T. J., Jr. (2003). The extended genotype: The heritability of personality accounts for the heritability of recalled family environments in twins reared apart. *Journal of Personality, 71,* 809–833.

Kruger, D. J. (2003). Evolution and altruism: Combining psychological mediators with naturally selected tendencies. *Evolution & Human Behavior, 24,* 118–125.

Kruger, J., & Dunning, D. (1999). Unskilled and unaware of it: How difficulties in recognizing one's own incompetence lead to inflated self-assessments. *Journal of Personality & Social Psychology, 77,* 1121–1134.

Krupinski, E., Nypaver, M., Poropatich, R., Ellis, D., Safwat, R., & Sapci, H. (2002). Clinical application in telemedicine/telehealth. *Telemedicine Journal and e-health, 8,* 13–34.

Krykouli, S. E., Stanley, B. G., Seirafi, R. D., & Leibowitz, S. F (1990). Stimulation of feeding by galanin: Anatomical localization and behavioral specificity of this peptide's effects in the brain. *Peptides, 11*(5), 995–1001.

Kuhs, H., & Tolle, R. (1991). Sleep deprivation therapy. *Biological Psychiatry, 29,* 1129–1148.

Kukull, W. A., Higdon, R., Bowen, J. D., McCormick, W. C., Teri, L., Schellenberg, G. D., et al. (2002). Dementia and Alzheimer disease incidence: A prospective cohort study. *Archives of Neurology, 59,* 1737–1746.

Kunda, Z.., & Spencer, S. J. (2003). When do stereotypes come to mind and when do they color judgment? A goal-based theoretical framework for stereotype activation and application. *Psychological Bulletin, 129,* 522–544.

Kunkel, D., Wilson, B. J., Linz, D., Potter, J., Donnerstein, E., Smith, S. L., et al. (1996). *The national television violence study.* Studio City, CA: Mediascope.

Kunz, P. R., & Woolcott, M. (1976). Season's greetings: From my status to yours. *Social Science Research, 5,* 269–278.

Kurzban, R., & Leary, M. R. (2001). Evolutionary origins of stigmatization: The functions of social exclusion. *Psychological Bulletin, 127,* 187–208.

Kushner, M. G., Thuras, P., Kaminski, J., Anderson, N., Neumeyer, B., & Mackenzie, T. (2000). Expectancies for alcohol to affect tension and anxiety as a function of time. *Addictive Behaviors, 25,* 93–98.

Kutchins, H., & Kirk, S. A. (1997). *Making us crazy: The psychiatric bible and the creation of mental disorders.* New York: Free Press.

Kwan, M., Greenleaf, W. J., Mann, J., Crapo, L., & Davidson, J. M. (1983). The nature of androgen action on male sexuality: A combined laboratory-self-report study on hypogonadal men. *Journal of Clinical Endocrinology and Metabolism, 57,* 557–562.

Kwate, N. O. A. (2001). Intelligence or misorientation? *Journal of Black Psychology, 27,* 221–238.

Kyrios, M., Sanavio, E., Bhar, S., & Liguori, L. (2001). Associations between obsessive-compulsive phenomena, affect, and beliefs: Cross-cultural comparisons of Australian and Italian data. *Behavioural and Cognitive Psychotherapy, 29,* 409–422.

Laan, E., Everaerd, W., Van Aanhold, M. T., & Rebel, M. (1993). Performance demand and sexual arousal in woman. *Behavior Research and Therapy, 31,* 25–36.

Labouvie-Vief, G. (1982). Discontinuities in development from childhood. In T. M. Field, A. Huston, H. C. Quay, L. Troll, & G. E. Finley (Eds.), *Review of human development.* New York: Wiley.

Labouvie-Vief, G. (1992). A new-Piagetian perspective on adult cognitive development. In R. J. Sternberg & C. A. Berg (Eds.), *Intellectual development.* New York: Cambridge University Press.

Lacayo, A. (1995). Neurologic and psychiatric complications of cocaine abuse. *Neuropsychiatry, Neuropsychology, and Behavioral Neurology, 8*(1), 53–60.

LaFrance, M., Hecht, M. A., & Paluck, E. L. (2003). The contingent smile: A meta-analysis of sex differences in smiling. *Psychological Bulletin, 129,* 305–334.

Lagerspetz, K. M. J., & Lagerspetz, K. Y. H. (1983). Genes and aggression. In E. C. Simmel, M. E. Hahn, & J. K. Walters (Eds.), *Aggressive behavior: Genetic and neural approaches.* Hillsdale, NJ: Erlbaum.

LaGreca, A. M., Silverman, W. K., Vernberg, E. M., & Prinstein, M. J. (1996). Symptoms of posttraumatic stress in children after Hurricane Andrew: A prospective study. *Journal of Consulting and Clinical Psychology, 64,* 712–723.

Lahey, B. B., Loeber, R., Hart, E. L., Frick, P. J., & Applegate, B. (1995). Four-year longitudinal study of conduct disorder in boys: Patterns and predictors of persistence. *Journal of Abnormal Psychology, 104,* 83–93.

Lai, C. S. L., Fisher, S. E., Hurst, J. A., Vargha-Khadem, F., & Monaco, A. P. (2001). A forkhead-domain gene is mutated in severe speech and language disorder. *Nature, 413,* 519–523.

Laird, R. D., Jordan, K. Y., Dodge, K. A., Pettit, G. S., & Gates, J. E. (2001). Peer rejection in childhood, involvement with antisocial peers in early adolescence, and the development of externalizing behavior problems. *Development and Psychopathology, 13,* 337–354.

Lalumière, M. L., Blanchard, R., & Zucker, K. J. (2000). Sexual orientation and handedness in men and women: A meta-analysis. *Psychological Bulletin, 126,* 575–592.

Lam, D. H., Watkins, E. R., Hayward, P., Bright, J., Wright, K., Kerr, N., Parr-Davis, G., & Sham, P. (2003). A randomized controlled study of cognitive therapy for relapse prevention for bipolar affective disorder: outcome of the first year. *Archives of General Psychiatry, 60,* 145–152.

Lamar, J. (2000). Suicides in Japan reach a record high. *British Medical Journal, 321,* 528.

Lamb, M. E. (Ed.). (1997). *The role of the father in child development* (3rd ed.). New York: Wiley.

Lamb, M. E. (1998). Assessments of children's credibility in forensic contexts. *Current Directions in Psychological Science, 7,* 43–46.

Lambert, M. J., & Barley, D. E. (2001). Research summary on the therapeutic relationship and psychotherapy outcome. *Psychotherapy, 38,* 357–361.

Lambert, M. J., & Bergin, A. E. (1994). The effectiveness of psychotherapy. In A. E. Bergin & S. L. Garfield (Eds.), *Handbook of psychotherapy and behavior change* (4th ed.). New York: Wiley.

Lambert, M. J., & Hill, C. E. (1994). *Assessing psychotherapy outcomes and processes. Assessing psychotherapy outcomes and processes.* New York: Wiley.

Lambert, N. M. (1999). Developmental trajectories in psychology: Applications to education and training. *American Psychologist, 54,* 991–1002.

Laming, P. R., Kimelberg, H., Robinson, S., Salm, A., Hawrylak, N., Muller, C., et al. (2000). Neuronal-glial interactions and behaviour. *Neuroscience and Biobehavioral Review, 24,* 295–340.

Landrine, H. (1991). Revising the framework of abnormal psychology. In P. Bronstein & K. Quina (Eds.), *Teaching a psychology of people.* Washington, DC: American Psychological Association.

Landsdale, M., & Laming, D. (1995). Evaluating the fragmentation hypothesis: The analysis of errors in cued recall. *Acta Psychologica, 88,* 33–77.

Lang, A. R., Goeckner, D. T., Adesso, V. J., & Marlatt, G. A. (1975). Effects of alcohol on aggression in male social drinkers. *Journal of Abnormal Psychology, 92,* 508–518.

Lang, P. J. (1995). The emotion probe: Studies of motivation and attention. *American Psychologist, 50*(5), 372–385.

Lang, P. J., & Melamed, B. G. (1969). Avoidance conditioning therapy of an infant with chronic ruminative vomiting. *Journal of Abnormal Psychology, 74,* 1–8.

Lange, C., & Byrd, M. (2002). Differences between students' estimated and attained grades in a first-year introductory psychology course as a function of identity development. *Adolescence, 37*(145), 93–108.

Langenberg, P., Ballesteros, M., Feldman, R., Damron, D., Anliker, J., Havas, S. (2000). Psychosocial factors and intervention-associated changes in those factors as correlates of change in fruit and vegetable consumption in the Maryland WIC 5 a day promotion program. *Annals of Behavioral Medicine, 22,* 307–315.

Langlois, J. H., Kalakanis, L., Rubenstein, A. J., Larson, A., Hallam, M., & Smoot, M. (2000). Maxims or myths of beauty: A meta-analytic and theoretical review. *Psychological Bulletin, 126,* 390–423.

Lansky, D., & Wilson, G. T. (1981). Alcohol, expectations and sexual arousal in males: An information processing analysis. *Journal of Abnormal Psychology, 89,* 528–538.

Lapointe, L. (1990). *Aphasia and related neurogenic language disorders.* New York: Thieme Medical.

Larsen, R. J., & Buss, D. M. (2002). *Personality psychology.* New York: Mc Graw-Hill.

Larson, J. R., Jr., Christensen, C., Franz, T. M., & Abbott, A. S. (1998). Diagnosing groups: The pooling, management, and impact of shared and unshared case information in team-based medical decision making. *Journal of Personality and Social Psychology, 75,* 93–108.

Larson, R. W., & Verma, S. (1999). How children and adolescents spend time across the world: Work, play, and developmental opportunities. *Psychological Bulletin, 125,* 701–736.

Latané, B. (1981). The psychology of social impact. *American Psychologist, 36,* 343–356.

Latané, B., & Rodin, J. (1969). A lady in distress: Inhibiting effects of friends and strangers on bystander intervention. *Journal of Experimental Social Psychology, 5,* 189–202.

Latham, G. P., Skarlicki, D., Irvine, D., & Siegel, J. P. (1993). The increasing importance of performance appraisals to employee effectiveness in organizational settings in North America. In C. L. Cooper & I. T. Robertson (Eds.), *International review of industrial and organizational psychology 1993* (pp. 87–132). Chichester, UK: Wiley.

Latkin, C. A., Sherman, S., & Knowlton, A. (2003). HIV prevention among drug users: Outcome of a network-oriented peer outreach intervention. *Health Psychology, 22,* 332–339.

Lau, M. A., Pihl, R. O., & Peterson, J. B. (1995). Provocation, acute alcohol intoxication, cognitive performance, and aggression. *Journal of Abnormal Psychology, 104,* 150–155.

Laughery, K. R. (1999). Modeling human performance during system design. In E. Salas (Ed.), *Human/technology interaction in complex systems* (Vol. 9, pp. 147–174). Stamford, CT: JAI Press.

Laughlin, P. L. (1999). Collective induction: Twelve postulates. *Organizational Behavior and Human Decision Processes, 80,* 50–69.

Laumann, E. O., Gagnon, J. H., Michael, R. T., & Michaels, S. (1994). *The social organization of sexuality: Sexual practices in the United States.* Chicago: University of Chicago Press.

Laumann, E. O., & Michael, R. T. (Eds.). (2000). *Sex, love, and health in America: Private choices and public policies.* Chicago: University of Chicago Press.

Laumann, E. O., Paik, A., Rosen, R. C. (1999). Sexual dysfunction in the United States: Prevalence and predictors. *Journal of the American Medical Association, 281,* 537–544.

Law, D. J., Pellegrino, J. W., & Hunt, E. B. (1993). Comparing the tortoise and the hare: Gender differences and experience in dynamic spatial reasoning tasks. *Psychological Science, 4,* 35–40.

Law, K. L., Stroud, L. R., LaGasse, L. L., Niaura, R., Liu, J., & Lester, B. M. (2003). Smoking during pregnancy and newborn neurobehavior. *Pediatrics, 111,* 1318–1323.

Lawford, B. R., Young, R. M., Rowell, J. A., Qualichefski, J., Fletcher, B. H., Syndulko, K., Ritchie, T., & Noble, E. P. (1995). Bromocriptine in the treatment of alcoholics with the D2 dopamine receptor A1 allele. *Nature Medicine, 1*(4), 337–341.

Lawless, H. T., & Engen, T. (1977). Associations to odors: Interference, memories and verbal learning. *Journal of Experimental Psychology, 3,* 52–59.

Lazarus, A. A. (1971). *Behavior therapy and beyond.* New York: McGraw-Hill.

Lazarus, R. S. (1966). *Psychological stress and the coping process.* New York: McGraw-Hill.

Lazarus, R. S. (1991). *Emotion and adaptation.* New York: Oxford University Press.

Lazarus, R. S. (1999). *Stress and emotion: A new synthesis.* New York: Springer.

Lazarus, R. S., & Folkman, S. (1984). *Stress, appraisal, and coping.* New York: Springer-Verlag.

Lazarus, R. S., Opton, E. M., Nomikos, M. S., & Rankin, M. O. (1965). The principle of short-circuiting of threat: Further evidence. *Journal of Personality, 33,* 622–635.

LeBlanc, M. M., & Barling, J. (in press). Understanding the many faces of workplace violence. In S. Fox & P. E. Spector (Eds.), *Counterproductive workplace behavior: An integration of both actor and recipient perspectives on causes and consequences.* Washington, DC: APA Books.

Lecrubier, Y., Clerc, G., Didi, R., & Kieser, M. (2002). Efficacy of St. John's wort extract WS 5570 in major depression: A double-blind, placebo-controlled trial. *American Journal of Psychiatry, 159,* 1361–1366.

LeDoux, J. E. (1995). Emotion: Clues from the brain. *Annual Review of Psychology, 46,* 209–235.

LeDoux, J. E. (1996). *The emotional brain.* New York: Simon & Schuster.

Lee, D. S., Lee, J. S., Oh, S. H., Kim, S. K., Kim, J. W., Chung, J. K., et al. (2001). Cross-modal plasticity and cochlear implants. *Nature, 409,* 149–150.

Lee, H. S., Nelms, J. L., Nguyen, M., Silver, R., & Lehman, M. N. (2003). The eye is necessary for a circadian rhythm in the suprachiasmatic nucleus. *Nature Neuroscience, 6,* 111–112.

Lee, M. C., Schiffman, S. S., & Pappas, T. N. (1994). Role of neuropeptides in the regulation of feeding behavior: A review of cholecystokinin, bombesin, neuropeptide Y, and galanin. *Neuroscience and Biobehavioral Reviews, 18*(3), 313–323.

Lee, T. M. C., Liu, H.-L., Tan, L.-H., Chan, C. C. H., Mahankali, S., Feng, C.-M., et al. (2002). Lie detection by functional magnetic resonance imaging. *Human Brain Mapping, 15,* 157–164.

Lee, V. E., Brooks-Gunn, J., & Schnur, E. (1988). Does Head Start work? A 1-year follow-up comparison of disadvantaged children attending Head Start, no preschool, and other preschool programs. *Developmental Psychology, 24,* 210–222.

Legerstee, M., Anderson, D., & Schaffer, A. (1998). Five- and eight-month-old infants recognize their faces and voices as familiar and social stimuli. *Child Development, 69,* 37–50.

Lehman, H. E. (1967). *Schizophrenia: IV. Clinical features.* Baltimore: Williams & Wilkins.

Leibel, R. L., Rosenbaum, M., & Hirsch, J. (1995). Changes in energy expenditure resulting from altered body weight. *New England Journal of Medicine, 332*(10), 621–628.

Leibowitz, S. F. (1992). Neurochemical-neuroendocrine systems in the brain controlling macronutrient intake and metabolism. *TINS, 15,* 491–497.

Leippe, M. R., Manion, A. P., & Romanczyk, A. (1992). Eyewitness persuasion: How and how well do fact finders judge the accuracy of adults' and children's memory reports? *Journal of Personality and Social Psychology, 63,* 181–197.

Lemly, B. (2000, February). Isn't she lovely? *Discover,* 43–49.

Lemmer, B., Kern, R. I., Nold, G., & Lohrer, H. (2002). Jet lag in athletes after eastward and westward time-zone transition. *Chronobiology International, 19,* 743–764.

Lenneberg, E. H. (1967). *Biological foundations of language.* New York: Wiley.

Leonard, B. E. (1992). *Fundamentals of psychopharmacology.* New York: Wiley.

Leonhardt, D. (2000, May 24). Makes sense to test for common sense. Yes? No? *New York Times.*

Lepore, S. J. (1995a). Measurement of chronic stressors. In S. Cohen, R. C. Kessler, & L. U. Gordon (Eds.), *Measuring stress: A guide for health and social scientists.* New York: Oxford University Press.

Lepore, S. J. (1995b). Cynicism, social support, and cardiovascular reactivity. *Health Psychology, 14,* 210–216.

Lerner, J. S., Gonzalez, R. M., Small, D. A., & Fischhoff, B. (2003). Effects of fear and anger on perceived risks of terrorism: A national field experiment. *Psychological Science, 14,* 144–150.

LeVay, S. (1991). A difference in hypothalamic structure between heterosexual and homosexual men. *Science, 253,* 1034–1037.

Levenson, H. (2003). Time-limited dynamic psychotherapy: An integrationist perspective. Journal of Psychotherapy Integration, 13, 300–333.

Levenson, R. W., Ekman, P., & Friesen, W. V. (1990). Voluntary facial action generates emotion-specific autonomic nervous system activity. *Psychophysiology, 27*(4), 363–384.

Levenson, R. W., Ekman, P., Heider, K., & Friesen, W. V. (1992). Emotion and autonomic nervous system activity in the Minangkabau of West Sumatra. *Journal of Personality and Social Psychology, 62*(6), 972–988.

Levenstein, S., Smith, M. W., & Kaplan, G. A. (2001). Psychosocial predictors of hypertension in men and women. *Archives of Internal Medicine, 161,* 1341–1346.

Leventhal, T., & Brooks-Gunn, J. (2000). The neighborhoods they live in: The effects of neighborhood residence on child and adolescent outcomes. *Psychological Bulletin, 126,* 309–337.

Levine, J. M., & Moreland, R. L. (1998). Small groups. In D. Gilbert, S. T. Fiske, & G. Lindzey (Eds.), *Handbook of social psychology* (Vol. 2, 4th ed., pp. 415–469). Boston: McGraw-Hill.

Levine, M. W., & Shefner, J. M. (1981). *Fundamentals of sensation and perception.* Reading, MA: Addison-Wesley.

Levine, R. V., Martinez, T. M., Brase, G., & Sorenson, K. (1994). Helping in 36 U.S. cities. *Journal of Personality and Social Psychology, 67,* 69–82.

Levine, S. (1999, February 1). In a loud and noisy world, baby boomers pay the consequences. *International Herald Tribune.*

Levinthal, C. F. (1996). *Drugs, behavior, and modern society.* Boston: Allyn & Bacon.

Levy, B. R., Slade, M. D., Kunkel, S. R., & Kasl, S. V. (2002). Longevity increased by positive self-perceptions of aging. *Journal of Personality & Social Psychology, 83*(2), 261–270.

Levy, R. L., Cain, K. C., Jarrett, M., & Heitkemper, M. M. (1997). The relationship between daily life stress and gastrointestinal symptoms in women with irritable bowel syndrome. *Journal of Behavioral Medicine, 20,* 177–194.

Levy-Shiff, R. (1994). Individual and contextual correlates of marital change across the transition to parenthood. *Developmental Psychology, 30,* 591–601.

Lewicki, P. (1992). Nonconscious acquisition of information. *American Psychologist, 47,* 796–801.

Lewinsohn, P. M., & Rosenbaum, M. (1987). Recall of parental behavior by acute depressives, remitted depressives, and nondepressives. *Journal of Personality and Social Psychology, 52,* 611–619.

Lewinsohn, P. M., Joiner, T. E., & Rohde, P. (2001). Evaluation of cognitive diathesis-stress models in precicting Major Depressive Disorder in adolescents. *Journal of Abnormal Psychology, 110,* 203–215.

Lewis, C. E., Jacobs, D. R., Jr., McCreath, H., Kiefe, C. I., Schreiner, P. J., Smith, D. E., & Williams, O. D. (2000). Weight gain continues in the 1990s: 10-year trends in weight and overweight from the CARDIA study. *American Journal of Epidemiology, 151,* 1172–1181.

Lewontin, R. (1976). Race and intelligence. In N. J. Block & G. Dworkin (Eds.), *The IQ controversy: Critical readings.* New York: Pantheon.

Ley, R. (1994) The "suffocation alarm" theory of panic attacks: A critical commentary. *Journal of Behavior Therapy and Experimental Psychiatry, 25,* 269–273.

Lezak, M. D. (1995). *Neuropsychological assessment* (3rd ed). New York: Oxford University Press.

Li, D-K., Petitti, D. B., Willinger, M., McMahon, R., Odouli, R., Vu, H., & Hoffman, H. J. (2003). Infant sleeping position and the risk of sudden infant death syndrome in California, 1997–2000. *American Journal of Epidemiology, 157,* 446–455.

Li, F., Harmer, P., McAuley, E., Duncan, T., Duncan, S. C., Chaumeton, N., & Fisher, K. J. (2001). An evaluation of the effects of Tai Chi exercise on physical function among older persons: A randomized controlled trial. *Annals of Behavioral Medicine, 23,* 139–146.

Li, S., Cullen, W., Anwyl, R., & Rowan, M. J. (2003). Dopamine-dependent facilitation of LTP induction in hippocampal CA1 by exposure to spatial novelty. *Nature Neuroscience, 6,* 526–531.

Liben, L. (1978). Perspective-taking skills in young children: Seeing the world through rose-colored glasses. *Developmental Psychology, 14,* 87–92.

Liberman, R. P., Wallace, C. J., Blackwell, G., Kopelowicz, A., Vaccaro, J. V., & Mintz, J. (1998). Skills training versus psychosocial occupational therapy for persons with persistent schizophrenia. *American Journal of Psychiatry, 155,* 1087–1091.

Lichtenstein, P., & Annas, P. (2000). Heritability and prevalence of specific fears and phobias in childhood. *Journal of Child Psychology and Psychiatry and Allied Disciplines, 41,* 927–937.

Lickey, M., & Gordon, B. (1991). *Medicine and mental illness: The use of drugs in psychiatry.* San Francisco: Freeman.

Lieberman, A., & Pawl, J. (1988). Clinical applications of attachment theory. In J. Bellsky & T. Nezworski (Eds.), *Clinical applications of attachment.* Hillsdale, NJ: Erlbaum.

Lieberman, J. A., Tollefson, G., Tohen, M., Green, A. I., Gur, R. E., Kahn, R., et al. (2003). Comparative efficacy and safety of atypical and conventional antipsychotic drugs in first-episode psychosis: A randomized, double-blind trial of olanzapine versus haloperidol. *The American Journal of Psychiatry, 160,* 1396–1404.

Lieberman, M. A., & Tobin, S. (1983). *The experience of old age.* New York: Basic Books.

Liebert, R. M., & Spiegler, M. D. (1994). *Personality: Strategies and issues.* Pacific Grove, CA: Brooks/Cole.

Liechti, M. E., Gamma, A., & Vollenweider, F. X. (2001). Gender differences in the subjective effects of MDMA. *Psychopharmacology, 154,* 161–168.

Liepert, J., Bauder, H., Miltner, W. H. R., Taub, E., & Weiller, C. (2000). Treatment-induced cortical reorganization after stroke in humans. *Stroke, 31,* 1210.

Lievens, F., Harris, M. M., Van Keer, E., & Bisqueret, C. (2003). Predicting cross-cultural training performance: The validity of personality, cognitive ability, and dimensions measured by an assessment center and a behavior description interview. *Journal of Applied Psychology, 88,* 476–489.

Light, K. C., Girdler, S. S., Sherwood, A., Bragdon, E. E., Brownley, K. A., West, S. G., & Hinderliter, A. L. (1999). High stress responsivity predicts later blood pressure only in combination with positive family history and high life stress. *Hypertension, 33,* 1458–1464.

Lilienfeld, S. O., & Marino, L. (1999). Essentialism revisited: Evolutionary theory and the concept of mental disorder. *Journal of Abnormal Psychology, 108,* 400–411.

Lilienfeld, S. O., Lynn, S. J., Kirsch, I., Chaves, J. F., Sarbin, T. R., Ganaway, G. K., & Powell, R. A. (1999). Dissociative identity disorder and the sociocognitive model: Recalling the lessons of the past. *Psychological Bulletin, 125,* 507–523.

Lilienfeld, S., Wood, J., & Garb, H. N. (2000). The scientific status of projective tests. *Psychological Science in the Public Interest, 1,* 27–66.

Lillywhite, A. R., Wilson, S. J., & Nutt, D. J. (1994). Successful treatment of night terrors and somnambulism with paroxetine. *British Journal of Psychiatry, 16,* 551–554.

Lin, L., Umahara, M., York, D. A., & Bray, G. A. (1998). Beta-casomorphins stimulate and enterostatin inhibits the intake of dietary fat in rats. *Peptides, 19,* 325–331.

Lin, S., Thomas, T. C., Storlien, L. H., & Huang, X. F. (2000). Development of high fat diet-induced obesity and leptin resistance in C57Bl/6J mice. *International Journal of Obesity Related Metabolic Disorders, 24,* 639–646.

Lindsey, K. P., & Paul, G. L. (1989). Involuntary commitments to public mental institutions: Issues involving the overrepresentation of blacks and assessment of relevant functioning. *Psychological Bulletin, 106,* 171–183.

Lindvall, O., & Hagell, P. (2001). Cell therapy and transplantation in Parkinson's disease. *Clinical Chemistry and Laboratory Medicine, 39,* 356–361.

Linnet, K. M., Dalsgaard, S., Obel, C., Wisborg, K., Henriksen, T. B., Rodriguez, A., et al. (2003). Maternal lifestyle factors in pregnancy risk of attention deficit hyperactivity disorder and associated behaviors: Review of the current evidence. *American Journal of Psychiatry, 160,* 1028–1040.

Linz, D., Donnerstein, E., & Penrod, S. (1987). The findings and recommendations of the Attorney General's Commission on Pornography: Do the psychological facts fit the political fury? *American Psychologist, 42,* 946–953.

Lippa, R. A. (2003). Are 2D:4D finger-length ratios related to sexual orientation?: Yes for men, no for women. *Journal of Personality and Social Psychology, 85,* 179–188.

Lisanby, S. H., Schlaepfer, T. E., Fisch, H. U., & Sackeim, H. A. (2001). Magnetic seizure therapy of major depression. *Archives of General Psychiatry, 58,* 303–305.

Littlepage, G. E., Schmidt, G. W., Whisler, E. W., & Frost, A. G. (1995). An input-output analysis of influence and performance in problem-solving groups. *Journal of Personality and Social Psychology, 69,* 877–889.

Littlewood, R. (1992). Psychiatric diagnosis and racial bias: Empirical and interpretative approaches. *Social Science & Medicine, 34,* 141–149.

Liu, C., Weaver, D. R., Jin, X., Shearman, L. P., Pieschl, R. L., Gribkoff, V. K., & Reppert, S. M. (1997). Molecular dissection of two distinct actions of melatonin on the suprachiasmatic circadian clock. *Neuron, 19,* 91–102.

Liu, S., Prince, M., Blizard, B., & Mann, A. (2002). The prevalence of psychiatric morbidity and its associated factors in general health care in Taiwan. *Psychological Medicine, 32,* 629–637.

Lively, W. M. (2001). Syncope and neurologic deficits in a track athlete: A case report. *Medicine and Science in Sports and Exercise, 33,* 345–347.

Lloyd-Richardson, E. E., Papandonatos, G., Kazura, A., Stanton, C., & Niaura, R. (2002). Differentiating stages of smoking intensity among adolescents: Stage-specific psychological and social influences. Journal of Consulting & Clinical Psychology, 70, 998–1009.

Locke, E. A. (2000). Motivation, cognition, and action: An analysis of studies of task goals and knowledge. *Applied Psychology: An International Review, 49,* 408–429.

Locke, E. A., & Latham G. P. (1990). *A theory of goal setting & task performance.* Englewood Cliffs, NJ: Prentice Hall.

Locke, E. A., & Latham, G. P. (2002). Building a practically useful theory of goal setting and task motivation: A 35-year odyssey. *American Psychologist, 57,* 705–717.

Lockhart, R. S., & Craik, F. I. M. (1990). (1990). *Canadian Journal of Psychology, 44,* 87–112.

Loeber, R. T., Cintron, C. M. B., & Yurgelun-Todd, D. A. (2001). Morphometry of individual cerebellar lobules in schizophrenia. *American Journal of Psychiatry, 158,* 952–954.

Loeber, R., & Stouthamer-Loeber, M. (1998). Development of juvenile aggression and violence. Some common misconceptions and controversies. *American Psychologist, 53,* 242–259.

Loehlin, J. C. (1989). Partitioning environmental and genetic contributions to behavioral development. *American Psychologist, 44,* 1285–1292.

Loehlin, J. C. (1992). *Genes and environment in personality development.* Newbury Park, CA: Sage.

Loehlin, J. C., Neiderhiser, J. M., & Reiss, D. (2003). The behavior genetics of personality and the NEAD study. *Journal of Research in Personality, 37,* 373–387.

Loewenstein, G. (1994). The psychology of curiosity: A review and reinterpretation. *Psychological Bulletin, 116*(1), 75–98.

Loftus, E. F. (1992). When a lie becomes memory's truth: Memory distortion after exposure to misinformation. *Psychological Science, 3,* 121–123.

Loftus, E. F. (1997a). Memory for a past that never was. *Current Directions in Psychological Science, 6,* 60–65.

Loftus, E. F. (1997b). Repressed memory accusations: Devastated families and devastated patients. *Applied Cognitive Psychology, 11,* 25–30.

Loftus, E. F. (1998). The price of bad memories. *Skeptical Inquirer, 22,* 23–24.

Loftus, E. F. (2003, January). *Illusions of memory.* Presentation at the 25th Annual National Institute on the Teaching of Psychology, St. Petersburg Beach, Florida.

Loftus, E., & Guyer, M. (2002). Who abused Jane Doe? The hazards of the single case history (Part 1). *Skeptical Inquirer, 26,* 24–32.

Loftus, E. F., & Hoffman, H. G. (1989). Misinformation and memory: The creation of new memories. *Journal of Experimental Psychology: General, 118,* 100–104.

Loftus, E. F., & Ketcham, K. (1991). *Witness for the defense.* New York: St. Martin's Press.

Loftus, E. F., & Ketcham, K. (1994). *The myth of repressed memory: False memories and allegations of sexual abuse.* New York: St. Martin's Press.

Loftus, E. F., & Palmer, J. C. (1974). Reconstruction of automobile destruction: An example of the interaction between language and memory. *Journal of Verbal Learning and Verbal Behavior, 13,* 585–589.

Loftus, E. F., & Pickrell, J. E. (1995). The formation of false memories. *Psychiatric Annals, 25,* 720–725.

Loftus, T. M., Jaworsky, D. E., Frehywot, G. L., Townsend, C. A., Ronnett, G. V., Lane, M. D., & Kuhajda, F. P. (2000). Reduced food intake and body weight in mice treated with fatty acid synthase inhibitors. *Science, 288,* 2379–2381.

Logue, A. W. (1985). Conditioned food aversion in humans. *Annals of the New York Academy of Sciences, 104,* 331–340.

Loher, B. T., Noe, R. A., Moeller, N. L., & Fitzgerald, M. P. (1985). A meta-analysis of the relation of job characteristics to job satisfaction. *Journal of Applied Psychology, 70,* 280–289.

LoLordo, V. M. (2001). Learned helplessness and depression. In M. E. Carroll & J. B. Overmier (Eds.), *Animal research and human health: Advancing human welfare through behavioral science* (pp. 63–77). Washington, DC: American Psychological Association.

London Daily Telegraph. (1998, September 19). " 'Cat' that turned out to be a clock." *London Daily Telegraph.*

Longo, N., Klempay, S., & Bitterman, M. E. (1964). Classical appetitive conditioning in the pigeon. *Psychonomic Science, 1,* 19–20.

Lopez, S. R. (1989). Patient variable biases in clinical judgment: Conceptual overview and methodological considerations. *Psychological Bulletin, 106,* 184–203.

Losh, S. C., Tavani, C. M., Njoroge, R., Wilke, R., & McAuley, M. (2003). What does education really do? Educational dimensions and pseudoscience support in the American general public, 1979–2001. *Skeptical Inquirer, 27,* 30–35.

Löw, K., Crestani, F., Keist, R., Benke, D., Brunig, I., Benson, J. A., et al. (2000). Molecular and neuronal substrate for the selective attenuation of anxiety. *Science, 290,* 131–134.

Lubinski, D., Benbow, C. P., Shea, D. L., Eftekhari-Sanjani, H., & Halverson, M. B. J. (2001). Men and women at promise for scientific achievement: Similarity not dissimilarity. *Psychological Science, 12,* 309–317.

Luborsky, L. (1972). Another reply to Eysenck. *Psychological Bulletin, 78,* 406–408.

Luborsky, L. (1997). The core conflictual relationship theme: A basic case formulation method. In T. D. Eells (Ed.), *Handbook of psychotherapy case formulation* (pp. 58–83). New York: Guilford.

Luborsky, L., Rosenthal, R., Diguer, L., Andrusyna, T. P., Berman, J. S., Levitt, J. T., et al. (2002). The dodo bird verdict is alive and well—mostly. *Clinical Psychology: Science and Practice, 9,* 2–12.

Luborsky, L., Singer, B., & Luborsky, L. (1975). Comparative studies of psychotherapies: Is it true that everyone has won and all must have prizes? *Archives of General Psychiatry, 32,* 995–1008.

Lucas, R. E., Diener, E., & Larsen, R. J. (2003). Measuring positive emotions. In S. J. Lopez & C. R. Snyder (Eds.), *Positive psychological assessment: A handbook of models and measures.* Washington, DC: American Psychological Association.

Luchins, A. S. (1942). Mechanization in problem solving: The effect of Einstellung. *Psychological Monographs, 54*(6, Whole No. 248).

Lucy, J. A. (1992). *Language diversity and thought: A reformulation of the linguistic relativity hypothesis.* Cambridge: Cambridge University Press.

Lue, T. F. (2000). Drug therapy: Erectile dysfunction. *The New England Journal of Medicine, 342,* 1802–1813.

Luntz, B. K., & Widom, C. S. (1994). Antisocial personality disorder in abused and neglected children grown up. *American Journal of Psychiatry, 151,* 670–674.

Luria, Z. (1992, February). *Gender differences in children's play patterns.* Paper presented at University of Southern California, Los Angeles.

Lutsky, N. (1995). When is "obedience" obedience? Conceptual and historical commentary. *Journal of Social Issues, 51,* 55–65.

Lutz, D. J., & Sternberg, R. J. (1999). Cognitive development. In M. H. Bornstein & M. E. Lamb (Eds.), *Developmental psychology: An advanced textbook* (4th ed.) Mahwah, NJ: Erlbaum.

Lykken, D. T. (1999). *Happiness: What studies on twins show us about nature, nurture, and the happiness set point.* New York: Golden Books.

Lynam, D. R. (1996). The early identification of chronic offenders: Who is the fledgling psychopath? *Psychological Bulletin, 120,* 209–234.

Lynam, D. R., & Widiger, T. A. (2001). Using the five-factor model to represent the *DSM-IV* personality disorders: An expert consensus approach. *Journal of Abnormal Psychology, 110,* 401–412.

Lynn, R. (1996). Racial and ethnic differences in intelligence in the U.S. on the Differential Ability Scale. *Personality and Individual Differences, 20,* 271–273.

Lynn, S. J., Lilienfeld, S. O., & Lohr, J. M. (Eds.). (2003). *Science and pseudoscience in clinical psychology.* New York: Guilford Press.

Lynn, S. J., Lock, T. G., Myers, B., & Payne, D. G. (1997). Recalling the unrecallable: Should hypnosis be used to recover memories in psychotherapy? *Current Directions in Psychological Science, 6,* 79–83.

Lynn, S. J., Myers, B., & Malinoski, P. (1997). Hypnosis, pseudomemories, and clinical guidelines: A sociocognitive perspective. In J. D. Read & D. S. Lindsay (Eds.), *Recollections of trauma: Scientific evidence and clinical practice. NATO ASI series: Series A: Life sciences* (Vol. 291, pp. 305–336). New York: Plenum Press.

Lynn, S. J., & Rhue, J. W. (1986). The fantasy-prone person: Hypnosis, imagination, and creativity. *Journal of Personality and Social Psychology, 51,* 404–408.

Lynn, S. J., Vanderhoff, H., Shindler, K., & Stafford, J. (2002). Defining hypnosis as a trance vs. cooperation: Hypnotic inductions, suggestibility, and performance standards. *American Journal of Clinical Hypnosis, 44,* 231–240.

Lynskey, M. T., Heath, A. C., Bucholz, K. K., Slutske, W. S., Madden, P. A. F., Nelson, E. C., et al. (2003). Escalation of drug use in early-onset cannabis users vs. co-twin controls. *Journal of the American Medical Association, 289,* 427–433.

Lyons, D., & McLoughlin, D. M. (2001). Clinical review: Psychiatry. *British Medical Journal, 323,* 1228–1231.

Lyubomirsky, S. (2001). Why are some people happier than others?: The role of cognitive and motivational processes in well-being. *American Psychologist, 56,* 239–249.

Lyubomirsky, S., & Nolen-Hoeksema, S. (1995). Effects of self-focused rumination on negative thinking and interpersonal problem solving. *Journal of Personality and Social Psychology, 69,* 176–190.

MacAndrew, C., & Edgerton, R. B. (1969). *Drunken comportment.* Chicago: Aldine.

MacArthur Foundation. (1999). *Research network on successful midlife development.* Vero Beach, FL: The John D. and Catherine T. MacArthur Foundation. Retrieved August 26, 2003, from http://midmac.med.harvard.edu/

MacDonald, M., & Bernstein, D. A. (1974). Treatment of a spider phobia with in vivo and imaginal desensitization. *Journal of Behavior Therapy and Experimental Psychiatry, 5,* 47–52.

Macey, P. M., Henderson, L. A., Macey, K. E., Alger, J. R., Frysinger, R. C., Woo, M. A., et al. (2002). Brain morphology associated with obstructive sleep apnea. *American Journal of Respiratory and Critical Care Medicine, 166,* 1382–1387.

Mack, A., & Rock, I. (1998). *Inattentional blindness.* Cambridge, MA: MIT Press.

MacMahon, K. M. A., & Lip, G. Y. H. (2002). Psychological factors in heart failure: A review of the literature. *Archives of Internal Medicine, 162,* 509–516.

MacMillan, H. L., Fleming, J. E., Steiner, D. L., Lin, E., Boyle, M. H., Jamieson, E., et al. (2001). Childhood abuse and lifetime psychopathology in a community sample. *American Journal of Psychiatry, 158,* 1878–1883.

MacMillan, M. (1997). *Freud evaluated: The completed arc.* Cambridge, MA: MIT Press.

MacQueen, G. M., Campbell, S., McEwen, B. S., Macdonald, K., Amano, S., Joffe, R. T., et al. (2003). Course of illness, hippocampal function, and hippocampal volume in major depression. *Proceedings of the National Academies of Science, 100,* 1387–1392.

Maddux, J. E. (1993). Social cognitive models of health and exercise behavior: An introduction and review of conceptual issues. *Journal of Applied Sport Psychology, 5,* 116–140.

Mahesh Yogi, M. (1994). *Science of being and art of living.* New York: NAL/Dutton.

Maier, S. F., & Watkins, L. R. (2000). The immune system as a sensory system: Implications for psychology. *Current Directions in Psychological Science, 9,* 98–102.

Maj, M., Gaebal, W., Lopez-Ibor, J. J., & Sartorius, N. (Eds.). (2002). *Psychiatric diagnosis and classification.* New York: Wiley.

Major, B., Sciacchtinano, A. M., & Crocker, J. (1993). In-group versus out-group comparisons and self-esteem. *Personality and Social Psychology Bulletin, 19,* 711–721.

Malamuth, N. M. (1998). The confluence model as an organizing framework for research on sexually aggressive men: Risk moderators, imagined aggression, and pornography consumption. In R. G. Geen & E. Donnerstein (Eds.), *Human aggression* (pp. 230–247). San Diego: Academic Press.

Malamuth, N., & Addison, T. (2001). Helping and altruism. In G. Fletcher & M. Clark (Eds.), *Blackwell handbook of social psychology: Interpersonal processes* (pp. 162–195). Oxford, England: Blackwell.

Malamuth, N. M., Addison, T., & Koss, M. (2000). Pornography and sexual aggression: Are there reliable effects and can we understand them? *Annual Review of Sex Research, 11,* 26–91.

Malamuth, N. M., & Check, J. V. P. (1983). Sexual arousal to rape depictions: Individual differences. *Journal of Abnormal Psychology, 92,* 55–67.

Malarkey, W. B., Kiecolt-Glaser, J. K., Pearl, D., & Glaser, R. (1994). Hostile behavior during marital conflict alters pituitary and adrenal hormones. *Psychosomatic Medicine, 56,* 41–51.

Malaspina, D., Goetz, R. R., Friedman, J. H., Kaufmann, C. A., Faraone, S. V., Tsuang, M., et al. (2001). Traumatic brain injury and schizophrenia in members of schizophrenia and bipolar disorder pedigrees. *American Journal of Psychiatry, 158,* 440–446.

Malatesta, C. Z., & Izard, C. E. (1984). The ontogenesis of human social signals: From biological imperative to symbol utilization. In N. A. Fox & R. J. Davidson (Eds.), *The psychobiology of affective development* (pp. 161–206). Hillsdale, NJ: Erlbaum.

Malenka, R. C. (1995). LTP and LTD: Dynamic and interactive processes of synaptic plasticity. *The Neuroscientist, 1,* 35–42.

Malenka, R. C., & Nicoll, R. A. (1999). Long-term potentiation—a decade of progress? *Science, 285,* 1870–1874.

Malgrange, B., Rigo, J. M., Van de Water, T. R., Staecker, H., Moonen, G., & Lefebvre, P. P. (1999). Growth factor therapy to the damaged inner ear: Clinical prospects. *International Journal of Pediatric Otorhinolaryngology, 49*(Suppl. 1), S19–S25.

Malleret, G., Haditsch, U., Genoux, D., Jones, M. W., Bliss, T. V. P., Vanhoose, A. M., et al. (2001). Inducible and reversible enhancement of learning, memory, and long-term potentiation by genetic inhibition of calcineurin. *Cell, 104,* 675–686.

Manderscheid, R., & Barrett, S. (Eds.). (1987). *Mental health, United States, 1987* (DHHS Pub. No. ADM 87–1518). Bethesda, MD: National Institute of Mental Health.

Maner, J. K., Luce, C. L., Neuberg, S. L., Cialdini, R. B., Brown, S., & Sagarin, B. J. (2002). The effects of perspective taking on motivations for helping: Still no evidence for altruism. *Personality and Social Psychology Bulletin, 28,* 1601–1610.

Manji, H. K., Bowden, C. L., & Belmaker, R. H. (Eds.). (2000). *Bipolar medications: Mechanisms of action.* Washington, DC: American Psychiatric Press.

Mann, K., Roschke, J., Nink, M., Aldenhoff, J., Beyer, J., Benkert, O., et al. (1992). Effects of corticotropin-releasing hormone administration in patients suffering from sleep apnea syndrome. *Society for Neuroscience Abstracts, 22,* 196.

Mannuzza, M., Schneider, F. R., Chapman, T. F., Liebowitz, M. R., Klein, D. F., & Fyer, A. J. (1995). Generalized social phobia. *Archives of General Psychiatry, 52,* 230–237.

Mansfield, P. K., Voda, A., & Koch, P. B. (1995). Predictors of sexual response changes in heterosexual midlife women. *Health Values, 19*(1), 10–20.

Maquet, P. (2001). The role of sleep in learning and memory. *Science, 294,* 1048–1052.

Marcotte, D. E., & Wilcox-Goek, V. (2001). Estimating the employment and earnings costs of mental illness: Recent developments in the United States. *Social Science and Medicine, 53,* 21–27.

Marcus, G. F. (1996). Why do children say "breaked"? *Current Directions in Psychological Science, 5,* 81–85.

Marenco, S., & Weinberger, D. R. (2000). The neurodevelopmental hypothesis of schizophrenia: Following a trail of evidence from cradle to grave. *Developmental Psychopathology, 12,* 501–527.

Margetic, S., Gazzola, C., Pegg, G. G., & Hill, R. A. (2002). Leptin: A review of its peripheral actions and interactions. *Obesity, 26,* 1407–1433.

Markman, E. M. (1994). Constraints children place on word meanings. In P. Bloom (Ed.), *Language acquisition: Core readings* (pp. 154–173). Cambridge, MA: MIT Press.

Markus, H. R., & Kitayama, S. (1991). Culture and the self: Implications for cognition, emotion, and motivation. *Psychological Review, 98,* 224–253.

Markus, H. R., & Kitayama, S. (1997). Culture and the self: Implications for cognition, emotion, and motivation. In L. A. Peplau & S. Taylor (Eds.), *Sociocultural perspectives in social psychology* (pp. 157–216). Upper Saddle River, NJ: Prentice-Hall.

Markus, H. R., Kitayama, S., & Heiman, R. J. (1996). Culture and "basic" psychological principles. In E. T. Higgins & A. W. Kruglanski (Eds.), *Social psychology: Handbook of basic principles* (pp. 857–913). New York: Guilford.

Marmar, C. R. (1990). Psychotherapy process research: Progress, dilemmas, and future directions. *Journal of Consulting and Clinical Psychology, 58,* 265–272.

Marshall, W. L. (1989). Pornography and sex offenders. In D. Zillmann & J. Bryant (Eds.), *Pornography: Research advances and policy considerations.* Hillsdale, NJ: Erlbaum.

Martin, B., & Hoffman, J. (1990). Conduct disorders. In M. Lewis & S. M. Miller (Eds.), *Handbook of developmental psychopathology.* New York: Plenum.

Martin, C. L., & Fabes, R. A. (2001). The stability and consequences of young children's same-sex peer interactions. *Developmental Psychology, 37,* 431–446.

Martin, D. J., Garske, J. P., & Davis, M. K. (2000). Relation of the therapeutic alliance with outcome and other variables: A meta-analytic review. *Journal of Consulting & Clinical Psychology, 68,* 438–450.

Martin, R. A. (2001). Humor, laughter, and physical health: Methodological issues and research findings. *Psychological Bulletin, 127,* 504–519.

Martin, R., Gardikiotis, A., & Hewstone, M. (2002). Levels of consensus and majority and minority influence. *European Journal of Social Psychology, 32,* 645–665.

Martindale, C. (1981). *Cognition and consciousness.* Homewood, IL: Dorsey Press.

Martindale, C. (1991). *Cognitive psychology: A neural-network approach.* Pacific Grove, CA: Brooks/Cole.

Martinez, C. R., & Forgatch, M. S. (2001). Preventing problems with boys' noncompliance: Effects of a parent training intervention for divorcing mothers. *Journal of Consulting and Clinical Psychology, 69,* 416–428.

Martinot, M.-L. P., Bragulat, V., Artiges, E., Dolle, F., Hinnen, F., Jouvent, R., et al. (2001). Decreased presynaptic dopamine function in the left caudate of depressed patients with affective flattening and psychomotor retardation. *American Journal of Psychiatry, 158,* 314–316.

Marzuk, P. M., Tardiff, K., Leon, A. C., Hirsch, C. S., Stajic, M., Portera, L., et al. (1995). Fatal injuries after cocaine use as a leading cause of death among young adults in New York City. *New England Journal of Medicine, 332*(26), 1753–1757.

Masand, P., Popli, A. P., & Welburg, J. B. (1995). Sleepwalking. *American Family Physician, 51*(3), 649–653.

Maslach, C., & Goldberg, J. (1995). Sleepwalking. *American Family Physician, 51*(3), 649–653.

Maslach, C., & Goldberg, J. (1998). Prevention of burnout: New perspectives. *Applied and Preventive Psychology, 7,* 63–74.

Masland, R. H. (2001). Neuronal diversity in the retina. *Current Opinion in Neurobiology, 11,* 431–436.

Masling, J., & Bornstein, R. F. (1991). Perception without awareness and electrodermal responding: A strong test of subliminal psychodynamic activation effects. *Journal of Mind and Behavior, 12,* 33–47.

Maslow, A. H. (1943). A theory of human motivation. *Psychological Review, 50,* 370–396.

Maslow, A. H. (1954). *Motivation and personality.* New York: Harper.

Maslow, A. H. (1970). *Motivation and personality* (2nd ed.). New York: Harper & Row.

Maslow, A. H. (1971). *Toward a psychology of being.* Princeton, NJ: Van Nostrand.

Mason, R. T., Fales, H. M., Jones, T. H., Pannell, L. K., Chinn, J. W., & Crews, D. (1989). Sex pheromones in snakes. *Science, 245,* 290–293.

Masters, J. C., Burish, T. G., Hollon, S. D., & Rimm, D. C. (1987). *Behavior therapy: Techniques and empirical findings* (3rd ed.). San Diego: Harcourt Brace Jovanovich.

Masters, W. H., & Johnson, V. E. (1966). *Human sexual response.* Boston: Little, Brown & Co.

Matlin, M. W. (1998). *Cognition* (4th ed.). Ft. Worth: Harcourt Brace College Publishers.

Matson, J., Sevin, J., Fridley, D., & Love, S. (1990). Increasing spontaneous language in autistic children. *Journal of Applied Behavior Analysis, 23,* 227–223.

Matsumoto, D. (2000) *Culture and psychology: People around the world.* Belmont, CA: Wadsworth.

Matsumoto, D., & Ekman, P. (1989). American-Japanese cultural differences in intensity ratings of facial expressions of emotion. *Motivation and Emotion, 13,* 143–157.

Matthews, G., & Dreary, I. J. (1998). *Personality traits.* Cambridge, England: Cambridge University Press.

Matthies, E., Hoeger, R., & Guski, R. (2000). Living on polluted soil: Determinants of stress symptoms. *Environment and Behavior, 32,* 270–286.

Maupin, H. E., & Fisher, J. R. (1989). The effects of superior female performance and sex-role orientation in gender conformity. *Canadian Journal of Behavioral Science, 21,* 55–69.

May, E. R., & Zelikow, P. D. (Eds.). (1997). *The Kennedy tapes: Inside the White House during the Cuban Missile Crisis.* New York: Belknap Press.

May, G. L., & Kahnweiler, W. M. (2000). The effect of a mastery practice design on learning and transfer in behavior modeling training. *Personnel Psychology, 53,* 353–373.

Mayberry, R. I., Lock, E., Kazmi, H. (2002). Linguistic ability and early language exposure. *Nature, 417,* 38.

Mayer, D. J., & Price, D. D. (1982). A physiological and psychological analysis of pain: A potential model of motivation. In D. W. Pfaff (Ed.), *The physiological mechanisms of motivation*. New York: Springer-Verlag.

Mayer, F. S., & Sutton, K. (1996). *Personality: An integrative approach*. Upper Saddle River, NJ: Prentice-Hall.

Mazoyer, B., Tzouri-Mazoyer, N., Mazard, A., Denis, M., Mellet, E. (2002). Neural basis of image and language interactions. *International Journal of Psychology, 37,* 204–208.

Mazzoni, G. A., & Loftus, E. F. (1996). When dreams become reality. *Consciousness and Cognition, 5,* 442–462.

Mazzoni, G., & Memon, A. (2003). Imagination can create false autobiographical memories. *Psychological Science, 14,* 186–188.

McAndrew, F. T. (2002). New evolutionary perspectives on altruism. Multilevel-selection and costly-signaling theories. *Current Directions in Psychological Science, 11,* 79–82.

McAuley, E. (1992). The role of efficacy cognitions in the prediction of exercise behavior in middle-aged adults. *Journal of Behavioral Medicine, 15,* 65–88.

McCarthy, H. D., Ellis, S. M., & Cole, T. J. (2003). Central overweight and obesity in British youth aged 11–16 years: Cross sectional surveys of waist circumference. *British Medical Journal, 326,* 624.

McClelland, D. C. (1958). Risk-taking in children with high and low need for achievement. In J. W. Atkinson (Ed.), *Motives in fantasy, action, and society*. Princeton, NJ: Van Nostrand.

McClelland, D. C. (1985). *Human motivation*. Glenview, IL: Scott, Foresman.

McCloskey, M. (1983). Naïve theories of motion. In D. Gentner & K. Stevens (Eds.), *Mental models* (pp. 299–324). Northvale, NJ: Erlbaum.

McClure, E. B. (2000). A meta-analytic review of sex differences in facial expression processing and their development in infants, children, and adolescents. *Psychological Bulletin, 126,* 424–453.

McCormick, D. A., & Thompson, R. F. (1984). Cerebellum essential involvement in the classically conditioned eyelid response. *Science, 223,* 296–299.

McCormick, E. J., Jeanneret, P. R., & Mecham, R. C. (1972). A study of job characteristics and job dimensions as based on the position analysis questionnaire (PAQ). *Journal of Applied Psychology, 56,* 347–368.

McCrae, R. R., & Costa, P. T. (1999). A five-factor theory of personality. In L. Pervin & O. John (Eds.), *Handbook of personality: Theory and research* (2nd ed., pp. 139–153). New York: Guilford.

McCrae, R. R., Costa, P. T., Jr., Osterndorf, F., Angleitner, A., Hrebickova, M., Avia, M. D., et al. (2000). Nature over nurture: Temperament, personality, and life-span.

McCrae, R. R., & John, O. (1992). An introduction to the five-factor model and its applications. *Journal of Personality, 60,* 175–215.

McCrae, R. R., Yik, M. S. M., Trapnell, P. D., Bond, M., & Paulhus, D. (1998). Interpreting personality profiles across cultures, bilingual, acculturation, and peer rating studies of Chinese undergraduates. *Journal of Personality and Social Psychology, 74,* 1041–1055.

McDaniel, M. A., Maier, S. F., & Einstein, G. O. (2002). "Brain-Specific" nutrients: A memory cure? *Psychological Science in the Public Interest, 3,* 12–38.

McDermott, K. B. (2000). Implicit memory. In A. E. Kazdin (Ed.), *The encyclopedia of psychology* (pp. 231–234). New York: American Psychological Association and Oxford University Press.

McDermott, K. B. (2002). Explicit and implicit memory. In V. S. Ramachandran (Ed.), *Encyclopedia of the human brain* (Vol. 2, pp. 773–781). New York: Academic Press.

McDermott, K. B., & Buckner, R. L. (2001). *Functional anatomic correlates of human memory retrieval*. New York: Guilford.

McDermott, K. B., & Roediger, H. L. (1998). Attempting to avoid illusory memories: Robust false recognition of associates persists under conditions of explicit warnings and immediate testing. *Journal of Memory and Language, 39,* 508–520.

McDougall, W. (1908). *An introduction to social psychology*. London: Methuen.

McEvoy, G. M., & Beatty, R. W. (1989). Assessment centers and subordinate appraisals of managers: A seven-year examination of predictive validity. *Personnel Psychology, 42,* 37–52.

McEwen, B. S. (1991). Steroid-hormones are multifunctional messengers to the brain. *Trends in Endocrinology and Metabolism, 2,* 62–67.

McEwen, B. S. (1998). Protective and damaging effects of stress mediators. *New England Journal of Medicine, 338,* 171–179.

McEwen, B. S., & Seeman, T. (1999). Protective and damaging effects of mediators of stress: Elaborating and testing concepts of allostasis and allostatic load. *Annals of the New York Academy of Sciences, 896,* 30–47.

McGehee, D. S., Heath, M. J. S., Gelber, S., Devay, P., & Role, L. W. (1995). Nicotine enhancement of fast excitatory synaptic transmissions in CNS by presynaptic receptors. *Science, 269,* 1692–1696.

McGlashan, T. H., & Hoffman, R. E. (2000). Schizophrenia as a disorder of reduced synaptic connectivity. *Archives of General Psychiatry, 57,* 637–648.

McGlynn, F. D., Moore, P. M., Lawyer, S., & Karg, R. (1999). Relaxation training inhibits fear and arousal during in vivo exposure to phobia-cue stimuli. *Journal of Behavior Therapy and Experimental Psychiatry, 30,* 155–168.

McGorry, P. D., Yung, A. R., Phillips, L. J., Yuen, H. P., Francey, S., Cosgrave, E. M., et al. (2002). Randomized controlled trial of interventions designed to reduce the risk of progression to first-episode psychosis in a clinical sample with subthreshold symptoms. *Archives of General Psychiatry, 59,* 921–928.

McGue, M. (1999). The behavioral genetics of alcoholism. *Current Directions in Psychological Science, 8,* 109–115.

McGuffin, P., Rijsdijk, F., Andrew, M., Sham, P., Katz, R., & Cardno, A. (2003). The heritability of bipolar affective disorder and the genetic relationship to unipolar depression. *Archives of General Psychiatry, 60,* 497–502.

McGuire, M. T., Wing, R. R., Klem, M. L., Lang., W., & Hill, J. O. (1999). What predicts weight regain in a group of successful weight losers? *Journal of Consulting and Clinical Psychology, 67,* 177–185.

McIntire, S. A., & Miller, L. A. (2000). *Foundations of psychological testing*. New York: McGraw-Hill.

McLaughlin, C. S., Chen, C., Greenberger, E., & Biermeier, C. (1997). Family, peer, and individual correlates of sexual experience among Caucasian and Asian-American late adolescents. *Journal of Research on Adolescence, 7,* 33–53.

McLeod, J. D., Kessler, R. C., & Landis, K. R. (1992). Speed of recovery from major depressive episodes in a community sample of married men and women. *Journal of Abnormal Psychology, 101,* 277–286.

McLoyd, V. C. (1998). Socioeconomic disadvantage and child development. *American Psychologist, 53,* 185–204.

McMahon, P. (2000). Oregon man leads life without frills, leaves $9 million to charities, children. *USA Today,* p. 4A.

McMullin, R. E. (2000). *The new handbook of cognitive therapy techniques*. New York: Norton.

McNally, R. J. (2003). Recovering memories of trauma: A view from the laboratory. *Current Directions in Psychological Science, 12,* 32–35.

McNally, R. J., Clancy, S. A., & Schacter, D. L. (2001). Directed forgetting of trauma cues in adults reporting repressed or recovered memories of childhood sexual abuse. *Journal of Abnormal Psychology, 110,* 151–156.

McNally, R. J., Clancy, S. A., Schacter, D. L., & Pittman, R. K. (2000a). Cognitive processing of trauma cues in adults reporting repressed, recovered, or continuous memories of childhood sexual abuse. *Journal of Abnormal Psychology, 109,* 355–359.

McNally, R. J., Clancy, S. A., Schacter, D. L., & Pittman, R. K. (2000b). Personality profiles, dissociation, and absorption in women reporting repressed, recovered, or continuous memories of childhood sexual abuse. *Journal of Consulting and Clinical Psychology, 68,* 1033–1037.

McNay, E. C., McCarty, R. C., & Gold, P. E. (2001). Fluctuations in brain glucose concentration during behavioral testing: Dissociations between brain areas and between brain and blood. *Neurobiology of Learning and Memory, 75,* 325–337.

McPhail, T. L., & Penner, L. A. (1995, August). *Can similarity moderate the effects of aversive racism?* Paper presented at the 103rd annual meeting of the American Psychological Association, New York.

McQuaid, J. R., Granholm, E., McClure, F. S., Roepke, S., Pedrelli, P., Patterson, T. L., et al. (2000). Development of an integrated cognitive-behavioral and social skills training intervention for older patients with schizophrenia. *Journal of Psychotherapy Practice and Research, 9,* 149–156.

McQuaid, J. R., Monroe, S. M., Roberts, J. E., Kupfer, D. J., & Frank, E. (2000). A comparison of two life stress assessment approaches: Prospective prediction of treatment outcome in recurrent depression. *Journal of Abnormal Psychology, 109,* 787–791.

Medin, D. L., & Bazerman, M. H. (1999). Broadening behavioral decision research: Multiple levels of cognitive processing. *Psychonomic Bulletin & Review, 6,* 533–546.

Medin, D. L., Ross, B. H., & Markman, A. B. (2001). *Cognitive psychology* (3rd ed.). Fort Worth, TX: Harcourt.

Mednick, S., Nakayama, K., & Stickgold, R. (2003). Sleep-dependent learning: A nap is as good as a night. *Nature Neuroscience, 6,* 697–698.

Meeus, W. H., & Raaijmakers, Q. A. W. (1995). Obedience in modern society. *Journal of Social Issues, 51,* 155–176.

Mehle, T. (1982). Hypothesis generation in an automobile malfunction inference task. *Acta Psychologica, 52,* 87–116.

Meichenbaum, D. (1977). *Cognitive behavior modification: An integrative approach*. New York: Plenum.

Meichenbaum, D. H. (1995). Cognitive-behavioral therapy in historical perspective. In B. Bongar & L. E. Beutler (Eds.), *Comprehensive textbook of psychotherapy: Theory and practice* (pp. 140–158). New York: Oxford University Press.

Melamed, S., Fried, Y., & Froom, P. (2001). *Journal of Occupational Health Psychology, 6,* 182–195.

Meltzer, H. Y. (1997). Treatment-resistant schizophrenia: The role of clozapine. *Current Medical Research Opinion, 14,* 1–20.

Melzack, R., & Wall, P. D. (1965). Pain mechanisms: A new theory. *Science, 150,* 971–979.

Menaker, M., & Vogelbaum, M. A. (1993). Mutant circadian period as a marker of suprachiasmatic nucleus function. *Journal of Biological Rhythms, 8,* 93–98.

Mendl, M. (1999). Performing under pressure: Stress and cognitive function. *Applied Animal Behaviour Science, 65,* 221–244.

Menini, A., Picco, C., & Firestein, S. (1995, February 2). Quantal-like current fluctuations induced by odorants in olfactory receptor cell. *Nature, 373,* 435–437.

Menkes, M. S., Matthews, K. A., Krantz, D. S., Lundberg, V., Mead, L. A., Qaqish, B., et al. (1989). Cardiovascular reactivity to the cold pressor as a predictor of hypertension. *Hypertension, 14,* 524–530.

Merchant, J. A., & Lundell, J. A. (2001). *Workplace violence: A report to the nation.* Iowa City: University of Iowa.

Merckelbach, H., Devilly, G. J., & Rassin, E. (2002). Alters in dissociative identity disorder: Metaphors or genuine entities? *Clinical Psychology Review, 22,* 481–497.

Mercer, C. H., Fenton, K. A., Johnson, A. M., Wellings, K., Macdowall, W., McManus, et al. (2003). Sexual function problems and help seeking behaviour in Britain: National probability sample survey. *British Medical Journal, 327,* 426–427.

Mereu, G., Fa, M., Ferraro, L., Cagiano, R., Antonelli, T., Tattoli, M., et al. (2003). Prenatal exposure to a cannabinoid agonist produces memory deficits linked to dysfunction in hippocampal long-term potentiation and glutamate release. *Proceedings of the National Academy of Sciences, 100,* 4915–4920.

Merzenich, M. (1998). Long-term change of mind. *Science, 282,* 1062–1063.

Mesman, J., & Koot, H. M. (2000). Common and specific correlates of preadolescent internalizing externalizing psychopathology. *Journal of Abnormal Psychology, 109,* 428–437.

Mesquita, B., & Frijda, N. H. (1992). Cultural variations in emotions: A review. *Psychological Bulletin, 112,* 179–204.

Messer, S. B., & Wampold, B. E. (2002). Let's face facts: Common factors are more potent than specific therapy ingredients. *Clinical Psychology: Science and Practice, 9,* 21–25.

Metzinger, T. (Ed.). (2000). *Neural correlates of consciousness: Empirical and conceptual questions.* Cambridge: MIT Press.

Meyer, B. H. F. L., Ehrhardt, A. A., Rosen, L. R., & Gruen, R. S. (1995). Prenatal estrogens and the development of homosexual orientation. *Developmental Psychology, 31*(1), 12–21.

Meyer, G. J., Finn, S. E., Eyde, L. D., Kay, G. G., Moreland, K. L., Dies, R. R., et al. (2001). Psychological testing and psychological assessment: A review of evidence and issues. *American Psychologist, 56,* 128–165.

Meyer, J. D., & Salovey, P. (1997). What is emotional intelligence? In P. Salovey & D. Sluyter (Eds.), *Emotional development and emotional intelligence* (pp. 3–31). New York: Basic Books.

Meyer, R. G. (1975). A behavioral treatment of sleepwalking associated with test anxiety. *Behavior Therapy and Experimental Psychiatry, 6,* 167–168.

Meyers, C., & Jones, T. B. (1993). *Promoting active learning: Strategies for the college classroom.* San Francisco: Jossey-Bass.

Mezey, E., Key, S., Vogelsang, G., Szalayova, I., Lange, G. D., & Crain, B. (2003). Transplanted bone marrow generates new neurons in human brains. *Proceedings of the National Academy of Sciences, 100,* 1364–1369.

Mezzacappa, E. S., Katkin, E. S., & Palmer, S. N. (1999). Epinephrine, arousal and emotion: A new look at two-factor theory. *Cognition and Emotion, 13,* 181–199.

Michael, R. T., Wadsworth, J., Feinleib, J., Johnson, A. M., Laumann, E. O., & Wellings, K. (1998). Private sexual behavior, public opinion, and public health policy related to sexually transmitted diseases: A US-British comparison. *American Journal of Public Health, 88,* 749–754.

Mick, E., Biederman, J., Prince, J., Fischer, M. J., & Faraone, S. V. (2002). Impact of low birth weight on attention-deficit hyperactivity disorder. *Journal of Developmental and Behavioral Pediatrics, 23,* 16–22.

Mikelson, K. D., Kessler, R. C., & Shaver, P. R. (1997). Adult attachment in a nationally representative sample. *Journal of Personality and Social Psychology, 72,* 1092–1106.

Miklowitz, D. J., & Alloy, L. B. (1999). Psychosocial factors in the course and treatment of bipolar disorder: Introduction to the special section. *Journal of Abnormal Psychology, 108,* 555–557.

Milberger, S., Biederman, J., Faraone, S. V., & Chen, L. (1997). Further evidence of an association between attention-deficit/hyperactivity disorder and cigarette smoking: Findings from a high-risk sample of siblings. *American Journal on Addictions, 6,* 205–217.

Milgram, S. (1963). Behavioral study of obedience. *Journal of Abnormal and Social Psychology, 67,* 371–378.

Milgram, S. (1965). Some conditions of obedience and disobedience to authority. *Human Relations, 18,* 57–76.

Milgram, S. (1974). *Obedience to authority.* New York: Harper & Row.

Milgram, S. (1977, October). Subject reaction: The neglected factor in the ethics of experimentation. *Hastings Center Report* (pp. 19–23).

Miller, G. (1956). The magical number seven, plus or minus two: Some limits on our capacity to process information. *Psychological Review, 63,* 81–97.

Miller, G. (2003). Spying on the brain, one neuron at a time. *Science, 300,* 78.

Miller, G. A. (1991). *The science of words.* New York: Scientific American Library.

Miller, G. A., Heise, G. A., & Lichten, W. (1951). The intelligibility of speech as a function of the context of the test materials. *Journal of Experimental Psychology, 41,* 329–335.

Miller, J. (2001). The cultural grounding of social psychological theory. In A. Tesser & N. Schwarz (Eds.), *Blackwell handbook of social psychology: Intraindividual processes* (pp. 22–43). Oxford, England: Blackwell.

Miller, J. G. (2002). Bringing culture to basic psychological theory—Beyond individualism and collectivism: Comment on Oyserman et al. *Psychological Bulletin, 128,* 97–109.

Miller, J. G., & Bersoff, D. M. (1994). Cultural influences on the moral status of reciprocity and the discounting of endogenous motivation. *Personality and Social Psychology Bulletin, 20,* 592–607.

Miller, K. F., Smith, C. M., Zhu, J., & Zhang, H. (1995). Preschool origins of cross-national differences in mathematical competence: The role of number-naming systems. *Psychological Science, 6,* 56–60.

Miller, L. C., Putcha-Bhagavatula, A., & Pedersen, W. C. (2002). Men's and women's mating preferences: Distinct evolutionary mechanisms? *Current Directions in Psychological Science, 11,* 88–93.

Miller, L. K. (1999). The savant syndrome: Intellectual impairment and exceptional skill. *Psychological Bulletin, 125,* 31–46.

Miller, L. T., & Vernon, P. A. (1997). Developmental changes in speed of information processing in young children. *Developmental Psychology, 33,* 549–554.

Miller, N. E. (1959). Liberalization of basic S-R concepts: Extensions to conflict behavior, motivation, and social learning. In S. Koch (Ed.), *Psychology: A study of science* (Vol. 2, pp. 196–292). New York: McGraw-Hill.

Millon, T., & Davis, R. D. (1996). *Disorders of personality.* DSM-IV *and beyond* (2nd ed.). New York: Wiley.

Mills, P. E., Cole, K. N., Jenkins, J. R., & Dale, P. S. (1998). Effects of differing levels of inclusion on preschoolers with disabilities. *Exceptional Children, 65,* 79–90.

Milner, B. (1966). Amnesia following operation on temporal lobes. In C. W. M. Whitty & O. L. Zangwill (Eds.), *Amnesia.* London: Butterworth.

Milner, D. (1983). *Children and race.* Beverly Hills, CA: Sage.

Miltenberger, R. G. (2001). *Behavior modification: Principles and procedures.* Pacific Grove, CA: Wadsworth.

Minsky, S., Vega, W., Miskimen, T., Gara, M., & Escobar, J. (2003). Diagnostic patterns in Latino, African American, and European American psychiatric patients. *Archives of General Psychiatry, 60,* 637–644.

Miotto, K., Darakjian, J., Basch, J., Murray, S., Zogg, J., & Rawson, R. (2001). Gamma-hydroxybutyric acid: Patterns of use, effects and withdrawal. *American Journal on Addictions, 10,* 232–241.

Miranda, J., & Green, B. L. (1999). The need for mental health services research focusing on poor young women. *Journal of Mental Health Policy and Economics, 2,* 73–89.

Mischel, W. (2002). *Introduction to personality* (7th ed.). Fort Worth, Texas: Harcourt Brace.

Mischel, W., & Shoda, Y. (1999). Integrating dispositions and processing dynamics. In L. Pervin & O. John (Eds.), *Handbook of personality: Theory and research* (2nd ed., pp. 197–218). New York: Guilford.

Mischel, W., Shoda, Y., & Mendoza-Denton, R. (2002). Situation-behavior profiles as a locus of consistency in personality. *Current Directions in Psychological Science, 11,* 50–54.

Mischel, W., Shoda, Y., & Smith, R. (2004). *Introduction to personality: Toward an integration* (7th ed.) New York: Wiley.

Mitchell, J. P., Heatherton, T. F., & Macrae, C. N. (2002). Distinct neural systems subserve person and object knowledge. *Proceedings of the National Academy of Sciences, 99,* 15238–15243.

Mitchell, K. J., & Zaragoza, M. S. (1996). Repeated exposure to suggestion and false memory: The role of contextual variability. *Journal of Memory and Learning, 35,* 246–260.

Moergen, S., Merkel, W., & Brown, S. (1990). The use of covert sensitization and social skills training in the treatment of an obscene telephone caller. *Journal of Behavior Therapy and Experimental Psychiatry, 21,* 269–275.

Moffitt, T. E. (2002). Teen-aged mothers in contemporary Britain. *Journal of Child Psychology & Psychiatry & Allied Disciplines, 43,* 727–742.

Mogenson, G. J. (1976). Neural mechanisms of hunger: Current status and future prospects. In D. Novin, W. Wyrwicka, & G. Bray (Eds.), *Hunger: Basic mechanisms and clinical applications.* New York: Raven.

Mohr, C., Rohrenbach, C. M., Landis, T., & Regard, M. (2001). Associations to smell are more pleasant than to sound. *Journal of Clinical and Experimental Neuropsychology, 23,* 484–489.

Mokdad, A. H., Ford, E. S., Bowman, B. A., Dietz, W. H., Vinicor, F., Bales, V. S., et al. (2003). Prevalence of obesity, diabetes, and obesity-related health risk factors, 2001. *Journal of the American Medical Association, 289,* 76–79.

Molden, D. C., & Dweck, C. S. (2000). Meaning and motivation. In C. Sansone & J. M. Harackiewicz (Eds.), *Intrinsic and extrinsic motivation: The search for optimal motivation and performance.* San Diego: Academic Press.

Moldin, S. O., & Gottesman, I. I. (1997). At issue: Genes, experience, and chance in schizophrenia—positioning for the 21st century. *Schizophrenia Bulletin, 23,* 547–561.

Molsa, P. K., Marttila, R. J., & Rinne, U. K. (1995). Long-term survival and predictors of mortality in Alzheimer's disease and multi-infarct dementia. *Acta Neurologica Scandinavica, 91,* 159–164.

Monane, M., Leichter, D., & Lewis, O. (1984). Physical abuse in psychiatrically hospitalized children and adolescents. *Journal of the American Academy of Child and Adolescent Psychiatry, 23,* 653–658.

Moncrief, W. C., Babakus, E., Cravens, D. W., & Johnston, M. W. (2000). Examining gender differences in field sales organizations. *Journal of Business Research, 49,* 245–257.

Monroe, S. M., Rohde, P., Seeley, J. R., & Lewinsohn, P. M. (1999). Life events and depression in adolescence: Relationship loss as a prospective risk factor for first onset of major depressive disorder. *Journal of Abnormal Psychology, 108,* 606–614.

Monroe, S., Thase, M., & Simons, A. (1992). Social factors and psychobiology of depression: Relations between life stress and rapid eye movement sleep latency. *Journal of Abnormal Psychology, 101,* 528–537.

Monteith, M. J., Sherman, J. W., & Devine, P. G. (1998). Suppression as a stereotype control strategy. *Personality & Social Psychology Review, 2,* 63–82.

Monteith, M. J., Zuwerink, J. R., & Devine, P. G. (1994). Prejudice and prejudice reduction: Classic challenges and contemporary approaches. In P. G. Devine, D. L. Hamilton, & T. M. Ostrom (Eds.), *Social cognition: Impact on social psychology* (pp. 324–346). San Diego, CA: Academic Press.

Moon, C., Cooper, R. P., & Fifer, W. P. (1993). Two-day-olds prefer their native language. *Infant Behavior and Development, 16,* 495–500.

Moore, J. W., Tingstom, D. H., Doggett, R. A., & Carlyon, W. D. (2001). Restructuring an existing token economy in a psychiatric facility for children. *Child & Family Behavior Therapy, 23,* 53–60.

Moos, R., Schaefer, J., Andrassy, J., & Moos, B. (2001). Outpatient mental health care, self-help groups, and patients' one-year treatment outcomes. *Journal of Clinical Psychology, 57,* 273–287.

Moran, C. C. (2002). Humor as a moderator of compassion fatigue. In C. R. Figley (Ed.), *Treating compassion fatigue* (pp. 139–154). New York: Brunner-Routledge.

Moran, D. R. (2000, June). *Is active learning for me?* Poster presented at APS Preconvention Teaching Institute, Denver.

Morgan, C. D., & Murray, H. A. (1935). A method for investigating fantasy: The Thematic Apperception Test. *Archives of Neurology and Psychiatry, 34,* 289–306.

Morganstern, J., Labouvie, E., McCrady, B. S., Kahler, C. W., & Frey, R. M. (1997). Affiliation with Alcoholics Anonymous after treatment: A study of its therapeutic effects and mechanism of action. *Journal of Consulting and Clinical Psychology, 65,* 768–777.

Morris, J. S., DeGelder, B., Weiskrantz, L., & Dolan, R. J. (2001). Differential extrageniculostriate and amygdala responses to presentation of emotional faces in a cortically blind field. *Brain, 124,* 1241–1252.

Morris, J. S., Friston, K. J., Buchel, C., Frith, C. D., Young, A. W., Calder, A. J., et al. (1998). A neuromodulatory role for the human amygdala in processing emotional facial expressions. *Brain, 121,* 47–57.

Morris, L. (2000, December 5). Hold the anaesthetic. I'll hypnotise myself instead. *Daily Mail,* p. 25.

Morris, M. W., & Peng, K. (1994). Culture and cause: American and Chinese attributions for social and physical events. *Journal of Personality and Social Psychology, 67,* 949–971.

Mortimer, R. G., Goldsteen, K., Armstrong, R. W., & Macrina, D. (1988). Effects of enforcement, incentives, and publicity on seat belt use in Illinois. *University of Illinois, Dept. of Health & Safety Studies, Final Report to Illinois Dept. of Transportation* (Safety Research Report 88–11).

Moscovici, S. (1985). Social influence and conformity. In G. Lindzey & E. Aronson (Eds.), *The handbook of social psychology* (Vol. 2, 3rd ed.). New York: Random House.

Muir, J. L. (1997). Acetylcholine, aging, and Alzheimer's disease. *Pharmacological and Biochemical Behavior, 56*(4), 687–696.

Mullen, B. (1986). Atrocity as a function of lynch mob composition: A self-attention perspective. *Personality and Social Psychology Bulletin, 12,* 187–197.

Mumme, D. L., & Fernald, A. (2003). The infant as onlooker: Learning from emotional reactions observed in a television scenario. *Child Development, 74,* 221–237.

Munroe, R. H., & Munroe, R. L. (1994). Behavior across cultures: Results from observational studies. In W. J. Lonner & R. S. Malpass (Eds.), *Psychology and culture.* Boston: Allyn & Bacon.

Munte, T. F., Altenmuller, E., & Jancke, L. (2002). The musician's brain as a model of neuroplasticity. *National Review of Neuroscience, 3,* 473–478.

Murphy, L., Gershon, R. M., & DeJoy, D. (1996). Stress and occupational exposure to HIV/AIDS. In C. L. Cooper (Ed.), *Handbook of stress, medicine, and health* (pp. 177–190). Boca Raton, FL: CRC Press.

Murray, B. (2000). Learning from real life. *APA Monitor, 31,* 72–73.

Murray, B. (2002). Good news for bachelor's grads? *Monitor on Psychology, 33,* 30–32.

Murray, E. A., & Mishkin, M. (1985). Amygdalectomy impairs crossmodal association in monkeys. *Science, 228,* 604–606.

Murray, H. A. (1938). *Explorations in personality.* New York: Oxford University Press.

Murray, H. A. (1971). *Thematic Apperception Test.* Cambridge: Harvard University Press.

Murray, J. A., & Terry, D. (1999). Parental reactions to infant death: The effects of resources and coping strategies. *Journal of Social and Clinical Psychology, 18,* 341–369.

Myers, B. J. (1987). Mother-infant bonding as a critical period. In M. H. Bornstein (Ed.), *Sensitive periods in development: Interdisciplinary perspectives.* Hillsdale, NJ: Erlbaum.

Myers, D. G. (2000a). *The American paradox: Spiritual hunger in an age of plenty.* New Haven, CT: Yale University Press.

Myers, D. G. (2000b). The funds, friends, and faith of happy people. *American Psychologist, 55,* 56–57.

Myers, M. G., Reeves, R. A., Oh, P. I., & Joyner, C. D. (1996). Overtreatment of hypertension in the community? *American Journal of Hypertension, 9,* 419–425.

Myers, S. L. (2001, March 12). Sub's crew may have hesitated to question a trusted captain. *New York Times.*

Nabeshima, T., & Yamada, K. (2000). Neurotrophic factor strategies for the treatment of Alzheimer disease. *Alzheimer Disease & Associated Disorders, 14*(Suppl. 1), S39–46.

Nader, K., Schafe, G. E., & Le Doux, J. E. (2000). Fear memories require protein synthesis in the amygdala for reconsolidation after retrieval. *Nature, 406,* 722–726.

Naëgelé, B., Thouvard, V., Pépin, J.-L., Lévy, P., Bonnet, C., Perret, J. E., et al. (1995). Deficits of cognitive functions in patients with sleep apnea syndrome. *Sleep, 18*(1), 43–52.

Nagy, T. F. (1999). *Ethics in plain English: An illustrative casebook for psychologists.* Washington, DC: American Psychological Association.

Naito, M., & Miura, H. (2001). Japanese children's numerical competencies: Age- and schooling-related influences on the development of number concepts and addition skills. *Developmental Psychology, 37,* 217–230.

Nakamura, J., & Csikszentmihalyi, M. (2001). Catalytic creativity. *American Psychologist, 56,* 337–341.

Nakano, K., & Kitamura, T. (2001). The relation of the anger subcomponent of Type A behavior to psychological symptoms in Japanese and foreign students. *Japanese Psychological Research, 43,* 50–54.

Narayanan, L., Menon, S., & Levine, E. L. (1995). Personality structure: A culture-specific examination of the five-factor model. *Journal of Personality Assessment, 64,* 51–62.

Narita, N., Narita, M., Takashima, S., Nakayama, M., Nagai, T., & Okado, N. (2001). Serotonin transporter gene variation is a risk factor for sudden infant death syndrome in the Japanese population. *Pediatrics, 107,* 690–692.

Narrow, W. E., Rae, D. S., Robins, L. N., & Regier, D. A. (2002). Revised prevalence based estimates of mental disorders in the United States: Using a clinical significance criterion to reconcile two survey estimates. *Archives of General Psychiatry, 59,* 115–123.

Nash, A. J., & Fernandez, M. (1996). P300 and allocation of attention in dual-tasks. *International Journal of Psychophysiology, 23,* 171–180.

Nash, I. S., Mosca, L., Blumenthal, R. S., Davidson, M. H., Smith, S. C., Jr., & Pasternak, R. C. (2003). Contemporary awareness and understanding of cholesterol as a risk factor: Results of an American Heart Association national survey. *Archives of Internal Medicine, 163,* 1597–1600.

Nathan, P. E., & Langenbucher, J. W. (1999). Psychopathology: Description and classification. *Annual Review of Psychology, 50,* 79–107.

Nathan, P. E., Stuart, S. P., & Dolan, S. L. (2000). Research on psychotherapy efficacy and effectiveness: Between Scylla and Charybdis? *Psychological Bulletin, 126,* 964–981.

National Advisory Mental Health Council. (1996). Basic behavioral science research for mental health: Vulnerability and resilience. *American Psychologist, 51,* 22–28.

National Association of Anorexia Nervosa and Associated Disorders. (2002). *Facts about eating disorders.* Retrieved August 26, 2003, from http://www.altrue.net/site/anadweb/content.php?type=1&id=6982

National Center for Chronic Disease Prevention and Health Promotion. (2002). Trends in Sexual Risk Behaviors Among High School Students—United States, 1991–2001. *Morbidity and Mortality Weekly Report, 51,* 856–859.

National Center for Education Statistics. (2000). *Trends in pregnancies and pregnancy rates by outcome: Estimates for the United States, 1976–1996.* Washington, DC: Centers for Disease Control and Prevention.

National Center for Education Statistics. (2002). *Digest of Education Statistics, 2001.* Washington, DC: Office of Educational Research & Improvement, U.S. Dept. of Education.

National Center for Health Statistics. (2000). *Health, United States, 2000: With adolescent health chartbook.* Hyattsville, Maryland: National Center for Health Statistics.

National Center for Health Statistics. (2001). *Births, marriages, divorces, and deaths: Provisional data for January–December 2000.* Hyattsville, Maryland: Public Health Service.

National Center for Injury Prevention and Control. (2002). *Ten leading causes of death, United States.* Washington, DC: Centers for Disease Control.

National Computer Systems. (1992). *Catalog of assessment instruments, reports, and services.* Minneapolis: National Computer Systems.

National Drug Intelligence Center. (2001, October 6). *Information bulletin oxycontin diversion and abuse.* Retrieved August 26, 2003, from http://www.usdoj.gov/ndic/pubs/651/

National Highway Traffic Safety Administration. (2003). *Motor vehicle traffic crash fatality and injury estimates for 2002.* Retrieved August 26, 2003, from http://www-nrd.nhtsa.dot.gov/pdf/nrd-30/NCSA/Rpts/2003/2002EARelease.pdf

National Institute for Occupational Safety and Health. (1999). *Stress at work.* Washington, DC: NIOSH Publication No. 99–101.

National Institute of Mental Health. (1995). *Medications.* Washington, DC: U.S. Department of Health and Human Services.

National Institute of Mental Health. (1998). *Genetics and mental disorders: Report of the National Institute of Mental Health's genetics workgroup.* Rockville, MD: Author.

National Institute on Alcohol Abuse and Alcoholism. (2000). *Tenth special report to the U.S. Congress on alcohol and health* (Publication No. 00–1583). Washington, DC: National Institutes of Health.

National Institute on Alcohol Abuse and Alcoholism. (2001). *Alcoholism: Getting the facts.* Bethesda, MD: Author.

National Institute on Drug Abuse. (2000). Facts about MDMA (Ecstacy). *NIDA Notes, 14.* Retrieved June 26, 2003, from http://drugabuse.gov/NIDA_Notes/NNVol14N4/tearoff.html

National Institutes of Health. (2001). *Eating disorders: Facts about eating disorders and the search for solutions* (NIH Publication No. 01–4901). Washington, DC: U.S. Department of Health and Human Services.

National Safety Council. (2001). *Reports on Injuries in America 2001.* Itasca, IL: Author.

National Science Foundation. (2000). *Women, minorities and persons with disabilities in science and engineering: 2000.* Arlington, VA: Author, 00–327.

National Science Foundation. (2001). *1999 survey of doctorate recipients.* Arlington, VA: Author.

National Science Foundation. (2002). *Science and engineering degrees: 1966–2000.* Washington, DC: Author, 02–327.

National Task Force on the Prevention and Treatment of Obesity. (2000). Dieting and the development of eating disorders in overweight and obese adults. *Archives of Internal Medicine, 160,* 2581–2589.

Needham, A., & Baillargeon, R. (1999). Effects of prior experience on 4.5 month-old infants' object segregation. *Infant Behavior & Development, 21,* 1–24.

Neher, A. (1991). Maslow's theory of motivation: A critique. *Journal of Humanistic Psychology, 31,* 89–112.

Nehra, A., & Kulaksizoglu, H. (2002). Combination therapy for erectile dysfunction: Where we are and what's in the future. *Current Urology Reports, 3,* 467–470.

Neisser, U. (1998). *The rising curve: Long-term gains in I.Q. and related measures.* Washington, DC: American Psychological Association.

Neisser, U. (2000a). Memorists. In U. Neisser & I. E. Hyman, Jr. (Eds.), *Memory observed* (2nd ed., pp. 475–478). New York: Worth.

Neisser, U. (2000b). Snapshots or benchmarks? In U. Neisser & I. E. Hyman, Jr. (Eds.), *Memory observed* (2nd ed., pp. 68 –74). New York: Worth.

Neisser, U., Boodoo, G., Bouchard, T. J., Boykin, A. W., Brody, N., Ceci, S. J., et al. (1996). Intelligence: Knowns and unknowns. *American Psychologist, 51,* 77–101.

Nelson, C. A. (1999). Neural plasticity and human development. *Current Directions in Psychological Science, 8,* 42–45.

Nelson, D. L. (1999). Implicit memory. In D. E. Morris & M. Gruneberg (Eds.), *Theoretical aspects of memory.* London: Routledge.

Nelson, K. (1986). Event knowledge and cognitive development. In K. Nelson (Ed.), *Event knowledge: Structure and function in development.* Hillsdale, NJ: Erlbaum.

Nelson-LeGall, S., & Resnick, L. (1998). Help seeking, achievement motivation, and the social practice of intelligence in school. In S. A. Karabenick (Ed.), *Strategic help seeking* (pp. 39–60). Mahwah, NJ: Erlbaum.

Nemeroff, C. B. (1998). Psychopharmacology of affective disorders in the 21st century. *Biological Psychiatry, 44,* 517–525.

Nestler, E. J. (2001). Molecular basis of long-term plasticity underlying addiction. *National Review of Neuroscience, 2,* 119–128.

Neugarten, B. L. (1977). Personality and aging. In J. E. Birren & K. W. Schaie (Eds.), *Handbook of the psychology of aging.* New York: Van Nostrand Reinhold.

Neumann, C. S., Grimes, K., Walker, E. F., & Baum, K. (1995). Developmental pathways to schizophrenia: Behavioral subtypes. *Journal of Abnormal Psychology, 104,* 558–566.

Newcombe, N. S., Drummey, A. B., Fox, N. A., Lie, E., & Ottinger-Alberts, W. (2000). Remembering early childhood: How much, how, and why (or why not). *Current Directions in Psychological Science, 9,* 55–58.

Newcombe, N. S., & Fox, N. A. (1994). Infantile amnesia: Through a glass darkly. *Child Development, 65,* 31–40.

Newell, A., & Simon, H. A. (1972). *Human problem solving.* Englewood Cliffs, NJ: Prentice-Hall.

Newsome, J. T. (1999). Another side to caregiving: Negative reactions to being helped. *Current Directions in Psychological Science, 8,* 183–187.

Newsome, J. T., & Schulz, R. (1998). Caregiving from the recipient's perspective: Negative reactions to being helped. *Health Psychology, 17,* 172–181.

NICHD Early Child Care Research Network. (1997). The effects of infant child care on infant-mother attachment security: Results of the NICHD Study of Early Child Care. *Child Development, 68,* 860–879.

NICHD Early Child Care Research Network. (1998). Early child care and self-control, compliance and problem behavior at 24 and 36 months. *Child Development, 69,* 1145–1170.

NICHD Early Child Care Research Network. (1999). Chronicity of maternal depressive symptoms, maternal sensitivity, and child functioning at 36 months. *Developmental Psychology, 35,* 1297–1310.

NICHD Early Child Care Research Network. (2001, April). *Further explorations of the detected effects of quantity of early child care on socioemotional adjustment.* Paper presented at the biennial meetings of the Society for Research in Child Development, Minneapolis.

NICHD Early Child Care Research Network (2002). Early child care and children's development prior to school entry: Results from the NICHD Study of Early Child Care. *American Educational Research Journal, 39,* 133–164.

Nicholson, I. R., & Neufeld, R. W. J. (1993). Classification of the schizophrenias according to symptomatology: A two factor model. *Journal of Abnormal Psychology, 102,* 259–270.

Nickell, J. (1997, January/February). Sleuthing a psychic sleuth. *Skeptical Inquirer, 21,* 18–19.

Nickell, J. (2001). Exorcism! Driving out the nonsense. *Skeptical Inquirer, 25,* 20–24.

Nickerson, R. A., & Adams, M. J. (1979). Long-term memory for a common object. *Cognitive Psychology, 11,* 287–307.

Niederhoffer, K. G., & Pennebaker, J. W. (2002). Sharing one's story: On the benefits of writing or talking about emotional experience. In C. R. Snyder & S. J. Lopez (Eds.), *Handbook of positive psychology* (pp. 573–583). London: Oxford University Press.

Nienhuys, J. W. (2001). Spontaneous human combustion: Requiem for Phyllis. *Skeptical Inquirer, 25,* 28–34.

Nietzel, M. T., & Bernstein, D. A. (1987). *Introduction to clinical psychology* (2nd ed.). New York: Prentice-Hall.

Nietzel, M. T., Bernstein, D. A., Kramer, G., & Milich, R. (2003). *Introduction to clinical psychology* (6th ed.). Englewood Cliffs, NJ: Prentice-Hall.

Nietzel, M. T., Speltz, M. L., McCauley, E. A., & Bernstein, D. A. (1998). *Abnormal psychology.* Boston: Allyn & Bacon.

Nigg, J. T. (2000). On inhibition/disinhibition in developmental psychopathology: Views from cognitive and personality psychology and a working inhibition taxonomy. *Psychological Bulletin, 126,* 220–246.

Nigg, J. T. (2001). Is ADHD a disinhibitory disorder? *Psychological Bulletin, 127,* 571–598.

NIH Consensus Conference. (1998). Acupuncture. *Journal of the American Medical Association, 280,* 1518–1524.

Nilsson, G. (1996, November). Some forms of memory improve as people age. *APA Monitor,* p. 27.

Nisbett, R. E. (2003). *The geography of thought.* New York: The Free Press.

Nisbett, R. E., & Masuda, T. (2003). Culture and point of view. *Proceedings of the National Academy of Sciences, 100,* 11163–11170.

Noble, H. B. (2000, January 25). Outgrowth of new field of tissue engineering. *New York Times.*

Nolan, R. P., Spanos, N. P., Hayward, A. A., & Scott, H. A. (1995). The efficacy of hypnotic and nonhypnotic response-based imagery for self-managing recurrent headache. *Imagination, Cognition, and Personality, 14*(3), 183–201.

Nolen-Hoeksema, S. (1990). *Sex differences in depression.* Stanford, CA: Stanford University Press.

Nolen-Hoeksema, S. (2001). Gender differences in depression. *Current Directions in Psychological Science, 10,* 173–176.

Nolen-Hoeksema, S., Larson, J., & Grayson, C. (1999). Explaining gender differences in depression. *Journal of Personality and Social Psychology, 77,* 1061–1072.

Nolen-Hoeksema, S., Morrow, J., & Fredrickson, N. (1993). Response styles and the duration of episodes of depressed mood. *Journal of Abnormal Psychology, 102,* 20–28.

Noll, R. B. (1994). Hypnotherapy for warts in children and adolescents. *Journal of Developmental and Behavioral Pediatrics, 15*(3), 170–173.

Norcross, J. C. (2001). Purposes, processes, and products of the task force on empirically supported therapy relationships. *Psychotherapy, 38,* 345–356.

Norcross, J. C., Hedges, M., & Prochaska, J. O. (2002). The face of 2010: A Delphi poll on the future of psychotherapy. *Professional Psychology: Research and practice, 33,* 316–322.

Norcross, J. C., Santrock, J. W., Campbell, L. F., Smith, T. P., Sommer, R., & Zuckerman, E. L. (2000). *Authoritative guide to self-help resources in mental health.* New York: The Guilford Press.

North, C., & Pfefferbaum, B. (2002). Research on the mental health effects of terrorism. *Journal of the American Medical Association, 288,* 633.

Nott, K. H., & Vedhara, K. (2002). Psychoneuroimmunology and HIV infection. In K. H. Nott & K. Vedhara (Eds.), *Psychosocial and biomedical interactions in HIV infection: Biobehavioural perspectives on health and disease prevention* (pp. 197–227). New York: Gordon & Breach.

Nowak, M. A., Komarova, N. L., & Niyogi, P. (2001). Evolution of universal grammar. *Science, 291,* 114–118.

Nurnberger, J. I., Jr., Foroud, T., Flury, L., Su, J., Meyer, E. T., Hu, K., et al. (2001). Evidence for a locus on chromosome 1 that influences vulnerability to alcoholism and affective disorder. *American Journal of Psychiatry, 158,* 718–724.

Nyberg, L., Petersson, K. M., Nilsson, L. G., Sandblom, J., Aberg, C., & Ingvar, M. (2001). Reactivation of motor brain areas during explicit memory for actions. *Neuroimage, 14,* 521–528.

Oatley, K. (1993). Those to whom evil is done. In R. S. Wyer & T. K. Srull (Eds.), *Toward a general theory of anger and emotional aggression: Advances in social cognition* (Vol. 6). Hillsdale, NJ: Erlbaum.

Ochsner, K. N., & Lieberman, M. D. (2001). The emergence of social cognitive neuroscience. *American Psychologist, 56,* 717–734.

O'Connor, T. G., Rutter, M., Beckett, C., Keaveney, L., Kreppner, J. M., & the English and Romanian Adoptees Study Team. (2000). The effects of global severe privation on cognitive competence: Extension and longitudinal follow-up. *Child Development, 71,* 376–390.

Oden, M. H. (1968). The fulfillment of promise: 40-year follow-up of the Terman gifted group. *Genetic Psychology Monographs, 17,* 3–93.

O'Donohue, W., Fisher, J. E., & Hayes, S. C. (2003). *Cognitive behavior therapy: Applying empirically supported techniques in your practice.* New York: Wiley.

Öhman, A., Dimberg, U., & Öst, L. G. (1985). Animal and social phobias: A laboratory model. In S. Reiss & R. R. Bootzin (Eds.), *Theoretical issues in behavior therapy.* Orlando, FL: Academic Press.

Öhman, A., & Mineka, S. (2001). Fears, phobias, and preparedness: Toward an evolved module of fear and fear learning. *Psychological Review, 108,* 483–522.

Öhman, A., & Mineka, S. (2003). The malicious serpent: Snakes as a prototypical stimulus for an evolved module of fear. *Current Directions in Psychological Science, 12,* 5–9.

Öhman, A., & Soares, J. F. (1994). "Unconscious anxiety": Phobic responses to masked stimuli. *Journal of Abnormal Psychology, 103*(2), 231–240.

Ohring, R., Graber, J. A., & Brooks-Gunn, J. (2002). Girls' recurrent and concurrent body dissatisfaction: Correlates and consequences over 8 years. *International Journal of Eating Disorders, 31*(4), 404–415.

Oishi, S., Diener, E., Lucas, R. E., & Suh, E. M. (1999). Cross-cultural variations in predictors of life-satisfaction: Perspectives from needs and values. *Personality and Social Psychology Bulletin, 25,* 980–990.

Oldenberg, P.-A., Zheleznyak, A., Fang, Y.-F., Lagenaur, C. F., Gresham, H. D., & Lindberg, F. P. (2000). Role of CD47 as a marker of self on red blood cells. *Science, 288,* 2051–2054.

Olds, J. (1973). Commentary on positive reinforcement produced by electrical stimulation of septal areas and other regions of rat brain. In E. S. Valenstein (Ed.), *Brain stimulation and motivation: Research and commentary.* Glenview, IL: Scott, Foresman.

Olds, J., & Milner, P. (1954). Positive reinforcement produced by electrical stimulation of septal areas and other regions of the rat brain. *Journal of Comparative and Physiological Psychology, 47,* 419–427.

O'Leary, D. S., Block, R. I., Koeppel, J. A., Flaum, M., Schulz, S. K., Andreason, N. C., et al. (2002). Effects of smoking marijuana on brain perfusion and cognition. *Neuropsychopharmacology, 26,* 802–816.

Olfson, M., Marcus, S. C., Druss, B., Elinson, L., Tanielian, T., & Pincus, H. A. (2002). National trends in the outpatient treatment of depression. *Journal of the American Medical Association, 287,* 203–209.

Olfson, M., Mechanic, D., Hansell, S., Boyer, C. A., & Walkup, J. (1999). Prediction of homelessness within three months of discharge among inpatients with schizophrenia. *Psychiatric Services, 50,* 667–673.

Oliner, S. P., & Oliner, P. M. (1988). *The altruistic personality: Rescuers of Jews in Nazi Europe.* New York: Free Press.

Olio, K. A. (1994). Truth in memory. *American Psychologist, 49,* 442–443.

Olson, L. (1997). Regeneration in the adult central nervous system. *Nature Medicine, 3,* 1329–1335.

Ölveczky, B. P., Baccus, S. A., & Meister, M. (2003). Segregation of object and background motion in the retina. *Nature, 423,* 401–408.

O'Neill, H. (2000, September 24). After rape, jail—a friendship forms. *St. Petersburg Times,* pp. 1A, 14A.

Ones, D. S., & Viswesvaran, C. (1996). Bandwidth-fidelity dilemma in personality measurement for personnel selection. *Journal of Organizational Behavior, 17,* 609–626.

Ones, D., & Viswesvaran, C. (2001). Personality at work: Criterion focused occupational personality scales used in personnel selection. In R. Hogan & B. Roberts (Eds.), *Personality psychology in the workplace* (pp. 63–92). Washington, DC: American Psychological Association.

Ones, D. S., Viswesvaran, C., & Schmidt, F. L. (1993). Comprehensive meta-analysis of integrity test validities: Findings and implications for personnel selection and theories of job performance. *Journal of Applied Psychology, 78,* 679–703.

Operario, D., & Fiske, S. T. (2001). Stereotypes: Processes, structures, content, and context. In R. Brown & S. Gaertner (Eds.), *Blackwell handbook in social psychology: Intergroup processes* (pp. 22–44). Oxford, England: Blackwell.

Oppel, S. (2000, March 5). Managing ABCs like a CEO. *St. Petersburg Times,* 1A, 12–13A.

Oquendo, M. A., Ellis, S. P., Greenwald, S., Malone, K. M., Weissman, M. M., & Mann, J. J. (2001). Ethnic and sex differences in suicide rates relative to major depression in the United States. *American Journal of Psychiatry, 158,* 1652–1658.

Oquendo, M. A., & Mann, J. J. (2000). The biology of impulsivity and suicidality. *Psychiatric Clinics of North America, 23,* 11–25.

Oquendo, M. A., & Mann, J. J. (2001). Identifying and managing suicide risk in bipolar patients. *Journal of Clinical Psychiatry, 62,* 31–34.

Organ, D. W., & Ryan, K. (1995). A meta-analytic review of attitudinal and dispositional predictors of organizational citizenship behavior. *Personnel Psychology, 48,* 775–802.

Orne, M. T., & Evans, F. J. (1965). Social control in the psychological experiment: Antisocial behavior and hypnosis. *Journal of Personality and Social Psychology, 1,* 189–200.

Orne, M. T., Sheehan, P. W., & Evans, F. J. (1968). Occurrence of posthypnotic behavior outside the experimental setting. *Journal of Personality and Social Psychology, 9,* 189–196.

Oskamp, S., & Schultz, P. W. (1998). *Applied social psychology* (2nd ed.). Upper Saddle River, NJ: Prentice-Hall.

Öst, L.-G. (1978). Behavioral treatment of thunder and lightning phobia. *Behavior Research and Therapy, 16,* 197–207.

Öst, L.-G. (1992). Blood and injection phobia: Background and cognitive, physiological and behavioral variables. *Journal of Abnormal Psychology, 101,* 68–74.

Öst, L.-G., Hellström, K., & Kåver, A. (1992). One- versus five-session exposure in the treatment of needle phobia. *Behavior Therapy, 23,* 263–282.

Öst, L.-G., Svensson, L., Hellström, K., & Lindwall, R. (2001). One-session treatment of specific phobias in youths: A randomized clinical trial. *Journal of Consulting and Clinical Psychology, 69,* 814–824.

Otsuka, R., Watanabe, H., Hirata, K., Tokai, K., Muro, T., Yoshiyama, M., et al. (2001). Acute effects of passive smoking on the coronary circulation in healthy young adults. *Journal of the American Medical Association, 286,* 436–441.

Otten, L. J., Henson, R. N., & Rugg, M. D. (2002). State-related and item-related neural correlates of successful memory encoding. *Nature Neuroscience, 5,* 1339–1344.

Otto, M. W., Pollack, M. H., Gould, R. A., Worthington, J. J., III, McArdle, E. T., Rosenbaum, J. F., et al. (2000). A comparison of the efficacy of clonazepam and cognitive-behavioral group therapy for the treatment of social phobia. *Journal of Anxiety Disorders, 14,* 345–358.

Ottosson, H., Ekselius, L., Grann, M., & Kullgren, G. (2002). Cross-system concordance of personality disorder diagnoses of *DSM-IV* and Diagnostic Criteria for Research of ICD-10. *Journal of Personality Disorders, 16,* 283–292.

Overmier, J. B. (2002). On learned helplessness. *Integrative Physiological & Behavioral Science, 37,* 4–8.

Overmier, J. B., & Seligman, M. E. P. (1967). Effects of inescapable shock upon subsequent escape and avoidance learning. *Journal of Comparative and Physiological Psychology, 63,* 23–33.

Overton, D. A. (1984). *State dependent learning and drug discriminations.* New York: Plenum.

Overton, P. G., Richards, C. D., Berry, M. S., & Clark, D. (1999). Long-term potentiation at excitatory amino acid synapses on midbrain dopamine neurons. *Neuroreport, 10,* 221–226.

Oyserman, D., Coon, H. M., & Kemmelmeier, M. (2002). Rethinking individualism and collectivism: Evaluation of theoretical assumptions and meta-analyses. *Psychological Bulletin, 128,* 3–72.

Oyserman, S. (2001). Self-concept and identity. In A. Tesser & N. Schwarz (Eds.), *Blackwell handbook of social psychology: Intraindividual processes* (pp. 499–517). Oxford, England: Blackwell.

Ozer, D. J. (1999). Four principles of personality assessment. In L. Pervin & O. John (Eds.), *Handbook of personality: Theory and research* (2nd ed., pp. 671–689). New York: Guilford.

Paik, H., & Comstock, G. (1994). The effects of television violence on antisocial behavior: A meta-analysis. *Communication Research, 21,* 516–546.

Paivio, S. C., & Greenberg, L. S. (1995). Resolving "unfinished business": Efficacy of experiential therapy using empty-chair dialogue. *Journal of Consulting and Clinical Psychology, 63,* 419–425.

Palkovitz, R., Copes, M. A., & Woolfolk, T. N. (2001). It's like . . . you discover a new sense of being: Involved fathering as an evoker of adult development. *Men & Masculinities, 4*(1), 49–69.

Palmer, S. E. (1999). *Vision science: Photons to phenomenology.* Cambridge, MA: MIT Press.

Palmisano, M., & Herrmann, D. (1991). The facilitation of memory performance. *Bulletin of the Psychonomic Society, 29,* 557–559.

Paoletti, M. G. (1995). Biodiversity, traditional landscapes and agroecosystem management. *Landscape and Urban Planning, 31*(1–3), 117–128.

Parish, C. L., Finkelstein, D. I., Tripanichkul, W., Satoskar, A. R., Drago, J., & Horne, M. K. (2002). The role of interleukin-1, interleukin-6, and glia in inducing growth of neuronal terminal arbors in mice. *Journal of Neuroscience, 22,* 8034–8041.

Park, D. C. (2001, August). *The aging mind.* Paper presented at the annual convention of the American Psychological Association, San Francisco.

Park, D. C., Lautenschlager, G., Hedden, T., Davidson, N. S., Smith, A. D., & Smith, P. (2002). Models of visuospatial and verbal memory across the adult life span. *Psychology & Aging, 17*(2), 299–320.

Park, J., White, A. R., & Ernst, E. (2001). New sham method in auricular acupuncture. *Archives of Internal Medicine, 161,* 894.

Park, M. Y., Matsumoto, K., Jin Seo, Y., Kang, M. J., & Nagashima, H. (2002). Effects of age and gender on sleep habits and sleep trouble for aged people. *Biological Rhythm Research, 33*(1), 39–51.

Park, W.-W. (2000). A comprehensive empirical investigation of the relationships among variables of the groupthink model. *Journal of Organizational Behavior, 21,* 873–887.

Parke, R. D. (2002). Fathers and families. In M. H. Bornstein (Ed.), *Handbook of parenting* (2nd ed., pp. 27–63).

Parke, R. D., & Buriel, R. (1998). Socialization in the family: Ethnic and ecological perspectives. In W. Damon & N. Eisenberg (Eds.), *Handbook of child psychology: Vol. 3. Social, emotional, and personality development* (5th ed., pp. 463–552). New York: Wiley.

Parke, R. D., & Buriel, R. (2002). Socializing processes. In N. Smelser & P. B. Baltes (Eds.), *International encyclopedia of social sciences.* New York: Elsevier.

Parke, R. D., & O'Neil, R. (2000). The influence of significant others on learning about relationships: From family to friends. In R. S. L. Mills & S. Duck (Eds.), *The developmental psychology of personal relationships.* New York: Wiley.

Parker, G., Gladstone, G., & Chee, K. T. (2001). Depression in the planet's largest ethnic group: The Chinese. *American Journal of Psychiatry, 158,* 857–864.

Parker, J. G., Saxon, J. L., Asher, S. R., & Kovacs, D. M. (2001). Dimensions of children's friendship adjustment: Implications for understanding loneliness. In K. J. Rotenberg & S. Hymel (Eds.), *Loneliness in childhood and adolescence.* New York: Cambridge University Press.

Parkes, C. M. P., & Weiss, R. S. (1983). *Recovery from bereavement.* New York: Basic Books.

Parnas, J., Cannon, T., Jacobsen, B., Schulsinger, H., Schulsinger, F., & Mednick, S. (1993). Lifetime *DSM-III-R* diagnostic outcomes in the offspring of schizophrenic mothers. *Archives of General Psychiatry, 50,* 707–714.

Parolaro, D., Massi, P., Rubino, T., & Monti, E. (2002). Endocannabinoids in the immune system and cancer. *Prostaglandins Leukotrienes & Essential Fatty Acids, 66,* 319–332.

Pascual-Leone, A., & Torres, F. (1993). Plasticity of the sensorimotor cortex representation of the reading finger in Braille readers. *Brain, 116,* 39–52.

Patel, S. R., White, D. P., Malhotra, A., Stanchina, M. L., & Ayas, N. T. (2003). Continuous positive airway pressure therapy for treating sleepiness in a diverse population with obstructive sleep apnea: Results of a meta-analysis. *Archives of Internal Medicine, 163,* 565–571.

Patkowski, M. (1994). The critical age hypothesis and interlanguage phonology. In M. Yavas (Ed.), *First and second language phonology* (pp. 205–221). San Diego, CA: Singular Publishing Group.

Patrick, C. J., Cuthbert, B. N., & Lang, P. J. (1994). Emotion in the criminal psychopath: Fear imaging processing. *Journal of Abnormal Psychology, 103,* 523–534.

Patterson, C. J. (2002). Lesbian and gay parenthood. In M. H. Bornstein (Ed.), *Handbook of parenting* (2nd ed., pp. 255–274). Mahwah, NJ: Erlbaum.

Patterson, D. R., Goldberg, M. L., & Ehde, D. M. (1996). Hypnosis in the treatment of patients with severe burns. *American Journal of Clinical Hypnosis, 38,* 200–212.

Patterson, D. R., & Jensen, M. P. (2003). Hypnosis and clinical pain. *Psychological Bulletin, 129,* 495–521.

Patton, G. C., Coffey, C., Carlin, J. B., Degenhardt, L., Lynskey, M., & Hall, W. (2002). Cannabis use and mental health in young people: Cohort study. *British Medical Journal, 325,* 1195–1198.

Pauk, W. (2002). *How to study in college.* Boston: Houghton Mifflin.

Pauk, W., & Fiore, J. P. (2000). *Succeed in college!* Boston: Houghton Mifflin.

Paul, G. L. (1969). Behavior modification research: Design and tactics. In C. M. Franks (Ed.), *Behavior therapy: Appraisal and status* (pp. 29–62). New York: McGraw-Hill.

Paul, G. L. (2000). Milieu therapy. In A. E. Kazdin (Ed.), *The encyclopedia of psychology*. Washington, DC: American Psychological Association.

Paul, G. L., & Lentz, R. J. (1977). *Psychosocial treatment of chronic mental patients: Milieu versus social learning programs*. Cambridge: Harvard University Press.

Paul, G. L., Stuve, P., & Cross, J. V. (1997). Real-world inpatient programs: Shedding some light—A critique. *Applied and Preventive Psychology, 6,* 193–204.

Paulhus, D. L., Trapnell, P., & Chen, D. (1999). Birth order effects on personality and achievement within families. *Psychological Science, 10,* 482–488.

Pauls, D. L., Alsobrook, J. P., II, Goodman, W., Rasmussen, S., & Leckman, J. F. (1995). A family study of obsessive-compulsive disorder. *American Journal of Psychiatry, 152,* 76–84.

Paulus, P. B. (1998). Developing consensus about groupthink after all these years. *Organizational Behavior and Human Decision Processes, 73,* 362–374.

Paus, T., Zijdenbos, A., Worsley, K., Collins, D. L., Blumenthal, J., Giedd, J. N., et al. (1999). Structural maturation of neural pathways in children and adolescents: In vivo study. *Science, 283,* 1908–1911.

Pavkov, T., Lewis, D., & Lyons, J. (1989). Psychiatric diagnosis and racial bias: An empirical investigation. *Professional Psychology: Research and Practice, 20,* 364–368.

Pavlov, I. P. (1927). *Conditioned reflexes.* Oxford: Oxford University Press.

Pear, J., & Martin, G. L. (2002). *Behavior modification: What it is and how to do it* (7th ed.). Englewood Cliffs, NJ: Prentice Hall.

Pearson, G. (2000, July 2). Rite-minded: Sports fans find rituals help them get through the game. *Milwaukee Journal-Sentinal.*

Pedersen, P. B., & Draguns, J. G. (2002). *Counseling across cultures.* Thousand Oaks, CA: Sage.

Peeters, A., Barendregt, J. J., Willekens, F., Mackenbach, J. P., Al Mamun, A., & Bonneux, L. (2003). Obesity in adulthood and its consequences for life expectancy: A life-table analysis. *Annals of Internal Medicine, 138,* 24–32.

Peiffer, L. C., & Trull, T. J. (2000). Predictors of suggestibility and false-memory production in young adult women. *Journal of Personality Assessment, 74,* 384–399.

Peigneux, P., Laureys, S., Delbeuck, X., & Maquet, P. (2001). Sleeping brain, learning brain: The role of sleep for memory systems. *Neuroreport, 12,* A111–A124.

Penfield, W., & Rasmussen, T. (1968). *The cerebral cortex of man: A clinical study of localization of function.* New York: Hafner.

Pennartz, C. M., McNaughton, B. L., & Mulder, A. B. (2000). The glutamate hypothesis of reinforcement learning. *Progress in Brain Research, 126,* 231–253.

Pennebaker, J. W. (1995). *Emotion, disclosure, and health.* Washington, DC: American Psychological Association.

Pennebaker, J. W. (2000). The effects of traumatic disclosure on physical and mental health: The values of writing and talking about upsetting events. In J. M. Violanti, D. Paton, & C. Dunning (Eds.), *Posttraumatic stress intervention: Challenges, issues, and perspectives* (pp. 97–114). Chicago: Charles C. Thomas.

Pennebaker, J. W., & Chew, C. H. (1985). Deception, electrodermal activity, and inhibition of behavior. *Journal of Personality and Social Psychology, 49,* 1427–1433.

Pennebaker, J. W., & O'Heeron, R. C. (1984). Confiding in others and illness rate among spouses of suicide and accidental death victims. *Journal of Abnormal Psychology, 93,* 473–476.

Penner, L. A. (2002). Dispositional and organizational influences on sustained volunteerism: An interactionist perspective. *Journal of Social Issues, 58,* 447–467.

Penner, L. A. (in press) Volunteerism and social problems: Making things better or worse? *Journal of Social Issues.*

Penner, L. A., Dovidio, J., & Albrecht, T. L. (2001). Helping victims of loss and trauma: A social psychological perspective. In J. Harvey & E. Miller (Eds.), *Loss and trauma: General and close relationship perspectives* (pp. 62–85). Philadelphia: Brunner Routledge.

Penner, L. A., Dovidio, J. F., Piliavin, J., & Schroeder, D. A. (in press). Prosocial behavior. *Annual Review of Psychology.* Palo Alto: Annual Reviews Inc.

Penner, L. A., & Finkelstein, M. A. (1998). Dispositional and structural determinants of volunteerism. *Journal of Personality and Social Psychology, 74,* 525–537.

Penner, L. A., Knoff, H., Batchshe, G., Nelson, D. L., & Spielberger, C. D. (Eds.). (1994). *Contributions of psychology to science and math education.* Washington, DC: American Psychological Association.

Penninx, B. W., Beekman, A. T., Honig, A., Deeg, D. J., Schoevers, R. A., van Eijk, J. T., van Tilburg, W. (2001). Depression and cardiac mortality: Results from a community-based longitudinal study. *Archives of General Psychiatry, 58,* 221–227.

Peña, M., Maki, A., Kovaci, D., Dehaene-Lambertz, G., Koizumi, H., Bouquet, F., & Mehler, J. (2003). Sounds and silence: An optical topography study of language recognition at birth. *Proceedings of the National Academy of Sciences,100,* 11702–11705.

Peplau, L. A. (2003). Human sexuality: How do men and women differ? *Current Directions in Psychological Science, 12,* 37–40.

Peplau, L. A., Fingerhut, A., & Beals, K. (in press). Sexuality in the relationships of lesbians and gay men. In J. Harvey, A. Wenzel, & S. Sprecher (Eds.), *Handbook of sexuality in close relationships.* Mahwah, NJ: Erlbaum.

Perlis, M. L., Sharpe, M., Smith, M. T., Greenblatt, D., & Giles, D. (2001). Behavioral treatment of insomnia: Treatment outcomes and the relevance of medical and psychiatric morbidity. *Journal of Behavioral Medicine, 24,* 281–296.

Perls, F. S. (1969). *Ego, hunger and aggression: The beginning of Gestalt therapy.* New York: Random House.

Perls, F. S., Hefferline, R. F., & Goodman, P. (1951). *Gestalt therapy.* New York: Julian Press.

Peroutka, S. J., Newman, H., & Harris, H. (1988). The subjective effects of 3,4-methylenedioxymethamphetamine in recreational users. *Neuropharmacology, 1*(4), 273–277.

Persons, J. B., Davidson, J., & Tompkins, M. A. (2001). *Essential components of cognitive-behavior therapy for depression.* Washington, DC: American Psychological Association.

Persons, J. B., & Silberschatz, G. (1998). Are results of randomized controlled trials useful to psychotherapists? *Journal of Consulting and Clinical Psychology, 66,* 126–135.

Pervin, L. A. (2003). *The science of personality.* New York: Oxford University Press.

Pervin, L. A., & John, O. P. (2001). *Personality: Theory and research* (8th ed.). Oxford, England: Wiley.

Peterson, A., Compas, B., Brooks-Gunn, J., Stemmler, M., Ey, S., & Grant, K. (1993). Depression in adolescence. *American Psychologist, 48,* 155–168.

Peterson, C. (1995, April). *The preschool child witness: Errors in accounts of traumatic injury.* Paper presented at the biennial meeting of the Society for Research in Child Development, Indianapolis.

Peterson, C., Maier, S. F., & Seligman, M. E. (1993). *Learned helplessness: A theory for the age of personal control.* New York: Oxford University Press.

Peterson, C., & Seligman, M. E. P. (1984). Causal explanations as a risk factor for depression: Theory and evidence. *Psychological Review, 91,* 347–374.

Peterson, C., & Seligman, M. E. P. (1995, April). *The preschool child witness: Errors in accounts of traumatic injury.* Paper presented at the biennial meeting of the Society for Research in Child Development, Indianapolis.

Peterson, C., Seligman, M. E. P., Yurko, K. H., Martin, L. R., & Friedman, H. S. (1998). Catastrophizing and untimely death. *Psychological Science, 9,* 127–130.

Peterson, L. R., & Peterson, M. J. (1959). Short-term retention of individual verbal items. *Journal of Experimental Psychology, 58,* 193–198.

Peterson, N. G., Mumford, M. D., Borman, W. C., Jeanneret, P. R., Fleishman, E. A., Levin, K. Y., et al. (2001). Understanding work using the Occupational Information Network (O*NET): Implications for practice and research. *Personnel Psychology, 54,* 451–492.

Petrill, S. A., Plomin, R., Berg, S., Johansson, B., Pederson, N. L., Ahern, F., & McClearn, G. E. (1998). The genetic and environmental relationship between general and specific cognitive abilities in twins age 80 and older. *Psychological Science, 9,* 183–189.

Petrocelli, J. V. (2002). Effectiveness of group cognitive-behavioral therapy for general symptomatology: A meta-analysis. *Journal of Specialists in Group Work, 27,* 92–115.

Petrovic, P., Kalso, E., Petersson, K. M., & Ingvar, M. (2002). Placebo and opioid analgesia: Imaging a shared neuronal network. *Science, 295,* 1737–1740.

Petry, N. M. (2001). Substance abuse, pathological gambling and impulsivity. *Drug and Alcohol Dependence, 63,* 29–38.

Pettigrew, T. F. (1979). The ultimate attribution error: Extending Allport's cognitive analysis of prejudice. *Personality and Social Psychology Bulletin, 5,* 461–476.

Pettigrew, T. F., & Tropp, L. R. (2000). Does intergroup contact reduce prejudice? Recent meta-analytic findings. In S. Oskamp (Ed.), *Reducing prejudice and discrimination* (pp. 93–114). Mahwah, NJ: Erlbaum.

Pettit, D. L., Shao, Z., & Yakel, J. L. (2001). Beta-amyloid (1–42) peptide directly modulates nicotinic receptors in the rat hippocampal slice. *Journal of Neuroscience, 21,* RC120.

Petty, R. E., & Wegener, D. T. (1998). Attitude change: Multiple roles for persuasion variables. In D. Gilbert, S. T. Fiske, & G. Lindzey (Eds.), *Handbook of social psychology* (Vol.1, 4th ed., pp. 323–390). Boston: McGraw-Hill.

Peyron, C., Faraco, J., Rogers, W., Ripley, B., Overeem, S., Charnay, Y., et al. (2000). A mutation in a case of early onset narcolepsy and a generalized absence of hypocretin peptides in human narcoleptic brains. *Nature Medicine, 6,* 991–997.

Pezdek, K., Finger, K., & Hodge, D. (1997). Planting false childhood memories: The role of event plausibility. *Psychological Science, 8,* 437–441.

Pfefferbaum, A., Rosenbloom, M., Deshmukkh, A., & Sullivan, E., (2001). Sex differences in the effects of alcohol on brain structure. *The American Journal of Psychiatry, 158,* 188–197.

Pham, L. B., Taylor, S. E., & Seeman, T. E. (2001) Effects of environmental predictability and personal mastery on self-regulatory and physiological processes. *Personality & Social Psychology Bulletin, 27,* 611–620.

Phares, E. J. (1976). *Locus of control in personality.* Morristown, NJ: General Learning Press.

Phares, E. J. (1991). *Introduction to personality* (3rd ed.). New York: Harper-Collins.

Phelan, J. C., Link, B. G., Stueve, A., & Pescosolido, B. A. (2000). Public conceptions of mental illness in 1950 and 1996: What is mental illness and is it to be feared? *Journal of Health and Social Behavior, 41,* 188–207.

Phelps, E. A., O'Connor, K. J., Cunningham, W. A., Funayama, E. S., Gatenby, J. C., Gore, J. C., & Banaji, M. R. (2000). Performance on indirect measures of race evaluation predicts amygdala activation. *Journal of Cognitive Neuroscience, 12,* 729–738.

Philip, P., Vervialle, F., Le Breton, P., Taillard, J., & Horne, J. A. (2001). Fatigue, alcohol, and serious road crashes in France: Factorial study of national data. *British Medical Journal, 322,* 829–830.

Phillips, D. P., & Cartensen, L. L. (1986). Clustering of teenage suicides after television news stories about suicide. *New England Journal of Medicine, 315,* 685–689.

Phillips, N. A. (2000). Female sexual dysfunction: Evaluation and treatment. *American Family Physician, 62,* 127–136, 141–142.

Phillips, P. E., Stuber, G. D., Heien, M. L., Wightman, R. M., & Carelli, R. M. (2003). Subsecond dopamine release promotes cocaine seeking. *Nature, 422,* 614–618.

Phinney, J. S., Ferguson, D. L., & Tate, J. D. (1997). Intergroup attitudes among ethnic minority adolescents: A causal model. *Child Development, 68,* 955–969.

Piaget, J. (1952). *The origins of intelligence in children.* New York: International Universities Press.

Pickering, A. D., & Gray, J. A. (1999). The neuroscience of personality. In L. Pervin & O. John (Eds.), *Handbook of personality: Theory and research* (2nd ed., pp. 277–299). New York: Guilford.

Pickler, N. (2002, November 19). *NTSB cites fatigue, sleep apnea in fatal train wreck.* Associated Press. Retrieved August 25, 2003, from http://newsobserver.com/24hour/nation/v-print/story/626769p-4807167c.html

Pietro, P., Guazzeli, M., Basso, G., Jaffe, K., & Grafman, J. (2000). Neural correlates of imaginal aggressive behavior assessed by positron emission tomography in healthy subjects. *American Journal of Psychiatry, 157,* 1772–1781.

Piliavin, J. A., Dovidio, J. F., Gaertner, S. L., & Clark, R. D., III. (1981). *Emergency intervention.* New York: Academic Press.

Pillard, R. C., & Bailey, J. M. (1998). Human sexual orientation has a heritable component. *Human Biology, 70,* 347–365.

Pilling, S., Bebbington, P., Kuipers, E., Garety, P., Geddes, J., Orbach, G., & Morgan, C. (2002). Psychological treatments in schizophrenia: I. Meta-analysis of family intervention and cognitive behavior therapy. *Psychological Medicine, 32,* 763–782.

Pincus, T., & Morley, S. (2001). Cognitive-processing bias in chronic pain: A review and integration. *Psychological Bulletin, 127,* 599–617.

Pinel, J. P. J. (1993). *Biopsychology.* Boston: Allyn & Bacon.

Pinker, S. (1994). *The language instinct: How the mind creates language.* New York: Morrow.

Pitman, R. K., Shin, L. M., & Rauch, S. L. (2001). Investigating the pathogenesis of posttraumatic stress disorder with neuroimaging. *Journal of Clinical Psychiatry, 62,* 47–54.

Pitschel-Walz, G., & Leutch, S., Bauml, J., Kissling, W., & Engel, R. R. (2001) The effect of family interventions on relapse and rehospitalization in schizophrenia: A meta-analysis. *Schizophrenia Bulletin, 27,* 73–92.

Plomin, R. (1994). *Genetics and experience: The developmental interplay between nature and nurture.* Newbury Park, CA: Sage.

Plomin, R., & Caspi, A. (1999). Behavioral genetics and personality. In L. Pervin & O. John (Eds.), *Handbook of personality research* (2nd ed.). New York: Guilford.

Plomin, R., Corley, R., Caspi, A., Fulker, D. W., & DeFries, J. C. (1998). Adoption results for self-reported personality: Not much nature or nurture? *Journal of Personality and Social Psychology, 75,* 211–218.

Plomin, R., & Crabbe, J. C. (2000). DNA. *Psychological Bulletin, 126,* 806–828.

Plomin, R., DeFries, J. C., Craig, I. W., & McGuffin, P. (2002). *Behavioral genetics in the postgenomic era.* Washington, DC: American Psychological Association.

Plomin, R., DeFries, J. C., McClearn, G. E., & McGuffin, P. (2001). *Behavioral genetics* (4th ed.). New York: Worth.

Ploner, M., Gross, J., Timmermann, L., & Schnitzler, A. (2002). Cortical representation of first and second pain sensation in humans. *Proceedings of the National Academy of Sciences, 99,* 12444–12448.

Plous, S. (1996). Attitudes toward the use of animals in psychological research and education: Results from a national survey of psychologists. *American Psychologist, 51,* 1167–1180.

Pluchino, S., Quattrini, A., Brambilla, E., Gritti, A., Salani, G., Dina, G., et al. (2003). Injection of adult neurospheres induces recovery in a chronic model of multiple sclerosis. *Nature, 422,* 688–694.

Plutchik, R., & Conte, H. R. (Eds.). (1997). *Circumplex models of personality and emotions.* Washington, DC: American Psychological Association.

Poczwardowski, A., & Conroy, D. E. (2002). Coping responses to failure and success among elite athletes and performing artists. *Journal of Applied Sport Psychology, 14,* 313–329.

Pol, H. E. H., Schnack, H. G., Bertens, M. G. B. C., van Haren, N. E. M., van der Tweel, I., Staal, W. G., et al. (2002). Volume changes in gray matter in patients with schizophrenia. *American Journal of Psychiatry, 159,* 244–250.

Polivy, J., & Herman, C. P. (2002). If at first you don't succeed: False hopes of self-change. *American Psychologist, 57,* 677–689.

Pollack, H. A., & Frohna, J. G. (2002). Infant sleep placement after the back to sleep campaign. *Pediatrics, 109,* 608–614.

Pollack, I. (1953). The assimilation of sequentially coded information. *American Journal of Psychology, 66,* 421–435.

Pollack, V. (1992). Meta-analysis of subjective sensitivity to alcohol in sons of alcoholics. *American Journal of Psychiatry, 149,* 1534–1538.

Polusny, M. A., & Follette, V. M. (1995). Long-term correlates of child sexual abuse: Theory and review of the empirical literature. *Applied and Preventive Psychology, 4,* 143–166.

Polusny, M. A., & Follette, V. M. (1996). Remembering childhood abuse: A national survey of psychologists' clinical practices, beliefs, and personal experiences. *Professional Psychology: Research and Practice, 27,* 41–52.

Poole, D. A., Lindsay, D. S., Memon, A., & Bull, R. (1995). Psychotherapy and the recovery of memories of childhood sexual abuse: U.S. and British practitioners' opinions, practices, and experiences. *Journal of Consulting and Clinical Psychology, 63,* 426–437.

Pope, H. G., Jr., Hudson, J. I., Bodkin, J. A., & Oliva, P. (1998). Questionable validity of "dissociative amnesia" in trauma victims: Evidence from prospective studies. *British Journal of Psychiatry, 172,* 210–215.

Pope, H. G., Jr., Kouri, E. M., & Hudson, J. I. (2000). Effects of supraphysiologic doses of testosterone on mood and aggression in normal men: A randomized controlled trial. *Archives of General Psychiatry, 57*(2), 133–140.

Pope, H. G., & Yurgelun-Todd, D. (1996). The residual cognitive effects of heavy marijuana use in college students. *Journal of the American Medical Association, 275,* 521–527.

Pope, K. S. (1998). Pseudoscience, cross-examination, and scientific evidence in the recovered memory controversy. *Psychology, Public Policy, and Law, 4,* 1160–1181.

Pope-Davis, D. B., Reynolds, A. L., Dings, J. G., & Nielson, D. (1995). Examining multicultural counseling competencies of graduate students in psychology. *Professional Psychology: Research and Practice, 26,* 322–329.

Porges, S. W., Doussard, R. J. A., & Maita, A. K. (1995). Vagal tone and the physiological regulation of emotion. *Monographs of the Society for Research on Child Development, 59*(2–3), 167–186, 250–283.

Porkka-Heiskanen, T., Strecker, R. E., Thakkar, M., Bjorkum, A. A., Greene, R. W., & McCarley, R. W. (1997). Adenosine: A mediator of the sleep-inducing effects of prolonged wakefulness. *Science, 276,* 1265–1268.

Port, C. L., Engdahl, B., & Frazier, P. (2001). A longitudinal and retrospective study of PTSD among older prisoners of war. *American Journal of Psychiatry, 158,* 1474–1479.

Porte, H. S., & Hobson, J. A. (1996). Physical motion in dreams: One measure of three theories. *Journal of Abnormal Psychology, 105,* 329–335.

Porter, R. H. (1998/1999). Olfaction and human kin recognition. *Genetica, 104,* 259–263.

Porter, R. H., Makin, J. W., Davis, L. B., & Christensen, K. M. (1992). Breast-fed infants respond to olfactory cues from their own mother and unfamiliar lactating females. *Infant Behavior and Development, 15,* 85–93.

Porter, S., Birt, A. R., Yuille, J. C., & Lehman, D. R. (2000). Negotiating false memories: Interviewer and rememberer characteristics relate to memory distortion. *Psychological Science, 11,* 507–510.

Porter, S., Yuille, J. C., & Lehman, D. R. (1999). The nature of real, implanted, and fabricated memories for emotional childhood events: Implications for the recovered memory debate. *Law & Human Behavior, 23,* 517–537.

Posener, J. A., DeBattista, C., Williams, G. H., Kraemer, H. C., Kalehzan, B. M., & Schatzberg, A. F. (2000). 24-hour monitoring of cortisol and corticotropin secretion in psychotic and nonpsychotic major depression. *Archives of General Psychiatry, 57,* 755–760.

Posner, M. I., & Peterson, S. E. (1990). The attention system of the human brain. *Annual Review of Neurosciences, 13,* 24–42.

Posner, M. I., & Raichle, M. E. (1994). *Images of mind.* New York: Scientific American Books.

Postmes, T., & Spears, R. (1998). Deindividuation and antinormative behavior: A meta-analysis. *Psychological Bulletin, 123,* 238–259.

Postmes, T., Spears, R., Sakhel, K., & de Groot, D. (2001). Social influence in computer-mediated communication: The effects of anonymity on group behavior. *Personality and Social Psychology Bulletin, 27,* 1243–1254.

Potkin, S. G., Saha, A. R., Kujawa, M. J., Carson, W. H., Ali, M., Stock, E., et al. (2003). Aripiprazole, an antipsychotic with a novel mechanism of action, and risperidone vs placebo in patients with schizophrenia and schizoaffective disorder. *Archives of General Psychiatry, 60,* 681–690.

Potter, P. T., & Zautra, A. J. (1997). Stressful life events' effects on rheumatoid arthritis disease activity. *Journal of Consulting and Clinical Psychology, 65,* 319–323.

Povinelli, D. J., & Bering, J. M. (2002). The mentality of apes revisited. *Current Directions in Psychological Science, 11,* 115–119.

Powch, I. G., & Houston, B. K. (1996). Hostility, anger-in, and cardiovascular activity in White women. *Health Psychology, 15,* 200–208.

Powell, L. H., Shahabi, L., & Thoresen, C. E. (2003). Religion and spirituality: Linkages to physical health. *American Psychologist, 58,* 36–52.

Powley, T. L., & Keesey, R. E. (1970). Relationship of body weight to the lateral hypothalamic feeding syndrome. *Journal of Comparative & Physiological Psychology, 70,* 25–36.

Pratkanis, A. R. (1992). The cargo-cult science of subliminal persuasion. *Skeptical Inquirer, 16,* 260–273.

Pratkanis, A., & Aronson, E. (2001). *The age of propaganda: The everyday use and abuse of propaganda.* New York: W. H. Freeman.

Pratkanis, A. R., Eskenazi, J., & Greenwald, A. G. (1994). What you expect is what you believe (but not necessarily what you get): A test of the effectiveness of self-help audiotapes. *Basic and Applied Social Psychology, 15,* 251–276.

Preciado, J. (1994). The empirical basis of behavior therapy applications with Hispanics. *The Behavior Therapist, 17,* 63–65.

Prentice, D. A., & Miller, D. T. (2002). The emergence of homegrown stereotypes. *American Psychologist, 57,* 352–359.

Prescott, J. W. (1996). The origins of human love and violence. *Pre- and Peri-Natal Psychology Journal, 10,* 143–188.

President's New Freedom Commission on Mental Health. (2003). *Achieving the promise: Transforming mental health care in America.* Rockville, Maryland: U.S. Department of Health and Human Services.

Preston, E. (2002). Detecting deception. *APS Observer,* 15, 19, 49.

Price, R. (1992). Psychosocial impact of job loss on individuals and families. *Current Directions in Psychological Sciences, 1,* 9–11.

Prinstein, M. J., & La Greca, A. M. (2002). Peer crowd affiliation and intrenalizing distress in childhood and adolescence: A longitudinal follow-back study. *Journal of Research on Adolescence, 12,* 35–351.

Prochaska, J. O. (1994). Strong and weak principles for progressing from precontemplation to action on the basis of twelve problem behaviors. *Health Psychology, 13,* 47–51.

Prochaska, J. O., DiClemente, C., & Norcross, J. (1992). In search of how people change: Application to addictive behaviors. *American Psychologist, 47,* 1102–1114.

Protinski, H., Sparks, J., & Flemke, K. (2001). Eye movement desensitization and reprocessing: Innovative clinical applications. *Journal of Contemporary Psychotherapy, 31,* 125–135.

Pryor, T. (1995). Diagnostic criteria for eating disorders: *DSM-IV* revisions. *Psychiatric Annals, 25*(1), 40–45.

Pulakos, E. D., Schmitt, N., Dorsey, D. W., Arad, S., Hedge, J. W., & Borman, W. C. (2002). Predicting adaptive performance: Further tests of a model of adaptability. *Human Performance, 15,* 299–324.

Putnam, F. W. (2003). Ten-year research update review: Child sexual abuse. *Journal of the American Academy of Child & Adolescent Psychiatry, 42,* 269–278.

Pyszczynski, T., Greenberg, J., & Solomon, S. (2001). Proximal and distal defense: A new perspective on unconscious motivation. *Current Directions in Psychological Science, 9,* 156–160.

Pyszczynski, T., Greenberg, J., & Solomon, S. (2003). *In the wake of 9/11: The psychology of terror.* Washington, DC: APA Books.

Quinn, G. E., Shin, C. H., Maguire, M. G., & Stone, R. A. (1999). Myopia and ambient lighting at night. *Nature, 399,* 113–114.

Quintana, S. M. (1998). Children's developmental understanding of ethnicity and race. *Applied and Preventive Psychology, 7,* 27–45.

Quintana, S. M., & Bernal, M. E. (1995). Ethnic minority training in counseling psychology: Comparisons with clinical psychology and proposed standards. *The Counseling Psychologist, 23*(1), 102–121.

Quitkin, F. M., Petkkova, E., McGrath, P. J., Taylor, B., Beasley, C., Stewart, J., et al. (2003). When should a trial of fluoxetine for major depression be declared failed? *American Journal of Psychiatry, 160,* 734–740.

Quitkin, F. M., Rabkin, J. G., Gerald, J., Davis, J. M., & Klein, D. F. (2000). Validity of clinical trials of antidepressants. *American Journal of Psychiatry, 157,* 327–337.

Rabasca, L. (1999). Behavioral interventions can cut the use of restraints. *APA Monitor,* July/August, p. 27.

Rabinowitz, J., De Smedt, G., Harvey, P. D., & Davidson, M. (2002). Relationship between premorbid functioning and symptom severity as assessed at first episode of psychosis. *American Journal of Psychiatry, 159,* 2021–2026.

Rabinowitz, J., Lichtenberg, P., Kaplan, Z., Mark, M., Nahon, D., & Davidson, M. (2001). Rehospitalization rates of chronically ill schizophrenic patients discharged on a regimen of risperidone, olanzapine, or conventional antipsychotics. *American Journal of Psychiatry, 158,* 266–269.

Racenstein, J. M., Harrow, M., Reed, R., Martin, E., Herbener, E., & Penn, D. L. (2002). The relationship between positive symptoms and instrumental work functioning in schizophrenai: A 10-year follow-up study. *Schizophrenia Research, 56,* 95–103.

Rachlin, H. (2000). *The science of self-control.* Cambridge: Harvard University Press.

Rada, J. B., & Rogers, R. W. (1973). *Obedience to authority: Presence of authority and command strength.* Paper presented at the annual convention of the Southeastern Psychological Association.

Radcliffe, N. M., & Klein, W. M. (2002). Dispositional, unrealistic and comparative optimism: Differential relations with the knowledge and processing of risk information and beliefs about personal risk. *Personality & Social Psychology Bulletin, 28,* 836–846.

Radvansky, G. A. (1999). Aging, memory, and comprehension. *Current Directions in Psychological Science, 8,* 49–53.

Rae, C., Harasty, J. A., Dzendrowskyj, T. E., Talcott, J. B., Simpson, J. M., Blamire, A. M., et al. (2002). Cerebellar morphology in developmental dyslexia. *Neuropsychologia, 40,* 1285–1292.

Raggatt, P. T. (1991). Work stress among long-distance coach drivers: A survey and correlational study. *Journal of Organizational Behavior, 12,* 565–579.

Raguram, R., & Bhide, A. (1985). Patterns of phobic neurosis: A retrospective study. *British Journal of Psychiatry, 147,* 557–560.

Raine, A., Brennan, P., & Mednick, S. (1994). Birth complications combined with early maternal rejection at age 1 year predispose to violent crime at age 18 years. *Archives of General Psychiatry, 51,* 984–988.

Raine, A., Lencz, T., Bihrle, S., LaCasse, L., & Colletti, P. (2000). Reduced prefrontal gray matter volume and reduced autonomic activity in antisocial personality disorder. *Archives of General Psychiatry, 57,* 119–127.

Rakic, P. (2002). Neurogenesis in adult primates. *Progress in Brain Research, 138,* 3–14.

Ramachandran, V. S. (1988, August). Perceiving shape from shading. *Scientific American,* pp. 76–83.

Ramey, C. T., Campbell, F. A., Burchinal, M., Skinner, M. L., Gardner, D. M., & Ramey, S. L. (2000). Persistent effects of early childhood education on high-risk children and their mothers. *Applied Developmental Science, 4,* 2–14.

Ramey, C. T., & Ramey, S. L. (1998). Early intervention and early experience. *American Psychologist, 53,* 109–121.

Ramey, S. L. (1999). Head Start and preschool education: Toward continued improvement. *American Psychologist, 54,* 344–346.

Ramirez, S. Z., Wassef, A., Paniagua, F. A., & Linskey, A. O. (1996). Mental health providers' perceptions of cultural variables in evaluating ethnically diverse clients. *Professional Psychology: Research and Practice, 27,* 284–288.

Ranta, S., Jussila, J., & Hynynen, M. (1990). Recall of awareness during cardiac anaesthesia: Influence of feedback information to the anaesthesiologists. *Acta Aneasthesiolgia Scandinavica, 40,* 554–560.

Rapee, R., Brown, T., Antony, M., & Barlow, D. (1992). Response to hyperventilation and inhalation of 5.5% carbon dioxide-enriched air across *DSM-III* anxiety disorders. *Journal of Abnormal Psychology, 101,* 538–552.

Rapp, S. R., Brenes, G., & Marsh, A. P. (2002). Memory enhancement training for older adults with mild cognitive impairment: A preliminary study. *Aging & Mental Health, 6*(1), 5–11.

Rasinski, K. A., Kuby, A., Bzdusek, S. A., Silvestri, J. M., & Weese-Mayer, D. E. (2003). Effect of a sudden infant death syndrome risk reduction education program on risk factor compliance and information sources in primarily black urban communities. *Pediatrics, 111,* 347–354.

Raskin, D. C. (1986). The polygraph in 1986: Scientific, professional and legal issues surrounding applications and acceptance of polygraph evidence. *Utah Law Review, 1,* 29–74.

Raskin, N. J., & Rogers, C. R. (2001). Person-centered therapy. In R. J. Corsini & D. Wedding (Eds.), *Current psychotherapies* (6th ed.) Itasca, IL: Peacock.

Ratcliff, R., & McKoon, G. (1989). Memory models, text processing, and cue-dependent retrieval. In H. L. Roediger & F. I. M. Craik (Eds.), *Varieties of memory and consciousness.* Hillsdale, NJ: Erlbaum.

Rathbone, D. B., & Huckabee, J. C. (1999). *Controlling road rage: A literature review and pilot study.* Washington, DC: American Automobile Association.

Ratner, C. (1994). The unconscious: A perspective from sociohistorical psychology. *Journal of Mind and Behavior, 15*(4), 323–342.

Rattenborg, N., Lima, S. L., & Amlaner, C. J. (1999). Half-awake to the risk of predation. *Nature, 397,* 397–398.

Raudenbush, B., & Meyer, B. (2002). Effect of nasal dilators on pleasantness, intensity and sampling behaviors of foods in the oral cavity. *Rhinology, 39,* 80–83.

Rauschecker, J. P., & Shannon, R. V. (2002). Sending sound to the brain. *Science, 295,* 1025–1029.

Ray, D. W., Wandersman, A., Ellisor, J., & Huntington, D. E. (1982). The effects of high density in a juvenile correctional institution. *Basic and Applied Social Psychology, 3,* 95–108.

Raynor, H. A., & Epstein, L. H. (2001). Dietary variety, energy regulation, and obesity. *Psychological Bulletin, 127,* 325–341.

Razali, S. M., Aminah, K., & Umeed, A. (2002). Religious-cultural psychotherapy in the management of anxiety patients. *Transcultural Psychiatry, 39,* 130–136.

Reber, A. S. (1992). The cognitive unconscious: An evolutionary perspective. *Consciousness and Cognition: An International Journal, 1*(2), 93–133.

Redd, W. H. (1984). Psychological intervention to control cancer chemotherapy side effects. *Postgraduate Medicine, 75,* 105–113.

Ree, M. J., & Carretta, T. R. (1998). General cognitive ability and occupational performance. In C. L. Cooper & I. T. Robertson (Eds.), *International review of industrial and organizational psychology 1998* (pp. 159–184). Chichester, UK: Wiley.

Reed, S. K. (2000). *Cognition* (5th ed.). Belmont, CA: Wadsworth.

Reedy, M. N. (1983). Personality and aging. In D. S. Woodruff & J. E. Birren (Eds.), *Aging: Scientific perspectives and social issues* (2nd ed.). Monterey, CA: Brooks/Cole.

Reeve, J. M. (1996). *Understanding motivation and emotion.* New York: Harcourt, Brace, Jovanovich.

Regan, P. C., & Berscheid, E. (1999). *Lust: What we know about human sexual desire.* Thousand Oaks, CA: Sage.

Regier, D. A., Farmer, M. E., Rae, D. S., Myers, J. K., Kramer, M., Robins, L. N., et al. (1993). One-month prevalence of mental disorders in the United States and sociodemographic characteristics: The Epidemiologic Catchment Area study. *Acta Psychiatrica Scandinavica, 88,* 35–47.

Regier, D. A., Narrow, W., Rae, D., Manderscheid, R., Locke, B., & Goodwin, F. (1993). The de facto U.S. mental and addictive disorders service system: Epidemiologic catchment area prospective 1-year prevalence rates of disorders and services. *Archives of General Psychiatry, 50,* 85–94.

Reich, T., Edenberg, H. J., Goate, A., Williams, J. T., Rice, J. P., Van Eerdewegh, P., et al. (1998). Genome-wide search for genes affecting the risk for alcohol dependence. *American Journal of Medical Genetics, 81,* 207–215.

Reinisch, J. M., Ziemba-Davis, M., & Sanders, S. A. (1991). Hormonal contributions to sexually dimorphic behavioral development in humans. *Psychoneuroendocrinology, 16,* 213–278.

Reisenzein, R. (1983). The Schachter theory of emotion: Two decades later. *Psychological Bulletin, 94,* 239–264.

Reiss, A. J., & Roth, J. A. (1993). *Understanding and preventing violence.* Washington, DC: National Academy Press.

Reiss, D., Neiderhiser, J. M., Hetherington, E. M., & Plomin, R. (2000). *The relationship code: Deciphering genetic and social influences on adolescent development.* Cambridge: Harvard University Press.

Reitman, D., & Drabman, R. S. (1999). Multifaceted uses of a simple timeout record in the treatment of a noncompliant 8-year-old boy. *Education and Treatment of Children, 22,* 136–145.

Ren, T. (2002). Longitudinal pattern of basilar membrane vibration in the sensitive cochlea. *Proceedings of the National Academy of Sciences, 99,* 17101–17106.

Rendall, D., Cheney, D. L., & Seyfarth, R. M. (2000). Proximate factors mediating "contact" calls in adult female baboons (*Papio cynocephalus ursinus*) and their infants. *Journal of Comparative Psychology, 114,* 36–46.

Rescorla, R. A. (1968). Probability of shock in the presence and absence of CS in fear conditioning. *Journal of Comparative and Physiological Psychology, 66,* 1–5.

Rescorla, L. A. (1981). Category development in early language. *Journal of Child Language, 8,* 225–238.

Resnick, M. (1997). Protecting adolescents from harm: Findings from the National Longitudinal Study of Adolescent Health. *Journal of the American Medical Association, 278,* 823–832.

Reynolds, C. F., III, Frank, E., Perel, J. M., Imber, S. D., Cornes, C., Miller, M. D., et al. (1999). Nortriptyline and interpersonal psychotherapy as maintenance therapies for recurrent major depression: A randomized controlled trial in patients older than 59 years. *Journal of the American Medical Association, 281,* 39–45.

Rheingold, H., & Cook, K. (1975). The contents of boys' and girls' rooms as an index of parents' behavior. *Child Development, 46,* 459–463.

Ricaurte, G. A., Yuan, J., Hatzidimitriou, G., Cord, B. J., & McCann, U. D. (2002). Severe dopaminergic neurotoxicity in primates after a common recreational dose regimen of MDMA ("ecstasy"). *Science, 297,* 2260–2263.

Riccio, D. C., Millin, P. M., & Gisquet-Verrier, P. (2003). Retrograde amnesia: Forgetting back. *Current Directions in Psychological Science, 12,* 41–44.

Rice, G., Anderson, C., Risch, H., & Ebers, G. (1999). Male homosexuality: Absence of linkage to microsatellite markers at Xq28. *Science, 284,* 665–667.

Rice, M. E. (1997). Violent offender research and implications for the criminal justice system. *American Psychologist, 52,* 414–423.

Richards, J. M., Beal, W. E., Seagal, J. D., & Pennebaker, J. W. (2000). Effects of disclosure of traumatic events on illness behavior among psychiatric prison inmates. *Journal of Abnormal Psychology, 109,* 156–160.

Richards, J. M., & Gross, J. J. (2000). Emotion regulation and memory: The cognitive costs of keeping one's cool. *Journal of Personality & Social Psychology, 79,* 410–424.

Richards, K. C., Anderson, W. M., Chesson, A. L. Jr., & Nagel, C. L. (2002). Sleep-related breathing disorders in patients who are critically ill. *Journal of Cardiovascular Nursing, 17,* 42–55.

Richards, P. S., & Bergin, A. E. (Eds.). (2000). *Handbook of psychotherapy and religious diversity* (pp. 105–129). Washington, DC: American Psychological Association Press.

Richardson, P. H., & Vincent, C. A. (1986). Acupuncture for the treatment of pain: A review of evaluative research. *Pain, 24,* 15–40.

Richardson-Klavehn, A., & Bjork, R. A. (1988). Measures of memory. *Annual Review of Psychology, 39,* 475–543.

Rickels, K., Schweizer, E., Weiss, S., & Zavodnick, S. (1993) Maintenance drug treatment of panic disorder: II. Short- and long-term outcome after drug taper. *Archives of General Psychiatry, 50,* 61–68.

Rickels, K., Zaninelli, R., McCafferty, J., Bellew, K., Iyengar, M., & Sheehan, D. (2003). Paroxetine treatment of generalized anxiety disorder: A double-blind, placebo-controlled study. *American Journal of Psychiatry, 160,* 749–756.

Ridley, M. (2000*). Genome: The autobiography of a species in 23 chapters.* New York: HarperCollins.

Riemsma, R. P., Pattenden, J., Bridle, C., Sowden, A. J., Mather, L., Watt, I. S., & Walker, A. (2003). Systematic review of the effectiveness of stage based interventions to promote smoking cessation. *British Medical Journal, 326,* 1175–1177.

Riggio, R. E. (1989). *Introduction to industrial/organizational psychology.* Glenview, IL: Scott, Foresman.

Rihmer, Z. (2001). Can better recognition and treatment of depression reduce suicide rates? A brief review. *European Psychiatry, 16,* 406–409.

Rind, B., & Tromovitch, P. (1997). A meta-analytic review of findings from national samples on psychological correlates of child sexual abuse. *Journal of Sex Research, 34,* 237–255.

Rind, B., Tromovitch, P., & Bauserman, R. (1998). A meta-analytic examination of assumed properties of child sexual abuse using college samples. *Psychological Bulletin, 124,* 22–53.

Rinn, W. E. (1984). The neuropsychology of facial expressions: A review of the neurological and psychological mechanisms for producing facial expressions. *Psychological Bulletin, 95,* 52–77.

Rioult-Pedotti, M.-S., Friedman, D., & Donoghue, J. P. (2000). Learning-induced LTP in neocortex. *Science, 290,* 533–536.

Rioux, S. M., & Penner, L. A. (2001). The causes of organizational citizenship behavior: A motivational analysis. *Journal of Applied Psychology, 86,* 1306–1314.

Ripple, C. H., Gilliam, W. S., Chanana, N., & Zigler, E. (1999). Will fifty cooks spoil the broth? The debate over entrusting Head Start to the states. *American Psychologist, 54,* 327–343.

Rips, L. J. (1994). *The psychology of proof: Deductive reasoning in human thinking.* Cambridge, MA: MIT Press.

Risen, J. (1998, July 7). CIA seeks "curmudgeon" to signal its mistakes. *New York Times.*

Rittenhouse, C. D., Stickgold, R., & Hobson, J. A. (1994). Constraint on the transformation of characters, objects, and settings in dream reports. *Consciousness and Cognition, 3*(1), 100–113.

Robbins, J. (2000, July 4). Virtual reality finds a real place as a medical aid. *New York Times.*

Robbins, T. W., & Everitt, B. J. (1999). Interaction of the dopaminergic system with mechanisms of associative learning and cognition: Implications for drug abuse. *Psychological Science, 10,* 199–202.

Roberts, B. W., Caspi, A., & Moffitt, T. E. (2001). The kids are alright: Growth and stability in personality development from adolescence to adulthood. *Journal of Personality & Social Psychology, 81*(4), 670–683.

Roberts, B. W., & DelVecchio, W. F. (2000). The rank-order consistency of traits from childhood to old-age: A quantitative review of longitudinal studies. *Psychological Bulletin, 126,* 3–25.

Roberts, M. C. (2002). The process and product of the Felix decree review of empirically supported treatments: Prospects for change. *Clinical Psychology: Science and Practice, 9,* 217–219.

Robertson, I. H., & Murre, J. M. J. (1999). Rehabilitation of brain damage: Brain plasticity and principles of guided recovery. *Psychological Bulletin, 125,* 544–575.

Robertson, J., & Robertson, J. (1971). Young children in brief separation: A fresh look. *Psychoanalytic Study of the Child, 26,* 264–315.

Robins, L. N., & Regier, D. A. (Eds.). (1991). *Psychiatric disorders in America: The Epidemiologic Catchment Area study.* New York: Free Press.

Robins, R. W., Gosling, S. D., & Craik, K. H. (1999). An empirical analysis of trends in psychology. *American Psychologist, 54,* 117–128.

Robins, R. W., Gosling, S., & Craik, K. H. (2000). Trends in psychology: An empirical issue. *American Psychologist, 55,* 277–278.

Robinson, J. H., & Pritchard, W. S. (1995). "The scientific case that nicotine is addictive": Reply. *Psychopharmacology, 117*(1), 16–17.

Robinson, T. N., Wilde, M. L., Navracruz, L. C., Haydel, K. F., & Varady, A. (2001). Effects of reducing children's television and video game use on aggressive behavior: A randomized controlled trial. *Archives of Pediatrics & Adolescent Medicine, 155,* 17–23.

Robinson, N. M., Zigler, E., & Gallagher, J. J. (2000). Two tails of the normal curve: Similarities and differences in the study of mental retardation and giftedness. *American Psychologist, 55,* 1413–1424.

Rock, I. (1978). *An introduction to perception.* New York: Macmillan.

Rock, I. (1983). *The logic of perception.* Cambridge, MA: MIT Press.

Rodier, P. M. (2000). The early origins of autism. *Scientific American, 282,* 56–63.

Rodriguez de Fonseca, F., Carrera, M. R. A., Navarro, M., Koob, G. F., & Weiss, F. (1997). Activation of corticotropin-releasing factor in the limbic system during cannabinoid withdrawal. *Science, 276,* 2050–2054.

Roe, K. V. (2001). Relationship between male infants' vocal responses to mother and stranger at three months and self-reported academic attainment and adjustment measures in adulthood. *Psychological Reports, 89*(2), 255–258.

Roediger, H. L., & Gallo, D. A. (2001). Levels of processing: Some unanswered questions. In M. Naveh-Benjamin, M. Moscovitch, & H.L. Roediger (Eds.), *Perspectives on human memory and cognitive aging: Essays in hounour of Fergus Craik* (pp. 28–47). New York: Psychology Press.

Roediger, H. L., III, Guynn, M. J., & Jones, T. C. (1995). Implicit memory: A tutorial review. In G. d'Ydewalle, P. Eelen, & P. Bertelson (Eds.), *International perspectives on psychological science: Vol. 2. The state of the art* (pp. 67–94). Hove, UK: Erlbaum.

Roediger, H. L., III, Jacoby, D., & McDermott, K. B. (1996). Misinformation effects in recall: Creating false memories through repeated retrieval. *Journal of Memory and Learning, 35,* 300–318.

Roediger, H. L., III, & McDermott, K. B. (1995). Creating false memories: Remembering words not presented in lists. *Journal of Experimental Psychology: Learning, Memory, and Cognition, 21,* 803–814.

Roediger, H. L., & McDermott, K. B. (2000). Tricks of memory. *Current Directions in Psychological Science, 9,* 123–127.

Roehrich, L., & Goldman, M. S. (1995). Implicit priming of alcohol expectancy memory processes and subsequent drinking behavior. *Experimental and Clincial Psychopharmocology, 3,* 402–410.

Roffwarg, H. P., Hermann, J. H., & Bowe-Anders, C. (1978). The effects of sustained alterations of waking visual input on dream content. In A. M. Arkin, J. S. Antrobus, & S. J. Ellman (Eds.), *The mind in sleep.* Hillsdale, NJ: Erlbaum.

Roffwarg, H. P., Muzio, J. N., & Dement, W. C. (1966). Ontogenetic development of the human sleep-dream cycle. *Science, 152,* 604–619.

Rogers, A. A., Aldrich, M. S., & Lin, A. (2001). A comparison of three different sleep schedules for reducing daytime sleepiness in narcolepsy. *Journal of Sleep and Sleep Disorders Research, 24,* 385–391.

Rogers, C. R. (1942). *Counseling and psychotherapy.* Boston: Houghton Mifflin.

Rogers, C. R. (1951). *Client-centered therapy.* Boston: Houghton Mifflin.

Rogers, C. R. (1961). *On becoming a person.* Boston: Houghton Mifflin.

Rogers, C. R. (1970). *Carl Rogers on encounter groups.* New York: Harper & Row.

Rogers, C. R. (1980) *A way of being.* Boston: Houghton Mifflin.

Rogers, J., Madamba, S. G., Staunton, D. A., & Siggins, G. R. (1986). Ethanol increases single unit activity in the inferior olivary nucleus. *Brain Research, 385,* 253–262.

Rogers, R. (1995). *Diagnostic and structured interviewing: A handbook for psychologists.* Odessa, FL: Psychological Assessment Resources.

Rogers, R. (2001). *Handbook of structured clinical interviewing* (2nd ed.). New York: Guilford.

Rogoff, B., & Waddell, K. J. (1982). Memory for information organized in a scene by children from two cultures. *Child Development, 53,* 1224–1228.

Rohan, M. J., & Zanna, M. P. (1996). Value transmission in families. In C. Seligman, J. M. Olson, & M. P. Zanna (Eds.), *The psychology of values: The Ontario symposium* (Vol. 8, pp. 253–276). Mahwah, NJ: Erlbaum.

Roid, G. H. (2003). *Stanford-Binet Intelligence Scales* (5th ed.). Itasca, IL: Riverside Publishing.

Rolland-Cachera1, M.-F., Castetbon, K., Arnault, N., Bellisle, F., Romano, M.-C., Lehingue, Y., et al. (2002). Body mass index in 7–9-y-old French children: frequency of obesity, overweight and thinness. *International Journal of Obesity, 26,* 1610–1616.

Rolls, E. T. (1997). Taste and olfactory processing in the brain and its relation to the control of eating. *Critical Review of Neurobiology, 11,* 263–287.

Rolls, E. T., Critchley, H. D., Browning, A., & Hernadi, I. (1998). The neurophysiology of taste and olfaction in primates, and umami flavor. *Annals of the New York Academy of Science, 855,* 426–437.

Rome, E. S., Ammerman, S., Rosen, D. S., Keller, R. J., Lock, J., Mammel, K. A., et al. (2003). Children and adolescents with eating disorders: The state of the art. *Pediatrics, 111,* e98–e108.

Roorda, A., & Williams, D. R. (1999). The arrangement of the three cone classes in the living human eye. *Nature, 397,* 520–522.

Rosch, E. (1975). Cognitive representations of semantic categories. *Journal of Experimental Psychology: General, 104,* 192–223.

Rosch, E., Mervis, C. B., Gray, W. D., Johnson, D. M., & Boyes-Braem, P. (1976). Basic objects in natural categories. *Cognitive Psychology, 8,* 382–439.

Rose, D., Fleischmann, P., Wykes, T., Leese, M., & Bindman, J. (2003). Patients' perspectives on electroconvulsive therapy: Systematic review. *British Medical Journal, 326,* 1363–1370.

Rosen, B. C., & D'Andrade, R. (1959). The psychosocial origins of achievement motivation. *Sociometry, 22,* 188–218.

Rosen, D., Stukenberg, K. W., & Saeks, S. (2001). The group-as-a-whole-object relations model of group psychotherapy. *Bulletin of the Menninger Clinic, 65,* 471–488.

Rosen, R. (1991). *The healthy company.* Los Angeles: Tarcher.

Rosenbaum, M., & Bennett, B. (1986). Homicide and depression. *American Journal of Psychiatry, 143,* 367–370.

Rosenbaum, R. S., Priselac, S. K., Black, S. E., Gao, F., Nadel, L., & Moscovitch, M. (2000). Remote spatial memory in an amnesiac person with extensive bilateral hippocampal lesions. *Nature Neuroscience, 3,* 1044–1048.

Rosenberg, H. J., Rosenberg, S. D., Ernstoff, M. S., Wolford, G. L., Amdur, R. J., Elshamy, M. R., et al. (2002). Expressive disclosure and health outcomes in a prostate cancer population. *International Journal of Psychiatry in Medicine, 32,* 37–53.

Rosenfarb, I. S., Goldstein, M. J., Mintz, J., & Nuechterlein, K. H. (1995). Expressed emotion and subclinical psychopathology observable within the transactions between schizophrenic patients and their family members. *Journal of Abnormal Psychology, 104,* 259–267.

Rosenfarb, I. S., Nuechterlein, K. H., Goldstein, M. J., & Subotnik, K. L. (2000). Neurocognitive vulnerability, interpersonal criticism, and the emergence of unusual thinking by schizophrenic patients during family transactions. *Archives of General Psychiatry, 57,* 1174–1179.

Rosenfeld, J. P. (1995). Alternative views of Bashore and Rapp's (1993) alternatives to traditional polygraphy: A critique. *Psychological Bulletin, 117*(1), 159–166.

Rosenstock, I. M. (1974). Historical origins of the health belief model. *Health Education Monographs, 2,* 328–335.

Rosenthal, R. (1996). *Initial report task force on statistical inference.* Washington, DC: Science Directorate of the American Psychological Association.

Rosenthal, R. R. (1966). *Experimenter effects in behavioral research.* New York: Appleton-Century-Crofts.

Rosenzweig, M. R., & Bennett, E. L. (1996). Psychobiology of plasticity: Effects of training and experience on brain and behavior. *Behavioural Brain Research, 78,* 57–65.

Rosmond, R., Bouchard, C., & Björntorp, P. (2001). Tsp509I polymorphism in exon 2 of the glucocorticoid receptor gene in relation to obesity and cortisol secretion: Cohort study. *British Medical Journal, 322,* 652–653.

Ross, C. A. (1997). *Dissociative identity disorder: Diagnosis, clinical features, and treatment of multiple personality.* New York: Wiley.

Ross, C. A., Anderson, G., Fleisher, W. P., & Norton, G. R. (1991). The frequency of multiple personality disorder among psychiatric inpatients. *American Journal of Psychiatry, 148,* 1717–1720.

Ross, M. W. (2002). Sexuality and health challenges: Responding to a public health imperative. *Journal of Sex Research, 39,* 7–9.

Ross, S. I., & Jackson, J. M. (1991). Teachers' expectations for Black males' and Black females' academic achievement. *Personality and Social Psychology Bulletin, 17,* 78–82.

Roth, H. L., Lora, A. N., & Heilman, K. M. (2002). Effects of monocular viewing and eye dominance on spatial attention. *Brain, 125,* 2023–2035.

Roth, P. L., Huffcutt, A. I., & Bobko, P. (2003). Ethnic group differences in measures of job performance: A new meta-analysis. *Journal of Applied Psychology, 88,* 694–706.

Rothbart, M. K., Ahadi, S. A., & Evans, D. E. (2000). Temperament and personality: Origins and outcomes. *Journal of Personality and Social Psychology, 78,* 122–135.

Rothbaum, B. O., Hodges, L. F., Alarcon, R., Ready, D., Shahar, F., Graap, K., et al. (1999). Virtual reality exposure therapy for PTSD Vietnam veterans: A case study. *Journal of Traumatic Stress, 12,* 263–271.

Rothbaum, B. O., Hodges, L., Anderson, P. L., Price, L., & Smith, S. (2002). Twelve-month follow-up of virtual reality and standard exposure therapies for fear of flying. *Journal of Consulting and Clinical Psychology, 70,* 428–432.

Rothbaum, B. O., Hodges, L. F., Kooper, R., & Opdyke, D. (1995). Effectiveness of computer-generated virtual reality graded exposure in the treatment of acrophobia. *American Journal of Psychiatry, 152,* 626–628.

Rothbaum, B. O., Hodges, L., Smith, S., Lee, J. H., & Price, L. (2000). A controlled study of virtual reality exposure therapy for the fear of flying. *Journal of Consulting and Clinical Psychology, 68,* 1020–1026.

Rothbaum, F., Pott, M., Azuma, H., Miyake, K., & Weisz, J. (2000). The development of close relationships in Japan and the United States: Paths of symbiotic harmony and generative tension. *Child Development, 71,* 1121–1142.

Rottenstreich, Y., & Tversky, A. (1997). Unpacking, repacking, and anchoring: Advances in support theory. *Psychological Review, 104,* 406–415.

Rotter, J. B. (1954). *Social learning and clinical psychology.* New York: Prentice Hall.

Rotter, J. B. (1982). *The development and application of social learning theory.* New York: Praeger.

Rotton, J. (1990). Individuals under stress. In C. E. Kimble (Ed.), *Social psychology: Living with people.* New York: W. C. Brown.

Rotton, J., & Kelly, I. W. (1985). Much ado about the full moon: A meta-analysis of lunar-lunacy research. *Psychological Bulletin, 97,* 286–306.

Rouéché, B. (1986, December 8). Cinnabar. *The New Yorker.*

Rovee-Collier, C. (1999). The development of infant memory. *Current Directions in Psychological Science, 8,* 80–85.

Rowe, D. C., Almeida, D. M., & Jacobson, K. C. (1999). School context and genetic influences on aggression in adolescence. *Psychological Science, 10,* 277–280.

Rowe, D. C., Jacobson, K. C., & Van den Oord, E. J. C. G. (1999). Genetic and environmental influences on vocabulary IQ: Parental education level as moderator. *Child Development, 70,* 1151–1162.

Roy, D. K., & Pentland, A. P. (2002). Learning words from sights and sounds: A computational model. *Cognitive Science, 26,* 113–146.

Roy-Byrne, P., Stang, P., Wittchen, H.-U., Ustun, B., Walters, E. E., & Kessler, R. (2000). Lifetime Panic-Depression comorbidity in the National Comorbidity Survey. *British Journal of Psychiatry, 176,* 229–235.

Rozin, P. (1982). "Taste-smell confusions" and the duality of the olfactory sense. *Perception and Psychophysics, 31,* 397–401.

Rozin, P. (1996). Sociocultural influences on human food selection. In E. D. Capaldi (Ed.), *Why we eat what we eat: The psychology of eating* (pp. 233–263). Washington DC: American Psychological Association.

Rubin, E. (1915). *Synsoplevede figure.* Copenhagen; Gyldendalske.

Rubin, K. H., Bukowski, W., & Parker, J. G. (1998). Peer interactions, relationships, and groups. In W. Damon & N. Eisenberg (Eds.), *Handbook of child psychology: Vol. 3. Social, emotional, and personality development* (5th ed., pp. 619–700). New York: Wiley.

Rubinstein, S., & Caballero, B. (2000). Is Miss America an undernourished role model? *Journal of the American Medical Association, 283,* 1569.

Ruble, D. N., & Martin, C. L. (1998). Gender development. In W. Damon & N. Eisenberg (Eds.), *Handbook of child psychology: Vol. 3. Social, emotional, and personality development* (5th ed., pp. 933–1016). New York: Wiley.

Rudman, L. A., Greenwald, A. G., Mellott, D. S., & Schwartz, J. L. K. (1999). Measuring the automatic components of prejudice: Flexibility and generality of the Implicit Association Test. *Social Cognition, 17,* 437–465.

Rudolph, K. D., Lambert, S. F., Clark, A. G., & Kurlakowsky, K. D. (2001). Negotiating the transition to middle school: The role of self-regulatory processes. *Child Development, 72,* 929–946.

Rudorfer, M. V., Henry, M. E., & Sackheim, H. A. (1997). Electroconvulsive therapy. In A. Tasman, J. Kay, & J. A. Lieberman (Eds.), *Psychiatry* (pp. 1535–1556). Philadelphia: Saunders.

Rueckert, L., Baboorian, D., Stavropoulos, K., & Yasutake, C. (1999). Individual differences in callosal efficiency: Correlation with attention. *Brain and Cognition, 41,* 390–410.

Rugg, M. D., & Wilding, E. L. (2000). Retrieval processing and episodic memory. *Trends in Cognitive Sciences, 4,* 108–115.

Rumelhart, D. E., & McClelland, J. L. (1986). *Parallel distributed processing: Explorations in the microstructure of cognition: Vol. 1. Foundations.* Cambridge, MA: Bradford.

Runyon, M., & Kenny, M. C. (2002). Relationship of attributional style, depression, and posttrauma distress among children who suffered physical or sexual abuse. *Child Maltreatment, 7,* 254–264.

Rusbult, C. E., Arriagi, X. B., & Agnew, C. R (2001). Interdependence in close relationships. In G. Fletcher & M. Clark (Eds.), *Blackwell handbook of social psychology: Interpersonal processes* (pp. 359–387). Oxford, England: Blackwell.

Rusbult, C. E., & Van Lange, P. A. M. (1996). Interdependence processes. In E. T. Higgins & A. W. Kruglanski (Eds.), *Social psychology: Handbook of basic principles* (pp. 564–596). New York: Guilford.

Russell, J. A. (1991). Culture and the categorization of emotions. *Psychological Bulletin, 110,* 426–450.

Russell, J. A. (1994). Is there universal recognition of emotion from facial expression? A review of the cross-cultural studies. *Psychological Bulletin, 155*(2), 102–141.

Russell, J. A. (1995). Facial expressions of emotion: What lies beyond minimal universality? *Psychological Bulletin, 118,* 379–391.

Rutkowski, G. K., Gruder, C. L., & Romer, D. (1983). Group cohesiveness, social norms, and bystander intervention. *Journal of Personality and Social Psychology, 44,* 545–552.

Rutter, M., Pickles, A., Murray, R., & Eaves, L. (2001). Testing hypotheses on specific environmental causal effects on behavior. *Psychological Bulletin, 127,* 291–324.

Rutter, M., & Schopler, E. (1992). Classification of pervasive developmental disorders: Some concepts and practical considerations. *Journal of Autism and Developmental Disorders, 22,* 459–482.

Ryan, R. H., & Geiselman, R. E. (1991). Effects of biased information on the relationship between eyewitness confidence and accuracy. *Bulletin of the Psychonomic Society, 29,* 7–9.

Rymer, R. (1992, April 23). A silent childhood. *The New Yorker,* pp. 41–81.

Rymer, R. (1993). *Genie: A scientific tragedy.* New York: HarperCollins.

Rynders, J., & Horrobin, J. (1980). Educational provisions for young children with Down's syndrome. In J. Gottlieb (Ed.), *Educating mentally retarded persons in the mainstream* (pp. 109–147). Baltimore: University Park Press.

Saarni, C., Mummer, D. L., & Campos, J. J. (1998). Emotional development: Action, communication, and understanding. In W. Damon & N. Eisenberg (Eds.), *Handbook of child psychology: Vol. 3. Social, emotional, and personality development* (5th ed., pp. 237–310). New York: Wiley.

Sabini, J., Siepmann, M., & Stein, J. (2001). The really fundamental attribution error in social psychological research. *Psychological Inquiry, 12,* 1–5.

Sachs, J. (1967). Recognition memory for syntactic and semantic aspects of connected discourse. *Perception and Psychophysics, 2,* 437–442.

Sack, R. L., Hughes, R. J., Edgar, D. M., & Lewy, A. J. (1997). Sleep-promoting effects of melatonin: At what dose, in whom, under what conditions, and by what mechanisms? *Sleep, 20,* 908–915.

Sackeim, H. A. (1994). Central issues regarding the mechanisms of action of electroconvulsive therapy: Directions for future research. *Psychopharmacology Bulletin, 30,* 281–308.

Sackeim, H. A., Haskett, R. F., Mulsant, B. H., Thase, M. E., Mann, J. J., Pettinati, H. M., et al. (2001). Continuation pharmacotherapy in the prevention of relapse following electroconvulsive therapy: A randomized controlled trial. *Journal of the American Medical Association, 285,* 1299–1307.

Sackeim, H. A., Prudic, J., Devanand, D. P., Nobler, M. S., Lisanby, S. H., Peyser, S., et al. (2000). A prospective, randomized, double-blind comparison of bilateral and right unilateral electroconvulsive therapy at different stimulus intensities. *Archives of General Psychiatry, 57,* 425–434.

Sackett, P. R., Schmitt, N., Ellington, J. E., & Kabin, M. B. (2001). High-stakes testing in employment, credentialing, and higher education: Prospects in a post-affirmative action world. *American Psychologist, 56,* 302–318.

Sacks, O. (1985). *The man who mistook his wife for a hat.* New York: Summit Books.

Sacks, O. (1992, July 27). The landscape of his dreams. *The New Yorker.*

Sacks, O. (2002, October 7). The case of Anna H. *The New Yorker,* pp. 62–73.

Saffran, J. R., Senghas, A., & Trueswell, J. C. (2001). The acquisition of language by children. *Proceedings of the National Academy of Science, 98,* 12874–12875.

Safren, S. A., Gershuny, B. S., Marzol, P., Otto, M. W., Pollack, M. H. (2002). History of childhood abuse in panic disorder, social phobia, and generalized anxiety disorder. *Journal of Nervous and Mental Disease, 190,* 453–456.

Sakairi, Y. (1992). Studies on meditation using questionnaires. *Japanese Psychological Review, 35*(1), 94–112.

Saks, M. J. (1992). Obedience versus disobedience to legitimate versus illegitimate authorities issuing good versus evil directives. *Psychological Science, 3,* 221–223.

Salin-Pascual, R., Gerashchenko, D., Greco, M., Blanco-Centurion, C., & Shiromani, P. J. (2001). Hypothalamic regulation of sleep. *Neuropsychopharmacology, 25*(Suppl. 5), S21.

Salloum, I. M., Cornelius, J. R., Thase, M. E., Daley, D. C., Kirisci, L., & Spotts, C. (1998). Naltrexone utility in depressed alcoholics. *Psychopharmacological Bulletin, 34,* 111–115.

Salovey, P., Mayer, J. D., & Rosenhan, D. L. (1991). Mood and helping: Mood as a motivator of helping and helping as a regulator of mood. In M. S. Clark (Ed.), *Review of personality and social psychology: Vol. 12. Prosocial behavior* (pp. 215–237). Newbury Park, CA: Sage.

Salzer, M. S., Rappaport, J., & Segre, L. (1999). Professional appraisal of professionally led and self-help groups. *American Journal of Ortho-Psychiatry, 69,* 536–540.

Sammons, M. T., Paige, R. U., & Levant, R. F. (Eds.). (2003). *Prescriptive authority for psychologists: A history and guide.* Washington, DC: APA Books.

Sampselle, C. M., Harris, V., Harlow, S. D., & Sowers, M. (2002). Midlife development and menopause in African American and Caucasian women. *Health Care for Women International, 23*(4), 351–363.

Sanchez-Ramos, J., Song, S., Cardozo-Pelaez, F., Hazzi, C., Stedeford, T., Willing, A., et al. (2000). Adult bone-marrow stromal cells differentiate into neural cells in vitro. *Experimental Neurology, 164,* 247–256.

Sanders, M. R., Markie-Dadds, C., Tully, L. A., & Bor, W. (2000). The triple p-positive parenting program: A comparison of enhanced, standard, and self-directed behavioral family intervention for parents of children with early onset conduct problems. *Journal of Consulting and Clinical Psychology, 68,* 624–640.

Sanderson, W. C., Rapee, R. M., & Barlow, D. H. (1989). The influence of an illusion of control on panic attacks induced via inhalation of 5.5% carbon dioxide-enriched air. *Archives of General Psychiatry, 46,* 157–162.

Sandin, R. H., Enlund, G., Samuelsson, P., & Lennmarken, C. (2000). Awareness during anaesthesia: A prospective case study. *Lancet, 355,* 707–711.

Saper, C. B., Chou, T. C., & Scammell, T. E. (2001). The sleep switch: Hypothalamic control of sleep and wakefulness. *Trends in Neurosciences, 24,* 726–731.

Sarafino, E. P., & Goehring, P. (2000). Age comparisons in acquiring biofeedback control and success in reducing headache pain. *Annals of Behavioral Medicine, 22,* 1–9.

Sarason, B. R., Sarason, I. G., & Gurung, R. A. R. (1997). Close personal relationships and health outcomes: A key to the role of social support. In S. Duck (Ed.), *Handbook of personal relationships* (pp. 547–573). New York: Wiley.

Sarason, I. G., Johnson, J., & Siegel, J. (1978). Assessing impact of life changes: Development of the life experiences survey. *Journal of Clinical and Consulting Psychology, 46,* 932–946.

Sasaki, Y., Jadjikhani, N., Fischl, B., Liu, A. K., Marret, S., Dale, A. M., & Tootell, R. B. H. (2001). Local and global attention are mapped retinotopically in human occipital cortex. *Proceedings of the National Academy of Science, 98,* 2077.

Sato, T. (1997). Seasonal affective disorder and phototherapy: A critical review. *Professional Psychology: Research and Practice, 28,* 164–169.

Satterfield, J. M., Folkman, S., & Acree, M. (2002). Explanatory style predicts depressive symptoms following AIDS-related bereavement. *Cognitive Therapy and Research, 26,* 393–403.

Sauter, S., Murphy, L., Colligan, M., Swanson, N., Hurrell, J., Jr., Scharf, F., Jr., et al. (1999). *Stress at work* (DHHS [NIOSH] Publication No. 99–101). Washington, DC: National Institute on Occupational Health and Safety.

Saveliev, S. V., Lebedev, V. V., Evgeniev, M. B., & Korochkin, L. I. (1997). Chimeric brain: Theoretical and clinical aspects. *International Journal of Developmental Biology, 41,* 801–808.

Savelkoul, M., Post, M. W. M., de Witte, L. P., & van den Borne, H. B. (2000). Social support, coping, and subjective well-being in patients with rheumatic diseases. *Patient Education and Counseling, 39,* 205–218.

Savic, I., Berglund, H., Gulyas, B., & Roland, P. (2001). Smelling of odorous sex hormone-like compounds causes sex-differentiated hypothalamic activations in humans. *Neuron, 31,* 661–668.

Savin-Williams, R. C., & Demo, D. H. (1984). Developmental change and stability in adolescent self-concept. *Developmental Psychology, 20,* 1100–1110.

Saxe, L., & Ben-Shakhar, G. (1999). Admissibility of polygraph tests: The application of scientific standards post-Daubert. *Psychology, Public Policy, and Law, 5,* 203–223.

Sayers, J. (1991). *Mother of psychoanalysis.* New York: Norton.

Scandura, T. A., & Lankau, M. J. (1997). Relationships of gender, family responsibility and flexible work hours to organizational commitment and job satisfaction. *Journal of Organizational Behavior, 18,* 377–391.

Scarr, S. (1998). How do families affect intelligence? Social environmental and behavior genetic prediction. In J. J. McArdle & R. W. Woodcock (Eds.), *Human cognitive abilities in theory and practice* (pp. 113–136). Mahwah, NJ: Erlbaum.

Scarr, S., & Carter-Saltzman, L. (1982). Genetics and intelligence. In R. Sternberg (Ed.), *Handbook of human intelligence* (pp. 792–896). Cambridge, England: Cambridge University Press.

Scarr, S., & Weinberg, R. A. (1976). IQ test performance of black children adopted by white families. *American Psychologist, 31,* 726–739.

Schachter, S., & Singer, J. (1962). Cognitive, social and physiological determinants of emotional state. *Psychological Review, 69,* 379–399.

Schacter, D. L. (1999). The seven sins of memory: Insights from psychology and cognitive neuroscience. *American Psychologist, 54,* 182–203.

Schacter, D. L. (2001). *The seven sins of memory.* Boston: Houghton Mifflin.

Schacter, D. L., Chiu, C.-Y. P., & Ochsner, K. N. (1993). Implicit memory: A selective review. *Annual Review of Neuroscience, 16,* 159–182.

Schacter, D. L., & Cooper, L. A. (1993). Implicit and explicit memory for novel visual objects: Structure and function. *Journal of Experimental Psychology: Learning, Memory, and Cognition, 19*(5), 995–1009.

Schacter, D. L., Cooper, L. A., Delaney, S. M., Peterson, M. A., & Tharan, M. (1991). Implicit memory for possible and impossible objects: Constraints on the construction of structural descriptions. *Journal of Experimental Psychology: Learning, Memory, and Cognition, 17,* 3–19.

Schacter, D. L., Norman, K. A., & Koutstaal, W. (1998). The cognitive neuroscience of constructive memory. *Annual Review of Psychology, 49,* 289–318.

Schaefer, J., Sykes, R., Rowley, R., & Baek, S. (1988, November). *Slow country music and drinking.* Paper presented at the 87th annual meeting of the American Anthropological Association, Phoenix, AZ.

Schafer, J., & Brown, S. A. (1991). Marijuana and cocaine effect expectancies and drug use patterns. *Journal of Consulting and Clinical Psychology, 59,* 558–565.

Schaffer, C. E., Davidson, R. J., & Saron, C. (1983). Frontal and parietal EEG asymmetry in depressed and non-depressed subjects. *Biological Psychiatry, 18,* 753–762.

Schaie, K. W. (1993). The Seattle longitudinal study of adult intelligence. *Current Directions in Psychological Science, 2*(6), 171–175.

Scharff, J. S., & Scharff, D. E. (1998). *Object relations individual psychotherapy.* Northvale, NJ: Aronson.

Schaubroeck, J., Jones, J. R., & Xie, J. J. (2001). Individual differences in utilizing control to cope with job demands: Effects on susceptibility to infectious disease. *Journal of Applied Psychology, 86,* 265–278.

Scheck, B., Neufeld, P., & Dwyer, J. (2000). *Actual innocence: Five days to execution and other dispatches from the wrongly convicted.* New York: Doubleday.

Scheerer, M., Rothmann, R., & Goldstein, K. (1945). A case of "idiot savant": An experimental study of personality organization. *Psychology Monograph, 58*(4), 1–63.

Scheier, M. F., Matthews, K. A., Owens, J. F., Magovern, G. J., Lefebvre, R. C., Abbott, R. A., et al. (1989). Dispositional optimism and recovery from coronary artery bypass surgery: The beneficial effects on physical and psychological well-being. *Journal of Personality and Social Psychology, 57,* 1024–1040.

Schenck, C. H., & Mahowald, M. W. (1992). Motor dyscontrol in narcolepsy: Rapid eye movement (REM) sleep without atonia and REM sleep behavior disorder. *Annals of Neurology, 32*(1), 3–10.

Scheufele, P. M. (2000). Effects of progressive relaxation and classical music on measurements of attention, relaxation, and stress responses. *Journal of Behavioral Medicine, 23,* 207–228.

Schiffman, S. S., Graham, B. G., Sattely-Miller, E. A., & Warwick, Z. (1999). Orosensory perception of dietary fat. *Current Directions in Psychological Science, 7,* 137–143.

Schlenger, W. E., Caddell, J. M., Ebert, L., Jordan, B. K., Rourke, K. M., Wilson, D., et al. (2002). Psychological reactions to terrorist attacks: Findings from the National Study of Americans' Reactions to September 11. *Journal of the American Medical Association, 288,* 581–588.

Schloss, P., & Williams, D. C. (1998) The serotonin transporter: A primary target for antidepressant drugs. *Journal of Psychopharmacology, 12,* 115–121.

Schmidt, N. B., Lerew, D. R., & Jackson, R. J. (1999). Prospective evaluation of anxiety sensitivity in the pathogenesis of panic: Replication and extension. *Journal of Abnormal Psychology, 108,* 532–537.

Schmidt, N. B., Storey, J., Greenberg, B. D., Santiago, H. T., Li, Q., & Murphy, D. L. (2000). Evaluating gene x psychological risk factor effects in the pathogenesis of anxiety: A new model approach. *Journal of Abnormal Psychology, 109,* 308–320.

Schmidtke, A., & Hafner, H. (1988). The Werther effect after television films: New evidence for an old hypothesis. *Psychological Medicine, 18,* 665–676.

Schmolck, H., Buffalo, E. A., & Squire, L. R. (2000). Memory distortions over time: Recollections of the O. J. Simpson trial verdict after 15 and 32 months. *Psychological Science, 11,* 39–47.

Schnabel, T. (1987). Evaluation of the safety and side effects of antianxiety agents. *American Journal of Medicine, 82*(Suppl. 5A), 7–13.

Schnall, S., & Laird, J. D. (2003). Keep smiling: Enduring effects of facial expressions and postures on emotional experience and memory. *Cognition & Emotion, 17,* 787–797.

Schneider, B. (1985). Organizational behavior. *Annual Review of Psychology, 36,* 573–611.

Schneider, B. H., Atkinson, L., & Tardif, C. (2001). Child-parent attachment and children's peer relations: A quantitative review. *Developmental Psychology, 37,* 86–100.

Schneider, T. R., Ring, C., & Katkin, E. S. (1998). A test of the validity of the method of constant stimuli as an index of heartbeat detection. *Psychophysiology, 35,* 86–89.

Schneider, W., & Bjorklund, D. F. (1998). Memory. In W. Damon, D. Kuhn, & R. Siegler (Eds.), *Handbook of child psychology: Vol. 2. Cognition, language and perception* (5th ed., pp. 467–521). New York: Wiley.

Schnurr, P. P., Ford, J. D., Friedman, M. J., Green, B. L., Dain, B. J., & Sengupta, A. (2000). Predictors and outcomes of posttraumatic stress disorder in World War II veterans exposed to mustard gas. *Journal of Consulting and Clinical Psychology, 68,* 258–268.

Schreiber, G. B., Robins, M., Striegel-Moore, R., Obarzanek, E., Morrison, J. A., & Wright, D. J. (1996). Weight modification efforts reported by black and white preadolescent girls: National Heart, Lung, and Blood Institute Growth and Health Study. *Pediatrics, 98,* 63–70.

Schroeder, D. A. (1995). An introduction to social dilemmas. In D. Schroeder (Ed.), *Social dilemmas: Perspectives on individuals and groups* (pp. 1–13). Westport, CT: Praeger.

Schroeder, D. A., Penner, L. A., Dovidio, J. F., & Piliavin, J. A. (1995). *The psychology of helping and altruism: Problems and puzzles.* New York: McGraw-Hill.

Schuckit, M. A. (1998). Biological, psychological, and environmental predictors of alcoholism risk: A longitudinal study. *Journal of Studies in Alcoholism, 59,* 485–494.

Schulteis, G., Ahmed, S. H., Morse, A. C., Koob, G. F., & Everitt, B. J. (2000). Conditioning and opiate withdrawal. *Nature, 405,* 1013–1014.

Schultheiss, O., & Brunstein, J. C. (2001). Assessment of implicit motives with a research version of the TAT: Picture profiles, gender differences, and relations to other personality measure. *Journal of Personality Assessment, 77,* 71–86.

Schultz, D. P., & Schultz, S. E. (1998). *Psychology and work today* (7th ed.). Upper Saddle River, NJ: Prentice-Hall.

Schultz, D. P., & Schultz, S. E. (2000). *A history of modern psychology* (7th ed.). Fort Worth, TX: Harcourt Brace.

Schultz, D. P., & Schultz, S. E. (2001). *Theories of personality.* Pacific Grove, CA: Brooks Cole.

Schultz, D. P., & Schultz, S. E. (2002). *A history of modern psychology* (8th ed.). Fort Worth, TX: Harcourt Brace.

Schulz, R. (1978). *The psychology of death, dying, and bereavement.* Reading, MA: Addison-Wesley.

Schulz, R., Beach, S. R., Lind, B., Martire, L. M., Zdaniuk, B., Hirsch, C., et al. (2001). Involvement in caregiving and adjustment to death of a spouse findings from the caregiver health effects study. *Journal of the American Medical Association, 285,* 3123–3129.

Schulz-Hardt, S., Frey, D., Luthgens, C., & Moscovici, S. (2000). Biased information search in group decision making. *Journal of Personality and Social Psychology, 78,* 665–669.

Schwartz, B., & Reisberg, D. (1991). *Learning and memory.* New York: Norton.

Schwartz, M. W., Woods, S. C., Porte, D., Jr., Seeley, R. J., & Baskin, D. G. (2000). Central nervous system control of food intake, *Nature, 404,* 661–671.

Schwarz, N., & Bohner, G. (2001). The construction of attitudes. In A. Tesser & N. Schwarz (Eds.), *Blackwell handbook of social psychology: Intraindividual processes* (pp. 436–457). Oxford, England: Blackwell.

Schwarz, N., & Scheuring, B. (1992). Frequency reports of psychosomatic symptoms: What respondents learn from response alternatives. *Zeutschrift fur Klinische Psychologie, 22,* 197–208.

Schwarzer, R. (2001). Social-cognitive factors in changing health-related behaviors. *Current Directions in Psychological Science, 10,* 47–51.

Schwender, D., Klasing, D., Daunderer, M., Maddler, C., Poppel, E., & Peter, K. (1995). Awareness during general anesthetic: Definition, incidence, clinical relevance, causes, avoidance, and medicolegal aspects. *Anaesthetist, 44,* 743–754.

Scott, S., Knapp, M., Henderson, J., & Maughan, B. (2001). Financial cost of social exclusion: Follow up study of antisocial children into adulthood. *British Medical Journal, 323,* 191.

Scribner, S. (1977). Modes of thinking and ways of speaking: Culture and logic reconsidered. In P. N. Johnson-Laird & P. C. Wason (Eds.), *Thinking: Readings in cognitive science.* Cambridge, England: Cambridge University.

Seamon, J. G., Williams, P. C., Crowley, M. J., Kim, I. J., Langer, S. A., Orne, P. J., et al. (1995). The mere exposure effect is based on implicit memory: Effects of stimulus type, encoding conditions, and number of exposures on recognition and affect judgements. *Journal of Experimental Psychology: Learning, Memory, and Cognition, 21*(3), 711–721.

Sears, R. (1977). Sources of satisfaction of the Terman gifted men. *American Psychologist, 32,* 119–128.

Sedikides, C., Campbell, W. K., Reeder, G., & Elliot, A. J. (1998). The self-serving bias in relational context. *Journal of Personality and Social Psychology, 74,* 378–386.

Seeman, T., & Chen, X. (2002). Risk and protective factors for physical functioning in older adults with and without chronic conditions: MacArthur studies of successful aging. *Journals of Gerontology: Series B. Psychological Sciences & Social Sciences, 57*(3), S135–S144.

Segal, Z. V., Gemar, M., & Williams, S. (2000). Differential cognitive response to a mood challenge following successful cognitive therapy or pharmacotherapy for unipolar depression. *Journal of Abnormal Psychology, 108,* 3–10.

Segall, M. H., Dasen, P. R., Berry, J. W., & Poortinga, Y. H. (1990). *Human behavior in global perspective: An introduction to cross-cultural psychology.* Elmwood, NY: Pergamon Press.

Segerstrom, S. C., Taylor, S. E., Kemeny, M. E., & Fahey, J. L. (1998). Optimism is associated with mood, coping, and immune change in response to stress. *Journal of Personality and Social Psychology, 74,* 1646–1655.

Seiger, A., Nordberg, A., Vonholst, H., Backman, L., Ebendal, T., Alafuzoff, I., et al. (1993). Intracranial infusion of purified nerve growth factor to an Alzheimer patient: The 1st attempt of a possible future treatment strategy. *Behavioral Brain Research, 57,* 255–261.

Sejnowski, T. J., & Destexhe, A. (2000). Why do we sleep? *Brain Research, 886,* 208–223.

Selemon, L. D., Mrzljak, J., Kleinman, J. E., Herman, M. M., & Goldman-Rakic, P. S. (2003). Regional specificity in the neuropathologic substrates of schizophrenia: A morphometric analysis of Broca's area 44 and area 9. *Archives of General Psychiatry, 60,* 69–77.

Seligman, M. E. P. (1975). *Helplessness: On depression, development, and death.* San Francisco: Freeman.

Seligman, M. E. P. (1991). *Learned optimism.* New York: Knopf.

Seligman, M. E. P. (1995). The effectiveness of psychotherapy: The *Consumer Reports* study. *American Psychologist, 50,* 965–974.

Seligman, M. E. P. (1996). Good news for psychotherapy: The *Consumer Reports* study. *Independent Practitioner, 16,* 17–20.

Seligman, M. E. P., Castellon, C., Cacciola, J., Shulman, P., Luborsky, L., Ollove, M., et al. (1988). Explanatory style change during cognitive therapy for unipolar depression. *Journal of Abnormal Psychology, 97,* 13–18.

Seligman, M. E. P., & Csikszentmihalyi, M. (2000). Positive psychology: An introduction. *American Psychologist, 55,* 5–14.

Seligman, M. E. P., & Schulman, P. (1986). Explanatory style as a predictor of productivity and quitting among life insurance agents. *Journal of Personality and Social Psychology, 50,* 832–838.

Sell, R. L., Wells, J. A., & Wypij, D. (1995). The prevalence of homosexual behavior and attraction in the United States, the United Kingdom, and France: Results of national population-based samples. *Archives of Sexual Behavior, 24*(3), 235–248.

Selye, H. (1956). *The stress of life.* New York: McGraw-Hill.

Selye, H. (1974). The general adaptation syndrome. In H. Selye, *Stress without distress.* New York: HarperCollins.

Selye, H. (1976). *The stress of life* (2nd ed.). New York: McGraw-Hill.

Senghas, A., & Coppola, M. (2001). Children creating language: How Nicaraguan sign language acquired a spatial grammar. *Psychological Science, 12,* 323–328.

Sergeant, J. A., Geurts, H., & Oosterlaan, J. (2002). How specific is a deficit of executive functioning for attention deficit/hyperactivity disorder? *Behavioural Brain Research, 130,* 3–28.

Serpell, R. (1994). The cultural construction of intelligence. In W. J. Lonner & R. S. Malpass (Eds.), *Psychology and culture.* Boston: Allyn & Bacon.

Servan-Schreiber, E., & Anderson, J. R. (1990). Learning artificial grammars with competitive chunking. *Journal of Experimental Psychology: Learning, Memory, and Cognition, 16,* 592–608.

Seto, M. C., Maric, A., & Barbaree, H. E. (2001). The role of pornography in the etiology of sexual aggression. *Aggression and Violent Behavior, 6,* 35–53.

Sevcik, R. A., & Savage-Rumbaugh, E. S. (1994). Language comprehension and use by great apes. *Language and Communication, 14,* 37–58.

Sewell, M. C., Goggin, K. J., Rabkin, J. G., Ferrando, S. J., McElhiney, M. C., & Evans, S. (2000). Anxiety syndromes and symptoms among men with AIDS: A longitudinal controlled study. *Psychosomatics, 41,* 294–300.

Shadish, W. R., Cook, T. D., & Campbell, D. T. (2002). *Experimental and quasi-experimental designs for generalized causal inference.* Boston: Houghton Mifflin.

Shadish, W. R., Matt, G. E., Navarro, A. M., & Phillips, G. (2000). The effects of psychological therapies under clinically representative conditions: A meta-analysis. *Psychological Bulletin, 126,* 512–529.

Shaffer, D. R. (1973). *Social and personality development* (Box 4–2). Pacific Grove, CA: Brooks/Cole.

Shaffer, D. R. (1999). *Developmental psychology: Childhood and adolescence.* Pacific Grove, CA: Brooks/Cole.

Shah, J. (2003). Automatic for the people: How representations of significant others implicitly affect goal pursuit. *Journal of Personality and Social Psychology, 84,* 661–681.

Shahinfar, A., Kupersmidt, J. B., & Matza, L. S. (2001). The relation between exposure to violence and social information processing among incarcerated adolescents. *Journal of Abnormal Psychology, 110,* 136–141.

Shand, M. A. (1982). Sign-based short-term memory coding of American Sign Language and printed English words by congenitally deaf signers. *Cognitive Psychology, 14,* 1–12.

Shapiro, A. F., Gottman, J. M., & Carrere, S. (2000). The baby and the marriage: Identifying factors that buffer against decline in marital satisfaction after the first baby arrives. *Journal of Family Psychology, 14,* 59–70.

Shapiro, D. H., & Walsh, R. N. (Eds.). (1984). *Meditation: Classical and contemporary perspectives.* New York: Aldine.

Shapiro, F. (1989a). Eye movement desensitization: A new treatment for post-traumatic stress disorder. *Journal of Behavior Therapy and Experimental Psychiatry, 20,* 211–217.

Shapiro, F. (1989b). Efficacy of the eye movement desensitization procedure in the treatment of traumatic memories. *Journal of Traumatic Stress, 2,* 199–223.

Shapiro, F. (1991). Eye movement desensitization and reprocessing procedure: From EMD to EMD/R—A new treatment model for anxiety and related traumata. *The Behavior Therapist, 15,* 133–135.

Shapiro, F. (2001). *Eye movement desensitization and reprocessing: Basic principles, protocols, and procedures* (2nd ed.). New York, NY: Guilford Press.

Shapiro, F., & Maxfield, L. (2002). Eye movement desensitization and reprocessing (EMDR): Information processing in the treatment of trauma. *Journal of Clinical Psychology, 58,* 933–936.

Shaw, D. S., Owens, E. B., Giovannelli, J., Winslow, E. B. (2001). Infant and toddler pathways leading to early externalizing disorders. *Journal of the American Academy of Child and Adolescent Psychiatry, 40,* 36–43.

Shaw, J. S., III. (1996). Increases in eyewitness confidence resulting from persistent questioning. *Journal of Experimental Psychology: Applied, 2,* 126–146.

Shaywitz, B. A., Shaywitz, S. E., Pugh, K. R., Constable, R. T., Skudlarski, P., Fulbright, R. K., et al. (1995). Sex differences in the functional organization of the brain for language. *Nature, 373,* 607–609.

Shea, M. T., Stout, R., Gunderson, J., Morey, L. C., Grilo, C. M., McGlashan, T., et al. (2002). Short-term diagnostic stability of schizotypal, borderline, avoidant, and obsessive-compulsive personality disorders. *American Journal of Psychiatry, 159,* 2036–2041.

Shechtman, Z. (1992). A group assessment procedure as a predictor of on-the-job performance of teachers. *Journal of Applied Psychology, 77,* 383–387.

Sheldon, K. M., Eliot, A. J., Kim, Y., & Kasser, T. (2001). What is satisfying about satisfying events? Testing 10 candidate psychological needs. *Journal of Personality and Social Psychology, 80,* 325–339.

Sheldon, K. M., & Kasser, T. (2001). Getting older, getting better? Personal striving and psychological maturity across the life span. *Developmental Psychology, 37,* 491–501.

Sheldon, K. M., & King, L. (2001). Why positive psychology is necessary. *American Psychologist, 56,* 216–217.

Shelton, R. C., Keller, M. B., Gelenberg, A., Dunner, D. L., Hirschfeld, R., Thase, M. E., et al. (2001). Effectiveness of St John's wort in major depression: A randomized controlled trial. *Journal of the American Medical Association, 285,* 1978–1986.

Shepard, R. N., & Metzler, J. (1971). Mental rotation of three-dimensional objects. *Science, 171,* 701–703.

Shepherd, C., Kohut, J. J., & Sweet, R. (1989). *News of the weird.* New York: New American Library.

Sher, K. J., Walitzer, K., Wood, P., & Brent, E. (1991). Characteristics of children of alcoholics: Putative risk factors, substance use and abuse, and psychopathology. *Journal of Abnormal Psychology, 100,* 427–448.

Sher, K. J., Wood, M. D., Wood, P. K., & Raskin, G. (1996). Alcohol outcome expectancies and alcohol use: A latent variable cross-lagged panel study. *Journal of Abnormal Psychology, 105,* 561–574.

Shera, C. A., Guinan, J. J., & Oxenham, A. J. (2002). Revised estimates of human cochlear tuning from otoacoustic and behavioral measurements. *Proceedings of the National Academy of Sciences, 99*(5), 3318–3323.

Sherif, M. (1937). An experimental approach to the study of attitudes. *Sociometry, 1,* 90–98.

Sherman, J. W., & Bessenoff, G. R. (1999). Stereotypes as source-monitoring cues: On the interaction between episodic and semantic memory. *Psychological Science, 10,* 106–110.

Sherman, J. W., & Klein, S. B. (1994). Development and representation of personality impressions. *Journal of Personality and Social Psychology, 67,* 972–983.

Sherman, S. J. (1980). On the self-erasing nature of errors of prediction. *Journal of Personality and Social Psychology, 39,* 211–221.

Sherwin, B. B., & Gelfand, M. M. (1987). The role of androgen in the maintenance of sexual functioning in oophorectomized women. *Psychosomatic Medicine, 49,* 397–409.

Sherwin, B. B., Gelfand, M. M., & Brender, W. (1985). Androgen enhances sexual motivation in females: A prospective crossover study of sex steroid administration in the surgical menopause. *Psychosomatic Medicine, 47,* 339–351.

Shiffman, S., Engberg, J. B., Paty, J. A., & Perz, W. G. (1997). A day at a time: Predicting smoking lapse from daily urge. *Journal of Abnormal Psychology, 106,* 104–116.

Shiller, R. J. (2001). *Irrational exuberance.* Princeton, NJ: Princeton University Press.

Shimamura, A. P., Berry, J. M., Mangels, J. A., Rusting, C. L., & Jurica, P. J. (1995). Memory and cognitive abilities in university professors: Evidence for successful aging. *Psychological Science, 6,* 271–277.

Shinohara, T., Bredberg, G., Ulfendahl, M., Pyykkö, I., Olivius, N. P., Kaksonen, R., et al. (2002). Neurotrophic factor intervention restores auditory function in deafened animals. *Proceedings of the National Academy of Sciences, 99*, 1657–1660.

Shiwach, R. S., Reid, W. H., & Carmody, T. J. (2001). An analysis of reported deaths following electroconvulsive therapy in Texas, 1993–1998. *Psychiatric Services, 52*, 1095–1097.

Shneidman, E. S. (1987). A psychological approach to suicide. In G. VandenBos & B. K. Bryant (Eds.), *Cataclysms, crises, and catastrophes: Psychology in action. The master lectures* (Vol. 6, pp. 147–183). Washington, DC: American Psychological Association.

Shoda, Y., & Tiernan, S. L. (2002). What remains invariant? Finding order within a person's thoughts, feelings, and behavior across situations. In D. Cervone & W. Mischel (Eds.), *Advances in personality science* (pp.241–270). New York: Guilford Press.

Shreeve, J. (1993, June). Touching the phantom. *Discover*, pp. 35–42.

Shu, S. Y., Wu, Y. M., Bao, X. M., Wen, Z. B., Huang, F. H., Li, S. X., et al. (2002). A new area in the human brain associated with learning and memory: Immunohistochemical and functional MRI analysis. *Molecular Psychiatry, 7*, 1018–1022.

Shweder, R. A., Much, N. C., Mahapatra, M., & Park, L. (1994). The "big three" of morality (autonomy, community, and divinity), and the "big three" explanations of suffering, as well. In A. Brandt & P. Rozin (Eds.), *Morality and health.* Stanford, CA: Stanford University Press.

Siebert, S. E., & Kraimer, M. L. (2001). The five-factor model of personality and career success. *Journal of Vocational Behavior, 58*, 1–21.

Siegal, M. (1997). *Knowing children: Experiments in conversation and cognition* (2nd ed.). Hove, England: Psychology Press/Erlbaum/Taylor & Francis.

Siegel, J. M., & Rogawski, M. A. (1988). A function for REM sleep: Regulation of noradrenergic receptor sensitivity. *Brain Research Review, 13*, 213–233.

Siegel, S., Hirson, R. E., Krank, M. D., & McCully, J. (1982). Heroin "overdose" death: The contribution of drug associated environmental cues. *Science, 216*, 430–437.

Siegler, R. S. (1994). Cognitive variability: A key to understanding cognitive development. *Current Directions in Psychological Science, 3*, 1–4.

Sigmundsson, T., Suckling, J., Maier, M., Bullmore, E., Greenwood, K., Ron, M., et al. (2001). Structural abnormalities in frontal, temporal, and limbic regions and interconnecting white matter tracts in schizophrenic patients with prominent negative symptoms. *The American Journal of Psychiatry, 158*, 234–243.

Silber, M. H. (2001). Sleep disorders. *Neurology Clinics, 19*, 173–186.

Silbersweig, D. A., Stern, E., Frith, C., Cahill, C., Holmes, A., Grootoonk, S., et al. (1995). A functional neuroanatomy of hallucinations in schizophrenia. *Nature, 378*, 176–179.

Silbert, M. H., & Pines, A. M. (1984). Pornography and sexual abuse of women. *Sex Roles, 10*, 857–868.

Silver, E. (1995). Punishment or treatment? Comparing the lengths of confinement of successful and unsuccessful insanity defendants. *Law and Human Behavior, 19*, 375–388.

Silver, E., Cirincione, C., & Steadman, H. J. (1994). Demythologizing inaccurate perceptions of the insanity defense. *Law and Human Behavior, 18*, 63–70.

Silverman, K., Evans, A. M., Strain, E. C., & Griffiths, R. R. (1992). Withdrawal syndrome after the double-blind cessation of caffeine consumption. *New England Journal of Medicine, 327*, 1109–1114.

Silverthorne, C. (2001) Leadership effectiveness and personality: A cross cultural evaluation. *Personality & Individual Differences, 30*, 303–309.

Simcock, G., & Hayne, H. (2002). Breaking the barrier?: Children fail to translate their preverbal memories into language. *Psychological Science, 13*, 225–231.

Simcock, G., & Hayne, H. (2003). Age-related changes in verbal and nonverbal memory during early childhood. *Developmental Psychology, 39*, 805–814.

Simeon, D., Greenberg, J., Knutelska, M., Schmeidler, J., & Hollander, E. (2003). Peritraumatic reactions associated with the World Trade Center disaster. *The American Journal of Psychiatry, 160*, 1702–1705.

Simons, D. J., & Levin, D. T. (1997). Failure to detect changes to attended objects. *Investigative Ophthalmology and Visual Science, 38*, S747.

Simons, T., & Roberson, Q. (2003). Why managers should care about fairness: The effects of aggregate justice perceptions on organizational outcomes. *Journal of Applied Psychology, 88*, 432–443.

Simonton, D. K. (1984). *Genius, creativity and leadership*. Cambridge: Harvard University Press.

Simonton, D. K. (1999). Creativity and genius. In L. Pervin & O. John (Eds.), *Handbook of personality research* (2nd ed., pp. 629–652). New York: Guilford.

Simonton, D. K. (2002). In C. R. Snyder & J. Shane (Eds.), *Handbook of positive psychology* (pp. 189–201). London: Oxford University Press.

Simpson, J. A., & Kenrick, D. T. (1997). *Evolutionary social psychology*. Mahwah, NJ: Erlbaum.

Simpson, J. A., & Rholes, W. S. (2000). Caregiving, attachment theory, and the connection theoretical orientation. *Psychological Inquiry, 11*, 114–117.

Simpson, J. A., Rholes, W. S., & Nelligan, J. S. (1992). Support seeking and support giving within couples in an anxiety-provoking situation: The role of attachment styles. *Journal of Personality and Social Psychology, 62*, 434–446.

Simpson, S., Hurtley, S. M., & Marx, J. (2000). Immune cell networks. *Science, 290*, 79.

Simpson, S. G., McMahon, F. J., McInnis, M. G., MacKinnon, D. F., Edwin, D., Folstein, S. E., et al. (2002). Diagnostic reliability of bipolar II disorder. *Archives of General Psychiatry, 59*, 736–740.

Sinclair, R. C., Hoffman, C., Mark, M. M., Martin, L. L., & Pickering, T. L. (1994). Construct accessibility and the misattribution of arousal. *Psychological Science, 5*(1), 15–19.

Singer, L. T., Arendt, R., Minnes, S., Farkas, K., Salvator, A., Kirchner, L., et al. (2002). Cognitive and motor outcomes of cocaine-exposed infants. *Journal of the American Medical Association, 287*(15), 1952–1960.

Singer, L. T., Arendt, R., Minnes, S., Salvator, A., Siegel, C., & Lewis, B. A. (2001). Developing language skills of cocaine-exposed infants. *Pediatrics, 107*, 1057–1064.

Sinha, R., & Parsons, O. A. (1996). Multivariate response patterning of fear and anger. *Cognition and Emotion, 10*, 173–198.

Sinton, C. M., & McCarley, R. W. (2000). Neuroanatomical and neurophysiological aspects of sleep: Basic science and clinical relevance. *Seminars in Clinical Neuropsychiatry, 5*, 6–19.

Sirvio, J. (1999). Strategies that support declining cholinergic neurotransmission in Alzheimer's disease patients. *Gerontology, 45*, 3–14.

Skinner, B. F. (1961). *Cumulative record* (3rd ed.). Englewood Cliffs, NJ: Prentice-Hall.

Skre, I., Onstad, S., Toregersen, S., Lyngren, S., & Kringlin, E. (2000). The heritability of common phobic fear: A twin study of a clinical sample. *Journal of Anxiety Disorders, 14*, 549–562.

Slamecka, N. J., & McElree, B. (1983). Normal forgetting of verbal lists as a function of their degree of learning. *Journal of Experimental Psychology: Learning, Memory, and Cognition, 9*, 384–397.

Slater, A., Mattock, A., Brown, E., & Bremner, J. G. (1991). Form perception at birth. *Journal of Experimental Child Psychology, 51*, 395–406.

Sleek, S. (1999, February). Programs aim to attract minorities to psychology. *APA Monitor*, p. 47.

Slife, B. D., & Reber, J. S. (2001). Eclecticism in psychotherapy: Is it really the best substitute for traditional theories? In B. D. Slife, R. N. Williams, & S. H. Barlow (Eds.), *Critical issues in psychotherapy* (pp. 213–234). Thousand Oaks, CA: Sage.

Sloan, D. M., Strauss, M. E., & Wisner, K. L. (2001). Diminished response to pleasant stimuli by depressed women. *Journal of Abnormal Psychology, 110*, 488–493.

Slomkowski, C., & Dunn, J. (1996). Young children's understanding of other people's beliefs and feelings and their connected communication with friends. *Developmental Psychology, 32*, 442–447.

Slutske, W., Eisen, S., Xian, H., True, W., Lyons, M. J., Goldberg, J., et al. (2001). A twin study of the association between pathological gambling and antisocial personality disorder. *Journal of Abnormal Psychology, 110*, 297–308.

Slutske, W. S., Heath, A. C., Dinwiddie, S. H., Madden, P. A., Bucholz, K. K., Dunne, M. P., et al. (1998). Common genetic risk factors for conduct disorder and alcohol dependence. *Journal of Abnormal Psychology, 107*, 363–374.

Small, B. J., & Bäckman, L. (1999). Time to death and cognitive performance. *Current Directions in Psychological Science, 8*, 168–172.

Small, D. M., Gregory, M. D., Mak, Y. E., Mesulam, M. M., & Parrish, T. (2003). Dissociation of neural representation of intensity and valuation in human gustation. *Neuron, 39*, 701–711.

Smeets, G., de Jong, P. J., & Mayer, B. (2000). If you suffer from a headache, then you have a brain tumor: Domain-specific reasoning 'bias' and hypochondriasis. *Behaviour Research and Therapy, 38*, 763–776.

Smit, A. B., Syed, N. I., Schaap, D., van Minnen, J., Klumperman, J., Kits, K. S., et al. (2001). A glia-derived acetylcholine-binding protein that modulates synaptic transmission. *Nature, 411*, 261–268.

Smith, A. P., & Maben, A. (1993). Effects of sleep deprivation, lunch, and personality on performance, mood, and cardiovascular function. *Physiology and Behavior, 54*(5), 967–972.

Smith, B. W., Pargament, K. I., Brant, C., & Oliver, J. M. (2000). Noah revisited: Religious coping by church members and the impact of the 1993 Midwest flood. *Journal of Community Psychology, 28,* 169–186.

Smith, D. (2003a). Angry thoughts, at-risk hearts. *Monitor on Psychology, 34,* 46.

Smith, D. (2003b). 10 ways practitioners can avoid ethical pitfalls. *Monitor on Psychology, 34,* 50–55.

Smith, E. E., Geva, A., Jonides, J., Miller, A., Reuter-Lorenz, P., & Koeppe, R. A. (2001). The neural basis of task-switching in working memory: Effects of performance and aging. *Proceedings of the National Academy of Sciences, 98,* 2095–2100.

Smith, E., & Mackie, D. (2000). *Social psychology.* Philadelphia: Taylor & Francis.

Smith, E., & Quellar, S. (2001). Mental representations. In A. Tesser & N. Schwarz (Eds.), *Blackwell handbook of social psychology: Intraindividual processes* (pp. 499–517). Oxford, England: Blackwell.

Smith, K. M., Larive, L. L., & Romananelli, F. (2002). Club drugs: Methylenedioxymethamphetamine, flunitrazepam, ketamine hydrochloride, and gamma-hydroxybutyrate. *American Journal of Health Systems Pharmacology, 59,* 1067–1076.

Smith, L. B., & Sera, M. D. (1992). A developmental analysis of the polar structure of dimensions. *Cognitive Psychology, 24,* 99–142.

Smith, M. L., Glass, G. V., & Miller, T. I. (1980). *The benefits of psychotherapy.* Baltimore: Johns Hopkins University Press.

Smith, M. U., & DiClemente, R. J. (2000). STAND: A peer educator training curriculum for sexual risk reduction in the rural South. Students Together Against Negative Decisions. *Preventive Medicine, 30,* 441–449.

Smith, N. T. (2002). A review of the published literature into cannabis withdrawal symptoms in human users. *Addiction, 97,* 621–632.

Smith, P. B., & Bond, M. (1999). *Social psychology across cultures.* Boston: Allyn & Bacon.

Smith, P. C., & Kendall, L. M. (1963). Retranslation of expectations: An approach to the construction of unambiguous anchors for rating scales. *Journal of Applied Psychology, 47,* 149–155.

Smith, S., & Donnerstein, E. (1998). Harmful effects of exposure to media violence: Learning of aggression, emotional desensitization, and fear. In R. Geen & E. Donnerstein (Eds.), *Human aggression: Theories, research, and implications for policy.* New York: Academic Press.

Smith, S., & Freedman, D. G. (1983, April). *Mother-toddler interaction and maternal perception of child temperament in two ethnic groups: Chinese-American and European-American.* Paper presented at the meeting of the Society for Research in Child Development, Detroit, MI.

Smith, S. M., Vela, E., & Williamson, J. E. (1988). Shallow input processing does not induce environmental context-dependent recognition. *Bulletin of the Psychonomic Society, 26,* 537–540.

Smith, S. S., O'Hara, B. F., Persico, A. M., Gorelick, D. A., Newlin, D. B., Vlahov, D., et al. (1992). Genetic vulnerability to drug abuse: The D2 dopamine receptor Taq i B1 restriction fragment length polymorphism appears more frequently in polysubstance abusers. *Archives of General Psychiatry, 49,* 723–727.

Smith, T. W., & Ruiz, J. M. (2002). Psychosocial influences on the development and course of coronary heart disease: Current status and implications for research and practice. *Journal of Consulting & Clinical Psychology, 70,* 548–568.

Snarey, J. (1987). A question of morality. *Psychological Bulletin, 97,* 202–232.

Snellingen, T., Evans, J. R., Ravilla, T., & Foster, A. (2002). Surgical interventions for age-related cataract. *Cochrane Database System Review, 2,* CD001323.

Snowden, L. R., & Cheung, F. (1990). Use of inpatient mental health services by members of ethnic minority groups. *American Psychologist, 45,* 347–355.

Soken, N. H., & Pick, A. D. (1992). Intermodal perception of happy and angry expressive behaviors by seven-month-old infants. *Child Development, 63,* 787–795.

Sokolowska, M., Siegel, S., & Kim, J. A. (2002). Intraadministration associations: Conditional hyperalgesia elicited by morphine onset cues. *Journal of Experimental Psychology: Animal Behavior Processes, 28,* 309–20.

Sohlberg, S., & Jansson, B. (2002). Unconscious responses to "mommy and I are one": Does gender matter? In R. F. Bornstein & J. M. Masling (Eds.), *The psychodynamics of gender and gender role. Vol. 10: Empirical studies in psychoanalytic theories* (pp. 165–201). Washington, DC, US: American Psychological Association.

Solomon, A. (1998, January 12). Anatomy of melancholy. *New Yorker,* pp. 46–61.

Solomon, P. R., Adams, F., Silver, A., Zimmer, J., & DeVeaux, R. (2002). Ginkgo for memory enhancement: a randomized controlled trial. *Journal of the American Medical Association, 288,* 835–840.

Solomon, R. L. (1980). The opponent-process theory of acquired motivation: The costs of pleasure and the benefits of pain. *American Psychologist, 35,* 691–712.

Solomon, R. L., Kamin, L. J., & Wynne, L. C. (1953). Traumatic avoidance learning: The outcomes of several extinction procedures with dogs. *Journal of Abnormal and Social Psychology, 48,* 291–302.

Solomonson, A. L., & Lance, C. E. (1997). Examination of the relationship between true halo and halo error in performance ratings. *Journal of Applied Psychology, 82,* 665–674.

Solowij, N., Stephens, R. S., Roffman, R. A., Babor, T., Kadden, R., Miller, M., et al. (2002). Cognitive functioning of long-term heavy cannabis users seeking treatment. *Journal of American Medical Association, 287,* 1123–1131.

Sommer, R. (1999). Applying environmental psychology. In D. A. Bernstein & A. M. Stec (Eds.), *The psychology of everyday life.* Boston: Houghton Mifflin.

Sorce, J., Emde, R., Campos, J., & Klinnert, M. (1981, April). *Maternal emotional signaling: Its effect on the visual cliff behavior of one-year-olds.* Paper presented at the meeting of the Society for Research in Child Development, Boston, MA.

Sørensen, H. J., Mortensen, E. L., Reinisch, J. M., & Mednick, S. A. (2003). Do hypertension and diuretic treatment in pregnancy increase the risk of schizophrenia in offspring? *American Journal of Psychiatry, 160,* 464–468.

Sorrentino, R. M., & Roney, C. J. R. (2000). *The uncertain mind: Individual differences in facing the unknown.* Philadelphia: Psychology Press.

Soumi, S. (1999). Attachment in rhesus monkeys. In J. Cassidy & P. Shaver (Eds.), *Handbook of attachment* (pp. 181–197). New York: Guilford.

Sowdon, J. (2001). Is depression more prevalent in old age? *Australian & New Zealand Journal of Psychiatry, 35,* 782–787.

Sowell, E. R., Delis, D., Stiles, J., & Jernigan, T. L. (2001). Improved memory functioning and frontal lobe maturation between childhood and adolescence: A structural MRI study. *Journal of the International Neuropsychological Society, 7,* 312–322.

Sowell, E. R., Peterson, B. S., Thompson, P. M., Welcome, S. E., Henkenius, A. L., & Toga, A. W. (2003). Mapping cortical change across the human life span. *Nature Neuroscience, 6,* 309–315.

Spanagel, R., & Weiss, F. (1999). The dopamine hypothesis of reward: Past and current status. *Trends in Neuroscience, 22,* 521–527.

Spangler, G., Fremmer-Bombik, E., & Grossman, K. (1996). Social and individual determinants of infant attachment security and disorganization. *Infant Mental Health Journal, 17,* 127–139.

Spanier, C., Frank, E., McEachran, A. B., Grochocinski, V. J., & Kupfer, D. J. (1996). The prophylaxis of depressive episodes in recurrent depression following discontinuation of drug therapy: Integrating psychological and biological factors. *Psychological Medicine, 26,* 461–475.

Spanos, N. P. (1994). Multiple identity enactments and multiple personality disorder: A sociocognitive perspective. *Psychological Bulletin, 116,* 143–165.

Spanos, N. P. (1996). *Multiple identities and false memories: A sociocognitive perspective.* Washington, DC: American Psychological Association.

Spanos, N. P., Burnley, M. C. E., & Cross, P. A. (1993). Response expectancies and interpretations as determinants of hypnotic responding. *Journal of Personality and Social Psychology, 65*(6), 1237–1242.

Sparks, K., Cooper, C., Fried, Y., & Shirom, A. (1997). The effects of hours of work on health: A meta-analytic review. *Journal of Occupational and Organizational Psychology, 70,* 391–408.

Speckhard, A. (2002). Voices from the inside: Psychological responses to toxic disasters. In J. M. Havenaar & J. G. Cwikel (Eds.), *Toxic turmoil: Psychological and societal consequences of ecological disasters* (pp. 217–236). New York: Plenum.

Spector, P. E. (1985). Measurement of human service staff satisfaction: Development of the Job Satisfaction Survey. *American Journal of Community Psychology, 13,* 693–713.

Spector, P. E. (2002). Employee control and occupational stress. *Current Directions in Psychological Science, 11,* 133–136.

Spector, P. E. (2003). *Industrial & organizational psychology: Research and practice* (3rd ed.). New York: Wiley.

Spelke, E. S., Breinlinger, K., Macomber, J., & Jacobson, K. (1992). Origins of knowledge. *Psychological Review, 99,* 605–632.

Spence, S. H., Donovan, C., Brechman-Toussaint, M. (2000). The treatment of childhood social phobia: The effectiveness of a social skills training-based, cognitive-behavioral intervention, with and without parental involvement. *Journal of Child Psychology and Psychiatry and Allied Disciplines, 41,* 713–726.

Spencer, T. J. (2002). Attention-deficit/hyperactivity disorder. *Archives of Neurology, 59,* 314–316.

Sperry, L. (1999). *Cognitive behavior therapy of DSM-IV personality disorders: Highly effective interventions for the most common personality disorders.* Bristol, PA: Bruner/Mazel.

Sperry, R. W. (1968). Hemisphere deconnection and unity in conscious awareness. *American Psychologist, 23,* 723–733.

Spiegel, D. (Ed.). (1994). *Dissociation: Culture, mind, and body*. Washington, DC: American Psychiatric Press.

Spiegel, D. A., & Bruce, T. J. (1997). Benzodiazepines and exposure-based cognitive behavior therapies for panic disorder: Conclusions from combined treatment trials. *American Journal of Psychiatry, 151,* 876–881.

Spiers, P. S., & Guntheroth, W. G. (2001). The black infant's susceptibility to sudden infant death syndrome and respiratory infection in late infancy. *Epidemiology, 12,* 33–37.

Spira, J. L. (2001). Study design casts doubt on value of St. John's wort in treating depression. *British Medical Journal, 322,* 493.

Spitzer, R. L., Gibbon, M., Skodol, A. E., & Williams, J. B. W., & First, M. B. (Eds.). (1994). *DSM-IV casebook: A learning companion to the* Diagnostic and Statistical Manual of Mental Disorders (4th ed.). Washington, DC: American Psychiatric Association.

Springer, K., & Belk, A. (1994). The role of physical contact and association in early contamination sensitivity. *Developmental Psychology, 30*(6), 864–868.

Squire, L. R. (1992). Memory and the hippocampus: A synthesis from findings with rats, monkeys, and humans. *Psychological Review, 99,* 195–231.

Srivastava, A., Locke, E. A., & Bartol, K. M. (2001). Money and subjective well-being: It's not the money, it's the motives. *Journal of Personality and Social Psychology, 80,* 959–971.

St. Clair, M. (1999). *Object relations and self-psychology: An introduction.* Pacific Grove, CA: Brooks/Cole.

St. Lawrence, J. S. (1993). African-American adolescents' knowledge, health-related attitudes, sexual behavior, and contraceptive decisions: Implications for the prevention of adolescent HIV infection. *Journal of Consulting Clinical Psychology, 61,* 104–112.

Stacey, J., & Biblarz, T. J. (2001). (How) Does the sexual orientation of parents matter? *American Sociological Review, 66,* 159–183.

Staddon, J. E. R., & Ettinger, R. H. (1989). *Learning: An introduction to the principles of adaptive behavior.* San Diego: Harcourt Brace Jovanovich.

Stafford, R. S., & Radley, D. C. (2003). National trends in antiobesity medication use. *Archives of Internal Medicine, 163,* 1046–1050.

Stahl, S. M. (2002). Selective actions on sleep or anxiety by exploiting GABA-A/benzodiazepine receptor subtypes. *Journal of Clinical Psychiatry, 63,* 179–180.

Stanley, B. G., Willett, V. L., Donias, H. W., & Ha-Lyen, H. (1993). The lateral hypothalamus: A primary site mediating excitatory aminoacid-elicited eating. *Brain Research, 63*(1–2), 41–49.

Stansfeld, S. A., & Marmot, M .G. (Eds.). (2002). *Stress and the heart: Psychosocial pathways to coronary heart disease.* London: BMJ Books.

Stanton-Hicks, M., & Salamon, J. (1997). Stimulation of the central and peripheral nervous system for the control of pain. *Journal of Clinical Neurophysiology, 14,* 46–62.

Stapleton, S. (2001, February 19). Miles to go before I sleep: America is becoming a culture of sleeplessness. *Amednews* [Online]. Available: http://www.ama-assn.org/sci-pubs/amnews/pick_01/hlsa0219.htm

Starkman, N., & Rajani, N. (2002). The case for comprehensive sex education. *AIDS Patient Care & STDs, 16,* 313–318.

Stasser, G. (1991). Pooling of unshared information during group discussion. In S. Worchel, W. Wood, & J. Simpson (Eds.), *Group processes and productivity.* Beverly Hills, CA: Sage.

Stasser, G., Stewart, D., & Wittenbaum, G. M. (1995). Expert roles and information exchange during discussion: The importance of knowing who knows what. *Journal of Experimental Social Psychology, 31,* 244–265.

Staudt, M., Grodd, W., Niemann, G., Wildgruber, D., Erb, M., & Krageloh-Mann, I. (2001). Early left periventricular brain lesions induce right hemispheric organization of speech. *Neurology 2001, 57,* 122–125.

Staw, B. M., Bell, N. E., & Clausen, J. A. (1986). The dispositional approach to job attitudes: A lifetime longitudinal test. *Administrative Science Quarterly, 31,* 56–77.

Steadman, H. J. (1993). *Reforming the insanity defense: An evaluation of pre- and post- Hinckley reforms.* New York: Guilford.

Steele, C. M. (1997). A threat in the air: How stereotypes shape intellectual identity and performance. *American Psychologist, 52,* 613–629.

Steele, T. D., McCann, U. D., & Ricaurte, G. A. (1994). 3,4-methylenedioxy-methamphetamine (MDMA, ecstasy): Pharmacology and toxicology in animals and humans. *Addiction, 89*(5), 539–551.

Steffen, P. R., McNeilly, M., Anderson, N., & Sherwood, A. (2003). Effects of perceived racism and anger inhibition on ambulatory blood pressure in African Americans. *Psychosomatic Medicine, 65,* 746–750.

Steiger, H., Young, S. N., Ng Ying Kin, N. M. K., Koerner, N., Israel, M., Lageix, P., et al. (2001). Implications of impulsive and affective symptoms for serotonin function in bulimia nervosa. *Psychological Medicine, 31,* 85–95.

Stein, D. J., Versiani, M., Hair, T., & Kumar, R. (2002). Efficacy of paroxetine for relapse prevention in social anxiety disorder: A 24-week study. *Archives of General Psychiatry, 59,* 1111–1118.

Stein, D. M., & Lambert, M. J. (1995). Graduate training in psychotherapy: Are therapy outcomes enhanced? *Journal of Consulting and Clinical Psychology, 63,* 182–196.

Stein, E. (1999). *The mismeasure of desire: The science, theory and ethics of sexual orientation.* New York: Oxford University Press.

Stein, K. D., Goldman, M. S., & Del Boca, F. K. (2000). The influence of alcohol expectancy priming and mood manipulation on subsequent alcohol consumption. *Journal of Abnormal Psychology, 109,* 106–115.

Stein, M. A. (1993, November 30). Spacewalking repair team to work on Hubble flaws; shower head inspires a device to improve focusing ability. *Los Angeles Times,* A1, A5.

Stein, M. B., Chavira, D. A., & Jang, K. L. (2001). Bringing up bashful baby: Developmental pathways to social phobia. *Psychiatric Clinics of North America, 24,* 661–675.

Steinberg, L. (1990). Autonomy, conflict, and harmony in the family relationship. In S. S. Feldman & G. R. Elliott (Eds.), *At the threshold: The developing adolescent* (pp. 255–276). Cambridge, MA: Harvard University Press.

Steinberg, L., Dornbusch, S. M., & Brown, B. B. (1992). Ethnic differences in adolescent achievement: An ecological perspective. *American Psychologist, 47,* 723–729.

Steinberg, L., Lamborn, S. D., Darling, N., Mounts, N. S., & Dornbusch, S. M. (1994). Over-time changes in adjustment and competence among adolescents from authoritative, authoritarian, indulgent, and neglectful families. *Child Development, 65,* 754–770.

Steindler, D. A., & Pincus, D. W. (2002). Stem cells and neuropoiesis in the adult human brain. *Lancet, 359,* 1047–1054.

Steiner, J. M., & Fahrenberg, J. (2000). Authoritarianism and social status of former members of the Waffen-SS and SS and of the Wehrmacht: An extension and reanalysis of the study published in 1970. *Koelner Zeitschrift fuer Soziologie und Sozialpsychologie, 52,* 329–348.

Stephan, K. E., Marshall, J. C., Friston, K. J., Rowe, J. B., Ritzl, A., Zilles, K., & Fink, G. R. (2003). Lateralized cognitive processes and lateralized task control in the human brain. *Science, 301,* 384–386.

Stephens, R. S., Roffman, R. A., & Simpson, E. E. (1994). Treating adult marijuana dependence: A test of the relapse prevention model. *Journal of Consulting and Clinical Psychology, 62*(1), 92–99.

Steriade, M., & McCarley, R. W. (1990). *Brainstem control of wakefulness and sleep.* New York: Plenum.

Stern, J., & Stern, M. (1992). Chiles (New Mexico). *The New Yorker,* p. 68.

Stern, K., & McClintock, M. K. (1998). Regulation of ovulation by human pheromones. *Nature, 392,* 177–179.

Stern, Y., Tang, M. X., Denaro, J., & Mayeux, R. (1995). Increased risk of mortality in Alzheimer's disease patients with more advanced educational and occupational attainment. *Annals of Neurology, 37,* 590–595.

Sternberg, R. J. (1985). *Beyond IQ: A triarchic theory of human intelligence.* Cambridge, England: Cambridge University Press.

Sternberg, R. J. (1988a). Triangulating love. In R. J. Sternberg & M. L. Barnes (Eds.), *The psychology of love.* New Haven: Yale University Press.

Sternberg, R. J. (1988b). *The triarchic mind.* New York: Cambridge Press.

Sternberg, R. J. (1996). *Successful intelligence.* New York: Simon & Schuster.

Sternberg, R. J. (1997a). Construct validation of a triangular love scale. *European Journal of Social Psychology, 27,* 313–335.

Sternberg, R. J. (1997b). *Thinking styles.* Cambridge, England: Cambridge University Press.

Sternberg, R. J. (1999, Spring). Ability and expertise: It's time to replace the current model of intelligence. *American Educator,* pp. 10–51.

Sternberg, R. J. (2000). Patterns of giftedness: A triarchic analysis. *Roeper Review, 22,* 231–236.

Sternberg, R. J. (2001). What is the common thread of creativity?: Its dialectical relation to intelligence and wisdom. *American Psychologist, 56,* 360–362.

Sternberg, R. J., & Dess, N. K. (2001). Creativity for the new millennium. *American Psychologist, 56,* 332.

Sternberg, R. J., & Kaufman, J. C. (1998). Human abilities. *Annual Review of Psychology, 49,* 479–502.

Sternberg, R. J., Lautrey, J., & Lubart, T. I. (2003). Where are we in the field of intelligence, how did we get here, and where are we going? In R. J. Sternberg, J. Lautrey, et al. (Eds.), *Models of intelligence: International perspectives* (pp. 3–25). Washington, DC: American Psychological Association.

Sternberg, R. J., & Lubart, T. I. (1992). Buy low and sell high: An investment approach to creativity. *Current Directions in Psychological Science, 1*(1), 1–5.

Sternberg, R. J., & O'Hara, L. A. (1999). Creativity and intelligence. In R. J. Sternberg, et al. (Eds.), *Handbook of creativity* (pp. 251–272). New York: Cambridge University Press.

Sternberg, R. J., Wagner, R. K., Williams, W. M., & Horvath, J. A. (1995). Testing common sense. *American Psychologist, 50,* 912–927.

Sternberg, R. J., & Williams, W. M. (1997). Does the graduate record examination predict meaningful success of graduate training of psychologists? A Case Study. *American Psychologist, 52,* 630–641.

Stevens, A. (1996). *Private myths: Dreams and dreaming.* Cambridge, MA: Harvard University Press.

Stevens, R. (1999, April 21). *Personal communication.*

Stevenson, H. (1992). *A long way from being number one: What we can learn from East Asia.* Washington, DC: Federation of Behavior, Psychological and Cognitive Sciences.

Stewart, R., & Przyborski, S. (2002). Non-neural adult stem cells: Tools for brain repair? *Bioessays, 24,* 708–713.

Stewart, W. F., Ricci, J. A., Chee, E., Hahn, S. R., & Morganstein, D. (2003). Cost of lost productive work time among US workers with depression. *Journal of the American Medical Association, 289,* 3135–3144.

Stice, E. (2001). A prospective test of the dual-pathway model of bulimic pathology: Mediating effects of dieting and negative affect. *Journal of Abnormal Psychology, 110,* 124–135.

Stickgold, R. (2002). EMDR: A putative neurobiological mechanism of action. *Journal of Clinical Psychology, 58,* 61–75.

Stickgold, R., Malia, A., Maguire, D., Roddenberry, D., & O'Connor, M. (2000). Replaying the game: Hypnagogic images in normals and amnesics. *Science, 290,* 350–353.

Stickgold, R., Rittenhouse, C. D., & Hobson, J. A. (1994). Dream splicing: A new technique for assessing thematic coherence in subjective reports of mental activity. *Consciousness and Cognition, 3*(1), 114–128.

Stillwell, M. E. (2002). Drug-facilitated sexual assault involving gamma-hydroxybutyric acid. *Journal of Forensic Science, 47,* 1133–1134.

Stoff, D. M., Breiling, J., & Maser, J. D. (Eds.). (1997). *Handbook of antisocial behavior.* New York: Wiley.

Stokes, P. E. (1998). Ten years of fluoxetine. *Depression and Anxiety, 8,* 1–4.

Stoleru, S., Gregoire, M. C., Gerard, D., Decety, J., Lafarge, E., Cinotti, L., et al. (1999). Neuroanatomical correlates of visually evoked sexual arousal in human males. *Archives of Sexual Behavior, 28,* 1–21.

Stone, J., & Cooper, J. (2001). A self-standards model of cognitive dissonance. *Journal of Experimental Social Psychology, 37,* 228–243.

Stoney, C. M., Bausserman, L., Niaura, R., Marcus, B., & Flynn, M. (1999b). Lipid reactivity to stress: II. Biological and behavioral influences. *Health Psychology, 18,* 251–261.

Stoney, C. M., & Finney, M. L. (2000). Social support and stress: Influences on lipid reactivity. *International Journal of Behavioral Medicine, 7,* 111–126.

Stoney, C. M., & Hughes, J. W. (1999). Lipid reactivity among men with a parental history of myocardial infarction. *Psychophysiology, 36,* 484–490.

Stoney, C. M., & Matthews, K. A. (1988). Parental history of hypertension and myocardial infarction predicts cardiovascular responses to behavioral stressors in middle-aged men and women. *Psychophysiology, 25,* 269–277.

Stoney, C. M., Niaura, R., Bausserman, L., & Matacin, M. (1999a). Lipid reactivity to stress: Comparison of chronic and acute stress responses in middle-aged airline pilots. *Health Psychology, 18,* 241–250.

Strain, E. C., Mumford, G. K., Silverman, K., & Griffiths, R. R. (1994). Caffeine dependence syndrome: Evidence from case histories and experimental evaluations. *Journal of the American Medical Association, 272*(13), 1043–1048.

Strang, J., Witten, J., & Hall, W. (2000). Improving the quality of the cannibis debate: Defining the different domains. *British Medical Journal, 320,* 108–110.

Strauss, R. S., & Pollack, H. A. (2001). Epidemic increases in childhood overweight: 1986–1998. *Journal of the American Medical Association, 286,* 2845–2848.

Streissguth, A. P., Barr, H. M., Bookstein, F. L., Sampson, P. D., & Olson, H. C. (1999). The long-term neurocognitive consequences of prenatal alcohol exposure: A 14-year study. *Psychological Science, 10,* 186–190.

Strongman, K. T., & Kemp, S. (1991). Autobiographical memory for emotion. *Bulletin of the Psychonomic Society, 29,* 195–198.

Stroop, J. R. (1935). Studies of interference in serial verbal reactions. *Journal of Experimental Psychology, 18,* 643–662.

Strote, J., Lee, J. E., & Wechsler, H. (2002). Increasing MDMA use among college students: Results of a national survey. *Journal of Adolescent Health, 30,* 64–72.

Sturm, R. (2003). Increases in clinically severe obesity in the United States, 1986–2000. *Archives of Internal Medicine, 163,* 2146–2148.

Sturm, R., & Wells, K. B. (2001). Does obesity contribute as much to morbidity as poverty or smoking? *Public Health, 115,* 229–235.

Sue, D. W., Bingham, R. P., Porché-Burke, L., & Vasquez, M. (1999). The diversification of psychology: A multicultural revolution. *American Psychologist, 54,* 1061–1069.

Sue, S. (1998). In search of cultural competence in psychotherapy and counseling. *American Psychologist, 53,* 440–448.

Sue, S., & Okazaki, S. (1990). Asian-American educational achievements: A phenomenon in search of an explanation. *American Psychologist, 45,* 913–920.

Sue, S., Zane, N., & Young, K. (1994). Research on psychotherapy with culturally diverse populations. In A. E. Bergin & S. L. Garfield (Eds.), *Handbook of psychotherapy and behavior change.* New York: Wiley.

Suh, E., Diener, E., & Fujita, F. (1996). Events and subjective well-being: Only recent events matter. *Journal of Personality and Social Psychology, 70,* 1091–1102.

Suinn, R. M. (2001). The terrible twos: Anger and anxiety. *American Psychologist, 56,* 27–36.

Sullivan, H. S. (1954). *The psychiatric interview.* New York: Norton.

Sullivan, J. W., & Horowitz, F. D. (1983). The effects of intonation on infant attention: The role of the rising intonation contour. *Journal of Child Language, 10,* 521–534.

Sullivan, P. F. (1995). Mortality in anorexia nervosa. *American Journal of Psychiatry, 152,* 1073–1074.

Suls, J., & Wan, C. K. (1993). The relationship between trait hostility and cardiovascular reactivity: A quantitative review and analysis. *Psychophysiology, 30,* 1–12.

Suzdak, P. D., Glowa, J. R., Crawley, J. N., Schwartz, R. D., Skolnick, P., & Paul, S. M. (1986). A selective imidazobenzodiazepine antagonist of ethanol in the rat. *Science, 234,* 1243–1247.

Swaab, D. F., Chung, W. C., Kruijver, F. P., Hofman, M. A., & Ishunina, T. A. (2001). Structural and functional sex differences in the human hypothalamus. *Hormones and Behavior, 40,* 93–98.

Swaab, D. F., & Hofman, M. A. (1995). Sexual differentiation of the human hypothalamus in relation to gender and sexual orientation. *Trends in Neuroscience, 18*(6), 264–270.

Swan, G. E. (1996, December). Some elders thrive on working into late life. *APA Monitor,* p. 35.

Swann, W. B., Jr., De La Ronde, C., & Hixon, J. G. (1994). Authenticity and positivity strivings in marriage and courtship. *Journal of Personality and Social Psychology, 66,* 857–869.

Sweller, J., & Gee, W. (1978). Einstellung: The sequence effect and hypothesis theory. *Journal of Experimental Psychology: Human Learning and Memory, 4,* 513–526.

Swets, J. A. (1992). The science of choosing the right decision threshold in high-stakes diagnostics. *American Psychologist, 47,* 522–532.

Swets, J. A. (1996). *Signal detection theory and ROC analysis in psychology and diagnostics.* New Jersey: Erlbaum.

Swets, J. A., Dawes, R. M., & Monahan, J. (2000). Psychological science can improve diagnostic decisions. *Psychological Science in the Public Interest, 1,* 1–26.

Swindle, R., Jr., Heller, K., Pescosolido, B., & Kikuzawa, S. (2000). Responses to nervous breakdowns in America over a 40-year period: Mental health policy implications. *American Psychologist, 55,* 740–749.

Swithers, S. E., & Hall, W. G. (1994). Does oral experience terminate ingestion? *Appetite, 23*(2), 113–138.

Szasz, T. S. (1987). *Insanity: The idea and its consequences.* New York: Wiley.

Szasz, T. (2002). *Liberation by oppression: A comparative study of slavery and psychiatry.* New Brunswick, NJ: Transaction Publishers.

Szatmari, P., Jones, M. B., Zwaigenbaum, L., & MacLean, J. E. (1998). Genetics of autism: Overview and new directions. *Journal of Autism and Developmental Disorders, 28,* 351–368.

Tabbarah, M., Crimmins, E., & Seeman, T. E. (2002). The relationship between cognitive and physical performance: MacArthur studies of successful aging. *Gerontological Society of America, US. Journals of Gerontology: Series A. Biological Sciences & Medical Sciences, 57*(4), M228–M235.

Tagliabue, J. (1999, January 28). Devil gets his due, but Catholic church updates exorcism rites. *International Herald Tribune,* p. 6.

Takei, N., Sham, P., O'Callaghan, E., Murray, G. K., Glover, G., & Murray, R. M. (1994). Prenatal exposure to influenza and the development of schizophrenia: Is the effect confined to females? *American Journal of Psychiatry, 151,* 117–119.

Takeuchi, N., Uchimura, N., Hashizume, Y., Mukai, M., Etoh, Y., Yamamoto, K., et al. (2001). Melatonin therapy for REM behavior disorder. *Psychiatry and Clinical Neurosciences, 55,* 267–269.

Tanaka, H., Taira, K., Arakawa, M., Toguti, H., Urasaki, C., Yamamoto, Y., et al. (2001). Effects of short nap and exercise on elderly people having difficulty sleeping. *Psychiatry and Clinical Neurosciences, 55,* 173–174.

Tanaka-Matsumi, J., & Higginbotham, H. N. (1994). Clinical application of behavior therapy across ethnic and cultural boundaries. *The Behavior Therapist, 17,* 123–126.

Tanda, G., Pontieri, F. E., & Di Chiara, G. (1997). Cannabinoid and heroin activation of mesolimbic dopamine transmission by a common mu1 opioid receptor mechanism. *Science, 276,* 2048–2050.

Tannen, D. (1994). *Gender and discourse.* New York: Oxford University Press.

Tanner, J. M. (1978). *Foetus into man: Physical growth from conception to maturity.* London: Open Books.

Task Force on Promotion and Dissemination of Psychological Procedures. (1995). Training in and dissemination of empirically validated psychological treatments: Report and recommendations. *Clinical Psychologist, 48,* 3–23.

Tasker, F., & Golombok, S. (1995). Adults raised as children in lesbian families. *American Journal of Orthopsychiatry, 65*(2), 203–215.

Tassi, P., & Muzet, A. (2001). Defining states of consciousness. *Neuroscience and Biobehavioral Reviews, 25,* 175–191.

Taub, A. (1998). Thumbs down on acupuncture. *Science, 279,* 159.

Tavris, C. (2003). Mind games: Psychological warfare between therapists and scientists. *The Chronicle of Higher Education, 49,* B7–B9.

Tavris, C. (2004, January 3). *From Dora to Jane Doe: The use and abuse of case studies.* Paper presented at the 26th Annual National Institute on the Teaching of Psychology, St. Petersburg, Florida.

Taylor, H. A., & Tversky, B. (1992). Spatial mental models derived from survey and route descriptions. *Journal of Memory and Language, 31,* 261–292.

Taylor, J. G. (2002). Paying attention to consciousness. *Trends in Cognitive Science, 6,* 206–210.

Taylor, R. L., & Richards, S. B. (1991). Patterns of intellectual differences of Black, Hispanic, and White children. *Psychology in the Schools, 28,* 5–8.

Taylor, S., Thordarson, D. S., Maxfield, L., Fedoroff, I. C., Lovell, K., & Ogrodniczuk, J. (2003). Comparative efficacy, speed, and adverse effects of three PTSD treatments: Exposure therapy, EMDR, and relaxation training. *Journal of Consulting and Clinical Psychology, 71,* 330–338.

Taylor, S. E. (1995). *Health psychology* (3rd ed.). New York: McGraw-Hill.

Taylor, S. E. (1999). *Health psychology* (4th ed.). New York: McGraw-Hill.

Taylor, S. E. (2002). *Health psychology* (5th ed.). New York: McGraw-Hill.

Taylor, S. E., & Aspinwall, L. G. (1996). Mediating processes in psychosocial stress: Appraisal, coping, resistance, and vulnerability. In H. B. Kaplan (Ed.), *Perspectives on psychosocial stress.* New York: Academic Press.

Taylor, S. E., Dickerson, S. S., & Klein, L. C. (2002). Toward a biology of social support. In C. R. Snyder & S. L. Lopez (Eds.), *Handbook of positive psychology* (pp. 556–569). London: Oxford University Press.

Taylor, S. E., Kemeny, M. E., Aspinwall, L. G., Schneider, S. G., Rodriguez, R., & Herbert, M. (1992). Optimism, coping, psychological distress, and high-risk sexual behavior among men at risk for acquired immunodeficiency syndrome (AIDS). *Journal of Personality and Social Psychology, 63,* 460–473.

Taylor, S. E., Kemeny, M. E., Reed, G. M., Bower, J. E., & Gruenewald, T. L. (2000). Psychological resources, positive illusions, and health. *American Psychologist, 55,* 99–109.

Taylor, S. E., Klein, L. C., Lewis, B. P., Gruenewald, T. L., Gurung, R. A. R., & Updegraff, J. A. (2000). Biobehavioral responses to stress in females: Tend-and-befriend, not fight-or-flight. *Psychological Review, 107,* 411–429.

Taylor, S. E., Lewis, B. P., Gruenewald, T. L., Gurung, R. A. R., Updegraff, J. A., & Klein, L. C. (2002). Sex differences in biobehavioral responses to threat: Reply to Geary and Flinn (2002). *Psychological Review, 109,* 751–753.

Taylor, S. E., & Lobel, M. (1989). Social comparison activity under threat: Downward evaluation and upward contacts. *Psychological Review, 96.*

Taylor, S., Peplau, A., & Sears, D. (2000). *Social psychology* (10th ed.). Upper Saddle River, NJ: Prentice-Hall.

Taylor, S., Peplau, A., & Sears, D. (2003). *Social psychology* (11th ed.). Upper Saddle River, NJ: Prentice-Hall.

Teigen, K. H. (1994). Yerkes-Dodson: A law for all seasons. *Theory and Psychology, 4*(4), 525–547.

Tellegen, A., Lykken, D. T., Bouchard, T. J., Wilcox, K. J., Segal, N. L., & Rich, S. (1988). Personality similarity in twins reared apart and together. *Journal of Personality and Social Psychology, 54,* 1031–1039.

Teng, Y. D., Lavik, E. B., Qu, X., Park, K. I., Ourednik, J., Zurakowski, D., et al. (2002). Functional recovery following traumatic spinal cord injury mediated by a unique polymer scaffold seeded with neural stem cells. *Proceedings of the National Academy of Science, 99,* 3024–3029.

Ter Riet, G., Kleijnen, J., & Knipschild, P. (1990). Acupuncture and chronic pain: A criteria-based meta-analysis. *Journal of Clinical Epidemiology, 43,* 1191–1199.

Terman, J. S., Terman, M., Lo, E. S., & Cooper, T. B. (2001). Circadian time of morning light administration and therapeutic response in winter depression. *Archives of General Psychiatry, 58,* 69–75.

Terman, L. M. (1916). *The measurement of intelligence.* Boston: Houghton Mifflin.

Terman, L. M., & Oden, M. H. (1947). *The gifted child grows up: Vol. 4. Genetic studies of genius.* Stanford, CA: Stanford University Press.

Terman, L. M., & Oden, M. H. (1959). *The gifted group at midlife.* Stanford, CA: Stanford University Press.

Tesser, A. (2001). Self-esteem: The frequency of temporal-self and social comparisons in people's personal appraisals. In A. Tesser & N. Schwarz (Eds.), *Blackwell handbook of social psychology: Intraindividual processes* (pp. 479–498). Oxford, England: Blackwell.

Thaker, G. K., & Carpenter, W. T., Jr. (2001). Advances in schizophrenia. *Nature Medicine, 7,* 667–671.

Thanos, P. K., Volkow, N. D., Freimuth, P., Umegaki, H., Ikari, H., Roth, G., et al. (2001). Overexpression of dopamine D2 receptors reduces alcohol self-administration. *Journal of Neurochemistry, 78,* 1094–1103.

't Hart, P. (1998). Preventing groupthink revisited: Evaluating and reforming groups in government. *Organizational Behavior and Human Decision Processes, 73,* 306–326.

Thase, M. E. (2002). Antidepressant effects: The suit may be small, but the fabric is real. *Prevention & Treatment, 5,* Article 32. Retrieved August 27, 2003, from http://www.journals.apa.org/prevention/volume5/pre0050032c.html

Thelen, E. (1995). Motor development: A new synthesis. *American Psychologist, 50,* 79–95.

Theofilopoulos, S., Goggi, J., Riaz, S. S., Jauniaux, E., Stern, G. M., & Bradford, H. F. (2001). Parallel induction of the formation of dopamine and its metabolites with induction of tyrosine hydroxylase expression in foetal rat and human cerebral cortical cells by brain-derived neurotrophic factor and glial-cell derived neurotrophic factor. *Brain Research: Developmental Brain Research, 127,* 111–122.

Thom, A., Sartory, G., & Jöhren, P. (2000). Comparison between one-session psychological treatment and benzodiazepine in dental phobia. *Journal of Consulting and Clinical Psychology, 68,* 378–387.

Thomas, A., & Chess, S. (1977). *Temperament and development.* New York: Brunner/Mazel.

Thomas, E. L., & Robinson, H. A. (1972). *Improving reading in every class: A sourcebook for teachers.* Boston: Allyn & Bacon.

Thompson, C., Koon, E., Woodwell, W., Jr., & Beauvais, J. (2002). *Training for the next economy: An ASTD state of the industry report on trend in employer-provided training in the United States.* Washington, DC: American Society for Training and Development.

Thompson, J. K., Heinberg, L. J., Altabe., M., & Tantleff-Dunn, S. (1999). *Exacting beauty: Theory, assessment and treatment of body image disturbance.* Washington, DC: American Psychological Association.

Thompson, J. K., & Stice, E. (2001). Thin-ideal internalization: Mounting evidence for a new risk factor for body-image disturbance and eating pathology. *Current Directions in Psychological Science, 10,* 181–183.

Thompson, P. M., Giedd, J. N., Woods, R. P., Macdonald, D., Evans, A. C., & Toga, A. W. (2000). Growth patterns in the developing brain detected by using continuum mechanical tensor maps. *Nature, 404,* 190–193.

Thompson, R. A. (1998). Early sociopersonality development. In W. Damon & N. Eisenberg (Eds.), *Handbook of child psychology: Vol. 3. Social, emotional, and personality development* (5th ed., pp. 25–104). New York: Wiley.

Thompson, W. G. (1995). Coffee: Brew or bane. *American Journal of the Medical Sciences, 308*(1), 49–57.

Thomson, C. P. (1982). Memory for unique personal events: The roommate study. *Memory & Cognition, 10,* 324–332.

Thorndike, E. L. (1898). Animal intelligence: An experimental study of the associative processes in animals. *Psychological Monographs, 2*(Whole No. 8).

Thorndike, E. L. (1905). *The elements of psychology.* New York: Seiler.

Thorngren, J. M., & Kleist, D. M. (2002). Multiple family group therapy: An interpersonal/postmodern approach. *Family Journal–Counseling and Therapy for Couples and Families, 10,* 167–176.

Thorpe, G. L., & Olson, S. L. (1997). *Behavior therapy: Concepts, procedures, and applications* (2nd ed.). Boston: Allyn & Bacon.

Tidwell, M. C. O., Reis, H. T., & Shaver, P. R. (1996). Attachment, attractiveness, and social interaction: A diary study. *Journal of Personality and Social Psychology, 71,* 729–745.

Tiihonen, J., Kuikka, J., Bergstrom, K., Hakola, P., Karhu, J., Ryynänen, O.-P., & Föhr, J. (1995). Altered striatal dopamine re-uptake site densities in habitually violent and non-violent alcoholics. Nature Medicine, 1(7), 654–657.

Tinbergen, N. (1989). *The study of instinct.* Oxford: Clarendon.

Todorov, C., Freeston, M. H., & Borgeat, F. (2000). On the pharmacotherapy of obsessive-compulsive disorder: is a consensus possible? *Canadian Journal of Psychiatry, 45,* 257–262.

Tolman, E. C., & Honzik, C. H. (1930). Introduction and removal of reward and maze performance in rats. *University of California Publication in Psychology, 4,* 257–275.

Tomasello, M. (2000). Culture and cognitive development. Current Directions in Psychological Science, 9, 37–40.

Tomes, H. (1999, April). The need for cultural competence. *APA Monitor,* p. 31.

Toni, N., Buchs, P. A., Nikonenko, I., Bron, C. R., & Muller, D. (1999). LTP promotes formation of multiple spine synapses between a single axon terminal and a dendrite. *Nature, 402,* 421–425.

Torasdotter, M., Metsis, M., Henriksson, B. G., Winblad, B., & Mohammed, A. H. (1998). Environmental enrichment results in higher levels of nerve growth factor mRNA in the rat visual cortex and hippocampus. *Behavior and Brain Research, 93,* 83–90.

Tower, R. B., Kasl, S. V., & Darefsky, A. S. (2002). Types of marital closeness and mortality risk in older couples. *Psychosomatic Medicine, 64*(4), 644–659.

Trabasso, T. R., & Bower, G. H. (1968). *Attention in learning.* New York: Wiley.

Tramer, M. R., Carroll, D., Campbell, F. A., Reynolds, D. J., Moore, R. A., & McQuay, H. J. (2001). Cannabinoids for control of chemotherapy induced nausea and vomiting: quantitative systematic review. *British Medical Journal, 323,* 16–21.

Treiber, F. A., Musante, L., Kapuku, G., Davis, C., Litaker, M., & Davis, H. (2001). Cardiovascular (CV) responsivity and recovery to acute stress and future CV functioning in youth with family histories of CV disease: A 4-year longitudinal study. *International Journal of Psychophysiology, 41,* 65–74.

Tremblay, R. E., Pagani-Kurtz, L., Mâsse, L., Vitaro, F., & Pihl, R. O. (1995). A bimodal preventive intervention for disruptive kindergarten boys: Its impact through mid-adolescence. *Journal of Consulting and Clinical Psychology, 63,* 560–568.

Tremblay, R. E., Pihl, R. O., Vitaro, F., & Dobkin, P. (1994). Predicting early onset of male antisocial behavior from preschool behavior. *Archives of General Psychiatry, 51,* 732–739.

Trevor, C. O. (2001). Interactions among actual ease-of-movement determinants and job satisfaction in the prediction of voluntary turnover. *Academy of Management Journal, 44,* 621–638.

Triandis, H. C. (1994). *Culture and social behavior.* New York: McGraw-Hill.

Triandis, H. C. (1998). Vertical and horizontal individualism and collectivism: Theory and research implications for international management. In J. L. C. Cheng, R. B. Peterson, et al. (Eds.), *Advances in international comparative management* (Vol. 12, pp. 7–35). Stamford, CT: JAI Press.

Trierweiler, S. J., Neighbors, H. W., Munday, C., Thompson, E. E., Binion, V. J., & Gomez, J. P. (2000). Clinician attributions associated with the diagnosis of schizophrenia in African American and non-African American patients. *Journal of Consulting and Clinical Psychology, 68,* 171–175.

Trillin, A. S. (2001, January 29). Betting your life. *The New Yorker,* pp. 38–41.

Trope, Y., Cohen, O., & Alfieri, T. (1991). Behavior identification as a mediator of dispositional inference. *Journal of Personality and Social Psychology, 61,* 873–883.

Trower, P. (1995). Adult social skills: State of the art and future directions. In W. O'Donohue & L. Krasner (Eds.), *Handbook of psychological skills training: Clinical techniques and applications* (pp. 54–80). Boston: Allyn & Bacon.

Trull, T. J., & Sher, K. J. (1994). Relationship between the five-factor model of personality and Axis I disorders in a nonclinical sample. *Journal of Personality and Social Psychology, 103,* 350–360.

Trunzo, J. J., & Pinto, B. M. (2003). Social support as a mediator of optimisim and distress in breast cancer survivors. *Journal of Consulting and Clinical Psychology, 71,* 805–811.

Tryon, W. W. (2002). Network models contribute to cognitive and social neuroscience. *American Psychologist, 57,* 728.

Tseng, W., Kan-Ming, M., Li-Shuen, L., Guo-Qian, C., Li-Wah, O., & Hong-Bo, Z. (1992). Koro epidemics in Guangdong China. *Journal of Nervous and Mental Disease, 180,* 117–123.

Tsuang, M. T., Stone, W. S., & Faraone, S. V. (2000). Toward reformulating the diagnosis of schizophrenia. *American Journal of Psychiatry, 157,* 1041–1950.

Tuch, S. A., & Martin, J. K. (1991). Race in the workplace: Black/white differences in the sources of job satisfaction. *The Sociological Quarterly, 32,* 103–116.

Tucker, C. M., & Herman, K. C. (2002). Using culturally sensitive theories and research to meet the academic needs of low-income African American children. *American Psychologist, 57,* 762–773.

Tulving, E. (1983). *Elements of episodic memory.* New York: Oxford University Press.

Tulving, E. (1995). Organization of memory: Quo vadis? In M. S. Gazzaniga (Ed.), *The cognitive neurosciences* (pp. 839–853). Cambridge: MIT Press.

Tulving, E. (2002). Episodic memory: From mind to brain. *Annual Review of Psychology, 53,* 1–25.

Tulving, E., & Psotka, J. (1971). Retroactive inhibition in free recall: Inaccessibility of information available in the memory store. *Journal of Experimental Psychology, 87,* 1–8.

Turiel, E. (1998). The development of morality. In W. Damon & N. Eisenberg (Eds.), *Handbook of child psychology: Vol. 3. Social, emotional, and personality development* (5th ed., pp. 863–932). New York: Wiley.

Turkheimer, E., & Waldron M. (2000). Nonshared environment: A theoretical, methodological, and quantitative review. *Psychological Bulletin, 126,* 78–108.

Turkkan, J. S. (1989). Classical conditioning: The new hegemony. *Behavioral & Brain Sciences, 12,* 121–179.

Turner, J. C. (1991). *Social influence.* Pacific Grove, CA: Brooks/Cole.

Turner, S. M., DeMers, S. T., Fox, H. R., & Reed, G. M. (2001). APA's guidelines for test user qualifications: An executive summary. *American Psychologist, 56,* 1099–1113.

Tuszynski, M. H., Grill, R., Jones, L. L., McKay, H. M., & Blesch, A. (2002). Spontaneous and augmented growth of axons in the primate spinal cord: Effects of local injury and nerve growth factor-secreting cell grafts. *Journal of Comparative Neurology, 449,* 88–101.

Tversky, A., & Kahneman, D. (1974). Judgment under uncertainty: Heuristics and biases. *Science, 185,* 1124–1131.

Tversky, A., & Kahneman, D. (1981). The framing of decisions and the psychology of choice. *Science, 211,* 453–458.

Tversky, A., & Kahneman, D. (1991). Loss aversion in riskless choice: A reference dependent model. *Quarterly Journal of Economics, 106,* 1039–1061.

Tversky, A., & Kahneman, D. (1993). Probabilistic reasoning. In A. Goldman (Ed.), *Readings in philosophy and cognitive science* (pp. 43–68). Cambridge: MIT Press.

Tversky, B., & Tuchin, M. (1989). A reconciliation of the evidence on eyewitness testimony: Comments on McCloskey and Zaragoza. *Journal of Experimental Psychology: General, 118,* 86–91.

U.K. Statistical Bulletin. (1999). *Electro convulsive therapy: Survey covering the period from January 1999 to March 1999, England.* London: Department of Health.

U.S. Bureau of Labor Statistics. (2001). *Census of fatal occupational injuries.* Retrieved August 27, 2003, from http://www.bls.gov/iif/oshcfoi1.htm

U.S. Census Bureau. (2003). *Poverty in the United States, 2002.* Washington, DC: U.S. Government Printing Office.

U.S Department of Health and Human Services. (2001). *Alzheimer's disease fact sheet.* Washington, DC: U.S. Public Health Service (NIH Publication No. 01–3431).

U.S. Department of Health and Human Services. (2001a). *Mental health: Culture, race, and ethnicity. A supplement to mental health: A report of the Surgeon General.* Washington, DC: United States Public Health Service.

U.S. Department of Health and Human Services. (2001b). *Women and smoking: A report of the Surgeon General.* Atlanta: Centers for Disease Control and Prevention.

U.S. Department of Justice. (1998). *Alcohol and crime: An analysis of national data on the prevalence of alcohol involved in crime.* Washington, DC: Author.

U.S. Department of Justice. (1999). *Eyewitness evidence: A guide for law enforcement.* Washington, DC: National Institute of Justice.

U.S. Department of Justice. (2002a). *Bureau of Justice statistics.* Washington, DC: United States Government.

U.S. Department of Justice. (2002b). *Recidivism of prisoners released in 1994*. Washington, DC: U.S. Department of Justice, Bureau of Justice Statistics.

U.S. Department of Labor. (2001–2002). *Occupational Outlook Quarterly Winter 2001–2002, 45*(4). Washington, DC: U.S. Government Printing Office.

U.S. Surgeon General. (1999). *Mental health: A report of the surgeon general*. Rockville, MD: U.S. Department of Health and Human Services.

Uchida, Y., Kitayama, S., Mesquita, B., & Reyes, J. A. (2001, June). *Interpersonal sources of happiness: The relative significance in Japan, the Philippines, and the United States*. Paper presented at Annual Convention of American Psychological Society, Toronto, Canada.

Uchino, B. N., Cacioppo, J. T., & Kiecolt-Glaser, J. K. (1996). The relationship between social support and physiological process: A review with emphasis on underlying mechanisms and implications for health. *Psychological Bulletin, 119*, 488–531.

Uhl, G. R., Sora, I., & Wang, Z. (1999). The mu opiate receptor as a candidate gene for pain: polymorphisms, variations in expression, nociception, and opiate responses. *Proceedings of the National Academy of Sciences, 96*, 7752–7755.

Ulett, G. A. (2003). Acupuncture, magic, and make-believe. *The Skeptical Inquirer, 27*(2), 47–50.

Ulrich, W. L., Richards, P. S., & Bergin, A. E. (2000). Psychotherapy with Latter-Day Saints. In P. S. Richards & A. E. Bergin (Eds.), *Handbook of psychotherapy and religious diversity* (pp. 185–209). Washington DC: American Psychological Association.

Ungless, M. A., Whistler, J. L., Malenka, R. C., & Bonci, A. (2001). Single cocaine exposure in vivo induces long-term potentiation in dopamine neurons. *Nature, 411*, 583–587.

Uniform guidelines on employee selection procedures. (1978, August 25). *Federal Register, 43*, Section 60–3, 38295.

Valent, F., Brusaferro, S., & Barbone, F. (2001). A case-crossover study of sleep and childhood injury. *Pediatrics, 107*, e23.

Valenza, E., Simion, F., Assia, V. M., & Umilta, C. (1996). Face preference at birth. *Journal of Experimental Psychology: Human Perception and Performance, 22*, 892–903.

Van Ameringen, M. A., Lane, R. M., Walker, J. R., Bowen, R. C., Chokka, P. R., Goldner, E. M., et al. (2001). Sertraline treatment of generalized social phobia: A 20-week, double-blind, placebo-controlled study. *American Journal of Psychiatry, 158*, 275–281.

Van Bezooijen, R., Otto, S. A., & Heenan, T. A. (1983). Recognition of vocal expression of emotion: A three-nation study to identify universal characteristics. *Journal of Cross-Cultural Psychology, 14*, 387–406.

Van Eerde, W., & Thierry, H. (1996). Vrooms's expectancy models and work-related criteria: A meta-analysis. *Journal of Applied Psychology, 81*, 575–586.

van IJzendoorn, M. H. (1995). Adult attachment representations, parental responsiveness, and infant attachment: A meta-analysis on the predictive validity of the Adult Attachment Interview. *Psychological Bulletin, 117*, 387–403.

Van Sickel, A. D. (1992). Clinical hypnosis in the practice of anesthesia. *Nurse Anesthesiologist, 3*, 67–74.

van Wel, F., ter Bogt, T., & Raaijmakers, Q. (2002). Changes in the parental bond and the well-being of adolescents and young adults. *Adolescence, 37*(146), 317–333.

VandeCreek, L., Janus, M.-D., Pennebaker, J. W., & Binau, B. (2002). Praying about difficult experiences as self-disclosure to God. International Journal for the Psychology of Religion, 12, 29–39.

Vandello, J. A., & Cohen, D. (1999). Patterns of individualism and collectivism across the United States. *Journal of Personality and Social Psychology, 77*, 279–292.

Vastag, B. (2001). Brain gene for autism? *Journal of the American Medical Association, 285*, 23.

Vattano, F. (2000). *The mind: Video teaching modules* (2nd ed.). Fort Collins, CO: Colorado State University and Annenberg/CPB.

Vecera, S. P., Vogel, E. K., & Woodman, G. F. (2002). Lower region: A new cue for figure-ground assignment. *Journal of Experimental Psychology: General, 131*, 194–205.

Velligan, D. I., Bow-Thomas, C. C., Huntzinger, C., Ritch, J., Ledbetter, N., Prihoda, T. J., & Miller, A. L. (2000). Randomized controlled trial of the use of compensatory strategies to enhance adaptive functioning in outpatients with schizophrenia. *American Journal of Psychiatry, 157*, 1317–1328.

Venter, J. C., et al. (2001). The sequence of the human genome. *Science, 291*, 1304–1351.

Verghese, J., Lipton, R. B., Katz, M. J., Hall, C. B., Derby, C. A., Kuslansky, G., et al. (2003). Leisure activities and the risk of dementia in the elderly. *The New England Journal of Medicine, 348*, 2508–2516.

Vernacchio, L., Corwin, M. J., Lesko, S. M., Vezina, R. M., Hunt, C. E., Hoffman, H. J., et al. (2003). Sleep position of low birth weight infants. *Pediatrics, 111*, 633–640.

Vernet, M. E., Robin, O., & Dittmar, A. (1995). The ohmic perturbation duration, an original temporal index to quantify electrodermal responses. *Behavioural Brain Research, 67*(1), 103–107.

Vilaseca, I., Morello, A., Montserrat, J. M., Santamaria, J., & Iranzo, A. (2002). Usefulness of uvulopalatopharyngoplasty with genioglossus and hyoid advancement in the treatment of obstructive sleep apnea. *Archives of Otolaryngology and Head and Neck Surgery, 128*, 435–440.

Vincent, C. A., & Richardson, P. H. (1986). The evaluation of therapeutic acupuncture: Concepts and methods. *Pain, 24*, 1–13.

Vingerhoets, G., Berckmoes, C., & Stroobant, N. (2003). Cerebral hemodynamics during discrimination of prosodic and semantic emotion in speech studied by transcranial Doppler ultrasonography. *Neuropsychology, 17*, 93--99.

Vink, T., Hinney, A., van Elburg, A. A., van Goozen, S. H. M., Sandkuijl, L. A., Sinke, R. J., et al. (2001). Association between an agouti-related protein gene polymorphism and anorexia nervosa. *Molecular Psychiatry, 6*, 325–328.

Vioque, J., Torres, A., & Quiles, J. (2000). Time spent watching television, sleep duration, and obesity in adults living in Valencia, Spain. *International Journal of Obesity, 24*, 1683–1688.

Visser, P. S., Krosnick, J. A., & Lavrakas, P. J. (2000). Survey research. In H. T. Reis & C. Judd (Eds.), *Handbook of research methods in social and personality psychology* (pp. 223–252) Cambridge, UK: Cambridge University Press.

Viswesvaran, C., & Ones, D. S. (2000). Measurement error in "Big Five factors" personality assessment: Reliability generalization across studies and measures. *Educational & Psychological Measurement, 60*, 224–235.

Voelker, R. (1997). "Decent research and closure" needed on medical marijuana, says head of NIH panel. *Journal of the American Medical Association, 278*, 802.

Vokey, J. R., & Read, J. D. (1985). Subliminal messages: Between the devil and the media. *American Psychologist, 40*, 1231–1239.

Volavka, J., Czobor, P., Sheitman, B., Lindenmayer, J. P., Citrome, L., McEvoy, J. P., et al. (2002). Clozapine, olanzapine, risperidone, and haloperidol in the treatment of patients with chronic schizophrenia and schizoaffective disorder. *American Journal of Psychiatry, 159*, 255–262.

Volkow, N. D., Chang, L., Wang, G. J., Fowler, J. S., Franceschi, D., Sedler, M. J., et al. (2001). Higher cortical and lower subcortical metabolism in detoxified methamphetamine abusers. *American Journal of Psychiatry, 158*, 383–389.

Vollebergh, W. A. M., Iedema, J., Bijl, R. V., de Graaf, R., Smit, F., & Ormel, J. (2001). The structure and stability of common mental disorders: The NEMESIS study. *Archives of General Psychiatry, 58*, 597–603.

Volz, H. P., & Laux, P. (2000). Potential treatment for subthreshold and mild depression: A comparison of St. John's wort extracts and fluoxetine. *Comprehensive Psychiatry, 41*, 133–137.

Volz, J. (2000). Successful aging: The second 50. *APA Monitor, 31*, 24–28.

Von Wright, J. M., Anderson, K., & Stenman, U. (1975). Generalization of conditioned GSRs in dichotic listening. In P. M. A. Rabbitt & S. Dornic (Eds.), *Attention and performance V*. New York: Academic Press.

Voracek, M., & Fisher, M. L. (2002). Shapely centrefolds? Temporal change in body measures: trend analysis. *British Medical Journal, 325*, 1447–1448.

Vroom, V. (1964). *Work and motivation*. New York: Wiley.

Vygotsky, L. S. (1991). Genesis of the higher mental functions. In P. Light, S. Sheldon, & M. Woodhead (Eds.), *Learning to think: Child development in social context* (Vol. 2, pp. 32–41). London: Routledge.

Vyse, S. A. (2000). *Believing in magic: The psychology of superstition*. New York: Oxford University Press.

Waagenaar, W. (1986). My memory: A study of autobiographical memory over six years. *Cognitive Psychology, 18*, 225–252.

Wachtel, S. R., ElSohly, M. A., Ross, S. A., Ambre, J., & de Wit, H. (2002). Comparison of the subjective effects of Delta-sup-9-tetrahydrocannabinol and marijuana in humans. *Psychopharmacology, 161*, 331–339.

Wadden, T. A., Berkowitz, R. I., Sarwer, D. B., Prus-Wisniewski, R., & Steinberg, C. (2001). Benefits of lifestyle modification in the pharmacologic treatment of obesity: A randomized trial. *Archives of Internal Medicine, 161*, 218–227.

Wade, C. (1988, April). *Thinking critically about critical thinking in psychology*. Paper presented at the annual meeting of the Western Psychological Association, San Francisco, CA.

Wade, W. A., Treat, T. A., & Stuart, G. L. (1998). Transporting an empirically supported treatment for panic disorder to a service clinic setting: A benchmarking strategy. *Journal of Consulting & Clinical Psychology, 66,* 231–239.

Waelti, P., Dickinson, A., & Schultz, W. (2001). Dopamine responses comply with basic assumptions of formal learning theory. *Nature, 412,* 43–48.

Wagner, K.D., Ambrosini, P., Rynn, M., Wohlberg, C., Yang, R., Greenbaum, M.S., et al. (2003). Efficacy of sertraline in the treatment of children and adolescents with major depressive disorder: Two randomized controlled trials. *Journal of the American Medical Association, 290,* 1033–1041.

Wagner, U., Gais, S., & Born, J. (2001). Emotional memory formation is enhanced across sleep intervals with high amounts of rapid eye movement sleep. *Learning and Memory, 8,* 112–119.

Wakefield, J. C. (1999). Evolutionary versus prototype analyses of the concept of disorder. *Journal of Abnormal Psychology, 108,* 374–399.

Walbeck, K., Forsen, T., Osmond, C., Barker, D. J., & Ericksson, J. G. (2001). Association of schizophrenia with low maternal body mass index, small size at birth, and thinness during childhood. *Archives of General Psychiatry, 58,* 48–52.

Walberg, H. J. (1987). Studies show curricula efficiency can be attained. *NASSP Bulletin, 71,* 15–21.

Walker, E. F., & Diforio, D. (1998). Schizophrenia: A neural diathesis-stress model. *Psychological Review, 104,* 667–685.

Walker, L. (1991). The feminization of psychology. *Psychology of Women Newsletter of Division, 35,* 1, 4.

Walker, L. J. (1989). A longitudinal study of moral reasoning. *Child Development, 60,* 157–166.

Walker, L. J. (1995). Sexism in Kohlberg's moral psychology? In W. M. Kurtines & J. L. Gewirtz (Eds.), *Moral development: An introduction* (pp. 83–107). Boston: Allyn & Bacon.

Walkup, J. T., Labellarte, M. J., Riddle, M. A., Pine, D. S., Greenhill, L., Klein, R., et al. (2001). Fluvoxamine for the treatment of anxiety disorders in children and adolescents. *The New England Journal of Medicine, 344,* 1279–1285.

Wall, T. L., Shea, S. H., Chan, K. K., & Carr, L. G. (2001). A genetic association with the development of alcohol and other substance use behavior in Asian Americans. *Journal of Abnormal Psychology, 110,* 173–178.

Wallace, R. K., & Benson, H. (1972). The physiology of meditation. *Scientific American, 226,* 84–90.

Wallen, K., & Lovejoy, J. (1993). Sexual behavior: Endocrine function and therapy. In J. Shulkin (Ed.), *Hormonal pathways to mind and brain*. New York: Academic Press.

Wallerstein, R. S. (2002). The growth and transformation of American ego psychology. *Journal of the American Psychoanalytic Association, 50,* 135–169.

Wampold, B. E., Ahn, H. & Coleman, H. L. K. (2001). Medical model as metaphor: Old habits die hard. *Journal of Counseling Psychology, 48,* 263–273.

Wampold, B. E., Lichtenberg, J. W., & Waehler, C. A. (2002). Principles of empirically supported interventions in counseling psychology. *Counseling Psychologist, 30,* 197–217.

Wang, X., Merzenich, M. M., Sameshima, K., & Jenkins, W. M. (1995). Remodelling of hand representation in adult cortex determined by timing of tactile stimulation. *Nature, 378,* 71–75.

Warburton, D. M. (1995). Effects of caffeine on cognition and mood without caffeine abstinence. *Psychopharmacology, 119,* 66–70.

Ward, C. (1994). Culture and altered states of consciousness. In W. J. Lonner & R. S. Malpass (Eds.), *Psychology and culture*. Boston: Allyn & Bacon.

Ward, L. M. (1997). Involuntary listening aids hearing. *Psychological Science, 8,* 112–118.

Warner, L., Kessler, R., Hughes, M., Anthony, J., & Nelson, C. (1995). Prevalence and correlates of drug use and dependence in the United States. *Archives of General Psychiatry, 52,* 219–229.

Wasserman, E. M., & Lisanby, S. H. (2001). Therapeutic application of repetitive transcranial magnetic stimulation: A review. *Clinical Neurophysiology, 112,* 1367–1377.

Watanabe, S., Sakamoto, J., & Wakita, M. (1995). Pigeons' discrimination of paintings by Monet and Picasso. *Journal of Experimental Analysis of Behavior, 63,* 165–174.

Watanabe, T., Náñez, J. E., & Sasaki, Y. (2001). Perceptual learning without perception. *Nature, 413,* 844–848.

Watanabe, T., & Sugita, Y. (1998). REM sleep behavior disorder (RBD) and dissociated REM sleep. *Nippon Rinsho, 56*(2), 433–438.

Waterman, A. S. (1982). Identity development from adolescence to adulthood: An extension of theory and a review of research. *Developmental Psychology, 18,* 341–358.

Watkins, T., & Barres, B. (2002). Nerve regeneration: Regrowth stumped by shared receptor. *Current Biology, 12,* R654.

Watson, J. B. (1913). Psychology as the behaviorist views it. *Psychological Review, 20,* 158–177.

Watson, J. B. (1919). *Psychology from the standpoint of a behaviorist.* Philadelphia: Lippincott.

Watson, J. B. (1925). *Behaviorism.* London: Kegan Paul, Trench, Trubner.

Watt, N. F., & Saiz, C. (1991). Longitudinal studies of premorbid development of adult schizophrenics. In E. F. Walker (Ed.), *Schizophrenia: A life-course in developmental perspective* (pp. 157–192). San Diego: Academic Press.

Wearden, A. J., Tarrier, N., Barrowclough, C., Zastowny, T. R., & Rahill, A. A. (2000). A review of expressed emotion research in health care. *Clinical Psychology Review, 20,* 633–666.

Weber, R. J. (1992). *Forks, phonographs, and hot air balloons: A field guide to inventive thinking.* New York: Oxford University Press.

Wechsler, D. (1939). *The measurement of adult intelligence.* Baltimore: Williams & Wilkins.

Wechsler, D. (1949). *The Wechsler Intelligence Scale for Children.* New York: Psychological Corporation.

Weekes, J. R., Lynn, S. J., Green, J. P., & Brentar, J. T. (1992). Pseudomemory in hypnotized and task-motivated subjects. *Journal of Abnormal Psychology, 101,* 356–360.

Weeks, D., & Weeks, J. (1995). *Eccentrics: A study of sanity and strangeness.* New York: Villard.

Weiler, B. L., & Widom, C. S. (1996). Psychopathy and violent behavior in abused and neglected young adults. *Criminal Behaviour & Mental Health, 6,* 253–271.

Weinberg, R. A., Scarr, S., & Waldman, I. D. (1992). The Minnesota transracial adoption study: A follow-up of IQ test performance at adolescence. *Intelligence, 16,* 117–135.

Weiner, B. (1980). *Human motivation.* New York: Holt, Rinehart & Winston.

Weiner, B. (1993). On sin versus sickness: A theory of perceived responsibility and social motivation. *American Psychologist, 48*(9), 957–965.

Weinraub, M., Horvath, D. L., & Gringlas, M. B. (2002). Single parenthood. In M. H. Bornstein (Ed.), *Handbook of parenting: Vol. 3. Being and becoming a parent* (2nd ed., pp. 109–140). Mahwah, NJ: Erlbaum.

Weinstein, D. (1999, July 24). Who are you? *Sunday Telegraph Magazine,* 24–26.

Weiss, B., & Weisz, J. R. (1995). Relative effectiveness of behavioral versus nonbehavioral child psychotherapy. *Journal of Consulting and Clinical Psychology, 63,* 317–320.

Weiss, F., Ciccocioppo, R., Parsons, L. H., Katner, S., Liu, X., Zorrilla, E. P., et al. (2001). Compulsive drug-seeking behavior and relapse: Neuro-adaptation, stress, and conditioning factors. *Annals of the New York Academy of Science, 937,* 1–26.

Weiss, S., & Moore, M. (1990). Cultural differences in the perception of magazine alcohol advertisements by Israeli Jewish, Moslem, Druze, and Christian high school students. *Drug and Alcohol Dependence, 26,* 209–215.

Weissberg, R. P., Kumpfer, K. L., & Seligman, M. E. P. (2003). Prevention that works for children and youth. *American Psychologist, 58,* 425–432.

Weissman, M. M., Bland, R., Joyce, P. R., Newman, S., Wells, J. E., & Wittchen, H. U. (1993). Sex differences in rates of depression: Cross-national perspectives. *Journal of Affective Disorders, 29,* 77–84.

Weissman, M. M., Markowitz, J. C., & Klerman, G. L. (2000). *Comprehensive guide to interpersonal psychotherapy.* New York: Basic Books.

Weisz, J. R., & Jensen, P. S. (1999). Efficacy and effectiveness of psychotherapy and pharmacotherapy with children and adolescents. *Mental Health Services Research, 1,* 125–157.

Weisz, J. R., Weiss, B., Han, S. S., Granger, D. A., & Morton, T. (1995). Effects of psychotherapy with children and adolescents revisited: A meta-analysis of treatment outcome studies. *Psychological Bulletin, 117,* 450–468.

Wells, G. L., & Bradfield, A. L. (1999). Distortions in eyewitness' recollections: Can the postidentification-feedback effect be moderated? *Psychological Science, 10,* 138–144.

Wells, G. L., Malpass, R. S., Lindsay, R. C. L., Fisher, R. P., Turtle, J. W., & Fulero, S. M. (2000). From the lab to the police station: A successful application of eyewitness research. *American Psychologist, 55,* 581–598.

Wells, G. L., & Olson, E. A. (2003). Eyewitness testimony. *Annual Review of Psychology, 54,* 277–295.

Wells, G. L., Olson, E. A., & Charman, S. D. (2002). The confidence of eyewitnesses in their identifications from lineups. *Current Directions in Psychological Science, 11,* 151–154.

Wells, G. L., Olson, E. A., & Charman, S. D. (2003). Distorted retrospective eyewitness reports as functions of feedback and delay. *Journal of Experimental Psychology: Applied, 9,* 42–52.

Wells, S., Graham, K., & West, P. (2000). Alcohol-related aggression in the general population. *Journal of Studies on Alcohol, 61,* 626–632.

Weltzin, T. E., Bulik, C. M., McConaha, C. W., & Kaye, W. H. (1995). Laxative withdrawal and anxiety in bulimia nervosa. *International Journal of Eating Disorders, 17*(2), 141–146.

Werner, E. (2003, January 28). Police: Sons kill mom, dismember her after seeing it done on "The Sopranos." *Naples Daily News.*

Wertheimer, M. (1987). *A brief history of psychology* (3rd ed.). New York: Holt, Rinehart & Winston.

Wesnes, K. A., Ward, T., McGinty, A., & Petrini, O. (2000). The memory enhancing effects of a Ginkgo biloba/Panax ginseng combination in healthy middle-aged volunteers. *Psychopharmacology (Berl), 152,* 353–361.

West, M. A., Borrill, C. S., & Unsworth, K. L. (1998). Team effectiveness in organizations. In C. L. Cooper & I. T. Robertson (Eds.), *International review of industrial and organizational psychology 1998* (pp. 1–48). Chichester, UK: Wiley.

Westen, D. (1998). The scientific legacy of Sigmund Freud: Toward a psychodynamically informed psychological science. *Psychological Bulletin, 124,* 333–371.

Westen, D., & Gabbard, G. O. (1999). Psychoanalytic approaches to personality. In L. Pervin & O. John (Eds), *Handbook of personality: Theory and research* (2nd ed., pp. 57–101). New York: Guilford.

Westen, D., & Morrison, K. (2001). A multidimensional meta-analysis of treatments for depression, panic, and generalized anxiety disorder: An empirical examination of the status of empirically supported therapies. *Journal of Consulting & Clinical Psychology, 69,* 875–899.

Weston, C., & Went, F. (1999). Speaking up for yourself: Description and evaluation of an assertiveness training program for people with learning disabilities. *Mental Handicap, 27,* 110–115.

Whalen, P. J. (1998). Fear, vigilance, and ambiguity: Initial neuroimaging studies of the human amygdala. *Current Directions in Psychological Science, 7,* 177–188.

Whaley, A. L. (2001). Cultural mistrust: An important psychological construct for diagnosis and treatment of African-Americans. *Professional Psychology: Research and Practice, 32,* 555–562.

Whalley, L. J., & Deary, I. J. (2001). Longitudinal cohort study of childhood IQ up to age 76. *British Medical Journal, 322,* 819.

Wharton, C. M., Grafman, J., Flitman, S. S., Hansen, E. K., Brauner, J., Marks, A., & Honda, M. (2000). Toward neuroanatomical models of analogy: A positron emission tomography study of analogical mapping. *Cognitive Psychology, 40,* 173–197.

Whimbey, A. (1976). *Intelligence can be taught.* New York: Bantam.

Whisman, M. A. (1999). Marital dissatisfaction and psychiatric disorders: Results from a national comorbidity study. *Journal of Abnormal Psychology, 108,* 701–706.

Whitam, F. L., Diamond, M., & Martin, J. (1993). Homosexual orientation in twins: A report on 61 pairs and three triplet sets. *Archives of Sexual Behavior, 22*(3), 187–206.

White, A. T., & Spector, P. E. (1987). An investigation of age-related factors in the age-job satisfaction relationship. *Psychology and Aging, 2,* 261–265.

White, F. J. (1998). Nicotine addiction and the lure of reward. *Nature Medicine, 4,* 659–660.

White, H. R., Pandina, R. J., & Chen, P. H. (2002). Developmental trajectories of cigarette use from early adolescence into young adulthood. *Drug & Alcohol Dependence, 65*(2), 167–178.

Whitney, P. (2001). Schemas, frames, and scripts in cognitive psychology. In N. J. Smelser & P. B. Baltes (Eds.), *International encyclopedia of the social and behavioral sciences.* The Netherlands: Elsevier.

Wickens, C. D. (1989). Attention and skilled performance. In D. Holding (Ed.), *Human skills* (pp. 71–105). New York: Wiley.

Wickens, C. D. (1992). *Engineering psychology and human performance* (2nd ed.) New York: HarperCollins.

Wickens, C. D. (2002). Situation awareness and workload in aviation. *Current Directions in Psychological Science, 11,* 128–133.

Wickens, C. D., & Carswell, C. M. (1997). Information processing. In G. Salvendy (Ed.), *Handbook of human factors and ergonomics* (2nd ed., pp. 89–122). New York: Wiley Interscience.

Wickens, C. D., Gordon, S. E., & Liu, Y. (1998). *An introduction to human factors engineering.* New York: Longman.

Wickens, C. D., Stokes, A., Barnett, B., & Hyman, F. (1992). The effects of stress on pilot judgment in a MIDIS simulator. In O. Svenson & J. Maule (Eds.), *Time pressure and stress in human judgment and decision making.* New York: Plenum.

Wickham, D. (2001, September 3). Castration often fails to halt offenders. *USA Today.*

Widiger, T. A. (1997). The construct of mental disorder. *Clinical Psychology: Science and Practice, 4,* 262–266.

Widiger, T. A., & Clark, L. A. (2000). Toward *DSM-V* and the classification of psychopathology. *Psychological Bulletin, 126,* 946–963.

Widiger, T. A., & Sanderson, C. J. (1995). Assessing personality disorders. In J. N. Butcher (Ed.), *Clinical personality assessment: Practical approaches* (pp. 380–394). New York: Oxford University Press.

Widiger, T. A., & Sankis, L. M. (2000). Adult psychopathology: Issues and controversies. *Annual Review of Psychology, 51,* 377–404.

Widom, C. S. (1989) The cycle of violence. *Science, 244,* 160–166.

Widom, C. S. (2000). *Childhood victimization: Early adversity, later psychopathology.* Washington, DC: National Institute of Justice Journal.

Wiens, S., Mezzacappa, E. S., & Katkin, E. S. (2000). Heartbeat detection and the experience of emotions. *Cognition & Emotion, 14,* 417–427.

Wiesner, W. H., & Cronshaw, S. F. (1988). A meta-analytic investigation of the impact of interview format and degree of structure on the validity of the employment interview. *Journal of Occupational Psychology, 61,* 275–290.

Wigfield, A., & Eccles, J. S. (2000). Expectancy-value theory of achievement motivation. *Contemporary Educational Psychology, 25,* 68–81.

Willams, R. B. (2001). Hostility and heart disease: Williams et al. (1980). *Advances in Mind-Body Medicine, 17,* 52–55.

Williams, J. E., & Best, D. L. (1990). *Measuring stereotypes: A multination study* (Rev. ed.). Newbury Park, CA: Sage.

Williams, K. D., & Sommer, K. L. (1997). Social ostracism by coworkers: Does rejection lead to loafing or compensation? *Personality and Social Psychology Bulletin, 23,* 693–706.

Williams, L. M. (1994). What does it mean to forget child sexual abuse? A reply to Loftus, Garry, and Feldman (1994). *Journal of Consulting and Clinical Psychology, 62,* 1182–1186.

Williams, S. (2000). What does it pay to be a psychologist? *Monitor on Psychology, 31,* 13.

Williams, T. J., Pepitone, M. E., Christensen, S. E., Cooke, B. M., Huberman, A. D., Breedlove, N. J., et al. (2000). Finger-length ratios and sexual orientation. *Nature, 404,* 455–456.

Willis, S. L., & Schaie, K. W. (1999). Intellectual functioning in midlife. In S. L. Willis & J. D. Reid (Eds.), *Life in the middle: Psychological and social development in middle age.* San Diego: Academic Press.

Wilson, G. T. (1985). Limitations of meta-analysis in the evaluation of the effects of psychological therapy. *Clinical Psychology Review, 5,* 35–47.

Wilson, G. T. (1995). Behavior therapy. In R. J. Corsini & D. Wedding (Eds.), *Current psychotherapies* (5th ed., pp. 197–228). Itasca, IL: Peacock.

Wilson, G. T. (1997). Dissemination of cognitive behavioral treatments: Commentary. *Behavior Therapy, 28,* 473–475.

Wilson, G. T., Loeb, K. L., Walsh, B. T., Labouvie, E., Petkova, E., Liu, X., & Waternaux, C. (1999). Psychological versus pharmacological treatments of bulimia nervosa: Predictors and processes of change. *Journal of Consulting and Clinical Psychology, 67,* 451–459.

Wilson, G. T., Nathan, P. E., O'Leary, K. D., & Clark, L. A. (1996). *Abnormal psychology.* Boston: Allyn & Bacon.

Wilson, R. S., Beckett, L. A., Barnes, L. L., Schneider, J. A., et al. (2002). Individual differences in rates of change in cognitive abilities of older persons. *Psychology & Aging, 17*(2), 179–193.

Wilson, R. S., Mendes de Leon, C. F., Barnes, L. L., Schneider, J. A., Bienias, J. L., Evans, D. A., & Bennett, D. A. (2002). Participation in cognitively stimulating activities and risk of incident Alzheimer disease. *Journal of the American Medical Association, 287,* 742–748.

Wilson, W. J. (1997). *When work disappears: The world of the new urban poor.* New York: Vintage Books.

Winer, G. A., Cottrell, J. E., Gregg, V., Fournier, J. S., & Bica, L. A. (2002). Fundamentally misunderstanding visual perception: Adults' belief in visual emissions. *American Psychologist, 57,* 417–424.

Winkielman, P., Bernston, G. G., & Cacioppo, J. T. (2001). The psychophysiological perspective on the social mind. In A. Tesser & N. Schwarz (Eds.), *Blackwell handbook of social psychology: Intraindividual processes* (pp. 89–109). Oxford, England: Blackwell.

Winn, P. (1995). The lateral hypothalamus and motivated behavior: An old syndrome reassessed and a new perspective gained. *Current Directions in Psychological Science, 4,* 182–187.

Winner, E. (2000). Giftedness: Current theory and research. *Current Directions in Psychological Science, 9,* 153–156.

Winson, J. (1990, November). The meaning of dreams. *Scientific American,* pp. 86–96.

Winter, D. G. (1996). *Personality: Analysis and interpretation of lives.* New York: McGraw-Hill.

Wisborg, K., Kesmodel, U., Bech, B. H., Hedegaard, M., & Henriksen, T. B. (2003). Maternal consumption of coffee during pregnancy and stillbirth and infant death in first year of life: Prospective study. *British Medical Journal, 326,* 420.

Wise, R. A. (1998). Drug-activation of brain reward pathways. *Drug & Alcohol Dependence, 51,* 13–22.

Wiseman, R., West, D., & Stemman, R. (1996, January/February). Psychic crime detectives: A new test for measuring their successes and failures. *Skeptical Inquirer, 21,* 38–58.

Witt, L. A., & Ferris, G. R. (2003). Social skills as a moderator of the conscientiousness-performance relationship: Convergent results across four studies. *Journal of Applied Psychology, 88,* 809–821.

Witt, L. A., & Nye, L. G. (1992). Gender and the relationship between perceived fairness of pay or promotion and job satisfaction. *Journal of Applied Psychology, 77,* 910–917.

Witt, S. D. (1997). Parental influence on children's socialization to gender roles. *Adolescence, 32,* 253–259.

Wittchen, H-U., & Hoyer, J. (2001). Generalized anxiety disorder: Nature and course. *Journal of Clinical Psychiatry, 62,* 15–19.

Wittchen, H. U., Zhao, S., Kessler, R. C., & Eaton, W. W. (1994). *DSM-III-R:* Generalized anxiety disorder in the national comorbidity survey. *Archives of General Psychiatry, 51,* 355–364.

Wittenbaum, G. M., & Stasser, G. (1996). Management of information in small groups. In J. L. Nye & A. M. Brower (Eds.), *What's social about cognition? Social cognition in small groups* (pp. 3–28). Newbury Park, CA: Sage.

Woehr, D. J., & Arthur, W., Jr. (2003). The construct-related validity of assessment center ratings: A review and meta-analysis of the role of methodological factors. *Journal of Management, 29,* 231–258.

Woelk, H. (2000). Comparison of St. John's wort and imipramine for treating depression: Randomised controlled trial. *British Medical Journal, 321,* 536–539.

Wolpe, J. (1958). *Psychotherapy by reciprocal inhibition.* Stanford, CA: Stanford University Press.

Wong, M. M., & Csikszentmihalyi, M. (1992). *Journal of Personality and Social Psychology, 60,* 154–164.

Wood, J. M., Nezworski, M. T., Lilienfeld, S. O., & Garb, H. N. (2003). *What's wrong with the Rorschach: Science confronts the controversial inkblot test.* New York: Jossey-Bass.

Wood, J. V., Michela, J. L., & Giordano, C. (2000). Downward comparison in everyday life: Reconciling self-enhancement models with the mood–cognition priming model. *Journal of Personality and Social Psychology, 79,* 563–579.

Wood, W. (2000). Attitude change: Persuasion and social influence. *Annual Review of Psychology, 51,* 539–570.

Wood, W., & Eagly, A. H. (2002). A cross-cultural analysis of the behavior of women and men: Implications for the origins of sex differences. *Psychological Bulletin, 128,* 699–727.

Wood, W., Wong, F. Y., & Chachere, G. (1991). Effects of media violence on viewers' aggression in unconstrained social interaction. *Psychological Bulletin, 109,* 371–383.

Woodbury, D., Schwarz, E. J., Prockop, D. J., & Black, I. B. (2000). Adult rat and human bone marrow stromal cells differentiate into neurons. *Journal of Neuroscience Research, 61,* 364–370.

Woods, S. C., Schwartz, M. W., Baskin, D. G., & Seeley, R. J. (2000). Food intake and the regulation of body weight. *Annual Review of Psychology, 51,* 255–277.

Woods, S. C., Seeley, R. J., Porte, D., Jr., & Schwartz, M. W. (1998). Signals that regulate food intake and energy homeostasis. *Science, 280,* 1378–1383.

Woodworth, R. S., & Schlosberg, H. (1954). *Experimental psychology.* New York: Holt.

Woolfolk-Hoy, A. (1999). Psychology applied to education. In A. Stec & D. Bernstein (Eds.), *Psychology: Fields of application.* Boston: Houghton Mifflin.

Woolley, J. D. (1997). Thinking about fantasy: Are children fundamentally different thinkers and believers from adults? *Child Development, 68,* 991–1011.

Worchel, S., Cooper, J., Goethals, G. R., & Olson, J. (2000). *Social psychology.* Belmont, CA: Wadsworth.

World Health Organization. (1998). *Communicable disease surveillance and response.* Geneva, Switzerland: Author.

World Health Organization. (2002a). *Nutrition: Controlling the global obesity epidemic.* Retrieved August 27, 2003, from http:www.who.int/nut/obs.htm

World Health Organization. (2002b). *WHO collaborative project on psychological problems in general health care.* Retrieved August 27, 2003, from http://www.who.int/msa/mnh/ems/primacare/ppghc/ppghc.htm

Worthington, J. J., III, Pollack, M. H., Otto, M. W., McLean, R. Y., Moroz, G., & Rosenbaum, J. F. (1998). Long-term experience with clonazepam in patients with a primary diagnosis of panic disorder. *Psychopharmacology Bulletin, 34,* 199–205.

Wren, C. S. (1998, September 22). For crack babies, a future less bleak. *New York Times.* Retrieved August 27, 2003, from http://query.nytimes.com/gst/abstract.html?res=F40715FA3B540C718EDDA00894D0494D81

Wren, C. S. (1999, February 24). U.N. drug board urges research on marijuana as medicine. *New York Times.* Retrieved August 27, 2003, from http://query.nytimes.com/gst/abstract.html?res=F10A13F83A590C778EDDAB0894D1494D81

Wright, E. F., Voyer, D., Wright, R. D., & Roney, C. (1995). Supporting audiences and performance under pressure: The home-ice disadvantage in hockey championships. *Journal of Sport Behavior, 18,* 21–28.

Wright, G. N., & Phillips, L. D. (1980). Cultural variation in probabilistic thinking: Alternative ways of dealing with uncertainty. *International Journal of Psychology, 15,* 239–257.

Wu, H. W., Cacioppo, J. T., Glaser, R., Kiecolt-Glaser, J. K., & Malarkey, W. B. (1999). Chronic stress associated with spousal caregiving of patients with Alzheimer's dementia is associated with downregulation of B-lymphocyte GH mRNA. *Journals of Gerontology, 54A,* M212–M215.

Wurtman, R. J., & Wurtman, J. J. (1995). Brain serotonin, carbohydrate-craving, obesity and depression. *Obesity Research, 3*(Suppl. 4), 477S–480S.

Yakimovich, D., & Saltz, E. (1971). Helping behavior: The cry for help. *Psychonomic Science, 23,* 427–428.

Yalom, I. D. (1995). Stimulus-driven attentional capture. *Current Directions in Psychological Science, 2,* 156–161.

Yang, C-M. & Spielman, A. J. (2001). The effect of delayed weekend sleep pattern on sleep and morning functioning. *Psychology and Health, 16,* 715–725.

Yang, S-Y., & Sternberg, Robert J. (1997). Taiwanese Chinese people's conceptions of intelligence. *Intelligence, 25,* 21–36.

Yantis, S. (1993). Stimulus-driven attentional capture. *Current Directions in Psychological Science, 2,* 156–161.

Yates, J. F., Lee, J. W., & Shinotsuka, H. (1992). *Cross-national variation in probability judgment.* Paper presented at the 33rd annual meeting of the Psychonomic Society, St. Louis.

Yates, J. F., Zhu, Y., Ronis, D. L., Wang, D. F., Shinotsuka, H., & Masanao, T. (1989). Probability judgment accuracy: China, Japan, and the United States. *Organizational Behavior and Human Decision Processes, 43,* 145–171.

Yates, W. R. (2000). Testosterone in psychiatry. *Archives of General Psychiatry, 57,* 155–156.

Yearta, S. K., Maitlis, S., & Briner, R. B. (1995). An exploratory study of goal setting in theory and practice: A motivational technique that works? *Journal of Occupational and Organizational Psychology, 68,* 237–252.

Yela, C., & Sangrador, J. L. (2001). Perception of physical attractiveness throughout loving relationships. *Current Research in Social Psychology, 6,* 57–75.

Yerkes, R. M. (Ed.). (1921). Psychological examining in the U.S. Army. *Memoirs of the National Academy of Sciences,* No. 15.

Yesavage, J. A., Leirer, V. O., Denari, M., & Hollister, L. E. (1985). Carry-over effects of marijuana intoxication on aircraft pilot performance: A preliminary report. *American Journal of Psychiatry, 142,* 1325–1329.

York, J. L., & Welte, J. W. (1994). Gender comparisons of alcohol consumption in alcoholic and nonalcoholic populations. *Journal of Studies on Alcohol, 55*(6), 743–750.

Yoshimasu, K., Washio, M., Tokunaga, S., Tanaka, K., Liu, Y., Kodama, H., et al. (2002). Relation between Type A behavior pattern and the extent of coronary atherosclerosis in Japanese women. *International Journal of Behavioral Medicine, 9,* 77–93.

Youm, Y., & Laumann, E. O. (2002). Social network effects on the transmission of sexually transmitted diseases. *Sexually Transmitted Diseases, 29,* 689–697.

Young, A. W., Aggleton, J. P., Hellawell, D. J., & Johnson, M. (1995). Face processing impairments after amygdalotomy. *Brain, 118*(1), 15–24.

Young, M. E. (1995). On the origin of causal theories. *Psychonomic Bulletin & Review, 2,* 83–104.

Yousif, Y., & Korte, C. (1995). Urbanization, culture, and helpfulness: Cross-cultural studies in England and the Sudan. *Journal of Cross-Cultural Psychology, 26,* 474–489.

Yukl, G., & Van Fleet, D. D. (1992). Theory and research on leadership in organizations. In M. D. Dunnette & L. M. Hough (Eds.), *Handbook of industrial and organizational psychology* (Vol. 3, 2nd ed., pp. 147–198). Palo Alto, CA: Consulting Psychologists Press.

Zadnik, K. (2001). Association between night lights and myopia: True blue or a red herring? *Archives of Ophthalmology, 119,* 146.

Zadra, A., & Donderi, D. C. (2000). Nightmares and bad dreams: Their prevalence and relationship to well-being. *Journal of Abnormal Psychology, 109,* 273–281.

Zahn-Waxler, C., Radke-Yarrow, E., Wagner, E., & Chapman, M. (1992). Development of concern for others. *Developmental Psychology, 28,* 1038–1047.

Zahrani, S. S., & Kaplowitz, S. A. (1993). Attributional biases in individualistic and collectivist cultures: A comparison of Americans with Saudis. *Social Psychology Quarterly, 56*(3), 223–233.

Zajonc, R. B. (1965). Social facilitation. *Science, 149,* 269–274.

Zajonc, R. B. (1998). Emotions. In D. Gilbert, S. T. Fiske, & G. Lindzey (Eds.), *Handbook of social psychology* (Vol. 1, 4th ed., pp. 591–634). Boston: McGraw-Hill.

Zajonc, R. B. (2001). Mere exposure: A gateway to the subliminal. *Current Directions in Psychological Science, 10,* 224–228.

Zald, D. H., & Pardo, J. V. (1997). Emotion, olfaction, and the human amygdala: Amygdala activation during aversive olfactory stimulation. *Proceedings of the National Academy of Sciences of the United States of America, 94*(8), 4119–4124.

Zambelis, T., Paparrigopoulos, T., & Soldatos, C. R. (2002). REM sleep behaviour disorder associated with a neurinoma of the left pontocerebral angle. *Journal of Neurology, Neurosurgery, and Psychiatry, 72,* 821–822.

Zammit, S., Allebeck, P., Andreasson, S., Lundberg, I., & Lewis, G. (2002). Self reported cannabis use as a risk factor for schizophrenia in Swedish conscripts of 1969: Historical cohort study. *British Medical Journal, 325,* 1199.

Zanarini, M. C., Skodol, A. E., Bender, D., Dolan, R., Sanislow, C., Schaefer, E., et al. (2000). The collaborative longitudinal personality disorders study: Reliability of axis I and II diagnoses. *Journal of Personality Disorders, 14,* 291–299.

Zaragoza, M. S., Payment, K. E., Ackil, J. K., Drivdahl, S. B., & Beck, M. (2001). Interviewing witnesses: Forced confabulation and confirmatory feedback increase false memories. *Psychological Science, 12,* 473–477.

Zelenski, J. M., & Larsen, R. J. (1999). Susceptibility to affect: A comparison of three taxonomies. *Journal of Personality, 67,* 761–791.

Zeman, A. (2001). Consciousness. *Brain, 124,* 1263–1289.

Zhang, Y., Hoon, M. A., Chandrashekar, J., Mueller, K. L., Cook, B., Wu, D., et al. (2003). Coding of sweet, bitter, and umami tastes: Different receptor cells sharing similar signaling pathways. *Cell, 112,* 293–301.

Zhao, M., Momma, S., Delfani, K., Carlen, M., Cassidy, R. M., Johansson, C. B., et al. (2003). Evidence for neurogenesis in the adult mammalian substantia nigra. *Proceedings of the National Academy of Sciences, 100,* 7925–7930.

Zhou, J.-N., Hofman, M. A., Gooren, L. J. G., & Swaab, D. F. (1995). A sex difference in the human brain and its relation to transsexuality. *Nature, 378,* 68–70.

Zhou, L., Yang, W., Liao, S., & Zou, H. (2000). A comparative study of event-related potentials between simulated crime condition and criminal field visiting condition in lie detection. *Chinese Journal of Clinical Psychology, 8,* 86–88.

Zigler, E., & Seitz, V. (1982). Social policy and intelligence. In R. J. Sternberg (Ed.), *Handbook of human intelligence* (pp. 586–641). Cambridge, England: Cambridge University Press.

Zigler, E., Taussig, C., & Black, K. (1992). Early childhood intervention: A promising preventive for juvenile delinquency. *American Psychologist, 47,* 997–1006.

Zillmann, D. (1984). *Connections between sexuality and aggression.* Hillsdale, NJ: Erlbaum.

Zillmann, D. (1998). *Connections between sexuality and aggression* (2nd ed.). Hillsdale, NJ: Erlbaum.

Zillmann, D., Katcher, A. H., & Milavsky, B. (1972). Excitation transfer from physical exercise to subsequent aggressive behavior. *Journal of Experimental Social Psychology, 8,* 247–259.

Zimbardo, P. G. (1973). The psychological power and pathology of imprisonment. In E. Aronson & R. Helmreich (Eds.), *Social psychology.* New York: Van Nostrand.

Zimmerman, M., McDermut, W., & Mattia, J. I. (2000). Frequency of anxiety disorders in psychiatric outpatients with major depressive disorder. *American Journal of Psychiatry, 157,* 1337–1340.

Zinbarg, R. E., & Barlow, D. H. (1996). Structure of anxiety and the anxiety disorders: A hierarchical model. *Journal of Abnormal Psychology, 105,* 181–193.

Zoellner, L. A., Foa, E. B., Brigidi, B. D., & Przeworski, A. (2000). Are trauma victims susceptible to "false memories"? *Journal of Abnormal Psychology, 109,* 517–524.

Zorumski, C., & Isenberg, K. (1991). Insights into the structure and function of GABA-benzodiazepine receptors: Ion channels and psychiatry. *American Journal of Psychiatry, 148,* 162–173.

Zsambok, C. E., & Klein, G. (1997). *Naturalistic decision making.* Hillsdale, NJ: Erlbaum.

Zubin, J., & Spring, B. (1977). Vulnerability—A new view of schizophrenia. *Journal of Abnormal Psychology, 86,* 103–126.

Zucker, A. N., Ostrove, J. M., & Stewart, A. J. (2002). College-educated women's personality development in adulthood: Perceptions and age differences. *Psychology & Aging, 17*(2), 236–244.

Zuckerman, M. (1984). Sensation seeking: A comparative approach to a human approach. *The Behavioral and Brain Sciences, 7,* 413–471.

Zuckerman, M. (1990). Some dubious premises in research and theory on racial differences. *American Psychologist, 45,* 1297–1303.

Zuckerman, M. (1993). Out of sensory deprivation and into sensation seeking: A personal and scientific journey. In G. G. Brannigan & M. R. Merrens (Eds.), *The undaunted psychologist: Adventures in research* (pp. 45–57). Philadelphia: Temple University Press.

Zuckerman, M. (1996). "Conceptual clarification" or confusion in "The study of sensation seeking" by J. S. H. Jackson and M. Maraun. *Personality and Individual Differences, 21,* 111–114.

Zuckerman, M. (1999). *Vulnerability to psychopathology: A biosocial model.* Washington, DC: American Psychological Association.

Zuger, A. (1998, July 28). A fistful of aggression is found among women. *New York Times,* pp. B8, B12.

Zungu-Dirwayi, N., Hugo, F., van Heerden, B. B., & Stein, D. J. (1999). Are musical obsessions a temporal lobe phenomenon? *Journal of Neuropsychiatry & Clinical Neurosciences, 11,* 398–400.

CREDITS

TEXT CREDITS

Chapter 1 **p. 4** *Figure 1.1* From *American Journal of Psychology*. Copyright © 1961 by the Board and Trustees of the University of Illinois. Used with permission of the University of Illinois Press. **p. 5** *Figure 1.2* From *Social and Personality Development* by David R. Shaffer. Copyright © 1973. Reprinted by permission of Wadsworth, a division of Thomson Publishing.

Chapter 2 **p. 65** *Figure 2.10* From *The Cerebral Cortex of Man: A Clinical Study of Localization Function* by Penfield & Rasmussen, © 1968 Gale Group. Reprinted by permission of The Gale Group. **p. 71** *Figure 2.13* Reprinted by permission of the publisher from *The Postnatal Development of the Human Cerebral Cortex*, Volume I-VIII by Jesse LeRoy Conel, Cambridge, MA: Harvard University Press, Copyright © 1939, 1975 by the President and Fellows of Harvard College.

Chapter 3 **p. 105** *Figure 3.18* From *Perplexing Puzzles and Tantalizing Teasers* (p. 75), by Martin Gardner, 1988, New York: Dover. **p. 114** *Figure 3.25* W. Hudson, "Pictorial Depth in Perception in Subcultural Groups in Africa," *Journal of Social Psychology, 52,* 183–208. Reprinted by permission of the University of Illinois Press. **p. 117** *Figure 3.29* From *Physiology and Behavior* by Johnson et al., Vol. 50, pp. 1245–1251. Copyright © 1991 by Elsevier with permission from Elsevier.

Chapter 4 **p. 132** *Figure 4.2* From D. L. Schacter, L. A. Cooper, S. M. Delaney, M. A. Peterson, and M. Tharan's article, "Implicit Memory for Possible and Impossible Objects: Constraints on the Construction of Structural Descriptions," (1991) from *Journal of Experimental Psychology: Learning, Memory, and Cognition, 17,* 3–19. Copyright © 1991 by the American Psychological Association. Reprinted with permission. **p. 138** *Figure 4.3* Horne, J. A., *Why We Sleep: The Functions of Sleep in Human and Other Mammals.* Copyright © 1988 James Horne. Reprinted by permission of Oxford University Press. **p. 139** *Figure 4.4* Adapted by permission of the author from *A Primer of Sleep and Dreaming* by Rosalind Cartwright. **p. 144** *Figure 4.6* Reprinted by permission of the author from *Hypnotic Age Susceptibility* by Ernest R. Hilgard. Copyright © 1965. Published by Harcourt, Brace, Jovanovich, Inc. **p. 144** *Figure 4.7* From E. R. Hilgard, *Divided Consciousness: Multiple Controls in Human Thought and Action.* Copyright © 1977. Reprinted by permission of John Wiley & Sons, Inc.

Chapter 5 **p. 173** *Figure 5.8* From *The Psychology of Learning and Memory* by Hintzman. Copyright © 1978 W. H. Freeman and Company. Used with permission of the author. **p. 176** *Figure 5.10* Adapted with permission from Teaching Machines, by B.F. Skinner. Copyright © 1961. **p. 186** *Figure 5.15* From Bandura, A., Ross, et al. (1963), "Imitation of film-mediated aggressive models." *Journal of Abnormal and Social Psychology, 66,* 3–11. Reprinted by permission of the American Psychological Association.

Chapter 6 **p. 204** *Figure 6.3* From *Cognitive Psychology: Memory, Language, and Thought* by Darlene V. Howard. © 1983 by Darlene V. Howard. Reprinted by permission of the author. **p. 206** *Figure 6.5* Figure from, "Long-Term Memory for a Common Object," by R. S. Nickerson and M. J. Adams from *Cognitive Psychology,* Volume 11, 287–307. Copyright © 1979 by Academic Press, reproduced by permission of the publisher. **p. 219** *Figure 6.12* Tulvin and Psotka, "Retroactive Inhibition in Free Recall: Inaccessibility of Information Available in the Memory Store," *Journal of Experimental Psychology*, 87, p. 1–8, 1971. Copyright © 1971 by the American Psychological Association. Reprinted with permission.

Chapter 7 **p. 240** *Figure 7.4* Shepard, R. N., & Metzler, J. (1971). "Mental rotation of three-dimensional objects. *Science*, 171, 701–703. Reprinted with permission from American Association for the Advancement of Science. **p. 262** *Figure 7.9* Simulated items similar to those in the Wechsler Intelligence Scales for Adults and Children. Copyright © 1949, 1955, 1974, 1981, 1991 by The Psychological Corpora-

tion, a Harcourt Assessment Company. Reproduced by permission. All rights reserved. **p. 273** *Figure 7.14* Reprinted with permission from Robert J. Sternberg, "Testing for Practical and Creative Intelligence," *New York Times,* November 8, 1997.

Chapter 8 **p. 287** *Figure 8.2* Adapted with permission from Schwartz, M. W., Woods, S. C., Porte Jr., D., Seeley, R. J., & Baskin, D. G. (2000). Central nervous system control of food intake, *Nature* 404, 661–671. **p. 294** *Figure 8.3* Adapted from W. H. Masters and V. E. Johnson, *Human Sexual Response,* p. 5 (Boston: Little, Brown & Company, 1966). Reprinted by permission from Masters and Johnson Institute. **p. 310** *Figure 8.9* From "Voluntary Facial Action Generates Emotion-Specific Autonomic Nervous System Activity," by R. W. Levenson, P. Ekman, and W. V. Friesen, *Psychophysiology*, 1990, 24, 363–384. Copyright © 1990 the Society for Psychophysiological Research. Reprinted with permission.

Chapter 9 **p. 335** *Figure 9.5* Baillargeon, R., "A model of physical reasoning in infancy." From C. Rovee-Collier & L.P. Lipsitt (Eds.), *Advances in infancy research.* Copyright © 1992. Reprinted by permission from ABLEX Publishing Corporation. **p. 359** *Figure 9.8* Adapted from Baltes (1994), *Life-span developmental psychology: On the overall landscape of human development.* Reprinted with permission of the author.

Chapter 10 **p. 374** *Table 10.2* C. S. Crandall, J. J. Preisler, and J. Aussprung, "Measuring life event stress in the lives of college students: The Undergraduate Stress Questionnaire (USQ)" from the *Journal of Behavioral Medicine, 15,* 627–662. Copyright © 1992 by Plenum Publishing Corp. **p. 376** *Figure 10.2* The General Adaptation Syndrome, from *Stress without Distress* by Hans Selye, M.D. Copyright © 1974 by Han Selye, M.D. Reprinted by permission of HarperCollins Publishers, Inc. **p. 381** *Figure 10.4* Adapted from Lazarus, Opton, Nornikos, and Rankin, *Journal of Personality*, 33:4. Copyright © Blackwell Publishers. Reprinted with permission.

Chapter 11 **p. 402** *Figure 11.1* From *Personality Strategies and Issues* by R. M. Liebert and M. D. Spiegler. Copyright © 1987, 1982, 1978, 1974, 1970 The Dorsey Press; © 1994, 1990 Brooks/Cole Publishing Company, Pacific Grove, CA 93950, a division of International Thomson Publishing Inc. **p. 408** *Figure 11.2* Reprinted by special permission of the publisher, Psychological Assessment Resource, Inc., Odessa, Florida 33556, from the *Structured Interview of Reported Symptoms* by Richard Rogers, Ph.D., Copyright © 1986, 1992 by PAR, Inc. Further reproduction is prohibited. **p. 409** *Table 11.2* From "An introduction to the five-factor model and its applications." *Journal of Personality, 60,* 175–215. Reprinted by permission of the American Psychological Association. **p. 410** *Figure 11.3* From "The Causes and Cures of Neurosis: An Introduction to Modern Behavior Therapy Based on Learning Theory and the Principle of Conditioning" by H. J. Eysenck and S. Rachman. © 1965 by Edits. **p. 414** *Figure 11.4* Reprinted from *Journal of Behavior Therapy and Experimental Psychiatry, 13,* A. Bandura, "The Assessment and Predictive Generality of Self-Precepts of Efficacy," pp. 195–199. Copyright © 1982 by Pergamon Press, with permission from Elsevier Science. **p. 424** *Table 11.3* From Trull, T. J., and Sher, J. K. "Relationship between the five-factor model of personality and Axis I disorders in a nonclinical sample." *Journal of Personality and Social Psychology, 103,* 350–360. Reprinted by permission of Duke University Press. **p. 425** *Figure 11.5* From *Minnesota Multiphasic Personality Inventory-2 Profile for Clinical Scales.* Copyright © by the Regents of the University of Minnesota 1942, 1943 (renewed 1970), 1989. All rights reserved. "MMPI-2" and "Minnesota Multiphasic Personality Inventory-2."

Chapter 12 **p. 441** *Table 12.2* Reprinted with permission from the *Diagnostic and Statistical Manual of Mental Disorders, Text Revision,* Copyright © 2000 American Psychiatric Association.

Chapter 13 **p. 487** *Figure 13.1* Reprinted with permission of the author from Matson, J., Sevin, J., Fridley, and Love, S. (1990). "Increasing Spontaneous Language in Autistic Children," *Journal of Applied Behavior Analysis, 23,* pp. 227–233.

Chapter 14   **p. 530** *Figure 14.6* Kenrick, D. T., Groth, G., Trost, M., & Sadalla, E. K. (1993), "Integrating Evolutionary and Social Exchange Perspectives on Relationships: Effects of Gender, Self-Appraisal, and Involvement Level on Mate Selection," *Journal of Personality and Social Psychology*.   **p. 537** *Figure 14.9* Adapted with permission from S. Milgram, "Behavioral Study of Obedience," from *Journal of Abnormal and Social Psychology, 67*, No. 4, p. 376. Copyright © 1963.   **p. 545** *Figure 14.12* Figure from, "Temperature and Aggression: Paradox, Controversy, and a (Fairly) Clear Picture," by C. A. Anderson, and K. P. Anderson, in *Human Aggression*, edited by R. G. Green and E. Donnerstein. Copyright © 1998 by Academic Press. Reprinted by permission of Academic Press.

Chapter 15   **p. 578** *Figure 15.2* Job Satisfaction Survey, Copyright Paul E. Spector, 1994, All rights reserved. Reprinted by permission.

PHOTO CREDITS

Chapter 1   **p. 1** © David Job/Stone/Getty Images.   **p. 5** © David Young-Wolff/PhotoEdit.   **p. 6** *(left)* © Kevin Horan/Stone/Getty Images. *(right)* © AFP/Corbis.   **p. 7** *(top)* © Will & Deni McIntyre/Photo Researchers. *(bottom)* © Charles Gupton 2002/Corbis Stock Market.   **p. 9** Photofest.   **p. 11** Archives of the History of American Psychology - The University of Akron.   **p. 12** Courtesy of the Harvard University Archives.   **p. 13** B. A. Shaywitz et al., 1995, NMR/Yale Medical School.   **p. 14** Courtesy Robert W. Levenson, Ph.D.   **p. 15** © Michael Newman/PhotoEdit.   **p. 16** © Bob Daemmrich/The Image Works.   **p. 18** *(top)* Courtesy of Wellesley College Archives, photo by Partridge. *(bottom)* Courtesy of Wilberforce University, Archives and Special Collections.   **p. 20** © Francis Dean/The Image Works.   **p. 24** © 2005 PhotoDisc, Inc.   **p. 26** © David Young-Wolff/PhotoEdit.   **p. 27** Everett Collection.   **p. 28** Getty Images.   **p. 31** © 2005 PhotoDisc, Inc.   **p. 32** © 1998 Joel Gordon.   **p. 36** © A. Ramey/PhotoEdit. **p. 37** © The New Yorker Collection 1981 Charles Addams from cartoonbank.com. All rights reserved.

Chapter 2   **p. 44** © Mary Kate Denny/PhotoEdit.   **p. 51** © Markel/Getty Images. **p. 56** AP/Wide World Photos.   **p. 59** D.N. Levin, H. Xiaoping, K.K. Tan, S. Galhotra, C.A. Palizzare, G.T.Y. Chen, R.N. Beck, C.T. Chen, M.D. Cooper, J.F. Mullan, J. Hekmatpanah, and J.-P. Spire (1989). *The Brain:* Integrated three-dimensional display of MR and PET images. *Radiology, 172:* 783–789.   **p. 61** © Bachmann/The Image Works.   **p. 67** © Bob Daemmrich/Stock Boston.   **p. 70** AP/Wide World Photos.

Chapter 3   **p. 78** © Peter Cade/Stone/Getty Images.   **p. 83** Getty Images.   **p. 86** © Omikron/Photo Researchers.   **p. 89** *(top)* © Michael Simpson/Index Stock Imagery. *(bottom)* Reprinted by permission from *Nature*. Roorda, A. & Williams, D.R. (1999). The arrangement of the three cone classes in the living human eye. *Nature, 397*, 520–522. Copyright 1999 Macmillan Magazines Ltd.   **p. 91** Vienot, Brettel, Mollon-MNHN, CNRS.   **p. 95** AP/Wide World Photos.   **p. 98** L. M. Bartoshuk and B. Duffy.   **p. 99** © Billy Hustace/Stone/Getty Images.   **p. 100** © Alain Evrard/Photo Researchers.   **p. 101** Mike Blake/Reuters.   **p. 109** *(bottom)* AP/Wide World Photos.   **p. 110** © David Young-Wolff/PhotoEdit.   **p. 111** *(top and bottom)* Phillip Kent/www.anamorphosis.com.   **p. 118** © Mark Richards /PhotoEdit.

Chapter 4   **p. 128** © Doug Martin/Photo Researchers.   **p. 129** © David Welling/Animals Animals.   **p. 131** Permission granted by International Creative Management Inc. Copyright © 1986 by Berke Breathed. Cartoon first appeared in *The Washington Post*.   **p. 134** AP/Wide World Photos.   **p. 136** *(top)* © Jacques Jangouz/Photo Researchers. *(bottom)* Nathan Benn/NGS Image Collection. **p. 139** © Bob Daemmrich/The Image Works.   **p. 140** © David Young-Wolff/PhotoEdit.   **p. 143** © David Parker/Photo Researchers.   **p. 145** © Grant Mason/ Manni Mason's Pictures.   **p. 148** The William H. Helfand Collection, New York. **p. 150** © Kenneth Murray/Photo Researchers.   **p. 151** © Barry King/Getty Images.   **p. 153** © Joel Gordon 1994.

Chapter 5   **p. 160** © Jack Monnier/Stone/Getty Images.   **p. 167** *(top)* © Steven Needham/Envision. *(bottom)* © Tom Stack & Assoc.   **p. 170** Nina Leen/Timepix/Getty Images.   **p. 173** © Frank Lotz Miller/Black Star.   **p. 174** © The New Yorker Collection 1993 Tom Cheney from cartoonbank.com. All Rights Reserved.   **p. 175** © Bob Daemmrich/The Image Works.   **p. 176** Courtesy of The Lincoln Electric Company.   **p. 177** Getty Images.   **p. 178** Lang, P. J., & Malamed,

B. G. (1969). Avoidance conditioning therapy of an infant with chronic ruminative vomiting. *Journal of Abnormal Psychology, 74*, 1–8.   **p. 180** © Lawrence Migdale/Stock Boston.   **p. 184** Kohler, W. 1976. *The Mentality of Apes*. London: Routledge and Kegan Paul Pic.   **p. 185** © Paul Chesley/Stone/Getty Images. **p. 186** Albert Bandura/Stanford University.   **p. 189** © Charles Gupton/Stock Boston.   **p. 190** © Hank Morgan/Rainbow.

Chapter 6   **p. 197** © Lawrence Migdale/Stock Boston. **p. 200** © Mary Kate Denny/Stone/Getty Images.   **p. 203** © Frank Siteman/Stock Boston.   **p. 207** *(left)* Franco Magnani, 1700 El Camino Real, Rue 21 Sp. 16, South San Francisco, CA 94080-1281. *(right)* S. Schwartzenberg, © Exploratorium, www.exploratorium.edu.   **p. 209** © Mary Kate Denny/PhotoEdit.   **p. 212** William F. Brewer, in Brewer, W. F., & Treyens, J. C. (1981), Role of schemata in memory for places. *Cognitive Psychology*, 13, 207–230.   **p. 214** © Todd Warshaw/Getty Images.   **p. 218** © Laurence Monneret/Stone/Getty Images.   **p. 221** © Paul Conklin.   **p. 223** Courtesy of Prof. Dominique Muller.   **p. 225** AP/Wide World Photos.   **p. 227** © Robert Burke/Getty Images.

Chapter 7   **p. 233** © Michael Newman/PhotoEdit.   **p. 237** © Vincent Besnault/Getty Images.   **p. 239** © Jeff Greenberg/PhotoEdit.   **p. 242** © Paul Howell/Getty Images.   **p. 245** AP/Wide World Photos.   **p. 251** Barbara L. Johnston/Reuters.   **p. 253** © Reuters NewMedia Inc./Corbis.   **p. 256** © Joe McNally/ Corbis Sygma.   **p. 258** © Michael Grecco/Stock Boston.   **p. 259** Dr. Ronald H. Cohn/Gorilla Foundation/Koko.org.   **p. 264** © The New Yorker Collection 1998 J. B. Handelsman from cartoonbank.com. All Rights Reserved.   **p. 272** Fraser Hale/St. Petersburg Times.

Chapter 8   **p. 280** © Bob Daemmrich/Stock Boston.   **p. 282** AP/Wide World Photos.   **p. 284** © Okoniewski/The Image Works.   **p. 287** © Richard Howard. **p. 288** © Peter Menzel/Stock Boston.   **p. 290** © UPPA/Topham/The Image Works. **p. 297** AP/Wide World Photos.   **p. 299** Reprinted by permission of the publishers from Henry A. Murray, *Thematic Apperception Test*, Cambridge, Mass.: Harvard University Press, © 1943 by the President and Fellows of Harvard College, © 1971 by Henry A. Murray.   **p. 300** © Mary Kate Denny/PhotoEdit.   **p. 302** © Ariel Skelley 2002/Corbis Stock Market.   **p. 305** © Kathy McLaughlin/The Image Works.   **p. 306** Joe Hoyle/The Daily Illini.   **p. 307** From *The Neurological Examination,* 4th edition, by R. N. Dejong, New York: Lipincott/Harper & Row, 1979. **p. 312** © Robert E. Daemmrich.   **p. 313** © Bob Daemmrich/Stock Boston. **p. 315** AP/Wide World Photos.   **p. 316** *(left)* © Eastcott/Momatiuk/Woodfin Camp. *(right)* © Rick Smolan/Stock Boston.

Chapter 9   **p. 323** © Myrleen Ferguson/PhotoEdit.   **p. 325** © Les Stone/Corbis Sygma.   **p. 327** © C. Salvador/Corbis Sygma.   **p. 328** Photo by Lennart Nilsson/Albert Bonniers Forlag AB, *Behold Man*, Little, Brown and Company. **p. 330** Nelson, C. A. (1987). "The recognition of facial expressions in the first two years of life: Mechanisms of development." *Child Development, 58*, 889–909.   **p. 331** © Petit Format/J. DaCunha/Photo Researchers.   **p. 333** © George Zimbel.   **p. 334** Courtesy of Carolyn Rovee-Collier.   **p. 337** © Pedrick/The Image Works. **p. 341** © Jose Polleross/The Image Works.   **p. 342** © Bob Daemmrich.   **p. 343** © Amy C. Etra/PhotoEdit.   **p. 344** © Martin Rogers/Stock Boston.   **p. 347** © B. Mahoney/ The Image Works.   **p. 350** © David Grossman/Photo Researchers. **p. 351** © Jeff Greenberg/Photo Researchers.   **p. 355** © Mary Kate Denny/PhotoEdit.   **p. 361** Steve Liss/TimePix/Getty Images.   **p. 362** © Bob Daemmrich/ Stock Boston.   **p. 363** *(top)* © Michael Newman/PhotoEdit. *(bottom)* Joe Skipper/ Reuters.

Chapter 10   **p. 370** © John Henley Photography/Corbis.   **p. 375** AP/Wide World Photos.   **p. 378** Photofest.   **p. 379** © Reuters NewMedia Inc./Corbis.   **p. 383** © Lauren Greenfield/Corbis Sygma.   **p. 388** Boehringer Ingelheim, International GmbH/photo Lennart Nilsson, *The Incredible Machine,* National Geographic Society.   **p. 389** © Esbin-Anderson/The Image Works.   **p. 391** © Bob Daemmrich/ PhotoEdit.   **p. 392** © Gustavo Gilabert/Corbis SABA.   **p. 393** © 1998 Steve Kelley/ Copley News Service.   **p. 394** Courtesy of American Psychological Association. **p. 395** © Leslie O'Shaughnessy/Medical Images.

Chapter 11   **p. 400** © Bonnie Kamin/PhotoEdit.   **p. 404** © Bob Daemmrich/Stock Boston.   **p. 405** Mary Evans Picture Library.   **p. 408** © John Neubauer/PhotoEdit.   **p. 409** © Robert Caputo/AURORA.   **p. 412** © Bruce Plotkin/Getty Images.   **p. 415** *(top)* © Titan Sports/Corbis Sygma. *(middle)*

Key terms, which appear in **boldface,** are followed by their definitions. Entries that appear in blue refer to the optional Industrial/Organizational Psychology chapter.

Brown, J., 205
Brown, J. R., 350
Brown, P. D., 498
Brown, R. A., 257
Brown, R., 211, 221
Brown, R. J., 527
Brown, S., 488
Brown, S. A., 149
Brown, T., 490
Brown, T. A., 442
Brownell, K. D., 289
Brown-Peterson procedure   *A method for determining how long unrehearsed information remains in short-term memory,* 205
Brownstein, A. L., 553
Bruce, D., 338
Bruce, T. J., 503, 505
Bruck, M., 207
Brunet, A., 144
Brüning, J. C., 286
Brunstein, J. C., 426
Brunvald, J. H., 22
Brusaferro, S., 141
Brush, D. H., 579, 580
Bryant, R. A., 145
Bryson, S. E., 468
Buckner, R. L., 225
Budney, A. J., 153
Buffalo, E. A., 207, 213
Bugental, D. B., 349
Bui, K.-V. T., 530
Bukowski, W., 350
Bulik, C. M., 290
Bulimia nervosa   *An eating disorder that involves eating massive quantities of food and then eliminating the food by self-induced vomiting or laxatives,* 288, 290, 441
Bullinger, M., 374, 378
Bullough, V. L., 295
Bupropion, 502
Burac, J. A., 468
Burchard, R. E., 288
Burger, J. M., 535
Buriel, R., 349
Burleson, B. R., 294, 383
Burman, B., 361
Burnley, M. C. E., 144
Burnout   *A pattern of physical and psychological dysfunctions in response to continuous stressors,* 379
Burnstein, E., 549
Burris, C. T., 517
Burrows, G. D., 145
Burton, A. M., 115
Bushman, B. J., 187, 188, 541, 542, 544
Bushnell, M. C., 100
Business organizations, 6
BuSpar, 503, 504
Buspirone, 503, 504
Buss, D., 2
Buss, D. M., 15, 283, 291, 352, 411, 421, 530, 549
Bustillo, J. R., 462
Buston, P. M., 529
Buswell, B. N., 310
Butcher, J. N., 423
Butler, R., 300, 301
Buunk, B., 514
Buxhoeveden, D. P., 259
Byrd, M., 355
Byrne, D., 523
Byrne, E., 2

Byrnes, G., 22
Bystander effect   *A phenomenon in which the chances that someone will help in an emergency decrease as the number of people present increases,* 547–548

Cabanac, M., 287
Cabeza, R., 225
Cabeza, R., 60
Cabot, P. J., 101
Cacioppo, J. T., 14, 376, 388, 390, 412, 413, 523, 524, 553, 554
Cadoret, R. J., 470
Caffeine, 146, 151, 154
Cahill, L., 53, 73
Cahill, S. P., 31, 485
Cain, D. J., 418, 483
Cairns, R. B., 540
Calkins, M. W., 18
Calle, E. E., 289
Calvert, G. A., 95
Camargo, C. A., 294
Campbell, D. P., 584
Campbell, D. T., 30
Campbell, F. A., 154
Campbell, J. P., 304, 416
Campbell, R. S., 389, 457
Campion, J. E., 565, 575
Campione, J. C., 274
Campos, J. J., 318, 342
Candia, V., 63
Cann, A., 209
Cannabis sativa, 153
Cannon, T. D., 462
Cannon, W. B., 286, 309, 312
Cannon-Bard theory, of emotion, 312, 314
Capaldi, D., 360
Capron, C., 265, 266
Capsaicin, 96
Captainitis, 538
Caramazza, A., 68
Carbohydrates, serotonin and, 50
Carbon monoxide, 52, 225
Cardena, E., 452
Cardinal, R. N., 177
Cardon, L. R., 265
Carli, L. L., 530
Carlo, G. L., 24
Carlsmith, J. M., 525
Carlson, N. R., 153, 288
Carmichael, L. L., 214
Carmody, T. J., 500
Carnegie Task Force on Learning in the Primary Grades, 189
Carney, R. M., 377
Carosa, D., 491
Carper, R. A., 468
Carr, J. E., 190
Carraher, D., 272
Carraher, T. N., 272
Carrere, S., 361
Carretta, T. R., 564
Carrigan, M. H., 31, 485
Carrillo, E., 498
Carroll, L., 134
Carstensen, L., 363

Carstensen, L. L., 363
Carswell, C. M., 119
Cartensen, L. L., 532
Carter, M. M., 446, 448
Carter-Saltzman, L., 265
Cartwright, R. D., 139, 142
Casacalenda, N., 503
Casagrande, 142
Casbon, T. S., 149
Case, L., 33
Case studies   *Research involving the intensive examination of some phenomenon in a particular individual, group, or situation,* 25–26, 28, 246
Caspi, A., 327, 343, 411, 412, 422, 360, 413, 421, 422, 455, 458, 523, 554
Cassel, E., 179, 351, 471, 583
Cassidy, J., 345
Castillo, S. R., 215
Castration, 294
Catabolic effects, 287
Catalano, M. C., 150
Catanese, K. R., 293
Cataplexy, 139
Cataracts, 86
Catastrophic events, 374
Catastrophizing, 378, 386, 394, 395
Catatonic schizophrenia, 460, 461
Catecholamines, 376, 377, 386
Cattell, R., 408
Cavaiola, A. A., 414
Cavallaro, S., 222
Cavanagh, P., 207
Ceci, S. J., 207, 220
Centers for Disease Control and Prevention, 372, 389, 391, 392, 454
Centerwall, L., 187
Centonze, D., 151
Central nervous system (CNS)   *The brain and spinal cord,* 54, 55, 56–72
   aggression and, 541
   emotions and, 306, 309, 312
   plasticity in, 69–71
   sensory systems and, 81
   see also Brain; Spinal cord
Central route, to attitude change, 524, 525
Central sulcus, 65
Central tendency, measures of, A-2
Central theory, of emotion, 312
Central traits, 407
Çeponien, R., 468
Cerbone, F. G., 469, 470
Cerebellar mutism, 60
Cerebellum   *The part of the hindbrain that controls finely coordinated movements,* 59–60, 61, 64, 103, 104, 141, 149, 223, 225
Cerebral cortex   *The outer surface of the forebrain,* 60, 61, 62–63, 64, 67, 71, 81, 100, 104, 141
   alcohol and, 149
   aggression and, 541
   chemical senses and, 96
   developmental changes in, 71
   dreams and, 143
   emotions and, 309, 312
   memory and, 223, 224, 225
   opiates and, 152
   visual processing and, 87, 114
Cerebral hemispheres, 62, 68–69, 87, 307
Cerletti, U., 500
Cerqueira, J., 546
Cervone, D., 413

fMRI. *See* Functional MRI
Foa, E. B., 380, 447, 448, 503
Folk, C. L., 119
Folkard, S., 584
Folkman, S., 380, 381, 382, 383, 384, 458
Follette, V. M., 221, 379
Fombonne, E., 468
Fontaine, K. R., 289
Food, 286. *See also* Eating; **Hunger**
Food culture, 288
Foot-in-the door technique, 535, 539
Forbes, S., 286
Ford, D. E., 138
Ford, J. K., 573
Forebrain *The part of the brain responsible for the most complex aspects of behavior and mental life,* 60–62, 64, 71
Forensic psychologists *Psychologists who are involved in many aspects of psychology and law,* 6
Forgatch, M. S., 507
Forgetting, 205, 217–222, 227
Forgetting curve, 217
Formal concept *A concept that can be clearly defined by a set of rules or properties,* 237–238
Formal operational period *According to Piaget, the fourth stage of cognitive development, characterized by the ability to engage in hypothetical thinking,* 332, 356, 358, 359, 364
Formal reasoning *A set of rigorous procedures for reaching valid conclusions,* 240–242
Foroud, T., 469
Fosse, R., 143
Foster, M. D., 383
Foulkes, D., 142
Fountain, D., 469
Fountain, J. W., 436
Foushee, H. C., 538
Fovea *A region in the center of the retina,* 85, 86–97, 118, 330
Fowler, R. D., 394
Fowles, D., 462
Fox, A. S., 286
Fox, M. J., 45
Fox, N. A., 339
Fox, S., 566, 582
Foxhall, K., 9, 498
Fozard, J., 358
Fraenkel, P., 31, 492
Fragile X syndrome, 272
France, C. R., 100
Francis, E. L., 457
Frank, J. B., 479
Frank, J. D., 479
Frank, J. S., 479
Frank, M. G., 317
Frankenberg, W. K., 326
Franklin, E., 219
Franklin, G., Sr., 219, 221
Franklin, N., 213
Franzoi, S., 519, 529
Fraser, S. C., 535
Frazier, P., 380
Fredrickson, N., 458
Free association, 481, 492
Free-floating anxiety, 446
Freed, C. R., 70
Freedland, R. L., 331
Freedman, D. G., 343
Freedman, J. L., 189, 535
Freedman, V. A., 360
Freeman, M. P., 455

Freeman, S. A., 455
Freeston, M. H., 503
Fremgen, A., 257
Fremmer-Bombik, E.,345
Frequency *The number of complete waves, or cycles, that pass a given point per unit of time,* 83, 84, 92, 93, 94, 95, 96
Frequency histogram *A pictorial presentation of how often each possible score on a dependent variable occurs in a set of research data,* A-1–A-2
Frequency matching, 96
Freres, D. R., 506
Frese, M., 589
Freud, A., 405
Freud, S., 10–11, 12, 13, 15–16, 26, 131, 143, 402–404, 405, 406, 417, 437, 480–481, 482, 540
Fridlund, A., 316
Fried, A. L., 500
Fried, P. A., 153
Fried, Y., 568, 578
Friedland, N., 378
Friedland, R. P., 54
Friedman, D., 223
Friedman, E., 447
Friedman, H. S., 10, 385–387, 416, 418
Friedman, M., 389
Friendships, 350
Friesen, W. V., 310, 317
Frigidity, 298
Frijda, N. H., 316
Fritzler, B. K., 488
Fritzsche, B., 547
Frohna, J. G., 140
Fromm, E., 405
Frone, M. R., 585
Frontal cortex, 71, 307
Frontal lobe, of brain, 63, 65, 67
Froom, P., 578
Frueh, B. C., 31
Frustration, 316, 542–543
Frustration-aggression hypothesis *A proposition stating that the existence of frustration always leads to some form of aggressive behavior,* 542–543
Fujita, F., 302
Fuligni, A. J., 355
Fulker, D. W., 265
Functional analysis of behavior, 12
Functional fixedness *The tendency to think about familiar objects in familiar ways,* 248, 249, 378
Functional MRI (fMRI), 58, 59, 71
Functionalism, 11, 12, 13
Fundamental attribution error *A bias toward overattributing the behavior of others to internal factors,* 520, 522
Fundamental frequency, 93
Funder, D., 402, 409, 412, 413, 414
Funtowicz, M. N., 444
Furedy, J. J., 311
Furey, M. L., 223
Furnham, A., 427

GABA. *See* Gamma-amino butyric acid
Gabbard, G. O., 405, 481, 482
Gabrieli, J. D. E., 225
Gabryel, B., 53
Gaertner, S. L., 527
Gaertner, S., 581
Gage, F. H., 70
Gais, S., 142
Galanin, 287

Galanter, E., 82
Galatzer-Levy, R. M., 494
Galea, S., 379, 380, 447
Gallagher, J. J., 272
Gallagher, M., 225, 346
Gallo, D. A., 201
Gallup, 577
Galotti, K. M., 239, 244
Galvanic skin resistance (GSR), 516
Gambler's fallacy, 253
Gamma hydroxybutyrate (GHB), 150, 150, 151, 154, 505
Gamma, A., 152
Gamma-amino butyric acid (GABA), 50–51, 52, 149, 151, 447
Ganchrow, J. R., 330
Ganglion cells, 87, 90
Ganley, R., 530
Garb, H. N., 426, 443, 444, 445
Garbarino, S., 141
Garber, J., 458
Garcia, J., 167
Garcia, S. M., 547
Garciaparra, N., 177
Gardikiotis, A., 534
Gardner, C. O., 458
Gardner, H., 105, 260, 271
Gardner, R., 190
Garfield, S. L., 496, 497
Gariepy, J., 540
Gariglietti, K. P., 490
Garland, A. F., 506, 532
Garry, M., 146, 149, 220
Garske, J. P., 495, 498
GAS. *See* **General adaptation syndrome**
Gases, as class of neurotransmitters, 50, 52
Gatchel, R. J., 374
Gate control theory *A theory suggesting the presence of a "gate" in the spinal cord that either permits or blocks the passage of pain impulses to the brain,* 100–101
Gates, G. A., 94
Gatewood, R. D., 582
Gatiss, J., 246–247, 248
Gatz, M., 54
Gauvain, M., 340
Gazzaniga, M. S., 68, 131
GDNF. *See* Glial cell line–derived neurotrophic factor
Ge, X., 353
Geary, D. C., 351
Geen, R. G., 540, 542, 543
Geiselman, R. E., 215
Gelabert-Gonzalez, M., 60
Gelfand, M. M., 294
Gelman, R., 337
Gemar, M., 503
Gender identity disorders, 441
Gender
    aggression and, 351
    alcohol and, 150, 438, 469
    conformity and, 534–535
    depression and, 438
    hormones and, 293–294
    job satisfaction and, 579
    leadership style and, 552
    mate selection preferences and, 15
    mood disorders and, 457
    moral reasoning and, 358
    self-esteem and, 420
    sexual behavior and, 293–294
    stress and, 385